Microsoft® Word

365 Complete

IN PRACTICE

2019

©Chris Ryan/Getty Images

Microsoft® Word
365 Complete

2019

Randy Nordell
AMERICAN RIVER COLLEGE

Mc
Graw
Hill

©Chris Ryan/Getty Images

MICROSOFT WORD 365 COMPLETE: IN PRACTICE, 2019

2 3 4 5 6 7 8 9 LMN 21 20

ISBN 978-1-260-81818-5 (bound edition)
MHID 1-260-81818-7 (bound edition)
ISBN 978-1-260-81819-2 (loose-leaf edition)
MHID 1-260-81819-5 (loose-leaf edition)

Managing Director: *Terry Schiesl*
Portfolio Manager: *Wyatt Morris*
Product Developers: *Alan Palmer*
Marketing Manager: *Corban Quigg*
Content Project Managers: *Harvey Yep*
Buyer: *Susan K. Culbertson*
Design: *Egzon Shaqiri*
Content Licensing Specialists: *Shawntel Schmitt*
Cover Image: *©Deklofenak/Getty Images*
Compositor: *SPi Global*

Library of Congress Control Number: 2019943541

mheducation.com/highered

dedication

Bob and Lanita, thank you for generously allowing me to use the cabin where I completed much of the work on this project. Don and Jennie, thank you for teaching me the value of hard work and encouraging me throughout the years. Kelsey and Taylor, thank you for keeping me young at heart. Kelly, thank you for your daily love, support, and encouragement. I could not have done this without you. I'm looking forward to spending more time together on our tandem!

—Randy

brief contents

contents

CHAPTER 4: USING TABLES, COLUMNS, AND GRAPHICS

CHAPTER 5: USING TEMPLATES AND MAIL MERGE

CHAPTER 7: ADVANCED TABLES AND GRAPHICS

CHAPTER 8: USING DESKTOP PUBLISHING AND GRAPHIC FEATURES

about the author

RANDY NORDELL, Ed.D.

AMERICAN RIVER COLLEGE

Dr. Randy Nordell is a Professor of Business Technology at American River College in Sacramento, California. He has been an educator for over 25 years and has taught at the high school, community college, and university levels. He holds a bachelor's degree in Business Administration from California State University, Stanislaus, a single subject teaching credential from Fresno State University, a master's degree in Education from Fresno Pacific University, and a doctorate in Education from Argosy University. Randy is the lead author of the *Microsoft Office 365: In Practice, Microsoft Office 2016: In Practice,* and *Microsoft Office 2013: In Practice* series of texts. He is also the author of *101 Tips for Online Course Success* and *Microsoft Outlook 2010.* Randy speaks regularly at conferences on the integration of technology into the curriculum. When not teaching and writing, he enjoys spending time with his family, cycling, skiing, swimming, backpacking, and enjoying the California weather and terrain.

preface

What We're About

We wrote *Microsoft Word 365 Complete: In Practice, 2019 Edition* to meet the diverse needs of both students and instructors. Our approach focuses on presenting Word topics in a logical and structured manner, teaching concepts in a way that reinforces learning with practice projects that are transferrable, relevant, and engaging. Our pedagogy and content are based on the following beliefs.

Students Need to Learn and Practice Transferable Skills

Students must be able to transfer the concepts and skills learned in the text to a variety of projects, not simply follow steps in a textbook. Our material goes beyond the instruction of many texts. In our content, students practice the concepts in a variety of current and relevant projects *and* are able to transfer skills and concepts learned to different projects in the real world. To further increase the transferability of skills learned, this text is integrated with SIMnet so students also practice skills and complete projects in an online environment.

Your Curriculum Drives the Content

The curriculum in the classroom should drive the content of the text, not the other way around. This book is designed to allow instructors and students to cover all the material they need to in order to meet the curriculum requirements of their courses no matter how the courses are structured. *Microsoft Word 365 Complete: In Practice, 2019 Edition* teaches the marketable skills that are key to student success. McGraw-Hill's Custom Publishing site, **Create,** can further tailor the content material to meet the unique educational needs of any school.

Integrated with Technology

Our text provides a fresh and new approach to an Office applications course. Topics integrate seamlessly with SIMnet with 1:1 content to help students practice and master concepts and skills using SIMnet's interactive learning philosophy. Projects in SIMnet allow students to practice their skills and receive immediate feedback. This integration with SIMnet meets the diverse needs of students and accommodates individual learning styles. Additional textbook resources found in SIMnet (Resources and Library sections) integrate with the learning management systems that are widely used in many online and onsite courses.

Reference Text

In addition to providing students with an abundance of real-life examples and practice projects, we designed this text to be used as a Microsoft Office 365 reference source. The core material, uncluttered with exercises, focuses on real-world use and application. Our text provides clear step-by-step instructions on how readers can apply the various features available in Microsoft Office in a variety of contexts. At the same time, users have access to a variety of both online (SIMnet) and textbook practice projects to reinforce skills and concepts. Both SIMnet and this text are updated with the most current Office 365 features. For the most current updates, please refer first to SIMnet.

instructor walkthrough

Textbook Learning Approach

Microsoft Word 365 Complete: In Practice, 2019 Edition uses the *T.I.P. approach:*
- **T**opic
- **I**nstruction
- **P**ractice

Topic
- Each Office application section begins with foundational skills and builds to more complex topics as the text progresses.
- Topics are logically sequenced and grouped by topics.
- Student Learning Outcomes (SLOs) are thoroughly integrated with and mapped to chapter content, projects, end-of-chapter review, and test banks.
- Reports are available within SIMnet for displaying how students have met these Student Learning Outcomes.

Instruction (How To)
- *How To* guided instructions about chapter topics provide transferable and adaptable instructions.
- Because *How To* instructions are not locked into single projects, this textbook functions as a reference text, not just a point-and-click textbook.
- Chapter content is aligned 1:1 with SIMnet.

Practice (Pause & Practice and End-of-Chapter Projects)
- Within each chapter, integrated Pause & Practice projects (three to five per chapter) reinforce learning and provide hands-on guided practice.
- In addition to Pause & Practice projects, each chapter has 10 comprehensive and practical practice projects: Guided Projects (three per chapter), Independent Projects (three per chapter), Improve It Project (one per chapter), and Challenge Projects (three per chapter). Additional projects can also be found in the Library or Resources section of SIMnet.
- Pause & Practice and end-of-chapter projects are complete content-rich projects, not small examples lacking context.
- Select auto-graded projects are available in SIMnet.

Chapter Features

All chapters follow a consistent theme and instructional methodology. Below is an example of chapter structure.

Main headings are organized according to the *Student Learning Outcomes (SLOs).*

SLO 1.1
Creating, Saving, and Opening Docume

In Microsoft Word, you can create a variety of document types of Word enables you to create, edit, and customize high-quality ments. You can create Word documents from a new blank doc plates, or from existing documents. Word enables you to save d

ate letters, memos, reports, flyers, brochures, and mailings without a va knowledge. This chapter covers the basics of creating and editing a Wo

STUDENT LEARNING OUTCOMES (SLOs)

After completing this chapter, you will be able to:

SLO 1.1 Create, save, and open a Word document (p. 3).

SLO 1.2 Customize a document by entering and selecting text, usin and using *AutoComplete*, *AutoCorrect*, and *AutoFormat* fe

SLO 1.3 Enhance a document using paragraph breaks, line breaks, non-breaking spaces (p. 10).

SLO 1.4 Edit a document using cut, copy, paste, the *Clipboard*, and and repeat features (p. 15).

SLO 1.5 Customize a document using different fonts, font sizes, and

SLO 1.6 Enhance a document using text alignment and line and pa (p. 28).

SLO 1.7 Finalize a document using Word's research, proofing, and tools (p. 32).

SLO 1.8 Apply custom document properties to a document (p. 38).

A list of Student Learning Outcomes begins each chapter. All chapter content, examples, and practice projects are organized according to the chapter SLOs.

WORD

CASE STUDY

Throughout this book, you have the opportunity to practice the application features presented in each chapter. Each chapter begins with a case study that introduces you to the Pause & Practice projects in the chapter. Pause & Practice projects provide a chance to apply and practice key skills in a realistic and practical context. Each chapter contains three to five Pause & Practice projects.

Placer Hills Real Estate (PHRE) is a real estate company with regional offices throughout central California. PHRE encourages agents to use standard formats for their business documents. This ensures consistency in document appearance while also allowing agents to personalize their correspondence to customers and colleagues. In the Pause & Practice projects for this chapter, you create a business document related to the real estate business.

The *Case Study* for each chapter is a scenario that establishes the theme for the entire chapter. Chapter content, examples, figures, Pause & Practice projects, SIMnet skills, and projects throughout the chapter closely related to this case study content. The three to five Pause & Practice projects in each chapter build upon each other and address key case study themes.

How To instructions enhance transferability of skills with concise steps and screen shots.

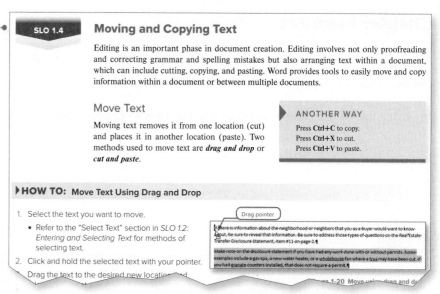

SLO 1.4

Moving and Copying Text

Editing is an important phase in document creation. Editing involves not only proofreading and correcting grammar and spelling mistakes but also arranging text within a document, which can include cutting, copying, and pasting. Word provides tools to easily move and copy information within a document or between multiple documents.

Move Text

Moving text removes it from one location (cut) and places it in another location (paste). Two methods used to move text are *drag and drop* or *cut and paste*.

ANOTHER WAY

Press **Ctrl+C** to copy.
Press **Ctrl+X** to cut.
Press **Ctrl+V** to paste.

HOW TO: Move Text Using Drag and Drop

1. Select the text you want to move.
   - Refer to the "Select Text" section in *SLO 1.2: Entering and Selecting Text* for methods of selecting text.
2. Click and hold the selected text with your pointer.
3. Drag the text to the desired new location and

How To instructions are easy-to-follow concise steps. Screen shots and other figures fully illustrate How To topics.

Students can complete hands-on exercises in either the Office application or in SIMnet.

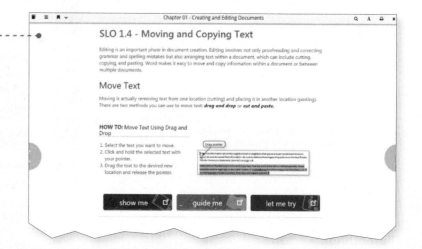

Pause & Practice 1-1: Create a business letter in block format with mixed punctuation.

Pause & Practice 1-2: Edit the business letter using copy, paste, and *Format Painter*. Modify the font, font size, color, style, and effects of selected text.

Pause & Practice 1-3: Finalize the business letter by modifying line spacing and paragraph spacing, changing paragraph alignment, translating text, using research and proofing tools, and adding document properties.

Pause & Practice projects, which each cover two to three of the student learning outcomes in the chapter, provide students with the opportunity to review and practice skills and concepts. Every chapter contains three to five Pause & Practice projects.

MORE INFO

The *launcher* (also referred to as the *dialog box launcher*) is referred to throughout this text. Click the launcher in the bottom-right corner of a group to open a dialog box or pane for additional options.

More Info provides readers with additional information about chapter content.

Another Way notations teach alternative methods of accomplishing
the same task or feature, such as
keyboard shortcuts.

ANOTHER WAY

Press **Ctrl+Z** to undo.
Press **Ctrl+Y** to redo or repeat.

Marginal notations present additional information and alternative methods.

End-of-Chapter Projects

Ten learning projects at the end of each chapter provide additional reinforcement and practice for
students. Many of these projects are available in SIMnet for completion and automatic grading.

- ***Guided Projects (three per chapter):*** Guided Projects provide guided step-by-step instructions to
  apply Word features, skills, and concepts from the chapter. Screen shots guide students through the
  more challenging tasks. End-of-project screen shots provide a visual of the completed project.
- ***Independent Projects (three per chapter):*** Independent Projects provide students further
  opportunities to practice and apply skills, instructing students what to do, but not how to do it.
  These projects allow students to apply previously learned content in a different context.
- ***Improve It Project (one per chapter):*** In these projects, students apply their knowledge and skills
  to enhance and improve an existing document. These are independent-type projects that instruct
  students what to do, but not how to do it.
- ***Challenge Projects (three per chapter):*** Challenge Projects are open-ended projects that encourage
  creativity and critical thinking by integrating Word concepts and features into relevant and engaging
  projects.

Appendix

- ***Office 365 Shortcuts:*** Appendix A covers the shortcuts available in Microsoft Office and within each
  of the specific Office applications. Information is in table format for easy access and reference.

Additional Resources
in SIMnet

Students and instructors can find the following resources in the Library or Resources sections in SIMnet.

Student Resources

- **Data Files:** Files contain start files for all Pause & Practice, Capstone, and end-of-chapter projects.
- **SIMnet Resources:** Resources provide getting started and informational handouts for instructors and students.
- **Check for Understanding:** A combination of multiple choice, fill-in, matching, and short answer questions are available at the end of each SIMbook chapter in SIMnet to assist students in their review of the skills and concepts covered in the chapter.

Capstone Projects

- **Integrating Applications:** Projects provide students with the opportunity to learn, practice, and transfer skills using multiple Office applications.
- **Integrating Skills:** Projects provide students with a comprehensive and integrated review of all of the topics covered in each application (Word, Excel, Access, and PowerPoint). Available in individual application texts.

Appendices

- **Business Document Formats:** Appendix B is a guide to regularly used business document formatting and includes numerous examples and detailed instructions.

Instructor Resources

- **Instructor's Manual:** An Instructor's Manual provides teaching tips and lecture notes aligned with the PowerPoint presentations for each chapter.
- **Test Bank:** The extensive test bank integrates with learning management systems (LMSs) such as Blackboard, WebCT, Desire2Learn, and Moodle.
- **PowerPoint Presentations:** PowerPoint presentations for each chapter can be used in onsite course formats for lectures or can be uploaded to LMSs.
- **SIMnet Resources:** These resources provide getting started and informational handouts for instructors.
- **Solution Files:** Files contain solutions for all Pause & Practice, Capstone, Check for Understanding, and end-of-chapter projects.

acknowledgments

REVIEWERS

Lori Mueller
Southeast Missouri State University

Scott Straub
College of Western Idaho

Philip Reaves
University of Western Georgia

B. Bhagyavati
Columbus State

Carolyn E. Johnson
Northern Oklahoma College

Dona Gibbons
Troy University

Denise Sullivan
Westchester Community College

Suzanne Marks
Bellevue College

Phyllis Fleming
Middlesex County College

Salli DiBartolo
Eastern Florida State College

Teresa Roberson
Northwest-Shoals Community College

Amy Chataginer
Mississippi Gulf Coast Community
College

Dr. Lucinda Stanley
Wor-Wic Community College

Bill Dorin
Indiana University Northwest

Anita Laird
Schoolcraft College

Sue Bajt
Harper College

Ralph Argiento
Guilford Technical Community
College

Annette D. Rakowski
Bergen Community College

Beth Deinert
Southeast Community College

Jo Stephens
University of Arkansas Community
College Batesville

Terry Beachy
Garrett College

Vincent Kayes
Mount Saint Mary College, Newburgh

Kimberly Madsen
Kellogg Community College

Nicolas Rouse
Phoenix College

Barbara Hearn
Community College of Philadelphia

Terribeth Gordon
University of Toledo

Stacy Martin
Southwestern Illinois College

Dr. Hamid Nemati
University of North Carolina at
Greensboro

Beverly Amer
Northern Arizona University

Michael L. Matuszek
San Antonio College

Sandra Metcalf
Grayson College

David Cook
Stephen F. Austin State University

Donnie W. Collins
Andrew College

Frank Whittle
Dutchess Community College

Robert LaRocca
Keiser University

Adnan Turkey
DeVry University

Sheryl S. Bulloch
Columbia Southern University

Richard Flores
Citrus College

Dmitriy Chulkov
Indiana University Kokomo

Mary Locke
Greenville Technical College

Sherrie Drye
North Carolina A&T State
University

Andrew Smith
Marian University Indianapolis

Crystal Theaker
Chandler-Gilbert Community College

Pam Cummings
Minnesota State Community and
Technical Colleg

Tina LePage
Chandler-Gilbert Community College

Darenda Kersey
Black River Technical College

Amy Rutledge
Oakland University

Brian Fox
Santa Fe College

Trey Cherry
Edgecombe Community College

Gigi N. Delk
The University of Texas at Tyler

Dr. Richard A. Warren
Vernon College

Debra Morgan
Eastern Washington University.

Pamela Bilodeau
Olympic College

Jim Hughes
Northern Kentucky University

Diane Shingledecker
Portland Community College

Hyo-Joo Han
Georgia Southern University

Becky McAfee
Hillsborough Community College
Home

Karen Donham
University of Arkansas at
Monticello

Craig Bradley
Shawnee Community College

Elodie Billionniere
Miami Dade College

Joan Rogers
Hillsborough Community College

Genalin F. Umstetter
Delta College

Michael Kato
University of Hawaii

Ann Konarski
St. Clair County Community College

Dr. Mark W. Huber
University of Georgia

Kathleen Morris
The University of Alabama

Rebecca Leveille
American River College

Dory Eddy
Colorado Christian University

Masoud Naghedolfeizi
Fort Valley State University

Joe Vargas
Santa Barbara Business College

Donna Kamen
Truckee Meadows Community College

David Sanford
Northwood University Home

Ken Werner
Alaska Vocational Technical Center

Gigi Simonsen
Northeast Community College

Paula Gregory
Yavapai College

Mordechai Adelman
Touro College

Ron Oler
Ivy Tech Community College of
Indiana

Sandra LaFevers
Joliet Junior College

Sherilyn Reynolds
San Jacinto College

Melissa Nemeth
Indiana University

Barbara Garrell
Delaware County Community College

Astrid Todd
Guilford Technical Community
College

Deedee Flax
Dodge City Community College

Elizabeth P. Sigman
Georgetown University

Preston Clark
Cornell University

Sara Rutledge
Mount Aloysius College

Robyn Barrett
St. Louis Community College

William Neiheisel
Gwinnett College

Sheila Gionfriddo
Luzerne County Community College

Teodoro Llallire
Fairleigh Dickinson University

Tracy Driscoll
Bishop State Community College

Sam McCall
St. Philip's College

Joyce King
Bay College

John Schrage
Southern Illinois University
Edwardsville

John Maloney
Miami Dade College

Lisa Friesen
Southwestern Oklahoma State
University

Shelley Ota
University of Hawaii

Heidi Eaton
Elgin Community College

LaVaughn Hart
Las Positas College

Sandy Keeter
Seminole State College

Kathy J. Schaefer
Southwest Minnesota State
University

Edward Hall
Seward County Community
College

Saiid Ganjalizadeh
The Catholic University of America

Melinda Norris
Coker College

Phillip Dickson
Black River Technical College

Kathy Powell-Case
Colorado Northwestern Community
College

Marianne Daugharthy
College of Western Idaho

Ann Taff
Tulsa Community College

Lydia Slater
Rock Valley College

Seyed Roosta
Albany State University

Pamela Silvers
Asheville-Buncombe Technical Community College

Phillip Davis
Del Mar College

Logan Phillips
Tulsa Community College

Dianne Hill
Jackson College

Jeff Harper
Indiana State University

Carla K. Draffen
West Kentucky Community & Technical College

Colin Onita
San Jose State University

N. T. Izuchi
Quinsigamond Community College

Camille Rogers
Georgia Southern University

Luy Parker
California State University, Northridge

Homer Sharafi
Prince George's Community College

Bill Courter
Jackson College

Robert Wardzala
University of Findlay

Lindsey Huber
Northern State University

David Rosenthal
Seton Hall University

Sandro Marchegiani
University of Pittsburgh

Linda Johnsonius
Murray State University

Barbara Bracken
Wilkes University

Marie Hassinger
Susquehanna University

Rich Cacace
Pensacola State College

Arcola Sullivan
Copiah-Lincoln Community College

Angela Mott
Northeast Mississippi Community College

Tony Hunnicutt
College of the Ouachitas

Stephen D. Ross
Mississippi Delta Community College

Alex Morgan
De Anza College

Aaron Ferguson
University of Maryland University College

Patricia White
University of Maryland University College

Anne Acker
Jacksonville University

Pam Shields
Mt. Hood Community College

Nancy Lilly
Central Alabama Community College

Mandy Reininger
Chemeketa Community College

Alison Rampersad
Lynn University

Jeanine Preuss
South Puget Sound Community College

Timothy J. Lloyd
University of Maryland University College

Betsy Boardwine
Virginia Western Community College

Meg Murray
Kennesaw State University

Lynne Lyon
Durham College

Peter Meggison
Massasoit Community College

Sujing Wang
Lamar University

Alla Zakharova
University of South Alabama

Rachel E. Hinton
SUNY Broome Community College

Rhoda A. M. James
Citrus College

Gena Casas
Florida State College at Jacksonville

James D. Powell
College of the Desert

Sue Joiner
Tarleton State University

Dawn Nelson
University of Dubuque

Carlos Jimenez
El Paso Community College

Diane Smith
Henry Ford College

Steven Brennan
Jackson College

Mehran Basiratmand
Florida Atlantic University

Sharolyn Sayers
Milwaukee Area Technical College

Charles Wunker
Webber International University

Doreen Palucci
Wilmington University

Kristy McAuliffe
San Jacinto College

Rob Lemelin
Eastern Washington University

Nancy Severe
Northern Virginia Community College

Julie Becker
Three Rivers Community College

David Childress
Kentucky Community & Technical College System

Carolyn Kuehne
Utah Valley University

Carolyn Carvalho
Kent State University

Irene Joos
La Roche College

Dr. Shayan Mirabi
American InterContinental University

Zhizhang Shen
Plymouth State University

Kirk Atkinson
Western Kentucky University: WKU

Nisheeth Agrawal
Calhoun Community College

Dr. Bernard Ku
Austin Community College

Jennifer Michaels
Lenoir-Rhyne University

William Barrett
Iowa Western Community College

Naomi Johnson
Dickinson State University

Gilliean Lee
Lander University

Clem Lundie
San Jose City College

Cynthia C. Nitsch
MiraCosta College

Beth Cantrell
Central Baptist College

Bernice Eng
Brookdale Community College

Paul Weaver
Bossier Parish Community College

William Penfold
Jamestown Community College

Kathrynn Hollis-Buchanan
University of Alaska

Carmen Morrison
North Central State College

Marie Campbell
Idaho State University

Jpann G. Becento
Navajo Technical University

Annette Yauney
Herkimer College

Judy Jernigan
Tyler Junior College

Elise Marshall
University of North Florida

Karen Waddell
Butler Community College

Allison Bryant
Howard University

William Spangler
Duquesne University

Henry Bradford
Massasoit Community College

Julie Haar
Alexandria Technical & Community College

Martha Balachandran
Middle Tennessee State University

Cheryl Jordan
San Juan College

Mary Kennedy
College of DuPage

Pengtao Li
California State University Stanislaus

Odemaris Valdivia
Santa Monica College

Joyce Quade
Saddleback College

Pam Houston
Oglala Lakota College

Marc Isaacson
Augsburg University

Penny Cypert
Tarrant County College

Manuel T. Uy
Peralta Colleges

Bonnie Smith
Fresno City College

Brenda Killingsworth
East Carolina University

Ember Mitchell
Dixie State University

Emily Holliday
Campbell University

Holly Bales
International Business College in Indianapolis

Elizabeth Sykes
Golden West College

TECHNICAL EDITORS

Karen May
Blinn College

Andrea Nevill
College of Western Idaho

Richard Finn
Moraine Valley Community College

Chris Anderson
North Central Michigan College

Gena Casas
Florida State College

Leon Blue
Pensacola State College

Amie Mayhall
Olney Central College

Patrick Doran
University of Wisconsin Milwaukeex

Thank you to the wonderful team at McGraw-Hill for your confidence in us and support throughout this project. Alan, Wyatt, Tiffany, Corban, Debbie, Harvey, and Julianna, we thoroughly enjoy working with you all! A special thanks to Debbie Hinkle for her thorough and insightful review of the series. Thank you to all of the reviewers and technical editors for your expertise and invaluable insight, which helped shape this book.

—Randy, Kathleen, Annette, and Pat

Windows 10, Office 365/2019, and File Management

CHAPTER OVERVIEW

Microsoft Office 2019 and Windows 10 introduce many new and enhanced features. Office 2019 includes the Office features added to Office 365 since the release of Office 2016. The integration of Office 2019 and Windows 10 improves file portability and accessibility when you use *OneDrive*, Microsoft's free online cloud storage. Office 2019, Office 365, Office Online, Office mobile apps, and Windows 10 enable you to work on tablet computers and smartphones in a consistent working environment that resembles your desktop or laptop computer.

STUDENT LEARNING OUTCOMES (SLOs)

After completing this chapter, you will be able to:

SLO Intro. 1   Explore select features of Windows 10 (p. Intro-2).

SLO Intro. 2   Use basic features of Microsoft Office and navigate the Office working environment (p. Intro-12).

SLO Intro. 3   Create, save, close, and open Office files (p. Intro-19).

SLO Intro. 4   Customize the view and display size in Office applications and work with multiple Office files (p. Intro-28).

SLO Intro. 5   Print, share, and customize Office files (p. Intro-32).

SLO Intro. 6   Use the *Ribbon*, tabs, groups, dialog boxes, task panes, galleries, and the *Quick Access* toolbar (p. Intro-37).

SLO Intro. 7   Use context menus, mini toolbar, keyboard shortcuts, and function keys in Office applications (p. Intro-41).

SLO Intro. 8   Organize and customize Windows folders and Office files (p. Intro-46).

CASE STUDY

Throughout this book, you have the opportunity to practice the application features presented in the text. Each chapter begins with a case study that introduces you to the Pause & Practice projects in the chapter. These Pause & Practice projects give you a chance to apply and practice key skills in a realistic and practical context. Each chapter contains three to five Pause & Practice projects.

American River Cycling Club (ARCC) is a community cycling club that promotes fitness. ARCC members include recreational cyclists who enjoy the exercise and camaraderie as well as competitive cyclists who compete in road, mountain, and cyclocross races throughout the cycling season. In the Pause & Practice projects, you incorporate many of the topics covered in the chapter to create, save, customize, manage, and share Office files.

Pause & Practice Intro-1: Customize the Windows *Start* menu and *Taskbar*, create and save a PowerPoint presentation, create a folder, open and rename an Excel workbook, and use Windows 10 features.

Pause & Practice Intro-2: Modify an existing document, add document properties,

customize the *Quick Access* toolbar, export the document as a PDF file, and share the document.

Pause & Practice Intro-3: Copy and rename files, create a folder, move files, create a zipped folder, and rename a zipped folder.

SLO INTRO. 1

Using Windows 10

Windows 10 is an *operating system* that controls computer functions and the working environment. Windows 10 uses the familiar *Windows desktop*, *Taskbar*, and *Start menu*. The Windows operating system enables you to customize the working environment and to install applications (apps), such as Microsoft Office. Visit the *Microsoft Store* to download additional apps similar to how you would add an app to your smartphone. Your *Microsoft account* stores your Microsoft settings, enabling you to download apps from the Microsoft Store, and to connect to Microsoft Office, *OneDrive*, and *Office Online.*

Windows 10

The Windows 10 operating system controls interaction with computer hardware and software applications (apps; also referred to as programs). *Windows 10* utilizes a *Start menu* where you select and open an app. Alternatively, you can open apps using the *Taskbar*, the horizontal bar that displays at the bottom of the Windows desktop. When you log in to Windows 10 using your Microsoft account, your Microsoft account synchronizes your Windows, Office, and *OneDrive* cloud storage among computers.

Microsoft Account

In Windows 10 and Office 365/2019, your files and account settings are portable. In other words, your Office settings and files travel with you and are accessible from different computers. You are not restricted to using a single computer. When you sign in to Windows 10 using your Microsoft account (user name and password), Microsoft uses this information to transfer your Windows and Office 2019 settings to the computer you are using. Different types of Microsoft accounts exist: Personal, Education, and Business.

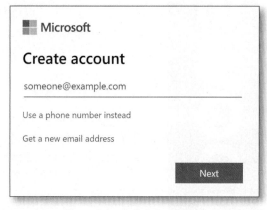

Figure Intro-1 Create a Microsoft account

Your Microsoft account not only signs in to Windows and Office but also to other free Microsoft online services, such as *OneDrive* and *Office Online*. As a student, you can get a free education Microsoft account at https://products.office.com/en-us/student/office-in-education. Also, you can create a free personal Microsoft account at https://signup.live.com (Figure Intro-1).

Windows Desktop and Taskbar

The Windows desktop is the working area of Windows. When you log in to Windows, the desktop displays (Figure Intro-2). The *Taskbar* displays horizontally at the bottom of the desktop. Click an icon on the *Taskbar* to open apps and folders (see Figure Intro-2). Pinning is used to add shortcuts to the *Taskbar* or the *Start* menu. You can pin the *Settings, File Explorer,* and other frequently used apps to the *Taskbar* (see "Customize the Taskbar" later in this section).

Figure Intro-2 Window desktop and *Taskbar*

Start Menu

Windows 10 utilizes a redesigned *Start* menu (Figure Intro-3) that you open by clicking the **Start button** located in the bottom left of the *Taskbar*. From the *Start* menu, you open apps, files, folders, or other Windows resources. The *Start* menu is divided into two main sections. The left side of the *Start* menu displays the *Account, Documents, Pictures, Settings,* and *Power* buttons. This section also displays *Recently added* and *Most used* items, as well as an alphabetical listing of all apps installed on your computer. The right side of the *Start* menu displays tiles (large and small buttons) you click to open an application or window.

Figure Intro-3 Windows *Start* menu

You can customize which apps and items appear on either side of the *Start* menu, arrange and group apps on the *Start* menu, resize the *Start* menu, and display the *Start* menu as a **Start page** when you log in to Windows. See "Customize the Start Menu" later in this section for information about customizing the *Start* menu.

Add Apps

Windows 10 uses the term *apps* generically to refer to applications and programs. Apps include the Windows 10 Weather app, Microsoft Excel program, Control Panel, Google Chrome, or *File Explorer.* Many apps are preinstalled on a Windows 10 computer, and additional apps can be installed on your computer. Install an app, such as Office 2019 or Quicken, by downloading it from a web site. These apps are referred to as *desktop apps* or *traditional apps*.

The *Microsoft Store* app is preinstalled on Windows 10 computers. Install apps such as Netflix, Yelp, and Spotify from the Microsoft Store. These apps are referred to as *modern apps* and look and function similar to apps you install on your smartphone. Many apps in the Microsoft Store are free, and others are available for purchase.

▶ **HOW TO: Add an App from the Microsoft Store**

1. Click the **Start** button to open the *Start* menu.
2. Click the **Microsoft Store** button (tile) to open the Microsoft Store app (Figure Intro-4) and click the **Apps** tab.
   - If the *Microsoft Store* tile is not available on the *Start* menu, locate the *Microsoft Store* button in the alphabetic listing of all apps.
3. Search for and select an app in the Microsoft Store (Figure Intro-5).
   - The Microsoft Store includes different categories of apps.
   - You can search for apps by typing keywords in the *Search* box in the upper-right corner.
   - When you select an app, information about the app displays.
4. Click the **Get**, **Buy**, or **Free trial** button to install the app.
   - You must have a payment method stored in your Microsoft account to purchase apps from the Microsoft Store.
5. Click **Launch** to open the installed app.
   - When you install an app, the app displays in the *Recently added* area on the *Start* menu and *All apps* list of applications.

Figure Intro-4 *Microsoft Store* app on the *Start* menu

Figure Intro-5 Install an app from the Microsoft Store

Customize the Start Menu

When you start using Windows 10 or after you have installed apps, you can customize what appears on your the *Start* menu. When you *pin* an app to the *Start* menu, the corresponding app tile remains on the right side of the *Start* menu. Pin the apps you most regularly use, unpin the apps you don't want displayed on the *Start* menu, and rearrange and resize app tiles to your preference.

1. Click the **Start** button to open the *Start* menu.

2. Move an app tile on the *Start* menu by clicking and dragging the app tile to a new location. The other app tiles shuffle to accommodate the placement of the moved app tile.

3. Remove an app tile from the *Start* menu by right-clicking the app tile and selecting **Unpin from Start** from the context menu (Figure Intro-6).
   - The app tile is removed from the right side of the *Start* menu, but the program or task is not removed from your computer.

4. Pin an app tile to the *Start* menu by right-clicking the app in the alphabetic listing of apps in the *Start* menu and selecting **Pin to Start** (Figure Intro-7).
   - Drag the newly added app tile to the desired location on the *Start* menu.

5. Resize an app tile by right-clicking the app tile, selecting **Resize**, and selecting **Small**, **Medium**, **Wide**, or **Large**.
   - Some apps only have *Small, Medium,* and *Wide* size options.

6. Turn on or off the live tile option by right-clicking the app tile, selecting **More**, and selecting **Turn Live Tile on** or **Turn Live Tile off**.
   - Live tile displays rotating graphics and options on the app tile. When this option is turned off, the name of the app displays on the tile.

7. Uninstall an app by right-clicking the app you want to uninstall and selecting **Uninstall**.
   - Unlike the unpin option, this option uninstalls the program from your computer, not just your *Start* menu.
   - The *Uninstall* option is not available for some pre-installed Microsoft Windows apps.

8. Resize the *Start* menu by clicking and dragging the top or right edge of the *Start* menu.

9. Customize *Start* menu settings by clicking the **Start** button, selecting **Settings** button (Figure Intro-8) to open the *Settings* window, clicking the **Personalization** button, and clicking the **Start** option at the left (Figure Intro-9).
   - Click the **X** in the upper-right corner to close the *Settings* window.

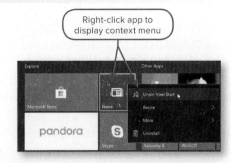

Figure Intro-6 Unpin an app from the *Start* menu

Figure Intro-7 Pin an app to the *Start* menu

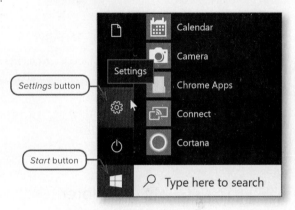

Figure Intro-8 *Settings* button on the *Start* menu

Figure Intro-9 Use full screen *Start* menu

Customize the Taskbar

The *Taskbar* is the horizontal bar located at the bottom of the Windows desktop, and you can quickly open an app by clicking an icon on the *Taskbar* rather than opening it from the *Start* menu. You can customize the *Taskbar* by pinning, unpinning, and rearranging apps. The right side of the *Taskbar* is the *System Tray,* which displays smaller icons of system applications that automatically run in the background of the Windows operating system.

▶HOW TO: Customize the Taskbar

1. Pin an app to the *Taskbar* by clicking the **Start** button, right-clicking an app, clicking **More**, and selecting **Pin to taskbar** (Figure Intro-10).

   - You can also pin an app to the *Taskbar* by right-clicking an app from the alphabetic listing of apps in the *Start* menu.

2. Unpin an app from the *Taskbar* by right-clicking an app icon on the *Taskbar* and selecting **Unpin from taskbar** (Figure Intro-11).

   - You can also unpin apps from the *Taskbar* by right-clicking an app in the *Start* menu, clicking **More**, and selecting **Unpin from taskbar**.

3. Rearrange apps on the *Taskbar* by clicking and dragging the app to the desired location on the *Taskbar* and releasing.

Figure Intro-10 Pin an app to the *Taskbar*

Figure Intro-11 Unpin an app from the *Taskbar*

> ▶ **MORE INFO**
>
> If using a touch screen, press and hold an app on the *Start* menu or *Taskbar* to display the app options.

File Explorer

The *File Explorer* in Windows 10 is a window that opens on your desktop where you browse files stored on your computer (Figure Intro-12). You can open a file or folder, move or copy items, create folders, and delete files or folders. Click the **Start** button and select **File Explorer** to open a *File Explorer* window. Alternatively, right-click the **Start** button and select **File Explorer**.

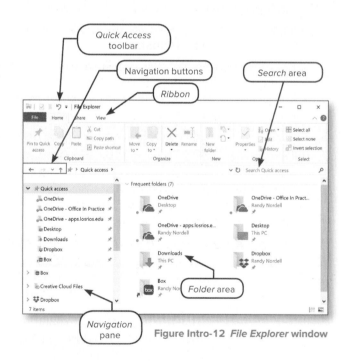

Figure Intro-12 *File Explorer* window

> ▶ **MORE INFO**
>
> You can pin the *File Explorer* to the *Taskbar* for easy access to this window.

The *File Explorer* has different areas:

- **Navigation pane**: The *Navigation* pane displays folders on the left. The **Quick access** area at the top of the *Navigation* pane displays shortcuts to favorite folders. You can pin or unpin folders in the *Quick access* area of the *Navigation* pane.
- **Navigation buttons**: The navigation buttons (*Back, Forward, Recent location,* and *Up*) are located directly above the *Navigation* pane and below the *Ribbon.* Use these buttons to navigate a File Explorer window.
- **Folder pane**: When you select a folder in the *Navigation* pane, the contents of the folder display in the *Folder* pane to the right of the *Navigation* pane. Double-click a folder or file in the *Folder* pane to open it.
- **Ribbon**: The *Ribbon* is located near the top of *File Explorer* and includes the *File, Home, Share,* and *View* tabs. When you click a tab on the *Ribbon,* the *Ribbon* displays the options for the selected tab. Other contextual tabs display when you select certain types of files. For example, the *Picture Tool Manage* tab opens when you select a picture file in the *Folder* pane.
- **Quick Access toolbar**: The *Quick Access* toolbar is above the *Ribbon.* From the *Quick Access* toolbar, click the **New Folder** button to create a new folder or click **Properties** to display the properties of a selected file or folder. You can add buttons, such as *Undo, Redo,* and *Rename,* to the *Quick Access* toolbar.
- **Search**: The *Search* text box is located on the right of the *File Explorer* window below the *Ribbon.* Type key words in the *Search* text box to find files or folders.

OneDrive

OneDrive is a cloud storage area where you store files in a private and secure online location that you access from any computer. With Windows 10, the **OneDrive folder** is one of your storage location folder options, similar to your *Documents* or *Pictures* folders (Figure Intro-13). You can save, open, and edit your *OneDrive* files from a *File Explorer* folder. Your *OneDrive* folder looks and functions similar to other Windows folders. *OneDrive* synchronizes your files so when you change a file stored in *OneDrive* it is automatically updated on the *OneDrive* cloud.

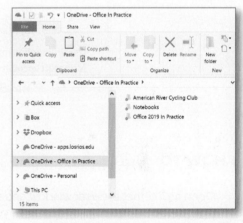

Figure Intro-13 *OneDrive* folder in a *File Explorer* window

When you store your files in *OneDrive,* you have the option of storing the files on *OneDrive* only (in the cloud) or syncing the files to your computer so they are saved on both your computer and on the cloud. You can customize which *OneDrive* folders and files are cloud only (not stored on your computer) and which folders and files are synced to your computer.

▶**HOW TO:** Customize OneDrive Settings

1. Open a *File Explorer* window using one of the following methods:
   - Click the **Start** button and select the **File Explorer** button.
   - Click the **File Explorer** button on the *Taskbar* (if available).
   - Right-click the **Start** button and select **File Explorer**.

2. Right-click the **OneDrive** folder in the *Navigation* pane of the *File Explorer* window and select **Settings** to open the *Microsoft OneDrive* dialog box.
   - Alternatively, right-click the **OneDrive** icon (if available) in the *System Tray* (right side of the *Taskbar*) and select **Settings**.
3. Click the **Account** tab and click the **Choose folders** button to open the *Sync your OneDrive files to this PC* dialog box (Figure Intro-14).
   - Check the **Sync all files and folders in OneDrive** box to sync all files and folders to your computer.
   - You can also select only those folders to sync in the *Or sync only these folders* area by selecting or deselecting the check boxes. Use this option to save storage space on your computer.
4. Click **OK** to close the *Sync your OneDrive files to this PC* dialog box and click **OK** to close the *Microsoft OneDrive* dialog box.

Figure Intro-14 Customize *OneDrive* folders to sync to your computer

OneDrive Online

In addition to the *OneDrive* folder on your computer, you can also access your *OneDrive* files online using an internet browser such as Microsoft Edge, Google Chrome, or Mozilla Firefox. When you access *OneDrive* online using a web browser, you can upload files, create folders, move and copy files and folders, and create Office files using *Office Online* (*Office Online* is discussed in *SLO Intro.2: Using Microsoft Office 2019*).

 MORE INFO

OneDrive online may display differently and include different features depending on the type of Microsoft account you have: personal, education, or business.

▶ HOW TO: Use OneDrive Online

1. Open an internet browser window and navigate to the *OneDrive* web site (www.onedrive.live.com), which takes you to the *OneDrive* sign-in page.
   - Use any internet browser to access *OneDrive* (Microsoft Edge, Google Chrome, Mozilla Firefox).
2. Click the **Sign in** button in the upper-right corner of the browser window.
3. Type your Microsoft account email address and click **Next** (Figure Intro-15).
4. Type your Microsoft account password and click **Sign in**. The *OneDrive* page displays.
   - If you are on your own computer, check the **Keep me signed in** box to stay signed in to *OneDrive* when you return to the page.
   - The different areas of *OneDrive* are listed under the *OneDrive* heading on the left (Figure Intro-16).
   - Click **Files** to display your folders and files in the folder area.
   - At the top of the page, buttons and drop-down menus list the different actions you can perform on selected files and folders.

Figure Intro-15 Log in to *OneDrive* online

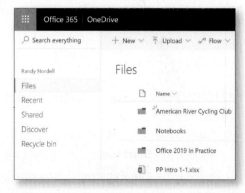

Figure Intro-16 *OneDrive* online environment

Cortana

In addition to using the search tools in *File Explorer,* you can also use **Cortana**, which is the Windows search feature. While the search feature in *File Explorer* searches only for content on your computer, *Cortana* searches for content on your computer, on the internet, and in the Microsoft Store. You can either type keywords for a search or use voice commands to search for content.

When you open *Cortana,* other content, such as weather, upcoming appointments, and popular news stories, displays in the *Cortana* pane.

▶ HOW TO: Search Using Cortana

1. Click the **Cortana** search area on the *Taskbar* to open the *Cortana* pane (Figure Intro-17).

   - If the *Cortana* search area is not on the *Taskbar,* click the **Start** button, right-click **Cortana** in the list of apps, and select **Pin to taskbar**.

2. Type keywords for your search in the **Type here to search** area at the bottom of the *Cortana* pane.

   - You can also click the microphone icon and speak to enter keywords as the search.
   - Content from your computer, the internet, and the Microsoft Store displays in the *Cortana* pane (Figure Intro-18).
   - The search results are grouped into categories such as *Best match, Photos, Search suggestions, Store,* and *Places.* These categories vary depending on the search results.

3. Click a result in the *Cortana* pane to view a file, search the internet, or view apps in the Microsoft Store.

   - The buttons at the top of the *Cortana* pane filter your search by *Apps, Documents, Email,* and *web.*
   - The *More* button displays a drop-down list of additional filter options.

4. Click the **Menu** button at the top left to display other content options in the *Cortana* pane (see Figure Intro-18).

   - The other content options are *Home, Notebook,* and *Devices.*

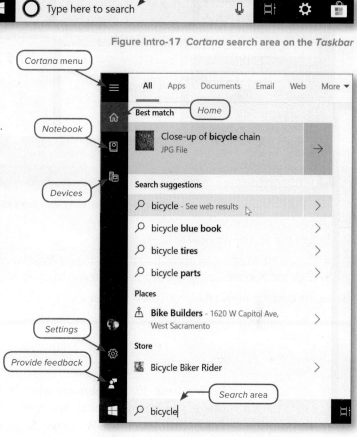

Figure Intro-17 *Cortana* search area on the *Taskbar*

Figure Intro-18 Use *Cortana* to search your computer, the internet, and the Microsoft Store

Task View

Task View displays all open apps and windows as tiles on your desktop, and you can choose which item to display or close. This feature is very helpful when you have multiple items open and need to select or close one. Additionally, *Task View* displays a timeline of tasks you've worked on in Windows. Scroll down in *Task View* to display previous days.

▶HOW TO: Use Task View

1. Click the **Task View** button on the *Taskbar* (Figure Intro-19).
   - All open apps and windows display on the desktop (Figure Intro-20).

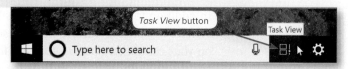

Figure Intro-19 *Task View* button on the *Taskbar*

Figure Intro-20 *Task View* with open apps and windows displayed on the desktop

2. Select the app or window to open or close.
   - Click a tile to open an app. The app opens and *Task View* closes.
   - Click the **X** in the upper-right corner of an app to close an app. *Task View* remains open when you close an app.
3. Scroll down to view tasks from previous days.

Settings

In Windows 10, the ***Settings*** window is where you change global Windows settings, customize the Windows environment, add devices, and manage your Microsoft account. Click the **Settings** button (Figure Intro-21) on the *Taskbar* or *Start* menu to open the *Settings* window (Figure Intro-22). The following categories are typically available in the *Settings* window. *Settings* categories and options may vary depending on the version of Windows you are using and updates to Windows.

- ***System***: Display, notifications, and power
- ***Devices***: Bluetooth, printers, and mouse

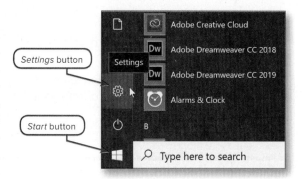

Figure Intro-21 *Settings* button on the Start menu

- **Phone**: Link your Android and iPhone
- **Network & internet**: Wi-Fi, airplane mode, and VPN
- **Personalization**: Background, lock screen, and colors
- **Apps**: Uninstall, defaults, and optional features
- **Accounts**: Your account, email, sync, work, and family
- **Time & Language**: Speech, region, and date
- **Gaming**: Game bar, DVR, broadcasting, and Game Mode
- **Ease of Access**: Narrator, magnifier, and high contrast
- **Cortana**: Cortana languages, permissions, and notifications
- **Privacy**: Location and camera
- **Update & Security**: Windows Update, recovery, and backup

Figure Intro-22 *Settings* window

> **MORE INFO**
>
> If you can't find an item in *Settings,* use the *Search* dialog box (*Find a setting*) to type keywords. If *Settings* is not available on the *Taskbar,* you can find it in the list of apps on the *Start* menu.

Action Center

The **Action Center** in Windows 10 provides a quick glance of notifications and buttons to open other commonly used settings and features in Windows. The *Action Center* displays notifications such as emails and Windows notifications. Click an action button to turn on or off features or open other windows or apps such as the *Settings* menu (*All Settings* button) or OneNote (*Note* button). Click the **Action Center** button on the right side of the *Taskbar* (last button in the *System Tray*) to open the *Action Center* pane, which displays on the right side of your screen (Figure Intro-23).

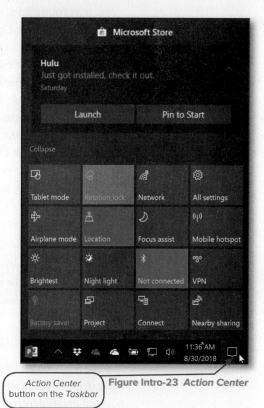

> **ANOTHER WAY**
>
> **Windows+A** opens the *Action Center.* The *Windows* key is typically located near the bottom-left corner of the keyboard.

Action Center button on the *Taskbar*

Figure Intro-23 *Action Center*

Using Microsoft Office

Microsoft Office includes common software applications such as Word, Excel, Access, and PowerPoint. These applications give you the ability to work with word processing documents, spreadsheets, presentations, and databases in your personal and business projects. Microsoft offers a variety of Office products and gives users the ability to work with these productivity apps on different technology devices.

Figure Intro-24 Microsoft Office application tiles on the *Start* menu

Office 2019 and Office 365

Microsoft Office is a suite of personal and business software applications (Figure Intro-24). *Microsoft Office 2019* and *Microsoft Office 365* are similar software products; the difference is how you purchase the software. Office 2019 is the traditional model of purchasing the software, and you own that software for as long as you want to use it. Office 365 is a subscription that you pay monthly or yearly, similar to how you purchase Netflix or Spotify. If you subscribe to Office 365, you automatically receive updated versions of the applications when they are released.

The common applications typically included in Microsoft Office 2019 and 365 are described in the following list:

- *Microsoft Word*: Word processing software used to create, format, and edit documents such as reports, letters, brochures, and resumes
- *Microsoft Excel*: Spreadsheet software used to perform calculations on numerical data such as financial statements, budgets, and expense reports
- *Microsoft Access*: Database software used to store, organize, compile, and report information such as product information, sales data, client information, and employee records
- *Microsoft PowerPoint*: Presentation software used to graphically present information in slides such as a presentation on a new product or sales trends
- *Microsoft Outlook*: Email and personal management software used to create and send email and to create and store calendar items, contacts, and tasks
- *Microsoft OneNote*: Note-taking software used to take and organize notes, which can be shared with other Office applications
- *Microsoft Publisher*: Desktop publishing software used to create professional-looking documents containing text, pictures, and graphics such as catalogs, brochures, and flyers

 MORE INFO

Office 365 includes regular updates that include new and enhanced features, while Office 2019 does not include these regular updates. So, differences in features may exist between the Office 2019 and Office 365.

Office 365 Products, Versions, and Update Channels

Office 365 is a subscription to the Office applications and can be purchased for home or business. Also, as a student, you can get Office 365 for education free (https://products.office.com/en-us/student/office-in-education). The Office applications that come with an Office 365 subscription can vary depending on the Office 365 product subscription you have. With an Office 365 subscription, you can install the Office applications (both PC and Mac) on multiple computers and mobile devices.

Another advantage of an Office 365 subscription is regular updates that enhance the functionality of the apps. The version and build of your Office 365 is determined by the update channel, which is the frequency of updates. This is typically set by your school or business. If you have Office 365 Home or Personal, you determine the update channel. If you have an Office 365 for education or business, the college or business determines the update channel. The following are common update channels:

- *Semi-annual Channel*: Receives updates two times a year in January and July
- *Semi-annual Channel (Targeted)*: Receives new feature updates earlier than the Semi-annual Channel. These semi-annual updates are rolled out in March and September.
- *Monthly Channel*: Receives new feature updates as soon as they are available, which is typically every month

▶ HOW TO: View Your Office 365 Product Information

1. Open an Office application and open a blank or existing file if necessary.
2. Click the **File** tab to open the *Backstage* view.
3. Click **Account** at the left to display *User Information* and *Product Information*.

   - The *Product Information* area displays the Office 365 product installed on your computer (Figure Intro-25).
   - The *About [Application]* area displays the version, build, and update channel.
   - The *Version* number indicates the year and month of the most recent update. For example, "Version 1808" means 2018 and the eighth month (August).

4. Click the **Update Options** button to select an update option: *Update Now, Disable Updates, View Updates,* or *About Updates.*

   - Click the **Update Now** button to manually check for Office 365 updates.

5. Click the **What's New** button to view the new features included in the most recent Office 365 updates for your update channel.
6. Close the **Back** arrow to close the *Backstage* view and return to the file.

Figure Intro-25 *Product Information* displayed in the *Account* area on the *Backstage* view

Office Desktop Apps, Office Mobile Apps, and Office Online

Office desktop apps are the full-function Office 2019 or 365 programs installed on your computer (PC or Mac). Both Office 2019 and Office 365 are considered Office desktop apps. Because of the increased popularity and capabilities of tablets and mobile devices, Office software is also available for both tablets and smartphones. *Office mobile apps* are the Office 365 programs that can be installed on tablets or other mobile devices. Office mobile apps do not have the full range of advanced features available in Office desktop applications, but Office mobile apps provide users the ability to create, edit, save, and share Office files using many of the most common features in the Office suite of programs.

The *Office Online* apps are free online apps from Microsoft that work in conjunction with your Microsoft account and *OneDrive* (Figure Intro-26). With *Office Online*, you can work with Office files online through a web browser, even on computers that do not have Office 2019 or 365 installed. Click the **App** launcher in the upper-left corner of *OneDrive* to display the *Office Online* applications. This list of *Office Online* apps may display differently depending on the type of Microsoft account you are using.

Figure Intro-26 *Office Online*

You can access *Office Online* from your *OneDrive* web page to create and edit Word documents, Excel workbooks, PowerPoint presentations, and OneNote notebooks. *Office Online* is a scaled-down version of Office and not as robust in terms of features, but you can use it to create, edit, print, share, and collaborate on files. If you need more advanced features, you can open *Office Online* files in the desktop version of Office.

▶ HOW TO: Create an Office Online File

1. Open an internet browser Window, navigate to the *OneDrive* web site (www.onedrive.live.com), and log in to *OneDrive*. If you are not already logged in to *OneDrive*, use the following steps.

   - Click the **Sign in** button, type your Microsoft account email address, and click **Next**.
   - Type your Microsoft account password and click **Sign in** to open your *OneDrive* page.

2. Click the **New** button and select the type of *Office Online* file to create (Figure Intro-27).

   - A new file opens in the *Office Online* program.
   - The new file is saved in your *OneDrive* folder (both online and on your computer).

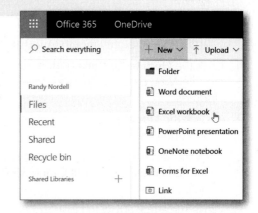

Figure Intro-27 Create an *Office Online* file from your online *OneDrive* page

3. Rename the file by clicking the file name at the top of the file, typing a new file name, and pressing **Enter** (Figure Intro-28).

   - You can also click the **File** tab to open the *Backstage* view, select **Save As**, and choose **Save As** or **Rename**.
   - Click the **Open in [Office application]** button (for example, **Open in Excel**) to open the file in the Office desktop application (see Figure Intro-28).

4. Close the browser tab or window to close the file.

   - *Office Online* automatically saves the file as you make changes.

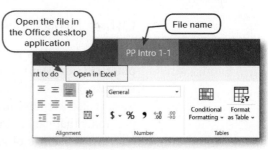

Figure Intro-28 Rename an *Office Online* file

Open an Office Desktop Application

When using Windows 10, you open an Office desktop application by clicking the application tile on the *Start* menu or the application icon on the *Taskbar*. If your *Start* menu and *Taskbar* do not display the Office applications, click the **Start** button and select **Word**, **Excel**, **Access**, or **PowerPoint** from the alphabetic list of apps to launch the application (Figure Intro-29).

You can also use *Cortana* to quickly locate an Office desktop app (Figure Intro-30).

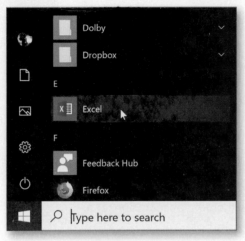

Figure Intro-29 Open an Office desktop app from the *All apps* area on the *Start* menu

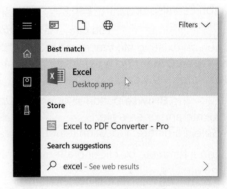

Figure Intro-30 Use *Cortana* to find and open an app

> ▶ **MORE INFO**
>
> Add commonly used apps to your Windows *Start* menu and/or *Taskbar* to save time. See the "Customize the *Start* Menu" and "Customize the *Taskbar*" sections in *SLO Intro.1: Using Windows 10*.

Office Start Page

Most of the Office applications (except Outlook and OneNote) display a ***Start page*** when you launch the application (Figure Intro-31). From this *Start* page, you can create a new blank file (for example, a Word document, an Excel workbook, an Access database, or a PowerPoint presentation), create a file from an online template, search for an online template, open a recently used file, or open another file. These options vary depending on the Office application.

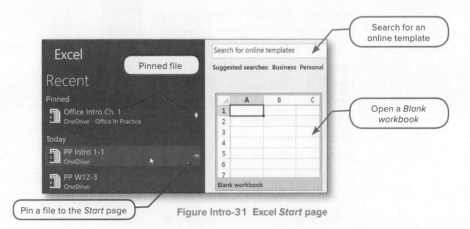

Figure Intro-31 Excel *Start* page

▶ HOW TO: Use the Office Start Page

1. Open an Office application from the *Start* page or *Taskbar*.
2. Open a file listed in the *Recent* area on the left side of the *Start* menu by clicking the file name. The file opens in the working area of the Office application.

   - The *Recent* area on the left side of the *Start* page displays recently used and pinned files.

3. Open a new blank file by clicking the **Blank *[file type]*** tile (*Blank workbook, Blank document,* etc.) to the right of the *Recent* area (see Figure Intro-31).

   - You can also press the **Esc** key to exit the *Start* page and open a new blank file.

4. Open an existing file that is not listed in the *Recent* area by clicking the **Open Other *[file type]*** link (Figure Intro-32). The *Open* area on the *Backstage* view displays.

   - Click the **Browse** button to open the *Open* dialog box where you can locate and open a file.
   - Select a different location (*OneDrive* or *This PC*) and select a file to open.

Figure Intro-32 *Open Other Workbooks* link on the *Start* page

5. Open a template by clicking a template file on the right or searching for a template.

   - Search for a template by typing keywords in the *Search* area on the *Start* page.
   - Click a link to one of the categories below the *Search* area to display templates in that category.

6. Pin a frequently used file to the *Start* page by clicking the **pin** icon (see Figure Intro-31).

   - The pin icon is on the right side of items listed in the *Recent* area and at the bottom right of templates displayed in the *Templates* area (to the right of the *Recent* area).
   - Pinned files display at the top of the *Recent* area.

> ▶ **MORE INFO**
>
> In Access, you have to open an existing database or create a new one to enter the program.

Backstage View

Office incorporates the ***Backstage view*** into all Office applications (including *Office Online* apps). Click the **File** tab on the *Ribbon* to open the *Backstage* view (Figure Intro-33). *Backstage* options vary depending on the Office application. The following list describes common tasks you can perform from the *Backstage* view:

Figure Intro-33 *Backstage* view in Excel

- ***Info***: Displays document properties and other protection, inspection, and version options.

- *New*: Creates a new blank file or a new file from a template or theme.
- *Open*: Opens an existing file from a designated location or a recently opened file.
- *Save*: Saves a file. If the file has not been named, the *Save As* dialog box opens when you select this option.
- *Save As*: Opens the *Save As* dialog box.
- *Print*: Prints a file, displays a preview of the file, or displays print options.
- *Share*: Invites people to share a file or email a file.
- *Export*: Creates a PDF file from a file or saves it as a different file type.
- *Close*: Closes an open file.
- *Account*: Displays your Microsoft account information.
- *Options*: Opens the *[Application] Options* dialog box (for example, *Excel Options*).

> **MORE INFO**
>
> Options on the *Backstage* view vary depending on the Office application you are using.

Office Help—Tell Me

In all the Office 2019/365 applications, **Tell Me** is the help feature (Figure Intro-34). This feature displays the commands in the Office application related to your search. The *Help* feature in older versions of Office displayed articles describing the feature and how to use it. The *Tell Me* feature provides command options that take you directly to a command or dialog box. For example, if you type *PivotTable* in the *Tell Me* search box in Excel, the results include the option to open the *Create PivotTable* dialog box, as well as other options such as *Recommended PivotTables* and *Summarize with PivotTable*.

Figure Intro-34 *Tell Me* search box

> ▶**HOW TO: Use Tell Me**

1. Place the insertion point in the **Tell me what you want to do** search box at the top of the *Ribbon* (see Figure Intro-34).
2. Type keywords for the command or feature for which you are searching.
3. Select an option from the search results list (Figure Intro-35).
   - When you select a search result, it may apply a command, open a dialog box, or display a gallery of command choices.

Figure Intro-35 *Tell Me* search results

> **ANOTHER WAY**
>
> **Alt+Q** places the insertion point in the *Tell Me* dialog box.
> The previous *Help* feature is still available in Office. Press **F1** to open the *Help* pane on the right.

Mouse and Pointers

If you are using Office on a desktop or laptop computer, use your mouse (or touchpad) to navigate around files, click tabs and buttons, select text and objects, move text and objects, and resize objects. Table Intro-1 lists mouse and pointer terminology used in Office.

Table Intro-1: Mouse and Pointer Terminology

Term	Description
Pointer	Move your mouse to move the pointer on your screen. A variety of pointers are used in different contexts in Office applications. The following pointers are available in most of the Office applications (the appearance of these pointers varies depending on the application and the context used): • *Selection pointer:* Select text or an object. • *Move pointer:* Move text or an object. • *Copy pointer:* Copy text or an object. • *Resize pointer:* Resize objects or table columns or rows. • *Crosshair:* Draw a shape.
Insertion point	The vertical flashing line indicating where you type text in a file or text box. Click the left mouse button to position the insertion point.
Click	Click the left mouse button. Used to select an object or button or to place the insertion point in the selected location.
Double-click	Click the left mouse button twice. Used to select text.
Right-click	Click the right mouse button. Used to display the context menu and the mini toolbar.
Scroll	Use the scroll wheel on the mouse to scroll up and down through your file. You can also use the horizontal or vertical scroll bars at the bottom and right of an Office file window to move around in a file.

Touch Mode and Touch-Screen Gestures

The user interface in Windows 10 and Office 2019 has improved touch features to facilitate the use of Windows and the Office applications on a tablet computer or smartphone. On tablets and smartphones, you can use a touch screen rather than using a mouse, so the process of selecting text and objects and navigating around a file is different from a computer without a touch screen.

In Office 2019/365, *Touch mode* optimizes the Office working environment when using a computer with a touch screen to provide more space between buttons and commands. Click the **Touch/Mouse Mode** button on the *Quick Access* toolbar (upper left of the Office app window) and select **Touch** from the drop-down list to enable *Touch* mode (Figure Intro-36). To turn off *Touch* mode, select **Mouse** from the *Touch/ Mouse Mode* drop-down list.

Figure Intro-36 Turn on *Touch* mode

> ### MORE INFO
>
> The *Touch/Mouse Mode* button displays on the *Quick Access* toolbar when using a touch-screen computer.

Table Intro-2 lists common gestures used when working on a tablet or smartphone (these gestures vary depending on the application used and the context).

Table Intro-2: Touch-Screen Gestures

Gesture	Used To	How To
Tap	Select text or an object or position the insertion point. Double tap to edit text in an object or cell.	
Pinch	Zoom in or resize an object.	
Stretch	Zoom out or resize an object.	
Slide	Move an object or selected text.	
Swipe	Select text or multiple objects.	

> **MORE INFO**
>
> Window 10 has a *Tablet mode* that optimizes all of Windows and apps for touch screens. When you turn on the *Tablet mode* feature in Windows, the *Touch mode* in Office apps turns on automatically. Click the **Action Center** button on the Windows *Taskbar* and click the **Tablet mode** button to turn on this feature in Windows.

SLO INTRO. 3

Creating, Saving, Closing, and Opening Office Files

Creating, saving, opening, and closing files is primarily done from the *Start* page or *Backstage* view of the active Office application. Both the *Start* page and the *Backstage* view provide many options and a central location to perform these tasks. You can also use shortcut commands to create, save, and open files.

Create a New File

When you create a new file in an Office application, you can create a new blank file or a new file based on a template (in PowerPoint, you can also create a presentation based on a theme). On the *Start* page, click **Blank** *[file type]* to create a new blank file in the application you are using (in Word, you begin with a blank document; in Excel, a blank workbook; in Access, a blank desktop database; and in PowerPoint, a blank presentation).

▶HOW TO: Create a New File from the Start Page

1. Open an Office application. The *Start* page displays when the application opens (Figure Intro-37).

2. Click **Blank *[file type]*** to open a new file.

   - The new file displays a generic file name (for example, *Document1, Book1,* or *Presentation1*). You can rename and save this file later.
   - When creating a new Access database, you are prompted to name the new file when you create it.
   - A variety of templates (and themes in PowerPoint only) display on the *Start* page, and you can search for additional online templates and themes using the *Search* text box at the top of the *Start* page.

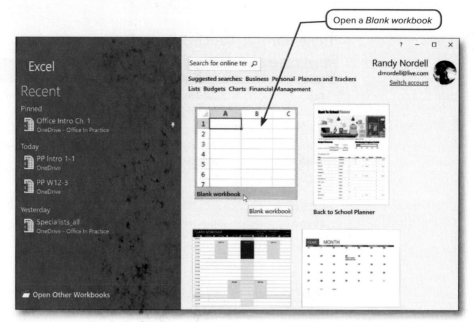

Open a *Blank workbook*

Figure Intro-37 *Start* page in Excel

> ### MORE INFO
>
> **Esc** closes the *Start* page opens a blank file in the Office application (except in Access).

If you have been using an application already and want to create a new file, you create it from the *Backstage* view. From the *Backstage* view, the new file options are available in the *New* area.

▶HOW TO: Create a New File from the Backstage View

1. Click the **File** tab to display the *Backstage* view.

2. Select **New** on the left to display the *New* area (Figure Intro-38).

3. Click **Blank *[file type]*** to open a new blank file or select a template or theme to use.

   - The new file displays a generic file name (*Document1, Book1,* or *Presentation1*). You can name and save this file later.
   - When you are creating a new Access database, you are prompted to name the new file when you create it.

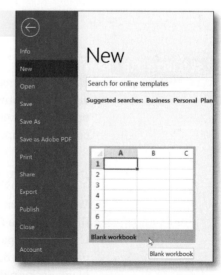

Figure Intro-38 *New* area on the *Backstage* view in Excel

Save a File

In Access, you name a file as you create it, but in Word, Excel, and PowerPoint, you name a file after you have created it. When you save a file, you type a name for the file and select the location to save the file. You can save a file on your computer, an online storage location such as *OneDrive,* or portable device, such as a USB drive.

▶HOW TO: Save a File

1. Click the **File** tab to display the *Backstage* view.
2. Select **Save** or **Save As** on the left to display the *Save As* area (Figure Intro-39).
   - If the file has not already been saved, clicking *Save* or *Save As* takes you to the *Save As* area on the *Backstage* view.
3. Click the **Browse** button to open the *Save As* dialog box (Figure Intro-40).
   - Alternatively, type the file name in the *Enter file name here* text box and click **Save**. To change the save location, click the **More options** link to open the *Save As* dialog box or select a save location at the left (*OneDrive* or *This PC*) and select a folder from the list of folders (see Figure Intro-39).
4. Select a location to save the file in the *Folder* list on the left.
5. Type a name for the file in the *File name* area.
   - By default, Office selects the file type, but you can change the file type from the *Save as type* drop-down list.
6. Click **Save** to close the dialog box and save the file.

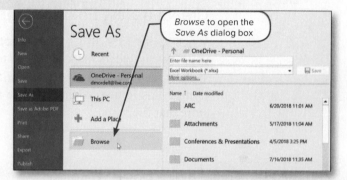

Figure Intro-39 *Save As* area on the *Backstage* view in Excel

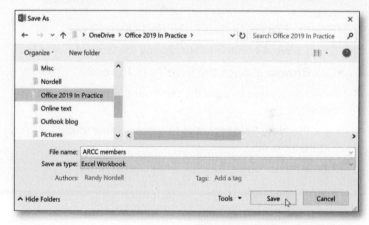

Figure Intro-40 *Save As* dialog box

AutoSave

AutoSave is a new feature that automatically saves a file that is stored on *OneDrive,* Microsoft's cloud storage area. The *AutoSave* feature turns on by default when you save a file to *OneDrive,* and changes made to the file are automatically saved as you work on a file.

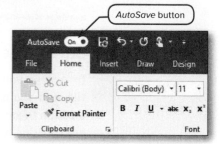

Office 2019 Note: The *AutoSave* feature is not available in Office 2019.

This feature displays in the upper-left corner of the file (Figure Intro-41). Click the **AutoSave** button to turn it on or off. When *AutoSave* is on, the save options on the *Backstage* view change from *Save* and *Save As* to *Save a Copy.*

Figure Intro-41 *AutoSave* feature

Create a New Folder When Saving a File

When saving files, it is a good practice to create folders to organize your files. Organizing your files in folders makes it easier to find files and saves time when you are searching for a specific file (see *SLO Intro.8: Organizing and Customizing Folders and Files* for more information on this topic). When you save an Office file, you can also create a folder in which to store that file.

> ▶ **HOW TO:** Create a New Folder When Saving a File

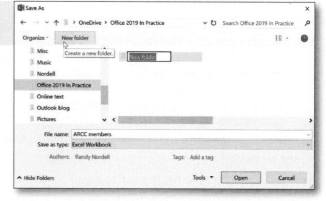

1. Click the **File** tab to display the *Backstage* view.
2. Select **Save As** on the left to display the *Save As* area.
3. Click **Browse** to open the *Save As* dialog box.
4. Select a location to save the file from the *Folder* list on the left.
5. Click the **New Folder** button to create a new folder (Figure Intro-42).
6. Type a name for the new folder and press **Enter**.

Figure Intro-42 Create a new folder

> ▶ **ANOTHER WAY**
>
> **F12** opens the *Save As* dialog box (except in Access). On a laptop, you might have to press **Fn+F12**. See more about the *Fn* (Function) key in *SLO Intro. 7: Using Context Menus, the Mini Toolbar, and Keyboard Shortcuts.*

Save As a Different File Name

After you have saved a file, you can save it again with a different file name. If you do this, you preserve the original file, and you can continue to revise the second file for a different purpose.

▶ HOW TO: Save As a Different File Name

1. Click the **File** tab to display the *Backstage* view.
2. Select **Save As** on the left to display the *Save As* area.
3. Click the **Browse** button to open the *Save As* dialog box (see Figure Intro-42).
4. Select a location to save the file from the *Folder* list on the left.
5. Type a new name for the file in the *File name* area.
6. Click **Save** to close the dialog box and save the file.

 MORE INFO

If *AutoSave* is turned on, *Save a Copy* is the save option on the *Backstage* view rather than *Save* and *Save As*.

Office File Types

By default, Office saves a file in the most current file format for that application. You also have the option of saving files in older versions of the Office application. For example, you can save a Word document as an older version to share with or send to someone who uses an older version of Word. Each file has an extension at the end of the file name that determines the file type. The *file name extension* is automatically added to a file when you save it. Table Intro-3 table lists common file types used in the different Office applications.

Table Intro-3: Office File Types

File Type	Extension	File Type	Extension
Word Document	.docx	Access Database	.accdb
Word Template	.dotx	Access Template	.accdt
Word 97-2003 Document	.doc	Access Database (2000-2003 format)	.mdb
Rich Text Format	.rtf	PowerPoint Presentation	.pptx
Excel Workbook	.xlsx	PowerPoint Template	.potx
Excel Template	.xltx	PowerPoint 97-2003 Presentation	.ppt
Excel 97-2003 Workbook	.xls	Portable Document Format (PDF)	.pdf
Comma Separated Values (CSV)	.csv		

Close a File

You can close a file using the following different methods:

- Click the **File** tab and select **Close** on the left.
- Press **Ctrl+W**.
- Click the **X** in the upper-right corner of the file window. This method closes the file and the program if only one file is open in the application.

When you close a file, you are prompted to save the file if it has not been named or if changes were made after the file was last saved (Figure Intro-43). Click **Save** to save and close the file or click **Don't Save** to close the file without saving. Click **Cancel** to return to the file.

Figure Intro-43 Prompt to save a document before closing

Open an Existing File

You can open an existing file from the *Start* page when you open an Office application or while you are working on another Office file.

▶HOW TO: Open a File from the Start Page

1. Open an Office application to display the *Start* page.
2. Select a file to open in the *Recent* area on the left (Figure Intro-44).
   - If you select a file in the *Recent* area that has been renamed, moved, or is on a storage device not connected to the computer, you receive an error message.
3. Alternatively, click **Open Other [*file type*]** (for example, *Open Other Presentations*) to display the *Open* area of the *Backstage* view (see Figure Intro-44).
   - Click the **Browse** button to open the *Open* dialog box (Figure Intro-45).
   - Select a location from the *Folder* list on the left.
   - Select the file to open and click the **Open** button.
   - If the file opens in *Protected View*, click the **Enable Editing** button to enable you to edit the file.

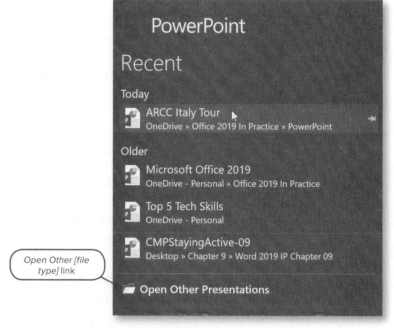

Open Other [file type] link

Figure Intro-44 Open a *Recent* file from the *Start* page

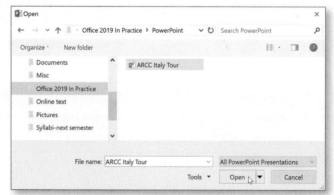

Figure Intro-45 *Open* dialog box

When working on a file in an Office application, you might want to open another file. You can open an existing file from within an Office application using the *Open* area on the *Backstage* view.

▶ HOW TO: Open a File from the Backstage View

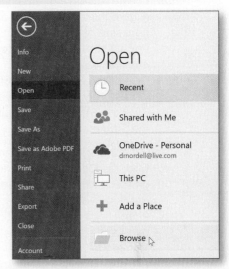

1. Click the **File** tab from within an open Office application to display the *Backstage* view.
2. Click **Open** on the left to display the *Open* area on the *Backstage* view (Figure Intro-46).
3. Click the **Browse** button to open the *Open* dialog box.
   - Alternatively, select a file to open from the list of *Recent* files on the right of the *Open* area on the *Backstage* view.
4. Select a location from the *Folder* list on the left.
5. Select the file to open and click the **Open** button.
   - If the file opens in *Protected View,* click the **Enable Editing** button to enable you to edit the file.

Figure Intro-46 *Open* area on the *Backstage* view

You can also open a file from a *File Explorer* folder. When you double-click a file in a *File Explorer* folder, the file opens in the appropriate Office application. Windows recognizes the file name extension and launches the correct Office application.

PAUSE & PRACTICE: INTRO-1

For this project, you log in to Windows using your Microsoft account, customize the Windows *Start* menu and *Taskbar,* create and save a PowerPoint presentation, create a folder, open and rename an Excel workbook, and use Windows 10 features.

File Needed: ***ARCC2020Budget-Intro.xlsx*** *(Student data files are available in the* Library *of your SIMnet account.)*
Completed Project File Names: *[your initials] PP Intro-1a.pptx* and *[your initials] PP Intro-1b.xlsx*

1. Log in to Windows using your Microsoft account if you are not already logged in.
   a. If you don't have a Microsoft account, you can create a free account at https://signup.live.com.
   b. If you are using a computer on your college campus, you may be required to log in to the computer using your college user name and password.

2. Pin the Office apps to the *Start* menu. If these apps tiles are already on the *Start* menu, skip steps 2a–e. You can pin other apps of your choice to the *Start* menu.
   a. Click the **Start** button at the bottom left of your screen to open the *Start* menu.
   b. Locate *Access* in the alphabetic list of apps, right-click the **Access** app, and select **Pin to Start** (Figure Intro-47). The app displays as a tile on the right side of the *Start* menu.
   c. Repeat step 2b to pin **Excel**, **PowerPoint**, and **Word** apps to the *Start* menu.
   d. Display the *Start* menu and drag these Office app tiles so they are close to each other.
   e. Click the **Start** button (or press the **Esc** key) to close the *Start* menu.

Figure Intro-47 Pin *Access* to the *Start* menu

3. Use *Cortana* and the *Start* menu to pin Office apps to the *Taskbar.*
   a. Click the **Cortana** button (to the right of the *Start* button) on the *Taskbar* and type *Access*. *Cortana* displays content matching your search.
   b. Right-click the **Access** option near the top of the *Cortana* pane and select **Pin to taskbar** (Figure Intro-48). The app pins to the *Taskbar.*
   c. Click the **Start** button to open the *Start* menu.
   d. Right-click the **Excel** tile on the right side of the *Start* menu, click **More**, and select **Pin to taskbar**. The app pins to the *Taskbar.*
   e. Use either of the methods described above to pin the **PowerPoint** and **Word** apps to the *Taskbar.*
   f. Drag the Office apps on the *Taskbar* to rearrange them to your preference.

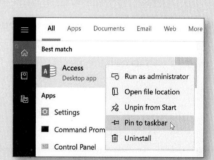

Figure Intro-48 Use *Cortana* to find an Office app and pin it to the *Taskbar*

4. Create a PowerPoint presentation and save the presentation in a new folder.
   a. Click the **PowerPoint** app tile on your *Start* menu to open the application.
   b. Click **Blank Presentation** on the PowerPoint *Start* page to create a new blank presentation.
   c. Click the **Click to add title** placeholder and type American River Cycling Club to replace the placeholder text.
   d. Click the **File** tab to open the *Backstage* view and click **Save As** on the left to display the *Save As* area.
   e. Click **Browse** to open the *Save As* dialog box (Figure Intro-49).
   f. Select a location to save the file from the *Folder* list on the left. If the *OneDrive* folder is an option, select **OneDrive**. If it is not, select the **Documents** folder in the *This PC* folder. You can also save to a portable storage device if you have one.
   g. Click the **New Folder** button to create a new folder.

Figure Intro-49 *Save As* area on the *Backstage* view in PowerPoint

h. Type American River Cycling Club as the name of the new folder and press **Enter** (Figure Intro-50).

i. Double-click the ***American River Cycling Club*** folder to open it.

j. Type [your initials] PP Intro-1a in the *File name* area.

k. Click **Save** to close the dialog box and save the presentation. Leave the file and PowerPoint open. If you saved your file to OneDrive, you may receive a notification about automatic saving.

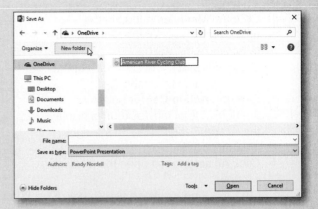

Figure Intro-50 Create a new folder from the *Save As* dialog box

5. Open an Excel file and save as a different file name.

a. Click the **Excel 2019** app button on the *Taskbar* to open the *Start* page in Excel.

b. Click the **Open Other Workbooks** link on the bottom left of the Excel *Start* page to display the *Open* area of the *Backstage* view.

c. Click **Browse** to open the *Open* dialog box (Figure Intro-51).

d. Browse to your student data files and select the ***ARCC2020Budget-Intro*** file.

e. Click **Open** to open the workbook. If the file opens in *Protected View,* click the **Enable Editing** button.

f. Click the **File** tab to open the *Backstage* view.

g. Click **Save As** on the left to display the *Save As* area and click **Browse** to open the *Save As* dialog box. If this file is stored on OneDrive, click **Save a Copy** rather than *Save As.*

Figure Intro-51 *Open* area on the *Backstage* view

h. Locate the ***American River Cycling Club*** folder (created in step 4h) in the *Folder* list on the left and double-click the folder to open it.

i. Type [your initials] PP Intro-1b in the *File name* area.

j. Click **Save** to close the dialog box and save the workbook. Leave the file and Excel open.

6. Use the *Tell Me* feature in Excel to find a command.

a. Click the **Tell Me** search box on the *Ribbon* of the Excel window and type PivotTable (Figure Intro-52).

b. Click **PivotTable** to open the *Create PivotTable* dialog box.

c. Click the **X** in the upper-right corner of the *Create PivotTable* dialog box to close it.

7. Open the *Microsoft Store* app, the *Action Center*, and the *Settings* window.

a. Click the **Cortana** search area and type Microsoft Store.

b. Click **Microsoft Store** at the top of the *Cortana* pane to open the *Microsoft Store* app.

c. Click the **Apps** tab in the top left and browse the available apps in the Microsoft Store.

Figure Intro-52 Use the *Tell Me* feature to find a command

d. Click the **Minimize** button in the
    upper-right corner of the *Store* window
    to minimize this app
    (Figure Intro-53). The app is still open,
    but it is minimized on the *Taskbar.*

Acton Center button

e. Click the **Action Center** button on
    the right side of the *Taskbar* to display
    the *Action Center* pane on the right
    (Figure Intro-54).

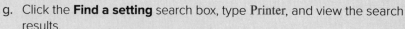

Minimize button

f. Click **All settings** to open the *Settings*
    window.

Figure Intro-53 *Minimize*
button on an app window

g. Click the **Find a setting** search box, type Printer, and view the search
    results.

Figure Intro-54 Windows 10
Action Center

h. Click the **Minimize** button to minimize the *Settings* windows to the
    Taskbar.

8. Use the *Task View* feature to open and close apps and windows.

a. Click the **Task View** button on the left side of the *Taskbar*
    (Figure Intro-55). All open apps and windows display tiled on the Windows desktop.

b. Click the **Store** app to open it. *Task
    View* closes and the *Store* app dis-
    plays on your Windows desktop.

c. Click the **Task View** button again.

d. Click the **X** in the upper-right corner
    to close each open app and win-
    dow. You may be prompted to save
    changes to a file.

Task View button

e. Click the **Task View** button again or
    press **Esc** to return to the desktop.

Figure Intro-55 *Task View* button on the *Taskbar*

SLO INTRO. 4

Working with Files

When you work with Office files, a variety of display views are available. You can change how
a file displays, adjust the display size, work with multiple files, and arrange windows to view
multiple files. Because most people work with multiple files at the same time, Office makes it
easy and intuitive to move from one file to another or to display multiple document windows
at the same time.

File Views

Each of the different Office applications provides
you with a variety of ways to view your document. In
Word, Excel, and PowerPoint, the different views are
available on the *View tab* (Figure Intro-56). You can
also change views using the buttons on the right side
of the *Status bar* at the bottom of the file window (Figure Intro-57). In Access, the different
views for each object are available in the *Views*
group on the *Home* tab.

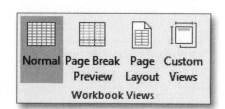

Normal Page Break   Page   Custom
        Preview   Layout   Views

Workbook Views

Figure Intro-56 *Workbook Views* group
on the *View* tab in Excel

Figure Intro-57 PowerPoint views on the *Status* bar

Table Intro-4 lists the views that are available in each of the different Office applications.

Table Intro-4: File Views

Office Application	Views	Office Application	Views
Word	*Read Mode* *Print Layout* *web Layout* *Outline* *Draft*	**Access** *(Access views vary* *depending on active* *object)*	*Layout View* *Design View* *Datasheet View* *Form View* *SQL View* *Report View* *Print Preview*
Excel	*Normal* *Page Break Preview* *Page Layout* *Custom Views*	**PowerPoint**	*Normal* *Outline View* *Slide Sorter* *Notes Page* *Reading View* *Presenter View*

Change Display Size

Use the ***Zoom*** feature to increase or decrease the display size of your file. Using *Zoom* to change the display size does not change the actual size of text or objects in your file; it only changes the size of your display. For example, if you change the *Zoom* level to 120%, you increase the display of your file to 120% of its normal size (100%), but changing the display size does not affect the actual size of text and objects in your file. Decrease the *Zoom* level to 80% to display more of your file on the screen.

You can increase or decrease the *Zoom* level several different ways. Your *Zoom* options vary depending on the Office application.

- ***Zoom level*** *on the Status* bar (Figure Intro-58): Click the + or − button to increase or decrease *Zoom* level in 10% increments.
- ***Zoom group*** *on the View tab* (Figure Intro-59): The *Zoom* group includes a variety of *Zoom* options. The options vary depending on the Office application.
- ***Zoom dialog box*** (Figure Intro-60): Click the **Zoom** button in the *Zoom* group on the *View* tab or click the **Zoom level** on the *Status* bar to open the *Zoom* dialog box.

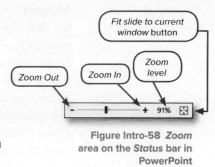

Figure Intro-58 *Zoom* area on the *Status* bar in PowerPoint

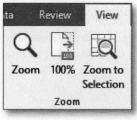

Figure Intro-59 *Zoom* group in Excel

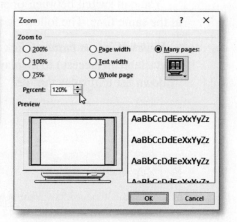

Figure Intro-60 *Zoom* dialog box in Word

Manage Multiple Open Files and Windows

When you are working on multiple files in an Office application, each file is opened in a new window. *Minimize* an open window to place the file on the Windows *Taskbar* (the bar at the bottom of the Windows desktop), *restore down* an open window so it does not fill the entire computer screen, or *maximize* a window so it fills the entire computer screen. The *Minimize, Restore Down/Maximize,* and *Close* buttons are in the upper-right corner of a file window (Figure Intro-61).

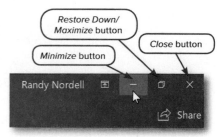

Figure Intro-61 Window options buttons

- *Minimize*: Click the **Minimize** button (see Figure Intro-61) to hide the active window. When a document is minimized, it is not closed. It is reduced to a button on the *Taskbar* and the window does not display. Place your pointer on the application icon on the Windows *Taskbar* to display thumbnails of open files. Click an open file thumbnail to display the file (Figure Intro-62).

- *Restore Down/Maximize*: Click the **Restore Down/ Maximize** button (see Figure Intro-61) to decrease the size of an open window or to maximize the window to fill the entire screen. This button toggles between *Restore Down* and *Maximize*. When a window is restored down, change the size of a window by clicking and dragging a border of the window. You

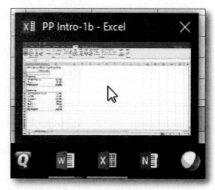

Figure Intro-62 Display minimized file on the *Taskbar*

can also move the window by clicking and dragging the title bar at the top of the window.

- *Close*: Click the **Close** button (see Figure Intro-61) to close the window. If there is only one open file, the Office application also closes when you click the *Close* button on the file.

You can switch between open files or arrange open files to display more than one window at the same time. The following are several methods to do this:

- *Switch Windows button*: Click the **Switch Windows** button [*View* tab, *Window* group] (not available in Access) to display a drop-down list of open files. Click a file from the drop-down list to display the file.

- **Windows Taskbar.** Place your pointer on an Office application icon on the Windows *Taskbar* to display the open files in that application. Click a file thumbnail to display it (see Figure Intro-62).
- **Arrange All button**: Click the **Arrange All** button [*View* tab, *Window* group] to display all windows in an application. You can resize or move the open file windows.

Snap Assist

The *Snap Assist* feature in Windows provides the ability to position an open window to the left or right side of your computer screen and fill half the screen. When you snap an open window to the left or right side of the screen, the other open windows tile on the opposite side where you can select another window to fill the opposite side of the computer screen (Figure Intro-63).

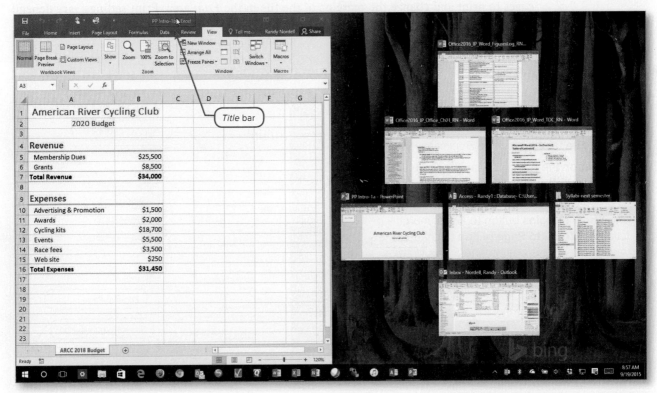

Figure Intro-63 Windows *Snap Assist* feature

▶HOW TO: Use Snap Assist

1. Click the **title bar** of an open window.
2. Drag it to the left or right edge of the computer screen and release the pointer.
   - The window snaps to the side of the screen and fills half of the computer screen (see Figure Intro-63).
   - The other open windows and apps display as tiles on the opposite side.
   - If you use a touch-screen computer, press and hold the title bar of an open window and drag to either side of the computer screen.
3. Select a tile of an open window or app to fill the other half of the screen.

> MORE INFO
>
> *Snap Assist* also enables you to snap a window to a quadrant (quarter rather than half) of your screen. Drag the **title bar** of an open window to one of the four corners of your computer screen.

Printing, Sharing, and Customizing Files

SLO INTRO. 5

Use *Backstage* view in any of the Office applications, to print a file and to customize how a file is printed. You can also export an Office file as a PDF file in most of the Office applications. In addition, you can add and customize document properties for an Office file and share a file in a variety of formats.

Print a File

Print an Office file if you need a hard copy. The *Print* area on the *Backstage* view displays a preview of the open file and many print options. For example, you can choose which page or pages to print and change the margins of the file in the *Print* area. Print settings vary depending on the Office application you are using and what you are printing.

> **HOW TO: Print a File**

1. Open the file you want to print from a Windows folder or within an Office program.
2. Click the **File** tab to open the *Backstage* view.
3. Click **Print** on the left to display the *Print* area (Figure Intro-64).
   - A preview of the file displays on the right. Click the **Show Margins** button to adjust margins or click the **Zoom to Page** button to change the view in the *Preview* area. The *Show Margins* button is only available in Excel.
4. Change the number of copies to print in the *Copies* area.
5. Click the **Printer** drop-down list to choose from available printers.
6. Customize what is printed and how it is printed in the *Settings* area.
   - The *Settings* options vary depending on the Office application and what you print.
   - In the *Pages* area (*Slides* area in PowerPoint), select a page or range of pages (slides) to print.
   - By default, all pages (slides) are printed when you print a file.
7. Click the **Print** button to print your file.

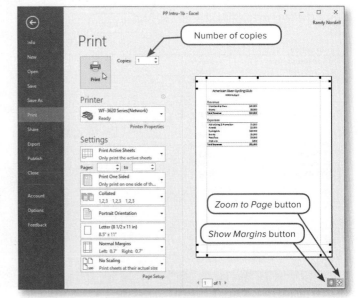

Figure Intro-64 *Print* area on the *Backstage* view

> **ANOTHER WAY**
>
> Press **Ctrl+P** to open the *Print* area on the *Backstage* view.

Export as a PDF File

Portable document format, or ***PDF***, is a specific file format that is often used to share files that are not to be changed, or to post files on a web site. When you create a PDF file from an Office application file, you are actually exporting a static image of the original file, similar to taking a picture of the file.

The advantage of working with a PDF file is that the format of the file is retained no matter who opens the file. PDF files open in the Windows Reader app or Adobe Reader, which is free software that is installed on most computers. Because a PDF file is a static image of a file, it is not easy for other people to edit your files. When you want people to be able to view a file but not change it, PDF files are a good choice.

> **HOW TO:** Export a File as a PDF File

1. Open the file you want to export as a PDF file.
2. Click the **File** tab and click **Export** to display the *Export* area on the Backstage view (Figure Intro-65).
3. Select **Create PDF/XPS Document** and click the **Create PDF/ XPS** button. The *Publish as PDF or XPS* dialog box opens.
   - XPS (XML Paper Specification) format is an alternative to a PDF file. XPS is a Microsoft format and is not widely used.
4. Select a location to save the file.
5. Type a name for the file in the *File name* area.
6. Click **Publish** to close the dialog box and save the PDF file.

Figure Intro-65 *Export* a file as a PDF file

> MORE INFO
>
> Microsoft Word can open PDF files, and you can edit and save the file as a Word document.
>
> If Adobe Acrobat is installed on your computer, *Save as Adobe PDF* displays as an option on the *Backstage* view.

Document Properties

Document properties are hidden codes in a file that store identifying information about that file. Each piece of document property information is called a *field*. You can view and modify document properties in the *Info* area of the *Backstage* view.

Some document properties fields are automatically generated when you work on a file, such as *Size*, *Total Editing Time*, *Created*, and *Last Modified*. Other document properties fields, such as *Title*, *Comments*, *Subject*, *Company*, and *Author*, can be modified. You can use document property fields in different ways such as inserting the *Company* field in a document footer.

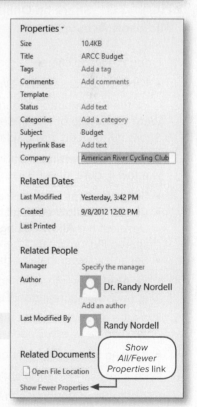

> **HOW TO:** View and Modify Document Properties

1. Click the **File** tab and click **Info** (if not already selected). The document properties display on the right (Figure Intro-66).
2. Click the text box area of a field that can be edited and type your custom document property information.

Figure Intro-66 Document properties

3. Click the **Show All Properties** link at the bottom to display additional document properties.
   - Click **Show Fewer Properties** to collapse the list and display fewer properties.
   - This link toggles between *Show All Properties* and *Show Fewer Properties.*
4. Click the **Back** arrow to return to the file.

Share a File

Windows 10 and Office have been enhanced to help you share files and collaborate with others. Because collaboration is so important and commonly used, the *Share* button is available in the upper-right corner of the application window, except on Access. When sharing a file with others, you can send a sharing email or get a sharing link to paste into an email message or post in an online location.

To share a file, it must first be saved in *OneDrive*. If you try to share a file that is not saved in *OneDrive*, Word prompts you to save your document to *OneDrive* before sharing it. Depending on the type of Microsoft account you're using, the sharing options display in a *Send Link* window (education and business Microsoft accounts) (Figure Intro-67) or the *Share* pane (personal Microsoft account). The *Send Link* window or *Share* pane displays a variety of sharing options.

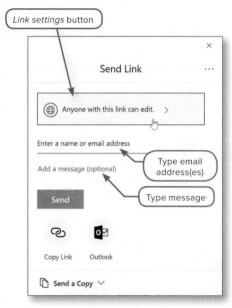

Figure Intro-67 *Send Link* window

▶ HOW TO: Share an Online File (Education and Business Microsoft Accounts)

Figure Intro-68 *Share* button

1. Open the file to share.
   - If the file is not saved in *OneDrive*, save the file to *OneDrive*.
2. Click the **Share** button (Figure Intro-68) in the upper-right corner of the Word window to open the *Send Link* window (see Figure Intro-67). The *Share* button icon may display differently in Office 2019.
3. Click the **Link settings** button (see Figure Intro-67) to open the *Link settings* window (Figure Intro-69).
   - Select who can use the sharing link.
   - Check the **Allow editing** box to enable recipients to edit the shared file. Deselect the **Allow editing** box to enable recipients to open and view the shared file, but restrict them from editing it.
   - Set an expiration date for the sharing link if desired (optional).
4. Click **Apply** to set the sharing link options and to return to the *Send Link* window (see Figure Intro-67).
5. Type the email address of the person with whom you are sharing the file in the *Enter a name or email address* area.
   - If typing multiple email addresses, separate each with a semicolon.
6. Type a message to recipient(s) in the *Add a message* area. This is optional.
7. Click the **Send** button. An email is sent to people you invited.
8. Click the **X** to close the confirmation window.

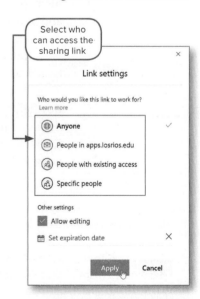

Figure Intro-69 *Link settings* window

If you're using a personal Microsoft account, the *Share* pane opens at the right after you click the *Share* button.

Figure Intro-70 Share a *OneDrive* file

▶ **HOW TO: Share an Online File (Personal Microsoft Account)**

1. Open the file to share.
   - If the file is not saved in *OneDrive,* save the file to *OneDrive*.
2. Click the **Share** button in the upper-right corner of the Word window to open the *Share* pane to the right of the Word window (Figure Intro-70). The *Share* button icon may display differently in Office 2019.
3. Type or select the email address of the person with whom you are sharing the file in the *Invite people* area.
4. Select **Can edit** or **Can view** from the *Permission* drop-down list.
   - *Can edit* enables users to edit a shared document.
   - *Can view* enables users to open and view a shared document but restricts users from editing the document.
5. Type a message to recipient(s) in the *Message* area.
6. Click the **Share** button. An email is sent to people you invited.
7. Click the **X** to close the *Share* pane.

Creating a sharing link (hyperlink) is another way to share a file with others rather than sending an email through Word. You can create and copy a sharing link and email the sharing link to others. You have the option of creating an ***Edit link*** or a ***View-only link***.

▶ **HOW TO: Create a Sharing Link (Education and Business Microsoft Accounts)**

1. Open the file to share.
   - If the file is not saved in *OneDrive*, you are prompted to save the file to *OneDrive*.
2. Click the **Share** button in the upper right of the Word window to open the *Send Link* window.
3. Click the **Link settings** button to open the *Link settings* window (see Figure Intro-69).
   - Select who can use the sharing link.
   - Check the **Allow editing** box to enable recipients to edit the shared file. Deselect the **Allow editing** box to enable recipients to open and view the shared file, but restrict them from editing it.
   - Set an expiration date for the sharing link if desired (optional).
4. Click **Apply** to set the sharing link options and to return to the *Send Link* window.
5. Click the **Copy Link** button to open the window that displays the sharing link (Figure Intro-71).
6. Click the **Copy** button to copy the sharing link.
7. Click the **X** to close the confirmation window.
8. Paste the copied sharing link in an email, Word document, or other online location.

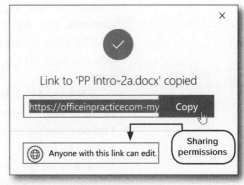
Figure Intro-71 Copy sharing link

If you're using a personal Microsoft account, the *Share* pane opens at the right after you after you click the *Share* button.

▶ HOW TO: Create a Sharing Link (Personal Microsoft Account)

1. Open the file to share.
   - If the file is not saved in *OneDrive*, you are prompted to save the file to *OneDrive*.
2. Click the **Share** button in the upper right of the Word window to open the *Share* pane to the right of the Word window.
3. Click **Get a sharing link** at the bottom of the *Share* pane (see Figure Intro-70).
4. Click the **Create an edit link** or **Create a view-only link** button (Figure Intro-72) to create a sharing link.
   - *Can edit* enables users to open, view, and edit a shared document.
   - *Can view* enables users to open and view a shared document but restricts users from editing the document.
5. Click the **Copy** button to copy the sharing link (Figure Intro-73).
6. Click the **Back** arrow to the left of *Get a sharing link* at the top of the *Share* pane to return to the main *Share* pane, or click the **X** to close the *Share* pane.
7. Paste the copied sharing link in an email, Word document, or other online location.

Figure Intro-72 Create a sharing link

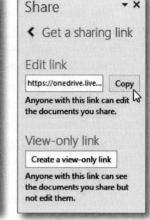

Figure Intro-73 Copy a sharing link

▶ **ANOTHER WAY**

You can also share a file through email by clicking the **Send as attachment** link at the bottom of the *Share* pane. The email share options require the use of Microsoft Outlook (email and personal management Office application) to share the selected file through email.

Program Options

Use program options to apply global changes to the Office program. For example, you can change the default save location to the *OneDrive* folder or you can turn off the opening of a *Start* page.

Click the **File** tab and select **Options** on the left to open the *[Program]* **Options** dialog box (Word Options, Excel Options, etc.) (Figure Intro-74). Click one of the categories on the left to display the category options on the right. The categories and options vary depending on the Office application.

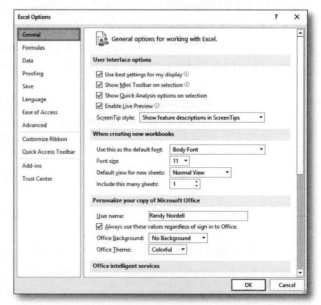

Figure Intro-74 *Excel Options* dialog box

Using the Ribbon, Tabs, and Quick Access Toolbar

Use the *Ribbon*, tabs, groups, buttons, drop-down lists, dialog boxes, task panes, galleries, and the *Quick Access* toolbar to modify your Office files. This section describes different tools used to customize your files.

The Ribbon, Tabs, and Groups

The **Ribbon**, which appears at the top of an Office file window, displays the many features available. The *Ribbon* is a collection of **tabs**. Each tab includes **groups** of commands. The tabs and groups available vary for each Office application. Click a tab to display the groups and commands available on that tab.

Some tabs always display on the *Ribbon* (for example, the *File* tab and *Home* tabs). Other tabs are contextual, which means that they only appear on the *Ribbon* when you select a specific object. Figure Intro-75 displays the contextual *Table Tools Fields* tab that displays in Access when you open a table.

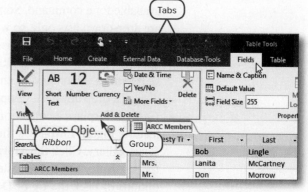

Figure Intro-75 Contextual *Table Tools Fields* tab displayed

> **MORE INFO**
>
> The *Ribbon* may appear slightly different depending on the version of Office you are using.

Ribbon Display Options

The *Ribbon* displays by default in Office applications, and you can customize the appearance of the *Ribbon*. The **Ribbon Display Options** button is in the upper-right corner of an Office application window (Figure Intro-76). Click the **Ribbon Display Options** button to select one of the three options:

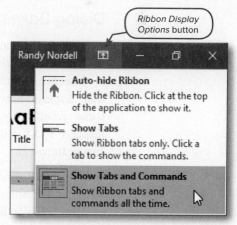

Figure Intro-76 *Ribbon Display Options*

- *Auto-Hide Ribbon*: Hides the *Ribbon*. Click at the top of the application to display the *Ribbon*.
- *Show Tabs*: Displays *Ribbon* tabs only. Click a tab to open the *Ribbon* and display the tab.
- *Show Tabs and Commands*: Displays the *Ribbon* and tabs, which is the default setting in Office applications.

> **MORE INFO**
>
> **Ctrl+F1** collapses or expands the *Ribbon*. Also, double-click a tab name on the *Ribbon* to collapse or expand it.

Buttons, Drop-Down Lists, and Galleries

Groups on each of the tabs contain a variety of *buttons*, *drop-down lists*, and *galleries*. The following list describes each of these features and how they are used:

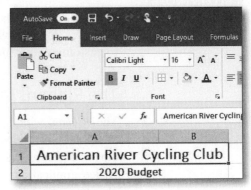

- **Button**: Applies a feature to selected text or an object. Click a button to apply the feature (Figure Intro-77).
- **Drop-down list**: Displays the various options available for a command. Some buttons are drop-down lists only, so when you click these buttons a drop-down list of options appears (Figure Intro-78). Other buttons are *split buttons*, which have both a button you click to apply a feature and an arrow you click to display a drop-down list of options (Figure Intro-79).
- **Gallery**: Displays a collection of option buttons. Click an option in a gallery to apply the

Figure Intro-77 *Bold* button in the *Font* group on the *Home* tab

feature. Figure Intro-80 is the *Styles* gallery. Click the **More** button to display the entire gallery of options or click the **Up** or **Down** arrow to display a different row of options.

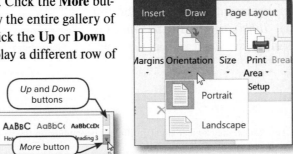

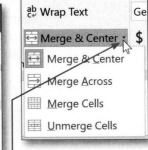

Figure Intro-80 *Styles* gallery in Word

Figure Intro-78 *Orientation* drop-down list

Figure Intro-79 *Merge & Center* split button—button and drop-down list

Click the arrow on a split button to display the drop-down list

Dialog Boxes, Task Panes, and Launchers

Office application features are also available in a *dialog box* or *task pane*. A *launcher*, which is a small square that displays in the bottom right of some groups, opens a dialog box or displays a task pane when clicked (see Figure Intro-82).

- **Dialog box**: A new window that opens to display additional features. Move a dialog box by clicking and dragging the title bar. The title bar appears at the top of the dialog box and displays the title. Figure Intro-81 shows the *Format Cells* dialog box that opens after you click the *Alignment* launcher in Excel.
- **Task pane**: Opens on the left or right of an Office application window. Figure Intro-82 shows the *Clipboard* pane, which is available in all Office applications. Task panes are named

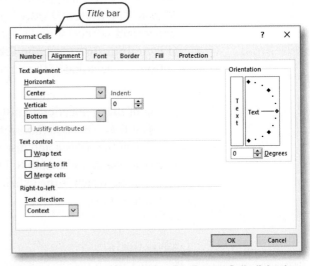

Figure Intro-81 *Format Cells* dialog box

according to their purpose (for example, *Clipboard* pane or *Navigation* pane). You can resize a task pane by clicking and dragging its left or right border. Click the **X** in the upper-right corner to close a task pane.

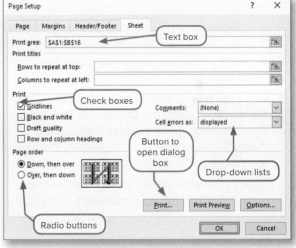

Figure Intro-83 *Align Left ScreenTip*

Figure Intro-82 *Clipboard* pane

ScreenTips

ScreenTips display descriptive information about a button, drop-down list, launcher, or gallery selection. When you place your pointer on an item on the *Ribbon*, a *ScreenTip* displays information about the selection (Figure Intro-83). The *ScreenTip* appears temporarily and displays the command name, keyboard shortcut (if available), and a description of the command.

Radio Buttons, Check Boxes, and Text Boxes

Dialog boxes and task panes contain a variety of options you can apply using **radio buttons**, **check boxes**, **text boxes**, **drop-down lists**, and other buttons (Figure Intro-84).

Figure Intro-84 *Page Setup* dialog box in Excel

- **Radio button**: A round button you click to select one option from a group of options. A selected radio button displays a solid dot inside the round button. Radio buttons are mutually exclusive.
- **Check box**: A square button you click to select one or more options. A check appears in a selected check box.
- **Text box**: An area where you type text.

A task pane or dialog box may also include drop-down lists or other buttons that open additional dialog boxes. Figure Intro-84 shows the *Page Setup* dialog box in Excel, which includes a variety of radio buttons, check boxes, text boxes, drop-down lists, and command buttons that open additional dialog boxes (for example, the *Print* and *Options* buttons).

Quick Access Toolbar

The **Quick Access toolbar** is located above the *Ribbon* on the upper left of each Office application window. It contains buttons to apply commonly used commands such as *Save*, *Undo*, *Redo*, and *Open*. The *Undo* button is a split button (Figure Intro-85). You can

Figure Intro-85 *Quick Access* toolbar

click the button to undo the last action performed, or you can click the drop-down arrow to display and undo multiple previous actions.

Customize the Quick Access Toolbar

You can customize the *Quick Access* toolbar to include commands you regularly use, such as *Quick Print*, *New*, and *Spelling & Grammar*. The following steps show how to customize the *Quick Access* toolbar in Word. The customization process is similar for the *Quick Access* toolbar in the other Office applications.

▶ **HOW TO:** **Customize the Quick Access Toolbar**

1. Click the **Customize Quick Access Toolbar** drop-down list on the right edge of the *Quick Access* toolbar (Figure Intro-86).

2. Select a command to add to the *Quick Access* toolbar. The command displays on the *Quick Access* toolbar.

   - Items on the *Customize Quick Access Toolbar* drop-down list with a check display on the *Quick Access* toolbar.
   - Select a checked item to remove it from the *Quick Access* toolbar.

3. Add a command that is not listed on the *Customize Quick Access Toolbar* by clicking the **Customize Quick Access Toolbar** drop-down list and selecting **More Commands**. The *Word Options* dialog box opens with the *Customize the Quick Access Toolbar* area displayed (Figure Intro-87).

4. Click the **Customize Quick Access Toolbar** drop-down list on the right and select **For all documents** or the current document.

   - If you select *For all documents*, the change is made to the *Quick Access* toolbar for all documents you open in Word.
   - If you select the current document, the change is made to the *Quick Access* toolbar in that document only.

5. Select the command to add from the alphabetic list of commands on the left and click the **Add** button.

   - If you can't find a command, click the **Choose commands from** drop-down list and select **All Commands**.
   - The list on the right contains the commands that display on the *Quick Access* toolbar.

6. Rearrange commands on the *Quick Access* toolbar by selecting a command in the list on the right and clicking the **Move Up** or **Move Down** button.

7. Click **OK** to close the *Word Options* dialog box.

Figure Intro-86 Add a command to the *Quick Access* toolbar

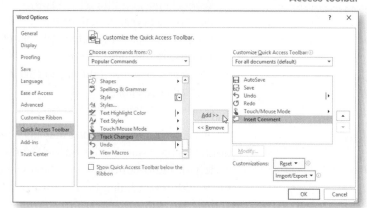

Figure Intro-87 Customize the *Quick Access* toolbar in the *Word Options* dialog box

Using Context Menus, the Mini Toolbar, and Keyboard Shortcuts

Most of the commands used for formatting and editing your files display in groups on the tabs. But many of these features are also available using context menus, the mini toolbar, and keyboard shortcuts. Use these tools to quickly apply formatting or other options to text or objects.

Context Menu

A *context menu* displays when you right-click text, a cell, or an object such as a picture, drawing object, chart, or *SmartArt* (Figure Intro-88). The context menu is a vertical list of options, and the options are contextual, which means they vary depending on what you right-click. Context menus include options that perform an action (*Cut* or *Copy*), open a dialog box or task pane (*Format Cells* or *Insert*), or display a drop-down list of selections (*Filter* or *Sort*).

Mini Toolbar

The *mini toolbar* is another context menu that displays when you right-click or select text, a cell, or an object in your file (see Figure Intro-88). The mini toolbar is a horizontal rectangular menu that lists a variety of formatting options. These options vary

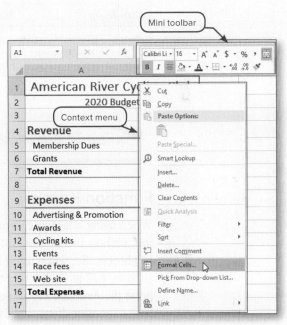

Figure Intro-88 Context menu and mini toolbar

depending on what you select or right-click. The mini toolbar contains a variety of buttons and drop-down lists. The mini toolbar typically displays above the context menu, and it automatically displays when you select text or an object, such as when you select a row of a table in Word or PowerPoint.

Keyboard Shortcuts

You can also use a *keyboard shortcut* to quickly apply formatting or perform commands. A keyboard shortcut is a combination of keyboard keys that you press at the same time. These can include the **Ctrl**, **Shift**, **Alt**, letter, number, and function keys (for example, **F1** or **F7**). Table Intro-5 lists common Office keyboard shortcuts.

Table Intro-5: Common Office Keyboard Shortcuts

Keyboard Shortcut	Action or Displays	Keyboard Shortcut	Action or Displays
Ctrl+S	Save	Ctrl+Z	Undo
F12	*Save As* dialog box	Ctrl+Y	Redo or Repeat
Ctrl+O	*Open* area on the *Backstage* view	Ctrl+1	Single space
Shift+F12	*Open* dialog box	Ctrl+2	Double space
Ctrl+N	New blank file	Ctrl+L	Align left
Ctrl+P	*Print* area on the *Backstage* view	Ctrl+E	Align center
Ctrl+C	Copy	Ctrl+R	Align right
Ctrl+X	Cut	F1	*Help* pane
Ctrl+V	Paste	F7	*Spelling* pane
Ctrl+B	Bold	Ctrl+A	Select All
Ctrl+I	Italic	Ctrl+Home	Move to the beginning
Ctrl+U	Underline	Ctrl+End	Move to the end

> **MORE INFO**
>
> See *Appendix A: Microsoft Office Shortcuts* (online resource) for additional Office keyboard shortcuts.

Function Keys on a Laptop

When using a laptop computer, function keys perform specific Windows actions on your laptop, such as increase or decrease speaker volume, open Windows *Settings*, or adjust the screen brightness. So, when using a numbered function key in an Office application, such as *F12* as a shortcut to open the *Save As* dialog box, you may need to press the *Function key* (**Fn** or **fn**) on your keyboard in conjunction with a numbered function key to activate the Office command (Figure Intro-89). The *Function key* is typically located near the bottom left of your laptop keyboard next to the *Ctrl* key.

Figure Intro-89
Function key

PAUSE & PRACTICE: INTRO-2

For this project, you work with a document for the American River Cycling Club. You modify the existing document, add document properties, customize the *Quick Access* toolbar, export the document as a PDF file, and share the document.

File Needed: ***ARCCTraining-Intro.docx*** (*Student data files are available in the* Library *of your SIMnet account.*)
Completed Project File Names: *[your initials] PP Intro-2a.docx* and *[your initials] PP Intro-2b.pdf*

1. Open Word and open the ***ARCCTraining-Intro*** file from your student data files. If the file opens in *Protected View*, click the **Enable Editing** button.

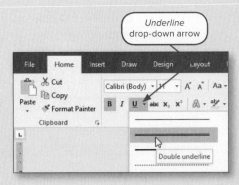

2. Save this document as [your initials] PP Intro-2a in the *American River Cycling Club* folder in your *OneDrive* folder.
   a. In *Pause & Practice Intro-1*, you created the *American River Cycling Club* folder in *OneDrive* or other storage area. Save this file in the same location.
   b. If you don't save this file in *OneDrive*, you will not be able to complete steps 7 and 9 in this project.

3. Use a button, drop-down list, and dialog box to modify the document.
   a. Select the first heading, "**What is Maximum Heart Rate?**"
   b. Click the **Bold** button [*Home* tab, *Font* group].
   c. Click the **Underline** drop-down arrow and select **Double underline** (Figure Intro-90).
   d. Click the **launcher** in the *Font* group [*Home* tab] to open the *Font* dialog box (Figure Intro-91).
   e. Select **12** from the *Size* area list or type 12 in the text box.
   f. Click the **Small caps** check box in the *Effects* area to select it.
   g. Click **OK** to close the dialog box and apply the formatting changes.
   h. Select the next heading, "**What is Target Heart Rate?**"
   i. Repeat steps 3b–g to apply formatting to selected text.

Figure Intro-90 Apply *Double underline* to selected text

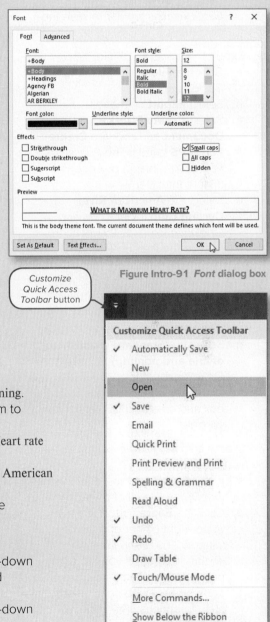

Figure Intro-91 *Font* dialog box

4. Add document properties.
   a. Click the **File** tab to display the *Backstage* view.
   b. Select **Info** on the left (if not already selected). The document properties display on the right.
   c. Click the **Add a title** text box and type ARCC Training.
   d. Click the **Show All Properties** link near the bottom to display additional document properties.
   e. Click the **Specify the subject** text box and type Heart rate training.
   f. Click the **Specify the company** text box and type American River Cycling Club.
   g. Click the **Back** arrow on the upper left to close the *Backstage* view and return to the document.

5. Customize the *Quick Access* toolbar.
   a. Click the **Customize Quick Access Toolbar** drop-down arrow and select **Open** if it is not already selected (Figure Intro-92).
   b. Click the **Customize Quick Access Toolbar** drop-down arrow again and select **Spelling & Grammar**.

Figure Intro-92 *Customize Quick Access Toolbar* drop-down list

c.   Click the **Customize Quick Access Toolbar** drop-down arrow again and select **More Commands**. The *Word Options* dialog box opens (Figure Intro-93).

d.   Select **Insert Comment** in the list of commands on the left.

e.   Click the **Add** button to add it to your *Quick Access* toolbar list on the right.

f.   Click **OK** to close the *Word Options* dialog box.

g.   Click the **Save** button on the *Quick Access* toolbar to save the document.

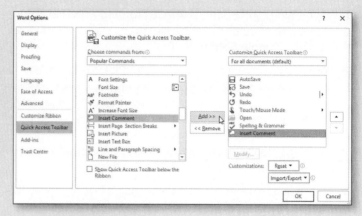

Figure Intro-93 Customize the *Quick Access* toolbar in the *Word Options* dialog box

6.   Export the file as a PDF file.

a.   Click the **File** tab to go to the *Backstage* view.

b.   Select **Export** on the left.

c.   Select **Create PDF/XPS Document** and click the **Create PDF/XPS** button. The *Publish as PDF or XPS* dialog box opens (Figure Intro-94).

d.   Select the **American River Cycling Club** folder in your *OneDrive* folder as the location to save the file.

e.   Type [your initials] PP Intro-2b in the *File name* area.

f.   Deselect the **Open file after publishing** check box if it is checked.

g.   Select the **Standard (publishing online and printing)** radio button in the *Optimize for* area.

h.   Click **Publish** to close the dialog box and create a PDF version of your file.

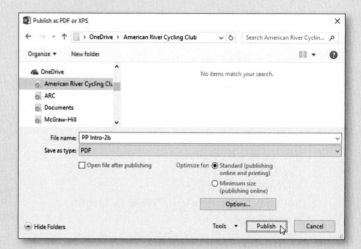

Figure Intro-94 *Publish as PDF or XPS* dialog box

7.   Create a sharing link to share this file with your instructor.

a.   If you don't have the ability to save to *OneDrive*, skip all of step 7.

b.   Click the **Share** button in the upper-right corner of the Word window. The *Send Link* window opens (Figure Intro-95). If you are using a personal Microsoft account, the *Share* pane opens at the right, and the sharing options differ slightly.

c.   Click the **Link settings** button to open the *Link settings* window.

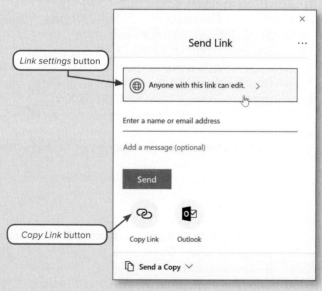

Figure Intro-95 *Send Link* window

d. Click the **Anyone** button and check the **Allow editing** box (if necessary) (Figure Intro-96).

e. Click **Apply** to return to the *Send Link* window.

f. Click the **Copy Link** button to create a sharing link.

g. Click **Copy** to copy the sharing link and click the **X** in the upper-right corner to close the sharing link window (Figure Intro-97).

h. Use your email account to create a new email to your instructor. Include an appropriate subject line and a brief message in the body.

i. Press **Ctrl+V** to paste the sharing link to your document in the body of the email and send the email message.

8. Save and close the document (Figure Intro-98).

Figure Intro-97 Copy a sharing link

Figure Intro-96 *Link settings* window

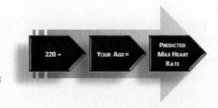

American River Cycling Club

www.arcc.org   Cycling...a way of life   info@arcc.org

WHAT IS MAXIMUM HEART RATE?

The maximum heart rate is the highest your pulse rate can get. To calculate your **predicted maximum heart rate**, use this formula:

(Example: a 40-year-old's predicted maximum heart rate is 180.)

Your actual maximum heart rate can be determined by a graded exercise test. Please note that some medicines and medical conditions might affect your maximum heart rate. If you are taking medicines or have a medical condition (such as heart disease, high blood pressure, or diabetes), always ask your doctor if your maximum heart rate/target heart rate will be affected.

220 – | Your Age = | Predicted Max Heart Rate

WHAT IS TARGET HEART RATE?

You gain the most benefits and decrease the risk of injury when you exercise in your target heart rate zone. Usually this is when your exercise heart rate (pulse) is 60 percent to 85 percent of your maximum heart rate. Do not exercise above 85 percent of your maximum heart rate. This increases both cardiovascular and orthopedic risk and does not add any extra benefit.

When beginning an exercise program, you might need to gradually build up to a level that is within your target heart rate zone, especially if you have not exercised regularly before. If the exercise feels too hard, slow down. You will reduce your risk of injury and enjoy the exercise more if you don't try to over-do it.

To find out if you are exercising in your target zone (between 60 percent and 85 percent of your maximum heart rate), use your heart rate monitor to track your heart rate. If your pulse is below your target zone (see the chart below), increase your rate of exercise. If your pulse is above your target zone, decrease your rate of exercise.

MAX AND TARGET HEART RATES	AGE	PREDICTED MAX HEART RATE	TARGET HEART RATE (60-85% OF MAX)
	20	✓ 200	120-170
	25	✓ 195	117-166
	30	✓ 190	114-162
	35	✓ 185	111-157
	40	✓ 180	108-153
	45	✓ 175	105-149
	50	✓ 170	102-145
	55	✓ 165	99-140
	60	✓ 160	96-136
	65	✓ 155	93-132
	70	✓ 150	90-128

Figure Intro-98 PP Intro-2a completed

Organizing and Customizing Folders and Files

The more you use your computer to create and edit files, the more important it is to create an organized system to locate and manage files. Use *folders* to store related files to make it easier to find, edit, and share your files. For example, you can create a folder for the college you attend. Inside the college folder, create a folder for each of your courses. Inside each of the course folders, create a folder for student data files, solution files, and group projects. Folders can store any type of files; you are not limited to Office files.

Create a Folder

In *SLO Intro. 3: Creating, Saving, Closing, and Opening Office Files*, you learned how to create a new folder when saving an Office file in the *Save As* dialog box. You can also create a Windows folder using *File Explorer*. You can create folders inside other folders.

▶HOW TO: Create a Windows Folder

1. Click the **File Explorer** on the *Taskbar* or click the **Start** button and select **File Explorer** to open a *File Explorer* window.
   - Your folders and computer locations display on the left in the *Navigation* pane.
2. Select the location in the *Navigation* pane where you want to create a new folder.
3. Click the **Home** tab and click the **New folder** button [*New* group]. A new folder is created (Figure Intro-99).
   - The *New Folder* button is also on the *Quick Access* toolbar in the *File Explorer* window.
4. Type the name of the new folder and press **Enter**.

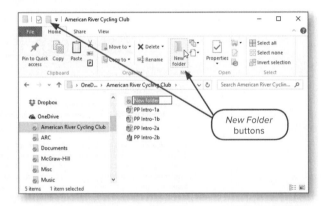

Figure Intro-99 Create a new Windows folder

> **ANOTHER WAY**
>
> **Ctrl+Shift+N** creates a new folder in a Windows folder.

Move and Copy Files and Folders

Moving a file or folder is cutting it from one location and pasting it in another location. Copying a file or folder creates a copy, and you can paste in another location so the file or folder is in two or more locations. If you move or copy a folder, the files in the folder are moved or copied with the folder. Move or copy files and folders using the *Move to* or *Copy to* buttons on the *Home* tab of *File Explorer*, keyboard shortcuts (**Ctrl+X, Ctrl+C, Ctrl+V**), or the drag-and-drop method.

To move or copy multiple folders or files at the same time, press the **Ctrl** key and select multiple items to move or copy. Use the **Ctrl** key to select or deselect multiple non-adjacent files or folders. Use the **Shift** key to select a range of files or folders. Click the first file or folder in a range, press the **Shift** key, and select the last file or folder in the range to select all of the items in the range.

▶ HOW TO: Move or Copy a File or Folder

1. Click the **File Explorer** on the *Taskbar* or click the **Start** button and select **File Explorer** to open a *File Explorer* window.

2. Select a file or folder to move or copy.
   - Press the **Ctrl** key or the **Shift** key to select multiple files or folders.

3. Click the **Home** tab in the *File Explorer* window.

4. Click the **Move to** or **Copy to** button [*Organize* group] and select the location where you want to move or copy the file or folder (Figure Intro-100).

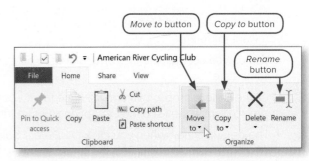

Figure Intro-100 Move or copy a selected file or folder

   - If the folder is not available, select **Choose location** to open the *Move Items* or *Copy Items* dialog box.
   - To use keyboard shortcuts, press **Ctrl+X** to cut the file or folder or **Ctrl+C** to copy the file or folder from its original location, go to the desired new location, and press **Ctrl+V** to paste it.
   - To use the drag-and-drop method to move a file or folder, select the file or folder and drag and drop to the new location.
   - To use the drag-and-drop method to copy a file or folder, press the **Ctrl** key, select the file or folder, and drag and drop to the new location.

> ▶ **ANOTHER WAY**
>
> Right-click a file or folder to display the context menu and select **Cut**, **Copy**, or **Paste**.

Rename Files and Folders

You can rename a file or folder in a *File Explorer* window. When you rename a file or folder, only the file or folder name changes. The contents of the file or folder do not change.

▶ HOW TO: Rename a File or Folder

1. Click the **File Explorer** on the *Taskbar* or click the **Start** button and select **File Explorer** to open a *File Explorer* window.
2. Select the file or folder you want to rename.
3. Click the **Rename** button [*Home* tab, *Organize* group] (see Figure Intro-100).
4. Type the new name of the file or folder and press **Enter**.

> ▶ **ANOTHER WAY**
>
> Select a file or folder to rename, press **F2**, type the new name, and press **Enter**. You can also right-click a file or folder and select **Rename** from the context menu.

Delete Files and Folders

You can easily delete files and folders. When you delete a file or folder, it is moved from its current location to the *Recycle Bin* on your computer. The *Recycle Bin* stores deleted items. If a file or folder is in the *Recycle Bin*, you can restore it to its original location or move it to a different location. You also have the option to permanently delete a file or folder. If an item is permanently deleted, you do not have the restore option.

▶ HOW TO: Delete Files and Folders

1. Open a *File Explorer* window and select the file or folder you want to delete.
   - You can select multiple files and folders to delete at the same time.

2. Click the **Delete** drop-down arrow [*Home* tab, *Organize* group] to display the list of delete options (Figure Intro-101).
   - The default action when you click the *Delete* button (not the drop-down arrow) is *Recycle*.

3. Delete a file by selecting **Recycle**, which moves it to the *Recycle Bin*.
   - *Recycle* deletes the item(s) and moves it (them) to the *Recycle Bin*.
   - When you *Recycle* an item, you are not prompted to confirm the deletion. To change the default setting, select **Show recycle confirmation** from the *Delete* drop-down list. A confirmation dialog box displays each time you delete or recycle an item.

4. Delete a file permanently by clicking the **Delete** drop-down arrow and selecting **Permanently delete**. A confirmation dialog box opens. Click **Yes** to confirm the deletion.
   - *Permanently delete* deletes the item(s) from your computer.

Figure Intro-101 Delete selected folder

> ▶ **ANOTHER WAY**
>
> Press **Ctrl+D** or the **Delete** key on your keyboard to recycle selected item(s).
> Press **Shift+Delete** to permanently delete selected item(s).

Create a Zipped (Compressed) Folder

If you want to share multiple files or a folder of files with classmates, coworkers, friends, or family, you can *zip* the files into a *zipped folder* (also called a *compressed folder*). For example, you can't attach an entire folder to an email message, but you can attach a zipped folder to an email message. Compressing files and folders decreases their size. You can zip a group of selected files, a folder, or a combination of files and folders, and then share the zipped folder with others through email or in a cloud storage location such as *OneDrive*.

▶ HOW TO: Create a Zipped (Compressed) Folder

1. Open a *File Explorer* window.
2. Select the file(s) and/or folder(s) you want to zip (compress).
3. Click the **Zip** button [*Share* tab, *Send* group] (Figure Intro-102). A zipped folder is created.
   - The default name of the zipped folder is the name of the first item you selected to zip.
4. Type a name for the zipped folder and press **Enter**. Alternatively, press **Enter** to accept the default name.
   - The icon for a zipped folder looks similar to the icon for a folder except it has a vertical zipper down the middle of the folder.

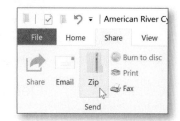

Figure Intro-102 Create a zipped folder

Extract a Zipped (Compressed) Folder

If you receive a zipped folder via email or download a zipped folder, save the zipped folder to your computer and then *extract* its contents. Extracting a zipped folder creates a regular Windows folder from the zipped folder.

▶ HOW TO: Extract a Zipped (Compressed) Folder

1. Select the zipped folder to extract.
2. Click the **Compressed Folder Tools** tab.
3. Click the **Extract all** button (Figure Intro-103). The *Extract Compressed (Zipped) Folders* dialog box opens (Figure Intro-104).
4. Click **Extract** to extract the folder.
   - Both the extracted folder and the zipped folder display.
   - If you check the **Show extracted files when complete** check box, the extracted folder will open after extracting.

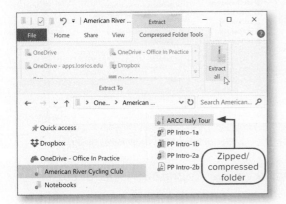

Figure Intro-103 Extract files from a zipped folder

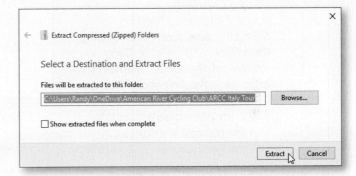

Figure Intro-104 *Extract Compressed (Zipped) Folders* dialog box

For this project, you copy and rename files in your *OneDrive* folder on your computer, create a folder, move files, create a zipped folder, and rename a zipped folder.

Files Needed: *[your initials] PP Intro-1a.pptx, [your initials] PP Intro-1b.xlsx, [your initials] PP Intro-2a.docx, [your initials] PP Intro-2b.docx,* and ***ARCC_Membership-Intro.accdb*** *(Student data files are available in the* Library *of your SIMnet account.)*

Completed Project File Names: *[your initials] PP Intro-1a.pptx, [your initials] PP Intro-1b.xlsx, [your initials] PP Intro-2a.docx, [your initials] PP Intro-2b.docx, [your initials] PP Intro-3.accdb,* and ***ARCC Italy Tour-2020*** (zipped folder)

1. Copy and rename a file.
    a. Click the **File Explorer** on the *Taskbar* or click the **Start** button and select **File Explorer** to open a *File Explorer* window. If *File Explorer* is not available on the *Taskbar* or *Start* menu, use *Cortana* to find and open a *File Explorer* window.
    b. Browse the *File Explorer* window to locate your student data files.
    c. Select the ***ARCC_Membership-Intro*** file.
    d. Click the **Copy to** button [*Home* tab, *Organize* group] and select **Choose location** from the drop-down list to open the *Copy Items* dialog box.
    e. Browse to locate the *American River Cycling Club* folder you created in *Pause & Practice: Intro-1.*
    f. Select the ***American River Cycling Club*** folder and click the **Copy** button to copy the ***ARCC_Membership-Intro*** file to the *American River Cycling Club* folder (Figure Intro-105). The *Copy Items* dialog box closes and the copied file displays.

    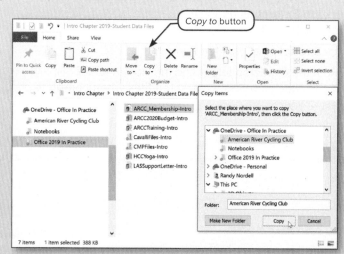
    Figure Intro-105 *Copy Items* dialog box

    g. Use the *File Explorer* window to browse and locate the *American River Cycling Club* folder. Double-click the folder to open it.
    h. Click the ***ARCC_Membership-Intro*** file in the *American River Cycling Club* folder to select it.
    i. Click the **Rename** button [*Home* tab, *Organize* group], type [your initials] PP Intro-3 as the new file name, and press **Enter** (Figure Intro-106).

2. Create a new folder and move files.
    a. With the *American River Cycling Club* folder still open, click the **New folder** button [*Home* tab, *New* group] (see Figure Intro-106).

    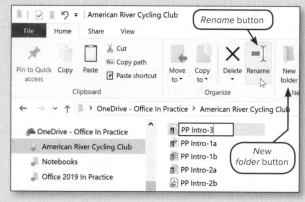
    Figure Intro-106 Rename a file

    b. Type ARCC Italy Tour as the name of the new folder and press **Enter**.
    c. Select the ***[your initials] PP Intro-1a*** file.

d. Press the **Ctrl** key, select the *[your initials] PP Intro-1b*, *[your initials] PP Intro-2a*, *[your initials] PP Intro-2b*, and *[your initials] PP Intro-3* files, and release the **Ctrl** key. All five files should be selected.

e. Click the **Move to** button [*Home* tab, *Organize* group] and select **Choose location** to open the *Move Items* dialog box (Figure Intro-107).

f. Browse to locate the *ARCC Italy Tour* folder in the *Move Items* dialog box.

g. Select the **ARCC Italy Tour** folder and click the **Move** button to move the selected files to the *ARCC Italy Tour* folder.

h. Double-click the **ARCC Italy Tour** folder to open it and confirm the five files are moved.

i. Click the **Up** or **Back** arrow above the *Navigation* pane to return to the *American River Cycling Club* folder (see Figure Intro-107).

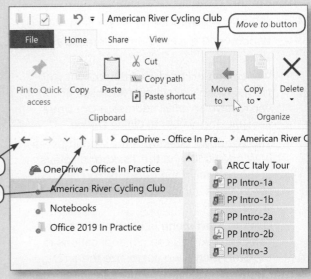

Figure Intro-107 Move selected files to a different folder

3. Create a zipped folder.
   a. Select the **ARCC Italy Tour** folder.
   b. Click the **Zip** button [*Share* tab, *Send* group]. A zipped (compressed) folder is created.
   c. Place the insertion point at the end of the zipped folder name, type –2020, and press **Enter** (Figure Intro-108).

4. Email the zipped folder to your instructor.
   a. Use your email account to create a new email to send to your instructor.
   b. Include an appropriate subject line and a brief message in the body.
   c. Attach the **ARCC Italy Tour-2020** zipped folder to the email message and send the email message.

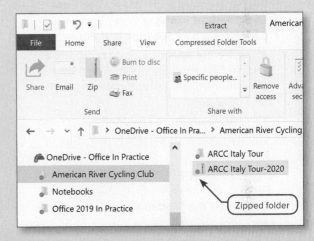

Figure Intro-108 Create a zipped folder

Chapter Summary

Intro. 1 Explore select features of Windows 10 (p. Intro-2).

- **Windows 10** is a computer operating system.
- A **Microsoft account** is a free account you create. When you create a Microsoft account, you receive an email address, a **OneDrive** account, and access to **Office Online**.
- The **Windows desktop** is the working area of Windows 10, and the **Taskbar** displays at the bottom of the desktop. You can rearrange icons and pin applications to the *Taskbar*.
- Use the **Start menu** in Windows 10 to select a task. You can pin applications to the *Start* menu and customize the arrangement of apps.
- The left side of the **Start menu** displays **Recently added** apps, **Most used** apps, an alphabetic listing of apps, and other buttons, such as **Settings** and **Power**.
- **Apps** are the applications or programs installed on your computer. App buttons are arranged in tiles on the Windows 10 *Start* menu.
- The **Microsoft Store** is a Windows 10 app you use to search for and install apps on your computer.
- Install both **traditional apps** and **modern apps** in Windows 10.
- Customize the *Start* menu and *Taskbar* to add, remove, or arrange apps.
- *File Explorer* is a window that displays files and folders on your computer.
- *OneDrive* is the cloud storage area where you can store files in a private and secure online location.
- The **OneDrive folder** in Windows 10 is one of your file storage location options.
- Access *OneDrive* folders and files using an internet browser window.
- **Cortana** is a search tool in Windows 10 used to locate information on your computer and the internet.
- **Task View** displays all open apps and windows as tiles on your desktop. Select an app or window to display or close.
- Use the **Settings** window to customize the Windows environment.
- The **Action Center** displays notifications and buttons to open many common Windows settings and features.

Intro. 2 Use basic features of Microsoft Office and navigate the Office working environment (p. Intro-12).

- **Office 2019/365** is application software that includes **Word**, **Excel**, **Access**, **PowerPoint**, **Outlook**, **OneNote**, and **Publisher**.
- **Office 2019** and **Office 365** include the same application products, but they differ in how you purchase them. Office 365 includes features that may not be available in Office 2019.
- **Office desktop apps** are the full-function Office 2019 or 365 products you install on your laptop or desktop computer.
- **Office universal apps** are a scaled-down version of Office applications installed on a tablet or mobile device.
- **Office Online** is free online software that works in conjunction with your online *Microsoft* account.
- A **Start page** displays when you open each of the Office applications. You can open an existing file or create a new file.
- The **Backstage view** in each of the Office applications performs many common tasks such as saving, opening an existing file, creating a new file, printing, and sharing.
- **Tell Me** is the Office help feature that displays Office commands related to specific topics.
- Use the mouse (or touchpad) on your computer to navigate the pointer on your computer screen. Use the pointer or click buttons to select text or objects.
- When using Office 2019/365 on a touchscreen computer, use the touch screen to perform actions. You can choose between **Touch Mode** and **Mouse Mode** in Office applications.

Intro. 3 Create, save, close, and open Office files (p. Intro-19).

- Create a new Office file from the *Start* page or *Backstage* view of the Office application.

- Assign a file name when you save a file for the first time.
- *AutoSave* is a new feature that automatically saves a file stored in *OneDrive*.
- Create folders to organize saved files, and you can save a file as a different file name.
- Office applications use a variety of different file types.
- Close an Office file when finished working on it. If the file has not been saved or changes have been made to the file, you are prompted to save the file before closing.
- Open an existing file from the *Start* page or from the *Open* area on *Backstage* view in each of the Office applications.

Intro. 4 Customize the view and display size in Office applications and work with multiple Office files (p. Intro-28).

- Each Office application has a variety of display views.
- Select an application view from the options on the *View tab* or the view buttons on the *Status bar*.
- The *Zoom* feature changes the display size of your file.
- *Minimize*, *restore down*, or *maximize* an open Office application window.
- Work with multiple Office files at the same time and switch between open files.
- *Snap Assist* enables you to arrange an open window on one side of your computer screen and select another window to fill the other side of the screen.

Intro. 5 Print, share, and customize Office files (p. Intro-32).

- Print a file in a variety of formats. The *Print* area on the *Backstage* view lists print options and displays a preview of your file.
- Export a file as a *PDF (portable document format)* file and save the PDF file to post to a web site or share with others.
- *Document properties* store information about a file.
- Share Office files in a variety of ways and enable others to view or edit shared files. To share a file with others, save the file in *OneDrive*.

- Program options are available on the *Backstage* view. Use program options to apply global changes to an Office application.

Intro. 6 Use the *Ribbon,* tabs, groups, dialog boxes, task panes, galleries, and the *Quick Access* toolbar (p. Intro-37).

- The *Ribbon* appears at the top of an Office window. It contains *tabs* and *groups* with commands to format and edit files.
- The *Ribbon Display Options* provides different ways to display the *Ribbon* in Office applications.
- A variety of *buttons*, *drop-down lists*, and *galleries* display within groups on each tab.
- *Dialog boxes* contain additional features not always displayed on the *Ribbon*.
- Click the *launcher* in the bottom-right corner of selected groups to open a dialog box.
- A *ScreenTip* displays information about commands on the *Ribbon*.
- Dialog boxes contain *radio buttons*, *check boxes*, *drop-down lists*, and *text boxes*.
- The *Quick Access toolbar* contains buttons that enable you to perform commands and displays in all Office applications. It is located in the upper left.
- Add or remove commands on the *Quick Access* toolbar.

Intro. 7 Use context menus, mini toolbar, keyboard shortcuts, and function keys in Office applications (p. Intro-41).

- A *context menu* displays when you right-click text or an object. A context menu contains different features depending on what you right-click.
- A *mini toolbar* is another context menu that displays formatting options.
- Use *keyboard shortcuts* to apply features or initiate commands.
- Numbered *function keys* perform commands in Office applications. On laptops, you may have to press the **Function key** (**Fn** or **fn**) to activate the numbered function keys.

Intro. 8 Organize and customize Windows folders and Office files (p. Intro-46).

- *Folders* store and organize files.
- Create, move, or copy files and folders. Files stored in a folder are moved or copied with that folder.
- Rename a file to change the file name.
- A deleted file or folder moves to the *Recycle Bin* on your computer by default. Alternatively, you can permanently delete files and folders.
- *Zip* files and/or folders into a *zipped (compressed) folder* to email or to share multiple files as a single file.
- *Extract* a zipped folder to create a regular Windows folder and to access its contents.

Check for Understanding

The SIMbook for this text (within your SIMnet account) provides the following resources for concept review:

- Multiple-choice questions
- Short answer questions
- Matching exercises

For these projects, you use your *OneDrive* to store files. If you don't already have a Microsoft account, see *SLO Intro.1: Using Windows 10* for information about creating a free personal Microsoft account.

Guided Project Intro-1

For this project, you organize and edit files for Emma Cavalli at Placer Hills Real Estate. You extract a zipped folder, rename files, manage multiple documents, apply formatting, and export as a PDF file. [Student Learning Outcomes Intro.1, Intro.2, Intro.3, Intro.4, Intro.5, Intro.6, Intro.7, Intro.8]

Files Needed: ***CavalliFiles-Intro*** (zipped folder) *(Student data files are available in the* Library *of your SIMnet account.)*
Completed Project File Names: ***PHRE*** folder containing the following files: ***BuyerEscrowChecklist-Intro***, ***CavalliProspectingLetter-Intro***, *[your initials] **Intro-1a.accdb**, [your initials] **Intro-1b.xlsx**, [your initials] **Intro-1c.docx**, [your initials] **Intro-1d.docx**,* and ***[your initials] Intro-1e.pdf***.

Skills Covered in This Project

- Copy and paste a zipped folder.
- Create a new folder in your *OneDrive* folder.
- Extract a zipped folder.
- Move a file.
- Rename a file.
- Open a Word document.

- Use *Task View* to switch between two open Word documents.
- Turn off *AutoSave*.
- Save a Word document with a different file name.
- Change display size.
- Use a mini toolbar, keyboard shortcut, context menu, and dialog box to apply formatting to selected text.
- Export a document as a PDF file.

---

1. Copy a zipped folder and create a new *OneDrive* folder.
    a. Click the Windows **Start** button and click **File Explorer** to open the *File Explorer* window. If *File Explorer* is not available on the *Start* menu, use *Cortana* to find and open the *File Explorer* window.
    b. Browse in the *File Explorer* window to locate your student data files.
    c. Select the ***CavalliFiles-Intro*** zipped folder from your student data files and press **Ctrl+C** or click the **Copy** button [*Home* tab, *Clipboard* group] to copy the folder.
    d. Select your ***OneDrive*** folder on the left of the *File Explorer* window, and click the **New folder** button [*Home* tab, *New* group] to create a new folder. If you don't have *OneDrive* available, create the new folder in a location where you store your files.
    e. Type PHRE and press **Enter**.
    f. Press **Enter** again to open the *PHRE* folder or double-click the folder to open it.
    g. Press **Ctrl+V** or click the **Paste** button [*Home* tab, *Clipboard* group] to paste the copied ***CavalliFiles-Intro*** zipped folder in the *PHRE* folder.

2. Extract a zipped folder.
    a. Select the ***CavalliFiles-Intro*** zipped folder.
    b. Click the **Compressed Folder Tools Extract** tab and click the **Extract all** button (Figure Intro-109). The *Extract Compressed (Zipped) Folders* dialog box opens.
    c. Uncheck the **Show extracted files when complete** box if it is checked.
    d. Click the **Extract** button. The zipped folder is extracted, and the *PHRE* folder now contains two *CavalliFiles-Intro* folders. One folder is zipped and the other is a regular folder.

e. Select the zipped **CavalliFiles-Intro** folder and click the **Delete** button [*Home* tab, *Organize* group] to delete the zipped folder.

3. Move and rename files.
   a. Double-click the **CavalliFiles-Intro** folder to open it.
   b. Click the first file, press and hold the **Shift** key, and click the last file to select all four files.
   c. Press **Ctrl+X** or click the **Cut** button [*Home* tab, *Clipboard* group] to cut the files from the current location (Figure Intro-110).
   d. Click the **Up** arrow to move up to the *PHRE* folder.
   e. Press **Ctrl+V** or click the **Paste** button [*Home* tab, *Clipboard* group] to paste and move the files.
   f. Select the **Cavalli files-Intro** folder and press **Delete** to delete the folder.
   g. Select the **CavalliPHRE-Intro** file and click the **Rename** button [*Home* tab, *Organize* group].
   h. Type [your initials] Intro-1a and press **Enter**.
   i. Right-click the **FixedMortgageRates-Intro** file and select **Rename** from the context menu.
   j. Type [your initials] Intro-1b and press **Enter**.

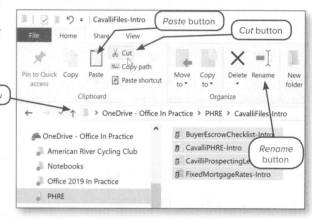

Figure Intro-109 Extract a zipped folder

Figure Intro-110 *Cut* files to move from a folder

4. Open two Word documents and rename a Word document.
   a. Click the **BuyerEscrowChecklist-Intro** file, press the **Ctrl** key, and click the **CavalliProspectingLetter-Intro** file to select both files.
   b. Press the **Enter** key to open both files in Word. If the files open in *Protected View,* click the **Enable Editing** button.
   c. Click the **Task View** button on your *Taskbar* (Figure Intro-111). All open windows display as tiles on your desktop.
   d. Select the **BuyerEscrowChecklist-Intro** document.
   e. Click the **AutoSave** button [*Quick Access* toolbar] to turn *AutoSave* off (if *AutoSave* is on).
   f. Click the **File** tab to open the *Backstage* view and select **Save As** on the left.
   g. Click the **Browse** button to open the *Save As* dialog box.
   h. Type [your initials] Intro-1c in the *File name* text box and click **Save**. The file is saved in the *PHRE* folder.
   i. Click the **X** in the upper-right corner of the Word window to close the document. The *CavalliProspectingLetter-Intro* document remains open.

Figure Intro-111 *Task View* button on the *Taskbar*

5. Change display size and edit and rename a Word document.
   a. Press the **Task View** button on your *Taskbar* and select the **CavalliProspectingLetter-Intro** document.

b. Click the **Zoom In** or **Zoom Out** button in the bottom right of the document window to change the display size to **120%** (Figure Intro-112).

c. Select "**Placer Hills Real Estate**" in the first body paragraph of the letter. The mini toolbar displays (Figure Intro-113).

d. Click the **Bold** button on the mini toolbar to apply bold formatting to the selected text.

Figure Intro-113 Use the mini toolbar to apply formatting

e. Select "**Whitney Hills resident**" in the first sentence in the second body paragraph and press **Ctrl+I** to apply italic formatting to the selected text.

f. Select the text that reads "**Emma Cavalli**," below "Best regards,".

g. Right-click the selected text and select **Font** from the context menu to open the *Font* dialog box.

h. Check the **Small Caps** box in the *Effects* area and click **OK** to close the *Font* dialog box.

i. Select "**Emma Cavalli**" (if necessary) and click the **Bold** button [*Home* tab, *Font* group].

j. Click the **File** tab and select **Save As** on the left. If the file is saved in *OneDrive* and *AutoSave* is turned on, select **Save a Copy**.

Figure Intro-114 *Save* area on the *Backstage* view.

k. Type [your initials] Intro-1d in the *File name* text box and click **Save** (Figure Intro-114).

6. Export a Word document as a PDF file.
   a. With the ***[your initials] Intro-1d*** still open, click the **File** tab to open the *Backstage* view.
   b. Select **Export** on the left, select **Create PDF/XPS Document** in the *Export* area, and click the **Create PDF/XPS** button (Figure Intro-115). The *Publish as PDF or XPS* dialog box opens.
   c. Deselect the **Open file after publishing** check box if it is checked.
   d. Select the **Standard (publishing online and printing)** radio button in the *Optimize for* area.
   e. Type [your initials] Intro-1e in the *File name* text box, select a location to save the file, and click **Publish**.
   f. Click the **Save** button on the *Quick Access* toolbar or press **Ctrl+S** to save the document.
   g. Click the **X** in the upper-right corner of the Word window to close the document and Word.

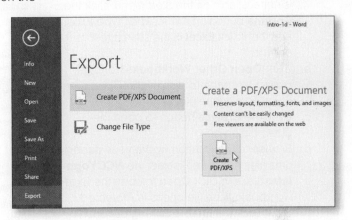

Figure Intro-115 Export as a PDF file

7. Your *PHRE* folder should contain the files shown in Figure Intro-116.

Figure Intro-116 Intro-1 completed

Guided Project Intro-2

For this project, you modify an Excel file for Hamilton Civic Center. You create a folder, rename a file, add document properties, use *Tell Me* to search for a topic, share the file, and export a file as a PDF file. [Student Learning Outcomes Intro.1, Intro.2, Intro.3, Intro.5, Intro.6, Intro.7, Intro.8]

File Needed: ***HCCYoga-Intro.xlsx*** *(Student data files are available in the* Library *of your SIMnet account.)*
Completed Project File Names: ***[your initials] Intro-2a.xlsx*** and ***[your initials] Intro-2b.pdf***

Skills Covered in This Project

- Open Excel and an Excel workbook.
- Create a new folder.
- Save an Excel workbook with a different file name.
- Add document properties to a file.
- Use *Tell Me* to search for a topic.
- Open a Word document.
- Share a file.
- Export a file as a PDF file.

1. Open Excel and open an Excel workbook.
   a. Click the Windows **Start** button and click **Excel** to open this application. If Excel 2019 is not available on the *Start* menu, click the **Cortana** button on the *Taskbar*, type Excel, and then click **Excel** in the search results to open it.
   b. Click **Open Other Workbooks** from the Excel *Start* page to display the *Open* area of the *Backstage* view.
   c. Click the **Browse** button to open the *Open* dialog box.
   d. Browse to the location where your student data files are stored, select the ***HCCYoga-Intro*** file, and click **Open** to open the Excel workbook. If the file opens in *Protected View,* click the **Enable Editing** button.

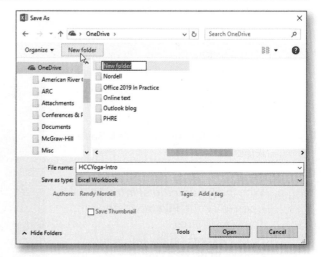

Figure Intro-117 Create a new folder from the *Save As* dialog box

2. Save a file as a different file name in your *OneDrive* folder.
   a. Click the **File** tab to open the *Backstage* view and select **Save As** (or **Save a Copy**) on the left.
   b. Click the **Browse** button to open the *Save As* dialog box.
   c. Select the **OneDrive** folder on the left and click the **New folder** button to create a new folder (Figure Intro-117). If *OneDrive* is not a storage option, select another location to create the new folder.
   d. Type HCC and press **Enter**.
   e. Double-click the **HCC** folder to open it.
   f. Type [your initials] Intro-2a in the *File name* area and click **Save** to close the dialog box and save the file.

3. Add document properties to the Excel workbook.
   a. Click the **File** button to open the *Backstage* view and select **Info** on the left if it is not already selected. The document properties display on the right.
   b. Place your insertion point in the *Title* text box ("Add a title") and type Yoga Classes as the worksheet title.
   c. Click the **Show All Properties** link at the bottom of the list of properties to display more properties (Figure Intro-118).

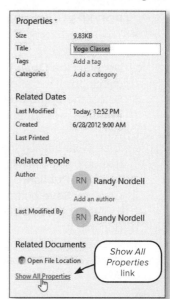

Figure Intro-118 Add document properties

d. Place your insertion point in the *Company* text box and type **Hamilton Civic Center** as the company name.

e. Click the **Back** arrow in the upper left of the *Backstage* window to return to the Excel workbook.

4. Use *Tell Me* to search for a topic.

a. Click the **Tell Me** search box at the top of the *Ribbon* and type **Cell formatting** (Figure Intro-119).

b. Select **Get Help on "Cell formatting"** and click **More Results for "Cell formatting"** to open the *Help* pane at the right.

c. Click the first result link to display information about the topic.

d. Click the **Back** arrow to return to the search list.

e. Click the **X** in the upper-right corner to close the *Help* pane.

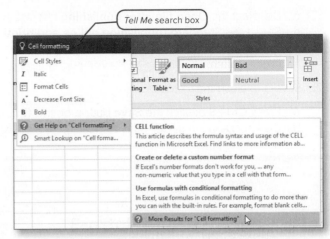

Figure Intro-119 Use *Tell Me* to search for a topic

5. Share an Excel workbook with your instructor. If your file is not saved on *OneDrive*, skip step 5.

a. Click the **Share** button in the upper-right corner of the Word window to open the *Send Link* window (Figure Intro-120). If you're using a personal Microsoft account, the *Share* pane displays at the right, and the sharing options differ slightly.

b. Click the **Link settings** button to open the *Link settings* window (Figure Intro-121).

c. Click the **Anyone** button and check the **Allow editing** box (if necessary).

d. Click **Apply** to close the *Link settings* window and return to the *Send Link* window.

e. Type your instructor's email address in the *Enter a name or email address* area (see Figure Intro-120).

f. Type a brief message to your instructor and click the **Send** button.

g. Click the **X** in the upper-right corner of the confirmation window to close it.

Figure Intro-120 *Send Link* window

Figure Intro-121 *Link settings* window

6. Export an Excel file as a PDF file.

a. Click the **File** tab to open the *Backstage* view.

b. Select **Export** on the left, select **Create PDF/XPS Document** in the *Export* area, and click the **Create PDF/XPS** button (Figure Intro-122). The *Publish as PDF or XPS* dialog box opens.

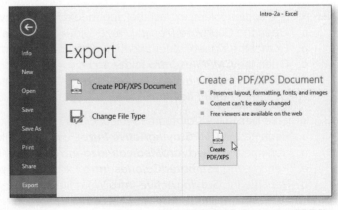

Figure Intro-122 Export as a PDF file

c. Deselect the **Open file after publishing** check box if it is checked.
   d. Select the **Standard (publishing online and printing)** radio button in the *Optimize for* area.
   e. Type [your initials] Intro-2b in the *File name* text box, select a location to save the file, and click **Publish**.

7. Save and close the Excel file.

   a. Press **Ctrl+S** or click the **Save** button on the *Quick Access* toolbar to save the worksheet.
   b. Click the **X** in the upper-right corner of the Excel window to close the file and Excel.

Independent Project Intro-3

For this project, you organize and edit files for Courtyard Medical Plaza. You extract a zipped folder, delete a folder, move files, rename files, export a file as a PDF file, and share a file.
[Student Learning Outcomes Intro.1, Intro.2, Intro.3, Intro.5, Intro.8]

File Needed: **CMPFiles-Intro** (zipped folder) *(Student data files are available in the* Library *of your SIMnet account.)*
Completed Project File Names: ***[your initials] Intro-3a.pptx***, ***[your initials] Intro-3a-pdf.pdf***, ***[your initials] Intro-3b.accdb***, ***[your initials] Intro-3c.xlsx***, and ***[your initials] Intro-3d.docx***

Skills Covered in This Project

- Copy and paste a zipped folder.
- Create a new folder in your *OneDrive* folder.
- Extract a zipped folder.
- Delete a folder.
- Move a file.
- Rename a file.
- Open a PowerPoint presentation.
- Export a file as a PDF file.
- Open a Word document.
- Share a file.

1. Copy a zipped folder and create a new *OneDrive* folder.
   a. Open a *File Explorer* window, browse to locate the **CMPFiles-Intro** zipped folder in your student data files and **Copy** the zipped folder.
   b. Go to your *OneDrive* folder and create a new folder named Courtyard Medical Plaza within the *OneDrive* folder. If *OneDrive* is not a storage option, select another location to create the new folder.

2. Paste a copied folder, extract the zipped folder, and move files.
   a. Open the *Courtyard Medical Plaza* folder and **Paste** the zipped folder.
   b. Extract the zipped folder and then delete the zipped folder.
   c. Open the **CMPFiles-Intro** folder and move all of the files to the *Courtyard Medical Plaza* folder.
   d. Return to the *Courtyard Medical Plaza* folder to confirm the four files were moved.
   e. Delete the **CMPFiles-Intro** folder.

3. Rename files in the *Courtyard Medical Plaza* folder.
   a. Rename the **CMPStayingActive-Intro** PowerPoint file as [your initials] Intro-3a.
   b. Rename the **CourtyardMedicalPlaza-Intro** Access file as [your initials] Intro-3b.
   c. Rename the **EstimatedCalories-Intro** Excel file as [your initials] Intro-3c.
   d. Rename the **StayingActive-Intro** Word file as [your initials] Intro-3d.

4. Export a PowerPoint file as a PDF file.
   a. Open the *[your initials] Intro-3a* file from the *Courtyard Medical Plaza* folder. The file opens in PowerPoint. If the file opens in *Protected View,* click the **Enable Editing** button.
   b. Export this file as a PDF file. Don't have the PDF file open after publishing and optimize for **Standard** format.
   c. Save the file as [your initials] Intro-3a-pdf and save in the *Courtyard Medical Plaza* folder.
   d. Close the PowerPoint file and exit PowerPoint.

5. Share a file with your instructor. If your files are not saved in *OneDrive*, skip step 5.
   a. Return to your *Courtyard Medical Plaza* folder and open the ***Intro-3d*** file. The file opens in Word. If the file opens in *Protected View*, click the **Enable Editing** button.
   b. Click the **Share** button in the upper-right corner of the Word window to open the *Send Link* window. If you're using a personal Microsoft account, the *Share* pane displays at the right, and the sharing options differ slightly.
   c. Click the **Link settings** button to open the *Link settings* window, click the **Anyone** button, check the **Allow editing** box (if necessary), and click **Apply** to close the *Link settings* window and return to the *Send Link* window.

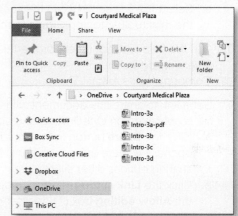

   d. Type your instructor's email address in the *Enter a name or email address* area.
   e. Type a brief message to your instructor and click the **Send** button.
   f. Click the **X** in the upper-right corner of the confirmation window to close it.

6. Save and close the document and exit Word.

7. Close the *File Explorer* window containing the files for this project (Figure Intro-123).

Figure Intro-123 Intro-3 completed

Independent Project Intro-4

For this project, you modify a Word file for Life's Animal Shelter. You create a folder, rename a document, add document properties, modify a document, create a sharing link, export a document as a PDF file, and create a zipped folder.
[**Student Learning Outcomes Intro.1, Intro.2, Intro.3, Intro.5, Intro.6, Intro.7, Intro.8**]

File Needed: ***LASSupportLetter-Intro.docx*** *(Student data files are available in the* Library *of your SIMnet account.)*
Completed Project File Names: *[your initials] Intro-4a.docx*, *[your initials] Intro-4b.pdf*, and ***LAS files*** (zipped folder)

Skills Covered in This Project

- Open a Word document.
- Create a new folder.
- Save a file with a different file name.

- Apply formatting to selected text.
- Add document properties to the file.
- Create a sharing link.
- Export a file as a PDF file.
- Create a zipped folder.

1. Open a Word document, create a new folder, and save the document with a different file name.
   a. Open Word.
   b. Open the **LASSupportLetter-Intro** Word document from your student data files. If the file opens in *Protected View*, click the **Enable Editing** button.
   c. Open the **Save As** dialog box and create a new folder named LAS in your *OneDrive* folder. If *OneDrive* is not a storage option, select another location to create the new folder.
   d. Save this document in the *LAS* folder and use [your initials] Intro-4a as the file name.

2. Apply formatting changes to the document using a dialog box, keyboard shortcut, and mini toolbar.
   a. Select "**To:**" in the memo heading and use the launcher to open the *Font* dialog box.
   b. Apply **Bold** and **All caps** to the selected text.
   c. Repeat the formatting on the other three memo guide words "**From:**", "**Date:**", and "**Subject:**".
   d. Select "**Life's Animal Shelter**" in the first sentence of the first body paragraph and press **Ctrl+B** to apply bold formatting.
   e. Select the first sentence in the second body paragraph ("**Would you again consider** . . . ") and use the mini toolbar to apply **italic** formatting.

3. Add the following document properties to the document:
   Title: Support Letter
   Company: Life's Animal Shelter

4. Get a link to share this document with your instructor and email your instructor the sharing link. If your file is not saved on *OneDrive*, skip step 5.
   a. Click the **Share** button in the upper-right corner of the Word window. The *Send Link* window opens. If you are using a personal Microsoft account, the *Share* pane opens at the right, and the sharing options differ slightly.
   b. Click the **Link settings** button to open the *Link settings* window, click the **Anyone** button, check the **Allow editing** box (if necessary), and click **Apply** to return to the *Send Link* window.
   c. Click the **Copy Link** button to create sharing link.
   d. Click **Copy** to copy the sharing link and click the **X** in the upper-right corner to close the sharing link window.
   e. Use your email account to create a new email to your instructor. Include an appropriate subject line and a brief message in the body.
   f. Press **Ctrl+V** to paste the sharing link to your document in the body of the email and send the email message.
   g. Click the **Task View** button on the Windows *Taskbar* and select the **Intro-4a** document to display this document.
   h. Use the **Save** command on the *Quick Access* toolbar to save the file before continuing.

5. Export this document as a PDF file.
   a. Export this file as a PDF file. Don't have the PDF file open after publishing and optimize for **Standard** format.
   b. Save the file as [your initials] Intro-4b and save in the *LAS* folder.
   c. Save and close the document and exit Word.

6. Create a zipped folder.
   a. Use *File Explorer* to open the **LAS** folder in your *OneDrive* folder.
   b. Select the two files and create a zipped folder.
   c. Name the zipped folder LAS files.

7. Close the open *File Explorer* window (Figure Intro-124).

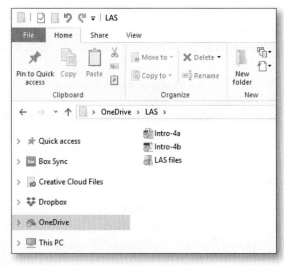

Figure Intro-124 Intro-4 completed

Challenge Project Intro-5

For this project, you create folders to organize your files for this class and share a file with your instructor.
[Student Learning Outcomes Intro.1, Intro.5, Intro.8]

Files Needed: Student data files for this course
Completed Project File Name: Share a file with your instructor

Using *File Explorer*, create *OneDrive* folders to contain all of the student data files for this class. Organize your files and folders according to the following guidelines:

- Create a *OneDrive* folder for this class.
- Create a *Student data files* folder inside the class folder.
- Copy and paste the student data files in the *Student data files* folder.
- Extract student data files and delete the zipped folder.
- Create a *Solution files* folder inside the class folder.
- Inside the *Solution files* folder, create a folder for each chapter.
- Create a folder to store miscellaneous class files such as the syllabus and other course handouts.
- Open one of the student data files and share the file with your instructor.

Challenge Project Intro-6

For this project, you save a file as a different file name, customize the *Quick Access* toolbar, share a file with your instructor, export a file as a PDF file, and create a zipped folder.
[Student Learning Outcomes Intro.1, Intro.2, Intro.3, Intro.5, Intro.6, Intro.8]

File Needed: Use an existing Office file
Completed Project File Names: *[your initials] Intro-6a* and *[your initials] Intro-6b*

Open an existing Word, Excel, or PowerPoint file. Save this file in a *OneDrive* folder and name it [your initials] Intro-6a. If you don't have any of these files, use one from your Pause & Practice projects or select a file from your student data files.

With your file open, perform the following actions:

- Create a new folder on *OneDrive* and save the file to this folder using a different file name.
- Customize the *Quick Access* toolbar to add command buttons. Add commands such as *New*, *Open*, *Quick Print*, and *Spelling* that you use regularly in the Office application.
- Share your file with your instructor. Enable your instructor to edit the file.
- Export the document as a PDF file. Save the file as [your initials] Intro-6b and save it in the same *OneDrive* folder as your open file.
- Zip the files in the folder.

Source of screenshots Microsoft Office 365 (2019): Word, Excel, Access, Powerpoint.

Microsoft® Office

IN PRACTICE

word

©Chris Ryan/Getty Images

Creating and Editing Documents

CHAPTER OVERVIEW

Microsoft Word (Word) has been and continues to be the leading word processing software in both the personal and business markets. Word improves with each new version and is used for creating and editing personal, business, and educational documents. Word enables you to create letters, memos, reports, flyers, brochures, and mailings without a vast amount of computer knowledge. This chapter covers the basics of creating and editing a Word document.

STUDENT LEARNING OUTCOMES (SLOs)

After completing this chapter, you will be able to:

SLO 1.1 Create, save, and open a Word document (p. 3).

SLO 1.2 Customize a document by entering and selecting text, using word wrap, and using *AutoComplete*, *AutoCorrect*, and *AutoFormat* features (p. 7).

SLO 1.3 Enhance a document using paragraph breaks, line breaks, spaces, and non-breaking spaces (p. 10).

SLO 1.4 Edit a document using cut, copy, paste, the *Clipboard*, and the undo, redo, and repeat features (p. 15).

SLO 1.5 Customize a document using different fonts, font sizes, and attributes (p. 18).

SLO 1.6 Enhance a document using text alignment and line and paragraph spacing (p. 28).

SLO 1.7 Finalize a document using Word's research, proofing, and learning tools (p. 32).

SLO 1.8 Apply custom document properties to a document (p. 38).

CASE STUDY

Throughout this book, you have the opportunity to practice the application features presented in each chapter. Each chapter begins with a case study that introduces you to the Pause & Practice projects in the chapter. Pause & Practice projects provide a chance to apply and practice key skills in a realistic and practical context. Each chapter contains three to five Pause & Practice projects.

Placer Hills Real Estate (PHRE) is a real estate company with regional offices throughout central California. PHRE encourages agents to use standard formats for their business documents. This ensures consistency in document appearance while also allowing agents to personalize their correspondence to customers and colleagues. In the Pause & Practice projects for this chapter, you create a business document related to the real estate business.

Pause & Practice 1-1: Create a business letter in block format with mixed punctuation.

Pause & Practice 1-2: Edit the business letter using copy, paste, and *Format Painter*. Modify the font, font size, color, style, and effects of selected text.

Pause & Practice 1-3: Finalize the business letter by modifying line spacing and paragraph spacing, changing paragraph alignment, translating text, using research and proofing tools, and adding document properties.

> **MORE INFO**
>
> *Appendix B: Business Document Formats* (online resource) contains examples of business documents.

SLO 1.1 Creating, Saving, and Opening Documents

In Microsoft Word, you can create a variety of document types. Your creativity and knowledge of Word enables you to create, edit, and customize high-quality and professional-looking documents. You can create Word documents from a new blank document, from existing Word templates, or from existing documents. Word enables you to save documents in a variety of formats.

Create a New Document

All new documents are based on the ***Normal template*** (*Normal.dotm*). When you create a Word document, a blank document displays in the Word window. This document has default fonts, font sizes, line and paragraph spacing, and margins—all of which are controlled by the *Normal* template.

▶ **HOW TO: Create a New Document**

1. Click the **File** tab to open the *Backstage* view.
   - When you first open Word, the *Start* page displays. You can open a new blank document from the *Start* page by clicking **Blank document**.
2. Click the **New** button (Figure 1-1).
3. Select **Blank document**. A new blank document opens in Word.

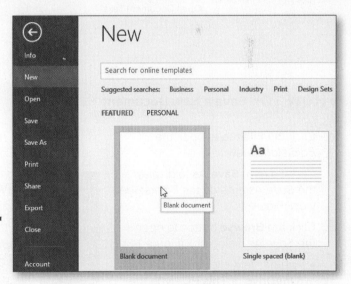

Figure 1-1 Open a new blank document

> **ANOTHER WAY**
>
> **Ctrl+N** opens a new blank document.

Save a Document

When you create a blank document, Word automatically assigns a generic file name to this document, such as *Document1*. Use the ***Save As dialog box*** to name and save a new document. You can save a Word document in a variety of file formats. By default, a Word document is saved as a ***.docx*** file. Other types of Word files are discussed throughout this text. Table 1-1 lists the more commonly used file formats.

Table 1-1: Save Formats

Type of File	File Extension	Uses
Word Document	.docx	Standard Word document.
Word Macro-Enabled Document	.docm	Word document with embedded macros.
Word 97-2003 Document	.doc	Word document that is compatible with previous versions of Microsoft Word.
Word Template	.dotx	Create a new document based upon a template.
Word Macro-Enabled Template	.dotm	Create a new document based upon a template with embedded macros.
Portable Document Format (PDF)	.pdf	Similar to a picture of a document that is used to preserve the formatting of a document.
Rich Text Format (RTF)	.rtf	Generic file format read by many different types of word processing programs while retaining the basic format of the document.
Plain Text	.txt	Files contain only text with no special formatting and open with most word processing programs.
Open Document Text	.odt	Format used in the Open Office word processing program.

▶ HOW TO: Save a New Document

1. Click the **File** tab to open the *Backstage* view.

2. Click **Save** or **Save As** to display the *Save As* area on the *Backstage* view (Figure 1-2).

3. Click the **Browse** button to open the *Save As* dialog box (Figure 1-3).

   - Alternatively, click a save location (**OneDrive** or **This PC**), type the file name in the *Enter file name here* text box, and click **Save**. To change the save location, click the **More options** link to open the *Save As* dialog box (see Figure 1-2).

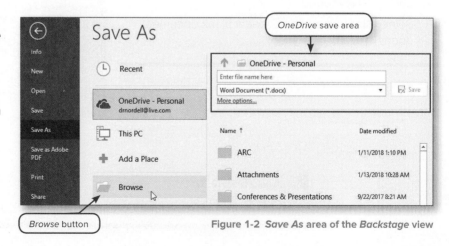

Figure 1-2 *Save As* area of the *Backstage* view

- You can also click the **Recent** button and select a recently used folder to open the *Save As* dialog box.

4. Use the folder list on the left side of the *Save As* dialog box to browse to a location to save the file (see Figure 1-3).

5. Type the file name in the *File name* area.

6. Click the **Save** button.

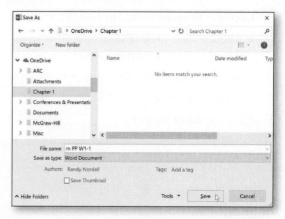

Figure 1-3 *Save As* dialog box

> **ANOTHER WAY**
>
> **F12** opens the *Save As* dialog box. When using a laptop computer, you might have to press the **Fn** (Function) key and the **F12** key to open the *Save As* dialog box.

After you have named and saved a document, you can save changes to the document without opening the *Save As* dialog box in the following ways:

- Press **Ctrl+S**.
- Click the **Save** button on the *Quick Access* toolbar.
- Select **Save** from the *Backstage* view.

AutoSave

AutoSave is a new feature that automatically saves a document that is stored on *OneDrive*, Microsoft's cloud storage area. The *AutoSave* feature turns on by default when you save a document to *OneDrive*, and the document is automatically saved as you change it.

This feature displays in the upper-left corner of the document (Figure 1-4). Click the **AutoSave** button to turn it on or off. When *AutoSave* is on, the save options on the *Backstage* view change from *Save* and *Save As* to **Save a Copy**.

Office 2019 Note: The *AutoSave* feature is not available in Office 2019.

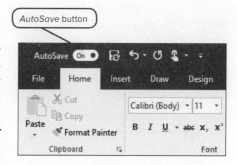

Figure 1-4 *AutoSave* feature

Save As a Different File Name

You can save a document as a different name by opening the *Save As* dialog box and typing a new file name. When you save a file with a different file name, the original document is not changed and is still available. Saving with a different file name creates a new version of the original document, but the new document has a different file name.

▶ **HOW TO:** Save As a Different File Name

1. Click the **File** tab to open the *Backstage* view.

2. Click the **Save As** button to display the *Save As* area.

- If *AutoSave* is turned on, *Save a Copy* is the save option on the *Backstage* view rather than *Save* and *Save As*.

3. Click the **Browse** button or select a recent folder to open the *Save As* dialog box (see Figure 1-3).
   - Alternatively, press **F12** to open the *Save As* dialog box from within Word (not the *Backstage* view). You may have to press the **Fn** (Function) key and the **F12** key to open the *Save As* dialog box when using a laptop.
4. Use the folder list on the left side of the *Save As* dialog box to browse to a location to save the file.
5. Type the file name in the *File name* area.
6. Click the **Save** button.

> **MORE INFO**
>
> Avoid saving too many different versions of the same document. Rename only when you have a good reason to have multiple versions of a document.

Open a Document

You can open an existing document from your computer, *OneDrive*, other storage location, or an attachment from an email. After you open a document, edit the content and save the changes to the document.

▶HOW TO: Open a Document

1. Click the **File** tab to open the *Backstage* view.
2. Click the **Open** button to display the *Open* area on the *Backstage* view.
3. Select the location where the document is stored.
   - The *Recent* area displays a list of recently used documents or folders.
   - You can also open a document from *OneDrive* or *This PC*.
4. Select a file or folder to open or click **Browse** to open the *Open* dialog box (Figure 1-5).
5. Select the file and click the **Open** button.
   - If the document opens in *Protected View*, click the **Enable Editing** button.

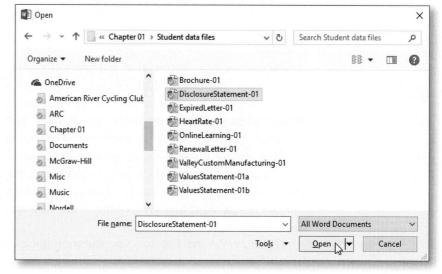

Figure 1-5 *Open* dialog box

> **ANOTHER WAY**
>
> **Ctrl+F12** opens the *Open* dialog box. Laptops may require **Fn+Ctrl+F12**.

Pin a Frequently Used Document

If you use a document frequently, pin it to the *Open* area on the *Backstage* view. Pinned documents appear at the top of the *Recent* documents list so you can quickly open the document.

In the *Open* area on the *Backstage* view, click **Recent** and then click the **pin** icon to the right of a file name to add the document to the *Pinned* area (Figure 1-6). Pinned files display in the *Pinned* area of the *Start* page and *Open* area of the *Backstage* view. Click the pinned file to open it.

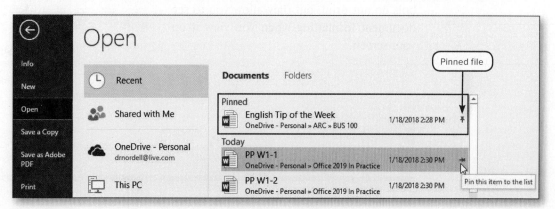

Figure 1-6 The *Pinned* area in the *Open* area on the *Backstage* view

Entering and Selecting Text

When creating or editing a document, you can type new text, insert text from another document, or copy text from a web page or another document. It is important to understand how to enter text, use word wrap, select text, show or hide formatting symbols, and use *AutoComplete* and *AutoCorrect* options to create professional-looking documents.

Type Text and Use Word Wrap

Word inserts text where the insertion point is flashing in the document. By default, text is aligned at the left margin and the text wraps to the next line when it reaches the right margin. This feature is called ***word wrap***. Press **Enter** to begin a new paragraph or line of text.

Show/Hide Formatting Symbols

The ***Show/Hide*** feature displays or hides formatting symbols in your document. By default, *Show/Hide* is turned off and formatting symbols do not display in your document. When the *Show/Hide* feature is turned on, you can see paragraph breaks, line breaks, spaces, tabs, and other formatting symbols to help you create clean documents and to edit existing documents (Figure 1-7).

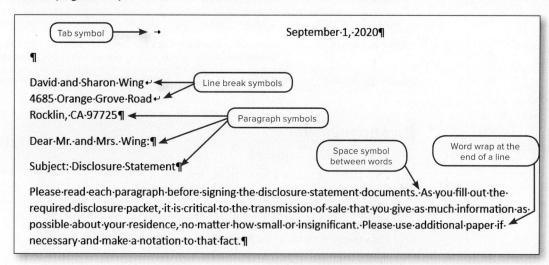

Figure 1-7 Document with *Show/Hide* turned on

Click the **Show/Hide** button in the *Paragraph* group on the *Home* tab to toggle on and off *Show/Hide* (Figure 1-8). These symbols do not print, but they allow you to see document formatting when you view it on your screen.

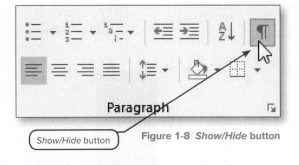

Show/Hide button

Figure 1-8 *Show/Hide* button

> ### ANOTHER WAY
> **Ctrl+Shift+8** turns on and off *Show/Hide*.

> ### MORE INFO
> When editing a document that has inconsistent formatting, begin by turning on **Show/Hide**.

Select Text

Word enables you to select words, lines, sentences, paragraphs, or the entire document. Select text to apply formatting, copy, move, or delete selected text. One way to select text is to click and drag the pointer over text. Word provides a variety of additional quick methods to select text. Table 1-2 lists ways to select text.

Table 1-2: Selecting Text

Select	Method
Word	Double-click the word.
Line	Click the *Selection* area, which is to the left of the left margin. Your pointer becomes a right-pointing arrow.
Multiple lines of text	Click the *Selection* area and drag up or down.
Sentence	Press **Ctrl+Click**. Hold down the **Ctrl** key and click the sentence.
Paragraph	Double-click the *Selection* area to the left of the paragraph.
Multiple paragraphs	Click the *Selection* area to the left of the first line of the paragraph and drag down.
Entire document	Press **Ctrl+A** or **Ctrl+Click** the *Selection* area. An alternative is to click the **Select** button [*Home* tab, *Editing* group] and choose **Select All**.
Non-adjacent text	Select text, press and hold the **Ctrl** key, and select non-adjacent text.

> ### ANOTHER WAY
> **F8** is the selection function key.
>
> Press once: Use the arrow keys to select text.
> Press twice: Select word.
> Press three times: Select sentence.
> Press four times: Select paragraph.
> Press five times: Select entire document.
>
> Press **Esc** to turn off **F8** selection.

AutoComplete

When you type a day, month, or date, Word uses the *AutoComplete* feature to automatically complete typing the date. AutoComplete saves you a few key strokes and enables you to be more efficient and accurate when entering dates. As you begin to type the date, Word displays the information in an *AutoComplete tag* (Figure 1-9). Press **Enter** to accept the *AutoComplete* entry. If you do not want this *AutoComplete* entry, keep typing and the *AutoComplete* entry disappears.

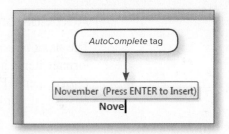

Figure 1-9 *AutoComplete* tag

AutoCorrect and AutoFormat

When you're typing, do you ever misspell a word by transposing letters or omitting a letter or adding a letter? Because we all regularly type errors, the *AutoCorrect* feature recognizes and corrects commonly misspelled words and grammatical errors. Word automatically inserts the following corrections:

- Eliminates two initial capitals in a word
- Capitalizes the first letter of a sentence
- Capitalizes the first letter of table cells
- Capitalizes the names of days
- Corrects accidental usage of the *Caps Lock* key
- Changes fractions such as 3/4 to ¾ and numbers such as 2nd to 2nd

Word's *AutoFormat* controls the formatting of items such as numbered and bulleted lists, fractions, ordinal numbers, hyphens and dashes, quotes, indents, and hyperlinks. For example, when you type 3/4 followed by a space, *AutoFormat* automatically changes the format of the fraction to ¾.

AutoCorrect Smart Tag

When Word automatically applies a correction or formatting change, you have the option to accept the change, undo the change, stop Word from making the change, or control *AutoCorrect* using the *AutoCorrect Options* dialog box. If you continue typing, the change is accepted. Often when Word automatically corrects a word, you don't even recognize that a change has been made.

If you do not want to accept a change, click the *AutoCorrect Options smart tag* on the changed word to open the *AutoCorrect Options* menu (Figure 1-10). For example, when you type reference initials at the end of a business letter, Word automatically capitalizes the first letter. Undo this automatic capitalization by clicking the *AutoCorrect Options* smart tag and selecting **Undo Automatic Capitalization**.

> ▶ **ANOTHER WAY**
>
> Press **Ctrl+Z** to reverse an automatic correction made by Word.

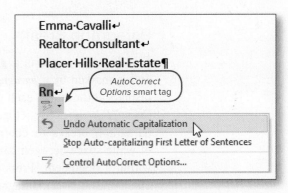

Figure 1-10 *AutoCorrect Options* smart tag

Add Custom AutoCorrect Entry

The *AutoCorrect* dialog box enables you to customize how Word automatically corrects and formats items in a document. In this dialog box, you can also add custom items to the *AutoCorrect* menu. For example, you can add a custom entry to the *AutoCorrect* menu to correct a misspelled word or type your name every time you type your initials.

▶**HOW TO:** Add a Custom AutoCorrect Entry

1. Click the **File** tab to open the *Backstage* view.
2. Choose the **Options** button to open the *Word Options* dialog box.
3. Click the **Proofing** button on the left.
4. Select the **AutoCorrect Options** button. The *AutoCorrect* dialog box opens (Figure 1-11).
5. Type the text you want to replace in the *Replace* box.
6. Type the word(s) to replace the original text in the *With* box.
7. Choose **Add** to add this custom *AutoCorrect* entry.
   - Delete an *AutoCorrect* entry in the *AutoCorrect* dialog box by selecting the entry and clicking **Delete**.
   - Add exceptions to *AutoCorrect* by clicking the **Exceptions** button.
8. Click **OK** to close the *AutoCorrect* dialog box.
9. Click **OK** to close the *Word Options* dialog box.

Figure 1-11 *AutoCorrect* dialog box

Using Paragraph Breaks, Line Breaks, and Non-Breaking Spaces

Use paragraph and line breaks to organize a document into more readable groups of text. Several types of breaks are available to create attractive and readable documents.

Paragraph Breaks

The **Enter** key inserts a **paragraph break** and is marked by a **paragraph symbol** that displays at the end of each paragraph when *Show/Hide* is active (Figure 1-12). Use paragraph breaks to control the amount of white space between paragraphs of text within a document. Press **Enter** to create blank lines between paragraphs.

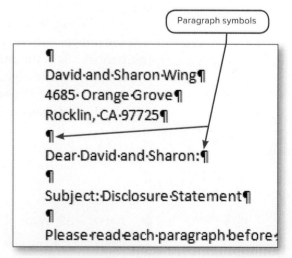

Figure 1-12 Paragraph breaks after and between lines

Many formatting features, such as indents, numbering, bullets, text alignment, line spacing, and paragraph spacing, apply to an entire paragraph. For example, if the insertion point is within a paragraph and you change the line spacing to double space, the entire paragraph is formatted with double spacing. It is not applied to the entire document or just the line where the insertion point is located. For more on line and paragraph spacing, see *SLO 1.6: Changing Text Alignment, Line Spacing, and Paragraph Spacing.*

Line Breaks

Use *line breaks* to control breaks between lines or sentences of text. The distinction between a paragraph break and a line break is that when line breaks are used, the text separated by line breaks is treated as one paragraph. Press **Shift+Enter** to insert a line break.

Use line breaks within a numbered or bulleted list to allow for multiple lines of text on separate lines or blank lines between the text without creating a new number or bullet (Figure 1-13). The line break symbol is different from the paragraph symbol.

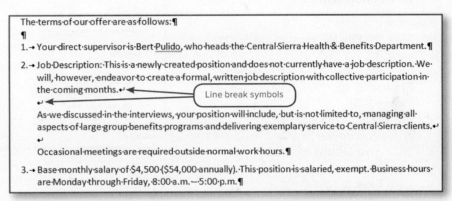

Figure 1-13 Line breaks used in a numbered list

Spaces and Non-Breaking Spaces

Use the *spacebar* to insert a space between words. Current practice now dictates one space after most punctuation marks, including periods, commas, semicolons, and ending quotation marks. Do not use spaces after a beginning quotation mark, before or after a hyphen in a hyphenated word, or when using a dash.

Occasionally, word wrap separates words that you may want to keep together. For example, you might want to keep a person's first and last name or a date together on the same line. In this case, use a *non-breaking space* to keep these words together. To insert a non-breaking space, press **Ctrl+Shift+Spacebar** between words rather than inserting a regular space. In Figure 1-14, a non-breaking space is used between 8:00 and a.m., which keeps this information together.

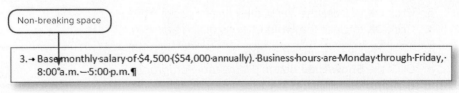

Figure 1-14 Non-breaking space used to keep text together

In this project, you create a block format business letter for Emma Cavalli, a realtor consultant for Placer Hills Real Estate. In a block format business letter, all lines begin at the left margin. For more examples of business documents, see *Appendix B* (online resource).

File Needed: None
Completed Project File Name: ***[your initials] PP W1-1.docx***

1. Open a new document.
   a. Open Microsoft Word and click **Blank document** on the *Start* page. If Word is already open, click the **File** tab to open the *Backstage* view, click **New**, and click **Blank document**.

2. Save the document.
   a. Click the **File** tab to open the *Backstage* view.
   b. Click **Save As** on the left and then click **Browse** to open the *Save As* dialog box (Figure 1-15).
   c. Browse to the location on your computer or storage device to save the document.
   d. Type [your initials] PP W1-1 in the *File name* area.
   e. Click **Save** to save the document.

Figure 1-15 *Save As* dialog box

> **ANOTHER WAY**
>
> **F12** opens the *Save As* dialog box. When using a laptop computer, you might have to press the **Fn** (Function) key and the **F12** key to open the *Save As* dialog box.

3. Create an *AutoCorrect* entry.
   a. Click the **File** tab to open the *Backstage* view and select **Options** on the left to open the *Word Options* dialog box.
   b. Click the **Proofing** button on the left and select **AutoCorrect Options** to open the *AutoCorrect* dialog box (Figure 1-16).
   c. Click the **AutoCorrect** tab if it is not already selected.
   d. Type Cavali in the *Replace* area.
   e. Type Cavalli in the *With* area.
   f. Click the **Add** button to add the *AutoCorrect* entry.
   g. Click **OK** to close the *AutoCorrect* dialog box.
   h. Click **OK** to close the *Word Options* dialog box.

4. Use *AutoComplete* to insert a date.
   a. Click the **Show/Hide** button [*Home* tab, *Paragraph* group] to turn on the *Show/Hide* feature.

Figure 1-16 Add an *AutoCorrect* entry

b. Begin typing the current date on the first line of the document (use September 1, 2020 format) and press **Enter** when the *AutoComplete* tag appears. The month is automatically inserted (Figure 1-17).

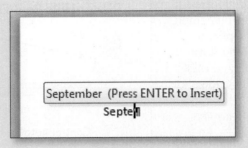

Figure 1-17 *AutoComplete* tag

c. Continue typing the rest of the date; press **Enter** if the *AutoCorrect* tag displays the current date.
d. Press **Enter** two times after typing the date.

5. Type the inside address, salutation, and subject line of the letter.
  a. Type **David and Sharon Wing** and press **Shift+Enter** to insert a line break.
  b. Type 4685 Orange Grove Road and press **Shift+Enter** to insert a line break.
  c. Type Rocklin, CA 97725 and press **Enter** to insert a paragraph break.
  d. Type Dear Mr. and Mrs. Wing: as the salutation and press **Enter**.
  e. Type Subject: Disclosure Statement as the subject and press **Enter**.

> ### MORE INFO
>
> In the salutation of a business letter, use "Dear" followed by a courtesy title (Mr., Mrs., Ms., Miss, or Dr.) and the person's last name.

6. Type the body paragraphs of the business letter and insert a non-breaking space.
  a. Type the following paragraph and press **Enter** once at the end of the paragraph. You will not need to press *Enter* at the end of each line because word wrap automatically moves text to the next line as you reach the right margin.

   Please read each paragraph before signing the disclosure statement documents. As you fill out the required disclosure packet, it is critical to the transmission of sale that you give as much information as possible about your residence, no matter how small or insignificant. Please use additional paper if necessary and make a notation to that fact.

  b. Type the following second paragraph and press **Enter** once at the end of the paragraph.

   If there is information about the neighborhood or neighbors that you as a buyer would want to know about, be sure to reveal that information. Be sure to address those types of questions on the Real Estate Transfer Disclosure Statement, item #11 on page 2.

  c. Delete the space between the words "Real" and "Estate" in the second paragraph and press **Ctrl+Shift+Spacebar** to insert a non-breaking space between.

7. Type the closing lines of the business letter.
  a. Place your insertion point on the blank line below the second body paragraph, type Best regards, and then press **Enter** two times.
  b. Type Emma Cavalli and press **Shift+Enter** to insert a line break.
  c. Type Realtor Consultant and press **Shift+Enter** to insert a line break.
  d. Type Placer Hills Real Estate and press **Enter** to insert a paragraph break.

e. Type your initials in lowercase letters and press **Shift+Enter** to insert a line break. Word automatically capitalizes the first letter because it is the first letter in a new paragraph.

f. Click the **AutoCorrect Options** smart tag and select **Undo Automatic Capitalization** (Figure 1-18) or press **Ctrl+Z** to undo automatic capitalization.

g. Type Enclosure on the blank line below the reference initials. An enclosure notation indicates to the reader that something is enclosed with the letter.

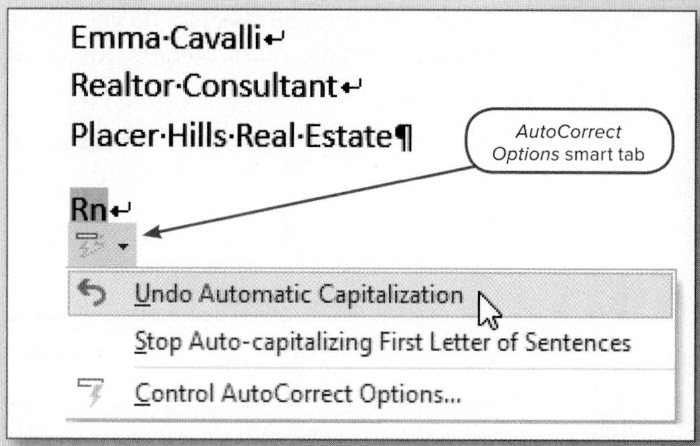

Emma·Cavalli↵

Realtor·Consultant↵

Placer·Hills·Real·Estate¶

AutoCorrect Options smart tab

Rn↵

↶ Undo Automatic Capitalization

Stop Auto-capitalizing First Letter of Sentences

⚡ Control AutoCorrect Options...

Figure 1-18 *AutoCorrect Options* smart tag

8. Press **Ctrl+S** to save the document (Figure 1-19). You can also save the document by clicking the **Save** button on the *Quick Access* toolbar or in the *Backstage* view.

9. Click the **File** tab and select **Close** (or press **Ctrl+W**) to close the document.

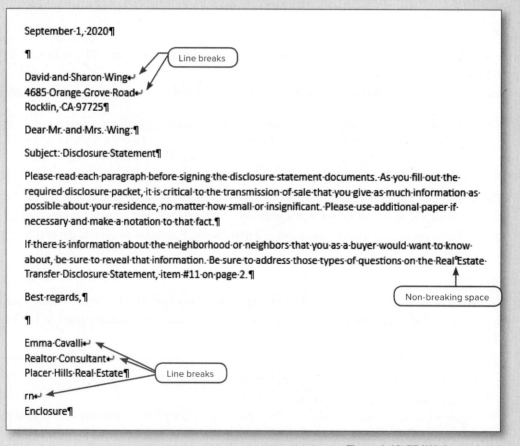

Figure 1-19 PP W1-1 completed

SLO 1.4

Moving and Copying Text

Editing is an important phase in document creation. Editing involves not only proofreading and correcting grammar and spelling mistakes but also arranging text within a document, which can include cutting, copying, and pasting. Word provides tools to easily move and copy information within a document or between multiple documents.

Move Text

Moving text removes it from one location (cut) and places it in another location (paste). Two methods used to move text are *drag and drop* or *cut and paste*.

> **ANOTHER WAY**
>
> Press **Ctrl+C** to copy.
> Press **Ctrl+X** to cut.
> Press **Ctrl+V** to paste.

▶ HOW TO: Move Text Using Drag and Drop

1. Select the text you want to move.
   - Refer to the "Select Text" section in *SLO 1.2: Entering and Selecting Text* for methods of selecting text.
2. Click and hold the selected text with your pointer.
3. Drag the text to the desired new location and release the pointer (Figure 1-20).

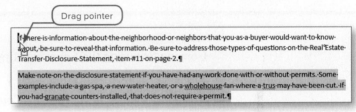

Figure 1-20 Move using drag and drop

The following are ways to move text using *Cut* and *Paste*:

- *Cut and Paste buttons*: Click the **Cut** and **Paste** buttons in the *Clipboard* group on the *Home* tab.
- *Shortcut commands*: Press **Ctrl+X** to cut and **Ctrl+V** to paste.
- *Context menu*: Right-click the selected text to display this menu.

▶ HOW TO: Move Text Using Cut and Paste

1. Select the text you want to move.
2. Click the **Cut** button [*Home* tab, *Clipboard* group].
   - You can also press **Ctrl+X** or right-click the selected text and choose **Cut** from the context menu.
3. Place your insertion point in the desired location.
4. Click the **Paste** button [*Home* tab, *Clipboard* group].
   - Alternatively, press **Ctrl+V** or right-click and choose from one of the *Paste Options* from the context menu. *Note:* See the "Paste Text and Paste Options" section below for the different paste options available.

Copy Text

An efficient method of inserting text into a document is to copy it from another location, such as a web page or a different document, and paste it into your document. Copying text leaves the text in its original location and places a copy of the text in a new location.

You can *copy* text by using the drag-and-drop method or the *Copy* and *Paste* buttons. Use the drag-and-drop method when copying text within the same document. The drag-and-drop method for copying is similar to the method for moving, except that you press the **Ctrl** key when dragging the text to be copied to another location.

▶ **HOW TO:** Copy Text Using Drag and Drop

1. Select the text you want to copy.
2. Press the **Ctrl** key and click and hold the selected text with your pointer.
   - A + (plus sign) appears next to your pointer, indicating this text is being copied.
3. Drag to the desired new location and release the pointer (Figure 1-21). Release the **Ctrl** key after you have released the pointer.

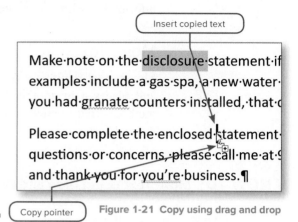

Figure 1-21 Copy using drag and drop

Copying text using the following copy and paste method is similar to moving text using the cut and paste method:

- *Copy and Paste buttons*: Press the **Copy** and **Paste** buttons in the *Clipboard* group on the *Home* tab.
- *Shortcut commands*: Press **Ctrl+C** to copy and **Ctrl+V** to paste.
- *Context menu*: Right-click the selected text to display this menu.

Paste Text and Paste Options

Word provides multiple paste options. You may want to paste plain text without formatting into a document or merge the format from the source document into the new document. You have three primary paste options when you use the *Paste* button in the *Clipboard* group (Figure 1-22) or from the context menu:

- *Keep Source Formatting*: Retains formatting from source document (the document where the text was copied)
- *Merge Formatting*: Merges formatting from source document and current document
- *Keep Text Only*: Pastes only unformatted text

The default paste option is *Keep Source Formatting*. In addition to these paste options, other contextual paste options are available when you paste information from lists, tables, or graphic objects.

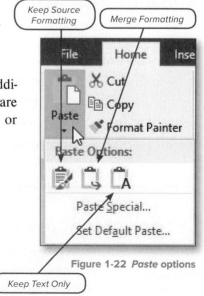

Figure 1-22 *Paste* options

▶ MORE INFO

If you have trouble with the format of pasted text, try pasting the text as plain text and formatting the text *after* you have pasted it into the document.

Clipboard Pane

When you copy or cut an item from a document, Word stores this information on the **Clipboard**. The *Clipboard* stores text, pictures, tables, lists, and graphics. When Word is open, the *Clipboard* stores multiple items copied from Word documents and also items from web pages or other applications. From the *Clipboard*, you can select a previously copied item and paste it into a document.

The **Clipboard pane** displays all the items stored on *Clipboard*. To display the *Clipboard* pane, click the **Clipboard** launcher in the bottom-right corner of the *Clipboard* group on the *Home* tab (Figure 1-23). The *Clipboard* pane displays on the left side of the Word window and stores up to 24 copied items.

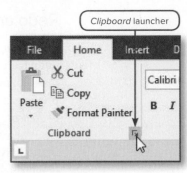

Figure 1-23 *Clipboard* launcher

> **MORE INFO**
>
> The *launcher* (also referred to as the *dialog box launcher*) is referred to throughout this text. Click the launcher in the bottom-right corner of a group to open a dialog box or pane for additional options.

▶ HOW TO: Use the Clipboard Pane to Paste Text

1. Select the text you want to copy or cut and click the **Copy** or **Cut** button [*Home* tab, *Clipboard* group].
   - Alternatively, press **Ctrl+C** to copy or **Ctrl+X** to cut selected text.
2. Place the insertion point in the document where you want to paste the text.
3. Click the **Clipboard** launcher to open the *Clipboard* pane on the left side of the Word window (see Figure 1-23).
4. Click the item to paste or click the drop-down arrow to the right of the item and choose **Paste** (Figure 1-24). The selected content from the *Clipboard* is inserted in the document.
   - *Paste All* pastes all the items in the *Clipboard* at the insertion point in the document.
   - *Clear All* empties the contents of the *Clipboard*.
5. Click the **X** in the upper-right corner of the *Clipboard* pane to close it.

Figure 1-24 *Clipboard* pane

Undo Change

You can undo, redo, or repeat previous actions. All these commands are available on the **Quick Access toolbar**, which is above the *Ribbon* on the upper left.

When you click the *Undo* button, the last action you performed is reversed. Undo multiple actions by clicking the **Undo** drop-down arrow to the right of the button and selecting the actions to undo (Figure 1-25). For example, if you select the third item in the list to undo, the previous two items will also undo.

Figure 1-25 *Undo* button on the *Quick Access* toolbar

Redo and Repeat Change

The **Redo** and **Repeat** features are similar to the undo feature. The same button is used for both commands, and it is context sensitive. Depending on the previous action performed, the button is either *Redo* or *Repeat*.

Figure 1-26 *Redo* button on the *Quick Access* toolbar

When you use the *Undo* button, the *Redo* button is activated so you can redo the previous change (Figure 1-26).

When you perform an action or apply formatting in a document, the *Repeat* button is activated (the icon changes) so you can repeat the previous action or formatting (Figure 1-27). For example, if you need to copy the date or a name into a document in multiple places, use the *Repeat* feature to accomplish this task quickly and accurately.

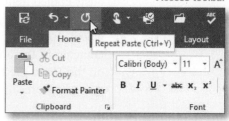

Figure 1-27 *Repeat* button on the *Quick Access* toolbar

> **ANOTHER WAY**
>
> Press **Ctrl+Z** to undo.
> Press **Ctrl+Y** to redo or repeat.

SLO 1.5

Changing Fonts, Font Sizes, and Attributes

Word has many features to customize the appearance of text within a document. You can change the font and font size; add font styles such as bold, italic, and underlining; change the case of text; add font and text effects; adjust the scale, spacing, and position of text; and change the default font settings. You can use buttons in the *Font* group on the *Home* tab, the *Font* dialog box, and the mini toolbar to apply formatting to text.

Font and Font Size

The two main categories of fonts are serif and sans serif. **Serif fonts** have structural details (flair) at the top and bottom of most of the letters. Commonly used serif fonts include Cambria, Times New Roman, and Courier New. **Sans serif fonts** have no structural details on the letters. Commonly used sans serif fonts include Calibri, Arial, and Century Gothic.

Font size is measured in **points** (pt.); the larger the point, the larger the font. Most documents use between 10 and 12 pt. font sizes. Titles and headings generally are larger font sizes.

When creating a new document, choose a font and font size before you begin typing, and it applies to the entire document. If you want to change the font or font size of existing text, select the text before applying the change.

> **MORE INFO**
>
> The default font and font size in Microsoft Word are Calibri and 11 pt.

▶**HOW TO: Change Font and Font Size**

1. Select the text you want to format.
2. Click the **Font** drop-down list to display the list of available fonts (Figure 1-28).
   - The *Font* drop-down list has three sections: *Theme Fonts*, *Recently Used Fonts*, and *All Fonts*.
3. Select the font to apply to the selected text.
4. Click the **Font Size** drop-down list to display the list of available font sizes (Figure 1-29).

Figure 1-28 *Font drop-down list*

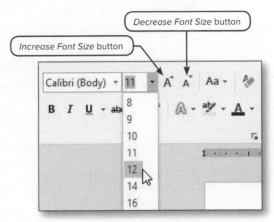

Figure 1-29 *Font size drop-down list*

5. Select a font size to apply to selected text.
   - You can also click the **Font Size** text box and type a size.
   - Click the **Increase Font Size** and **Decrease Font Size** buttons to increase or decrease the size of the font in small increments.

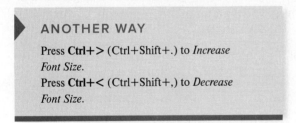

ANOTHER WAY

Press **Ctrl+>** (Ctrl+Shift+.) to *Increase Font Size*.
Press **Ctrl+<** (Ctrl+Shift+,) to *Decrease Font Size*.

Figure 1-30 Select or right-click text to display the mini toolbar

The *mini toolbar* displays when you select or right-click text (Figure 1-30). Use the mini toolbar to apply text formatting. Similar to the context menu, the mini toolbar is contextual and displays different options depending on the selection.

Bold, Italic, and Underline Font Styles

Add *font styles* such as **Bold**, *Italic*, and <u>Underline</u> to fonts to improve their appearance or call attention to specific text. The font style buttons for *Bold*, *Italic*, and *Underline* are available in the *Font* group on the *Home* tab.

To apply a font style, select the desired text, and click the **Bold, Italic,** or **Underline** button in the *Font* group on the *Home* tab (Figure 1-31). You can also click a font style button to turn on a style, type the text, and click the font style button again to turn off the style.

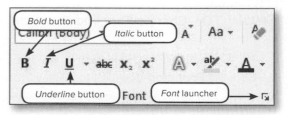

Figure 1-31 *Font* group on the *Home* tab

> ### ANOTHER WAY
>
> **Ctrl+B** applies *Bold* formatting.
> **Ctrl+I** applies *Italic* formatting.
> **Ctrl+U** applies *Underline* formatting.

Other Font Style Buttons

The following are other font styles and effects in the *Font* group on the *Home* tab (see Figure 1-31). Several style and effect features display on the mini toolbar when you select or right-click text:

- *Strikethrough*
- *Subscript*
- *Superscript*
- *Text Effects and Typography*, which includes *Outline, Shadow, Reflection, Glow, Number Styles, Ligatures,* and *Stylistic Sets*
- *Text Highlight Color*
- *Font Color*

Change Case

The ***Change Case*** feature provides a quick and easy way to change the case of a single word or group of words. The *Change Case* button is in the *Font* group on the *Home* tab (Figure 1-32). The different case options are:

- *Sentence case* (capitalizes the first letter of the sentence)
- *lowercase*
- *UPPERCASE*
- *Capitalize Each Word*
- *tOGGLE cASE* (changes letters that are uppercase to lowercase and lowercase letters to uppercase)

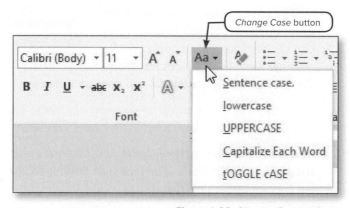

Figure 1-32 *Change Case* options

Font Dialog Box

The ***Font dialog box*** combines many of the *font style* and *effect options* in one location for easy access. Click the **Font** launcher in the bottom-right corner of the *Font* group to open the *Font* dialog box (Figure 1-33).

In addition to the *Font*, *Font Style*, and *Size* commands on the *Font* tab, use the *Font* dialog box to change *Font Color*, *Underline Style*, *Underline Color*, and *Effects*. The *Preview* area displays a preview of selected changes, styles, and effects.

The *Advanced* tab lists *Character Spacing* options such as *Scale*, *Spacing*, *Position*, and *Kerning*. From this tab, you can also open the *Format Text Effects* dialog box.

Figure 1-33 *Font* dialog box

> ANOTHER WAY
>
> **Ctrl+D** opens the *Font* dialog box.

Font Color

By default, the font color in a Word document is black. You can change the font color of selected text to add emphasis. The ***Font Color*** drop-down list in the *Font* dialog box displays a list of available font colors.

> **HOW TO:** Change Font Color

1. Select the text you want to be a different color.
2. Click the **Font** launcher [*Home* tab, *Font* group]. The *Font* dialog box opens (Figure 1-34).
3. Click the **Font Color** drop-down arrow to display the list of font colors.
   - The drop-down list of font color options includes *Theme Colors*, *Standard Colors*, and *More Colors*. Theme colors are those colors associated with the theme of the document. For more on themes, see *SLO 2.7: Using Styles and Themes*.
4. Choose **OK** to close the *Font* dialog box.

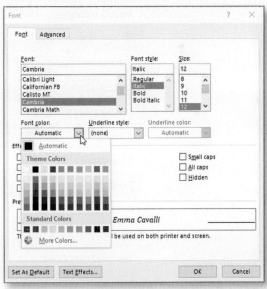

Figure 1-34 Change font color in the *Font* dialog box

> ANOTHER WAY
>
> Change the font color by clicking the **Font Color** button [*Home* tab, *Font* group].

Underline Style and Color

When you underline selected text, the default underline style is a solid black underline. Word provides a variety of additional underline styles. You can also change the color of the underline.

The *Underline style* and *Underline color* drop-down lists are available in the *Font* dialog box (Figure 1-35). A preview of the formatted text displays in the *Preview* area of the *Font* dialog box.

Font Effects

Use the *Font* dialog box to apply font effects from a variety of options in the *Effects* section. Several font effects are also available in the *Font* group on the *Home* tab. Table 1-3 lists the different font styles and effects.

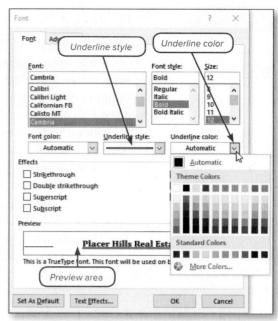

Figure 1-35 Change underline style and color

Table 1-3: Font Styles and Effects

Style/Effect	Example
Bold	This **word** is in bold.
Italic	This *word* is in italic.
Bold and Italic	This ***word*** is in bold and italic.
Underline	This sentence is underlined.
Double underline	This word is double underlined.
Underline Words only	This sentence is words only underlined.
Thick underline with color	This word has a thick, colored underline.
Strikethrough	This ~~word~~ has a strikethrough.
Double strikethrough	~~This sentence has a double strikethrough.~~
Subscript	H_2O uses a subscript number.
Superscript	Footnotes and endnotes use superscript numbers or letters.[1]
Small caps	MICROSOFT WORD is in small caps.
All caps	THIS SENTENCE IS IN ALL CAPS.
Hidden	
Text Highlight Color	This word has a highlight color.
Font Color	This sentence has a font color applied.

> **MORE INFO**
>
> *Hidden* text appears in your on-screen document, but it does not print or display in print preview.

Character Spacing

Character Spacing options allow you to add more or less space between letters and words. You can also vertically raise and lower letters and words (Figure 1-36).

- ***Scale***: Changes the horizontal spacing of a word or group of words by a percentage. Choose from preset percentages or type a custom percentage for scaling.
- ***Spacing***: Increases or decreases the space between letters. Choose from three options: *Normal*, *Expanded*, and *Condensed*. For *Expanded* and *Condensed*, choose the amount of points to expand or condense the selected text.
- ***Position***: Vertically raises or lowers text by a selected number of points.
- ***Kerning***: Adjusts the space between letters in a proportional font.

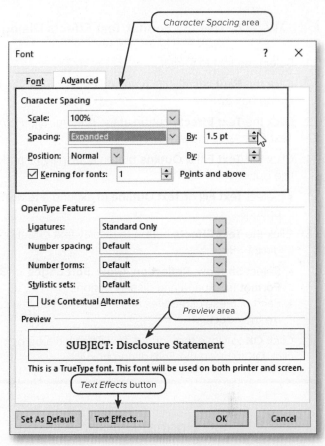

Figure 1-36 *Font* dialog box *Advanced* tab

Text Effects

Text Effects add special formatting features to selected text, such as *Outline*, *Shadow*, *Reflection*, and *Glow* (Figure 1-37). The *Text Effects* button is in the *Font* group on the *Home* tab. Many preset options are available for the different text effects, and more custom text effect options are available in the *Format Text Effects* pane.

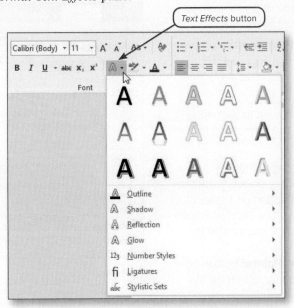

Figure 1-37 *Text Effects* button in the *Font* group

▶ HOW TO: Use the Format Text Effects Dialog Box

1. Select the text to format.

2. Click the **Font** launcher [*Home* tab, *Font* group]. The *Font* dialog box opens.

3. Click the **Text Effects** button at the bottom. The *Format Text Effects* dialog box opens.

4. Click the **Text Fill & Outline** button to display fill and outline options.

   • Select **Text Fill** or **Text Outline** to expand and display options.

5. Click the **Text Effects** button to display text effect options (Figure 1-38).

   • Select **Shadow**, **Reflection**, **Glow**, **Soft Edges**, or **3-D Format** to expand and display options.
   • Each of these categories has *Presets*, or you can customize the effect.

6. Click **OK** to close the *Format Text Effects* dialog box and click **OK** to close the *Font* dialog box.

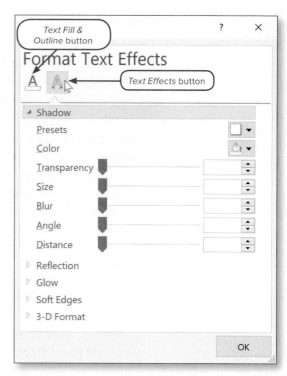

Figure 1-38 *Format Text Effects* dialog box

Format Painter

The ***Format Painter*** copies text formatting from selected text and applies the same formatting to other text in the same document or a different document. The *Format Painter* copies font, font size, line spacing, indents, bullets, numbering, styles, and other formatting features in Word. This feature saves time in applying formats and ensures consistency in document format.

▶ HOW TO: Use the Format Painter

1. Select the formatted text you want to copy.

2. Click the **Format Painter** button [*Home* tab, *Clipboard* group] (Figure 1-39). The *Format Painter* icon displays (Figure 1-40).

3. Select the text you want to format, and Word applies the formatting to the selected text.

   • To apply formatting to multiple non-adjacent selections, double-click the **Format Painter** button and select the text to format. The *Format Painter* remains active until you turn off the feature.
   • Click the **Format Painter** button again or press the **Esc** key to turn off the *Format Painter*.

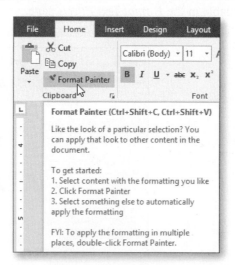

Figure 1-39 *Format Painter* button

Figure 1-40 *Format Painter* icon

Clear All Formatting

The **Clear All Formatting** feature removes all formatting for the selected text and returns it to plain text (Figure 1-41). For example, if you applied multiple formatting styles and effects to text, use the *Clear Formatting* feature rather than individually deselecting all the formatting options previously selected.

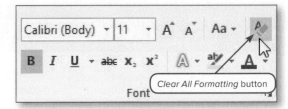

Figure 1-41 *Clear All Formatting* button in the *Font* group

> **MORE INFO**
>
> Be careful when using the *Clear Formatting* feature. It not only clears all text formatting but also clears line and paragraph spacing, numbering, bullets, and style formatting.

Change Default Font and Font Size

Recall that the default font in Microsoft Word is Calibri and the default font size is 11 pt. This *default* setting applies to each new blank document you create. Each new document is based on the *Normal.dotm* template. This template stores default settings for documents and controls document elements such as font, font size, line spacing, paragraph spacing, alignment, and styles.

You can change default settings on the current document only or change default settings in the *Normal* template. If you change the default settings for the *Normal* template, each new blank document uses the new default font and font size.

> ▶ **HOW TO: Change the Default Font and Font Size**
>
> 1. Select the text you want to format.
> 2. Click the **Font** launcher [*Home* tab, *Font* group]. The *Font* dialog box opens (Figure 1-42).
> 3. Click the **Font** tab if it is not already selected.
> 4. Select the font and font size to set as the default.
> 5. Click the **Set As Default** button on the bottom left. A confirmation dialog box opens with two options (Figure 1-43):
>   - *This document only?*
>   - *All documents based on the Normal template?*
> 6. Select an option and click **OK** to close the dialog box.
> 7. Click **OK** to close the *Font* dialog box.

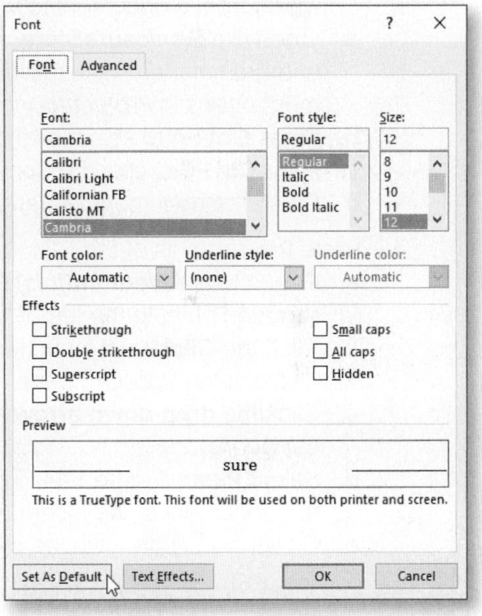

Figure 1-42 *Set As Default* button in the *Font* dialog box

> **MORE INFO**
>
> Be careful about changing default settings in the *Normal* template. Do this only when you are sure you want to change global default settings.

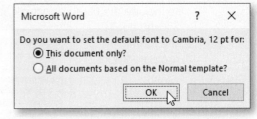

Figure 1-43 Change default settings confirmation options

In this Pause & Practice project, you customize the content of the block format letter Emma created for Placer Hills Real Estate using cut, copy, paste, and the *Clipboard*. You also enhance your document by changing the font and applying font attributes.

Files Needed: ***[your initials] PP W1-1.docx*** and ***DisclosureStatement-01.docx*** *(Student data files are available in the* Library *of your SIMnet account.)*
Completed Project File Name: ***[your initials] PP W1-2.docx***

1. Open the ***[your initials] PP W1-1*** document completed in *Pause & Practice 1-1*.
   a. Click the **File** tab to open the *Backstage* view and click **Open** on the left.
   b. Click **Browse** to open the *Open* dialog box.
   c. Browse to locate the ***[your initials] PP W1-1*** document, select the document, and click **Open**.

2. Save this document as ***[your initials] PP W1-2***.
   a. Click the **File** tab to open the *Backstage* view and select **Save As** on the left. If the document is saved on *OneDrive* and *AutoSave* is on, select **Save a Copy**.
   b. Click **Browse** to open the *Save As* dialog box and select the desired location to save the file.
   c. Change the file name to [your initials] PP W1-2.
   d. Click **Save** to rename the document and close the *Save As* dialog box.

3. Copy text from a document to the *Clipboard*.
   a. Open the ***DisclosureStatement-01*** document from your student date files. Ignore any spelling and grammar errors in this document; you will correct these in *Pause & Practice 1-3*. If the document opens in *Protected View*, click the **Enable Editing** button.
   b. Press **Ctrl+A** to select all the text.
   c. Press **Ctrl+C** or click the **Copy** button [*Home* tab, *Clipboard* group].
   d. Close the document without saving.

4. Paste the contents of the *Clipboard*.
   a. Return to the ***[your initials] PP W1-2*** document and place your insertion point to the left of "Best regards,".
   b. Click the **Clipboard** launcher [*Home* tab, *Clipboard* group] to display the *Clipboard* pane.
   c. Click the **drop-down arrow** to the right of the copied text in the *Clipboard*.
   d. Select **Paste** (Figure 1-44). The paragraphs of text are pasted in the document at the insertion point.
   e. Close the *Clipboard* pane by clicking the **X** in the upper-right corner.

Figure 1-44 Paste text from the *Clipboard*

5. Copy the formatting of the first paragraph to the two new paragraphs.
   a. Place your insertion point in the first body paragraph of the letter.
   b. Click the **Show/Hide** button [*Home* tab, *Paragraph* group] to display formatting symbols if necessary.
   c. Click the **Format Painter** button [*Home* tab, *Clipboard* group].
   d. Select the last two paragraphs in the body of the letter (don't select "Best regards,"). Be sure to include the paragraph mark at the end of the last body paragraph (Figure 1-45). The *Format Painter* applies the formatting to the paragraphs.

> Make note on the disclosure statement if you have had any work done with or without permits. Some examples include a gas spa, a new water heater, or a wholehouse fan where a trus may have been cut. If you had granate counters installed, that does not require a permit.¶
> Please complete the enclosed statement by [date] and return it to me. As always, if you have any questions or concerns, please call me at 916-450-3334 or email me at ecavalli@phre.com. Best wishes and thank you for you're business.¶ A⌐ ← *Format Painter* pointer
> Best regards,¶

Figure 1-45 Use the *Format Painter* to apply formatting to selected text

6. Copy text using the drag-and-drop method.
   a. Double-click the word "**disclosure**" in the first sentence of the third body paragraph to select it.
   b. Press the **Ctrl** key and click and hold the selected text with your pointer.
   c. Drag and drop the text between the words "enclosed" and "statement" in the first sentence in the last body paragraph (Figure 1-46). Confirm one space displays before and after the copied word.

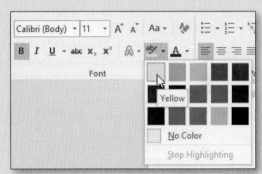

Make·note·on·the·disclosure·statement·if
examples·include·a·gas·spa,·a·new·water·
you·had·granate·counters·installed,·that·o

Copy pointer

Please·complete·the·enclosed·statement·
questions·or·concerns,·please·call·me·at·9
and·thank·you·for·you're·business.¶

Figure 1-46 Copy text using drag and drop

7. Move a paragraph in the body of the letter.
   a. Select the entire third paragraph in the body of the letter ("**Make note . . .**"), including the paragraph mark at the end of the paragraph.
   b. Click the **Cut** button [*Home* tab, *Clipboard* group] or press **Ctrl+X**. The selected paragraph is cut from the document and stored on the *Clipboard*.
   c. Place your insertion point at the beginning of the second body paragraph ("**If there is . . .**").
   d. Click the top half of the **Paste** button [*Home* tab, *Clipboard* group] or press **Ctrl+V**.

8. Insert and format a date.
   a. Delete the placeholder "[date]" (including the brackets) in the last paragraph and type the date that is one week from today (use January 1, 2020 format).
   b. Select the date you just typed.
   c. Click the **Text Highlight Color** drop-down list button [*Home* tab, *Font* group or on the mini toolbar] and choose the **Yellow** text highlight color (Figure 1-47).

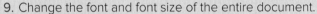

9. Change the font and font size of the entire document.
   a. Press **Ctrl+A** to select all the text in the document.
   b. Click the **Font** drop-down list button [*Home* tab, *Font* group] and select **Cambria**.
   c. Click the **Font Size** drop-down list button [*Home* tab, *Font* group] and select **12**.

Figure 1-47 Apply text highlight color

10. Change the case and spacing of selected text.
    a. Select the word "**Subject**" in the subject line of the document.
    b. Click the **Change Case** button [*Home* tab, *Font* group] and select **UPPERCASE**. Do not use the *Font* dialog box to change the case.
    c. Select the entire subject line.
    d. Click the **Font** launcher [*Home* tab, *Font* group] to open the *Font* dialog box. **Ctrl+D** also opens the *Font* dialog box.
    e. Click the **Advanced** tab.
    f. Click the **Spacing** drop-down list in the *Character Spacing* area and select **Expanded**.
    g. Click the up arrow in the *By* area to the right of *Spacing* to change the character spacing to expanded by **1.5 pt** (Figure 1-48).
    h. Click **OK** to close the *Font* dialog box.

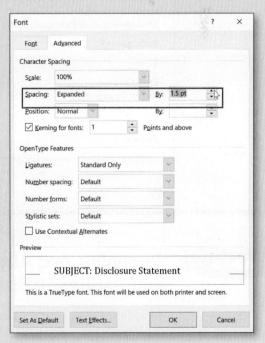

Figure 1-48 Change character spacing

11. Apply font styles to selected text.
    a. Select the email address "**ecavalli@phre.com**" in the last body paragraph.
    b. Click the **Font Color** drop-down list button [*Home* tab, *Font* group] and select the **ninth color** (**Dark Blue**) in the *Standard Colors* area.
    c. Click the **Underline** button or press **Ctrl+U** to apply an underline to the selected email address.
    d. Select the writer's name "**Emma Cavalli**" (below "Best regards,").
    e. Click the **Font** launcher in the bottom-right corner of the *Font* group to open the *Font* dialog box.
    f. Click the **Font** tab and check the **Small caps** box in the *Effects* area.
    g. Click **OK** to close the *Font* dialog box.
    h. Select the writer's title "**Realtor Consultant**" and click the **Italic** button or press **Ctrl+I**.
    i. Select the company name "**Placer Hills Real Estate**" and click the **Bold** button or press **Ctrl+B**.

12. Save and close the document (Figure 1-49).

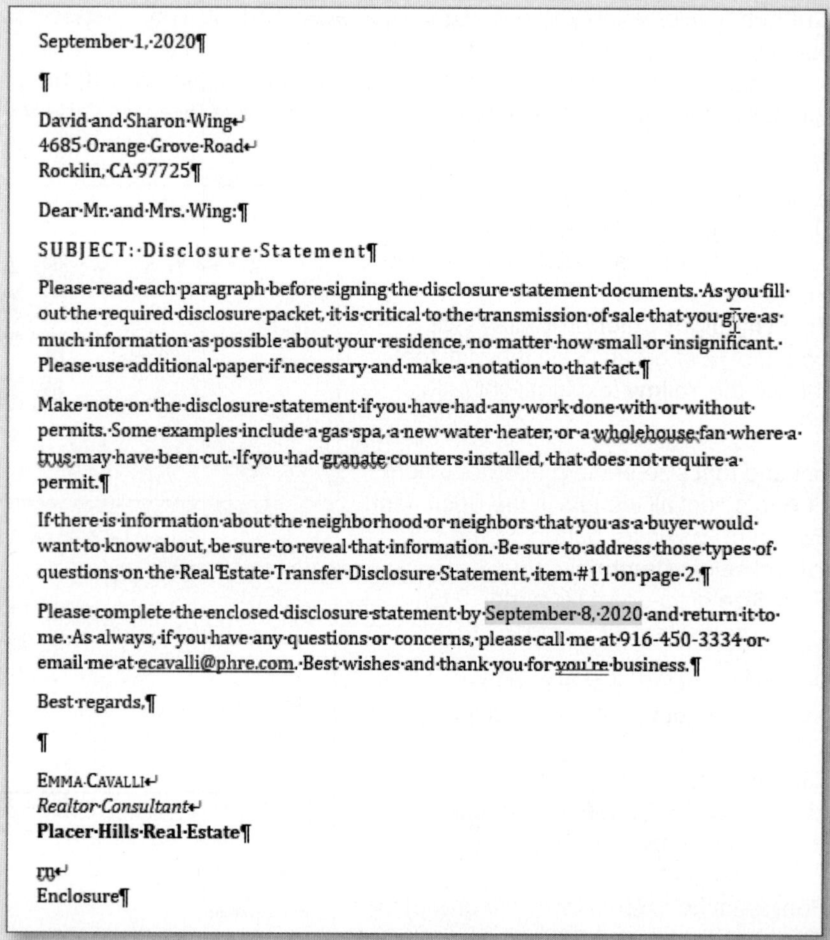

September·1,·2020¶

¶

David·and·Sharon·Wing↵
4685·Orange·Grove·Road↵
Rocklin,·CA·97725¶

Dear·Mr.·and·Mrs.·Wing:¶

SUBJECT:·Disclosure·Statement¶

Please·read·each·paragraph·before·signing·the·disclosure·statement·documents.·As·you·fill·out·the·required·disclosure·packet,·it·is·critical·to·the·transmission·of·sale·that·you·give·as·much·information·as·possible·about·your·residence,·no·matter·how·small·or·insignificant.·Please·use·additional·paper·if·necessary·and·make·a·notation·to·that·fact.¶

Make·note·on·the·disclosure·statement·if·you·have·had·any·work·done·with·or·without·permits.·Some·examples·include·a·gas·spa,·a·new·water·heater,·or·a·wholehouse·fan·where·a·truss·may·have·been·cut.·If·you·had·granate·counters·installed,·that·does·not·require·a·permit.¶

If·there·is·information·about·the·neighborhood·or·neighbors·that·you·as·a·buyer·would·want·to·know·about,·be·sure·to·reveal·that·information.·Be·sure·to·address·those·types·of·questions·on·the·Real·Estate·Transfer·Disclosure·Statement,·item·#11·on·page·2.¶

Please·complete·the·enclosed·disclosure·statement·by·September·8,·2020·and·return·it·to·me.·As·always,·if·you·have·any·questions·or·concerns,·please·call·me·at·916-450-3334·or·email·me·at·ecavalli@phre.com.·Best·wishes·and·thank·you·for·you're·business.¶

Best·regards,¶

¶

EMMA·CAVALLI↵
Realtor·Consultant↵
Placer·Hills·Real·Estate¶

rn↵
Enclosure¶

Figure 1-49 PP W1-2 completed

SLO 1.6

Changing Text Alignment, Line Spacing, and Paragraph Spacing

In addition to word wrap, line breaks, and paragraphs breaks, you can use text alignment, line spacing, and paragraph spacing to control the layout and white space between the parts of your document.

Default Settings

Just as font and font size have default settings, Word has default settings for paragraph alignment, line spacing, and paragraph spacing. These default settings are stored in the *Normal* template on which all new blank documents are based. Table 1-4 summarizes font, line spacing, and paragraph default settings:

Table 1-4: Normal Template Default Settings

Setting	Default Setting
Font	Calibri
Font Size	11 pt.
Horizontal Paragraph Alignment	Left
Line Spacing	1.08 lines
Paragraph Spacing—Before	0 pt.
Paragraph Spacing—After	8 pt.

Paragraph Alignment

Paragraph alignment controls the horizontal alignment of paragraphs. A paragraph is a single word, a group of words, a sentence, or multiple sentences. Paragraphs are separated by paragraph breaks. A group of words using word wrap and line breaks is considered one paragraph.

The four different paragraph alignment options are:

- *Left* (default): The paragraph is aligned on the left margin.
- *Center*: The paragraph is centered between the left and right margins.
- *Right*: The paragraph begins and is aligned on the right margin.
- *Justify*: The paragraph is aligned flush with both the left and right margins.

> **ANOTHER WAY**
>
> Press **Ctrl+L** to *Align Text Left*.
> Press **Ctrl+E** to *Center* text.
> Press **Ctrl+R** to *Align Text Right*.
> Press **Ctrl+J** to *Justify* text.

Change the alignment of a paragraph by clicking a paragraph alignment button in the *Paragraph* group on the *Home* tab (Figure 1-50). When changing the alignment of a single paragraph, the entire paragraph need not be selected; the insertion point only needs to be within the paragraph for the alignment to be applied. Text alignment can also be changed in the *Paragraph* dialog box.

Figure 1-50 Paragraph alignment options in the *Paragraph* group

Line Spacing

Line spacing refers to the amount of blank space between lines of text within a paragraph. The default setting in Word is 1.08 lines, which is slightly more than single spacing. Most documents you type are single-spaced or 1.08 line spacing, but you may want to use double-spacing (two lines) when needed, such as when typing an academic report.

As with paragraph alignment, you can apply line spacing to an individual paragraph, multiple paragraphs, or an entire document.

To change line spacing, click the **Line and Paragraph Spacing** button in the *Paragraph* group on the *Home* tab and select an option (Figure 1-51). Choose from the preset line spacing options or select **Line Spacing Options** to open the *Paragraph* dialog box and set custom line spacing.

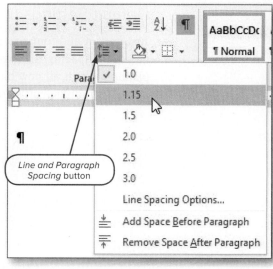

Figure 1-51 *Line and Paragraph Spacing* button in the *Paragraph* group

> **ANOTHER WAY**
>
> **Ctrl+1** applies single-space (1 line).
> **Ctrl+5** applies 1.5 line spacing.
> **Ctrl+2** applies double-space (2 lines).

The *Paragraph* dialog box includes additional line spacing options (Figure 1-52). The *At Least* and *Exactly* options allow you to specify points of spacing, rather than lines of spacing, between lines of text. The *Multiple* option enables you to set a line spacing option that is not a whole number, such as 1.3 or 2.25 line spacing.

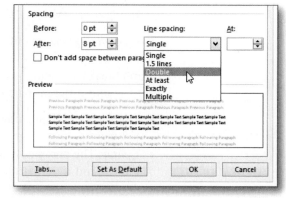

Figure 1-52 *Line spacing* options in the *Paragraph* dialog box

> **MORE INFO**
>
> If a document has inconsistent line spacing, it looks unprofessional. Select the entire document and set the line spacing to enhance consistency and improve readability.

Paragraph Spacing

While line spacing controls the amount of space between lines of text in a paragraph, *paragraph spacing* controls the amount of spacing before and after paragraphs. For example, you might want the text of a document to be single-spaced but prefer to have more blank space before and after paragraphs. Use paragraph spacing to accomplish this task.

Before and ***After*** paragraph spacing is set in points. The default *After* paragraph spacing is 8 pt., which is a little less than one blank line. The default *Before* paragraph spacing is 0 pt.

Change *Before* and *After* paragraph spacing in the *Paragraph* group on the *Layout* tab (Figure 1-53). You can also change *Before* and *After* paragraph spacing in the *Paragraph* dialog box and from the *Line and Paragraph Spacing* button in the *Paragraph* group on the *Home* tab.

Use the *Line and Paragraph Spacing* button in the *Paragraph* group on the *Home* tab to **Add/Remove Space Before Paragraph** or **Add/Remove Space After Paragraph** (Figure 1-54). These options are contextual and change depending on whether *Before* or *After* paragraph spacing is already applied on the text.

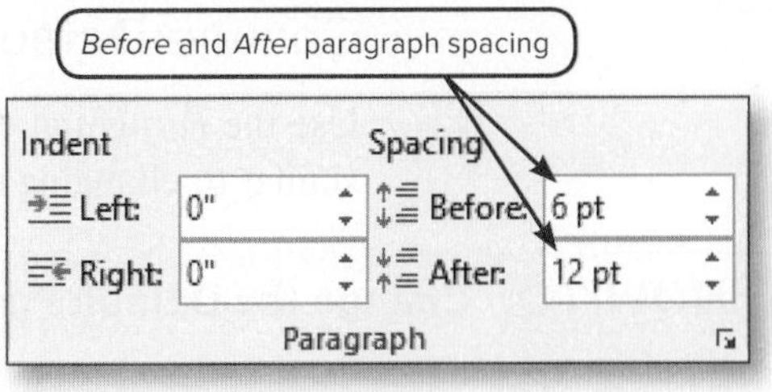

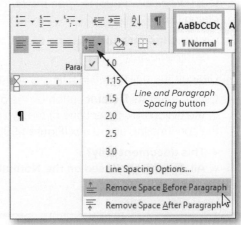

Figure 1-53 *Paragraph group on the Layout tab*

> **MORE INFO**
>
> Insert line breaks to keep lines of text as a single paragraph. *Before* and *After* paragraph spacing is not applied to individual lines of text when line breaks are used to create a paragraph.

Figure 1-54 *Add/Remove paragraph spacing options*

Paragraph Dialog Box

The **Paragraph dialog box** combines many of the alignment and spacing options included in the *Paragraph* groups on the *Home* and *Layout* tabs.

▶ HOW TO: Change Alignment and Spacing in the Paragraph Dialog Box

1. Select the text to format.
2. Click the **Paragraph** launcher [*Home* or *Layout* tab, *Paragraph* group] to open the *Paragraph* dialog box (Figure 1-55).
3. Click the **Alignment** drop-down list in the *General* area and select **Left**, **Centered**, **Right**, or **Justified**.
   - The *Indentation* section of this dialog box controls indents. Indents are covered in *SLO 2.3: Using Indents*.
4. Change **Before** and **After** paragraph spacing in the *Spacing* section.
   - Type the number of points of spacing or use the spinner (up and down) arrows.
   - The *Don't add space between paragraphs of the same style* check box controls paragraph spacing between paragraphs of the same style, which is primarily used with numbered and bulleted lists and outlines.
5. Click the **Line spacing** drop-down list to select a line spacing option.
   - Alternatively, type a custom line spacing in the **At** text box. The Line spacing changes to *Multiple*.
6. Notice the *Preview* area displays how your document will look with changes.
7. Click **OK** to close the *Paragraph* dialog box.

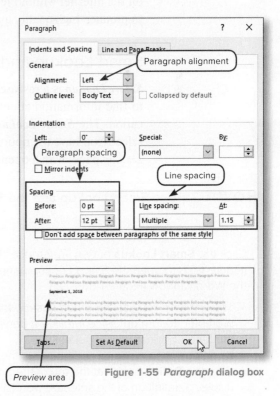

Figure 1-55 *Paragraph dialog box*

Change Default Line and Paragraph Spacing

Use the *Paragraph* dialog box to set default paragraph alignment and spacing. This process is similar to changing the default font and font size settings.

▶**HOW TO:** Change the Default Paragraph Alignment and Spacing

1. Click the **Paragraph** launcher [*Home* or *Layout* tab, *Paragraph* group] to open the *Paragraph* dialog box.

2. Click the **Indents and Spacing** tab if it is not already selected.

3. Change the paragraph and line spacing settings.

4. Click the **Set As Default** button on the bottom left of the dialog box. Select one of the two options in the confirmation dialog box (Figure 1-56):

   - **This document only?**
   - **All documents based on the Normal template?**

5. Click **OK**.

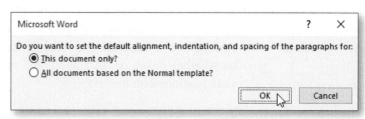

Figure 1-56 Change default setting confirmation options

SLO 1.7

Using Smart Lookup and Proofreading Tools

The words and grammar you use in a document reflect your professionalism and the reputation of your organization. Word provides many proofing and editing tools to improve the quality of the documents you produce. The *Smart Lookup* feature enables you to search for information on the internet without leaving Word. The spelling, grammar, and thesaurus features help you to produce high-quality and professional-looking documents.

Smart Lookup and the Smart Lookup Pane

Smart Lookup is a research feature in Word. This feature uses Bing, an internet search engine, to find information about a selected word or words in a document without leaving the application. The ***Smart Lookup pane*** displays information from the internet about the words you select. You have the option to find additional information by clicking a hyperlink in the *Smart Lookup* pane, which opens an internet browser displaying additional internet content.

▶**HOW TO:** Use Smart Lookup and the Smart Lookup Pane

1. Select the word or words to research.

2. Click the **Smart Lookup** button [*References* tab, *Research* group] (Figure 1-57) to open the *Smart Lookup* pane on the right side of the Word window (Figure 1-58).

   - The first time you use the *Smart Lookup* feature, you may be prompted to turn on *Office Intelligent Services*. Click **Turn on** in the *Smart Lookup* pane if necessary.
   - By default, the *Explore* area displays in the *Smart Lookup* pane.
   - Click the **Define** button at the top of the *Smart Lookup* pane to display a definition of the selected word(s).
   - A privacy notice may appear in the *Smart Lookup* pane upon first time use.

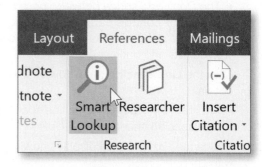

Figure 1-57 *Smart Lookup* button

3. View the research results in the *Smart Lookup* pane.

   - To view additional information about a research result, click one of the results, which is a hyperlink that will open an internet browser window displaying additional information about the topic.
   - To perform additional research on a different word, select the word in the document and click the **Smart Lookup** button again. The new results appear in the *Smart Lookup* pane.

4. Click the **X** in the upper-right corner of the *Smart Lookup* pane to close the pane.

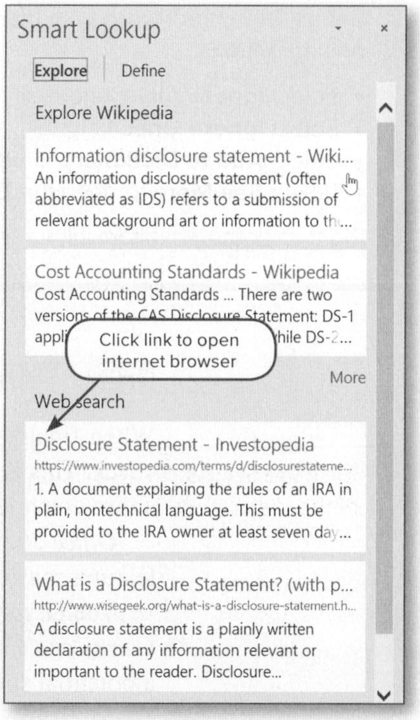

> **ANOTHER WAY**
>
> Right-click a word or selected words and choose **Smart Lookup** from the context menu to open the *Smart Lookup* pane.

Automatic Spelling and Grammar Notifications

Recall that Word uses *AutoCorrect* to automatically correct many commonly misspelled words. When typing a document, Word constantly compares the words you type with the words in its dictionary. When Word doesn't recognize a word, it marks the potential ***spelling error*** with a ***red wavy underline***. Word also checks the grammar of your document and marks potential word choice or ***grammatical errors*** with a ***blue double underline*** and ***clarity and conciseness errors*** with a ***light brown dotted line***.

Figure 1-58 *Smart Lookup* pane

> **MORE INFO**
>
> When Word marks a word as a possible spelling error, it does not necessarily mean that the word is misspelled. Many proper nouns are not included in the Word dictionary.

When you right-click a potential spelling or grammar error, the context menu displays options for correction and provides additional information, such as word definitions and a reason for grammatical errors.

> **▶ HOW TO: Correct Spelling and Grammatical Errors**

1. Right-click a word that has a red wavy underline, blue double underline, or light brown dotted line.

   - A context menu opens that provides editing options depending on the type of potential error (Figure 1-59).
   - For potential spelling errors, a list of possible corrections displays. The definition of the word displays below some options.
   - Click the arrow to the right of a word in the context menu to select *Read Aloud*, *Add to AutoCorrect*, or *AutoCorrect Options*.
   - Potential grammar errors display possible corrections and a reason for the grammatical error. Click the arrow to the right of a correction in the context menu to *Read Aloud*.

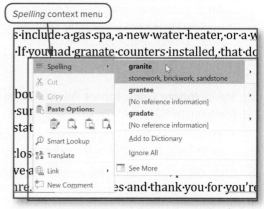

Figure 1-59 **Correct a spelling error**

2. Select the correct word from the list to replace the misspelled word. You can also choose from the following editing options:

- Select **Ignore All** to ignore all instances of this spelling throughout the document.
- Select **Ignore Once** to ignore a potential grammar error.
- Select **Add to Dictionary** to add the word to the Word dictionary.
- Select **See More** to open the *Editor* pane at the right

3. Right-click the next item with a red or blue underline to repeat the editing process.

Editor Pane

When finalizing a document, proofread it one last time and use the spelling and grammar check. This is especially true with longer documents. You can use the ***Editor pane*** to check an entire document for potential spelling, grammatical, and clarity and conciseness errors.

    Office 2019 Note: This pane is labeled ***Proofing*** rather than *Editor* in Office 2019 and some features may differ slightly.

    The *Editor* pane is contextual. The label below the *Editor* pane title (*Spelling*, *Grammar*, or *Clarity and Conciseness*) and the available options change depending on whether Word detects a potential spelling or grammatical error.

▶ HOW TO: Use the Editor Pane

1. Press **Ctrl+Home** to move to the beginning of your document. When checking a document for correct spelling and grammar, it is best to start at the beginning of the document.

2. Click the **Spelling & Grammar** button [*Review* tab, *Proofing* group] to open the *Editor* pane (Figure 1-60).

   - The first potential spelling or grammatical error displays in the *Editor* pane.
   - Click the **Read Aloud** button (speaker icon) to have Word read the sentence containing the error.

3. Select the correct word from the *Suggestions* list to replace the incorrect word.

   - A definition of each suggested word displays below each word in the list of suggestions.
   - Click the drop-down list to the right of a word and select **Change All** to change all instances of the misspelled word. Other options on the drop-down list include *Read Aloud*, *Spell Out*, *Add to AutoCorrect*, and *AutoCorrect Options*.
   - If no word options are available, retype the word in the body of the document.

4. Select **Ignore Once**, **Ignore All**, or **Add to Dictionary** if the word does not need to be changed.

   - If you select *Add to Dictionary*, the selected word is added to the dictionary, so it is not detected as a potential error in the future.

5. Click **OK** to finish when the dialog box opens indicating the spelling and grammar check is complete.

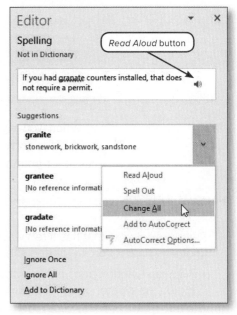

Figure 1-60 *Editor* pane

Customize the Dictionary

When you spell check a document, you can easily add a word to the *Word Dictionary*. When you add a word to the dictionary, Word creates a custom dictionary. You can manually add or delete words from the custom dictionary. Many proper nouns are marked as a misspelled word during a spell check. You can add commonly used proper nouns to the dictionary so they won't be marked as a misspelled word each time you spell check a document.

▶ **HOW TO: Add Words to the Custom Dictionary**

1. Click the **File** tab to open the *Backstage* view.
2. Click the **Options** button to open the *Word Options* dialog box.
3. Click the **Proofing** button.
4. Click the **Custom Dictionaries** button. The *Custom Dictionaries* dialog box opens (Figure 1-61).
5. Select the dictionary to edit in the *Dictionary List*.
    *   The *RoamingCustom.dic* is typically the default custom dictionary.
6. Click the **Edit Word List** button. Your custom dictionary dialog box opens (Figure 1-62). Words previously added to your dictionary display in the *Dictionary* area.
7. Click the **Word(s)** text box, type a word to add to your dictionary, and click the **Add** button to add the word to your dictionary.
    *   To delete a word from the dictionary, select the word and click the **Delete** button.
8. Click **OK** when finished to close the dialog box.
9. Click **OK** to close the *Custom Dictionaries* dialog box.
10. Click **OK** to close the *Word Options* dialog box.

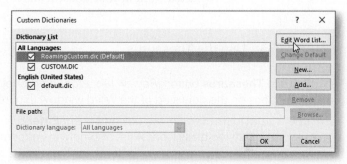

Figure 1-61 *Custom Dictionaries* dialog box

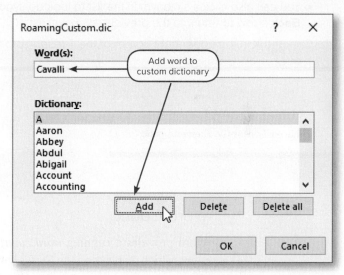

Figure 1-62 Add word to custom dictionary

The Thesaurus

Word provides a *Thesaurus* feature to help you find *synonyms* to add variety to your writing. A varied vocabulary indicates a more educated and professional writer.

Word provides two ways to use the *Thesaurus* to find synonyms. The first and quickest way is to select a word in the document and use the context menu (right-click) to replace a selected word with an appropriate synonym.

▶HOW TO: Find Synonyms Using the Context Menu

1. Right-click the word you want to replace with an appropriate synonym. The context menu displays.

2. Place your pointer on **Synonyms**. Another context menu appears with a list of synonym choices.

3. Select the synonym you prefer (Figure 1-63). The selected synonym replaces the selected word in the text and the menus close.

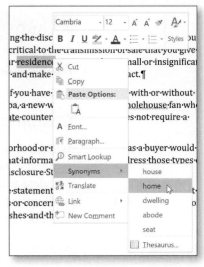

You can also use the *Thesaurus* feature in the *Thesaurus* pane. This method enables you to search for synonyms for any word, not just a selected word in your document.

Figure 1-63 Use *Thesaurus* to find synonyms

▶HOW TO: Use the Thesaurus

1. Click the **Thesaurus** button [*Review* tab, *Proofing* group]. The *Thesaurus* pane opens on the right side of the Word window (Figure 1-64).

2. Type a word in the *Search* text box and press **Enter** or click the **Search** button (magnifying glass icon). A list of synonyms appears in the *Thesaurus* area.

3. Click the **drop-down arrow** to the right of the synonym and select **Insert** or **Copy**.

   • You can also click a synonym in the list to look up synonyms for that word. Click the **Back** arrow to return to the previous synonym list.

4. Click the **X** in the upper-right corner of the *Thesaurus* pane to close this pane.

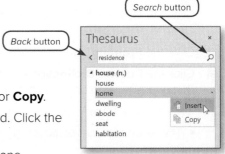

Figure 1-64 *Thesaurus* pane

> **ANOTHER WAY**
>
> **Shift+F7** opens the *Thesaurus* pane.

Figure 1-65 *Word Count* area on the *Status* bar

Word Count

Word provides a running ***word count*** in each document, which displays on the *Status* bar in the bottom-left corner of the Word window (Figure 1-65). Click the **Word Count** area to open the *Word Count* dialog box to display more detailed information: number of pages, words, characters (no spaces), characters (with spaces), paragraphs, and lines (Figure 1-66). You can also choose whether to have Word count words in textboxes, footnotes, and endnotes.

Figure 1-66 *Word Count* dialog box

Read Aloud

The ***Read Aloud*** feature increases accessibility and adds another proofreading tool to your Word documents. This feature reads a word, selected text, or an entire document. You can control the speed in which text is read and select a voice to read your text.

▶ HOW TO: Use the Read Aloud Feature

1. Select a word or group of words to read aloud.
   - Alternatively, place your insertion point at a location in your document where you want the reading to begin.
2. Click the **Read Aloud** button [*Review* tab, *Speech* group].
   - Word reads the selected word or words. If no words are selected, Word begins reading from the insertion point.
   - The *Read Aloud* controls appear in the upper-right corner (Figure 1-67).
3. Click the **Pause** button to pause the reading. Click the **Play** button to resume reading.
4. Click the **Settings** button to change *Reading speed* or *Voice Selection*.
5. Click the **Next** or **Previous** button to move to and read the next or previous paragraph.
6. Click the **X** in the upper-right corner of the *Read Aloud* controls to close the controls.

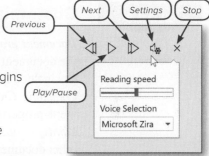

Figure 1-67 *Read Aloud controls*

Learning Tools

In addition to the *Read Aloud* feature, Word provides a set of ***Learning Tools***. These tools increase accessibility by enabling users to view a document at different widths, change the page color, change the text spacing, view spaces between syllables in words, and use the *Read Aloud* feature.

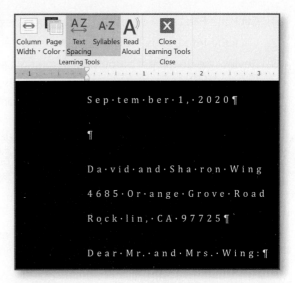

▶ HOW TO: Use the Learning Tools

1. Click the **Learning Tools** button [*View* tab, *Immersive* group]. The *Immersive Learning Tools* contextual tab displays (Figure 1-68).
2. Click the **Column Width** button [*Immersive Learning Tools* tab, *Learning Tools* group] and select **Very Narrow**, **Narrow**, **Moderate**, or **Wide** to change the display width.

Figure 1-68 *Learning Tools*

3. Click the **Page Color** button [*Immersive Learning Tools* tab, *Learning Tools* group] and select **None**, **Sepia**, or **Inverse** to change the display color.

4. Click the **Text Spacing** button [*Immersive Learning Tools* tab, *Learning Tools* group] to increase or decrease the spacing between letters and words.

5. Click the **Syllables** button [*Immersive Learning Tools* tab, *Learning Tools* group] to display a space between syllables in words. Click the **Syllables** button again to hide the space between syllables.

6. Click the **Read Aloud** button [*Immersive Learning Tools* tab, *Learning Tools* group] to read selected words or begin reading from the insertion point.

   - The *Read Aloud* controls appear in the upper-right corner.

7. Click the **Close** button [*Immersive Learning Tools* tab, *Close* group] to close the *Learning Tools* view and return to your document.

Customizing Document Properties

Document properties are details about a document. These details are not visible in the text of the document but are included as hidden information within the document. Document properties include fields such as *Title, Author, Comments, Subject, Company, Created,* and *Last Modified.* Several document properties are automatically generated, such as *Words, Total Editing Time,* and *Last Modified,* whereas other document property details are edited individually.

Document Properties

Document properties are viewed and edited in the *Info* area on the *Backstage* view. Document properties are saved within the document and can be viewed by others.

Figure 1-69 Document properties on the *Backstage* view

▶HOW TO: Add Document Properties

1. Click the **File** tab to display the *Backstage* view.

2. Click the **Info** button if it is not already selected.

3. Review the document properties on the right side of the window (Figure 1-69).

   - Document property field names are listed on the left, and the information in these fields displays on the right.

4. Click a field and type information to edit the document property.

   - Several properties cannot be changed because they are automatically generated by Word.

5. Click the **Show All/Fewer Properties** link at the bottom to display more or fewer document property fields.

6. Click the **Back** arrow in the upper-left corner of the *Backstage* view to return to the document when you finish entering and reviewing document properties.

Advanced Properties

In addition to viewing and editing the document properties on the *Backstage* view, you can also display document properties in the **Properties dialog box** (Figure 1-70). In the *Info* area on the *Backstage* view, click the **Properties** button (see Figure 1-69) and select **Advanced Properties** to open the *Properties* dialog box.

You can modify the document properties on the *Summary* tab. The title of the *Properties* dialog box is contextual. The file name displays before *Properties* in the title bar of the dialog box.

Print Document Properties

You can print document properties using the *Backstage* view. When you print document properties, only a page listing the document properties prints, not the document itself.

Figure 1-70 *Properties* dialog box

▶HOW TO: Print Document Properties

1. Click the **File** tab to open the *Backstage* view.
2. Select **Print** on the left.
3. Click **Print All Pages** and select **Document Info** from the drop-down list (Figure 1-71).
4. Click the **Print** button to print the document properties.

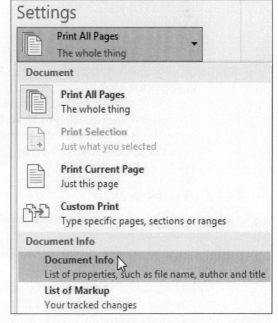

Figure 1-71 Print document properties

PAUSE & PRACTICE: WORD 1-3

In the final Pause & Practice project in this chapter, you add the finishing touches on a document for Placer Hills Real Estate. You customize paragraph and line spacing, change paragraph alignment, and use spelling and grammar checkers to produce an error-free document. You also modify the document properties.

File Needed: ***[your initials] PP W1-2.docx***
Completed Project File Name: ***[your initials] PP W1-3.docx***

1. Open the ***[your initials] PP W1-2*** document completed in *Pause & Practice 1-2*.
   a. Click the **File** tab to open the *Backstage* view and click **Open** on the left.
   b. Click **Browse** to open the *Open* dialog box.
   c. Browse to locate the ***[your initials] PP W1-2*** document, select the document, and click **Open**.

2. Save this document with a different file name.
   a. Click the **File** tab to open the *Backstage* view and select **Save As** on the left. If your document is saved on *OneDrive* and *AutoSave* is turned on, select **Save a Copy**.
   b. Click **Browse** to open the *Save As* dialog box and select the desired location to save the file.
   c. Change the file name to [your initials] PP W1-3.
   d. Click **Save** to save the document with a different file name and close the *Save As* dialog box.

3. Change the line and paragraph spacing for the entire document.
   a. Press **Ctrl+A** to select the entire document.
   b. Click the **Paragraph** launcher [*Home* or *Layout* tab, *Paragraph* group] to open the *Paragraph* dialog box (Figure 1-72).
   c. Change the *Line spacing* to **Single**.
   d. Change the *After* spacing to **12 pt**. Use the up arrow or type the amount of spacing.
   e. Click **OK** to close the dialog box.

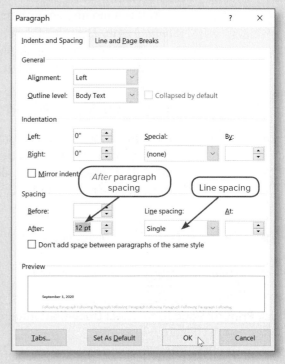

Figure 1-72 Change *Line spacing* and *After* paragraph spacing in the *Paragraph* dialog box

> ▶ **ANOTHER WAY**
>
> Change line spacing in the *Paragraph* group on the *Home* tab. Change *Before* and *After* paragraph spacing in the *Paragraph* group on the *Layout* tab.

4. Add paragraph spacing before the date line of the business letter.
   a. Select or place your insertion point in the first line (date line) of the business letter.
   b. Click the **Layout** tab.
   c. Change the *Before* spacing to **72 pt**. (Figure 1-73). *Note:* 72 pt. is approximately 1", which is commonly used as the spacing before the date line on business letters.

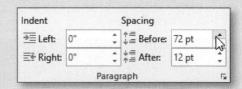

Figure 1-73 Change *Before* paragraph spacing in the *Paragraph* group

5. Change the paragraph alignment of selected text.
   a. Select or place your insertion point in the subject line of the business letter.
   b. Click the **Center** button [*Home* tab, *Paragraph* group] or press **Ctrl+E**.

6. Use the *Thesaurus* to find synonyms for selected words.
   a. Select the word "**reveal**" in the third body paragraph.

W1-40

b. Click the **Thesaurus** button [*Review* tab, *Proofing* group]. The *Thesaurus* pane opens on the right with a list of synonyms for the selected word (Figure 1-74).

c. Click the **drop-down arrow** to the right of the word "divulge" and choose **Insert**. The word "divulge" replaces "reveal."

d. Click the **X** in the upper-right corner of the *Thesaurus* pane to close the pane.

e. Right-click the word "**residence**" in the first body paragraph. A context menu opens.

f. Point to **Synonyms** and a list of synonyms appears.

g. Select "**home**" from the list of synonyms. The word "home" replaces "residence."

Figure 1-74 Insert a synonym from the *Thesaurus* pane

7. Add a word to the custom dictionary.

a. Click the **File** tab to open the *Backstage* view.

b. Click the **Options** button to open the *Word Options* dialog box.

c. Click **Proofing** on the left.

d. Click the **Custom Dictionaries** button in the *When correcting spelling in Microsoft Office programs* area. The *Custom Dictionaries* dialog box opens.

e. Select **RoamingCustom.dic** in the *Dictionary List*. If this dictionary is not available, select the available custom dictionary.

f. Click the **Edit Word List** button. The *RoamingCustom.dic* dialog box opens (Figure 1-75).

g. Type your last name in the *Word(s)* area and click the **Add** button. If your last name is already in the dictionary, the *Add* button is shaded gray.

h. Click **OK** to close the *RoamingCustom.dic* dialog box.

i. Click **OK** to close the *Custom Dictionaries* dialog box.

j. Click **OK** to close the *Word Options* dialog box.

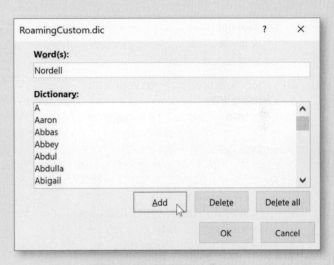

Figure 1-75 Add a word to the custom dictionary

8. Spell and grammar check the document.

a. Right-click the word "**wholehouse**" in the second paragraph. A context list of words appears (Figure 1-76).

b. Select "**whole house**." The correctly spelled word replaces the incorrectly spelled word.

c. Place your insertion point at the beginning of the document or press **Ctrl+Home**.

d. Click the **Spelling & Grammar** button [*Review* tab, *Proofing* group] or press **F7** to open the *Editor* pane on the right (Figure 1-77).
    Office 2019 Note: This pane is labeled **Proofing** rather than *Editor* in Office 2019 and some features may differ slightly.

e. Click "**truss**" in the *Suggestions* area in *Editor* pane to replace the misspelled word.

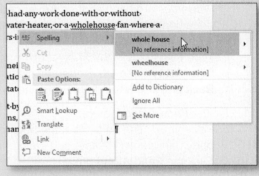

Figure 1-76 Correct spelling using the context menu

f. Continue spell checking the remainder of the document. Change "granate" to "**granite**" and "you're" to "**your**."

g. Click **Add to Dictionary** for "Cavalli" if it is marked as incorrect.

h. Click **Ignore Once** for your reference initials if it is marked as incorrect.

i. Click **OK** to close the dialog box that opens and informs you that the spelling and grammar check is complete. The *Editor* pane closes.

9. Use *Smart Lookup* to research selected words.

a. Select "**Transfer Disclosure Statement**" in the third body paragraph.

b. Click the **Smart Lookup** button [*References* tab, *Research*]. The *Smart Lookup* pane opens on the right. If you are using this feature for the first time, you may receive a message about privacy and must click the **Got it** button before data will display.

c. Review the research results on the *Smart Lookup* pane.

d. Click the **X** in the upper-right corner of the *Smart Lookup* pane to close the pane.

10. Add document properties to your letter.

a. Click the **File** tab to open the *Backstage* view.

b. Click **Info** on the left if it is not already selected. The document properties display on the right side of the *Backstage* view (Figure 1-78).

c. Click the *Title* field and type **Disclosure Statement**.

d. Right-click the existing author in the *Author* area and select **Remove Person**.

e. Click **Add an author** in the *Author* area, type **Emma Cavalli**, and press **Tab**.

f. Click the **Show All Properties** link at the bottom. Additional document properties display.

g. Click the *Company* area and type **Placer Hills Real Estate**.

h. Click the **Properties** drop-down list at the top of the *Properties* area and choose **Advanced Properties**. The document properties display in the *Summary* tab of the *Properties* dialog box.

i. Type **Real Estate** in the *Subject* text box.

j. Click **OK** to close the *Properties* dialog box and click the **Back** arrow to return to the document.

11. Use the *Read Aloud* feature.

a. Place your insertion point at the beginning of the first body paragraph ("Please read each paragraph. . .").

b. Click the **Read Aloud** button [*Review* tab, *Speech* group]. Word begins reading the first paragraph and the *Read Aloud* controls display at the left.

c. Click the **Pause** button in the *Read Aloud* controls.

d. Click the **Settings** button and change the **Reading speed** and **Voice Selection** as desired (Figure 1-79).

e. Press **Esc** to close the *Settings* menu.

f. Click the **Next** button to skip to the next paragraph.

g. Click the **Stop** button to stop the reading and close the *Read Aloud* controls.

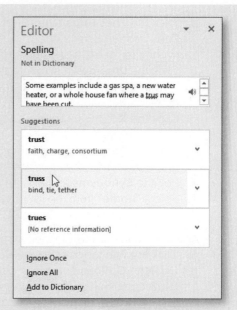

Figure 1-77 *Editor* pane

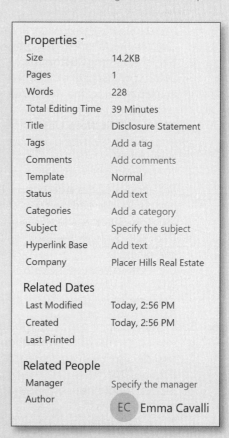

Figure 1-78 Document properties on the *Backstage* view

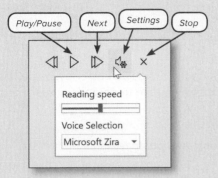

Play/Pause Next Settings Stop

Reading speed

Voice Selection

Microsoft Zira

Figure 1-79 *Read Aloud controls*

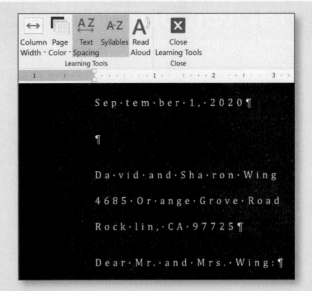

Column Width Page Color Text Spacing Syllables Read Aloud Close Learning Tools

Learning Tools   Close

Sep·tem·ber·1,·2020¶

¶

Da·vid·and·Sha·ron·Wing

4685·Or·ange·Grove·Road

Rock·lin,·CA·97725¶

Dear·Mr.·and·Mrs.·Wing:¶

Figure 1-80 *Learning Tools*

12. Use the *Learning Tools*.
    a. Click the **Learning Tools** button [*View* tab, *Immersive* group]. The *Immersive Learning Tools* contextual tab displays.
    b. Click the **Column Width** button [*Immersive Learning Tools* tab, *Learning Tools* group] and select **Moderate** to change the display width.
    c. Click the **Page Color** button and select **Inverse**.
    d. Click the **Text Spacing** button if necessary to display wide spacing. This button toggles between wide and normal spacing.
    e. Click the **Syllables** button to display a space between syllables in words (Figure 1-80).
    f. Click the **Close Learning Tools** button [*Immersive Learning Tools* tab, *Close* group] to close the *Learning Tools* view and return to your document.

13. Save and close the document (Figure 1-81).

September·1,·2020¶

¶

David·and·Sharon·Wing↵
4685·Orange·Grove·Road↵
Rocklin,·CA·97725¶

Dear·Mr.·and·Mrs.·Wing:¶

SUBJECT:·Disclosure·Statement¶

Please·read·each·paragraph·before·signing·the·disclosure·statement·documents.·As·you·fill·out·the·required·disclosure·packet,·it·is·critical·to·the·transmission·of·sale·that·you·give·as·much·information·as·possible·about·your·home,·no·matter·how·small·or·insignificant.·Please·use·additional·paper·if·necessary·and·make·a·notation·to·that·fact.¶

Make·note·on·the·disclosure·statement·if·you·have·had·any·work·done·with·or·without·permits.·Some·examples·include·a·gas·spa,·a·new·water·heater,·or·a·whole·house·fan·where·a·truss·may·have·been·cut.·If·you·had·granite·counters·installed,·that·does·not·require·a·permit.¶

If·there·is·information·about·the·neighborhood·or·neighbors·that·you·as·a·buyer·would·want·to·know·about,·be·sure·to·divulge·that·information.·Be·sure·to·address·those·types·of·questions·on·the·Real·Estate·Transfer·Disclosure·Statement,·item·#11·on·page·2.¶

Please·complete·the·enclosed·disclosure·statement·by·September·8,·2020·and·return·it·to·me.·As·always,·if·you·have·any·questions·or·concerns,·please·call·me·at·916-450-3334·or·email·me·at·ecavalli@phre.com.·Best·wishes·and·thank·you·for·your·business.¶

Best·regards,¶

¶

EMMA·CAVALLI↵
Realtor·Consultant↵
Placer·Hills·Real·Estate¶

rn↵
Enclosure¶

Figure 1-81 PP W1-3 completed

Chapter Summary

1.1 Create, save, and open a Word document (p. W1-3).

- New Word documents are based on the **Normal template** (*Normal.dotm*).
- Save documents with the existing file name or with a different file name.
- **AutoSave** automatically saves documents saved in *OneDrive*.
- A **Word document** (*.docx*) is the standard file format. Word documents can be saved in a variety of file formats.
- Open, edit, and save existing Word documents.

1.2 Customize a document by entering and selecting text, using word wrap, and using *AutoComplete*, *AutoCorrect*, and *AutoFormat* features (p. W1-7).

- **Word wrap** automatically wraps text to the next line as you reach the right margin of the document.
- The **Show/Hide** button displays formatting symbols in the document to enable properly and consistently formatted documents.
- Select text in a variety of ways: select individual words, an entire line, multiple lines of text, a sentence, a paragraph, multiple paragraphs, or the entire document.
- **AutoComplete** automatically completes a day, month, or date when entering text.
- **AutoCorrect** automatically corrects commonly misspelled words and capitalization errors.
- **AutoFormat** automatically controls the formatting of items such as numbered and bulleted lists.
- Add, delete, and edit *AutoCorrect* entries and customize *AutoCorrect* options in Word.

1.3 Enhance a document using paragraph breaks, line breaks, spaces, and non-breaking spaces (p. W1-10).

- The **Enter** key on the keyboard inserts a **paragraph break**. Click the *Show/Hide* button to display the **paragraph symbol**.
- **Line breaks** control breaks between lines or sentences to retain paragraph formatting between lines.
- **Non-breaking spaces** keep related words together.

1.4 Edit a document using cut, copy, paste, the *Clipboard*, and the undo, redo, and repeat features (p. W1-15).

- Word provides a variety of methods to **cut**, **copy**, and **paste** text in a document.
- The **Clipboard** stores cut or copied text. Use the *Clipboard* to paste text into a document.
- Use **Undo**, **Redo**, and **Repeat** when working on a document. These features are available on the **Quick Access toolbar**.

1.5 Customize a document using different fonts, font sizes, and attributes (p. W1-18).

- **Serif** and **sans serif** are the two main categories of **fonts**.
- Fonts are measured in **points** (pt.). Most documents use between 10 and 12 pt. font size.
- Change fonts and font size for specific text or the entire document.
- **Bold**, **Italic**, and **Underline** are font styles.
- Other font effects include **Strikethrough**, **Subscript**, **Superscript**, **Small caps**, and **All caps**.
- Change the case of text in Word using the **Change Case** button or the **Font** dialog box.
- The **Font dialog box** provides many **font**, **size**, **style**, and **effect options**.
- Modify the **scale**, **spacing**, **position**, and **kerning** of selected text using the **Advanced** tab in the *Font* dialog box.
- The **Format Painter** applies formatting from selected text to other text.
- The **Clear Formatting** feature removes all formatting applied to selected text.
- Change the **default** font and font size in Word by opening the *Font* dialog box.

1.6 Enhance a document using text alignment and line and paragraph spacing (p. W1-28).

- **Paragraph alignment** describes how text is aligned horizontally between the margins of a document: **Left**, **Center**, **Right**, or **Justified**.
- **Line spacing** refers to the amount of blank space between lines of text in a paragraph.
- **Paragraph spacing** is the amount of space between paragraphs. Paragraph spacing is measured in points.

- Modify alignment, line spacing, and paragraph spacing on the *Home* or *Layout* tab or in the **Paragraph dialog box**.
- Change the default line and paragraph spacing in Word by opening the *Paragraph* dialog box.

1.7 Finalize a document using Word's research, proofing, and learning tools (p. W1-32).

- **Smart Lookup** is used to research selected word(s) without leaving Word. Research results display in the **Smart Lookup pane**.
- Word automatically checks documents for **spelling** and **grammatical errors**.
- Word marks potential spelling, incorrect word, or grammatical errors with a colored line under the words. Correct errors by selecting options in the context menu.
- Manually spell and grammar check a document using the *Editor* pane.
- Customize the **Word dictionary** by adding, deleting, or modifying words in the word list.
- Use the **Thesaurus** to find synonyms for words in your document.

- Word includes a **Word Count** feature.
- The **Read Aloud** feature reads text in a document.
- **Learning Tools** enables users to change page width, page color, text spacing; view spaces between syllables in words; and use the *Read Aloud* feature.

1.8 Apply custom document properties to a document (p. W1-38).

- Add **document properties**, such as *Title*, *Author*, *Company*, *Subject*, *Created*, and *Last Modified*.
- Add document properties on the *Backstage* view or in the *Properties* dialog box.

Check for Understanding

The SIMbook for this text (within your SIMnet account) provides the following resources for concept review:

- Multiple-choice questions
- Short answer questions
- Matching exercises

Guided Project 1-1

In this project, Jennie Owings at Central Sierra Insurance writes a business letter to Hartford Specialty regarding the renewal of the insurance policy for Valley Custom Manufacturing. This business letter appears in block format and uses open punctuation. See *Appendix B* (online resource) for examples of business document formats and mixed and open punctuation.
[Student Learning Outcomes 1.1, 1.2, 1.3, 1.4, 1.5, 1.6, 1.7, 1.8]

File Needed: ***ValleyCustomManufacturing-01.docx*** *(Student data files are available in the* Library *of your* SIMnet *account.)*
Completed Project File Name: *[your initials] **Word 1-1.docx***

Skills Covered in This Project

- Add document properties.
- Use block business letter format using open punctuation.
- Change line spacing.
- Change paragraph spacing.
- Use *AutoComplete*.
- Use paragraph breaks for proper spacing between the parts of a business letter.
- Copy and paste text from another document using the *Clipboard*.
- Use *Show/Hide*.
- Undo automatic capitalization.
- Change font size.
- Apply font styles.
- Use *Smart Lookup*.
- Use spelling and grammar checker.
- Add words to the dictionary.

1. Open a new Word document.
   a. Click the **File** tab to open the *Backstage* view.
   b. Click **New** on the left and click **Blank document**. You can also click **Blank document** from the *Start* page when you first open Word.

2. Save the document as *[your initials] **Word 1-1***.
   a. Click the **File** tab to open the *Backstage* view and select **Save As** on the left.
   b. Click **Browse** to open the *Save As* dialog box and select the desired location to save the file.
   c. Change the file name to [your initials] Word 1-1.
   d. Click **Save** to rename the document and close the *Save As* dialog box.

3. Add document properties.
   a. Click the **File** tab to open *Backstage* view and click the **Info** button on the left if it is not already selected.
   b. Click the **Show All Properties** link at the bottom of the *Properties* area.
   c. Type Valley Custom Manufacturing in the *Title* field.
   d. Type Central Sierra Insurance in the *Company* field.
   e. Click the **Back** arrow in the upper left of the *Backstage* view to return to the document.

4. Change the line and paragraph spacing of the document.
    a. Click the **Paragraph** launcher [*Home* or *Layout* tab, *Paragraph* group] to open the *Paragraph* dialog box (Figure 1-82).
    b. Change the *Line spacing* to **Single**.
    c. Change the *After* paragraph spacing to **0 pt**.
    d. Choose **OK** to close the *Paragraph* dialog box.

5. Use *AutoComplete* to type a date.
    a. Turn on **Show/Hide** [*Home* tab, *Paragraph* group] if it is not already turned on.
    b. Type the current date using month, day, year format (September 1, 2020). As you begin typing the date, *AutoComplete* completes the month and current date. Press **Enter** to accept the *AutoComplete* date.
    c. Press **Enter** four times (quadruple space) after the date.

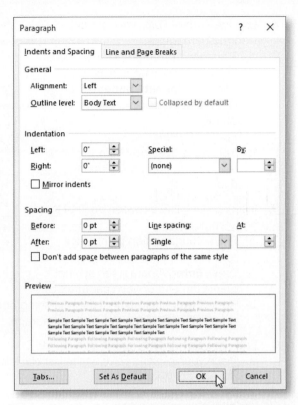

Figure 1-82 *Paragraph* dialog box

6. Type the inside address, salutation, and subject line.
    a. Type Mrs. Cammie Speckler and press **Enter** once at the end of the line.
    b. Type Hartford Specialty and press **Enter** once.
    c. Type 4788 Market Street, Suite A205 and press **Enter** once.
    d. Type San Francisco, CA 95644 and press **Enter** two times.
    e. Type Dear Mrs. Speckler as the salutation and press **Enter** two times. No colon is used after the salutation when using open punctuation.
    f. Type RE: Valley Custom Manufacturing as the subject line and press **Enter** two times.

7. Copy text from another document and paste it into the current document.
    a. Click the **File** to open the *Backstage* view and select **Open** at the left.
    b. Click the **Browse** button to open the *Open* dialog box.
    c. Locate and select the ***ValleyCustomManufacturing-01*** document from your student data files and click **Open**. If the document opens in *Protected View*, click the **Enable Editing** button.
    d. Press **Ctrl+A** to select the entire document.
    e. Click the **Copy** button [*Home* tab, *Clipboard* group] or press **Ctrl+C**.
    f. Close ***ValleyCustomManufacturing-01*** without saving the document.
    g. Return to the ***[your initials] Word 1-1*** document and place your insertion point on the last blank line of the document.
    h. Click the **Clipboard** launcher [*Home* tab, *Clipboard* group] to open the *Clipboard* pane (Figure 1-83).
    i. Click the **drop-down arrow** to the right of the copied text in the *Clipboard* and click **Paste**. The paragraphs of text are pasted in the body of the document.
    j. Click the **X** in the upper-right corner of the *Clipboard* pane to close it.

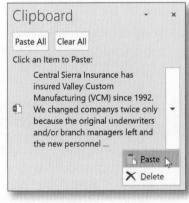

Figure 1-83 Paste from the *Clipboard*

8. Use the *Format Painter* to format the inserted paragraphs.
   a. Place your insertion point on the first line of the document (date line).
   b. Click the **Format Painter** button [*Home* tab, *Clipboard* group] to turn on the *Format Painter*.
   c. Select the five body paragraphs of the letter to apply the formatting (Figure 1-84).

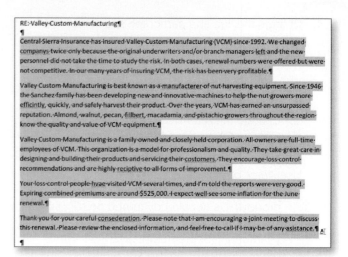

Figure 1-84 Use the *Format Painter* to copy formatting

9. Insert a blank line between each of the body paragraphs.
   a. Place your insertion point at the end of the first body paragraph and press **Enter**. A paragraph symbol marks the end of each paragraph.
   b. Press **Enter** after each of the remaining body paragraphs including the last body paragraph.

10. Enter the closing lines of the document.
    a. Place your insertion point on the last blank line below the body of the letter.
    b. Type **Sincerely** and press **Enter** four times. Type **Jennie Owings, Vice President** and press **Enter**.
    c. Type **Central Sierra Insurance** and press **Enter** two times.
    d. Type your reference initials (your first and last initials in lowercase letters with no punctuation).
    e. Press **Enter**. *AutoCorrect* automatically capitalizes the first letter of your reference initials.
    f. Click the **AutoCorrect Options** smart tag (Figure 1-85). The *AutoCorrect Options* smart tag appears when you place your pointer below your reference initials.

Figure 1-85 *AutoCorrect Options* smart tag

    g. Select **Undo Automatic Capitalization** to undo the automatic capitalization of your reference initials.
    h. Place your insertion point on the blank line below your reference initials and type **Enclosure** as an enclosure notation.

11. Select the entire document (**Ctrl+A**) and change the font size to **10 pt**. [*Home* tab, *Font* group].

12. Add *Before* paragraph spacing to the date line.
    a. Select or place your insertion point in the date line.
    b. Change the *Before* spacing to **72 pt**. [*Layout* tab, *Paragraph* group] (Figure 1-86).

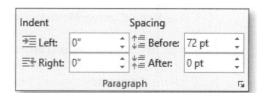

Figure 1-86 Change *Before* paragraph spacing on the date line

13. Apply a font style to selected text.
    a. Select the words "**Central Sierra Insurance**" in the first body paragraph.
    b. Click the **Font** launcher [*Home* tab, *Font* group] to open the *Font* dialog box.
    c. Select **Bold** in the *Font style* area, check the **Small caps** box in the **Effects** area, and click **OK** to close the *Font* dialog box.
    d. Select the words "**Valley Custom Manufacturing (VCM)**" in the first body paragraph.
    e. Click the **Bold** button [*Home* tab, *Font* group] or press **Ctrl+B**.

14. Use *Smart Lookup* to research selected words.
    a. Select "**harvesting equipment**" in the second body paragraph.
    b. Click the **Smart Lookup** button [*References* tab, *Research* group]. The *Smart Lookup* pane opens on the right.
    c. Review the research results on the *Smart Lookup* pane.
    d. Click the **X** in the upper-right corner of the *Smart Lookup* pane to close the pane.

15. Spell and grammar check the entire document.
    a. Place your insertion point at the top of the document (or press **Ctrl+Home**).
    b. Click the **Spelling & Grammar** button [*Review* tab, *Proofing* group]. The *Editor* pane opens at the right (Figure 1-87).

    Office 2019 Note: This pane is labeled **Proofing** rather than *Editor* in Office 2019 and some features may differ slightly.

Figure 1-87 Select correct word from the *Editor* pane

    c. Add "Cammie" and "Speckler" to the dictionary if they are marked as potential spelling errors. Click **Add to Dictionary** to add each name.
    d. Select the correct word in the *Editor* pane for the remaining spelling and grammatical errors (see Figure 1-87).
    e. Continue checking the document from the beginning if prompted. Choose **Yes**.
    f. Click **Ignore Once** if your reference initials are marked as a potential spelling or grammatical error.
    g. Click **OK** to close the dialog box that informs you the spelling and grammar check is complete.

16. Save and close the document (Figure 1-88).

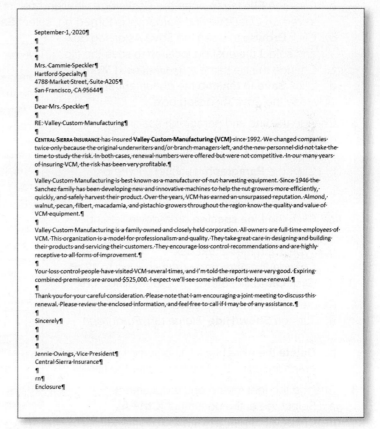

Figure 1-88 Word 1-1 completed

Guided Project 1-2

Sierra Pacific Community College District is a multi-campus community college district. In this project, you format an informational handout regarding online learning.
[Student Learning Outcomes 1.1, 1.2, 1.3, 1.4, 1.5, 1.6, 1.7, 1.8]

File Needed: **OnlineLearning-01.docx** *(Student data files are available in the* Library *of your SIMnet account.)*
Completed Project File Name: ***[your initials] Word 1-2.docx***

Skills Covered in This Project

- Open and edit an existing document.
- Change line spacing.
- Change paragraph spacing.
- Use *Show/Hide.*
- Change font size and apply color, styles, and effects.

- Cut and paste to move a paragraph.
- Use drag and drop to move a paragraph.
- Apply a shadow text effect.
- Use the *Format Painter.*
- Use spelling and grammar checker.
- Use *Read Aloud.*
- Add document properties.

1. Open the **OnlineLearning-01** document from your student data files.
   a. Click the **File** tab to open the *Backstage* view and click **Open** on the left.
   b. Click **Browse** to open the *Open* dialog box.
   c. Browse to locate the **OnlineLearning-01** document, select the document, and click **Open**. If the document opens in *Protected View*, click the **Enable Editing** button.

2. Save the document as *[your initials] Word 1-2.*
   a. Click the **File** tab to open the *Backstage* view and select **Save As** on the left. If your document is saved on *OneDrive* and *AutoSave* is turned on, select **Save a Copy**.
   b. Click **Browse** to open the *Save As* dialog box and select the desired location to save the file.
   c. Change the file name to [your initials] Word 1-2.
   d. Click **Save** to rename the document and close the *Save As* dialog box.

3. Change the line and paragraph spacing for the entire document.
   a. Press **Ctrl+A** to select the entire document.
   b. Click the **Paragraph** launcher [*Home* or *Layout* tab, *Paragraph* group] to open the *Paragraph* dialog box (Figure 1-89).
   c. Click the **Line spacing** drop-down list and select **Multiple**.
   d. Type 1.2 in the *At* text box.
   e. Change the *After* paragraph spacing to **12 pt**.
   f. Click **OK** to close the *Paragraph* dialog box.

4. Delete blank lines in the document.
   a. Turn on **Show/Hide** [*Home* tab, *Paragraph* group].
   b. **Delete** the extra blank line between each paragraph including the blank line after the title.

5. Change the font for the entire document.
   a. Select the entire document (**Ctrl+A**).
   b. Change the font to **Cambria** [*Home* tab, *Font* group].

Figure 1-89 Change *Line spacing* and *After* paragraph spacing

6. Change the paragraph spacing, alignment, font size, styles, effects, and color of the title.
   a. Select the title of the document ("**Online Learning Information**").
   b. Click the **Layout** tab.
   c. Change the *Before* spacing to **36 pt**. and the *After* spacing to **18 pt**. [*Paragraph* group].
   d. Click the **Center** button [*Home* tab, *Paragraph* group].
   e. Click the **Font** launcher [*Home* tab, *Font* group]. The *Font* dialog box opens (Figure 1-90).
   f. Change the *Font* style to **Bold** and change the *Font Size* to **24**.
   g. Click the **Small caps** check box in the *Effects* area.
   h. Click the **Font color** drop-down list and choose the **fourth color** in the **first row** of the *Theme Colors* (**Blue-Gray**, **Text 2**).
   i. Click the **Advanced** tab.
   j. Click the **Spacing** drop-down list and select **Expanded**. Change the *By* to **1.2 pt**.
   k. Click **OK** to close the *Font* dialog box.

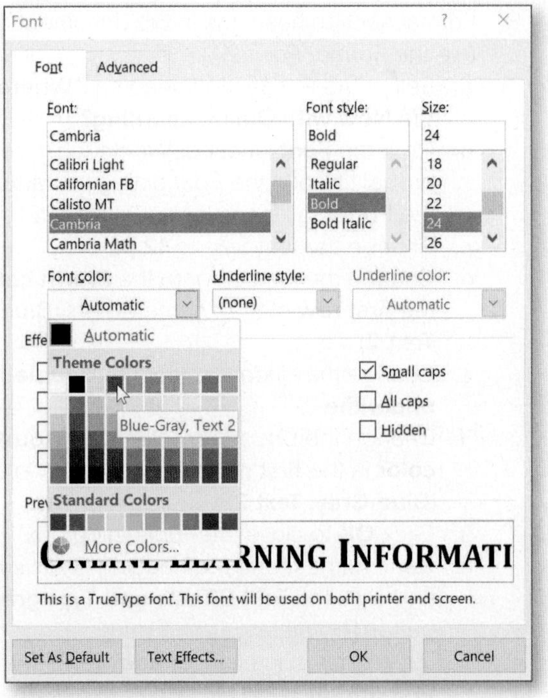

Figure 1-90 Change font style, size, effects, and color

7. Move paragraphs in the document and insert a heading.
   a. Select the last paragraph in the document, including the paragraph mark at the end of the paragraph.
   b. Click the **Cut** button [*Home* tab, *Clipboard* group] or press **Ctrl+X**.
   c. Place your insertion point before the second line of the document ("Definition of Online Learning Modalities").
   d. Click the top half of the **Paste** button [*Home* tab, *Clipboard* group] or press **Ctrl+V**.
   e. Click at the beginning of the pasted paragraph and type Where Are We Now with Online Learning? and press **Enter**.
   f. Select the paragraph that begins "Hybrid Course:" including the paragraph mark at the end of the paragraph.
   g. Move this paragraph using the drag-and-drop method (click, hold, and drag) so it appears before the paragraph that begins with "Television or Tele-web Course:" (Figure 1-91).

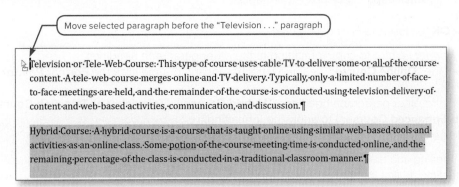

Figure 1-91 Move paragraph using drag and drop

8. Format section headings in the document and use the *Format Painter*.
   a. Select the first section heading ("**Where Are We Now with Online Learning?**").
   b. Click the **Font** launcher [*Home* tab, *Font* group] to open the *Font* dialog box and click the **Font** tab if necessary (Figure 1-92).
   c. Change the font *Size* to **12 pt**.
   d. Change the *Font color* to the **fourth color** in the **first row** of the *Theme Colors* (**Blue-Gray, Text 2**).
   e. Change the *Underline style* to **Double underline**.
   f. Change the *Underline color* to the **fourth color** in the **first row** of the *Theme Colors* (**Blue-Gray, Text 2**).
   g. Click **OK** to close the *Font* dialog box.
   h. Confirm the formatted heading is still selected and click the **Text Effects and Typography** button [*Home* tab, *Font* group].
   i. Place your pointer on **Shadow** and select the **first option** in the *Outer* category (**Offset: Bottom Right**) (Figure 1-93).
   j. Confirm the formatted heading still selected and click the **Format Painter** button [*Home* tab, *Clipboard* group].
   k. Select the next heading ("**Definition of Online Learning Modalities**") to apply the formatting.

9. Format paragraph headings in the document.
   a. Select the first paragraph heading ("**Online Course:**"), including the colon.
   b. Click the **Font** launcher [*Home* tab, *Font* group] to open the *Font* dialog box.
   c. Change the *Font style* to **Bold**.
   d. Change the *Font color* to the **fourth color** in the **first row** of the *Theme Colors* (**Blue-Gray, Text 2**).
   e. Click the **Small caps** check box in the *Effects* area.
   f. Click **OK** to close the *Font* dialog box.

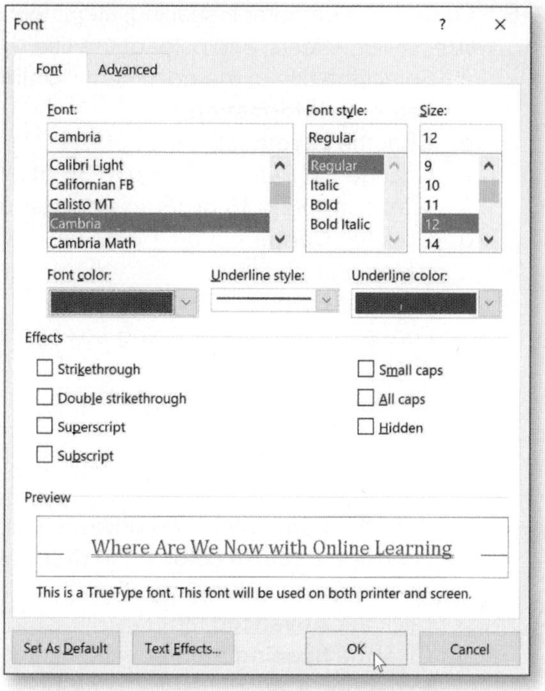

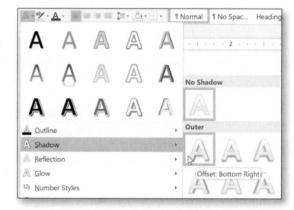

Figure 1-92 Format heading using the *Font* dialog box

Figure 1-93 Apply *Shadow* text effect

10. Use the *Format Painter* to copy formatting to the other paragraph headings.
    a. Select the "**Online Course:**" heading if necessary and double click the **Format Painter** button.
    b. Select the other paragraph headings ("**Hybrid Course:**", "**Television or Tele-web Course:**", and "**web-Enhanced Course:**") to apply the formatting.
    c. Click the **Format Painter** button again to turn off the *Format Painter*.

11. Correct spelling and grammar in the document using the context menu.
    a. Right-click the first misspelled word ("**managment**") and choose the correct spelling from the list of options.
    b. Repeat this process for "**potion.**"
    c. Click **Ignore All** or **Ignore Once** if other words are marked as potentially incorrect.

12. Select the sentence in parentheses at the end of the document, including the parentheses, and click the **Italic** button [*Home* tab, *Font* group] or press **Ctrl+I**.

13. Use the *Read Aloud* feature.
    a. Place your insertion point at the beginning of the first body paragraph ("SPCCD was a pioneer. . .").
    b. Click the **Read Aloud** button [*Review* tab, *Speech* group]. Word begins reading the first paragraph and the *Read Aloud* controls display at the left.
    c. Click the **Pause** button in the *Read Aloud* controls.
    d. Click the **Settings** button and change the **Reading speed** and **Voice Selection** as desired (Figure 1-94).
    e. Press **Esc** to close the *Settings* menu.
    f. Click the **Next** button to skip to the next paragraph.
    g. Click the **Stop** button to stop the reading and close the *Read Aloud* controls.

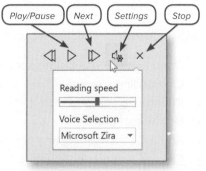

Figure 1-94 *Read Aloud* controls

14. Add document properties using the *Properties* dialog box.
    a. Click the **File** tab to open the *Backstage* view and click the **Info** button if it is not already selected.
    b. Click the **Properties** button on the right and choose **Advanced Properties**. The *Properties* dialog box opens.
    c. Click the **Summary** tab if necessary.
    d. Type Online Learning Information in the *Title* text box.
    e. Type Online Learning in the *Subject* text box.
    f. Delete the existing author name in the *Author* area and type Tanesha Morris as the author.
    g. Click **OK** to accept changes and close the *Properties* dialog box.
    h. Click the **Back** arrow in the upper left of the *Backstage* view to return to the document.

15. Save and close the document (Figure 1-95).

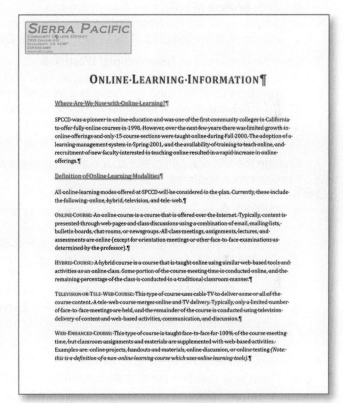

Figure 1-95 Word 1-2 completed

Guided Project 1-3

In this project, you create a memo for American River Cycling Club about using heart rate to increase the effectiveness of training. See *Appendix B* (online resource) for examples of business document formats.
[**Student Learning Outcomes 1.1, 1.2, 1.3, 1.5, 1.6, 1.7, 1.8**]

File Needed: ***HeartRate-01.docx*** *(Student data files are available in the* Library *of your SIMnet account.)*
Completed Project File Name: ***[your initials] Word 1-3.docx***

Skills Covered in This Project

- Open and edit an existing document.
- Change line spacing.
- Change paragraph spacing.
- Use *Show/Hide.*
- Add a memo heading to a document.
- Change paragraph alignment.

- Change font size and apply styles and effects.
- Use the *Format Painter.*
- Add text highlight color.
- Use non-breaking space.
- Use *Thesaurus.*
- Add words to the dictionary.
- Add document properties.

1. Open the ***HeartRate-01*** document from your student data files.
   a. Click the **File** tab to open the *Backstage* view and click **Open** on the left.
   b. Click **Browse** to open the *Open* dialog box.
   c. Browse to locate the ***HeartRate-01*** document, select the document, and click **Open**. If the document opens in *Protected View*, click the **Enable Editing** button.

2. Save the document as ***[your initials] Word 1-3.***
   a. Click the **File** tab to open the *Backstage* view and select **Save As** on the left. If your document is saved on *OneDrive* and *AutoSave* is turned on, select **Save a Copy**.
   b. Click **Browse** to open the *Save As* dialog box and select the desired location to save the file.
   c. Change the file name to [your initials] Word 1-3.
   d. Click **Save** to rename the document and close the *Save As* dialog box.

3. Change the line and paragraph spacing for the entire document and insert a paragraph break between each paragraph.
   a. Press **Ctrl+A** to select the entire document.
   b. Click the **Paragraph** launcher [*Home* or *Layout* tab, *Paragraph* group]. The *Paragraph* dialog box opens.
   c. Click the **Line spacing** drop-down list and select **Single**.
   d. Change the *After* paragraph spacing to **0 pt**.
   e. Click **OK** to close the *Paragraph* dialog box.
   f. Turn on **Show/Hide** [*Home* tab, *Paragraph* group] if it is not already on.
   g. Click at the end of each paragraph and press **Enter** once to add a blank line between each of the paragraphs. Don't press *Enter* after the last body paragraph. A paragraph symbol marks the end of each paragraph.

4. Add a memo heading to the document.
   a. Place your insertion point at the beginning of the first paragraph ("What is Maximum Heart Rate?") and press **Enter**.
   b. Place the insertion point on the blank line above the first paragraph.
   c. Type **TO:** and press **Tab** two times.
   d. Type **All ARCC Club Members** and press **Enter** two times.
   e. Type **FROM:** and press **Tab** two times.
   f. Type **Taylor Mathos, ARCC Coach** and press **Enter** two times.
   g. Type **DATE:** and press **Tab** two times.
   h. Type the current date in month, day, year format (January 1, 2020) and press **Enter** two times.
   i. Type **SUBJECT:** and press **Tab** once.
   j. Type **Heart Rate Training** and press **Enter** two times.

5. Change the paragraph alignment and font styles of selected text.
   a. Select the second and third paragraphs in the body of the memo (beginning with "**220 – Your Age . . .**" and ending with "**. . . heart rate is 180.)**"), including the paragraph mark at the end of the third paragraph.

b. Click the **Center** button [*Home* tab, *Paragraph* group] or press **Ctrl+E**.
c. Select the paragraph beginning "**220 – Your Age . . .**" and click the **Bold** button [*Home* tab, *Font* group] or press **Ctrl+B**.
d. Select the next paragraph and click the **Italic** button [*Home* tab, *Font* group] or press **Ctrl+I**.
e. **Delete** the blank line between the second and third paragraphs (Figure 1-96).

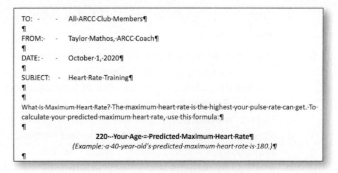

Figure 1-96 Memo heading added and paragraphs formatted

6. Change the font and style of selected text.
   a. Press **Ctrl+A** to select the entire document.
   b. Click the **Increase Font Size** button [*Home* tab, *Font* group] to increase the font size to 12 pt. (Figure 1-97).
   c. Select the words "**What is Maximum Heart Rate?**" in the first sentence of the first body paragraph.

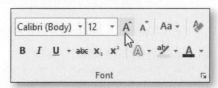

Figure 1-97 *Increase Font Size* button

   d. Click the **Font** launcher [*Home* tab, *Font* group] to open the *Font* dialog box (Figure 1-98).
   e. Change the *Font style* to **Bold**.
   f. Change the *Underline style* to **Words only**.
   g. Change the *Underline color* to the **tenth color** in the **first row** of the *Theme Colors* (**Green, Accent 6**).
   h. Select the **Small caps** check box in the *Effects* area.
   i. Click **OK** to close the *Font* dialog box.
   j. Select the text if necessary and click the **Format Painter** button [*Home* tab, *Clipboard* group].
   k. Select the words "**Target Heart Rate Zone**" in the first sentence of the fifth paragraph in the body ("You gain the most benefits . . ."). The *Format Painter* applies the formatting to the selected words.
   l. Select the last sentence of the fifth body paragraph ("**Do not exercise above 85 percent . . .**") including the period at the end of the second sentence.

Figure 1-98 Change font style and effects

   m. Click the **Text Highlight Color** drop-down arrow [*Home* tab, *Font* group] (Figure 1-99) and select the **fourth option** in the **third row** (**Gray-25%**).

7. Use a non-breaking space to keep words together.
   a. **Delete** the space between the words "Target" and "Heart" in the first sentence of the fifth paragraph in the body ("You gain the most benefits . . .").
   b. Place your insertion point between these two words and press **Ctrl+Shift+Spacebar** to insert a non-breaking space. "Target" is wrapped to the next line so the words do not break between lines.
   c. Delete the space between "80" and "percent" in the next sentence and press **Ctrl+Shift+Spacebar** to insert a non-breaking space.

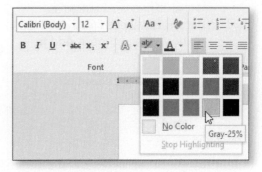

Figure 1-99 *Text Highlight Color* drop-down list

8. Add *Before* paragraph spacing to the first line of the memo heading.
   a. Place the insertion point in the first line of the memo heading ("**TO: . . .**").

b. Change the *Before* spacing to **72 pt**. [*Layout* tab, *Paragraph* group].

9. Use the *Thesaurus* to find synonyms for selected words.
   a. Right-click the word "**medicines**" in the third sentence of the fourth body paragraph ("Your actual maximum . . .").
   b. Point to **Synonyms** to display a list of synonyms.
   c. Select "**medications**" as the synonym (Figure 1-100).
   d. Right-click the word "**added**" in the last sentence of the fifth paragraph ("You gain the most benefits . . .").
   e. Point to **Synonyms** and select "**additional**."

10. Add reference initials to the document.
    a. Click at the end of the last paragraph and press **Enter** two times.
    b. Type your reference initials in lowercase letters.

11. Add document properties.
    a. Click the **File** tab to open the *Backstage* view.
    b. Click the **Info** button if necessary to display the document properties on the right.
    c. Type Heart Rate Training in the *Title* text box.
    d. Right-click the existing author in the *Author* area and select **Remove Person**.
    e. Type Taylor Mathos in the *Author* text box.
    f. Click the **Show All Properties** link at the bottom of the document properties.
    g. Type ARCC in the *Company* text box.
    h. Click the **Back** arrow in the upper left of the *Backstage* view to return to the document.

12. Add words to the dictionary.
    a. Right-click "**Mathos**" in the second line of the memo heading if it is marked as a potential spelling error and choose **Add to Dictionary** from the context menu.
    b. Right-click your reference initials if they are marked as incorrectly spelled (red wavy underline) and choose **Add to Dictionary**.

13. Save and close the document (Figure 1-101).

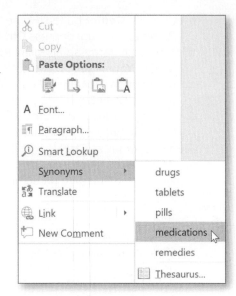

Figure 1-100 Select synonym from context menu

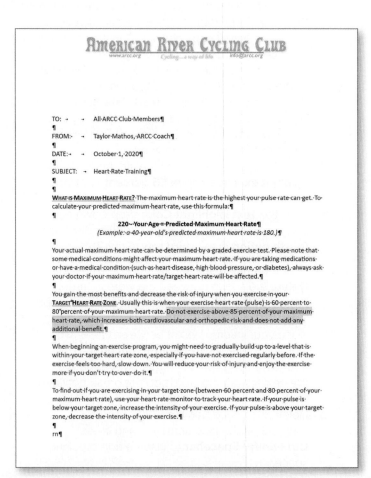

Figure 1-101 Word 1-3 completed

Independent Project 1-4

In this project, you format a business letter for Emma Cavalli to send to clients whose current home listings are expiring. See *Appendix B* (online resource) for examples of business document formats and mixed and open punctuation.
[Student Learning Outcomes 1.1, 1.2, 1.3, 1.4, 1.5, 1.6, 1.7, 1.8]

File Needed: ***ExpiredLetter-01.docx*** *(Student data files are available in the* Library *of your SIMnet account.)*
Completed Project File Name: *[your initials]* **Word 1-4.docx**

Skills Covered in This Project

- Open and edit an existing document.
- Change line spacing.
- Change paragraph alignment and spacing.
- Change font and font size.
- Use *Show/Hide.*

- Format document as a block format business letter with mixed punctuation.
- Move text.
- Change font styles and effects.
- Use *Smart Lookup.*
- Use *Read Aloud.*
- Add document properties.
- Use spelling and grammar checker.

---

1. Open the ***ExpiredLetter-01*** document from your student data files. If the document opens in *Protected View*, click the **Enable Editing** button.

2. Save this document as *[your initials]* **Word 1-4.**

3. Apply the following formatting changes to the entire document:
   a. Select the entire document.
   b. Change the *Before* and *After* paragraph spacing to **0 pt**.
   c. Change the line spacing to **Single**.
   d. Change the paragraph alignment to **Left**.
   e. Change the font and font size to **Calibri** and **11 pt**.

4. Turn on **Show/Hide** and press **Enter** at the end of each paragraph to add a blank line after each paragraph (including the last paragraph).

5. Type and format the opening lines of the business letter.
   a. Press **Ctrl+Home** or move your insertion point to the top of the document.
   b. Type the current date (use January 1, 2020 format) and press **Enter** four times.
   c. Type the following inside address and press **Enter** two times after the last line:

      Mr. Rick Hermann
      9035 Masi Drive
      Fair Oaks, CA 95528

   d. Type Dear Mr. Hermann: as the salutation and press **Enter** two times after the salutation. One blank line displays between the salutation and the body of the letter.
   e. Add **72 pt**. *Before* paragraph spacing to the date line.

6. Type the closing lines of the business letter.
   a. Place your insertion point on the blank line below the last body paragraph and press **Enter**.
   b. Type Best regards, and press **Enter** four times.
   c. Type the following closing lines:

      Emma Cavalli
      Realtor Consultant
      Placer Hills Real Estate

   d. Press **Enter** two times after the company name and type your reference initials in lowercase letters.

7. Move a paragraph and sentence.
   a. Move the third body paragraph so it appears before the second body paragraph. Confirm one blank line displays between each of the body paragraphs. If a blank space displays in front of the first word in the third paragraph, delete it.
   b. Move the last two sentences in the new second body paragraph ("A lot of detail . . .") to the beginning of the paragraph. Verify proper spacing displays between sentences.

8. Apply formatting to text in the business letter.
   a. Select "**Placer Hills Real Estate**" in the first body paragraph and apply **Bold** and **Small caps** formatting.
   b. Select the first sentence in the third paragraph including the period ("The service and experience . . .") and apply **Italic** formatting.
   c. Select the writer's name at the bottom and apply **Small caps** formatting.
   d. Select the writer's title and apply **Italic** formatting.
   e. Select the company name below the writer's title and apply **Bold** formatting.

9. Use *Smart Lookup* to research selected words.
   a. Select "**Fair Oaks**" in the first body paragraph.
   b. Click the **Smart Lookup** button [*References* tab, *Research* group]. The *Smart Lookup* pane opens on the right.
   c. Review the research results in the *Smart Lookup* pane.
   d. Click the **X** in the upper-right corner of the *Smart Lookup* pane to close the pane.

10. Use the **Read Aloud** feature [*Review* tab, *Speech* group] to read the first two body paragraphs.

11. Add the following document properties:
    a. *Title*: Expired Letter
    b. *Company*: Placer Hills Real Estate
    c. *Manager*: Kelsey Kroll
    d. *Author*: Emma Cavalli (right-click and choose **Remove Person** to remove existing author)

12. Spell and grammar check the entire document, apply changes where necessary, and ignore proper nouns.

13. Save and close the document (Figure 1-102).

Figure 1-102 Word 1-4 completed

Independent Project 1-5

In this project, you combine information from different documents to create a memo for Sierra Pacific Community College District. This memo is a draft of the values statement for the district. See *Appendix B* (online resource) for examples of business document formats.
[Student Learning Outcomes 1.1, 1.2, 1.3, 1.4, 1.5, 1.6, 1.7, 1.8]

File Needed: ***ValuesStatement-01a.docx*** and ***ValuesStatement-01b.docx*** *(Student data files are available in the* Library *of your SIMnet account.)*
Completed Project File Name: *[your initials]* **Word 1-5.docx**

Skills Covered in This Project

- Open and edit an existing document.
- Change line spacing.
- Change paragraph spacing.
- Change font and font size.
- Use *Show/Hide*.

- Format a document as a memo.
- Use spelling and grammar checker.
- Change font styles and effects.
- Use the *Format Painter*.
- Move text.
- Add document properties.

---

1. Open the ***ValuesStatement-01a*** document from your student data files. If the document opens in *Protected View*, click the **Enable Editing** button.

2. Save this document as *[your initials]* **Word 1-5**.

3. Copy text from another document and paste it into the current document.
   a. Open the ***ValuesStatement-01b*** document from your student data files.
   b. Select and **copy** all the text in this document.
   c. Close the ***ValuesStatement-01b*** document without saving.
   d. Return to the *[your initials]* **Word 1-5** document.
   e. Place your insertion point at the end of the document and press **Enter**.
   f. **Paste** the copied text below the existing paragraphs.
   g. **Delete** the extra paragraph breaks between the first four paragraphs and at the end of the document.

4. Select the entire document and apply the following formatting changes:
   a. Change *After* paragraph spacing to **12 pt**.
   b. Change the line spacing to **1.15**.
   c. Change the font and font size to **Calibri** and **10 pt**.

5. Type and format the heading lines in the memorandum.
   a. Turn on **Show/Hide**.
   b. Place your insertion point at the beginning of the document and press **Enter**.
   c. Place your insertion point on the blank line at the beginning of the document and type the following memo information. Press **Tab** (once or twice) after the guidewords to align information at 1" and press **Enter** once at the end of each of the first three lines of the memo heading (don't press *Enter* after the SUBJECT line).

TO:	All SPCCD Faculty, Staff, and Managers
FROM:	Lanita Morrow, Chancellor
DATE:	type current date (use January 1, 2020 format)
SUBJECT:	Draft of SPCCD Values Statement

   d. Change the *Before* paragraph spacing on the "TO:" line of the memo heading to **24 pt**.
   e. Change the *After* paragraph spacing on the "SUBJECT:" line of the memo heading to **18 pt**.

6. Spell and grammar check the entire document.
   a. Add the chancellor's first and last names to the dictionary if they are marked as potential spelling errors.
   b. Correct other spelling and grammar errors as necessary.

7. Apply formatting to a paragraph heading and use the *Format Painter* to copy formatting.
   a. Select the first paragraph heading ("**Access**") in the body of the memo and apply the following formatting:

   Font style: **Bold**
   Font color: **Fourth color** in the **first row** of *Theme Colors* (**Blue-Gray, Text 2**)
   Underline: **Double Underline**
   Underline color: **Fourth color** in the **first row** of *Theme Colors* (**Blue-Gray, Text 2**)
   Effects: **Small caps**

   b. Use the *Format Painter* to apply this formatting to each of the other paragraph headings in the body of the memo.

8. Move body paragraphs.
   a. Use cut and paste or drag and drop to move the body paragraphs so they are ordered alphabetically by paragraph heading. Exclude the first body paragraph ("Below is a draft . . ."). Be sure to include the paragraph symbol at the end of each paragraph when cutting or dragging.
   b. Verify that no extra *Enters* (paragraph marks) display after the last paragraph.
   c. Verify that no extra spaces display before the first word in each of the paragraphs.

9. Delete any extra blank lines at the end of the document so this document fits on one page if necessary.

10. Add the following document properties:
    a. *Title*: SPCCD Values Statement
    b. *Company*: Sierra Pacific Community College District
    c. *Author*: Yoon Soo Park (right-click and choose **Remove Person** to remove existing author)

11. Save and close the document (Figure 1-103).

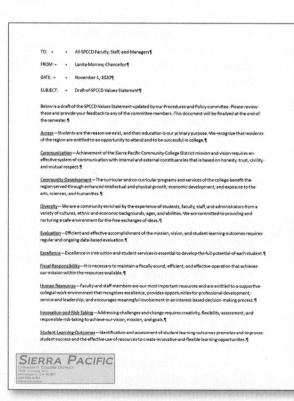

Figure 1-103 Word 1-5 completed

Independent Project 1-6

In this project, you create a professional and appealing brochure for Emma Cavalli at Placer Hills Real Estate using formatting features in Word.
[Student Learning Outcomes 1.1, 1.2, 1.3, 1.4, 1.5, 1.6, 1.7, 1.8]

File Needed: ***Brochure-01.docx*** *(Student data files are available in the* Library *of your SIMnet account.)*
Completed Project File Name: *[your initials] Word 1-6.docx*

Skills Covered in This Project

- Open and edit an existing document.
- Change font and font size.
- Change paragraph spacing.
- Change line spacing.
- Use *Show/Hide*.
- Change paragraph alignment.

- Change font styles and effects.
- Use the *Format Painter*.
- Move text.
- Use the thesaurus to find synonyms.
- Use *Smart Lookup*.
- Use *Read Aloud*.
- Add document properties.

---

1. Open the **Brochure-01** document from your student data files. If the document opens in *Protected View*, click the **Enable Editing** button.

2. Save this document as *[your initials] Word 1-6.*

3. Select the entire document and apply the following formatting changes:
   a. Change the font and font size to **Cambria** and **10 pt**.
   b. Change the *After* paragraph spacing to **6 pt**.
   c. Change the line spacing to **Single**.

4. Apply formatting to the opening lines of the document.
   a. Select the first five lines of the document ("**Emma Cavalli**" to "**Email: ecavalli@phre.com**") and change the *After* paragraph spacing to **2 pt**.
   b. Select the first six lines of the document ("**Emma Cavalli**" to "**web: www.phre.com/ecavalli**") and **Center** these lines.
   c. Select the first line of the document ("**Emma Cavalli**") and apply the following changes:
      Font size: **12 pt**.
      Font style: **Bold**
      Font color: **tenth color** in the **last row** of *Theme Colors* (**Green, Accent 6, Darker 50%**)
   d. Select the second line of the document ("**Realtor Consultant**") and apply **Bold** formatting.
   e. Select the third line of the document ("**Putting Your Needs First**") and apply **Italic** formatting.

5. Apply formatting to a section heading and use the *Format Painter*.
   a. Select the first section heading, "**Personal Statement**," and apply **Bold**, **Underline**, and **Small Caps** formatting.
   b. Change the *Before* paragraph spacing to **12 pt**. and the *After* paragraph spacing to **3 pt**.
   c. Use the *Format Painter* to copy this formatting to the other section headings:

      "**Real Estate Experience**"
      "**Why I Am a Real Estate Agent**"
      "**What Clients are Saying**"
      "**Professional Credentials**"
      "**Education & Training**"

6. Turn on **Show/Hide** and combine the four sentences in the "Why I Am a Real Estate Agent" section into one paragraph. Delete paragraph marks and insert spaces as needed.

7. Apply the following changes in the "What Clients are Saying" section:
   a. Select the second paragraph ("It was a pleasure . . ."), apply **Italic**, and change the *After* spacing to **0 pt**.
   b. Select the source of the quote ("-**Rod & Luisa Ellisor, Rocklin, CA**") and right-align this text.
   c. Repeat the above two steps for the second quote ("Emma is conscientious . . .") and the source of the quote ("-Jon & Robin Anderson . . .").

8. Move the third section heading and the paragraph below it ("Why I Am a Real Estate Agent") so it appears before the second section ("Real Estate Experience").

9. Select the lines of text in the "Professional Credentials" section (don't include the heading) and change the *After* paragraph spacing to **3 pt**.

10. Use the *Format Painter* to repeat the above formatting to the lines of text (excluding the heading) in the "Education & Training" section.

11. Use the thesaurus to find an appropriate synonym for the following words:
    a. Replace "surpass" (in the "Personal Statement" section) with "**exceed**."
    b. Replace "emotions" (in the "Why I Am a Real Estate Agent" section) with "**sentiments**."

12. Use *Smart Lookup* to research selected words.
    a. Select "**University of Nevada, Reno**" in the "Education & Training" section.
    b. Click the **Smart Lookup** button [*References* tab, *Research* group]. The *Smart Lookup* pane opens on the right.
    c. Review the research results in the *Smart Lookup* pane.
    d. Click the **X** in the upper-right corner of the *Smart Lookup* pane to close the pane.

13. Use the *Read Aloud* feature [*Review* tab, *Speech* group] to read the first two body paragraphs.

14. Add the following document properties:
    a. *Title*: Brochure
    b. *Company*: Placer Hills Real Estate
    c. *Author*: Emma Cavalli (right-click and choose **Remove Person** to remove existing author)

15. Save and close the document (Figure 1-104).

Figure 1-104 Word 1-6 completed

Improve It Project 1-7

In this project, you create a block format business letter for Margaret Jepson, an insurance agent at Central Sierra Insurance. You improve the formatting and text in this document and add opening and closing lines to create a properly formatted business letter. For more information on creating a correctly formatted block format business letter, see *Appendix B* (online resource).
[Student Learning Outcomes 1.1, 1.2, 1.3, 1.5, 1.6, 1.7, 1.8]

File Needed: ***RenewalLetter-01.docx*** *(Student data files are available in the* Library *of your SIMnet account.)*
Completed Project File Name: *[your initials] Word 1-7.docx*

Skills Covered in This Project

- Open and edit an existing document.
- Change font and font size.
- Change paragraph spacing.
- Change line spacing.
- Use spelling and grammar checker.
- Format a business letter.
- Change paragraph alignment.
- Change font styles and effects.
- Use the *Format Painter.*
- Add document properties.

1. Open the ***RenewalLetter-01*** document from your student data files. If the document opens in *Protected View*, click the **Enable Editing** button.

2. Save this document as *[your initials] Word 1-7*.

3. Select the entire document and apply the following formatting:
   a. *Line spacing*: **Single**
   b. *Before* and *After paragraph spacing*: **0 pt**.
   c. *Font*: **Calibri**
   d. *Font size*: **11 pt**.

4. Correct spelling and grammar as needed.

5. Type the opening lines of the business letter.
   a. Turn on **Show/Hide** if it is not already on.
   b. Place your insertion point at the top of the document and press **Enter**.
   c. Place your insertion point on the blank line at the beginning of the document, type the current date (use January 1, 2020 format), and press **Enter** four times.
   d. Type the following inside address and press **Enter** two times after the last line:

   Mr. Rick DePonte
   8364 Marshall Street
   Granite Bay, CA 95863

   e. Type Dear Mr. DePonte: as the salutation press **Enter** two times.
   f. Type Subject: Policy HO-2887-5546-B as the subject line and press **Enter** once.
   g. Apply **72 pt**. *Before* paragraph spacing on the date line.

6. Type the closing lines of the business letter.
   a. Place the insertion point on the last blank line of the document and type Best regards, as the complimentary close.
   b. Press **Enter** four times.
   c. Type the following information below as the writer's name, title, and company and press **Enter** two times after the last line:

   Margaret Jepson, ARM, CIC, CRM
   Insurance Agent
   Central Sierra Insurance

   d. Type your initials in lowercase letters as the reference initials, press **Enter** once, and **Undo** the automatic capitalization of your reference initials.

   e. Type Enclosure as the enclosure notation at the end of the business letter.

7. Apply formatting to the renewal premium information.

   a. **Center** the four lines of renewal premium information in the body of the letter.

   b. Apply **Bold** and **Small caps** formatting to the headings (including the colons) for each of these four lines of renewal premium information.

   c. Format the "Total Premium" dollar amount as **Bold**, **Italic**, and **Double Underline**.

8. Type Hartford Specialty to replace the "*[Company Name]*" placeholder (delete brackets also) in the second body paragraph.

9. Type Rick to replace the "*[First Name]*" placeholder in the last body paragraph.

10. Add the following document properties:

   a. *Title*: Renewal Letter

   b. *Company*: Central Sierra Insurance

   c. *Author*: Margaret Jepson (right-click and choose **Remove Person** to remove existing author)

11. Save and close the letter (Figure 1-105).

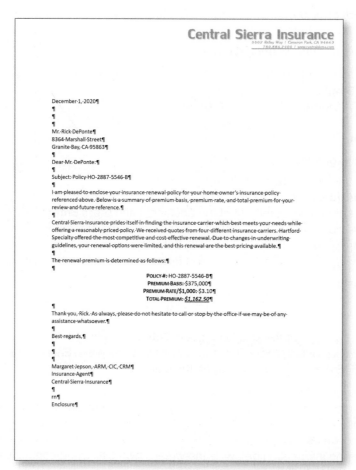

Figure 1-105 Word 1-7 completed

Challenge Project 1-8

Create a cover letter for a job application. A cover letter typically accompanies a resume to introduce an applicant to a prospective employer. You can use and modify an existing cover letter, or you can create a new one. It is important to customize each cover letter for each job for which you are applying.
[Student Learning Outcomes 1.1, 1.2, 1.3, 1.4, 1.5, 1.6, 1.7, 1.8]

File Needed: None
Completed Project File Name: *[your initials] Word 1-8.docx*

Open a new document and save this document as *[your initials] Word 1-8.*

Type this document as a personal business letter in block format. For more information on formatting a personal business letter, see *Appendix B* (online resource). Many online resources are available to help you with both content and format. One of the best online resources for writing is the Online Writing Lab (OWL) from Purdue University (http://owl.english.purdue.edu/owl/). Search this site for helpful information about cover letters.

Modify your document according to the following guidelines:

- Move sentences and paragraphs as needed to produce a well-organized cover letter.
- Add words to the dictionary as needed.
- Use the *Thesaurus* to find synonyms as needed.
- Include document properties, and spell and grammar check the document.

Challenge Project 1-9

Create a list of five places you would like to visit in the next five years. For each of the places you list, compose a short paragraph about that place and why it is interesting to you. Research each of the places you choose using the internet. Use your own words when composing the paragraphs about each place.
[Student Learning Outcomes 1.1, 1.2, 1.3, 1.4, 1.5, 1.6, 1.7, 1.8]

File Needed: None
Completed Project File Name: *[your initials] Word 1-9.docx*

Open a new document and save it as *[your initials] Word 1-9.*

Modify your document according to the following guidelines:

- Create and format a title for the document.
- Format each of the headings by modifying the font, style, and attributes.
- Change line and paragraph spacing as needed to create an attractive and readable document.
- Use consistent line and paragraph spacing throughout the document.
- Use the *Format Painter* to apply consistent formatting throughout the document.
- Move the paragraphs so the places are listed in priority order.
- Include document properties, and spell and grammar check the document.

Challenge Project 1-10

Create a flyer for an upcoming event for an organization to which you belong. Be sure to include all the relevant information for this event and arrange it attractively and professionally on the page.
[Student Learning Outcomes 1.1, 1.2, 1.3, 1.5, 1.6, 1.7, 1.8]

File Needed: None
Completed Project File Name: *[your initials] Word 1-10.docx*

Open a new document and save it as *[your initials] Word 1-10.*

Modify your document according to the following guidelines:

- Create and format a title for the document.
- Format the information by modifying the fonts, styles, and attributes.
- Change line and paragraph spacing as needed to create an attractive and readable document.
- Change the text alignment as desired.
- Use the *Format Painter* to keep formatting consistent throughout the document.
- Include document properties, and spell and grammar check the document.

Source of screenshots Microsoft Office 365 (2019): Word, Excel, Access, Powerpoint.

Formatting and Customizing Documents

CHAPTER OVERVIEW

In addition to creating common business documents, Microsoft Word provides formatting and editing tools to customize a variety of documents. Formatting features such as custom margins, tab stops, indents, page numbering, headers, footers, breaks, lists, styles, themes, borders, and shading help you produce readable and attractive professional and personal documents.

STUDENT LEARNING OUTCOMES (SLOs)

After completing this chapter, you will be able to:

SLO 2.1 Format a document by customizing margins, page orientation, paper size, vertical alignment, and page movement (p. W2-68).

SLO 2.2 Improve alignment and page layout by setting, using, and editing tab stops in a document (p. W2-72).

SLO 2.3 Apply indents to control text alignment (p. W2-76).

SLO 2.4 Enhance document layout by inserting page numbers, headers, and footers (p. W2-82).

SLO 2.5 Control pagination with page and section breaks (p. W2-89).

SLO 2.6 Use customized bulleted and numbered lists to effectively present information (p. W2-91).

SLO 2.7 Apply styles and themes to improve consistency in document format (p. W2-95).

SLO 2.8 Use find and replace to edit a document and use the *Resume Assistant* to customize a resume (p. W2-100).

SLO 2.9 Improve overall document design and format with borders, shading, horizontal lines, and hyperlinks (p. W2-103).

CASE STUDY

Courtyard Medical Plaza has a preschool for its employees' children. The preschool is currently looking for qualified applicants to fill a vacant teacher position. In the Pause & Practice projects, you modify a resume for Richelle Wilkinson. You apply features covered in this chapter to create an attractive and informative resume.

Pause & Practice 2-1: Edit a resume to change margins and set tab stops and indents.

Pause & Practice 2-2: Modify a resume to include a header with text and a page number.

Pause & Practice 2-3: Enhance a resume by using bulleted lists, a page break, and a theme.

Pause & Practice 2-4: Finalize a resume by using find and replace, borders, shading, horizontal line, hyperlinks, and *Resume Assistant.*

Customizing Margins and Page Layout

Use margins to create *white space* around the edges of a document. White space improves the readability of a document and prevents the document from appearing cluttered. The document type and content influence the margin settings you apply. Other ways to customize a document include changing the page orientation, page size, vertical alignment, or page movement.

Page Layout Settings

When you open a new Word document, the default settings control margins, page orientation, paper size, and vertical alignment. Table 2-1 lists the default page layout settings for a new document.

Table 2-1: Default Page Layout Settings

Page Layout Option	Default Setting
Margins	1" top, bottom, left, and right
Page Orientation	Portrait
Paper Size	8.5"×11" (Letter)
Vertical Alignment	Top

Page layout settings apply to the entire Word document, and you can easily change all of these settings using the *Layout* tab.

Margin Settings

Margin settings are measured in inches; the default margin settings for a new Word document are 1". Word provides a variety of *preset margin settings*. You can choose and change margins from the *Margins* drop-down list.

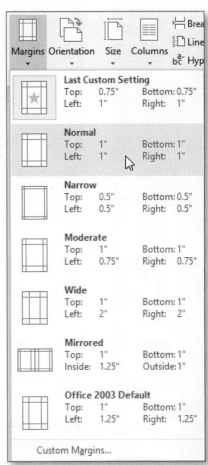

▶ **HOW TO:** Change Margin Settings

1. Click the **Layout** tab.
2. Click the **Margins** button [*Page Setup* group]. Preset margin options appear in the *Margins* drop-down list (Figure 2-1).
3. Select the desired margin settings from the drop-down list of options.

The *Margins* drop-down list provides preset margin options. You are not limited to these preset options; you can also create your own custom margin settings in the *Page Setup* dialog box.

> **MORE INFO**
>
> The top of the *Margins* list displays the **Last Custom Setting** option, which is the most recent custom margin settings applied.

Figure 2-1 *Margins* drop-down list

Page Setup Dialog Box

If you want to apply margin settings that are not listed in the preset margin settings in the *Margins* drop-down list, use the **Page Setup dialog box** (Figure 2-2) to change one or more of the margin settings and to create custom margins.

▶ HOW TO: Set Custom Margins

1. Click the **Layout** tab.

2. Click the **Page Setup** launcher [*Page Setup* group] to open the *Page Setup* dialog box (see Figure 2-2).
   - Alternatively, click the **Margins** button and select **Custom Margins**.

3. Click the **Margins** tab if it is not already selected.

4. Change the *Top*, *Bottom*, *Left*, and *Right* margin settings using one of the following methods:
   - Click the **Top**, **Bottom**, **Left**, or **Right** margin box and type the desired margin setting.
   - Click the **up** or **down arrow** to increase or decrease the margin size. Each click of the up or down arrow increases or decreases the margins by 0.1".
   - Press **Tab** to move from one text box to another in the *Margins* area.
   - The *Preview* area displays a document thumbnail with the customized margin settings.

5. Click the **Apply to** drop-down list and select an option to apply margin settings: **Whole document**, **This point forward**, or **This section**.

6. Click **OK** to apply the custom margin settings.

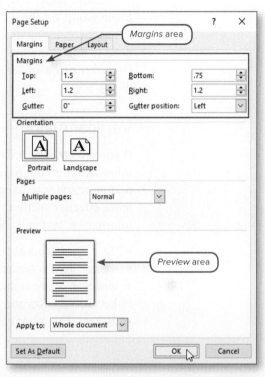

Figure 2-2 *Page Setup* dialog box

> **MORE INFO**
>
> Margin settings apply to the entire document by default. However, you can apply different margin settings to different sections of a document. Sections and section breaks are covered later in this chapter.

Page Orientation

Page orientation refers to the direction of the page. The two different orientation options in Word are **Portrait** and **Landscape**. Portrait is the tall orientation (8.5" × 11"), which is the default page orientation in Word. Landscape is the wide orientation (11" × 8.5"). Change page orientation by clicking the **Orientation** button in the *Page Setup* group on the *Layout* tab (Figure 2-3).

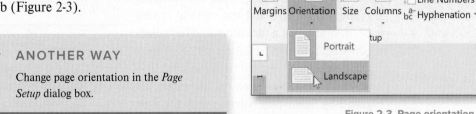

Figure 2-3 Page orientation settings

> **ANOTHER WAY**
>
> Change page orientation in the *Page Setup* dialog box.

Paper Size

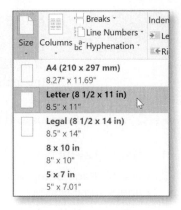

Figure 2-4 Paper size preset options

Paper size refers to the actual size of the paper of your final printed document. A new document in Word is standard letter size, which is 8.5"×11" by default. Word also provides other preset paper size settings, as shown in Figure 2-4.

Change paper size by clicking the **Size** button in the *Page Setup* group on the *Layout* tab. When a different paper size is set, the margins of the document do not change. You may need to adjust the margin setting when you change the paper size. You can also set a custom paper size in the *Page Setup* dialog box.

Vertical Alignment

If you are creating a flyer or a title page for a report, you might want to vertically center the information on the page. *Vertical alignment* controls the position of text between the top and bottom margins. Changing the vertical alignment of a page, section, or document is a much more effective method than using paragraph breaks (pressing *Enter* multiple times) to align information vertically. Word has four vertical alignment options.

- *Top*: Text begins at the top margin of the document, which is the default setting in Word.
- *Center*: Text is centered vertically between the top and bottom margins.
- *Justified*: Space is automatically added between lines to fill the entire vertical space between the top and bottom margins.
- *Bottom*: Text begins at the bottom margin of the document.

▶ HOW TO: Change Vertical Alignment

1. Click the **Layout** tab.
2. Click the **Page Setup** launcher [*Page Setup* group]. The *Page Setup* dialog box opens.
3. Click the **Layout** tab.
4. Click the **Vertical alignment** drop-down list in the *Page* area (Figure 2-5).
5. Select a vertical alignment option and click **OK**.

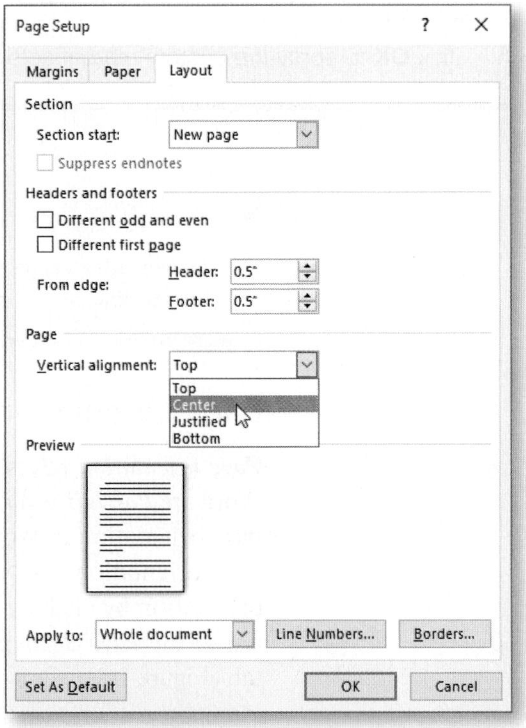

Figure 2-5 Change vertical alignment

Use the Ruler

Microsoft Word provides horizontal and vertical *rulers* that display both the horizontal typing line length and the vertical typing space available in a document. The rulers are divided into 1/8" increments. Half-inch markers are longer vertical or horizontal lines (depending on the ruler) and inch markers are numerical. The typing area on the rulers displays in white, while the margin area is shaded (Figure 2-6). To display rulers, check the **Ruler** box in the *Show* group on the *View* tab.

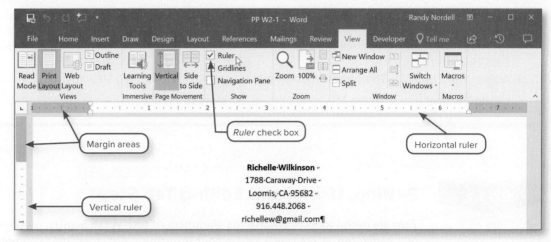

Figure 2-6 Horizontal and vertical rulers displayed

> MORE INFO

The rulers are increasingly important and useful as you begin using tab stops, indents, columns, tables, and section breaks.

Page Movement

By default, you move vertically through a multi-page document. The **Side to Side** option enables you to scroll horizontally through a document with multiple pages. Scrolling horizontally resembles the look of a book and displays multiple pages on the screen. Additionally, the *Side to Side* page movement includes an option to view your document as **Thumbnails**, which display multiple pages tiled on the screen. Click a thumbnail to navigate to a page in your document.

▶ HOW TO: Use Side to Side Page Movement

1. Click the **View** tab.
2. Click the **Side to Side** button [*Page Movement* group]. The document displays pages horizontally on the screen (Figure 2-7).
3. Use the left and right arrow keys or the mouse scroll wheel to scroll horizontally through the pages.

Figure 2-7 *Side to Side* page movement view

4. Click the **Thumbnails** button [*Zoom* group] to display all pages of the document as thumbnail icons.
   - A page number displays below each page thumbnail.
   - Click a page thumbnail to display the page. The *Thumbnail* option turns off and the page displays in *Side to Side* view.
   - Alternatively, click the **Thumbnail** button again to return to *Side to Side* view.
5. Click the **Vertical** button [*Page Movement* group] to return to *Vertical* page movement view.

Setting, Using, and Editing Tab Stops

Tabs are useful tools to control the alignment of text. A tab is often used to indent the first line of a paragraph. A *tab stop* is where your insertion point stops after you press the *Tab* key. Tabs can also be used to align text in columns or to begin the date at the horizontal midpoint on a modified block business letter. The five different types of tab stops are described in Table 2-2.

Table 2-2: Types of Tab Stops

Type of Tab Stop	Description	Tab Stop Indicator	Tab Stop in Use	
Left	Text is left-aligned at the tab stop.	⌞	Left tab	
Center	Text is centered on the tab stop.	⊥	Center tab	
Right	Text is right-aligned at the tab stop.	⌟	Right tab	
Decimal	Decimal point is aligned at the tab stop.	⊥	Decimal tab 620.50 8.375	
Bar	A vertical bar (line) is inserted at the tab stop.	I	A bar tab between	displays these words

Set a Tab Stop

Tabs are different from margins because tab stops apply to a paragraph or selected paragraphs rather than an entire document or sections of a document. This is important to keep in mind when setting, using, and editing tab stops.

By default, Word includes tab stops every 0.5" on the ruler. You can set custom tab stops in a new document before text is typed or set tab stops for existing text. If you open a new blank document and set a left tab stop at 3.25", the tab stop applies to the entire document. On the other hand, if you open an existing document and set a tab stop for the first paragraph of the document, the tab stop is only set for a single paragraph. When setting a tab stop in an existing document or for selected text, remember to select all the text or paragraphs before you apply the tab settings.

The following are two ways to set a tab stop in Word.

- *Tabs* dialog box
- Ruler

Set a Tab Stop Using the Tabs Dialog Box

The *Tabs dialog box* is an effective and easy method to set single or multiple tab stops. Access the *Tabs* dialog box from the *Paragraph* dialog box. Open the *Paragraph* dialog box by clicking the **Paragraph** launcher from the *Paragraph* group on either the *Home* or *Layout* tabs.

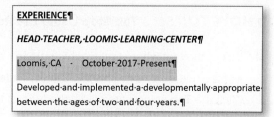

Figure 2-8 Select text before setting tab stops

Figure 2-9 *Tabs* button in *Paragraph* dialog box

▶ **HOW TO: Set a Tab Stop Using the Tabs Dialog Box**

1. Select the text where you want to set a tab stop (Figure 2-8).
2. Click the **Home** or **Layout** tab.
3. Click the **Paragraph** launcher to open the *Paragraph* dialog box.
4. Click the **Tabs** button (Figure 2-9) to open the *Tabs* dialog box.
5. Type the desired tab stop position in the **Tab stop position** text box.
6. Select the **Left**, **Center**, **Right**, **Decimal**, or **Bar** radio button in the *Alignment* area.
7. Click the **Set** button (Figure 2-10). The tab stop appears in the list of tab stops below the *Tab stop position* text box.
8. Click **OK** to close the *Tabs* dialog box.
    - The tab stop is applied to the selected text.
    - The tab stop is visible on the ruler.

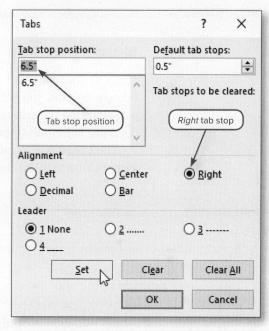

Figure 2-10 Set a right tab stop in the *Tabs* dialog box

> **MORE INFO**
>
> Set and use tab stops to align and balance columns of text rather than pressing *Tab* multiple times between columns.

Set a Tab Stop Using the Ruler

Using the ruler to set tab stops is a quick way to add them to a document. You can also easily move or remove tab stops using the ruler. Use the *Tab selector* to select the type of tab stop you want to insert. The *Tab* selector is located at the top of the vertical ruler on the left side of the Word window (Figure 2-11). When setting tab stops in an existing document, it is very important to select the text or paragraphs where you want the tab stop to apply before setting the tab stop.

▶HOW TO: Set a Tab Stop Using the Ruler

1. Select the text where you want to set the new tab stop(s).
   - If the rulers do not display, check the **Ruler** box [*View* tab, *Show* group].
2. Click the **Tab** selector to select the type of tab stop to set (see Figure 2-11).
   - The *Tab* selector toggles through the different types of tabs and indents: left, center, right, decimal, bar, first line indent, and hanging indent.
3. Click the ruler to set a tab stop.
   - When setting tab stops using the ruler, click the bottom edge of the ruler to set a tab stop (Figure 2-12).

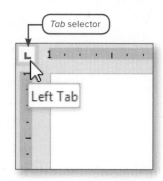

Figure 2-11 *Tab* selector

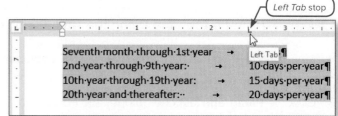

> **MORE INFO**
>
> Use the *Format Painter* to copy tab stops from one area of your document to another area.

Figure 2-12 Set a left tab stop at 2.5" on the ruler

Move a Tab Stop

It can be challenging to align text correctly and balance space between columns. As you practice setting tabs, you will become more comfortable selecting the correct type of tab stop to use, adjusting the settings of existing tab stops, and removing tab stops. When using multiple columns, adjust tab stops so you have the same amount of white space between columns.

The easiest way to move tab stops is by using the ruler. When using the ruler to adjust a tab stop, be sure to select the appropriate text before moving a tab stop.

▶HOW TO: Move a Tab Stop

1. Select the text or paragraphs containing the tab stops you want to edit.
2. Left-click the **tab stop** on the ruler and drag it to the new location (Figure 2-13).
   - When you click the tab stop to be moved, a vertical alignment guide appears. This alignment guide displays the position of the tab stop.
   - Press the **Alt** key when you are moving a tab stop to display a vertical guide and horizontal ruler settings to assist in moving a tab stop to a specific measurement (Figure 2-14).
3. Release the pointer to set the tab stop in the new location.
4. Repeat this process until you are satisfied with the placement of your tab stops.

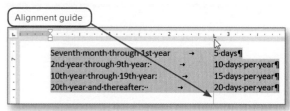

Figure 2-13 Move a tab stop using the ruler

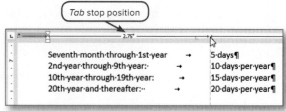

Figure 2-14 Use the *Alt* key to adjust a tab stop

> **ANOTHER WAY**
>
> Adjust tab stops in the *Tabs* dialog box by clearing an existing tab stop and setting a new tab stop.

Remove a Tab Stop

When setting tab stops using the ruler, you may unintentionally add a tab stop. Or, you may want to remove unwanted tab stops. When removing tab stops from existing text, it is very important to select the text or paragraphs before deleting the tabs. When you remove or clear a tab stop, the tabbed text realigns to the default 0.5" tab stop or nearest remaining custom tab stop. Following are three different ways to remove tab stops:

- Drag a tab stop off (below) the ruler.
- Clear a single tab stop in the *Tabs* dialog box.
- Clear all tab stops in the *Tabs* dialog box.

To clear a single tab stop using the ruler, select the text or paragraphs, select the tab stop to remove, drag the tab stop down below the ruler, and release the pointer.

When using the *Tabs* dialog box to remove tab stops, you can clear a single tab stop or clear all existing tab stops on the selected text or paragraphs.

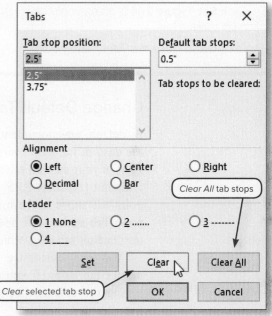

Figure 2-15 Clear a tab stop in the *Tabs* dialog box

▶ HOW TO: Clear a Tab Stop Using the Tabs Dialog Box

1. Select the text or paragraphs containing the tab stops to remove.
2. Click the **Paragraph** launcher [*Home* or *Layout* tab] to open the *Paragraph* dialog box.
3. Click the **Tabs** button to open the *Tabs* dialog box.
4. Select the tab stop to remove in the list of existing tab stops, and click the **Clear** button to remove a single tab stop (Figure 2-15). Repeat on any other tab stops you want to remove.
   - Click the **Clear All** button to clear all tab stops.
5. Click **OK** to close the *Tabs* dialog box.

Add a Tab Leader

Tab leaders insert dots or a line between text when using tab stops. The most common type of leader is the dot leader, which is regularly used in a table of contents. In a table of contents, a dot leader displays between the text and the right-aligned page number. You can also use leaders to insert a dashed line in the blank space between columns or to create a solid under-line when creating a printed form.

Word has three different types of tab leaders. Examples of each type appear in Table 2-3.

Table 2-3: Types of Leaders

Leader	Example of Use
Dot	Chapter 1 4
Dash	Vacation Days ------ 10 days per year
Solid underline	Name _____

Use the *Tabs* dialog box to add tab leaders to existing tabbed text or to set new tab stops.

▶HOW TO: Add a Tab Leader

1. Select the text or paragraphs where you want to add a tab leader.

2. Click the **Paragraph** launcher [*Home* or *Layout* tab] to open the *Paragraph* dialog box.

3. Click the **Tabs** button to open the *Tabs* dialog box.

4. Select an existing tab stop or type a number in the *Tab stop position* text box to set a new tab stop.

5. Select the type of leader to apply in the *Leader* area (see Figure 2-15).

6. Click **Set**. Figure 2-16 is an example of a dash leader.

7. Click **OK** to close the *Tabs* dialog box.

Figure 2-16 Tab stop with a dash leader

Change Default Tab Stops

By default, new documents include a left tab stop every 0.5". When you set a tab stop in Word, the custom tab stop overrides all preceding default tab stop, but the default tab stops to the right of your custom tab stop remain. For example, if you set a left tab stop at the horizontal midpoint (typically 3.25") and press **Tab** to move to the horizontal midpoint, your insertion point will move to the midpoint, not 0.5". But if you press **Tab** again, your insertion point will stop at the next default tab stop, which is 3.5".

You can customize the half-inch interval for default tab stops. If you change the default tab stop setting, this change affects only the current document, not all new documents.

▶HOW TO: Change Default Tab Stops

1. Click the **Paragraph** launcher [*Home* or *Layout* tab] to open the *Paragraph* dialog box.

2. Click the **Tabs** button to open the *Tabs* dialog box.

3. Type a value or use the up or down arrow to change the default tab stop setting in the *Default tab stops* area (Figure 2-17).

4. Click **OK** to close the *Tabs* dialog box.

Figure 2-17 Change default tab stops

SLO 2.3

Using Indents

Indents are another powerful tool to control how text aligns between the left and right margins. Consider indents to be temporary margins, which apply to selected paragraphs. Use indents to indent the first line of each paragraph, set off a long quote in a report, or indent the carry-over lines of bulleted or numbered lists.

Similar to setting tab stops, it is important to select the text where you want to apply indent settings. Set indents using the ruler, the *Paragraph* group on the *Layout* tab, or the *Paragraph* dialog box. Table 2-4 describes the four different types of indents.

Table 2-4: Types of Indents

Indent	Example of Use	Ruler Indent Marker
Left Indent	This paragraph has a left indent.	Left Indent
Right Indent	This paragraph has a right indent.	Right Indent
First Line Indent	This paragraph has a first line indent.	First Line Indent
Hanging Indent	This paragraph has a hanging indent.	Hanging Indent

Left and Right Indents

Indents apply to an entire paragraph or multiple paragraphs, not just lines of text within a paragraph. When setting an indent, select the paragraph(s) on which to apply the indent. If your insertion point is in a paragraph, the indent you set applies to that paragraph only.

▶ **HOW TO:** Set a Left and Right Indent

1. Select the text or paragraph where you want to apply the indent. If it is just one paragraph, place your insertion point in that paragraph.

2. Click the **Layout** tab.
   - Alternatively, click the **Paragraph** launcher to open the *Paragraph* dialog box.

3. Change the *Left* and *Right* indent settings [*Paragraph* group on the *Layout* tab or Indentation area in the *Paragraph* dialog box]. The change applies to the selected text (Figure 2-18).

   - When you apply an indent to a paragraph and press *Enter* at the end of the paragraph, the indent carries over to the next paragraph.

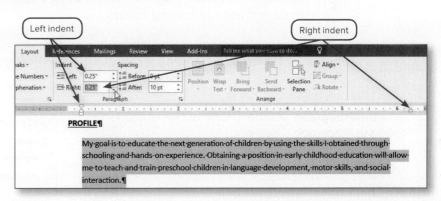

Figure 2-18 Change left and right indents

Indents can also be set using the ruler. Select the text to indent and drag the indent marker to the desired location. As you drag the indent marker, an alignment guide displays the location where your text aligns.

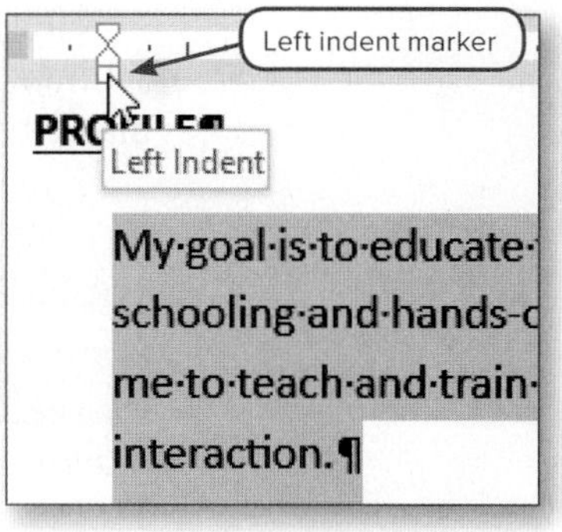

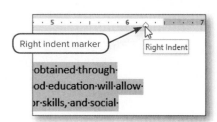

Figure 2-19 Change left indent using the ruler

▶**HOW TO:** Set Indents Using the Ruler

1. Select the text or paragraph to indent. If it is just one paragraph, place your insertion point in that paragraph.

2. Left click the **left indent marker** (bottom square), drag to the desired location, and release the pointer. The left indent applies to the selected text (Figure 2-19).

3. Left click the **right indent marker**, drag to the desired location, and release the pointer. The right indent applies to the selected text (Figure 2-20).

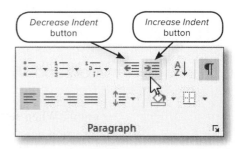

Figure 2-20 Change right indent using the ruler

The ***Decrease Indent*** and ***Increase Indent*** buttons in the *Paragraph* group on the *Home* tab increase or decrease the left indent in increments of 0.5" (Figure 2-21). Remove a left indent by positioning the insertion point at the beginning of the paragraph and pressing **Backspace** or clicking the **Decrease Indent** button.

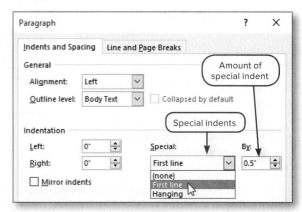

Figure 2-21 *Decrease Indent* and *Increase Indent* buttons

First Line and Hanging Indents

Add a ***First line indent*** to indent the first line of a paragraph instead of pressing *Tab*. A ***Hanging indent*** is typically used with bulleted and numbered lists but can be used effectively to indent text that wraps to a second or additional lines, such as entries on a references page. Use the *Paragraph* dialog box to set first line and hanging indents.

▶**HOW TO:** Set a First Line or a Hanging Indent Using the Paragraph Dialog box

1. Select the paragraph(s) to indent.

2. Click the **Paragraph** launcher [*Home* or *Layout* tab] to open the *Paragraph* dialog box.

3. Click the **Special** drop-down list in the *Indentation* area and choose the type of indent: **First line** or **Hanging** (Figure 2-22).

4. Type the indent amount or use the up or down buttons in the *By* area to increase or decrease the amount of the indent.

   • The *Preview* area displays the text with the indent applied.

5. Click **OK** to close the *Paragraph* dialog box.

Figure 2-22 Set first line or hanging indent using the *Paragraph* dialog box

To set a first line indent using the ruler, select the paragraph(s) to indent and drag the first line indent marker (top triangle) to the desired location (Figure 2-23). The alignment guide displays where the first line of each paragraph aligns.

To set a hanging indent using the ruler, select the paragraph(s) to indent and drag the hanging indent marker (bottom triangle) to the desired location (Figure 2-24). The alignment guide displays where the carryover lines of the paragraph align.

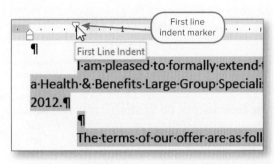

Figure 2-23 Set a first line indent using the ruler

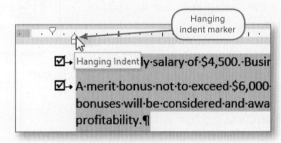

Figure 2-24 Set a hanging indent using the ruler

An *outdent* aligns text outside the left or right margins. Outdents can be used to emphasize section headings so they display slightly to the left of the left margin. To apply an outdent, set a ***negative value*** (−0.25") in the indents area in the *Paragraph* dialog box or *Paragraph* group on the *Layout* tab or by dragging the indent marker outside of the left or right margins.

Remove Indents

Removing indents moves the indent markers back to either the left or right margin, so the margins control the alignment of text rather than the indents. Remember to select the paragraph or paragraphs before removing the indents. To remove an indent, set the indent value to **0"** using the *Paragraph* dialog box or the *Paragraph* group on the *Layout* tab (Figure 2-25).

The ruler can also be used to remove indents. When using this method, select the text or paragraphs on which to remove the indents and drag the indent marker(s) to the margin.

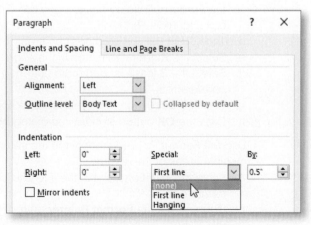

Figure 2-25 Remove indents using the *Paragraph* dialog box

In this Pause & Practice project, you format a resume for Richelle Wilkinson. This resume is a two-page document, and you change the margins, set tab stops and leaders, and use indents.

File Needed: **Resume-02.docx** *(Student data files are available in the* Library *of your SIMnet account.)*
Completed Project File Name: **[your initials] PP W2-1.docx**

1. Open the **Resume-02** document from your student data files.

2. Save this document as [your initials] PP W2-1.

3. Change the margins of the resume.
   a. Click the **Layout** tab.
   b. Click the **Page Setup** launcher [*Page Setup* group] to open the *Page Setup* dialog box (Figure 2-26). Alternatively, click the **Margins** button and select **Custom Margins**.
   c. Type .75 in the **Top** text box in the *Margins* area and press **Tab** to move to the *Bottom* text box.
   d. Type .75 in the *Bottom* text box.
   e. Click the **down arrow** to the right of the *Left* text box to change the left margin to **1"**.
   f. Click the **down arrow** to the right of the *Right* text box to change the right margin to **1"**.
   g. Click the **Apply to** drop-down list at the bottom of the dialog box and select **Whole document** if it is not already selected.
   h. Click **OK** to apply the new margin settings and close the dialog box.

Figure 2-26 Change margins in the *Page Setup* dialog box

4. Set a right tab stop with a dash leader.
   a. Select the "**Loomis, CA October 2017 Present**" text below "*HEAD TEACHER, LOOMIS LEARNING CENTER.*"
   b. Click the **Paragraph** launcher [*Layout* or *Home* tab] to open the *Paragraph* dialog box.
   c. Click the **Tabs** button in the bottom-left corner of the *Paragraph* dialog box to open the *Tabs* dialog box (Figure 2-27).
   d. Type 6.5 in the *Tab stop position* area.
   e. Select the **Right** radio button in the *Alignment* area.
   f. Select the **3** (dash leader) radio button in the *Leader* area.
   g. Click the **Set** button to set this tab stop and leader.
   h. Click the **OK** button to close the dialog box.

5. Use the *Format Painter* to apply the tab setting to multiple areas of the resume.
   a. Place the insertion point in the line you just formatted.
   b. Double-click the **Format Painter** button [*Home* tab, *Clipboard* group].

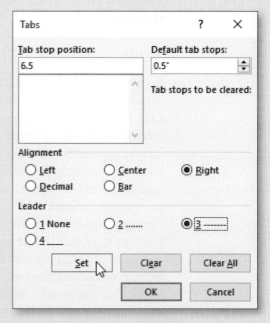

Figure 2-27 Set a right tab stop with a dash leader

c. Click each of the city, state, and date lines in the "EXPERIENCE" and "EDUCATION" sections to apply the tab settings as shown in Figure 2-28.
d. Click the **Format Painter** button to turn off copy format.

6. Remove an existing tab stop and set a left tab stop.
   a. Select the lines of text below the "REFERENCES" heading on the second page.
   b. Click the **Paragraph** launcher [*Layout* or *Home* tab] to open the *Paragraph* dialog box.
   c. Click the **Tabs** button to open the *Tabs* dialog box.
   d. Select the existing tab stop (**2.5"**) in the *Tab stop position* area and click the **Clear** button to remove the existing tab.
   e. Type 3.75 in the *Tab stop position* area.
   f. Select the **Left** radio button in the *Alignment* area if it is not already selected.
   g. Select the **1 None** radio button in the *Leader* area if it is not already selected.
   h. Click the **Set** button to set the left tab stop (Figure 2-29).
   i. Click the **OK** button to close the dialog box.

7. Apply a left and right indent to selected text.
   a. Place the insertion point in the paragraph below the "PROFILE" heading on the first page.
   b. Click the **Layout** tab.
   c. Type .25 in the **Left** indent area [*Paragraph* group] and press **Tab**.
   d. Type .25 in the **Right** indent area [*Paragraph* group] and press **Enter**.

8. Save and close this document (Figure 2-30).

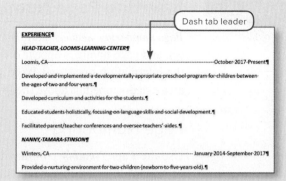

Figure 2-28 Use the *Format Painter* to apply tab settings

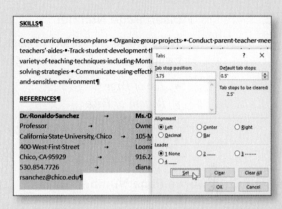

Figure 2-29 Set a left tab stop on selected text

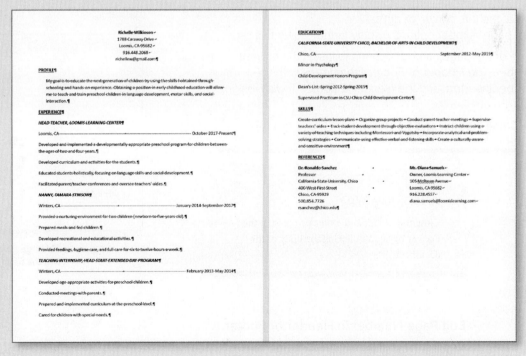

Figure 2-30 PP W2-1 completed

Inserting Page Numbers, Headers, and Footers

Page numbering, *headers*, and *footers* are regularly used in multiple-page documents. Headers, footers, and page numbers appear on each page of the document, which means you only have to type the information once, and Word repeats that information on each subsequent page. The header area of a document is above the top margin, and the footer area is below the bottom margin.

Page Numbering

Use the *Page Number* command in Word to insert a *page number field* in the header, footer, or current location in a document. The page number field displays the current page number. When inserting a page number, specify the page number location and the page number format.

Insert Page Number

Word provides a variety of page number locations, horizontal alignment options, and number format options. The following is a list of the basic page number placement options:

- *Top of Page*
- *Bottom of Page*
- *Page Margins*
- *Current Position*

▶ **HOW TO: Insert a Page Number**

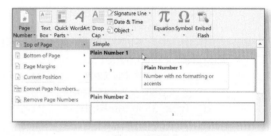

Figure 2-31 Insert page number

1. Click the **Insert** tab.

2. Click the **Page Number** button [*Header & Footer* group]. A drop-down list of options appears (Figure 2-31).

3. Click either **Top of Page** or **Bottom of Page**. Another drop-down list of page number options appears.
   - The top three options in this list are simple page numbers aligned at the left, center, or right.
   - Custom page number options display further down this list.

4. Select one of the page number options to insert the current page number. The *Header* or *Footer* area opens with the page number inserted, and the *Header & Footer Tools Design* tab opens (Figure 2-32).

5. Click the **Close Header and Footer** button [*Close* group].

▶ **ANOTHER WAY**

Close the header and footer by pressing the **Esc** key or double-clicking the body of the document.

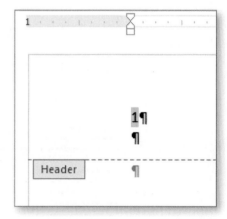

Figure 2-32 Page number inserted in the header on the left

Edit Page Number in Header or Footer

When you close the header or footer, the page number appears in gray rather than black like the text of the document. The header and footer areas are outside the boundaries of the margins.

If you want to edit the page number or contents of the header or footer, you must open the header or footer. The following are three ways to do this:

- Right-click the header or footer and select **Edit Header** or **Edit Footer**.
- Click the **Insert** tab, click the **Header** or **Footer** button in the *Header & Footer* group, and choose **Edit Header** or **Edit Footer**.
- Double-click the header or footer area of the document.

Different First Page

Occasionally, you may not want the page number, header, or footer to print on the first page of the document, but you want these page elements to appear on the second and continuing pages. For example, on both multiple-page business letters and reports, the page number typically does not display on the first page but displays on the second and subsequent pages. Use the *Different First Page* option to control the display of page numbers, headers, and footers on page one.

▶HOW TO: Set a Different First Page Header and Footer

1. Go to the first page of the document.
2. Open the header or footer if it is not already open. Use one of the following methods to open the header or footer if it is not already open:
   - Right-click the header or footer and select **Edit Header** or **Edit Footer**.
   - Click the **Insert** tab, click the **Header** or **Footer** button in the *Header & Footer* group, and choose **Edit Header** or **Edit Footer**.
   - Double-click the header or footer area of the document.
3. Click the **Different First Page** check box [*Header & Footer Tools Design* tab, *Options* group] (Figure 2-33).
4. Click the **Close Header and Footer** button [*Close* group]. The page number, header, and footer no longer display on the first page but display on the second and continuing pages.

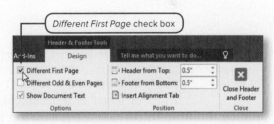

Figure 2-33 *Different First Page* check box

> **MORE INFO**
>
> When inserting a page number, header, or footer, it is best to insert it on the first page of the document. This becomes increasingly important as you add section breaks to a document.

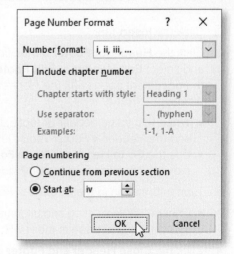

Figure 2-34 *Page Number Format* dialog box

Page Number Format

After adding page numbers, specify the page number format, select a different starting page number, or add a chapter number before the page number. The *Page Number Format* dialog box provides a variety of page numbering options (Figure 2-34).

1. Click the **Page Number** button [*Insert* tab or *Header & Footer Tools Design, Header & Footer* group] and select **Format Page Numbers** to open the *Page Number Format* dialog box (see Figure 2-34).

2. Click the **Number format** drop-down list and select a page number format. Choose from six preset page numbering options.

3. Select **Continue from previous section** (default setting) or **Start at** a different page number in the *Page numbering* section.

   • Click the **Start at** radio button to set a different starting page number.
   • Type the starting page number or use the up or down arrow to set the starting page number.

4. Click **OK** to close the *Page Number Format* dialog box.

5. Click the **Close Header and Footer** button [*Close* group] if necessary.

Remove Page Number

To remove page numbering from a document, use one of the following options:

• Select **Remove Page Numbers** from the *Page Number* drop-down list (Figure 2-35).
• Open the header or footer and manually delete the page number.

Insert Header and Footer Content

In addition to inserting page numbers into the header or footer of a document, you might want to include the number of pages in the document, date or time, title of the document, company name, or other custom content. You can enter information manually into the header or footer, or insert document property fields.

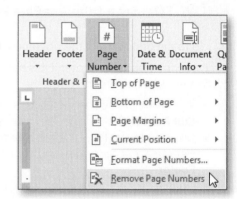

Figure 2-35 Remove page numbers

1. Click the **Insert** tab.

2. Click the **Header** or **Footer** button [*Insert* tab, *Header & Footer* group] and select **Edit Header** or **Edit Footer**. The header or footer of the document opens and the *Header & Footer Tools Design* tab displays.

   • When you edit a header or footer, both the header and footer open and the *Header & Footer Tools Design* tab displays.
   • Use the **Go to Header** or **Go to Footer** buttons [*Navigation* group] to move to the header or footer (Figure 2-36).

3. Type information in the *Header* or *Footer* area (Figure 2-37).

   • Change the formatting and alignment as desired.
   • You can insert a page number with the header or footer open.

4. Click the **Close Header and Footer** button [*Close* group].

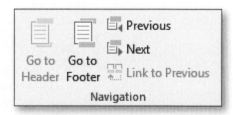

Figure 2-36 *Navigation* group on the *Header & Footer Tools Design* tab

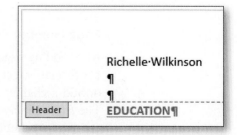

Figure 2-37 Enter custom information in the header

Number of Pages Field

In addition to inserting the current page number in a document, you can add a field code to automatically insert the total number of pages in a document (*NumPages* field).

▶ **HOW TO:** Insert the Number of Pages Field

1. Open the header or footer. The page number should already be inserted in the document.
2. Click before the page number, type Page, and press the **spacebar**.
3. Click after the page number, press the **spacebar**, type of, and press the **spacebar**.

Figure 2-38 Insert field code

4. Click the **Document Info** button [*Header & Footer Tools Design* tab, *Insert* group] (Figure 2-38).
   - Alternatively, click the **Quick Parts** button.
5. Select **Field** from the drop-down list. The *Field* dialog box opens (Figure 2-39).
6. Scroll down the *Field names* area and select **NumPages**. The field description displays in the *Description* area.
7. Select a page number format in the *Format* area.
8. Click **OK** to close the *Field* dialog box. The number of pages in the document displays (Figure 2-40).
9. Click the **Close Header and Footer** button [*Close* group].

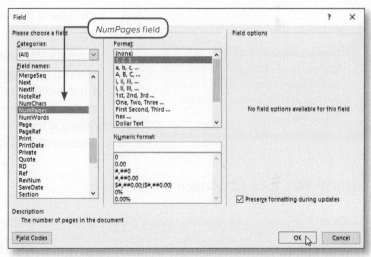

Figure 2-39 Insert *NumPages* field from the *Field* dialog box

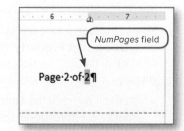

Figure 2-40 Page number and number of pages field inserted into the header

Date and Time

Word can automatically insert a date and/or time in your document. When you insert the date or time, choose from a variety of date and time formats. The date and time can be set to update automatically each time you open the document.

▶HOW TO: Insert the Date and Time

1. Open the header or footer area and position the insertion point at the location to insert the date.

   • Use alignment buttons or tabs to position the date and/or time in the header or footer.

2. Click the **Date & Time** button [*Header & Footer Tools Design* tab, *Insert* group]. The *Date and Time* dialog box opens (Figure 2-41).

3. Select the date or time format to use in the *Available formats* area.

4. Check the **Update automatically** check box if you want the date to update automatically.

   • Do not check *Update automatically* on documents where the date should remain constant.

5. Click **OK** to close the *Date and Time* dialog box. The date displays in the header.

6. Click the **Close Header and Footer** button [*Close* group].

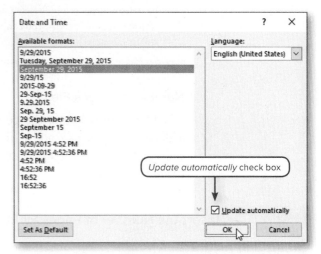

Figure 2-41 *Date and Time* dialog box

MORE INFO

Inserting a date or time is not limited to headers and footers. You can insert the date or time in the body of a document by clicking **Date & Time** [*Insert* tab, *Text* group].

Document Properties

After you enter document properties in a Word document, you can automatically insert this information in the header or footer. For example, you might want to include the title of the document, name of the author, or date last modified. One of the advantages of inserting document properties rather than typing this information is that when you update the document properties, these fields automatically update in the header or footer and throughout the document.

▶HOW TO: Insert Document Properties

1. Open the header or footer and place the insertion point at the location to insert the document property.

   • Use alignment buttons or tabs to position document property fields in the header or footer.

2. Click the **Document Info** button [*Header & Footer Tools Design* tab, *Insert* group] (Figure 2-42).

3. Select the document property field or click **Document Property** to select from additional fields. The document property displays in the document (Figure 2-43).

   • Alternatively, click the **Quick Parts** button [*Header & Footer Tools Design* tab, *Insert* group] and select **Document Property**.

   • Press the **right arrow** key on your keyboard to deselect a document property field.

4. Click the **Close Header and Footer** button [*Close* group].

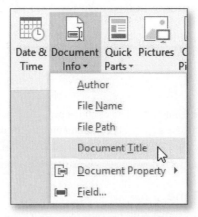

Figure 2-42 Insert document property field

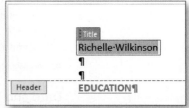

Figure 2-43 *Title* document property field inserted in the header

Built-In Headers, Footers, and Page Numbers

In addition to inserting basic page numbers, manually adding header or footer content, and inserting date and time, Word provides you with a variety of built-in custom header, footer, and page number format options. Many of the header and footer options include document properties that are automatically inserted and updated.

▶ **HOW TO: Insert a Built-In Header, Footer, or Page Number**

1. Click the **Insert** tab.
2. Click the **Header**, **Footer**, or **Page Number** button [*Header & Footer* group] and select a built-in header, footer, or page number from the drop-down list (Figure 2-44).
   - Document property fields update automatically with document property information.
   - Some fields, such as *Pick the date,* require you to input or select information.
3. Click the **Close Header and Footer** button [*Close* group].

Figure 2-44 List of built-in headers

Some of Word's built-in headers, footers, and page numbers include tables, graphics, and advanced formatting. Editing the elements may be challenging without a thorough understanding of this type of content.

PAUSE & PRACTICE: WORD 2-2

In this Pause & Practice project, you modify the resume from *Pause & Practice 2-1*. You add a header that appears only on the second page of the document and insert a document property field, page number, and Word field into the header.

File Needed: *[your initials] PP W2-1.docx*
Completed Project File Name: *[your initials] PP W2-2.docx*

1. Open the *[your initials] PP W2-1* document completed in *Pause & Practice 2-1*.
2. Save this document as [your initials] PP W2-2.

3. Edit the document properties.
   a. Click the **File** tab to open the *Backstage* view and select **Info** if necessary.
   b. Type Richelle Wilkinson in the **Title** document property text box.
   c. Click the **Back** arrow to return to the resume.

4. Insert a document property field in the header of the resume.
   a. Place the insertion point at the beginning of the first page.
   b. Click the **Insert** tab.
   c. Click the **Header** button [*Header & Footer* group] and select **Edit Header** from the drop-down list. The header on the first page opens.
   d. Click the **Document Info** button [*Header & Footer Tools Design* tab, *Insert* group] and select **Document Title** from the drop-down list. The *Title* document property displays in the header.
   e. Leave the header open for the next instruction.

5. Insert a page number and number of pages field in the header and set it to display only on the second page.
   a. Press the **right arrow** key once to deselect the inserted document property field.
   b. Press **Tab** two times to move to the right margin.
   c. Type Page and **space** once.
   d. Click the **Page Number** button [*Header & Footer* group], select **Current Position** from the drop-down list, and select **Plain Number**. The page number displays in the header.
   e. **Space** once, type of, and **space** once.
   f. Click the **Document Info** (or **Quick Parts**) button [*Header & Footer Tools Design* tab, *Insert* group] and select **Field** from the drop-down list. The *Field* dialog box opens (Figure 2-45).
   g. Select **NumPages** in the *Field names* area (this is the field code to insert the total number of pages in the document).
   h. Select **1, 2, 3** in the *Format* area and click **OK** to insert the number of pages in the header.
   i. Press **Enter** two times to insert two blank lines after the header.
   j. Check to ensure proper spacing is used between each of the words and page numbers.

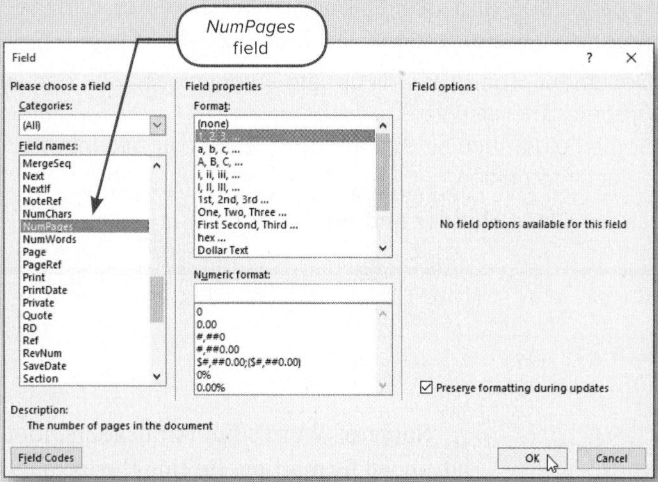

   Figure 2-45 Insert *NumPages* field

   k. Check the **Different First Page** check box [*Header & Footer Tools Design* tab, *Options* group]. This removes the header content from the first page, but the header content displays on the second page (Figure 2-46).

Figure 2-46 Header with document property field, page number, and number of pages field

   l. Click the **Close Header and Footer** button [*Close* group] to close the header and return to the document.

6. Save and close the document (Figure 2-47).

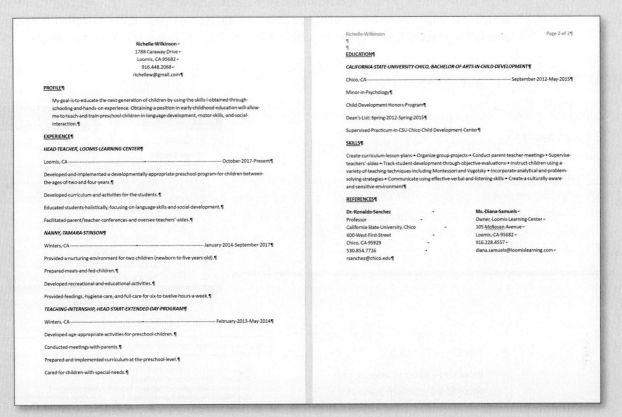

Figure 2-47 PP W2-2 completed

Using Page and Section Breaks

As you're typing a document and get to the bottom of the page, Word automatically moves to the top of the next page so you can continue typing; this is referred to as a *soft page break*. The document's content and margins determine how much information fits on a page and what information flows to a new page.

Occasionally, you may want to start a new page before you get to the bottom margin, or you may want different margins or page orientation in a different section of a document. Word provides options for page and section breaks to control page endings and formatting (Figure 2-48).

> **MORE INFO**
>
> Turn on **Show/Hide** [*Home* tab, *Paragraph* group] when working with page and section breaks, so you can view the placement of page and section breaks.

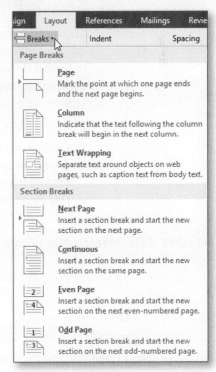

Figure 2-48 Page and section breaks

Page Breaks

Page breaks end one page and begin a new page. When you insert a *Page* break, you control where one page ends and a new page begins. This type of page break is called a *hard page break*. The three different types of page breaks are *Page*, *Column*, and *Text Wrapping*.

▶HOW TO: Insert a Page Break

1. Position the insertion point where you want to insert a page break.
2. Click the **Layout** tab.
3. Click the **Breaks** button [*Page Setup* group].
4. Select **Page** from the drop-down list. A page break displays in the document (Figure 2-49).

   • Turn on **Show/Hide** [*Home* tab, *Paragraph* group].
   • The *Page Break* indicator displays when *Show/Hide* is on (Figure 2-50).

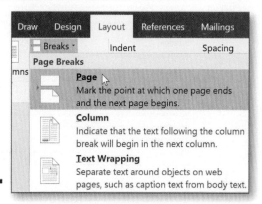

Figure 2-49 Insert *Page* break

> **ANOTHER WAY**
>
> Press **Ctrl+Enter** to insert a page break at the insertion point or click the **Insert** tab and click **Page Break** in the *Pages* group.

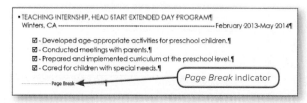

Figure 2-50 *Page* break inserted in a document

Section Breaks

Section breaks provide more formatting control over your document than page breaks. Insert a section break to control the format of an individual section of a document. Use section breaks to format different headers, footers, and page numbering. If you want one page in your document to be landscape orientation, insert a section break and change the orientation for that section. The following are the four different types of section breaks:

• *Next Page*: Insert a section break and start the new section on the next page.
• *Continuous*: Insert a section break and start the new section on the same page.
• *Even Page*: Insert a section break and start the new section on the next even-numbered page.
• *Odd Page*: Insert a section break and start the new section on the next odd-numbered page.

▶HOW TO: Insert a Next Page Section Break

1. Position the insertion point at the location in your document to end one page and begin a new section on a new page.
2. Click the **Layout** tab.
3. Click the **Breaks** button [*Page Setup* group].
4. Select **Next Page** from the drop-down list. A next page section break displays in the document.

   • Turn on **Show/Hide** [*Home* tab, *Paragraph* group].

- The *Section Break (Next Page)* indicator displays when *Show/Hide* is on (Figure 2-51).

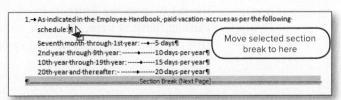

Figure 2-51 *Next Page* section break inserted in a document

Edit Page and Section Breaks

When finalizing a document, you may need to change the placement of a page or section break or remove a page or section break from the document. Delete and move breaks the same way you delete and move text from a document.

To delete a page or section break, select the break and press **Delete**.

To move a section or page break to a new location, first select the **Page Break** or **Section Break**, and then use **Cut** and **Paste** or the drag-and-drop method (Figure 2-52).

Figure 2-52 Move a section break using drag and drop

SLO 2.6

Using Bulleted, Numbered, and Multilevel Lists

Bulleted and *numbered lists* highlight important information. Generally, use bulleted lists when the order of information is not important, and use numbered lists for sequential information. A *Multilevel list* combines a variety of numbers, letters, and bullets. Word provides built-in bulleted, numbered, and multilevel lists, but you can customize how the information in the list displays and aligns.

> **MORE INFO**
>
> When using bulleted and numbered lists, do not use a period at the end of lists containing only words or short phrases. If you are using complete sentences in your list, use a period at the end of each sentence.

Create a Bulleted List

You can create a bulleted list from existing text or create a new bulleted list by typing text. Choose the type of bullet to use from the *Bullet Library* in the *Bullets* drop-down list.

▶ HOW TO: Create a Bulleted List

1. Place the insertion point at the location to begin the list or select the text to convert to a bulleted list.
2. Click the **Bullets** drop-down arrow [*Home* tab, *Paragraph* group] to display the library of bullet options (Figure 2-53).
   - If you click the *Bullets* button (not the *Bullets* drop-down arrow), the most recently used bullet is used for the bulleted list.

3. Select a bullet from the list of options.

4. Type your information after the bullet if you are typing a new bulleted list.

5. Press **Enter** after typing a bulleted item to add another bullet.

6. Press **Enter** two times after the last bullet or click the **Bullets** button to turn off bullets.

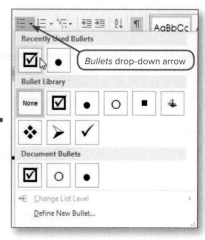

Figure 2-53 *Bullets* drop-down list

By default, bulleted lists are formatted with a hanging indent. The first line is indented 0.25" and the hanging indent is set at 0.5". Adjust the indent using the *Decrease Indent* or *Increase Indent* buttons, ruler, or *Paragraph* dialog box.

Add new bulleted items in the middle or at the end of the list by pressing **Enter** in front of or at the end of an existing bulleted item. To add a bulleted item before the first item in the list, click at the beginning of the first item and press **Enter**.

> **MORE INFO**
>
> To add a blank line between bulleted items, use a line break (**Shift+Enter**) at the end of a bulleted item.

Customize a Bulleted List

In addition to using the bullets listed in the *Bullets Library*, you can select and use a custom bullet. You have the option of using a symbol from one of the font groups or using a picture. If you use a picture, use *Bing Image Search* to find a picture or select a graphic file of your own.

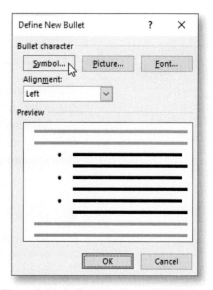

Figure 2-54 *Define New Bullet* dialog box

▶**HOW TO:** Customize a Bulleted List

1. Select the bulleted list.

2. Click the **Bullets** drop-down arrow [*Home* tab, *Paragraph* group] and select **Define New Bullet**. The *Define New Bullet* dialog box opens (Figure 2-54).

3. Click the **Symbol**, **Picture**, or **Font** button to open a dialog box.

   - If you click **Symbol**, the *Symbol* dialog box opens (Figure 2-55). From the *Font* drop-down list, select a font set (the most common are *Symbol*, *Wingdings*, and *Webdings*) or *Recently used symbols*.
   - Each symbol has a character code to identify the symbol (see Figure 2-55).
   - If you click **Picture**, the *Insert Pictures* dialog box opens. Use *Bing Image Search* to find a picture or select a graphic file of your own.
   - If you click **Font**, the *Font* dialog box opens where you change the font size of the bullet. Changing the bullet font size does not change the size of the bulleted text.

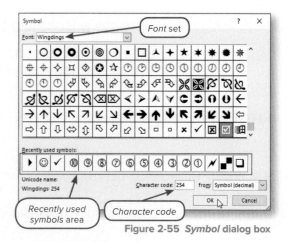

Figure 2-55 *Symbol* dialog box

4. Select the bullet to use and click **OK** (or **Insert** or **Open** depending on the open dialog box) to close the dialog box.

5. Click **OK** to close the *Define New Bullet* dialog box.

You also have the option of formatting text with multiple levels of bullets with a different bullet for each level. Each subsequent bullet level is indented to distinguish it from the previous level. The following are methods to increase or decrease the bullet level.

Figure 2-56 Change bulleted list level

- Click the **Bullets** drop-down arrow [*Home* tab, *Paragraph* group] and select a bullet list level from the **Change List Level** drop-down list (Figure 2-56).
- Select or click at the beginning of a bulleted item and press **Tab** to increase the bullet level.
- Select or click at the beginning of a bulleted item and click the **Increase Indent** button [*Home* tab, *Paragraph* group] to increase the bullet level.
- Press **Shift+Tab** or click the **Decrease Indent** button to decrease the bullet level.

Create a Numbered List

Creating a numbered list is similar to creating a bulleted list. The *Numbering Library* in the *Numbering* drop-down list contains number format options.

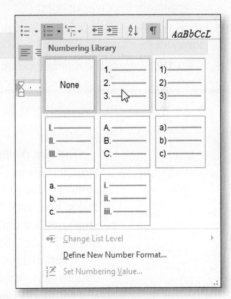

Figure 2-57 Numbering format options

▶**HOW TO:** Create a Numbered List

1. Place the insertion point at the location to begin the list or select the text to convert to a numbered list.

2. Click the **Numbering** drop-down arrow [*Home* tab, *Paragraph* group] to display the library of numbering options (Figure 2-57).

   - If you click the *Numbering* button, the most recently used number format is applied to the numbered list.

3. Select a number style from the list of options.

4. Type your information after the number if you are typing a new numbered list.

5. Press **Enter** after a numbered item to add another numbered item.

6. Press **Enter** two times after the last numbered item or click the **Numbering** button to turn off numbering.

Customize a Numbered List

In addition to being able to select a format from the *Numbering Library*, you also have the options to *Change List Level*, *Define New Number Format*, and *Set Numbering Value*.

The ***Change List Level*** option in the *Numbering* drop-down list enables you to select the level of the list. The numbering of each subsequent level of the list is dependent upon the number format you select.

You are not limited to the numbering formats available in the *Numbering* drop-down list. The ***Define New Number Format*** option enables you to customize how the numbered list displays.

▶HOW TO: Customize a Numbered List

1. Select the numbered list.
2. Click the **Numbering** drop-down arrow [*Home* tab, *Paragraph* group] and select **Define New Number Format**. The *Define New Number Format* dialog box opens (Figure 2-58).
3. Click the **Number style** drop-down list and select a number format.
   - Click the **Font** button to change the numbering font, size, or style.
4. Use the *Number format* area to customize how the numbers display.
   - Typically, a period follows the numbers, but you can change this to an ending parenthesis, hyphen, other character, or no punctuation.
5. Click the **Alignment** drop-down arrow to change number alignment.
   - Numbers align on the left by default, but you can change the number alignment to center or right.
6. View the *Preview* area to see how the number format will display in the document.
7. Click **OK** to apply the number format and close the dialog box.

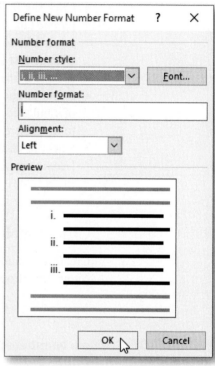

Figure 2-58 *Define New Number Format* dialog box

The ***Set Numbering Value*** dialog box includes options to *Start new list* or *Continue from previous list*. You can also set the number value to begin a new list. Open the *Set Numbering Value* dialog box from the *Numbering* drop-down list or right-click a numbered list and select *Set Numbering Value* from the context menu (Figure 2-59).

When using numbering, the context menu (right-click) lists options to *Adjust List Indents*, *Restart at 1*, *Continue Numbering*, and *Set Numbering Value* (Figure 2-60).

Figure 2-59 *Set Numbering Value* dialog box

▶ MORE INFO

Use the *Format Painter* to copy numbered or bulleted list formatting to other areas in a document.

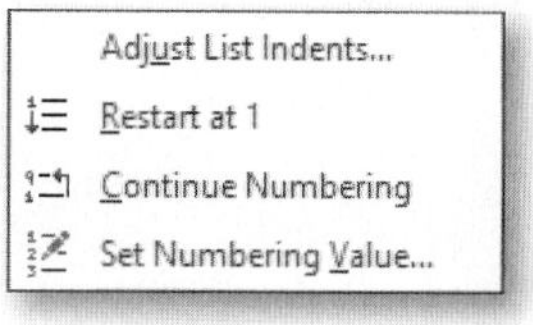

Figure 2-60 Context menu numbering options

Multilevel Lists

Multilevel lists enable you to customize a list using a combination of numbers, letters, or bullets. Word provides a *List Library* from which to select a multilevel list. You can customize an existing multilevel list or define your own list.

As you define a new multilevel list, you have the following options to customize each level of the list:

- Number format including font and starting number
- Number style, which can be a number, letter, Roman numeral, or bullet
- Position of the number and the text that follows

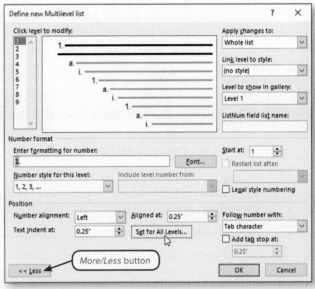

Figure 2-61 *Define new Multilevel list dialog box*

▶ HOW TO: Define a New Multilevel List

1. Select the text or the beginning point on which to apply a multilevel list.

2. Click the **Multilevel List** drop-down arrow [*Home* tab, *Paragraph* group].

3. Select **Define New Multilevel list** from the drop-down list. The *Define new Multilevel list* dialog box opens (Figure 2-61).

4. Click the **More** button in the bottom left of the dialog box to display all formatting options.

5. Select the level to modify in the *Click level to modify* area.

6. Select the *Number format, Start at* number, and *Number style for this level* in the *Number format* area.

7. Set the *Number alignment,* the *Aligned at* measurement (which is the first line indent), and *Text indent at* measurement (which is the hanging indent) in the *Position* area.

8. Click the **Set for All Levels** button to open the *Set for All Levels* dialog box where you set the indents for all levels (Figure 2-62). Click **OK** to close the *Set for All Levels* dialog box.

9. Select the next level to modify in the *Click level to modify* area and change settings as described in the steps above.

10. Click **OK** to apply the multilevel list settings after customizing the levels.

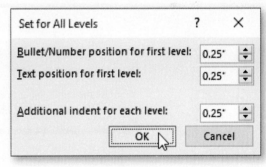

Figure 2-62 *Set for All Levels dialog box*

Using Styles and Themes

Styles are a collection of preset formatting to apply to a paragraph or selected text. A style controls the font, font size, style, color, effects, indents, line spacing, paragraph spacing, and borders applied to text. Use styles to apply preset formatting to titles, section headings, paragraph headings, text, lists, and tables. *Themes* are a collection of fonts, colors, and effects to apply to an entire document. Use both styles and themes to maintain consistent formatting throughout a single document or multiple documents.

Style Gallery

The *Style gallery* in the *Styles* group on the *Home* tab provides numerous built-in styles to apply to selected text in a document (Figure 2-63). The *Style* gallery does not display all the available styles but rather displays the more commonly used styles.

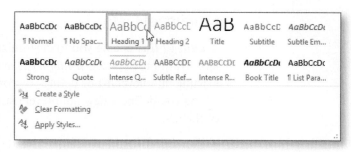

Figure 2-63 *Style* gallery

Apply a Built-In Style

You can quickly preview or apply styles to selected text or paragraphs. To preview a style, place the pointer on a style in the *Style* gallery. A live preview of the style displays on the selected text or paragraph. Apply a style to the text by choosing a style in the *Style* gallery.

> ▶ **HOW TO:** Apply a Built-In Style from the Style Gallery

1. Select the text or paragraph where you want to apply the style.
2. Select a style from the *Style* gallery [*Home* tab, *Styles* group].
   - Click the **More** button to see all the styles in the *Style* gallery (Figure 2-64).
   - Click the **down arrow** on the right side of the gallery to see the next row of styles available in the *Style* gallery.

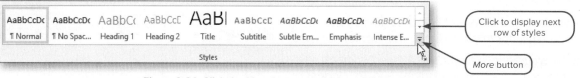

Figure 2-64 Click the *More* button to display additional styles

> ▶ **ANOTHER WAY**
>
> Use the mini toolbar to apply a style to selected text by selecting or right-clicking text, choosing **Styles** from the mini toolbar, and selecting the style to apply.

Modify a Style

Once a style has been applied to text, the style can be modified. One way to do this is changing the font, font size, color, style, or effects on the selected text without actually changing the style.

The other option is to modify the style. The advantage of modifying a style is that the formatting will be consistent when the style is applied to other text in a document. When you modify a style, all other text with this style applied updates automatically. The following are two ways to modify a style:

- *Update [style name] to Match Selection*
- *Modify* style

▶ HOW TO: Update Style to Match Selection

1. Apply a style to selected text.
2. Apply formatting changes on the text where the style was applied.
3. Select the text you changed.
4. Right-click the style in the *Style* gallery and choose **Update [style name] to Match Selection** (Figure 2-65).
   - The style updates to match the selected text.
   - All other text with this style applied updates automatically.

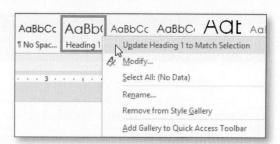

Figure 2-65 Update style to match selected text

You can also modify a style using the *Modify Style* dialog box.

▶ HOW TO: Modify an Existing Style

1. Right-click the style to modify in the *Style* gallery and select **Modify**. The *Modify Style* dialog box opens (Figure 2-66).
2. Make basic formatting changes in the *Formatting* area of the dialog box.
   - The updated style displays in the *Preview* area, and a summary of the style formatting displays below the *Preview* area.
3. Click the **Format** button at the bottom-left corner to open other dialog boxes, such as *Font*, *Paragraph*, *Tabs*, and *Borders*, for additional formatting changes.
   - Change the style formatting, and click **OK** to apply changes and to close the dialog box.
4. Click **OK** to apply the style change and to close the *Modify Style* dialog box.

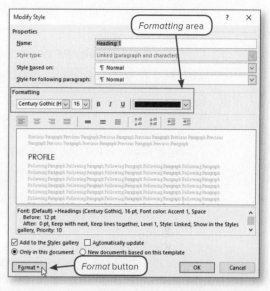

Figure 2-66 *Modify Style* dialog box

Apply a Theme

A theme is a collection of fonts, colors, and effects. Themes are similar to styles, but instead of applying a format to selected text, themes apply formatting to an entire document. All documents have a theme; the default theme for a new document is *Office*. You can change the theme of a document or individually change the *Theme Colors*, *Theme Fonts*, or *Theme Effects* in a document.

▶ HOW TO: Apply a Document Theme

1. Click the **Design** tab.
2. Click the **Themes** button [*Document Formatting* group].
3. Select the theme to apply from the *Themes* gallery (Figure 2-67).
4. Click the **Colors**, **Fonts**, or **Effects** buttons [*Design* tab, *Document Formatting* group] to change each of these options individually within the existing theme.

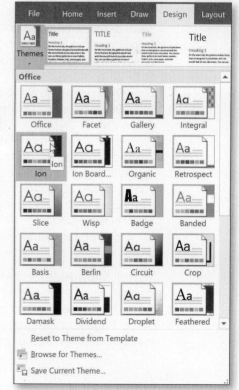

Figure 2-67 Change the *Theme* of a document

In this Pause & Practice project, you modify the resume you edited in *Pause & Practice 2-2*. You add a bulleted list, customize the bulleted list, insert a page break, apply and modify styles, and apply a document theme.

File Needed: *[your initials] PP W2-2.docx*
Completed Project File Name: *[your initials] PP W2-3.docx*

1. Open the *[your initials] PP W2-2* document completed in *Pause & Practice 2-2*.

2. Save this document as [your initials] PP W2-3.

3. Convert text to a bulleted list, customize the bullet, and use the *Format Painter*.

   a. Select the four paragraphs of text below the "EXPERIENCE" heading and below the city, state, and date line.

   b. Click the **Bullets** button [*Home* tab, *Paragraph* group]. The selected text converts to a bulleted list (Figure 2-68).

   c. Confirm the bulleted paragraphs are still selected, click the **Bullets** drop-down arrow, and select **Define New Bullet**. The *Define New Bullet* dialog box opens.

   d. Click the **Symbol** button. The *Symbol* dialog box opens (Figure 2-69).

   e. Click the **Font** drop-down list and scroll down to select **Wingdings**.

   f. Scroll down the list of symbols and select the **check box** symbol (*Character code* 254).

   g. Click **OK** to close the *Symbol* dialog box.

   h. Click **OK** to close the *Define New Bullet* dialog box.

   i. Double-click the **Format Painter** button and apply this bullet format to lines of text in the other "EXPERIENCE" sections and the "EDUCATION" section (see Figure 2-71). Don't apply bullet formatting to the city, state, and date lines where the tab stops and leaders display.

   j. Click the **Format Painter** button again to turn off this feature.

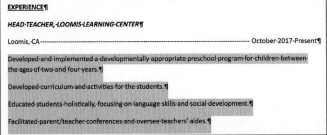

Figure 2-68 Apply bullets to selected text

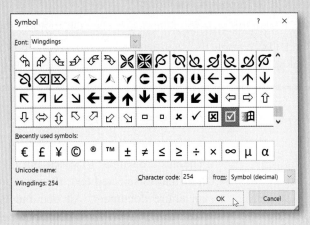

Figure 2-69 *Symbol* dialog box

4. Insert a page break in the document.

   a. Turn on **Show/Hide** [*Home* tab, *Paragraph* group] if necessary.

   b. Place the insertion point in front of the "EDUCATION" heading.

   c. Select the **Layout** tab and click the **Breaks** button [*Page Setup* group].

   d. Select **Page** from the drop-down list. A page break displays at the bottom of the first page, and the "EDUCATION" section moves to the next page.

5. Change the theme and theme color of the document.
   a. Click the **Design** tab.
   b. Click the **Themes** button [*Document Formatting* group] and select **Ion** from the *Themes* gallery.
   c. Click the **Colors** button [*Document Formatting* group] and select **Red** from the *Theme Colors*.

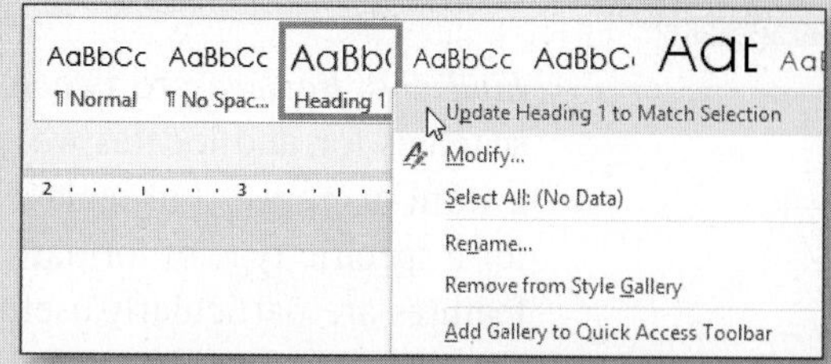

6. Apply styles from the *Style* gallery to selected text.
   a. Select "**Richelle Wilkinson**" on the first page of the resume (don't select the line break character).
   b. Click the **Title** style in the *Style* gallery [*Home* tab].
   c. Change the font size to **20 pt**.
   d. Apply the **Heading 1** style to each of the underlined main headings ("PROFILE," "EXPERIENCE," "EDUCATION," "SKILLS," and "REFERENCES").
   e. Apply the **Heading 2** style to each of the bold and italicized subheadings in the "EXPERIENCE" and "EDUCATION" sections.

7. Modify a style.
   a. Select the "**PROFILE**" heading.
   b. Change the *Before* paragraph spacing to **16 pt**.
   c. Right-click the **Heading 1** style in the *Style* gallery [*Home* tab, *Styles* group] and select **Update Heading 1 to Match Selection** (Figure 2-70). This style change applies to all text with *Heading 1* style.
   d. Select "**CALIFORNIA STATE UNIVERSITY CHICO, BACHELOR OF ARTS IN CHILD DEVELOPMENT**" in the "EDUCATION" section (not "REFERENCES" section) on the second page and change the font size to **11 pt**.
   e. Right-click the **Heading 2** style in the *Style* gallery [*Home* tab, *Styles* group] and select **Update Heading 2 to Match Selection**.

8. Save and close the document (Figure 2-71).

Figure 2-70 Update style to match selection

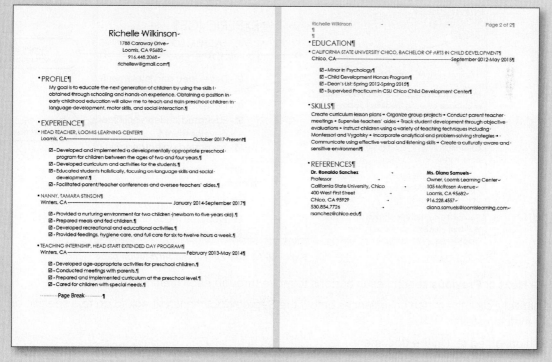

Figure 2-71 PP W2-3 completed

Using Find and Replace and Resume Assistant

Find and *Replace* are two extremely useful and powerful tools in Word. The *Find* feature searches for and locates words and phrases in a document. The *Replace* feature searches for a word or phrase and replaces it with other text. You can also use *Find* and *Replace* to search for a specific type of formatting in a document and replace it with different formatting. These features are particularly useful in longer documents. When using *Find* or *Replace*, it is best to position your insertion point at the top of the document so Word searches from the beginning of your document. The ***Resume Assistant*** connects with *LinkedIn* and provides assistance in Word when working on a resume.

Find

When you use the ***Find*** feature, the ***Navigation pane*** opens on the left and displays all instances of text matching your search (Figure 2-72). Word also highlights in yellow each instance of the matching text in the document. Navigate through the document to view each instance and edit as desired.

> ### HOW TO: Use Find in the Navigation Pane

1. Place your insertion point at the beginning of the document.
2. Click the **Find** button [*Home* tab, *Editing* group]. The *Navigation* pane opens on the left.
3. Click the **Search document** text box at the top of the *Navigation* pane and type the text for which to search (see Figure 2-72).
   - The matching results display below the text box.
   - Word highlights the matching text in the document.

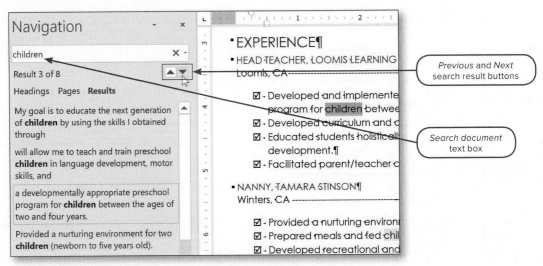

Figure 2-72 Use *Find* in the *Navigation* pane

4. Click the **Next** or **Previous** search result buttons to move through each matching instance in the document.
   - Alternatively, click the matching instances below the *Search document* text box to go to a specific occurrence of the matching text.
5. Edit the highlighted text in the document.
6. Click the **X** to the right of the *Search Document* text box to clear the current search.
7. Click the **X** in the upper-right corner of the *Navigation* pane to close the pane.

Find and Replace

The *Find and Replace* dialog box includes three different advanced options for searching your document: *Find, Replace,* and *Go To.* The *Find* tab of the *Find and Replace* dialog box not only searches for text in your document but also searches for specific formatting (such as font styles, line spacing, or paragraph spacing). For example, search for all text that is bold or italic, or that has 6 pt. *After* paragraph spacing.

Use the *Replace* feature to search for text, formatting, or a combination of text and formatting and to replace the matching text with other text, formatting, or formatted text. This feature is a quick and efficient way to find and replace text in a document.

▶HOW TO: Use Replace

1. Place your insertion point at the beginning of the document.
2. Click the **Replace** button [*Home* tab, *Editing* group] or press **Ctrl+H**. The *Find and Replace* dialog box opens with the *Replace* tab displayed (Figure 2-73).
3. Click the **Find what** text box and type the text for which you are searching.
4. Click the **Replace with** text box and type the text to replace the found text.
5. Click the **More** button to display advanced find options. The *Less* button hides the advanced find options.
6. Click the **Format** or **Special** button to add formatting options or special characters to either the text for which you are searching or the replacement text.

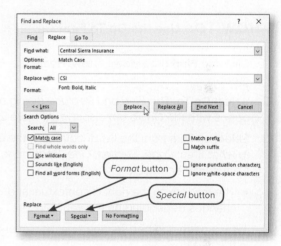

Figure 2-73 Replace text

   • Place the insertion point in the **Find what** or **Replace with** text box before selecting a format or special character.
7. Click the **Find Next** button to locate the first occurrence of the text (and formatting) for which you are searching.

   • It is best to click the **Less** button to collapse this dialog box when finding and replacing content in your document.
8. Select **Replace** (this occurrence), **Replace All** (all occurrences), or **Find Next** (skip this occurrence without replacing and move to the next) to apply an action on each occurrence.

   • When you select one of these options, Word moves to the next occurrence.
   • When you finish finding and replacing text in the document, a dialog box opens informing you that Word has finished searching the document. Click **OK** to close this dialog box.
9. Click the **X** in the upper-right corner to close the *Find and Replace* dialog box.

When using *Find* or *Replace*, wildcards are helpful to find information. You can use wildcards before, after, or between words.

   • *Question mark (?):* A wildcard for a single character. For example, *w???* finds any words that begins with "w" and contains four letters (for example, when, with, warm, or wish).
   • *Asterisk (*):* A wildcard for a string of characters. For example, **search*** finds any form of the word "search" (for example, searches, searching, or searched).

> **MORE INFO**
>
> It is a good idea to use *Match Case* when replacing acronyms (capital letters) with words so the replaced words will not be all uppercase. Also, use *Find whole words only* to refine your search.

Go To

The *Go To* feature enables you to move quickly to specific items or locations in your document. This feature is different from *Find* because *Go To* moves to specific objects or locations in your document such as a page, section, or bookmark. This feature is available on the *Go To* tab in the *Find and Replace* dialog box.

▶ HOW TO: Use the Go To Feature

1. Click the **Find** drop-down arrow [*Home* tab, *Editing* group].

2. Select **Go To**. The *Find and Replace* dialog box opens with the *Go To* tab displayed (Figure 2-74).

3. Select an item from the list of options in the *Go to what* area: *Page*, *Section*, *Line*, *Bookmark*, *Comment*, *Footnote*, etc.

   - The text box to the right is contextual and changes depending on the item chosen.

4. Type a page number, section, line, bookmark, etc., in the text box.

5. Click the **Go To** button.

6. Click **Close** to close this dialog box.

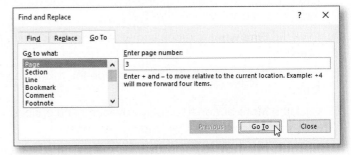

Figure 2-74 *Go To* in the *Find and Replace* dialog box

Resume Assistant

The new **Resume Assistant** feature connects with *LinkedIn* and provides assistance when working on a resume. When you open a document that Word believes is a resume, a notification opens and asks if you want to see resume suggestions (Figure 2-75). Based on the content of the resume, the *Resume Assistant* provides examples of resumes and other information to help you customize your resume.

Office 2019 Note: The *Resume Assistant* feature is not available in Office 2019 and some versions of Office 365.

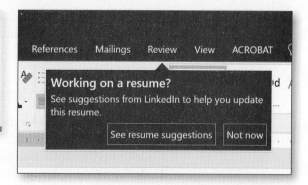

Figure 2-75 *Resume Assistant* notification

▶ HOW TO: Use the Resume Assistant

1. Open an existing resume and click **See resume suggestions** to open the *Resume Assistant* pane on the right (Figure 2-76).

    - If this notification does not display, click the **Resume Assistant** button [*Review* tab, *Resume* group].
    - If the *Resume Assistant* button is not active, turn on the *LinkedIn Features*. Click the **File** tab to open the *Backstage* view, click **Options** to open the *Word Options* dialog box, and check the **Enable LinkedIn features in my Office applications** box in the *LinkedIn Features* area.

2. Click **Get started** if necessary. This menu may not display in the *Resume Assistant* pane if you've used the *Resume Assistant* previously.

3. Type a role and industry (optional) if necessary and click **See examples**. Resume examples display in the *Resume Assistant* pane (Figure 2-77). This menu may not display in the *Resume Assistant* pane if you've used the *Resume Assistant* previously.

    - The *Role* area may already be populated with text based upon your resume. You can change the role if necessary.
    - The *Resume Assistant* pane displays examples of resumes, top skills for the type of job, articles on resume writing, and suggested jobs.

4. Click the **Read more** link on an example resume to view detailed information.

    - Click the **Back** arrow to return to the main *Resume Assistant* pane.
    - Click the **Filter examples by top skills** drop-down list to filter resume examples.

5. Click the **X** in the upper-right corner of the *Resume Assistant* pane to close this pane.

Figure 2-76 Get started using the *Resume Assistant*

SLO 2.9

Using Borders, Shading, and Hyperlinks

Borders and ***shading*** are excellent ways to highlight or emphasize important information in a document. Word provides preset border options, as well as custom border and shading options.

A ***hyperlink*** functions like a button and is used to take a reader to a web page, open an existing or

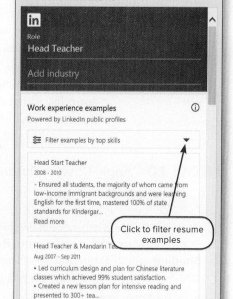

Figure 2-77 *Resume Assistant* pane

new document, open an email message, or move to another location in the current document. You can add a hyperlink to text or a graphic object.

Apply Built-In Borders

Use the **Borders drop-down list** in the *Paragraph* group on the *Home* tab to quickly apply borders to selected text. Borders are typically applied to paragraphs, but they can also be applied to selected text. Borders, by default, apply to the paragraph where your insertion point is located. Figure 2-78 shows the different types of built-in borders.

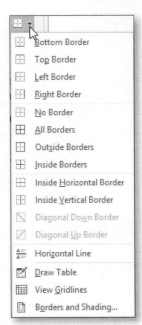

▶ HOW TO: Apply Built-In Borders

1. Select the paragraph or place the insertion point in the paragraph to apply the border.
2. Click the **Home** tab.
3. Click the **Borders** drop-down arrow [*Paragraph* group] (see Figure 2-78).
4. Click the border option to apply to the selected paragraph.

Figure 2-78 *Borders drop-down list*

Customize Borders

The **Borders and Shading dialog box** provides many more options to customize the type of borders you use. Not only can you customize the style, width, and color of a border line but also customize where the border is placed in relation to the selected text. The *Borders and Shading* dialog box is available from the *Borders* drop-down list in the *Paragraph* group on the *Home* tab.

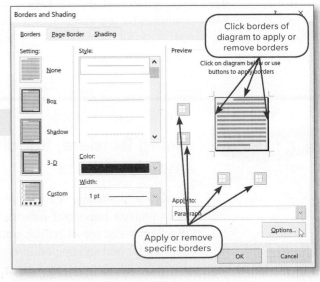

▶ HOW TO: Apply Custom Borders

1. Select the paragraph(s) to apply a border.
2. Click the **Borders** drop-down arrow [*Home* tab, *Paragraph* group] and choose the **Borders and Shading** option at the bottom of the list. The *Borders and Shading* dialog box opens (Figure 2-79).
   - In the *Apply to* area, select *Text* or *Paragraph*.
3. Select the type of border to use in the *Setting* area. Your options are *None*, *Box*, *Shadow*, *3-D*, and *Custom*.

Figure 2-79 *Borders and Shading dialog box*

4. Select a style of the line from the list of options in the *Style* area.

5. Click the **Color** drop-down arrow and select line color.

6. Click the **Width** drop-down arrow and select the width of the border line. The width of the line is measured in points.

7. View the *Preview* area to see how the border will appear in your document.

   - In the *Preview* area, customize how the borders appear by clicking the *Top*, *Bottom*, *Left*, or *Right* border buttons to turn a border on or off (see Figure 2-79).
   - Alternatively, click a border preview icon to turn a border on or off.

8. Click the **Options** button to open the *Border and Shading Options* dialog box (Figure 2-80).

   - This dialog box includes the option to add additional space (padding) between the border and the text at the *Top*, *Bottom*, *Left*, and *Right*.
   - The spacing is measured in points.
   - Click **OK** to close the *Border and Shading Options* dialog box.

9. Click **OK** to close the *Borders and Shading* dialog box.

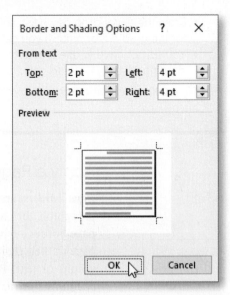

Figure 2-80 *Border and Shading Options dialog box*

Apply Shading

Applying shading to a paragraph or text is similar to applying borders. **Shading** applies a background color to selected text. *Shading* color options are available from the *Shading* drop-down list in the *Paragraph* group on the *Home* tab or the *Shading* tab in the *Borders and Shading* dialog box.

The shading colors available are dependent upon the theme of the document. Click the **Shading** drop-down list and select from *Theme Colors* or *Standard Colors* (Figure 2-81). If you want a color that is not available in the menu, click *More Colors* to select from a color palette.

Figure 2-81 Shading color options from the *Shading* drop-down list

▶HOW TO: Apply Shading from the Borders and Shading Dialog Box

1. Select the paragraph(s) to apply a shade.

2. Click the **Borders** drop-down arrow [*Home* tab, *Paragraph* group] and choose the **Borders and Shading** option at the bottom of the list. The *Borders and Shading* dialog box opens (Figure 2-82).

3. Click the **Shading** tab.

4. Click the **Fill** drop-down arrow and select a shading fill color.

   - Alternatively, select a shading *Style* or *Color* in the *Patterns* area.
   - From the *Style* drop-down list, select a gradient percent or a fill pattern as the shading style.

- From the *Color* drop-down list, select a fill color for the gradient or pattern you selected.
- You do not have to use a pattern style or color for shading. Usually just a fill color is sufficient.

5. Click **OK** to close the *Borders and Shading* dialog box.

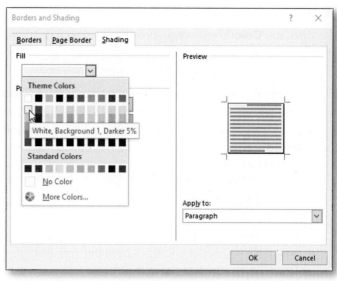

Figure 2-82 Shading options in the *Borders and Shading* dialog box

Apply a Page Border

Page borders are different from paragraph or text borders. A page border surrounds the entire page rather than selected paragraphs or text. Page borders are useful and attractive when creating flyers or handouts. A page border consists of a line with varying styles, widths, and colors, or you can use art graphics as a page border.

▶HOW TO: Apply a Page Border

1. Click the **Design** tab.
2. Click the **Page Borders** button [*Page Background* group]. The *Borders and Shading* dialog box opens with the *Page Border* tab displayed (Figure 2-83).
3. Select the type of page border to apply in the *Setting* area.
4. Select a border style in the *Style* list.
   - Alternatively, select an art design to apply as the border from the **Art** drop-down list.
5. Select a border color and width from the **Color** and **Width** drop-down lists.
6. Customize page borders by clicking the **Top**, **Bottom**, **Left**, or **Right** border buttons in the *Preview* area to turn on or off borders if desired.
7. Click the **Apply to** drop-down list and select the page(s) to apply the page border. Your options are:
   - *Whole document*
   - *This section*
   - *This section – First page only*
   - *This section – All except first page*
8. Click **OK** to close the *Borders and Shading* dialog box.

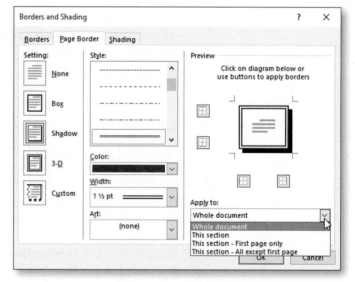

Figure 2-83 Apply a page border

> **MORE INFO**
>
> When you apply a page border, the text in the document is not affected because the page border is placed outside the margin boundaries.

W2-106

Insert a Horizontal Line

In addition to inserting top and bottom borders on selected text, you can also insert a *horizontal line* to use as a border to separate information on a page. A horizontal line is a graphic object inserted into the document. When you insert a horizontal line, the line is the width of the page. More information about using and customizing graphics is covered in *SLO 4.5: Working with Graphics*.

▶**HOW TO:** Insert a Horizontal Line

1. Place your insertion point at the location to insert a horizontal line.
2. Click the **Borders** drop-down arrow [*Home* tab, *Paragraph* group].
3. Select **Horizontal Line** from the drop-down list (Figure 2-84).
   - The horizontal line is treated as a separate paragraph and has a paragraph mark to the right.

Figure 2-84 Insert a horizontal line

Create a Hyperlink

A hyperlink is an excellent way to direct users to information on a web site, another document, or a location in the same document. Hyperlink can also be used for an email address, which automatically opens a new Microsoft Outlook email message addressed to the recipient. When creating a hyperlink, you can also customize the *ScreenTip* and the target frame.

> **MORE INFO**
>
> Typically, hyperlinks are underlined and a different color to distinguish them from regular text in a document. In a Word document, Press **Ctrl+Click** to follow a hyperlink.

The *ScreenTip* is the text that displays when you place your pointer over a hyperlink in the document. The *target frame* is the window where the hyperlink document or web site opens. Word provides many different target frame options from which to choose. Usually, it is best to choose **New window** if the link is to a different document or a web page. An email hyperlink always opens in a new window.

▶**HOW TO:** Create a Hyperlink

1. Select the text or graphic to create a hyperlink.
   - If you are creating a hyperlink to a web page, copy (**Ctrl+C**) the web page address (URL) before selecting the text or graphic.
2. Click the top half of the **Link** button [*Insert* tab, *Links* group] to open the *Insert Hyperlink* dialog box (Figure 2-85).

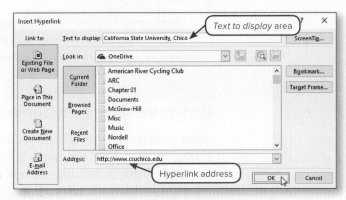

Figure 2-85 *Insert Hyperlink* dialog box

- The text you selected in the document displays as the hyperlink in the *Text to display* area. If you type other text in this text box, it will replace the text you selected in the document.
- Alternatively, click the **Link** drop-down list (bottom half) and select a copied URL to apply a hyperlink on the selected text without opening the *Insert Hyperlink* text box (Figure 2-86). To customize the hyperlink, open the *Insert Hyperlink* dialog box.

3. Select the type of hyperlink in the *Link to* area. Your options are *Existing File or web Page*, *Place in This Document*, *Create New Document*, or *E-mail Address*.

   - If you are linking to a file, browse your computer in the *Look in* area to locate and select the file.
   - If you are linking to a web page, type or paste (**Ctrl+V**) a web address in the *Address* area.
   - If you are linking to a place in the document, a list of headings from which to choose displays.
   - If you are inserting a link to create a new document, options for the new document display.
   - If you are linking to an email address, type the email address, and create a subject line for the email (optional).

4. Click the **ScreenTip** button to insert text that displays when you place the pointer over the hyperlink (Figure 2-87).

   - Type the *ScreenTip* text and click **OK** to close the *Set Hyperlink ScreenTip* dialog box.

5. Click the **Target Frame** button to open the *Set Target Frame* dialog box (Figure 2-88).

   - From the drop-down list of options, select where the hyperlink destination will open.
   - Check the **Set as default for all hyperlinks** box to make your target frame selection the default for all hyperlinks in your document.
   - Click **OK** to close the *Set Target Frame* dialog box.

6. Click **OK** to insert the hyperlink and close the *Insert Hyperlink* dialog box.

Figure 2-86 Insert hyperlink from *Link* drop-down list

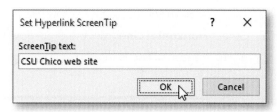

Figure 2-87 *Set Hyperlink ScreenTip* dialog box

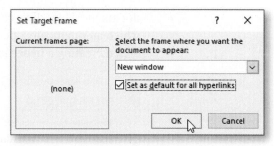

Figure 2-88 *Set Target Frame* dialog box

> **ANOTHER WAY**
>
> **Ctrl+K** opens the *Insert Hyperlink* dialog box. *Link* options are also available in the context menu when you right-click a word, selected text, or an object.

Edit or Remove a Hyperlink

Word enables you to quickly edit hyperlinks to change hyperlink information, add a *ScreenTip*, or change the target frame. Also, you can quickly remove a hyperlink from a document without deleting the text in the document. When you remove a hyperlink from existing text or an object, the text or object in your document is not deleted. Only the hyperlink is removed.

▶HOW TO: Edit or Remove a Hyperlink

1. Select or click the hyperlink to edit.
2. Click the top half of the **Link** button [*Insert* tab, *Links* group]. The *Edit Hyperlink* dialog box opens.
   - Alternatively, press **Ctrl+K** to open the *Edit Hyperlink* dialog box.
3. Change hyperlink information or options as needed.
4. Click the **Remove Link** button to remove an existing hyperlink (Figure 2-89).
   - When you click **Remove Link**, the *Edit Hyperlink* dialog box closes automatically.
5. Click **OK** to close the *Edit Hyperlink* dialog box if necessary.

Figure 2-89 Edit or remove a hyperlink

▶ **ANOTHER WAY**

Right-click a hyperlink and select **Edit Hyperlink** or **Remove Hyperlink**.

PAUSE & PRACTICE: WORD 2-4

In this Pause & Practice project, you finalize the resume you edited in *Pause & Practice 2-3*. You use *Find and Replace*, apply borders and shading to selected text, add hyperlinks to the document, and use the *Resume Assistant*.

File Needed: *[your initials] PP W2-3.docx*
Completed Project File Name: *[your initials] PP W2-4.docx*

1. Open the *[your initials] PP W2-3* document completed in *Pause & Practice 2-3*.
2. Save this document as [your initials] PP W2-4.
3. Use *Find and Replace* to replace the hyphen between dates with an en dash.
   a. Place your insertion point at the top of the document (or press **Ctrl+Home**).
   b. Click the **Replace** button [*Home* tab, *Editing* group] or press **Ctrl+H** to open the *Find and Replace* dialog box.
   c. Type **–** (hyphen) in the *Find what* text box.
   d. Place the insertion point in the *Replace with* text box.
   e. Click the **More** button if the *Search Options* are not already displayed.
   f. Click the **Special** button and select **En Dash** (Figure 2-90). The en dash is used between dates.

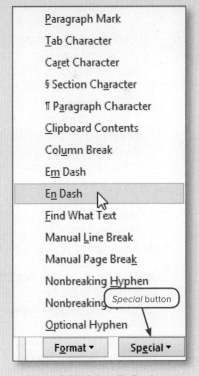

Figure 2-90 Select *En Dash* as the special character to replace a hyphen

g. Click the **Less** button to collapse the **Find and Replace** dialog box (Figure 2-91).

h. Click the **Find Next** button to locate the first instance of a hyphen.

Figure 2-91 Use *Find and Replace*

i. Choose **Find Next** to skip the hyphenated word in the first paragraph.

j. Click the **Replace** button to replace each occurrence of a hyphen between the dates with an en dash; choose **Find Next** to skip and not replace each occurrence of a hyphenated word.

k. Click **OK** when Word has finished searching the document.

l. Click **Close** to close the *Find and Replace* dialog box.

4. Add borders and shading to a paragraph.

   a. Turn on **Show/Hide** [*Home* tab, *Paragraph* group] if necessary.

   b. Select the paragraph after the "PROFILE" heading on the first page, including the paragraph mark at the end of the paragraph.

   c. Click the **Borders** drop-down arrow [*Home* tab, *Paragraph* group] and select **Borders and Shading** to open the *Borders and Shading* dialog box.

   d. Select **Shadow** in the *Setting* area.

   e. Select the **solid line** (first option) in the *Style* area.

   f. Click the **Color** drop-down list and select **fifth color** in the **first row** of the *Theme Colors* (**Dark Red, Accent 1**) (Figure 2-92).

   g. Click the **Width** drop-down list and select **1 pt**.

   h. Select **Paragraph** in the *Apply to* area if necessary.

   i. Click the **Options** button to open the *Border and Shading Options* dialog box and change *Top* and *Bottom* to **2 pt**.

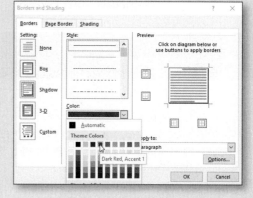

Figure 2-92 Select border color in the *Borders and Shading* dialog box

   j. Click **OK** to close the *Border and Shading Options* dialog box.

   k. Click the **Shading** tab.

   l. Click the **Fill** drop-down list and select the **first color** in the **second row** of the *Theme Colors* (**White, Background 1, Darker 5%**) (Figure 2-93).

   m. Click **OK** to close the *Borders and Shading* dialog box.

5. Add a bottom border to the header.

   a. Right-click the header on the second page and select **Edit Header** to open the *Header* area on the second page.

   b. Place the insertion point in the first line of the header.

   c. Click the **Borders** drop-down arrow [*Home* tab, *Paragraph* group].

   d. Select **Bottom Border**. A 1 pt. red border displays because that is the last border setting you used.

   e. Click the **Close Header and Footer** button [*Header & Footer Tools Design* tab, *Close* group].

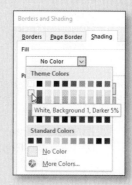

Figure 2-93 Apply shading to selected text

6. Insert a hyperlink to an email address.
   a. Select the email address in the heading information near the top of the first page.
   b. Click the top half of the **Link** button [*Insert* tab, *Links* group] or press **Ctrl+K** to open the *Insert Hyperlink* dialog box (Figure 2-94).
   c. Click the **E-mail Address** button in the *Link to* area.
   d. Type richellew@outlook.com in the *Text to display* area.
   e. Type richellew@outlook.com in the *E-mail address* area. Word automatically inserts "mailto:" before the email address.
   f. Click the **ScreenTip** button. The *Set Hyperlink ScreenTip* dialog box opens (Figure 2-95).
   g. Type Email Richelle in the *ScreenTip text* area and click **OK** to close the *Set Hyperlink ScreenTip* dialog box.
   h. Click **OK** to close the *Insert Hyperlink* dialog box.

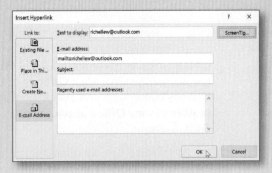

Figure 2-94 Insert hyperlink to an email address

Figure 2-95 *Set Hyperlink ScreenTip* dialog box

7. Insert a hyperlink to a web site.
   a. Select "**California State University, Chico**" in the "REFERENCES" section on the second page. Don't select this text in the "EDUCATION" section.
   b. Click the top half of the **Link** button or press **Ctrl+K** to open the *Insert Hyperlink* dialog box (Figure 2-96).
   c. Select **Existing File or web Page** in the *Link to* area. The *Text to display* area has *California State University, Chico* already filled in.
   d. Type www.csuchico.edu in the *Address* text box of the dialog box. Word automatically inserts "http://" before the web address.
   e. Click the **ScreenTip** button, type CSU Chico web site, and click **OK** to close the *Set Hyperlink ScreenTip* dialog box.
   f. Click the **Target Frame** button in the *Insert Hyperlink* dialog box to open the *Set Target Frame* dialog box.
   g. Select **New window** from the drop-down list and check the **Set as default for all hyperlinks** box (Figure 2-97).
   h. Click **OK** to close the *Set Target Frame* dialog box and click **OK** to close the *Insert Hyperlink* dialog box.

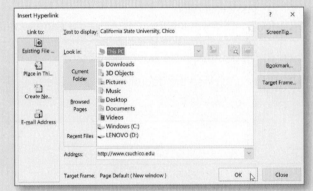

Figure 2-96 Insert hyperlink to a web page

Figure 2-97 *Set Target Frame* dialog box

8. Add hyperlinks to email addresses.
   a. Place the insertion point after "rsanchez@chico.edu" in the "REFERENCES" section on the second page.
   b. Press the **spacebar** once to automatically convert the text to a hyperlink to the email address.
   c. Place the insertion point after "diana.samuels@loomislearning.com" in the "REFERENCES" section and press the **spacebar** once to convert it to a hyperlink.

9. Use the *Resume Assistant*.

   a. Click the **Resume Assistant** button [*Review* tab, *Resume* group]. If the *Resume Assistant* button is not active, turn on the *LinkedIn Features*. Click the **File** tab to open the *Backstage* view, click **Options** to open the *Word Options* dialog box, and check the **Enable LinkedIn features in my Office applications** box in the *LinkedIn Features* area.

   Office 2019 Note: The *Resume Assistant* feature is not available in Office 2019 and some versions of Office 365.

   b. Click **Get started** if necessary. This menu may not display in the *Resume Assistant* pane if you've used the *Resume Assistant* previously.

   c. Click **See examples** if necessary. This menu may not display in the *Resume Assistant* pane if you've used the *Resume Assistant* previously. Resume examples display in the *Resume Assistant* pane (Figure 2-98).

   d. Click the **Read more** link on an example resume to view detailed information.

   e. Click the **Back** arrow to return to the main *Resume Assistant* pane.

   f. Scroll down the *Resume Assistant* pane to view the other information in this pane.

   g. Click the **X** in the upper-right corner of the *Resume Assistant* pane to close this pane.

10. Save and close the document (Figure 2-99).

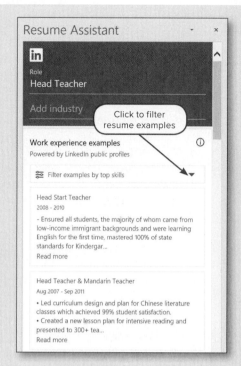

Figure 2-98 *Resume Assistant* pane

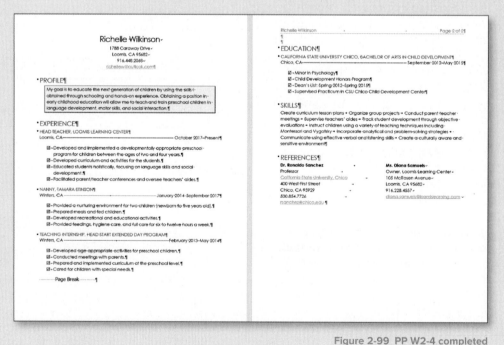

Figure 2-99 PP W2-4 completed

Chapter Summary

2.1 Format a document by customizing margins, page orientation, paper size, vertical alignment, and page movement (p. W2-68).

- Adjust the *margins* of a document to increase or decrease the *white space* surrounding the text. Adjust the top, bottom, left, and right margins of a document.
- *Landscape* and *Portrait* are the two *page orientation* options.
- A standard sheet of paper is 8½"×11". Select other paper sizes or create a custom paper size.
- *Vertical alignment* controls text alignment between the top and bottom margins. By default, text aligns vertically at the top of the document. Other vertical alignment options include center, justified, or bottom vertical alignment.
- Use horizontal and vertical *rulers* to display the typing area on a document.
- Change default page settings using the *Page Setup dialog box*.
- Change the page movement to *Side to Side* to view and scroll through your document horizontally rather than vertically.
- Use the *Thumbnails* feature to display your document as miniature page icons.

2.2 Improve alignment and page layout by setting, using, and editing tab stops in a document (p. W2-72).

- Five different types of *tab stops* are available: *Left*, *Center*, *Right*, *Decimal*, and *Bar*.
- Set, modify, or remove tab stops using the ruler or the *Tabs dialog box*.
- Use the *Tab selector* on the left side of the ruler to select a type of tab stop to set.
- Add *Leaders* with tab stops. Three different types of leaders are available: *Dot*, *Dash*, and *Solid underline*.
- In a Word document, default tab stops are set every 0.5". Customize default tab stops using the *Tabs* dialog box.

2.3 Apply indents to control text alignment (p. W2-76).

- *Indents* function as temporary margins and enable you to arrange paragraphs horizontally between the margins.
- Word provides four types of indents: *left*, *right*, *first line*, and *hanging*.

- Apply, modify, and remove indents with the ruler, *Layout* tab, or *Paragraph* dialog box.

2.4 Enhance document layout by inserting page numbers, headers, and footers (p. W2-82).

- Insert a *page number* into the header or footer in various locations or use default tab settings.
- *Headers* and *footers* are areas above and below a document's top and bottom margins.
- The *Different First Page* option enables you to remove or have different first page content in the header or footer.
- Header and footer content is typed once, and it appears on subsequent pages.
- Customize headers and footers with text, page numbers, the date, and other document property fields.
- A variety of built-in header, footer, and page numbering options are available.

2.5 Control pagination with page and section breaks (p. W2-89).

- Use *page breaks* to control the ending and beginning of pages in a document.
- Use *section breaks* for different page setup formatting in different sections of a document.
- Word provides four different section break options: *Next Page*, *Continuous*, *Even Page*, and *Odd Page*.
- Section breaks are visible in a document when the *Show/Hide* feature is turned on.

2.6 Use customized bulleted and numbered lists to effectively present information (p. W2-91).

- Use *bulleted* and *numbered lists* to emphasize important information.
- Customize lists by using different symbols or pictures as bullets.
- Use numbering to display an ordered list.
- Customize lists by changing number format and levels.
- Use *Multilevel lists* to customize a list using a combination of numbers, letters, or bullets.

2.7 Apply styles and themes to improve consistency in document format (p. W2-95).

- A *style* is a collection of preset formatting applied to selected text.
- The *Style gallery* is a collection of built-in styles.

- Existing styles can be modified.
- A *theme* is a collection of fonts, colors, and effects applied to a document.

2.8 Use find and replace to edit a document and use the *Resume Assistant* to customize a resume. (p. W2-100).

- The *Find* feature in Word searches for specific text or format in a document.
- The *Navigation pane* displays all occurrences of the text for which you are searching.
- The *Replace* feature searches for specific text in a document and replaces it with other text.
- Both *Find* and *Replace* search for and replace formatting in a document.
- Use the *Go To* feature to go directly to a page, section, line, or other area in your document.
- The *Resume Assistant* connects with *LinkedIn* and provides assistance in Word when working on a resume.

2.9 Improve overall document design and format with borders, shading, horizontal lines, and hyperlinks (p. W2-103).

- Apply *borders* and *shading* to text and paragraphs in a document.
- Word provides a variety of built-in border and shading options. Customize borders and shading using the *Borders and Shading dialog box*.
- Apply *page borders* to an individual page or all pages in a document.
- A *horizontal line* is a graphic object.
- A *hyperlink* takes readers to a web page, a different document, a different location in a document, or an email address. An email hyperlink opens Microsoft Outlook and places the recipient's email address in the email message.

Check for Understanding

The SIMbook for this text (within your SIMnet account) provides the following resources for concept review:

- Multiple-choice questions
- Short answer questions
- Matching exercises

Guided Project 2-1

In this project, you create a form for contractors seeking insurance coverage at Central Sierra Insurance. You apply a theme, styles, a multilevel list, tab stops, leaders, indents, borders and shading, a page break, and page numbering.
[Student Learning Outcomes 2.1, 2.2, 2.3, 2.4, 2.5, 2.6, 2.7, 2.9]

File Needed: *InsuranceQuestionnaire-02.docx* (Student data files are available in the Library of your SIMnet account.)
Completed Project File Name: *[your initials] Word 2-1.docx*

Skills Covered in This Project

- Modify an existing document.
- Change margins.
- Apply a document theme and theme color.
- Change font size, line spacing, and paragraph spacing.
- Apply a style to selected text.
- Modify an existing style.
- Apply borders and shading to selected text.
- Set and use a tab stop with an underline leader.
- Apply and modify a multilevel list.
- Insert a page break.
- Insert a built-in page number in the footer.
- View the document in *Side to Side* view.

1. Open the *InsuranceQuestionnaire-02* document from your student data files.

2. Save this document as [your initials] Word 2-1.

3. Change the margins of the document.
   a. Click the **Page Setup** launcher [*Layout* tab, *Page Setup* group] to open the *Page Setup* dialog box.
   b. Change the *Left* and *Right* margins to **0.75"**.
   c. Click **OK** to close the *Page Setup* dialog box.

4. Change the theme and theme color of the document.
   a. Click the **Themes** button [*Design* tab, *Document Formatting* group].
   b. Select **Integral** from the drop-down list.
   c. Click the **Colors** button [*Document Formatting* group] (Figure 2-100).
   d. Select **Aspect** from the drop-down list.

5. Change the font size, paragraph spacing, and line spacing of the entire document.
   a. Press **Ctrl+A** to select the entire document.
   b. Change the font size to **11 pt**.
   c. Change the line spacing to **Single (1.0)**.
   d. Change the *After* paragraph spacing to **6 pt**.

6. Apply styles to selected text.
   a. Place the insertion point in the first line of text ("Contractor's Insurance Questionnaire").

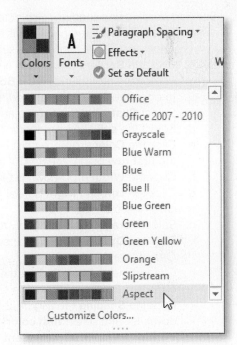

Figure 2-100 *Theme Colors* drop-down list

b. Click the **Title** style [*Home* tab, *Styles* group] in the *Style* gallery.

c. Select the second line of the document ("**Please carefully . . .**").

d. Right-click the selected text, click **Styles** on the mini toolbar, and select **Book Title** from the *Style* gallery.

e. Click the **Change Case** button [*Home* tab, *Font* group] and select **UPPERCASE**.

f. Select "**Applicant's Instructions**" and apply the **Intense Quote** style from the *Style* gallery. If necessary, click the **More** button in the *Style* gallery (bottom-right corner) to display all styles.

g. Apply the **Strong** style to the three words in all caps ("**ALL**," "**NONE**," and "**NONE**") in the next paragraph ("Please answer ALL questions . . .").

h. Select "**Insurance Application Disclaimer**" on the second page of the document and apply the **Intense Quote** style.

7. Modify an existing style.

a. Click the **More** button [*Home* tab, *Styles* group] to display all the styles in the *Style* gallery.

b. Right-click the **Intense Quote** style in the *Style* gallery and select **Modify** (Figure 2-101). The *Modify Style* dialog box opens.

Figure 2-101 Modify an existing style

c. Change the font size to **12 pt**. in the *Formatting* area.

d. Click the **Format** button on the bottom-left corner and select **Paragraph**. The *Paragraph* dialog box opens.

e. Change the *Left* and *Right* indent to **0**.

f. Click **OK** to close the *Paragraph* dialog box.

g. Click the **Only in this document** radio button if it is not already selected to apply the style changes to only this document.

h. Click **OK** to close the *Modify Style* dialog box. The style changes apply to all text formatted with the *Intense Quote* style on both the first and second pages.

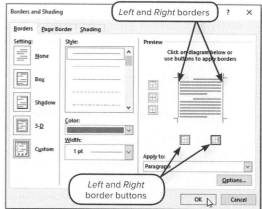

Figure 2-102 Apply a left and right border

8. Add borders and shading to selected text.

a. Select the first three paragraphs below "Insurance Application Disclaimer" on the second page.

b. Click the **Borders** drop-down arrow [*Home* tab, *Paragraph* group] and select **Borders and Shading** to open the *Borders and Shading* dialog box (Figure 2-102).

c. Select **Custom** in the *Setting* area.

d. Select the **solid line** border (first option) in the *Style* area.

e. Click the **Color** drop-down list and select the **fifth color** in the **first row** of the *Theme Colors* (**Orange, Accent 1**).

f. Click the **Width** drop-down list and select **1 pt**.

g. Click the **Left** and **Right** border buttons in the *Preview* area (see Figure 2-102).

h. Select **Paragraph** in the *Apply to* area if necessary.

i. Click the **Options** button to open the *Border and Shading Options* dialog box.

j. Change the *Left* and *Right* settings to **5 pt**. and click **OK** to close the *Border and Shading Options* dialog box.

k. Click the **Shading** tab (Figure 2-103), click the **Fill** drop-down list, and select **fifth color** in the **second row** of the *Theme Colors* (**Orange, Accent 1, Lighter 80%**).

l. Click **OK** to close the *Borders and Shading* dialog box.

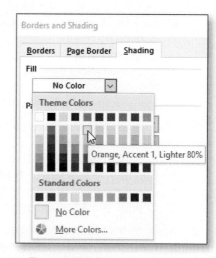

Figure 2-103 Select shading *Fill* color

W2-116

9. Change the paragraph spacing and add a tab stop with an underline leader to selected text.
   a. Select the last three lines of text on the second page.
   b. Click the **Paragraph** launcher [*Home* or *Layout* tab] to open the *Paragraph* dialog box.
   c. Change the *Before* paragraph spacing to **12 pt**.
   d. Click the **Tabs** button to open the *Tabs* dialog box (Figure 2-104).
   e. Type 7 in the *Tab stop position* text box.
   f. Click the **Right** radio button in the *Alignment* area.
   g. Click the **4** (solid underline) radio button in the *Leader* area.
   h. Click the **Set** button to set this tab stop and click **OK** to close the *Tabs* dialog box.
   i. Click at the end of the "Name and Title of the Insured" line and press **Tab**. A solid underline displays across the page to the right margin.
   j. Repeat step i on the next two lines.

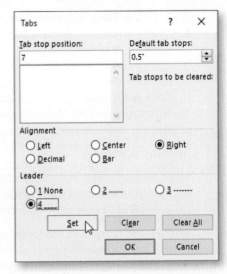

Figure 2-104 Set a right tab stop with an underline leader

10. Add a multilevel list to selected text and modify lists settings.
    a. Select the lines of text beginning with "**Applicant**" on the first page and ending with the last "**If yes, please explain:**" on the second page.
    b. Click the **Multilevel List** button [*Home* tab, *Paragraph* group] and select the **1), a), i)** option.
    c. Click the **Multilevel List** button again and select **Define New Multilevel List**. The *Define new Multilevel list* dialog box opens.
    d. Click the **Set for All Levels** button to open the *Set for All Levels* dialog box (Figure 2-105).
    e. Set the *Bullet/Number position for first level* to **0"**.
    f. Set the *Text position for first level* to **0.3"**.
    g. Set the *Additional indent for each level* to **0.3"**.
    h. Click **OK** to close the *Set for All Levels* dialog box and click **OK** to close the *Define new Multilevel list* dialog box.

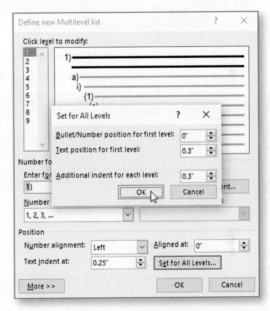

Figure 2-105 Change settings for a multilevel list

11. Increase indent on selected lines.
    a. Click anywhere in the list to deselect it.
    b. Place your insertion point in 13 in the numbered list ("If yes, . . .") and click the **Increase Indent** button [*Home* tab, *Paragraph* group]. This line is now letter *a)*.
    c. Repeat step b on each of the lines in the list that begin with "If yes, . . ." The list should display 28 numbered items when you finish this process.

12. Change paragraph spacing on the multilevel list and add a right tab stop with an underline leader.
    a. Select the entire multilevel list.
    b. Click the **Paragraph** launcher [*Home* or *Layout* tab] to open the *Paragraph* dialog box.
    c. Deselect the **Don't add space between paragraphs of the same style** check box (Figure 2-106).

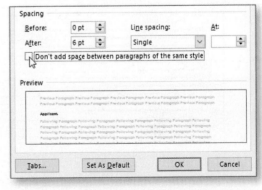

Figure 2-106 Add spacing between lines of text with the same style

d. Click the **Tabs** button to open the *Tabs* dialog box.

e. Type 7 in the *Tab stop position* text box.

f. Click the **Right** radio button in the *Alignment* area.

g. Click the **4** (solid underline) radio button in the *Leader* area.

h. Click the **Set** button to set this tab stop and click **OK** to close the *Tabs* dialog box.

i. Click at the end of the first numbered item ("Applicant:") and press **Tab**. A solid underline displays across the page to the right margin.

j. Repeat step i on each of the numbered and lettered paragraphs.

13. Save the document.

14. Insert a page break in the document.
    a. Place the insertion point before the text in number 22 in the multilevel list.
    b. Press **Ctrl+Enter** to insert a page break.

15. Add a page number in the footer of the document.
    a. Place your insertion point at the beginning of the document or press **Ctrl+Home**.
    b. Click the **Page Number** button [*Insert* tab, *Header & Footer* group].
    c. Select **Bottom of Page** to display the drop-down list.
    d. Scroll down and choose **Bold Numbers 3** in the *Page X of Y* section. The page numbers display at the right of the footer.
    e. Click the blank line below the page numbers in the footer and press **Backspace** to delete the blank line.
    f. Click the **Close Header and Footer** button [*Header & Footer Tools Design* tab, *Close* group].

16. View the document in *Side to Side* page movement.
    a. Click the **Side to Side** button [*View* tab, *Page Movement* group].
    b. Click the **Vertical** button to return to your document [*View* tab, *Page Movement* group].

17. Save and close the document (Figure 2-107).

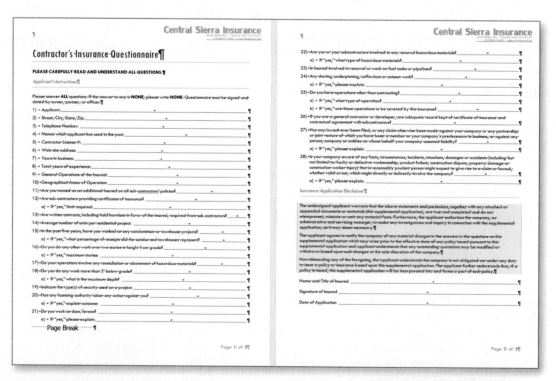

Figure 2-107 Word 2-1 completed

Guided Project 2-2

In this project, you create a checklist for employees at Placer Hills Real Estate to track the tasks they need to complete when a house enters escrow. You create a bulleted list, modify a bullet in a list, set and modify tab stops, apply and modify styles, and insert document properties in the footer.
[Student Learning Outcomes 2.1, 2.2, 2.3, 2.4, 2.6, 2.7, 2.9]

File Needed: ***SellerEscrowChecklist-02.docx*** *(Student data files are available in the* Library *of your* SIMnet account.)
Completed Project File Name: *[your initials] **Word 2-2.docx***

Skills Covered in This Project

- Modify an existing document.
- Change margins, line spacing, font, and font size.
- Set a tab stop using the ruler.
- Set a tab stop with leader.
- Apply a style to selected text.
- Modify an existing style.
- Apply and customize a bulleted list.
- Use the *Format Painter.*
- Insert a document property field and date in the footer.
- Apply a border in the footer.

1. Open the ***SellerEscrowChecklist-02*** document from your student data files.

2. Save this document as [your initials] Word 2-2.

3. Change margins, vertical alignment, line spacing, font, and font size, and delete blank lines.
   a. Click the **Margins** button [*Layout* tab, *Page Setup* group] and select **Normal** from the drop-down list.
   b. Click the **Page Setup** launcher to open the *Page Setup* dialog box and click the **Layout** tab.
   c. Change *Vertical alignment* in the *Page* area to **Center** and click **OK** to close the dialog box.
   d. Press **Ctrl+A** to select the entire document.
   e. Change the font to **Calibri** and change the font size to **12 pt**.
   f. Change the line spacing to **2.0** (Double).
   g. Turn on **Show/Hide**.
   h. Delete all the blank lines between the lines of text.

4. Add text to the document.
   a. Place the insertion point after "Seller" in the second line of the document and press **Tab** once.
   b. Type Property Address.
   c. Place the insertion point after "Escrow Company" and press **Tab** once.
   d. Type Escrow #.
   e. Place the insertion point after "Tasks to be Completed" and press **Tab** once.
   f. Type Date Completed.

5. Set tab stops using the ruler to align information. If the ruler does not display, check the **Ruler** box [*View* tab, *Show* group].
   a. Select the second and third lines of text (beginning with "**Seller**" and ending with "**Escrow #**").
   b. Verify that the **Left Tab** is selected in the *Tab* selector area to the left of the horizontal ruler.
   c. Click the ruler at **3.5"** to set a left tab stop. If you click the wrong location on the ruler, drag the tab stop to the correct location (Figure 2-108).

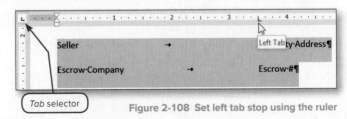

Figure 2-108 Set left tab stop using the ruler

     d. Select the fourth line of text (beginning with "Tasks").

     e. Click the **Tab** selector to change to a **Center Tab** stop (Figure 2-109).

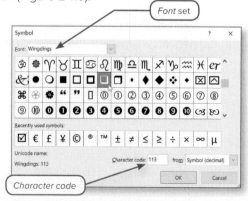

Figure 2-109 Center tab stop

     f. Click the ruler at **5.5"** to set a center tab stop.

6. Set tab stops and add leaders to create lines for users to fill in information.
     a. Select the second and third lines of text (beginning with "**Seller**" and ending with "**Escrow #**").
     b. Click the **Paragraph** launcher to open the *Paragraph* dialog box.
     c. Click the **Tabs** button to open the *Tabs* dialog box.
     d. Type 3 in the *Tab stop position* area.
     e. Click the **Right** radio button in the *Alignment* area.
     f. Click the **4** (solid underline) radio button in the *Leader* area.
     g. Click the **Set** button to set this tab stop.
     h. Type 6.5 in the *Tab stop position* area.
     i. Click the **Right** radio button in the *Alignment* area.
     j. Click the **4** (solid underline) radio button in the *Leader* area.
     k. Click the **Set** button to set this tab stop.
     l. Click **OK** to close the *Tabs* dialog box.

7. Use tab stops to align text and insert underline leader.
     a. Place the insertion point before "Property Address" and press **Tab** once.
     b. Place the insertion point to the right of "Property Address" and press **Tab** once.
     c. Place the insertion point before "Escrow #" and press **Tab** once.
     d. Place the insertion point to the right of "Escrow #" and press **Tab** once.

8. Apply styles to selected text and update a style.
     a. Place the insertion point in the first line of text ("Seller Escrow Checklist").
     b. Select **Title** style in the *Style* gallery [*Home* tab, *Styles* group].
     c. Change the *After* paragraph spacing to **24 pt**. [*Layout* tab, *Paragraph* group].
     d. Click the **Center** alignment button [*Home* tab, *Paragraph* group] to center the title.
     e. Select "**Tasks to be Completed**" and apply the **Book Title** style from the *Style* gallery.
     f. Change the font size of the selected text to **14 pt**. and apply a **Double underline**.
     g. Right-click the **Book Title** style in the *Style* gallery and select **Update Book Title to Match Selection**. The *Book Title* style is updated.
     h. Select "**Date Completed**" and apply the **Book Title** style.

9. Create a bulleted list to selected text and apply a custom bullet.
     a. Select the lines of text beginning with "**Open Escrow . . .**" and ending with "**Disclosures Sent to Agent**."
     b. Click the **Bullets** drop-down arrow [*Home* tab, *Paragraph* group] and select **Define New Bullet**. The *Define New Bullet* dialog box opens.
     c. Click the **Symbol** button to open the *Symbol* dialog box (Figure 2-110).
     d. Click the **Font** drop-down arrow and select **Wingdings**.
     e. Locate and select the **open square** bullet with a shadow (Character code 113).
     f. Click **OK** to close the *Symbol* dialog box.
     g. Click the **Font** button in the *Define New Bullet* dialog box. The *Font* dialog box opens.
     h. Change the *Size* to **14 pt**.
     i. Click **OK** to close the *Font* dialog box and click **OK** to close the *Define New Bullet* dialog box.
     j. Confirm the bulleted list is still selected and click the **Decrease Indent** button [*Home* tab, *Paragraph* group] to align the bulleted list at the left margin.

Figure 2-110 Select a symbol for a custom bullet

10. Change the hanging indent and add tab stops.
    a. Select the bulleted list if it is not already selected.
    b. Click the **Paragraph** launcher to open the *Paragraph* dialog box.
    c. Change the *Hanging* indent to **0.3"**.
    d. Click the **Tabs** button to open the *Tabs* dialog box (Figure 2-111).
    e. Type 4.5 in the *Tab stop position* area.
    f. Click the **Left** radio button in the *Alignment* area, click the **1 None** radio button in the *Leader* area, and click the **Set** button to set this tab stop.
    g. Type 6.5 in the *Tab stop position* area.
    h. Click the **Right** radio button in the *Alignment* area, click the **4** (solid underline) radio button in the *Leader* area, and click the **Set** button to set this tab stop, and click **OK** to close the *Tabs* dialog box.
    i. Place the insertion point after "Open Escrow with Escrow Company" and press **Tab** two times. A solid underline displays between 4.5" and 6.5".
    j. Repeat step i on the remaining lines in the bulleted list.

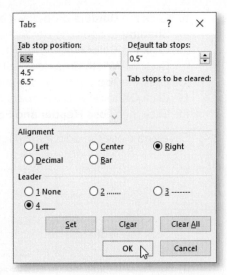
Figure 2-111 *Tabs* dialog box

11. Add text to the document.
    a. Place the insertion point at the end of the document (after the solid underline in the last line of text) and press **Enter**.
    b. Click the **Bullets** button [*Home* tab, *Paragraph* group] to turn off the bullet format for this line.
    c. Type Fax/Email Clear Pest Report and press **Enter**.
    d. Type Title and press **Enter**.
    e. Type Lender and press **Enter**.
    f. Type Buyer's Agent.

12. Apply a style to selected text and use the *Format Painter*.
    a. Select "**Fax/Email Clear Pest Report**" and apply the **Book Title** style from the *Style* gallery or mini toolbar.
    b. Place the insertion point in one of the bulleted items.
    c. Click the **Format Painter** button [*Home* tab, *Clipboard* group] to copy the formatting of this bulleted item.
    d. Select the last three lines of text (beginning with "**Title . . .**"). The *Format Painter* copies the bullet formatting and tab settings to these lines of text.
    e. Press **Tab** two times after each of these last three lines to insert the tabs and leaders.

13. Insert a document property field, the date, and a border in the footer of the document.
    a. Click the **Footer** button [*Insert* tab, *Header & Footer* group] and select **Edit Footer** from the drop-down list to open the footer.
    b. Click the **Document Info** button [*Header & Footer Tools Design* tab, *Insert* group], click **Document Property**, and select **Company**. The *Company* document property field displays in the footer.
    c. Press the **right arrow** key once to deselect the *Company* field.
    d. Press **Tab** two times, type Last updated:, and **space** once. The text aligns at the right side of the footer.
    e. Click the **Date & Time** button [*Header & Footer Tools Design* tab, *Insert* group] to open the *Date and Time* dialog box.
    f. Select the spelled-out month, day, year option (January 1, 2020), check the **Update automatically** box, and click **OK** to insert the date and close the dialog box.
    g. Select all the text in the footer and change the font to **Calibri** and the font size to **10 pt**.

h. Click the **Borders** drop-down arrow [*Home* tab, *Paragraph* group] and select **Borders and Shading** to open the *Borders and Shading* dialog box.

i. Click the **Color** drop-down list and select **Automatic** (if it is not already selected).

j. Click the **Width** drop-down list and select **½ pt**.

k. Click the **Top** border button in the *Preview* area to apply a top border to the footer.

l. Click **OK** to close the *Borders and Shading* dialog box.

m. Click the **Close Header and Footer** button [*Header & Footer Tools Design* tab, *Close* group].

14. Save and close the document (Figure 2-112).

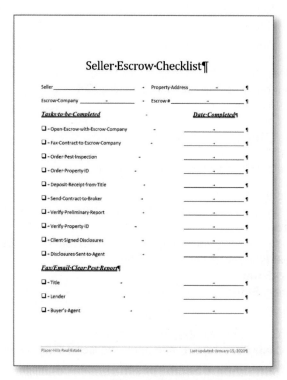

Figure 2-112 Word 2-2 completed

Guided Project 2-3

In this project, you edit and format the personal training guide for the American River Cycling Club to improve readability and effectiveness. You use find and replace, apply a document theme, modify styles, customize numbered and bulleted lists, apply borders and shading, and insert headers, footers, and document properties.
[Student Learning Outcomes 2.1, 2.3, 2.4, 2.6, 2.7, 2.8, 2.9]

File Needed: ***PersonalTrainingProgram-02.docx*** (*Student data files are available in the* Library *of your SIMnet account.*)

Completed Project File Name: *[your initials]* **Word 2-3.docx**

Skills Covered in This Project

- Modify an existing document.
- Apply a document theme.
- Change margins.
- Change line spacing and paragraph spacing.
- Apply a style to selected text.
- Apply borders and shading to selected text.
- Update an existing style.
- Customize a multilevel bulleted list.
- Use *Find*.
- Use *Find* and *Replace*.
- Insert a hyperlink.
- Insert header, footer, page number, and document properties.
- Use *Side to Side* page movement and *Thumbnails*.

1. Open the **PersonalTrainingProgram-02** document from your student data files.

2. Save this document as [your initials] Word 2-3.

3. Apply a document theme and change the line and paragraph spacing.
   a. Click the **Themes** button [*Design* tab, *Document Formatting* group] and select **Slice** from the drop-down list of theme options.
   b. Click the **Page Setup** launcher [*Layout* tab, *Page Setup* group] to open the *Page Setup* dialog box.
   c. Change the *Left* and *Right* margins to **1"** and click **OK** to close the *Page Setup* dialog box.
   d. Press **Ctrl+A** to select the entire document.
   e. Change the line spacing to **1.15** using the *Line and Paragraph Spacing* drop-down list.
   f. Change the *After* paragraph spacing to **10 pt**. on the entire document.
   g. Turn on **Show/Hide**.

4. Apply styles to the title, subtitle, and section headings.
   a. Select the title (first line) of the document.
   b. Apply the **Title** style from the *Style* gallery [*Home* tab, *Styles* group].
   c. Change the font size to **20 pt**. and apply **bold** and **center** alignment.
   d. Select the subtitle (second line) of the document.
   e. Apply the **Subtitle** style from the *Style* gallery [*Home* tab, *Styles* group].
   f. Change the font size to **16 pt**. and apply **center** alignment.
   g. Select the first section heading ("**General Guidelines**").
   h. Apply the **Heading 1** style from the *Style* gallery.
   i. Apply the **Heading 1** style to the remaining bold section headings in the document ("**Personal Training Program Guidelines**," "**More About Long Rides**," "**Training Intensity and Heart Rate**," "**Tracking Training Miles or Hours**," and "**Using a Training Log**").

5. Update a style in the document.
   a. Select the first section heading ("**General Guidelines**") including the paragraph mark at the end of the line.
   b. Change the *Before* paragraph spacing to **12 pt**. and the *After* paragraph spacing to **6 pt**.
   c. Click the **Borders** drop-down arrow [*Home* tab, *Paragraph* group] and select **Borders and Shading** to open the *Borders and Shading* dialog box.
   d. Select **Shadow** in the *Setting* area.
   e. Select the **solid line** (first option) in the *Style* area.
   f. Click the **Color** drop-down list and select the **fifth color** in the **last row** of the *Theme Colors* (**Dark Blue, Accent 1, Darker 50%**) (Figure 2-113).
   g. Click the **Width** drop-down list and select **1 pt**.
   h. Click the **Apply to** drop-down list and select **Paragraph** if necessary.
   i. Click the **Shading** tab, click the **Fill** drop-down list, and select the **fifth color** in the **second row** of the *Theme Colors* (**Dark Blue, Accent 1, Lighter 80%**).

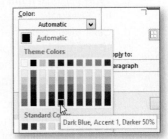

Figure 2-113 Select border line color

j. Click the **Apply to** drop-down list and select **Paragraph** if necessary.

k. Click **OK** to close the *Borders and Shading* dialog box. Confirm that "**General Guidelines**" is still selected.

l. Right-click the **Heading 1** style in the *Style gallery*, and select **Update Heading 1 to Match Selection**. All the headings in the document with the *Heading 1* style applied update automatically.

6. Customize the bullets and indents for the bulleted list.

a. Right-click the first bulleted item on the first page and select **Adjust List Indents**. The *Define new Multilevel list* dialog box opens.

b. Click **1** in the *Click level to modify* area.

c. Click the **Number style for this level** drop-down list and select **New Bullet** (Figure 2-114) to open the *Symbol* dialog box.

d. Click the **Font** drop-down list, select **Webdings**, click the **right pointing triangle** (Character code 52), and click **OK** to close the *Symbol* dialog box (Figure 2-115).

e. Click **2** in the *Click level to modify* area in the *Define new Multilevel list* dialog box.

f. Click the **Number style for this level** drop-down list and select **New Bullet** to open the *Symbol* dialog box.

g. Click the **Font** drop-down list, select **Webdings**, click the **double right pointing triangle** (Character code 56), and click **OK** to close the *Symbol* dialog box.

h. Click the **Set for All Levels** button in the *Define new Multilevel list* dialog box. The *Set for All Levels* dialog box opens (Figure 2-116).

i. Change the *Bullet/Number position for first level* to **0.25"**, change the *Text position for first level* to **0.5"**, and change *Additional indent for each level* to **0.25"**.

j. Click **OK** to close the *Set for All Levels* dialog box and click **OK** to close the *Define new Multilevel list* dialog box. All the first and second level bullets and indents in the entire document are changed.

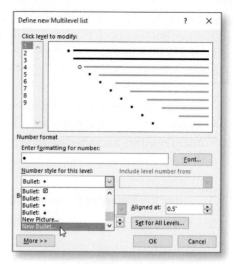

Figure 2-114 Customize bulleted list

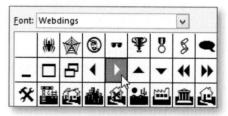

Figure 2-115 Select bullet from *Webdings* font set

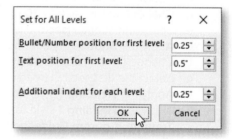

Figure 2-116 Set indents for all levels

7. Use the *Find* feature to find text in the document.

a. Place your insertion point at the beginning of the document (or press **Ctrl+Home**).

b. Click the **Find** button [*Home* tab, *Editing* group] or press **Ctrl+F** to open *Find* in the *Navigation* pane.

c. Type **personal training program** in the *Search Document* area. All instances of this text appear in the *Navigation* pane and are highlighted in the document.

d. Click after "personal training program" in the first body paragraph on the first page and type **(PTP)**. Verify one space displays before and after "(PTP)".

e. Select "**PTP**" (not the parentheses) and apply **italic** format.

f. Click the **X** in the upper-right corner of the *Navigation* pane to close this pane.

8. Use the replace feature to find and replace text in the document.

a. Place your insertion point at the beginning of the document (or press **Ctrl+Home**).

b. Click the **Replace** button [*Home* tab, *Editing* group] to open the *Find and Replace* dialog box with the *Replace* tab selected (Figure 2-117).

c. Type **personal training program** in the *Find what* area.

d. Type **PTP** in the *Replace with* area.

e. Click the **More** button to display more search options.

f. Click the **Format** button and select **Font** to open the *Replace Font* dialog box.

g. Click **Italic** in the *Font style* area and click **OK** to close the *Replace Font* dialog box.

h. Click the **Less** button to collapse the *Find and Replace* dialog box.

i. Click the **Find Next** button to find the first occurrence of "personal training program" in the document.

j. Do not replace this text in the title, first body paragraph, or section heading. Replace all other occurrences of "personal training program" with "PTP". Click the **Replace** button to replace the highlighted occurrence or click the **Find Next** button to skip and not replace an occurrence.

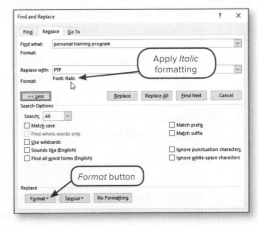

Figure 2-117 Replace text with text and formatting

k. Click **OK** when you are finished searching the document and click **Close** to close the *Find and Replace* dialog box.

9. Add a hyperlink to the document.

a. Select the subtitle of the document ("**American River Cycling Club**").

b. Click the top half of the **Link** button [*Insert* tab, *Links* group] or press **Ctrl+K** to open the *Insert Hyperlink* dialog box.

c. Click the **Existing File or web Page** button in the *Link to* area.

d. Type www.arcc.org in the *Address* area. Word automatically inserts "http://" before the web address.

e. Click the **ScreenTip** button to open the *Set Hyperlink ScreenTip* dialog box.

f. Type American River Cycling Club and click **OK** to close the *Set Hyperlink ScreenTip* dialog box.

g. Click the **Target Frame** button to open the *Set Target Frame* dialog box.

h. Select **New window** from the drop-down list.

i. Click **OK** to close the *Set Target Frame* dialog box and click **OK** to close the *Insert Hyperlink* dialog box.

10. Insert header and footer on the second and continuing pages.

a. Place your insertion point at the beginning of the document (or press **Ctrl+Home**).

b. Click the **Page Number** button [*Insert* tab, *Header & Footer* group].

c. Click **Top of Page** and select **Accent Bar 2** from the drop-down list. The page number displays in the header area.

d. Check the **Different First Page** check box [*Header & Footer Tools Design* tab, *Options* group] to remove the header from the first page so it only displays on the second and continuing pages.

11. Insert document property fields in the footer.

a. Open the header (if necessary) and click the **Go to Footer** button [*Navigation* group].

b. Click the **Next** button [*Navigation* group] to move to the footer on the second page.

c. Click the **Document Info** button [*Insert* group], click **Document Property**, and select **Company** to insert the company document property field.

d. Press the **right arrow** key once to deselect the property field.

e. Press **Tab** two times to move the insertion point to the right margin in the footer.

f. Click the **Document Info** button [*Insert* group] and select **Document Title** to insert the title document property field.

g. Press **Ctrl+A** to select all the text in the footer.

h. Apply **bold** and **italic** formatting and change the font size to **10 pt**.

     i.   Click the **Go to Header** button [*Header & Footer Tools Design* tab, *Navigation* group] to move to the header on the second page.

     j.   Press **Ctrl+A** to select all the text in the header and change the font size to **10 pt**.

     k.   Click the **Close Header and Footer** button [*Header & Footer Tools Design* tab, *Close* group]. The header and footer information should appear on the second and continuing pages in the document.

12. View the document in *Side to Side* page movement and view as *Thumbnails*.

     a.   Click the **Side to Side** button [*View* tab, *Page Movement* group] to display your document horizontally.

     b.   Scroll through the pages of your document using the left and right arrows keys or the scroll wheel on the mouse.

     c.   Click the **Thumbnails** button [*View* tab, *Zoom* group] to display all pages as thumbnails.

     d.   Select page **3** to view this page in *Side to Side* page movement view.

     e.   Click the **Vertical** button [*View* tab, *Page Movement* group] to return to your document.

13. Save and close the document (Figure 2-118).

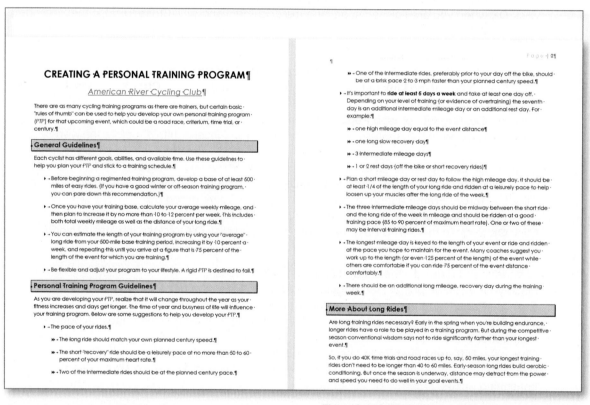

Figure 2-118 Word 2-3 completed (pages 1 and 2 of 5)

Independent Project 2-4

In this project, you use styles, indents, lists, tab stops, the replace feature, footers, and document properties to customize the Emergency Procedures document for Sierra Pacific Community College District. [Student Learning Outcomes 2.1, 2.2, 2.3, 2.4, 2.6, 2.7, 2.8, 2.9]

File Needed: ***EmergencyProcedures-02.docx*** *(Student data files are available in the* Library *of your SIMnet account.)*
Completed Project File Name: *[your initials] Word 2-4.docx*

Skills Covered in This Project

- Modify an existing document.
- Apply a document theme and theme color.
- Change margins and font size.
- Apply and modify a style.
- Apply a border to selected text.
- Apply and customize a numbered and bulleted list.
- Use the *Format Painter.*
- Set and modify tab stops.
- Use *Replace.*
- Insert a footer with document properties and current date.
- Insert a page border.
- Center text vertically.
- Use *Side to Side* page movement.

1. Open the ***EmergencyProcedures-02*** document from your student data files.

2. Save this document as [your initials] Word 2-4.

3. Change the theme to **Integral** and the theme color to **Red**.

4. Change the top, bottom, left, and right margins to **0.75"**.

5. Select the entire document and change the font size to **12 pt**.

6. Format the title of the document.
   a. Select the title of the document and apply **Heading 1** style.
   b. Open the *Font* dialog box, apply **All caps** effect, and change the font size to **16 pt**.
   c. Change the *Before* paragraph spacing to **0 pt**.
   d. Add a **bottom border** to the title using the **Borders** drop-down list.

7. Apply and modify the *Heading 2* style and delete blank lines.
   a. Apply the **Heading 2** style to each of the bold section headings.
   b. Select the first section heading ("**Emergency Telephones [Blue Phones]**").
   c. Change *Before* paragraph spacing to **12 pt**. and *After* paragraph spacing to **3 pt**.
   d. Apply **small caps** effect.
   e. Update **Heading 2** style to match selection. All the section headings are updated.
   f. Turn on **Show/Hide** and delete all the blank lines in the document.

8. Select the bulleted list in the first section and change it to a numbered list.

9. Apply numbering format and formatting changes, and use the *Format Painter.*
   a. Apply numbering to the text below the section headings in the following sections: "*Assaults, Fights, or Emotional Disturbances*"; "*Power Failure*"; "*Fire*"; "*Earthquake*"; and "*Bomb Threat.*"
   b. Select the numbered list in the "Bomb Threat" section.
   c. Open the *Paragraph* dialog box, set *Before* and *After* paragraph spacing to **2 pt**., deselect the **Don't add space between paragraphs of the same style** check box, and click **OK** to close the dialog box.
   d. Use the *Format Painter* to copy this numbering format to each of the other numbered lists.
   e. Reset each numbered list so it begins with **1** (right-click the first item in each numbered list and select **Restart at 1** from the context menu).

10. Customize a bulleted list and use the *Format Painter.*
   a. Select the text in the "Accident or Medical Emergency" section.
   b. Create a custom bulleted list and use a **double right-pointing triangle** symbol (*Webdings,* Character code 56).

    c. Open the *Paragraph* dialog box and confirm the left indent is **0.25"** and hanging indent is **0.25"**. If not, change the settings.

    d. Set *Before* and *After* paragraph spacing to **2 pt**. and deselect the **Don't add space between paragraphs of the same style** check box.

    e. Use the *Format Painter* to apply this bulleted list format to the following text in the following sections: "*Tips to Professors and Staff*" and "*Response to Students*."

11. Change indent and paragraph spacing and apply a style.
    a. Select the text below the "Emergency Telephone Locations" heading.
    b. Set a **0.25"** left indent.
    c. Set *Before* and *After* paragraph spacing to **2 pt**.
    d. Confirm the **Don't add space between paragraphs of the same style** box is unchecked (*Paragraph* dialog box).
    e. Apply **Book Title** style to each of the telephone locations in the "Emergency Telephone Locations" section. Select only the location, not the text in parentheses or following text.

12. Change left indent and paragraph spacing and set a tab stop with a dot leader.
    a. Select the text below the "Emergency Phone Numbers" heading.
    b. Open the *Paragraph* dialog box and set a **0.25"** left indent for this text.
    c. Set *Before* and *After* paragraph spacing to **2 pt**. and confirm the **Don't add space between paragraphs of the same style** box is unchecked.
    d. Open the *Tabs* dialog box, set a right tab stop at **7"**, and use a **dot leader (2)**.
    e. Press **Tab** before the phone number (after the space) on each of these lines. The phone numbers align at the right margin with a dot leader between the text and phone number.

13. Apply the **Intense Reference** style to the paragraph headings in the "Accident or Medical Emergency" section ("*Life-Threating Emergencies*" and "*Minor Emergencies*"). Include the colon when selecting the paragraph headings.

14. Use the *Replace* feature to replace all instances of "Phone 911" with "CALL 911" with **bold** font style. *Note*: If previous *Find* or *Replace* criteria displays in the *Replace* dialog box, remove this content before performing this instruction.

15. Insert a footer with document property fields and the current date that appears on every page.
    a. Edit the footer on the first page and use the ruler to move the center tab stop to **3.5"** and the right tab stop to **7"**.
    b. Insert the **Title** document property field on the left. Use the **right arrow** key to deselect the document property field.
    c. **Tab** to the center tab stop and insert the **Company** document property field at center. Use the **right arrow** key to deselect the document property field.
    d. **Tab** to the right tab stop, insert (not type) the date (use January 1, 2020 format), and set it to update automatically.
    e. Change the font size of all the text in the footer to **10 pt**.
    f. Add a **top border** to the text in the footer using the **Borders** drop-down list and close the footer.

16. Use the *Borders and Shading* dialog box to insert a **Page Border** on the entire document. Use **Shadow** setting and **solid line** style. Select the **fifth color** in the **first row** of the *Theme Colors* (**Dark Red, Accent 1**) and **1 pt**. line width.

17. Center the entire document vertically. (Hint: Use the *Page Setup* dialog box.)

18. View the document in **Side to Side** page movement view [*View* tab, *Page Movement* group] and then return to **Vertical** page movement view.

19. Save and close the document (Figure 2-119).

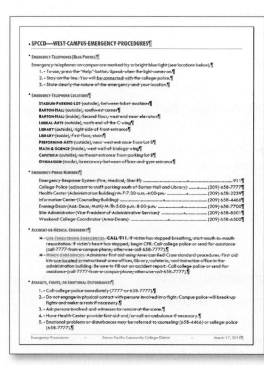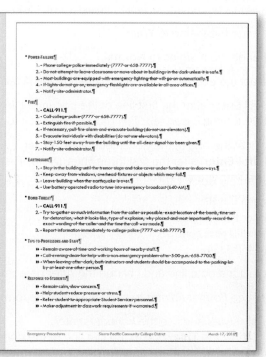

Figure 2-119 Word 2-4 completed

Independent Project 2-5

In this project, you format a bank authorization letter for Placer Hills Real Estate. You modify the formatting of an existing document, apply a theme, apply and modify styles, set tab stops, apply borders, and insert and edit hyperlinks.
[Student Learning Outcomes 2.1, 2.2, 2.7, 2.9]

File Needed: **BankAuthorization-02.docx** (Student data files are available in the Library of your SIMnet account.)
Completed Project File Name: **[your initials] Word 2-5.docx**

Skills Covered in This Project

- Modify an existing document.
- Apply a document theme.
- Change margins.
- Insert an automatically updated date.
- Apply and modify a style.

- Expand font spacing.
- Change paragraph spacing.
- Use the *Format Painter*.
- Set and use tab stops.
- Apply borders and shading to selected text.
- Insert a hyperlink.
- Edit a hyperlink.

1. Open the ***BankAuthorization-02*** document from your student data files.

2. Save this document as [your initials] Word 2-5.

3. Change the theme to **Wisp**.

4. Change the margins to **Normal**.

5. Select the entire document and change the *After* paragraph spacing to **18 pt**.

6. Press **Enter** after the first line of the document, insert (don't type) the current date (use January 1, 2020 format) [*Insert* tab, *Text* group], and set it to update automatically.

7. Click at the end of the document, press **Enter**, and type the following information. Use line breaks (**Shift+Enter**) after the first three lines. (*Note:* The email address is automatically converted to a hyperlink; you will edit this later.)

    Emma Cavalli
    Placer Hills Real Estate
    ecavalli@phre.com
    916-450-3334

8. Select the date line and change the *After* paragraph spacing to **30 pt**.

9. Use the *Format Painter* to copy the date line format to the "**Sincerely**," line.

10. Apply styles and use the *Format Painter*.
    a. Apply the **Title** style to the first line of the document and change the *Before* paragraph spacing to **36 pt**.
    b. Select "**Authorization Letter to Lender**," apply the **Intense Reference** style, and expand the font *Spacing* to **1 pt**.
    c. Select the five lines of text beginning with "**Bank/Financial Institution:**" and ending with "**Borrower Name(s):**" and apply the **Book Title** style.
    d. Use the *Format Painter* to copy the "Bank/Financial Institution" format to "**Seller/Borrower Signature(s)**".

11. Set a tab stop with a leader.
    a. Select the five lines of text beginning with "**Bank/Financial Institution:**" and ending with "**Borrower Name(s):**."
    b. Set a right tab stop at **6.5"** with a **solid underline leader (4)**.
    c. Press **Tab** after each of these five lines to insert the solid underline leader to the right margin.

12. Apply a border and shading to the paragraph.
    a. Select the paragraph beginning "**Please consider . . .**".
    b. Apply a border with **Shadow** setting, **solid line** style.
    c. Select the **second color** in the **second row** in the *Theme Colors* (**Black, Text 1, Lighter 50%**) and **1½ pt**. line width.
    d. Change the border **Options** so there is **4 pt**. from text on the top, bottom, left, and right.
    e. Set the shading **Fill** color to the **first color** in the **second row** in the *Theme Colors* (**White, Background 1, Darker 5%**).

13. Select the "**Seller/Borrower Signature(s)**" line and apply a **Custom** border that is **solid line**, **Automatic** color, and **2¼ pt**. width, and apply it to the **top** of the selected paragraph.

14. Insert and customize a hyperlink.
    a. Select "**Placer Hills Real Estate**" in the closing lines and insert a hyperlink.
    b. Type www.phre.com as the web page address.
    c. Type Placer Hills Real Estate as the *ScreenTip*.
    d. Set the target frame to **New window** and make this the default for all hyperlinks.

15. Edit the "ecavalli@phre.com" email hyperlink and type **Email Emma Cavalli** as the *ScreenTip*.

16. Save and close the document (Figure 2-120).

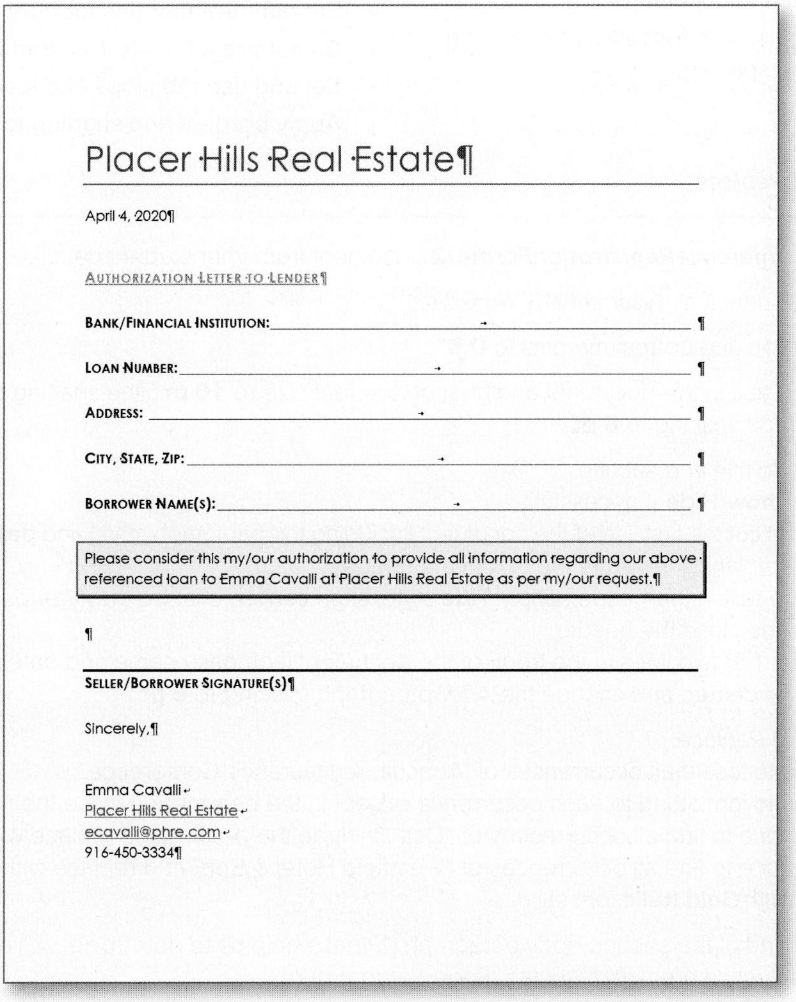

Placer Hills Real Estate¶

April 4, 2020¶

AUTHORIZATION LETTER TO LENDER¶

BANK/FINANCIAL INSTITUTION:_____¶

LOAN NUMBER: _____¶

ADDRESS: _____¶

CITY, STATE, ZIP: _____¶

BORROWER NAME(S): _____¶

Please consider this my/our authorization to provide all information regarding our above referenced loan to Emma Cavalli at Placer Hills Real Estate as per my/our request.¶

¶

SELLER/BORROWER SIGNATURE(S)¶

Sincerely,¶

Emma Cavalli
Placer Hills Real Estate
ecavalli@phre.com
916-450-3334¶

Figure 2-120 Word 2-5 completed

Independent Project 2-6

In this project, you edit, format, and customize the conference registration form for Central Sierra Insurance's Agriculture Insurance Conference. You use a continuous section break, find and replace text, set tab stops and leaders, apply styles, bullets, indents, borders, shading, and hyperlinks.
[Student Learning Outcomes 2.1, 2.2, 2.3, 2.4, 2.5, 2.6, 2.7, 2.8, 2.9]

File Needed: ***ConferenceRegistrationForm-02.docx*** *(Student data files are available in the* Library *of your SIMnet account.)*
Completed Project File Name: ***[your initials] Word 2-6.docx***

Skills Covered in This Project

- Modify an existing document.
- Change margins, font, font size, line spacing, and paragraph spacing.
- Insert a header.
- Apply a style.
- Use *Find and Replace*.
- Insert a continuous section break.
- Insert a horizontal line.
- Set different margins for different sections.
- Customize a bulleted list and indents.
- Set and use tab stops and leaders.
- Apply borders and shading to selected text.
- Insert hyperlinks.

---

1. Open the **ConferenceRegistrationForm-02** document from your student data files.

2. Save this document as [your initials] Word 2-6.

3. Change the top and bottom margins to **0.5"**.

4. Select all the text in the document and change the font size to **10 pt.**, line spacing to **1** (Single), and *After* paragraph spacing to **6 pt**.

5. Apply styles to title and subtitle.
   a. Turn on **Show/Hide** if necessary.
   b. Select and **cut** the first line of the document (including the paragraph mark) and **paste** it in the header.
   c. Delete the blank line below the text in the header.
   d. Select the text in the header, apply **Title** style, align **center**, change the *After* paragraph spacing to **6 pt.**, and close the header.
   e. Select the first two lines in the body of the document (company name and date), apply **Subtitle** style, align **center**, and change the *After* paragraph spacing to **6 pt**.

6. Use *Find* and *Replace*.
   a. Use *Find* to locate all occurrences of "Agriculture Insurance Conference."
   b. Apply **italic** formatting to each occurrence except in the header and close the *Navigation* pane.
   c. Use *Replace* to find all occurrences of "Oct." (include the period) and replace with "**May**".
   d. Use *Replace* to find all occurrences of "Westfield Hotel & Spa" and replace with "***Northgate Resort***" with **Bold Italic** font style.

7. Click at the end of the second body paragraph ("Please help us to determine . . .") and insert a **continuous** section break [*Layout* tab, *Page Setup* group].

8. Click the blank line below the section break and insert a **Horizontal Line** from the **Borders** drop-down list (see "Insert a Horizontal Line" in *SLO 2.9: Using Borders, Shading, and Hyperlinks*).

9. Place the insertion point in the document below the section break and change the left and right margins to **1.25"** and *Apply to* **This section**.

10. Set a tab stop with a leader.
    a. Select the first two lines of text below the horizontal line.
    b. Set a **right** tab stop at **6"** with a **solid underline leader (4)**.
    c. Press **Tab** after each of these lines to insert the solid underline leader to the right margin.

11. Define a new multilevel list and customize bullets and indents.
    a. Press the **Ctrl** key and select the four different bulleted lists in the document. The *Ctrl* key enables you to select non-adjacent text in the document. Don't select the text between each of the bulleted lists, and confirm all bulleted items are selected.
    b. Open the **Define new Multilevel list** dialog box (in the *Multilevel List* drop-down list).
    c. Change the level **1** *Number style* to a **New Bullet** and select the **shaded open square bullet** (*Wingdings,* Character code 113).
    d. Change levels **2** and **3** to the same bullet used on level 1.
    e. Change the **Font** size of the bullets on each of the first three levels to **12 pt**.
    f. **Set for All Levels** the indents so the first level begins at **0"**, the text position for first level begins at **0.25"**, and the additional indent for each level is **0.25"**.

12. Set tab stops with a leader.
   a. Select the "**Flying—Arrival time:**" line.
   b. Set a **right** tab stop at **3"** with a **solid underline leader (4)**.
   c. Press **Tab** after this line to insert the leader.
   d. Select the "**I need directions to *Northgate Resort* from:**" line.
   e. Set a **right** tab stop at **5"** with a **solid underline leader (4)**.
   f. Press **Tab** after this line to insert the leader.

13. Change indents and apply custom borders and shading to selected text.
   a. Select the last two lines in the document, align **center**, and change the left and right indents to **1"**.
   b. Open the *Borders and Shading* dialog box and select **Custom** in the *Settings* area.
   c. Apply a **double line** border, select the **fourth color** in the **first row** of the *Theme Colors* (**Dark Blue, Text 2**), select **¾ pt**. width, and apply to the **top** and **bottom** borders in the *Preview* area.
   d. Select the **Shading** tab, apply a **Fill** color, and select the **fourth color** in the **second row** of the *Theme Colors* (**Dark Blue, Text 2, Lighter 80%**).

14. Insert and customize hyperlinks to email addresses.
   a. Use *Find* to locate the first occurrence of "apelandale@centralsierra.com."
   b. Select this email address and insert a hyperlink to an email address.
   c. Type apelandale@centralsierra.com as the *Text to display* and *E-mail address*. In the *E-mail address* text box, "mailto:" is automatically inserted in front of the email address.
   d. Type **Email Asia Pelandale** as the *ScreenTip*.
   e. Repeat steps b–d above on the second occurrence of this email address.

15. Save and close the document (Figure 2-121).

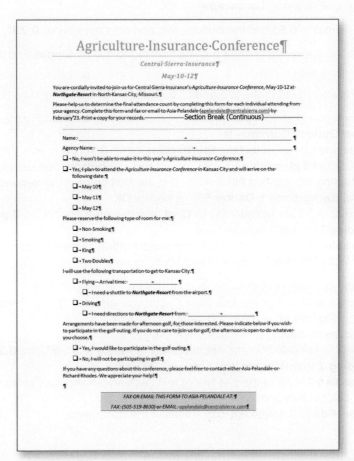

Figure 2-121 Word 2-6 completed

Improve It Project 2-7

In this project, you modify a document that contains shortcuts for Microsoft Outlook. Courtyard Medical Plaza wants to distribute the document to all of its employees. You use tab stops, styles, and many other page layout features that you have learned in this chapter to create a professional and attractive reference document.
[Student Learning Outcomes 2.1, 2.2, 2.4, 2.5, 2.7, 2.9]

File Needed: **OutlookShortcuts-02.docx** (Student data files are available in the Library of your SIMnet account.)
Completed Project File Name: **[your initials] Word 2-7.docx**

Skills Covered in this Project

- Modify an existing document.
- Change margins, line spacing, and paragraph spacing.
- Apply and modify a style.
- Apply borders and shading to selected text.
- Set and modify tab stops and leaders.
- Use the *Format Painter*.
- Insert a page break.
- Edit footer content and tab stops.

1. Open the **OutlookShortcuts-02** document from your student data files.
2. Save this document as [your initials] Word 2-7.
3. Change the page orientation to **Landscape**.
4. Change the top margin to **0.5"** and the bottom, left, and right margins to **0.75"**.
5. Select the entire document and change the line spacing to **1.0** (or **Single**) and the *After* paragraph spacing to **4 pt**.
6. Remove the bottom border from the title and change the *After* paragraph spacing to **0 pt**.
7. Apply custom borders and shading, change paragraph spacing, and modify the *Heading 1* style.
   a. Select "**Global Outlook Commands**."
   b. Apply a **single line** border, select the **fourth color** in the **first row** of the *Theme Colors* (**Dark Blue, Text 2**), select **1 pt**. width, and apply to the **top** and **bottom** borders in the *Preview* area.
   c. Select the **Shading** tab, apply a **Fill** color, select the **first color** in the **second row** of the *Theme Colors* (**White, Background 1, Darker 5%**), and click **OK**.
   d. Change the *Before* paragraph spacing to **12 pt**. and the *After* spacing to **0 pt**.
   e. Update **Heading 1** to match selected text.
   f. Apply the **Heading 1** style to each of the remaining bolded section headings ("*Mail,*" "*Calendar,*" "*Contacts,*" "*Tasks,*" "*Notes,*" "*Journal,*" and "*Formatting*").
8. Change paragraph spacing, set tab stops, and modify the *Heading 2* style.
   a. Select the third line of text on the first page ("Activity Shortcut . . .") and change the *Before* paragraph spacing to **6 pt**. and the *After* spacing to **3 pt**.
   b. Apply **Small caps** formatting to the selected text.
   c. Confirm the text is still selected and set three **left** tab stops at **3"**, **5"**, and **8.25"**.
   d. Update **Heading 2** to match selected text.
   e. Apply the **Heading 2** style to the first line of text ("Activity Shortcut . . .") after each section heading to create column headings.
   f. Turn on **Show/Hide** and delete any blank lines in the document.

9. Set tab stops and leaders to align text under the column headings and use the *Format Painter* to copy formatting.
   a. Select all the tabbed text in the first section ("Global Outlook Commands") below the column headings ("ACTIVITY SHORTCUT . . .") beginning with "**Go to Mail**" and ending with "**Delete selected item Ctrl+D**."
   b. Set the following tabs stops:
      3" left tab stop with **dot leader (2)**
      5" left tab stop with **no leader (1)**
      8.25" left tab stop with **dot leader (2)**
   c. Use the *Format Painter* to apply these tab settings to the remaining text below the column headings ("ACTIVITY SHORTCUT . . .") in all the other sections.

10. Remove the existing footer and insert a custom footer.
    a. Place your insertion point at the beginning of the document.
    b. Edit the footer and remove all content.
    c. Open the *Tabs* dialog box, **Clear All** existing tab stops, set a **center** tab stop at **4.75"**, and a **right** tab stop at **9.5"**.
    d. Insert the **Company** document property field on the left side of the footer.
    e. Press the **right arrow** key to deselect the document property field, **tab** to the center tab stop, and insert the **Title** (or **Document Title**) document property field.
    f. Press the **right arrow** key to deselect the document property field, **tab** to the right tab stop.
    g. Type Page, **space** once, insert a plain page number in the current position.
    h. **Space** once, type of, **space** once, and insert the **NumPages** field (use **1,2,3. . .** format).
    i. Apply a **single line** border, select the **fourth color** in the **first row** of the *Theme Colors* (**Dark Blue, Text 2**), select **1 pt**. width, and apply to the **top** border in the *Preview* area.
    j. Change the font size of all of the text in the footer to **10 pt**.
    k. Set the footer so it does not appear on the first page and close the footer.

11. Insert a **Page** break on the third page before the "Formatting" heading. This document fits on four pages.

12. Save and close the document (Figure 2-122).

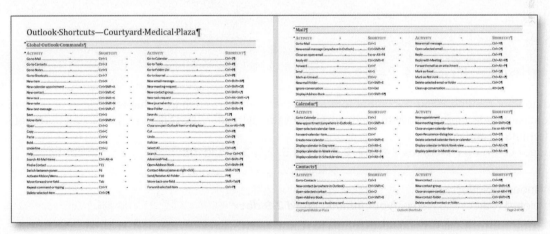

Figure 2-122 Word 2-7 completed (pages 1 and 2 of 4)

Challenge Project 2-8

Create an agenda for an upcoming meeting for an organization you are a member of, such as a club, church committee, volunteer organization, student group, or neighborhood association. Research online to find the common components of agendas. Robert's Rules of Order is a good source of information about meetings and guidelines for meeting protocol.
[Student Learning Outcomes 2.1, 2.2, 2.3, 2.6, 2.7, 2.9]

File Needed: None
Completed Project File Name: *[your initials] Word 2-8.docx*

Create a new document and save it as [your initials] Word 2-8. An agenda can include, but is not limited to, the following items:

- Organization name as the title
- Meeting date, start time, and end time
- Meeting location
- Meeting attendees
- Topic headings
- Topic subheadings (include details for each topic heading)
- The time each topic is expected to last

Modify your document according to the following guidelines:

- Apply styles.
- Use a multilevel list for the agenda items and subheadings.
- Customize number or bullet format and indents as needed.
- Use a right tab stop with a leader to align the amount of time allocated for each main topic heading.
- Apply borders, shading, and/or a horizontal line to create an attractive agenda.
- Adjust margins as needed.
- Include an appropriate header and/or footer.

Challenge Project 2-9

Update your resume using document formatting features learned in this chapter. Edit your resume so it is consistently formatted, easy to read, and professional looking. Research resumes online to get ideas for formatting and content.
[Student Learning Outcomes 2.1, 2.2, 2.3, 2.4, 2.5, 2.6, 2.7, 2.8, 2.9]

File Needed: None
Completed Project File Name: *[your initials] Word 2-9.docx*

Open an existing resume or create a new document and save it as [your initials] Word 2-9. Modify your document according to the following guidelines:

- Apply a document theme.
- Use the *Resume Assistant* (if available) to find examples of similar resumes.

- Apply styles to headings and subheadings to improve consistency in format.
- Adjust margins as needed.
- Use bulleted lists with customized bullets and indents to attractively arrange information.
- Set and use tab stops and indents as necessary to align information.
- Apply borders, shading, and/or a horizontal line to emphasize information in your resume.
- Use page or section breaks as needed.
- Use *Find and Replace* as needed.
- Insert hyperlinks for appropriate information (email address and company names).
- Include a header and/or footer on the second and continuing pages if your resume is more than one page.

Challenge Project 2-10

Format your favorite recipe using some of the formatting features learned in this chapter. Review online recipes using the Food Network, Epicurious, Simply Recipes, or other food web sites.
[Student Learning Outcomes 2.1, 2.2, 2.3, 2.6, 2.7, 2.9]

File Needed: None
Completed Project File Name: *[your initials] Word 2-10.docx*

Create a new document and save it as [your initials] Word 2-10. Your recipe should include, but is not limited to, the following:
- Recipe title
- Descriptive paragraph about the recipe
- Tab stops to arrange quantity and ingredients (and special instructions if needed)
- Numbered, step-by-step instructions
- Recipe source and/or additional information

Modify your document according to the following guidelines:
- Apply a document theme.
- Apply styles.
- Adjust margins as needed.
- Set and use a combination of tab stops (left, right, center, decimal, bar, and leaders) as necessary to attractively line up information.
- Use a numbered list for instructions.
- Use left, right, first line, and/or hanging indents as necessary.
- Apply borders, shading, page border, and/or a horizontal line to highlight or emphasize information in your recipe.
- Insert hyperlinks to appropriate information (link to online recipe).

Collaborating with Others and Working with Reports

CHAPTER OVERVIEW

Creating a long report with a table of contents, citations, footnotes or endnotes, a reference page, and headers and footers can be a challenging task. Word includes numerous tools to automatically create components in a report or a multipage document. Using these tools not only saves you time, it also improves consistency within your documents. Word also provides a variety of collaboration tools to help you more efficiently and effectively work with others on documents.

STUDENT LEARNING OUTCOMES (SLOs)

After completing this chapter, you will be able to:

SLO 3.1 Insert, review, edit, and customize comments (p. 139).

SLO 3.2 Modify and review a document using *Track Changes* and share an online document (p. 142).

SLO 3.3 Insert and edit footnotes and endnotes in a document (p. 151).

SLO 3.4 Create a bibliography with properly formatted sources and insert citations into a document (p. 156).

SLO 3.5 Create and edit a table of contents based on headings (p. 168).

SLO 3.6 Insert a cover page and modify content and content control fields (p. 172).

SLO 3.7 Apply and customize headers and footers in a multipage document (p. 175).

CASE STUDY

American River Cycling Club (ARCC) is a community cycling club that promotes fitness for the entire region. ARCC members include recreational cyclists who enjoy the exercise and camaraderie, as well as competitive cyclists who compete in road, mountain, and cyclocross races throughout the cycling season.

For the Pause & Practice projects, you create a report for club members to describe how to develop a personal training program. In this report, you incorporate many of the report features covered in the chapter to produce a professional-looking and useful report.

Pause & Practice 3-1: Review a report that includes comments and edits marked with tracked changes.

Pause & Practice 3-2: Insert endnotes into the report, convert endnotes to footnotes, add reference sources, insert citations, and create a bibliography page.

Pause & Practice 3-3: Apply styles to headings, create a table of contents based on the headings in the document, modify the table of contents, insert a cover page, customize headers and footers, and share an online file.

WORD

Using Comments

When you are collaborating with others on a report or document, use *comments* to provide feedback in the document without making changes to the text of the document. For example, use comments to ask a question, include a suggestion, record notes to yourself, or provide additional information. You can also customize how comments appear in a document, review comments in a document, edit comments, and delete comments.

Change User Name

Each comment and tracked change in a document is attributed to the user name stored in Office. When you sign in to Word with your Microsoft Account, Word uses this information as the *user name*. Word uses your user name as the *author* of each new document created. Each person editing a document is referred to as a *reviewer*.

If you are using a public computer, such as in a computer lab on your college campus, the user name is a generic name assigned to Office for that computer. To make sure the comments you add in a document are attributed to you, change your user name and initials in Office.

▶HOW TO: Change User Name

1. Click the **Tracking** launcher [*Review* tab, *Tracking* group] to open the *Track Changes Options* dialog box.

2. Click the **Change User Name** button to open the *Word Options* dialog box (Figure 3-1).

3. Type your name in the *User name* text box in the *Personalize your copy of Microsoft Office* area.

4. Type your initials in the *Initials* text box.

5. Check the **Always use these values regardless of sign in to Office** box.

6. Click **OK** to close the *Word Options* dialog box.

7. Click **OK** to close the *Track Changes Options* dialog box.

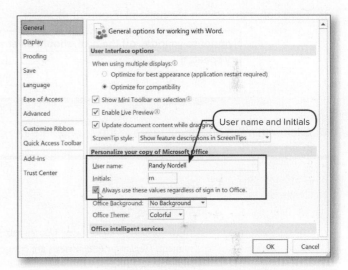

Figure 3-1 Change user name and initials in the *Word Options* dialog box

---

> ▶ **ANOTHER WAY**
>
> Click the **File** tab to open the *Backstage* view. Click **Options** to open the *Word Options* dialog box to change user name and initials.

Insert a Comment

When you insert a comment, the comment appears in a *balloon* in the *Markup area*, which is the area to the right of a document. The *Markup* area opens when a document has comments or tracked changes (we discuss tracking changes in *SLO 3.2: Using Track Changes and Sharing*). Comments in a document are marked with the name of the author of the comment and the time or date the comment was created. The text of the comment appears below the author's name in the balloon.

▶ HOW TO: Insert a Comment

1. Select the text at the location to insert a comment.
   - When you place your insertion point at the beginning of a word or within a word, the comment is attached to the entire word.

2. Click the **New Comment** button [*Review* tab, *Comments* group] (Figure 3-2).

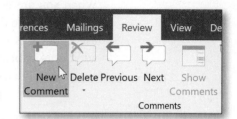

Figure 3-2 *New Comment* button

   - Alternatively, right-click text in the document and select **New Comment** from the context menu.
   - Additionally, in Office 365, click the **Comments** icon in the upper-right corner of the Word window and select **New Comment** (Figure 3-3). This button is not available in Office 2019.
   - The comment balloon appears in the *Markup* area to the right of the Word window.
   - The comment time or date displays as either minutes or hours ago (for example, *4 minutes ago*), or if it was created more than 24 hours ago, the date displays.
   - The word or words in the document with the comment attached are highlighted.

Figure 3-3 Insert *New Comment*

3. Type comment text in the balloon (Figure 3-4).

Figure 3-4 Comment in a balloon in the *Markup* area

4. Click within the document to leave the *Markup* area.

> ▶ **MORE INFO**
>
> The *Display for Review* view [*Review* tab, *Tracking* group] determines how comments display in the document. *Display for Review* views are covered in the next section, *SLO 3.2: Using Track Changes and Sharing*.

Ink Comments

Another option to insert a comment is to use *Ink Comment*. **Ink Comment** is used to hand write a comment or note using a stylus or your finger on a touch-screen computer. Ink comments function similarly to comments except they display larger in the *Markup* area, and an eraser is used to remove text from the comment. This feature is not available on computers without a touch screen.

Figure 3-5 *Ink Comment* in the *Markup* area

▶ HOW TO: Use Ink Comments

1. Select the text at the location to insert a comment.

2. Click the **Ink Comment** button [*Review* tab, *Comments* group] (Figure 3-5).
   - The comment balloon appears in the *Markup* area to the right of the Word window.

3. Use your finger or stylus to write a comment in the *Ink Comment* area.
   - To remove text in an ink comment, click the **Eraser** button [*Review* tab, *Comments* group] and use your finger, stylus, or pointer to erase the text in the comment.
4. Click within the document to return to the document.

Review Comments

Each comment in a document is attributed to the reviewer who made the comment. When you place your pointer on text in a document where a comment is attached, a tag displays with the reviewer's name, the date and time of the comment, and the comment text (Figure 3-6).

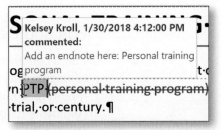

Figure 3-6 Comment details displayed in a tag

If you are working on a long document with multiple comments, Word provides navigation tools to move to the next or previous comment in the document. Click the **Next** or **Previous** button in the *Comments* group on the *Review* tab (Figure 3-7) to move to the next or previous comment in your document.

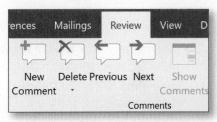

Figure 3-7 Move to the next or previous comment

> **ANOTHER WAY**
>
> Click the **Comments** icon in the upper-right corner of the Word window and select **Previous** or **Next**.

Reply to a Comment

To reply to a comment, click the **Reply** button on the right side of the comment in the *Markup* area (Figure 3-8). A reply area opens within the existing comment. Type a reply below the original comment.

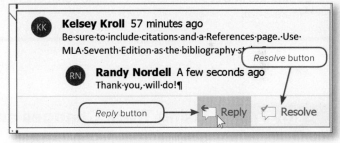

Figure 3-8 Reply to a comment

> **ANOTHER WAY**
>
> Right-click an existing comment in the *Markup* area or the highlighted text in a document with a comment attached. Select **Reply To Comment** from the context menu.

Resolve Comment

You can also resolve a comment after you take action on the comment and when you don't want the comment deleted. When a comment is resolved, the text of the comment changes to a light gray color, and the highlighted text in the document where the comment is attached is a lighter shade of the comment color.

To resolve a comment, click the **Resolve** button on the comment (see Figure 3-8). Alternatively, right-click a comment in the *Markup* area and select **Resolve Comment** from the context menu (Figure 3-9). Reopen a resolved comment by clicking the **Reopen** button on the comment or right-clicking the comment and selecting **Reopen Comment**.

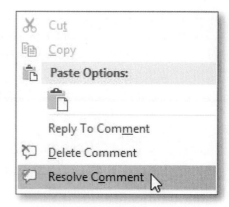

Figure 3-9 *Resolve Comment* from the context menu

Edit and Delete Comments

Edit a comment by clicking the comment balloon and editing existing text or typing new text. Once you finish reviewing comments, you can delete them. Delete comments individually or delete all the comments in the document at once.

▶**HOW TO: Delete Comments**

1. Click the comment balloon in the *Markup* area.
   - Alternatively, click **Next** or **Previous** [*Review* tab, *Comments* group] to select a comment (see Figure 3-7).
2. Click the top half of the **Delete** button [*Review* tab, *Comments* group] to delete the selected comment.
   - Alternatively, right-click a comment and select **Delete Comment** from the context menu.
3. Click the bottom half of the **Delete** button and select **Delete All Comments in Document** to delete all the comments in the document (Figure 3-10).

Figure 3-10 Delete all comments in the document

SLO 3.2

Using Track Changes and Sharing

Track Changes is a valuable editing tool in Word that marks changes in a document. All reviewers can see changes to the document. This feature is very useful when working with a group on a report or project. As you review tracked changes in a document, accept, reject, or skip the marked changes. Different options are available for viewing how tracked changes display in the document. Word also provides the ability to share online documents with others and use real-time collaboration.

Track Changes

To mark editing changes in a document, you must first turn on *Track Changes*. Once *Track Changes* is turned on, all editing and formatting changes are marked in the document. Tracked changes display in the body of the document and in balloons in the *Markup* area. Each line in the document that has a change is marked with a vertical gray or red line (depending on *Display for Review* view, which is covered in the next section) to the left of the line. Reviewers can easily see where changes have been made.

▶ HOW TO: Use Track Changes

1. Click the top half of the **Track Changes** button [*Review* tab, *Tracking* group] (Figure 3-11).
   - When *Track Changes* is turned on, the button is highlighted.
   - Alternatively, click the bottom half of the **Track Changes** button and select **Track Changes** to turn on *Track Changes*.
2. Edit, delete, insert, or format text in the document.
   - The *Display for Review* view determines how editing changes appear in the document. The *Display for Review* views are covered in the next section.
3. Click the top half of the **Track Changes** button to turn off *Track Changes*.

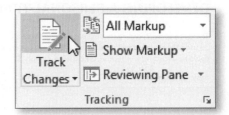

Figure 3-11 Turn on *Track Changes*

▶ **ANOTHER WAY**

Ctrl+Shift+E toggles *Track Changes* on and off.

Display for Review Views

The ***Display for Review*** view determines the appearance of editing changes in a document when using *Track Changes*. Click the **Display for Review** drop-down list in the *Tracking* group on the *Review* tab to select a *Display for Review* view (Figure 3-12). Table 3-1 lists and describes each of these different views.

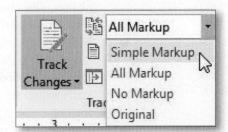

Figure 3.12 *Display for Review* views

Table 3-1: Display for Review Views

Display for Review View	Description
Simple Markup	Displays a final version of the document with the proposed changes incorporated. A red line to the left of a line marks changed lines in the document. Click the **Show Comments** button [*Review* tab, *Comments* group] to display or hide comments in the document.
All Markup	Displays added, deleted, and edited text in the body of the document. Formatting changes and comments display in balloons on the right. A gray line to the left of a line marks changed lines in the document.
No Markup	Displays a final version of the document with the proposed changes incorporated. All editing changes and comments are hidden.
Original	Displays the original document with proposed changes not incorporated. All editing changes and comments are hidden.

All Markup view is typically used when reviewing a document with changes tracked (Figure 3-13). When using *Simple Markup*, *No Markup*, or *Original* view, the tracked changes are still in the document, but they are hidden so you can view the final or original version without markup displayed. It is important to understand these different views when using *Track Changes* to edit a document.

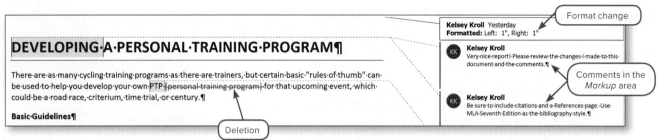

Figure 3-13 Changes tracked in a document displayed in *All Markup* view

Accept and Reject Changes

After a document has been marked with editing changes, you can review each proposed change and either accept or reject the change. It's best to work in *All Markup* view when reviewing a document with changes tracked. When you accept an editing or formatting change, the change is applied to the document, and the inline markup and/or balloon is removed. When you reject an editing or formatting change, the text and formatting revert back to their original form.

Similar to comments, each editing change is attributed to a reviewer. Place your pointer on a change in the body of the text or on a balloon to display a tag containing the reviewer's name, the date and time of the change, and a description of the change (Figure 3-14).

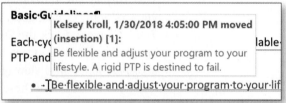

Figure 3-14 Tracked changes details displayed in a tag

▶HOW TO: Accept and Reject Changes

1. Place the insertion point at the beginning of the document (**Ctrl+Home**).

2. Click the **Display for Review** drop-down list [*Review* tab, *Tracking* group] and select **All Markup** if this is not the current view.

3. Click the **Next** button [*Review* tab, *Changes* group] to select the next change made to the document (Figure 3-15).

   - Click the **Previous** button to select the previous revision.
   - If you are in *No Markup* or *Original* view and click the *Next* or *Previous* button, the view automatically changes to *All Markup*.

4. Click the **Accept** or **Reject** button [*Review* tab, *Changes* group] to accept or reject the change and move to the next revision.

   - Click the bottom half of the **Accept** button to display additional options: *Accept and Move to Next, Accept This Change, Accept All Changes Shown, Accept All Changes,* and *Accept All Changes and Stop Tracking* (Figure 3-16).

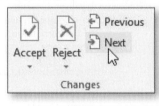

Figure 3-15 Move to the next revision in the document

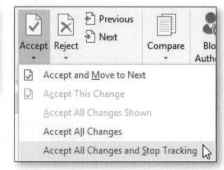

Figure 3-16 *Accept All Changes and Stop Tracking* option

- Click the bottom half of the **Reject** button to display additional options: *Reject and Move to Next*, *Reject Change*, *Reject All Changes Shown*, *Reject All Changes*, and *Reject All Changes and Stop Tracking*.
- When accepting and rejecting changes, Word also stops on comments. Click **Accept** to leave the comment in the document or **Reject** to delete the comment.
- Click **Next** to skip a comment or revision in the document.

5. Continue accepting or rejecting changes in the document.

6. Click **OK** in the dialog box that confirms no more comments or tracked changes are in the document. (Figure 3-17).

- When all changes have been accepted or rejected, no vertical lines display to the left of the text in the body of the document.

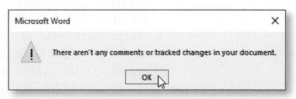

Figure 3-17 Dialog box that appears after reviewing the document

---

Reviewing Pane

When working with a document that has many tracked changes or comments, the ***Reviewing pane*** is a useful tool. The *Reviewing* pane is a separate pane that includes all tracked changes and comments. It can be displayed vertically on the left side of the Word window or horizontally at the bottom of the Word window (Figure 3-18). If many changes and comments display in a document and all the balloons cannot fit in the *Markup* area, the *Reviewing* pane automatically opens.

To open the *Reviewing* pane, click the **Reviewing Pane** button in the *Tracking* group on the *Review* tab and select either **Reviewing Pane Vertical** or **Reviewing Pane Horizontal**.

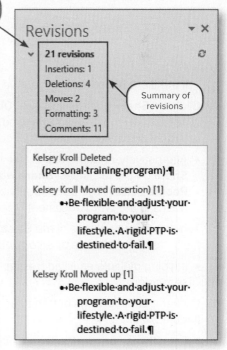

Figure 3-18 *Reviewing* pane displayed vertically

At the top of the *Reviewing* pane, a summary displays the number of revisions in the document. Click the arrow to the left of the revision summary to display the number of insertions, deletions, moves, formatting changes, and comments in the document. Right-click any of the revisions in the *Reviewing* pane and select **Accept** or **Reject** from the context menu.

Share an Online File

In addition to collaborating with others on a document using *Comments* and *Track Changes*, Word also provides you with the option of sharing an online file with others. Sharing an online file gives you the ability to work with others on the same file at the same time, which is called *real-time collaboration*.

To share a file, it must first be saved in *OneDrive*. If you try to share a file that is not saved in *OneDrive*, Word prompts you to save your document to *OneDrive* before sharing it. Depending on the type of Microsoft account you're using, the sharing options display in a ***Send Link*** window (education and business Microsoft accounts) (Figure 3-19) or the ***Share*** pane (personal Microsoft account). The *Send Link* window or *Share* pane provides options to type or select recipients, set the permission level of the shared file, type a message recipients receive through email, or get a sharing link.

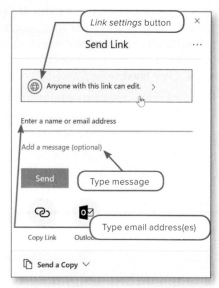

Figure 3-19 *Send Link* window

▶HOW TO: Share an Online File (Education and Business Microsoft Accounts)

1. Open the file to share.
   - If the file is not saved in *OneDrive*, save the file to *OneDrive*.

2. Click the **Share** button (Figure 3-20) in the upper-right corner of the Word window to open the *Send Link* window (see Figure 3-19). The *Share* button icon may display differently in Office 2019.

   Figure 3-20 *Share* button

   - Alternatively, click the **File** button to open the *Backstage* view, click **Share** on the left, select **Share with People**, and click the **Share with People** button. The *Backstage* view closes and the *Send Link* window opens in the Word document.

3. Type the email address of the person with whom you are sharing the file in the *Enter a name or email address* area.
   - If typing multiple email addresses, separate each with a semicolon.

4. Click the **Link settings** button to open the *Link settings* window (Figure 3-21).
   - Select who can use the sharing link.
   - Check the **Allow editing** box to enable recipients to edit the shared file. Deselect the **Allow editing** box to enable recipients to open and view the shared file, but restrict them from editing it.
   - Set an expiration date for the sharing link if desired (optional).

5. Click **Apply** to set the sharing link options and to return to the *Send Link* window.

6. Type a message to recipient(s) in the *Add a message* area. This is optional.

7. Click the **Send** button. An email is sent to people you invited.

8. Click the **X** to close the confirmation window.

Figure 3-21 *Link settings* window

If you're using a personal Microsoft account, the *Share* pane opens at the right after you click the *Share* button.

▶HOW TO: Share an Online File (Personal Microsoft Account)

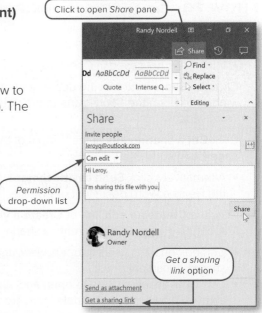

Click to open *Share* pane

1. Open the file to share.
   - If the file is not saved in *OneDrive*, save the file to *OneDrive*.
2. Click the **Share** button in the upper-right corner of the Word window to open the *Share* pane to the right of the Word window (Figure 3-22). The *Share* button icon may display differently in Office 2019.
3. Type or select the email address of the person with whom you are sharing the file in the *Invite people* area.
4. Select **Can edit** or **Can view** from the *Permission* drop-down list.
   - *Can edit* enables users to edit a shared document.
   - *Can view* enables users to open and view a shared document but restricts users from editing the document.

   Permission drop-down list

5. Type a message to recipient(s) in the *Message* area.
6. Click the **Share** button. An email is sent to people you invited.
7. Click the **X** to close the *Share* pane.

Get a sharing link option

Figure 3-22 Share a *OneDrive* file using the *Share* pane

Create a Sharing Link

Creating a sharing link (hyperlink) is another way to share a file with others rather than sending an email through Word. You can create and copy a sharing link and email the sharing link to others. You have the option of creating an *Edit link* or a *View-only link*.

▶HOW TO: Create a Sharing Link (Education and Business Microsoft Accounts)

1. Open the file to share.
   - If the file is not saved in *OneDrive*, you are prompted to save the file to *OneDrive*.
2. Click the **Share** button in the upper right of the Word window to open the *Send Link* window.
3. Click the **Link settings** button to open the *Link settings* window (see Figure 3-21).
   - Select who can use the sharing link.
   - Check the **Allow editing** box to enable recipients to edit the shared file. Deselect the **Allow editing** box to enable recipients to open and view the shared file, but restrict them from editing it.
   - Set an expiration date for the sharing link if desired (optional).
4. Click **Apply** to set the sharing link options and to return to the *Send Link* window.
5. Click the **Copy Link** button to open the window that displays the sharing link (Figure 3-23).
6. Click the **Copy** button to copy the sharing link.
7. Click the **X** to close the confirmation window.
8. Paste the copied sharing link in an email, Word document, or other online location.

Link to 'PP W3-3.docx' copied

https://officeinpracticecom-my   Copy

Anyone with this link can edit.

Figure 3-23 Copy sharing link

Sharing permissions

If you're using a personal Microsoft account, the *Share* pane opens at the right after you click the *Share* button.

▶HOW TO: Create a Sharing Link (Personal Microsoft Account)

1. Open the file to share.
   - If the file is not saved in *OneDrive*, you are prompted to save the file to *OneDrive*.

2. Click the **Share** button in the upper right of the Word window to open the *Share* pane to the right of the Word window.

3. Click **Get a sharing link** at the bottom of the *Share* pane (see Figure 3-22).
   - Alternatively, click **Send as attachment** to email the file as a Word document or PDF file.

4. Click the **Create an edit link** or **Create a view-only link** button (Figure 3-24) to create a sharing link.
   - *Can edit* enables users to open, view, and edit a shared document.
   - *Can view* enables users to open and view a shared document but restricts users from editing the document.

5. Click the **Copy** button to copy the sharing link (Figure 3-25).

6. Click the **Back** arrow to the left of *Get a sharing link* at the top of the *Share* pane to return to the main *Share* pane, or click the **X** to close the *Share* pane.

7. Paste the copied sharing link in an email, Word document, or other online location.

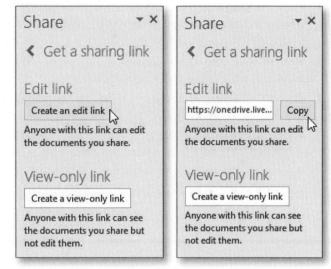

Figure 3-24 Create a sharing link   Figure 3-25 Copy a sharing link

PAUSE & PRACTICE: WORD 3-1

For this Pause & Practice project, you modify the *Developing a Personal Training Program* report for American River Cycling Club using comments and *Track Changes*.

Files Needed: ***PersonalTrainingProgram-03.docx*** (*Student data files are available in the* Library *of your SIMnet account.*)
Completed Project File Names: ***[your initials] PP W3-1.docx***

1. Open the ***PersonalTrainingProgram-03*** document from your student data files.

2. Save the document as [your initials] PP W3-1.

3. Change user name and initials.
   a. Click the **Tracking** launcher [*Review* tab, *Tracking* group] to open the *Track Changes Options* dialog box.
   b. Click the **Change User Name** button to open the *Word Options* dialog box.
   c. Type your first and last name in the *User name* text box in the *Personalize your copy of Microsoft Office* area.
   d. Type your first and last initials in lowercase letters in the *Initials* text box.
   e. Check the **Always use these values regardless of sign in to Office** box.

f. Click **OK** to close the *Word Options* dialog box.

g. Click **OK** to close the *Track Changes Options* dialog box.

4. Change *Display for Review* view.

   a. Click the **Display for Review** drop-down list [*Review* tab, *Tracking* group] and select **Original** to view the original document without changes (Figure 3-26).

   b. Click the **Display for Review** drop-down list again and select **No Markup** to view the final document with proposed changes applied.

   c. Click the **Display for Review** drop-down list again and select **Simple Markup** to view the document with proposed changes applied. A red line on the left indicates changes in the document.

   d. Click the **Show Comments** button [*Review* tab, *Comments* group] to hide comment text if the text displays in the balloons. Only comment balloons display.

   e. Click the **Display for Review** drop-down list again and select **All Markup** to view the final document with proposed changes visible inline and comments in balloons in the *Markup* area.

Figure 3-26 Change *Display for Review* view

5. Display the *Reviewing* pane and reject changes.

   a. Click the **Reviewing Pane** drop-down arrow [*Review* tab, *Tracking* group] and select **Reviewing Pane Vertical**. The *Reviewing* pane displays on the left side of the Word window.

   b. Find the moved bulleted item ("Kelsey Kroll Moved (insertion) [1]") in the *Reviewing* pane.

   c. Right-click "**Kelsey Kroll Moved (insertion) [1]**" and select **Reject Move** from the context menu (Figure 3-27).

   d. Click the **X** in the upper-right corner of the *Reviewing* pane to close it.

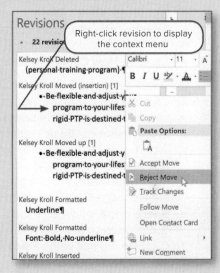

Figure 3-27 Reject moved text in the *Reviewing* pane

6. Accept changes in the document.

   a. Place your insertion point at the beginning of the document (or **Ctrl+Home**).

   b. Click the **Next** button [*Review* tab, *Changes* group] to select the first change (left and right margins changed).

   c. Click the top half of the **Accept** button [*Review* tab, *Changes* group] to accept the change. Word automatically moves to the next item, which is a comment.

   d. Click the **Next** button [*Review* tab, *Changes* group] three times to skip the first three comments and to locate the next tracked change ("personal training program" deleted).

   e. Click the top half of the **Accept** button to accept the change.

   f. Click the bottom half of the **Accept** button and select **Accept All Changes** from the drop-down list (Figure 3-28). All of the remaining changes in the document are accepted and disappear from view. Only comments remain in the *Markup* area.

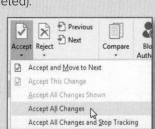

Figure 3-28 Accept all changes in the document

7. Resolve a comment and reply to a comment.

   a. Place your insertion point at the beginning of the document.

   b. Click the **Next** button [*Review* tab, *Comments* group] to move to the first comment.

   c. Click the **Resolve** button on the comment in the *Markup* area or right-click the comment and select **Resolve Comment** from the context menu (Figure 3-29). A resolved comment becomes grayed out text.

   d. Click the **Next** button to move to the next comment ("Be sure to include . . .").

   e. Click the **Reply** button on the comment in the *Markup* area (see Figure 3-29).

   f. Type Thank you, will do!

8. Delete selected comments in the document.
   a. Click the **Next** button [*Review* tab, *Comments* group] to move to the next (third) comment.
   b. Click the top half of the **Delete** button [*Review* tab, *Comments* group] to delete the comment.
   c. Continue clicking **Next** and **Delete** to delete the remaining comments. Don't delete the first two comments on the first page.

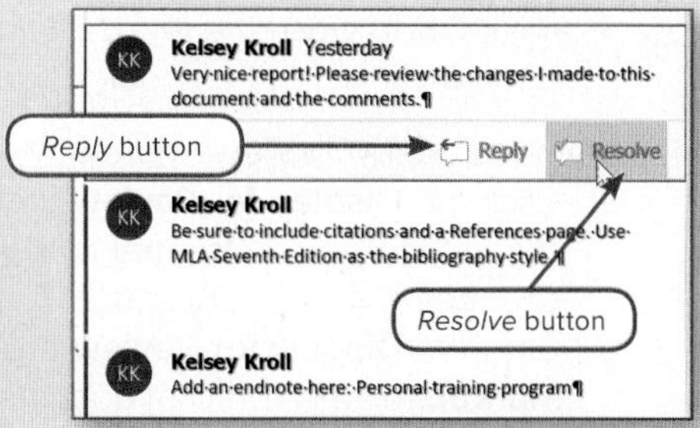

9. Add comments to the document.
   a. Place the insertion point at the top of the document (**Ctrl+Home**).
   b. Click the **New Comment** button [*Review* tab, *Comments* group] to insert a new comment.
   c. Type Insert a cover page and table of contents in the new comment.
   d. Select the first word in the first body paragraph ("**There**").
   e. Click the **New Comment** button and type Proofread this report one more time in the new comment.

10. Use *Track Changes* to revise the document.
    a. Click the top half of the **Track Changes** button [*Review* tab, *Tracking* group] to turn on track changes (or press **Ctrl+Shift+E**).
    b. Select the word "**Basic**" in the first section heading below the first body paragraph.
    c. Type General to replace the selected word. Verify one space displays after the word (turn on **Show/Hide** if necessary).
    d. Place your insertion point after "Training" (and before the space) in the second section heading on the first page ("Personal Training Guidelines").
    e. **Space** once and type Program to insert the word between "Training" and "Guidelines." Verify one space displays between the words.
    f. Click the top half of the **Track Changes** button to turn off *Track Changes*.

11. Save and close the document (Figure 3-30).

Figure 3-29 Resolve and reply to comments

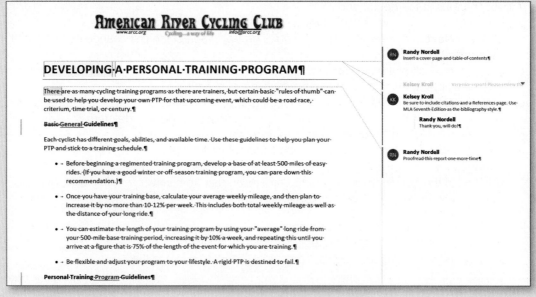

Figure 3-30 PP W3-1 completed

Using Footnotes and Endnotes

Footnotes and *endnotes* cite reference sources used in a document. Footnotes and endnotes can also be used to include additional information. Footnotes display at the bottom of each page, while endnotes display at the end of the document.

As you insert footnotes and endnotes, Word numbers them consecutively. If you insert a footnote or endnote before or between existing notes, Word automatically reorders notes. You can customize the number format and convert footnotes to endnotes or endnotes to footnotes.

Insert a Footnote

When you insert a footnote into a document, a *reference marker*, which is a number or letter in superscript format (smaller font size and slightly raised above the typed line), displays directly after the word. Word then places the insertion point at the bottom of the page where you type the text of the footnote. A thin top border above the note separates the note from the text in the body of the document.

Footnotes display in the body of the document at the bottom of the page, not in the footer area, and the text on a page with a footnote adjusts to allow space for the footnote.

▶ HOW TO: Insert a Footnote

1. Position the insertion point directly after the word where the footnote is to be inserted.
2. Click the **References** tab.
3. Click the **Insert Footnote** button [*Footnotes* group] (Figure 3-31).
   A reference marker displays in the body of the document (Figure 3-32), and the insertion point is positioned after the corresponding reference marker in the footnote area near the bottom of the page.
4. Type the footnote text in the footnote area of the page (Figure 3-33).

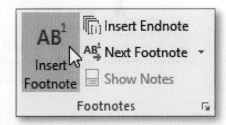

Figure 3-31 *Insert Footnote* button

Figure 3-32 Footnote reference marker in the body of the document

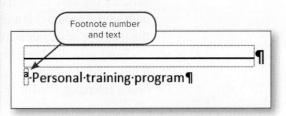

Figure 3-33 Footnote text at the bottom of the page

5. Click the body of the document to leave the footnote area and to return to the document.

Insert an Endnote

Inserting endnotes is similar to inserting footnotes. The main difference is the text for the endnote displays after the text at the end of the document rather than at the bottom of the page where the note appears.

1. Position the insertion point directly after the word where the endnote is to be inserted.
2. Click the **References** tab.
3. Click the **Insert Endnote** button [*Footnotes* group] (Figure 3-34). The reference marker displays in the body of the document, and the insertion point is positioned after the corresponding reference marker at the end of the document.
4. Type the endnote text.
5. Click the body of the document to leave the endnote area and to return to the document.

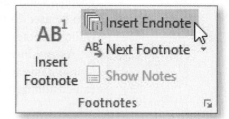

Figure 3-34 *Insert Endnote* button

> ▶ **ANOTHER WAY**
>
> **Alt+Ctrl+F** inserts a footnote. **Alt+Ctrl+D** inserts an endnote.

View Footnotes and Endnotes

Once you insert footnotes or endnotes in your document, it is easy to see the footnote or endnote text at the bottom of a page or at the end of the document. However, you might have a difficult time locating the reference markers in the body of the document. Word provides you with a tool to easily locate footnote reference markers in your document.

Click the **Next Footnote** button in the *Footnotes* group on the *References* tab to move to the next footnote (Figure 3-35). Click the **Next Footnote** drop-down arrow to display a list of options to move to the next or previous footnote or endnote. Click the **Show Notes** button in the *Footnotes* group to toggle between the note reference markers (in the body of the document) and the note text (in the footnote or endnote area).

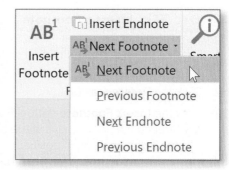

Figure 3-35 *Next Footnote* drop-down list

Word also displays the text of the footnote or endnote when you place your pointer over a reference marker (Figure 3-36).

Figure 3-36 Footnote text displayed as a tag

> ▶ **ANOTHER WAY**
>
> Use the *Go To* feature in the *Find and Replace* dialog box to go to a specific note. Press **Ctrl+G** to open the *Find and Replace* dialog box with the *Go To* tab displayed.

Customize Footnotes and Endnotes

By default, footnotes are numbered consecutively with numbers (1, 2, 3) and endnotes are numbered with lowercase Roman numerals (i, ii, iii). Letters or symbols such as an asterisk (*), section mark (§), or number symbol (#) are other reference marker options. You can customize how notes are numbered and where they display in a document.

▶ HOW TO: Customize Footnotes and Endnotes

1. Click the **Footnotes** launcher [*Reference* tab, *Footnotes* group] to open the *Footnote and Endnote* dialog box (Figure 3-37).
2. Select the **Footnotes** or **Endnotes** radio button in the *Location* area.
   - In the drop-down list for *Footnotes*, you have the option to position the footnote text at the *Bottom of page* (default) or *Below text*.
   - In the drop-down list for *Endnotes*, you have the option to position the endnote text at the *End of document* (default) or *End of section*.
3. Customize *Number format*, *Custom mark*, *Start at*, or *Numbering* in the *Format* area.
4. Click the **Apply changes to** drop-down list and select where to apply changes: *Whole document* or *This section* (if multiple sections exist in your document).
5. Click **Apply** to close the dialog box and apply the changes. Do not click *Insert*, which inserts a footnote or endnote in the document.

Figure 3-37 *Footnote and Endnote* dialog box

▶ **MORE INFO**

Use the *Footnote and Endnote* dialog box to insert a footnote or endnote.

Modify Footnote and Endnote Format

In addition to customizing note placement and format, you can also change the format of footnote and endnote text. Apply formatting to footnote or endnote text the same way you format regular text in the document.

Select the footnote or endnote text and apply formatting changes such as font, font size, style, line or paragraph spacing, or text effects (Figure 3-38). Use the buttons on the *Home* or *Layout* tab, the context menu (right-click selected text), the mini toolbar, or keyboard shortcuts to apply formatting changes.

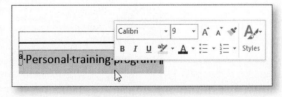

Figure 3-38 Apply formatting to footnote text

Modify Footnote and Endnote Styles

Styles determine the appearance of the footnotes and endnotes in your document. Styles include the font, font size, text styles and effects, and paragraph formatting. When you insert a footnote, Word applies the *Footnote Text* style.

Modify the *Footnote Text* or *Endnote Text* style to automatically update all of your footnote or endnote text.

▶HOW TO: Modify the Footnote or Endnote Style

1. Right-click the footnote or endnote text and select **Style** from the context menu. The *Style* dialog box opens, and the name of the style displays in the *Styles* area (Figure 3-39).

2. Click the **Modify** button to open the *Modify Style* dialog box (Figure 3-40).

3. Change the font formatting in the *Formatting* area.

4. Click the **Format** button to display a list of other formatting options (see Figure 3-40).

   • When you select a format option, another dialog box opens.
   • Apply formatting changes and click **OK** to close the dialog box.

5. Click **OK** to close the *Modify Style* dialog box.

6. Click **Apply** to apply changes to the style and close the *Style* dialog box.

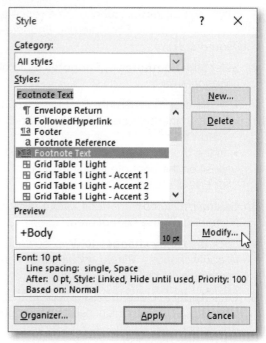

Figure 3-39 *Style* dialog box

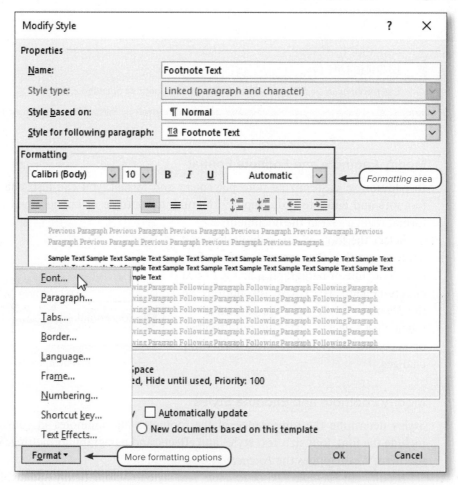

Figure 3-40 *Modify Style* dialog box

Convert Footnotes and Endnotes

At times, you may want to convert footnotes to endnotes or endnotes to footnotes. Rather than deleting and re-creating the notes, Use the *Convert Notes* feature. When you convert notes, Word automatically renumbers the reference markers and moves the note text to the correct location in the document.

▶HOW TO: Convert Footnotes and Endnotes

1. Click the **Footnotes** launcher [*References* tab, *Footnotes* group] to open the *Footnote and Endnote* dialog box.
2. Click the **Convert** button in the *Location* area. The *Convert Notes* dialog box opens (Figure 3-41).
3. Select from one of the three convert options: **Convert all footnotes to endnotes**, **Convert all endnotes to footnotes**, or **Swap footnotes and endnotes**.
4. Click **OK** to close the *Convert Notes* dialog box.
5. Click **Close** to close the *Footnote and Endnote* dialog box.

   • Do not click *Insert* or Word will insert a footnote or endnote.

Figure 3-41 *Convert Notes* dialog box

> **MORE INFO**
>
> All three of the convert options are active *only* if you have both footnotes and endnotes in your document. Otherwise, only one option is active.

Convert individual notes using the context menu. Right-click a footnote or endnote (*not* the reference marker in the text of the document) and select **Convert to Endnote** or **Convert to Footnote** (Figure 3-42).

Move Footnotes and Endnotes

Move footnotes and endnotes in the same way you move text in a document. To move a note, select the **reference marker** in the body of the document (Figure 3-43) and use one of the following methods:

Figure 3-42 Convert individual note

• Drag and drop
• **Ctrl+X** to cut and **Ctrl+V** to paste
• *Cut* and *Paste* buttons [*Home* tab, *Clipboard* group]
• *Cut* and *Paste* options in the context menu

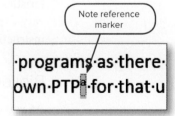

Figure 3-43 Select note reference marker to move

> **MORE INFO**
>
> When moving a note, select the note carefully to ensure that you are only moving the note and not any spaces, text, or paragraph marks.

Delete Footnotes and Endnotes

When you delete a note, Word removes the reference marker and the text of the note. Your remaining notes renumber and remain in consecutive order. To delete a note, always delete the note reference marker in the body of the document, which also deletes the note text in the footnote or endnote area.

> **HOW TO:** Delete a Note

1. Select the **reference marker** in the body of the document (*not* the text of the footnote or endnote at the bottom of the page or end of the document).
2. Press **Delete** on the keyboard. Both the note marker and the note in the footnote or endnote area are deleted.
   - Deleting footnote or endnote text in the footnote or endnote area will not delete the note reference marker in the body of the document.
3. Check to ensure proper spacing around text where the note was deleted.

Creating a Bibliography and Inserting Citations

Typically, the most tedious and time-consuming aspect of writing a research paper is compiling sources, creating a bibliography page, and citing sources in the body of the report. A *source* is the complete bibliographic reference for a book, journal article, or web page. A *citation* is the abbreviated source information that you place in the body of the report to credit the source of the information you use. A *bibliography* or *works cited* page lists the sources used in the report. Word includes tools to create sources, insert citations, and create a bibliography or works cited page at the end of your report.

Report Styles

A variety of report styles exist, and each differs not only in the overall format of the report but also in the format for sources and citations. The most common report styles are the following:

- *APA* (American Psychological Association)
- *Chicago* (*The Chicago Manual of Style*)
- *MLA* (Modern Language Association)
- *Turabian* (*Manual for Writers of Research Papers, Theses, and Dissertations*)

MLA and APA are the two most common report formats. Table 3-2 lists the general characteristics of each of these two report styles. Within each of these report formats, the format can vary depending on the preference of your college or instructor. Always follow the formatting instructions your instructor provides.

Bibliography Styles

As you begin compiling the sources for your report, the first step is to select the *bibliography style* of the report. The bibliography style determines how citations display in the body of the report and how references appear on a references, bibliography, or works cited page.

Table 3-2: Common Report Styles

Report Features	APA	MLA
Font	11 or 12 pt.	11 or 12 pt.
Line Spacing	Academic APA is double-spaced and business APA is single spaced.	Double-space.
Margins	For an unbound report, use 1" for all margins. For a left-bound report, use 1.5" left margin and 1" top, bottom, and right margins.	Use 1" margins.
Heading Information	Heading information is typically typed on a title page.	Left align at the top of the first page and include author's name, instructor's name, class, and date on separate lines.
Title	The title is either on the title page or horizontally centered on the first page of the report.	Center on the first page of the report.
Header	Include report title and page number on the right.	Include author's last name and page number on the right.
Uses	Typically used in social and behavioral sciences, business, and nursing.	Typically used in humanities.

▶HOW TO: Select the Bibliography Style of the Report

1. Click the **Reference** tab.
2. Click the **Style** drop-down arrow [*Citations & Bibliography* group].
3. Select the style of the report from the drop-down list of report styles (Figure 3-44).

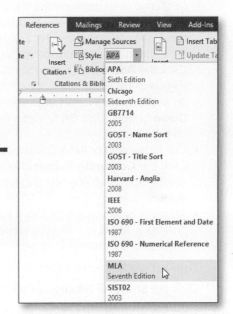

Figure 3-44 Select bibliography style

Add a New Source

When writing a report, gather bibliographic information about sources used in your report (author; title of book, journal, or article; publication date and edition; publisher or online location). When you use the *Add New Source* feature, Word inserts a citation in your report at the insertion point and stores this source information. Use stored sources to insert additional citations and to create a bibliography page.

▶HOW TO: Add a New Source

1. Position the insertion point at the location to insert a citation.

2. Click the **Insert Citation** button [*References* tab, *Citations & Bibliography* group].

3. Select **Add New Source**. The *Create Source* dialog box opens (Figure 3-45).

4. Click the **Type of Source** drop-down list and select the type of source.

   - The fields for the source change depending on the type of source you choose.

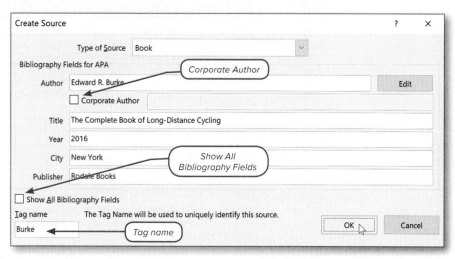

Figure 3-45 *Create Source* dialog box

5. Type the author information in the *Author* area. Enter this information differently depending on the author(s) of the source.

   - *Individual Author*: Type first name, middle initial, and last name (with no commas) in the *Author* field.
   - *Multiple Authors*: Click the **Edit** button to the right of the *Author* area to open the *Edit Name* dialog box. Type the author information in the *Add name* fields. Click the **Add** button to add additional authors (Figure 3-46). Reorder multiple authors by selecting an author in the *Names* area and clicking the **Up** or **Down** button. Click **OK** to close the *Edit Name* dialog box.
   - *Corporate Author* (USA Cycling or Velo News): Click the **Corporate Author** check box in the *Create Source* dialog box and type the corporate author.
   - After you type the author, Word automatically creates a *Tag name* for your source. Edit the *Tag name* if desired.

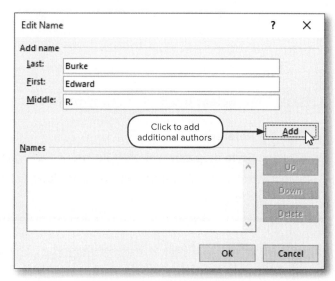

Figure 3-46 *Edit Name* dialog box

6. Type additional source information as needed (see Figure 3-45).

7. Click the **Show All Bibliography Fields** check box to display more fields, such as the edition of the book.

8. Click **OK** to close the *Create Source* dialog box.

   - The citation displays in the document in the report style you selected (Figure 3-47).
   - The *Researcher* pane may open on the right. If necessary, click the **X** in the upper-right corner to close the pane. The *Researcher* is discussed later in this section.

Figure 3-47 Citation inserted in text

Insert a Citation

Often, you cite a source more than once in a report. Once a source is added to your document, insert the same citation without re-entering the source information. When inserting a citation, choose from citations you have previously created.

Citations available in the document

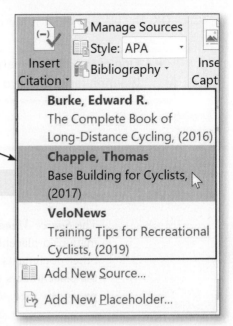

Figure 3-48 Insert citation from a previously created source

▶ HOW TO: Insert a Citation

1. Position the insertion point at the location to insert a citation.
2. Click the **Insert Citation** button [*References* tab, *Citations & Bibliography* group].
   - A list of previously used or created sources displays in the drop-down list (Figure 3-48).
3. Select from your list of sources.
   - The citation is inserted in the document.
   - When you insert a citation, Word automatically inserts a space between the citation and the preceding word.

▶ MORE INFO

When inserting citations, the citation typically is placed one space after the preceding word and directly before the punctuation mark. Always check your document to ensure proper spacing.

Insert a Placeholder

Occasionally, you may need to insert a citation but do not have all the bibliographic information to create the source. A *placeholder* temporarily marks a spot where a citation needs to be completed. Later, you can add bibliographic source information for any placeholders inserted in the document.

▶ HOW TO: Insert a Placeholder

1. Position the insertion point at the location to insert a placeholder.
2. Click the **Insert Citation** button [*References* tab, *Citations & Bibliography* group].
3. Select **Add New Placeholder**. The *Placeholder Name* dialog box opens (Figure 3-49).
4. Type the name of the placeholder.
   - Do not use spaces between words in the placeholder text because the placeholder name is the tag name of the source.
   - If necessary, use an underscore between words when naming a placeholder.

Figure 3-49 Insert a placeholder

5. Click **OK**. The placeholder displays in the document and looks similar to a citation (Figure 3-50).

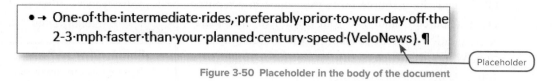

Figure 3-50 **Placeholder in the body of the document**

Manage Sources

The *Source Manager* dialog box enables you to edit existing sources, add bibliographic information to placeholders, create new sources, and copy sources that were created and used in other documents. The *Source Manager* dialog box displays the sources used in your report, the placeholders that need bibliographic information, and a master list of all sources you have previously used.

▶**HOW TO:** Manage Sources

1. Click the **Manage Sources** button [*References* tab, *Citations & Bibliography* group]. The *Source Manager* dialog box opens (Figure 3-51).

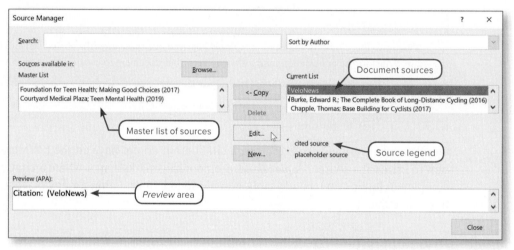

Figure 3-51 *Source Manager* dialog box

- The *Master List* of sources on the left displays *all* available sources. Some of these may have been created in other Word documents.
- The *Current List* displays the sources available in your current document.
- Sources that are cited in the document have a checkmark next to them.
- Sources that are placeholders have a question mark next to them and require additional information.
- The *Preview* area displays the contents of your source.

2. Copy a source from the *Master List* to the *Current List* by selecting the source on the left and clicking the **Copy** button. The copied source remains in the *Master List*.

3. Edit a source from either list by selecting a source and clicking the **Edit** button (see Figure 3-51). The *Edit Source* dialog box opens.

- Edit the source and click **OK**.
- Word automatically updates citations in your document after changes to the source are completed.

4. Add bibliographic information to a placeholder by selecting the placeholder and clicking the **Edit** button. The *Edit Source* dialog box opens.

- Add bibliographic information to the placeholder and click **OK**.
- When bibliographic information is added to a placeholder, it becomes a complete source, and the question mark next to it changes to a check.
- Word automatically replaces the placeholder with a citation in your document when you add bibliographic information.

5. Create a new source by clicking the **New** button. The *Create Source* dialog box opens.

- Type the bibliographic information and click **OK**.
- This source is now available as a citation to insert in your document.
- This source is also added to the *Master List*.

6. Delete a source from either list by selecting the source and clicking the **Delete** button.

- You cannot delete a source from the *Current List* if it is cited in the document. You must first delete the citation in the document before deleting a source in the *Source Manager* dialog box.
- If a source is in both lists and you delete it from one list, it is not deleted from the other list.

7. Click **Close** to close the *Source Manager* dialog box and apply any changes made.

Edit Citations and Sources

After citations and placeholders are inserted into the document, edit the citation or source without using the *Source Manager* dialog box. When you click a citation or placeholder in your document, a drop-down list of editing options displays (Figure 3-52):

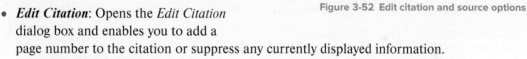

Figure 3-52 Edit citation and source options

- *Edit Citation*: Opens the *Edit Citation* dialog box and enables you to add a page number to the citation or suppress any currently displayed information.
- *Edit Source*: Opens the *Edit Source* dialog box and enables you to update source bibliographic information.
- *Convert citation to static text*: Changes the citation from a Word field that is automatically generated and updated to static text that is not updated.
- *Update Citations and Bibliography*: Updates your bibliography page to reflect any changes to citations or sources.

> **MORE INFO**
>
> Edit citations and placeholders using either the drop-down list or the context menu.

You can move or delete a citation or placeholder in the body of the text by clicking the citation or placeholder handle on the left and dragging it to a new location (to move) or by pressing **Delete** (to delete) on your keyboard (Figure 3-53).

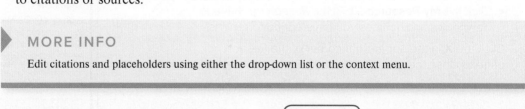
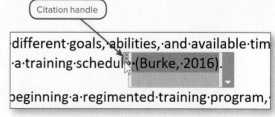

Figure 3-53 Select a citation to move or delete

Use the Researcher

The *Researcher* enables you to search for quotes, citable sources, and images about a topic in your report and displays information from journals and web sites in the *Researcher* pane on the right side of the Word window. From the results in the *Researcher* pane, you can review topics to gather information, add citations to the report, and add topic headings to the report. When you add a citation to the report, the complete bibliographic information is saved as a source in the *Source Manager*, and this source is saved in the *My Research* area of the *Researcher* pane for future reference.

Office 2019 Note: The *Researcher* feature is not available in Office 2019.

▶ HOW TO: Use the Researcher and Research Pane

1. Click the **Researcher** button [*References* tab, *Research* group]. The *Researcher* pane opens on the right side of the Word window (Figure 3-54).

2. Type key words of the search topic in the search text box and press **Enter**. Search results display in the *Researcher* pane (Figure 3-55).

   - *Relevant topics* and *Top sources for [search topic]* display in the *Researcher* pane.

3. Click a topic or source to view detailed information.

   - Click the **Back** arrow to return to search results in the *Researcher* pane.

4. Click the plus sign (**+**) in the upper-right corner of a *topic* result to add a heading to the report.

   - A heading is added to the report and a comment is attached to the heading.
   - The heading is formatting in *Heading 1* style.
   - The comment includes a link to the topic.

5. Click the plus sign (**+**) in the upper-right corner of a *source* result to add a citation to the report.

   - A dialog box may open in the *Researcher* pane asking if you want to "*Create a bibliography?*" Select **Create** or **No thanks**.
   - When a citation is added to a report from the *Researcher* pane, the complete bibliographic information is saved as a source in the *Source Manager*.
   - Click the **My Research** tab in the *Researcher* pane to view topics and sources you have added to reports.

6. Click the **X** in the upper-right corner of the *Researcher* pane to close the pane.

Figure 3-54 *Researcher* pane

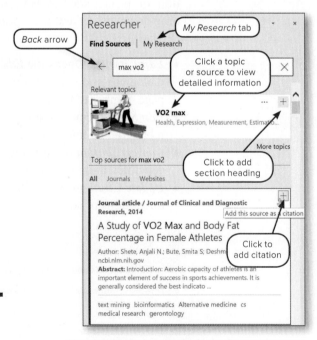

Figure 3-55 Search results in the *Researcher* pane

Insert a Bibliography

Once you create sources and insert citations in the body of the report, you are ready to create a bibliography page. The bibliography page is automatically generated from the sources in your document and is formatted according to the selected *Bibliography Style*. Word provides a variety of bibliography options.

The *Bibliography*, *References*, and *Works Cited* built-in options insert a page title above the list of sources. The *Insert Bibliography* option inserts only the sources; you can add a title of your choice. If you plan to include a table of contents in your report, it is best to use one of the built-in options. Word applies a style to the bibliography title and automatically includes the bibliography page in the table of contents.

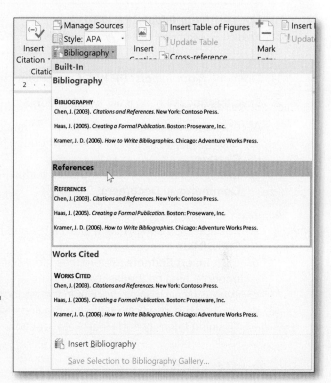

Figure 3-56 Insert *References* page

▶HOW TO: Insert a Bibliography

1. Position the insertion point at the location to insert the bibliography.
   - It is usually best to insert a page break (**Ctrl+Enter**) at the end of the document and begin the bibliography on a new page.

2. Click the **Bibliography** button [*References* tab, *Citations & Bibliography* group] to display the list of options (Figure 3-56).

3. Select a bibliography option. The bibliography displays in the document.

If changes are made to sources after the bibliography page has been inserted, you must update the bibliography. Click one of the references on the bibliography page to select the entire bibliography and click **Update Citations and Bibliography** (Figure 3-57).

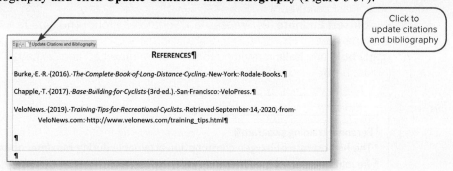

Figure 3-57 *References* page inserted into the document

▶ ANOTHER WAY

Right-click the bibliography and choose **Update Field** or press **F9** to update the bibliography.

For this Pause & Practice project, you modify the *Developing a Personal Training Program* report for American River Cycling Club. You accept tracked changes, delete comments, add and modify notes, select the report style, add sources and citations, use the *Researcher*, and insert a bibliography page.

File Needed: *[your initials] PP W3-1.docx*
Completed Project File Name: *[your initials] PP W3-2.docx*

1. Open the *[your initials] PP W3-1* document completed in *Pause & Practice 3-1*.

2. Save this document as [your initials] PP W3-2.

3. Accept tracked changes and delete all comments in the document.
    a. Click the bottom half of the **Accept** button [*Review* tab, *Changes* group] and select **Accept All Changes**.
    b. Click the bottom half of the **Delete** button [*Review* tab, *Comments* group] and select **Delete All Comments in Document**.

4. Insert endnotes into the report.
    a. Position the insertion point after "PTP" and before the space (page 1, first body paragraph). Turn on **Show/Hide** if necessary.
    b. Click **Insert Endnote** [*References* tab, *Footnotes* group]. Word moves the insertion point to the endnote area on the last page.
    c. Type Personal training program in the endnote area.
    d. Position the insertion point after the first instance of "Max VO2" and before the space (page 3, "Training Intensity and Heart Rate" section, second sentence).

> **MORE INFO**
>
> Use the *Find* feature in the *Navigation* pane to locate specific words.

    e. Click **Insert Endnote** [*References* tab, *Footnotes* group] and type The highest rate of oxygen consumption attainable during maximal or exhaustive exercise in the endnote area.
    f. Position the insertion point after "RPM" and before the period (page 3, "Sample Session" section, end of last paragraph).
    g. Click **Insert Endnote** [*References* tab, *Footnotes* group] and type Revolutions per minute in the endnote area.
    h. Apply **bold** and *italic* formatting to the words "maximal" and "exhaustive" in the second endnote (Figure 3-58).

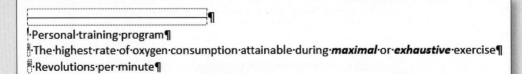

Figure 3-58 Endnotes added to report

5. Convert endnotes to footnotes and change numbering.
    a. Click the **Footnotes** launcher [*References* tab, *Footnotes* group]. The *Footnote and Endnote* dialog box opens.

b. Click the **Convert** button to open the *Convert Notes* dialog box (Figure 3-59).

c. Select **Convert all endnotes to footnotes** if necessary and click **OK**.

d. Click **Close** to close the *Footnote and Endnote* dialog box.

e. Click the **Footnotes** launcher again to open the *Footnote and Endnote* dialog box.

f. Click the **Footnotes** radio button if necessary.

g. Click the **Number format** drop-down arrow and select **a, b, c . . .** (Figure 3-60). Don't change any of the other *Format* settings.

h. Choose **Apply** to close the *Footnote and Endnote* dialog box and apply the changes.

i. Check your document to confirm that endnotes have been converted to footnotes and that the number format has been changed.

6. Change the style of the footnotes.

a. Right-click the footnote text at the bottom of the first page.

b. Select **Style** from the context menu (not mini toolbar). The *Style* dialog box opens.

c. Click the **Modify** button to open the *Modify Style* dialog box (Figure 3-61).

d. Change the font size to **9 pt**.

e. Change line spacing to **1.5** (see Figure 3-61).

f. Click **OK** to close the *Modify Style* dialog box.

g. Choose **Apply** to close the *Style* dialog box.

7. Select the report style for sources and citations.

a. Click the **Style** drop-down list [*References* tab, *Citations & Bibliography* group].

b. Select **MLA Seventh Edition**.

Figure 3-59 Convert endnotes to footnotes

Figure 3-60 Change the number format of footnotes

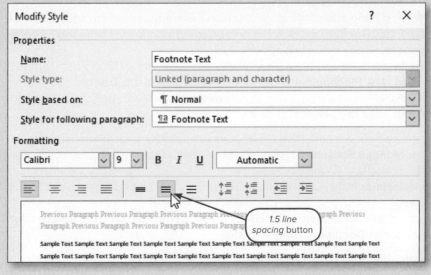

Figure 3-61 Modify *Footnote Text* style

8. Add a new source and insert a citation.
   a. Position the insertion point after the word "schedule" and before the period (page 1, "General Guidelines" section, end of first paragraph).
   b. Click the **Insert Citation** button [*References* tab, *Citations & Bibliography* group].
   c. Select **Add New Source**. The *Create Source* dialog box opens (Figure 3-62).

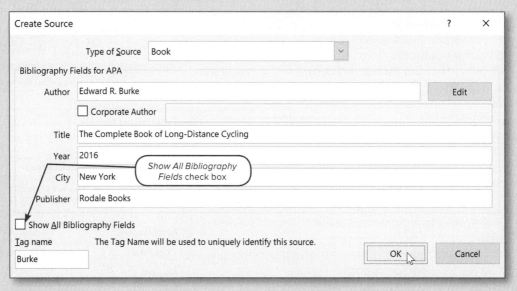

Figure 3-62 *Create Source* dialog box

   d. Select **Book** as the type of source.
   e. Type Edward R. Burke in the *Author* field.
   f. Type the following source information in the *Create Source* dialog box:

   Title: The Complete Book of Long-Distance Cycling
   Year: 2016
   City: New York
   Publisher: Rodale Books
   Tag name: Burke

   g. Click **OK** to add the source, insert the citation, and close the dialog box.

9. Add a placeholder to the report.
   a. Go to the first page and position the insertion point after the word "speed" and before the period ("Pace of Rides" section, last bulleted item). **Ctrl+G** opens the *Go To* tab in the *Find and Replace* dialog box to quickly move to a specific page.
   b. Click the **Insert Citation** button [*References* tab, *Citations & Bibliography* group].
   c. Select **Add New Placeholder**. The *Placeholder Name* dialog box opens.
   d. Type VeloNews (no space between words) as the placeholder text.
   e. Click **OK** to insert the placeholder and close the dialog box.

10. Manage sources to add a new source and complete bibliographic information for the placeholder.
    a. Click the **Manage Sources** button [*References* tab, *Citations & Bibliography* group]. The *Source Manager* dialog box opens.
    b. Select **VeloNews** in the *Current List* area and click the **Edit** button to open the *Edit Source* dialog box.
    c. Check the **Show All Bibliography Fields** box and type the following source information:
    Type of Source: **Document from web site**

    Corporate Author (check **Corporate Author** check box): VeloNews
    Name of web Page: Training Tips for Recreational Cyclists
    Name of web Site: VeloNews.com

Year: 2019
Year Accessed: 2020
Month Accessed: September
Day Accessed: 14
URL: http://www.velonews.com/training_tips.html

  d. Click **OK** to close the *Edit Source* dialog box. The placeholder is updated as a complete source.
  e. Click the **New** button in the *Source Manager* dialog box to create a new source.
  f. Check the **Show All Bibliography Fields** box and type the following source information:

> *Type of Source*: **Book**
> *Author*: Thomas Chapple
> *Title*: Base Building for Cyclists
> *Year*: 2017
> *City*: San Francisco
> *Publisher*: VeloPress
> *Edition*: 3rd
> *Tag name*: Chapple

  g. Click **OK** to close the *Create Source* dialog box.
  h. Click **Close** to close the *Source Manager* dialog box.

11. Insert citations into the report.
  a. Go to the top of the second page and position the insertion point after "rest day" and before the period (second sentence of first paragraph).
  b. Click the **Insert Citation** button [*References* tab, *Citations & Bibliography* group] (Figure 3-63).
  c. Select the **Chapple, Thomas** source. The citation displays in the report.
  d. Use the **Insert Citation** button to insert the following citations:
    Burke, Edward, R.: after "training week" and before the period (page 2, "Duration of Rides" section, last bulleted item).
    VeloNews: after "overtraining" and before the period (page 3, "Other Heart Rate Factors" section, end of the paragraph).

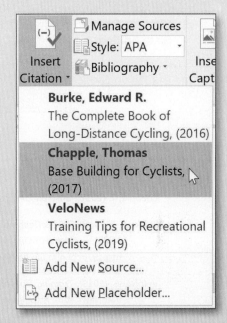

Figure 3-63 Insert a citation

12. Use the *Researcher* to insert a citation. If you are using Office 2019, skip all of step 12 because the *Researcher* is not available in Office 2019.
  a. Place your insertion point after "maximum heart rate" and before the period (page 3, "Training Intensity and Heart Rate" section, first paragraph).
  b. Click the **Researcher** button [*References* tab, *Research* group] to open the *Researcher* pane.
  c. Type max vo2 in the search text box and press **Enter**.
  d. Review the results in the *Top sources for max vo2* area (Figure 3-64).
  e. Click the plus sign (**+**) in the upper-right corner of one of the *Top sources* (not *Relevant topics*) to insert a citation at the insertion point in the report. If a dialog box opens and asks to "*Update a bibliography?*" click **No thanks**.

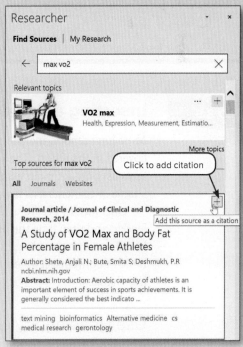

Figure 3-64 Add a citation from the *Researcher* pane

f. Review the citation you inserted in the report. The bibliographic information for this citation was also added as a source in the *Source Manager*.

g. Click the **X** in the upper-right corner of *Researcher* pane to close it.

13. Insert a bibliography and change report style.

a. Position the insertion point on the blank line at the end of the document and press **Ctrl+Enter** to insert a page break.

b. Click the **Bibliography** button [*References* tab, *Citations & Bibliography* group] and select **References** from the drop-down list. The *Reference* page displays on the blank page at the end of the document.

c. **Center** the "*References*" title and apply **10 pt** after paragraph spacing.

d. Click the **Style** drop-down list [*References* tab, *Citations & Bibliography* group] and select **APA Sixth Edition**.

14. Save and close the document (Figure 3-65). Your *References* page may be different depending on the citation you added using the *Researcher*.

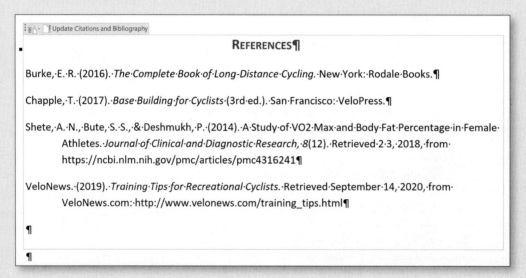

Figure 3-65 PP W3-2 References page

SLO 3.5

Inserting a Table of Contents

Most long reports include a *table of contents* to provide readers with an overview of the material covered in the report. The table of contents reflects the headings in the report; some tables of contents list only the main headings, while others might list second- and third-level headings. Typically, a table of contents lists headings on the left and page numbers on the right with a dot leader.

One way to create a table of contents is to manually type headings, set a tab with a dot leader, and then type the page number. But Word can automatically generate a table of contents based upon the headings in your report, which saves you time. When using Word to generate a table of contents, it automatically updates if headings are changed or moved or if page numbering changes.

Use Heading Styles for a Table of Contents

Word automatically generates a table of contents listing the headings in your report if you apply *heading styles* to each heading. Styles control the appearance of text by applying a specific font,

font size, color, font styles and effects, and spacing to the text on which a style is applied. The document *theme* determines the appearance of the styles. The *Style* gallery displays commonly used styles.

▶ MORE INFO

Styles and themes were introduced in Chapter 2 (see *SLO 2.7: Using Styles and Themes*).

The first step in automatically generating a table of contents in a report is to apply a heading style to each heading in the document. Word provides multiple levels of heading styles (*Heading 1*, *Heading 2*, etc.).

▶ **HOW TO:** Apply Heading Styles

1. Select the heading where you want to apply a style.
2. Click the heading style to apply [*Home* tab, *Styles* group] (Figure 3-66). The style is applied to the heading.

Figure 3-66 Document styles displayed in the *Style* gallery

- Apply *Heading 1* to main headings, *Heading 2* to second level headings, and other heading styles as needed.
- When you place the insertion point on a style, Word displays a live preview of the style and temporarily applies the style to the selected text.
- Click the **More** button to expand the *Style* gallery to display additional styles.

3. Continue to select headings and apply styles. Apply a heading style to every heading you want to display in the table of contents.

- When a heading style has been applied to text, an *Expand/Collapse* button displays to the left of the heading (Figure 3-67). Click the **Expand/ Collapse** button to expand or collapse the text below the heading.

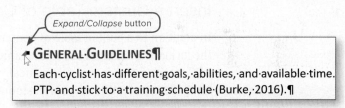

Figure 3-67 Expand or collapse text below a heading

Insert a Built-In Table of Contents

Word inserts the table of contents where you position the insertion point in the report. Therefore, it is a good idea to insert a blank page before the first page of your report and to position your insertion point on the blank page. Use a page break to insert the blank page at the top of your document.

▶ **HOW TO:** Insert a Built-In Table of Contents

1. Place the insertion point before the first line of the report and press **Ctrl+Enter** to insert a page break.
2. Position the insertion point at the top of the new first page.
3. Click the **References** tab.

4. Click the **Table of Contents** button [*Table of Contents* group] (Figure 3-68).

5. Select a built-in table of contents to insert. The table of contents displays in your report (Figure 3-69).

    • Each heading in the table of contents is a hyperlink. Press the **Ctrl** key and click a heading in the table of contents to move to the heading in the body of the document.

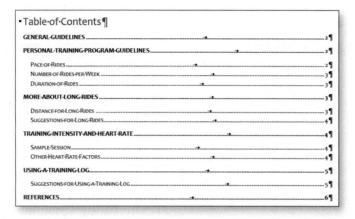

Figure 3-69 Table of contents inserted into the report

Figure 3-68 Insert built-in table of contents

Insert a Custom Table of Contents

In addition to a built-in table of contents, you can insert a custom table of contents and modify the format and appearance of the table. When you insert a custom table of contents, the "Table of Contents" title is not automatically inserted as it is when you insert a built-in table of contents. To insert a title on your custom table of contents page, type it before inserting your table of contents.

> **MORE INFO**
>
> It is usually best to apply font formatting (not a heading style) to the table of contents title. If you apply a heading style to the table of contents title, the table of contents title displays as an item in the table of contents when it is updated.

▶ HOW TO: Insert a Custom Table of Contents

1. Place the insertion point before the first line of your report and press **Ctrl+Enter** to insert a page break.

2. Position the insertion point at the top of the new first page.

    • If desired, type a title for the table of contents and press **Enter**.
    • Do not apply a heading style to the table of contents title.

3. Click the **Table of Contents** button [*References* tab, *Table of Contents* group].

4. Select **Custom Table of Contents**. The *Table of Contents* dialog box opens (Figure 3-70).

   - A preview of the table of contents appears in the *Print Preview* area.

5. Click the **Formats** drop-down list in the *General* area and select a table of contents format.

6. Select the number of heading levels to display in the *Show levels* area.

7. Customize the table of contents using the options below the *Print Preview* area where you can choose to not show page numbers, choose to not right align page numbers, and choose the type of tab leader to use with right-aligned page numbers.

8. Click **OK** to insert the table of contents.

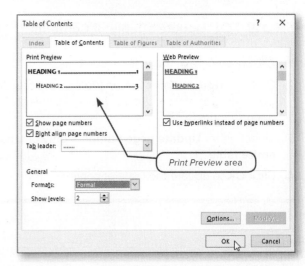

Figure 3-70 *Table of Contents* dialog box

Modify a Table of Contents

After inserting a table of contents, you may decide to use a different format or change the levels of headings that display. When you update a table of contents, you are actually replacing the old table of contents with a new one.

▶ HOW TO: Modify a Table of Contents

1. Click anywhere in the table of contents.

2. Click the **Table of Contents** button [*References* tab, *Table of Contents* group].

3. Select **Custom Table of Contents**. The *Table of Contents* dialog box opens.

4. Customize the table of contents.

5. Click **OK**. A dialog box opens, confirming you want to replace the existing table of contents (Figure 3-71).

6. Click **Yes** to replace the table of contents.

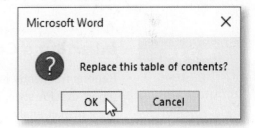

Figure 3-71 Replace an existing table of contents

Update a Table of Contents

When you change your report, such as adding or modifying headings, content, or page breaks, the content and page numbers in the table of contents may no longer be accurate. You must update the table of contents to reflect these changes. You have the option of updating only page numbers or updating the entire table of contents, which includes both headings and page numbers.

▶HOW TO: Update a Table of Contents

1. Click anywhere in the table of contents.
2. Click the **Update Table** button [*References* tab, *Table of Contents* group]. The *Update Table of Contents* dialog box opens (Figure 3-72).
3. Select either **Update page numbers only** or **Update entire table**.
4. Click **OK** to update the table of contents.

Figure 3-72 Update a table of contents

> ▶ ANOTHER WAY
>
> Press **F9** or right-click the table of contents and select **Update Field** to update the table of contents.

Remove a Table of Contents

If you no longer want a table of contents in your report, you can easily remove it. Click the **Table of Contents** button in the *Table of Contents* group on the *References* tab and select **Remove Table of Contents**. The table of contents is removed from your document (Figure 3-73).

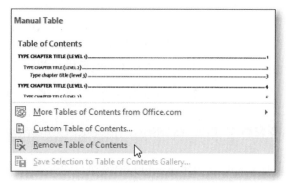

Figure 3-73 Remove a table of contents

SLO 3.6

Inserting a Cover Page

Reports frequently include a title page as the cover or introduction. If you're writing a formal report in APA style, the title page includes specific content and format. But if you're presenting a market analysis or product feasibility report, you may choose to include a *cover page* to introduce the report with professional appeal. Word provides a variety of cover page options.

Insert a Built-In Cover Page

When you insert a cover page into a document, Word automatically inserts it at the beginning of the document and inserts a page break to move the existing first page content to the second page.

To insert a cover page, click the **Cover Page** button in the *Pages* group on the *Insert* tab and select one of the built-in cover pages from the drop-down list (Figure 3-74). Additional custom cover pages are available on Office.com. Select **More Cover Pages from Office.com** to display a list of additional cover pages.

Customize Cover Page Content

The built-in cover pages in Word include graphics, text boxes, and Word fields. Some of the fields are *document property fields* and others are *content control fields*, fields where you type custom information. Customize the content of the fields, delete unwanted fields, and modify the graphics and text boxes on the cover page. The theme of your document controls the format of cover pages. Colors and fonts in a cover page change based on the selected theme.

Customize Document Property Content

If you add information to the document properties of your document, Word automatically populates the document properties fields in the cover page. When you type information into a document property field on the cover page, Word adds this information to your document properties.

Figure 3-74 Insert a built-in cover page

▶HOW TO: Customize Document Properties

1. Click the **File** tab to open the *Backstage* view and select **Info** to display document properties (Figure 3-75).
2. Click the **Show All Properties** link at the bottom to display additional document property fields.
   - This link toggles between *Show All Properties* and *Show Fewer Properties*.
3. Add or modify document property content.
   - Fields, such as *Last Modified* and *Created*, cannot be modified.
   - To remove the *Author*, right-click the author and select **Remove Person**.
4. Click the **Back** arrow to return to the document. Word updates the document property fields on the cover page.

Add or Remove Document Property Fields

You can also add document property fields to the cover page or remove them. When you add a document property field to a cover page, the content of the field is automatically populated with the information from your document properties.

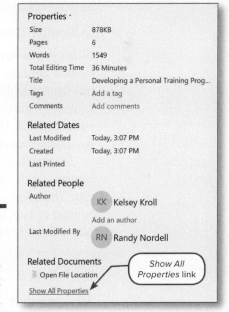

Figure 3-75 Document properties in the *Backstage* view

1. Position the insertion point at the place where you want to insert the document property field.

2. Click the **Insert** tab.

3. Click the **Quick Parts** button [*Text* group] (Figure 3-76).

4. Choose **Document Property**.

5. Select a document property field from the drop-down list. The document property field displays in the document.

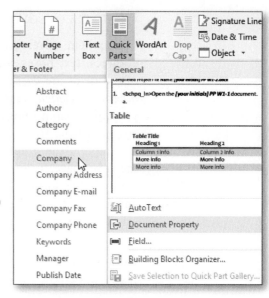

> **MORE INFO**
>
> You can insert document property fields anywhere in a document.

Figure 3-76 Insert a document property field

To remove a document property field, click the **field handle** to select the field and press **Delete** (Figure 3-77). Check for proper spacing and paragraph breaks when you delete a document property field.

Field handle

Figure 3-77 Select and delete a document property field

> **MORE INFO**
>
> Deleting the contents of a document property or content control field does not delete the field. To remove a field, click the **field handle** to select the field and press **Delete**.

Customize Content Control Fields

When you insert a cover page, the page may include content control fields. Content control fields enable you to type or select custom content (Figure 3-78). Remove Word content control fields the same way you remove a document property field (see Figure 3-77).

Figure 3-78 Type text into a content control field

To insert custom content in a content control field, click the field and type the text. The information you type is not restricted by the content control field label. For example, you can type a web address in an *Address* field (see Figure 3-78).

Remove a Cover Page

After inserting a cover page, you may decide that you no longer need one or you want a different one. Removing a cover page is similar to removing a table of contents. Click the **Cover Page** button on the *Insert* tab and select **Remove Current Cover Page** (Figure 3-79).

Figure 3-79 Remove a cover page

When you remove a cover page, Word deletes the entire contents of the cover page and removes the page break.

SLO 3.7

Using Advanced Headers and Footers

Headers and footers are used to include page numbers and document information at the top or bottom of each page in a report or multipage document. Headers appear at the top of the page, and footers appear at the bottom. Type headers and footers just once, and they automatically display on subsequent pages. You can automatically insert page numbers in the header or footer, and add custom content such as text, document property fields, the date, or borders.

Page and Section Breaks

For multipage documents, it is a good idea to insert page or section breaks to control page endings or special formatting in different sections. A *Page* break controls where one page ends and another begins. Use a *Next Page* section break when special document layout formatting is applied to a whole page or multiple pages of a document, such as landscape orientation to one page of the document. Use a *Continuous* section break when you apply special formatting to a section of the document, such as the two-column format to specific text on one page.

> **MORE INFO**
>
> Do not use a section break to control page endings.

HOW TO: Insert a Page or Section Break

1. Place the insertion point in the document at the location to insert a *Page* break or *Next Page* section break.
   - When inserting a *Continuous* section break, select the text on which to apply the section break.
   - When you insert a *Continuous* section break for selected text, Word inserts a *Continuous* section break before and after the selected text.
2. Click the **Breaks** button [*Layout* tab, *Page Setup* group] (Figure 3-80).
3. Select the type of break from the drop-down list.

> **ANOTHER WAY**
>
> **Ctrl+Enter** inserts a page break.

When working with page and section breaks, it is best to have the *Show/Hide* feature turned on to display breaks in a document. To delete a page or section break, select the break and press **Delete**.

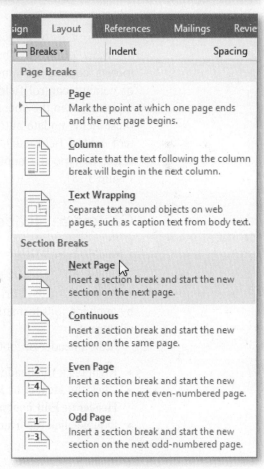

Figure 3-80 Insert a page or section break

Built-In Headers, Footers, and Page Numbers

Word provides a variety of built-in headers, footers, and page numbering options to insert and customize. Insert built-in header and footer content with the header or footer open or while you are in the main document.

▶ HOW TO: Insert a Built-In Header, Footer, or Page Number

1. Click the **Insert** tab.
2. Click the **Header**, **Footer**, or **Page Number** button [*Header & Footer* group].
3. Select a built-in header, footer, or page number from the drop-down list (Figure 3-81). The content displays and the header or footer area opens.
   - When inserting a page number, select the position (*Top of Page*, *Bottom of Page*, *Page Margins*, or *Current Position*) to insert the page number.
   - Additional built-in headers, footers, and page numbers display when you place your pointer on *More Headers (Footer* or *Page Numbers) from Office.com.*

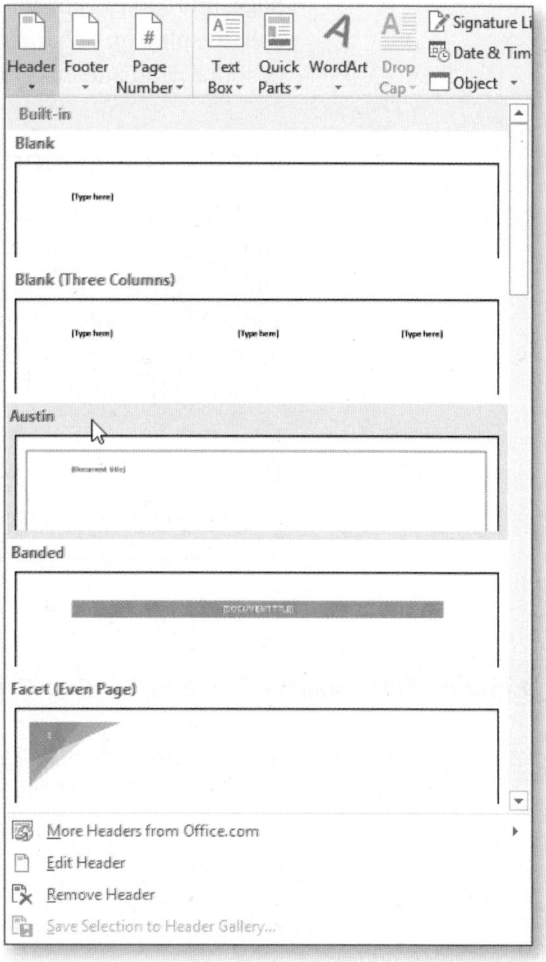

Figure 3-81 Insert a built-in header

Many of Word's built-in headers and footers contain document property fields or content control fields. When you enter information in the document property area, these fields update automatically. For content control fields such as *Date* or *Address*, select or type the content to display (see Figure 3-78).

Customize Header and Footer Content

In addition to the built-in header and footer content, you can type text or insert or delete content control fields. Format header and footer text as you would other text in your document by applying font formatting and borders, inserting graphics, and modifying or setting tabs for alignment.

Edit a header or footer in the following ways:

- Right-click the header or footer area and select **Edit Header** or **Edit Footer**.
- Click the **Header** or **Footer** button [*Insert* tab, *Header & Footer* group] and select **Edit Header** or **Edit Footer**.
- Double-click the header or footer area of the document.

▶**HOW TO:** Insert Custom Content in the Header or Footer

1. Edit the header or footer. See above for different ways to edit the header or footer. The *Header & Footer Tools Design* tab opens (Figure 3-82).

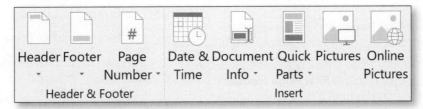

Figure 3-82 Insert content from the *Header & Footer Tools Design* tab

2. Insert content from the *Header & Footer Tools Design* tab.

3. Type content, insert a document property field, insert the date, or insert built-in header, footer, or page number content to display in the header or footer (Figure 3-83).

Figure 3-83 A built-in footer and document property field inserted in the footer

4. Align information in the header or footer by using horizontal alignment buttons (*Center* or *Align Right*) or tabs.

   • By default, a center tab stop is set at the horizontal midpoint, and a right tab stop is set at the right margin.
   • Insert a tab stop by clicking the **Insert Alignment Tab** button [*Header & Footer Tools Design* tab, *Position* group] (Figure 3-84).
   • Alternatively, modify, add, or remove tabs on the *Ruler* or in the *Tabs* dialog box [*Paragraph* dialog box, *Tabs* button].

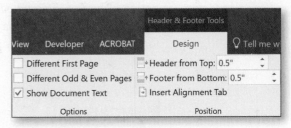

Figure 3-84 Header and footer position options

5. Apply formatting to header and footer content.

6. Change the position of the header and footer in the *Position* group.

   • By default, the header and footer are positioned 0.5" from the top and bottom of the page (see Figure 3-84).
   • Alternatively, change these settings in the *Page Setup* dialog box on the *Layout* tab.

7. Click **Close Header and Footer** to return to the main document.

Different First Page Header and Footer

For many reports, the page number or header and footer content should not display on the first page, but it does display on subsequent pages. When you select the ***Different First Page*** option, Word removes existing content from the header and footer on the first page. You can choose to leave the first page header and footer blank or insert content that is different from the header and footer on second and subsequent pages.

▶HOW TO: Insert a Different First Page Header and Footer

1. Edit the header or footer on the first page of the document.

2. Check the **Different First Page** check box [*Header & Footer Tools Design* tab, *Options* group] (Figure 3-85).

   - When the *Different First Page* check box is checked, the header (or footer) label displays ***First Page Header*** (or ***First Page Footer***) to distinguish it from other headers and footers in the document, which are labeled *Header* (or *Footer*) (Figure 3-86).
   - The header (or footer) label changes when you apply other header and footer formatting such as odd and even pages or have different headers for different sections of your document.

3. Click **Close Header and Footer**.

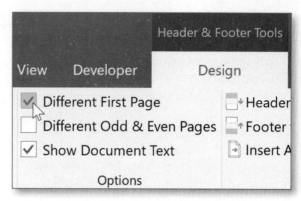

Figure 3-85 Apply *Different First Page* header and footer

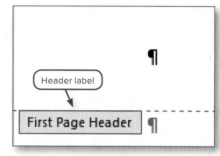

Figure 3-86 First page header

Different Odd and Even Pages

Just as you can have different header and footer content on the first page, Word provides the option of having ***different odd and even pages*** header and footer content on a multipage document. For example, you may want the title of the report to appear on all even pages in the footer and the page number and a company name to appear on odd pages.

> ▶ MORE INFO
>
> It is best to insert header and footer content on the first page of your document and then make any desired header and footer option changes.

▶HOW TO: Insert Different Odd and Even Headers and Footers

1. Edit the header or footer on the first page of the document.

2. Check the **Different Odd & Even Pages** check box [*Header & Footer Tools Design* tab, *Options* group] (see Figure 3-85).

   - When the *Different Odd & Even Pages* check box is checked, the header (or footer) label displays *Odd* (or *Even*) *Page Header* (or *Footer*) to distinguish it from other headers and footers in the document (Figure 3-87).

3. Click **Close Header and Footer**.

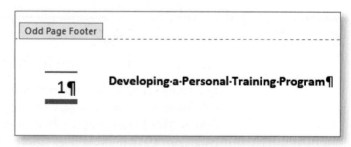

Figure 3-87 Odd page footer

Link to Previous Header or Footer

Section breaks separate your document into different sections. When you have different sections in your document, the headers and footers are by default linked to previous headers and footers. For example, a page number that appears in the footer of the first section of a document will also appear in the same position in the next section footer because it is linked to the previous footer. Break this link to format header and footer content in one section independently of the header or footer in another section. To break the link, click the **Link to Previous** button.

▶ HOW TO: Link or Unlink a Header or Footer

1. Edit the header or footer to be unlinked from the previous section.
   - By default, the *Link to Previous* button is on (shaded).
   - The *Same as Previous* label displays on the right of the header or footer.
2. Click the **Link to Previous** button [*Header & Footer Tools Design* tab, *Navigation* group] to unlink it from the previous section (Figure 3-88).

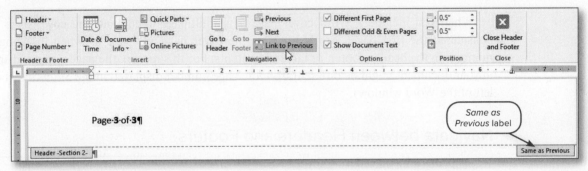

Figure 3-88 *Link to Previous* button

   - The *Same as Previous* label no longer displays.
   - The header or footer content still displays, but you can edit it without it changing the header or footer content in the previous section.
3. Click the **Link to Previous** button to link header or footer content to a previous section after it has been unlinked.
   - Click **Yes** in the dialog box that opens asking if you want to link the header or footer to the previous section (Figure 3-89).
4. Click the **Close Header and Footer** button.

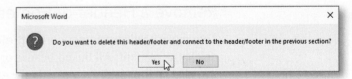

Figure 3-89 Link header or footer content to the previous section

Format Page Numbers

When using page numbers in your document, you can change the page number format and the starting page number. For example, reports typically use Roman numerals on the front matter pages (title page, table of contents, executive summary) and regular numbers on the body pages. If you are using different numbering for different sections of a document, insert a next page section break between sections. This allows you to format the page numbering of each section differently.

▶HOW TO: Format Page Numbers

1. Select the page number to format in the header or footer.
2. Click the **Page Number** button [*Header & Footer Tools Design* tab, *Header & Footer* group].
3. Select **Format Page Numbers** from the drop-down list. The *Page Number Format* dialog box opens (Figure 3-90).
4. Click the **Number format** drop-down list and select the number format.
5. Select either the **Continue from previous section** or **Start at** radio button in the *Page numbering* area.
   - If you select *Continue from previous section*, the numbering continues consecutively from the previous section.
   - If you select *Start at*, select the starting page number for the section.
6. Click **OK** to close the *Page Number Format* dialog box.

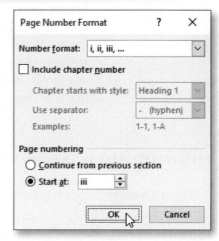

Figure 3-90 *Page Number Format* dialog box

When you include a Word cover page in a multipage document, the cover page is *not* considered the first page. Word considers the cover page as "page 0" when inserting page numbers in the header, footer, or table of contents. For this reason, the page number displayed in your document might be different from the page number displayed in the *Status* bar (bottom left of the Word window).

Navigate between Headers and Footers

When you are in a header or footer of a document, Word provides a variety of buttons to navigate the header or footer areas: ***Go to Header***, ***Go to Footer***, ***Previous***, and ***Next***. These navigation buttons are in the *Navigation* group on the *Header & Footer Tools Design* tab (Figure 3-91).

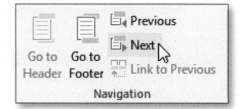

Figure 3-91 Header and footer navigation buttons

Remove a Header or Footer

To remove header or footer content from a document, open the header or footer and manually delete the content. All linked header or footer content is also removed when you do this. Word can also automatically remove the header or footer from a document.

▶HOW TO: Remove a Header or Footer

1. Click the **Insert** button.
2. Click the **Header or Footer** button [*Header & Footer* group].
3. Select **Remove Header** or **Remove Footer** from the drop-down list (Figure 3-92). The header or footer content is removed.

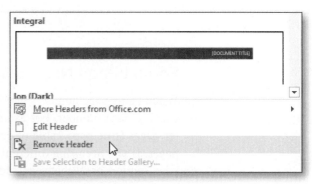

Figure 3-92 Remove header

For this Pause & Practice project, you continue to modify the *Personal Training Program* report for the American River Cycling Club. You apply styles to headings in the report, insert and modify a table of contents, insert and modify a cover page, and insert customized footers.

File Needed: *[your initials] PP W3-2.docx*
Completed Project File Name: *[your initials] PP W3-3.docx*

1. Open the *[your initials] PP W3-2* document completed in *Pause & Practice 3-2*.

2. Save this document as [your initials] PP W3-3.

3. Apply styles to the headings in the report.
   a. Select the "**General Guidelines**" heading on the first page.
   b. Click the **Heading 1** style [*Home* tab, *Styles* group] to apply this style to the selected heading (Figure 3-93). If the *Heading 1* style is not visible, click the **More** button to display the entire *Styles* gallery.

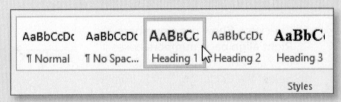

Figure 3-93 Apply *Heading 1* style

   c. Apply the **Heading 1** style to the following headings (bolded headings in the document):

      Personal Training Program Guidelines
      More about Long Rides
      Training Intensity and Heart Rate
      Using a Training Log

   d. Apply the **Heading 2** style to the following subheadings (underlined headings in the document):

      Pace of Rides
      Number of Rides per Week
      Duration of Rides
      Distance for Long Rides
      Suggestions for Long Rides
      Sample Session
      Other Heart Rate Factors
      Suggestions for Using a Training Log

4. Add a table of contents at the beginning of the report.
   a. Turn on **Show/Hide** [*Home* tab, *Paragraph* group] if necessary.
   b. Position the insertion point at the beginning of the document before the title ("Developing a Personal Training Program").
   c. Click the **Breaks** button [*Layout* tab, *Page Setup* group] and select **Page** or press **Ctrl+Enter** to insert a page break.
   d. Position the insertion point before the page break on the new first page.
   e. Click the **Table of Contents** button [*References* tab, *Table of Contents* group] (Figure 3-94).

Figure 3-94 Insert table of contents

f. Select **Automatic Table 2** from the drop-down list. The table of contents displays on the first page of the report.

5. Customize the table of contents.
    a. Position the insertion point in the body of the table of contents.
    b. Click the **Table of Contents** button [*References* tab, *Table of Contents* group].
    c. Select **Custom Table of Contents** to open the *Table of Contents* dialog box (Figure 3-95).
    d. Click the **Formats** drop-down list and select **Formal**.
    e. Set the number of levels to **2** in the *Show levels* area.
    f. Check the **Show page numbers** and **Right align page numbers** boxes if they are not already checked.
    g. Select the dot leader option from the *Tab leader* drop-down list if it is not already selected.
    h. Click **OK** to close the dialog box. A dialog box opens, confirming you want to replace the existing table of contents (Figure 3-96).
    i. Click **OK** to replace the existing table of contents.

6. Insert page breaks and update the table of contents.
    a. Position the insertion point in front of the "Number of Rides per Week" heading on the second page.
    b. Click the **Breaks** button [*Layout* tab, *Page Setup* group] and select **Page** to insert a page break (or press **Ctrl+Enter**).
    c. Repeat this process on the following headings:
        Suggestions for Long Rides
        Using a Training Log
    d. Place the insertion point in the table of contents at the beginning of the document.
    e. Click the **Update Table** button [*References* tab, *Table of Contents* group]. The *Update Table of Contents* dialog box opens.
    f. Select the **Update entire table** radio button and click **OK** (Figure 3-97). If a blank line displays above the table of contents, select the **paragraph mark** and press **Delete**.
    g. Select the entire table of contents (including the heading) and change the font to **Calibri**.

7. Customize document properties.
    a. Click the **File** tab to open the *Backstage* view and select **Info** (if necessary) to display document properties.
    b. Click the **Show All Properties** link in the document properties area.
    c. Add the following document properties:

        Title: Developing a Personal Training Program
        Company: American River Cycling Club
        Manager: Olesia Sokol

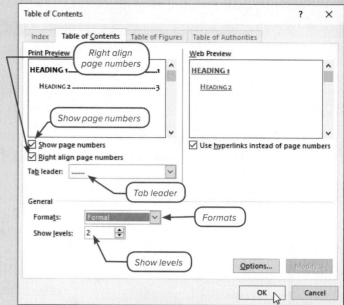

Figure 3-95 Customize table of contents

Figure 3-96 Replace existing table of contents

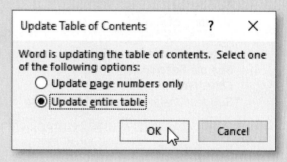

Figure 3-97 Update entire table of contents

d. Right-click the author's name in the *Author* area and select **Remove Person**.

e. Click the **Back** arrow to return to the report.

8. Add a cover page and customize fields.

   a. Click the **Cover Page** button [*Insert* tab, *Pages* group] and select **Semaphore**. The cover page displays on the page before the table of contents.

   b. Click the **Date** field, click the **Date** drop-down arrow, and select the current date.

   c. Click the **Author** document property field near the bottom of the cover page, select the field handle (Figure 3-98), and press **Delete** to delete the field. The insertion point is on the blank line where the *Author* field was removed, although it may not be visible.

Figure 3-98 Select and delete the document property field

   d. Click the **Quick Parts** button [*Insert* tab, *Text* group], select **Document Property**, and select **Manager** from the drop-down list to insert the *Manager* field above the company name.

   e. Click the **Company Address** field and type **www.arcc.org** in the field.

   f. Right-click the **Subtitle** field ("[Document Subtitle]") and select **Remove Content Control** from the context menu.

   g. Click the **Title** field and apply **bold** format. Bold formatting applies to the entire *Title* field.

   h. Save the document.

9. Insert odd page and even page footers.

   a. Place your insertion point at the beginning of the document (cover page).

   b. Click the **Footer** button [*Insert* tab, *Header & Footer* group] and select **Edit Footer** to open the footer area.

   c. Check the **Different First Page** box (if it is not already checked) and check the **Different Odd & Even Pages** box [*Header & Footer Tools Design* tab, *Options* group].

   d. Click the **Next** button [*Navigation* group] (Figure 3-99) to move to the odd page footer on the second page (table of contents).

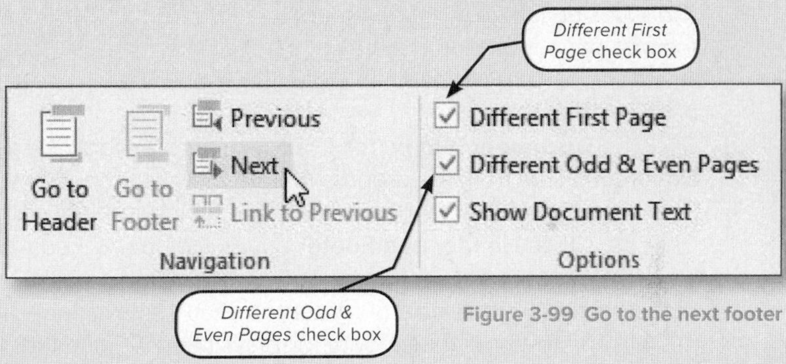

Figure 3-99 Go to the next footer

   e. Click the **Page Number** button [*Header & Footer* group].

   f. Select **Bottom of Page** and select **Two Bars 1** from the drop-down list (Figure 3-100). The page number "1" displays on the second page.

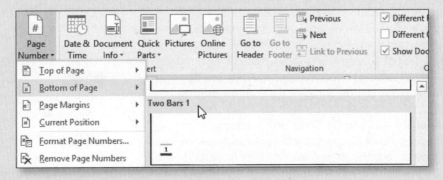

Figure 3-100 Select a built-in page number

▶ MORE INFO

Word considers the cover page as page 0. The table of contents page is page 1.

g. Click the **Next** button [*Navigation* group] to move to the even page footer on the next page.
h. Click the **Page Number** button [*Header & Footer* group], select **Bottom of Page**, and select **Two Bars 2** from the drop-down list. The page number "2" displays on the right.
i. Leave the footer open to add custom content in the next step.

10. Add custom content to the odd and even footers.
    a. Place the insertion point in the even page footer.
    b. Press **Ctrl+R** or click the **Align Right** button [*Home* tab, *Paragraph* group] to position the insertion point on the right.
    c. Click the **Document Info** button [*Header & Footer Tools Design* tab, *Insert* group] (Figure 3-101).
    d. Select **Document Property** and choose **Company** from the drop-down list. The *Company* document property field displays on the right side of the footer area.
    e. Select the **Company** document property field, change the font size to **10 pt**, and apply **bold** formatting.
    f. Click the **Previous** button [*Header & Footer Tools Design* tab, *Navigation* group] to move to the odd page footer on the previous page. The insertion point should be on the left after the page number "1."

Figure 3-101 Insert a document property field

    g. Click the **Document Info** button [*Header & Footer Tools Design* tab, *Insert* group] and select **Document Title** from the drop-down list. The *Title* document property field displays in the footer.
    h. Select the **Title** document property field, change the font size to **10 pt**, and apply **bold** formatting.
    i. Click the **Close Header and Footer** button [*Header & Footer Tools Design* tab, *Close* group].
    j. Review the document to ensure correct page numbering. No footer displays on the cover page of the document. The table of contents footer displays page "1" and the title of the report at the left. The first body page footer displays page "2" and the company name at the right. Each subsequent page should be numbered consecutively with odd and even footers.

11. Create a sharing link to share this file with your instructor.
    a. Save this document on *OneDrive* if you haven't already. If you don't have the ability to save to *OneDrive*, skip all of step 11.
    b. Click the **Share** button in the upper-right corner of the Word window. The *Send Link* window opens (Figure 3-102). If you are using a personal Microsoft account, the *Share* pane opens at the right, and the sharing options differ slightly.
    c. Click the **Link settings** button to open the *Link settings* window.
    d. Click the **Anyone** button and check the **Allow editing** box (if necessary) (Figure 3-103).
    e. Click **Apply** to return to the *Send Link* window.
    f. Click the **Copy Link** button to create a sharing link.
    g. Click **Copy** to copy the sharing link and click the **X** in the upper-right corner to close the sharing link window (Figure 3-104).

Figure 3-102 *Send Link* window

h. Use your email account to create a new email to your instructor. Include an appropriate subject line and a brief message in the body.

i. Press **Ctrl+V** to paste the sharing link to your document in the body of the email and send the email message.

12. Save and close the document (Figure 3-105).

Figure 3-104 Copy sharing link

Figure 3-103 *Link settings* window

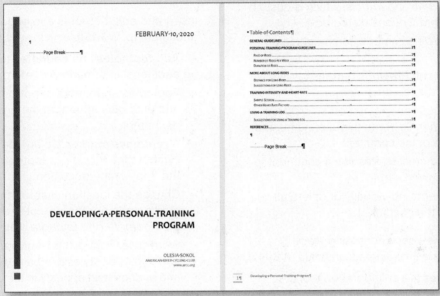

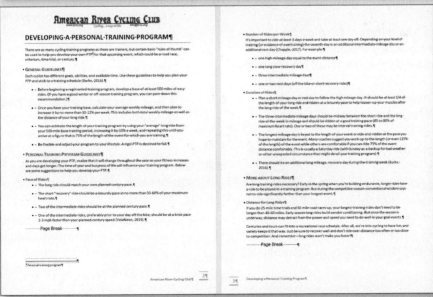

Figure 3-105 PP W3-3 completed (pages 1–4 of 7)

Chapter Summary

3.1 Insert, review, edit, and customize comments (p. W3-139).

- Use **comments** to insert a note or provide feedback in a document. The content and format of the document does not change.
- Use **Ink Comment** to insert a handwritten comment using a stylus or finger on a touch-screen computer.
- Users can add, edit, or delete comments. Comments appear to the right of the document in the **Markup area**.
- Comments are numbered sequentially in a document and are associated with a Microsoft Office **user name** and **initials**, which is customized in the *Word Options* dialog box.
- Multiple reviewers can add comments to a document.
- Use the **Next** and **Previous** buttons to review the comments in the document.
- When you place your pointer on a comment, a tag provides details about the user name and date and time of the comment.
- **Reply** to a comment or **Resolve** a comment to mark it as resolved.
- Delete comments individually or delete all comments in the document.

3.2 Modify and review a document using *Track Changes* and share an online document (p. W3-142).

- **Track Changes** is a collaboration tool that enables reviewers to make and track changes in a document.
- Word provides four different **Display for Review views** to display changes in a document: **All Markup**, **Simple Markup**, **No Markup**, and **Original**.
- When *Track Changes* is on, each change is attributed to a reviewer and his or her user name.
- Review changes using the **Previous** and **Next** buttons.
- Accept or reject individual changes in the document, or accept or reject all of the changes in the document.
- The **Reviewing pane** displays vertically on the left side of the document or horizontally at the bottom of the document and shows all the changes in the document.

- Customize which markup displays in the document.
- Use the *Track Changes Options* dialog box to customize how tracked changes appear in a document.
- Share online files with others. More than one user can edit an online file at the same time, which enables **real-time collaboration** on documents.
- The **Send Link** or **Share pane** provides different options for sharing an online document.

3.3 Insert and edit footnotes and endnotes in a document (p. W3-151).

- Add **footnotes** and **endnotes** to include additional information or reference sources.
- Footnotes appear at the bottom of the page, and endnotes appear at the end of the document.
- A **reference marker** is a number, letter, or symbol that indicates a footnote or endnote in the body of the document.
- Change the location, number format, and starting number for footnotes and endnotes in the *Footnote and Endnote* dialog box.
- Word styles control the format of footnotes and endnotes. Edit styles to modify how your footnote and endnote text appears in the document.
- Convert footnotes to endnotes or endnotes to footnotes using the **Convert Notes** dialog box.
- Move footnotes and endnotes using the drag and drop method or using cut and paste.
- When you delete a footnote or endnote reference marker in the body of the document, the associated footnote and endnote text is also deleted. Footnotes and endnotes automatically renumber if one is deleted or inserted.

3.4 Create a bibliography with properly formatted sources and insert citations into a document (p. W3-156).

- A **source** is the complete bibliographic information for a reference (book, web page, journal article) used in a report.

- A *citation* is the abbreviated source information used in the body of a report.
- The *bibliography style* controls the format of the sources on the bibliography page and citations in the body of the document.
- Add a *placeholder* to temporarily mark a citation in the body of a report.
- Use the *Source Manager* dialog box to create and edit sources, edit placeholders, and view available sources.
- Use the *Researcher* to search for quotes, citable sources, and images about a topic and to display information from journals and web sites in the *Researcher* pane.
- Insert a *bibliography* or *works cited* page to list the sources in your document.

3.5 Create and edit a table of contents based on headings in a document (p. W3-168).

- Word can automatically generate a *table of contents* for a document.
- *Heading styles* (Heading 1, Heading 2, etc.) determine the content for a table of contents.
- Use built-in table of contents formats or customize the format of the table of contents.
- Use the *Table of Contents* dialog box to customize the format and the number of levels displayed in the table of contents.
- When document headings or pagination change, update the table of contents to reflect the changes.

3.6 Insert a cover page and modify content and content control fields (p. W3-172).

- Word provides a variety of built-in *cover pages* available to add to your documents.
- A cover page has graphics, colors, text boxes, and Word fields that you can customize. The document theme controls the colors and fonts on the cover page.
- Use *document property* and *content control fields* to display information on the cover page. Customize or delete this content.

3.7 Apply and customize headers and footers in a multipage document (p. W3-175).

- *Headers* and *footers* provide information and page numbers in a document. Headers are located at the top, and footers are located at the bottom of a document.
- *Page* and *section breaks* control pagination and page numbering in a document.
- Insert a variety of built-in headers, footers, and page numbers into a document.
- Customize content and page numbering in headers and footers.
- *Different first page* headers and footers enable you to include different information on the first page of a document.
- Use *odd and even page* headers and footers to display different information on odd and even pages in a document.
- Change the page number format and starting page number in the *Page Number Format* dialog box.

Check for Understanding

The SIMbook for this text (within your SIMnet account) provides the following resources for concept review:

- Multiple-choice questions
- Short answer questions
- Matching exercises

Guided Project 3-1

For this project, you customize the *Online Learning Plan* for Sierra Pacific Community College District. You review comments and tracked changes, add document properties, apply styles, create a table of contents, insert and modify footnotes, insert headers and footers, and add a customized cover page. [Student Learning Outcomes 3.1, 3.2, 3.3, 3.5, 3.6, 3.7]

File Needed: ***OnlineLearningPlan-03.docx*** *(Student data files are available in the* Library *of your SIMnet account.)*
Completed Project File Name: *[your initials]* **Word 3-1.docx**

Skills Covered in This Project

- Modify user name and initials.
- Reject and accept tracked changes.
- Reply to a comment and resolve a comment.
- Customize document properties.
- Apply styles to selected text.
- Insert page breaks.

- Insert a table of contents.
- Insert footnotes.
- Modify footnote number format.
- Insert built-in page numbers and document property fields in the footer.
- Insert a cover page and remove and add document property fields.
- Update a table of contents.

1. Open the ***OnlineLearningPlan-03*** document from your student data files.

2. Save this document as [your initials] Word 3-1.

3. Change user name and initials.
   a. Click the **Tracking** launcher [*Review* tab, *Tracking* group] to open the *Track Changes Options* dialog box.
   b. Click the **Change User Name** button to open the *Word Options* dialog box.
   c. Type your first and last name in the *User name* text box in the *Personalize your copy of Microsoft Office* area.
   d. Type your first and last initials in lowercase letters in the *Initials* text box.
   e. Check the **Always use these values regardless of sign in to Office** box.
   f. Click **OK** to close the *Word Options* dialog box and click **OK** to close the *Track Changes Options* dialog box.

4. Display the *Reviewing* pane and reject changes.
   a. Click the **Display for Review** drop-down list [*Review* tab, *Tracking* group] and select **All Markup** to view the document with comments and proposed changes visible.
   b. Click the **Reviewing Pane** drop-down arrow [*Review* tab, *Tracking* group] and select **Reviewing Pane Vertical**. The *Reviewing* pane displays on the left side of the Word window.
   c. Find where "Hasmik Kumar Deleted **Television or Tele-Web course—**" in the *Reviewing* pane.
   d. Right-click this deletion and select **Reject Deletion** from the context menu (Figure 3-106).
   e. Click the **X** in the upper-right corner of the *Reviewing* pane to close it.

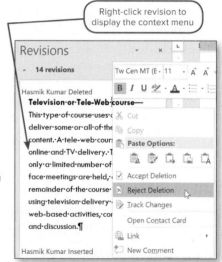

Figure 3-106 Reject a deletion in the *Reviewing* pane

5. Accept changes in the document.
   a. Place your insertion point at the top of the document.
   b. Click the **Next** button [*Review* tab, *Changes* group] to select the first change (Left: 1").
   c. Click the top half of the **Accept** button [*Review* tab, *Changes* group] to accept the change and move to the next change.
   d. Click the top half of the **Accept** button again to accept the change (delete CCD).
   e. Click the bottom half of the **Accept** button and select **Accept All Changes** from the drop-down list (Figure 3-107). All of the remaining changes in the document are accepted. Only comments remain in the *Markup* area.

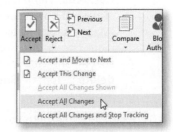

Figure 3-107 Accept all changes in the document

6. Reply to a comment, resolve a comment, and delete a comment.
   a. Place your insertion point at the top of the document and click the **Next** button [*Review* tab, *Comments* group] to move to the first comment.
   b. Click the **Reply** button in the *Markup* area.
   c. Type **Done!**
   d. Click the **Resolve** button on the comment in the *Markup* area (Figure 3-108). The comment and reply become grayed out.
   e. Click the **Next** button [*Review* tab, *Comments* group] to move to the second comment (not the reply to the first comment).
   f. Click the top half of the **Delete** button [*Review* tab, *Comments* group] to delete the comment.
   g. Click the **Display for Review** drop-down list [*Review* tab, *Tracking* group] and select **No Markup** so comments are not visible.

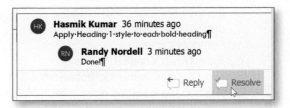

Figure 3-108 *Resolve* button on a comment

7. Add document properties.
   a. Click the **File** tab to open the *Backstage* view.
   b. Click **Show All Properties** in the *Properties* area.
   c. Add the following document properties:

   Title: Online Learning Plan
   Company: Sierra Pacific Community College District
   Manager: Hasmik Kumar

   d. Click the **Back** arrow to return to the document.

8. Apply styles to the document.
   a. Go to the first page of the document, select the title ("**Online Learning Plan**"), and apply the **Title** style.
   b. Select the subtitle ("**Sierra Pacific Community College District**") and apply the **Subtitle** style.
   c. Apply the **Heading 1** style to all the main headings (all caps and bold) in the document.
   d. Apply the **Heading 2** style to all subheadings (underlined) in the document.

9. Insert a table of contents into the report.
   a. Place your insertion point in front of the first main heading in the document ("Purpose of this Plan") and press **Ctrl+Enter** to insert a page break.
   b. Go to the new first page of the document, place the insertion point directly after the subtitle and press **Enter**.
   c. Click the **Table of Contents** button [*References* tab, *Table of Contents* group] (Figure 3-109).
   d. Select **Automatic Table 2**. The table of contents displays below the subtitle.

e. Select the words "**Table of Contents**" in the table of contents, click the **Font Color** drop-down list, and select **Automatic**. If a blank line displays between the subtitle and "Table of Contents," **delete** it. Turn on **Show/Hide** if necessary.

10. Insert footnotes into the document.
    a. Go to the second page of the document and position the insertion point after "web-Enhanced course" and before the dash.
    b. Click the **Insert Footnote** button [*References* tab, *Footnotes* group]. A footnote reference marker appears after the text and the insertion point moves to the bottom of the page in the *Footnotes* area.
    c. Type This is a non-OL course that uses OL tools. in the footnote area.
    d. Position the insertion point after "(OL)" and before the space (page 2, "Purpose of This Plan" section, second sentence).
    e. Click the **Insert Footnote** button and type Online learning is referred to as OL throughout this report. in the footnote area. This footnote becomes footnote 1, and the other footnote automatically becomes number 2.

11. Modify footnote number format.
    a. Click the **Footnotes** launcher to open the *Footnote and Endnote* dialog box (Figure 3-110).
    b. Click the **Number format** drop-down list and select **i, ii, iii, . . .**.
    c. Click **Apply** to close the dialog box and apply the number format change.

12. Insert and modify content in the footer.
    a. Place your insertion point at the beginning of the document.
    b. Click the **Footer** button [*Insert* tab, *Header & Footer* group] and select **Edit Footer**.
    c. Click the **Document Info** button [*Header & Footer Tools Design* tab, *Insert* group] and select **Document Title** from the drop-down list to insert the *Title* document property field.
    d. Press the **right arrow** once to deselect the document property field and press **Tab** to move to the center preset tab stop.
    e. Click the **Document Info** button, select **Document Property**, and select **Company** from the drop-down list.
    f. Press the **right arrow** once to deselect the document property field and press **Tab** to move to the right preset tab stop.

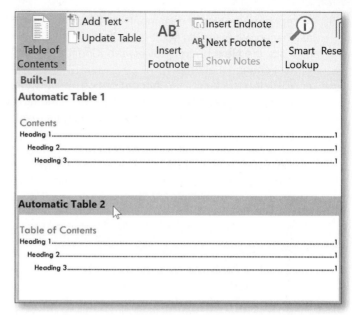

Figure 3-109 Insert a table of contents

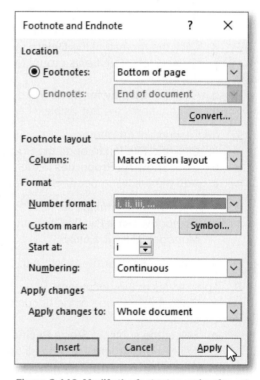

Figure 3-110 Modify the footnote number format

g. Click the **Page Number** button [*Insert* tab, *Header & Footer* group], select **Current Position**, and select **Bold Numbers** from the drop-down list.

h. Select all of the text in the footer and change the font size to **10 pt** (Figure 3-111).

Figure 3-111 Document properties and built-in page number inserted into the footer

i. Click the **Close Header and Footer** button [*Header & Footer Tools Design* tab, *Close* group].

13. Insert a page break.
    a. Position the insertion point before the last subheading ("How are Courses and Programs Selected for Online Learning Delivery?") on page 2 of the report.
    b. Press **Ctrl+Enter** to insert a page break.

14. Insert a cover page and modify content control fields.
    a. Place your insertion point at the top of the document.
    b. Click the **Cover Page** button [*Insert* tab, *Pages* group].
    c. Select the **Retrospect** built-in cover page from the drop-down list. The cover page displays before the first page of the document.
    d. Click the **Subtitle** ("Document Subtitle") content control field handle and press **Delete** (Figure 3-112) to delete the entire content control field.
    e. Click the **Author** content control field handle and press **Delete**.

Figure 3-112 Select and delete a content control field

    f. Confirm the insertion point is on the blank line where the *Author* field was deleted.
    g. Click the **Quick Parts** button [*Insert* tab, *Text* group], select **Document Property**, and select **Manager** from the drop-down list.
    h. Apply **bold** formatting to the *Company* document property field.
    i. Type **www.spccd.edu** in the *Address* ("Company Address") field. The web address displays in all caps; you will fix this in the next step.
    j. Select the **Address** document property field, open the *Font* dialog box, deselect the **All caps** check box, and click **OK**. The web address changes to lowercase (Figure 3-113).

Figure 3-113 Document property fields modified on the cover page

15. Update the table of contents.
    a. Click the table of contents.

b. Click the **Update Table** button [*References* tab, *Table of Contents* group]. The *Update Table of Contents* dialog box opens (Figure 3-114).

c. Select the **Update entire table** radio button.

d. Click **OK** to close the dialog box and update the table.

16. Save and close the document (Figure 3-115).

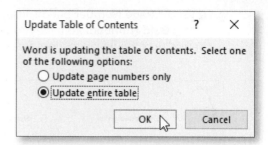

Figure 3-114 *Update Table of Contents* dialog box

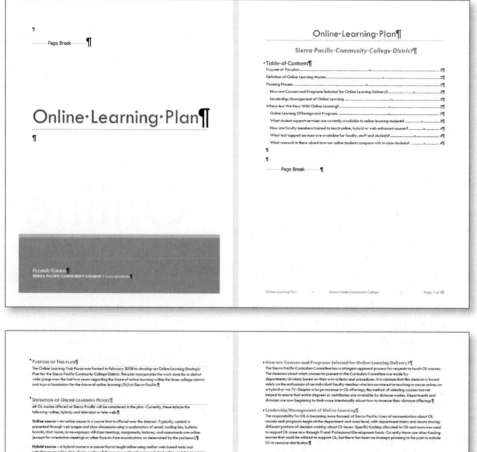

Figure 3-115 **Word 3-1 completed (first four of six pages)**

Guided Project 3-2

For this project, you create a multipage insurance renewal letter that Central Sierra Insurance will send on behalf of Valley Custom Manufacturing. You review comments and tracked changes, use *Track Changes*, format the document as a business letter, insert a document property field, insert and customize header content, use footnotes and endnotes, and insert a page and section break.
[**Student Learning Outcomes 3.1, 3.2, 3.3, 3.7**]

File Needed: ***ValleyCustomManufacturing-03.docx*** *(Student data files are available in the Library of your SIMnet account.)*
Completed Project File Name: ***[your initials] Word 3-2.docx***

Skills Covered in This Project

- Review tracked changes and comments.
- Use *Track Changes*.
- Change *Display for Review* view.
- Format the document as a block format business letter.
- Insert a next page section break.
- Change margins and header location on a section of a document.
- Use a different first page header.

- Insert a document property, date, and page number in the header.
- Format the page number in the header.
- Apply a bottom border.
- Insert footnotes.
- Convert footnotes to endnotes and change number format.
- Insert a page break to control pagination.
- Accept tracked changes.
- Share a document.

---

1. Open the ***ValleyCustomManufacturing-03*** document from your student data files.

2. Save this document as [your initials] Word 3-2.

3. Review a comment, accept tracked changes, and delete a comment.
   a. Click the **Display for Review** drop-down list [*Review* tab, *Tracking* group] and select **All Markup**.
   b. Read the comment in the *Markup* area at the top of the document and review the tracked changes in the document.
   c. Click the **Next** button [*Review* tab, *Changes* group] to move to the first tracked change (not comment).
   d. Click the bottom half of the **Accept** button [*Review* tab, *Changes* group] and select **Accept and Move to Next**.
   e. Click the bottom half of the **Accept** button and select **Accept All Changes**.
   f. Click the bottom half of the **Delete** button [*Review* tab, *Comments* group] and select **Delete All Comments in Document**.

4. Change user name and initials.
   a. Click the **Tracking** launcher [*Review* tab, *Tracking* group] to open the *Track Changes Options* dialog box.
   b. Click the **Change User Name** button to open the *Word Options* dialog box.
   c. Type your first and last name in the *User name* text box in the *Personalize your copy of Microsoft Office* area.
   d. Type your first and last initials in lowercase letters in the *Initials* text box.
   e. Check the **Always use these values regardless of sign in to Office** box.
   f. Click **OK** to close the *Word Options* dialog box and click **OK** to close the *Track Changes Options* dialog box.

5. Turn on *Track Changes* and format the first page of the document as a block format business letter.
   a. Click the top half of the **Track Changes** button [*Review* tab, *Tracking* group] to turn on *Track Changes* and turn on **Show/Hide**. All changes will be tracked.
   b. Place your insertion point in front of "LIABILITY" on the first page.
   c. Click the **Breaks** button [*Layout* tab, *Page Setup* group] and select **Next Page** in the *Section Breaks* area.
   d. Move to the last blank line on the first page (in front of the paragraph mark and section break), type Sincerely, and press **Enter** four times.
   e. Type Jennie Owings, Vice President and press **Enter** once.
   f. Type Central Sierra Insurance and press **Enter** two times.
   g. Type your initials in lowercase letters with no spaces or punctuation and press **Enter**. Word automatically capitalizes the first letter of your initials. Use the **smart tag** to undo automatic capitalization (Figure 3-116).

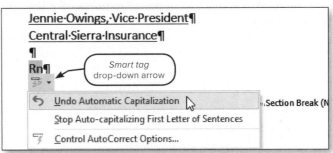

Figure 3-116 Use the smart tag to undo automatic capitalization

   h. Type Enclosure on the line after your reference initials.
   i. Place your insertion point at the top of the document and press **Enter** four times.
   j. Place the insertion point on the first blank line at the top and click the **Date & Time** button [*Insert* tab, *Text* group]. The *Date and Time* dialog box opens.
   k. Select the *January 1, 2020* date format, check the **Update automatically** box, and click **OK** to close the dialog box and insert the date.
   l. Select the dateline and apply **24 pt** *Before* paragraph spacing.

6. Modify the margins and header position in the second section of the document.
   a. Place your insertion point in the second section of the document (page 2 or 3).
   b. Click the **Page Setup** launcher [*Layout* tab, *Page Setup* group] to open the *Page Setup* dialog box.
   c. Change the *Top* margin to **1.5"** and the *Left* and *Right* margins to **1.25"**.
   d. Click the **Layout** tab.
   e. Change the *From edge: Header* setting to **1"** in the *Headers and footers* area.
   f. Click the **Apply to** drop-down list and select **This section** (if not already selected) (Figure 3-117).
   g. Click **OK** to close the dialog box and apply the settings.

7. Insert header content on the second and continuing pages.
   a. Place your insertion point at the top of the document.

Figure 3-117 Change the header position in this section of the document

b. Click the **Header** button [*Insert* tab, *Header & Footer* group] and select **Edit Header** from the drop-down list.

c. Check the **Different First Page** box [*Header & Footer Tools Design* tab, *Options* group].

d. Click the **Next** button [*Header & Footer Tools Design* tab, *Navigation* group] to move to the header in section 2.

e. Click the **Document Info** button [*Header & Footer Tools Design* tab, *Insert* group] and select **Document Title**.

f. Press the **right arrow** on the keyboard to deselect the document property field and press **Enter**.

g. Click the **Date & Time** button [*Header & Footer Tools Design* tab, *Insert* group]. The *Date and Time* dialog box opens.

h. Select the *January 1, 2020* date format, check the **Update automatically** check box, and click **OK** to close the dialog box and insert the date.

i. Leave the header open for the next instructions.

8. Insert the page number in the header and format the page number.

a. Press **Enter** after the date in the header.

b. Type Page and **space** once.

c. Click the **Page Number** button [*Header & Footer Tools Design* tab, *Header & Footer* group], click **Current Position**, and select **Plain Number** from the drop-down list.

d. Click the **Page Number** button and select **Format Page Numbers** to open the *Page Number Format* dialog box (Figure 3-118).

e. Click the **Start at** radio button in the *Page numbering* area and change the page number to **2**.

f. Click **OK** to close the dialog box.

g. Place the insertion point after the page number and press **Enter** two times.

h. Select the page number line, click the **Borders** drop-down arrow [*Home* tab, *Paragraph* group], and select **Bottom Border**.

i. Click the **Close Header and Footer** button [*Header & Footer Tools Design* tab, *Close* group]. The header appears on the second and continuing pages.

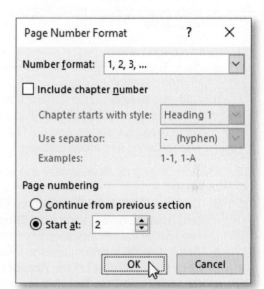

Figure 3-118 Change the *Start at* page number

9. Insert footnotes.

a. Go to page 4 and place the insertion point after the period at the end of the last line of text (after "reports are included.").

b. Click the **Insert Footnote** button [*References* tab, *Footnotes* group].

c. Type A list of drivers was faxed as a separate attachment. in the footnotes area.

d. Go to the first page and place the insertion point after the period at the end of the fourth body paragraph (after "2020 renewal.").

e. Click the **Insert Footnote** button and type Inflation is anticipated to be 2 percent. in the footnotes area.

10. Convert footnotes to endnotes and change number format.

a. Click the **Footnotes** launcher to open the *Footnote and Endnote* dialog box.

b. Click the **Convert** button. The *Convert Notes* dialog box opens (Figure 3-119).

Figure 3-119 Convert footnotes to endnotes

c. Select the **Convert all footnotes to endnotes** radio button and click **OK** to close the *Convert Notes* dialog box.

d. Click **Close** to close the *Footnote and Endnote* dialog box.

e. Click the **Footnotes** launcher again to open the *Footnote and Endnote* dialog box (Figure 3-120).

f. Select the **Endnotes** radio button if it is not selected.

g. Click the **Number format** drop-down list and select **a, b, c, . . .**.

h. Click the **Apply changes to** drop-down list and select **Whole document**.

i. Click **Apply** to close the dialog box and apply the changes.

11. Insert a page break.
    a. Go to page 2 and place the insertion point in front of the "PROPERTY" heading.
    b. Click the **Breaks** button [*Layout* tab, *Page Setup* group] and select **Page** in the *Page Breaks* area. A page break is inserted, and the "PROPERTY" heading and following text move to page 3.

12. Change *Display for Review* view and accept all tracked changes.
    a. Click the **Display for Review** drop-down list [*Review* tab, *Tracking* group] and select **Simple Markup**. A red line on the left indicates where changes were made.
    b. Scroll through the four pages to review the document.
    c. Click the bottom half of the **Accept** button [*Review* tab, *Tracking* group] and select **Accept All Changes and Stop Tracking**.

13. Save the document.

14. Share the document with your instructor.
    a. Save this document on *OneDrive* if you haven't already. If you don't have the ability to save to *OneDrive*, skip all of step 14.
    b. Click the **Share** button in the upper-right corner of the Word window to open the *Send Link* window (Figure 3-121). If you're using a personal Microsoft account, the *Share* pane displays at the right, and the sharing options differ slightly.
    c. Click the **Link settings** button to open the *Link settings* window (Figure 3-122).

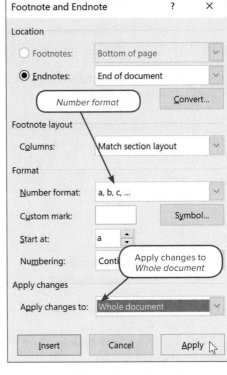
Figure 3-120 Change endnote number format

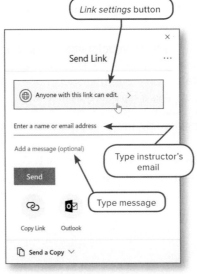
Figure 3-121 *Send Link* window

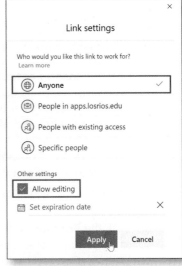
Figure 3-122 *Link settings* window

d. Click the **Anyone** button and check the **Allow editing** box (if necessary).

e. Click **Apply** to close the *Link settings* window and return to the *Send Link* window.

f. Type your instructor's email address in the *Enter a name or email address* area (see Figure 3-121).

g. Type a brief message to your instructor and click the **Send** button.

h. Click the **X** in the upper-right corner of the confirmation window to close it.

15. Save and close the document (Figure 3-123).

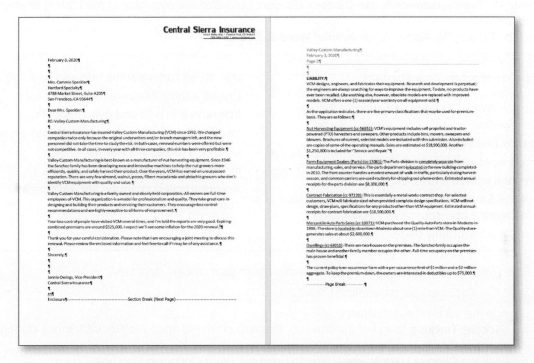

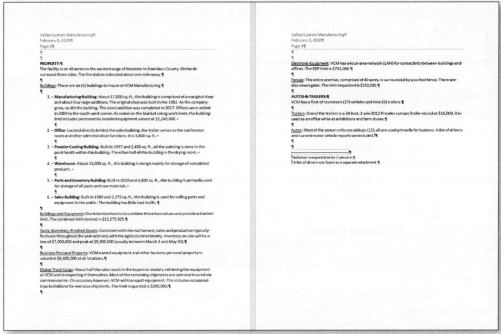

Figure 3-123 Word 3-2 completed

Guided Project 3-3

For this project, you customize the *Teen Substance Abuse* report for Courtyard Medical Plaza. You use *Comments* and *Track Changes*, and you add citations, a bibliography page, table of contents, headers and footers, and a cover page.
[Student Learning Outcomes 3.1, 3.2, 3.4, 3.5, 3.6, 3.7]

File Needed: ***TeenSubstanceAbuse-03.docx*** *(Student data files are available in the* Library *of your SIM-net account.)*
Completed Project File Name: ***[your initials] Word 3-3.docx***

Skills Covered in This Project

- Turn on *Track Changes* and change *Display for Review* view.
- Set the bibliography style.
- Insert a placeholder for a citation.
- Create a source and insert a citation.
- Use the *Source Manager* to edit a placeholder and create a new source.
- Insert a bibliography page.

- Use styles to format the title and headings.
- Create a table of contents.
- Insert built-in odd and even headers.
- Insert a document property field into a header.
- Update a table of contents.
- Insert and customize a cover page.
- Accept tracked changes and resolve a comment.
- Share a document.

1. Open the ***TeenSubstanceAbuse-03*** document from your student data files.

2. Save this document as [your initials] Word 3-3.

3. Change the user name and initials.
   a. Click the **Tracking** launcher [*Review* tab, *Tracking* group] to open the *Track Changes Options* dialog box.
   b. Click the **Change User Name** button to open the *Word Options* dialog box.
   c. Type your first and last name in the *User name* text box in the *Personalize your copy of Microsoft Office* area.
   d. Type your first and last initials in lowercase letters in the *Initials* text box.
   e. Check the **Always use these values regardless of sign in to Office** box.
   f. Click **OK** to close the *Word Options* dialog box and click **OK** to close the *Track Changes Options* dialog box.

4. Turn on *Track Changes* and change the *Display for Review* view.
   a. Click the top half of the **Track Changes** button [*Review* tab, *Tracking* group] to turn on *Track Changes* and turn on **Show/Hide**. All changes will be tracked.
   b. Click the **Display for Review** drop-down list [*Review* tab, *Tracking* group] and select **Simple Markup**. A red line on the left indicates tracked changes.

5. Select the report style and insert placeholders for a citation.
   a. Click the **Style** drop-down list [*References* tab, *Citations & Bibliography* group].
   b. Select **Chicago Sixteenth Edition**.
   c. Go to the "What Problems Can Teen Substance Abuse Cause?" section on page 1 and place the insertion point at the end of the last sentence in the second paragraph ("unsafe substances") and before the period.
   d. Click the **Insert Citation** button [*References* tab, *Citations & Bibliography* group] and select **Add New Placeholder**. The *Placeholder Name* dialog box opens.
   e. Type Foundation and click **OK**. The placeholder for the citation displays in the report.
   f. Go to the "Can Teen Substance Use and Abuse Be Prevented?" section on page 2 and place the insertion point at the end of the last sentence in the first paragraph ("and drugs") and before the period.

g. Click the **Insert Citation** button and select the **Foundation** placeholder from the drop-down list (Figure 3-124).

6. Insert a citation into the report.

   a. Go to the "What Is Teen Substance Abuse?" section on page 1 and place the insertion point at the end of the last sentence in the second paragraph ("most often") and before the period.

   b. Click the **Insert Citation** button [*References* tab, *Citations & Bibliography* group] and select **Add New Source**. The *Create Source* dialog box opens (Figure 3-125).

   c. Check the **Show All Bibliography Fields** box and create a new source with the following information:

Figure 3-124 Insert a placeholder for a citation

   Type of Source: **Journal Article**
   Author: Kelly L. Sanchez
   Title: Examining High School Drug Use
   Journal Name: Journal of Secondary Education
   Year: 2018
   Pages: 22-26
   Volume: XXI
   Issue: 2
   Tag Name: Sanchez

   d. Click **OK** to close the dialog box and insert the citation. The citation displays in the report.

7. Use the *Source Manager* to create a new source and provide source information for a placeholder.

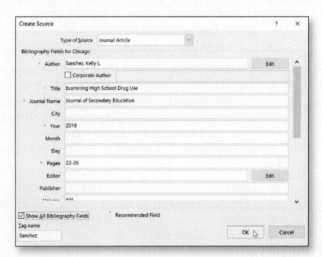

Figure 3-125 *Create Source* dialog box

   a. Click the **Manage Sources** button [*References* tab, *Citations & Bibliography* group] to open the *Source Manager* dialog box.

   b. Select the **Foundation** placeholder in the *Current List* area and click **Edit**. The *Edit Source* dialog box opens.

   c. Use the following information to edit the placeholder source:

   Type of Source: **web site**
   Corporate Author: Foundation for Teen Health
   Name of web Page: Making Good Choices
   Year: 2017
   Year Accessed: 2020
   Month Accessed: June
   Day Accessed: 25
   URL: http://www.foundationforteenhealth.org/choices.htm

   d. Click **OK** to close the dialog box and update the placeholders. The placeholders in the report are updated with the proper citation from the source information. Leave the *Source Manager* dialog box open.

   e. Click the **New** button in the *Source Manager* dialog box. The *Create Source* dialog box opens.

   f. Create a new source with the following information:

   Type of Source: **Document From web site**
   Corporate Author: Courtyard Medical Plaza
   Name of web Page: Teen Mental Health
   Name of web Site: Courtyard Medical Plaza
   Year: 2019

Month: March
Day: 6
URL: http://www.cmp.com/Teen_Mental_Health.pdf
Tag Name: CMP

    g. Click **OK** to close the dialog box and click **Close** to close the *Source Manager* dialog box.

8. Insert citations into the report.
    a. Go to the "Why Do Teens Abuse Drugs and Alcohol?" section on page 1 and place the insertion point at the end of the last sentence in the second paragraph ("increased risk") and before the period.
    b. Click the **Insert Citation** button [*References* tab, *Citations & Bibliography* group] and select the **Courtyard Medical Plaza** citation from the drop-down list.
    c. Go to the "What Should You Do if You Discover Your Teen Is Using?" section on page 2 and place the insertion point at the end of the last sentence in the second paragraph ("or both") and before the period.
    d. Click the **Insert Citation** button and select the **Sanchez, Kelly L.** citation from the drop-down list.

9. Insert a bibliography page at the end of the document.
    a. Place your insertion point on the blank line at the end of the document.
    b. Click the **Breaks** button [*Layout* tab, *Page Setup* group] and select **Page** in the *Page Breaks* section to insert a page break (or press **Ctrl+Enter**).
    c. Click the **Bibliography** button [*References* tab, *Citations & Bibliography* group] and select **Bibliography** to insert the built-in bibliography into the document.

10. Apply styles to the title and section headings and insert a table of contents.
    a. Apply the **Title** style to the title of the report on the first page.
    b. Apply the **Heading 1** style to each of the bold section headings in the report.
    c. Place your insertion point at the beginning of the report.
    d. Click the **Blank Page** button [*Insert* tab, *Pages* group] to insert a blank page before the first page of the report.
    e. Place your insertion point at the top of the new first page, type Teen Substance Abuse, and press **Enter**. The text should be formatted as *Title* style. If it's not, apply the **Title** style.
    f. Click the **Table of Contents** button [*References* tab, *Table of Contents* group] and select **Automatic Table 1** from the drop-down list. The table of contents is inserted below the title.

11. Insert odd and even page headers and customize content.
    a. Confirm the insertion point is on the first page, click the **Header** button [*Insert* tab, *Header & Footer* group], and select **Edit Header** from the drop-down list.
    b. Check the **Different Odd & Even Pages** check box [*Header & Footer Tools Design* tab, *Options* group].
    c. Select **Motion (Odd Page)** from the drop-down list of built-in headers [*Header & Footer* group].
    d. Delete the existing text in the text box to the left of the page number. Don't delete the text box.
    e. Click the **Document Info** button [*Header & Footer Tools Design* tab, *Insert* group], click **Document Property**, and select **Company** from the drop-down list (Figure 3-126).

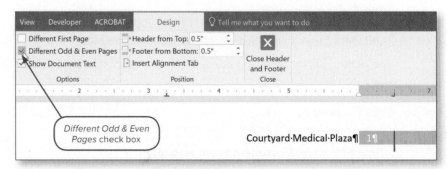

Figure 3-126 Odd page header inserted and content customized

    f. Click the **Next** button to move to the *Even Page Header*.

g. Click the **Header** button [*Header & Footer Tools Design* tab, *Header & Footer* group] and select **Motion (Even Page)** from the drop-down list.

h. Click the **Close Header and Footer** button [*Close* group].

12. Insert page breaks to control page endings.
   a. Go to the second page, click in front of the last section heading ("What Are the Signs of Substance Abuse"), and insert a **Page** break.
   b. Go to the third page, click in front of the last section heading ("Can Teen Substance Use and Abuse Be Prevented"), and insert a **Page** break.

13. Update the table of contents.
   a. Click the table of contents on the first page.
   b. Click the **Update Table** button at the top of the content control field. The *Update Table of Contents* dialog box opens (Figure 3-127).
   c. Select the **Update entire table** radio button and click **OK**.

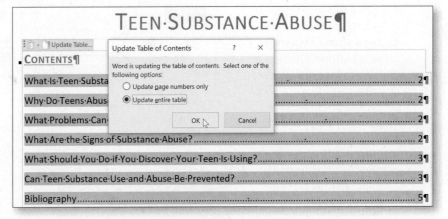

Figure 3-127 Update the table of contents

14. Insert and customize a cover page.
   a. Place your insertion point at the beginning of the document.
   b. Click the **Cover Page** button [*Insert* tab, *Pages* group].
   c. Select the **Slice (Dark)** built-in cover page from the drop-down list. The cover page displays on a new page before the table of contents.
   d. Select the **Title** document property field, apply **Bold** formatting, and change the font size to **40 pt**.
   e. Click the **Subtitle** content control field handle and press **Delete**.
   f. Press **Ctrl+Home** to move the insertion point to the top of the cover page.
   g. Click the **Quick Parts** button [*Insert* tab, *Text* group], select **Document Property**, and select **Company** from the drop-down list.
   h. Select the **Company** document property field, apply **Bold** and **Small Caps** formatting, and change the font size to **36 pt**.

15. Review comments and track changes.
   a. Click the **Display for Review** drop-down list [*Review* tab, *Tracking* group] and select **All Markup**.
   b. Right-click the comment in the *Markup* area at the top of the third page and select **Resolve Comment**.
   c. Click the bottom half of the **Accept** button [*Changes* group] and select **Accept All Changes and Stop Tracking**.
   d. Click the **Display for Review** drop-down list [*Review* tab, *Tracking* group] and select **No Markup**.
   e. Save the document.

16. Share the document with your instructor.
   a. Save this document on *OneDrive* if you haven't already. If you don't have the ability to save to *OneDrive*, skip all of step 16.
   b. Click the **Share** button in the upper-right corner of the Word window to open the *Send Link* window (Figure 3-128). If you're using a personal Microsoft account, the *Share* pane displays at the right, and the sharing options differ slightly.

c. Click the **Link settings** button to open the *Link settings* window (Figure 3-129).

d. Click the **Anyone** button and check the **Allow editing** box (if necessary).

e. Click **Apply** to close the *Link settings* window and return to the *Send Link* window.

f. Type your instructor's email address in the *Enter a name or email address* area (see Figure 3-128).

g. Type a brief message to your instructor and click the **Send** button.

h. Click the **X** in the upper-right corner of the confirmation window to close it.

17. Save and close the document (Figure 3-130).

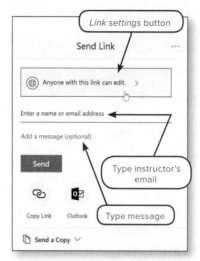

Figure 3-128 *Send Link* window

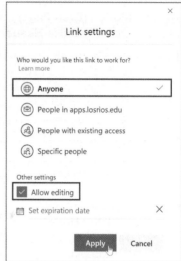

Figure 3-129 *Link settings* window

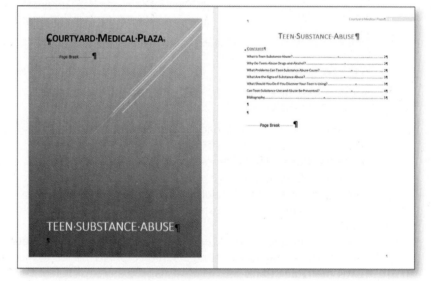

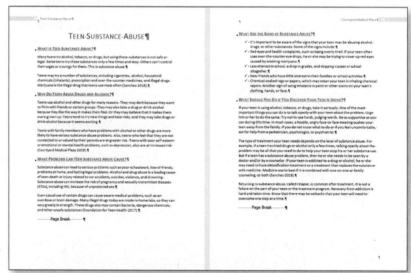

Figure 3-130 Word 3-3 completed (first four of six pages)

Independent Project 3-4

For this project, you modify the *Tips for Better Heart Rate Monitor Training* document from the American River Cycling Club. You use *Track Changes* and comments, insert and modify endnotes, insert place-holders, create sources, insert a bibliography page, insert a table of contents and cover page, and use custom headers and footers.
[Student Learning Outcomes 3.1, 3.2, 3.3, 3.4, 3.5, 3.6, 3.7]

File Needed: ***HeartRateMonitorTraining-03.docx*** *(Student data files are available in the* Library *of your SIMnet account.)*
Completed Project File Name: *[your initials]* **Word 3-4.docx**

Skills Covered in This Project

- Use comments and *Track Changes*.
- Insert endnotes.
- Insert a placeholder for a citation.
- Use the *Source Manager* to edit placeholders and create a new source.
- Change the bibliography style.
- Insert a bibliography page.

- Convert endnotes to footnotes.
- Insert a table of contents.
- Insert and modify a cover page.
- Insert custom headers and footers.
- Insert a document property field.
- Insert page breaks.
- Change the footnote number format.
- Resolve a comment.
- Accept tracked changes.

---

1. Open the ***HeartRateMonitorTraining-03*** document from your student data files.
2. Save this document as [your initials] Word 3-4.
3. Change user name and initials.
   a. Open the *Track Changes Options* dialog box (**Tracking** launcher) and click the **Change User Name** button to open the *Word Options* dialog box.
   b. Type your first and last name in the *User name* text box and your first and last initials in lowercase letters in the *Initials* text box.
   c. Check the **Always use these values regardless of sign in to Office** box, click **OK** to close the *Word Options* dialog box, and click **OK** to close the *Track Changes Options* dialog box.
4. Turn on *Track Changes* and insert a comment.
   a. Turn on **Track Changes** and change the *Display for Review* view to **Simple Markup**.
   b. Select the title, insert a **New Comment**, and type Insert endnotes, citations, a references page, a table of contents, and a cover page in the new comment.
   c. Click the **Show Comments** button (if necessary) to close the *Markup* area on the right and display only the comment balloon and not the comment text.
5. Insert endnotes.
   a. Insert an endnote at the end of the first body paragraph on the first page (after the period after "your training rides.").
   b. Type See the References page for related book and articles. in the endnote area.
   c. Go to the "Analyze Your Heart Rate Data" section on page 1 and insert an endnote at the end of the body paragraph (after the period after "and duration.").
   d. Type See the ARCC web site (www.arcc.org) for information about specific heart rate monitors. in the endnote area.
   e. Go to the "Comparing Heart Rate Values with Others" section on page 2 and insert an endnote at the end of the second body paragraph (after the period after "predict performance.").
   f. Type 220-age is an estimate of maximum heart rate. in the endnote area.
6. Insert placeholders for citations.
   a. Go to the "Know Your Resting Heart Rate" section on page 1, place the insertion point at the end of the second body paragraph and before the period ("psychological stress"), and insert a placeholder named **RoadCycling**.

b. Go to the "Perform a Threshold Test" section on page 1, place the insertion point at the end of the second body paragraph and before the period ("threshold test"), and insert a placeholder named **Segura**.

c. Go to the "Not Analyzing Heart Rate Data" section on page 2, place the insertion point at the end of the body paragraph and before the period ("cycling training"), and insert a placeholder named **Wallace**.

7. Use the *Source Manager* dialog box to provide source information for the three placeholders. Check the **Show All Bibliography Fields** box, if necessary to display additional fields.

a. **Edit** the **RoadCycling** placeholder to include the following information.

Type of Source: **Document from web site**
Corporate Author: Road Cycling
Name of web Page: Training with a Heart Rate Monitor
Name of web Site: RoadCycling.com
Year: 2018
Year Accessed: 2020
Month Accessed: January
Day Accessed: 25
URL: http://www.roadcycling.com/heart_rate.html

b. **Edit** the **Segura** placeholder to include the following information.

Type of Source: **Article in a Periodical**
Author: Manuel A. Segura
Title: Maximizing Threshold Training
Periodical Title: Cycling Weekly
Year: 2019
Month: March
Day: 1
Pages: 35-41

c. **Edit** the **Wallace** placeholder to include the following information.

Type of Source: **Book**
Author: Ingrid L. Wallace
Title: Understanding Heart Rate
Year: 2017
City: Chicago
Publisher: Penguin Books

8. Convert all endnotes to footnotes.

9. Change the bibliography style and insert a references page at the end of the document.
a. Change the bibliography style of the report to **APA**.
b. Place your insertion point on the blank line at the end of the document and insert a **page break**.
c. Insert a **References** bibliography on the last page.
d. **Center** the *References* heading and apply **10 pt** *After* paragraph spacing.

10. Insert a table of contents.
a. Place the insertion point at the top of the document and insert a **page break**.
b. Place the insertion point in front of the page break at the top of the new first page.
c. Type Table of Contents and press **Enter** two times.
d. Select text you just typed, change the font size to **14 pt**, apply **bold** and **small caps** formatting.
e. Place your insertion point on the blank line below "Table of Contents."
f. Insert a **Custom Table of Contents** and use **Simple** format, show **2** levels of headings, show page numbers, right align page numbers, and use a dot tab leader.

11. Insert a cover page.
a. Insert the **Ion (Dark)** built-in cover page.
b. Select the **Year** field and choose the current date.

c. Select the **Title** field, change the font size to **44 pt**, apply **bold** formatting, and align **center**.

d. Delete the **Subtitle** and **Author** fields. Be sure to delete the entire fields, not just the text.

e. Select the **Company** field, change the font size to **12 pt**, and apply **bold** formatting.

f. Select the **Company Address** field and type www.arcc.org.

12. Insert a header and footer.
    a. Place the insertion point in the table of contents on the second page.
    b. Edit the header, type Page, **space** once, and insert a plain page number in the current position.
    c. **Align Right** the header information (use **Align Right**, not a tab).
    d. Go to the footer on the second page and insert the **Company** document property field.
    e. Press the right arrow key to deselect the field and press **Tab** two times.
    f. Type www.arcc.org on the right.
    g. Use the *Borders and Shading* dialog box to apply a **solid line**, **Automatic** color, **¾ pt** width, **top** and **bottom border** to the information in the footer.
    h. Change the font size of the information in the header and footer to **10 pt**.
    i. Close the header and footer. No header or footer should appear on the cover page.

13. Insert a **page break** before the "Analyze Your Heart Rate Data" and "Not Being Aware of Factors Affecting Heart Rate" headings.

14. Change the footnote number format to **A, B, C**.

15. Resolve a comment and accept all tracked changes.
    a. Click the **Show Comments** button to display comments.
    b. **Resolve** the comment near the top of the third page.
    c. Accept all changes in the document and stop tracking changes.
    d. Click the **Show Comments** button again so the text of the comment does not display.

16. **Update** the entire table of contents.

17. Save and close the document (Figure 3-131).

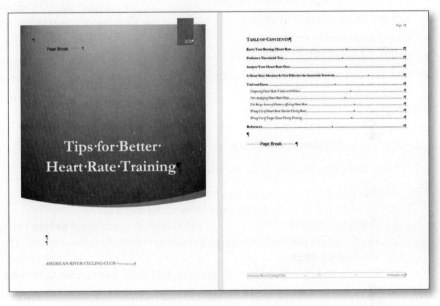
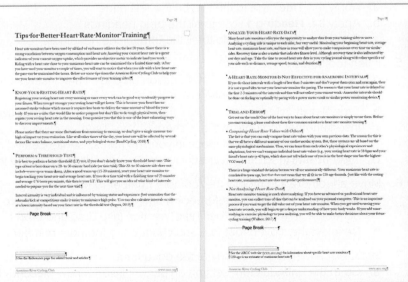

Figure 3-131 Word 3-4 completed (first four of six pages)

Independent Project 3-5

Sierra Pacific Community College District gives incoming college students a *Student Success Tips* document. For this project, you review comments and tracked changes, apply heading styles, and insert footnotes, placeholders, and a works cited page, table of contents, and cover page.
[Student Learning Outcomes 3.1, 3.2, 3.3, 3.4, 3.5, 3.6, 3.7]

File Needed: **StudentSuccess-03.docx** *(Student data files are available in the Library of your SIMnet account.)*
Completed Project File Name: **[your initials] Word 3-5.docx**

Skills Covered in This Project

- Review and delete a comment.
- Reject and accept tracked changes.
- Apply title and heading styles.
- Insert and modify footnotes.
- Insert a placeholder.
- Use the *Source Manager* to update a reference.
- Change the bibliography style.

- Insert a works cited page.
- Insert a table of contents.
- Use different odd and even page footers.
- Insert page numbers and a document property field into the footer.
- Insert and customize a cover page.
- Insert a page break.
- Update a table of contents.
- Share a document.

---

1. Open the **StudentSuccess-03** document from your student data files.

2. Save this document as [your initials] Word 3-5.

3. Review and delete selected comments and tracked changes.
   a. Change the *Display for Review* view to **All Markup**.
   b. Read the comment at the top of the document and then **delete** the comment.
   c. Find the first tracked change in the document (left, right, and top margin changed) and **Reject Format Change**.
   d. Review the changes in the document and then **Accept All Changes** in the document.

4. Apply styles to the title and headings.
   a. Apply the **Title** style to the title on the first page.
   b. Apply the **Heading 1** style to all the bold headings
   c. Apply the **Heading 2** style to all the underlined headings.

5. Insert footnotes.
   a. Go to the "Schedule Your Time" section on page 1 and insert a footnote after "Weekly Schedules" in the first sentence.
   b. Type Weekly Schedules are available from your counselor or in the college bookstore. as the footnote text.
   c. Insert another footnote in the "Schedule Your Time" section at the end of the "Be sure to schedule your time for all these in your 119 hours." sentence and after the period.
   d. Type Be sure to schedule recreational time in your 119 hours. as the footnote text.

6. Move a footnote and modify the footnote number format.
   a. Select the first footnote reference marker (in the body) and move it so it appears after "Weekly Schedule" in the "Track Your Time" section (use drag and drop or cut and paste).
   b. Deselect the moved footnote and change the footnote number format to **a, b, c**.

7. Insert placeholders in the body of the document.
   a. Go to the "Introduction" section on page 1, insert a new placeholder named Navarro at the end of the body paragraph (after "your advantage" and before the period).

b. Go to the "Test Anxiety" section on page 2 and insert a new placeholder named **Sierra** at the end of the body paragraph (after "become a problem" and before the period).

c. Go to the "Goal Setting" section on page 4 and insert the **Navarro** placeholder (not a new placeholder) at the end of the intro paragraph (after "your goals" and before the period).

8. Use the *Source Manager* dialog box to provide source information for the two placeholders. Check the **Show All Bibliography Fields** box if necessary.
   a. **Edit** the **Navarro** placeholder to include the following information.

   Type of Source: **Book**
   Author: Tessa C. Navarro
   Title: Study Skills for College Students
   Year: 2018
   City: Chicago
   Publisher: McGraw-Hill

   b. **Edit** the **Sierra** placeholder to include the following information.

   Type of Source: **Document from web site**
   Corporate Author: Sierra Pacific Community College District
   Name of web Page: Tips for Student Success
   Name of web Site: spccd.edu
   Year: 2019
   Year Accessed: 2020
   Month Accessed: February
   Day Accessed: 2
   URL: http://www.spccd.edu/tips4success.pdf

9. Use the *Researcher* to insert a citation.
   a. Go to the "Procrastination" section on page 1 and place your insertion point at the end of the third sentence and before the period ("a million disguises").
   b. Open the *Researcher* pane, type **procrastination** in the search box, and press **Enter**.
   c. Review the *Top sources for procrastination*.
   d. Locate one of the journal articles and click the plus sign (**+**) in the upper-right corner to add a citation to your document. The source is also added to the *Source Manager*. Click **No thanks** if a dialog box opens and asks if you want to update your bibliography.
   e. Close the *Researcher* pane.

10. Change bibliography style and insert a works cited page.
    a. Change the bibliography style to **MLA**.
    b. Place your insertion point on the blank line at the end of the document and insert a **page break**.
    c. Insert a **Works Cited** bibliography.

11. Insert a table of contents.
    a. Place your insertion point at the beginning of the document and insert a **page break**.
    b. Place your insertion point before the page break on the new first page.
    c. Type Student Success Tips and press **Enter**.
    d. Insert the **Automatic Table 1** table of contents.
    e. Apply the **Title** style to "**Student Success Tips**" on the new first page.

12. Insert a footer and add custom content.
    a. Edit the footer on the first page of the document (table of contents).
    b. Check the **Different Odd & Even Pages** box. The insertion point displays in the odd page footer.
    c. Insert the **Accent Bar 2** from the *Page Number*, *Current Position* drop-down list.
    d. Press **Tab** two times and insert the **Document Title** (or **Title**) document property field.
    e. Go to the even page footer and insert the **Accent Bar 2** from the *Page Number*, *Current Position* drop-down list.

     f. Press **Tab** two times and insert the **Company** document property field.

     g. Change the font size to **10 pt** and apply **bold** formatting to all footer content in both the even and odd page footers.

     h. Close the footer.

13. Insert and customize a cover page.

     a. Insert the **Slice (Light)** cover page.

     b. Delete the **Subtitle** ("Document subtitle") and **Course** ("Course title") document property fields.

     c. Change the font size of the title on the cover page to **40 pt** and apply **bold** formatting.

14. Insert a **page break** before the "Physical Signs of Test Anxiety" heading.

15. Update the entire table of contents and save your document.

16. Share the document with your instructor.

     a. Save this document on *OneDrive* if you haven't already. If you don't have the ability to save to *OneDrive*, skip all of step 16.

     b. Click the **Share** button in the upper-right corner of the Word window to open the *Send Link* window. If you are using a personal Microsoft account, the *Share* pane opens at the right, and the sharing options differ slightly.

     c. Edit the **Link settings** to **Allow editing** to **Anyone** and **Apply** these link settings.

     d. Type your instructor's email address in the email area.

     e. Type a brief message to your instructor and **Send** the sharing link.

     f. Click the **X** in the upper-right corner of the confirmation window to close it.

17. Save and close the document (Figure 3-132).

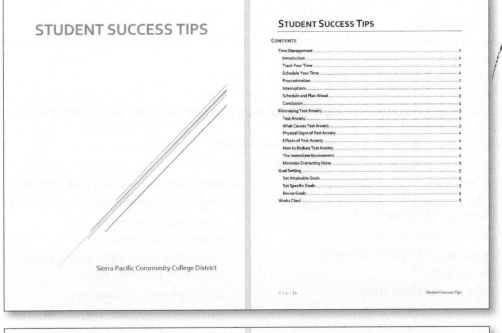

Figure 3-132 Word 3-5 completed (first four of seven pages)

Independent Project 3-6

Courtyard Medical Plaza works closely with the Skiing Unlimited winter ski program. For this project, you modify the *Skiing Unlimited Training Guide* using *Track Changes* to include footnotes, a table of contents, cover page, and headers and footers.
[Student Learning Outcomes 3.1, 3.2, 3.3, 3.5, 3.6, 3.7]

File Needed: ***SkiingUnlimitedTrainingGuide-03.docx*** *(Student data files are available in the Library of your SIMnet account.)*
Completed Project File Name: *[your initials] Word 3-6.docx*

Skills Covered in This Project

- Review and delete a comment.
- Change the *Display for Review* view.
- Review and accept tracked changes.
- Change margins.
- Apply title and heading styles.
- Insert a custom table of contents.

- Insert a page number in the header.
- Insert a document property field into the footer.
- Insert page breaks.
- Insert a cover page.
- Customize cover page content and insert a document property field.
- Update a table of contents.

---

1. Open the **SkiingUnlimitedTrainingGuide-03** document from your student data files.

2. Save this document as [your initials] Word 3-6.

3. Change user name and initials.
   a. Open the *Track Changes Options* dialog box (**Tracking** launcher) and click the **Change User Name** button to open the *Word Options* dialog box.
   b. Type your first and last name in the *User name* text box and your first and last initials in lowercase letters in the *Initials* text box.
   c. Check the **Always use these values regardless of sign in to Office** box, click **OK** to close the *Word Options* dialog box, and click **OK** to close the *Track Changes Options* dialog box.

4. Change *Display for Review* view, review and delete a comment, and accept *Tracked Changes*.
   a. Change the *Display for Review* view to **All Markup** and review tracked changes in the document.
   b. Read the comment on the first page and then **delete** the comment.
   c. **Accept All Changes** in the document.

5. Change the left and right margins to **1"**.

6. Apply styles to the title and headings.
   a. Apply the **Title** style to the title on the first page.
   b. Apply the **Heading 1** style to all the bold headings.
   c. Apply the **Heading 2** style to all the underlined headings.
   d. Apply the **Heading 3** style to all the italicized headings.

7. Insert and customize footnotes.
   a. Insert a footnote after the "Skiing Procedures" heading on the first page.
   b. Type **Skiing procedures vary depending on the clients' needs.** as the footnote text.
   c. Insert a footnote after the "Guiding Techniques" heading on the second page.
   d. Type **A minimum of two guides is required for all clients.** as the footnote text.
   e. Change the footnote *Number format* to **A, B, C** and change *Numbering* to **Continuous**.

8. Insert a custom table of contents.
   a. Place your insertion point at the beginning of the document and insert a **page break**.
   b. Type Table of Contents at the beginning of the first line (before the page break) on the new first page and press **Enter**.
   c. Insert a **Custom Table of Contents**, use **Fancy** format, show **2** levels of headings, show page numbers, right align page numbers, and do not include a tab leader.
   d. Apply the **Title** style to the "**Table of Contents**" heading on the table of contents page.

9. Insert header and footer.
   a. Edit the header on the first page (table of contents) and insert the **Bold Numbers 3** built-in page number at the **Top of Page**.
   b. Remove the blank line below the page numbers.
   c. Go to the footer on the same page and insert the **Title** document property field on the left. Use the right arrow key to deselect the document property field.
   d. Press **Tab** two times and insert the **Company** field on the right.
   e. **Bold** the text in the footer and close the footer.

10. Insert page breaks to keep headings with the text below.
    a. Insert a **page break** before the "Beginning Wedge Christie Turns" heading (page 4).
    b. Insert a **page break** before the "Introduction to Equipment" heading (page 5).

11. Insert and modify a cover page.
    a. Insert the **Grid** cover page.
    b. Delete the **Subtitle** field.
    c. Place the insertion point on the blank line between the *Title* and *Abstract* fields and insert the **Company** document property field.
    d. Delete the **Abstract** field.
    e. Select the **Company** document property field, change the font size to **20 pt**, apply **bold** formatting, and change the text color to the **fourth color** in the **first row** of the *Theme Colors* (**Blue-Gray, Text 2**).

12. Update the entire table of contents.

13. Save and close the document (Figure 3-133).

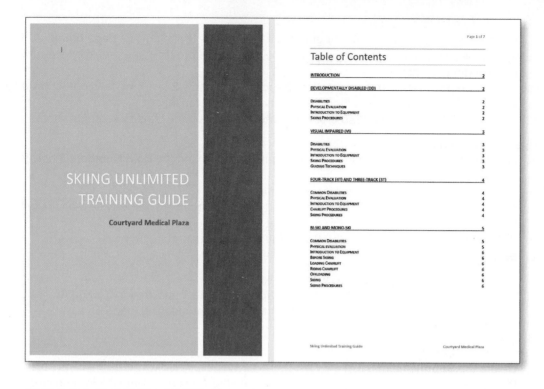

Figure 3-133 Word 3-6 completed (first four of eight pages)

Improve It Project 3-7

American River Cycling Club is working with a cycling tour company to arrange a trip to cycle through the Tuscany region of Italy. The original document from the cycling tour company needs to be improved and updated. Modify the document to remove content and add a cover page, table of contents, footnotes, and a footer.
[Student Learning Outcomes 3.1, 3.2, 3.3, 3.5, 3.6, 3.7]

File Needed: ***ItalyTourItinerary-03.docx*** *(Student data files are available in the* Library *of your SIMnet account.)*
Completed Project File Name: ***[your initials] Word 3-7.docx***

1. Open the ***ItalyTourItinerary-03*** document from your student data files.

Skills Covered in This Project

- Delete a comment and review tracked changes.
- Change the *Display for Review* view.
- Edit a document using *Track Changes*.
- Remove the existing cover page, table of contents, and header and footer.
- Apply a style and update a style.
- Insert page breaks.

- Move and delete an endnote.
- Convert endnotes to footnotes.
- Insert and customize footnotes.
- Insert a custom table of contents.
- Edit document properties.
- Insert and modify a cover page.
- Insert custom footer content.
- Review and accept tracked changes.
- Share a document.

2. Save this document as [your initials] Word 3-7.

3. Change user name and initials.
   a. Open the *Track Changes Options* dialog box (**Tracking** launcher) and click the **Change User Name** button to open the *Word Options* dialog box.
   b. Type your first and last name in the *User name* text box and your first and last initials in lower-case letters in the *Initials* text box.
   c. Check the **Always use these values regardless of sign in to Office** box, click **OK** to close the *Word Options* dialog box, and click **OK** to close the *Track Changes Options* dialog box.

4. Change *Display for Review* view, review and delete a comment, and turn on *Track Changes*.
   a. Change the *Display for Review* view to **All Markup** and review the changes in the document.
   b. Read the comment on the first page and then delete the comment.
   c. Turn on **Track Changes** and change the *Display for Review* view to **Simple Markup**.

5. Remove the existing cover page, table of contents, and header and footer content.
   a. Click the **Cover Page** button [*Insert* tab, *Pages* group] and select **Remove Current Cover Page**.
   b. Click the **Table of Contents** button [*References* tab, *Table of Contents* group] and select **Remove Table of Contents**.
   c. Use **Remove Header** and **Remove Footer** to remove all header and footer content.

6. Change the page orientation to **Landscape**.

7. Apply a heading style and update a style.
   a. Apply the **Day** style to the "Day 1: . . ." heading on the first page.
   b. Place your insertion point in the "Day 1" heading and **Update Heading 1 to Match Selection**. The new *Heading 1* style applies to all day headings in the document.

8. Insert page breaks.
   a. Click in front of "Day 3" and insert a **page break**.
   b. Insert a **page break** for each of the odd-numbered days so only two days appear on each page.

9. Add text and apply style.
   a. Place your insertion point on the blank line after "*Distance*:" in the "Day 2" section.
   b. Press **Enter** and type Notes and Questions at the insertion point.
   c. Apply the **Day** style to the text you just typed.
   d. Repeat steps b and c to insert this information at the end of the "Day 4" and "Day 6" sections.
   e. Go to the "Day 8" section, place your insertion point on the blank line below the "Kilometers to Miles Conversion" information and above the endnotes.
   f. Press **Enter**, type Notes and Questions, and apply the **Day** style to the text you just typed.

10. Move and delete endnotes and convert endnotes to footnotes.
    a. Move the first endnote marker (after the distance on "Day 3") to appear in the "Day 2" section after "*Distance*: 83 km".
    b. Change the text to Day 2 is the longest day of the tour. in the endnote text area.
    c. Delete the endnote reference marker after "Day 4." The endnote text is removed when you delete the reference marker.
    d. Convert all endnotes to footnotes.

11. Insert and customize footnotes.
    a. Place your insertion point after "*Distance*: 0-26 km" in the "Day 4" section, insert a footnote, and type Day 4 is an optional riding day. in the footnote text area. *Note*: The footnote number may not be consecutive until you accept tracked changes, which you will do later.
    b. Place your insertion point after "*Distance*: 42-58 km" in the "Day 5" section, insert a footnote, and type Day 5 has two routes from which to choose. in the footnote text area.
    c. Place your insertion point after "*Distance*: 52-68 km" in the "Day 6" section, insert a footnote, and type Day 6 has three routes from which to choose. in the footnote text area.
    d. Change the footnote *Number format* to **a, b, c** and change *Numbering* to **Continuous** if it is not already selected. *Note*: The footnote number may not be consecutive until you accept tracked changes, which you will do later.

12. Insert a custom table of contents.
    a. Place your insertion point at the beginning of the document and insert a **page break**.
    b. Type Contents on the first line on the new first page (before the page break) and press **Enter**.
    c. Insert a **Custom Table of Contents**, use **Distinctive** format, show **1** level of headings, show page numbers, right align page numbers, and include a solid line tab leader.
    d. Select the "Day 1" through "Day 8" lines of text in the table of contents and apply **12 pt** *After* paragraph spacing.

13. Edit the following document properties.

    Title: Cycling Classic Tuscany: Tour Itinerary
    Company: American River Cycling Club

14. Insert and modify a cover page.
    a. Insert the **Semaphore** cover page.
    b. Select the current date in the **Publish Date** field.
    c. Change the font size of the *Title* field to **48 pt** and apply **bold** format.
    d. Delete the **Subtitle** (*Document Subtitle*) and **Author** fields.
    e. Change the font size of the *Company* field to **14 pt** and apply **bold** format.
    f. Select the *Address* field and type www.arcc.org in the field.

15. Insert footers on the second and continuing pages.
    a. Go to the second page of the document (table of contents) and edit the footer.
    b. Change the alignment to **right**, insert the **Company** document property field, deselect the field (right arrow key), and **space** once.

   c. Type | (press **Shift+** to type a vertical line) and **space** once.

   d. Type Page and **space** once.

   e. Insert a plain page number in the current position.

   f. **Bold** all the text in the footer and close the footer.

16. Change *Display for Review* view, accept tracked changes, and turn off *Track Changes*.

   a. Change the *Display for Review* view to **All Markup**.

   b. Review the tracked changes in the document.

   c. Turn off **Track Changes** and **Accept All Changes** in the document.

   d. Save the document.

17. Share the document with your instructor.

   a. Save this document on *OneDrive* if you haven't already. If you don't have the ability to save to *OneDrive*, skip all of step 17.

   b. Click the **Share** button in the upper-right corner of the Word window to open the *Send Link* window. If you are using a personal Microsoft account, the *Share* pane opens at the right, and the sharing options differ slightly.

   c. Edit the **Link settings** to **Allow editing** to **Anyone** and **Apply** these link settings.

   d. Type your instructor's email address in the email area.

   e. Type a brief message to your instructor and **Send** the sharing link.

   f. Click the **X** in the upper-right corner of the confirmation window to close it.

18. Save and close the document (Figure 3-134).

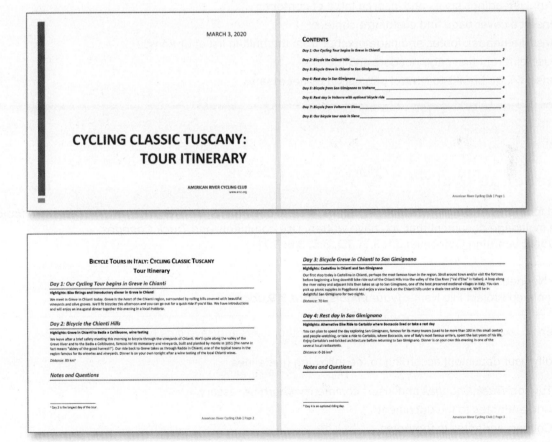

Figure 3-134 Word 3-7 completed (first four of six pages)

Challenge Project 3-8

Modify a report you have written for another class to include citations, a bibliography or works cited page, a table of contents, a cover page, and headers and footers. Use comments and *Track Changes*.
[Student Learning Outcomes 3.1, 3.2, 3.4, 3.5, 3.6, 3.7]

File Needed: None
Completed Project File Name: *[your initials] Word 3-8.docx*

Open an existing report you have created and save it as [your initials] Word 3-8.

Modify your document according to the following guidelines:

- Turn on *Track Changes* and insert comments where necessary.
- Select the citation style to use for your report (APA, MLA, Chicago).
- Add citations to the body of your report and create sources.
- Add placeholders for citations in the body of your report.
- Use the *Researcher* to find sources of information and insert citations.
- Insert a bibliography or works cited page at the end of your report.
- Use the *Source Manager* to edit placeholders and sources and add new sources if necessary.
- Insert other citations in the body as necessary.
- Update the bibliography page.
- Apply headings styles and insert a table of contents.
- Insert a cover page and customize content.
- Insert a header, footer, and page number from the built-in list of options.
- Use different first page headers and footers.
- Insert page breaks to control pagination as necessary.

Challenge Project 3-9

Add footnotes and endnotes, heading styles, a table of contents, a cover page, and headers and footers to a multipage document that you have written. Use comments and *Track Changes*.
[Student Learning Outcomes 3.1, 3.2, 3.3, 3.5, 3.6, 3.7]

File Needed: None
Completed Project File Name: *[your initials] Word 3-9.docx*

Open an existing report you have written for another class and save it as [your initials] Word 3-9.

Modify your document according to the following guidelines:

- Turn on *Track Changes* and insert comments where necessary.
- Add endnotes to the document.
- Convert endnotes to footnotes.
- Change the number format for footnotes.
- Move a footnote to a new location and delete a footnote.

- Insert a custom header or footer in your document.
- Add a page number in the header or footer of the document.
- Insert page breaks to control pagination as necessary.
- Apply headings styles and insert a table of contents.
- Insert a cover page and customize content.
- Insert custom header and footer content.
- Use different first page or odd and even page headers and footers.
- Accept all tracked change and turn off *Track Changes*.
- Insert page breaks to control pagination as necessary.

Challenge Project 3-10

Modify a report or multipage document you have written for another class to include a table of contents, a cover page, and headers and footers. Use comments and *Track Changes*.
[Student Learning Outcomes 3.1, 3.2, 3.5, 3.6, 3.7]

File Needed: None
Completed Project File Name: *[your initials] Word 3-10.docx*

Open an existing report or multipage document and save it as [your initials] Word 3-10.

Modify your document according to the following guidelines:

- Turn on *Track Changes* and insert comments where necessary.
- Apply *Heading 1* and *Heading 2* styles to the headings of your document. If the document does not have headings, add two levels of headings to the document.
- Insert a built-in or custom table of contents as the first page of your document.
- Include two levels of headings in the table of contents.
- Customize the *Title*, *Company*, and *Author* document property fields.
- Insert a cover page of your choice.
- Customize the cover page by adding or removing a document property or content control fields.
- Add custom information to content control fields.
- Insert a header, footer, and page number from the built-in list of options.
- Use different first page or odd and even page headers and footers.
- Insert page breaks to control pagination as necessary.
- Update the table of contents.

Source of screenshots Microsoft Office 365 (2019): Word, Excel, Access, Powerpoint.

Using Tables, Columns, and Graphics

CHAPTER OVERVIEW

Tables, columns, and graphics enhance the appearance and readability of your Word documents. For example, use tables to attractively arrange and align information in column and row format. Format documents with columns to improve readability and provide additional white space. You can also insert and manipulate graphics to add attention-grabbing visual elements to your documents. This chapter introduces you to the Word tools used to add and customize tables, columns, and graphics.

STUDENT LEARNING OUTCOMES (SLOs)

After completing this chapter, you will be able to:

SLO 4.1 Improve the design and readability of a document by using tables to present and arrange information (p. W4-219).

SLO 4.2 Modify a table by changing the column and row size, aligning text, using the *Table Properties* dialog box, sorting data, and using *AutoFit* (p. W4-223).

SLO 4.3 Enhance the appearance and function of a table by applying borders and shading, using table styles, inserting formulas, and converting text into a table (p. W4-229).

SLO 4.4 Modify the layout and design of a document using columns to present information (p. W4-236).

SLO 4.5 Improve a document by adding, modifying, and arranging pictures (p. W4-240).

SLO 4.6 Enrich a document by adding and customizing graphic objects such as shapes, *SmartArt*, *WordArt*, symbols, icons, 3D models, and online video (p. W4-248).

CASE STUDY

For the Pause & Practice projects in this chapter, you modify a brochure for Emma Cavalli, a realtor consultant with Placer Hills Real Estate (PHRE). In the past, Emma distributed brochures that were poorly designed and negatively impacted the effectiveness of her message. You modify one of Emma's brochures to include tables, columns, and graphics to improve the overall layout and effectiveness of the document.

Pause & Practice 4-1: Modify an existing brochure to include a table that presents information attractively.

Pause & Practice 4-2: Enhance the table in the brochure by using borders, shading, and table styles.

Pause & Practice 4-3: Improve the readability of the brochure by arranging text in columns.

Pause & Practice 4-4: Add visual elements to the brochure to improve the overall design of the document.

WORD

SLO 4.1

Creating and Editing Tables

In chapter 2, you learned to align information into column and row format using tab stops. *Tables* are another tool to organize information into column and row format. In addition to aligning data, tables enable you to apply additional formatting options.

> **MORE INFO**
>
> Most web pages organize information into table and row format even though you might not see the table borders or structure.

Tables

A table consists of individual *cells* where you enter information. Cells are grouped into *columns* and *rows*. When using tables, it is important to distinguish between cells, columns, and rows (Figure 4-1).

- *Cell*: The area where a column and row intersect
- *Column*: A vertical grouping of cells (think of vertical columns that support a building)
- *Row*: A horizontal grouping of cells (think of horizontal rows of seating in a stadium or auditorium)

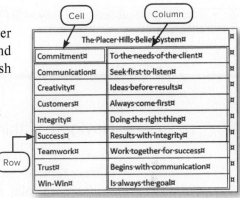

Figure 4-1 Table

▶**HOW TO: Insert a Table**

1. Place your insertion point at the location to insert a table.
2. Click the **Insert** tab.
3. Click the **Table** button [*Tables* group] to open the drop-down list.
4. Click and drag across the *Insert Table* grid to select the number of columns and rows you want in the table (Figure 4-2). The table is inserted into your document.

   - As you drag across the grid, the *Insert Table* label changes to display the size of the table (*3×7 Table*).

> **MORE INFO**
>
> Word lists table dimensions in column and row format. For example, a three-column and seven-row table is a 3 × 7 table.

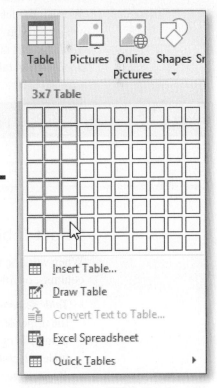

Figure 4-2 *Insert Table* drop-down list

Another way to insert a table is to use the ***Insert Table*** dialog box.

▶**HOW TO:** Insert a Table Using the Insert Table Dialog Box

1. Place your insertion point at the location to insert a table.
2. Click the **Table** button [*Insert* tab, *Tables* group] to open the drop-down list.
3. Select **Insert Table** to open the *Insert Table* dialog box (Figure 4-3).
4. Type or select the desired number of columns and rows in the *Table size* area.
5. Select how the table is distributed horizontally between the left and right margins in the *AutoFit behavior* area.
   - *AutoFit* is discussed more fully in *SLO 4.2: Arranging Text in Tables.*
6. Click **OK** to insert the table.

Figure 4-3 *Insert Table* dialog box

Navigate within a Table

To move the insertion point within a table, press **Tab** (or the **right arrow** key on your keyboard) to move forward one cell in the current row. When you get to the end of a row and press *Tab*, the insertion point moves to the first cell in the next row. **Shift+Tab** (or the **left arrow** key) moves you back one cell at a time. You can also use your pointer to click a cell.

Table Tools Layout Tab

When you insert a table into a document, the contextual ***Table Tools tabs*** display on the *Ribbon*. Word provides two *Table Tools* tabs: ***Design*** and ***Layout***. These contextual toolbars display whenever you place the insertion point in the table or select a region of the table. The *Table Tools Layout* tab provides a variety of formatting options (Figure 4-4). For more on the *Table Tools Design* tab, see *SLO 4.3: Formatting and Editing Tables.*

Figure 4-4 *Table Tools Layout* tab

Select Table and Text

When working with tables, you can select the entire table; a cell, column, or row; or multiple cells, columns, or rows to apply formatting changes. Word provides a variety of table selection tools.

- ***Table selector handle***: This handle appears above the upper-left corner of the table when the pointer is on the table (Figure 4-5). Click the **table selector** to select the entire table.
- ***Row selector***. The row selector is the right-pointing arrow when your pointer is just to the

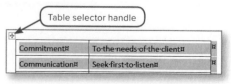

Figure 4-5 Table selector handle

left of the table row (Figure 4-6). When the pointer becomes the row selector, click to select a single row. To select multiple rows, click and drag up or down.

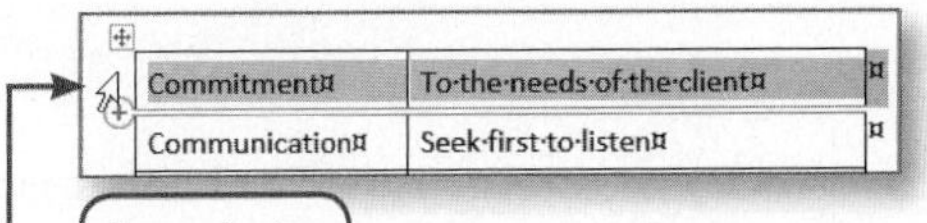

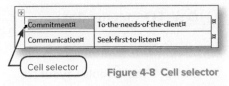

Figure 4-6 Row selector

- *Column selector*. The column selector is the thick, black down arrow when your pointer is on the top border of a column (Figure 4-7). When the pointer becomes the column selector, click to select a single column. To select multiple columns, click and drag left or right.

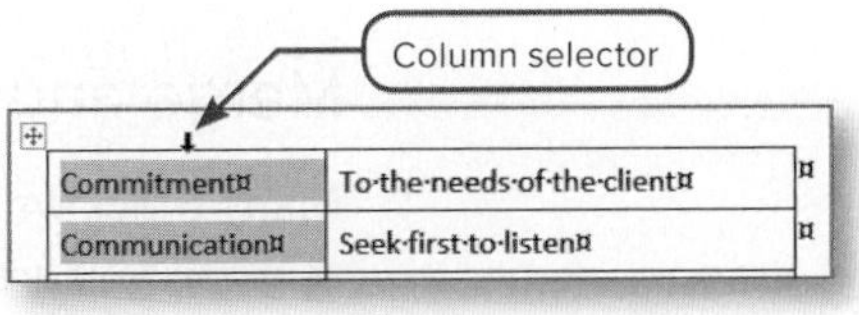

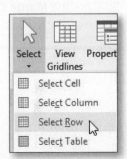

Figure 4-7 Column selector

- *Cell selector*. The cell selector is the thick, black right-pointing arrow when your pointer is just inside the left border of a cell (Figure 4-8). When the pointer becomes the cell selector, click to select a single cell. To select multiple cells, click and drag left, right, up, or down. When the cell selector displays, double-click to select the entire row.

Figure 4-8 Cell selector

- *Select button*: The *Select* button is located on the *Table Tools Layout* tab in the *Table* group. Click the **Select** button to access a drop-down list of table selection options (Figure 4-9).

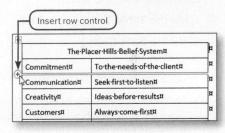

Add Rows and Columns

When you insert a table into a document, you are not limited to your original table dimensions. The following are methods to insert columns and rows in a table.

Figure 4-9 *Select drop-down list*

- *Insert Control*: Place your pointer on the left outside edge of a row or top outside edge of a column to display the insert row or column control (plus sign). Click the **insert control** to add a row or column (Figure 4-10). Select multiple rows or columns and click the insert control to add the number or rows or columns selected.
- *Table Tools Layout tab*: In the *Rows & Columns* group, you can insert a row above or below the current row or a column to the left or right of the current column (see Figure 4-10).
- *Mini toolbar*. Select a cell, row, column, or table to display the mini toolbar. You can also right-click the table to display the mini toolbar. Click the **Insert** button to display a list of insert options (Figure 4-11).

Figure 4-10 Insert row control

- *Insert Cells dialog box*: Open this dialog box by clicking the **Rows & Columns** launcher on the *Table Tools Layout* tab (Figure 4-12).
- *Tab*: When your insertion point is in the last cell in the last row, press **Tab** to insert a new row below the last row.

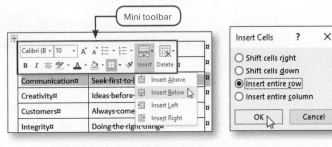

Figure 4-11 Use the mini toolbar to insert a row

Figure 4-12 *Insert Cells* dialog box

Merge and Split Cells

Many times when you use tables you want information to span across multiple columns, such as when you are inserting a title or subtitle in a table. Use the *Merge Cells* feature to combine multiple columns, rows, and cells into one cell.

▶HOW TO: Merge Cells

1. Select the cells to merge.
2. Click the **Table Tools Layout** tab.
3. Click the **Merge Cells** button [*Merge* group] (Figure 4-13). The cells merge into one cell.

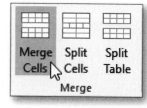

Figure 4-13 *Merge Cells* button

Word also enables you to split a cell into multiple cells. Split cells that were previously merged or split a single cell into multiple columns and rows. When splitting cells, the *Split Cells* dialog box prompts you to specify the number of columns and rows.

▶HOW TO: Split Cells

1. Select the cell(s) to split.
2. Click the **Table Tools Layout** tab.
3. Click the **Split Cells** button [*Merge* group]. The *Split Cells* dialog box opens (Figure 4-14).
4. Select the number of columns and rows.
   - By default, the *Merge cells before split* check box is selected. When you select this check box, Word merges the selected cells before splitting them into the desired number of columns and rows.
5. Click **OK** to split the cells.

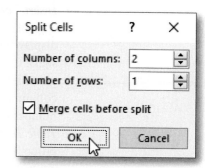

Figure 4-14 *Split Cells* dialog box

Copy or Move Columns and Rows

Copying or moving columns and rows in a table is similar to how you copy or move text in a document. Select the column or row to copy or move, and use one of the following methods:

- *Keyboard Shortcuts*: **Ctrl+C** (copy), **Ctrl+X** (cut), and **Ctrl+V** (paste).
- *Context menu*: Right-click the selected column or row and select **Cut**, **Copy**, or **Paste**.

- **Drag and drop**: Drag and drop the column or row to the new location to move it. Hold the **Ctrl** key while dragging and dropping to copy a column or row.
- **Clipboard group on the Home tab**: Use the **Cut**, **Copy**, and **Paste** buttons in this group.

Delete Columns and Rows

At times, you may need to remove columns or rows from your table. Click the **Delete** button in the *Rows & Columns* group on the *Table Tools Layout* tab or the mini toolbar to remove cells, columns, rows, or an entire table. You have the following options (Figure 4-15):

- *Delete Cells. . .* (opens the *Delete Cells* dialog box)
- *Delete Columns*
- *Delete Rows*
- *Delete Table*

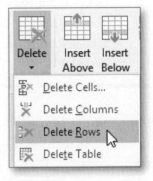

Figure 4-15 *Delete* options

Delete a Table

If you select an entire table and press *Delete* on your keyboard, only the information in the table is deleted; the blank table remains in your document. To delete a table, select the **Delete Table** option from the *Delete* drop-down on the *Table Tool Layout* tab or mini toolbar (see Figure 4-15). The **Delete Table** option is also available on the context menu when you select and right-click a table.

SLO 4.2

Arranging Text in Tables

You can adjust the width of columns and the height of rows and control how text is aligned within the cells of a table. Word provides a variety of table resizing and text alignment options. You also can sort information automatically within a table.

Resize Columns and Rows

When you insert a table into a document, the default size for the table is the width of the document. You can manually adjust the width of columns and the height of rows.

Drag the column or row borders to increase or decrease the size of a column or row. When you place your pointer on the vertical border of a column, the pointer changes to a *resizing pointer* (Figure 4-16). Drag the column border to the left or right to adjust the size of the column. Use the same method to adjust the height of a row by dragging the top or bottom border of a row up or down.

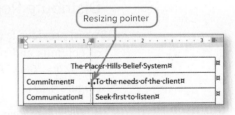

Figure 4-16 Manually adjust column width

> **MORE INFO**
>
> When you manually adjust the height of a row, it adjusts the height of the selected row only. Usually, it is best to keep the height of rows consistent.

Word also enables you to set a specific size for columns and rows. Adjust the size of columns and rows before merging cells. When adjusting the size of columns or rows after merging cells, be very careful when selecting cells.

▶ HOW TO: Resize Columns and Rows

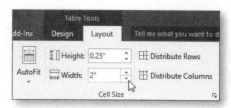

1. Select the cells, columns, or rows to resize.
2. Click the **Table Tools Layout** tab.
3. Change the height or width to the desired size [*Cell Size* group] (Figure 4-17).
   - Manually type the specific size or use the up or down arrows (spinner box) to resize.

Figure 4-17 Set cell *Height* and *Width*

AutoFit a Table

When you insert a table into a document, the table is automatically set to the width of the typing line (inside the left and right margins). Word has three different *AutoFit* options to adjust the column width of the table. Click the **AutoFit** button in the *Cell Size* group on the *Table Tools Layout* tab to display the *AutoFit* options (Figure 4-18).

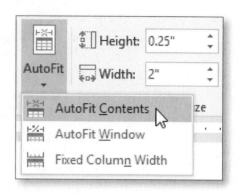

Figure 4-18 *AutoFit* options

- *AutoFit Contents*: Adjusts column widths to fit the contents of the table.
- *AutoFit Window*: Distributes the column widths so the table fits across the width of the page. (This is the default setting when you insert a table into a document.)
- *Fixed Column Width*: Adjusts columns to a fixed column width.

> ### MORE INFO
>
> When you insert a table, the table has the same formatting as the text in the document. If your rows seem too tall, the text in the table may contain *Before* or *After* paragraph spacing that controls the height of the rows in your table.

Distribute Rows and Columns

Word provides features to evenly distribute rows and columns, which is useful when the sizes of columns and rows in a table are uneven. **Distribute Rows** and **Distribute Columns** are on the *Table Tools Layout* tab in the *Cell Size* group (Figure 4-19).

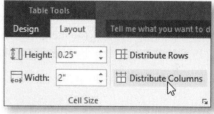

- *Distribute Rows*: This feature evenly distributes the rows based on the height of the existing table, adjusting all rows to a consistent height.
- *Distribute Columns*: This feature evenly distributes the columns based on the width of the existing table, adjusting all columns to the same width.

Figure 4-19 Distribute rows and columns

> ### ANOTHER WAY
>
> *AutoFit* and *Distribute* options are available from the context menu when a table is selected.

Text Alignment

In chapter 1, you learned paragraph alignment and how to left align, right align, center, or justify text. In chapter 2, you learned how to change the vertical alignment of a page or section. Similarly, when using tables, you have both horizontal and vertical alignment options. Align all text in the table or select individual cells, columns, or rows. Table 4-1 displays nine alignment options that are available in the *Alignment* group on the *Table Tools Layout* tab (Figure 4-20).

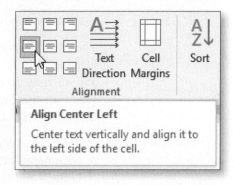

Align Center Left

Center text vertically and align it to the left side of the cell.

Figure 4-20 Text alignment options within a table

Table 4-1: Alignment Options

Align Top Left	Align Top Center	Align Top Right
Align Center Left	Align Center	Align Center Right
Align Bottom Left	Align Bottom Center	Align Bottom Right

> **MORE INFO**
>
> For horizontal alignment, text in the table is usually aligned on the left and numbers are aligned on the right. If you increase row height, it's generally best to vertically center text within a cell.

Cell Margins

In addition to being able to change alignment in cells, you can also adjust ***cell margins***. Just like the margins on a Word document, the cells of a table have top, bottom, left, and right margins. Cell margins add space around text within a cell. The default cell margins are 0" top and bottom, and 0.08" left and right.

▶HOW TO: Change Cell Margins

1. Select the entire table to change the cell margins for all cells in the table.
   - Click the table selector handle to select the entire table or click the **Select** button [*Table Tools Layout* tab, *Table* group] and click **Select Table**.
   - You can also change cell margins on individual cells.
2. Click the **Table Tools Layout** tab.
3. Click the **Cell Margins** button [*Alignment* group]. The *Table Options* dialog box opens (Figure 4-21).
4. Enter the desired changes to the *Top*, *Bottom*, *Left*, and *Right* cell margins.
   - You can also add spacing between cells in the *Default cell spacing* area. This puts padding (space) around the outside of the cells.
   - If you don't want the size of your table to be automatically adjusted, deselect the **Automatically resize to fit contents** check box.
5. Click **OK** to apply the cell margin settings.

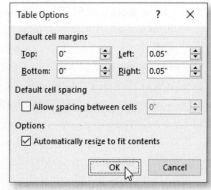

Figure 4-21 *Table Options* dialog box

Table Properties Dialog Box

The *Table Properties* dialog box consolidates many table sizing and alignment options in one location. The *Table Properties* dialog box includes separate tabs for *Table*, *Row*, *Column*, *Cell*, and *Alt Text*. To open the *Table Properties* dialog box, click the **Properties** button in the *Table* group on the *Table Tools Layout* tab (Figure 4-22). You can also open the *Table Properties* dialog box from the context menu.

- *Table tab*: Adjusts the size of the table, alignment, text wrapping, positioning, borders and shading, and cell margins.
- *Row tab*: Adjusts the height of rows and controls how rows break between pages.
- *Column tab*: Adjusts the width of columns.
- *Cell tab*: Adjusts the width of cells, vertical alignment of information in cells, and cell margins.
- *Alt Text tab*: Alternative text (alt text) is an information tag that displays when you place your pointer on the table. Screen readers use alt text in tables to accommodate those with visual impairments. Alt text is very common on web pages.

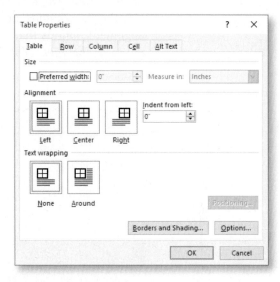

Figure 4-22 *Table Properties* dialog box

Sort Data in Tables

Word also provides the ability to sort information within a table. For example, use the *Sort* feature to arrange the text in the first column of a table alphabetically or sort numbers in descending order. When using the *Sort* feature on a table, rows of information rearrange according to how you specify the sort.

▶**HOW TO:** Sort Data in a Table

1. Place your insertion point in the table.
2. Select the **Table Tools Layout** tab.
3. Click the **Sort** button [*Data* group]. The entire table is selected and the *Sort* dialog box opens (Figure 4-23).
4. Click the **Sort by** drop-down list and select the column to use to sort the table.
   - Sort using any of the columns in the table.
5. Click the **Type** drop-down list and select the type of sort to perform: *Text*, *Number*, or *Date*.
6. Click the **Using** drop-down list and select the cell information to use in the sort.
   - *Paragraphs* is the default option, and usually, this is the only option available.

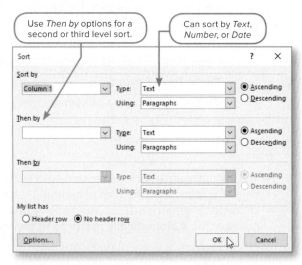

Figure 4-23 *Sort* dialog box

7. Select **Ascending** (A to Z or 1 to 10) or **Descending** (Z to A or 10 to 1) for the sort order.
   - To add a second- or third-level sort on different columns, click the **Then by** drop-down list and add additional sorts.
   - If your table has a header row (title or column headings), click the **Header row** radio button to omit this row from the sort.
8. Click **OK** to perform the sort. The table sorts according to the settings in the *Sort* dialog box.

> ### MORE INFO
> If your table has both a title and column headings, select the rows of the table to be sorted before clicking the **Sort** button so that only the data in the table is sorted.

> ### ANOTHER WAY
> Manually sort or arrange rows using copy (**Ctrl+C**), cut (**Ctrl+X**), and paste (**Ctrl+V**), or the drag and drop method.

PAUSE & PRACTICE: WORD 4-1

For this Pause & Practice project, you begin modifying Emma Cavalli's brochure. You add a table to the end of this document and then modify the table.

File Needed: ***Brochure-04.docx*** *(Student data files are available in the* Library *of your SIMnet account.)*
Completed Project File Name: ***[your initials] PP W4-1.docx***

1. Open the ***Brochure-04*** document from your student data files.
2. Save this document as [your initials] PP W4-1.
3. Move to the end of the document and insert a table.
   a. Place the insertion on the blank line at the end of the document (or press **Ctrl+End**).
   b. Click the **Insert** tab.
   c. Click the **Table** button [*Tables* group] and select a **3×7 Table** using the table grid. The table displays in the document.
4. Type the following information in Table 4-2. Press **Tab** to move from one cell to the next cell in the row. Leave the third column blank. *Note*: Table 4-2 is formatted for readability and will display differently in Word.

Table 4-2

Commitment	To the needs of the client	
Communication	Seek first to listen	
Integrity	Doing the right thing	
Customers	Always come first	
Teamwork	Work together for success	
Success	Results with integrity	
Creativity	Ideas before results	

5. Delete a column and insert rows.
   a. Place the insertion point in any cell in the last column.
   b. Click the **Delete** button [*Table Tools Layout* tab, *Rows & Columns* group] and select **Delete Columns**.
   c. Place the insertion point in the second row and click the **Insert Below** button [*Table Tools Layout* tab, *Rows & Columns* group]. A blank row is inserted below the second row.
   d. Type the following information in the new third row:

Trust	Begins with communication

   e. Click the last cell of the table (bottom right cell) and press **Tab** to insert a new row at the bottom of the table.
   f. Type the following information in the new last row:

Win-Win	Is always the goal

6. *AutoFit* the table and adjust the column and row size.
   a. Place your insertion point in the table.
   b. Click the **AutoFit** button [*Table Tools Layout* tab, *Cell Size* group] and select **AutoFit Contents**. The column widths adjust to fit the contents of the table.
   c. Place the insertion point in the first column.
   d. Change the *Width* to **1.2"** [*Table Tool Layout* tab, *Cell Size* group]
   e. Place the insertion point in the second column.
   f. Change the *Width* to **2"**.
   g. Use the table selector handle (upper-left corner) to select the entire table.
   h. Click the **Properties** button [*Table Tool Layout* tab, *Table* group] to open the *Table Properties* dialog box (Figure 4-24).
   i. Click the **Row** tab and check the **Specify height** box.
   j. Type .25 in the *Specify height* field and select **Exactly** from the *Row height is* drop-down list.
   k. Click **OK** to close the *Tables Properties* dialog box and apply these settings.

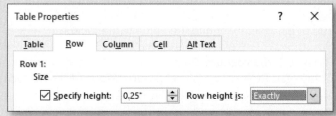

Figure 4-24 Change row height on the selected table

7. Insert a row and merge cells.
   a. Click anywhere in the table so the entire table is no longer selected.
   b. Select the first row of the table. The mini toolbar displays.
   c. Click the **Insert** button on the mini toolbar and select **Insert Above** to insert a new row at the top of the table.
   d. Select the new first row (if it is not already selected) and click the **Merge Cells** button [*Table Tools Layout* tab, *Merge* group]. The cells in the first row merge into one cell.
   e. Type **The Placer Hills Belief System** in the merged first row.

8. Sort the table by text in the first column.
   a. Select the **second through tenth (last) rows** of the table. Don't select the first merged row.
   b. Click the **Sort** button [*Table Tools Layout* tab, *Data* group]. The *Sort* dialog box opens (Figure 4-25).

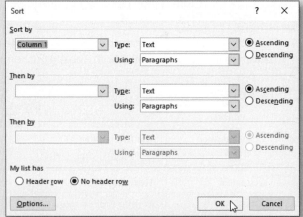

Figure 4-25 Sort the table by the first column in ascending order

c. Click the **Sort by** drop-down list and select **Column 1**.

d. Click the **Ascending** radio button if necessary. Leave *Type* as **Text** and *Using* as **Paragraphs**.

e. Click **OK** to sort the rows below the title in alphabetical order.

9. Change cell margins and text alignment.

a. Select the entire table.

> **MORE INFO**
>
> Click the **table selector** handle in the upper left of the table or click the **Select** button in the *Table* group on the *Table Tool Layout* tab and choose **Select Table**.

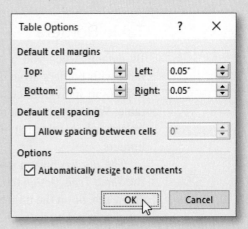

Figure 4-26 Change cell margins

b. Click the **Cell Margins** button [*Table Tools Layout* tab, *Alignment* group]. The *Table Options* dialog box opens (Figure 4-26).

c. Change the *Left* and *Right* cell margins **0.05"**.

d. Check the **Automatically resize to fit contents** box (if it is not already checked) and click **OK**. Keep the table selected for the next instruction.

e. Click the **Align Center Left** button (**first alignment button** in the **second row**) [*Table Tools Layout* tab, *Alignment* group] to align text left horizontally and center vertically within each cell.

f. Place the insertion point in the first row of the table to deselect the table.

g. Click the **Align Center** button (**second alignment button** in the **second row**) [*Table Tools Layout* tab, *Alignment* group] to center the title horizontally and vertically.

10. Save and close this document (Figure 4-27).

Figure 4-27 PP W4-1 completed (table only displayed)

Formatting and Editing Tables

In addition to the ability to adjust the structure of tables, Word provides you with many tools to enhance the appearance of tables. For example, add custom borders, shading, and table styles to tables. You can also add formulas to tables and convert text into tables.

Table Tools Design Tab

Word provides two *Table Tools* tabs when working with tables: *Design* and *Layout*. Both tabs are contextual and only display when the table or a portion of the table is selected or when the insertion point is in the table. The ***Table Tools Design tab*** enables you to apply table style options, table styles, and borders (Figure 4-28).

Figure 4-28 *Table Tools Design* tab

Table Borders

By default, when you insert a table, Word formats the table with borders around each cell. You can apply borders to an individual cell, a group of cells, or an entire table. When applying borders, it is important to be very precise when selecting the area of the table to apply borders.

The *Borders* button is located in the *Borders* group on the *Table Tools Design* tab, in the *Paragraph* group on the *Home* tab, or on the mini toolbar. The *Borders* drop-down list displays a variety of border options (Figure 4-29). You can also apply borders using the *Borders and Shading* dialog box.

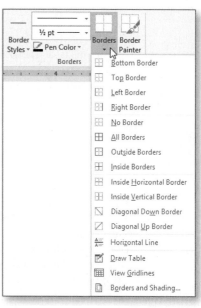

Figure 4-29 *Borders* drop-down list

▶ HOW TO: Apply Borders to a Table Using the Borders and Shading Dialog Box

1. Select the entire table or the desired area of the table to apply borders.
2. Click the **bottom half** of the **Borders** button [*Table Tools Design* tab, *Borders* group] and select **Borders and Shading** to open the *Borders and Shading* dialog box (Figure 4-30).
   - Alternatively, click the **Borders** drop-down list [*Home* tab, *Paragraph* group] or the **Borders** drop-down list on the mini toolbar.
   - The selection in the *Apply to* area depends on whether you are applying borders to the entire table or selected cells or rows.
3. Select the type of border from the list of options in the *Setting* area.
   - Remove all borders by selecting **None**.
4. Select the *Style* of the border from the list of options.
5. Click the **Color** drop-down list and select the color of the border.
6. Click the **Width** drop-down list and select the width of the border.
7. View the *Preview* area to see how borders display.
   - Click the border buttons in the *Preview* area or click the diagram borders to turn borders on or off.
8. Click **OK** to apply the border settings and close the *Borders and Shading* dialog box.

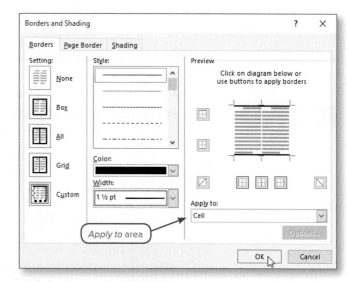

Figure 4-30 *Borders and Shading* dialog box

View Gridlines

When borders are removed from a table, it is difficult to see the column and row structure of your table. When a table format does not include borders, click the **View Gridlines** button [*Table Tools Layout* tab, *Table* group] to display cell boundaries. Gridlines display in the document only; they do not print (Figure 4-31).

THE·PLACER·HILLS·BELIEF·SYSTEM¤		¤
COMMITMENT¤	To·the·needs·of·the·client¤	¤
COMMUNICATION¤	Seek·first·to·listen¤	¤
CREATIVITY¤	Ideas·before·results¤	¤
CUSTOMERS¤	Always·come·first¤	¤
INTEGRITY¤	Doing·the·right·thing¤	¤
SUCCESS¤	Results·with·integrity¤	¤
TEAMWORK¤	Work·together·for·success¤	¤
TRUST¤	Begins·with·communication¤	¤
WIN-WIN¤	Is·always·the·goal¤	¤

Figure 4-31 Table displayed with *View Gridlines* and no borders

Table Shading

You can apply shading to specific cells or to an entire table. Click the **bottom half** of the **Shading** button in the *Table Styles* group on the *Table Tools Design* tab to display a color palette. Choose from *Theme Colors* or *Standard Colors* (Figure 4-32). Theme colors change depending on the theme of your document. Choose a custom color by selecting **More Colors**, which opens the *Colors* dialog box. Remove shading by selecting **No Color**.

You can also apply, change, or remove shading using the *Shading* tab in the *Borders and Shading* dialog box.

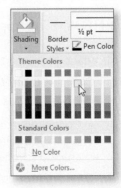

Figure 4-32 Table *Shading* options

> **ANOTHER WAY**
>
> Apply borders and shading from the mini toolbar by right-clicking the table or a portion of the table.

Table Styles

Table Styles are built-in styles for tables and are similar to text styles (see *SLO 2.7: Using Styles and Themes*). Table styles include a variety of borders, shading, alignment, and formatting options. Word provides a wide variety of built-in table styles in the *Table Styles* group on the *Table Tools Design* tab. Click the **More** button on the bottom right to display the *Table Styles* gallery (Figure 4-33).

After you apply a table style, you can customize all aspects of

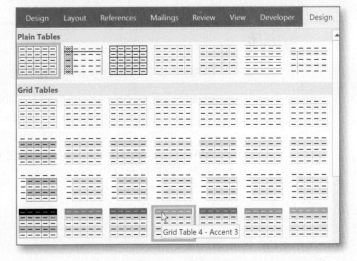

Figure 4-33 *Table Styles* gallery

the table. Remove all formatting of a table by selecting the **Clear** option at the bottom of the *Table Styles* gallery.

Table Style Options

Word offers a variety of *Table Style Options* to customize tables (Figure 4-34). For example, many tables have a header row or column, or a total or last row, where you may want to apply special formatting for emphasis. When you select one or more of the *Table Style Options*, Word applies special formatting to the table style you select. Select your table style options before applying a table style.

☑ Header Row	☑ First Column
☐ Total Row	☐ Last Column
☑ Banded Rows	☐ Banded Columns

Table Style Options

Figure 4-34 *Table Style Options* group

> ► **MORE INFO**
>
> *Banded Rows* apply shading to every other row. *Banded Columns* apply shading to every other column.

►HOW TO: Apply a Table Style and Table Style Options

1. Place your insertion point in the table.
2. Click the **Table Tools Design** tab.
3. Select the *Table Style Options* to apply to the table [*Table Style Options* group] (see Figure 4-34).
   - Consider the content of your table when deciding the table style options to apply.
   - When you select or deselect table style options, the thumbnails of the table styles in the *Table Styles* gallery change to reflect the options you have chosen.
4. Click the **More** button to display the *Table Styles* gallery.
   - Scroll down the *Table Styles* gallery to view additional table styles.
5. Choose a table style. Word applies the style and options to your table.
   - When you point to a table style in the *Table Styles* gallery, Word temporarily displays the table style on your table to preview your table with the style applied.

Insert a Formula in a Table

In addition to formatting tables to be more attractive and easier to read, you can add *formulas* to tables. Add formulas to automatically calculate amounts. For example, insert a formula in a total row of the table to total the numbers in the rows above (Figure 4-35).

Formula that adds the numbers above

Figure 4-35 Formula in a table

> ► **MORE INFO**
>
> Remember, it's best to align amount figures on the right in a table.

Most formulas used in tables in Word are simple formulas that calculate numbers in a column or row. When you insert a formula, Word, by default, inserts the *SUM* formula, which adds the range of numbers in the column or row. Word also enables you to insert more complex formulas.

▶HOW TO: Insert a Formula in a Table

1. Place the insertion point in the cell to insert the formula.
2. Click the **Formula** button [*Table Tools Layout* tab, *Data* group]. The *Formula* dialog box opens, and the formula displays in the *Formula* text box (Figure 4-36).
3. Adjust the formula and the range as necessary.
   - Select different formula functions from the **Paste function** drop-down list.
4. Click the **Number format** drop-down list and select a number format.
5. Click **OK** to insert the formula.

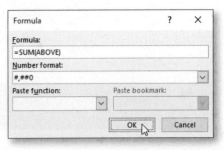

Figure 4-36 *Formula* dialog box

Update a Formula

A formula performs calculations on values in a table. If values in the table change, update the formula. Update a formula in one of two ways:

- Right-click the formula and select **Update Field**.
- Select the formula and press the **F9** function key (you might have to press **Fn+F9** if using a laptop).

Convert Text to a Table

Occasionally, you may want to create a table from existing text. For example, you may want to convert text that is arranged using tabs into a table or convert an existing table into text. Word provides ***Convert Text to Table*** or ***Convert Table to Text*** options.

When converting text into a table, the selected text must be separated by tabs, commas, paragraph breaks, or other characters. Word uses these characters to separate text into individual cells in the table.

▶HOW TO: Convert Text to a Table

1. Select the text to be converted to a table.
2. Click the **Insert** tab.
3. Click **Tables** [*Tables* group] and select **Convert Text to Table**. The *Convert Text to Table* dialog box opens (Figure 4-37).
4. Select the number of columns or rows in the *Table size* area.
   - Word automatically detects the size of the table you need.
   - You may not be able to change one or both values, depending on the text you selected.
5. Select an *AutoFit* option in the *AutoFit behavior* area.
   - The default setting is *Fixed column width*.
6. Select how you want Word to separate columns and rows in the *Separate text at* area.
   - Word automatically picks an option based on the selected text.
7. Click **OK** to convert the text to a table.

Figure 4-37 *Convert Text to Table* dialog box

PAUSE & PRACTICE: WORD 4-2

For this Pause & Practice project, you continue to modify Emma's brochure. You apply a table style and table style options to the table you created in the previous Pause & Practice project. You also convert text to a table and apply borders and shading.

File Needed: *[your initials] PP W4-1.docx*
Completed Project File Name: *[your initials] PP W4-2.docx*

1. Open the *[your initials] PP W4-1* document completed in *Pause & Practice 4-1*.

2. Save this document as [your initials] PP W4-2.

3. Apply table style options and a table style.
   a. Place your insertion point in the table at the end of the document.
   b. Click the **Table Tools Design** tab.
   c. Select **Header Row**, **Banded Rows**, and **First Column** [*Table Style Options* group] if they are not already selected. The other check boxes should not be selected.
   d. Click the **More** button in the *Table Styles* group to open the *Table Styles* gallery.
   e. Select the **Grid Table 5 Dark – Accent 3** style (Figure 4-38) to apply the style to the table.

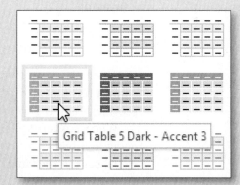

Figure 4-38 Select table style

4. Apply a custom top and bottom border to the table.
   a. Select the **first row** (title) of the table.
   b. Click the **Borders** drop-down arrow [*Table Tools Design* tab, *Borders* group] and select **Borders and Shading**. The *Borders and Shading* dialog box opens.
   c. Select **Custom** in the *Setting* area.
   d. Click the **Color** drop-down list and select the **second option** in the **first row** of *Theme Colors* (**Black, Text 1**).
   e. Click the **Width** drop-down list and select **1½ pt**.
   f. Select the **solid line** (first line style in the list) in the *Style* area if it is not already selected.
   g. Click the **top boundary** of the example cell in the *Preview* area to add a modified top border (Figure 4-39).

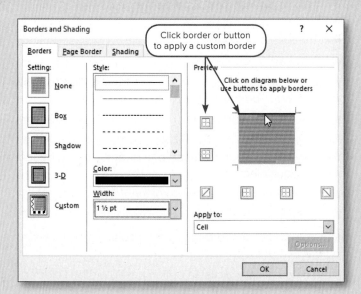

Figure 4-39 Apply custom borders

    h. Click **OK** to close the dialog box and add the border.

    i. Select the entire **bottom row** of the table.

    j. Open the *Borders and Shading* dialog box and apply the same custom border to the **bottom boundary** of the selected row (**Black, Text 1**; **1½ pt**; **solid line**).

    k. Click **OK** to add the border and close the dialog box.

5. Vertically align text in cells.

    a. Select the entire table and click the **Properties** button [*Table Tools Layout* tab, *Table* group] to open the *Table Properties* dialog box.

    b. Click the **Cell** tab and select **Center** in the *Vertical alignment* area.

    c. Click **OK** to close the dialog box.

6. Apply formatting changes to the text in the table.

    a. Select the first row (title).

    b. Open the *Font* dialog box, change *Size* to **12** and *Font color* to the **second option** in the **first row** of *Theme Colors* (**Black, Text 1**), and check **All caps** in the *Effects* area.

    c. Click **OK** to close the *Font* dialog box.

    d. Select the text in the first column, not including the title.

    e. Open the *Font* dialog box and check **Small caps** in the *Effects* area.

    f. Click **OK** to close the *Font* dialog box.

7. Convert text to a table.

    a. Go to the first page and select the three lines of text after "Realtor Consultant" ("**Phone**" through "**www.phre.com/ecavalli**"). Be sure to include the paragraph mark at the end of the third line, but don't select the blank line below the three lines of text.

    b. Click the **Insert** tab.

    c. Click the **Table** button [*Tables* group] and select **Convert Text to Table**. The *Convert Text to Table* dialog box opens (Figure 4-40).

    d. Change the *AutoFit behavior* to **AutoFit to contents**.

    e. Click **OK** to convert selected text to a table.

Figure 4-40 *Convert Text to Table* dialog box

8. Remove all borders, add custom borders and shading, and display table gridlines.

    a. Select the table if necessary, click the **Borders** drop-down arrow [*Table Tools Design* tab, *Borders* group], and select **No Border** to remove all borders.

    b. Click the **Borders** drop-down arrow again and select **Top Border**.

    c. Click the **Borders** drop-down arrow again and select **Bottom Border**.

    d. Select the table if necessary, click the **Shading** drop-down arrow [*Table Tools Design* tab, *Table Styles* group], and select the **seventh option** in the **second row** of *Theme Colors* (**Olive Green, Accent 3, Lighter 80%**) (Figure 4-41).

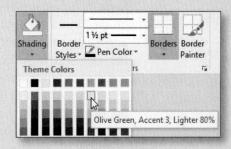

Figure 4-41 Select *Shading* color

    e. Click the **View Gridlines** button [*Table Tools Layout* tab, *Table* group] to display non-printing gridlines on the table.

9. Save and close the document (Figure 4-42).

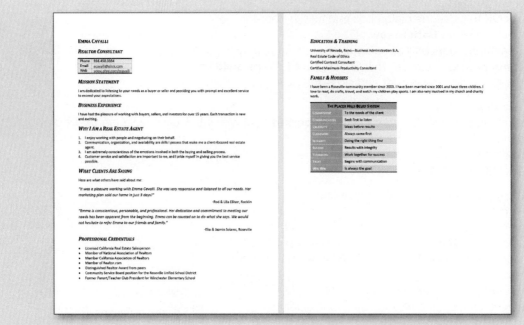

Figure 4-42 PP W4-2 completed

SLO 4.4

Using Columns

Columns are used to arrange text and tables to improve the readability, layout, and design of a document. By default, Word documents display text in a single column. You can apply columns to an entire document or to selected sections of a document. Word includes preset column setting options, or you can customize column settings to control the number of columns, column width, and space between columns. Use column and section breaks to control column endings and to balance columns.

Preset Column Settings

Apply column settings to a new document or to an existing document. To apply preset column settings, click the **Columns** button on the *Layout* tab in the *Page Setup* group (Figure 4-43). The *Two* and *Three* column options set columns with equal width, while the *Left* and *Right* column options format documents in two columns of unequal width.

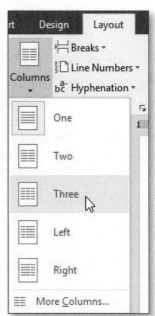

Figure 4-43 Preset column options

When you apply columns to a document, the column settings apply only to that section of the document. If your document contains no section breaks, columns apply to the entire document.

Customize Columns

Use the ***Columns dialog box*** to apply column settings or to customize current column settings. In the *Columns* dialog box, select the number of columns, adjust the column width and space between columns, insert a line between columns, and select the portion of the document to apply the column settings.

▶ HOW TO: Customize Columns Using the Columns Dialog Box

1. Click the **Layout** tab.
2. Click the **Columns** button [*Page Setup* group].
3. Select **More Columns**. The *Columns* dialog box opens (Figure 4-44).
4. Select column settings from the *Presets* options or *Number of columns* box.

   - Based on the number of columns you choose, Word automatically sets the column width and spacing.
   - The default spacing between columns is 0.5".
   - You can choose to have more than three columns in the *Number of columns* area.

5. Adjust the column widths and spacing as desired in the *Width and spacing* area.

   - Deselect the **Equal column widths** check box to apply unequal column widths.
   - When *Equal column width* is deselected, adjust the width and spacing of each column individually.
   - When *Equal column width* is selected, adjust the width and spacing to apply to all columns.

6. Click the **Apply to** drop-down list and select the portion of the document where you want to apply column settings: **Whole document** or **This point forward**.

   - When *This point forward* is selected, Word inserts a continuous section break at the insertion point in the document and applies column settings to the text after the continuous section break.
   - If you selected text before opening the *Columns* dialog box, *Selected text* is the default selection in the *Apply to* drop-down list.

7. Check the **Line between** check box to insert a vertical line between columns if desired.
8. View the *Preview* area to see a diagram of how your columns will display.
9. Click **OK** to apply column settings.

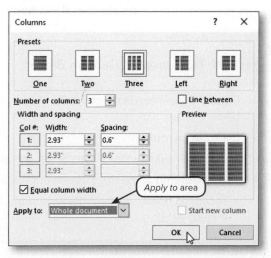

Figure 4-44 *Columns* dialog box

Convert Text to Columns

Apply column settings to the *Whole document*, from *This point forward*, or to *Selected text*. Depending on the portion of the document where you are applying column settings, Word applies the column settings and inserts any needed section breaks. Use the *Apply to* drop-down list in the *Columns* dialog box to select an option (see Figure 4-44). Table 4-3 describes how Word handles each of the options.

Table 4-3: Apply to Column Options

Columns Applied to	Actions
Whole Document	Word applies column settings to the entire document. No section breaks are added.
This point forward	Word inserts a continuous section break before the insertion point in the document and applies the column setting beginning at the insertion point, which becomes a new section of the document.
Selected text	When text is selected and column settings are applied, Word inserts a continuous section break before and after the selected text. The column settings apply only to that section.

Insert a Column Break

Column widths control the horizontal text wrapping, while the top and bottom margins or section breaks control where a column ends and wraps to the next column. Insert ***column breaks*** to end a column and move subsequent text to the next column.

▶ HOW TO: Insert a Column Break

1. Place the insertion point at the location to end a column or begin the next column.
2. Click the **Layout** tab.
3. Click the **Breaks** button [*Page Setup* group].
4. Select **Column** in the *Page Breaks* options (Figure 4-45).
   - A column break indicator displays when *Show/Hide* is on (Figure 4-46).

Breaks
Indent
Spacing
Page Breaks
Page
Mark the point at which one page ends and the next page begins.
Column
Indicate that the text following the column break will begin in the next column.

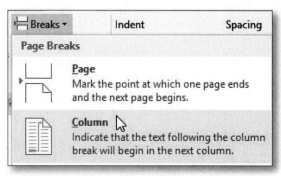

Figure 4-45 Insert *Column* break

> **ANOTHER WAY**
>
> **Ctrl+Shift+Enter** inserts a column break. The *Columns* dialog box also includes an option to start a new column.

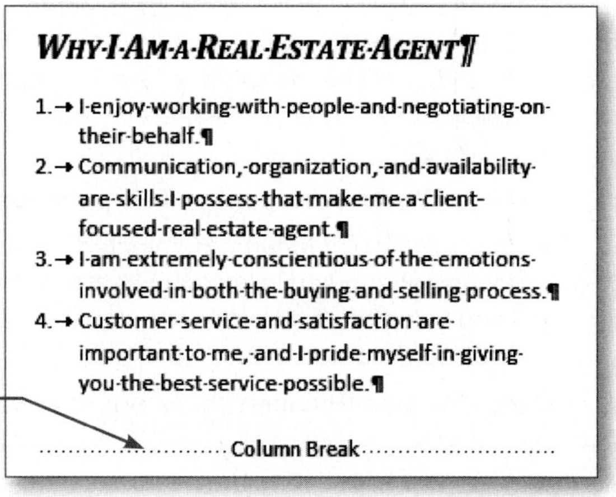

Why·I·Am·a·Real·Estate·Agent¶
1.→ I·enjoy·working·with·people·and·negotiating·on·their·behalf.¶
2.→ Communication,·organization,·and·availability·are·skills·I·possess·that·make·me·a·client-focused·real·estate·agent.¶
3.→ I·am·extremely·conscientious·of·the·emotions·involved·in·both·the·buying·and·selling·process.¶
4.→ Customer·service·and·satisfaction·are·important·to·me,·and·I·pride·myself·in·giving·you·the·best·service·possible.¶
Column Break
Column break indicator

Figure 4-46 *Column* break inserted

> **MORE INFO**
>
> Always turn on **Show/Hide (Ctrl+Shift+8)** when using page, section, or column breaks to help you see these elements in your document.

Balance Columns

Column breaks are one way to balance columns on a page. Another way is to use a ***continuous section break***. To format columns with equal length on a page, insert a continuous section break at the end of the last column on the page. Word automatically adjusts columns so they are approximately the same length.

▶ HOW TO: Balance Columns Using a Continuous Section Break

1. Place the insertion point at the end of the last column in your document.
2. Click the **Layout** tab.

3. Click the **Breaks** button [*Page Setup* group].
4. Select **Continuous** in the *Section Breaks* options.
   - A continuous section break indicator displays when *Show/Hide* is turned on.

PAUSE & PRACTICE: WORD 4-3

For this Pause & Practice project, you apply columns to Emma's brochure. With the use of columns and column breaks, you arrange the columns and format the document to fit on one page.

File Needed: ***[your initials] PP W4-2.docx***
Completed Project File Name: ***[your initials] PP W4-3.docx***

1. Open the ***[your initials] PP W4-2*** document completed in *Pause & Practice 4-2*.

2. Save this document as [your initials]

3. Change the page orientation and margins.
   a. Click the **Orientation** button [*Layout* tab, *Page Setup* group] and select **Landscape**.
   b. Click the **Page Setup** launcher to open the Page Setup dialog box.
   c. Change the *Top* margin to **1.2"**, and the *Bottom*, *Left*, and *Right* margins to **0.5"**.
   d. Click **OK** to close the dialog box and apply the margin settings. If a dialog box opens informing you that the margins are outside the printable area, click **Ignore**.

4. Arrange the text in columns and customize columns.
   a. Place your insertion point at the top of the document.
   b. Click the **Columns** button [*Layout* tab, *Page Setup* group] and select **Two**. The text displays in two columns.
   c. Click the **Columns** button again [*Layout* tab, *Page Setup* group] and select **More Columns**. The *Columns* dialog box opens (Figure 4-47).
   d. Select **Three** in the *Presets* area.
   e. Change the *Spacing* to **0.6"** in the *Width and spacing* area.
   f. Click the **Apply to** drop-down list and select **Whole document** if necessary.
   g. Click **OK** to apply custom column settings.

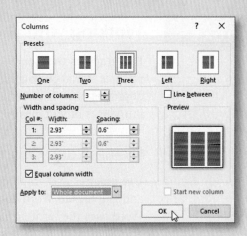

Figure 4-47 Customize column settings

5. Use column breaks to control column endings.
   a. Place the insertion point in front of "What Clients Are Saying."
   b. Click the **Breaks** button [*Layout* tab, *Page Setup* group] and select **Column** to insert a column break.

c. Place the insertion point in front of "Education & Training."

d. Press **Ctrl+Shift+Enter** to insert a column break.

6. Save and close the document (Figure 4-48).

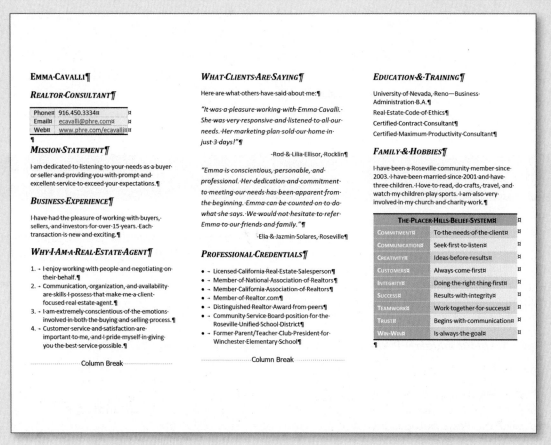

Figure 4-48 PP W4-3 completed

SLO 4.5

Working with Graphics

Use graphics to visually present information and to enhance a document. Graphics include pictures stored on your computer, online pictures, shapes, *SmartArt*, and *WordArt*. This section describes how to insert and arrange picture graphics. *SLO 4.6: Working with Other Graphics* introduces other types of graphic objects available in Word.

Pictures and Online Pictures

Use pictures and graphics to add visual elements to your documents. Add your own pictures and graphics to Word documents or use Bing images to find a wide variety of online pictures. Word uses the term *picture* generically to refer to any type of visual image that is saved as a graphic file. Table 4-4 describes common types of graphic formats.

Table 4-4: Types of Graphics

Format	Full Name	Extension	Details
PNG	Portable Network Graphics	.png	Used with pictures and editing pictures; high-quality resolution
JPEG	Joint Photographic Experts Group	.jpeg or .jpg	Relatively small file size; many pictures are saved and distributed in JPEG format
TIFF	Tagged Image File Format	.tiff	Used with high-quality digital photos and has a larger file size than JPEG or PNG
GIF	Graphics Interchange Format	.gif	Used with graphics with fewer colors
WMF	Windows Metafile	.wmf	Windows format used with many graphic images
BMP	Windows Bitmap	.bmp	Proprietary Windows format used with many Microsoft graphic images

Insert a Picture

To enhance a document, insert your own picture or a picture you have saved. See the steps below to insert a picture into a document.

> **HOW TO:** Insert a Picture

1. Place the insertion point in the document where you want the picture inserted.
2. Click the **Insert** tab.
3. Click the **Pictures** button [*Illustrations* group]. The *Insert Picture* dialog box opens (Figure 4-49).

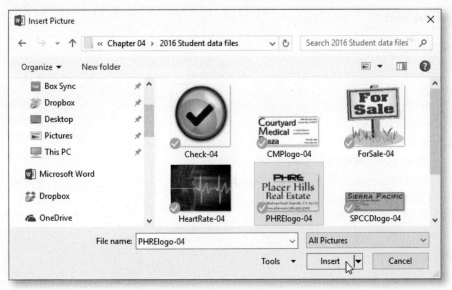

Figure 4-49 *Insert Picture* dialog box

4. Browse to the location on your computer and select a picture.
5. Click the **Insert** button to insert the picture and close the *Insert Picture* dialog box.

When you find a picture on the internet you want to include in a document, you can either save the picture and insert it, or copy and paste the picture into your document. Press **Ctrl+C** to copy the picture and **Ctrl+V** to paste the picture.

Include pictures obtained from the web only if you have permission from the image owner to avoid copyright infringement. For academic purposes, you may include images if you reference their sources as you would any other research citation.

> **ANOTHER WAY**
>
> Use the context menu (right-click) to both copy a picture and paste it into a document.

Use Alt Text

Alternative text, referred to as *alt text*, is text used to describe a picture, table, or graphic object. In Word documents, alt text is used by screen readers to provide an audio description of the graphic for those with visual impairments.

Depending on the type of picture you insert, Word may automatically generate alt text based upon the content of the picture and temporarily display the alt text at the bottom of the picture (Figure 4-50). Customize the alt text description in the *Alt Text* pane. Alt text does not permanently display on the graphic or in your document; it is hidden text attached to the graphic, similar to document properties.

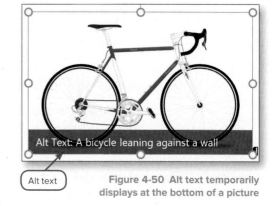

Figure 4-50 **Alt text temporarily displays at the bottom of a picture**

▶HOW TO: Edit Alt Text

1. Insert a picture into your document.
   - Alt text may temporarily display at the bottom of the picture (see Figure 4-50).
   - Some versions of Word automatically generate alt text based on the content of the picture.
2. Click the **Alt Text** button [*Picture Tools Format* tab, *Accessibility* group]. The *Alt Text* pane opens on the right (Figure 4-51).
   - Alternatively, right-click the picture and select **Edit Alt Text** from the context menu or click the alt text that temporarily displays at the bottom of the picture to open the *Alt Text* pane.
3. Edit the alt text as desired.
4. Click the **X** in the upper-right corner to close the *Alt Text* pane.

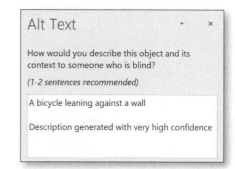

Figure 4-51 *Alt Text* pane

Insert an Online Picture

Word provides a variety of online picture choices using *Bing Image Search*. When using an image from *Bing Image Search*, make sure you have the permission of the image owner to avoid copyright infringement.

1. Place the insertion point in the document where you want the picture inserted.
2. Click the **Insert** tab.
3. Click the **Online Pictures** button [*Illustrations* group] to open the *Insert Pictures* dialog box.
4. Click the *Bing* text box, type keywords for the image you want to find, and press **Enter**.

   - Thumbnails of pictures appear below the search box (Figure 4-52).
   - By default, the *Creative Commons only* box is checked, which displays only those pictures that require no license or fee. Deselect this check box to display all pictures that match the search keywords.
   - Click the **Filter** drop-down lists to refine your search.

5. Select the picture to insert into your document.

   - Click the link below a picture to view a larger picture in a browser window. Close the browser window and return to the Word document.

6. Click the **Insert** button to insert the picture into your document.

   - Pictures may include a caption below the inserted picture.
   - Click the border of the caption text box to select it and press **Delete** to remove the caption if desired.

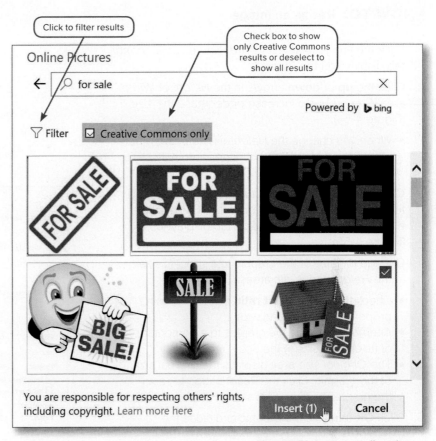

Figure 4-52 Insert an online picture

Resize a Graphic

In most cases, you will need to resize a graphic to fit properly in your document. Manually change the size of a graphic by dragging the top, bottom, side, or corner handles. Alternatively, enter a precise measurement in the *Layout* dialog box or the *Height* and *Width* text boxes in the *Size* group on the *Picture Tools Format* tab.

When you select (click) a graphic, *sizing handles* appear on each side and in each corner (Figure 4-53). To resize the graphic, click and hold one of the handles and drag in or out to decrease or increase the

Figure 4-53 Resize a graphic using the sizing handles

size of the graphic. Use the corner handles to maintain the horizontal and vertical proportion of the image. If you use the side, top, or bottom handles to resize, the proportions of the image may become distorted.

You can also resize the image to a specific size or to a percentage of its original size.

▶ HOW TO: Resize an Image

1. Click the image to select it. The *Picture Tools Format* tab displays on the *Ribbon*.

2. Click the **up** or **down** arrows in the *Height* or *Width* area [*Size* group] to increase or decrease the size (Figure 4-54).

   - When you change the *Height* or *Width*, the other setting (*Height* or *Width*) changes automatically to keep the graphic proportional.

3. Click the **Size** launcher [*Picture Tools Format* tab] to display additional sizing options. The *Layout* dialog box opens with the *Size* tab displayed (Figure 4-55).

4. Change the size of the graphic to a specific size in the *Height* and *Width* areas.

   - Check the **Lock aspect ratio** box to maintain proportional height and width.
   - Alternatively, scale the graphic to a percentage of its original size in the *Scale* area.
   - The *Original size* area displays the original size of the graphic. Click the **Reset** button to reset the graphic to its original size.

5. Click **OK** to resize the graphic and close the dialog box.

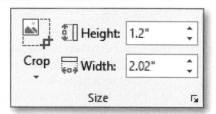

Figure 4-54 *Size* group on the *Picture Tools Format* tab

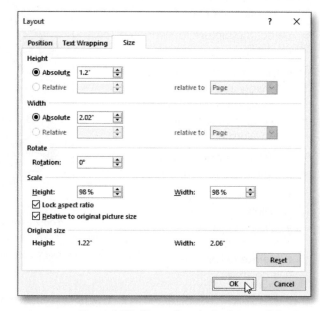

Figure 4-55 *Size* options in the *Layout* dialog box

> **ANOTHER WAY**
>
> Open the *Layout* dialog box by right-clicking the graphic and selecting **Size and Position**.

Wrap Text around a Graphic

Use the ***text wrapping*** options to control how the text aligns or wraps around a graphic. You can also choose to position the graphic in front of or behind text.

▶HOW TO: Wrap Text around a Graphic

1. Click the graphic to select it.
2. Click the **Wrap Text** button [*Picture Tools Format* tab, *Arrange* group] (Figure 4-56).
3. Select a text wrapping option.

- Select **More Layout Options** to display additional text wrapping options. The *Layout* dialog box opens with the *Text Wrapping* tab displayed (Figure 4-57).
- Use the *Layout* dialog box to customize text wrapping [*Text Wrapping* tab], specify the position of the graphic [*Position* tab], and resize the graphic [*Size* tab].
- In the *Wrap text* area, choose *Both sides*, *Left only*, *Right only*, or *Largest only*.
- In the *Distance from text* area, set a specific distance from the graphic to wrap text.
- Click **OK** to close the *Layout* dialog box.

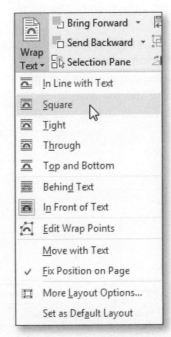

Figure 4-56 *Wrap Text* options

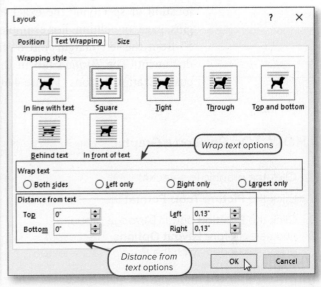

Figure 4-57 *Text Wrapping* tab in the *Layout* dialog box

You can also click the **Layout Options** button to the right of a selected graphic and select a text wrapping option (Figure 4-58). Click the **See more** link to open the *Layout* dialog box.

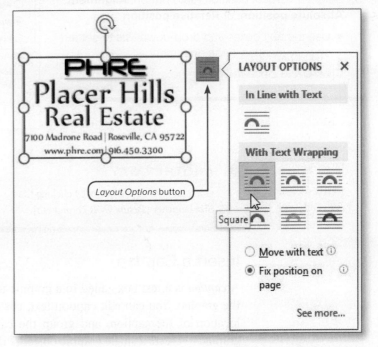

Figure 4-58 *Layout Options* menu

Position a Graphic

In addition to adjusting the size of a graphic and specifying how text wraps around a graphic, you can also control the position of the graphic in your document. Select the graphic, click the **Align** button in the *Arrange* group on the *Picture Tools Format* tab, and select an alignment option from the drop-down list (Figure 4-59).

Position a graphic by dragging the graphic to the desired location or specifying the exact location relative to the margins, page, or column. For example, you can position a graphic 5" from the left margin and 6" from the top margin of the document. The *Position* tab in the *Layout* dialog box offers customization options (Figure 4-60).

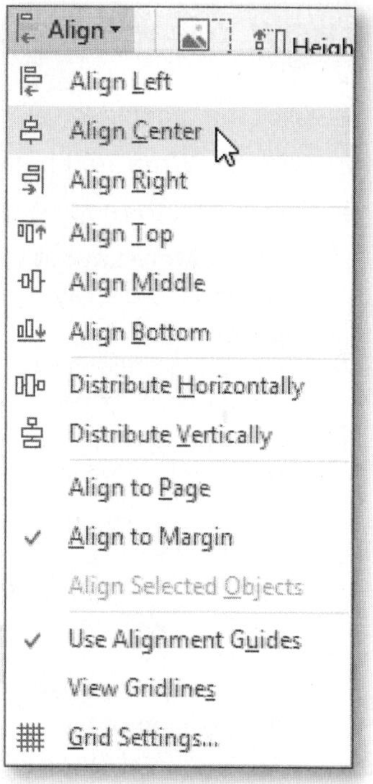

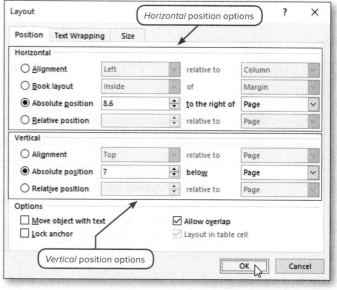

Figure 4-59 *Align* options

▶ HOW TO: Position a Graphic

1. Click the graphic to select it.
2. Click the **Picture Tools Format** tab.
3. Click the **Position** button [*Arrange* group] and select **More Layout Options**. The *Layout* dialog box opens with the *Position* tab selected (see Figure 4-60).
4. Select a *Horizontal* position radio button: **Alignment**, **Book layout**, **Absolute position**, or **Relative position**.
   - Use the text boxes and drop-down lists to set a specific location in the document.
5. Select a *Vertical* position radio button: **Alignment**, **Absolute position**, or **Relative position**.
   - Use the text boxes and drop-down lists to set a specific location in the document.
6. Click **OK** to close the dialog box.

Figure 4-60 *Position* tab in the *Layout* dialog box

▶ ANOTHER WAY

Open the *Layout* dialog box by clicking the **Size** launcher [*Picture Tools Format* tab].

Insert a Caption

A *caption* is a text box added to a graphic to describe the graphic. You can edit caption text, customize the location of the caption, and group the caption and graphic to create a single graphic object (Figure 4-61). Grouping graphic objects is covered in the next section.

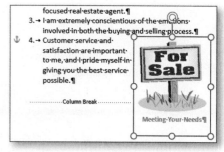

Figure 4-61 Graphic with caption below

▶ HOW TO: Insert a Caption

1. Right-click the graphic and select **Insert Caption** from the context menu. The *Caption* dialog box opens (Figure 4-62).

   - Alternatively, click the **Insert Caption** button [*References* tab, *Captions* group] to open the *Caption* dialog box.
   - Word automatically creates a caption for the selected object. Add a description after the label in the *Caption* text box. You cannot delete the label in the *Caption* text box.
   - After adding a caption to a graphic, you can edit or delete the caption text within the document.

2. Click the **Label** drop-down list and choose **Equation**, **Figure**, or **Table**.

   - Add a custom label by clicking the **New Label** button and typing a custom label.
   - Check the **Exclude label from caption** box to remove the label (but not the number).

3. Click the **Position** drop-down list and select the location of the caption.

4. Click **OK** to insert the caption.

5. Edit the caption in the text box after it is added to the graphic (Figure 4-63).

   - Customize the size and color of the caption text and adjust the size and position of the text box.

Figure 4-62 *Caption* dialog box

Figure 4-63 Caption added to graphic

Group Graphic Objects

When you work with graphics, you can ***group*** related graphics and objects. For example, group a picture and its caption or group the graphic objects that comprise a company logo. The advantage of grouping graphics is to create one object that can be resized and positioned.

▶ HOW TO: Group and Ungroup Graphics

1. Press the **Ctrl** key and click the graphics to be grouped (Figure 4-64).

2. Click the **Group** button [*Picture Tools Format* tab, *Arrange* group].

3. Select **Group**. The selected objects become one grouped object (Figure 4-65).

   - Notice that the number of sizing handles changes from 16 handles for two separate objects to 8 handles on the grouped object.
   - To ungroup grouped items, select the grouped object, click the **Group** button in the *Arrange* group on the *Picture Tools Format* tab, and select **Ungroup**.

Figure 4-64 Multiple objects selected to be grouped together

Figure 4-65 Grouped objects

> ▶ **ANOTHER WAY**
>
> *Group* and *Ungroup* options are available in the context menu by right-clicking selected graphics or a grouped object.

SLO 4.6

Working with Other Graphic Objects

In addition to inserting and customizing pictures, Word provides a variety of other graphic objects. Add shapes, *SmartArt*, *WordArt*, symbols, icons, 3D models, and videos as visual elements. Each of these graphic objects include design and format options to customize the appearance and position of the objects.

Insert and Customize a Shape

Word provides a variety of **shapes** to insert into your document. Word's *Shapes* gallery groups shapes into eight categories (Figure 4-66). The *Recently Used Shapes* categories collects shapes you recently selected. When inserting a shape or line, you actually draw the object in your document. After drawing a shape, you can edit the size, position, alignment, and text wrapping.

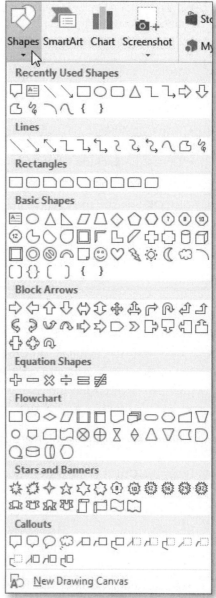

Figure 4-66 *Shapes* drop-down list

> **HOW TO:** Insert a Shape

1. Click the **Insert** tab.
2. Click the **Shapes** button [*Illustrations* group] to display the gallery of shape options.
3. Select the shape to use. The pointer becomes a drawing crosshair (large, dark plus sign) when you position the pointer in the document.
4. Click and drag to create the shape (Figure 4-67). When you release the pointer, the shape displays in the document.
   - You don't have to be perfectly accurate when drawing the shape because you can easily resize and position it.
   - The document theme controls the format of the shape.
   - Use text wrapping to position the shape on top or behind text or wrap text around a shape.

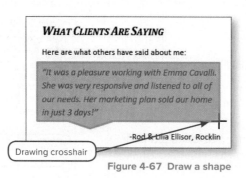

Figure 4-67 Draw a shape

> **MORE INFO**
>
> To create an exact square or circle or to draw a straight line, press the **Shift** key while drawing.

After a shape has been inserted, it can be moved or resized. You can customize the shape fill color, outline color and weight, or shape effect. See Figure 4-68 and its callouts for examples of the available selection and sizing handles. The following is a list of those options:

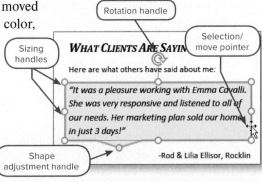

Figure 4-68 Shape selected with handles displayed

- *Selection/move pointer*. This pointer (four-pointed arrow) enables you to select and move objects. Select multiple objects by pressing the **Ctrl** key and selecting the objects.
- *Sizing handles*: Eight sizing handles are located on corners and sides of the shape. When you point to a handle, the pointer becomes a sizing pointer (two-pointed arrow).
- *Rotation handle*: The rotation handle is the circular arrow at the top of the selected shape. Rotate a shape by clicking and dragging this handle to the left or right.
- *Shape adjustment handle*: This handle is the yellow circle and is not available for all shapes. Use this handle to change the shape of an object. Also, use this handle to change the size or location of a callout, corner roundness, and other shape elements.

When you select a shape, the *Drawing Tools Format* tab displays on the *Ribbon* with options to format the shape (Figure 4-69).

Figure 4-69 *Drawing Tools Format* tab

Insert and Customize SmartArt

SmartArt graphics are a combination of shapes and text boxes. *SmartArt* includes a variety of categories, and within each category, numerous options are available (Figure 4-70). After inserting a *SmartArt* graphic, use **SmartArt Tools Design** and **SmartArt Tools Format** tabs to customize the text content and the graphic's structure.

▶ **HOW TO: Insert and Customize SmartArt**

1. Position your insertion point at the location to insert the *SmartArt*.

2. Click the **SmartArt** button [*Insert* tab, *Illustrations* group]. The *Choose a SmartArt Graphic* dialog box opens (see Figure 4-70).

3. Select a *SmartArt* graphic.
   - *SmartArt* categories display on the left side of the dialog box.

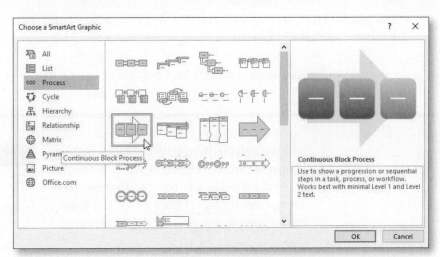

Figure 4-70 *Choose a SmartArt Graphic* dialog box

- A preview and description of the selected *SmartArt* displays on the right of the dialog box.

4. Click **OK** to insert the *SmartArt*.

5. Type text in the *SmartArt* graphic objects (Figure 4-71).

   - Alternatively, click the arrow on the left side of the *SmartArt* graphic to display the *Text* pane to type text in the *SmartArt* graphic.
   - Format the text in the *SmartArt*.

6. Customize text in the *SmartArt* using *Text Fill*, *Text Outline*, and *Text Effects* on the *SmartArt Tools Format* tab.

7. Customize the graphic objects in a *SmartArt* graphic using the *SmartArt Tools Design* and *Format* tabs.

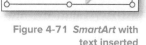

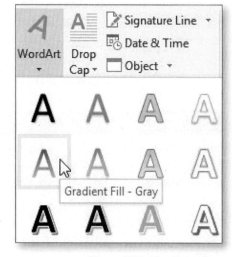 (top portion)

Figure 4-71 *SmartArt* with text inserted

- The *SmartArt Tools Design* tab controls the overall design and colors of the *SmartArt* objects.
- The *SmartArt Tools Format* tab provides options to customize the shape of objects, colors, borders, fill, and effects.

Insert and Customize WordArt

Use *WordArt* to create special effects with text. Select text in a document or type text to create the *WordArt* object. When you insert *WordArt*, you are actually inserting a text box that can be manipulated as a graphic. Modify *WordArt* by editing the text or changing the size, position, color, fill, or effects of this object.

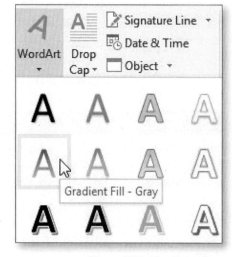

Figure 4-72 *WordArt* gallery

▶**HOW TO:** Insert WordArt

1. Position your insertion point at the location to insert the *WordArt*.

   - Alternatively, select text in the document to convert text to a *WordArt* object.

2. Click the **WordArt** button [*Insert* tab, *Text* group] and select a *WordArt* style from the gallery of options (Figure 4-72). The *WordArt* text box displays in your document.

3. Type text in the *WordArt* text box.

   - The placeholder text (*Your text here*) is selected when you insert the *WordArt* (Figure 4-73). Type to replace the placeholder text. If the placeholder text is not selected, select it before typing text.

4. Click anywhere in your document away from the text box to deselect the *WordArt* graphic.

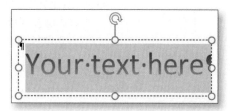

Figure 4-73 *WordArt* inserted into a document

Customizing *WordArt* is similar to customizing other graphic objects in Word. When you select the *WordArt* text box, the **Drawing Tools Format** tab displays (Figure 4-74). The following are ways to customize a *WordArt* graphic:

Figure 4-74 *Drawing Tools Format* tab

- Use the **Drawing Tools Format** tab to change the *WordArt* style, add a border, and change the fill, outline, and effects of the *WordArt* text.

- Resize the *WordArt* graphic using the sizing handles on the corners and sides.
- Rotate the *WordArt* text box using the rotation handle.
- Change the position and text wrapping of the *WordArt* in the same way you manipulate other graphics.

Modify Graphics with Styles

You can apply a variety of styles, fills, outlines, and effects to each of the different types of graphic objects. Contextual tabs display when you select a graphic object, and each tab includes a variety of *style galleries* (Figure 4-75).

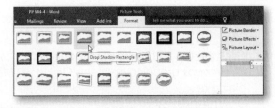

Figure 4-75 *Picture Styles* gallery

When applying styles to graphics, Word provides a *live preview*. When you place the pointer on a style from one of the style galleries, Word temporarily applies the style to the selected graphic to preview how it will appear in the document.

Insert Icons and 3D Models

In addition to inserting pictures, shapes, and other graphic objects, Word provides a variety of icons and 3D models. *Icons* are small images you insert into a document and can be resized and positioned similar to other graphic objects.

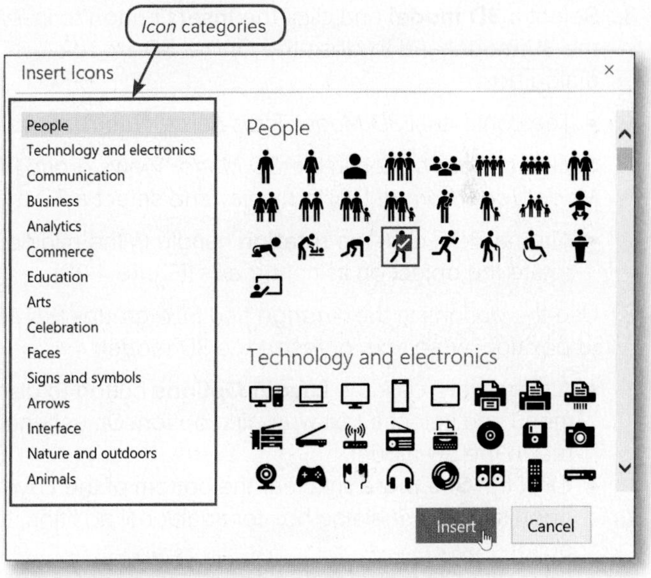

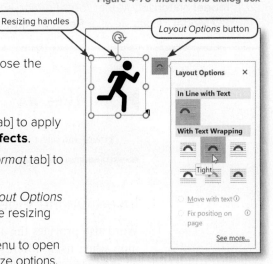

Figure 4-76 *Insert Icons* dialog box

▶HOW TO: Insert an Icon

1. Position the insertion point at the location to insert an icon.

2. Click the **Icon** button [*Insert* tab, *Illustrations* group] to open the *Insert Icons* dialog box (Figure 4-76).
   - Categories of icons display on the left.

3. Select an **icon** and click the **Insert** button to insert the icon and close the *Insert Icons* dialog box.
   - The contextual *Graphic Tools Format* tab displays.

4. Use options in the *Graphics Styles* group [*Graphic Tools Format* tab] to apply **Graphics Styles**, **Graphics Fill**, **Graphics Outline**, or **Graphics Effects**.

5. Use the options in the *Arrange* and *Size* groups [*Graphic Tools Format* tab] to position, wrap text, or resize the icon.
   - Alternatively, click the **Layout Options** button to display the *Layout Options* menu and select a text wrapping option (Figure 4-77). Or, use the resizing handles to resize the icon.
   - Click the **See more** link near the bottom of the *Layout Options* menu to open the *Layout* dialog box for additional position, text wrapping, and size options.

Figure 4-77 Icon with *Layout Options* menu displayed

A **3D model** is a graphic object similar to a picture, but it can be rotated on its center axis to display the object at different angles and tilt. Insert and customize 3D models similar to other graphic objects.

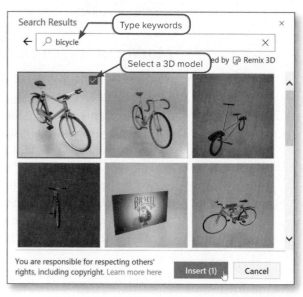

Figure 4-78 Search results in the *Online 3D Models* dialog box

▶**HOW TO:** Insert a 3D Model from Online Sources

1. Position the insertion point at the location to insert a 3D model.
2. Click the top half of the **3D Models** button [*Insert* tab, *Illustrations* group] to open the *Online 3D Models* dialog box.
   - Categories of 3D models display in the dialog box. Select a category to display 3D models.
   - Alternatively, type keywords in the *Type a keyword here* text box and press **Enter** or click the **search** icon (magnifying glass) to display 3D models (Figure 4-78).
3. Select a **3D model** and click the **Insert** button to insert the 3D model and to close the *Online 3D Models* dialog box.
   - The contextual *3D Model Tools Format* tab displays.
4. Click the **More** button in the *3D Model Views* group [*3D Model Tools Format* tab] to display and select a 3D model view.
   - Alternatively, click the **rotation** handle in the middle of the 3D model and rotate the object on its center axis (Figure 4-79).
5. Use the options in the *Arrange* and *Size* groups [*3D Model Tools Format* tab] to position, wrap text, or resize the 3D model.
   - Alternatively, click the **Layout Options** button to display the *Layout Options* menu and select a text wrapping option. Or, use the resizing handles to resize the 3D model.
   - Click the **See more** link near the bottom of the *Layout Options* menu to open the *Layout* dialog box for additional position, text wrapping, and size options.
   - To reset a 3D model to its original view and/or position, click the **Reset 3D Model** button [*3D Model Tools Format* tab, *Adjust* group] and select **Reset 3D Model** (resets view) or **Reset 3D Model and Size** (resets view and size).

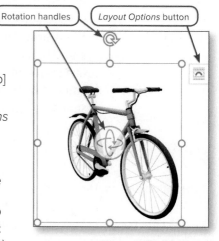

Figure 4-79 3D model

▶ ANOTHER WAY

To insert a 3D model that is already saved as a file, click the **3D Models** button [*Insert* tab, *Illustrations* group] and select **From a File**.

Insert Online Video

Word also provides the ability to insert videos. Although, inserting videos is much more common when using Microsoft PowerPoint or developing web sites, you may have a document where a video clip would be appropriate and useful. An **online video** in a Word document is a graphic object that links to an online video and is played from within Word.

▶ **HOW TO:** Insert an Online Video

1. Position the insertion point at the location to insert a video.

2. Click the **Online Video** button [*Insert* tab, *Media* group] to open the *Insert Video* dialog box (Figure 4-80).

3. Type keywords in the **YouTube** text box.

   • Alternatively, if you have already copied a video embed code, paste the code (**Ctrl+V**) in the *From a Video Embed Code* text box and press **Enter**. The video displays in the document.

4. Select a video in the search results and click **Insert**. The video displays in the document (Figure 4-81) and the contextual *Picture Tools Format* tab displays.

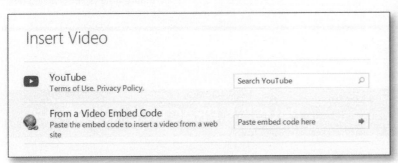

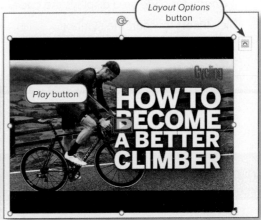

Figure 4-80 *Insert Video* dialog box   Figure 4-81 Video inserted into a document

5. Use the options on the *Picture Tools Format* tab to apply a style or border, position the video in the document, apply text wrapping, or resize the video.

   • Alternatively, click the **Layout Options** button to display the *Layout Options* menu and select a text wrapping option. Or, use the resizing handles to resize the video.
   • Click the **See more** link near the bottom of the *Layout Options* menu to open the *Layout* dialog box for additional position, text wrapping, and size options.

6. Click the **Play** button in the middle of the video to open the video in a new window.

   • Click the **Play** button again to begin the video.

Insert Symbols and Special Characters

Word also has a variety of symbols and other special characters to insert into a document (Figure 4-82). The *Symbols*, *Wingdings*, and *Webdings* font sets have an assortment of symbols and small graphics to insert into a document. Additional special characters are available, such as the em dash, en dash, and copyright symbols.

Figure 4-82 *Symbol* button on the *Insert* tab

▶ **HOW TO:** Insert a Symbol

1. Position the insertion point at the location to insert a symbol.

2. Click the **Symbol** button [*Insert* tab, *Symbols* group] to display a drop-down list of recently used symbols.

3. Select **More Symbols** (see Figure 4-82) to open the *Symbol* dialog box (Figure 4-83).

4. Click the **Font** drop-down list on the *Symbols* tab to select the font set.

   • Alternatively, click the **Special Character** tab to display the list of available special characters.

5. Select a symbol or special character to insert.

   • Each character has a numerical code for identification. The *Character code* area displays the code.

6. Click **Insert** to insert the symbol.

7. Click **Close** to close the dialog box.

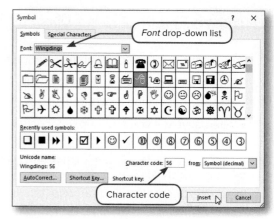

Figure 4-83 *Symbol* dialog box

PAUSE & PRACTICE: WORD 4-4

For this Pause & Practice project, you finalize Emma's brochure by inserting a picture, shapes, and *Word-Art*. You format and arrange these graphic objects attractively in the document.

Files Needed: *[your initials] PP W4-3.docx*, *PHRElogo-04.png*, and *ForSale-04.png* (*Student data files are available in the* Library *of your SIMnet account.*)
Completed Project File Name: *[your initials] PP W4-4.docx*

1. Open the *[your initials] PP W4-3* document completed in *Pause & Practice 4-3*.

2. Save this document as [your initials] PP W4-4.

3. Insert the Placer Hills Real Estate logo at the bottom-right corner of the document.
   a. Position the insertion point below the table in the third column.
   b. Click the **Pictures** button [*Insert* tab, *Illustrations* group]. The *Insert Picture* dialog box opens.
   c. Select the *PHRElogo-04* file from the student data files and click **Insert**. Word may automatically insert alt text. You will edit alt text later in this project.

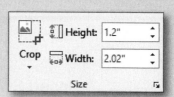

Figure 4-84 Adjust size of graphic

4. Arrange and format the logo.
   a. Select the logo (if necessary), click the **Wrap Text** button [*Picture Tools Format* tab, *Arrange* group], and choose **In Front of Text**.
   b. Type 1.2 in the *Height* box [*Size* group] and press **Enter** (Figure 4-84). The width automatically adjusts to keep the picture proportional.
   c. Click the middle of the picture and drag the graphic near the bottom-right corner of the document.
   d. Click the **Picture Border** button [*Picture Styles* group] and select the **seventh option** in the **first row** of the *Theme Colors* (**Olive Green, Accent 3**) (Figure 4-85).

Figure 4-85 Select *Picture Border* color

e. Click the **Picture Border** again, click **Weight**, and select **1½ pt**.

f. Click the **Position** button [*Arrange* group] and select **More Layout Options**. The *Layout* dialog box opens with the *Position* tab displayed (Figure 4-86).

g. Select the **Absolute position** radio button in the *Horizontal* area, type 8.6, click the **to the right of** drop-down list, and select **Page**.

h. Select the **Absolute position** radio button in the *Vertical* area, type 7, click the **below** drop-down list, and select **Page**.

i. Click **OK** to close the dialog box.

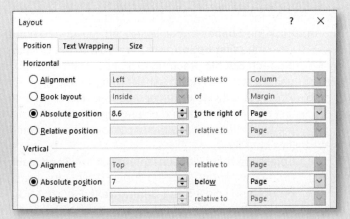

Figure 4-86 Customize position of the logo

5. Add a picture near the bottom of the first column.

a. Place the insertion point at the end of the fourth numbered item in the first column.

b. Click the **Pictures** button [*Insert* tab, *Illustrations* group]. The *Insert Picture* dialog box opens.

c. Select the **ForSale-04** picture from the student data files and click **Insert**.

d. Change the *Height* [*Picture Tools Format* tab, *Size* group] to **1.2"** and press **Enter**.

e. Right-click the picture, choose **Wrap Text**, and select **Square**.

f. Click the middle of the picture and drag it to the right of the fourth numbered item in the first column (Figure 4-87).

Figure 4-87 Picture and caption grouped

6. Insert a caption for the picture.

a. Right-click the picture and choose **Insert Caption** to open the *Caption* dialog box.

b. Click **OK** to insert a caption and close the *Caption* dialog box. Word inserts the default caption that serves as placeholder text.

c. Delete the placeholder text in the caption text box and type **Meeting Your Needs** as the caption. If the caption covers the bottom of the graphic, select the border of the caption and use the down keyboard arrow to move it down slightly.

d. Press **Ctrl+E** or click the **Center** button [*Home* tab, *Paragraph* group] to center the text in the caption.

e. With the caption still selected, press the **Ctrl** key and click the picture to select it also. Both the picture and the caption should be selected.

f. Click the **Group** button [*Picture Tools Format* tab, *Arrange* group] and choose **Group**. The two objects are grouped into one object (see Figure 4-87).

7. Change the paragraph spacing on the two quotes in the second column.

a. Place your insertion point in the first quoted paragraph in the second column (beginning with "It was a pleasure . . .").

b. Change the *After* paragraph spacing to **12 pt**.

c. Place your insertion point in the second quoted paragraph in the second column (beginning with "Emma is conscientious . . .").

d. Change the *After* paragraph spacing to **12 pt**.

8. Add and format a shape to the quoted text.
   a. Click the **Shapes** button [*Insert* tab, *Illustration* group] and select the **first option** in the **first row** in the *Callouts* area (**Speech Bubble**: **Rectangle**) (Figure 4-88). Your pointer becomes a drawing crosshair (dark plus sign).

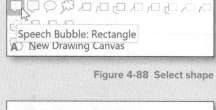

Figure 4-88 Select shape

   b. Place the drawing crosshair near the upper left of the first quote in the second column and click and drag to the lower right to draw the shape over the quoted text (Figure 4-89).
   c. Select the shape (if necessary), click the **Send Backward** drop-down arrow [*Drawing Tools Format* tab, *Arrange* group], and select **Send Behind Text** (Figure 4-90). The text displays on top of the shape.
   d. Click the *Shape Styles* **More** button [*Drawing Tools Format* tab, *Shape Styles* group] to display the gallery of shape styles.

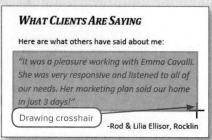

Figure 4-89 Draw rectangular shape

   e. Select the **fourth option** in the **first row** of the *Theme Styles* (**Colored Outline – Olive Green, Accent 3**) (Figure 4-91).
   f. Click the **Shape Fill** button [*Drawing Tools Format* tab, *Shape Styles* group] and select the **seventh option** in the **second row** of the *Theme Colors* (**Olive Green, Accent 3, Lighter 80%**).
   g. Click the **Shape Effects** button [*Drawing Tools Format* tab, *Shape Styles* group], select **Shadow**, and choose the first option in the first row of the *Outer* category (**Offset: Bottom Right**) (Figure 4-92).

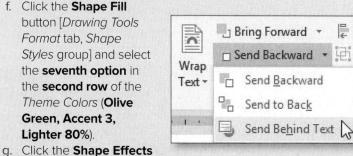

Figure 4-90 *Send Behind Text*

Figure 4-91 Apply a shape style

   h. Change the *Shape Height* to **1"** and the *Shape Width* to **3.1"** [*Drawing Tools Format* tab, *Size* group].
   i. Drag the shape to position it evenly behind the text. You can also use the keyboard arrow keys to position a selected shape.

9. Replicate and align the callout shape.
   a. Select the shape (if necessary), press **Ctrl+C** to copy it, and **Ctrl+V** to paste the copy of the shape into the document.
   b. Drag the new shape over the second quote.
   c. Change the *Shape Height* to **1.4"** [*Drawing Tools Format* tab, *Size* group].
   d. Drag the shape to position it evenly behind the text.
   e. Select the second shape (if necessary), press the **Shift** key, and click the right edge of the first shape to select both shapes (Figure 4-93).

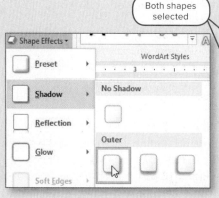

Figure 4-92 Select a shape *Shadow* option

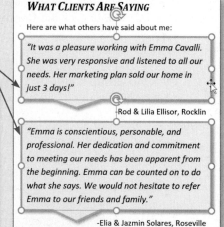

Figure 4-93 Shapes positioned behind text

f. Click the **Align** button [*Drawing Tools Format* tab, *Arrange* group] and select **Align Center**.

g. Use the up or down arrow keys to adjust the vertical position of the selected shape if necessary.

10. Add *WordArt* to the brochure and customize it.

a. Select the text "**Emma Cavalli**" including the paragraph mark at the top of the first column (turn on **Show/Hide** if necessary).

b. Click the **WordArt** button [*Insert* tab, *Text* group].

c. Select the **first option** in the **second row** to convert the selected text to *WordArt* (Figure 4-94).

d. Select the *WordArt* (if necessary) and change the *Shape Height* to **0.8"** and the *Shape Width* to **3.6"** [*Drawing Tools Format* tab, *Size* group]. Document content is temporarily adjusted and will be corrected in the following steps.

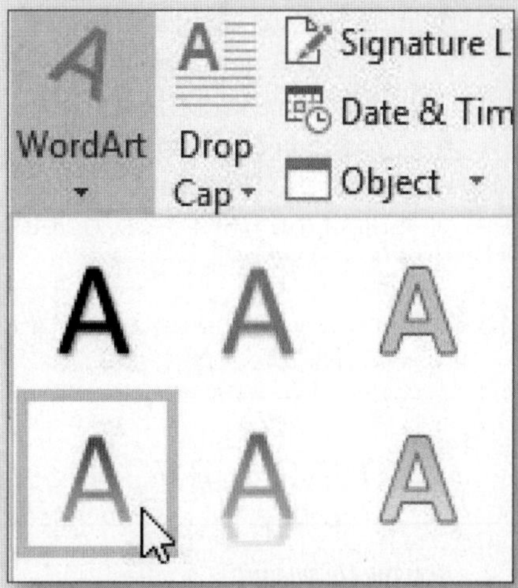

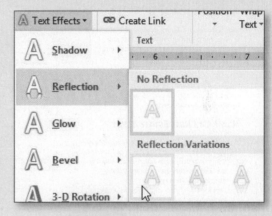

Figure 4-94 Select *WordArt* style

e. Click the **Text Effects** button [*Drawing Tools Format* tab, *WordArt Styles* group], click **Reflection**, and select the **first option** in the **first row** of the *Reflection Variations* category (**Tight Reflection: Touching**) (Figure 4-95).

f. Click the **Position** button [*Drawing Tools Format* tab, *Arrange* group] and select **More Layout Options**. The *Layout* dialog box opens.

g. Change the **Absolute position** in the *Horizontal* area to **0.2"** *to the right of* **Page**.

h. Change the **Absolute position** in the *Vertical* area to **0.2"** *below* **Page**.

i. Click **OK** to close the *Layout* dialog box.

Figure 4-95 Apply a *Reflection* text effect

11. Insert, resize, and position an icon.

a. Place the insertion point at the beginning of the second column.

b. Click the **Icons** button [*Insert* tab, *Illustrations* group] to open the *Insert Icons* dialog box.

c. Click the **Buildings** category on the left, select the **fourth option** in the **first row**, and click **Insert** (Figure 4-96). You may have to scroll down the categories on the left to locate the *Buildings* category.

d. Change the *Height* [*Graphic Tools Format* tab, *Size* group] to **0.8"**. The width adjusts automatically.

e. Click the **Wrap Text** button [*Graphic Tools Format* tab, *Arrange* group] and select **In Front of Text**.

Figure 4-96 *Insert Icons* dialog box

f. Click the **Position** button [*Graphic Tools Format* tab, *Arrange* group] and select **More Layout Options**. The *Layout* dialog box opens.

g. Change the **Absolute position** in the *Horizontal* area to **3.7"** *to the right of* **Page**.

h. Change the **Absolute position** in the *Vertical* area to **0.2"** *below* **Page**.

i. Click **OK** to close the *Layout* dialog box.

12. Edit the alt text on all three images in the document.
   a. Select the home icon near the top of the document and click the **Alt Text** button [*Graphic Tools Format* tab, *Accessibility* group]. The *Alt Text* pane opens.
   b. Type Icon of a home in the text box in the *Alt Text* pane.
   c. Select the "**For Sale**" graphic and type For Sale sign in the text box in the *Alt Text* pane.
   d. Select the *PHRE logo*, delete existing alt text if necessary, type PHRE logo in the text box, and close the *Alt Text* pane.

13. Save and close the document (Figure 4-97).

Emma Cavalli

REALTOR CONSULTANT

Phone	916.450.3334
Email	ecavalli@phre.com
Web	www.phre.com/ecavalli

MISSION STATEMENT

I am dedicated to listening to your needs as a buyer or seller and providing you with prompt and excellent service to exceed your expectations.

BUSINESS EXPERIENCE

I have had the pleasure of working with buyers, sellers, and investors for over 15 years. Each transaction is new and exciting.

WHY I AM A REAL ESTATE AGENT

1. I enjoy working with people and negotiating on their behalf.
2. Communication, organization, and availability are skills I possess that make me a client-focused real estate agent.
3. I am extremely conscientious of the emotions involved in both the buying and selling process.
4. Customer service and satisfaction are important to me, and I pride myself in giving you the best service possible.

Meeting Your Needs

WHAT CLIENTS ARE SAYING

Here are what others have said about me:

"It was a pleasure working with Emma Cavalli. She was very responsive and listened to all our needs. Her marketing plan sold our home in just 3 days!"

-Rod & Lilia Ellisor, Rocklin

"Emma is conscientious, personable, and professional. Her dedication and commitment to meeting our needs has been apparent from the beginning. Emma can be counted on to do what she says. We would not hesitate to refer Emma to our friends and family."

-Elia & Jazmin Solares, Roseville

PROFESSIONAL CREDENTIALS

- Licensed California Real Estate Salesperson
- Member of National Association of Realtors
- Member California Association of Realtors
- Member of Realtor.com
- Distinguished Realtor Award from peers
- Community Service Board position for the Roseville Unified School District
- Former Parent/Teacher Club President for Winchester Elementary School

EDUCATION & TRAINING

University of Nevada, Reno—Business Administration B.A.
Real Estate Code of Ethics
Certified Contract Consultant
Certified Maximum Productivity Consultant

FAMILY & HOBBIES

I have been a Roseville community member since 2003. I have been married since 2001 and have three children. I love to read, do crafts, travel, and watch my children play sports. I am also very involved in my church and charity work.

THE PLACER HILLS BELIEF SYSTEM	
COMMITMENT	To the needs of the client
COMMUNICATION	Seek first to listen
CREATIVITY	Ideas before results
CUSTOMERS	Always come first
INTEGRITY	Doing the right thing first
SUCCESS	Results with integrity
TEAMWORK	Work together for success
TRUST	Begins with communication
WIN-WIN	Is always the goal

Figure 4-97 PP W4-4 completed

Chapter Summary

4.1 Improve the design and readability of a document by using tables to present and arrange information (p. W4-219).

- *Tables* organize information in column and row format. A *column* is a vertical grouping of cells, and a *row* is a horizontal grouping of cells.
- A *cell* is the intersection of a column and row.
- Press **Tab** to move forward to the next cell and **Shift+Tab** to move to the previous cell.
- *Table Tools Layout* and *Table Tools Design* tabs provide many table formatting features.
- Copy or move columns or rows in a table.
- Add or delete columns and rows in tables.
- When working with tables, select individual cells, a range of cells, rows, columns, or an entire table.
- Merge a group of cells to create one cell. Cells can also be split into multiple cells.

4.2 Modify a table by changing the column and row size, aligning text, using the *Table Properties* dialog box, sorting data, and using *AutoFit* (p. W4-223).

- Resize columns and rows in a table.
- Use the *AutoFit* feature to automatically resize the table to fit the contents of the table, the window, or a fixed width.
- Align text in a cell both horizontally and vertically.
- *Cell margins* control the amount of spacing around the text within a cell.
- The *Table Properties* dialog box provides size and alignment options for cells, rows, columns, or an entire table.
- Sort table information in ascending or descending order.

4.3 Enhance the appearance and function of a table by applying borders and shading, using table styles, inserting formulas, and converting text into a table (p. W4-229).

- Apply borders and shading to parts of a table or to the entire table.
- *Table Styles* are collections of borders, shading, and formatting applied to a table. Word provides a gallery of table styles.
- Apply *Table Style Options* to a header row, total row, banded rows, first column, last column, or banded columns.

- *Formulas* in a table perform mathematical calculations.
- Convert existing text into a table or convert an existing table to text.

4.4 Modify the layout and design of a document using columns to present information (p. W4-236).

- Arrange text in a document in columns.
- Choose from preset column settings or customize column settings and space between columns using the *Columns dialog box*.
- *Column breaks* control column endings.
- Balance columns with column breaks or a *continuous section break*.

4.5 Improve a document by adding, modifying, and arranging pictures (p. W4-240).

- Pictures and graphics add visual appeal to a document. Insert a variety of graphic file types.
- *Alt text* is used by screen readers to provide an audio description of a graphic to assist individuals who are visually impaired.
- Resize a graphic and position it at a specific location in a document.
- *Text wrapping* controls how text wraps around graphics.
- The *Layout* dialog box includes options to change the position, text wrapping, and size of graphic objects.
- Add a *caption* to a graphic object.
- *Group* graphic objects together to create one graphic object, for easier resizing and positioning.

4.6 Enrich a document by adding and customizing graphic objects such as shapes, *SmartArt*, *WordArt*, symbols, icons, 3D models, and online video (p. W4-248).

- Insert shapes using the *Shapes* gallery. Customize shapes by changing size, position, fill color, outline color and width, and shape effects.
- *SmartArt* graphically presents information in a document.
- *WordArt* is special text formatting.
- Word provides a variety of formatting options and styles for *SmartArt*, *WordArt*, and other graphic objects.

- Use the *Symbols* dialog box to insert a variety of symbols and special characters.
- Use **icons** and **3D models** to visually enhance a document.
- An **online video** is a graphic object that links to an online video and can be played from within Word.

Check for Understanding

The SIMbook for this text (within your SIMnet account) provides the following resources for concept review:

- Multiple-choice questions
- Short answer questions
- Matching exercises

Guided Project 4-1

For this project, you modify the values statement document for Sierra Pacific Community College District to arrange text in columns, insert the company logo, and insert shapes.
[Student Learning Outcomes 4.4, 4.5, 4.6]

Files Needed: ***ValuesStatement-04.docx*** and ***SPCCDlogo-04.png*** *(Student data files are available in the* Library *of your SIMnet account.)*
Completed Project File Name: *[your initials] Word 4-1.docx*

Skills Covered in This Project

- Change page orientation.
- Change margins.
- Apply columns to text.
- Modify column settings.
- Insert a column break.

- Insert a picture.
- Change picture color.
- Modify picture size and position.
- Insert a shape.
- Modify shape size and position.
- Modify shape fill and outline.
- Edit alt text.

1. Open the ***ValuesStatement-04*** document from your student data files.

2. Save this document as [your initials] Word 4–1.

3. Change the orientation and margins of the document.
   a. Change the orientation of the document to **Landscape**.
   b. Change the top and bottom margins to **0.5"**.
   c. Change the left and right margins to **0.75"**.

4. Apply column formatting to the text in the body of the document.
   a. Place the insertion point in front of the first paragraph heading ("Access").
   b. Click the **Columns** button [*Layout* tab, *Page Setup* group] and select **More Columns**. The *Columns* dialog box opens (Figure 4-98).
   c. Select **Three** in the *Presets* area.
   d. Change the *Spacing* to **0.4"** in the *Width and spacing* area.
   e. Click the **Apply to** drop-down list and select **This point forward**.
   f. Click **OK** to close the *Columns* dialog box.

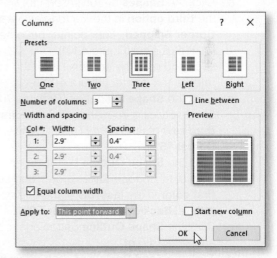

Figure 4-98 *Columns* dialog box

5. Insert a column break to balance the columns on the page.
   a. Place the insertion point in front of the "Student Learning Outcomes" paragraph heading in the first column.
   b. Click the **Breaks** button [*Layout* tab, *Page Setup* group] and select **Column**.

6. Insert, resize, and position the company logo on the bottom left of the document.
    a. Place the insertion point at the end of the last paragraph in the first column.
    b. Click the **Pictures** button [*Insert* tab, *Illustrations* group].
    c. Select the **SPCCDlogo-04** file from the student data files and click **Insert**.
    d. Click the **Wrap Text** button [*Picture Tools Format* tab, *Arrange* group] and select **Behind Text**.
    e. Right-click the logo and choose **Size and Position**. The *Layout* dialog box opens (Figure 4-99).
    f. Change the *Height* to **120%** in the *Scale* area on the *Size* tab and press **Tab**. The width automatically adjusts to keep the logo proportional.
    g. Click the **Position** tab.
    h. Change the **Absolute position** in the *Horizontal* area to **0.3"** *to the right of* **Page**.
    i. Change the **Absolute position** in the *Vertical* area to **7.2"** *below* **Page**.
    j. Click **OK** to close the *Layout* dialog box.

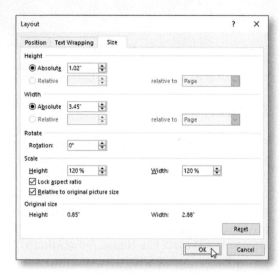

Figure 4-99 Resize logo as a percentage of its original size

7. Change the color of the logo.
    a. Select the logo (if necessary) and click the **Color** button [*Picture Tools Format* tab, *Adjust* group].
    b. Select the **first option** in the *Color Saturation* area (**Saturation: 0%**) (Figure 4-100).

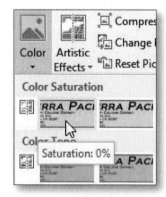

Figure 4-100 Change *Color Saturation*

8. Add a shape around the title, resize the shape, and modify the outline and fill.
    a. Click the **Shapes** button [*Insert* tab, *Illustrations* group] and select the **third option** in the *Rectangles* area (**Rectangle: Single Corner Snipped**). Your pointer becomes a crosshair (dark plus sign) (Figure 4-101).
    b. Click and drag the crosshair over the title and then release the pointer (Figure 4-102).
    c. Click the **Shape Fill** button [*Drawing Tools Format* tab, *Shape Styles* group] and select the **first color** in the **third row** of the *Theme Colors* (**White, Background 1, Darker 15%**).
    d. Click the **Shape Outline** button [*Drawing Tools Format* tab, *Shape Styles* group] and select the **first color** in the **last row** of the *Theme Colors* (**White, Background 1, Darker 50%**).
    e. Click the **Shape Outline** button again, select **Weight**, and select **1½ pt**.
    f. Click the **Send Backward** drop-down arrow [*Drawing Tools Format* tab, *Arrange* group] and select **Send Behind Text** from the drop-down list.
    g. Change the *Shape Height* [*Drawing Tools Format* tab, *Size* group] to **0.4"** and the *Shape Width* to **6.3"**.

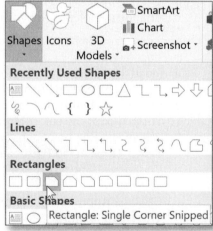

Figure 4-101 Select shape

Figure 4-102 Draw shape around the title

h. Click the **Align** button [*Drawing Tools Format* tab, *Arrange* group] and select **Align Center**.

i. Use the up and down keyboard arrow keys to vertically center the shape behind the title.

9. Edit the alt text on the shape and graphic in the document.

a. Select the border of the shape at the top of the document and click **Alt Text** button [*Drawing Tools Format* tab, *Accessibility* group]. The *Alt Text* pane opens.

b. Type Shape around the title in the text box in the *Alt Text* pane.

c. Select the *Sierra Pacific logo*, type Sierra Pacific logo in the text box in the *Alt Text* pane, and close the *Alt Text* pane.

10. Save and close the document (Figure 4-103).

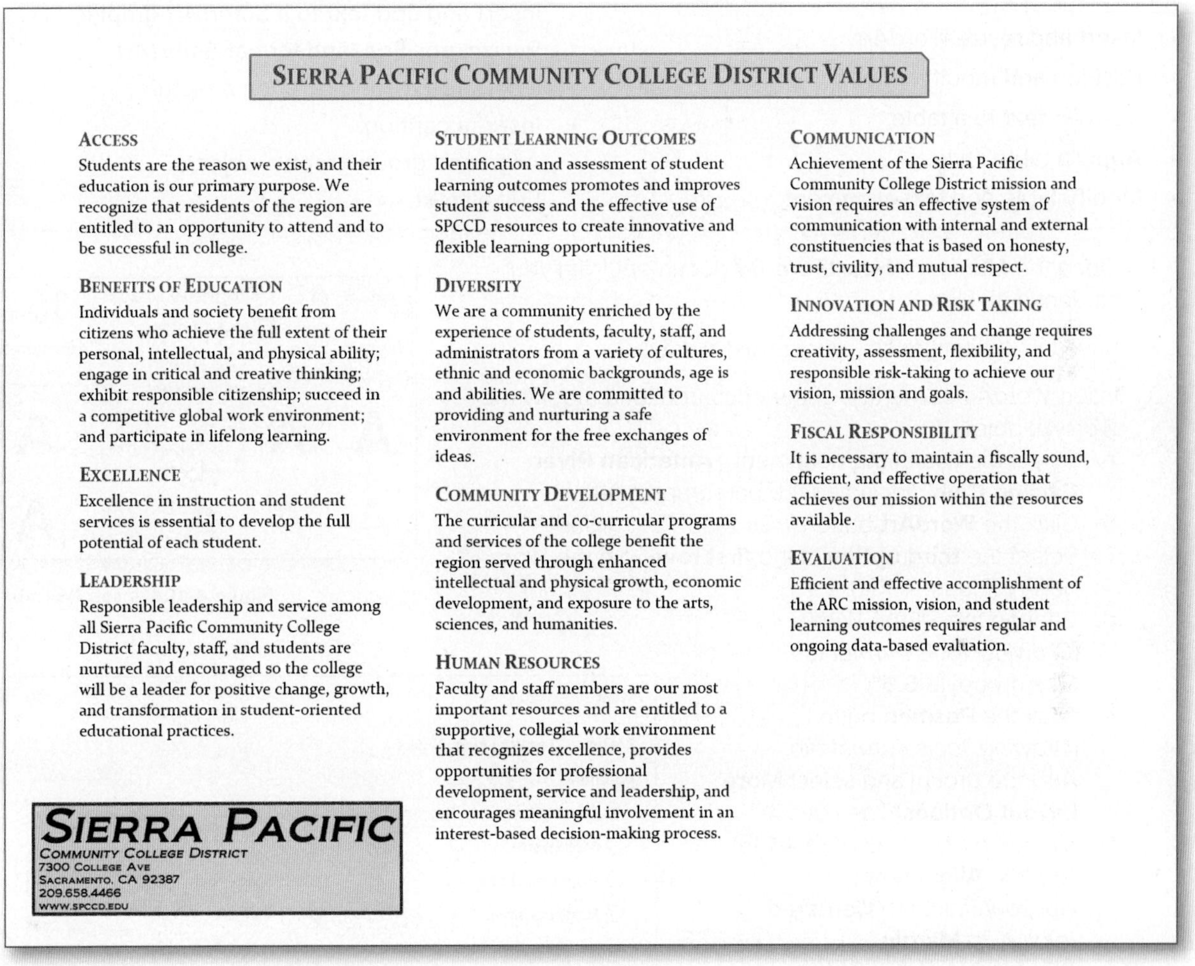

SIERRA PACIFIC COMMUNITY COLLEGE DISTRICT VALUES

ACCESS

Students are the reason we exist, and their education is our primary purpose. We recognize that residents of the region are entitled to an opportunity to attend and to be successful in college.

BENEFITS OF EDUCATION

Individuals and society benefit from citizens who achieve the full extent of their personal, intellectual, and physical ability; engage in critical and creative thinking; exhibit responsible citizenship; succeed in a competitive global work environment; and participate in lifelong learning.

EXCELLENCE

Excellence in instruction and student services is essential to develop the full potential of each student.

LEADERSHIP

Responsible leadership and service among all Sierra Pacific Community College District faculty, staff, and students are nurtured and encouraged so the college will be a leader for positive change, growth, and transformation in student-oriented educational practices.

STUDENT LEARNING OUTCOMES

Identification and assessment of student learning outcomes promotes and improves student success and the effective use of SPCCD resources to create innovative and flexible learning opportunities.

DIVERSITY

We are a community enriched by the experience of students, faculty, staff, and administrators from a variety of cultures, ethnic and economic backgrounds, age is and abilities. We are committed to providing and nurturing a safe environment for the free exchanges of ideas.

COMMUNITY DEVELOPMENT

The curricular and co-curricular programs and services of the college benefit the region served through enhanced intellectual and physical growth, economic development, and exposure to the arts, sciences, and humanities.

HUMAN RESOURCES

Faculty and staff members are our most important resources and are entitled to a supportive, collegial work environment that recognizes excellence, provides opportunities for professional development, service and leadership, and encourages meaningful involvement in an interest-based decision-making process.

COMMUNICATION

Achievement of the Sierra Pacific Community College District mission and vision requires an effective system of communication with internal and external constituencies that is based on honesty, trust, civility, and mutual respect.

INNOVATION AND RISK TAKING

Addressing challenges and change requires creativity, assessment, flexibility, and responsible risk-taking to achieve our vision, mission and goals.

FISCAL RESPONSIBILITY

It is necessary to maintain a fiscally sound, efficient, and effective operation that achieves our mission within the resources available.

EVALUATION

Efficient and effective accomplishment of the ARC mission, vision, and student learning outcomes requires regular and ongoing data-based evaluation.

SIERRA PACIFIC
COMMUNITY COLLEGE DISTRICT
7300 COLLEGE AVE
SACRAMENTO, CA 92387
209.658.4466
WWW.SPCCD.EDU

Figure 4-103 Word 4-1 completed

Guided Project 4-2

For this project, you modify a document about maximum and target heart rate for the American River Cycling Club. You arrange text in a table and insert and modify *SmartArt* and a picture.
[Student Learning Outcomes 4.1, 4.2, 4.3, 4.5, 4.6]

File Needed: ***MaximumHeartRate-04.docx*** and ***HeartRate-04.png*** *(Student data files are available in* the Library *of your SIMnet account.)*
Completed Project File Name: *[your initials]* ***Word 4-2.docx***

Skills Covered in This Project

- Insert and resize *WordArt*.
- Position and modify *WordArt*.
- Convert text to a table.
- Apply a table style.
- Modify table and text alignment.

- Change cell margins in a table.
- Insert and add text to a *SmartArt* graphic.
- Resize, position, and format *SmartArt*.
- Insert, resize, and position a picture.
- Insert a caption.
- Align and group graphic objects.
- Edit alt text.

1. Open the ***MaximumHeartRate-04*** document from your student data files.

2. Save this document as [your initials] Word 4-2.

3. Insert *WordArt* as the title of the document and modify the *WordArt* object.
   a. Select the title of the document, "**American River Cycling Club**" (including the paragraph mark).
   b. Click the **WordArt** button [*Insert* tab, *Text* group].
   c. Select the **third option** in the **first row** from the *WordArt* gallery (Figure 4-104).
   d. Change the *Shape Width* [*Drawing Tools Format* tab, *Size* group] to **6.5"**.
   e. Click the **Position** button [*Drawing Tools Format* tab, *Arrange* group] and select **More Layout Options**. The *Layout* dialog box opens (Figure 4-105).
   f. Change **Alignment** in the *Horizontal* area to **Centered** *relative to* **Margin**.
   g. Change **Absolute position** in the *Vertical* area to **0.2"** *below* **Page**.
   h. Click **OK** to close the *Layout* dialog box.
   i. Click the **Text Effects** button [*Drawing Tools Format* tab, *WordArt Styles* group], select **Reflection**, and select the **first option** in the **first row** of the *Reflection Variations* area (**Tight Reflection: Touching**) (Figure 4-106).

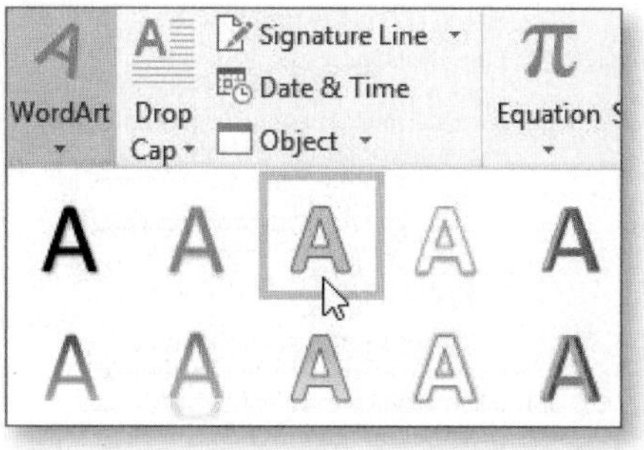

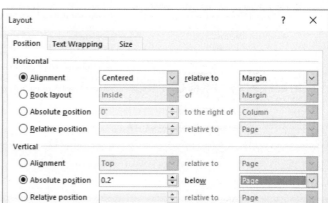

Figure 4-104 Insert *WordArt*

Figure 4-105 Adjust position of *WordArt*

4. Convert text into a table and format the table.
   a. Select all the tabbed text at the bottom of the document (including the last paragraph mark).
   b. Click the **Table** button [*Insert* tab, *Tables* group] and select **Convert Text to Table**. The *Convert Text to Table* dialog box opens.
   c. Click the **AutoFit to contents** radio button in the *AutoFit behavior* area.
   d. Click **OK** to close the dialog box.
   e. Click the **Table Tools Design** tab.
   f. Check the **Header Row** and **Banded Rows** boxes [*Table Style Options* group] (if necessary) and deselect the other check boxes.
   g. Click the **More** button in the *Table Styles* group to display the *Table Styles* gallery.
   h. Select **Grid Table 4 – Accent 2** in the *Grid Tables* section (Figure 4-107).
   i. Place the insertion point before "Zone" in the second column in the first row, press **Backspace** to delete the space between words, and press **Enter**.
   j. Place the insertion point before "Heart" in the third column in the first row, press **Backspace** to delete the space between words, and press **Enter**.

5. Adjust the size and alignment of the table.
   a. Use the table selector handle to select the entire table.
   b. Click the **Align Center** button [*Table Tool Layout* tab, *Alignment* group] (Figure 4-108). All text in the table is centered vertically and horizontally.
   c. Click the **Properties** button [*Table Tools Layout* tab, *Table* group].
   d. Click the **Table** tab, select **Center** in the *Alignment* area, and click **OK** to close the dialog box. The entire table is centered horizontally on the page.
   e. Click the **Cell Margins** button [*Table Tools Layout* tab, *Alignment* group]. The *Table Options* dialog box opens.
   f. Change the *Top* and *Bottom* cell margins to **0.03"** and the *Left* and *Right* cell margins to **0.1"**.
   g. Click **OK** to close the *Table Options* dialog box.

6. Insert and modify a *SmartArt* graphic.
   a. Place the insertion point at the end of the second body paragraph, "(*Example*: . . .)," in the first section.
   b. Click the **SmartArt** button [*Insert* tab, *Illustrations* group]. The *Choose a SmartArt Graphic* dialog box opens (Figure 4-109).

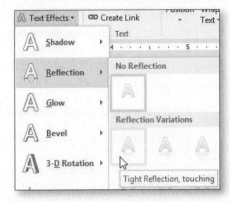

Figure 4-106 Apply *Reflection* option

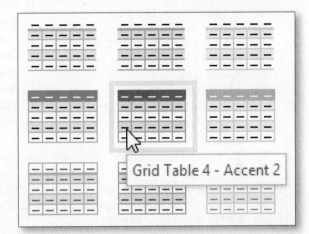

Figure 4-107 *Table Styles* gallery

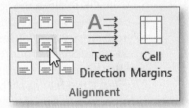

Figure 4-108 *Align Center* the text in the table

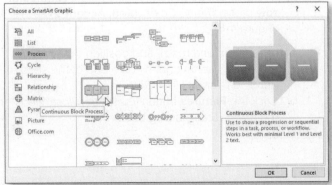

Figure 4-109 *Choose a SmartArt Graphic* dialog box

    c. Click **Process** in the list of *SmartArt* types.

    d. Select **Continuous Block Process** and click **OK** to insert the *SmartArt*. If the *Text* pane displays on the left of the *SmartArt* graphic, click the **X** in the upper-right corner to close it.

    e. Click the placeholder text (*[Text]*) in the first rectangle graphic, type 220, **space** once, and type - (hyphen or minus).

    f. Click the next placeholder text, type Your Age, **space** once, and type =.

    g. Click the last placeholder text, type Predicted Maximum Heart Rate.

7. Format, resize, and position the *SmartArt*.

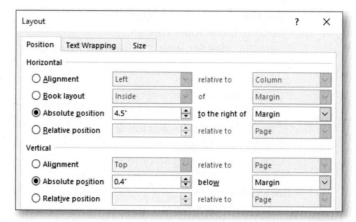

Figure 4-110 Adjust *SmartArt* position

    a. Click the outside frame of the *SmartArt* graphic to select the entire *SmartArt* graphic. *Note*: Select the entire *SmartArt* and not an object within the graphic.

    b. Change the *Shape Height* to **1.5"** and the *Shape Width* to **2.6"** in the *Size* group [*SmartArt Tools Format* tab].

    c. Click the **Wrap Text** button [*SmartArt Tools Format* tab, *Arrange* group] and select **Square**.

    d. Click the **Position** button [*SmartArt Tools Format* tab, *Arrange* group] and select **More Layout Options**. The *Layout* dialog box opens (Figure 4-110).

    e. Change the **Absolute position** in the *Horizontal* area to **4.5"** *to the right of* **Margin**.

    f. Change **Absolute position** in the *Vertical* area to **0.4"** *below* **Margin**.

    g. Click **OK** to close the *Layout* dialog box.

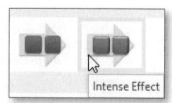

Figure 4-111 Apply *SmartArt* style

    h. Select the *SmartArt* (if necessary), select **Intense Effect** from the *SmartArt Styles* gallery [*SmartArt Tools Design* tab, *SmartArt Styles* group] (Figure 4-111).

    i. Click the edge of the first text box ("220 -") to select it and press **Ctrl+B** to apply bold format. Repeat this format on the other two text boxes.

    j. Select the last text box (if it is not already selected) and click the **SmartArt Tools Format** tab.

    k. Click the **Shape Fill** button and select **sixth color** in the **first row** of the *Theme Colors* (**Red, Accent 2**) as the fill color (Figure 4-112).

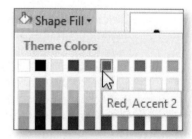

Figure 4-112 Change *Shape Fill* color

8. Insert a picture and resize and position the graphic.

    a. Place the insertion point at the end of the second section heading ("Target Heart Rate").

    b. Click the **Pictures** button [*Insert* tab, *Illustrations* group] to open the *Insert Picture* dialog box.

    c. Locate the ***HeartRate-04*** picture from your student data files and click **Insert**.

    d. Change the *Height* [*Picture Tools Format* tab, *Size* group] to **1"** (the width adjusts automatically).

    e. Click the **Wrap Text** button [*Picture Tools Format* tab, *Arrange* group] and select **Tight**.

    f. Click the **Align** button [*Picture Tools Format* tab, *Arrange* group] and select **Align Right**.

9. Format the picture and insert a caption.

    a. Select the picture (if necessary), click the **More** button in the *Pictures Styles* group [*Picture Tools Format* tab] to display the gallery of styles.

    b. Select the **Bevel Rectangle** picture style (Figure 4-113).

    c. Right-click the picture and select **Insert Caption** from the context menu. The *Insert Caption* dialog box opens.

    d. Click **OK** to insert the caption.

    e. Select and delete the caption placeholder text, and type Know your target heart rate as the caption text.

    f. Select the caption text, click the **Text Fill** button [*Drawing Tools Format* tab, *WordArt Styles* group], and select the **sixth color** in the **first row** of the *Theme Colors* (**Red, Accent 2**) as the text color.

    g. Change the caption *Height* to **0.2"** and the *Width* to **1.5"** in the *Size* group [*Drawing Tools Format* tab].

    h. Press the **Ctrl** key and click the picture. Both the caption and picture should be selected.

    i. Click the **Align** button [*Drawing Tools Format* tab, *Arrange* group] and select **Align Center**.

    j. Click the **Group** button [*Arrange* group] and select **Group**. The picture and caption are grouped into one object.

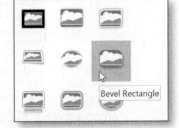

Figure 4-113 Apply *Picture Style*

10. Edit the alt text on the graphics in the document.

    a. Select the border of the *SmartArt* to select the entire *SmartArt* graphic.

    b. Right-click the *SmartArt* graphic and select **Edit Alt Text** from the context menu. The *Alt Text* pane opens.

    c. Type Graphic of predicted maximum heart rate in the text box in the *Alt Text* pane.

    d. Select the picture of a heart, type Picture of a heart in the text box in the *Alt Text* pane, and close the *Alt Text* pane.

11. Save and close the document (Figure 4-114).

American River Cycling Club

WHAT IS MAXIMUM HEART RATE?

The maximum heart rate is the highest your pulse rate can get. To calculate your **predicted maximum heart rate**, use this formula:

(Example: a 40-year-old's predicted maximum heart rate is 180.)

Your actual maximum heart rate can be determined by a graded exercise test. Please note that some medicines and medical conditions might affect your maximum heart rate. If you are taking medicines or have a medical condition (such as heart disease, high blood pressure, or diabetes), always ask your doctor if your maximum heart rate/target heart rate will be affected.

TARGET HEART RATE

You gain the most benefits and decrease the risk of injury when you exercise in your target heart rate zone. Usually this is when your exercise heart rate (pulse) is 60 percent to 80 percent of your maximum heart rate. Do not exercise above 85 percent of your maximum heart rate. This increases both cardiovascular and orthopedic risk and does not add any extra benefit.

Know your target heart rate

When beginning an exercise program, you might need to gradually build up to a level that is within your target heart rate zone, especially if you have not exercised regularly before. If the exercise feels too hard, slow down. You will reduce your risk of injury and enjoy the exercise more if you don't try to over-do it.

To find out if you are exercising in your target zone (between 60 percent and 80 percent of your maximum heart rate), use your heart rate monitor to track your heart rate. If your pulse is below your target zone (see the chart below), increase your rate of exercise. If your pulse is above your target zone, decrease your rate of exercise.

Age	Target Heart Rate (HR) Zone (60-85%)	Predicted Maximum Heart Rate
20	120-170	200
25	117-166	195
30	114-162	190
35	111-157	185
40	108-153	180
45	105-149	175
50	102-145	170
55	99-140	165
60	96-136	160
65	93-132	155
70	90-128	150

Figure 4-114 Word 4-2 completed

Guided Project 4-3

For this project, you format a buyer escrow checklist for Placer Hills Real Estate. You convert text to a table, format the table, and insert a picture.
[Student Learning Outcomes 4.1, 4.2, 4.3, 4.5, 4.6]

Files Needed: ***BuyerEscrowChecklist-04.docx***, ***Check-04.png***, and ***PHRElogo-04.png*** (Student data files are available in the Library of your SIMnet account.)
Completed Project File Name: ***[your initials] Word 4-3.docx***

Skills Covered in This Project

- Convert text to a table.
- Add columns to a table.
- Apply bullets and modify alignment.
- *AutoFit* a table.
- Apply table styles and borders.
- Modify row width and column height.
- Center text vertically in a table.
- Insert, resize, and position a picture.
- Change picture color.
- Use absolute position and text wrapping.
- Apply border and effects to a picture.
- Edit alt text.

1. Open the **BuyerEscrowChecklist-04** document from your student data files.

2. Save this document as [your initials] Word 4–3.

3. Convert text to a table.
   a. Select the text beginning with "**Task**" through "**Verify Preliminary Report with Lender**" (including the last paragraph mark).
   b. Click the **Table** button [*Insert* tab, *Tables* group].
   c. Click the **Convert Text to Table** button. The *Convert Text to Table* dialog box opens.
   d. Click **OK** to accept the default settings. The text converts to a table with 1 column and 14 rows.

4. Add columns and column headings to the table.
   a. Select the entire table (if necessary), click the **Table Tools Layout** tab.
   b. Click the **Insert Right** button [*Rows & Columns* group] to insert a blank column to the right of the existing column.
   c. Click the **Insert Right** button two more times to insert two more columns. Your table should now have four columns.
   d. Type the following column headings in the first row:
   Column 2: Date Completed
   Column 3: Initials
   Column 4: Notes

5. Add bullets to selected text.
   a. Select all of the text in the first column below "Task."
   b. Apply an **open square bullet** to these items (*Wingdings*, Character code 111).
   c. Click the **Decrease Indent** button once so the first line indent is 0" and the hanging indent is 0.25".

6. Apply table style and apply formatting.
   a. Place your insertion point in the first cell in the first column.
   b. Click the **AutoFit** button [*Table Tools Layout* tab, *Cell Size* group] and select **AutoFit Contents**.
   c. Click the **Table Tools Design** tab.
   d. Check the **Header Row** and **Banded Rows** boxes in the *Table Style Options* group. The other options should be unchecked.
   e. Click the **More** button in the *Table Styles* group to open the *Table Styles* gallery.
   f. Select **Grid Table 5 Dark** style (Figure 4-115).
   g. Select the column headings (first row of the table).
   h. **Bold** and **center** the column headings. You might have to click the **Bold** button more than once to bold all column headings.

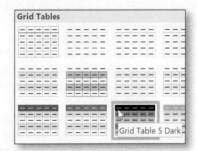

Figure 4-115 Apply table style

7. Modify cell size and alignment.
   a. Use the table selector handle to select the entire table or use the **Select** button [*Table Tools Layout* tab, *Table* group] and click **Select Table**.
   b. Change the *Height* [*Table Tools Layout* tab, *Cell Size* group] to **0.35"**. The row height changes on the entire table.

c. Click the **Properties** button [*Table Tools Layout* tab, *Table* group]. The *Table Properties* dialog box opens.

d. Click the **Cell** tab, select **Center** in the *Vertical alignment* area, and click **OK** to close the *Table Properties* dialog box.

e. Place your insertion point in the fourth column and change the *Width* [*Table Tools Layout* tab, *Cell Size* group] to **1.5"**.

8. Insert a picture, customize it, and position it in the document.

a. Place your insertion point at the end of the "Buyer(s):" line after the solid underline tab leader.

b. Click the **Pictures** button [*Insert* tab, *Illustrations* group]. The *Insert Pictures* dialog box opens.

c. Locate the **Check-04** file from your student data files and click **Insert**.

d. Change the *Height* to **1.5"** [*Picture Tools Format* tab, *Size* group] (the width adjusts automatically).

e. Click the **Wrap Text** button [*Picture Tools Format* tab, *Arrange* group] and select **Tight**.

f. Click the **Color** button [*Picture Tools Format* tab, *Adjust* group] and select the **third option** in the **second row** in the *Recolor* area (**Olive Green, Accent color 2 Dark**) (Figure 4-116).

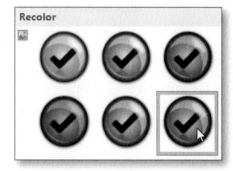

Figure 4-116 Change picture color

g. Click the **Position** button [*Picture Tools Format* tab, *Arrange* group] and select **More Layout Options** to open the *Layout* dialog box (Figure 4-117).

h. Change the **Absolute position** in the *Horizontal* area to **5.5"** *to the right of* **Margin**.

i. Change the **Absolute position** in the *Vertical* area to **0.7"** *below* **Margin**.

j. Click **OK** to close the *Layout* dialog box.

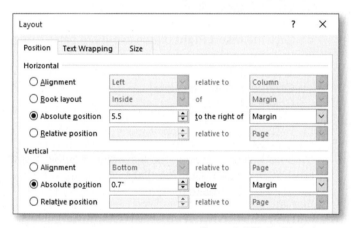

Figure 4-117 Position picture

9. Insert a picture, position it in the document, and customize it.

a. Place your insertion point at the end of the title.

b. Click the **Pictures** button [*Insert* tab, *Illustrations* group]. The *Insert Picture* dialog box opens.

c. Select the **PHRElogo-04** file from the student data files and click **Insert**.

d. Right-click the picture, select **Wrap Text**, and choose **In Front of Text**.

e. Click the **Position** button [*Picture Tools Format* tab, *Arrange* group] and select **More Layout Options** to open the *Layout* dialog box.

f. Change the **Absolute position** in the *Horizontal* area to **6.2"** *to the right of* **Page**.

g. Change the **Absolute position** in the *Vertical* area to **0.2"** *below* **Page**.

h. Click **OK** to close the *Layout* dialog box.

i. Click the **Picture Border** button [*Picture Tools Format* tab, *Picture Styles* group] and select the **sixth color** in the **first row** of the *Theme Colors* (**Olive Green, Accent 2**) (Figure 4-118).

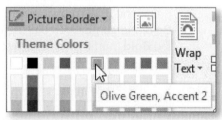

Figure 4-118 Apply *Picture Border* color

j. Click the **Picture Border** button again, click **Weight**, and select **1½ pt**.

k. Click the **Picture Effects** button [*Picture Tools Format* tab, *Picture Styles* group], select **Shadow**, and select **second option** in the **first row** of the *Outer* category (**Offset: Bottom**).

10. Edit the alt text on the graphics in the document.

   a. Select the *PHRE* logo near the top and click **Alt Text** button [*Picture Tools Format* tab, *Accessibility* group]. The *Alt Text* pane opens.

   b. Type PHRE logo in the text box in the *Alt Text* pane.

   c. Select the checkmark picture, type Picture of a checkmark in the text box in the *Alt Text* pane, and close the *Alt Text* pane.

11. Save and close the document (Figure 4-119).

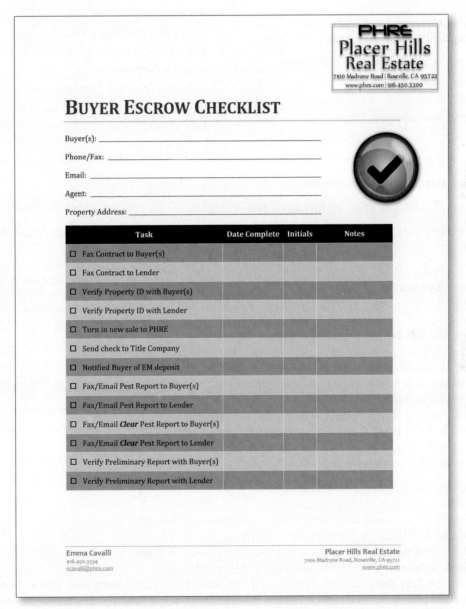

Figure 4-119 Word 4-3 completed

Independent Project 4-4

For this project, you format a vaccination schedule for Courtyard Medical Plaza by converting text to a table, formatting the table, and inserting a picture.
[Student Learning Outcomes 4.1, 4.2, 4.3, 4.5, 4.6]

Files Needed: **VaccinationSchedule-04.docx**, **CMPLogo-04.png**, and **Vaccination-04.png** (Student data files are available in the Library of your SIMnet account.)
Completed Project File Name: **[your initials] Word 4-4.docx**

Skills Covered in This Project

- Convert text to a table.
- Apply a table style.
- *AutoFit* the table and change row height.
- Center text vertically.
- Sort text in a table.
- Insert rows and add text.
- Merge cells.

- Apply custom borders.
- Apply a style to text.
- Insert and position a picture.
- Adjust the size and position of a picture.
- Apply a picture effect.
- Add and format a caption.
- Group a caption and picture.
- Edit alt text.

---

1. Open the **VaccinationSchedule-04** document from your student data files.

2. Save this document as [your initials] Word 4–4.

3. Select the tabbed text in the middle of the document and convert it to a table (accept default settings). Don't include the blank line below the tabbed text.

4. Select the entire table and apply the following changes:
   a. Select **Banded Rows** in the *Table Style Options* group [*Table Tools Design* tab] and deselect all other check boxes.
   b. Apply the **List Table 1 Light – Accent 2** table style (Figure 4-120).
   c. Change the font size on all the text in the table to **10 pt**.
   d. **AutoFit** the table and choose **AutoFit Window**.
   e. Change row height to **0.25"**.
   f. Center all text vertically within each cell. (*Hint*: Use the *Cell* tab in the *Table Properties* dialog box.)
   g. Sort the table by **Name of Vaccine** in **Ascending** order. Be sure to select **Header row** in the *My list has* area of the *Sort* dialog box.

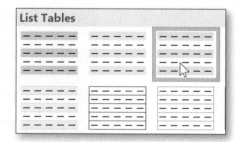

Figure 4-120 Apply a table style

5. Make the following changes to the table:
   a. Insert a row above the first row.
   b. Merge the three cells in the new first row and type the following:
      RECOMMENDED VACCINATION SCHEDULE
   c. **Bold** and **center** the first row and change the font size to **11 pt**.
   d. **Bold** and **italicize** the column headings in the second row.
   e. Select the **first row** and apply borders with the following settings: **solid line**, **Black, Text 1** color (**second color** in the **first row** of **Theme Colors**), **1½ pt**. width, and apply a **top** and **bottom** border.
   f. Select the second row and apply a border with the following settings: **solid line**, **Black, Text 1** color, **1½ pt**. width, and apply a **bottom** border. Do not remove the top border applied in the previous step.

g. Select the last row and apply a border with the following settings: **solid line**, **Black, Text 1** color, **1½ pt.** width, and apply a **bottom** border.

h. **Align Center** [*Table Tools Layout* tab, *Alignment* group] the column headings.

i. **Align Center** the text in the third column.

6. Insert the Table 4-5 information alphabetically into the table. Insert rows where needed.

Table 4-5

Meningococcal conjugate (MCV)	At 11-12 years	1
Hepatitis B (HepB)	At birth, 1-2 months, and 6 months	3

7. Modify the title of the document ("Vaccination Schedule").
   a. Apply the **Title** style to the title of the document.
   b. Change the *After* paragraph spacing to **8 pt**.
   c. **Center** the title horizontally.
   d. Apply **small caps** and **bold** formatting to the title.

8. Insert and modify a picture.
   a. Place the insertion point after the title and insert the **CMPLogo-04** picture from your student data files. Use the *Insert Picture* dialog box.
   b. Change text wrapping to **Top and Bottom**.
   c. Change the height of the logo to **1"**. Verify the logo remains proportional.
   d. Apply the **Offset: Bottom Right** shadow picture effect (*Outer* category).
   e. Set the *Horizontal* **Absolute position** to **0.2"** *to the right of* **Page**.
   f. Set the *Vertical* **Absolute position** to **0.2"** *below* **Page**.

9. Insert a picture and add a caption.
   a. Place the insertion point at the end of the first body paragraph and insert the **Vaccination-04** picture from your student data files. Use the *Insert Picture* dialog box.
   b. Change the text wrapping to **Square**.
   c. Change the height of the picture to **1.3"**. Verify the graphic remains proportional.
   d. Drag the picture to the right of the first and second paragraphs.
   e. Insert a caption, delete the caption placeholder text, and type Don't neglect your vaccinations! as the caption text.
   f. **Center** the caption text, change the font color to **Red, Accent 2** (**sixth color** in the **first row** of *Theme Colors*), and turn off italics if it is applied to the text.
   g. Select the caption and the picture and **Align Center**.
   h. **Group** the caption and the picture.
   i. Set the *Horizontal* **Absolute position** to **6"** *to the right of* **Margin**.
   j. Set the *Vertical* **Absolute position** to **0.8"** *below* **Margin**.

10. Edit the alt text of the graphic objects.
    a. Edit the alt text of the CMP logo and type Courtyard Medical Plaza logo as the alt text.
    b. Edit the alt text of the graphic of a doctor, type Graphic of a doctor as the alt text, and close the *Alt Text* pane.

11. Save and close the document (Figure 4-121).

VACCINATION SCHEDULE

Think of vaccines as a coat of armor for your child. To keep it shiny and strong, you have to make sure your child's immunizations are up to date. Timely vaccinations help to prevent disease and keep your family and the community healthy. Some immunizations are given in a single shot, while others require a series of shots over a period of time.

Vaccines for children and teenagers are listed alphabetically below with their routinely recommended ages. Missed doses will be assessed by your child's physician and given if necessary. Keep a personal record of all immunizations and bring it with you to each office visit.

Don't neglect your vaccinations!

RECOMMENDED VACCINATION SCHEDULE

Name of Vaccine	When It's Recommended	Total Doses
Chickenpox (varicella)	At 12 months and 4-6 years	2
Diphtheria, tetanus, and pertussis (DTaP)	At 2, 4, 6 and 12-15 months, and 4-6 years	5
Haemophilus influenzae type b (Hib)	At 2, 4, 6, and 12 months	4
Hepatitis A (HepA)	At 12 and 18 months	3
Hepatitis B (HepB)	At birth, 1-2 months, and 6 months	3
Human papillomavirus (HPV)	3-dose series for girls at age 11-12 years	3
Inactivated influenza (flu shot)	Annually starting at age 6 months	Annually
Inactivated poliovirus (IPV)	At 2, 4, 6 months, and 4-6 years	4
Live intranasal influenza	Annually starting at age 2 years	Annually
Measles, mumps, and rubella (MMR)	At 12 months and 4-6 years	2
Meningococcal conjugate (MCV)	At 11-12 years	1
Pneumococcal conjugate (PCV)	At 2, 4, 6, and 12 months	4
Pneumococcal polysaccharide (PPSV)	At 2, 4, 6, and 12 months	4
Rotavirus (RV)	At 2, 4, and 6 months	3
Tetanus and diphtheria (Td)	At 11-12 years	1

These recommendations are for generally healthy children and teenagers and are for information only. If your child has ongoing health problems, special health needs or risks, or if certain conditions run in your family, talk with your child's physician. He or she may recommend additional vaccinations or schedules based on earlier immunizations and special health needs.

Figure 4-121 Word 4-4 completed

Independent Project 4-5

For this project, you create an emergency telephone information sheet for Sierra Pacific Community College District (SPCCD). You add and modify a *SmartArt* graphic, convert text to a table, insert a new table, format the tables, and insert the company logo.
[Student Learning Outcomes 4.1, 4.2, 4.3, 4.5, 4.6]

Files Needed: ***EmergencyTelephones-04.docx*** and ***SPCCDlogo.png*** (Student data files are available in the Library of your SIMnet account.)
Completed Project File Name: ***[your initials] Word 4-5.docx***

Skills Covered in This Project

- Modify an existing document.
- Insert a *SmartArt* graphic.
- Add text to a *SmartArt* graphic.
- Resize, change the color of, and apply a style to *SmartArt*.
- Convert text to a table and *AutoFit*.
- Sort text in a table.
- Insert a row, merge cells, and add information.

- Apply a table style.
- Change cell margins and alignment.
- Apply a style to text.
- Insert a table and type text.
- Insert a picture.
- Adjust a picture size and position.
- Insert, modify, and position an icon.
- Insert a symbol and the current date.
- Edit alt text.

---

1. Open the **EmergencyTelephones-04** document from your student data files.

2. Save this document as [your initials] Word 4–5.

3. Insert a *SmartArt* graphic and add text.
   a. Place your insertion point in front of the second section heading ("Emergency Telephone Locations").
   b. Insert the **Vertical Chevron List** *SmartArt* graphic from the *List* category (Figure 4-122).
   c. Type 1 in the graphic text box in the upper-left corner of the *SmartArt* graphic (first chevron shape).
   d. Type 2 in the second graphic text box in the first column of the graphic.
   e. Type 3 in the third graphic text box in the first column of the graphic.

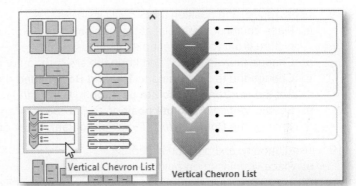

Figure 4-122 Insert *SmartArt* graphic

   f. Type the following text in the bulleted text boxes in the second column. You do not need to add bullets because bullets are already included in the *SmartArt*.

   - Press the "Help" button
   - Speak when the light comes on

   - Stay on the line
   - You will be connected with the college police

   - State clearly the nature of the emergency and your location

   g. Use **Backspace** to remove the extra bullet in the last graphic in the second column.

4. Resize and format the *SmartArt* graphic.
   a. Select the frame of the graphic to select the entire graphic.
   b. Change the height to **2.5"** and the width to **4.2"**.
   c. Change the text wrapping to **Top and Bottom**.
   d. **Change Colors** [*SmartArt Tools Design* tab] of the entire *SmartArt* graphic to **Dark 2 Fill** (Figure 4-123).
   e. Apply the **Intense Effect** *SmartArt* style.

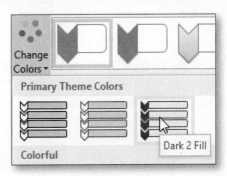

Figure 4-123 Change *SmartArt* colors

5. Convert text to a table.
   a. Select the tabbed text below the second section heading ("Emergency Telephone Locations"). Do not select the paragraph mark below the last row.
   b. **Convert Text to Table** and select **AutoFit to contents**.

6. Sort the table text by **Column 1** in **Ascending** order.

7. Add a title row and insert text.
   a. Add a row above the first row.
   b. Merge the cells in this row.
   c. Type **Blue Emergency Telephones** in the merged first row.

8. Format the table.
   a. Select **Header Row**, **First Column**, and **Banded Rows** in the *Table Style Options* group (if necessary). Deselect all other options.
   b. Apply the **List Table 2** table style.
   c. Select the entire table and change the top and bottom cell margins to **0.04"** and the left and right cell margins to **0.1"**.
   d. Vertically **center** all text in the table. (*Hint*: Use the *Cell* tab in the *Table Properties* dialog box.)
   e. Select the first row and horizontally **center** the text. This text should be centered vertically and horizontally.

9. Insert, resize, and position the SPCCD logo.
   a. Place your insertion point at the beginning of the document and insert the **SPCCDlogo_04** picture (from your student data files). Use the *Insert Picture* dialog box.
   b. Change the width to **3"** and keep the size proportional.
   c. Change the text wrapping to **Top and Bottom** and drag the logo above the title.
   d. Set the *Horizontal* **Absolute position** to **0.3"** *to the right of* **Page**.
   e. Set the *Vertical* **Absolute position** to **0.3"** *below* **Page**.
   f. Change the **Color** [*Picture Tools Format* tab, *Adjust* group] to **Saturation: 0%**.

10. Insert, modify, and position an icon.
    a. Place your insertion point at the end of the title.
    b. Insert an icon and select the phone in the *Communications* section (Figure 4-124).
    c. Change the width to **2"** and keep the size proportional.
    d. Change the text wrapping to **Tight**.
    e. Set the *Horizontal* **Alignment** to **Right** *relative to* **Margin**.
    f. Set the *Vertical* **Absolute position** to **1.1"** *below* **Margin**.
    g. Change the **Graphics Fill** color to **Dark Blue, Text 2** (**fourth color** in the **first row** of *Theme Colors*).

Figure 4-124 Insert an icon

11. Modify the footer to include a symbol and the current date.
    a. Edit the footer and **space** once at the end of the text on the right side of the footer.
    b. Insert a **solid circle** symbol from the *Symbol* font set (Character code 183) and **space** once after it.
    c. Type **Revised:** and **space** once.
    d. Insert the current date in MM/DD/YY format, set it so that it does not update automatically, and close the footer.

12. Edit the alt text of the graphic objects.
    a. Edit the alt text of the Sierra Pacific logo, type **Sierra Pacific logo** as the alt text.
    b. Select the entire *SmartArt* graphic, type **Graphic of emergency telephone instructions** as the alt text.
    c. Edit the alt text of the phone icon, type **Icon of a blue phone** as the alt text, and close the *Alt Text* pane.

13. Save and close the document (Figure 4-125).

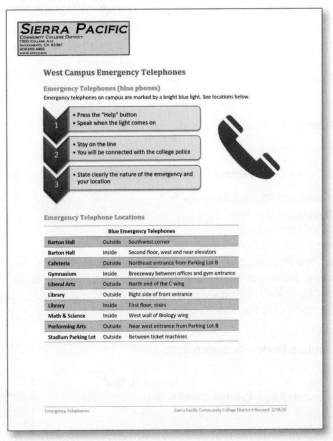

Figure 4-125 Word 4-5 completed

Independent Project 4-6

For this project, you modify a memo for Life's Animal Shelter. You edit an existing table, add rows and a column, format the table, insert formulas into the table, and insert and modify *WordArt* and a 3D model.
[Student Learning Outcomes 4.1, 4.2, 4.3, 4.6]

File Needed: **WeeklyExpenses-04.docx** *(Student data files are available in the Library of your SIMnet account.)*
Completed Project File Name: **[your initials] Word 4-6.docx**

Skills Covered in This Project

- Modify an existing document.
- Modify a table row height.
- Change cell alignment.

- Add rows and a column to a table.
- Merge table rows.
- Modify the borders and shading of a table.
- Insert formulas into a table.

- Set the formula number format.
- Update formulas.
- Format selected text.
- Insert *WordArt*.
- Modify and position *WordArt*.

- Change paragraph spacing.
- Insert a date.
- Insert and customize a 3D model.
- Edit alt text.

---

1. Open the **WeeklyExpenses-04** document from your student data files.

2. Save this document as [your initials] Word 4-6.

3. Select the table and **Sort** it by **Expenses** in **Ascending** order (the table has a header row).

4. Add rows, a column, and text to the table.
   a. Insert one row above the first row.
   b. Insert one row below the last row.
   c. Insert one column to the right of the last column.
   d. Merge the cells in the first row, type Life's Animal Shelter, press **Enter**, and type Weekly Expenses. If a paragraph symbol displays at the end of the subtitle text, delete the paragraph symbol.
   e. Type Totals in the last column in the second row.
   f. Type Totals in the last row in the first column.

5. Apply a table style and modify row height and text alignment.
   a. Apply the **Grid Table 5 Dark – Accent 6** table style (Figure 4-126).
   b. Select the entire table and change the row height to **0.3"**.
   c. Select the first row and **Align Center** (vertical and horizontal).
   d. Select the first column below the merged row and **Align Center Left**.
   e. Select columns 2–9 (including blank cells) below the merged row and **Align Center Right**.
   f. Select the column headings in the second row (beginning with "**Mon**" and ending with "**Totals**") and apply **Bold** formatting.

Figure 4-126 Apply a table style.

6. Insert formulas into the table.
   a. Place your insertion point in the last row of the second column, insert a **Formula** [*Table Tools Layout* tab, *Data* group] to add the figures above. The formula should be **=SUM(ABOVE)**. Use the **$#,##0.00;($#,##0.00)** number format (Figure 4-127).
   b. Insert the same formula and number format in remaining cells in the last row, except for the last column.
   c. Place your insertion point in the last column of the third row, insert a **Formula** to add the figures to the left. The formula should be **=SUM(LEFT)**. Use the **$#,##0.00;($#,##0.00)** number format.

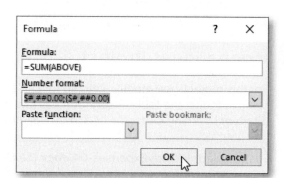

Figure 4-127 Insert a formula into the table

   d. Insert the same formula and number format in remaining rows in the last column. Verify the correct formula, **=SUM(LEFT)**, has been inserted in each of these cells. Replace "ABOVE" with "LEFT" in the formula, if needed.

7. Change expense data and update formulas.
   a. Change the "Wages" for "Wednesday" to 592.75.
   b. Right-click the total amount in this column and select **Update Field** from the context menu to update the total.
   c. Update the totals formulas in the last two rows in the last column. The total in the last cell in the last row should be $12,536.34.

8. Format text in the table and *AutoFit* the table.
   a. Apply **small caps**, and **12 pt.** font size to the text in the first row.
   b. **Bold** the total amounts in the last row.
   c. **Bold** the total amounts in the last column.
   d. AutoFit the table and select **AutoFit Window**.

9. Insert and customize *WordArt* for the company logo.
   a. Place the insertion point at the beginning of the document.
   b. Insert **WordArt** and select the **third option** in the **first row** (Figure 4-128).
   c. Type Life's Animal Shelter as the text for the *WordArt*.
   d. Select the text in the *WordArt* and change the text to **small caps** and **40 pt**.
   e. Change the **Text Fill** to **Orange, Accent 6** (**last color** in the **first row** of *Theme Colors*).
   f. Change the **Shadow** text effect to **Offset: Right** (**first option** in the **second row** of the *Outer* category).
   g. Set the *Horizontal* **Alignment** to **Left** *relative to* **Margin**.
   h. Set the *Vertical* **Absolute position** to **0.2"** *below* **Page**.

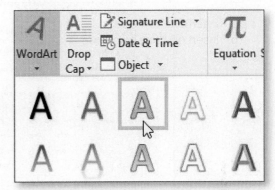

Figure 4-128 Insert *WordArt*

10. Modify the heading lines of the memo.
    a. Add **36 pt.** before paragraph spacing on the first line of the memo heading ("TO: . . .").
    b. Insert the current date on the date line in the memo heading to replace the placeholder text and set it to update automatically (use January 1, 2020 format).

11. Insert, rotate, resize, and position a 3D model.
    a. Place your insertion point before "TO:" in the memo heading lines.
    b. Click the bottom half of the **3D Models** button and select **From Online Sources**.
    c. Type dog in the search text box and press **Enter**.
    d. Select and insert a 3D model of your choice.
    e. Select and drag the 3D model near the right margin.
    f. Use the rotation handle in the middle of the 3D model to rotate the model to an angle of your choice
    g. Change the *Width* to **1.5"**.
    h. Click the **Position** button and select **Position in Top Right with Square Text Wrapping**.

12. Edit the alt text of the graphic objects.
    a. Edit the alt text of the Word Art near the top of the document and type Life's Animal Shelter Word Art as the alt text.
    b. Edit the alt text of the 3D model dog, type 3D model of a dog as the alt text, and close the *Alt Text* pane.

13. Save and close the document (Figure 4-129).

LIFE'S ANIMAL SHELTER

TO: Life's Animal Shelter Staff and Volunteers

FROM: Kelly Sung, Director of Services

DATE: April 3, 2020

SUBJECT: Weekly Expenses

Thank you for the time you have spent volunteering at Life's Animal Shelter. Our staff and volunteers have contributed countless hours making this shelter a safe environment for animals and providing adoption services for families in our community. You have been a part of hundreds of animal rescues and adoptions over the past year. Families throughout our region are enjoying their new pets thanks to your dedication and work at Life's Animal Shelter.

I'm providing you with our expenses update for the last week. Our operating funds come through donations and pet adoption fees. Thank you for your help in keeping our expenses at a moderate level. Because of you, we are able to offer reasonable adoption fees to animal lovers in our community.

Again, thank you for all of your hard work. Because of you, Life's Animal Shelter valuably serves our community providing shelter and adoption services.

LIFE'S ANIMAL SHELTER WEEKLY EXPENSES								
Expenses	Mon	Tue	Wed	Thurs	Fri	Sat	Sun	Totals
Electricity	19.45	20.09	21.75	19.02	19.99	23.56	19.45	$ 143.31
Equipment	199.03	209.25	198.90	229.05	245.09	351.98	205.55	$1,638.85
Food	340.45	344.05	350.51	340.01	341.48	359.75	340.02	$2,416.27
Heat	25.75	26.01	28.05	25.03	25.99	31.04	24.99	$ 186.86
Medicine	525.33	529.31	535.25	524.59	527.99	543.39	540.01	$3,725.87
Wages	675.21	580.91	592.75	579.55	680.81	750.05	565.90	$4,425.18
Totals	$1,785.22	$1,709.62	$1,727.21	$1,717.25	$1,841.35	$2,059.77	$1,695.92	$12,536.34

Life's Animal Shelter   Weekly Expenses

Figure 4-129 Word 4-6 completed

Improve It Project 4-7

For this project, you edit a document for Courtyard Medical Plaza. You arrange text in columns, position the company logo, and apply formatting to improve the overall layout of the document.
[Student Learning Outcomes 4.4, 4.5]

Files Needed: *StayingActive-04.docx* and *CMPlogo.png* (Student data files are available in the Library of your SIMnet account.)
Completed Project File Name: *[your initials] Word 4-7.docx*

Skills Covered in This Project

- Modify an existing document.
- Apply style formatting to the title and headings.
- Change font size and alignment.
- Change paragraph spacing.
- Use the *Format Painter*.
- Arrange text in columns.
- Change spacing between columns.
- Use a column break to balance columns.
- Insert a picture.
- Resize and position a picture.
- Edit alt text.

---

1. Open the ***StayingActive-04*** document from your student data files.

2. Save this document as [your initials] Word 4–7.

3. Modify the title of the document.
   a. Apply **Intense Reference** style to the title ("Tips for Staying Active").
   b. Change to **18 pt.** font size.
   c. Align **center**.
   d. Change the *Before* paragraph spacing to **36 pt.** and *After* paragraph spacing to **12**.

4. Modify section headings of the document.
   a. Apply **Subtle Reference** style to the first section heading ("**Try Some of the Following Suggestions**").
   b. Change the font size to **14 pt.** and **center** the section heading.
   c. Change *Before* paragraph spacing to **12 pt.** and *After* paragraph spacing to **6 pt**.
   d. Use the **Format Painter** to apply the formatting of the first section heading to the second section heading ("**To Keep Exercise Fun and Interesting**").

5. Format the last line of the document to make it part of the bulleted list that precedes it and format it consistently with the other bulleted items.

6. Apply column format to the multilevel list following the first section heading.
   a. Select the multilevel list in the first section and apply two-column format. Do not include the section heading. If the section break above the list has a number, turn off numbering on this line.
   b. Customize the space between columns to **0.75"**.

7. Apply column format to the bulleted list following the second section heading.
   a. Select the bulleted list in the second section and apply two-column format. Do not include the section heading. If the section break above the list has a bullet, turn off bullets on this line.
   b. Customize the space between columns to **0.75"**.
   c. Insert a **column break** before the third bulleted item to balance the columns.

8. Place the insertion point at the end of the first section heading ("Try Some of the Following Suggestions") and **delete** the paragraph mark.

9. Place the insertion point at the end of the second section heading ("To Keep Exercise Fun and Interesting") and **delete** the paragraph mark.

10. Insert, resize, and position a picture.
    a. Place your insertion point at the top of the document and insert the ***CMPlogo-04*** picture. Use the *Insert Picture* dialog box.
    b. Change the width to **2.5"** and keep the size proportional.
    c. Change the text wrapping to **In Front of Text**.
    d. Set the *Horizontal* **Absolute position** to **0.2"** *to the right of* **Page**.
    e. Set the *Vertical* **Absolute position** to **0.2"** *below* **Page**.
    f. Edit the alt text of the CMP logo, type Courtyard Medical Plaza logo as the alt text, and close the *Alt Text* pane.

11. Save and close the document (Figure 4-130).

TIPS FOR STAYING ACTIVE

Almost any activity that gets you moving and strengthens your muscles is good for your health and can help you meet your fitness and weight goal. If you haven't been exercising regularly, start out slowly and gradually increase duration, frequency, and intensity. If you have been exercising regularly, keep it up!

TRY SOME OF THE FOLLOWING SUGGESTIONS:

1) AIM FOR AT LEAST 30 TO 60 MINUTES OF MODERATE INTENSITY ACTIVITY ON MOST DAYS.
   a) You can get your exercise all at once or spread it out during the day.
      i) For example, exercising for three 10-minute periods is just as effective as exercising for 30 minutes at a time.
   b) The more physical activity you do, the more calories you burn and the greater the health benefit.

2) IF YOU DON'T LIKE COUNTING CALORIES, TRY COUNTING YOUR STEPS! WALKING 10,000 STEPS A DAY CAN HELP YOU MANAGE YOUR WEIGHT.
   a) Use a pedometer (an easy-to-wear device that senses your body's motion) to count your steps and motivate you to increase your activity.
   b) Use a journal to track your walking.

3) USE BOTH AEROBIC AND STRENGTHENING ACTIVITIES ARE IMPORTANT TO LOSING WEIGHT AND KEEPING IT OFF.
   a) As you grow older, your body slows down and your metabolism—the rate at which your body burns calories—naturally decreases.
   b) Taking a brisk walk will boost your metabolism and keep you burning calories for hours afterward.

4) REMEMBER THAT ANY FORM OF EXERCISE IS GOOD FOR YOU.
   a) Household chores
      i) Cleaning windows
      ii) Vacuuming
      iii) Folding clothes
   b) Yard work and gardening
   c) Using stairs rather than an elevator
   d) Getting up and moving regularly at work

TO KEEP EXERCISE FUN AND INTERESTING:

✓ PICK ONE OR MORE ACTIVITIES YOU ENJOY. Regular exercise is more likely to become a healthy habit when it's fun as well as rewarding. Varying your activities can help prevent boredom.

✓ EXERCISE WITH A FRIEND. The support and companionship will help keep you going.

✓ THINK ABOUT THE PAYOFFS. Exercise not only helps control weight, it is beneficial to the body and mind in a number of ways. It improves health, boosts your immune system, helps control appetite, helps you feel more energetic and relaxed, and raises your self-confidence!

✓ SET REALISTIC EXERCISE GOALS. Reward yourself in healthy ways when you achieve them.

Figure 4-130 Word 4-7 completed

Challenge Project 4-8

A budget tracks actual or anticipated spending and compares the amount you spend with your earnings. For this project, use skills learned in this chapter to create a weekly or monthly budget.
[Student Learning Outcomes 4.1, 4.2, 4.3, 4.5, 4.6]

File Needed: None
Completed Project File Name: *[your initials] Word 4-8.docx*

Create a new document and save it as [your initials] Word 4-8.

A budget can include, but is not limited to, the following elements:

- Document title
- Time frame of the budget
- Expenditure categories
- Days in the week or weeks in the month
- Row and column totals

Modify your document according to the following guidelines:

- Format your budget in a table.
- Use column headings for days or weeks.
- Use row headings for expense categories.
- Use formulas to total rows and columns.
- Sort table by expenditure amounts.
- Apply table style formatting.
- Adjust shading and borders as needed.
- Adjust column width and row height.
- Modify cell margins.
- Format row and column totals.
- Insert a picture, icon, 3D model, or other graphic.
- Format, resize, and position a graphic.
- Edit alt text.
- Adjust document margins as needed.
- Include an appropriate header and/or footer.

Challenge Project 4-9

Newspapers and magazines arrange text in column format to improve readability and overall attractiveness of the publication. For this project, you arrange an existing document you have written (an essay, blog entry, article for a newspaper, or posting for Craigslist) in column format.
[Student Learning Outcomes 4.4, 4.5, 4.6]

File Needed: None
Completed Project File Name: *[your initials] Word 4-9.docx*

Open an existing document you have created and save it as [your initials] Word 4-9.

A document in column format can include, but is not limited to, the following elements:

- Document title
- Byline (Author name)
- Section headings
- Graphics

Modify your document according to the following guidelines:

- Format your article in column format. Don't include the title as part of the columns.
- Change spacing between columns and/or add a vertical line between columns.
- Use a column or continuous section break to balance the columns.
- Insert a graphic.
- Adjust size, wrapping, and position of the graphic.
- Add a caption to the graphic.
- Edit alt text.
- Adjust margins as needed.
- Include an appropriate header and/or footer.

Challenge Project 4-10

A weekly schedule helps you organize and manage work, school, family, and personal time more effectively. For this project, use a table to create a weekly schedule and calculate the time you spend on each daily activity.
[Student Learning Outcomes 4.1, 4.2, 4.3, 4.5, 4.6]

File Needed: None
Completed Project File Name: *[your initials] Word 4-10.docx*

Create a new document and save it as [your initials] Word 4–10.

A weekly schedule can include, but is not limited to, the following elements:

- Document title
- Days of the week
- Time commitment categories
- Row and column totals

Modify your document according to the following guidelines:

- Format your weekly schedule as a table.
- Use column headings for days of the week.
- Use row headings for time commitment categories.
- Use formulas to total rows and columns.
- Apply table style formatting.
- Adjust shading and borders as needed.
- Adjust column width and row height.
- Adjust cell margins as needed.
- Format row and column totals.
- Insert a graphic.
- Format, resize, and position a graphic.
- Edit alt text.
- Adjust document margins as needed.
- Include an appropriate header and/or footer.

Source of screenshots Microsoft Office 365 (2019): Word, Excel, Access, Powerpoint.

Using Templates and Mail Merge

CHAPTER OVERVIEW

Templates and mail merge are two valuable, time-saving features in Microsoft Word. *Templates* are documents on which other documents are based, such as memos, form letters, and fax cover sheets. You can create a new document based upon a template that can be edited and customized without changing the original template.

The *Mail Merge* features enable you to create form letters, labels, or envelopes without having to retype or create a separate document for each recipient. For example, you may want to create mailing labels for an annual holiday card list or send a yearly letter to volunteers at an organization. Mail merge enables you to merge existing information, such as a letter or labels, with addresses and other information from Access, Outlook, or Excel data files.

STUDENT LEARNING OUTCOMES (SLOs)

After completing this chapter, you will be able to:

SLO 5.1 Create and customize a template based upon a Word sample template (p. W5-286).

SLO 5.2 Create and use a template from a blank document or an existing Word document (p. W5-291).

SLO 5.3 Use Word to create envelopes and mailing labels (p. W5-296).

SLO 5.4 Understand the types of merges and how to select or create a recipient list (p. W5-302).

SLO 5.5 Create a merged document using the *Mailings* tab (p. W5-303).

SLO 5.6 Use the *Mail Merge Wizard* to create a merged document (p. W5-315).

CASE STUDY

Kelly McFarland is the community services coordinator for Courtyard Medical Plaza (CMP). She is also the director of volunteers for Skiing Unlimited, an adaptive snow ski program for disabled children and adults. CMP is a proud sponsor of the Skiing Unlimited program and encourages its employees to volunteer for this valuable community outreach program.

In the Pause & Practice projects in this chapter, you create a fax template, form letter template, a merged form letter, and mailing labels for Ms. McFarland.

Pause & Practice 5-1: Use a Word template to create a fax template.

Pause & Practice 5-2: Create a form letter template from an existing document.

Pause & Practice 5-3: Create mailing labels from a recipient list.

Pause & Practice 5-4: Use mail merge to create a form letter.

Pause & Practice 5-5: Use the *Mail Merge Wizard* to create mailing labels.

Using and Customizing Templates

All documents created in Word are based upon a template. Template files contain default fonts, margins, line and paragraph spacing, styles, themes, and other preset formatting options. Templates provide consistency and efficiency in creating documents. Another advantage of using a template is that the original template remains unchanged when you create and edit a new document based upon the template.

Word Normal Template

All new Word documents are based upon the *Normal template*. The *Normal* template defines one-inch margins, Calibri font, 11 pt font size, left alignment, and line and paragraph spacing formatting. One way to identify a template file is the file name extension. A *file name extension* follows the name of the file and typically consists of a period and three to five letters. A regular Word document has a *.docx* extension (for example, "*Document1.docx*"), while a template file has a *.dotx* extension (for example, "*Document1.dotx*"). See Table 5.1 for a list of file types and file name extensions.

Table 5-1: Word File Types

File Name Extension	File Type	Sample File Name
.docx	Word Document	*Document1.docx*
.dotx	Word Template	*Document1.dotx*
.doc	Word 97-2003 Document	*Document1.doc*
.dot	Word 97-2003 Template	*Document1.dot*

> **MORE INFO**
>
> Although many other types of files are available in Word (such as .pdf, .rtf, .txt, and .xml), documents (.docx) and templates (.dotx) are most commonly used.

Usually, the document extension for a Word file does not display in the *Title* bar of Word, nor does it display in a *File Explorer* window. However, you can change the settings of *File Explorer*, so the file name extension displays after the file name.

▶ HOW TO: Display File Name Extensions in a File Explorer Window

1. Click **File Explorer** on the *Taskbar* or click the **Start** button and select **File Explorer** to open a *File Explorer* window.
   - The *File Explorer* button is typically on the Windows *Taskbar* or *Start* menu.
2. Click the **View** tab.
3. Check the **File name extensions** box [*Show/hide* group] (Figure 5-1).
   - The file name extension displays after the file name in the *File Explorer* window (Figure 5-2).
   - Change how files display in the folder by selecting an option in the *Layout* group [*View* tab] (see Figure 5-1).

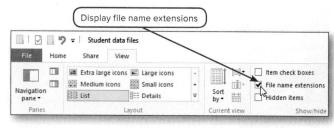

Figure 5-1 Display file name extensions in a *File Explorer* window

- Depending on the display view, you may have to widen the column to display the file name extension.

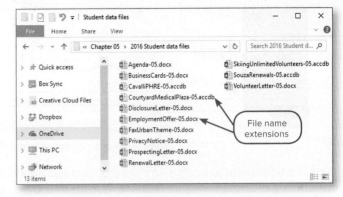

Figure 5-2 *File Explorer* window with file name extensions displayed

In Chapter 1, we discussed changing default settings on a document such as font, size, margins, and line spacing or paragraph spacing. When you change the default settings for a document, you are actually making changes to the *Normal* template (Figure 5-3). All new blank Word documents are based upon the *Normal* template, and changes made to this template are applied to all new blank Word documents.

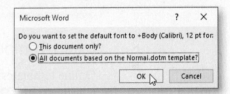

Figure 5-3 Options for changing default document settings

Online Templates

In addition to the *Normal* template, Word has a variety of online templates you can download and customize. The *New* area on the *Backstage* view displays a variety of templates. Online templates are grouped into categories, and each category contains a variety of templates. Click one of the *Suggested searches* links or use *Search for online templates* to locate and use an online template.

You can create a document based upon a fax, letter, agenda, resume, or other online template. A template provides the basic structure and formatting for the document, and you can customize it to meet your needs.

HOW TO: Open an Online Template in Word

1. Click the **File** tab to display the *Backstage* view.
2. Click the **New** button on the left. Sample templates display in the *New* area.
3. Click one of the template category links in the *Suggested searches* area or type key words to search for a template in the *Search for online templates* text box (Figure 5-4).

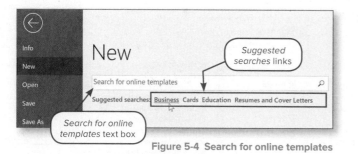

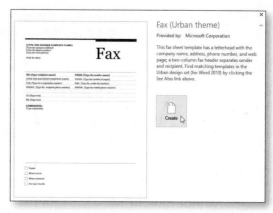

Figure 5-4 Search for online templates

4. Click a template to open a window that contains information about the template (Figure 5-5).

5. Click the **Create** button. A document (.docx) based upon the Word template opens in a new Word window.

Figure 5-5 Create a document from an online template

> MORE INFO
>
> After creating a document based upon a template, save the document as a document (.docx) or a template (.dotx).

Insert Template Content

Online templates include a combination of text, tables, document property fields, and content control fields. The text functions as headings or content descriptions, while the document property and content control fields are areas where you enter personalized text. After creating a document based upon an online template, you can insert content, modify the format of the template, and remove content fields that are not needed.

▶ **HOW TO:** Insert Content in a Template

1. Click the **File** tab to open the *Backstage* view and select **New** on the left.

2. Select an online template and click the **Create** button. A document based upon the template opens in a new Word window.

3. Customize the text or formatting as desired.

4. Select a content control field and enter the desired text (Figure 5-6). Repeat for other control fields in the template.

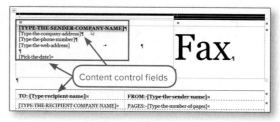

Figure 5-6 Insert content in a template

- When you enter document properties such as *Author* or *Company* in your document, the document property fields automatically display this information.
- Change document property information in the *Info* area on the *Backstage* view.

Remove Template Content

After creating a document based upon a Word template, you may need to delete one or more of the content control fields in the template. The following are two methods to remove the unneeded content control fields.

- Click the content control field handle to select the entire field and press **Delete** (Figure 5-7).

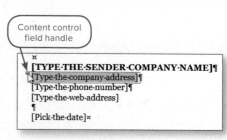

Figure 5-7 Select content control field

- Right-click the middle of the content control field and select **Remove Content Control** from the context menu (Figure 5-8).

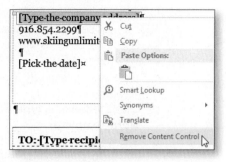

Figure 5-8 Remove content control field

Modify Template Content and Format

After creating a document based upon an online template, you can add content control fields and remove any unnecessary fields. In addition to adding and removing fields, you can also change or remove any of the descriptive text used in the document. Knowledge of line and paragraph spacing, indents, tables, and borders and shading helps when modifying your template format.

Before modifying a template, ask yourself the following questions:

- Are tables used in my template? (Use the table selection handle to select each table in your template.)
- How many columns and rows are in each table? (Use *View Gridlines* [*Table Tools Format* tab, *Table* group] to display gridlines to better view the table structure.)
- Are any of the cells merged?
- How is the text aligned within each cell?
- Are borders and/or shading used in the table or template?
- Are tabs and indents used in the template? (Turn on *Show/Hide*.)
- What is the line and paragraph spacing?

Taking the time to ask yourself these questions will help you understand the structure and format of the template if you need to modify the template.

PAUSE & PRACTICE: WORD 5-1

In this Pause & Practice project, you create a fax template for Kelly McFarland's Skiing Unlimited correspondence. You create a fax template from a sample template, edit the content and structure, and save the revised template.

File Needed: ***Fax (Urban theme).dotx*** (from online templates) or ***FaxUrbanTheme-05.docx*** (*Student data files are available in the* Library *of your SIMnet account.*)
Completed Project File Name: ***[your initials] PP W5-1 template.dotx***

1. Create a template based upon a Word sample template.
   a. Click the **File** button to open the *Backstage* view.
   b. Click the **New** button on the left.
   c. Type Fax in the *Search for online templates* text box and press **Enter**. Online fax templates display in the *New* area.
   d. Select **Fax (Urban theme)** and click **Create** (Figure 5-9). A document based upon the template opens in a new Word window. If this online template is not available, open the ***FaxUrbanTheme-05*** document from your student data files.

2. Save the document as a *Word Template* file.
   a. Open the *Save As* dialog box from the *Backstage* view.
   b. Type [your initials] PP W5-1 template in the *File name* text box.
   c. Click the **Save as type** drop-down list and select **Word Template**.
   d. Browse to the folder on your computer where you save your completed projects. Be very specific about the save location when saving Word template files.
   e. Click **Save** to save the template and to close the dialog box. If a dialog box opens informing you the document will be upgraded to the newest file format, click **OK**.

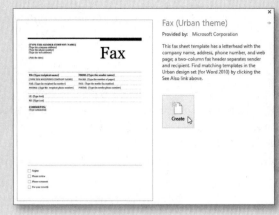

Figure 5-9 Create document based upon *Fax (Urban theme)* template

3. Modify a document property and type text in content control fields.
   a. Click the **File** tab to open the *Backstage* view and click **Info** on the left if it is not already selected.
   b. Right-click the existing author in the *Properties* area (if one exists) and select **Remove Person**.
   c. Type Kelly McFarland in the *Author* document property field.
   d. Click the **Back** arrow to return to the document.
   e. Fill the following content control fields with the information in the table:

Content Control Field	Enter Content
Type the sender company name	SKIING UNLIMITED
Type the phone number	916.854.2299
Type the web address	www.skiingunlimited.org
Type the sender fax number	916.854.2288
Type the sender phone number	916.854.2299

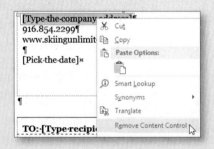

Figure 5-10 Remove content control field

4. Remove content control fields.
   a. Right-click the **Type the company address** field and select **Remove Content Control** from the context menu (Figure 5-10). The field is removed, leaving a blank line between "SKIING UNLIMITED" and the phone number.
   b. Place your insertion point anywhere in the "CC: [Type text]" row.
   c. Click the **View Gridlines** button [*Table Tools Layout* tab, *Table* group] if necessary.
   d. Click the **Delete** button [*Table Tools Layout* tab, *Rows & Columns* group] and select **Delete Rows** (Figure 5-11). The content control field and the entire row are removed.

Figure 5-11 Delete row

5. Modify table format.
   a. Select the second table in the template (beginning "TO: [Type recipient name"]).
   b. Change the row height to **0.3"** [*Table Tools Layout* tab, *Cell Size* group] (Figure 5-12).
   c. Change the alignment to **Align Center Left** [*Table Tools Layout* tab, *Alignment* group] (see Figure 5-12).

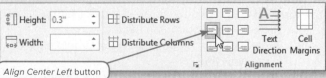

Figure 5-12 Modify row height and cell alignment

6. Modify template format and content.
   a. Select the field containing "**SKIING UNLIMITED**" and change the font size to **16 pt**.
   b. Select "**Fax**" (in the second column in the first table) and apply **small caps**.
   c. Delete "**Please comment**" in the third table at the bottom of the template and type Please complete and return.

7. Save and close this template (Figure 5-13).

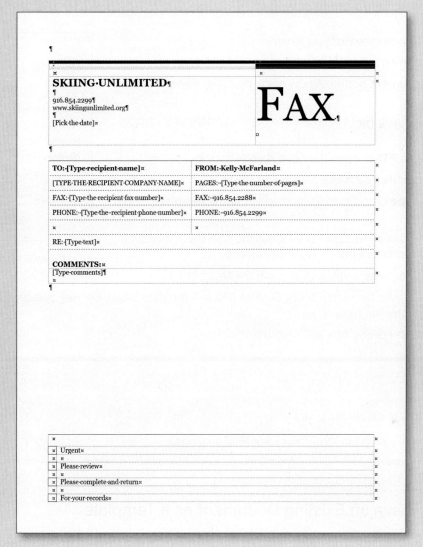

Figure 5-13 PP W5-1 template completed

Creating Templates

Word provides a variety of online templates you can customize to meet your needs, but you may want to create a template from a blank document or use an existing document. For example, you can create a template from a letter you use on a regular basis or create a new template for a monthly travel report. The main advantage of using templates is to create a standardized document to use and customize without modifying the original template file.

Create a Template from a Blank Document

When you create a new blank document in Word, it is a Word document based upon the *Normal* template. You can convert a blank document into a template by saving it as a *Word Template*.

▶ **HOW TO:** Create a Template from a Blank Document

1. Click the **File** tab to open the *Backstage* view.
2. Click the **New** button on the left.
3. Click the **Blank document** button. A new blank document opens in the Word window.
4. Open the *Save As* dialog box from the *Save As* area on the *Backstage* view.
   - Alternatively, press **F12** to open the *Save As* dialog box.
5. Type the file name in the *File name* area.
6. Click the **Save as type** drop-down list and select **Word Template** (Figure 5-14).
   - When viewing files in a *File Explorer* window, the document icon for a *Word Template* is different from a *Word Document*.
7. Browse to the location where you want to save the file.
   - By default, Word saves templates in the *Custom Office Templates* folder. Be very specific about the location where you save template files.
8. Click **Save** to close the dialog box and save the template.

Figure 5-14 Save as a *Word Template*

> **ANOTHER WAY**
>
> Press **Ctrl+N** to create a new blank document.

Save an Existing Document as a Template

Occasionally, you may want to save an existing file as a template. For example, you might save a course assignment sheet with your name, course title, and professor's name in the header as a template. Saving an existing document as a template is similar to saving a new document as a template.

▶ **HOW TO:** Save an Existing Document as a Template

1. Open an existing Word document.
2. Open the *Save As* dialog box from the *Save As* area on the *Backstage* view.
   - Alternatively, press **F12** to open the *Save As* dialog box.
3. Type the file name in the *File name* area.

4. Click the **Save as type** drop-down list and select **Word Template** (see Figure 5-14).
5. Browse to the location where you want to save the file.
6. Click **Save** to close the dialog box and save the template. The Word document is saved as a *Word Template*.

Create a Document Based upon a Template

One of the most confusing aspects of using templates is determining how to open each of the different files. You can create a new Word document based upon an existing template, or you can open and edit an existing template file. When you create a document based upon a template, open the file from a *File Explorer* folder.

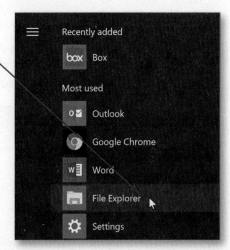

Open a *File Explorer* window from the *Start* menu

▶HOW TO: Create a Document Based upon a Template

1. Click **File Explorer** on the *Taskbar* or click the **Start** button and select **File Explorer** to open a *File Explorer* window (Figure 5-15).
2. Open the *File Explorer* folder containing the template file (Figure 5-16).
3. Double-click the template file to create a document based upon that template or select the template file (click once) and press **Enter**.
   - When you create a document based upon a template file, Word assigns the document a generic file name, such as *Document1*, which displays in the *Title* bar of the Word window.
4. Save the document.
   - When you save the document based upon a template, the *Save As* dialog box opens so you can type a unique name for the document.
   - Notice that *Word Document* is already selected in the *Save as type* area of the *Save As* dialog box.

Figure 5-15 Open a *File Explorer* window

Double-click to create a document based upon a template

Figure 5-16 Create a document based upon a template

> ### MORE INFO
> Do not use the *Open* feature from within Word to create a document based upon a template. This always opens the template file, not a document based upon the template.

Edit a Template

You can also edit a template file. Opening a template to edit the template is different from creating a document based upon a template. The following are two different ways to open a template to edit it.

- *Open the template file from within Word.* Click the **Browse** button in the *Open* area on the *Backstage view* to display the *Open* dialog box. Browse to find and select the template file and click **Open**.
- *Open the template file from a File Explorer window.* Right-click the template file and select **Open** from the context menu.

When you open a template file to edit it, the template file name displays in the Word *Title* bar rather than the generic document name (*Document1*) that Word generates when you open a document based upon a template.

 MORE INFO

When editing a template, open the template from within Word. When creating a document based upon a template, locate the template in a *File Explorer* window and double-click the template file.

PAUSE & PRACTICE: WORD 5-2

For this Pause & Practice project, you create a volunteer letter template file from an existing document for Kelly McFarland to send to all the Skiing Unlimited program volunteers. You then modify the template and create a document based upon this template.

The document you create based upon this template is used in *Pause & Practice 5-4*. This document contains placeholder text that you will replace when you perform a mail merge in *Pause & Practice 5-4*.

File Needed: ***VolunteerLetter-05.docx*** *(Student data files are available in the* Library *of your SIMnet account.)*
Completed Project File Names: ***[your initials] PP W5-2 template.dotx*** and ***[your initials] PP W5-2.docx***

1. Open the ***VolunteerLetter-05*** document from your student data files.
2. Save the document as a *Word Template* file.
   a. Open the *Save As* dialog box.
   b. Type [your initials] PP W5-2 template as the file name in the *File name* area.
   c. Click the **Save as type** drop-down list and select **Word Template**.
   d. Browse to the location on your computer where you save your solution files. Be very specific about the location where you save a template file.
   e. Click **Save** to close the dialog box and save the template.
3. Add content to the template.
   a. Place your insertion point at the beginning of the first paragraph and click the **Date & Time** button [*Insert* tab, *Text* group] to open the *Date and Time* dialog box.
   b. Insert the current date (use January 1, 2020 format), set to update automatically, and click **OK** to close the *Date and Time* dialog box.
   c. Press **Enter** four times.
   d. Type [Address Block] and press **Enter** two times.
   e. Type [Greeting Line] and press **Enter** two times.
   f. Press **Ctrl+End** or place your insertion point at the end of the document (last blank line in the document). Turn on **Show/Hide** if necessary.

g. Type Sincerely, and press **Enter** four times.

h. Type Kelly McFarland and press **Enter** once.

i. Type Community Services Coordinator.

4. Apply formatting changes to the template.

   a. Place your insertion point in the date line at the top of the document and change the *Before* paragraph spacing to **24 pt**.

   b. Select "**Courtyard Medical Plaza**" in the first body paragraph and apply **bold** and **italic** formatting.

   c. Use the **Find** feature to find all occurrences of "Skiing Unlimited" and apply **italic** formatting to each occurrence.

   d. See Figure 5-18 to compare with your document.

5. Save and close the template.

6. Create a document based upon the *[your initials] PP W5-2 template* file (Figure 5-17).

   a. Click **File Explorer** on the *Taskbar* or click the **Start** button and select **File Explorer** to open a *File Explorer* window.

   b. Open the *File Explorer* folder containing the *[your initials] PP W5-2 template* file.

   c. Double-click the *[your initials] PP W5-2 template* file or select the file (click once) and press **Enter** to create a document based upon the template. A new document based upon the template opens, and it has a generic file name such as *Document 1*.

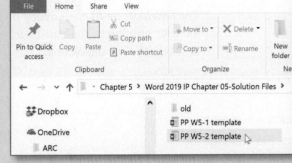

Figure 5-17 Create a document based upon a template

7. Save the document as a **Word Document** named [your initials] PP W5-2 (Figure 5-18).

8. Close the document. If prompted to save the *[your initials] PP W5-2 template* file, click **No**.

Figure 5-18 PP W5-2 completed

Creating Envelopes and Labels

In your professional or personal life, you may need to create *envelopes* or *mailing labels* for letters, cards, or packages. If you only have a couple to do, it's not a problem to write them by hand. But when sending invitations to 100 people for a grand opening of a new store or to 50 friends for a graduation party, addressing envelopes by hand can be very time consuming. Also, printed envelopes and labels look more professional. Word provides features to quickly create envelopes and mailing labels.

Create an Envelope

The *Envelopes and Labels* dialog box provides an area to type the delivery and return addresses for your envelope. You can select the type of envelope or a specific size of envelope in the *Envelope Options* dialog box.

▶ HOW TO: Create an Envelope

1. Create a new blank document.
2. Click the **Mailings** tab.
3. Click the **Envelopes** button [*Create* group] (Figure 5-19). The *Envelopes and Labels* dialog box opens, and the *Envelopes* tab displays (Figure 5-20).

Figure 5-19 Create an envelope

Figure 5-20 *Envelopes and Labels* dialog box

4. Type the mailing address in the *Delivery address* area.
5. Type the return address in the *Return address* area.
   - To change the font, size, and style of the text for both the delivery and return addresses, select the text, right-click the selected text, and select **Font** from the context menu. In the *Font* dialog box, select formatting options to apply to the address.
6. Click the **Print** button.
   - If prompted to save the return address as the default return address, click **No**.
   - You may be prompted to load an envelope in the printer prior to printing.

Envelope Options

When creating and printing envelopes, specify the type or size of envelope. Word provides an *Envelope Options* dialog box to select the type or size of the envelope, the font and size of the delivery and return address, and the position of the addresses on the envelope (Figure 5-21).

In the *Envelopes and Labels* dialog box, click the **Options** button to open the *Envelope Options* dialog box. Click the **Envelope size** drop-down list and select the envelope you will use. You can also change the font and adjust the position of the addresses.

Figure 5-21 *Envelope Options* dialog box

Envelope Printing Options

A *Printing Options* tab is also available in the *Envelope Options* dialog box (Figure 5-22). Use this tab to specify how the envelope is fed into the printer. Word provides a recommended setting for printing, but you can select a different feed method depending on the printer you are using.

Add an Envelope to an Existing Document

Word also gives you the option of adding an envelope to an existing document. Word uses the delivery address from the letter to automatically populate the *Delivery address* field in the envelope.

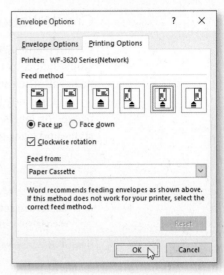

Figure 5-22 Envelope printing options

▶**HOW TO:** Add an Envelope to a Document

1. Open a letter document where you want to add an envelope.
2. Click the **Envelopes** button [*Mailings* tab, *Create* group]. The *Envelopes and Labels* dialog box opens (Figure 5-23).
   - If the letter contains a delivery address, it displays in the *Delivery address* area.
   - If the letter does not have a delivery address, type the address in the *Delivery address* area.
3. Type the return address in the *Return address* area.
4. Click the **Options** button to set the envelope size and printing options and click **OK**.
5. Click the **Add to Document** button.
   - A dialog box opens asking if you want to set the return address as the default return address (Figure 5-24).

Figure 5-23 Add an envelope to an existing document

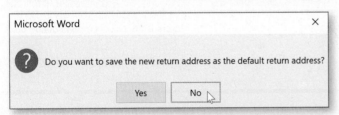

Figure 5-24 Set the default return address

   - Click **Yes** if you want to save this address as the default return address, or click **No** if you do not want this address as the default return address.
   - The envelope is added as a separate page before the existing document (Figure 5-25).
6. Save and close the document.

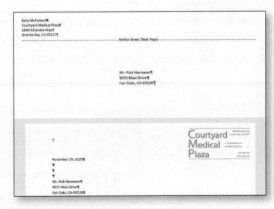

Figure 5-25 Envelope added to an existing document

Create Labels

Creating and printing labels saves time and produces a professional look. You can create individual labels by typing the delivery address or other information on each label or create a full page with the same information on every label, such as a page of return address labels.

You are not limited to mailing labels only. Labels can also be used for conference name badges or labels to identify project folders. Most office supply stores offer a variety of label styles and sizes to meet your needs.

> ### MORE INFO
>
> Labels and envelopes can also be merged with a database or other data sources rather than typing each label or envelope individually. Merging is covered later in this chapter.

Label Options

Before creating and printing labels, it is important to select the correct type and size of label in the *Label Options* dialog box.

▶ HOW TO: Set Label Options

1. Create a new blank document and click the **Labels** button [*Mailings* tab, *Create* group]. The *Envelopes and Labels* dialog box opens, and the *Labels* tab displays.

2. Click the **Options** button to open the *Label Options* dialog box (Figure 5-26).

3. Select the type of printer and the printer tray you are using in the *Printer information* area.

4. Click the **Label vendors** drop-down list and select the vendor of the labels you are using.

5. Select the specific label product number in the *Product number* list.

   - If you can't find your specific label, click the **Find updates on Office.com** link for an updated list of labels.
   - Click the **Details** button to change the label dimensions.
   - Alternatively, click the **New Label** button and type the label dimensions to create a custom label.

6. Click **OK** to close the *Label Options* dialog box.

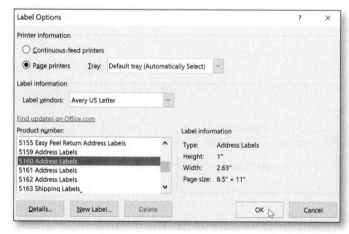

Figure 5-26 *Label Options* dialog box

> ### MORE INFO
>
> Avery 5160 is one of the most common types of labels used for delivery and return address labels.

Create Individual Labels

When creating individual labels, Word inserts a table in a new document based upon the type of label you select. You type the information for each label in the cells of the table.

▶HOW TO: Create Individual Labels

1. Create a new blank document and click the **Labels** button [*Mailings* tab, *Create* group]. The *Envelopes and Labels* dialog box opens with the *Labels* tab selected (Figure 5-27).

2. Click the **Options** button and select the type of label you want to use.

3. Click **OK** to close the *Label Options* dialog box.

4. Leave the *Address* area blank.

5. Select the **Full page of the same label** radio button in the *Print* area.

   - This option creates a full page of blank labels where you type the information for each label.

6. Click the **New Document** button. A new document opens with an empty table inserted in the document.

   - Turn on **View Gridlines** [*Table Tools Layout* tab, *Table* group] (if necessary) to view individual labels.

7. Type the information for each label (Figure 5-28).

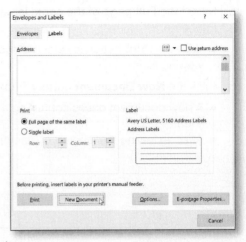

Figure 5-27 Create individual labels

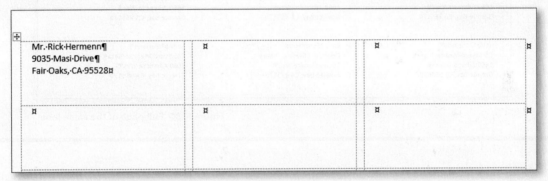

Figure 5-28 Type individual labels

- Press **Enter** after each line of the label.
- Press **Tab** twice to move to the next label. A blank column is added between each label to allow for spacing between labels.
- After typing the labels, you can print, save, and close the labels document.

> ### MORE INFO
>
> After creating labels, it may be necessary to adjust the left indent, line spacing, and *Before* and *After* paragraph spacing to arrange the label content.

Create a Full Page of the Same Label

You can also print a full sheet of the same label. This saves you the time of typing the same label over and over or copying and pasting the same label information in each cell.

▶HOW TO: Create a Full Page of the Same Label

1. Create a new blank document and click the **Labels** button [*Mailings* tab, *Create* group]. The *Envelopes and Labels* dialog box opens, and the *Labels* tab displays.

2. Click the **Options** button and select the type of label to use.

3. Click **OK** to close the *Label Options* dialog box.

4. Type the label information in the *Address* area.

5. Select the **Full page of the same label** radio button in the *Print* area.

   - Click the **Print** button to print the document without viewing it.

6. Click the **New Document** button (Figure 5-29).

   - A new document opens containing a full page of the same label (Figure 5-30).
   - After reviewing the labels, you can print, save, and close the labels document.

Figure 5-29 Create a full page of the same label

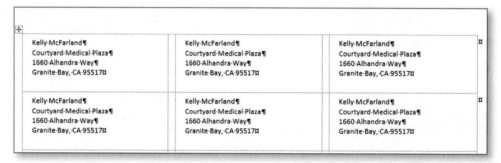

Figure 5-30 Full page of the same label

> **MORE INFO**
>
> If you previously saved your return address, you can use this address for labels by checking the **Use return address** check box in the upper-right corner of the *Envelopes and Labels* dialog box.

PAUSE & PRACTICE: WORD 5-3

In this Pause & Practice project, you create mailing labels for Kelly McFarland to use when sending out volunteer letters for the Skiing Unlimited program. You also create individual labels for delivery addresses and a full page of the same label for return addresses.

File Needed: None
Completed Project File Names: ***[your initials] PP W5-3a.docx*** and ***[your initials] PP W5-3b.docx***

1. Create a new blank Word document.

2. Select the mailing label format.
   a. Click the **Labels** button [*Mailings* tab, *Create* group].
   b. Click the **Options** button. The *Label Options* dialog box opens.

c. Click the **Label vendors** drop-down list and select **Avery US Letter**.

d. Select **5160 Address Labels** in the *Product number* area (Figure 5-31).

e. Click **OK** to close the *Label Options* dialog box.

3. Create individual mailing labels.

a. Leave the *Address* area blank (Figure 5-32).

b. Click the **Full page of the same label** radio button in the *Print* area.

c. Click the **New Document** button. A new Word document opens with the labels table inserted.

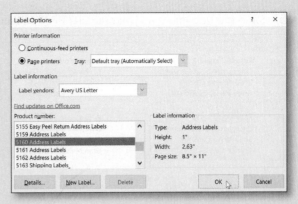

Figure 5-31 Select label type

4. Save the document as [your initials] PP W5-3a.

5. Type individual mailing labels.

a. Use the information in the following table to type six mailing labels.

b. Press **Tab** two times after each label to move to the next label cell on the same row. At the end of the row, press **Tab** once to move to the label cell in the new row.

Mr. Rick Hermenn 9035 Masi Drive Fair Oaks, CA 95528	Dr. Karen Draper 784 Ehrlich Road Carmichael, CA 96774	Mr. Ty Han 1272 Eastwood Court Auburn, CA 95236
Dr. Seth Uribe 8263 Wales Avenue Roseville, CA 95722	Mr. Sawyer Petrosky 2741 Lake Road Granite Bay, CA 95517	Ms. Kallyn Nickols 7336 Ebony Way Auburn, CA 95236

Figure 5-32 Create individual mailing labels

6. Save and close this document (Figure 5-33).

7. Return to the open blank Word document.

8. Create a full page of the same label for return address labels.

a. Click the **Labels** button [*Mailings* tab, *Create* group]. The *Envelopes and Labels* dialog box opens.

b. Confirm that **Avery US Letter** and **5160 Address Labels** are selected. If not, click the **Options** button and select this label.

c. Type the following information in the *Address* area:

Kelly McFarland Courtyard

Medical Plaza

1660 Alhandra Way

Granite Bay, CA 95517

d. Click the **Full page of the same label** radio button in the *Print* area.

e. Click the **New Document** button (Figure 5-34). A new Word document opens, and a full page of the same label displays in the labels table (Figure 5-35).

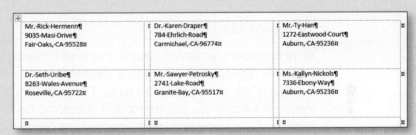

Figure 5-33 PP W5-3a completed

Figure 5-34 Create a full page of the same label

9. Save the document as [your initials] PP W5-3b and close the document.

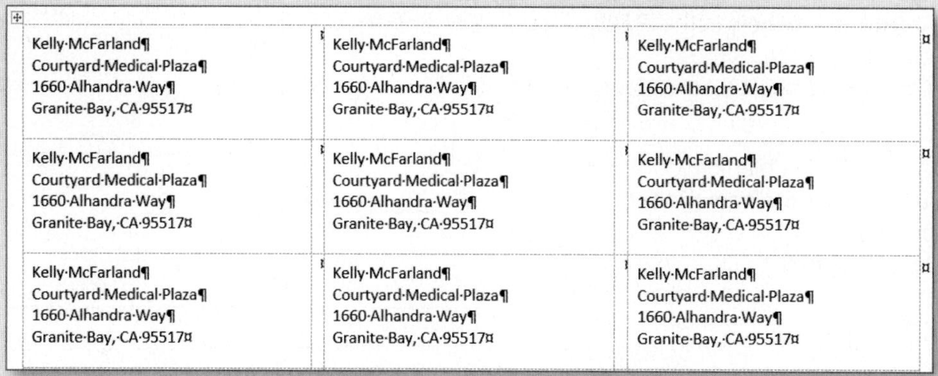

Kelly·McFarland¶ Courtyard·Medical·Plaza¶ 1660·Alhandra·Way¶ Granite·Bay,·CA·95517¤	Kelly·McFarland¶ Courtyard·Medical·Plaza¶ 1660·Alhandra·Way¶ Granite·Bay,·CA·95517¤	Kelly·McFarland¶ Courtyard·Medical·Plaza¶ 1660·Alhandra·Way¶ Granite·Bay,·CA·95517¤
Kelly·McFarland¶ Courtyard·Medical·Plaza¶ 1660·Alhandra·Way¶ Granite·Bay,·CA·95517¤	Kelly·McFarland¶ Courtyard·Medical·Plaza¶ 1660·Alhandra·Way¶ Granite·Bay,·CA·95517¤	Kelly·McFarland¶ Courtyard·Medical·Plaza¶ 1660·Alhandra·Way¶ Granite·Bay,·CA·95517¤
Kelly·McFarland¶ Courtyard·Medical·Plaza¶ 1660·Alhandra·Way¶ Granite·Bay,·CA·95517¤	Kelly·McFarland¶ Courtyard·Medical·Plaza¶ 1660·Alhandra·Way¶ Granite·Bay,·CA·95517¤	Kelly·McFarland¶ Courtyard·Medical·Plaza¶ 1660·Alhandra·Way¶ Granite·Bay,·CA·95517¤

Figure 5-35 PP W5-3b completed

SLO 5.4

Understanding Mail Merge

Mail Merge is one of Word's most helpful and time-saving features. Mail merge provides the ability to merge a document, such as a form letter, labels, or envelopes, with a data source such as a database file or contact records from Microsoft Outlook. Merges range from very simple to complex. You can create a list of mailing labels from your Outlook contacts or create a more sophisticated merge where you merge address and account information for a client's insurance renewal letter. Before working with mail merge, it is important to understand the various components of a merge.

Types of Mail Merge

Word performs a variety of merges. The most common types of merges are letters, labels, and envelopes. The category of *Letters* is somewhat misleading because you can merge content into any type of document, not just a letter. For example, you can merge information into a report, memo, or form. When you start a mail merge, the first step is to select the type of merge to be performed (for example, *Letters*, *Envelopes*, or *Labels*).

Main Document

The ***main document*** is the Word document where you insert merge fields that will be replaced with recipient information from a data source. Main documents include text and other information that does not change when the merge is performed, such as the date and body of the letter. When you perform a letter mail merge, you can begin with an existing document, such as a business letter, or start with a blank document. When you perform a labels or envelopes mail merge, you specify the type of label or envelope to use.

Recipients

Recipients refer to a data source that can contain names, addresses, and other variable information. The recipients' data source can be an existing Microsoft Access or Excel file or contacts from Microsoft Outlook. You can also create a new recipient list to merge into the main document.

The data source used for mail merge is essentially a database of information. It is important to understand database terminology used in the mail merge process.

- *Field*: A field is an individual piece of information such as title, first name, last name, or street address.
- *Record*: A record is a collection of related fields. It is all the information about one recipient, such as name, address, and other contact information.
- *File*, *Table*, or *Contacts Folder*: A file, table, or Microsoft Outlook *Contacts* folder is a group of related records.

Figure 5-36 displays a Microsoft Access table. The information in each cell is a *field*. Each column heading is a *field name*. A row of information is a *record*. All of the information displayed is a *table*.

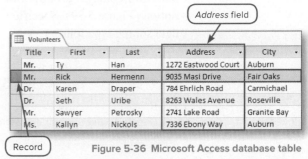

Figure 5-36 Microsoft Access database table

SLO 5.5

Merging Using the Mailings Tab

One method to perform a mail merge is to use the *Mailings* tab. Another method is to use the *Mail Merge Wizard*. This section demonstrates a mail merge using the *Mailings* tab (Figure 5-37). The *Mail Merge Wizard* is discussed in the next section.

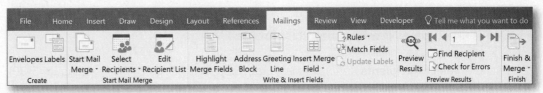

Figure 5-37 *Mailings* tab

Start the Mail Merge

The first step in a mail merge is to select the type of merge to be performed.

▶**HOW TO: Start the Mail Merge**

1. Click the **Mailings** tab.
2. Click the **Start Mail Merge** button [*Start Mail Merge* group] and select the type of merge to be performed (Figure 5-38).
   - If you are performing a mail merge using an existing document, make sure the document is open before clicking the *Start Mail Merge* button.
   - If you are performing a labels or envelopes mail merge, you are prompted to select the type of labels or envelopes in the *Labels Options* or *Envelope Options* dialog box.

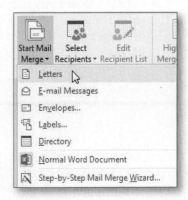

Figure 5-38 Types of mail merges

Select Recipients

The next step in the mail merge process is to select the recipients, which is the data source to be merged into the main document. Word enables you to select from a variety of file types, type a new list as the source data, or use Outlook Contacts.

Click the **Select Recipients** button [*Mailings* tab, *Start Mail Merge* group] and select a data source option (Figure 5-39). Specific information about each data source type follows.

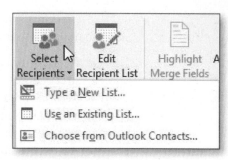

Figure 5-39 Select recipient source file

> **MORE INFO**
>
> Proofread and edit your data source before beginning a mail merge.

Type a New List

The *Type a New List* option enables you to define fields, arrange or order fields, and type recipients' information. Save the data source using a descriptive file name. Once the data source has been created and saved, it can be selected as a recipient option for other mail merges.

▶**HOW TO:** Type a New Recipient List for Mail Merge

1. Click the **Select Recipients** button [*Mailings* tab, *Start Mail Merge* group] (see Figure 5-39).

2. Select **Type a New List**. The *New Address List* dialog box opens (Figure 5-40).

   • Word provides you with default fields (*Title*, *First Name*, *Last Name*).
   • Edit these fields by clicking the **Customize Columns** button.

3. Type recipients' information.

   • Press **Tab** to move from field to field.
   • You do not have to type information in every field.
   • Click the **New Entry** button to begin a new record or press **Tab** after typing the last field of information.

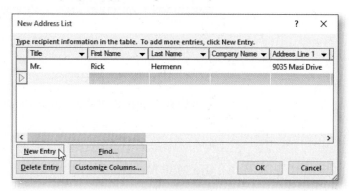

Figure 5-40 *New Address List* dialog box

4. Click **OK** after typing all recipient information. The *Save Address List* dialog box opens.

5. Type a name for the new address list, browse to the location to save the file, and click **Save**.

> **MORE INFO**
>
> When creating a new address list for a mail merge, Word will save the document as a *Microsoft Office Address Lists* file (.mdb), which you can edit and use for other mail merges.

Use an Existing List

When using an existing source file containing the recipients' information, browse to select the source file. You can use a variety of database file types for a mail merge.

▶ **HOW TO:** Use an Existing List for Mail Merge

1. Click the **Select Recipients** button [*Mailings* tab, *Start Mail Merge* group].

2. Select **Use an Existing List**. The *Select Data Source* dialog box opens (Figure 5-41).

3. Browse to locate the data source file, select the data source file, and click **Open**.

    - If your data source is a database file with multiple tables, a dialog box opens and prompts you to select the table to use in the merge.

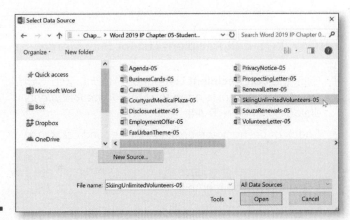

Figure 5-41 *Select Data Source* dialog box

Select from Outlook Contacts

If you use Microsoft Outlook, you probably have many contacts saved in the *Contacts* area of Outlook. The information stored in the Outlook *Contacts* folder is used to perform a mail merge.

▶ **HOW TO:** Select from Outlook Contacts for Mail Merge

1. Click the **Select Recipients** button [*Mailings* tab, *Start Mail Merge* group].

2. Select **Choose from Outlook Contacts**.

    - If the *Choose Profile* dialog box opens (Figure 5-42), select the Outlook profile to use and click **OK**. The *Select Contacts* dialog box opens.
    - Typically, people only have one Outlook profile, but if you have more than one Outlook profile, choose the correct profile to use.

3. Select the contacts folder to use for the mail merge in the *Select Contacts* dialog box (Figure 5-43).

4. Click **OK** to close the *Select Contacts* dialog box. The *Mail Merge Recipients* dialog box opens.

    - From within this dialog box, select the recipients to include in the merge, sort recipients, and filter recipients.

5. Click **OK** to close the *Mail Merge Recipients* dialog box.

Figure 5-42 Select *Outlook* profile

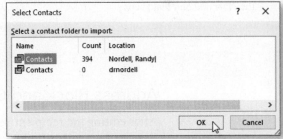

Figure 5-43 Select Outlook *Contacts* folder

Edit Recipients

After selecting or creating the recipient list, the next step in mail merge is to edit your recipient list. During this process, select the records (recipients) to include in the merge, *sort* the records, and *filter* the records. Sorting arranges records in alphabetical order by a specific field, such as last name. Filtering enables you to display only those records that match a specific condition, such as from a specific town or zip code.

▶ HOW TO: Edit Recipient List for Mail Merge

1. Click the **Edit Recipient List** button [*Mailings* tab, *Start Mail Merge* group] to open the *Mail Merge Recipients* dialog box (Figure 5-44).

2. Check or uncheck the boxes in the second column to select or deselect recipients.

   - By default, all recipients in the data source file are included in the merge.

3. Sort the recipient list by clicking a column heading drop-down arrow and selecting **Sort Ascending** or **Sort Descending** (Figure 5-45).

   - Alternatively, click the **Sort** link in the *Refine recipient list* area to open the *Filter and Sort* dialog box.

4. Filter the recipient list by clicking a column heading drop-down arrow and selecting a criterion by which to filter the recipient list.

   - Alternatively, click the **Filter** link in the *Refine recipient list* area to open the *Filter and Sort* dialog box.
   - When you filter a data source, only those recipient records that match the filter criterion display in the recipient list. To display all of the recipient records, select **(All)** from the column heading drop-down list.

5. Click **OK** to close the *Mail Merge Recipients* dialog box.

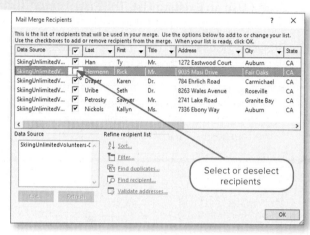

Figure 5-44 *Mail Merge Recipients* dialog box

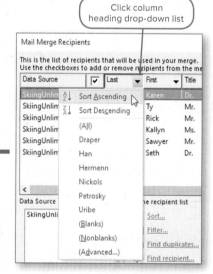

Figure 5-45 Sort or filter by field

MORE INFO

When performing a sort or filter on more than one field, use the *Filter and Sort* dialog box. Click the **Sort** or **Filter** link in the *Mail Merge Recipients* dialog box to open the *Filter and Sort* dialog box.

Address Block and Greeting Line Merge Fields

After editing the recipient list, the next step is to insert *merge fields* into your main document. You can insert an address block, greeting line, or individual merge fields into the main document. Both the *Address Block* and *Greeting Line* merge fields combine individual merge fields to create an acceptable mailing address and greeting line.

▶ HOW TO: Insert the Address Block and Greeting Line Merge Fields

1. Position the insertion point at the location in the main document to insert the address block merge field.
   - If the main document for the mail merge is not open, open the main document and select the recipients.
2. Click the **Address Block** button [*Mailings* tab, *Write & Insert Fields* group]. The *Insert Address Block* dialog box opens.
3. Select the format for the recipient's name in the *Specify address elements* area (Figure 5-46).
   - A preview of the address block displays in the *Preview* area on the right.
   - Click the **Next** or **Previous** arrow in the *Preview* area to view other recipients.
4. Click **OK** to close the *Insert Address Block* dialog box and to insert the address block merge field (<<*AddressBlock*>>) into the document (Figure 5-47).
   - Merge fields are shaded in gray when selected.
5. Position the insertion point at the location to insert the greeting line merge field.
6. Click the **Greeting Line** button [*Write & Insert Fields* group]. The *Insert Greeting Line* dialog box opens (Figure 5-48).
7. Select the format for the greeting line in the *Greeting line format* area.
   - In the *Greeting line for invalid recipient names* area, you can specify a generic greeting to use if a recipient name has an invalid format.
   - In the *Preview* area, click the **Next** or **Previous** arrow to preview the greeting line for each of your recipients.
8. Click **OK** to close the *Insert Greeting Line* dialog box and to insert the greeting line merge field (<<*GreetingLine*>>) into the document (Figure 5-49).

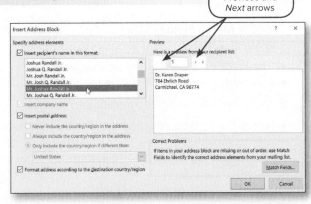

Figure 5-46 *Insert Address Block* dialog box

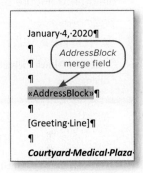

Figure 5-47 *Address-Block* merge field in the main document

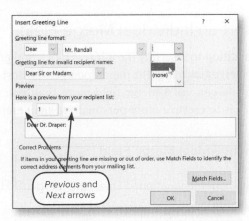

Figure 5-48 *Insert Greeting Line* dialog box

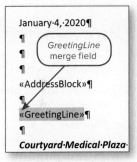

Figure 5-49 *GreetingLine* merge field in the main document

You can also manually build your address block and greeting line by using individual merge fields from your data source. To build an address block, typically use the following merge fields: *Courtesy Title*, *First Name*, *Last Name*, *Address 1*, *City*, *State*, and *Postal Code*.

To build a greeting line, use the following merge fields: *Courtesy Title* and *Last Name*. Type the word "Dear" or "To" before the recipient's name and punctuation after (colon) if needed.

Match Fields

If Word does not correctly build your address block or greeting line, use the **Match Fields** feature to manually match the field names from your data source to those field names recognized by Word.

▶HOW TO: Match Fields

1. Click the **Match Fields** button [*Mailings* tab, *Write & Insert Fields* group].
   The *Match Fields* dialog box opens (Figure 5-50).

   - The fields on the left are Word merge fields.
   - The fields on the right are from the merge data source.

2. Select a field at the right to match the Word field at the left.

   - Not all the fields on the right have to be matched. Word ignores fields that are not matched.
   - Each field drop-down list displays the available fields in the merge data source.

3. Click **OK** to close the *Match Fields* dialog box.

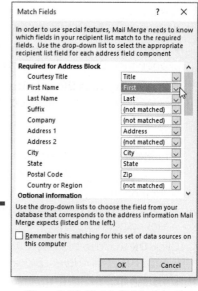

▶ **ANOTHER WAY**

Click the **Match Fields** button in the *Insert Address Block* or *Insert Greeting Line* dialog box.

Figure 5-50 *Match Fields* dialog box

Insert an Individual Merge Field

In addition to inserting the address block and greeting line merge fields, you can insert individual merge fields into the main document. Insert a merge field anywhere in the main document, and you can use a merge field more than one time. An advantage of using individual merge fields is to create a more personalized mail merge document.

▶HOW TO: Insert an Individual Merge Field

1. Position the insertion point at the location to insert the merge field.

2. Click the **Insert Merge Field** drop-down arrow [*Mailings* tab, *Write & Insert Fields* group] to display a list of merge fields from your data source (Figure 5-51).

   - Alternatively, click the top half of the **Insert Mail Merge** button to open the *Insert Merge Field* dialog box where you can select a merge field to insert.

3. Select the merge field to insert into the main document. The merge field displays in the document (Figure 5-52).

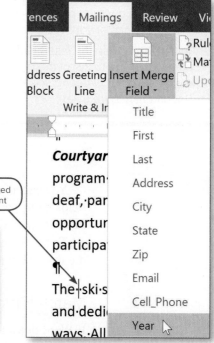

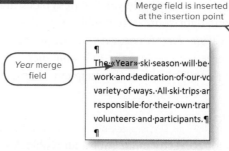

Figure 5-52 Individual merge field in the main document

Figure 5-51 Insert an individual merge field

Update Labels

When creating a labels mail merge, Word inserts the address block or merge field only in the first cell (label) of the labels main document. Click the **Update Labels** button in the *Write & Insert Fields* group to automatically update each label. Word inserts a next record (<<*Next-Record*>>) merge field code when performing a labels merge (Figure 5-53). When performing the mail merge, Word inserts recipient content from the data source into each subsequent label until all records are merged into the labels.

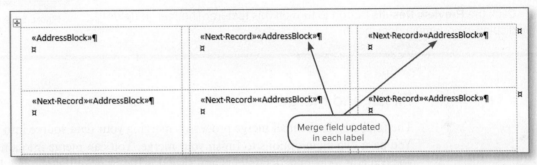

Figure 5-53 Labels updated in the main document

Highlight Merge Fields

Word enables you to highlight merge fields in a document so you can easily locate each merge field. Click the **Highlight Merge Fields** button in the *Write & Insert Fields* group to highlight each merge field in your main document and to verify proper spacing and punctuation around each merge field (Figure 5-54). Toggle this feature on or off by clicking the **Highlight Merge Fields** button.

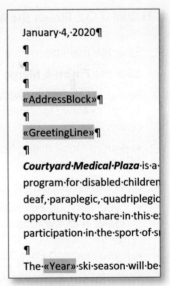

Figure 5-54 Merge fields highlighted in main document

Preview Mail Merge

Before finishing the mail merge, preview the merge. The ***Preview Results*** option displays data from the source file in merge fields in the final document. You can edit the main document if necessary before finalizing the merge. Word can also automatically check your mail merge for potential errors.

▶HOW TO: Preview Mail Merge

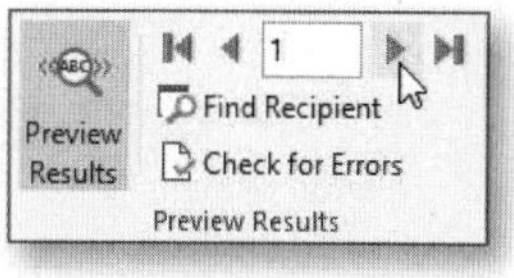

1. Click the **Preview Results** button [*Mailings* tab, *Preview Results* group] (Figure 5-55). The data from the first record of your data source displays in the main document.

2. Click the **Next Record** arrow to preview the next record from your data source.

3. Click the **Check for Errors** button [*Preview Results* group] to check for errors in the mail merge.

   • Three error checking options display. (Figure 5-56). The first and third options display merge errors in a new document. The second option pauses the merge and displays merge errors as they occur.

   • Select an error checking option and click **OK**.

   • Word displays any errors found, and you can correct the errors in the data source before finalizing the merge. If Word opened a new document, close this document.

4. Click the **Preview Results** button to turn off this feature. The merge fields display in your main document.

Figure 5-55 Preview the next record in the main document

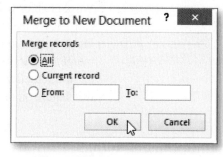

Figure 5-56 *Checking and Reporting Errors* dialog box

Finish and Merge

The final step in the mail merge process is merging your data source into the main document. You have two main options to finish your merge. You can merge into a new document where you can edit individual documents and save this file or print the merged document.

▶HOW TO: Finish the Mail Merge

1. Save the main document before beginning the merge.

2. Click the **Finish & Merge** button [*Mailings* tab, *Finish* group].

3. Select either **Edit Individual Documents** or **Print Documents**. The *Merge to New Document* (Figure 5-57) or *Merge to Printer* dialog box opens.

   • Both of these dialog boxes enable you to choose which records to include in the merge.

4. Select a *Merge records* radio button and click **OK**.

   • If you selected *Edit Individual Documents*, your completed merge opens in a new window. You can edit, save, or print the completed merge.

   • If you selected *Print Document*, your completed merge is sent to your printer.

5. Save and close any open documents.

Figure 5-57 *Merge to New Document* dialog box

> **MORE INFO**
>
> The third *Finish & Merge* option is *Send Email Messages*, which requires the use of Microsoft Outlook. This option sends an email to each recipient.

Open an Existing Merge Document

When working on a mail merge document, you may have to save and close it and return to it later. When you open a main document that is linked to a data source file, Word alerts you with a dialog box where you have three options (Figure 5-58):

- *Yes*: This option opens your merge document and keeps it linked to the data source file. If Word cannot locate your data source, the *Select Data Source* dialog box opens.
- *No*: This option opens your merge document; select the data source file by clicking the *Select Recipients* button.
- ***Show Help***: This option displays the *Word Help* information in the dialog box.

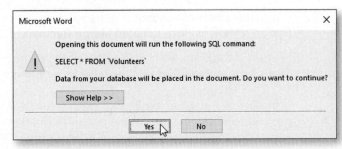

Figure 5-58 Alert dialog box when opening a merge document

> **MORE INFO**
>
> If the data source file linked to your merge main document was moved or deleted, you are prompted to select a data source for the main document.

PAUSE & PRACTICE: WORD 5-4

In this Pause & Practice project, you merge the Skiing Unlimited volunteer letter you created for Kelly McFarland in *Pause & Practice 5-2* with a Microsoft Access database to create a merged form letter. You select and edit the data source, insert merge fields into the main document, and finish the merge.

Files Needed: ***[your initials] PP W5-2.docx*** and ***SkiingUnlimitedVolunteers-05.accdb*** *(Student data files are available in the Library of your SIMnet account.)*
Completed Project File Names: ***[your initials] PP W5-4 main.docx*** and ***[your initials] PP W5-4 merge.docx***

1. Open the ***[your initials] PP W5-2*** document completed in *Pause & Practice 5-2*. Do not open the *[your initials] PP W5-2 template* file.

2. Save the document as [your initials] PP W5-4 main.

3. Begin the merge and select recipients.
   a. Click the **Mailings** tab.
   b. Click the **Start Mail Merge** button [*Start Mail Merge* group] and select **Letters** (Figure 5-59).
   c. Click the **Select Recipients** button [*Start Mail Merge* group] and select **Use an Existing List**. The *Select Data Source* dialog box opens.
   d. Locate your student data files, select ***SkiingUnlimitedVolunteers-05*** (Access database file), and click **Open**.

Figure 5-59 Select the type of mail merge

4. Select recipients and sort the recipient list.
   a. Click the **Edit Recipient List** button [*Start Mail Merge* group]. The *Mail Merge Recipients* dialog box opens.
   b. Confirm that the check box for each recipient is checked.
   c. Click the **Last** column heading drop-down arrow and select **Sort Ascending** (Figure 5-60).
   d. Click **OK** to close the **Mail Merge Recipients** dialog box.

5. Insert the address block merge field into the main document.
   a. Turn on **Show/Hide** [*Home* tab, *Paragraph* group] if it is not already on.
   b. Delete the "**[AddressBlock]**" placeholder text and brackets (do not delete the paragraph mark).
   c. Click the **Address Block** button [*Mailings* tab, *Write & Insert Fields* group]. The *Insert Address Block* dialog box opens (Figure 5-61).
   d. Select **Mr. Joshua Randall Jr.** as the format for the recipient's name in the *Specify address elements* area.
   e. Click the **Next** arrow in the *Preview* area to view the address block for each of the six recipients.
   f. Click **OK** to close the *Insert Address Block* dialog box. Three blank lines should display above and one blank line should display below the <<*AddressBlock*>> merge field in the main document.

6. Insert the greeting line merge field into the main document.
   a. Delete the "**[GreetingLine]**" placeholder text and brackets (do not delete the paragraph mark).
   b. Click the **Greeting Line** button [*Mailings* tab, *Write & Insert Fields* group]. The *Insert Greeting Line* dialog box opens (Figure 5-62).
   c. Select **Dear**, **Mr. Randall**, and **:** (colon) from the three drop-down lists in the *Greeting line format* area.
   d. Click the **Next** or **Previous** arrow in the *Preview* area to view the greeting line for each of the six recipients.
   e. Click **OK** to close the *Insert Greeting Line* dialog box. One blank line should display above and below the <<*GreetingLine*>> merge field in the main document.

7. Insert individual merge fields into the main document.
   a. Delete the "**[year]**" placeholder text and brackets in the second body paragraph. Do not delete the spaces before and after the placeholder text.

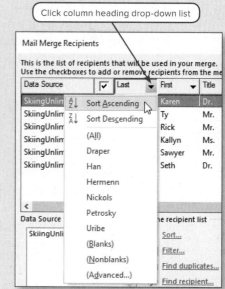

Click column heading drop-down list

Figure 5-60 Sort the recipient list

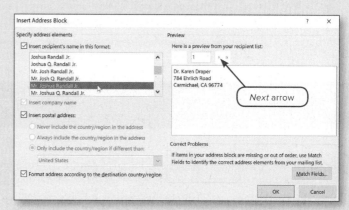

Next arrow

Figure 5-61 Insert address block into main document

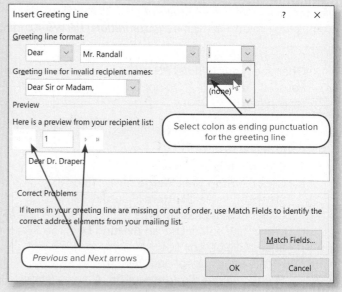

Select colon as ending punctuation for the greeting line

Previous and Next arrows

Figure 5-62 Insert greeting line into main document

b. Click the **Insert Merge Field** drop-down arrow [*Mailings* tab, *Write & Insert Fields* group] and select **Year** to insert the <<*Year*>> merge field (Figure 5-63). Confirm one space displays before and after the <<*Year*>> merge field.

c. Delete the other "**[year]**" placeholder text and brackets before the bulleted list and insert the **Year** merge field. Confirm one space displays before and after <<*Year*>> the merge field.

d. Click the **Highlight Merge Fields** button [*Write & Insert Fields* group] to highlight the merge fields in the main document.

e. Select the second occurrence of the <<**Year**>> merge field (before the bulleted list) and **italicize** the field.

f. Click the **Highlight Merge Fields** button again to turn off this feature.

Figure 5-63 Insert an individual merge field into the main document

8. Delete the placeholder text (including brackets) in the bulleted list and replace each with the following dates:

January 18
January 25
February 8
February 15
February 22

9. Preview the merge results and check for errors.

a. Click the **Preview Results** button [*Mailings* tab, *Preview Results* group] to display the recipient information in the main document.

b. Click the **Next Record** or **Previous Record** arrow [*Preview Results* group] to view each of the six recipients.

c. Click the **Check for Errors** button. The *Checking and Reporting Errors* dialog box opens (Figure 5-64).

d. Select the **Simulate the merge . . .** radio button and click **OK**. If no errors are found in the merge, a dialog box opens to verify no errors exist. If errors are found, a new document opens with the errors displayed. Fix errors if needed.

e. Click **OK** to close the dialog box that confirms no errors in the merge.

f. Click the **Preview Results** button [*Mailings* tab, *Preview Results* group] to display the merge fields in the main document.

Figure 5-64 *Checking and Reporting Errors* dialog box

10. Save the document.

11. Finish the mail merge and save the merged document.

a. Click the **Finish & Merge** button [*Mailings* tab, *Finish* group] and select **Edit Individual Documents**. The *Merge to New Document* dialog box opens.

b. Select the **All** radio button (if necessary) and click **OK**. The merge letters open in a new document.

c. Scroll through the document to make sure each of the six letters are correct.

12. Save the merged document as [your initials] PP W5-4 merge and close the document (Figure 5-65).

13. Save and close the *[your initials] PP W5-4 main* document.

¶

January·4,·2020¶
¶
¶
¶
Dr.·Karen·Draper¶
784·Ehrlich·Road¶
Carmichael,·CA·96774¶
¶
Dear·Dr.·Draper:¶
¶
Courtyard·Medical·Plaza·is·a·proud·sponsor·of·the·*Skiing·Unlimited*·program,·which·is·an·adaptive·snow·ski·
program·for·disabled·children·and·adults.·This·program·provides·access·to·the·sport·of·snow·skiing·for·many·blind,·
deaf,·paraplegic,·quadriplegic·and·developmentally·disabled·individuals·who·would·otherwise·be·not·have·the·
opportunity·to·share·in·this·exhilarating·sport.·With·the·help·of·trained·volunteers·and·adaptive·ski·equipment,·
participation·in·the·sport·of·snow·skiing·is·available·to·most·anyone.¶
¶
The·2020·ski·season·will·be·here·before·we·know·it,·and·this·program·is·only·able·to·continue·through·the·hard·
work·and·dedication·of·our·volunteers.·Regardless·of·your·level·of·snow·skiing·ability,·you·can·volunteer·in·a·
variety·of·ways.·All·ski·trips·are·held·at·Boulder·Creek·Canyon·Ski·Resort.·Volunteers·and·participants·are·
responsible·for·their·own·transportation.·Our·group·meets·in·the·Olympic·Room·at·9:00·a.m.·to·coordinate·
volunteers·and·participants.¶
¶
Below·are·the·dates·for·this·year's·*Skiing·Unlimited*·program.·Please·contact·me·at·916-854-2299·or·email·me·at·
kellym@skiingunlimited.org·to·let·me·know·the·dates·for·which·you·can·volunteer.·I·will·fax·or·e-mail·you·the·
volunteer·registration·packet.¶
¶
If·you·have·any·questions·regarding·the·*Skiing·Unlimited*·program,·please·feel·free·to·contact·me.·Thank·you·for·
your·commitment·to·the·*Skiing·Unlimited*·program·and·its·participants.¶
¶
Our·*2020·Skiing·Unlimited*·dates·are:¶
¶

- → January·18¶
- → January·25¶
- → February·8¶
- → February·15¶
- → February·22¶

¶
Sincerely,¶
¶
¶
¶
Kelly·McFarland¶
Community·Services·Coordinator-----------------------------Section Break (Next Page)----------------------------

Figure 5-65 PP W5-4 merge completed (page 1 of 6)

SLO 5.6 — Using the Mail Merge Wizard

Instead of using the *Mailings* tab to perform a mail merge, you can use the **Mail Merge Wizard**, which walks you through the mail merge process step by step. Using the *Mail Merge Wizard* is similar to using the *Mailings* tab. When you select the *Mail Merge Wizard* option, the *Mail Merge* pane opens on the right side of the Word window. The following are the six main steps in a mail merge:

- *Step 1*: Select document type.
- *Step 2*: Select starting document.
- *Step 3*: Select recipients.
- *Step 4*: Arrange your document. Note that the name of this step varies depending on the type of document you are merging and whether you are using an existing or new document.
- *Step 5*: Preview your document.
- *Step 6*: Complete the merge.

The following *How To* instructions and figures provide an example of using the *Mail Merge Wizard* to create mailing labels from a blank document. This example uses an Access database as the data source for the recipients. The options for each of the steps vary depending on the type of mail merge you perform with the *Mail Merge Wizard*.

Select Document Type

First, select the type of mail merge you want to perform.

▶ HOW TO: Select Document Type

1. Create a new blank Word document.
2. Click the **Start Mail Merge** button [*Mailings* tab, *Start Mail Merge* group].
3. Select **Step-by-Step Mail Merge Wizard**. The *Mail Merge* pane opens on the right (Figure 5-66).
4. Select the radio button for the type of document to merge in the *Select document type* area.
   - A description of the type of document appears in a section below the radio buttons.
5. Click the **Next: Starting document** link at the bottom of the *Mail Merge* pane.

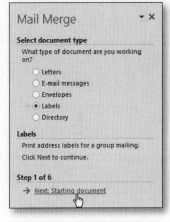

Figure 5-66 *Mail Merge Wizard*: Step 1

Select Starting Document

Next, select your starting document. The main document can be a new document or use an existing document. Depending on the type of merge, you may have to change the document options, such as changing label or envelope options.

▶ HOW TO: Select Starting Document

1. Click the **Change document layout** radio button in the *Select starting document* area if it is not already selected (Figure 5-67).
   - If you select *Start from existing document*, you are asked to select the document on which to perform the merge.

2. Click the **Label options** link in the *Change document layout* area. The *Label Options* dialog box opens.

3. Select the type of label to use.

4. Click **OK** to close the *Label Options* dialog box. A blank table of labels displays in the document.

5. Click the **Next: Select recipients** link to move to the next step in the *Mail Merge Wizard*.

   • Click the **Previous** link in *the Mail Merge Wizard* to return to the previous step if necessary.

Figure 5-67 *Mail Merge Wizard*: Step 2

Select Recipients

Next, select the recipients to merge into your main document. Use an existing data source, use contacts from a Microsoft Outlook Contacts folder, or type a new recipient list.

▶ HOW TO: Select Recipients

1. Click the **Use an existing list** radio button in the *Select recipients* area (Figure 5-68).

   • If you choose *Select from Outlook contacts*, you are prompted to select the Outlook *Contacts* folder.
   • If you select *Type a new list*, click the *Create* link and type the list of recipients.

2. Click the **Browse** link. The *Select Data Source* dialog box opens.

3. Select the data source file and click **Open**. The *Select Data Source* dialog box closes, and the *Mail Merge Recipients* dialog box opens (Figure 5-69).

Figure 5-68 *Mail Merge Wizard*: Step 3

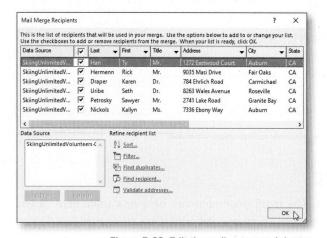

Figure 5-69 **Edit the mail merge recipients**

4. Select the recipients to be included in the merge, sort by a field in the data source, or filter the data source by specific criteria.

5. Click **OK** to close the *Mail Merge Recipients* dialog box after editing the recipient list.

6. Click the **Next: Arrange your labels** link to move to the next step.

Arrange Your Document

In the next step, insert an address block, greeting line, or other merge fields from your data source.

▶ HOW TO: Arrange Your Document

1. Click the **Address block** link to insert the merge field into your main document. The *Insert Address Block* dialog box opens.
   - You can also insert individual merge fields into the label. Click the **More items** link in the *Arrange your labels* area to open the *Insert Merge Field* dialog box where you can insert one or more merge fields.

2. Select the address block format, confirm that the address block structure is correct, and preview the recipients in the *Preview* area.
   - If the address block is not displayed correctly, click the **Match Fields** button to match the fields from your data source with the Word merge fields used in the address block.

3. Click **OK** to close the *Insert Address Block* dialog box and to insert the <<AddressBlock>> merge field into the first label in your document.

4. Click the **Update all labels** button in the *Replicate labels* area (Figure 5-70) to insert the <<AddressBlock>> merge field into each of the labels in your document (Figure 5-71).

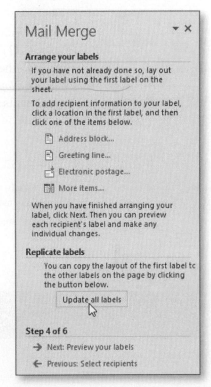

Figure 5-70 *Mail Merge Wizard*: Step 4

Figure 5-71 Address block inserted and labels updated

5. Click the **Next: Preview your labels** link to move to the next step.

Preview Your Document

The next-to-last step is previewing your mail merge to verify that the information from the recipient data source is correctly merged into the main document. In this step, the recipient information displays in the main document. Before completing the merge, you can preview each of the recipients, find a specific recipient, or edit the recipient list (Figure 5-72). Click the **Next: Complete the merge** link in the *Mail Merge* pane to finish the mail merge.

Figure 5-72 *Mail Merge Wizard*: Step 5

Complete the Merge

Select one of the following options to complete the merge: **Print** or **Edit individual labels** (or *letters* or *envelopes*) (Figure 5-73). Select *Print* to send the merged document directly to the printer. Select *Edit individual labels* (or *letters* or *envelopes*) to open a new document displaying the merge results. Review the document before printing.

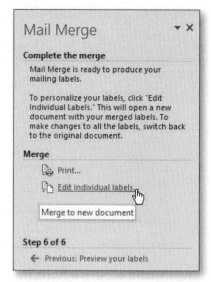

Figure 5-73 *Mail Merge Wizard:* Step 6

PAUSE & PRACTICE: WORD 5-5

In this Pause & Practice project, you create mailing labels for Kelly McFarland to use when she sends the volunteer letters for the Skiing Unlimited program. You create individual labels for delivery addresses using information from an Access database for the recipient list.

File Needed: **SkiingUnlimitedVolunteers-05.accdb** *(Student data files are available in the* Library *of your SIMnet account.)*
Completed Project File Names: **[your initials] PP W5-5 labels.docx** and
[your initials] PP W5-5 labels merge.docx

1. Create a new blank Word document.

2. Save the document as [your initials] PP W5-5 labels.

3. Start the *Mail Merge Wizard* (Figure 5-74).
    a. Click the **Mailings** tab.
    b. Click the **Start Mail Merge** button [*Start Mail Merge* group] and select **Step-by-Step Mail Merge Wizard**. The *Mail Merge* pane opens on the right side of the Word window.

4. Select the document type and starting document.
    a. Click the **Labels** radio button in the *Select document type* area.
    b. Click the **Next: Starting document** link at the bottom of the *Mail Merge* pane to move to *Step 2 of 6*.

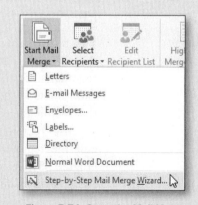

Figure 5-74 Open the *Mail Merge Wizard*

c. Click the **Change document layout** radio button in the *Select starting document* area.

d. Click the **Labels options** link in the *Change document layout* area. The *Labels Options* dialog box opens (Figure 5-75).

e. Select **Avery US Letter** from the *Label vendors* drop-down list.

f. Select **5160 Address Labels** in the *Product number* list.

g. Click **OK** to close the *Label Options* dialog box.

h. Click the **Next: Select recipients** link at the bottom of the *Mail Merge* pane to move to *Step 3 of 6*.

5. Select recipients for the labels.

a. Click the **Use an existing list** radio button in the *Select recipients* area.

b. Click the **Browse** link in the *Use an existing list* area. The *Select Data Source* dialog box opens.

c. Browse to the location on your computer containing your student data files.

d. Select the ***SkiingUnlimitedVolunteers-05*** database and click **Open**. The *Mail Merge Recipients* dialog box opens (Figure 5-76).

e. Click the **Last** column heading drop-down arrow and select **Sort Ascending** from the drop-down list.

f. Click **OK** to close the *Mail Merge Recipients* dialog box.

g. Click the **Next: Arrange your labels** link at the bottom of the *Mail Merge* pane to move to *Step 4 of 6*.

6. Insert an address block to arrange labels.

a. Place your insertion point in the first label cell and click the **Address block** link in the *Arrange your labels* area. The *Insert Address Block* dialog box opens (Figure 5-77).

b. Select the **Mr. Joshua Randall Jr.** option in the *Specify address elements* area.

c. Confirm that the **Insert postal address** check box is checked.

d. Click **OK** to close the *Insert Address Block* dialog box and to insert the merge field.

e. Click the **Update all labels** button in the *Replicate labels* area of the *Mail Merge* pane to automatically insert the <<*AddressBlock*>> field code in each of the labels in the document.

f. Click the **Next: Preview your labels** link at the bottom of the *Mail Merge* pane to move to *Step 5 of 6*.

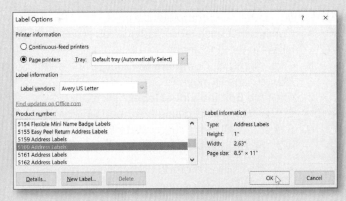

Figure 5-75 *Label Options* dialog box

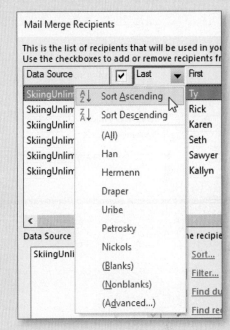

Figure 5-76 Sort mail merge recipients

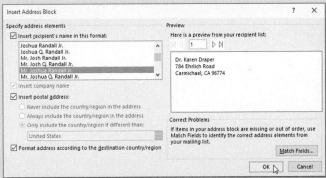

Figure 5-77 Insert address block into labels document

7. Preview labels and complete the merge.
   a. Confirm that each label displays correctly in the preview of the labels in the document.
   b. Click the **Next: Complete the merge** link at the bottom of the *Mail Merge* pane to move to *Step 6 of 6*.
   c. Click the **Edit individual labels** link in the *Merge* area. The *Merge to New Document* dialog box opens (Figure 5-78).
   d. Select the **All** radio button and click **OK**. A new document opens with the recipients merged into the labels.

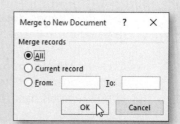

Figure 5-78 *Merge to New Document* dialog box

8. Save the completed merged document as [your initials] PP W5-5 labels merge and close the document (Figure 5-79).

9. Save and close the *[your initials] PP W5-5 labels* document.

Figure 5-79 PP W5-5 labels merge completed

Chapter Summary

5.1 Create and customize a template based upon a Word sample template (p. W5-286).

- **Templates** control default font and size, margins, line and paragraph spacing, themes, and other formatting options.
- All new blank Word documents are based upon the **Normal** template.
- Word template files have a **.dotx** extension.
- Change and save defaults in the *Normal* template; all new documents based upon this template incorporate these changes.
- Word also has a variety of templates from Office.com in the *Backstage* view.
- Insert, delete, or customize template content.

5.2 Create and use a template from a blank document or an existing Word document (p. W5-291).

- Save a new Word document or an existing document (.docx) as a template (.dotx).
- Open a new document based upon a template and edit this new document without affecting the content and format of the template.
- Templates can also be edited.

5.3 Use Word to create envelopes and mailing labels (p. W5-296).

- Create individual **envelopes** in Word or add an envelope to an existing document.
- Select the type or specific size of envelope to create and select how the envelope will print.
- Create **mailing labels** in Word by typing individual labels or creating a full sheet of the same label.

5.4 Understand the types of merges and how to select or create a recipient list (p. W5-302).

- **Mail Merge** enables you to combine a document with a **data source** such as an Access database or Outlook Contacts.
- The **main document** is the document into which information from a data source is merged.
- The data source consists of fields and records. A **field** is an individual piece of information, and a **record** is a group of related fields.

5.5 Create a merged document using the *Mailings* tab (p. W5-303).

- Use the **Mailings** tab to create and customize a mail merge.
- Begin the mail merge by selecting the type of merge to perform.
- Select the **recipients** from an existing data source or type a new list of recipients.
- **Sort**, **filter**, or select specific recipients from a recipient list.
- Insert an **Address Block** or **Greeting Line** merge field into a document. These blocks combine individual fields from the data source to create a standard address block or greeting line for a letter or labels.
- Insert individual **merge fields** from the data source into the main document.
- Preview the results of the merge in the main document before finalizing the merge.
- Send the finished merge results to the printer or to a new document.

5.6 Use the *Mail Merge Wizard* to create a merged document (p. W5-315).

- The **Mail Merge Wizard** is another method to create and customize a mail merge.
- The **Mail Merge pane** appears on the right side of the Word window.
- The *Mail Merge Wizard* walks you through each step of the merge process, providing you with links and buttons to customize your merge.

Check for Understanding

The SIMbook for this text (within your SIMnet account) provides the following resources for concept review:

- Multiple-choice questions
- Short answer questions
- Matching exercises

Guided Project 5-1

For this project, you create a disclosure statement form letter for Emma Cavalli. You merge this letter with a Microsoft Access database containing a recipient list table. You also use the *Mail Merge Wizard* to create mailing labels.
[Student Learning Outcomes 5.3, 5.4, 5.5, 5.6]

Files Needed: ***DisclosureLetter-05.docx*** and ***CavalliPHRE-05.accdb*** (*Student data files are available in the* Library *of your SIMnet account.*)
Completed Project File Names: *[your initials] Word 5-1 letter.docx, [your initials] Word 5-1 letter merge.docx, [your initials] Word 5-1 labels.docx,* and *[your initials] Word 5-1 labels merge.docx*

Skills Covered in This Project

- Use the *Mailings* tab to create merged letters.
- Use an Access database table as the data source.
- Filter and sort a data source.
- Insert an address block and greeting line merge fields.
- Insert an individual merge field.
- Apply bold and italic formatting to a merge field.
- Highlight merge fields.
- Preview and complete a merge.
- Use the *Mail Merge Wizard* to create labels.
- Select label type and recipients.
- Filter and sort label recipients.
- Insert an address block and update labels.
- Preview and complete a label merge.

1. Open the ***DisclosureLetter-05*** document from your student data files.

2. Save the document as [your initials] Word 5-1 letter.

3. Start the mail merge and select recipients.
   a. Click the **Mailings** tab.
   b. Click the **Start Mail Merge** button [*Start Mail Merge* group] and select **Letters**.
   c. Click the **Select Recipients** button [*Start Mail Merge* group] and select **Use an Existing List**. The *Select Data Source* dialog box opens.
   d. Browse to locate your student data files, select the ***CavalliPHRE-05*** database file, and click **Open**. The *Select Table* dialog box opens (Figure 5-80).
   e. Select **Current Clients** and click **OK**.

4. Filter and sort the recipient list.
   a. Click the **Edit Recipient List** button [*Start Mail Merge* group]. The *Mail Merge Recipients* dialog box opens.
   b. Click the **City** column heading drop-down arrow and select **Roseville** (Figure 5-81). Only the records that match the filter (City = Roseville) display.

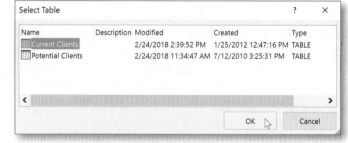

Figure 5-80 Select the database table to use as recipient list

c. Click the **Last** column heading drop-down arrow and select **Sort Ascending** to sort the filtered records by last name.

d. Click **OK** to close the *Mail Merge Recipients* dialog box.

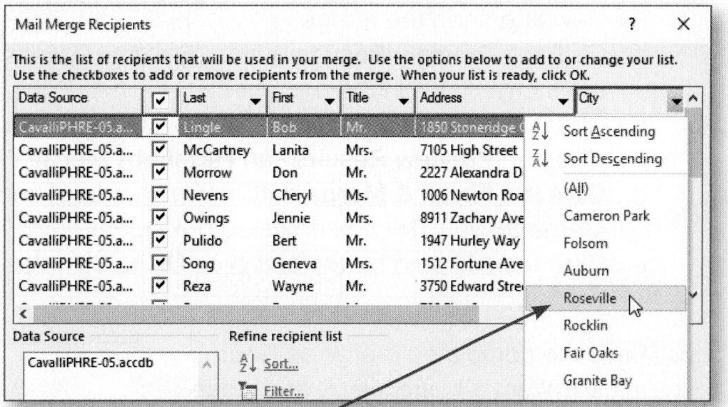

5. Insert address block and greeting line merge fields.

a. Turn on **Show/Hide** [*Home* tab, *Paragraph* group] if it is not already on.

b. Delete the "**[Address]**" placeholder text (including the brackets). Don't delete the paragraph mark at the end of the line.

c. Click the **Address Block** button [*Mailings* tab, *Write & Insert Fields* group]. The *Insert Address Block* dialog box opens (Figure 5-82).

d. Select the **Mr. Joshua Randall Jr.** option in the *Specify address elements* area.

e. Click **OK** to close the *Insert Address Block* dialog box and to insert the <<*AddressBlock*>> merge field in the document.

f. Delete the "**[Salutation]**" placeholder text (including the brackets). Don't delete the paragraph mark at the end of the line.

g. Click the **Greeting Line** button [*Write & Insert Fields* group]. The *Insert Greeting Line* dialog box opens (Figure 5-83).

h. Select **Dear**, **Mr. Randall**, and **(none)** from the three drop-down lists in the *Greeting line format* area.

i. Click **OK** to close the *Insert Greeting Line* dialog box and to insert the <<*GreetingLine*>> merge field in the document.

6. Insert an individual merge field in the body of the document.

a. Delete the "**[date]**" placeholder text (including the brackets) in the first sentence of the fourth body paragraph. Don't delete the space before or after the placeholder text.

b. Click the **Insert Merge Field** drop-down arrow [*Write & Insert Fields* group] and select **ReturnDate** from the drop-down list to insert the <<*ReturnDate*>> merge field.

c. Verify one space displays before and after the <<*ReturnDate*>> merge field.

d. Select the <<**ReturnDate**>> merge field and apply **bold** and **italic** formatting.

e. Click the **Highlight Merge Fields** button [*Write & Insert Fields* group] to highlight the merge fields in the document.

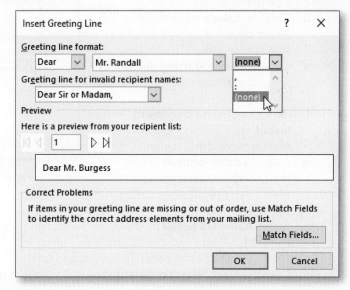

Figure 5-81 Filter recipient list

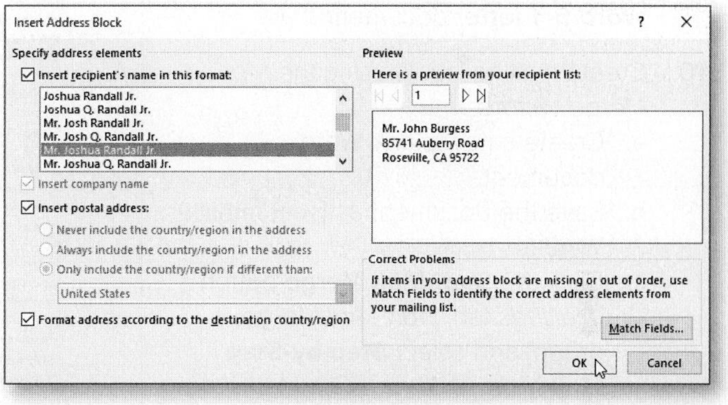

Figure 5-82 *Insert Address Block* dialog box

Figure 5-83 *Insert Greeting Line* dialog box

7. Preview and finish the merge.
   a. Click the **Preview Results** button [*Preview Results* group]. The recipient information displays in the merge fields in the document.
   b. Click the **Next Record** button to view the next recipient. Repeat this for each of the five recipients.
   c. Click the **Preview Results** and **Highlight Merge Fields** buttons to turn off these features.
   d. Click the **Finish & Merge** button [*Finish* group] and select **Edit Individual Documents**. The *Merge to New Document* dialog box opens.
   e. Click the **All** radio button and click **OK** to complete the merge. The completed merge opens in a new document.

8. Save the completed merge as [your initials] Word 5-1 letter merge and close this document (Figure 5-84).

9. Save and close the *[your initials] Word 5-1 letter* document.

10. Create mailing labels using the *Mail Merge Wizard*.
    a. Create a new blank Word document.
    b. Save the document as [your initials] Word 5-1 labels.
    c. Click the **Start Mail Merge** button [*Mailings* tab, *Start Mail Merge* group] and select **Step-by-Step Mail Merge Wizard**. The *Mail Merge* pane opens on the right side of the Word window.
    d. Click the **Labels** radio button in the *Select document type* area of the *Mail Merge* pane.
    e. Click the **Next: Starting document** link at the bottom of the *Mail Merge* pane.
    f. Click the **Change document layout** radio button if it is not already selected.
    g. Click the **Label options** link in the *Change document layout* area. The *Label Options* dialog box opens.
    h. Select **Avery US Letter** as the *Label vendor* and select **5160 Address Labels** as the *Product number*.
    i. Click **OK** to close the *Label Options* dialog box.
    j. Click the **Next: Select recipients** link at the bottom of the *Mail Merge* pane.

Figure 5-84 Word 5-1 letter merge completed (page 1 of 5)

11. Select and edit recipient list.
    a. Click the **Use an existing list** radio button in the *Select recipients* area.
    b. Click the **Browse** button in the *Use an existing list* area. The *Select Data Source* dialog box opens.
    c. Browse to your student data files, select the ***CavalliPHRE-05*** database, and click **Open**. The *Select Table* dialog box opens.
    d. Select **Current Clients** and click **OK**. The *Mail Merge Recipients* dialog box opens.

e. Click the **Filter** link in the bottom half of the *Mail Merge Recipients* dialog box. The *Filter and Sort* dialog box opens (Figure 5-85).

f. On the *Filter Records* tab, click the **Field** drop-down arrow and select **City**.

g. Click the **Comparison** drop-down arrow and select **Equal to**.

h. Type Roseville in the *Compare to* field.

i. Click the **Sort Records** tab (Figure 5-86).

j. Click the **Sort by** drop-down arrow and select **Last**.

k. Click the **Ascending** radio button.

l. Click **OK** to close the *Filter and Sort* dialog box and click **OK** to close the *Mail Merge Recipients* dialog box.

m. Click the **Next: Arrange your labels** link at the bottom of the *Mail Merge* pane.

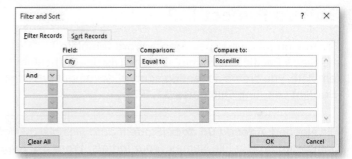

Figure 5-85 *Filter and Sort* dialog box

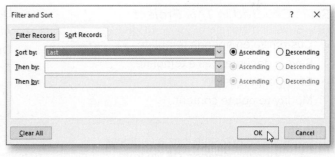

Figure 5-86 Sort records

12. Insert merge field and update labels.

a. Click the **Address block** link in the *Arrange your labels* area. The **Insert Address Block** dialog box opens.

b. Select the **Mr. Joshua Randall Jr.** option in the *Specify address elements* area.

c. Click **OK** to close the *Insert Address Block* dialog box and to insert the *<<AddressBlock>>* merge field in the first label in the document.

d. Click the **Update all labels** button in the *Replicate labels* area to automatically insert the *<<AddressBlock>>* merge field in each label in the document.

e. Click the **Next: Preview your labels** link at the bottom of the *Mail Merge* pane.

13. Preview and finish the merge.

a. Preview the recipients in the labels document. Five labels display with client information.

b. Click the **Next: Complete the merge** link at the bottom of the *Mail Merge* pane.

c. Click the **Edit individual labels** link in the *Complete the merge* area. The *Merge to New Document* dialog box opens.

d. Click the **All** radio button and click **OK** to complete the merge. The completed merge opens in a new document.

14. Save the completed merge as [your initials] Word 5-1 labels merge and close this document (Figure 5-87).

15. Save and close the *[your initials] Word 5-1 labels* document.

Figure 5-87 Word 5-1 labels merge completed

Guided Project 5-2

For this project, you customize a Word template to create a curriculum meeting agenda template for the Sierra Pacific Community College District Curriculum Committee. After customizing and saving this template, you create a meeting agenda document based upon this template.
[Student Learning Outcomes 5.1, 5.2]

File Needed: ***Agenda-05.docx*** *(Student data files are available in the* Library *of your SIMnet account.)*
Completed Project File Names: *[your initials]* **Word 5-2 template.dotx** and
[your initials] **Word 5-2 agenda.docx**

Skills Covered in This Project

- Customize an agenda template.
- Save a document as a template.
- Change margins.
- Modify template content.

- Delete a column in a table.
- *AutoFit* table contents.
- Open a document based upon a template.
- Add content to a document based upon a template.

1. Open a file and save it as a template.
   a. Open the ***Agenda-05*** file from your student data files.
   b. Open the *Save As* dialog box.
   c. Type [your initials] Word 5-2 template in the *File name* area.
   d. Click the **Save as type** drop-down list and select **Word Template**.
   e. Browse to the location on your computer to save this template.
   f. Click **Save** to save the document as a Word template.

2. Customize the template content and format.
   a. Turn on **Show/Hide**.
   b. Change the top and bottom margins to **0.5"**. If a dialog opens and alerts you about margins, click **Ignore**.
   c. Place the insertion point before the title ("AGENDA"), type SPCCD CURRICULUM, and **space** once.
   d. **Left** align this line.
   e. Click the **Meeting Title** field and type Full Curriculum Committee Meeting.
   f. Click the **Start Time** field (below the "Click to select date" field) and type 3.
   g. Click the **End Time** field and type 5 p.m..
   h. Click the **Facilitator Name** field and type Dr. Manuel Chavez.
   i. Click the **Attendee Names** field and type Melissa Rogan, Roietta Jones, Tony Parsons, Ravi Singh, Rachel Salazar, Rebecca Frank, Kai Sung, and Heidi Anderson.
   j. Click the **Reading List** field and type Curriculum printouts (Figure 5-88).
   k. Turn on **View Gridlines** (if necessary) [*Table Tools Layout* tab, *Table* group].

Figure 5-88 Customize a template

W5-326

Microsoft Word 365 Chapter 5: Using Templates and Mail Merge

l. Delete the third row of the first table ("Please bring").

m. Replace "Additional Instructions:" near the bottom with **Follow-up Notes:**.

3. Customize the second table content and format.

   a. Delete the third column of the second table.

   b. Select the entire second table and **AutoFit Window**.

   c. Select and remove the **Continental Breakfast** field in the second column in the first row and delete the blank line above the *Topic* field.

   d. Select and remove the **Speaker** field in the second column in the first row and delete the tab after the *Topic* field.

   e. Type the following information in the *Start Time, End Time, Introduction,* and *Item* content control fields. Don't remove or type any content in the *Topic* fields. Word automatically converts "1st" and "2nd" to superscript format.

Start Time	End Time	Introduction/Item
3:00	3:10	Preliminaries
3:10	4:00	1st Readings
4:00	4:40	2nd Readings
4:40	5:00	Degrees and Certificates

4. Save and close the template (Figure 5-89).

5. Create a document based upon the **[your initials] Word 5-2 template**.
   Note: Do not open this template from within Word; open from a File Explorer *window.*

   a. Open a **File Explorer** window.

   b. Browse to the folder on your computer containing the **[your initials] Word 5-2 template** file.

   c. Double-click the **[your initials] Word 5-2 template** file to create a new document based upon this template.

   d. Save this Word document as [your initials] Word 5-2 agenda. Confirm that *Save as type* is **Word Document**; if it's not, change it.

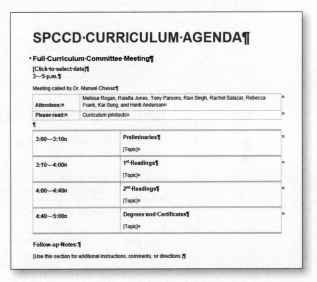

Figure 5-89 Word 5-2 template completed

6. Insert content into the agenda.

   a. Click the **Click to select date** field and select the next Wednesday.

   b. Click the **Topic** field below the "Preliminaries" heading and type the following content. Press **Enter** after the first line, but don't press *Enter* after the last item.

   Approve minutes

   State Curriculum Committee updates

   c. Click the **Topic** field below the "1st Readings" heading and type the following and press **Enter** after each line except the last line:

   BIO 334

   BUS 300

   FITN 120

   PSCH 310

d. Click the **Topic** field below the "2nd Readings" heading and type the following and press **Enter** after each line except the last line:

HUM 330
HUM 335
PSCH 315
PSCH 320

e. Click the **Topic** field below the *Degrees and Certificates* field and type the following and press **Enter** after each line except the last line:

ACCT Accounting Degree
BUSTEC Office Professional Degree
ARTNM Animation Certificate

f. Click the field below the "Follow-up Notes" heading, type the following:
State Curriculum Committee Conference applications due next Wednesday.

7. Save and close the document (Figure 5-90).

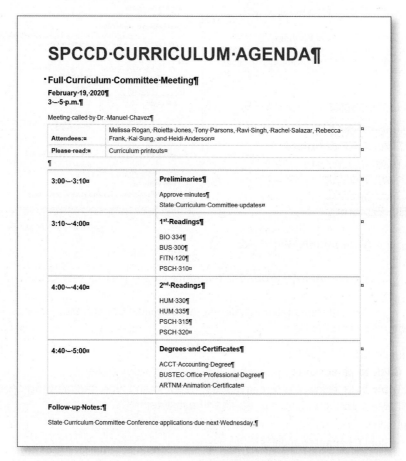

Figure 5-90 Word 5-2 agenda completed

Guided Project 5-3

For this project, you create an insurance renewal letter template for Gretchen Souza at Central Sierra Insurance. You then create a renewal letter based upon the template and merge the letter with recipients and renewal information from an Excel file.
[Student Learning Outcomes 5.1, 5.2, 5.4, 5.5]

Files Needed: **RenewalLetter-05.docx** and **SouzaRenewals-05.xlsx** *(Student data files are available in the* Library *of your SIMnet account.)*
Completed Project File Names: *[your initials] Word 5-3 template.dotx*,
[your initials] Word 5-3 renewals.docx, and *[your initials] Word 5-3 renewals merge.docx*

Skills Covered in This Project

- Open an existing document and save as a template.
- Insert date field and set the date to update automatically.
- Create a new Word document based upon a template.
- Use the *Mailings* tab to create merged letters.

- Use an Excel file as a data source.
- Sort and filter a data source.
- Deselect recipients.
- Insert address block and greeting line merge fields.
- Insert individual merge fields.
- Highlight merge fields.
- Preview a merge and check for errors.
- Complete the merge.

1. Open a document and save as a template.
   a. Open the **RenewalLetter-05** document from your student data files.
   b. Open the *Save As* dialog box.
   c. Type [your initials] Word 5-3 template in the *File name* area.
   d. Click the **Save as type** drop-down list and select **Word Template**.
   e. Browse to the location on your computer to save this template.
   f. Click **Save** to save the document as a Word template.

2. Insert a current date field into the letter.
   a. Delete the "**[Insert current date]**" placeholder text (including the brackets). Don't delete the paragraph mark at the end.
   b. Click the **Date & Time** button [*Insert* tab, *Text* group] to open the *Date and Time* dialog box.
   c. Select the date option (use January 1, 2020 format), check the **Update automatically** box, and click **OK** to insert the current date and to close the dialog box.
   d. Save and close the template.

3. Create a document based upon the *[your initials] Word 5-3 template*. *Note: Do not open this template from within Word; open from a* File Explorer *window.*
   a. Open a **File Explorer** window.
   b. Browse to the folder on your computer containing the *[your initials] Word 5-3 template* file.
   c. Double-click the *[your initials] Word 5-3 template* file to create a new Word document based upon this template.
   d. Save this Word document as [your initials] Word 5-3 renewals. Confirm that the *Save as type* is **Word Document**; if it's not, change it. If prompted to save the template file, click **No**.

4. Start the mail merge and select the recipients.
   a. Click the **Start Mail Merge** button [*Mailings* tab, *Start Mail Merge* group] and select **Letters**.
   b. Click the **Select Recipients** button [*Start Mail Merge* group] and select **Use an Existing List**. The *Select Data Source* dialog box opens.

c. Browse to locate your student data files, select the **SouzaRenewals-05** Excel file, and click **Open**. The *Select Table* dialog box opens.

d. Select the **Renewals$** table, check the **First row of data contains column headers** box (if necessary), and click **OK**.

e. Click the **Edit Recipient List** button [*Start Mail Merge* group] to open the *Mail Merge Recipients* dialog box.

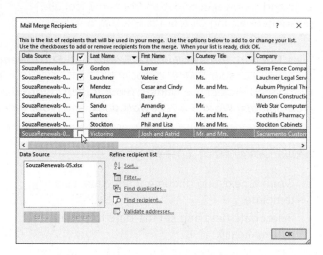

f. Click the **Last Name** column heading drop-down arrow and select **Sort Ascending**. The records are sorted by last name.

g. Deselect the check box on the last four recipients so they are not included in the merge (Figure 5-91).

h. Click **OK** to close the *Mail Merge Recipients* dialog box.

Figure 5-91 Deselect recipients

5. Insert the address block and greeting line merge fields into the letter.

a. Turn on **Show/Hide** [*Home* tab, *Paragraph* group].

b. Delete the "**[Address]**" placeholder text (including the brackets). Don't delete the paragraph mark at the end of the line.

c. Click the **Address Block** button [*Write & Insert Fields* group] to open the *Insert Address Block* dialog box.

d. Select the **Mr. Joshua Randall Jr.** option in the *Specify address elements* area. Click the **Next** button in the *Preview* area to view each of the four recipients.

e. Click **OK** to close the *Insert Address Block* dialog box and to insert the <<*AddressBlock*>> merge field in the document.

f. Delete the "**[Greeting]**" placeholder text (including the brackets). Don't delete the paragraph mark at the end of the line.

g. Click the **Greeting Line** button [*Write & Insert Fields* group] to open the *Insert Greeting Line* dialog box (Figure 5-92).

h. Select **Dear**, **Mr. and Mrs. Randall**, and **:** (colon) from the three drop-down lists in the *Greeting line format* area.

Figure 5-92 *Insert Greeting Line* dialog box

i. Click **OK** to close the *Insert Greeting Line* dialog box and to insert the <<*GreetingLine*>> merge field in the document.

6. Insert other merge fields in the body and table of the document.

a. Click the **Highlight Merge Fields** button [*Write & Insert Fields* group] to highlight the merge fields in the document.

b. Delete the "**[Policy Number]**" placeholder text (including the brackets) in the subject line. Don't delete the space before or after the placeholder text.

c. Click the **Insert Merge Field** drop-down arrow [*Write & Insert Fields* group] and select **Policy_Number** from the drop-down list.

d. Verify one space displays before and after the <<*Policy_Number*>> merge field.

e. Continue inserting merge fields in the document to replace the placeholder text (including the brackets) using the information in the following table. Verify proper spacing and punctuation around merge fields (Figure 5-93).

Placeholder Text	Location	Merge Field
[Company]	First body paragraph	**Company**
[Insurance Company]	Second body paragraph	**Insurance_Company**
[Policy Description]	First column of table	**Policy_Description**
[Premium Basis]	Second column of table	**Premium_Basis**
[Rate per $1000]	Third column of table	**Rate_per_1000**
[Total Premium]	Fourth column of table	**Total_Premium**
[First Name]	Last body paragraph	**First_Name**

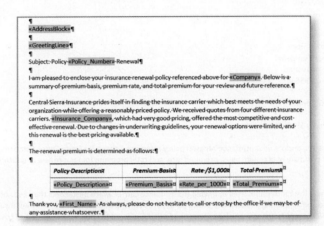

Figure 5-93 Merge fields inserted into the letter

7. Preview and check for errors in the merge.
   a. Click the **Preview Results** button [*Preview Results* group] to display the recipient information in the merge fields in the document.
   b. Click the **Next Record** or **Previous Record** button to preview all four recipients.
   c. Click the **Preview Results** button to turn off the previewing and to display the merge fields in the document.
   d. Click the **Highlight Merge Fields** button to turn off this feature.
   e. Click the **Check for Errors** button [*Preview Results* group]. The *Checking and Reporting Errors* dialog box opens (Figure 5-94).
   f. Click the **Simulate the merge . . .** radio button and click **OK**. A dialog box opens confirming that no errors exist (Figure 5-95). If errors exist, the errors are reported in a new document.
   g. Click **OK** to close the dialog box.
   h. Save the document.

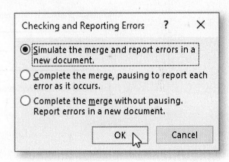

Figure 5-94 *Checking and Reporting Errors dialog box*

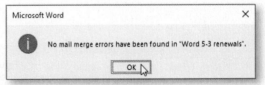

Figure 5-95 Dialog box confirming no errors in the merge

8. Finish and save the merge.
   a. Click the **Finish & Merge** button [*Finish* group] and select **Edit Individual Documents**. The *Merge to New Document* dialog box opens.

b. Click the **All** radio button and click **OK** to complete the merge. The completed merge opens in a new document.

c. Save the completed merge as [your initials] Word 5-3 renewals merge and close this document (Figure 5-96). If prompted to save the template file, click **Don't Save**.

Central Sierra Insurance
5502 Ridley Way | Cameron Park, CA 94663
780.886.2400 | www.centralsierra.com

February 25, 2020

Mr. Lamar Gordon
Sierra Fence Company
2405 Eureka Avenue
Fair Oaks, CA 95636

Dear Mr. Gordon:

Subject: Policy SF752284 Renewal

I am pleased to enclose your insurance renewal policy referenced above for Sierra Fence Company. Below is a summary of premium basis, premium rate, and total premium for your review and future reference.

Central Sierra Insurance prides itself in finding the insurance carrier which best meets the needs of your organization while offering a reasonably priced policy. We received quotes from four different insurance carriers. West Coast Insurance, which had very good pricing, offered the most competitive and cost-effective renewal. Due to changes in underwriting guidelines, your renewal options were limited, and this renewal is the best pricing available.

The renewal premium is determined as follows:

Policy Description	Premium Basis	Rate /$1,000	Total Premium
Construction	$325,000	$21	$6,825

Thank you, Lamar. As always, please do not hesitate to call or stop by the office if we may be of any assistance whatsoever.

Sincerely,

Gretchen Souza, ARM, CIC, CRM
Central Sierra Insurance
gretchen@centralsierra.com

Figure 5-96 Word 5-3 renewals merge completed (page 1 of 4)

9. Save and close the *[your initials] Word 5-3 renewals* document. If prompted to save the template file, click **Don't Save**.

Independent Project 5-4

For this project, you create a letter for Emma Cavalli at Placer Hills Real Estate to send to prospective clients. You merge this letter with recipient information from an Access database and create mailing labels. [Student Learning Outcomes 5.3, 5.4, 5.5, 5.6]

Files Needed: ***ProspectingLetter-05.docx*** and ***CavalliPHRE-05.accdb*** *(Student data files are available in the* Library *of your SIMnet account.)*
Completed Project File Names: *[your initials]* **Word 5-4 letter.docx**, *[your initials]* **Word 5-4 letter merge.docx**, *[your initials]* **Word 5-4 labels.docx**, and *[your initials]* **Word 5-4 labels merge.docx**

Skills Covered in This Project

- Insert a date field and set to update automatically.
- Use the *Mailings* tab or *Mail Merge Wizard* to create merged letters and labels.
- Use an Access database table as the data source for the merged letters and labels.
- Filter and sort a recipient list.
- Insert address block and greeting line merge fields.
- Insert individual merge fields.
- Highlight merge fields.
- Preview a merged document.
- Complete a letter and label merge.

1. Open the ***ProspectingLetter-05*** document from your student data files.

2. Save the document as [your initials] Word 5-4 letter.

3. Insert the current date.
   a. Delete the "**[Current date]**" placeholder text and brackets (don't delete the paragraph mark).
   b. Insert the current date (use January 1, 2020 format) and set the date to update automatically.

4. Use either the *Mailings* tab or the *Mail Merge Wizard* to start a **Letters** mail merge.

5. Select the ***CavalliPHRE-05*** database as the existing recipient list.
   a. Use the **Potential Clients** table in this database.
   b. Edit the recipient list and filter for those recipients who live in the city of **Rocklin**.
   c. Sort the recipients by last name in ascending order.

6. Replace the "**[Address]**" placeholder text and brackets with an address block merge field.
   a. Use the **Mr. Joshua Randall Jr.** format.
   b. View the recipients in the *Preview* area to ensure the address block is formatted correctly.

7. Replace the "**[Salutation]**" placeholder text and brackets with a greeting line merge field.
   a. Use **Dear Mr. and Mrs. Randall**: format.
   b. View the recipients in the *Preview* area to ensure the greeting line is formatted correctly.

8. Insert merge fields in the body of the letter.
   a. Replace the "**[City]**" placeholder text and brackets with the **City** merge field.
   b. Replace the "**[First name]**" placeholder text and brackets with the **First** merge field.
   c. Turn on **Highlight Merge Fields** and verify spacing and punctuation around merge fields.

9. Replace "xx" with your reference initials at the end of the document.

10. Preview the merged letters. After previewing the letters, turn off both preview and highlight merge fields.

11. Finish the merge and save the documents.
    a. Select **Edit Individual Documents** to finish the merge.
    b. Save the merged letters as [your initials] Word 5-4 letter merge and close the document (Figure 5-97).
    c. Save and close the *[your initials] Word 5-4 letter* document.

12. Create a new blank Word document and save the document as [your initials] Word 5-4 labels.

13. Use either the *Mailings* tab or the *Mail Merge Wizard* to start a **Labels** merge.
    a. Use **Avery US Letter**, **5160 Address Labels** as the label type.
    b. Select the ***CavalliPHRE-05*** database as the existing recipient list.
    c. Use the **Potential Clients** table in this database.
    d. Edit the recipient list and filter for those recipients who live in the city of **Rocklin**.
    e. Sort the recipients by last name in ascending order.
    f. Insert address block merge field. Use the **Mr. Joshua Randall Jr.** format.
    g. **Update Labels** so the address block merge field appears in each of the label cells.

14. Preview the merged labels. After previewing the labels, turn off preview.

15. Finish the merge to edit individual labels and save and close the documents.
    a. Save the merged document as [your initials] Word 5-4 labels merge and close the document (Figure 5-98).
    b. Save and close the *[your initials] Word 5-4 labels* document.

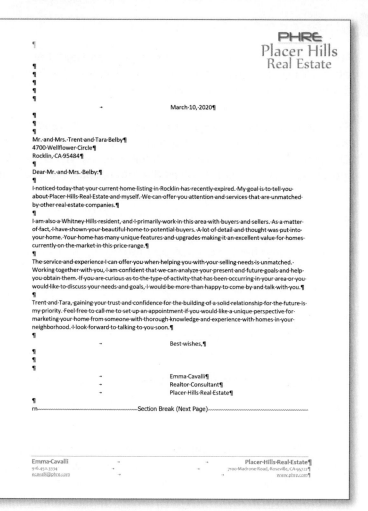

Figure 5-97 Word 5-4 letter merge completed (page 1 of 4)

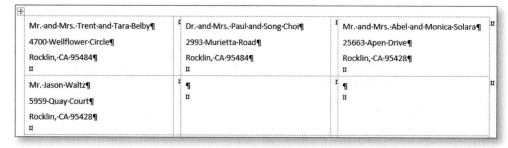

Figure 5-98 Word 5-4 labels merge completed

Independent Project 5-5

For this project, you create a business card template for the members of the American River Cycling Club. You use an online business card template, customize it, and save the document as a template. You then create a document based upon this template and customize the business cards for Kelsey Kroll. [Student Learning Outcomes 5.1, 5.2]

Files Needed: ***Business card (general format).dotx*** (from online templates) or ***BusinessCards-05.docx*** *(Student data files are available in the* Library *of your SIMnet account.)*
Completed Project File Names: ***[your initials] Word 5-5 template.dotx*** and
[your initials] Word 5-5 business cards.docx

Skills Covered in This Project

- Download an online business card template.
- Save a document as a template.
- Modify template content.

- Remove a content control field.
- Open a document based upon a template.
- Add content to a document based upon a template.

1. Create a document based upon a business card template.
   a. Display the *New* area on the *Backstage* view and search for business cards.
   b. Select the **Business cards (Burgundy Wave design, 10 per page)** business card format as shown in Figure 5-99.

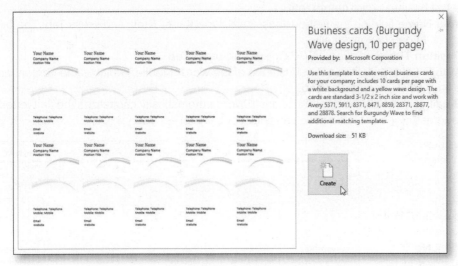

Figure 5-99 Create business cards from an online template

   c. **Create** a document based upon this business card template. If this template is not available, open the ***BusinessCards-05*** document from your student data files.

2. Save the document as a **Word Template**, name it [your initials] Word 5-5 template, and select the specific location to save the template. If prompted, update the file to the newest file format.

3. Customize template content.
   a. Turn on the **Show/Hide** feature and **View Gridlines** [*Table Tools Layout* tab, *Table* group].
   b. Click the **Company Name** field on the first business card (upper left), type American River Cycling Club, and press **Tab**. The *Company Name* fields on each business card update automatically.

    c. Apply **bold**, **small caps**, and **10 pt** font size formatting to "American River Cycling Club" on the first business card.

    d. Use the **Format Painter** to apply this formatting to "American River Cycling Club" on each of the other business cards.

    e. Select "**Telephone: Telephone**" (including the paragraph mark at the end of the line) on the first business card and delete the selected label and content control field. Delete this information on each of the other business cards.

    f. Click the **Website** field at the bottom of the first business card, type www.arcc.org, and press **Tab**. The *Website* fields on each business card update automatically.

4. Save and close the template (Figure 5-100). If a dialog box opens and prompts you to save styles and building blocks, click **Don't Save**.

5. Create a document based upon a template and save the document.

    a. Open a *File Explorer* window, browse to the folder containing the *[your initials] Word 5-5 template* file, and double-click the file to create a document based upon the template file. Do not open the template file from within Word.

    b. Save the Word document as [your initials] Word 5-5 business cards. Make sure you save the document as a **Word Document**. If prompted to save the template file, click **No**.

6. Customize the first business card (upper left).

    a. Click the **Your Name** field on the first business card, type Kelsey Kroll, and press **Tab**. The other business cards update automatically.

    b. Click the **Position Title** field, type ARCC Coach, and press **Tab**.

    c. Click the **Mobile** field (click the second instance of the word "Mobile," which is the content control field), type 916.522.7741, and press **Tab**.

    d. Click the **Email** field, type kelsey.kroll@arcc.org (if Word automatically capitalizes the first letter in the email address, undo this automatic capitalization), and press **Tab**.

7. Verify each business card displays the same information.

8. Save and close the document (Figure 5-101). If prompted to save the template file, click **No**. If a dialog box opens and prompts you to save styles and building blocks, click **Don't Save**.

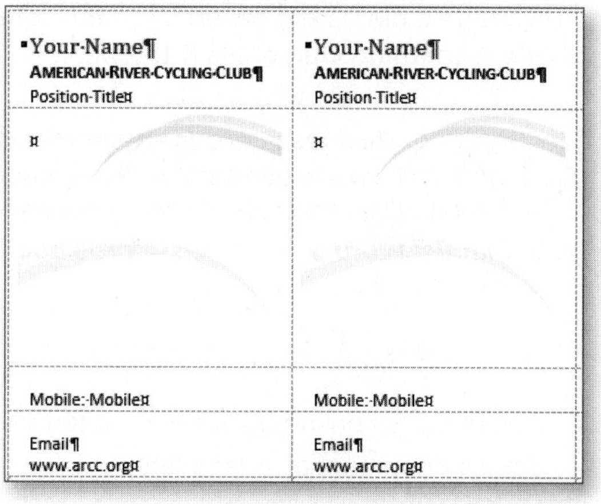

Figure 5-100 Modified business card template

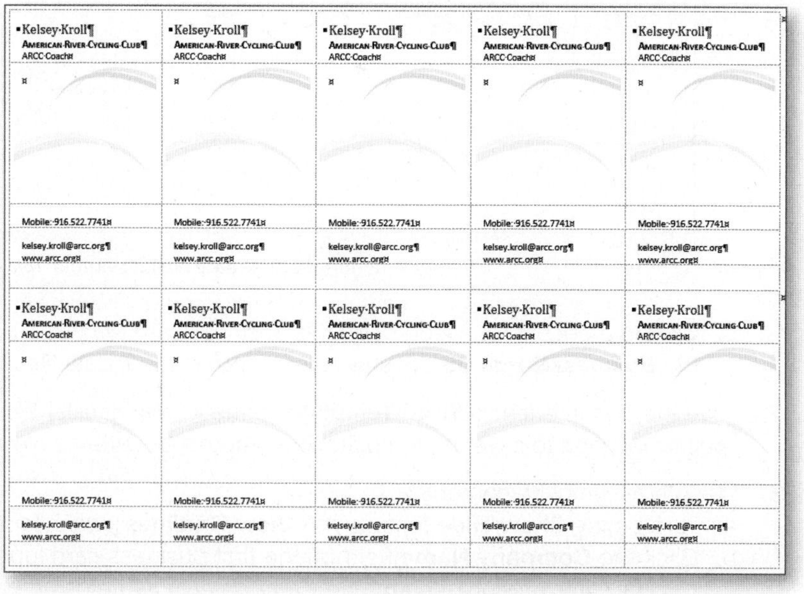

Figure 5-101 Word 5-5 business cards completed

Independent Project 5-6

For this project, you customize a privacy notice for Courtyard Medical Plaza that includes merge fields for recipients' names and employee information. You also create file folder labels for individual employees. [Student Learning Outcomes 5.3, 5.4, 5.5, 5.6]

Files Needed: ***PrivacyNotice-05.docx*** and ***CourtyardMedicalPlaza-05.xlsx*** *(Student data files are available in the* Library *of your SIMnet account.)*
Completed Project File Names: *[your initials]* **Word 5-6 main.docx**, *[your initials]* **Word 5-6 merge.docx**, *[your initials]* **Word 5-6 labels.docx**, and *[your initials]* **Word 5-6 labels merge.docx**

Skills Covered in This Project

- Edit an existing document.
- Set a left tab stop.
- Use the *Mailings* tab or *Mail Merge Wizard* to create merged letters and labels.
- Use an Excel file as the data source for merged letters and labels.
- Filter and sort a recipient list.
- Insert individual merge fields.
- Apply formatting to merge fields.
- Insert a date field and set to update automatically.
- Preview merge documents.
- Complete a letter and label merge.

1. Open the ***PrivacyNotice-05*** document from your student data files.

2. Save the document as [your initials] Word 5-6 main.

3. Use either the *Mailings* tab or the *Mail Merge Wizard* to start a **Letters** mail merge.

4. Select the ***CourtyardMedicalPlaza-05*** Excel file as the recipient list and select the **Employees$** table in this file. Verify the **First row of data contains column headers** box is checked.

5. Edit the recipient list.

6. Filter for those recipients whose **Department** is **Equal to** Accounting **Or** Marketing. *Hint: Use the* Filter and Sort *dialog box.*
   a. Sort the recipients by last name in ascending order.
   b. Verify five recipients display in the *Mail Merge Recipients* dialog box.

7. Set a tab stop to align the merge fields.
   a. Select the four lines at the beginning of the document ("Name" through "Date") and set a **1.25"** left tab stop.
   b. Press **Tab** once at the end of each of these four lines.

8. Insert merge fields.
   a. Insert the **Title**, **First**, and **Last** merge fields after the tab on the "Name:" line. **Space** once after the *Title* and *First* fields; don't use commas after the fields.
   b. Select these three merge fields and apply **bold** formatting.
   c. Insert the **EmpNumber** merge field after the tab on the "Employee Number:" line.
   d. Insert the **Department** merge field after the tab on the "Department:" line.

9. Insert the current date after the tab after "Date:" (use January 1, 2020 format) and set the date so it does not update automatically.

10. Preview the results.
    a. Check to ensure proper spacing between employee name merge fields.
    b. Preview each of the five recipients. After previewing the documents, turn off preview.
    c. Save the document.

11. Complete the merge to edit individual documents.

12. Save the merged document as [your initials] Word 5-6 merge (Figure 5-102) and close the document.

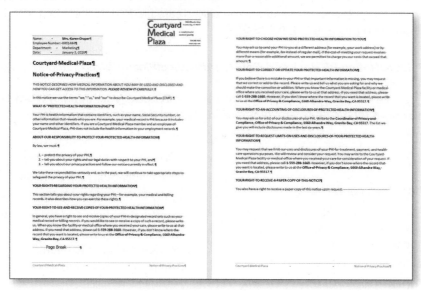

Figure 5-102 Word 5-6 merge completed (recipient 1 of 5)

13. Save and close the *[your initials] Word 5-6 main* document.

14. Create a new blank Word document and save the document as [your initials] Word 5-6 labels.

15. Use either the *Mailings* tab or the *Mail Merge Wizard* to start a **Labels** mail merge.
    a. Select **Avery US Letter**, **45366 EcoFriendly File Folder Labels**.
    b. Select the ***CourtyardMedicalPlaza-05*** Excel file as the recipient list and select the **Employees$** table in this file. Verify the **First row of data contains column headers** box is checked.
    c. Edit the recipient list and sort the recipients by last name in ascending order.
    d. Select the entire document and change the font to **Cambria** and the size to **10 pt**.

16. Insert merge fields and text in the labels.
    a. Place the insertion point in the first cell (upper left) in the labels table, insert the **Last** and **First** fields. Separate the last and first name merge fields with a comma and space.
    b. Press **Enter** and type Employee Number:.
    c. **Space** once and insert the **EmpNumber** merge field.
    d. Press **Enter** and insert the **Department** merge field.
    e. **Space** once and type Department.
    f. Select the first line of the label (<<Last>>, <<First>>) and apply **bold**, **italic**, and **small caps** formatting.

17. **Update Labels** and preview the merge. After previewing the labels, turn off preview and save the document.

18. Complete the merge to edit individual documents. Ten labels with merged information display.

19. Save the merged document as [your initials] Word 5-6 labels merge (Figure 5-103) and close the document.

20. Save and close the *[your initials] Word 5-6 labels* document.

DRAPER, KAREN¶ Employee·Number:·0001484¶ Marketing·Department¶		*FALLON, TRISHA*¶ Employee·Number:·0001736¶ Medicine·Department¶	
FAN, KAI¶ Employee·Number:·0001984¶ Medicine·Department¶		*HAN, TY*¶ Employee·Number:·0001325¶ Accounting·Department¶	
HERMENN, RICK¶ Employee·Number:·0000552¶ Personnel·Department¶		*KIM, JAMIE*¶ Employee·Number:·0000954¶ Accounting·Department¶	
NICKOLS, KALLYN¶ Employee·Number:·0007746¶ Accounting·Department¶		*PETROSKY, SAWYER*¶ Employee·Number:·0001080¶ Marketing·Department¶	
SOLARA, RAMON¶ Employee·Number:·0000825¶ Personnel·Department¶		*URIBE, SETH*¶ Employee·Number:·0006985¶ Medicine·Department¶	
Employee·Number:·¶ ·Department¶		Employee·Number:·¶ ·Department¶	

Figure 5-103 Word 5-6 labels merge completed

Improve It Project 5-7

For this project, you create an employment letter template from an existing employment letter from Central Sierra Insurance. You delete specific employment information, insert placeholder text, and modify the structure of the letter.
[Student Learning Outcomes 5.1, 5.2]

File Needed: **EmploymentOffer-05.docx** (*Student data files are available in the* Library *of your SIMnet account.*)
Completed Project File Name: **[your initials] Word 5-7 template.dotx**

Skills Covered in This Project

- Save an existing document as a template.
- Delete numbered and lettered items from a document.
- Move numbered and lettered items.
- Change the level of an item in a multilevel list.
- Delete and insert a page break.
- Insert a date.
- Delete text and insert placeholder text.
- Apply text highlight color.
- Modify header content.

---

1. Open the **EmploymentOffer-05** document from your student data files.

2. Save the document as a **Word Template** named [your initials] Word 5-7 template. Select the specific location to save the template.

3. Delete text from the employment letter. Be sure to delete the paragraph mark at the end of the paragraphs being deleted and delete items in the order they are listed below.
   a. Delete item **16**.
   b. Delete item **11**, including the three lettered items below the number. The numbered items following these deleted lines will automatically renumber.
   c. Delete items **7–9**, including the lettered item on item **8**.
   d. Delete the page break at the end of the second page.

4. Move text from the employment letter. Be sure to include the paragraph mark at the end of the items being moved.
   a. Move item **5** so it displays before item 7 ("Eligibility for health benefits. . .").
   b. Move item **9** so it displays before item 8 ("Your retirement benefits") and click the **Increase Indent** button to make this the third lettered item (c) of item 7. This letter should now display ten numbered items.

5. Insert a **page break** at the beginning of item 7.

6. Delete the date at the beginning of the first page (don't delete the paragraph mark), insert the current date (use January 1, 2020 format), and set the date so it updates automatically.

7. Delete text and insert placeholder text. Be sure to include appropriate spacing and punctuation around placeholder text.
   a. Delete all three lines of the inside address and type [Employee's name and address] as the placeholder text. Three blank lines should display above this placeholder text, and one blank line should display below it.
   b. Delete "**Mrs. Skaar**" in the salutation (do not delete the colon) and type [Employee]. Confirm proper spacing before placeholder text.
   c. Delete "**Health & Benefits Large Group Specialist**" in the first body paragraph and type [Job title].
   d. Delete "**Cameron Park**" in the first body paragraph and type [Office location].
   e. Delete "**April 1, 2020**" In the first body paragraph and type [Start date].
   f. Delete "**Bert Pulido**" on item 1 and type [Supervisor].

g. Delete "**Central Sierra Health & Benefits**" in item 1 and type [Department].

h. Delete all of the text after "Job Description:" on item 2 (don't delete the period or paragraph mark at the end of the paragraph) and type [Job description].

i. Delete "**$4,500**" on item 3 (don't delete the period after "$4,500") and type [Salary].

8. Apply yellow text highlight color (not text color) to all of the placeholder text. Highlight only the placeholder text and brackets, not the spaces or punctuation around the placeholder text.

9. Delete the date in the header on the second page, insert the current date (use January 1, 2020 format), and set the date so it updates automatically.

10. Proofread the document to check for proper business letter formatting, spacing between parts, and spacing and punctuation around placeholder text.

11. Save and close the template (Figure 5-104).

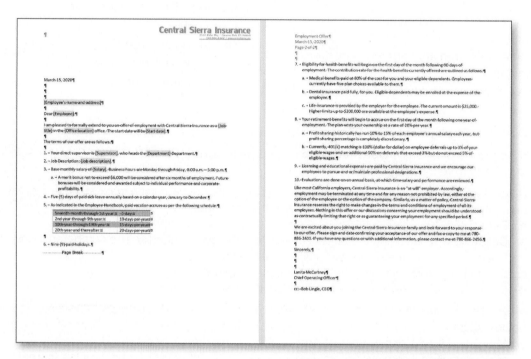

Figure 5-104 Word 5-7 template completed

Challenge Project 5-8

For this project, you create a form letter to use in a mail merge. You can merge information from a data source into any kind of document. The following is a list of examples for potential mail merge projects (you are not limited to these examples):

- A letter to your instructors informing them of an upcoming project and soliciting their input
- A letter to family and friends inviting them to an upcoming event
- A letter to your college's alumni soliciting scholarship donations

Use an existing database as your data source or type a new list with recipient information. Complete the merge to a new document to edit individual documents.

[Student Learning Outcomes 5.4, 5.5, 5.6]

File Needed: None
Completed Project File Names: **[your initials] Word 5-8 main.docx**, **[your initials] Word 5-8 data.accdb**, and **[your initials] Word 5-8 merge.docx**

Create a new document and save it as [your initials] Word 5-8 main. Modify your document according to the following guidelines:

- Use proper business letter formatting if applicable.
- Change line and paragraph spacing as needed to create an attractive and readable document. Use consistent line and paragraph spacing throughout the document.
- Insert placeholder text where the merge fields are inserted.
- Select recipients or create a new list for recipients. Save the data source as [your initials] Word 5-8 data.
- Sort and/or filter the merge. Include at least five recipients in your merge.
- Insert merge fields as needed. Check for proper spacing and punctuation around merge fields.
- Highlight merge fields in the main document.
- Apply font formatting to at least one of the merge fields.
- Complete the mail merge to a new document and save as [your initials] Word 5-8 merge.

Challenge Project 5-9

For this project, you create a Word template based upon one of the Word templates on Office.com. Choose from a brochure, business cards, an invitation, a schedule, or any of the other templates available from Office.com on the *Backstage* view.
[Student Learning Outcomes 5.1, 5.2]

File Needed: None
Completed Project File Names: **[your initials] Word 5-9 template.dotx** and **[your initials] Word 5-9.docx**

Open a Word template of your choice and save the document as a Word template named [your initials] Word 5-9 template. Modify the template according to the following guidelines:

- Customize the template by adding text and placeholder text.
- Delete any placeholder text not needed.
- Apply formatting as needed.
- Save and close the template.
- Create a Word document based upon the template and save this document as [your initials] Word 5-9.
- Replace placeholder text with custom content.
- Check for consistent and attractive formatting.

Challenge Project 5-10

For this project, you create a full sheet of return mailing labels and merged labels.
[Student Learning Outcomes 5.3, 5.4, 5.5, 5.6]

File Needed: None
Completed Project File Names: *[your initials]* **Word 5-10 return labels.docx**, *[your initials]* **Word 5-10 mailing labels.docx**, and *[your initials]* **Word 5-10 mailing labels merge.docx**

Create a full sheet of return mailing labels.

- Select the types of labels to be used for your return labels. Look online to find specific label information.
- Type the information to be included on the return labels and create a full page of the same label.
- Save the return labels as [your initials] Word 5-10 return labels.

Use an existing database as your data source or type a new list with recipient information. Complete the merge to a new document to edit individual labels. Modify your document according to the following guidelines:

- Select the types of labels to be used for your return labels.
- Select and sort recipients.
- Insert address block or individual merge fields.
- Change font and size as desired.
- Update all labels.
- Preview the labels
- Save the document as [your initials] Word 5-10 mailing labels.
- Complete the merge to edit individual documents.
- Save the merged mailing labels as [your initials] Word 5-10 mailing labels merge.

Using Custom Styles and Building Blocks

CHAPTER OVERVIEW

In Chapter 2, you learned about styles and how to apply styles to text. This chapter provides additional information about creating and managing custom styles. You will also create building blocks, which are saved blocks of information or graphics. Building blocks, like styles, save time and help produce documents that are consistent in format. This chapter also covers *Quick Parts* building blocks, *AutoText* building blocks, document property fields, and Word fields.

STUDENT LEARNING OUTCOMES (SLOs)

After completing this chapter, you will be able to:

SLO 6.1 Create and modify styles using the *Style* gallery and *Styles* pane (p. W6-344).

SLO 6.2 Customize a document by managing styles and using a styles template (p. W6-353).

SLO 6.3 Use the *Building Blocks Organizer* to create and save information in a document (p. W6-364).

SLO 6.4 Create *AutoText* building blocks to save text and objects and insert building blocks into a document (p. W6-368).

SLO 6.5 Use the *Quick Parts* gallery to store building blocks and insert building blocks into a document (p. W6-374).

SLO 6.6 Customize and use document properties and Word fields in a document (p. W6-375).

CASE STUDY

In the Pause & Practice projects in this chapter, you create a styles template and a document detailing flexibility exercises for the American River Cycling Club. In these documents, you apply many of the features you learn in this chapter to create, save, and insert information in a document.

Pause & Practice 6-1: Create, save, and modify styles in a new document.

Pause & Practice 6-2: Create a style template to create, save, and manage styles, and attach a styles template to a document.

Pause & Practice 6-3: Use the *Building Blocks Organizer* and *AutoText* entries to save information and insert it into a document.

Pause & Practice 6-4: Customize the *Quick Parts* gallery and use document property fields in a document.

Creating and Using Custom Styles

Recall from *SLO 2.7: Using Styles and Themes* that **styles** are a collection of preset formatting that you apply to selected text. Use styles to apply preset formatting to titles, section headings, paragraph headings, text, lists, and tables. You can apply or modify existing Word styles or create new styles. When you modify a style, Word automatically updates all text where that style is applied.

Themes are a collection of fonts, colors, and effects that apply to an entire document. Use styles and themes to apply consistent formatting throughout a single document or multiple documents. The default theme of a new document is *Office*. When you change the theme of a document, the font, size, color, and other attributes of each style change.

Style Gallery

The **Style gallery** is in the *Styles* group on the *Home* tab and contains commonly used styles. Click the **More** button in the *Style* gallery to display all of the styles in the gallery (Figure 6-1). Use the **Styles** down arrow to scroll through the styles in the *Style* gallery.

Figure 6-1 *Style* gallery

Apply a style to selected text or a paragraph by clicking a style in the *Style* gallery. When you place your pointer on a style, Word temporarily applies the style to the selected text for a preview of how the text will appear with the style applied.

> **ANOTHER WAY**
>
> Apply a style from the mini toolbar when you select or right-click text.

Styles Pane

The **Styles pane** lists many of the available styles in the document and in the *Style* gallery. By default, this pane does not list all of the available styles in a document. Use the *Styles* pane to apply a style, modify a style, or create a new style from the *Styles* pane.

▶ **HOW TO:** Use the Styles Pane

1. Select the text where you want to apply a style.
2. Click the **Styles** launcher [*Home* tab, *Styles* group] (see Figure 6-1) to open the *Styles* pane (Figure 6-2).

3. Place your pointer on a style to display the attributes of the style.

   - Check the **Show Preview** box to display a preview of styles in the *Styles* pane.

4. Click a style to apply the style to selected text.

   - Click the style drop-down arrow to display additional options.

5. Resize the *Styles* pane by clicking and dragging the top, bottom, left, or right edge.

6. Move the *Styles* pane by clicking and dragging the top bar of the pane.

   - Alternatively, click the **Task Pane Options** drop-down arrow to move, size, or close the *Styles* pane.
   - Drag the *Styles* pane to the right edge of the Word window to dock the *Styles* pane at the right.

7. Click the **X** in the upper-right corner to close the *Styles* pane.

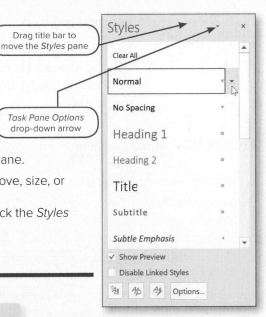

Figure 6-2 *Styles* pane

▶ ANOTHER WAY

Press **Alt+Ctrl+Shift+S** to open the *Styles* pane.

Types of Styles

Word documents include different types of styles. Apply styles to selected text or to an entire paragraph. You can also create styles for lists and tables. An icon to the right of the style in the *Styles* pane indicates the type of style (Figure 6-3). Table 6-1 lists the different types of styles and a description of each type:

Table 6-1: Types of Styles

Style Type	Description
Paragraph	Style applies to the entire paragraph.
Character	Style applies to selected text.
Linked	Style applies to selected text or an entire paragraph.
Table	Style applies to an entire table. Table styles are in the *Table Styles* gallery on the *Table Tools Design* tab.
List	Style applies to a paragraph or selected paragraphs.

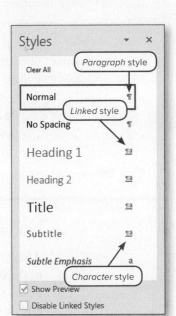

Figure 6-3 *Styles* pane with *Show Preview* turned on

▶ MORE INFO

By default, table and list styles do not display in the *Styles* pane.

Modify a Style

Use the *Modify Style* dialog box to easily modify or update a style. In the *Modify Style* dialog box, you can quickly change the name of the style, font format, and alignment. The *Format* button in the *Modify Style* dialog box displays a list of other formatting options to further customize a style.

▶**HOW TO:** Modify a Style

1. Right-click a style in the *Style* gallery or the *Styles* pane.
2. Select **Modify** from the context menu (Figure 6-4). The *Modify Style* dialog box opens (Figure 6-5).

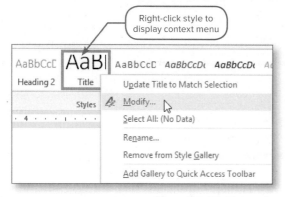

Figure 6-4 Modify a style

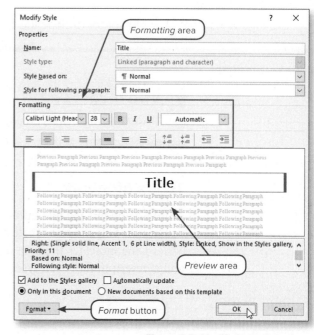

Figure 6-5 *Modify Style* dialog box

3. Type a new name for the style in the *Name* text box to rename the style.
4. Change the font, size, color, style, alignment, and line spacing in the *Formatting* area.

   - The *Preview* area displays how text appears in your document.

5. Click the **Format** button to display a list of additional formatting options (Figure 6-6).

   - When you select one of the options from the *Format* drop-down list, a dialog box opens where you select options to modify the style.

   - If you open and apply changes in one of these dialog boxes, click **OK** to close the dialog box and return to the *Modify Style* dialog box.

6. Click **OK** to close the *Modify Style* dialog box.

Update a Style

After you apply a style to text, you may need to change the format of the styled text. If you want the format changes to become a part of the style, update the style to match the new format. When you update a style, the style updates are based on the formatting of the selected text. For example, if you select text formatted with a *Heading 1* style and change the font, size, color, or paragraph spacing, you can update the *Heading 1* style to match the format applied to the selected text. When you update or modify a style, all text in the document formatted with the style updates automatically.

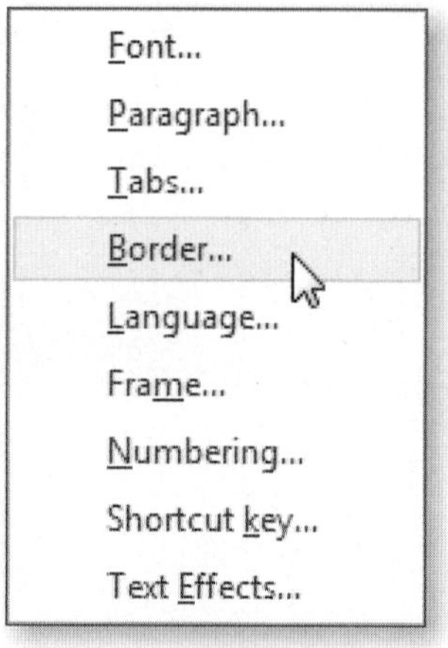

Figure 6-6 Style formatting options available from the *Format* button

▶ HOW TO: Update a Style

1. Format selected text and select the formatted text.
2. Right-click the style name to update in the *Style* gallery or the *Styles* pane.
3. Select **Update *[Style Name]* to Match Selection** from the context menu to update the style to match the selected text (Figure 6-7).

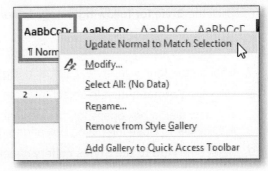

Figure 6-7 Update a style

▶ ANOTHER WAY

Right-click selected text to update a style from the *Styles* context menu on the mini toolbar.

Create a New Style

You can create a new style from scratch or create a new style based upon text that is already formatted. When creating a new style, name the style and select a style type (*Paragraph, Character, Linked, Table,* or *List*). You have the option to base the new style on an existing style, which uses the formatting of the existing style as a starting point for the new style. You also set the style for the paragraph following the text with a style applied. For example, when you press *Enter* after a *Heading 1* style, you can set *Normal* to be the style of the next paragraph.

▶ HOW TO: Create a New Style

1. Click the **Styles** launcher to open the *Styles* pane.

2. Click the **New Style** button in the bottom left of the *Styles* pane (Figure 6-8). The *Create New Style from Formatting* dialog box opens (Figure 6-9).

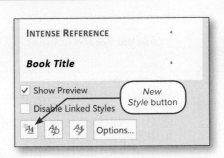

Figure 6-8 Create a new style

3. Click the **Name** text box and type the name of the style.

4. Click the **Style type** drop-down list and select the type of style.

5. Click the **Style based on** drop-down list and select a style as the starting point for the new style.

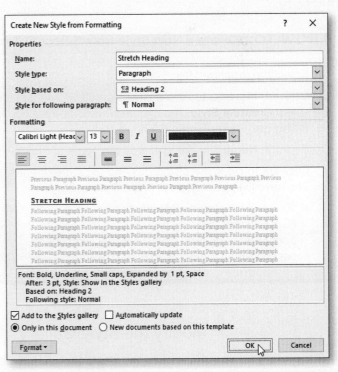

Figure 6-9 *Create New Style from Formatting* dialog box

6. Click the **Style for following paragraph** drop-down list and select the style for the paragraph following the style.

    - This option controls the style applied to the next paragraph.

7. Change the font, size, style, color, and alignment in the *Formatting* area.

8. Click the **Format** button to select from other formatting options.

    - A new dialog box opens for each format option you choose.
    - Click **OK** to close the dialog box and to return to the *Create New Style from Formatting* dialog box.

9. Select the **Add to the Styles gallery** check box to add the new style to the *Style* gallery.

    - By default, this box is checked when you create a new style.

10. Select the **Only in this document** radio button.

    - If you select **New documents based upon this template**, this style is added to the *Normal* template and is available for all new documents.

11. Click **OK** to close the dialog box.

> **▶ MORE INFO**
>
> Recall from Chapter 1 that each new document is based on the *Normal* template. This template stores the default settings for documents and controls document elements such as font, size, line spacing, paragraph spacing, alignment, and styles.

Create a New Style from Selected Text

You can also create a style based on formatted text. When you do this, Word uses the existing text format to create the new style, and you can modify the format of this style.

▶ HOW TO: Create a New Style from Selected Text

1. Select the formatted text.

2. Click the **More** button in the *Styles* group [*Home* tab] and select **Create a Style**. The *Create New Style from Formatting* dialog box opens (Figure 6-10).

3. Click the **Name** text box and type the name of the new style.

4. Click **OK** to close the dialog box and to create the new style. The new style also displays in the *Style* gallery.

    - You can also click the **Modify** button in the *Create New Style from Formatting* dialog box to open the *Create New Style from Formatting* dialog box to display additional customization options (see Figure 6-9).

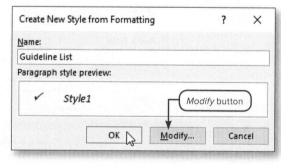

Figure 6-10 *Create New Style from Formatting dialog box*

Modify the Style Gallery

Customize the styles that display in the *Style* gallery by adding or removing styles. When you create a new style, you have the option to add it to the *Style* gallery by checking the

Add to the Styles gallery box. If you didn't check this box when you created the style, you can add a style to the *Style* gallery two different ways.

- Click the style drop-down list or right-click a style in the *Styles* pane and select **Add to Style Gallery** (Figure 6-11).
- Click the style drop-down list or right-click a style in the *Styles* pane and select **Modify** to open the *Modify Style* dialog box. Check the **Add to the Styles gallery** box and click **OK**.

To remove a style from the *Style* gallery, right-click the style in the *Style* gallery or in the *Styles* pane and select **Remove from Style Gallery**.

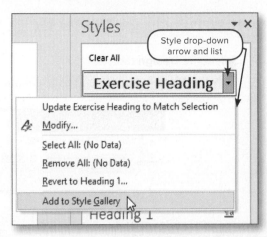

Figure 6-11 Add a style to the *Style* gallery

Clear Formatting

After you create, modify, and apply styles, you may need to remove style formatting from text in your document. You can modify style formatting or remove specific formatting such as font, size, style, color, borders, etc. Use the ***clear formatting*** option to quickly remove style formatting. When you clear formatting, the *Normal* style is applied to the text.

Select the text where you want to remove formatting and clear the formatting in one of the following ways:

- Click the **Clear All Formatting** button [*Home* tab, *Font* group] (Figure 6-12).

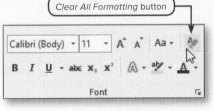

Figure 6-12 *Clear All Formatting* button in the *Font* group

- Click the **More** button in the *Styles* group [*Home* tab] and select **Clear Formatting** (Figure 6-13).
- Click the **Clear All** option in the *Styles* pane (Figure 6-14).

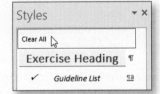

Figure 6-14 Clear formatting from the *Styles* pane

Figure 6-13 *Clear Formatting* from the *Style* gallery

- Select **Styles** from the mini toolbar and choose **Clear Formatting**.

Change Document Style Set

In addition to individual styles, Word provides ***style sets***, which are groups of styles. When you change the style set of your document, the format of all the styles in the document changes based on the style set you select. Style sets display in the *Style Sets* gallery in the *Document Formatting* group on the *Design* tab. Style sets control the font, size, styles, colors, borders, and line and paragraph spacing of a document. By default, a new Word document uses the *Word* style set.

▶HOW TO: Change the Style Set

1. Select the **Design** tab.
2. Click the **More** button [*Document Formatting* group] to display the *Style Sets* gallery (Figure 6-15).

Figure 6-15 Style Sets in the Document Formatting group

3. Select a style set from the gallery. The format of styles in your document changes based on the style set you choose.

You can also select different ***theme colors***, ***theme fonts***, and ***paragraph spacing*** to apply to your document. Click the **Colors**, **Fonts**, or **Paragraph Spacing** button in the *Document Formatting* group on the *Design* tab to display options (see Figure 6-15). Change these options to modify the existing theme in your document.

PAUSE & PRACTICE: WORD 6-1

In this Pause & Practice project, you create a Word template, modify existing styles, and create new styles. You also customize the *Style* gallery and change theme colors. You will apply the new and modified styles in *Pause & Practice 6-2*.

File Needed: None
Completed Project File Name: ***[your initials] ARCC styles.dotx***

1. Create a new Word document.
2. Save the document as a Word template.
   a. Open the *Save As* dialog box.
   b. Type [your initials] ARCC styles in the *File name* text box.
   c. Select **Word Template** in the *Save as type* drop-down list. By default, Word changes the save location to a templates folder when you select *Word Template* as the file type.
   d. Browse to the location where you save your completed files.
   e. Click **Save** to close the dialog box and save the template.
3. Change the theme color of the document.
   a. Click the **Colors** button [*Design* tab, *Document Formatting* group].
   b. Select **Orange Red** from the drop-down list.
4. Type the following text, pressing **Enter** after each line (including the last line):
   Title
   Normal
   Subtle Emphasis
   Exercise Heading
   Stretch Heading
   Guideline List

5. Apply styles to selected text.
   a. Select the word "**Title**" and click the **Title** style in the *Style* gallery [*Home* tab, *Styles* group].
   b. Select "**Subtle Emphasis**," click the **Styles** button on the mini toolbar, and select **Subtle Emphasis** from the drop-down list.

6. Modify an existing style.
   a. Select the word "**Title**" and click the **Styles** launcher to open the *Styles* pane.
   b. Right-click the **Title** style or click the **Title** drop-down arrow in the *Styles* pane and select **Modify** to open the *Modify Style* dialog box.
   c. Click the **Format** button and select **Border** to open the *Borders and Shading* dialog box (Figure 6-16).
   d. Click the **Color** drop-down list and select the **fifth color** in the **first row** of *Theme Colors* (**Orange, Accent 1**).
   e. Click the **Width** drop-down list and select **1 pt**.
   f. Click the **Top Border** and **Bottom Border** buttons in the *Preview* area to apply a **1 pt** top and bottom border.
   g. Click the **Width** drop-down arrow and select **6 pt**.
   h. Click the **Left Border** and **Right Border** buttons in the *Preview* area to apply a **6 pt** left and right border.
   i. Click **OK** to close the *Borders and Shading* dialog box and to return to the *Modify Style* dialog box.
   j. Click the **Format** button and select **Paragraph** to open the *Paragraph* dialog box.
   k. Change the *After* paragraph spacing to **24 pt** and click **OK** to close the *Paragraph* dialog box and to return to the *Modify Style* dialog box.
   l. Click the **Bold** button and the **Center** alignment button in the *Formatting* area (Figure 6-17).
   m. Click **OK** to close the *Modify Style* dialog box.

7. Modify text and update styles to match.
   a. Select the word "**Normal**" and change the line spacing to **single** (**1.0**) and the *After* paragraph spacing to **10 pt**.
   b. Right-click the **Normal** style in the *Style* gallery and select **Update Normal to Match Selection** (Figure 6-18).
   c. Select the words "**Subtle Emphasis**" and apply **bold** formatting.
   d. Right-click the **Subtle Emphasis** style in the *Styles* pane and select **Update Subtle Emphasis to Match Selection**.

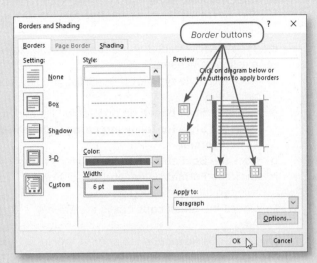

Figure 6-16 *Borders and Shading* dialog box

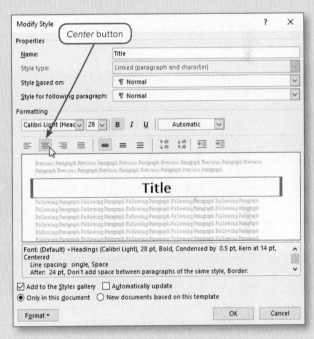

Figure 6-17 Modify the *Title* style

Figure 6-18 Update style to match selection

8. Create a new style.
   a. Select the "**Stretch Heading**" text in your document.
   b. Click the **New Style** button at the bottom left of the *Styles* pane (Figure 6-19) to open the *Create New Style from Formatting* dialog box.
   c. Type Stretch Heading in the *Name* text box to replace the existing style name.
   d. Click the **Style type** drop-down list and select **Paragraph** if necessary.
   e. Click the **Style based on** drop-down list and select **Heading 2**.
   f. Click the **Style for following paragraph** drop-down list and select **Normal**.
   g. Click the **Bold** and **Underline** buttons in the *Formatting* area.
   h. Click the **Format** button and select **Font** to open the *Font* dialog box.
   i. Check the **Small caps** box in the *Effects* area.
   j. Select the *Advanced* tab and set the *Spacing* to be **Expanded** by **1 pt** and click **OK** to close the *Font* dialog box and return to the *Create New Style from Formatting* dialog box.
   k. Click the **Format** button and select **Paragraph** to open the *Paragraph* dialog box.
   l. Change the *After* paragraph spacing to **3 pt** and click **OK** to close the *Paragraph* dialog box and return to the *Create New Style from Formatting* dialog box.
   m. Confirm the **Add to Styles gallery** box is checked and click **OK** to close the dialog box and to create the new style. The *Stretch Heading* style applies to the selected text, and the style appears in the *Style* gallery and the *Styles* pane (Figure 6-20).

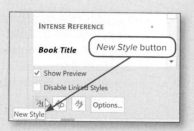

Figure 6-19 *New Style* button in the *Styles* pane

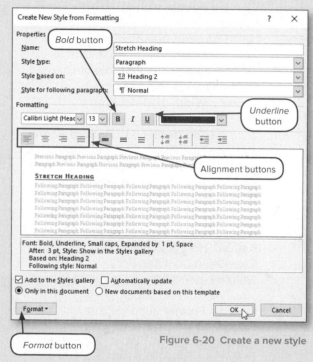

Figure 6-20 Create a new style

9. Create another new style.
   a. Select the "**Exercise Heading**" text in your document and click the **New Style** button in the *Styles* pane. The *Create New Style from Formatting* dialog box opens.
   b. Enter the following information to create the new style:
      Name: Exercise Heading
      Style type: **Paragraph**
      Style based on: **Heading 1**
      Style for following paragraph: **Stretch Heading**
      Formatting area: **Bold** and **Center** alignment
   c. Click the **Format** button and select **Border** to open the *Borders and Shading* dialog box.
   d. Change the border *Color* to **Orange, Accent 1** (**fifth color** in the **first row** of *Theme Colors*), the *Width* to ½ pt, and click the **Top Border** and **Bottom Border** buttons in the *Preview* area.
   e. Click the **Shading** tab, click the **Fill** drop-down list, select the **first color** in the **second row** of *Theme Colors* (**White, Background 1, Darker 5%**), and click **OK** to close the *Borders and Shading* dialog box.
   f. Click the **Format** button and select **Paragraph** to open the *Paragraph* dialog box.
   g. Change the *After* paragraph spacing to **12 pt** and click **OK** to close the *Paragraph* dialog box.
   h. Click **OK** to close the *Create New Style from Formatting* dialog box and to create the new style.

10. Create a new style based on formatted text.
    a. Select the "**Guideline List**" text in your document and apply **italic** formatting.
    b. Click the **Bullets** drop-down arrow [*Home* tab, *Paragraph* group] and select **Define New Bullet** to open the *Define New bullet* dialog box.
    c. Click the **Symbol** button to open the *Symbol* dialog box and select **Wingdings** from the *Font* drop-down list.
    d. Select the **check mark** symbol (*Character code* 252), click **OK** to close the *Symbol* dialog box, and click **OK** to close the *Define New Bullet* dialog box.
    e. Open the *Paragraph* dialog box, confirm that the *Left* and *Hanging* indents are **0.25"** (change them if they are not), change the *After* paragraph spacing to **12 pt**, and click **OK** to close the dialog box.
    f. Click the **More** button [*Home* tab, *Styles* group] to display the *Style* gallery, and select **Create a Style**. The *Create New Style from Formatting* dialog box opens (Figure 6-21).
    g. Type Guideline List in the *Name* text box to replace the existing style name and click **OK** to close the dialog box.

11. Remove styles from the *Style* gallery.
    a. Right-click the **Heading 1** style in the *Style* gallery and select **Remove from Style Gallery** from the context menu (Figure 6-22).
    b. Right-click the **Heading 2** style in the *Styles* pane and select **Remove from Style Gallery** from the context menu.

12. Save and close the document (Figure 6-23).

Figure 6-21 *Create New Style from Formatting* dialog box

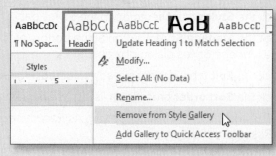

Figure 6-22 Remove a style from the *Style* gallery

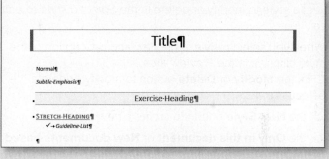

Figure 6-23 *ARCC styles* completed

Managing Styles

After creating and modifying styles, you can choose which styles display in the *Styles* pane, delete styles from a document, modify or rename styles, and reorder styles in the *Styles* pane and *Style* gallery. You can also import styles from or export styles to another document. Recall from Chapter 5 that templates store styles you have created or modified, and templates can be attached to other Word files.

Manage Styles Dialog Box

In the previous section of this chapter, you modified existing styles in the *Style* gallery and *Styles* pane and created new styles. In this section, you use the ***Manage Styles dialog box*** to customize how styles display in the *Style* gallery or the *Styles* pane.

Edit a Style

The following options are available on the *Edit* tab in the *Manage Styles* dialog box:

- Change sort order.
- Preview a style.
- Modify a style.
- Delete a style.
- Create a new style.
- Import and export styles.

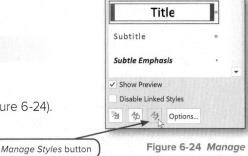

▶ HOW TO: Edit Styles in the Manage Styles Dialog Box

1. Click the **Styles** launcher to open the *Styles* pane.
2. Click the **Manage Styles** button at the bottom of the *Styles* pane (Figure 6-24). The *Manage Styles* dialog box opens.
3. Click the **Edit** tab if it is not already selected (Figure 6-25).
4. Click the **Sort order** drop-down list and select a sort option.
   - The sort options are *Alphabetical*, *As Recommended*, *Font*, *Based on*, and *By type*.
   - To display more styles, deselect the **Show recommended styles only** check box.
   - On the *Recommend* tab, you can change which styles are recommended.
5. Select a style to modify or delete in the *Select a style to edit* area.
   - When you select a style, a preview and description of the style displays in the *Preview* area.
   - Click the **Modify** or **Delete** button to modify or delete the selected style.
6. Click the **New Style** button to create a new style.
7. Click the **Only in this document** or **New documents based on this template** radio button to specify where these styles are available.
8. Click the **Import/Export** button to open the *Organizer* dialog box where you import styles from or export styles to another Word document.
   - Importing and exporting styles is covered later in this section.
9. Click **OK** to close the *Manage Styles* dialog box.

Figure 6-24 *Manage Styles* button in the *Styles* pane

Figure 6-25 Edit styles in the *Manage Styles* dialog box

> **MORE INFO**
>
> The *Import/Export* button is available on all the tabs in the *Manage Styles* dialog box.

Recommended Styles

Recommended styles are those styles that display in the *Style* gallery and *Styles* pane by default. You can modify the recommended styles list.

▶ HOW TO: Modify the Recommended Styles List

1. Click the **Styles** launcher to open the *Styles* pane.
2. Click the **Manage Styles** button to open the *Manage Styles* dialog box.
3. Select the **Recommend** tab (Figure 6-26).
4. Deselect the **Show recommended styles only** check box to display all available styles.
5. Reorder styles by selecting a style and clicking the **Move Up** or **Move Down** button.
   - Sort order determines the order of styles displayed in the *Styles* gallery and *Styles* pane.
6. Modify the recommended styles list by selecting a style and clicking the **Show**, **Hide until used**, or **Hide** button.
   - When you click *Hide until used* on a selected style, the style does not display until you apply the previous style. For example, the *Heading 2* style does not display in the *Style* gallery or *Styles* pane until you apply the *Heading 1* style in a document.
7. Click the **Only in this document** or **New documents based on this template** radio button to determine where these styles are available.
8. Click **OK** to close the *Manage Styles* dialog box.

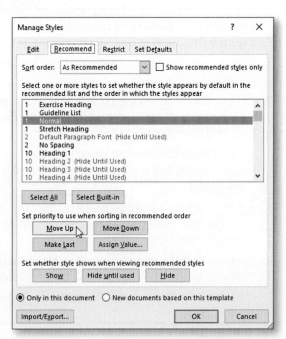

Figure 6-26 Recommended styles in the *Manage Styles* dialog box

Style Pane Options

Use the ***Style Pane Options dialog box*** to control which styles display and their order. The options in this dialog box control only the styles in the *Styles* pane, not those in the *Style* gallery. If you display additional styles in the *Styles* pane, you can always add a style to the *Style* gallery (see *SLO 6.1: Creating and Using Custom Styles*).

▶ HOW TO: Modify Style Pane Options

1. Click the **Styles** launcher to open the *Styles* pane.
2. Check the **Show Preview** box in the *Styles* pane to display a preview of the format of each style.
3. Click the **Options** link (Figure 6-27) to open the *Style Pane Options* dialog box (Figure 6-28).
4. Click the **Select styles to show** drop-down list and select which styles to display in the *Styles* pane.
   - The available options are *Recommended*, *In use*, *In current document*, and *All styles*.
5. Click the **Select how list is sorted** drop-down list and select how to sort the styles in the *Styles* pane.
   - The sort options are *Alphabetical*, *As Recommended*, *Font*, *Based on*, and *By type*.

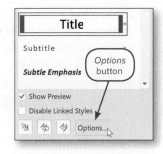

Figure 6-27 *Options* link in the *Styles* pane

6. Display text formatting as a style in the *Styles* pane by selecting one or more of the options in the *Select formatting to show as styles* area: **Paragraph level formatting**, **Font formatting**, or **Bullet and numbering formatting** (see Figure 6-28).

   - These options display text formatting similar to how a style displays (Figure 6-29).

7. Control how built-in styles display in the *Styles* pane by selecting one or more of the options in the *Select how built-in style names are shown* area.

   - The *Show next heading when previous level is used* check box controls the availability of styles that are marked as *Hide until used*.

   - If the *Hide built-in name when an alternate name exists* box is checked, built-in styles that have been renamed are not listed in the *Styles* pane.

8. Click the **Only in this document** or **New documents based on this template** radio button to determine where these styles are available.

9. Click **OK** to close the *Style Pane Options* dialog box.

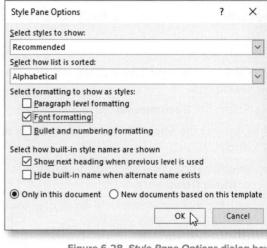

Figure 6-28 *Style Pane Options* dialog box

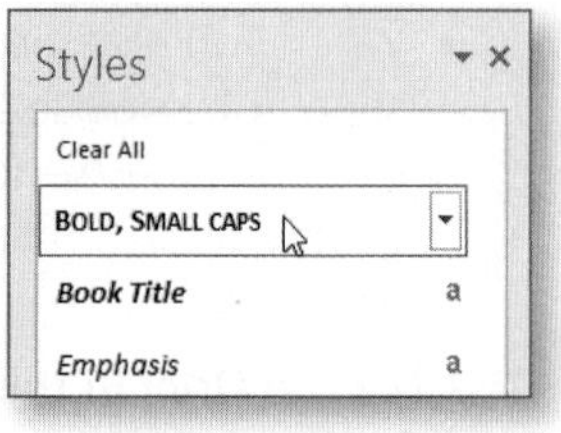

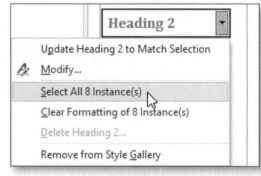

Figure 6-29 Formatting displayed as styles

Select and Clear All Styles

In a document, you may want to replace all of one style with another style or clear all formatting of one style. Word enables you to select all instances of a specific style in your document. This is an excellent way to modify all text formatted with a specific style at one time rather than change each occurrence individually.

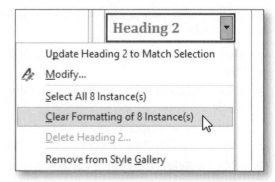

Figure 6-30 Select all instances of a style in a document

▶**HOW TO:** Select All Formatting

1. Right-click a style in the *Style* gallery or *Styles* pane.

2. Choose **Select All** (Figure 6-30) to select all instances of the style in the document.

   - The number of instances this style is used in the document displays after the words "*Select All.*"
   - If the selected style is not used in the document, the *Select All* option is not active.

3. Apply a different style, change formatting and update the style to match selection, or clear formatting for the selected style.

4. Remove all formatting on all instances of a specific style by selecting **Clear Formatting of Instances** (Figure 6-31).

   - The *Clear Formatting* option is also available from the *Styles* drop-down list on the mini toolbar and in the *Styles* pane.

5. Click anywhere in the document to deselect the selected text.

Figure 6-31 Clear formatting for all instances of a style

Find and Replace Styles

Recall from Chapter 2 that you use *Find and Replace* to find text or formatting in a document and replace it with different text or formatting. You can also use *Find and Replace* to find a specific style and replace it with a different one.

Figure 6-32 *Find Style* dialog box

▶ HOW TO: Find and Replace Styles

1. Click the **Replace** button [*Home* tab, *Editing* group] to open the *Find and Replace* dialog box.
2. Click the **More** button to display additional search options if they are not already displayed.
3. Click the **Find what** text box.
4. Click the **Format** button and select **Styles** to open the *Find Style* dialog box (Figure 6-32).
5. Select the style to find and click **OK** to close the *Find Style* dialog box.
6. Click the **Replace with** text box.
7. Click the **Format** button and select **Style** to open the *Replace Style* dialog box.
8. Select the style you want to find and click **OK** to close the dialog box.
9. Click the **Find Next** button to highlight the first occurrence of the style in the document (Figure 6-33).
10. Click the **Replace** or **Replace All** button to replace an individual occurrence or all of the occurrences of a style with a different style.
11. Click **Cancel** (or the **X** in the upper-right corner) when you are finished.

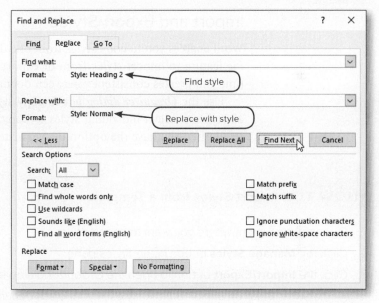

Figure 6-33 Find and replace styles

Expand or Collapse Headings

After applying styles to the headings in a document, use the ***Expand/Collapse*** feature to display or hide the text below headings. When you collapse a heading, the information below the heading does not display. Collapse or expand a single heading or all headings in the document. This feature is useful to collapse headings in a multi-page document and display only the headings in the document.

▶ HOW TO: Expand or Collapse Headings

1. Right-click the heading to collapse.
2. Click **Expand/Collapse** from the context menu.

3. Select from the available options: **Expand Heading**, **Collapse Heading**, **Expand All Headings**, and **Collapse All Headings** (Figure 6-34).

- Alternatively, click the **Expand/Collapse** button (small gray triangle) to the left of the heading to collapse or expand a heading (see Figure 6-34).

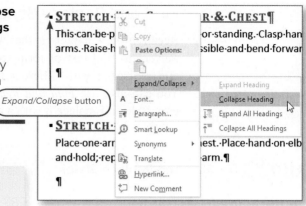

Figure 6-34 *Collapse Heading* option

> **MORE INFO**
>
> When *Show/Hide* is turned on, a small, black square displays to the left of a heading where a style has been applied. This indicator helps you locate heading styles in a document.

Import and Export Styles

Word enables you to copy styles from one document to another. Use the ***importing and exporting*** feature to import styles from or export styles to a different document. This feature saves time and creates consistency between documents.

Use the ***Organizer dialog box*** to copy styles from one document to another. You can copy all styles or select individual styles to copy. When copying built-in styles from one document to another, you have the option to overwrite the existing built-in styles with the copied styles.

▶ HOW TO: Import Styles from a Template

1. Open the document where you want to import styles.
2. Click the **Manage Styles** button in the *Styles* pane.
3. Click the **Import/Export** button to open the *Organizer* dialog box.
   - The styles listed on the left are the styles in your open document.
   - The styles listed on the right are the styles in the *Normal* template.
4. Click the **Close File** button on the right to close the *Normal* template.
5. Click the **Open File** button to open the file containing the styles to import. The *Open* dialog box displays.
6. Browse to find the file containing the styles to import and click **Open**.
   - If you are importing from a regular Word document (.docx) or a file other than a template file, select the appropriate file type from the list of options available to the right of the *File name* text box.
7. Select the styles from the list on the right to copy (import) into your open document (style list on the left) (Figure 6-35).
8. Click the **Copy** button.

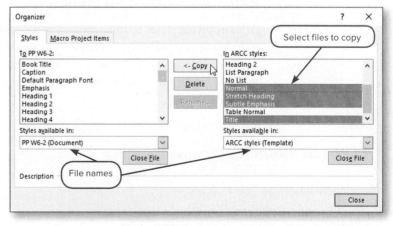

Figure 6-35 Copy styles using the *Organizer* dialog box

- If you are importing styles that have the same names as the styles in the open document, a dialog box opens asking if you want to overwrite the existing styles. Select **Yes to All** to overwrite existing styles (Figure 6-36).

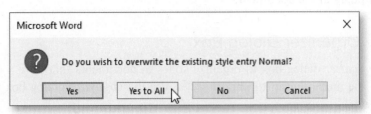

Figure 6-36 Overwrite existing styles

9. Click **Close** to close the *Organizer* dialog box.
- The imported styles display in the *Style* gallery and the *Styles* pane (Figure 6-37).

Figure 6-37 Imported styles displayed in the *Styles* pane

The process to export styles is similar to the importing process. When importing or exporting styles, always verify you are using the correct files to import and export styles. The name of the file displays above each of the styles lists in the *Organize* dialog box (see Figure 6-35).

Styles Template

In *Pause & Practice 6-1*, you created a template containing new styles and modified styles. This is called a ***styles template***. When you attach a styles template to a document, the styles in the template are available in that document. The advantage of using a styles template is that, when you update styles in the styles template, these changes automatically update in all the documents where the styles template is attached.

Attach a Template to a Document

All new Word documents are, by default, based on the *Normal* template, which contains the theme and styles for the document. You can attach a different template to a document and set the styles from the template to update automatically in the document(s) where the template is attached.

▶ **HOW TO: Attach a Template to a Document**

1. Open the document where you want to attach a template.
2. Click the **Document Template** button [*Developer* tab, *Templates* group] to open the *Templates and Add-ins* dialog box (Figure 6-38).
   - If the *Developer* tab is not available, click the **File** tab, select **Options**, click **Customize Ribbon**, check the **Developer** box under *Main Tabs* in the *Customize the Ribbon* area, and click **OK**.
3. Click the **Attach** button. The *Attach Template* dialog box opens.
4. Browse to find the template and click **Open**.
5. Check the **Automatically update document styles** check box.
   - If you do not check this box, styles in the document will not update when you modify styles in the template.
6. Click **OK** to close the *Templates and Add-ins* dialog box.

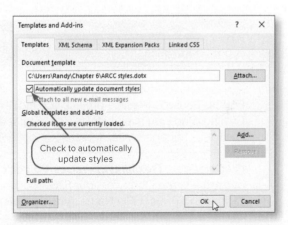

Figure 6-38 Attach a template to a document

When modifying styles in a template attached to other documents, make sure the other documents are closed. After modifying the styles in the template, save and close the template. When you open a document based on the modified template, the styles from the template automatically update in the document.

Use the Organizer Dialog Box

Use the *Organizer* dialog box to organize styles in documents that have a template attached. Similar to the method used to import styles, use the *Organizer* dialog box to copy, delete, or rename styles.

▶**HOW TO:** Use the Organizer Dialog Box

1. Open the document that has a template attached.
2. Click the **Document Template** button [*Developer* tab, *Templates* group] to open the *Templates and Add-ins* dialog box (see Figure 6-38).
3. Click the **Organizer** button to open the *Organizer* dialog box.
4. Click the **Styles available in** drop-down arrow on the left to select from the available documents and templates (Figure 6-39).
5. Select a style from the style list and **Copy**, **Rename**, or **Delete** the style.
6. Click **Close** to close the *Organizer* dialog box.

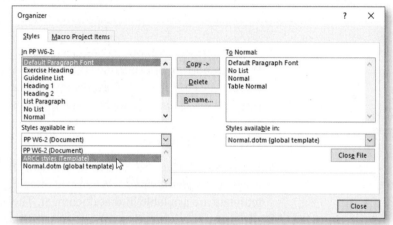

Figure 6-39 *Organizer* dialog box

▶ MORE INFO

If you accidentally create a style and add it to the *Normal* template, use the *Organizer* dialog box to delete the style.

PAUSE & PRACTICE: WORD 6-2

For this Pause & Practice project, you modify a document about flexibility exercises for the American River Cycling Club. You import styles from a template, attach a styles template to a document, replace and modify styles, manage styles, and change options in the *Styles* pane.

Files Needed: **FlexibilityExercises-06.docx** and **[your initials] ARCC styles.dotx** *(Student data files are available in the* Library *of your SIMnet account.)*
Completed Project File Name: **[your initials] PP W6-2.docx**

1. Open the **FlexibilityExercises-06** document from your student data files.

2. Save the document as [your initials] PP W6-2.

3. Import styles from the **[your initials] ARCC styles** template you created in *Pause & Practice 6-1*.

   a. Click the **Styles** launcher [*Home* tab, *Styles* group] to open the *Styles* pane.
   b. Click the **Manage Styles** button at the bottom of the *Styles* pane to open the *Manage Styles* dialog box (Figure 6-40).
   c. Click the **Import/Export** button to open the *Organizer* dialog box.
   d. Click the **Close File** button at the right to close the *Normal* template.
   e. Click the **Open File** button to open the *Open* dialog box.
   f. Browse to locate the **[your initials] ARCC Styles** template and click **Open**.
   g. Click **Exercise Heading** in the list of styles on the right, press the **Ctrl** key, and select the following styles (Figure 6-41):
      Guideline List
      Normal
      Stretch Heading
      Subtle Emphasis
      Title

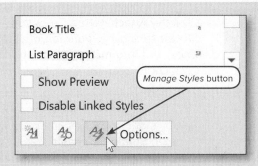

Figure 6-40 *Manage Styles* button in the *Styles* pane

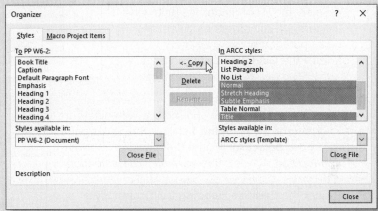

Figure 6-41 Copy styles using the *Organizer* dialog box

 MORE INFO

Use the **Ctrl** key to select multiple, non-adjacent items in a list.

   h. Click the **Copy** button to copy the selected styles to **PP W6-2**. A dialog box opens asking if you want to overwrite the existing styles.
   i. Select **Yes to All** to overwrite existing styles.
   j. Click **Close** to close the *Organizer* dialog box.

4. Attach the **[your initials] ARCC styles** template to your document.
   a. Click the **Document Template** button [*Developer* tab, *Templates* group] to open the *Templates and Add-ins* dialog box (Figure 6-42). If the *Developer* tab is not available, click the **File** tab, select **Options**, click **Customize Ribbon**, check the **Developer** box under *Main Tabs* in the *Customize the Ribbon* area, and click **OK**.

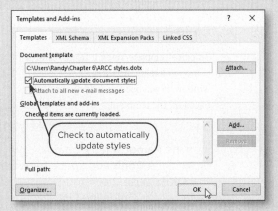

Figure 6-42 Attach the styles template to the document

b. Click the **Attach** button. The *Attach Template* dialog box opens.

c. Browse to find the *[your initials] **ARCC styles*** template and click **Open**.

d. Check the **Automatically update document styles** box.

e. Click **OK** to close the *Templates and Add-ins* dialog box.

5. Change the theme color and apply styles.

a. Click the **Colors** button [*Design* tab, *Document Formatting* group] and choose **Orange Red**.

b. Select "**static stretches**" in the second paragraph on the first page.

c. Click the **Subtle Emphasis** style from the *Style* gallery or the *Styles* pane.

d. Select the one-line paragraph that begins "**Here are some general guidelines . . .**" on the first page.

e. Click the **Intense Reference** style from the *Style* gallery or the *Styles* pane.

f. Select the list of guidelines below the "Here are some general guidelines . . ." paragraph.

g. Click the **Guideline List** style from the *Style* gallery or the *Styles* pane (Figure 6-43).

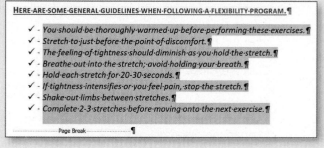

Figure 6-43 Apply a style to selected text

6. Select instances of styles and replace with different styles.

a. Right-click the **Heading 1** style in the *Styles* pane.

b. Choose **Select All** (Figure 6-44). All the text with *Heading 1* style is selected. *Note: This selection might be displayed as "Select All: (No Data)."*

c. Click the **Exercise Heading** style in the *Style* gallery or the *Styles* pane to apply the *Exercise Heading* style to selected text.

d. Right-click the **Heading 2** style and choose **Select All** to select all instances of the *Heading 2* style.

e. Click the **Stretch Heading** style in the *Style* gallery or the *Styles* pane.

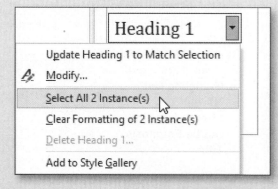

7. Save and close the document.

Figure 6-44 Select all instances of the *Heading 1* style

8. Modify a style in the styles template.

a. Display the *Open* dialog box in Word.

b. Browse to find the *[your initials] **ARCC styles*** template and click **Open**.

c. Select the "**Guideline List**" text.

> ▶ MORE INFO
>
> To edit a template, open it from Word. If you open a template from a *File Explorer* window, it will open as a document based on the template.

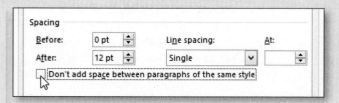

Figure 6-45 Apply formatting changes to the bulleted list

d. Open the **Paragraph** dialog box.

e. Deselect the **Don't add space between paragraphs of the same style** check box (Figure 6-45).

f. Click **OK** to close the *Paragraph* dialog box.

g. Right-click the **Guideline List** style in the *Style* gallery and select **Update Guideline List to Match Selection** to update the style (Figure 6-46).

h. Save and close the template.

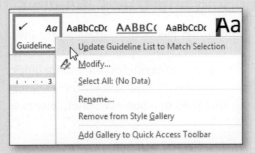

Figure 6-46 Update style to match selection

9. Open a document and change options in the *Styles* pane.
   a. Open the **[your initials] PP W6-2** document. Notice that *12 pt. After* paragraph spacing now applies to the bulleted list on the first page.
   b. Open the *Styles* pane if it is not already open.
   c. Check the **Show Preview** box if it is not already checked.
   d. Click the **Options** link in the *Styles* pane to open the *Style Pane Options* dialog box (Figure 6-47).
   e. Click the **Select how list is sorted** drop-down list and select **Alphabetical**.
   f. Click **OK** to close the dialog box.
   g. Verify the changes in the *Styles* pane.

10. Save and close the document (Figure 6-48). If prompted to save changes to the template, click **No** (or **Don't Save**).

Figure 6-47 Change sort order in the *Style Pane Options* dialog box

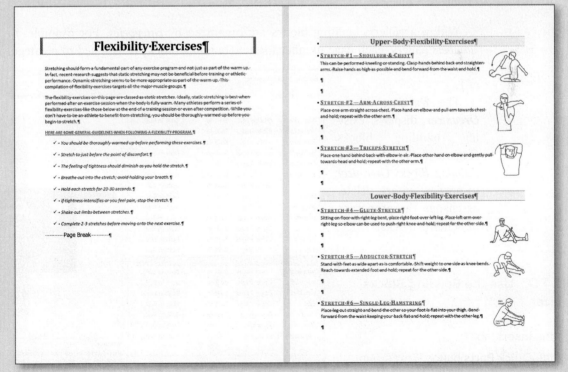

Figure 6-48 PP W6-2 completed (pages 1 and 2 of 3 pages)

SLO 6.3

Understanding and Using Building Blocks

Building blocks are stored pieces of information to insert in documents. The built-in headers and footers, page numbers, cover pages, tables of contents, and bibliographies that you have used in previous projects are examples of building blocks. In addition to using Word's built-in building blocks, you can create and save custom building blocks such as company logos, paragraphs of text, closing lines of a business letter, letterhead information, or footers.

Building Blocks Organizer

Building blocks are grouped into galleries. The following built-in ***building block galleries*** are available in Word:

- *Bibliography* gallery
- *Cover Pages* gallery
- *Equations* gallery
- *Footers* gallery
- *Headers* gallery
- *Page Numbers* gallery
- *Table of Contents* gallery
- *Tables* gallery
- *Text Boxes* gallery
- *Watermarks* gallery

> **MORE INFO**
>
> *Quick Parts* and *AutoText* building block galleries are covered later in this chapter.

Within a gallery, building blocks are organized by ***categories***. For example, in the *Page Numbers* gallery, each page number format (building block) is assigned to a category such as *Simple*, *Page X*, or *Page X of Y*.

The ***Building Blocks Organizer*** displays existing building blocks (Figure 6-49). Use the *Building Blocks Organizer* to preview, insert, delete, or change the properties of building blocks.

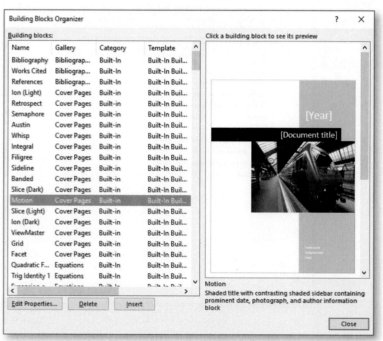

Figure 6-49 *Building Blocks Organizer* dialog box

▶ HOW TO: Use the Building Blocks Organizer

1. Click the **Insert** tab.
2. Click the **Quick Parts** button [*Text* group].
3. Select **Building Blocks Organizer** to open the *Building Blocks Organizer* dialog box (see Figure 6-49).

- The *Name*, *Gallery*, *Category*, and *Template* of each building block display.
- By default, building blocks display in alphabetical order by gallery.
- Click a column heading to change the sort order.

4. Select a building block to preview it on the right side of the dialog box.

- You can change the properties of a building block or delete or insert a building block by clicking the **Edit Properties**, **Delete**, or **Insert** button.

5. Click **Close** to close the *Building Blocks Organizer*.

Create a Building Block

By default, built-in building blocks are stored in the *Building Block* template. The built-in building blocks are available in all new documents. You can create your own building block, add it to a gallery, assign it to a category, and select the template where you want to save it.

When you create a new building block, it is important to decide where to save it. If you are using a styles template and attaching it to other documents, save your custom building blocks in this template. The custom building blocks are then available in all documents where you attach the styles template.

▶ HOW TO: Create a Building Block

1. Select the information to save as a building block (Figure 6-50).

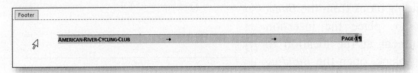

Figure 6-50 Select information to save as a building block

2. Click the button of the gallery where you want to save the building block.

- For example, if you are saving a footer building block to the *Footer* gallery, click the **Footer** button [*Header & Footer* group].

3. Select **Save Selection to [gallery name] Gallery** (Figure 6-51). The *Create New Building Block* dialog box opens (Figure 6-52).

4. Type a name for the building block in the **Name** text box.

5. Click the **Gallery** drop-down list and select a gallery to store the building block.

- This step is only necessary if you want to save the building block in a different gallery.

6. Click the **Category** drop-down list and select a category for the building block.

- By default, new building blocks are saved in the *General* category.
- You can create a new category or choose a different category.

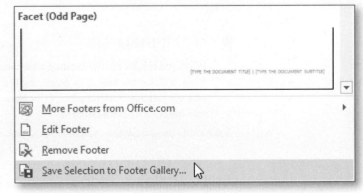

Figure 6-51 Save selection to *Footer Gallery*

7. Type a description in the *Description* text box if desired; a description is optional.

8. Click the **Save in** drop-down list and choose where to save the building block.

   • Typically, your *Save in* options are *Building Blocks* or the *Normal* template.
   • If you are working on a file that is a template or has a template attached, this template is also a *Save in* option.

9. Click the **Options** drop-down list and select how you want to insert content into a document.

   • The three options are *Insert content only*, *Insert content in its own paragraph*, and *Insert content in its own page*.

10. Click **OK** to save the new building block.

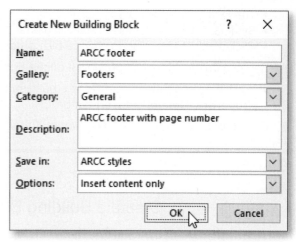

Figure 6-52 *Create New Building Block* dialog box

Insert a Building Block

After you save a building block, insert it by selecting the building block in the gallery where you saved it. For example, if you saved a *Footer* building block in the *Footers* gallery, it is available in the *Footer* drop-down list (Figure 6-53).

To insert a building block from the *Building Blocks Organizer*, place the insertion point in the document at the location to insert the building block, open the *Building Blocks Organizer*, select the building block to insert, and click the **Insert** button. The building block content is inserted in the document, and the *Building Blocks Organizer* closes (Figure 6-54).

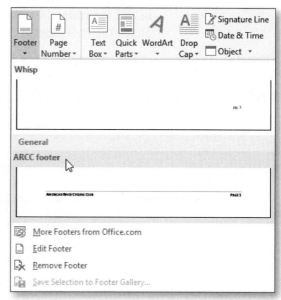

Figure 6-53 Insert *Footer* building block

> **MORE INFO**
>
> When you exit Word after creating a building block, a dialog box may open prompting you to save the building block template. Click **Save** to save the building block template.

Figure 6-54 Insert building block from the *Building Blocks Organizer*

Edit a Building Block

Use the *Building Blocks Organizer* to change building block properties. Edit the properties of a building block to change the name, assign it to a different gallery or category, or save it in a different location. You can also create a new category within a gallery.

▶ HOW TO: Edit Building Block Properties and Create a New Category

1. Click the **Quick Parts** button [*Insert* tab, *Text* group] and select **Building Blocks Organizer**.

2. Select the building block to edit and click the **Edit Properties** button to open the *Modify Building Block* dialog box.

3. Edit the building block properties as desired.

4. Click the **Category** drop-down list (Figure 6-55) and select **Create New Category**. The *Create New Category* dialog box opens (Figure 6-56).

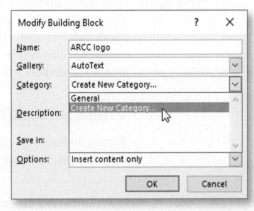

Figure 6-55 Create a new category

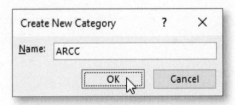

Figure 6-56 *Create New Category* dialog box

5. Type a name for the new category and click **OK**.

6. Click **OK** to close the *Modify Building Block* dialog box and to save the changes to the building block.

7. Click **Yes** in the dialog box that asks if you want to redefine the building block (Figure 6-57).

8. Click **Close** to close the *Building Blocks Organizer*.

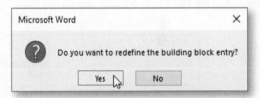

Figure 6-57 Redefine a building block

Delete a Building Block

When you no longer need a building block, use the *Building Blocks Organizer* to delete it. You cannot change the content of a building block, but you can delete the existing building block and re-create it as a new building block.

▶ HOW TO: Delete a Building Block

1. Click the **Quick Parts** button [*Insert* tab, *Text* group] and select **Building Blocks Organizer**.

2. Select a building block to delete.

3. Click the **Delete** button (Figure 6-58). A dialog box opens confirming you want to delete the building block.

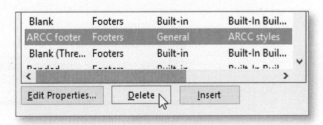

Figure 6-58 Delete a building block

4. Click **Yes** to delete the building block.

5. Click **Close** to close the *Building Blocks Organizer*.

Creating and Using AutoText Building Blocks

AutoText is another gallery where you save custom building blocks to use in documents. Use the *AutoText* gallery when the information you want to store does not belong in other building block galleries such as the *Footers* gallery or *Page Numbers* gallery. For example, you may want to save specific text or a graphic you regularly use, such as a company logo graphic, the closing lines of a business letter, the opening lines of a memo, or a paragraph of text.

Create an AutoText Building Block

Similar to how you created other building blocks, select the text or object to save as *AutoText* and save this selection as an *AutoText* building block in the *AutoText* gallery.

▶HOW TO: Create an AutoText Building Block

1. Select the text or object to save as an *AutoText* building block.
2. Click the **Quick Parts** button [*Insert* tab, *Text* group].
3. Click **AutoText** and select **Save Selection to AutoText Gallery** (Figure 6-59). The *Create New Building Block* dialog box opens (Figure 6-60).
   - The selection is assigned to the *AutoText* gallery.

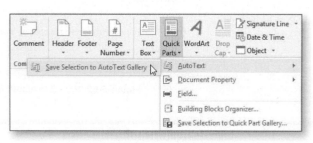

Figure 6-59 Save selection in the *AutoText* gallery

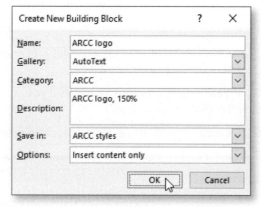

Figure 6-60 *Create New Building Block* dialog box

4. Click the **Name** text box and type a name for the *AutoText*.
5. Click the **Category** drop-down list and select a category or create a new category.
6. Click the **Description** text box and type a description of the *AutoText*. A description is optional.
7. Click the **Save in** drop-down list and select the location where you want to save the *AutoText*.
8. Click **OK** to close the dialog box and save the *AutoText*.

▶ **ANOTHER WAY**

Select the text or object to save as an *AutoText* building block and press **Alt+F3** to open the *Create New Building Block* dialog box.

Insert an AutoText Building Block

AutoText building blocks are saved in the *AutoText* gallery, which is available from the *Quick Parts* drop-down list. You can also insert an *AutoText* building block from the *Building Blocks Organizer* dialog box.

▶HOW TO: Insert an AutoText Building Block

1. Place the insertion point at the location to insert the *AutoText*.

2. Click the **Quick Parts** button and select **AutoText**. The *AutoText* gallery displays (Figure 6-61).

   - The category and name of the *AutoText* building blocks display above the building block.
   - Place your pointer on the *AutoText* building block to display its description.

3. Click the *AutoText* building block to insert it into the document.

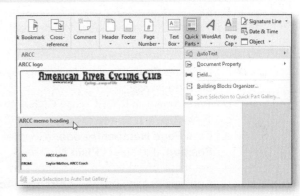

Figure 6-61 Insert *AutoText* building block from the *AutoText* gallery

Edit or Delete an AutoText Building Block

The process of editing or deleting an *AutoText* building block is similar to the process of editing other building blocks. Open the *Building Blocks Organizer* to locate the *AutoText* building blocks. Select the building block to edit or delete and click the **Edit Properties** or **Delete** button (Figure 6-62).

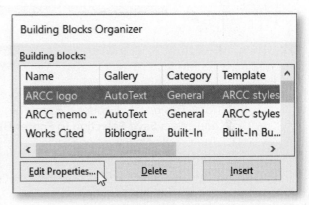

Figure 6-62 Edit *AutoText* building block properties

> **ANOTHER WAY**
>
> Right-click an *AutoText* building block and select **Edit Properties** to open the *Modify Building Block* dialog box or select **Organize and Delete** to open the *Building Blocks Organizer*.

PAUSE & PRACTICE: WORD 6-3

For this Pause & Practice project, you modify the *[your initials] ARCC styles* template you created in *Pause & Practice 6-1* to include building blocks and *AutoText* building blocks. You also insert building blocks into the flexibility document you modified in *Pause & Practice 6-2*.

Files Needed: *[your initials] ARCC styles.dotx*, *[your initials] PP W6-2.docx*, and *ARCC-logo-06.png* *(Student data files are available in the* Library of your SIMnet account.)
Completed Project File Name: *[your initials] PP W6-3.docx*

1. Open the **[your initials] ARCC styles** template you created in *Pause & Practice 6-1* and modified in *Pause & Practice 6-2*. Open the template from within Word to edit the template. Do not open the file from a *File Explorer* window, which creates a document based on the template.

2. Create a *Footer* building block.
    a. Click the **Footer** button [*Insert* tab, *Header & Footer* group] and select **Edit Footer** from the drop-down list.
    b. Type American River Cycling Club at the left margin and press **Tab** two times.
    c. Type Page and **space** once.
    d. Click **Page Number** [*Header & Footer Tools Design* tab, *Header & Footer* group], select **Current Position**, and select **Plain Number**.
    e. Select all of the text in the footer and apply **bold**, **small caps**, and **10 pt** formatting.
    f. Apply a ½ pt top border in **Orange, Accent 1** color (**fifth option** in the **first row** of *Theme Colors*).
    g. Select all the text in the footer if it is not already selected (Figure 6-63).

Figure 6-63 Select text to save as a *Footer* building block

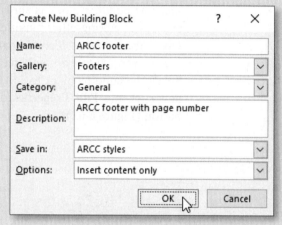

Figure 6-64 *Create New Building Block* dialog box

    h. Click the **Footer** button [*Header & Footer Tools Design* tab, *Header & Footer* group] and select **Save Selection to Footer Gallery**. The *Create New Building Block* dialog box opens.
    i. Enter the following properties for the building block (Figure 6-64):
        Name: ARCC footer
        Gallery: **Footers**
        Category: **General**
        Description: ARCC footer with page number
        Save in: **[your initials] ARCC styles**
        Options: **Insert content only**
    j. Click **OK** to close the dialog box and to save the building block.
    k. Close the footer.

3. Create a memo heading.
    a. Place the insertion point on the blank line after "Guideline List." If a blank line does not display after this line, press **Enter** after this line.
    b. Apply the **Normal** style to the blank line.
    c. Type TO:, press **Tab**, type ARCC Cyclists, and press **Enter**.
    d. Type FROM:, press **Tab**, type Taylor Mathos, ARCC Coach, and press **Enter**.
    e. Type DATE:, press **Tab**, insert (don't type) current date (use January 1, 2020 format), and set to update automatically.
    f. Press **Enter** after the inserted date.
    g. Type SUBJECT: and press **Tab**.
    h. Select the first line of the memo heading ("**TO: . . .**") and change the *Before* paragraph spacing to **72 pt**.
    i. Select the last line of the memo heading ("**SUBJECT**:") and change the *After* paragraph spacing to **24 pt**.
    j. Select all four lines of the memo heading and set a **1"** left tab stop.

4. Save a memo heading as an *AutoText* building block.
   a. Select all four lines of the memo heading if they are not already selected.
   b. Click the **Quick Parts** button [*Insert* tab, *Text* group], click **AutoText**, and select **Save Selection to AutoText Gallery**. The *Create New Building Block* dialog box opens (Figure 6-65).
   c. Enter the following properties for the building block:
      Name: ARCC memo heading
      Gallery: **AutoText**
      Category: **General**
      Description: ARCC memo heading
      Save in: **[your initials] ARCC styles**
      Options: **Insert content only**
   d. Click **OK** to close the dialog box and to save the building block.

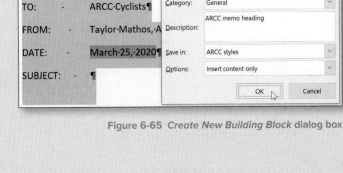

Figure 6-65 *Create New Building Block* dialog box

5. Insert a picture in the document.
   a. Place the insertion point after the tab on the last line of the memo heading and press **Enter**.
   b. Insert as a picture the ***ARCC-logo-06*** file from your student data files.
   c. Click the **Size** launcher [*Picture Tools Format* tab, *Size* group] to open the *Layout* dialog box.
   d. Change the *Height* and *Width* to **150%** in the *Scale* area on the *Size* tab.
   e. Click the **Text Wrapping** tab and change the *Wrapping style* to **Tight**.
   f. Click the **Position** tab (Figure 6-66) and change the *Horizontal* **Alignment** to **Centered** *relative to* **Page**.
   g. Change the *Vertical* **Absolute position** to **0.3** *below* **Page**.
   h. Click **OK** to close the *Layout* dialog box.

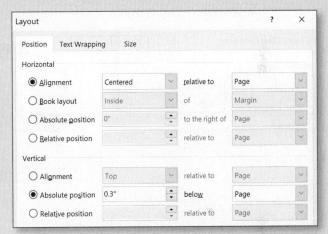

Figure 6-66 *Layout* dialog box

6. Save a graphic as an *AutoText* building block.
   a. Select the graphic at the top of the document, click the **Quick Parts** button [*Insert* tab, *Text* group], click **AutoText**, and select **Save Selection to AutoText Gallery**. The *Create New Building Block* dialog box opens.
   b. Enter the following properties for the building block:
      Name: ARCC logo
      Gallery: **AutoText**
      Category: **General**
      Description: ARCC logo, 150%
      Save in: **[your initials] ARCC styles**
      Options: **Insert content only**
   c. Click **OK** to close the dialog box and save the building block.

7. Edit building blocks to create a category.
   a. Click the **Quick Parts** button [*Insert* tab, *Text* group] and select **Building Blocks Organizer**. The *Building Blocks Organizer* dialog box opens.

b. Select the **ARCC logo** *AutoText* building block and click the **Edit Properties** button to open the *Modify Building Block* dialog box.

c. Click the **Category** drop-down list and select **Create New Category** (Figure 6-67). The *Create New Category* dialog box opens.

Figure 6-67 Create a new category

d. Type ARCC and click **OK** to close the *Create New Category* dialog box (Figure 6-68).

e. Click **OK** to close the *Modify Building Block* dialog box.

f. Click **Yes** when the dialog opens confirming you want to redefine the building block.

g. Select the **ARCC memo heading** *AutoText* building block in the *Building Blocks Organizer* and click the **Edit Properties** button.

h. Click the **Category** drop-down list and select **ARCC**.

i. Click **OK** to close the *Modify Building Block* dialog box and click **Yes** to confirm the change.

j. Click **Close** to close the *Building Blocks Organizer*.

8. Save and close the *[your initials] **ARCC** styles* template (Figure 6-69).

Figure 6-68 Name the new category

Figure 6-69 *ARCC styles* template completed

9. Open the *[your initials] **PP W6-2*** file you created in *Pause & Practice 6-2*.

10. Save the document as [your initials] PP W6-3.

11. Move the first page heading to the second page.
    a. Select "**Flexibility Exercises**" heading (including the paragraph mark) and cut (**Ctrl+X**) from the first page.
    b. Place the insertion point before "Upper-Body Flexibility Exercises" on the second page.
    c. Paste (**Ctrl+V**) the heading you cut from the first page.

12. Insert building blocks into the document.
    a. Place the insertion point at the beginning of the first page.
    b. Click the **Quick Parts** button [*Insert* tab, *Text* group] and select **AutoText**.

c. Click the **ARCC memo heading** *AutoText* building block to insert it into the document (Figure 6-70). The memo heading displays at the top of the document.

d. Place the insertion point at the beginning of the first body paragraph below the memo heading lines if it is not already at that location.

e. Insert the **ARCC logo** *AutoText* building block into the document. The logo displays at the top of the document.

f. Click the **Footer** button [*Insert* tab, *Header & Footer* group].

g. Scroll down the list of footers and select the **ARCC footer** building block (Figure 6-71).

h. Delete the blank line below the footer text and close the footer.

13. Save and close the document (Figure 6-72). If prompted to save changes to the template, click **No** (or **Don't Save**).

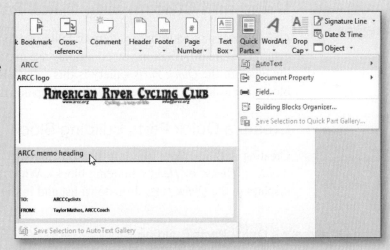

Figure 6-70 Insert *ARCC memo heading* building block

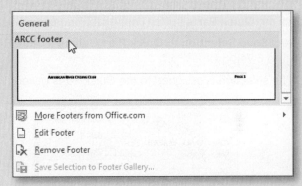

Figure 6-71 Insert *ARCC footer* building block

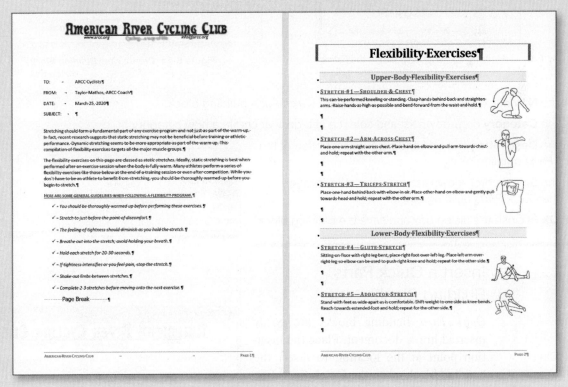

Figure 6-72 PP W6-3 completed (pages 1 and 2 of 3 pages)

Using and Customizing Quick Parts Building Blocks

Quick Parts is an additional gallery of building blocks available in Word. Use the *Quick Parts* gallery to store information you commonly use in documents. The advantage of saving a building block in the *Quick Parts* gallery is this gallery is very easy to access. *Quick Parts* building blocks are available from the *Quick Parts* drop-down list on the *Insert* tab.

Create a Quick Parts Building Block

Creating a *Quick Parts* building block is similar to creating other building blocks such as *AutoText*, *Footer*, or *Header* building blocks. When you create a *Quick Parts* building block, it displays in the *Quick Parts* drop-down list and in the *Building Blocks Organizer*.

▶**HOW TO:** Create a Quick Parts Building Block

1. Select the text or object you want to save as a *Quick Parts* building block.
2. Click the **Quick Parts** button [*Insert* tab, *Text* group].
3. Select **Save Selection to Quick Part Gallery** (Figure 6-73). The *Create New Building Block* dialog box opens (Figure 6-74).
   - The selection is assigned to the *Quick Parts* gallery.

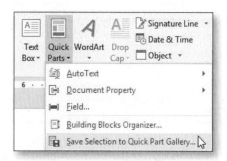

Figure 6-73 Save selection in the *Quick Parts* gallery

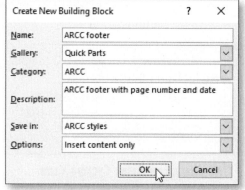

Figure 6-74 *Create New Building Block* dialog box

4. Click the **Name** text box and type a name for the *Quick Parts* building block.
5. Click the **Category** drop-down list and select a category or create a new category.
6. Click the **Description** text box and type a description of the *Quick Parts* building block.
7. Click the **Save in** drop-down list and select the location to save the *Quick Parts* building block.
8. Click **OK** to close the dialog box and save the building block.

Insert a Quick Parts Building Block

Quick Parts building blocks are easily inserted into a document. Place the insertion point at the location to insert the building block, click the **Quick Parts** button in the *Text* group on the *Insert* tab, and select the *Quick Parts* building block to insert (Figure 6-75).

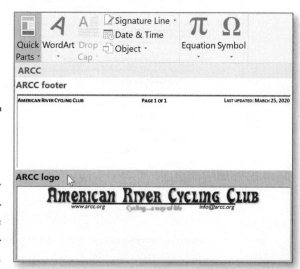

Figure 6-75 Insert *Quick Parts* building block from the *Quick Parts* gallery

Edit or Delete a Quick Parts Building Block

Edit and delete *Quick Parts* building blocks the same way you edit and delete other building blocks. You can also edit regularly used building blocks stored in other galleries so they are available in the *Quick Parts* gallery.

> **HOW TO: Add a Building Block to the Quick Parts Gallery**

1. Click the **Quick Parts** button [*Insert* tab, *Text* group] and select **Building Blocks Organizer**. The *Building Blocks Organizer* dialog box opens.
2. Select the building block to add to the *Quick Parts* gallery.
3. Click the **Edit Properties** button to open the *Modify Building Block* dialog box.
4. Click the **Gallery** drop-down list and select **Quick Parts** (Figure 6-76).
5. Edit the building block properties as desired.
   - Create a new category in *Quick Parts* if desired.
   - You can have multiple *Quick Parts* categories, and *Quick Parts* are grouped by the categories in the drop-down list.
6. Click **OK** to save the changes to the *Quick Parts* building block.
7. Click **Yes** when the dialog box opens asking you to confirm that you want to redefine the style.
8. Click **Close** to close the *Building Blocks Organizer* dialog box.

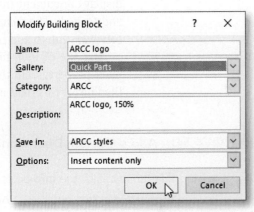

Figure 6-76 Add a building block to the *Quick Parts* gallery

---

> **SLO 6.6**

Using Document Properties and Word Fields

Each document you create and save includes *document properties*. Document properties are a category of Word *fields*. Word fields are special codes you insert into a document. Word fields, such as the *Company* document property field, the *NumPages* field (number of pages in the document), or a formula field, automatically insert content into a document.

> ### MORE INFO
>
> Chapter 7 describes how to insert a custom formula field.

Document Properties

To view and edit document properties, use the *Backstage* view. You can edit document properties such as *Title, Company*, and *Comments*, while others are automatically generated and cannot be changed, such as *Size, Pages, Words*, and *Last Modified*.

> **HOW TO: Edit Document Properties**

1. Click the **File** tab to open the *Backstage* view (Figure 6-77).
   - If necessary, click the **Info** button on the left to display the document properties on the right.

Figure 6-77 Document properties on the *Backstage* view

2. Click a document property field text box to add or edit information.

3. Click the **Show All Properties** link at the bottom to display all document properties.

   • When all properties display, the link changes to *Show Fewer Properties*.

4. Click the **Back** arrow or press **Esc** to return to the document.

Custom Document Properties

You can also view and edit document properties in the ***Properties dialog box***. This dialog box displays document information on five different tabs: *General, Summary, Statistics, Contents,* and *Custom.* The *General, Statistics,* and *Contents* tabs display document information. Use the *Summary* tab to add or edit document properties.

Use the *Custom* tab to add a custom document property field. For example, add a document property field that is not normally available in a document such as *Department.* You can then insert this field into a document.

▶HOW TO: Add a Custom Document Property Field

1. Click the **File** tab and click the **Info** button if it is not already selected.

2. Click the **Properties** button and select **Advanced Properties**. The *[File name] Properties* dialog box opens.

3. Click the **Custom** tab.

4. Select the custom document property field to add from the list in the *Name* area.

5. Click the **Type** drop-down list and select the type of information to store in this field: **Text, Date, Number,** or **Yes or no**.

6. Click the **Value** text box and type the information you want to store in this field.

7. Click **Add** to add the custom document property field (Figure 6-78). The custom field displays in the *Properties* area.

8. Click **OK** to close the *[File name] Properties* dialog box and click the **Back** arrow to return to the document.

Figure 6-78 Add custom document properties in the *[File name] Properties* dialog box

▶ MORE INFO

Insert a custom document property field using the *Field* dialog box, which is discussed in the *Insert a Word Field* section in this chapter.

Insert a Document Property Field

You can insert document property fields in the body of a document or in the header or footer. When you insert a document property field into a document, Word inserts the content stored in that field. If you edit the contents of a document property field on the *Backstage* view or in the *Properties* dialog box, Word automatically updates the document property field in your document.

▶HOW TO: Insert a Document Property Field

1. Place the insertion point at the location to insert the document property field.
2. Click the **Quick Parts** button [*Insert* tab, *Text* group].
3. Select **Document Property** (Figure 6-79).
4. Select the document property from the list of document properties. The document property field displays in the document (Figure 6-80).
   - Use the right arrow key to deselect a document property field.

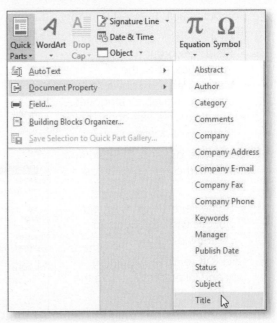

Figure 6-79 Insert document property field

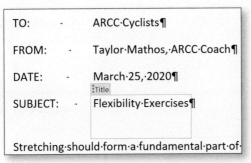

Figure 6-80 Document property field inserted into document

Insert a Word Field

You can also insert Word fields into a document. Insert a Word field using the ***Field dialog box***. Table 6-2 lists commonly used fields.

The *Field* dialog box displays the available fields. Many of the fields have field properties, which determine how the content of the field displays in the document.

Table 6-2: Commonly Used Fields

Field	Description
DocProperty	Inserts a document property or custom document property field
FileName	Inserts the document file name
NumPages	Inserts the number of pages in a document
SaveDate	Inserts the date the document was last saved
UserInitials	Inserts your initials from your Office personalization options
UserName	Inserts your name from your Office personalization options

▶HOW TO: Insert a Word Field

1. Place the insertion point in your document where you want to insert the field.
2. Click the **Quick Parts** button [*Insert* tab, *Text* group].
3. Select **Field** to open the *Field* dialog box (Figure 6-81).

4. Select the field to insert from the list in the *Field names* area.

   - Fields are grouped into categories. Click the **Categories** drop-down list to view the available categories.
   - The fields in a category display in the *Field names* area.

5. Select the format of the field from the list in the *Field properties* area.

   - Some fields also have *Field options* where you further customize fields.

6. Click **OK** to close the dialog box and insert the field into the document (Figure 6-82).

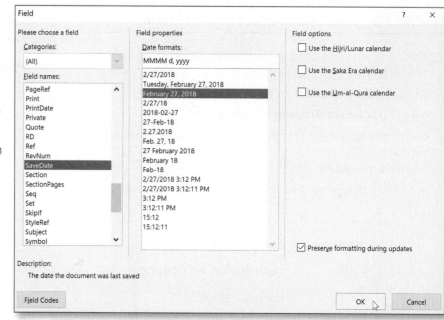

Figure 6-81 *Field* dialog box

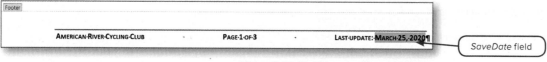

Figure 6-82 Field inserted into the footer

Personalize Microsoft Office

When you originally install and register Microsoft Office on your computer, you are prompted to provide your user name and initials to personalize Microsoft Office. These entries are Word fields that can be inserted in your documents. You can change this personalization information after Microsoft Office has been installed on your computer.

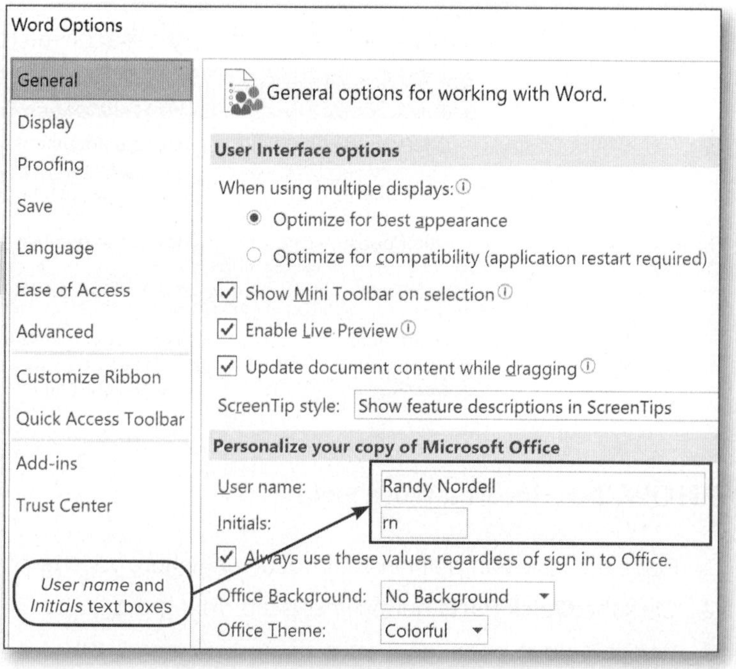

▶ **HOW TO:** Personalize Microsoft Office

1. Click the **File** tab to open the *Backstage* view.
2. Click the **Options** button to open the *Word Options* dialog box (Figure 6-83).
3. Click the **General** button.
4. Type your information in the *User name* and *Initials* text boxes in the *Personalize your copy of Microsoft Office*.
5. Click **OK** to close the *Word Options* dialog box.

Figure 6-83 Personalize Microsoft Office

Edit and Update Fields

When you insert a field in your document, you select the field and set the field properties. You can edit a field to change how it displays in your document, such as the format of a page number or a date. Right-click a field and select **Edit Field** from the context menu (Figure 6-84) to open the *Field* dialog box.

Fields in a document update automatically each time you open a document, but you may need to update a field after editing a document, such as updating a formula field when values are changed. Manually update a field by right-clicking the field and selecting **Update Field** from the context menu.

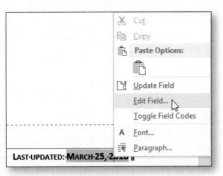

Figure 6-84 Select *Edit Field* from the context menu

> **ANOTHER WAY**
>
> Press **F9** to update a field.

For this Pause & Practice project, you delete and modify existing building blocks, add building blocks to the *Quick Parts* gallery, customize and insert document properties, and insert Word fields to finalize the flexibility document for the American River Cycling Club.

File Needed: *[your initials] PP W6-3.docx*
Completed Project File Name: *[your initials] PP W6-4.docx*

1. Open the *[your initials] PP W6-3* document completed in *Pause & Practice 6-3*.

2. Save the document as [your initials] PP W6-4.

3. Delete and modify building blocks.
    a. Click the **Quick Parts** button [*Insert* tab, *Text* group] and select **Building Blocks Organizer** to open the *Building Blocks Organizer* dialog box.
    b. Select the **ARCC footer** *Footers* building block, click the **Delete** button, and click **Yes** when the dialog box opens asking if you want to delete the building block.
    c. Select the **ARCC memo heading** *AutoText* building block, click the **Delete** button, and click **Yes** in the dialog box that asks if you want to delete the building block.
    d. Select the **ARCC logo** *AutoText* building block and click the **Edit Properties** button. The *Modify Building Block* dialog box opens.
    e. Click the **Gallery** drop-down list and select **Quick Parts** to move this building block to the *Quick Parts* gallery.
    f. Click the **Category** drop-down list and select **Create New Category**. The *Create New Category* dialog box opens.
    g. Type ARCC and click **OK** to create the new category.
    h. Select **ARCC** from the *Category* drop-down list if it is not already selected (Figure 6-85).
    i. Click **OK** to close the *Modify Building Block* dialog box and click **Yes** to confirm you want to redefine the building block.
    j. Click **Close** to close the *Building Blocks Organizer* dialog box.

4. Customize and insert document properties.
   a. Click the **File** tab to open the *Backstage* view and click **Info** on the left if it is not already selected.
   b. Type Flexibility Exercises in the *Title* document property field.
   c. Click the **Show All Properties** link at the bottom of the document properties.
   d. Type American River Cycling Club in the *Company* document property field.
   e. Click the **Back** arrow to close the *Backstage* view and to return to the document.
   f. Place the insertion point after the tab on the subject line of the memo heading.
   g. Click the **Quick Parts** button [*Insert* tab, *Text* group], click **Document Property**, and select **Title** from the list of document properties to insert the *Title* document property field (Figure 6-86).

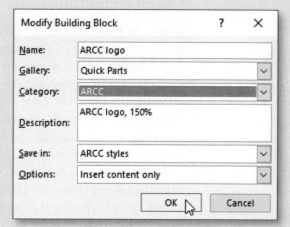

Figure 6-85 *Modify Building Block* dialog box

5. Modify the footer to include document properties and Word fields.
   a. Edit the footer on the first page of the document.
   b. Select "**American River Cycling Club**."
   c. Click the **Document Info** button [*Header & Footer Tools Design* tab, *Insert* group], click **Document Property**, and select **Company** from the list of document properties. The *Company* document property field replaces the selected text.
   d. Place the insertion point directly before "Page" in the footer and press **Backspace** to remove one tab.
   e. Place the insertion point after the page number, **space** once, type of, and **space** once.
   f. Click the **Quick Parts** button and select **Field**. The *Field* dialog box opens (Figure 6-87).

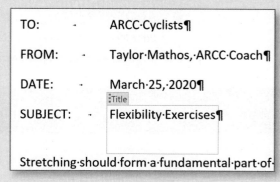

Figure 6-86 *Title* document property inserted

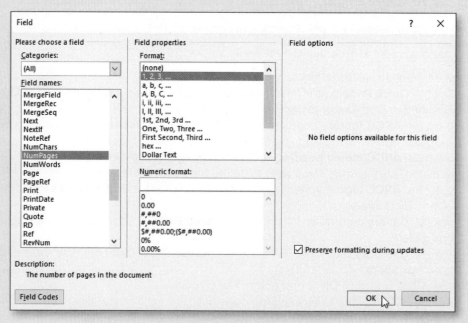

Figure 6-87 Insert *NumPages* field in the footer

g. Select **NumPages** in the *Field* names area.

h. Select **1**, **2**, **3** in the *Format* area and click **OK** to close the *Field* dialog box and to insert the field.

i. Press **Tab** after the *NumPages* field, type **Last updated:** and **space** once.

j. Click the **Quick Parts** button and select **Field**. The *Field* dialog box opens.

k. Select **SaveDate** in the *Field* names area, select the date format (use January 1, 2020 format) in the *Date formats* area, and click **OK** to close the *Field* dialog box and to insert the field.

 MORE INFO

When you insert document property and Word fields, include proper spacing before and after the field.

6. Add the footer and memo heading to the *Quick Parts* gallery.

a. Select the entire footer (Figure 6-88).

Footer

AMERICAN·RIVER·CYCLING·CLUB · PAGE·1·OF·3 · LAST·UPDATED:·MARCH·25,·2020¶

Figure 6-88 Select footer to save in the *Quick Parts* gallery

b. Click the **Quick Parts** button and select **Save Selection to Quick Part Gallery**. The *Create New Building Block* dialog box opens.

c. Enter the following properties for the building block (Figure 6-89):
Name: ARCC footer
Gallery: **Quick Parts**
Category: **ARCC**
Description: ARCC footer with page number and date
Save in: **[your initials] ARCC styles**
Options: **Insert content only**

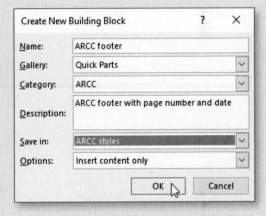

Create New Building Block ? ✕

Name: ARCC footer
Gallery: Quick Parts
Category: ARCC
Description: ARCC footer with page number and date
Save in: ARCC styles
Options: Insert content only

OK Cancel

d. Click **OK** to close the dialog box and save the building block.

e. Close the footer.

Figure 6-89 Create a new building block

f. Select the four memo heading lines.

g. Click the **Quick Parts** button and select **Save Selection to Quick Part Gallery**. The *Create New Building Block* dialog box opens.

h. Enter the following properties for the building block:
Name: ARCC memo heading
Gallery: **Quick Parts**
Category: **ARCC**
Description: ARCC memo heading
Save in: **[your initials] ARCC styles**
Options: **Insert content only**

i. Click **OK** to close the dialog box and to save the building block.

7. Save and close the document. Click **Yes** if a dialog box opens asking if you want to save changes to the **ARCC styles** template file (Figures 6-90 and 6-91).

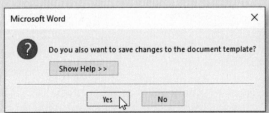
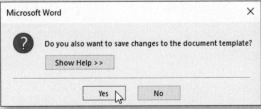

Microsoft Word ✕

? Do you also want to save changes to the document template?

Show Help >>

Yes No

Figure 6-90 Save changes in the template file

American River Cycling Club

www.arcc.org   Cycling...a way of life   info@arcc.org

TO: →   ARCC·Cyclists¶

FROM: →   Taylor·Mathos,·ARCC·Coach¶

DATE: →   March·25,·2020¶

SUBJECT: →   Flexibility·Exercises¶

Stretching·should·form·a·fundamental·part·of·any·exercise·program·and·not·just·as·part·of·the·warm-up.· In·fact,·recent·research·suggests·that·static·stretching·may·not·be·beneficial·before·training·or·athletic· performance.·Dynamic·stretching·seems·to·be·more·appropriate·as·part·of·the·warm-up.·This· compilation·of·flexibility·exercises·targets·all·the·major·muscle·groups.¶

The·flexibility·exercises·on·this·page·are·classed·as·*static·stretches*.·Ideally,·static·stretching·is·best·when· performed·after·an·exercise·session·when·the·body·is·fully·warm.·Many·athletes·perform·a·series·of· flexibility·exercises·like·those·below·at·the·end·of·a·training·session·or·even·after·competition.·While·you· don't·have·to·be·an·athlete·to·benefit·from·stretching,·you·should·be·thoroughly·warmed·up·before·you· begin·to·stretch.¶

HERE·ARE·SOME·GENERAL·GUIDELINES·WHEN·FOLLOWING·A·FLEXIBILITY·PROGRAM.¶

✓ → You·should·be·thoroughly·warmed·up·before·performing·these·exercises.¶

✓ → Stretch·to·just·before·the·point·of·discomfort.¶

✓ → The·feeling·of·tightness·should·diminish·as·you·hold·the·stretch.¶

✓ → Breathe·out·into·the·stretch;·avoid·holding·your·breath.¶

✓ → Hold·each·stretch·for·20-30·seconds.¶

✓ → If·tightness·intensifies·or·you·feel·pain,·stop·the·stretch.¶

✓ → Shake·out·limbs·between·stretches.¶

✓ → Complete·2-3·stretches·before·moving·onto·the·next·exercise.¶

------------Page Break------------¶

Flexibility·Exercises¶

Upper-Body·Flexibility·Exercises¶

- **STRETCH·#1 — SHOULDER·&·CHEST**¶
This·can·be·performed·kneeling·or·standing.·Clasp·hands·behind·back·and·straighten· arms.·Raise·hands·as·high·as·possible·and·bend·forward·from·the·waist·and·hold.¶
¶
¶

- **STRETCH·#2 — ARM·ACROSS·CHEST**¶
Place·one·arm·straight·across·chest.·Place·hand·on·elbow·and·pull·arm·towards·chest· and·hold;·repeat·with·the·other·arm.¶
¶
¶

- **STRETCH·#3 — TRICEPS·STRETCH**¶
Place·one·hand·behind·back·with·elbow·in·air.·Place·other·hand·on·elbow·and·gently·pull· towards·head·and·hold;·repeat·with·the·other·arm.¶
¶
¶

Lower-Body·Flexibility·Exercises¶

- **STRETCH·#4 — GLUTE·STRETCH**¶
Sitting·on·floor·with·right·leg·bent,·place·right·foot·over·left·leg.·Place·left·arm·over- right·leg·so·elbow·can·be·used·to·push·right·knee·and·hold;·repeat·for·the·other·side.¶
¶
¶

- **STRETCH·#5 — ADDUCTOR·STRETCH**¶
Stand·with·feet·as·wide·apart·as·is·comfortable.·Shift·weight·to·one·side·as·knee·bends.· Reach·towards·extended·foot·and·hold;·repeat·for·the·other·side.¶
¶
¶

Figure 6-91 PP W6-4 completed (pages 1 and 2 of 3 pages)

Chapter Summary

6.1 Create and modify styles using the *Style* gallery and *Styles* pane (p. W6-344).

- A **style** is a set of formatting commands that are grouped together and applied to text. Use styles to apply consistent formatting in documents.
- The **Style gallery** on the *Home* tab and the **Styles pane** contain commonly used styles.
- The different types of styles available are **Paragraph**, **Character**, **Linked**, **Table**, and **List**.
- Apply styles to selected text using the *Style* gallery, *Styles* pane, or context menu.
- Modify an existing style, create a new style, or update a style based on the formatting of selected text.
- Add or remove styles from the *Style* gallery.
- Clear all formatting on text by clicking the **Clear Formatting** button [*Home* tab, *Font* group] or selecting **Clear Formatting** in the *Style* gallery or from the context menu. Alternatively, apply the *Clear All* style from the *Styles* pane.
- Change the **Style Set** or **theme fonts**, **theme colors**, and **paragraph spacing** to control the formatting of your document.

6.2 Customize a document by managing styles and using a styles template (p. W6-353).

- Use the **Manage Styles dialog box** to customize which styles display, change the display order of styles, edit and create styles, and import and export styles.
- **Recommended styles** display in the *Style* gallery and the *Styles* pane.
- The **Style Pane Options dialog box** also controls which styles display and the order they display in the *Styles* pane.
- Select all instances or clear formatting of instances of styles in a document. Select all instances of a style and apply formatting to these instances or replace each instance with another style.
- Use the *Find and Replace* dialog box to find and replace styles in a document.
- **Import** or **export** styles from a template or document to another template or document.

- A **styles template** contains styles that can be attached or imported to other documents.
- Use the **Organizer dialog box** to copy styles from one document to another.

6.3 Use the *Building Blocks Organizer* to create and save information in a document (p. W6-364).

- A **building block** is information that is saved and inserted into other documents.
- Building blocks are grouped into a variety of **building block galleries**. Commonly used building block galleries include **Footers gallery**, **Headers gallery**, and **Page Numbers gallery**.
- Create a building block by saving selected text or an object, such as a graphic or table, to a gallery.
- Use the **Building Blocks Organizer** to edit, insert, or delete building blocks.
- Edit the properties of a building block and create a **category** to group building blocks.

6.4 Create *AutoText* building blocks to save text and objects and insert building blocks into a document (p. W6-368).

- Use the **AutoText gallery** to store specialized text or objects.
- Modify, insert, and delete **AutoText building blocks** using the *Building Blocks Organizer*.
- Display the *AutoText* gallery by clicking the **Quick Parts** button [*Insert* tab, *Text* group] and selecting **AutoText**.

6.5 Use the *Quick Parts* gallery to store building blocks and insert building blocks into a document (p. W6-374).

- The **Quick Parts gallery** is an easy access area to store building blocks.
- Modify, insert, and delete **Quick Parts building blocks** using the *Building Blocks Organizer*.
- Display the *Quick Parts* gallery by clicking the **Quick Parts** button [*Insert* tab, *Text* group].

6.6 Customize and use document properties and Word fields in a document (p. W6-375).

- **Document property fields** are included in each document you create.

- Create custom document properties to insert into a document.
- View and customize document properties from the *Backstage* view or the **Properties dialog box**.
- **Word fields** are special codes used to insert content in a document.
- Use Word fields to insert a file name, user name, save date, and number of pages in a document.
- Insert Word fields using the **Field dialog box**.
- The *Field* dialog box lists available fields. Customize the properties of many fields, which determines how the field displays in the document.
- Edit fields using the context menu and update fields using the context menu or by pressing **F9**.

Check for Understanding

The SIMbook for this text (within your SIMnet account) provides the following resources for concept review:

- Multiple-choice questions
- Matching exercises
- Short answer questions

Guided Project 6-1

In this project, you modify the *Staying Active* document from Courtyard Medical Plaza to create new styles, modify existing styles, create a building block, and customize and insert document properties and Word fields.
[**Student Learning Outcomes 6.1, 6.2, 6.3, 6.5, 6.6**]

Files Needed: **StayingActive-06.docx** and **CMP-logo-06.png** *(Student data files are available in the Library of your SIMnet account.)*
Completed Project File Name: *[your initials] Word 6-1.docx*

Skills Covered in This Project

*   Change the theme color set.
*   Modify existing styles.
*   Select all instances of a style.
*   Replace an existing style with a different style.
*   Create a new style based on selected text.
*   Update styles to match a selection.
*   Insert and position a picture.
*   Save a picture as a *Quick Parts* building block.
*   Insert a footer.
*   Add a Word field to a footer.

1. Open the **StayingActive-06** document from your student data files.

2. Save the document as [your initials] Word 6-1.

3. Change the color set of the document.
    a. Click the **Colors** button [*Design* tab, *Document Formatting* group].
    b. Select **Red** from the drop-down list of colors.

4. Modify existing styles.
    a. Right-click **Title** in the *Style* gallery [*Home* tab, *Styles* group] or *Styles* pane and select **Modify** to open the *Modify Style* dialog box.
    b. Click the **Center** alignment button in the *Formatting* area.
    c. Click the **Format** button and select **Font** to open the *Font* dialog box.
    d. Apply **Bold** font style, change the font size to **20 pt**, and click **OK** to close the *Font* dialog box.
    e. Click **OK** to close the *Modify Style* dialog box (Figure 6-92).
    f. Right-click the **Heading 1** style in the *Style* gallery or *Styles* pane and select **Modify** to open the *Modify Style* dialog box.
    g. Click the **Underline** button in the *Formatting* area.

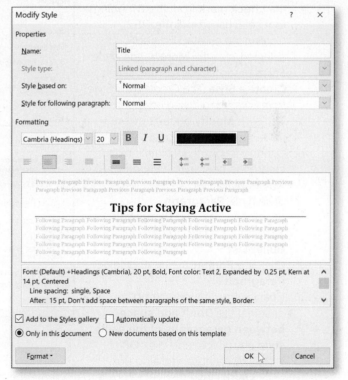

Figure 6-92 Modify *Title* style

h. Click the **Format** button and select **Font** to open the *Font* dialog box.

i. Apply **Small Caps** and click **OK** to close the *Font* dialog box.

j. Click the **Format** button and select **Paragraph** to open the *Paragraph* dialog box.

k. Apply the following changes:
   Before paragraph spacing: **12 pt**
   After paragraph spacing: **3 pt**
   Line spacing: **Single**

l. Click **OK** to close the *Paragraph* dialog box.

m. Click **OK** to close the *Modify Style* dialog box.

5. Select all instances of a style and apply a different style.

   a. Click the **Styles** launcher [*Home* tab, *Styles* group] to open the *Styles* pane if it is not already open.

   b. Right-click the **Heading 2** style in the *Styles* pane and choose **Select All** to select all the text with the *Heading 2* style applied (Figure 6-93).

   c. Click the **Heading 1** style in the *Styles* panes or *Style* gallery to replace the *Heading 2* style with the *Heading 1* style.

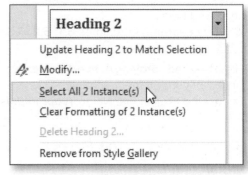

Figure 6-93 Select all instances of the *Heading 2* style

6. Create a new style based on selected text.

   a. Select all the text after the "Keep Exercise Fun and Interesting" heading.

   b. Apply a **check mark bullet** to the selected text. If this bullet is not available from the *Bullet* drop-down list, **Define New Bullet**, and select the **check mark** from the *Wingdings* font set (character code: 252).

   c. Confirm the bulleted list is still selected, click the **More** button in the *Styles* group [*Home* tab] and select **Create a Style**. The *Create New Style from Formatting* dialog box opens.

   d. Click the **Modify** button to view more formatting options.

   e. Use the following information to create the new style (Figure 6-94):
   Name: Bullet List
   Style type: **Paragraph**
   Style based on: **List Paragraph**
   Style for following paragraph: **Bullet List**

   f. Click the **Format** button and select **Paragraph**.

   g. Change the *Left* indent to **0"**, deselect the **Don't add space between paragraphs of the same style** check box, and click **OK** to close the *Paragraph* dialog box.

   h. Click **OK** to close the dialog box and to create the new style.

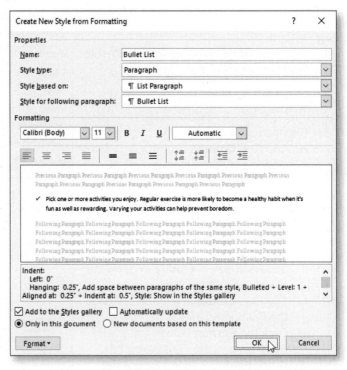

Figure 6-94 Create a new style from selected text

7. Update styles to match a selection and apply a style.

   a. Select the paragraph after the title of the document.

   b. Change the font size to **10 pt**.

   c. Right-click the **Normal** style in the *Styles* pane and choose **Update Normal to Match Selection**. All of the body text, including the numbered and bulleted lists, changes to 10 pt.

   d. Select the title and change the *Before* paragraph spacing to **48 pt**.

   e. Right-click the **Title** style in the *Style* gallery and select **Update Title to Match Selection**.

8. Insert a picture and change text wrapping and position.

   a. Place the insertion point at the beginning of the document.

   b. Insert the ***CMP-logo-06*** picture from your student data files.

   c. Click the **Wrap Text** button [*Picture Tools Format* tab, *Arrange* group] and select **In Front of Text**.

   d. Click the **Position** button and select **More Layout Options** to open the *Layout* dialog box.

   e. Change the *Horizontal* **Absolute position** to **0.3"** *to the right of* **Page**.

   f. Change the *Vertical* **Absolute position** to **0.3"** *below* **Page**.

   g. Click **OK** to close the *Layout* dialog box.

9. Save the CMP logo in the *Quick Parts* gallery.

   a. Click the **CMP logo** picture to select it.

   b. Click the **Quick Parts** button [*Insert* tab, *Text* group] and select **Save Selection to Quick Part Gallery**. The *Create New Building Block* dialog box opens (Figure 6-95).

   c. Add the following properties for the new building block:
      Name: CMP logo
      Gallery: **Quick Parts**
      Category: **General**
      Description: Insert CMP logo
      Save in: **Building Blocks**
      Options: **Insert content only**

   d. Click **OK** to close the dialog box and create the new building block.

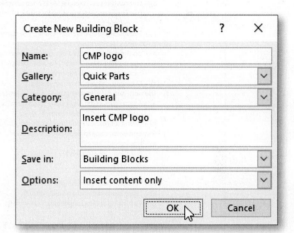

Figure 6-95 Save the CMP logo in the *Quick Parts* gallery

10. Insert a Word field in the footer.

   a. Edit the footer.

   b. Press **Tab** two times to move to the right margin.

   c. Type Last modified: and **space** once.

   d. Click the **Quick Parts** button and select **Field**. The *Field* dialog box opens.

   e. Select **SaveDate** in the *Field names* area and select the short number date format (1/1/20) in the *Date formats* area (Figure 6-96).

   f. Click **OK** to close the *Field* dialog box.

   g. Select all the text in the footer and apply **Italic** font style.

   h. Close the footer.

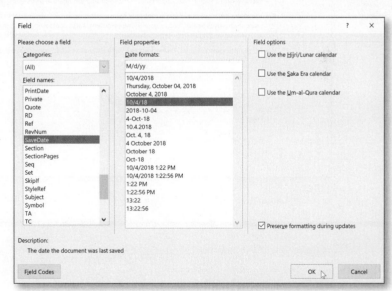

Figure 6-96 Insert the *SaveDate* field

11. Save and close the document (Figure 6-97). When you exit Word after creating and saving building blocks, you might be prompted to save these changes. Click **Save** to save changes.

Tips·for·Staying·Active¶

Almost·any·activity·that·gets·you·moving·and·strengthens·your·muscles·is·good·for·your·health·and·can·help·you· meet·your·fitness·and·weight·goal.·If·you·haven't·been·exercising·regularly,·start·out·slowly·and·gradually·increase· duration,·frequency,·and·intensity.·If·you·have·been·exercising·regularly,·keep·it·up!¶

STAYING·ACTIVE¶

1) → Aim·for·at·least·30·to·60·minutes·of·moderate·intensity·activity·on·most·days.¶
   a) → You·can·get·your·exercise·all·at·once·or·spread·it·out·during·the·day.¶
      i) → For·example,·exercising·for·three·10-minute·periods·is·just·as·effective·as·exercising·for·30·minutes·at· a·time.¶
   b) → The·more·physical·activity·you·do,·the·more·calories·you·burn·and·the·greater·the·health·benefit.¶
2) → If·you·don't·like·counting·calories,·try·counting·your·steps!¶
   a) → Walking·10,000·steps·a·day·can·help·you·manage·your·weight.¶
   b) → Use·a·pedometer·(an·easy-to-wear·device·that·senses·your·body's·motion)·to·count·your·steps·and· motivate·you·to·increase·your·activity.¶
   c) → Use·a·journal·to·track·your·walking.¶
3) → Use·both·aerobic·and·strengthening·activities·are·important·to·losing·weight·and·keeping·it·off.¶
   a) → As·you·grow·older,·your·body·slows·down·and·your·metabolism—the·rate·at·which·your·body·burns· calories—naturally·decreases.¶
   b) → Taking·a·brisk·walk·will·boost·your·metabolism·and·keep·you·burning·calories·for·hours·afterward.¶
4) → Remember·that·any·form·of·exercise·is·good·for·you.¶
   a) → Household·chores¶
      i) → Cleaning·windows¶
      ii) → Vacuuming¶
      iii) → Folding·clothes¶
   b) → Yard·work·and·gardening¶
   c) → Using·stairs·rather·than·an·elevator¶
   d) → Getting·up·and·moving·regularly·at·work¶

KEEP·EXERCISE·FUN·AND·INTERESTING¶

✓ → Pick·one·or·more·activities·you·enjoy.·Regular·exercise·is·more·likely·to·become·a·healthy·habit·when·it's·fun· as·well·as·rewarding.·Varying·your·activities·can·help·prevent·boredom.¶

✓ → Exercise·with·a·friend.·The·support·and·companionship·will·help·keep·you·going.¶

✓ → Think·about·the·payoffs.·Exercise·not·only·helps·control·weight,·it·is·beneficial·to·the·body·and·mind·in·several· ways.·It·improves·health,·boosts·your·immune·system,·helps·control·appetite,·helps·you·feel·more·energetic· and·relaxed,·and·raises·your·self-confidence!¶

✓ → Set·realistic·exercise·goals.·Reward·yourself·in·healthy·ways·when·you·achieve·them.¶

Last·modified:·1/12/20¶

Figure 6-97 Word 6-1 completed

Guided Project 6-2

For this project, you create a styles template for Sierra Pacific Community College District. You modify existing styles, create new styles, and create building blocks. You attach this styles template to the *Emergency Procedures* document, import styles, apply styles to text, and insert building blocks.
[Student Learning Outcomes 6.1, 6.2, 6.3, 6.5, 6.6]

Files Needed: ***SPCCDstyles-06.dotx*** and ***EmergencyProcedures-06.docx*** *(Student data files are available in the* Library *of your SIMnet account.)*
Completed Project File Names: ***[your initials] Word 6-2 styles.dotx*** and ***[your initials] Word 6-2.docx***

Skills Covered in This Project

- Edit a styles template.
- Modify text and update styles to match selected text.
- Create a new style based on selected text.
- Save a picture as a *Quick Parts* building block.
- Create a footer and insert document properties and a Word field.

- Create a *Footer* building block.
- Modify a document style set.
- Attach a template to a document.
- Insert a *Quick Parts* building block.
- Insert a footer from the *Footer* gallery.
- Import styles from the styles template.
- Apply styles.
- Modify before and after paragraph spacing.

1. Open the ***SPCCDstyles-06*** template from your student data files. Open this template from within Word, not from a *File Explorer* window.

2. Save this template as [your initials] Word 6-2 styles. Be sure to save as a template.

3. Modify text and update styles.
   a. Select the "**Heading 1**" text and change the font size to **14 pt**.
   b. Right-click the **Heading 1** style in the *Style* gallery and select **Update Heading 1 to Match Selection**.

4. Create new styles.
   a. Select "**Text with Tab**" including the tab.
   b. Click the **Styles** launcher [*Home* tab, *Styles* group] to open the *Styles* pane.
   c. Click the **New Style** button in the *Styles* pane (Figure 6-98). The *Create New Style from Formatting* dialog box opens.

Figure 6-98 *New Style* button in the *Styles* pane

   d. Enter the following properties for the new style (Figure 6-99):
      Name: Text with Tab
      Style type: **Paragraph**
      Style based on: **Normal**
      Style for following paragraph: **Text with Tab**
   e. Click the **Format** button and select **Tabs** to open the *Tabs* dialog box.
   f. Set a **6.5" right** tab stop with a **dot leader** (2).
   g. Click **OK** to close the *Tabs* dialog box and click **OK** to close the *Create New Style from Formatting* dialog box.
   h. Select the "**Number List**" text.
   i. Click the **More** button in the *Style* gallery [*Home* tab, *Styles* group] and select **Create a Style** to open the *Create New Style from Formatting* dialog box.
   j. Type **Number List** in the *Name* text box.
   k. Click **OK** to close the dialog box and create the new style.

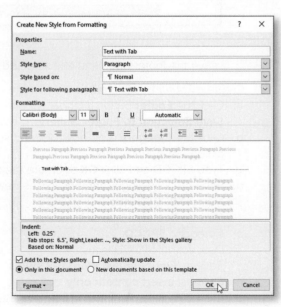

Figure 6-99 Create a new style from selected text

5. Save the Sierra Pacific logo in the *Quick Parts* gallery.
   a. Click the **Sierra Pacific logo** picture to select it.
   b. Click the **Quick Parts** button [*Insert* tab, *Text* group] and select **Save Selection to Quick Part Gallery**. The *Create New Building Block* dialog box opens (Figure 6-100).
   c. Enter the following properties for the new building block:
      Name: SPCCD logo
      Gallery: **Quick Parts**
      Category: **General**
      Description: Insert SPCCD logo
      Save in: *[your initials]* **Word 6-2 styles**
      Options: **Insert content only**
   d. Click **OK** to close the dialog box and create the new building block.

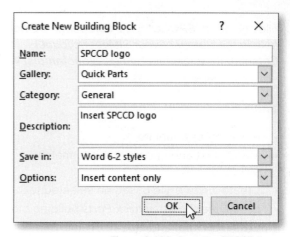

Figure 6-100 Save the SPCCD logo in the *Quick Parts* gallery

6. Create a footer and insert document properties and Word fields.
   a. Edit the footer.
   b. Click the **Document Info** button [*Header & Footer Tools Design* tab, *Insert* group] and select **Document Title** to insert this document property field in the footer.
   c. Press the **right arrow** key once to deselect the document property field and press **Tab**.
   d. Insert the **Company** document property field.
   e. Press the **right arrow** key once to deselect the document property field and press **Tab**.
   f. Type Revised and **space** once.
   g. Click the **Quick Parts** button and select **Field** to open the *Field* dialog box.
   h. Select **SaveDate** in the *Field names* area, select the date format in the *Date formats* area (use January 1, 2020 format), and click **OK** to close the *Field* dialog box.
   i. Select all the text in the footer, change the font size to **10 pt**, and apply a **Top Border** from the *Borders* drop-down list [*Home* tab, *Paragraph* group] (Figure 6-101).

Figure 6-101 Footer with document property and Word fields

   j. Leave the footer open and text selected for the next instruction.

7. Create a *Footer* building block.
   a. Click the **Footer** button [*Header & Footer Tools Design* tab, *Header & Footer* group] and select **Save Selection to Footer Gallery**. The *Create New Building Block* dialog box opens.
   b. Click the **Category** drop-down list and select **Create New Category**. The *Create New Category* dialog box opens (Figure 6-102).
   c. Type SPCCD and click **OK** to create the new category.
   d. Enter the following properties for the new building block:
      Name: SPCCD footer
      Gallery: **Footers**
      Category: **SPCCD**
      Description: SPCCD footer
      Save in: *[your initials]* **Word 6-2 styles**
      Options: **Insert content only**
   e. Click **OK** to close the dialog box and create the new building block.
   f. Close the footer.

Figure 6-102 Create a new building block category

8. Save and close the template.

9. Open the ***EmergencyProcedures-06*** document from your student data files.

10. Save the document as [your initials] Word 6-2.

11. Change the style set of the document.
    a. Click the **Design** tab and click the **More** button [*Document Formatting* group] to display *Style Set* gallery.
    b. Select the **Shaded** style set from the list of options (Figure 6-103).

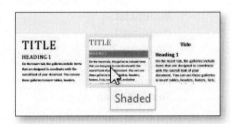
Figure 6-103 Select a style set

12. Customize the document properties in the *Info* area on the *Backstage* view.
    a. Type Emergency Procedures in the *Title* document property field.
    b. Type Sierra Pacific Community College District in the *Company* document property field.
    c. Click the **Back** button to return to the document.

13. Attach a template to the document.
    a. Click the **Document Template** button [*Developer* tab, *Templates* group] to open the *Template and Add-ins* dialog box (Figure 6-104). If the *Developer* tab is not available, click the **File** tab, select **Options**, click **Customize Ribbon**, and check the **Developer** box under *Main Tabs* in the *Customize the Ribbon* area.
    b. Click the **Attach** button, browse to find and select the ***[your initials] Word 6-2 styles*** template, and click **Open** to attach the template.
    c. Check the **Automatically update document styles** box.
    d. Click **OK** to close the *Templates and Add-ins* dialog box.

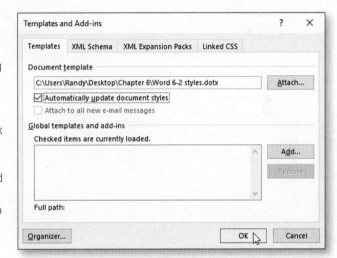
Figure 6-104 Attach styles template to document

14. Insert building blocks.
    a. Place the insertion point at the beginning of the document.
    b. Click the **Quick Parts** button [*Insert* tab, *Text* group] and select the **SPCCD logo** to insert the picture at the top of the document.
    c. Click the **Footer** button [*Header & Footer* group].
    d. Select the **SPCCD footer** from the drop-down list (bottom of the list) to insert the footer with the document property fields into the document.
    e. Delete the blank line below the text in the footer.
    f. Close the footer.

15. Import styles from a template.
    a. Click the **Styles** launcher [*Home* tab, *Styles* group] to open the *Styles* pane.
    b. Click the **Manage Styles** button in the *Styles* pane to open the *Manage Styles* dialog box (Figure 6-105).
    c. Click the **Import/Export** button to open the *Organizer* dialog box.

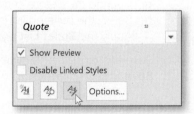
Figure 6-105 *Manage Styles* button in the *Styles* pane

d. Click the **Close File** button at the right to close the *Normal* template.
e. Click the **Open File** button, browse to find and select the *[your initials] Word 6-2 styles* template, and click **Open**.
f. Copy the following styles from the *[your initials] Word 6-2 styles* template (list on the right). Press the **Ctrl** key to select multiple non-adjacent styles (Figure 6-106):

    Bullet List
    Heading 1
    Heading 2
    Normal
    Number List
    Text with Tab

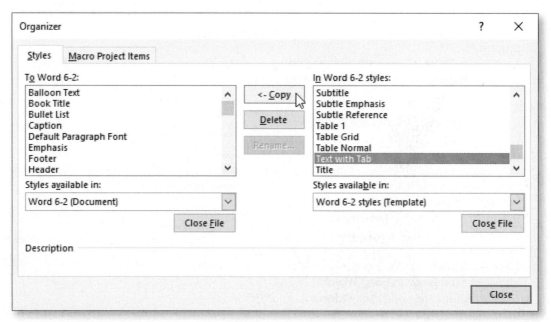

Figure 6-106 Import styles from styles template

g. Click the **Copy** button.
h. Click **Yes to All** in the dialog box that asks if you want to overwrite existing styles.
i. Click **Close** to close the *Organizer* dialog box.

16. Apply styles to selected text.
    a. Select the bulleted list in the "Emergency Telephones [Blue Phones]" section.
    b. Apply the **Number List** style.
    c. Select the lines of text below the "Emergency Telephone Locations" heading.
    d. Change the *Before* and *After* paragraph spacing to **0 pt**.
    e. Select the lines of text below the "Emergency Phone Numbers" heading.
    f. Apply the **Text with Tab** style. Keep the text selected.
    g. Change the *Before* and *After* paragraph spacing to **0 pt**.
    h. Select the bulleted list in the last section ("Accident or Medical Emergency").
    i. Apply the **Bullet List** style.

17. Save and close the document (Figure 6-107). If prompted to save changes in the template, select **Save** to save changes.

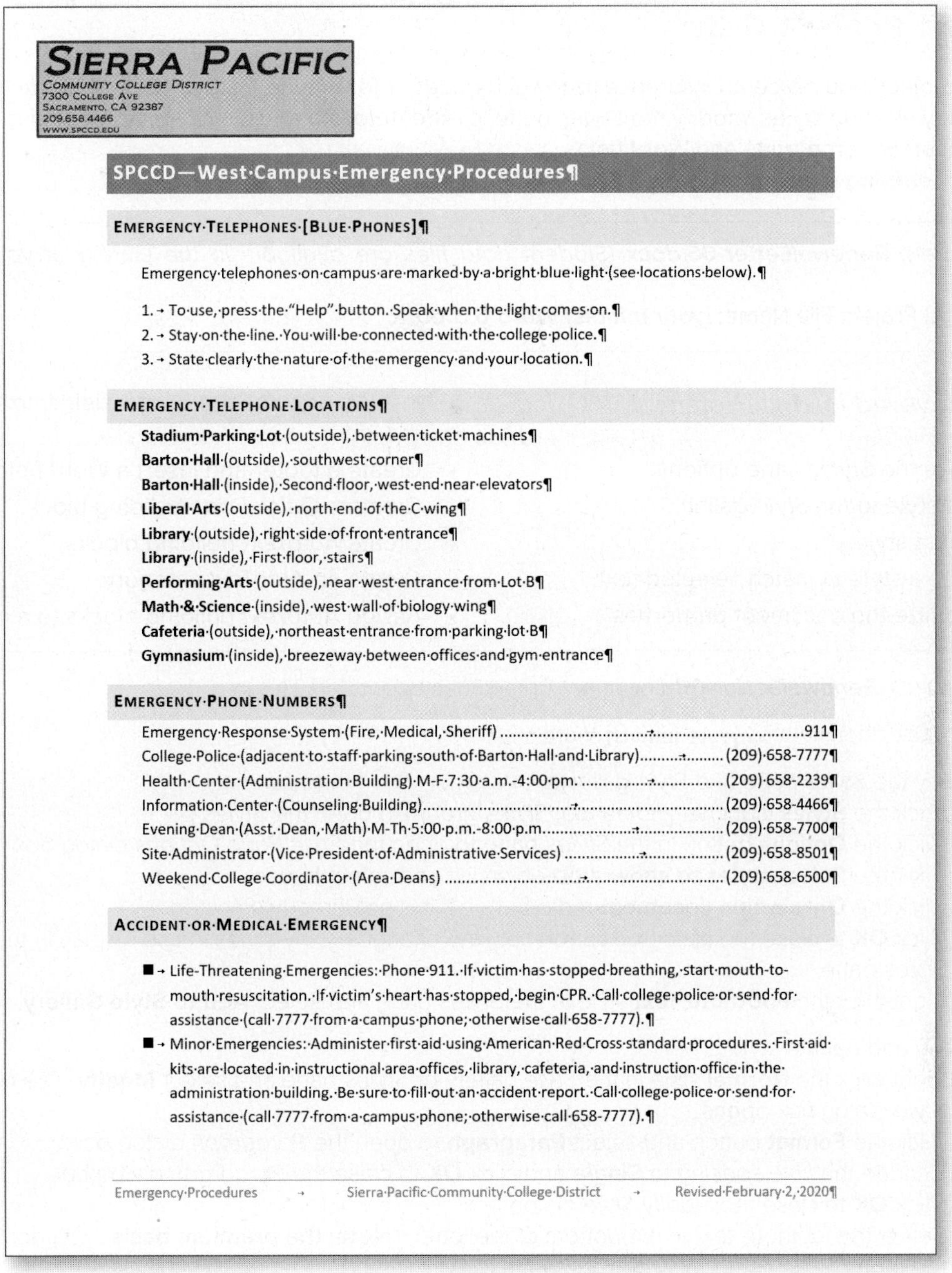

SIERRA PACIFIC
COMMUNITY COLLEGE DISTRICT
7300 College Ave
Sacramento, CA 92387
209.658.4466
WWW.SPCCD.EDU

SPCCD—West·Campus·Emergency·Procedures¶

EMERGENCY·TELEPHONES·[BLUE·PHONES]¶

Emergency·telephones·on·campus·are·marked·by·a·bright·blue·light·(see·locations·below).¶

1. → To·use,·press·the·"Help"·button.·Speak·when·the·light·comes·on.¶
2. → Stay·on·the·line.·You·will·be·connected·with·the·college·police.¶
3. → State·clearly·the·nature·of·the·emergency·and·your·location.¶

EMERGENCY·TELEPHONE·LOCATIONS¶

Stadium·Parking·Lot·(outside),·between·ticket·machines¶
Barton·Hall·(outside),·southwest·corner¶
Barton·Hall·(inside),·Second·floor,·west·end·near·elevators¶
Liberal·Arts·(outside),·north·end·of·the·C·wing¶
Library·(outside),·right·side·of·front·entrance¶
Library·(inside),·First·floor,·stairs¶
Performing·Arts·(outside),·near·west·entrance·from·Lot·B¶
Math·&·Science·(inside),·west·wall·of·biology·wing¶
Cafeteria·(outside),·northeast·entrance·from·parking·lot·B¶
Gymnasium·(inside),·breezeway·between·offices·and·gym·entrance¶

EMERGENCY·PHONE·NUMBERS¶

Emergency·Response·System·(Fire,·Medical,·Sheriff) ....911¶
College·Police·(adjacent·to·staff·parking·south·of·Barton·Hall·and·Library).........(209)·658-7777¶
Health·Center·(Administration·Building)·M-F·7:30·a.m.-4:00·pm. ....(209)·658-2239¶
Information·Center·(Counseling·Building)...(209)·658-4466¶
Evening·Dean·(Asst.·Dean,·Math)·M-Th·5:00·p.m.-8:00·p.m. ....(209)·658-7700¶
Site·Administrator·(Vice·President·of·Administrative·Services) ....(209)·658-8501¶
Weekend·College·Coordinator·(Area·Deans) ....(209)·658-6500¶

ACCIDENT·OR·MEDICAL·EMERGENCY¶

■ → Life-Threatening·Emergencies:·Phone·911.·If·victim·has·stopped·breathing,·start·mouth-to-mouth·resuscitation.·If·victim's·heart·has·stopped,·begin·CPR.·Call·college·police·or·send·for·assistance·(call·7777·from·a·campus·phone;·otherwise·call·658-7777).¶

■ → Minor·Emergencies:·Administer·first·aid·using·American·Red·Cross·standard·procedures.·First·aid·kits·are·located·in·instructional·area·offices,·library,·cafeteria,·and·instruction·office·in·the·administration·building.·Be·sure·to·fill·out·an·accident·report.·Call·college·police·or·send·for·assistance·(call·7777·from·a·campus·phone;·otherwise·call·658-7777).¶

Emergency·Procedures → Sierra·Pacific·Community·College·District → Revised·February·2,·2020¶

Figure 6-107 Word 6-2 completed

Guided Project 6-3

For this project, you revise an insurance renewal form letter for Wayne Reza at Central Sierra Insurance. You modify existing styles, modify the *Styles* pane, create *AutoText* and *Quick Parts* building blocks, and insert document properties and Word fields.
[Student Learning Outcomes 6.1, 6.2, 6.3, 6.4, 6.5, 6.6]

File Needed: ***RenewalLetter-06.docx*** *(Student data files are available in the* Library *of your SIMnet account.)*
Completed Project File Name: *[your initials]* ***Word 6-3.docx***

Skills Covered in This Project

- Change the *Styles* pane options.
- Add a style to the *Style* gallery.
- Modify a style.
- Update a style to match selected text.
- Customize the document properties.

- Insert a document property field into the letter.
- Create a footer and insert a Word field.
- Create a *Quick Parts* building block.
- Create *AutoText* building blocks.
- Create an *AutoText* category.
- Assign *AutoText* building blocks to a category.

1. Open the ***RenewalLetter-06*** document from your student data files.

2. Save the document as [your initials] Word 6-3.

3. Modify the *Styles* pane and *Style* gallery.
   a. Click the **Styles** launcher [*Home* tab, *Styles* group] to open the *Styles* pane.
   b. Click the **Options** button in the *Styles* pane to open the *Style Pane Options* dialog box.
   c. Click the **Select styles to show** drop-down list and select **In use**.
   d. Click the **Only in this document** radio button if it is not already selected.
   e. Click **OK** to close the dialog box and apply the changes. Only styles in use display in the *Styles* pane.
   f. Right-click the **Footnote Text** style in the *Styles* pane and select **Add to Style Gallery**.

4. Modify and update styles.
   a. Right-click the **Normal** style in the *Style* gallery or *Styles* pane and select **Modify**. The *Modify Style* dialog box opens.
   b. Click the **Format** button and select **Paragraph** to open the *Paragraph* dialog box.
   c. Change the *Line spacing* to **Single** and click **OK** to close the *Paragraph* dialog box.
   d. Click **OK** to close the *Modify Style* dialog box.
   e. Select the footnote text at the bottom of the letter ("**Note: the premium basis . . .**"); don't select the footnote number that precedes the text.
   f. Change the font to **Cambria** and apply **italic** formatting.
   g. Change the before and after paragraph spacing to **3 pt**.
   h. Right-click the **Footnote Text** style in the *Style* gallery and select **Update Footnote Text to Match Selection** to update this style.

5. Customize and insert document properties.
   a. Click the **File** tab to open the *Backstage* view and select **Info** if necessary.
   b. Customize the following document properties:
      Title: Renewal Letter
      Subject: type policy #
      Company: Central Sierra Insurance
   c. Click the **Back** arrow to return to the letter.

d. Select "**Number**" in the subject line of the letter.

e. Click the **Quick Parts** button [*Insert* tab, *Text* group].

f. Click **Document Property** and select **Subject** to insert this field (Figure 6-108). Deselect the document property field and verify one space displays before and after the *Subject* field.

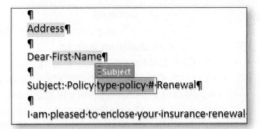

Figure 6-108 Insert *Subject* document property field

6. Create a footer and insert a Word field.

a. Edit the footer.

b. Click the **Align Right** button [*Home* tab, *Paragraph* group], type File name:, and **space** once.

c. Click the **Quick Parts** button [*Header & Footer Tools Design* tab, *Insert* group] and select **Field** to open the *Field* dialog box (Figure 6-109).

d. Select **FileName** in the *Field* names area.

e. Select **(none)** in the *Format* area.

f. Click **OK** to close the dialog box and insert the field.

g. Select all of the text in the footer and change the font size to **9 pt**.

h. Close the footer.

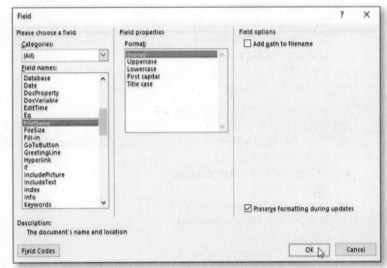

Figure 6-109 Insert *FileName* field in the footer

7. Add the Central Sierra Insurance logo to the *Quick Part* gallery.

a. Edit the header and select the **Central Sierra Insurance logo**.

b. Click the **Quick Parts** button and select **Save Selection to Quick Part Gallery**. The *Create New Building Block* dialog box opens (Figure 6-110).

c. Enter the following properties for the new building block:
Name: CSI logo
Gallery: **Quick Parts**
Category: **General**
Description: Insert CSI logo
Save in: **Building Blocks**
Options: **Insert content only**

d. Click **OK** to close the dialog box and save the *Quick Part* building block.

e. Close the header.

Figure 6-110 Save picture to *Quick Parts* gallery

8. Create new *AutoText* building blocks.

a. Select the opening lines of the letter beginning with the date and ending with the blank line after the subject line.

b. Click the **Quick Parts** button [*Insert* tab, *Text* group], select **AutoText**, and choose **Save Selection to AutoText Gallery**. The *Create New Building Block* dialog box opens.

c. Enter the following properties for the new building block:
Name: CSI letter opening
Gallery: **AutoText**

Category: **General**
Description: Insert opening lines of letter
Save in: **Building Blocks**
Options: **Insert content only**

d. Click **OK** to close the dialog box and to save the *AutoText* building block.
e. Select the closing lines of the letter beginning with "**Sincerely**" and ending with the email address.
f. Click the **Quick Parts** button, select **AutoText**, and choose **Save Selection to AutoText Gallery**. The *Create New Building Block* dialog box opens.
g. Enter the following properties for the new building block:
Name: CSI letter closing
Gallery: **AutoText**
Category: **General**
Description: Insert closing lines of letter
Save in: **Building Blocks**
Options: **Insert content only**

h. Click **OK** to close the dialog box and to save the *Auto-Text* building block.

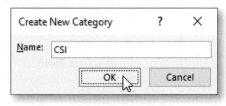

Figure 6-111 Create new *AutoText* category

9. Create a new *AutoText* category and assign *AutoText* build-ing blocks to this category.

a. Click the **Quick Parts** button and select **Building Blocks Organizer** to open the *Building Blocks Organizer* dialog box.
b. Select the **CSI letter closing** in the *Building blocks* area and click the **Edit Properties** button to open the *Modify Building Block* dialog box.
c. Click the **Category** drop-down list and select **Create New Category**. The *Create New Category* dialog box opens (Figure 6-111).
d. Type CSI and click **OK** to create the new category and assign this category to the *AutoText* building block.
e. Click **OK** to close the *Modify Building Block* dialog box and click **Yes** in the dialog box that opens asking if you want to redefine the building block.
f. Use the *Building Blocks Organizer* to edit the properties of the **CSI letter opening** *AutoText* building block and assign this building block to the **CSI** category.
g. Close the *Building Blocks Organizer* dialog box.

10. Save and close the document (Figure 6-112). When you exit Word after creating and saving building blocks, you might be prompted to save these changes. Click **Save** to save changes.

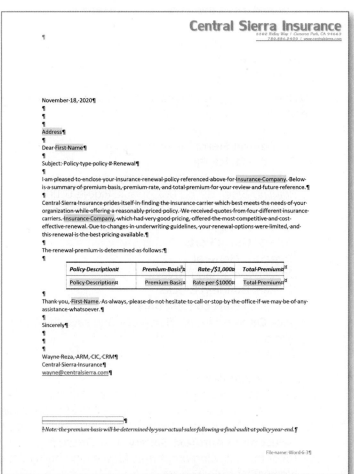

Figure 6-112 Word 6-3 completed

Independent Project 6-4

For this project, you revise the vaccination schedule for Courtyard Medical Plaza. You update an existing style, create *AutoText* and *Quick Parts* building blocks, and insert document properties and Word fields. [Student Learning Outcomes 6.1, 6.3, 6.4, 6.5, 6.6]

Files Needed: ***VaccinationSchedule-06.docx*** and ***CMP-logo-06.png*** *(Student data files are available in the Library of your SIMnet account.)*
Completed Project File Name: ***[your initials] Word 6-4.docx***

Skills Covered in This Project

- Customize document properties.
- Insert a document property field.
- Modify text and update a style to match selected text.
- Insert and position a picture.

- Create a *Quick Parts* building block.
- Create an *AutoText* building block.
- Create a new *AutoText* category.
- Assign *AutoText* building blocks to a category.
- Create a footer and insert a Word field.

---

1. Open the ***VaccinationSchedule-06*** document from your student data files.

2. Save the document as [your initials] Word 6-4.

3. Customize the following document properties:
   Title: Vaccination Schedule
   Company: Courtyard Medical Plaza

4. Insert a document property field and apply a style.
   a. Insert the **Title** document property field on the blank line at the beginning of the document.
   b. Apply the **Title** style to the *Title* document property field.

5. Modify text and update a style.
   a. Select the title and change the alignment to **Center**.
   b. Apply **Bold** and **Small Caps** formatting.
   c. Change the font color to the **sixth color** in the **first row** of *Theme Colors* (**Red, Accent 2**).
   d. Use the *Borders and Shading* dialog box to change the border color to the **second color** in the **first row** of *Theme Colors* (**Black, Text 1**), change the border width to 2¼ pt, and apply the border to the **bottom**.
   e. Update the *Title* style to match the formatted title text.

6. Insert a picture at the bottom left of the document.
   a. Place the insertion point at the end of the document.
   b. Insert the ***CMP-logo-06*** picture from your student data files.
   c. Change text wrapping to **Tight**.
   d. Change the *Horizontal* **Absolute position** to **0.3"** *to the right of* **Page**.
   e. Change the *Vertical* **Absolute position** to **9.6"** *below* **Page**.

7. Select the **CMP logo** and create a *Quick Part* building block using the following properties:
   Name: CMP logo bottom
   Gallery: **Quick Parts**
   Category: **General**
   Description: Insert CMP logo at the bottom left
   Save in: **Building Blocks**
   Options: **Insert content only**

8. Select the entire table and save it as an *AutoText* building block using the following properties:
   Name: Vaccination table
   Gallery: **AutoText**
   Category: **CMP** (create new category)
   Description: Insert Vaccination table
   Save in: **Building Blocks**
   Options: **Insert content only**

9. Edit the footer and insert a Word field.
   a. Edit the footer, change alignment to **Align Right**, type Last updated:, and **space** once.
   b. Insert the **SaveDate** field (use January 1, 2020 format).
   c. Change the font size of all the information in the footer to **10 pt** and apply **italic** formatting.
   d. Close the footer.

10. Save and close the document (Figure 6-113). When you exit Word after creating and saving building blocks, you might be prompted to save these changes. Click **Save** to save changes.

VACCINATION SCHEDULE

Think of vaccines as a coat of armor for your child. To keep it shiny and strong, you must make sure your child's immunizations are up to date. Timely vaccinations help to prevent disease and keep your family and the community healthy. Some immunizations are given in a single shot, while others require a series of shots over a period of time.

Vaccines for children and teenagers are listed alphabetically below with their routinely recommended ages. Missed doses will be assessed by your child's physician and given if necessary. Keep a personal record of all immunizations and bring it with you to each office visit.

Don't neglect your vaccinations!

RECOMMENED VACCINATION SCHEDULE		
Name of Vaccine	*When It's Recommended*	*Total Doses*
Chickenpox (varicella)	At 12 months and 4-6 years	2
Diphtheria, tetanus, and pertussis (DTaP)	At 2, 4, 6 and 12-15 months, and 4-6 years	5
Haemophilus influenzae type b (Hib)	At 2, 4, 6, and 12 months	4
Hepatitis A (HepA)	At 12 and 18 months	3
Hepatitis B (HepB)	At birth, 1-2 months, and 6 months	3
Human papillomavirus (HPV)	3-dose series for girls at age 11-12 years	3
Inactivated influenza (flu shot)	Annually starting at age 6 months	Annually
Inactivated poliovirus (IPV)	At 2, 4, 6 months, and 4-6 years	4
Live intranasal influenza	Annually starting at age 2 years	Annually
Measles, mumps, and rubella (MMR)	At 12 months and 4-6 years	2
Meningococcal conjugate (MCV)	At 11-12 years	1
Pneumococcal conjugate (PCV)	At 2, 4, 6, and 12 months	4
Pneumococcal polysaccharide (PPSV)	At 2, 4, 6, and 12 months	4
Rotavirus (RV)	At 2, 4, and 6 months	3
Tetanus and diphtheria (Td)	At 11-12 years	1

These recommendations are for generally healthy children and teenagers and are for information only. If your child has ongoing health problems, special health needs or risks, or if certain conditions run in your family, talk with your child's physician. He or she may recommend additional vaccinations or schedules based on earlier immunizations and special health needs.

Courtyard Medical Plaza
1660 Alhandra Way
Granite Bay, CA 95517
a comprehensive medical facility
559.288.1660
www.cmp.com

Last updated: March 1, 2020

Figure 6-113 Word 6-4 completed

Independent Project 6-5

For this project, you create a styles template for Sierra Pacific Community College District, attach the styles template to a document, and import styles from a template into a document. You modify and update existing styles, create new styles, create a *Quick Parts* building block, and insert document property and Word fields.
[Student Learning Outcomes 6.1, 6.2, 6.3, 6.5, 6.6]

Files Needed: new template file, ***OnlineLearningPlan-06.docx***, and ***SPCCD-logo-06.png*** *(Student data files are available in the* Library *of your SIMnet account.)*
Completed Project File Names: *[your initials] **Word 6-5 styles.dotx*** and *[your initials] **Word 6-5.docx***

Skills Covered in This Project

- Create a styles template.
- Modify a style set and theme colors.
- Update styles to match selected text.
- Create new styles based on selected text.
- Save a picture as a *Quick Parts* building block.
- Create a footer and insert document properties and a Word field.
- Create a *Footer* building block.
- Attach a template to the document.
- Insert a *Quick Parts* building block.
- Insert a footer from the *Footer* gallery.
- Import styles from the styles template.
- Select all instances of a style and replace with a different style.

1. Create a new blank document and save it as a **Word Template** named [your initials] Word 6-5 styles.

2. Change the *Style Set* to **Shaded** and the *Theme Colors* to **Grayscale** [*Design* tab, *Document Formatting* group].

3. Type the following lines of text and press **Enter** after each line (including the last line):
   Heading 1
   Heading 2
   Learning Mode
   Bullet List

4. Apply the **Heading 1** style to the "Heading 1" text and the **Heading 2** style to the "Heading 2" text.

5. Update styles.
   a. Select the "**Heading 1**" text, change the font size to **12 pt**, change the font color to the **second color** in the **first row** of *Theme Colors* (**Black, Text 1**), and apply **bold** formatting.
   b. Update the **Heading 1** style to match the selected text.
   c. Select the "**Heading 2**" text and change to **12 pt** font size and **small caps**.
   d. Update the **Heading 2** style to match the selected text.

6. Modify the *Normal* style and set line spacing to **single**.

7. Create new styles.
   a. Select the "**Learning Mode**" text, apply **Bold** and **Small Caps** formatting, and change the *Character spacing* to **Expanded** by **1 pt** [*Font* dialog box, *Advanced* tab].
   b. Select the "**Learning Mode**" text (if necessary) and open the *Styles* pane.
   c. Create a new style, name the new style Learning Mode, and change the *Style type* to **Linked (paragraph and character)** if it is not already selected. Don't change any other settings.
   d. Select the "**Bullet List**" text in the template and apply a **solid square bullet** (Wingdings, character code 110).

e. Select the "**Bullet List**" text, create a new style, name the new style Bullet List, and change the *Style type* to **Linked (paragraph and character)** if it is not already selected. Don't change any other settings.

8. Insert a picture, position it, and create a *Quick Parts* building block.
   a. Place the insertion point on the blank line below the bulleted list. If a blank line does not display below the bulleted list, position the insertion point at the end of the bulleted list, press **Enter** two times, and apply the **Normal** style.
   b. Insert the ***SPCCD-logo-06*** picture from your student data files.
   c. Change text wrapping to **Top and Bottom**.
   d. Change the *Horizontal* **Absolute position** to **0.3"** *to the right of* **Page**.
   e. Change the *Vertical* **Absolute position** to **0.3"** *below* **Page**.
   f. Select the logo and create a *Quick Parts* building block with the following properties:
      Name: SPCCD logo top
      Gallery: **Quick Parts**
      Category: **General**
      Description: Insert SPCCD logo
      Save in: ***[your initials]* Word 6-5 styles**
      Options: **Insert content only**

9. Add document properties and Word fields to the footer and create a footer building block.
   a. Edit the footer.
   b. Insert the **Title** document property field on the left side of the footer. Use the **right arrow** key to deselect the document property field.
   c. **Tab** to the center and insert the **Company** document property field. Use the **right arrow** key to deselect the document property field.
   d. **Tab** to the right, type Page, **space** once, and insert a plain page number in the current position.
   e. **Space** once, type of, **space** once, and insert a **NumPages** field. Use **1**, **2**, **3** as the format for the *NumPages* field.
   f. Use the *Borders and Shading* dialog box to change the border color to the **second color** in the **first row** of *Theme Colors* (**Black, Text 1**), change the border width to ½ pt, and apply the border to the **top**.
   g. Select the entire footer and **Save Selection to Footer Gallery** using the following information:
      Name: SPCCD footer
      Gallery: **Footers**
      Category: **General**
      Description: Footer with document properties
      Save in: ***[your initials]* Word 6-5 styles**
      Options: **Insert content only**
   h. Close the footer.

10. Save and close the template.

11. Open the ***OnlineLearningPlan-06*** document from your student data files.

12. Save the document as [your initials] Word 6-5.

13. Customize the following document properties:
    Title: Online Learning Plan
    Company: Sierra Pacific Community College District

14. Change *Theme Colors* [*Design* tab, *Document Formatting* group] to **Grayscale**.

15. Attach the ***[your initials]* Word 6-5 styles** template to the document and set it to automatically update styles.

16. Insert building blocks on the first page of the document.
    a. Place the insertion point at the beginning of the document and insert the **SPCCD logo top** building block from the *Quick Parts* gallery.

b. Insert the **SPCCD footer** building block from the *Footer* gallery.

c. Delete the blank line below the footer text and close the footer.

17. Import styles from the **[your initials] Word 6-5 styles** template and copy the following styles (**Yes to All** to overwrite existing styles):

Bullet List

Heading 1

Heading 2

Learning Mode

Normal

18. Select all instances of the **Intense Reference** style and apply the **Learning Mode** style.

19. Select the bulleted list on the last page and apply the **Bullet List** style.

20. Save and close the document (Figure 6-114).

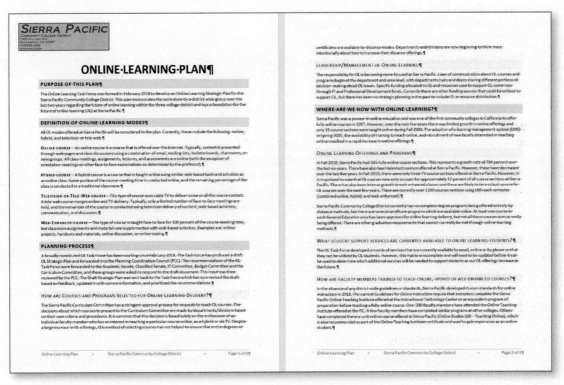

Figure 6-114 Word 6-5 completed (pages 1 and 2 of 3 pages)

Independent Project 6-6

For this project, you revise a brochure for Emma Cavalli at Placer Hills Real Estate. You update existing styles, create new styles, apply styles, and create *Header*, *AutoText*, and *Quick Parts* building blocks. [Student Learning Outcomes 6.1, 6.2, 6.3, 6.4, 6.5, 6.6]

File Needed: ***CavalliBrochure-06.docx*** *(Student data files are available in the* Library *of your SIMnet account.)*

Completed Project File Name: ***[your initials] Word 6-6.docx***

Skills Covered in This Project

- Add document properties.
- Modify text and update a style to match selected text.
- Create new styles.
- Apply styles to selected text.
- Create a *Quick Parts* building block.
- Create an *AutoText* building block.
- Insert a document property field.
- Create a *Header* building block.
- Create a new *Header* category.
- Assign *AutoText* building blocks to a category.
- Modify the *Styles* pane options.

---

1. Open the **CavalliBrochure-06** document from your student data files.

2. Save the document as [your initials] Word 6-6.

3. Customize the following document properties:
   Title: Brochure
   Company: Placer Hills Real Estate
   Author: Emma Cavalli (remove existing author)

4. Update and apply styles.
   a. Select "**Emma Cavalli**" near the upper left and update the *Heading 1* style to match the selected text.
   b. Select "**Realtor Consultant**" and change the *After* paragraph spacing to **6 pt**.
   c. Update the *Heading 2* style to match the selected text.
   d. Apply the **Heading 2** style to the other section headings in the document.

5. Modify a bulleted list, create a new style, and apply a style.
   a. Select the bulleted list in the second column.
   b. Change the bullet to a **check mark** (Wingdings, character code 252).
   c. Create a style based on the selected text and name the style Check Bullet.
   d. Apply the **Check Bullet** style to the numbered list in the first column.
   e. Apply the **Check Bullet** style to the lines of text in the "Education & Training" section. Do not select the "Education & Training" heading.

6. Save the PHRE logo (bottom right) as a *Quick Parts* building block with the following properties:
   Name: PHRE logo bottom right
   Gallery: **Quick Parts**
   Category: **General**
   Description: Insert PHRE logo
   Save in: **Building Blocks**
   Options: **Insert content only**

7. Select the entire table in the third column and save as an *AutoText* building block with the following properties:
   Name: PHRE beliefs
   Gallery: **AutoText**
   Category: **General**
   Description: Insert PHRE table
   Save in: **Building Blocks**
   Options: **Insert content only**

8. Edit the header, select "**Placer Hills**," and replace it with the **Company** document property field.

9. Select the table in the header and save it in the *Headers* gallery with the following properties:
   Name: PHRE header landscape
   Gallery: **Headers**
   Category: **PHRE** (create new category)
   Description: Insert PHRE header
   Save in: **Building Blocks**
   Options: **Insert content only**

10. Modify the *Styles Pane Options* to show only those styles in use, sort styles alphabetically, and apply these settings only in this document.

11. Save and close the document (Figure 6-115). When you exit Word after creating and saving building blocks, you may be prompted to save these changes. Click **Save** to save changes.

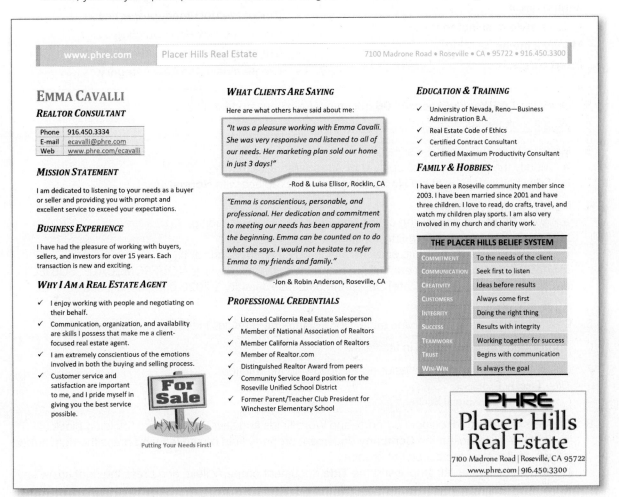

Figure 6-115 Word 6-6 completed

Improve It Project 6-7

For this project, you revise an existing weekly expense memo for Life's Animal Shelter to convert it into a form. You update an existing style, create *AutoText*, *Quick Parts*, and *Footer* building blocks, and insert document properties and Word fields.
[Student Learning Outcomes 6.1, 6.3, 6.4, 6.5, 6.6]

File Needed: ***LASWeeklyExpenses-06.docx*** *(Student data files are available in the* Library *of your SIMnet account.)*
Completed Project File Name: *[your initials] Word 6-7.docx*

Skills Covered in This Project

- Modify a style.
- Find all instances of a style and replace with another style.
- Apply a style to selected text.
- Modify a memo heading.
- Insert a date.
- Update Word fields.
- Create a footer and insert document properties and Word fields.
- Create a *Footer* building block.
- Customize document properties.
- Create a *Quick Parts* building block.
- Create an *AutoText* building block.
- Create a new *AutoText* category.

1. Open the **LASWeeklyExpenses-06** document from your student data files.

2. Save the document as [your initials] Word 6-7.

3. Modify a style and replace a style.
   a. Modify the *Normal* style to apply **0 pt** *After* paragraph spacing.
   b. Select all instances of the **No Spacing** style and replace with **Normal** style.

4. Modify the memo heading.
   a. Apply **36 pt** *Before* spacing on the first line of the memo heading.
   b. Select the four memo heading lines and set a **1"** left tab stop.
   c. Delete extra tabs so all info after the memo guide words aligns at 1".
   d. Apply the **Strong** style to each of the memo heading guide words (TO:, FROM:, DATE:, SUBJECT:).
   e. Delete "**[Insert Current Date]**", insert the date (use January 1, 2020 date format), and set it to update automatically.

5. Delete the expense values in the table. Don't delete the formulas in the *Totals* column or row.

6. Update each of the formulas in the table.

7. Customize document properties using the following information:
   Title: **Weekly Expenses**
   Company: **Life's Animal Shelter**

8. Create a footer with document property and Word fields and save it as a *Footer* building block.
   a. Edit the footer, insert the **Company** document property field on the left, and press the right arrow key to deselect the document property field.
   b. **Tab** to the center tab stop, insert the **Title** document property field, and press the right arrow key to deselect the document property field.
   c. **Tab** to the right tab stop, type Updated:, **space** once, and insert the **SaveDate** Word field (use January 1, 2020 date format).
   d. Change the font of all footer text to **10 pt**.
   e. Use the *Borders and Shading* dialog box to change the border color to the **second color** in the **first row** of *Theme Colors* (**Black, Text 1**), change the border width to ½ pt, and apply the border to the **top**.
   f. Select the entire footer and save it in the *Footers* gallery using the following properties:
      Name: **LAS footer**
      Gallery: **Footers**
      Category: **LAS** (create new category)
      Description: **Insert LAS footer**
      Save in: **Building Blocks**
      Options: **Insert content only**

9. Save the *WordArt* at the top of the document as a *Quick Parts* building block with the following properties:
   Name: **LAS WordArt**
   Gallery: **Quick Parts**

Category: **General**
Description: Insert LAS WordArt
Save in: **Building Blocks**
Options: **Insert content only**

10. Select the memo heading lines (include the two blank lines after "SUBJECT") and save as an *Auto-Text* building block with the following properties:
Name: LAS memo heading
Gallery: **AutoText**
Category: **General**
Description: Insert memo heading
Save in: **Building Blocks**
Options: **Insert content only**

11. Replace "xx" at the end of the document with your initials in lowercase.

12. Save and close the document (Figure 6-116). When you exit Word after creating and saving building blocks, you might be prompted to save these changes. Click **Save** to save changes.

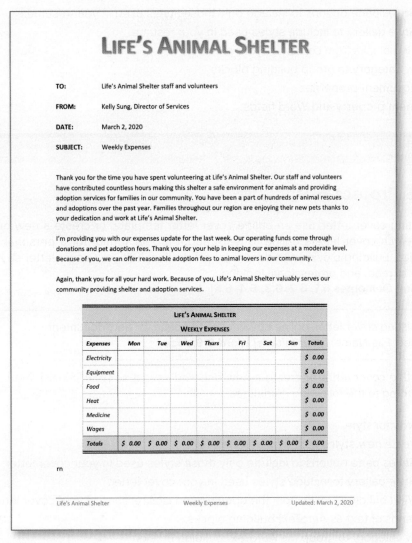

Figure 6-116 Word 6-7 completed

Challenge Project 6-8

Update your resume using document formatting features learned in this chapter. If you don't have an existing resume, create a new one based on an online resume template or use a blank document to create a resume. Incorporate styles, building blocks, and document properties. Edit your resume so it is consistently formatted, easy to read, and professional looking. Research resumes online to get ideas about formatting and content.
[Student Learning Outcomes 6.1, 6.2, 6.3, 6.4, 6.5, 6.6]

File Needed: Existing resume, online resume template, or new document
Completed Project File Name: *[your initials] Word 6-8.docx*

Open your existing resume or create a new resume and save it as [your initials] Word 6-8. Modify your document according to the following guidelines:

- Modify and apply existing styles to headings, subheadings, and lists to improve consistency in your resume.
- Update or create new styles based on selected text.
- Modify the *Styles* pane options to include only those styles used in your resume.
- Modify the *Style* gallery to include styles used in your resume.
- Create building blocks from content in your resume.
- Create a new category to group building blocks.
- Customize document properties.
- Insert document property and Word fields.

Challenge Project 6-9

Update an existing cover letter, use an online cover letter template, or create a new one from a blank document. Research cover letters online to learn about proper format for a personal business letter. Incorporate styles, building blocks, and document properties. Edit your cover letter so it is consistently formatted, easy to read, and professional looking.
[Student Learning Outcomes 6.1, 6.2, 6.3, 6.4, 6.6]

File Needed: Existing cover letter, online cover letter template, or new document
Completed Project File Name: *[your initials] Word 6-9.docx*

Open your existing cover letter or create a new one and save it as [your initials] Word 6-9. Modify your document according to the following guidelines:

- Modify the *Normal* style.
- Update or create new styles based on selected text.
- Modify the *Styles* pane options to include only those styles used in your cover letter.
- Modify the *Style* gallery to include styles used in your cover letter.
- Create *AutoText* building blocks from the opening and closing lines of your cover letter.
- Save paragraphs of text as *AutoText* building blocks.
- Create a new category to group the *AutoText* building blocks.
- Customize document properties.
- Insert document property fields.

Challenge Project 6-10

Create an agenda or meeting outline for an upcoming meeting for an organization you belong to, such as a club, church, volunteer organization, student group, or neighborhood association. Incorporate styles, building blocks, and document property and Word fields. Use the internet to research required and optional components of a meeting agenda. Robert's Rules of Order is a good source of information about meetings and guidelines for meeting protocol.
[Student Learning Outcomes 6.1, 6.2, 6.3, 6.4, 6.5, 6.6]

File Needed: None
Completed Project File Name: *[your initials] Word 6-10.docx*

Create a new document and save it as [your initials] Word 6-10. Agendas or meetings can include, but are not limited to, the following items:

- Organization name as the title
- Meeting date, start time, and end time
- Meeting location
- Meeting attendees
- Topic headings
- Topic subheadings (include details for each topic heading)
- The time each topic is expected to last

Modify your document according to the following guidelines:

- Modify and apply existing styles to headings, subheadings, and lists to improve consistency in format.
- Update or create new styles based on selected text.
- Modify the *Styles* pane options to include only those styles used in your document.
- Modify the *Style* gallery to include styles used in your document.
- Create building blocks from content in your document.
- Create a new category to group building blocks.
- Customize document properties.
- Insert document property and Word fields.

Source of screenshots Microsoft Office 365 (2019): Word, Excel, Access, PowerPoint.

W6-407

Using Microsoft Word 365

CHAPTER

7

Advanced Tables and Graphics

CHAPTER OVERVIEW

In Chapter 4, we covered the basics of tables, columns, and graphics. This chapter introduces the advanced features that are available when working with tables, columns, and graphics. The advanced topics in this chapter enable you to effectively customize table content, layout, and styles. The final two sections in this chapter introduce advanced picture and shape features.

STUDENT LEARNING OUTCOMES (SLOs)

After completing this chapter, you will be able to:

SLO 7.1 Customize table content using sorting, formulas, bullets and numbers, tabs and indents, and text direction (p. W7-409).

SLO 7.2 Customize table layouts using table properties, cell margins, the split table feature, nested tables, and a repeated header row (p. W7-418).

SLO 7.3 Enhance a table design using shading, borders, and a table style (p. W7-422).

SLO 7.4 Modify a picture using advanced layout and picture format options (p. W7-432).

SLO 7.5 Adjust pictures to remove background, apply corrections, change colors, and add artistic effects, and compress, change, and reset a picture (p. W7-438).

SLO 7.6 Create, group, align, and modify a shape in a document (p. W7-444).

CASE STUDY

In the Pause & Practice projects, you modify a document about maximum and target heart rates for the American River Cycling Club. You use tables, columns, graphics, and shapes to effectively communicate this information.

Pause & Practice 7-1: Customize table content by converting text to a table, sorting information in the table, adding formulas, and changing text direction.

Pause & Practice 7-2: Enhance tables in the document by customizing the table layout and applying, modifying, and creating table styles.

Pause & Practice 7-3: Insert, modify, and arrange pictures in the document.

Pause & Practice 7-4: Insert, modify, arrange, and group shapes to present information graphically in the document.

WORD

Customizing Table Content

Use tables to display information in an attractive, organized arrangement. This section reviews the basics of formatting table content and introduces advanced features to customize tables, such as sorting table content, creating custom formulas, adding bullets and numbering, modifying tab stops and indents, and changing text direction.

When the insertion point is in a table or when you select a table, two contextual *Table Tools* tabs display on the *Ribbon*: **Table Tools Design tab** and **Table Tools Layout tab**. The *Table Tools Layout* tab provides options to customize the layout and table content. The *Table Tools Design* tab includes options to apply and customize table styles and borders, which are covered in *SLO 7.3: Customizing Table Design*.

Convert Text to a Table

You can convert existing text into a table if it is formatted with tabs or separated with other characters. When converting text to a table, Word uses the existing structure of the text to create the table. You can then modify the table to meet your needs.

▶ **HOW TO:** Convert Text into a Table

Figure 7-1 *Convert Text to Table* dialog box

1. Select the text to convert to a table.
2. Click the **Table** button [*Insert* tab, *Tables* group] and select **Convert Text to Table**. The *Convert Text to Table* dialog box opens (Figure 7-1).
3. Adjust the number of columns and rows as necessary in the *Table size* area.
   - Word automatically determines the number of columns and rows based upon the structure of the text you select.
   - Modify the number of columns and rows in this area.
4. Select from the radio buttons in the *AutoFit behavior* area to specify how the column widths of the table are set.
5. Select from the radio buttons in the *Separate text at* area to specify how the columns and rows are separated.
   - Word automatically selects a separation option based upon the structure of the text you select.
6. Click **OK** to close the dialog box and convert the text to a table.

Convert a Table to Text

You can also convert an existing table into text. The procedure for converting a table to text is similar to the process for converting text to a table.

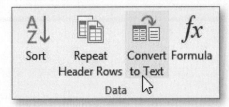

Figure 7-2 *Convert to Text* button

▶ **HOW TO:** Convert a Table to Text

1. Select the table to convert to text.
2. Click the **Convert to Text** button [*Table Tools Layout* tab, *Data* group] (Figure 7-2). The *Convert Table to Text* dialog box opens.

3. Select from the radio buttons in the *Separate text with* area to determine how the text will be separated (Figure 7-3).

   - Word inserts paragraph marks, tabs, commas, or a custom separator, such as a hyphen or other symbol, to separate the text when converting a table to text.
   - Tabs are the most commonly used separator when converting a table to text.

4. Click **OK** to close the dialog box and convert the table to text.

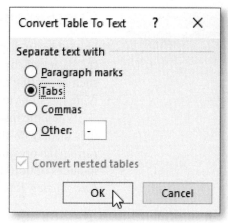

Figure 7-3 *Convert Table To Text* dialog box

Sort Text in a Table

Sorting text in a table is a common method of reorganizing the content. You can sort any of the columns in a table in ascending or descending order. Word automatically moves entire rows of information when you perform a sort. You can also perform a multi-level sort, such as sorting a table by city and then within each city sorting by last name.

▶**HOW TO:** Sort Text in a Table

1. Place the insertion point in the table or select the entire table.
2. Click the **Sort** button [*Table Tools Layout* tab, *Data* group]. The *Sort* dialog box opens (Figure 7-4).
3. Determine whether the table has a header row (column headings) and select the appropriate radio button in the *My list has* area.

   - If your table has a header row, the *Sort by* options are the column headings.
   - If your table does not have a header row, the *Sort by* options are the column numbers (*Column 1*, *Column 2*, etc.).

4. Click the **Sort by** drop-down list and select the column heading or column to sort.
5. Click the **Type** drop-down list and select **Text**, **Number**, or **Date**.

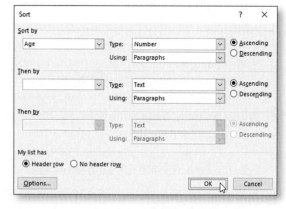

Figure 7-4 *Sort dialog box*

   - When sorting text in a table, the text is sorted using paragraphs, which means entire rows are moved rather than individual cells.

6. Click the **Ascending** or **Descending** radio button to select the sort order.
7. Perform a secondary sort by clicking the **Then by** drop-down list, selecting the column heading or column to sort, and selecting the type and sort order.
8. Click **OK** to close the dialog box and perform the sort.

> ▶ MORE INFO
>
> The *Sort* feature is not limited to tables. You can also sort selected paragraphs of information or a bulleted list.

Formulas and Functions

In Chapter 4, you learned how to create a simple formula in a table to add values in columns and rows. Insert *Formulas* to perform simple or complex mathematical calculations. Formulas add, subtract, multiply, or divide values in a table. Additionally, use *functions*, such as *SUM* (add values) or *AVG* (average values), to calculate the sum or average of the values in a column or row.

Create a Formula

Formulas are constructed in a specific order, which is called *syntax*. Formula syntax refers to the rule or rules that dictate how the various parts of a formula are written. For example, the equals sign (=) is always the first character you enter when creating a formula. The other parts of a formula include cell references, operators, and values.

Remember that tables are grouped into columns (vertical) and rows (horizontal). Columns are referenced with letters, and rows are referenced with numbers. For example, the first column is A, the second column is B, the first row is 1, and the second row is 2. These column and row references are not visible in Word tables as they are in Excel.

A *cell* is where a column and row intersect. Each cell has a *cell address*, which is the column and row reference. In Table 7-1, the cell address displays in each cell. When creating a formula, you refer to a cell using its cell address, which is called a *cell reference* in a formula.

Table 7-1: Cell References

A1	B1	C1
A2	B2	C2
A3	B3	C3

Operators are the symbols for mathematical operations. Table 7-2 lists the mathematical operators and their order of precedence (the order they are performed in a formula):

Table 7-2: Formula Operators

Operator	Operator Name	Order of Precedence
()	Parenthesis	First
^	Exponent	First
*	Multiplication	Second
/	Division	Second
−	Subtraction	Third
+	Addition	Third

You can also use *values* in formulas. For example, multiply a cell reference by 85% or subtract a cell reference from 220. Table 7-3 displays the proper syntax for formulas that use cell references, operators, and values:

Table 7-3: Formula Syntax

Formula	Explanation
=A1+B1	Adds cells A1 and B1.
=220-B3	Subtracts cell B3 from 220.
=B3*85%	Multiplies cell B3 by 85% (0.85).
=(A1+A2)/2	Adds cells A1 and A2 and then divides by 2.

▶HOW TO: Create a Formula

1. Place the insertion point in the cell where you want to insert a formula.

2. Click the **Formula** button [*Table Tools Layout* tab, *Data* group] to open the *Formula* dialog box (Figure 7-5).

3. Delete the existing formula in the *Formula* area if necessary.
   * Word typically inserts a function in the *Formula* area.

4. Type = followed by the new formula.
   * Do not include spaces between the parts of a formula.

5. Click the **Number format** drop-down list to select a number format.

6. Click **OK** to close the dialog box and insert the formula.

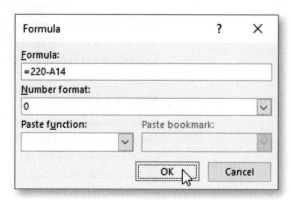

Figure 7-5 *Formula* dialog box

> ### ANOTHER WAY
>
> Click **Quick Parts** [*Insert* tab, *Text* group] and select **Field** to open the *Field* dialog box. Click **Formula** to open the *Formula* dialog box.

> ### MORE INFO
>
> Formulas created in Word tables are similar to formulas in Excel, with a few exceptions. One difference is you cannot select a cell in Word to automatically insert a cell reference in a formula as you can in Excel. Another difference is that formulas in Word do not update automatically when data changes.

Use a Function in a Formula

Functions are built-in formulas created for common types of calculations, such as *SUM* and *AVERAGE*. Functions require a specific syntax and save time once you understand how to build them. Functions typically are performed on a ***range*** of values. A range contains more than one cell. For example, use a function to add or average the values in a column or row. Table 7-4 displays the syntax for the *SUM* and *AVERAGE* functions.

Table 7-4: Formula Syntax

Function	Explanation
=SUM(B1:B5)	Adds values in cells B1 through B5. The colon between cell references is the syntax to represent a range of cells.
=SUM(ABOVE)	Adds all the values in the column above. "*Above*" is the syntax used to reference all the cells in the column above the formula.
=AVERAGE(A2:A5)	Averages the values in cells A2 through A5. The colon between cell references is the syntax to represent a range of cells.
=AVERAGE(LEFT)	Averages all the values in the row to the left. "*Left*" is the syntax used to reference all the cells in the row to the left of the formula.

▶ HOW TO: Use a Function in a Formula

1. Place the insertion point in the cell where you want to insert a formula.

2. Click the **Formula** button [*Table Tools Layout* tab, *Data* group] to open the *Formula* dialog box.

3. Delete the existing formula in the *Formula* area.

4. Type = and click the **Paste function** drop-down list and select the function.
   - Alternatively, type the function after the equals sign (=) using the proper syntax.

5. Type the range in the parentheses (Figure 7-6).
   - Use a colon (:) between cell references to create a range.
   - Alternatively, type **above** or **left** to use the cells above or to the left of the formula.

6. Click the **Number format** drop-down list to select the formula number format.

7. Click **OK** to close the dialog box and insert the formula.

Figure 7-6 Insert *AVERAGE* function

Edit a Formula

You may need to edit a formula to change the formula or the number format. The following are two ways to edit a formula:

- Select the formula and click the **Formula** button [*Table Tools Layout* tab, *Data* group] to open the *Formula* dialog box.
- Right-click the formula, select **Edit Field** from the context menu to open the *Field* dialog box, and click the **Formula** button to open the *Formula* dialog box.

Update a Formula

Each time you open a document, all the Word fields in the document update automatically (a formula is a Word field). But, when a document is open and the values in a table change, formulas do not update automatically; you must update the formulas manually. The following are two ways to update a formula:

- Right-click the formula and select **Update Field** from the context menu.
- Select the formula and press **F9**.

Change Text Direction

You can change the direction of text in a cell of the table. For example, change the direction of a title column on the left side of the table to display vertically.

▶ HOW TO: Change Text Direction

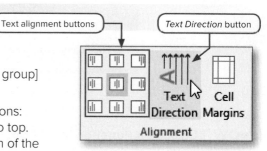

Text alignment buttons   *Text Direction* button

1. Select the cell or cells to change the text direction.
2. Click the **Text Direction** button [*Table Tools Layout* tab, *Alignment* group] (Figure 7-7).
   - The *Text Direction* button cycles through three text direction options: horizontal, vertical from top to bottom, and vertical from bottom to top.
   - Text displays on the *Text Direction* button to indicate the direction of the text in the cell.
   - Merging cells may be necessary before changing text direction.
3. Use the alignment buttons [*Table Tools Layout* tab, *Alignment* group] to adjust text alignment in the cell (see Figure 7-7).

Figure 7-7 Change text direction

Tabs and Indents in Tables

Pressing the *Tab* key in a table functions differently from using the tab key in paragraph text or a list. When you press the **Tab** key in a table, your insertion point moves to the next cell. But what if you need to align text or numbers in a cell using a tab stop? To move to a tab stop in the cell of a table, press **Ctrl+Tab**. Set tab stops in a table using the ruler or the *Tabs* dialog box. Tabs were covered in Chapter 2 in *SLO 2.2: Setting, Using, and Editing Tab Stops.*

▶ HOW TO: Set and Use Tab Stops in a Table

1. Select the entire table or the cells in the table where you want to set a tab stop.
2. Click the **Paragraph** launcher [*Layout* tab, *Paragraph* group] to open the *Paragraph* dialog box.
   - Alternatively, use the ruler to set tab stops. Select the type of tab stop from the *Tab* selector on the left side of the ruler. Click the ruler to set a tab stop.
3. Click the **Tabs** button to open the *Tabs* dialog box (Figure 7-8).
4. Type the tab stop position, select an alignment option, and click **Set**.
5. Click **OK** to close the dialog box.
6. Press **Ctrl+Tab** to move to the tab stop in the cell.

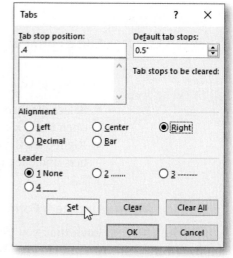

Figure 7-8 Set a tab stop in a table

Use indents in tables to control text alignment and alignment of carryover lines the same way you use indents in the body of a document. Set or modify indents in a table using one of the following methods:

- *Paragraph* group on the *Layout* tab
- *Paragraph* dialog box
- *Ruler*

> ▶ **MORE INFO**
>
> When setting or modifying tab stops or indents in a table, select the area of the table to change before modifying tab stops or indents.

Bullets and Numbering in Tables

Add bulleted and numbered lists to a table to display multiple lines of text in a cell or to itemize text in rows. The major difference when using lists in tables is the use of the *Tab* key. In lists that are not in a table, use the *Tab* key to increase the level of the list. For example, press **Tab** before typing a list to indent text to the next level; press **Shift+Tab** to decrease the level. Remember, pressing **Tab** in a table moves the insertion point to the next cell and **Shift+Tab** moves to the previous cell.

The following are two ways to adjust the level of a list in a table:

- Press the **Increase Indent** or **Decrease Indent** button [*Home* tab, *Paragraph* group].
- Click the **Bullets** or **Numbering** button [*Home* tab, *Paragraph* group], select **Change List Level**, and select the level.

> **ANOTHER WAY**
>
> Options to change the list level are available from the context menu when you right-click text in a list.

PAUSE & PRACTICE: WORD 7-1

For this Pause & Practice project, you modify a document from the American River Cycling Club about maximum and target heart rates. You convert text to a table, sort information in a table, change text direction, and create formulas.

File Needed: **HeartRate-07.docx** (*Student data files are available in the* Library *of your SIMnet account.*)
Completed Project File Name: **[your initials] PP W7-1.docx**

---

1. Open the **HeartRate-07** document from your student data files.

2. Save the document as [your initials] PP W7-1.

3. Convert text to a table.
   a. Select all the text aligned with tabs beginning with the "**Age**" column heading and ending with "**120-170**" in the third column.
   b. Click the **Table** button [*Insert* tab, *Tables* group] and select **Convert Text to Table** to open the *Convert Text to Table* dialog box (Figure 7-9).
   c. Confirm the number of columns in the *Table size* area is **3**.
   d. Click the **AutoFit to contents** radio button in the *AutoFit behavior* area.
   e. Click the **Tabs** radio button in the *Separate text at* section if it is not already selected.
   f. Click **OK** to close the dialog box and convert the text to a table.

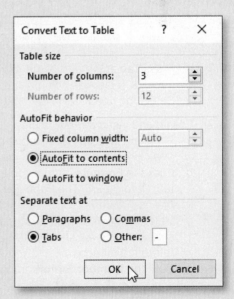

Figure 7-9 Convert selected text to a table

4. Sort the table in ascending order by age.
   a. Select the entire table if necessary and click the **Sort** button [*Table Tools Layout* tab, *Data* group]. The *Sort* dialog box opens (Figure 7-10).
   b. Select the **Header row** radio button in the *My list has* area.
   c. Click the **Sort by** drop-down list and select **Age**.
   d. Click the **Type** drop-down list and select **Number**.
   e. Click the **Using** drop-down list and select **Paragraphs**.
   f. Click the **Ascending** radio button.
   g. Click **OK** to close the dialog box and to sort the table.

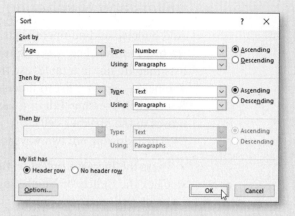

Figure 7-10 Sort the table in ascending order by age

5. Add a column, merge cells, add text, and change text direction.
   a. Place the insertion point in the first column of the table.
   b. Click the **Insert Left** button [*Table Tools Layout* tab, *Rows & Columns* group] to insert a column to the left of the first column.
   c. Click the **Merge Cells** button [*Table Tools Layout* tab, *Merge* group] to merge all the cells in the first column.
   d. Type Max and Target, press **Enter**, and type Heart Rates in the first column.
   e. Click the **Text Direction** button [*Table Tools Layout* tab, *Alignment* group] two times to change the text to vertical from the bottom (Figure 7-11).
   f. Click the **Align Center** button [*Table Tools Layout* tab, *Alignment* group] to align the text vertically and horizontally in the cell.
   g. Change the font size of the text in the first column to **20 pt** and the format to **small caps**.

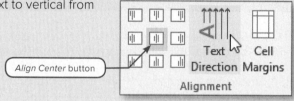

Figure 7-11 Change text direction

6. Add rows to the table and insert text.
   a. Place the insertion point in the last cell of the last row and press **Tab** to insert a new row.
   b. Type the following information in the new row:

| Age | Max Heart Rate | 60% of Max | 85% of Max |

   c. Press **Tab** at the end of the row to insert a new row.
   d. Type 28 in the *Age* column and press **Tab**.
   e. Select the headings in the next to the last row in the table and apply **bold** format.

7. Create and insert three formulas.
   a. Place the insertion point in the cell below "Max Heart Rate" in the last row of the table.
   b. Click the **Formula** button [*Table Tools Layout* tab, *Data* group]. The *Formula* dialog box opens (Figure 7-12).
   c. Delete the existing formula in the *Formula* area and type =220–A14. A14 is the cell reference for age.
   d. Click the **Number format** drop-down arrow and select **0**.
   e. Click **OK** to close the dialog box and to insert the formula.

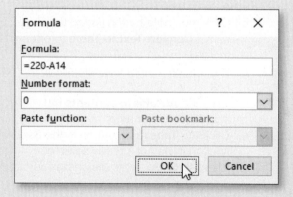

Figure 7-12 Insert a formula

f. Place the insertion point in the cell below "60% of Max" and create the following formula: =B14*60%. Use **0** as the number format. B14 is the cell containing the max heart rate formula.
   g. Place the insertion point in the cell below "85% of Max" and create the following formula: =B14*85%. Use **0** as the number format.

8. Edit a value and update formulas.
   a. Change the age in the first cell in the last row to 33.
   b. Select the formula in the last row below "Max Heart Rate" and press **F9** to update the formula. You might have to press **Fn+F9** if you are using a laptop computer.
   c. Right-click the formula below "60% of Max" and select **Update Field** from the context menu to update the formula.
   d. Update the formula below the "85% of Max" heading using one of the update methods.

9. Add bullets to selected text and adjust indents.
   a. Select the numbers in the column below the "Predicted Max Heart Rate" column heading beginning with "**200**" and ending with "**150**". Do not select the text in the last two rows.
   b. Apply a **check mark** bullet (Wingdings, character code 252).
   c. Confirm the bulleted list is still selected and change the left indent to **0"** [*Layout* tab, *Paragraph* group].
   d. Use the **Format Painter** to apply this bullet format to the value below "Max Heart Rate" in the last row of the table.

10. Save and close the document (Figure 7-13).

WHAT IS MAXIMUM HEART RATE?

Maximum heart rate is the highest your pulse rate can get. To calculate your **predicted maximum heart rate**, use this formula:

(Example: a 40-year-old's predicted maximum heart rate is 180.)

Your actual maximum heart rate can be determined by a graded exercise test. Please note that some medicines and medical conditions might affect your maximum heart rate. If you are taking medicines or have a medical condition (such as heart disease, high blood pressure, or diabetes), always ask your doctor if your maximum heart rate/target heart rate will be affected.

WHAT IS TARGET HEART RATE?

You gain the most benefits and decrease the risk of injury when you exercise in your target heart rate zone. Target heart rate (pulse) is generally defined as 60 percent to 85 percent of your maximum heart rate. Exercising above 85 percent of your maximum heart rate increases both cardiovascular and orthopedic risk and does not add any extra benefit.

When beginning an exercise program, gradually build up to a level that is within your target heart rate zone, especially if you have not exercised regularly before. If the exercise feels too hard, slow down. You will reduce your risk of injury and enjoy the exercise more if you don't over-do it.

To determine if you are exercising in your target zone (between 60 and 85 percent of your maximum heart rate), use a heart rate monitor to track your heart rate. If your pulse is below your target zone (see the chart below), increase your rate of exercise. If your pulse is above your target zone, decrease your rate of exercise.

MAX AND TARGET HEART RATE

Age	Predicted Max Heart Rate	Target Heart Rate (60-85% of Max)
20	✓ 200	120-170
25	✓ 195	117-166
30	✓ 190	114-162
35	✓ 185	111-157
40	✓ 180	108-153
45	✓ 175	105-149
50	✓ 170	102-145
55	✓ 165	99-140
60	✓ 160	96-136
65	✓ 155	93-132
70	✓ 150	90-128

Age	Max Heart Rate	60% of Max	85% of Max
33	✓ 187	112	159

Figure 7-13 PP W7-1 completed

Customizing Table Layout

After entering the content of a table, customize the table layout, such as adjusting the size of the table, columns, or rows. You can also modify table alignment on the page and how text aligns within the cells. Cell margins and spacing control space around the text in cells and space between cells. Tables can be split into multiple tables or combined into nested tables, which are tables within tables.

Table Size

Use the *Table Properties* dialog box to set a specific table width and row height. Use the *Table* tab in the *Table Properties* dialog box to set the table width, and use the *Row* tab to set row height.

▶ HOW TO: Resize a Table Using the Table Properties Dialog Box

1. Click the **table selector** in the upper-left corner of the table to select the entire table (see Figure 7-15).

   - Alternatively, click the **Select** button [*Table Tools Layout* tab, *Table* group] and select **Table**.

2. Click the **Properties** button [*Table Tools Layout* tab, *Table* group] to open the *Table Properties* dialog box (Figure 7-14).

3. Click the **Table** tab, check the **Preferred width** box, and type the width of the table.

4. Click the **Row** tab, check the **Specify height** box, and type the row height.

   - The height of all rows in the table changes.
   - Alternatively, click the **Previous Row** or **Next Row** button to individually set the height of each row.

5. Click **OK** to close the *Table Properties* dialog box.

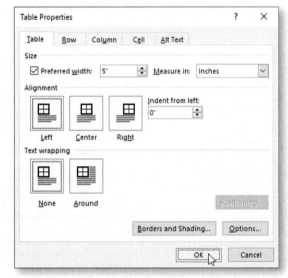

Figure 7-14 Change the width of a table

Manually resize a table by dragging the table sizing handle in the bottom-right corner of the table.

▶ HOW TO: Manually Resize a Table

1. Click the **table selector** in the upper-left corner of the table to select the entire table (Figure 7-15).

2. Click and drag the **table sizing handle** in the bottom-right corner of the table.

   - Your pointer becomes a diagonal sizing pointer.
   - Increase or decrease the height and width of the table using the table sizing handle.

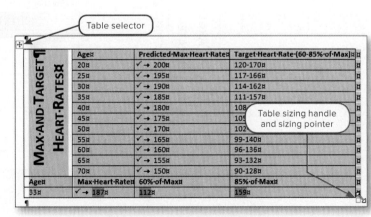

Figure 7-15 Resize a table using the table sizing handle

Row Height and Column Width

In addition to resizing the entire table, resize rows and columns individually using the following methods:

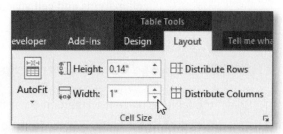

- Select the row or column to resize and change the size in the *Height* or *Width* area [*Table Tools Layout* tab, *Cell Size* group] (Figure 7-16).
- Use the *Row* and *Column* tabs in the *Table Properties* dialog box to change the height or width of specific columns and rows.
- Click and drag the right cell border to resize a column.
- Click and drag the bottom cell border to resize a row.

Figure 7-16 Resize columns and rows

Table Alignment and Position

Horizontally align a table the same way you align text in a document. Select the entire table and click an alignment button in the *Paragraph* group on the *Home* tab. You can also change the horizontal alignment of a table in the *Table Properties* dialog box (Figure 7-17).

By default, tables display in line with the text, which means the paragraph text aligns above or below the table. However, you can modify the table position to wrap paragraph text around a table. You can position a table anywhere in a document and specify how text wraps around a table as you have done with graphics (see *SLO 4.5: Working with Graphics*).

▶ HOW TO: Position a Table

1. Select the table or place the insertion point in the table.

2. Click the **Properties** button [*Table Tools Layout* tab, *Table* group] to open the *Table Properties* dialog box (see Figure 7-17).

3. Click the **Table** tab and click the **Around** button in the *Text wrapping* area.

   - The *Positioning* button becomes active when *Around* is selected, but it is not active if *None* is selected.

4. Click the **Positioning** button. The *Table Positioning* dialog box opens (Figure 7-18).

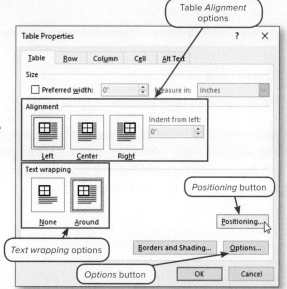

Figure 7-17 Set table to wrap around text

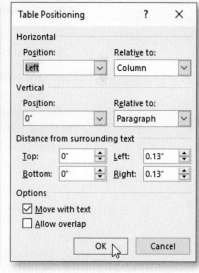

Figure 7-18 *Table Positioning* dialog box

5. Set the *Horizontal* and *Vertical* table position using the **Position** and **Relative to** drop-down lists.

6. Set the **Distance from surrounding** text, which is the minimum space between the table and surrounding text.

7. Click **OK** to close the *Table Positioning* dialog box.

8. Click **OK** to close the *Table Properties* dialog box.

Cell Margins and Spacing

In Chapter 4 you learned about cell margins, which are the margins in a cell around the text (see *SLO 4.2: Arranging Texts in Tables*). *Cell spacing* refers to the space between cells. Change cell margins and cell spacing in the *Table Options* dialog box.

▶ **HOW TO:** Change Cell Margins and Spacing

1. Select the table or place the insertion point in the table.
2. Click the **Cell Margins** button [*Table Tools Layout* tab, *Alignment* group] to open the *Table Options* dialog box (Figure 7-19).
3. Set the **Top**, **Bottom**, **Left**, and **Right** cell margins in the *Default cell margins* area.
4. Check the **Allow spacing between cells** box and set the amount of space between cells.
5. Check the **Automatically resize to fit contents** box so the table is resized based on the new cell margins and spacing.
6. Click **OK** to close the dialog box and apply the settings.

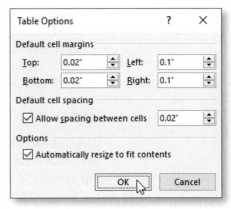

Figure 7-19 *Table Options* dialog box

> **ANOTHER WAY**
>
> Click the **Options** button on the *Table* tab in the *Table Properties* dialog box to open the *Table Options* dialog box to change cell margins and spacing.

Split a Table and Cells

The ***split table*** feature divides a table into one or more tables. When you split a table, it is split between rows, not columns. Position the insertion point in or select the row that will become the first row in the new table and click the **Split Table** button in the *Merge* group on the *Table Tools Layout* tab (Figure 7-20). The table becomes two tables with a blank line between the two tables.

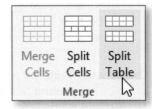

Figure 7-20 *Split Table* button

> **MORE INFO**
>
> When you split a table containing formulas with cell references, the cell references in the formulas in the split table may be incorrect. Edit the formulas and change the cell references if necessary.

You can also split cells into multiple rows or columns. Split a merged cell, an individual cell that has not been merged, or a range of cells in a table.

▶ HOW TO: Split a Cell

1. Select the cell or cells to be split.
2. Click the **Split Cells** button [*Table Tools Layout* tab, *Merge* group] to open the *Split Cells* dialog box (Figure 7-21).
3. Set the number of columns and rows.
    - When splitting a range of cells, the *Merge cells before split* check box is activated. Check this box to merge the cells before splitting the cells.
4. Click **OK** to close the dialog box and split the cells.

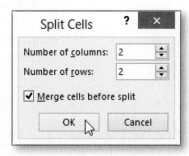

Figure 7-21 *Split Cells* dialog box

Nested Tables

Nested tables are tables within tables. Insert a table into a cell of another table the same way you insert a table into a document. In nested tables, the main table is called the ***parent table***, and the table within the parent table is the ***child table***. A parent table can contain more than one child table. Figure 7-22 displays an example of nested tables: the parent table has one column and two rows with the gridlines visible, and the parent table contains two child tables.

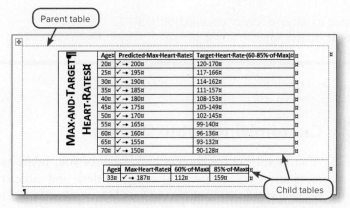

Figure 7-22 Nested tables

Repeat Header Rows

If a table spans multiple pages, improve readability by displaying column headings at the top of the second and continuing pages. The ***repeat header rows*** feature automatically displays the header row or rows at the beginning of each page. You can choose to have one or more rows repeat as the header row or rows. If information is inserted into or deleted from the table or page endings change, the header row still displays at the top of each page.

To use the feature, select the row or rows of the table to repeat at the top of each page and click the **Repeat Header Rows** button in the *Data* group on the *Table Tools Layout* tab (Figure 7-23). Turn off this feature by selecting the header row or rows and clicking the **Repeat Header Rows** button.

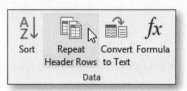

Figure 7-23 *Repeat Header Rows* button

Draw a Table

Another way to insert a table into a document is to use the **draw table** feature. Word provides a table drawing tool to create a table or add cells, rows, or columns to an existing table. When drawing a table, your pointer becomes a **pen**. Use the pen to draw a table or split cells into rows and columns. Use the **eraser** to erase cells, rows, or columns.

▶ **HOW TO:** Draw a Table

1. Click the **Table** button [*Insert* tab, *Tables* group] and select **Draw Table**. Your pointer becomes a pen.
2. Click and drag to draw the outside border of the table.
3. Draw vertical lines to create columns and draw horizontal lines to create rows (Figure 7-24).

    - Draw rows and columns outside the border of the table to add columns or rows to the table.
    - Draw diagonally within a table to create a new table (child table) inside the existing table (parent table).

4. Click the **Draw Table** button [*Table Tools Layout* tab, *Draw* group] or press **Esc** to turn off the draw table feature.
5. Click the **Eraser** button [*Table Tools Layout* tab, *Draw* group] and the pointer becomes an eraser.

    - Drag the eraser to remove row or column borders.
    - Click the **Eraser** button again to turn it off.

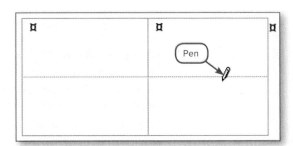

Figure 7-24 Create rows and columns using the pen

Customizing Table Design

After modifying the content and layout of your table, customize the table design to create a more attractive table. Use shading, borders, and table styles to improve the appearance and readability of your table. A **table style** is a collection of borders, shading, and fonts. You can apply table styles, modify table styles, and create custom table styles. Also, insert tables from the *Tables* building blocks gallery or add your own table to this gallery.

Border Painter

Use the **Border Painter** to draw borders on your table rather than selecting borders from the *Borders* drop-down list. The *Border Painter* is similar to drawing a table, except it draws borders on the table rather than creating new rows and columns.

▶ **HOW TO:** Use the Border Painter

1. Place the insertion point in the table to activate the *Table Tools* tabs.
2. Select the **Table Tools Design** tab.

3. Click the **Border Painter** button [*Borders* group] (Figure 7-25).

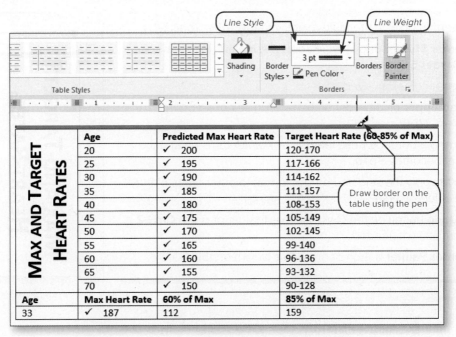

Figure 7-25 Draw a border using the *Border Painter*

- When you click the *Border Painter* button, the pointer becomes a pen to draw borders.
4. Click the **Line Style** drop-down arrow and select a border line style.
5. Click the **Line Weight** drop-down arrow and select a border line weight.
6. Click the **Pen Color** drop-down arrow and select a border color.
7. Click a border of the table to apply the selected border formatting.
   - Click and drag to apply the border across multiple columns or rows.
8. Click the **Border Painter** button or press **Esc** to turn off this feature.

Border Styles

The **Border Styles** gallery provides a variety of built-in border styles and colors (Figure 7-26). Selecting a border style from the *Border Styles* gallery turns on the *Border Painter* so you can draw borders on your table. Customize the border style using the *Line Style*, *Line Width*, and *Pen Color* drop-down lists.

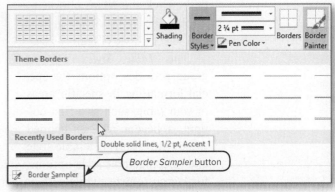

Figure 7-26 *Border Styles* gallery

Border Sampler

You previously used the *Format Painter* to copy text formatting and apply it to other text. The **Border Sampler** is similar to the *Format Painter*. Use the *Border Sampler* to select an existing border format from a table and apply it to other areas of the table or to a different table.

▶HOW TO: Use the Border Sampler

1. Place the insertion point in the table to activate the *Table Tools* tabs.
2. Click the **Border Styles** button [*Table Tools Design* tab, *Borders* group] and select **Border Sampler**.
   - The pointer becomes an eyedropper.
3. Click the **eyedropper** on a border of the table to select a border format (Figure 7-27).
   - After selecting a border format, the *Border Painter* turns on and the eyedropper becomes a pen.
4. Use the pen to apply the selected border format to other areas of the table or to a different table.
   - Click the **Undo** button on the *Quick Access* toolbar or press **Ctrl+Z** to undo formatting if needed.
5. Click the **Border Painter** button or press **Esc** to turn off this feature.

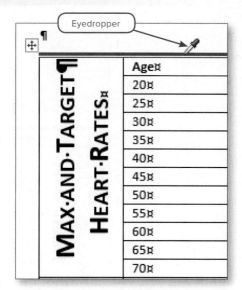

Figure 7-27 Use the eyedropper to select a border format

> **MORE INFO**
>
> Click the **Borders** launcher to open the *Borders and Shading* dialog box.

Table Styles

Table styles enhance the appearance of tables with borders, shading, and font formatting. The **Table Styles gallery** on the *Table Tools Design* tab displays the available table styles. To apply a table style to a selected table, click the **More** button to display the *Table Styles* gallery and select a style (Figure 7-28).

The **Table Styles Options** group provides options for special formatting in specific areas of your table, such as a first column, a header row, or banded rows. After applying a table style and selecting table style options,

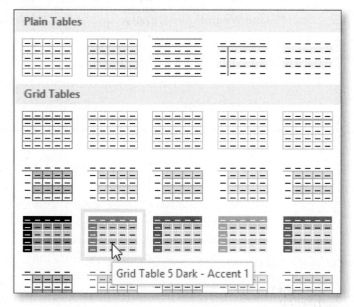

Figure 7-28 *Table Styles* gallery

further customize a table with borders, shading, font formatting, and paragraph formatting.

Modify a Table Style

Chapter 6 demonstrated the procedure to modify and create text styles (see *SLO 6.1: Creating and Using Custom Styles*). Similarly, you can modify and create table styles. Modify a table style after applying it to a table or modify a table style before applying it to a table. When you modify a table style, the changes apply to all tables in the document formatted with the table style.

W7-424

▶HOW TO: Modify a Table Style

1. Select a table and apply a table style from the *Table Styles* gallery [*Table Tools Design* tab, *Table Styles* group].
2. Click the **More** button in the *Table Styles* gallery and select **Modify Table Style**. The *Modify Style* dialog box opens (Figure 7-29).
   - Alternatively, right-click a style and select **Modify Table Style**.

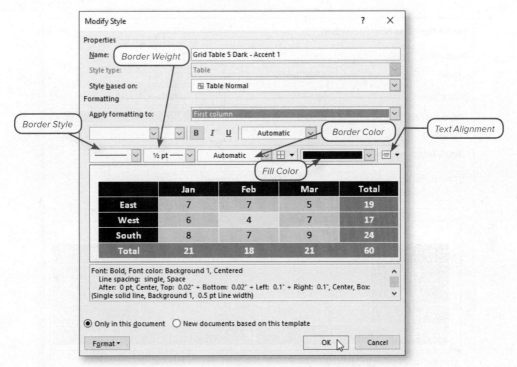

Figure 7-29 *Modify Style* dialog box

3. Type a name for the style in the *Name* text if you want to rename the style.
4. Click the **Apply formatting to** drop-down list and select an area of the table to modify formatting.
   - Apply changes to the *Whole table* or specific parts of the table, such as *Header row* or *First column*.
5. Use the **Border Style**, **Border Weight**, **Border Color**, **Fill Color**, and **Text Alignment** drop-down lists to modify the selected part of the table.
   - The *Preview* area displays the customized table style.
6. Click the **Format** button and select from additional formatting options.
   - Open any of the following dialog boxes and apply changes to the table style: *Table Properties*, *Borders and Shading*, *Banding*, *Font*, *Paragraph*, *Tabs*, and *Text Effects*.
   - Click **OK** to close any dialog box you opened and to return to the *Modify Style* dialog box.
7. Click **OK** to close the *Modify Style* dialog box and to apply the changes to the table style.

Create a New Table Style

Creating a new table style is similar to creating a text style. Most table styles are based on the *Table Normal* style. When creating a new style, you can base the style on any of the existing table styles and then apply changes as desired.

▶HOW TO: Create a New Table Style

1. Click the **More** button in the *Table Styles* gallery and select **New Table Style**. The *Create New Style from Formatting* dialog box opens (Figure 7-30).
   - Alternatively, right-click a style and select **New Table Style**.
   - By default, the *Only in this document* radio button is selected, which means this new style is only available in this document.
   - To make this style available in other documents, select **New documents based on this template**.

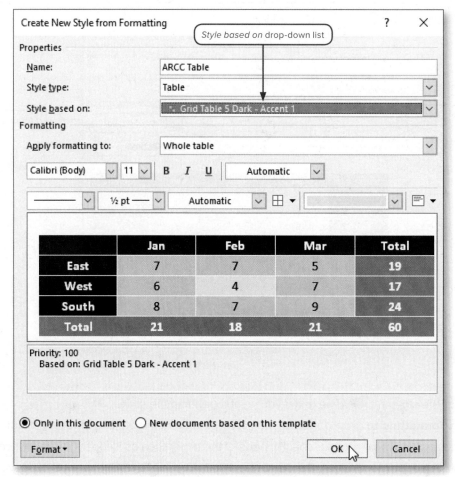

Figure 7-30 Create new table style

2. Type a name for the style in the *Name* text box.
3. Confirm the *Style type* is **Table**.
4. Click the **Style based on** drop-down list and select the table style on which to base the new style.
5. Click the **Apply formatting to** drop-down list and select an area of the table to modify formatting.
   - Apply changes to the *Whole table* or specific parts of the table, such as *Header row* or *First column*.
6. Use the **Border Style**, **Border Weight**, **Border Color**, **Fill Color**, and **Text Alignment** drop-down lists to modify the selected part of the table.
   - The *Preview* area displays the new table style.
7. Click the **Format** button and select from additional formatting options.
   - Open any of the following dialog boxes and apply changes to the table style: *Table Properties*, *Borders and Shading*, *Banding*, *Font*, *Paragraph*, *Tabs*, and *Text Effects*.
   - Click **OK** to close any dialog box you opened and to return to the *Create New Style from Formatting* dialog box.

8. Click **OK** to close the *Create New Style from Formatting* dialog box and apply the changes to the table style.
    - The new style is available in the *Table Styles* gallery in the *Custom* section (Figure 7-31).

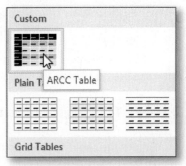

Figure 7-31 New custom style in the *Table Styles* gallery

Quick Tables Gallery

In Chapter 6, we covered building blocks (see *SLO 6.3: Understanding and Using Building Blocks*). Word includes *Table building blocks* to insert into your documents. *Table* building blocks are called *Quick Tables*. Insert a *Quick Table* from the gallery or save an existing table to the *Quick Tables* gallery.

▶ HOW TO: Insert a Quick Tables Building Block

1. Place the insertion point at the location to insert the table.
2. Click the **Table** button [*Insert* tab, *Tables* group].
3. Select **Quick Tables** to display the list of *Quick Tables* (Figure 7-32).

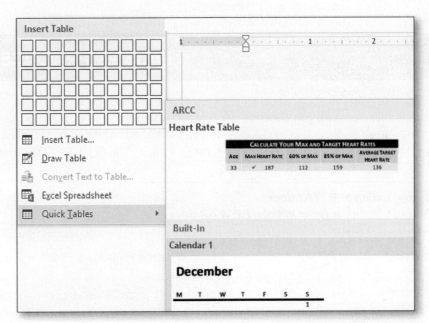

Figure 7-32 Insert *Quick Table*

4. Select a *Quick Table* to insert into your document.

> **ANOTHER WAY**
>
> Insert a *Quick Table* using the *Building Blocks Organizer*.

Save a table you use regularly as a *Table* building block, and the table displays in the *Quick Tables* gallery. Saving a table as a building block is similar to saving a *Header*, *Footer*, *AutoText*, or *Quick Part* building block.

▶ **HOW TO:** Save a Table to the Quick Tables Gallery

1. Select the table to save to the *Quick Tables* gallery.
2. Click the **Table** button [*Insert* tab, *Tables* group] and select **Quick Tables**.
3. Select **Save Selection to Quick Tables Gallery** at the bottom of the *Quick Tables* gallery. The *Create New Building Block* dialog box opens (Figure 7-33).
4. Fill in or select *Name*, *Gallery*, *Category*, *Description*, *Save in*, and *Options* information.
5. Click **OK** to close the dialog box.
   - The new *Table* building block displays in the *Quick Tables* gallery and the *Building Blocks Organizer*.

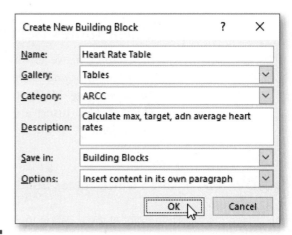

Figure 7-33 Save table as a building block in the *Quick Tables* gallery

PAUSE & PRACTICE: WORD 7-2

For this Pause & Practice project, you continue working with the document about maximum and target heart rates for the American River Cycling Club. You split a table, edit and create formulas, apply table styles, modify a table style, create a new table style, apply a custom table style, and save a table in the *Quick Tables* gallery.

File Needed: *[your initials] PP W7-1.docx*
Completed Project File Name: *[your initials] PP W7-2.docx*

1. Open the ***[your initials] PP W7-1*** document you completed in *Pause & Practice 7-1*.
2. Save the document as [your initials] PP W7-2.
3. Split the table into two tables.
   a. Place the insertion point in the next to the last row of the table.
   b. Click the **Split Table** button [*Table Tools Layout* tab, *Merge* group]. The last two rows split into a separate table.
4. Modify the new (second) table.
   a. Insert a column to the right of the last column in the new (second) table.
   b. Type Average Target in the last cell in the first row (second table), press **Enter**, and type Heart Rate.
   c. Insert a row above the first row in the second table.
   d. Merge the cells in the new first row.

e.   Turn on **Show/Hide** if it is not on, and if a paragraph mark displays in the merged row, delete the paragraph mark.

f.   Type Calculate Your Max and Target Heart Rates in the merged first row.

5.   Edit existing formulas and create a new formula.

a.   Select the maximum heart rate formula (second table, last row, second column) and click the **Formula** button [*Table Tools Layout* tab, *Data* group]. The *Formula* dialog box opens.

b.   Change the cell reference to A3 and click **OK** to close the dialog box (Figure 7-34). A3 is the cell reference for age in the new table.

c.   Edit the "60% of Max" and "85% of Max" formulas and type B3 as the cell reference. B3 is the cell reference for maximum heart rate in the new table.

d.   Place the insertion point in the last cell of the last column in the second table.

e.   Insert a formula to average the target heart rates. Use the following function syntax for your formula and use **0** number format.
=AVERAGE(C3:D3)

Figure 7-34 Edit existing formula

6.   Modify the first table and apply a style.

a.   Place the insertion point before "Heart" in the first table (first row, third column), press **Backspace** to delete the space, and press **Enter** to make a two-line column heading.

b.   Place the insertion point before "(60-85% of Max)" (first row, fourth column), press **Backspace** to delete the space, and press **Enter** to make a two-line column heading.

c.   Place the insertion point in the first table.

d.   Check the **Header Row**, **Banded Rows**, and **First Column** boxes in the *Table Styles Options* group [*Table Tools Design* tab] if they are not already checked. The other options should not be selected.

e.   Click the **More** button in the *Table Styles* gallery and select the **Grid Table 5 Dark - Accent 1** table style (Figure 7-35).

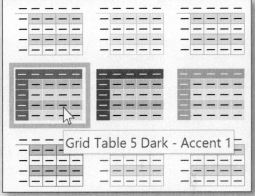

Figure 7-35 Apply a table style

7.   Modify a table style.

a.   Click the **More** button in the *Table Styles* gallery and select **Modify Table Style**. The *Modify Style* dialog box opens.

b.   Click the **Format** button and select **Table Properties** to open the *Table Properties* dialog box.

c.   Click the **Options** button to open the *Table Options* dialog box.

d.   Change the *Top* and *Bottom* cell margins to **0.02"** and the *Left* and *Right* cell margins to **0.1"**.

e.   Click **OK** to close the *Table Options* dialog box.

f.   Select **Center** in the *Alignment* area on the *Table* tab of the *Table Properties* dialog box.

g.   Click **OK** to close the *Table Properties* dialog box.

h.   Click the **Text Alignment** drop-down arrow and select **Align Center** (Figure 7-36).

i.   Click the **Apply formatting to** drop-down arrow and select **Header row**.

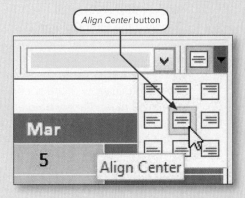

Figure 7-36 Change text alignment to *Align Center*

j. Click the **Fill Color** button and select the **fourth color** in the **last row** of *Theme Colors* (**Dark Blue, Text 2, Darker 50%**) (Figure 7-37).

k. Click the **Apply formatting to** drop-down arrow, select **First column**, and apply the same fill color to the first column.

l. Click **OK** to close the *Modify Style* dialog box.

8. Save your document, which saves the document and the modified table style.

9. Create a new table style.

    a. Select the first table, click the **More** button in the *Table Styles* gallery, and select **New Table Style**. The *Create New Style from Formatting* dialog box opens (Figure 7-38).

    b. Type **ARCC Table** in the *Name* area.

    c. Click the **Style based on** drop-down arrow and select **Grid Table 5 Dark - Accent 1**.

    d. Click **OK** to close the dialog box and create the new table style.

10. Apply custom table style and modify tables.

    a. Select the first table.

    b. Click the **More** button in the *Table Styles* gallery.

    c. Select the **ARCC Table** in the *Custom* area to apply the custom table style to the first table (Figure 7-39).

    d. Select the column headings in the first row of the first table (don't include the first column).

    e. Apply **small caps** format to the text. The text in this row should already be bold; if it is not, apply **bold**.

    f. Select all the text in the first column in the first table and apply **bold** (if it is not already bold).

    g. Select the second table.

    h. Deselect the **First Column** check box in the *Table Style Options* group [*Table Tools Design* tab]. *Header Row* and *Banded Rows* should be checked.

    i. Apply the **ARCC Table** custom table style.

    j. Select the first row of the second table, change the font size to **12 pt**, and apply **bold** and **small caps** format.

    k. Select the second row of the second table and apply **small caps** format. The text in this row should already be bold; if it is not, apply **bold**.

11. Save a table to the *Quick Tables* gallery.

    a. Select the entire second table.

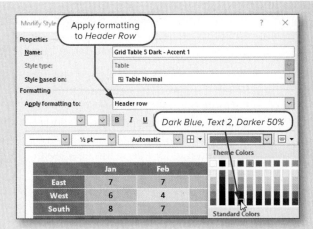

Figure 7-37 Change *Fill Color* of the header row

Figure 7-38 Create new table style

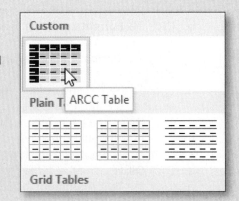

Figure 7-39 Apply custom table style

b. Click the **Table** button [*Insert* tab, *Tables* group], select **Quick Tables**, and select **Save Selection to Quick Tables Gallery** at the bottom of the *Quick Tables* list. The *Create New Building Block* dialog box opens (Figure 7-40).

c. Enter the following properties for the building block:
   Name: Heart Rate Table
   Gallery: **Tables**
   Category: ARCC (create new category)
   Description: Insert Heart Rate Table
   Save in: **Building Blocks**
   Options: **Insert content in its own paragraph**

d. Click **OK** to close the *Create New Building Block* dialog box.

12. Save and close the document (Figure 7-41). If prompted to save changes to building blocks, click **Save**.

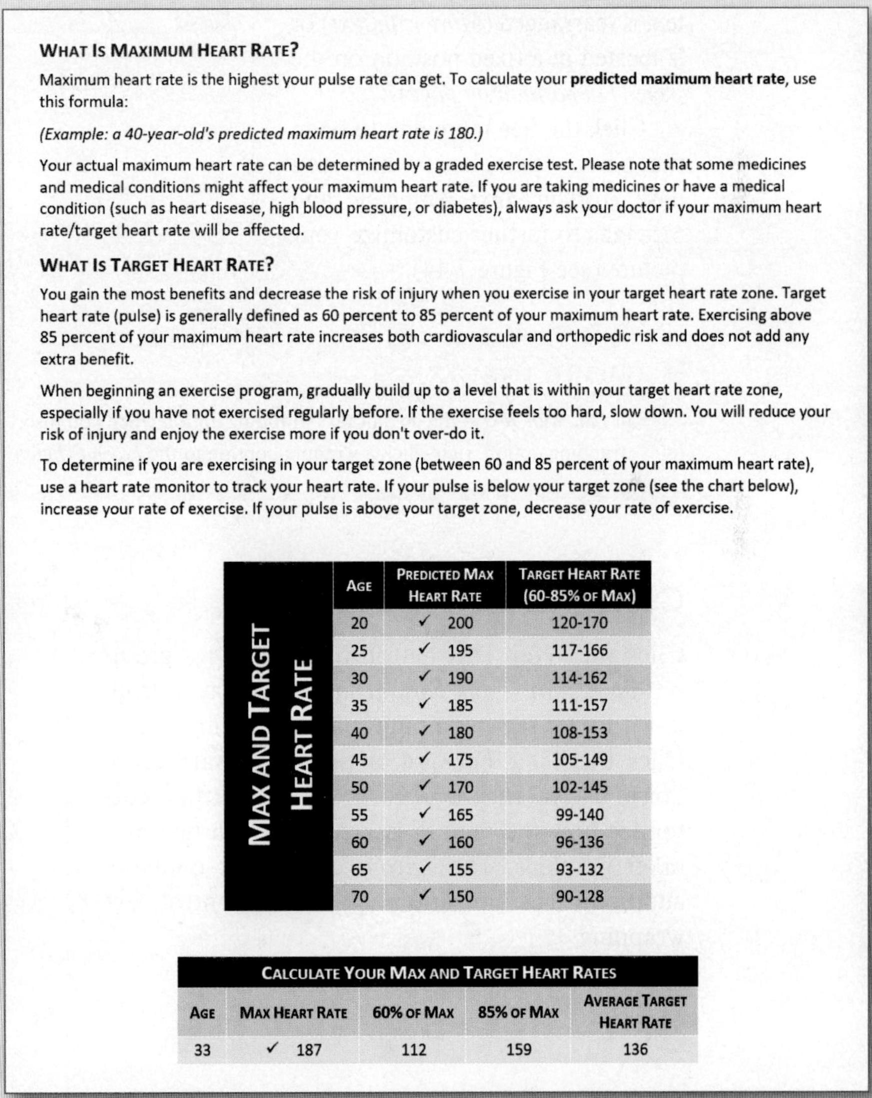

Create New Building Block ? ✕

Name:	Heart Rate Table
Gallery:	Tables
Category:	ARCC
Description:	Insert Heart Rate Table
Save in:	Building Blocks
Options:	Insert content in its own paragraph

OK   Cancel

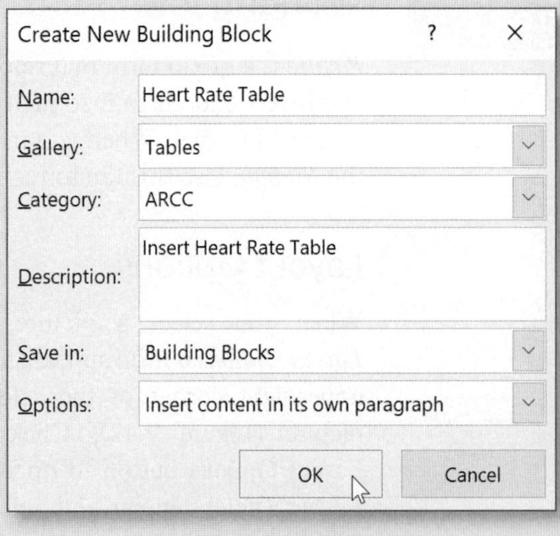

Figure 7-40 Create new table building block

WHAT IS MAXIMUM HEART RATE?

Maximum heart rate is the highest your pulse rate can get. To calculate your **predicted maximum heart rate**, use this formula:

(Example: a 40-year-old's predicted maximum heart rate is 180.)

Your actual maximum heart rate can be determined by a graded exercise test. Please note that some medicines and medical conditions might affect your maximum heart rate. If you are taking medicines or have a medical condition (such as heart disease, high blood pressure, or diabetes), always ask your doctor if your maximum heart rate/target heart rate will be affected.

WHAT IS TARGET HEART RATE?

You gain the most benefits and decrease the risk of injury when you exercise in your target heart rate zone. Target heart rate (pulse) is generally defined as 60 percent to 85 percent of your maximum heart rate. Exercising above 85 percent of your maximum heart rate increases both cardiovascular and orthopedic risk and does not add any extra benefit.

When beginning an exercise program, gradually build up to a level that is within your target heart rate zone, especially if you have not exercised regularly before. If the exercise feels too hard, slow down. You will reduce your risk of injury and enjoy the exercise more if you don't over-do it.

To determine if you are exercising in your target zone (between 60 and 85 percent of your maximum heart rate), use a heart rate monitor to track your heart rate. If your pulse is below your target zone (see the chart below), increase your rate of exercise. If your pulse is above your target zone, decrease your rate of exercise.

	AGE	PREDICTED MAX HEART RATE	TARGET HEART RATE (60-85% OF MAX)
MAX AND TARGET HEART RATE	20	✓ 200	120-170
	25	✓ 195	117-166
	30	✓ 190	114-162
	35	✓ 185	111-157
	40	✓ 180	108-153
	45	✓ 175	105-149
	50	✓ 170	102-145
	55	✓ 165	99-140
	60	✓ 160	96-136
	65	✓ 155	93-132
	70	✓ 150	90-128

CALCULATE YOUR MAX AND TARGET HEART RATES				
AGE	MAX HEART RATE	60% OF MAX	85% OF MAX	AVERAGE TARGET HEART RATE
33	✓ 187	112	159	136

Figure 7-41 PP W7-2 completed

Working with Pictures

Picture is a broad term that refers to many types of graphical images, including photos and clip art. Insert and customize pictures to enhance document layout and present information in a graphical format. When you insert or select a picture, the ***Picture Tools Format tab*** displays on the *Ribbon*. Use this tab to resize, arrange, and customize pictures.

Layout Options

When you select a picture, the ***Layout Options*** button appears in the upper-right corner of the selected picture (Figure 7-42). Click the **Layout Options** button to open the *Layout Options* menu and select a text wrapping option. In this menu, select whether the picture moves as text is rearranged (*Move with text*) or is located in a fixed position on the page (*Fix position on page*).

Click the **See more** link to open the *Layout* dialog box where you have *Position*, *Text Wrapping*, and *Size* tabs to further customize your picture (see Figure 7-44).

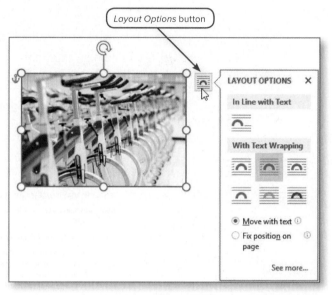

Figure 7-42 *Layout Options* menu

> ## MORE INFO
>
> *In Line with Text* is the default text wrapping option when you insert a picture. To change the default wrapping option, right-click a wrapping option in the *Layout Options* menu and select **Set as Default**.

Customize Text Wrapping

Click the **Wrap Text** button in the *Arrange* group on the *Picture Tools Format* tab to display a drop-down list of text wrapping options (Figure 7-43). Click the **Bring Forward** or **Send Backward** drop-down list in the *Arrange* group to further customize how the picture is arranged with text and other graphics. The *Layout* dialog box contains additional customization options to control text wrapping.

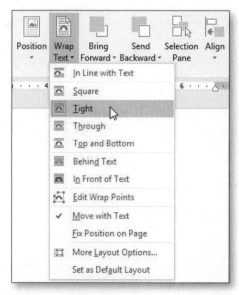

Figure 7-43 Text wrapping options from the *Wrap Text* drop-down list

▶ HOW TO: Customize Text Wrapping Options

1. Select the picture.

2. Click the **Wrap Text** button [*Picture Tools Format* tab, *Arrange* group] and select **More Layout Options**. The *Layout* dialog box opens and displays the *Text Wrapping* tab (Figure 7-44).

3. Select a *Wrapping style* to specify how the text wraps around the picture.

4. Select one of the *Wrap text* radio buttons to specify how the text wraps around the sides of the graphic.

5. Set the specific distance for text to wrap around the graphic in the *Distance from text* area.

   • The *Wrapping style* option you chose controls which options are available in the *Distance from text* area.

6. Click **OK** to close the *Layout* dialog box.

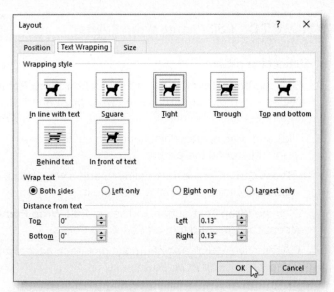

Figure 7-44 Text wrapping options in the *Layout* dialog box

Alignment Guides and Live Layout

After inserting a picture and selecting a text wrapping option, you can drag the picture to the desired location. Word provides features to help you accurately position pictures. *Alignment guides* are vertical and horizontal green lines that display to guide alignment (Figure 7-45). As you drag the picture to a location, the vertical alignment guide displays at the left and right margins and the center of the document. The horizontal alignment guide displays at the top and bottom margins and on lines of text.

Click the **Align** button in the *Arrange* group on the *Picture Tools Format* tab and select **Use Alignment Guides** from the drop-down list to display alignment guides. *Live layout* automatically rearranges text and other objects in your document as you move a picture to a new location.

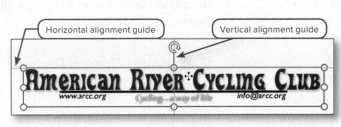

Figure 7-45 Alignment guides displayed

> **ANOTHER WAY**
>
> The *Align* drop-down list is also available in the *Arrange* group on the *Layout* tab.

Picture Wrap Points

Wrap points are the points around a picture that control the position of text in relationship to the picture. Edit these wrap points to more precisely position text around the picture.

1. Select the picture.
2. Click the **Wrap Text** button and select **Edit Wrap Points**. The selected picture displays the wrap point handles (Figure 7-46).
3. Click and drag a wrap point handle to customize text wrapping around the picture.
   - Press **Ctrl** and click the red line to add a wrap point. Press **Ctrl** and click a wrap point to delete it.
4. Click the **Wrap Text** button and select **Edit Wrap Points** to accept changes and turn off *Edit Wrap Points*.
   - Alternatively, click away from the picture to accept changes and turn off *Edit Wrap Points*.

Figure 7-46 Edit wrap points

Picture Anchor

The *picture anchor* is a blue anchor icon and displays where the picture is connected (anchored) to text (Figure 7-47). The picture anchor enables a picture to move with selected text if a document is modified and the text rearranges on the page. The picture anchor displays when you select a picture.

When you insert a picture, the picture anchor is automatically placed to the left of the paragraph closest to the picture. The picture anchor always displays at the beginning of a paragraph. Click and drag the **picture anchor** icon to anchor the picture to a different location.

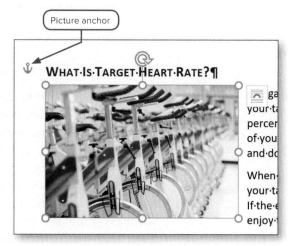

Figure 7-47 Picture anchor

Resize and Crop a Picture

The following list describes different ways to resize a picture:

- *Sizing handles*: Drag the sizing handles to increase or decrease the size of the picture.
- *Size group*: Type a specific size in the *Height* and *Width* areas in the *Size* group on the *Picture Tools Format* tab.
- *Layout dialog box*: Click the **Size** launcher to open the *Layout* dialog box. Click the **Size** tab and type a specific height and width or scale the picture to a percentage of its original size.

Aspect ratio is the relationship between the width and height of a picture. When resizing a picture, it is best to maintain picture proportion. This prevents distortion of the image. By default, when you change the size in the *Size* group or in the *Layout* dialog box, the aspect ratio is locked to keep the picture proportional to its original size. When resizing a picture using the sizing handles, the corner sizing handles resize the picture proportionally. However, the side sizing handles do not resize the picture proportionally.

Cropping is different from resizing a picture. While cropping does resize a picture, it does so by removing part of the picture. Use cropping to remove unwanted portions of a picture.

▶HOW TO: Crop a Picture

1. Select the picture to crop.
2. Click the top half of the **Crop** button [*Picture Tools Format* tab, *Size* group].
   - Cropping handles appear in the corners and on the sides (Figure 7-48).
   - Click the bottom half of the **Crop** button to display a drop-down list of cropping options (Figure 7-49). Select **Crop to Shape** or **Aspect Ratio** to crop a picture to a specific shape or aspect ratio. Select **Fill** or **Fit** to crop a picture to a specific size.

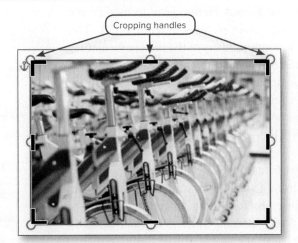

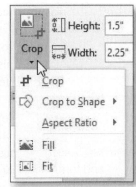

Figure 7-48 Picture with cropping handles displayed   Figure 7-49 Cropping options

3. Drag a cropping handle to edit the picture.
4. Click the **Crop** button again, press **Esc**, or click away from the picture to accept the changes and to turn off cropping.

▶ **ANOTHER WAY**

To crop a picture, right-click the picture and select **Crop** from the mini toolbar.

▶ **MORE INFO**

Click the **Undo** button on the *Quick Access* toolbar or press **Ctrl+Z** to undo changes made to a picture.

Rotate a Picture

Rotate a picture in a document to enhance its placement. Select the picture and use one of the following methods to rotate the picture:

- **Rotation handle**: Click the rotation handle at the top and drag to the left or right to rotate the picture (Figure 7-50).

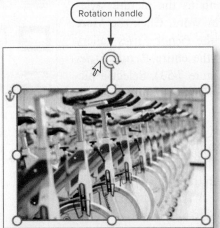

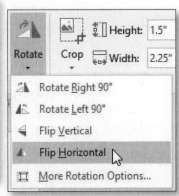

Figure 7-50 Picture with rotation handle displayed   Figure 7-51 Rotate options

- **Rotate drop-down list**: Click the **Rotate** button in the *Arrange* group on the *Picture Tools Format* tab to display the drop-down list of rotate options (Figure 7-51).
- **Layout dialog box**: Click the **Rotate** button and select **More Rotation Options** to open the *Layout* dialog box. Click the **Size** tab and change the degree of rotation in the *Rotate* area.

Format Picture Pane

Use the **Format Picture pane** to modify and enhance your pictures (Figure 7-52). This pane contains many of the picture formatting features that are available on the *Picture Tools Format* tab. Click the **Picture Styles** launcher to open the *Format Picture* pane. You can also open this pane from many of the drop-down lists on the *Picture Tools Format* tab.

The formatting categories display at the top of this pane. Click one of the category buttons to display the options in that category. The four main formatting categories and the different options in each category are listed below:

- **Fill & Line**: *Fill* and *Line*
- **Effects**: *Shadow, Reflection, Glow, Soft Edges, 3-D Format, 3-D Rotation,* and *Artistic Effects*
- **Layout & Properties**: *Text Box* and *Alt Text*
- **Picture**: *Picture Corrections, Picture Color,* and *Crop*

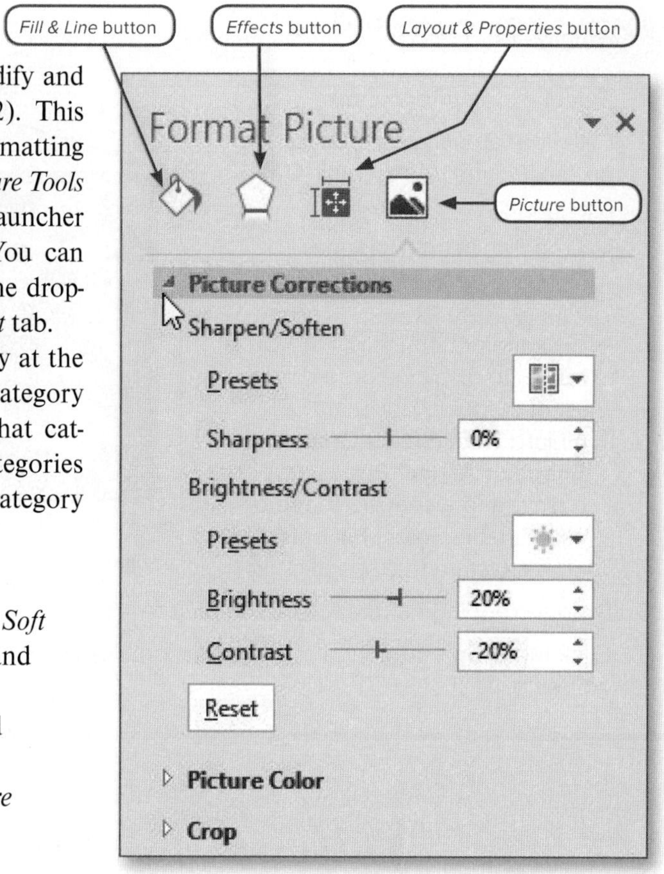

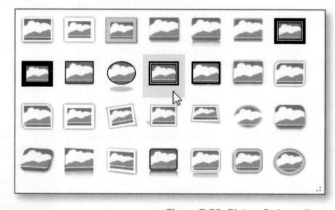

Fill & Line button   *Effects* button   *Layout & Properties* button

Format Picture

Picture button

◢ **Picture Corrections**

Sharpen/Soften

Presets

Sharpness ——|——— 0%

Brightness/Contrast

Presets

Brightness ———|—— 20%

Contrast ——|——— -20%

Reset

▷ **Picture Color**

▷ **Crop**

Figure 7-52 *Format Picture* pane

Picture Styles

Similar to text and table styles, **picture styles** apply preset borders and effects. The **Picture Styles gallery** contains the picture styles available in Word. Click the **More** button in the *Picture Styles* gallery to display the entire *Picture Styles* gallery (Figure 7-53). Select a picture and click a picture style to apply it to the picture. When you place your pointer on a picture style, the picture style temporarily applies to the picture to preview the picture with the style applied.

Figure 7-53 *Picture Styles* gallery

> **ANOTHER WAY**
> Right-click a picture and select a picture style from the mini toolbar.

Picture Borders

Apply a border to your pictures and customize the color of the border, the border weight (size of the border), and the type of border line.

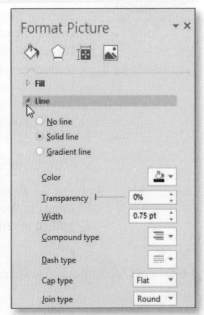

▶ HOW TO: Apply a Picture Border

1. Select the picture.
2. Click the **Picture Border** button [*Picture Tools Format* tab, *Picture Styles* group] to display the drop-down list of picture border options (Figure 7-54).
3. Select the border color in the *Theme Colors* or *Standard Colors* area.
   - Click **More Outline Colors** to open the *Colors* dialog box and choose from more border color options.
4. Select **Weight** and select the thickness of the border line.
5. Select **Dashes** and select the type of border line.
   - Select *More Lines* from the *Weight* or *Dashes* drop-down list to open the *Format Picture* pane that displays more line options (Figure 7-55).

Figure 7-54 Picture border options

Figure 7-55 Picture border line options in the *Format Picture* pane

Alternatively, apply a picture border from the *Format Picture* pane. Click the **Picture Styles** launcher to open the *Format Picture* pane (see Figure 7-55). Click the **Fill & Line** button at the top to customize the picture border. Click **Fill** or **Line** to display the customization options below each of these categories.

Picture Effects

Use ***picture effects*** to apply *Preset, Shadow, Reflection, Glow, Soft Edges, Bevel,* or *3-D Rotation* effects to a picture. Click the **Picture Effects** button in the *Picture Styles* group on the *Picture Tools Format* tab to display the picture effects categories. Select a picture effect category to display a drop-down list of options (Figure 7-56).

At the bottom of each drop-down list is an options button (for example, *Shadow Options*). Click an options button to open the *Format Picture* pane. The *Format Picture* pane contains the *Shadow, Reflection, Glow, Soft Edges, 3-D Format, 3-D Rotation,* and *Artistic Effects* categories.

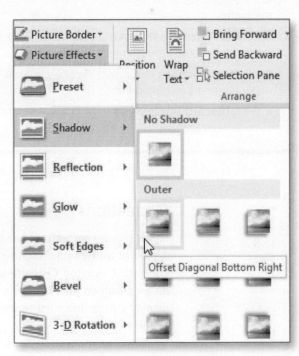

Figure 7-56 *Picture Effects* drop-down list

Adjusting and Changing Pictures

Remove background, apply corrections, change colors, or add artistic effects to adjust pictures. Also, compress pictures to reduce the file size, change a picture in the document, or reset a picture to its original size and appearance. Apply these adjustments from the *Adjust* group on the *Picture Tools Format* tab.

Remove Background

Use the ***Remove Background*** feature to apply transparency to selected areas of a picture. When using the *Remove Background* feature, Word automatically selects a portion of the picture background to remove. You can customize the areas of the picture to keep or remove.

▶ **HOW TO:** Remove Background from a Picture

1. Select the picture.
2. Click the **Remove Background** button [*Picture Tools Format* tab, *Adjust* group].
   - Word selects the background to remove and highlights it in pink (Figure 7-57).
   - The *Background Removal* tab displays (Figure 7-58).
3. Click **Mark Areas to Keep** [*Background Removal* tab] and draw around areas to retain on the picture.
4. Click **Mark Areas to Remove** [*Background Removal* tab] and draw around areas to remove on the picture.
5. Click **Keep Changes** to remove the selected background and make those areas transparent.
   - Click **Discard All Changes** to return the picture to its original state.

Figure 7-57 **Remove highlighted background from a picture**

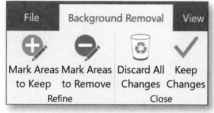

Figure 7-58 *Background Removal* tab

Corrections

Apply picture corrections to sharpen or soften a picture and change picture brightness and contrast. Click the **Corrections** button in the *Adjust* group on the *Picture Tools Format* tab to display a drop-down list of correction options (Figure 7-59).

The *Corrections* drop-down list displays two categories of correction options: *Sharpen/Soften*

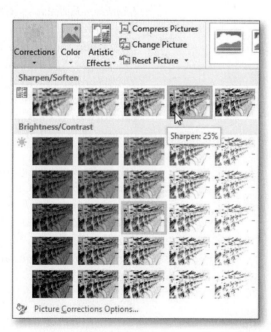

Figure 7-59 **Picture correction options**

and *Brightness/Contrast*. Each of the options in both categories changes the picture by a percentage of the original picture. Click **Picture Corrections Options** to open the *Format Picture* pane for additional correction options.

Color

Click the **Color** button in the *Adjust* group on the *Picture Tools Format* tab to display a drop-down list of color options (Figure 7-60). Adjust the color tone or color saturation of a picture or recolor a picture.

The *Color* drop-down list displays three categories of color options: *Color Saturation*, *Color Tone*, and *Recolor*. Click **Picture Color Options** to open the *Format Picture* pane for additional correction options. Click **More Variations** for additional color options.

You can also change a color in the picture to be transparent. Click **Set Transparent Color** and select the color or colors in the picture to make transparent.

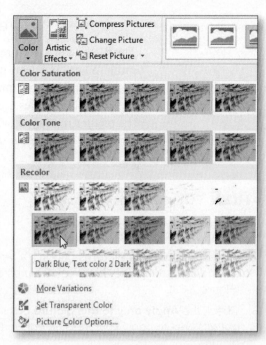

Figure 7-60 Picture color options

Artistic Effects

Word provides a variety of artistic effects to adjust pictures. Click the **Artistic Effects** button in the *Adjust* group on the *Picture Tools Format* tab to display a drop-down list of options (Figure 7-61). Click **Artistic Effects Options** to open the *Format Picture* pane to view additional artistic effect options.

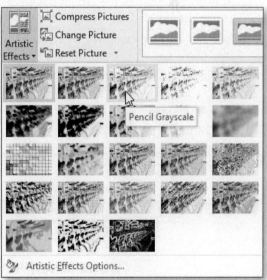

Figure 7-61 Artistic picture effects

Transparency

The *Transparency* feature is new to Word 365. This feature allows you to apply a percentage of transparency to a picture. The higher the percent of transparency, the more transparent the picture displays. Click the **Transparency** button in the *Adjust* group on the *Picture Tools Format* tab and choose from the preset transparency options (Figure 7-62). Click **Picture Transparency Options** to open the *Picture Format* pane on the right where you can specify a custom transparency percentage.

Office 2019 Note: The *Transparency* feature is not available in Office 2019.

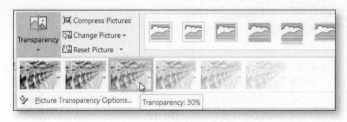

Figure 7-62 *Transparency* options

Compress Pictures

The file size of a picture can range from a few kilobytes (KB) up to a few megabytes (MB) or more. When you insert pictures into a document, the file size of the document increases. Word provides options to compress the file size of pictures to prevent the document from becoming too large (larger files are harder to send via email). When you compress a picture, it changes the picture *resolution*, which affects picture quality. Compressed picture files have lower resolution and are of lesser quality.

▶HOW TO: Compress Pictures

1. Select the picture to compress.
2. Click the **Compress Pictures** button [*Picture Tools Format* tab, *Adjust* group]. The *Compress Pictures* dialog box opens (Figure 7-63).
3. Check the **Apply only to this picture** box in the *Compression options* area to apply compression only to the selected picture.
   - Deselect this check box to apply the settings to all pictures in the document.
   - The *Delete cropped areas of pictures* is checked by default. This option removes the cropped area of pictures (if the picture has been cropped) and reduces the file size.
4. Select one of the picture resolution radio buttons in the *Resolution* area.
   - The default setting is *Use default resolution*.
   - The *Resolution* options available depend on the picture type and its original resolution.
5. Click **OK** to close the dialog box and compress the picture or pictures.

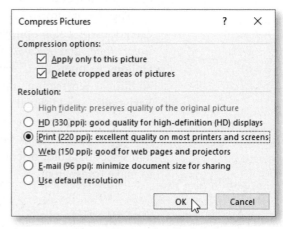

Figure 7-63 *Compress Pictures* dialog box

Change Picture

Use the *Change Picture* command to quickly replace a picture with another picture in a Word document. The *Change Picture* feature removes an existing picture and replaces it with a different picture while retaining the picture size and formatting.

▶HOW TO: Change a Picture in a Document

1. Select the picture to change.
2. Click the **Change Picture** button [*Picture Tools Format* tab, *Adjust* group] and select from the following options (Figure 7-64):
   - Select **From a file** to open the *Insert Picture* dialog box.
   - Select **From Online Sources** to open the *Online Pictures* dialog box. In this dialog box, you can search *Bing* or *OneDrive* for pictures.
   - Select **From Icons** to open the *Insert Icons* dialog box.

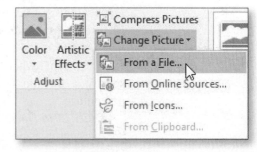

Figure 7-64 *Change Picture* drop-down list

- Select **From Clipboard** to replace the existing picture with a copied picture stored in the *Clipboard*.
- Alternatively, right-click a picture, select **Change Picture**, and select an option from the context menu.
3. Browse or search to find and select the picture or icon you want to insert to replace the selected picture.
4. Click the **Insert** button to insert the new picture.
- The size and formatting of the original picture applies to the new picture.

Reset Picture

After making changes to a picture, you might decide to discard the changes and return to the original picture. Click the **Reset Picture** drop-down arrow in the *Adjust* group on the *Picture Tools Format* tab and select from the following options (Figure 7-65):

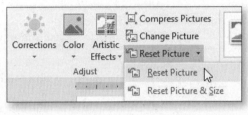

Figure 7-65 *Reset Picture* options

- ***Reset Picture***: Discards all formatting changes
- ***Reset Picture & Size***: Discards all formatting and sizing changes

PAUSE & PRACTICE: WORD 7-3

For this Pause & Practice project, you work with the American River Cycling Club document to insert two pictures and modify the size, arrangement, borders, and effects. You also apply adjustments to the pictures and compress the pictures.

Files Needed: ***[your initials] PP W7-2.docx, ARCC-logo-07.png***, and ***Bikes-07.png*** *(Student data files are available in the* Library *of your SIMnet account.)*
Completed Project File Name: ***[your initials] PP W7-3.docx***

1. Open the ***[your initials] PP W7-2*** document you completed in *Pause & Practice 7-2*.

2. Save the document as [your initials] PP W7-3.

3. Change the top and bottom margins to **0.5"** and the left and right margins to **0.75"**. If you are prompted about margins being outside printable area, click **Ignore**.

4. Select the "**What Is Maximum Heart Rate?**" heading and change the *Before* spacing to **12 pt**.

5. Insert, resize, and arrange a picture.
   a. Place the insertion point at the beginning of the document.
   b. Insert the **ARCC-logo-07** picture from your student data files.
   c. Click the **Alt Text** button [*Picture Tools Format* tab, *Accessibility* group], type ARCC logo in the text box to replace the existing alt text, and close the *Alt Text* pane.
   d. Click the **Size** launcher [*Picture Tools Format* tab, *Size* group] to open the *Layout* dialog box.
   e. Click the **Height** text box in the *Scale* area, type 150% to replace the existing setting, and press **Tab**. The *Width* automatically changes.
   f. Click the **Text Wrapping** tab and change the text wrapping to **Top and Bottom**.

g. Click **OK** to close the *Layout* dialog box.

h. Drag the picture so it is positioned at the top margin and centered horizontally. Use the alignment guides to position the picture accurately (Figure 7-66). If the alignment guides don't display, click **Align** [*Picture Tools Format* tab, *Arrange* group] and select **Use Alignment Guides**.

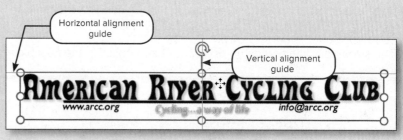

Figure 7-66 Use the alignment guides to position the picture

6. Use the *Format Picture* pane to modify a picture.

a. Select the logo and click the **Picture Styles** launcher to open the *Format Picture* pane.

b. Click the **Fill & Line** button at the top of the pane and select **Line** to display the *Line* setting options (Figure 7-67).

c. Select the **Solid line** radio button.

d. Click the **Color** drop-down arrow and select the **fourth color** in the **last row** of *Theme Colors* (**Dark Blue, Text 2, Darker 50%**).

e. Change the *Width* to **1.5 pt**.

f. Click the **Picture** button at the top of the pane and select **Picture Color** to open the *Picture Color* settings.

g. Click the **Recolor** drop-down list and select the **second option** in the **second row** (**Blue, Accent color 1 Dark**) (Figure 7-68).

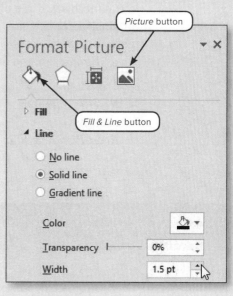

Figure 7-67 *Fill & Line* area of the *Format Picture* pane

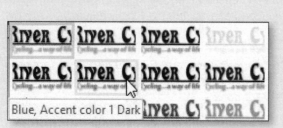

Figure 7-68 Recolor picture

h. Click the **Picture Corrections** category in the *Format Picture* pane to display the options.

i. Change the *Brightness* to **20%** and the *Contrast* to **−20%** in the *Brightness/Contrast* area. Use the up and down arrows or type the settings (Figure 7-69).

j. Click the **X** in the upper-right corner to close the *Format Picture* pane.

7. Insert, resize, arrange, and add alt text to a picture.

a. Place the insertion point in front of the "What Is Target Heart Rate?" heading.

b. Insert the ***Bikes-07*** picture from your student data files.

c. Right-click the bike picture and select **Edit Alt Text** from the context menu.

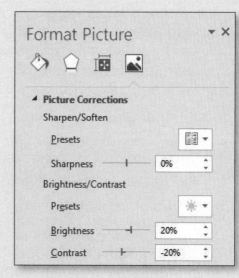

Figure 7-69 Adjust picture brightness and contrast

d. Type **Picture of bicycles** in the text box to replace the existing alt text and close the *Alt Text* pane.

e. Type 1.5 in the *Height* area [*Picture Tools Format* tab, *Size* group] and press **Enter**. The width automatically adjusts to maintain the aspect ratio.

f. Click the **Wrap Text** button [*Picture Tools Format* tab, *Arrange* group] and select **Tight**.

g. Click the **Align** button [*Picture Tools Format* tab, *Arrange* group] and select **Align Right**.

h. Drag the picture anchor to the first paragraph below "What Is Target Heart Rate?" (Figure 7-70).

What·Is·Target·Heart·Rate?¶

⚓ You·gain·the·most·benefits·and·decrease· your·target·heart·rate·zone.·Target·heart· percent·to·85·percent·of·your·maximum·h percent·of·your·maximum·heart·rate·incr orthopedic·risk·and·does·not·add·any·ext

Figure 7-70 Move picture anchor

8. Modify the picture.

a. Select the bike picture, click the **Picture Effects** button [*Picture Tools Format* tab, *Picture Styles* group], select **Shadow**, and select **Offset: Bottom Right** (**first option** in the *Outer* section) (Figure 7-71).

Figure 7-71 Apply shadow picture effect

b. Click the **Artistic Effects** button [*Picture Tools Format* tab, *Adjust* group] and select **Pencil Grayscale** (**third option** in the **first row**) (Figure 7-72).

c. Click the **Color** button [*Picture Tools Format* tab, *Adjust* group] and select **Dark Blue**, **Text color 2 Dark** (**first option** in the **second row** in the *Recolor* area) (Figure 7-73).

Figure 7-72 Apply artistic effect

Figure 7-73 Apply picture color

9. Compress the picture.

a. Select the bikes picture.

b. Click the **Compress Pictures** button [*Picture Tools Format* tab, *Adjust* group] to open the *Compress Pictures* dialog box.

c. Select the **Print (220 ppi)** radio button in the *Resolution* area.

d. Click **OK** to close the dialog box and compress the picture.

10. Save and close the document (Figure 7-74).

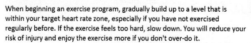

American River Cycling Club
www.arcc.org   Cycling...a way of life   info@arcc.org

WHAT IS MAXIMUM HEART RATE?

Maximum heart rate is the highest your pulse rate can get. To calculate your **predicted maximum heart rate**, use this formula:

(Example: a 40-year-old's predicted maximum heart rate is 180.)

Your actual maximum heart rate can be determined by a graded exercise test. Please note that some medicines and medical conditions might affect your maximum heart rate. If you are taking medicines or have a medical condition (such as heart disease, high blood pressure, or diabetes), always ask your doctor if your maximum heart rate/target heart rate will be affected.

WHAT IS TARGET HEART RATE?

You gain the most benefits and decrease the risk of injury when you exercise in your target heart rate zone. Target heart rate (pulse) is generally defined as 60 percent to 85 percent of your maximum heart rate. Exercising above 85 percent of your maximum heart rate increases both cardiovascular and orthopedic risk and does not add any extra benefit.

When beginning an exercise program, gradually build up to a level that is within your target heart rate zone, especially if you have not exercised regularly before. If the exercise feels too hard, slow down. You will reduce your risk of injury and enjoy the exercise more if you don't over-do it.

To determine if you are exercising in your target zone (between 60 and 85 percent of your maximum heart rate), use a heart rate monitor to track your heart rate. If your pulse is below your target zone (see the chart below), increase your rate of exercise. If your pulse is above your target zone, decrease your rate of exercise.

MAX AND TARGET HEART RATE

AGE	PREDICTED MAX HEART RATE	TARGET HEART RATE (60-85% OF MAX)
20	✓ 200	120-170
25	✓ 195	117-166
30	✓ 190	114-162
35	✓ 185	111-157
40	✓ 180	108-153
45	✓ 175	105-149
50	✓ 170	102-145
55	✓ 165	99-140
60	✓ 160	96-136
65	✓ 155	93-132
70	✓ 150	90-128

CALCULATE YOUR MAX AND TARGET HEART RATES			
AGE	MAX HEART RATE	60% OF MAX	85% OF MAX	AVERAGE TARGET HEART RATE
33	✓ 187	112	159	136

Figure 7-74 PP W7-3 completed

SLO 7.6

Working with Shapes

When working with shapes, you can modify their size, arrangement, style, fill color, border color, and effects. Customizing shapes is similar to modifying pictures, but instead of using the *Picture Tools Format* tab when working with pictures, use the ***Drawing Tools Format tab***.

Customize Shapes

As you learned in Chapter 4, insert a shape by clicking the **Shapes** button on the *Insert* tab (see *SLO 4.6: Working with Other Graphic Objects*). The *Shapes* gallery includes a variety of shapes to draw and customize.

▶HOW TO: Insert and Customize a Shape

1. Click the **Shapes** button [*Insert* group, *Illustrations* tab] and select a shape from the gallery.
   - The pointer becomes a drawing crosshair (large plus sign).
2. Use the drawing crosshair to draw a shape in the document.
   - After drawing a shape, use the *Drawing Tools Format* tab or *Format Shapes* pane to customize the shape.
   - Use the *Size* and *Align* groups, the *Layout* menu, and the *Layout* dialog box to change the size, text wrapping, and position of the shape.
   - The size and arrangement options available are the same options available when working with a picture.
3. Select a shape to edit. Shape handles appear on the selected shape (Figure 7-75).
   - Edit a shape using the sizing handles (white circles) on the sides and corners.
   - Use the shape rotation handle (circle with arrow) at the top to rotate a shape.
   - Use the shape adjustment handle (yellow circle) to change the contour of a shape.
4. Click the **Edit Shape** button in the *Insert Shapes* group to *Change Shape* or *Edit Points* of a shape (Figure 7-76).
   - When you click *Edit Points*, shape editing handles display on a red border. Drag the handles to change the appearance of the shape.
   - Press **Ctrl** and click the red border to add or delete editing handles.

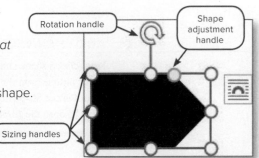

Figure 7-75 Selected shape with handles displayed

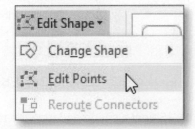

Figure 7-76 *Edit Shape* drop-down list

Shape Styles

Use the *Shape Styles* group on the *Drawing Tools Format* tab to apply a shape style or customize the *Shape Fill, Shape Outline,* and *Shape Effects.* The *Shape Styles* gallery contains a variety of built-in styles to apply a preset outline, fill color, and effects to shapes. The document theme controls the colors of built-in shape styles in a document. Click the **More** button in the *Shape Styles* gallery to display the available shape styles (Figure 7-77).

In addition to the built-in shape styles, customize shapes using the *Shape Fill, Shape Outline,* and *Shape Effects* drop-down lists in the *Shape Styles* group on the *Drawing Tools Format* tab. The following list details the options available in each of these areas:

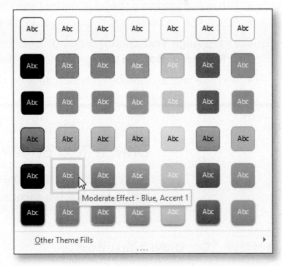

Figure 7-77 *Shape Styles* gallery

- **Shape Fill**: Customize and apply *Theme Colors, Standard Colors, No Fill, More Fill Colors, Picture, Gradient,* or *Texture* to a shape.

- *Shape Outline*: Customize and apply *Theme Colors*, *Standard Colors*, *No Outline*, *More Outline Colors*, *Weight*, *Dashes*, or *Arrows* to a shape.
- *Shape Effects*: Apply built-in *Preset*, *Shadow*, *Reflection*, *Glow*, *Soft Edges*, *Bevel*, or *3-D Rotation* effects to a shape.

Alternatively, use the *Format Shape* pane to apply and customize shape fill, outline, and effects. This pane is similar to the *Format Picture* pane and provides additional shape customization options. Click the **Shape Styles** launcher to open the *Format Shape* pane (Figure 7-78).

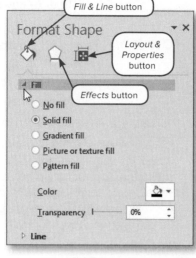

Figure 7-78 *Format Shape* pane

> **ANOTHER WAY**
>
> Right-click a shape and select a style, fill, or outline from the mini toolbar or select **Format Shape** from the context menu to open the *Format Shape* pane.

Add Text to a Shape

After drawing a shape, you can add text to a shape. When adding text to a shape, the text becomes part of the shape. Format the text in a shape using the *Font* dialog box, the ribbon, or keyboard shortcuts.

▶HOW TO: Add Text to a Shape

1. Select a shape and type the text in the shape (Figure 7-79).
   - Alternatively, right-click a shape and select **Add Text** from the context menu. The insertion point displays in the shape.
2. Select the text in the shape and customize the font, size, style, and effects.
   - The text added to a shape is *Normal* style text by default.
   - Adjust line and paragraph spacing to vertically center text in the shape.
3. Click the **Align Text** button [*Drawing Tools Format* tab, *Text* group] and select **Top**, **Middle**, or **Bottom** to align the text vertically on the shape.
   - Text in a shape is centered horizontally by default.

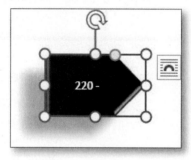

Figure 7-79 Add text to shape

Draw a Text Box

You can also add text to a shape by drawing a text box on a shape and typing text in the text box. A text box is a separate object that you can modify independently of the shape.

▶HOW TO: Draw a Text Box

1. Select a shape.
2. Click the **Draw Text Box** button [*Drawing Tools Format* tab, *Insert Shapes* group]. Your pointer becomes a drawing crosshair.

3. Draw a text box on the shape.

4. Type text in the text box (Figure 7-80).

5. Format and arrange the text box.

- Select the text in the text box and customize the font, size, style, and effects.
- Select the border of the text box and customize the outline, fill, and arrangement.
- You can group a text box and a shape so they become one object. Grouping objects is covered in the *Group Shapes* section.

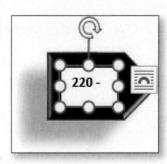

Figure 7-80 Type text in a text box

Customize text in shapes by changing the text direction or vertical alignment or by adding a hyperlink to text using the options in the *Text* group on the *Drawing Tools Format* tab (Figure 7-81).

Figure 7-81 *Text* group on the *Drawing Tools Format* tab

> **MORE INFO**
>
> To add a caption to a shape or picture, right-click the shape or picture and select **Insert Caption** from the context menu.

Drawing Tools

In addition to drawing shapes from the *Shapes* gallery, Word provides a ***Draw*** tab with a variety of drawing tools. Use the ***Ink Editor*** to mark a document with editing changes using one of the available pens (Figure 7-82). Use the ***Ink to Shape*** feature to draw a shape using a pen. Word converts the drawn image to a shape, such as a circle, oval, square, rectangle, or triangle. Use the pointer or your finger or stylus on a touch screen to draw.

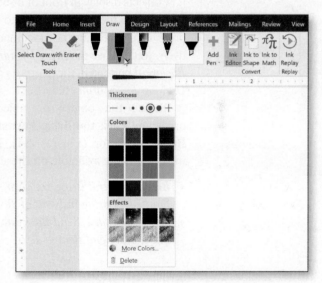

Figure 7-82 Use the *Draw* tab

After drawing editing marks or a shape, click the **Select** button to select and edit the object. Use the *Drawing Tools Format* tab, *Format Shape* pane, or *Format Ink* pane to edit the drawing object similar to how you edit shapes or other graphic objects. Press **Esc** to turn off the drawing tools.

Selection Pane

After inserting shapes, drawings, pictures, or other graphic objects, use the ***Selection pane*** to view, select, and order these objects in your document. The *Selection* pane displays on the right side of the Word window, and it displays all the objects in your document.

▶HOW TO: Use the Selection Pane

1. Select a shape, picture, or graphic object.

2. Click the **Selection Pane** button [*Drawing Tools Format, Picture Tools Format*, or *Layout* tab; *Arrange* group].

   - The *Selection* pane displays on the right side of the Word window (Figure 7-83).
   - All the objects in the document display in the *Selection* pane.
   - Each object has a default name.

3. Click an object in the *Selection* pane or document to select it.

   - Click an object name in the *Selection* pane to rename the object.
   - Use the **Ctrl** key and your pointer to select multiple objects.
   - Click the **Hide** button (eye) to the right of the object name to hide the object in the document.

4. Select an object and click the **Bring Forward** (up arrow) or **Send Backward** (down arrow) button to re-order objects.

   - Ordering determines which object appears in front of or behind other objects.

5. Click the **Selection Pane** button or the **X** in the upper-right corner of the *Selection* pane to close it.

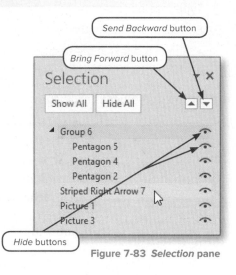

Figure 7-83 *Selection* pane

Order Shapes

Ordering is important when working with multiple shapes and pictures. Ordering determines how objects display in front of or behind other objects. Use the *Selection* pane to change the order of objects in your document. Alternatively, you can use the ***Bring Forward*** and ***Send Backward*** buttons in the *Arrange* group on the *Drawing Tools Format* tab.

Select the object or objects to re-order and click the **Bring Forward** or **Send Backward** button (Figure 7-84). The following options are available on these buttons:

- ***Bring Forward***: *Bring Forward, Bring to Front,* and *Bring in Front of Text*
- ***Send Backward***: *Send Backward, Send to Back,* and *Send Behind Text*

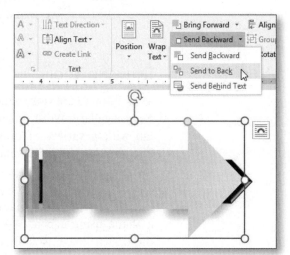

Figure 7-84 Re-order object to display the large arrow behind the shapes

Align Shapes

Word provides a variety of options to precisely align shapes (or pictures) in your document. When aligning multiple objects, use the **Ctrl** or **Shift** key and the pointer to select multiple objects in a document or use the **Ctrl** key and the pointer to select multiple objects in the *Selection* pane. Click

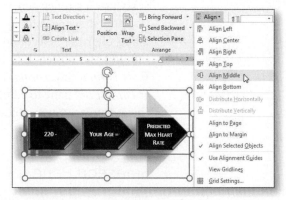

Figure 7-85 Align selected shapes

the **Align** button in the *Arrange* group and select from the alignment options (Figure 7-85). Table 7-5 describes each of the alignment options:

Table 7-5: Shape Alignment Options

Alignment Option	Description
Align Left	Horizontally aligns selected objects on the left edge of objects.
Align Center	Horizontally aligns selected objects in the center of objects.
Align Right	Horizontally aligns selected objects on the right edge of objects.
Align Top	Vertically aligns selected objects on the top edge of objects.
Align Middle	Vertically aligns selected objects in the middle of objects.
Align Bottom	Vertically aligns selected objects on the bottom edge of objects.
Distribute Horizontally	Equally distributes horizontal space between selected objects.
Distribute Vertically	Equally distributes vertical space between selected objects.
Align to Page	Aligns objects in relation to the page of the document. Turn on this option and then select one of the horizontal or vertical alignment options.
Align to Margin	Aligns objects in relation to document margins. Turn on this option and then select one of the horizontal or vertical alignment options.
Align Selected Objects	Automatically turns on when you select multiple objects to align.
Use Alignment Guides	Displays vertical and horizontal alignment guides to help you align objects when dragging an object.
View Gridlines	Displays gridlines in the document to help you precisely align objects.
Grid Settings	Opens the *Drawing Grid* dialog box to customize how gridlines appear in the document.

Group Shapes

After modifying and aligning objects in your document, combine multiple objects into one object to modify it as one object rather than individual objects. Use the ***Group*** feature to combine multiple objects into one object that you can resize, arrange, and modify. Also, use the group feature to group a text box with a shape or to group a caption with a picture.

▶ HOW TO: Group Multiple Objects

1. Select the objects to group.
   - In the document, use the **Ctrl** or **Shift** key and the pointer to select the objects.
   - In the *Selection* pane, use the **Ctrl** key and the pointer to select the objects.
2. Click the **Group** button [*Drawing Tools Format* tab, *Arrange* group] (Figure 7-86).
3. Select **Group**.
   - The individual objects become one grouped object.
   - To ungroup objects, select the grouped object, click the **Group** button, and select **Ungroup**.

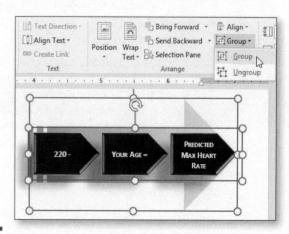

Figure 7-86 *Group* selected shapes

For this Pause & Practice project, you finalize the heart rate document for American River Cycling Club. You insert and customize shapes, add text to shapes, align and group shapes, and arrange the grouped object.

File Needed: *[your initials] PP W7-3.docx*
Completed Project File Name: *[your initials] PP W7-4.docx*

1. Open the *[your initials] PP W7-3* document you completed in *Pause & Practice 7-3*.

2. Save the document as [your initials] PP W7-4.

3. Insert, resize, and customize a shape.
   a. Click the **Shapes** button [*Insert* tab, *Illustrations* group].
   b. Select the **Arrow: Pentagon** shape (**seventh shape** in the **second row** in the *Block Arrows* category) (Figure 7-87). Your pointer becomes a drawing crosshair.
   c. Draw a shape approximately **1" square** on the right side of the text in the "What Is Maximum Heart Rate?" section. The shape displays on top of the text; you will modify text wrapping later.
   d. Select the shape and change the *Height* to **0.6"** and the *Width* to **1"** [*Drawing Tools Format* tab, *Size* group].
   e. Click the **Shape Fill** button [*Shape Styles* group] and select the **fourth color** in the **last row** of *Theme Colors* (**Dark Blue, Text 2, Darker 50%**).
   f. Click the **Shape Outline** button [*Shape Styles* group] and select **No Outline**.
   g. Click the **Shape Effects** button [*Shape Styles* group], select **Preset**, and select **Preset 5** (Figure 7-88).

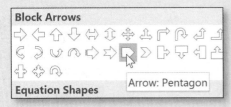

Figure 7-87 Select *Pentagon* shape

4. Add text to a shape and modify text.
   a. Right-click the shape and select **Add Text** from the context menu. The insertion point displays in the shape.
   b. Type 220, **space** once, and type - (hyphen).
   c. Select the text in the shape, change the font size to **9 pt**, and apply **bold** and **small caps** formatting.
   d. Change the line spacing to **single (1.0)** and the *After* paragraph spacing to **0 pt**.
   e. Move the shape so it is approximately in the middle of the page horizontally.

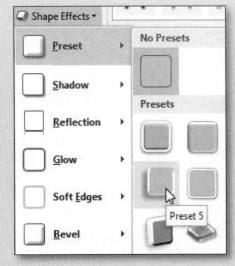

Figure 7-88 Select *Preset* shape effect

5. Copy shapes and modify text in shapes.
   a. Click the edge of the shape to select it.
   b. Press **Ctrl+C** to copy the shape, and press **Ctrl+V** to paste the shape.
   c. Drag the copied shape and move it to the right of the first shape.
   d. Press **Ctrl+V** again to paste another copy of the shape.
   e. Drag the third shape to the right of the second shape.
   f. Select the text in the second shape and type Your Age, **space** once, and type = to replace the existing text.
   g. Select the text in the third shape and type Predicted Max Heart Rate to replace the existing text.

6. Align and group shapes.
   a. Manually move the shapes horizontally so they are almost touching each other, leaving only a little white space between each. Use the **Ctrl** key and the **right** or **left** arrow key to move the shapes in small increments.
   b. Click the **Selection Pane** button [*Drawing Tools Format* tab, *Arrange* group] to display the *Selection* pane.
   c. Press the **Ctrl** key and select the three **Arrow**: **Pentagon** shapes in the *Selection* pane.
   d. Click the **Align** button [*Drawing Tools Format* tab, *Arrange* group] and select **Align Selected Objects** (if it is not already checked).
   e. Click the **Align** button again and select **Align Middle** to vertically center the selected shapes (Figure 7-89).
   f. Click the **Align** button again and select **Distribute Horizontally** to place equal space between the selected shapes.
   g. Click the **Group** button [*Arrange* group] and select **Group** to group the selected shapes.

Figure 7-89 Align selected shapes

7. Draw another shape and resize and position it.
   a. Click the **Shapes** button [*Insert* tab, *Illustrations* group].
   b. Select the **Arrow**: **Striped Right** shape (**fifth shape** in the **second row** in the *Block Arrows* category) (Figure 7-90). Your pointer becomes a drawing crosshair.
   c. Draw a shape approximately **3"** wide over the grouped shapes in your document.
   d. Select the new shape, change the *Height* to **1.6"** and the *Width* to **3"** [*Drawing Tools Format* tab, *Size* group].
   e. Right-click the new shape, click the **Outline** button on the mini toolbar, and select **No Outline**.
   f. Click the **Fill** button on the mini toolbar and select the **fourth color** in the **last row** of *Theme Colors* (**Dark Blue, Text 2, Darker 50%**).
   g. Click the **Fill** button on the mini toolbar, select **Gradient**, and select **Linear Right** (Figure 7-91).

Figure 7-90 Select *Arrow: Striped Right* shape

8. Order, align, and group shapes.
   a. Select the striped right arrow shape (if it is not selected), click the **Send Backward** button [*Drawing Tools Format* tab, *Arrange* group] to position the arrow behind the grouped shapes.
   b. Press the **Ctrl** key and click the **Group** and **Arrow**: **Striped Right** in the *Selection* pane to select both objects (Figure 7-92). *Note: The numbers to the right of the object names may vary.*

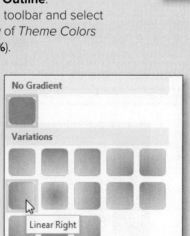
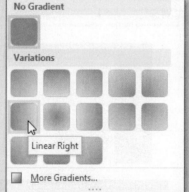

Figure 7-91 Select a *Gradient* shape fill

Figure 7-92 Select objects in the *Selection* pane

   c. Click the **Align** button [*Arrange* group] and select **Align Middle** to vertically center the selected objects.
   d. Click the **Align** button again and select **Align Right**.

e. Click the **Group** button [*Arrange* group] and select **Group** to group the selected shapes.

f. Click the **Selection Pane** button to close the *Selection* pane.

9. Adjust text wrapping and the position of the grouped shape.

   a. Select the grouped shape (if it is not selected), click the **Wrap Text** button [*Drawing Tools Format* tab, *Arrange* group] and select **Tight**.

   b. Click the **Position** button [*Arrange* group] and select **More Layout Options** to open the *Layout* dialog box.

   c. Change the *Horizontal* **Absolute position** to **5"** *to the right of* **Page**.

   d. Change the *Vertical* **Absolute position** to **1.6"** *below* **Page**.

   e. Click the **Text Wrapping** tab.

   f. Change *Top* and *Bottom* to **0.2"** and *Left* and *Right* to **0"** in the *Distance from text* area.

   g. Click **OK** to close the *Layout* dialog box.

10. Add alt text to the graphic.

    a. Select the grouped shapes graphic object, right-click the top border, and select **Edit Alt Text**.

    b. Type Predicted Max Heart Rate graphic in the *Description* text box.

11. Save and close the document (Figure 7-93).

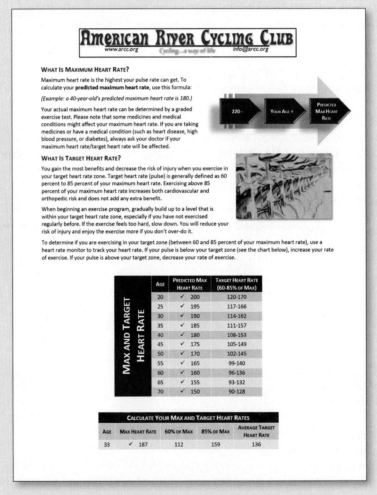

Figure 7-93 PP W7-4 completed

Chapter Summary

7.1 Customize table content using sorting, formulas, bullets and numbers, tabs and indents, and text direction (p. W7-409).

- Convert text to a table or convert a table to text.
- The **Table Tools Layout tab** includes options to customize the layout and contents of tables.
- Sort text in a table in ascending or descending order.
- Use **formulas** in tables to perform calculations.
- The **syntax** of a formula is the structure of a formula. All formulas begin with an equals sign (=) and include a combination of **cell references**, **operators**, and **values**.
- The **cell address** is the column letter and row number where a column and row intersect. A cell reference is a cell address used in a formula.
- **Functions**, such as **SUM** and **AVERAGE**, are built-in formulas used in common calculations.
- When values in a table change, manually update the formula.
- Change the text direction of text in a cell of a table.
- Modify text arrangement in a table using tabs and indents. Press **Ctrl+Tab** to move to a tab stop in the cell of a table.
- Modify text arrangement in a table using bulleted and numbered lists.

7.2 Customize table layouts using table properties, cell margins, the split table feature, nested tables, and a repeated header row (p. W7-418).

- Customize table layout by modifying the size, alignment, and position of a table.
- Use the **Table Properties** dialog box to modify an entire table, rows, columns, or individual cells.
- **Cell margins** place space around text in a cell; **cell spacing** is the amount of space between cells.
- Use **Split Table** to divide a table into multiple separate tables, and use **Split Cells** to divide cells into multiple rows or columns.
- **Nested tables** are tables within tables. The main table is the **parent table**, and tables within the parent table are **child tables**.

- Use **repeat header rows** to automatically display a header row or rows at the top of each page when a table spans more than one page.
- Draw a table using the table drawing tools.

7.3 Enhance a table design using shading, borders, and a table style (p. W7-422).

- Use the *Table Tools Design* tab to customize table style options, **table styles**, and borders and shading.
- Use the **Border Painter** to draw borders on a table.
- Use the **Border Sampler** to select an existing border from a table and use the *Border Painter* to apply the border format to other areas of the table or to a different table.
- Modify an existing table style or create a new table style.
- Built-in tables stored as building blocks display in the **Quick Tables gallery**. Also, create custom **Table building blocks**.

7.4 Modify a picture using advanced layout and picture format options (p. W7-432).

- Modify pictures using the **Picture Tools Format** tab or the **Format Picture** pane.
- Text wrapping controls how text wraps around a picture. Modify a picture's **wrap points** to customize how text wraps around a picture.
- Use **Alignment guides** and **live layout** to arrange pictures in a document.
- The **picture anchor** determines the text the picture is anchored to in the document. The picture anchor enables the picture to move with text when a document is modified.
- After inserting a picture into a document, resize the picture using the sizing handles, the *Size* group on the *Picture Tools Format* tab, or the *Layout* dialog box.
- **Aspect ratio** refers to the picture being proportional to its original size when it is resized.
- **Crop** a picture to remove an unwanted portion of a picture.
- Crop a picture to a shape or to a specific aspect ratio, or crop a picture to fit or fill a size.
- **Rotate** a picture in a document.
- **Picture styles** are built-in styles used to apply borders and effects to pictures.

- Customize a picture by applying *picture borders* and *picture effects*.

7.5 Adjust pictures to remove background, apply corrections, change colors, and add artistic effects, and compress, change, and reset a picture (p. W7-438).

- Use *Remove Background* to apply transparency to a portion of the picture.
- Apply picture *Corrections* to sharpen or soften a picture or adjust the brightness and contrast.
- Use the *Color* feature to adjust a picture's color saturation, tone, or color.
- Apply *Artistic Effects* to a picture to change how it displays.
- Use the *Transparency* feature to add transparency to a picture.
- *Compress* a picture file size, change the picture to a different picture, or reset the picture to its original form.

7.6 Create, group, align, and modify a shape in a document (p. W7-444).

- Use the drawing crosshair to draw a shape and customize its size and rotation using the *shape handles*.
- Use *edit points* of the shape to further customize the shape.

- Use built-in *shape styles* to apply *shape fill*, *shape outline*, and *shape effects* to shapes.
- Add text to a shape using the context menu or by drawing a text box on a shape.
- The *Selection pane* displays all objects in your document. Use the *Selection* pane to select and reorder objects.
- The order of shapes determines which shape appears in front of or behind other shapes.
- When working with multiple shapes, align them vertically and horizontally in relation to each other, the page, or the margins.
- *Group* multiple shapes into one object and then resize, align, position, or modify the grouped object as one object.
- *Ungroup* shapes to separate a grouped object into individual objects.

Check for Understanding

The SIMbook for this text (within your SIMnet account) provides the following resources for concept review:

- Multiple-choice questions
- Short answer questions
- Matching exercises

Guided Project 7-1

For this project, you modify a document from Sierra Pacific Community College. You convert text to tables, modify tables, apply a table style, modify a style, create a new style, draw and format a shape, and insert and format a picture.
[Student Learning Outcomes 7.1, 7.2, 7.3, 7.4, 7.5, 7.6]

Files Needed: **_EmergencyTelephones-07.docx_** and **_SPCCD-logo-07.png_** (Student data files are available in the Library of your SIMnet account.)
Completed Project File Name: **_[your initials] Word 7-1.docx_**

Skills Covered in This Project

- Convert text to a table.
- Sort information in a table.
- Modify a table and change text direction.
- Apply a table style.

- Modify a table style.
- Create a table style.
- Apply a custom table style.
- Draw, resize, and modify a shape.
- Insert, resize, and modify a picture.

1. Open the **_EmergencyTelephones-07_** document from your student data files.

2. Save the document as [your initials] Word 7-1.

3. Convert text to a table and sort information in a table.
   a. Select the tabbed text in the "Emergency Phone Locations" section.
   b. Click the **Table** button [_Insert_ tab, _Tables_ group] and select **Convert Text to Table**. The _Convert Text to Table_ dialog box opens (Figure 7-94).

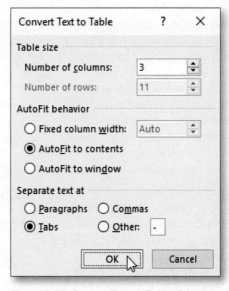

Figure 7-94 _Convert Text to Table_ dialog box

c. Enter the following settings to convert the text to a table:
   Number of columns: **3**
   AutoFit behavior: **AutoFit to contents**
   Separate text at: **Tabs**
d. Click **OK** to close the dialog box.
e. Select the table and click the **Sort** button [*Table Tools Layout* tab, *Data* group] to open the *Sort* dialog box (Figure 7-95).
f. Select the **Header row** radio button in the *My list has* area.
g. Click the **Sort by** drop-down list, select **Building**, and click the **Ascending** radio button.
h. Click the **Then by** drop-down list, select **Inside/Outside**, and click the **Ascending** radio button.
i. Click **OK** to close the dialog box.

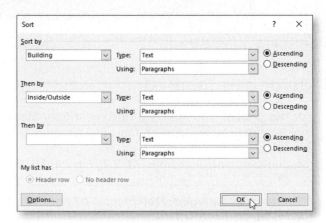

Figure 7-95 Sort information in a table

4. Convert text to a table and sort information in the table.
   a. Select the tabbed text in the "Emergency Phone Numbers" section.
   b. Click the **Table** button and select **Convert Text to Table**. The *Convert Text to Table* dialog box opens.
   c. Enter the following settings to convert the text to a table:
      Number of columns: **4**
      AutoFit behavior: **AutoFit to contents**
      Separate text at: **Tabs**
   d. Click **OK** to close the dialog box.
   e. Select the table and click the **Sort** button to open the *Sort* dialog box.
   f. Select the **Header row** radio button, *Sort by* **Emergency Contact** in **Ascending** order, and click **OK** to close the dialog box.

5. Modify tables and change text direction.
   a. Place the insertion point in the first cell in the first table, insert a column to the left of the first column, and merge the cells in the new first column.
   b. Type Emergency Phone Locations in the new first column.
   c. Click the **Text Direction** button [*Table Tools Layout* tab, *Alignment* group] two times to change the text direction to vertical from bottom to top.
   d. Click the **Align Center** button [*Table Tools Layout* tab, *Alignment* group].
   e. Place the insertion point in the first cell in the second table, insert a column to the left of the first column, and merge the cells in the new first column.
   f. Type Emergency Phone Numbers in the first column.
   g. Click the **Text Direction** button two times to change the text direction to vertical from bottom to top and click the **Align Center** button. Not all the text in the first column displays; you will fix this later in the project.

6. Apply a table style and modify the table.
   a. Select the first table and check the **Header Row**, **Banded Rows**, and **First Column** boxes in the *Table Style Options* group [*Table Tools Design* tab]. The other check boxes should not be checked.
   b. Apply the **List Table 4 - Accent 1** table style from the *Table Styles* gallery (Figure 7-96).

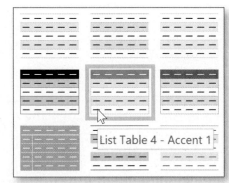

Figure 7-96 Apply a table style

c. Click the **More** button in the *Table Styles* gallery [*Table Tools Design* tab] and select **Modify Table Style**. The *Modify Style* dialog box opens.

d. Click the **Apply formatting to** drop-down list and select **Whole table** (if it is not already selected).

e. Change the font size to **10 pt** and the text alignment to **Align Center Left** (Figure 7-97).

f. Click the **Format** button and select **Table Properties** to open the *Table Properties* dialog box.

g. Click the **Table** tab and click the **Options** button to open the *Table Options* dialog box.

h. Set the *Top* and *Bottom* cell margins to **0.03"** and the *Left* and *Right* cell margins to **0.1"**.

i. Click **OK** to close the *Table Options* dialog box.

j. Click **OK** to close the *Table Properties* dialog box.

k. Click **OK** to close the *Modify Style* dialog box.

7. Save the document.

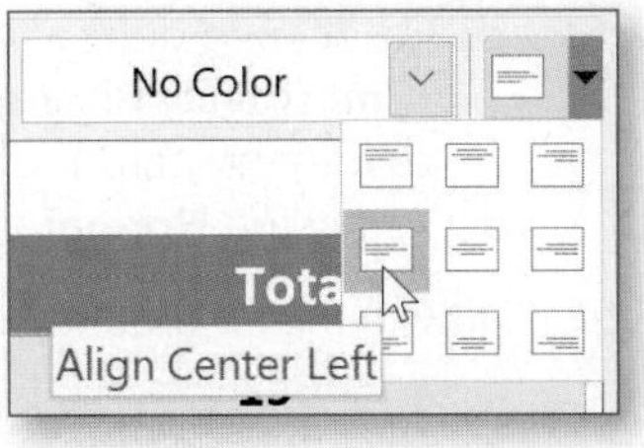

Figure 7-97 Change text alignment

8. Create a table style.
a. Place the insertion point in the first table.
b. Right-click one of the table styles in the *Table Styles* gallery and select **New Table Style**. The *Create New Style from Formatting* dialog box opens (Figure 7-98).
c. Type SPCCD table in the *Name* area.
d. Click the **Style based on** drop-down arrow and select **List Table 4 - Accent 1**.
e. Click the **Apply formatting to** drop-down list and select **First column**.
f. Click the **Format** button and select **Font** to open the *Font* dialog box.
g. Change the font size to **11 pt** and apply **small caps**.
h. Click **OK** to close the *Font* dialog box.
i. Click **OK** to close the *Create New Style from Formatting* dialog box and to create the new style.

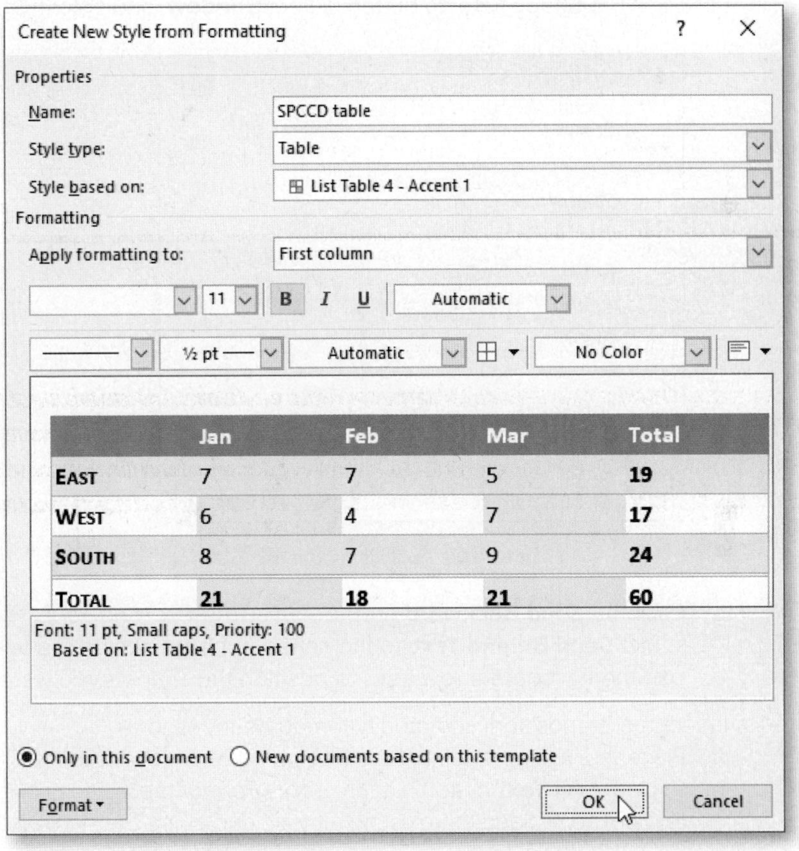

Figure 7-98 Create a new table style

9. Apply a custom table style to tables and delete text headings.
a. Select the first table and apply the **SPCCD table** style from the *Custom* area in the *Table Styles* gallery.
b. Select the second table and apply the **SPCCD table** style.

c. Select and delete the "**Emergency Phone Locations**" and "**Emergency Phone Numbers**" headings above the tables, but don't delete the paragraph marks.

d. Apply the **Normal** text style to the blank line above each table.

10. Draw a shape around the numbered list and resize, modify, and arrange the shape.

   a. Click the **Shapes** button [*Insert* tab, *Illustrations* group] and select the **Double Bracket** shape (**first shape** in the **fourth row** in the *Basic Shapes* area) (Figure 7-99).

   b. Draw a shape around the numbered list.

   c. Select the shape and change the *Height* to **0.8"** and the *Width* to **4.6"** [*Drawing Tools Format* tab, *Size* group].

   d. Click the **Shape Fill** button [*Drawing Tools Format* tab, *Shape Styles* group] and select **fifth color** in the **second row** of *Theme Colors* (**Blue**, **Accent 1**, **Lighter 80%**).

   e. Click the **Shape Outline** button, select **Weight**, and select **2¼ pt**.

   f. Click the **Shape Effects** button, select **Shadow**, and select **Offset: Bottom Right** (Figure 7-100).

Figure 7-99 Select shape to draw

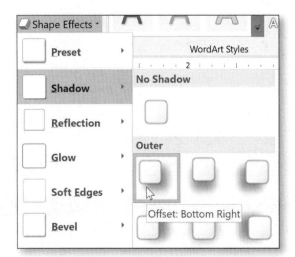

Figure 7-100 Apply a *Shadow* shape effect

   g. Click the **Send Backward** drop-down arrow [*Drawing Tools Format* tab, *Arrange* group] and select **Send Behind Text** so the shape appears behind the text.

   h. Use the keyboard arrow keys to position the shape evenly around the numbered list.

11. Insert, resize, position, and modify the company logo.

   a. Place the insertion point at the beginning of the document and insert the ***SPCCD-logo-07*** picture.

   b. Click the **Alt Text** button [*Picture Tools Format* tab, *Accessibility* group], type SPCCD logo in the text box to replace the existing alt text, and close the *Alt Text* pane.

   c. Click the **Wrap Text** button [*Picture Tools Format* tab, *Arrange* group] and select **Tight**.

   d. Click the **Size** launcher [*Picture Tools Format* tab, *Size* group] to open the *Layout* dialog box.

   e. Select the *Size* tab (if necessary), change the *Scale* to **120%** of its original height and width.

   f. Click the **Position** tab.

   g. Change the *Horizontal* **Absolute position** to **0.3"** *to the right of* **Page**.

   h. Change the *Vertical* **Absolute position** to **0.3"** *below* **Page** and click **OK** to close the *Layout* dialog box.

   i. Click the **Corrections** button and select **Picture Corrections Options** to open the *Format Picture* pane with *Picture Corrections* area opened.

j. Change the *Brightness* to **25%** and the *Contrast* to **25%**.

k. Click the **Picture Color** heading to expand this section in the *Format Picture* pane.

l. Click the **Recolor** button and select the **second option** in the **second row** (**Blue, Accent color 1 Dark**).

m. Click the **X** in the upper-right corner of the *Format Picture* pane to close the pane.

12. Save and close the document (Figure 7-101).

SPCCD—WEST CAMPUS EMERGENCY TELEPHONES

EMERGENCY PHONE [BLUE PHONES] PROCEDURES

1. Press the "Help" button. Speak when the light comes on.
2. Stay on the line. You will be connected with the college police.
3. State clearly the nature of the emergency and your location.

EMERGENCY PHONE LOCATIONS

Building	Inside/Outside	Location
Barton Hall	Inside	Second floor, west end near elevators
Barton Hall	Outside	Southwest corner
Cafeteria	Outside	Northeast entrance from parking lot B
Gymnasium	Inside	Breezeway between offices and gym entrance
Liberal Arts	Outside	North end of the C wing
Library	Inside	First floor, stairs
Library	Outside	Right side of front entrance
Math & Science	Inside	West wall of biology wing
Performing Arts	Outside	Near west entrance from Lot B
Stadium Parking Lot	Outside	Between ticket machines

EMERGENCY PHONE NUMBERS

Emergency Contact	Days	Hours	Phone Number
College Police	M-Su	7:00 a.m. – 7:00 p.m.	(209) 658-7777
Emergency Response System	M-Su	Available 24 hrs.	911
Evening Dean	M-Th	5:00 p.m. – 8:00 p.m.	(209) 658-7700
Health Center	M-F	7:30 a.m. – 4:00 pm.	(209) 658-2239
Information Center	M-F	8 a.m. – 5 p.m.	(209) 658-4466
Site Administrator	M-F	8:00 a.m. – 5:00 p.m.	(209) 658-8501
Weekend College Coordinator	S	8:00 a.m. – 5:00 p.m.	(209) 658-6500

Emergency Telephones   Sierra Pacific Community College District   Revised March 4, 2020

Figure 7-101 Word 7-1 completed

Guided Project 7-2

For this project, you modify an insurance renewal letter from Eva Skaar at Central Sierra Insurance. You create a table and insert text, insert formulas in the table, apply a table style, customize table borders, create a table building block, insert and format a picture, and update formulas.
[Student Learning Outcomes 7.1, 7.2, 7.3, 7.4, 7.5]

Files Needed: ***InsuranceRenewal-07.docx*** and ***CSI-logo-07.png*** *(Student data files are available in the Library of your SIMnet account.)*
Completed Project File Name: ***[your initials] Word 7-2.docx***

Skills Covered in This Project

- Insert a table and add text to a table.
- Insert formulas in a table.
- Apply a table style.
- Change cell margins and spacing.

- Change table and text alignment.
- Use the *Border Sampler* and *Border Painter.*
- Save a table as a building block.
- Insert, resize, and modify a picture.
- Update formulas in a table.

---

1. Open the ***InsuranceRenewal-07*** document from your student data files.

2. Save the document as [your initials] Word 7-2.

3. Insert a table into the document and type text into the table.
   a. Place the insertion point on the blank line below the "The renewal premium is . . ." paragraph and press **Enter**.
   b. Click the **Table** button [*Insert* tab, *Tables* group] and insert a **6×2** table (six columns and two rows) using the *Insert Table* grid.
   c. Type the following information in the table. Press **Enter** to create two-line column headings as shown in the following table:

Policy Description	Premium Basis	Rate per $1,000	Premium	Discount	Discounted Premium
Construction	$325,000	$21			

4. Insert formulas in the table to calculate the premium, discount, and discounted premium.
   a. Place the insertion point in the fourth cell of the second row and click the **Formula** button [*Table Tools Layout* tab, *Data* group]. The *Formula* dialog box opens (Figure 7-102).
   b. Delete the existing formula in the *Formula* area and type =B2/1000*C2.
   c. Click the **Number format** drop-down list and select **$#,##0.00;($#,##0.00)**.
   d. Click **OK** to insert the formula.

Figure 7-102 *Formula* dialog box

e. Place the insertion point in the fifth cell of the second row, create the following formula, and use the **$#,##0.00;($#,##0.00)** number format: $=D2*15\%$

f. Place the insertion point in the sixth cell of the second row, create the following formula, and use the **$#,##0.00;($#,##0.00)** number format: $=D2-E2$

5. Apply a table style and modify the table style.
   a. Select the table and **AutoFit Contents**.
   b. Check the **Header Row**, **Banded Rows**, and **Last Column** boxes in the *Table Style Option* group [*Table Tools Design* tab]. The other boxes should not be checked.
   c. Apply the **Grid Table 2** table style from the *Table Styles* gallery (Figure 7-103).
   d. Click the **Cell Margins** button [*Table Tools Layout* tab, *Alignment* group] to open the *Table Options* dialog box.
   e. Change the *Top* and *Bottom* margins to **0.05"** and the *Left* and *Right* margins to **0.15"** and click **OK** to close the dialog box.
   f. Click the **Properties** button [*Table Tools Layout* tab, *Table* group] to open the *Table Properties* dialog box and click the **Table** tab.
   g. Click the **Center** button in the *Alignment* area and click **OK** to close the *Table Properties* dialog box.
   h. Select the first row of the table and change text alignment to **Align Bottom Center** [*Table Tools Layout* tab, *Alignment* group].
   i. Select the second row of the table and change text alignment to **Align Center**.

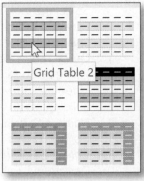

Figure 7-103 Apply a table style

6. Use the *Border Sampler* and *Border Painter* to apply borders to the table.
   a. Place the insertion point in the table and click the **View Gridlines** button [*Table Tools Layout* tab, *Table* group] to display table gridlines if they do not already display.
   b. Click the **Border Styles** drop-down arrow [*Table Tools Design* tab, *Border* group] and select **Border Sampler** from the drop-down list. Your pointer becomes an eyedropper.
   c. Use the eyedropper and click the horizontal border between the first and second rows (Figure 7-104). The eyedropper copies the border style, the *Border Painter* turns on, and the eyedropper becomes a pen.
   d. Use the pen to draw a horizontal border on the table gridline above the first row (Figure 7-105).

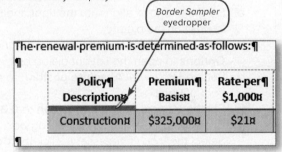

Figure 7-104 Use the *Border Sampler*

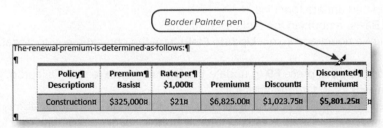

Figure 7-105 Use the *Border Painter*

e. Use the pen to draw a horizontal border on the table gridline below the second row.

f. Click the **Border Painter** button [*Table Tools Design* tab, *Border* group] to turn off the *Border Painter*.

g. Click the **View Gridlines** button [*Table Tools Layout* tab, *Table* group] to turn off table gridlines.

7. Save the table as a building block in the *Quick Tables* gallery.

a. Select the table.

b. Click the **Table** button [*Insert* tab, *Tables* group], select **Quick Tables**, and then select **Save Selection to Quick Tables Gallery**. The *Create New Building Block* dialog box opens (Figure 7-106).

c. Enter the following information to create a new table building block:
Name: CSI Premium table
Gallery: **Tables**
Category: CSI (create new category)
Description: Calculates insurance premium
Save in: **Building Blocks**
Options: **Insert content in its own paragraph**

d. Click **OK** to close the *Create New Building Block* dialog box.

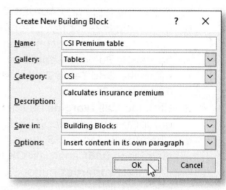

Figure 7-106 Create a new building block

8. Insert, resize, position, and modify company logo.

a. Place the insertion point at the beginning of the document and insert the ***CSI-logo-07*** picture.

b. Click the **Alt Text** button [*Picture Tools Format* tab, *Accessibility* group], type Central Sierra Insurance logo in the text box to replace the existing alt text, and close the *Alt Text* pane.

c. Click the **Wrap Text** button [*Picture Tools Format* tab, *Arrange* group] and select **Square**.

d. Change the *Width* to **4"** [*Picture Tools Format* tab, *Size* group].

e. Drag the logo to align with the right and top margins of the document. Use the alignment guides to position the picture.

f. Click the **Position** button [*Picture Tools Format* tab, *Arrange* group] and select **More Layout Options** to open the *Layout* dialog box.

g. Set the *Horizontal* **Absolute position** to **4.2"** *to the right of* **Page**.

h. Set the *Vertical* **Absolute position** to **0.3"** *below* **Page**.

i. Click **OK** to close the *Layout* dialog box.

j. Select the logo (if necessary), click the **Color** button [*Picture Tools Format* tab, *Adjust* group] and select **Red**, **Accent color 2 Dark** (**third option** in the **second row** in the *Recolor* area) (Figure 7-107).

Figure 7-107 Change picture color

9. Change a value in the table and update formulas.

a. Change the "Premium Basis" amount in the table to $350,000.

b. Right-click the "Premium" amount and select **Update Field** from the context menu to update the formula.

c. Select the "Discount" amount and press **F9** to update the formula (if you're using a laptop, you might have to press **Fn+F9** to update the formula).

d. Update the "Discounted Premium" formula using one of the two methods described above.

e. Select the "Discounted Premium" formula result and apply **bold** formatting. You may have to click the **bold** button two times.

10. Save and close the document (Figure 7-108). If prompted to save changes to building blocks, click **Save**.

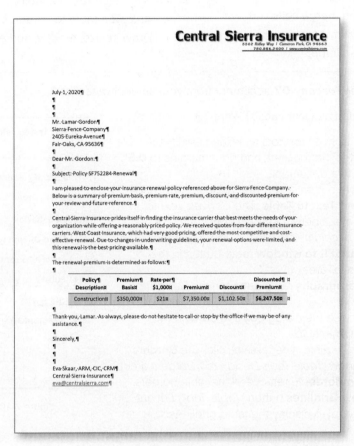

Figure 7-108 Word 7-2 completed

Guided Project 7-3

For this project, you modify the Tuscany cycling tour itinerary for the American River Cycling Club. You convert text to a table, modify the table, insert pictures, crop and modify pictures, and insert and modify a shape.
[Student Learning Outcomes 7.1, 7.2, 7.3, 7.4, 7.6]

Files Needed: *CyclingTuscany-07.docx*, *Day1-07.jpg*, *Day2-07.jpg*, *Day3-07.jpg*, *Day4-07.jpg*, *Day5-07.jpg*, *Day6-07.jpg*, *Day7-07.jpg*, and *Day8-07.jpg* (Student data files are available in the Library of your SIMnet account.)
Completed Project File Name: *[your initials] Word 7-3.docx*

Skills Covered in This Project

- Convert text to a table.
- Insert a column and merge cells.
- Remove borders from a table.
- Insert and resize a picture.
- Crop a picture to a shape and apply a shadow.
- Align pictures in a table.
- *AutoFit* a table to contents.
- Draw, resize, modify, and arrange a shape.

---

1. Open the **CyclingTuscany-07** document from your student data files.

2. Save the document as [your initials] Word 7-3.

3. Change margins, convert text to a table, and modify the table.
   a. Change the top, bottom, left, and right margins to **0.5"**.
   b. Select the entire document.
   c. Click the **Table** button [*Insert* tab, *Tables* group] and select **Convert Text to Table**. The *Convert Text to Table* dialog box opens (Figure 7-109).
   d. Set *Number of columns* to **1** in the *Table size* area.
   e. Select the **AutoFit to window** radio button in the *AutoFit behavior* area.
   f. Select the **Paragraphs** radio button in the *Separate text at* area.
   g. Click **OK** to close the dialog box and convert the selected text to a table.
   h. Select the entire table (if necessary), click the **Borders** drop-down arrow [*Table Tools Design* tab, *Borders* group] and select **No Border** to remove all the table borders.
   i. Click the **View Gridlines** button [*Table Tools Layout* tab, *Table* group] to display the table gridlines.

Figure 7-109 Convert text to a table

4. Insert a column and merge cells.
   a. Place the insertion point in the first cell and insert a column to the right of the existing column.
   b. Select the entire second column and apply the **Normal** text style.
   c. Select the two cells in the first row and click the **Merge Cells** button [*Table Tools Layout* tab, *Merge* group].
   d. Select the cells in the second column in rows 2–4 and click the **Merge Cells** button. This step merges the cells in the second column to the right of the "Day 1" heading, "Highlights," and description content.
   e. Repeat step 4d to merge the three cells in the second column to the right of each day, highlights, and description cell in the first column. Continue this process through the cells that contain the "Day 8" heading, highlights, and description (Figure 7-110).

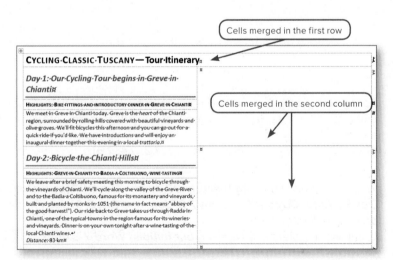

Figure 7-110 Cells merged in the first row and second column

5. Insert, resize, crop, modify, and align pictures.
   a. Place the insertion point in the cell in the second column to the right of the "Day 1" content.
   b. Insert the **Day1-07** picture [*Insert* tab, *Illustrations* group] from your student data files. Accept the default alt text for the pictures in this project.
   c. Change the *Width* of the picture to **2.5"** [*Picture Tools Format* tab, *Size* group]. The height automatically adjusts to maintain the aspect ratio.
   d. Click the **Crop** drop-down arrow [*Picture Tools Format* tab, *Size* group], select **Crop to Shape**, and then select **Rectangle: Rounded Corners** (**second shape** in the *Rectangles* area) (Figure 7-111). The picture is cropped to the size of the shape.

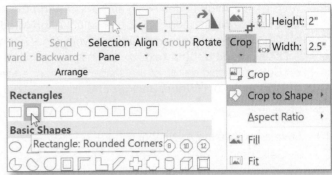

Figure 7-111 Crop picture to a shape

   e. Click the **Picture Effects** button [*Picture Tools Format* tab, *Picture Styles* group], select **Shadow**, and select **Offset: Center** (**second option** in the **second row** in the *Outer* area) (Figure 7-112).
   f. Click the **Align Center** button [*Table Tools Layout* tab, *Alignment* group] to center the picture vertically and horizontally in the cell.
   g. Repeat steps 5b–f to insert and format the following pictures in the cell to the right of the corresponding day: **Day2-07**, **Day3-07**, **Day4-07**, **Day5-07**, **Day6-07**, **Day7-07**, and **Day8-07**. Don't be concerned about pagination at this point; you address this in the next step.

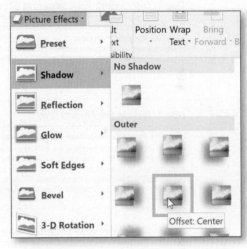

Figure 7-112 Apply a *Shadow* picture effect

6. *AutoFit* the table to contents.
   a. Select the entire table.
   b. Click the **AutoFit** button [*Table Tools Layout* tab, *Cell Size* group] and select **AutoFit Contents**.

7. Draw, resize, and modify a shape.
   a. Go to the first page of the itinerary and **center** the text in the first row.
   b. Click the **Shapes** button [*Insert* tab, *Illustrations* group] and select **Rectangle Rounded Corners** in the *Rectangles* area.
   c. Draw a shape around the text in the first row of the table.
   d. Change the *Height* to **0.35"** and the *Width* to **5.2"** [*Drawing Tools Format* tab, *Size* group].
   e. Click the **Shape Fill** button [*Drawing Tools Format* tab, *Shape Styles* group] and select the **sixth color** in the **first row** of *Theme Colors* (**Red, Accent 2**).
   f. Click the **Shape Fill** button again, select **Gradient**, and then select **Linear Up** (**second option** in the **third row** in the *Dark Variations* area) (Figure 7-113).
   g. Click the **Shape Outline** button [*Drawing Tools Format* tab, *Shape Styles* group] and select the **sixth color** in the *Standard Colors* area (**Green**).
   h. Click the **Shape Outline** button again, select **Weight**, and then select **2¼ pt**.

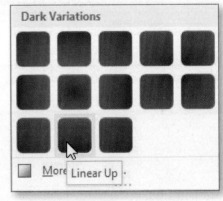

Figure 7-113 Apply a *Gradient* shape fill

8. Align and order a shape.
   a. Select the shape (if necessary), click the **Align** button [*Drawing Tools Format* tab, *Arrange* group] and select **Align to Margin** if it is not already selected. The *Align to Margin* option should have a check to the left of it.
   b. Click the **Align** button again and select **Align Center**.
   c. Click the **Align** button again and select **Align Middle**.
   d. Click the **Send Backward** drop-down arrow [*Drawing Tools Format* tab, *Arrange* group] and select **Send Behind Text**.
   e. Select the text on top of the shape and change the font color to the **first color** in the **first row** of *Theme Colors* (**White, Background 1**).

9. Place the insertion point before "Day 7" on page 2 and press **Ctrl+Enter** to insert a page break.

10. Save and close the document (Figure 7-114).

CYCLING CLASSIC TUSCANY—Tour Itinerary

Day 1: Our Cycling Tour begins in Greve in Chianti

HIGHLIGHTS: BIKE FITTINGS AND INTRODUCTORY DINNER IN GREVE IN CHIANTI

We meet in Greve in Chianti today. Greve is the *heart* of the Chianti region, surrounded by rolling hills covered with beautiful vineyards and olive groves. We'll fit bicycles this afternoon, and you can go out for a quick ride if you'd like. We have introductions and will enjoy an inaugural dinner together this evening in a local *trattoria*.

Day 2: Bicycle the Chianti Hills

HIGHLIGHTS: GREVE IN CHIANTI TO BADIA A COLTIBUONO, WINE TASTING

We leave after a brief safety meeting this morning to bicycle through the vineyards of Chianti. We'll cycle along the valley of the Greve River and to the Badia a Coltibuono, famous for its monastery and vineyards, built and planted by monks in 1051 (the name in fact means "abbey of the good harvest!"). Our ride back to Greve takes us through Radda in Chianti, one of the typical towns in the region famous for its wineries and vineyards. Dinner is on your own tonight after a wine tasting of the local Chianti wines.
Distance: 83 km

Day 3: Bicycle Greve in Chianti to San Gimignano

HIGHLIGHTS: CASTELLINA IN CHIANTI AND SAN GIMIGNANO

Our first stop today is Castellina in Chianti, perhaps the most famous town in the region. Stroll around town and/or visit the fortress before beginning a long downhill bike ride out of the Chianti Hills into the valley of the Elsa River ("Val d'Elsa" in Italian). A loop along the river valley and adjacent hills then takes us up to San Gimignano, one of the best preserved medieval villages in Italy. You can pick up picnic supplies in Poggibonsi and enjoy a view back on the Chianti hills under a shade tree while you eat. We'll be in delightful San Gimignano for two nights.
Distance: 70 km

American River Cycling Club | Page 1 of 3

Figure 7-114 Word 7-3 completed (page 1 of 3 with table gridlines visible)

Independent Project 7-4

For this project, you modify a memo detailing the weekly expenses of Life's Animal Shelter. You convert text to a table, add formulas, modify the table, insert a picture, crop and modify the picture, and insert and modify a shape.
[Student Learning Outcomes 7.1, 7.2, 7.3, 7.4, 7.5, 7.6]

Files Needed: **WeeklyExpenses-07.docx** and **LASfamily.jpg** (Student data files are available in the Library of your SIMnet account.)
Completed Project File Name: **[your initials] Word 7-4.docx**

Skills Covered in This Project

- Convert text to a table.
- Insert rows and columns and merge cells.
- Insert *SUM* and *AVERAGE* formulas.
- Create a table style.
- Apply a custom table style to a table.

- Insert, crop, and resize a picture.
- Crop a picture to a shape and apply a border.
- Position a picture in the document.
- Compress a picture.
- Draw, resize, and modify a shape.
- Add text to a shape and format the text.

1. Open the **WeeklyExpenses-07** document from your student data files.

2. Save the document as [your initials] Word 7-4.

3. Convert text to a table and modify the table.
   a. Select the lines of tabbed text below the body of the memo, convert the text to a table, and **AutoFit to contents** the table.
   b. Insert one column to the right of the last column.
   c. Insert two rows below the last row.
   d. Type Totals in the last cell in the first row.
   e. Type Totals in the next to last cell in the first column.
   f. Type Averages in the last cell in the first column.
   g. Insert a row above the first row and merge the cells in this row. If a paragraph symbol displays in this row, delete it.
   h. **Center** and type Life's Animal Shelter Weekly Expenses in the new first row.

4. Insert formulas to add and average expenses.
   a. Insert a **SUM** function in rows 3–8 in the last column to add the numbers to the left. Use "LEFT" as the range for the *SUM* functions (**=SUM(LEFT)**) and apply the **$#,##0.00;($#,##0.00)** number format.
   b. Insert a **SUM** function in the cells in the next to last row to add the numbers above. Use "ABOVE" as the range for the *SUM* functions and apply the **$#,##0.00;($#,##0.00)** number format.
   c. Insert an **AVERAGE** function in the cells in the last row to calculate the average of the amounts in rows 3–8 above. Type the cell reference range to average (for example, **=AVERAGE(B3:B8)**) and apply the **$#,##0.00;($#,##0.00)** number format. Don't include the *Totals* row in the range. The letter reference for the column changes in each of these formulas.

5. Create and customize a new table style.
   a. Create a **New Table Style** and name the new table style LAS Expenses.
   b. Base the new table style on **Grid Table 5 Dark - Accent 3**.
   c. Apply formatting to the **Whole table** and change the font size to **10 pt**.
   d. Open the *Table Properties* dialog box (*Format* drop-down list), change the top and bottom cell margins to **0.02"** and the left and right cell margins to **0.1"** (Hint: select **Options**), click **OK** to close the *Table Options* dialog box.
   e. Change the *Alignment* to **Center** on the *Table* tab and click **OK** to close the *Table Properties* dialog box.

f. Click **OK** to close the *Create New Style from Formatting* dialog box and to create the new style.

6. Set the table style options, apply a custom table style, and modify the table format.
   a. Select the table and set the *Table Style Options* to include the following: **Header Row**, **Banded Rows**, **First Column**, and **Last Column**.
   b. Apply the **LAS Expenses** custom table style to the table.
   c. **Center** the text in the first row of the table (if necessary) and change the font size to **12 pt**.
   d. Apply **bold** formatting to the column headings in the second row (columns B–G).
   e. Apply **bold** formatting to the average values in the last row (columns B–G).
   f. Change the alignment of all values and their corresponding column headings to **Align Top Right** (columns B–H).

Figure 7-115 Crop picture

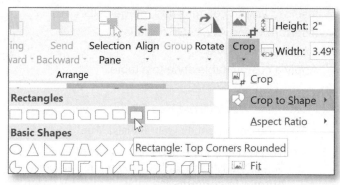

Figure 7-116 Crop picture to a shape

7. Insert, crop, and modify a picture.
   a. Insert the ***LASfamily-07*** picture at the bottom of the document. Accept the default alt text.
   b. Crop the picture so the edges are approximately ¼" from the individuals in the picture (Figure 7-115). Click the top half of the **Crop** button to accept the cropping changes.
   c. Change the picture height to **2"** and maintain aspect ratio.
   d. Crop the picture to the **Rectangle**: **Top Corners Rounded** (**eighth shape** in the *Rectangles* area) (Figure 7-116).
   e. Apply an **Olive Green, Accent 3** picture border (**seventh color** in the **first row** of *Theme Colors*) and change the picture border weight to **1 pt**.
   f. Apply the **Film Grain** *Artistic Effect* to the picture (**third option** in the **third row**).
   g. Change the *Position* of the picture to **Position in Bottom Center with Square Text Wrapping** (Figure 7-117).
   h. Compress the picture so the resolution is **Web (150 ppi)**.

8. Draw a shape, modify the shape, and add text to the shape.
   a. Draw a **Wave** shape (**seventh shape** in the **second row** of the *Stars and Banners* category) at the top of the document.
   b. Change the height to **1"** and the width to **4"**.
   c. Change the shape fill to **Olive Green, Accent 3** (**seventh color** in the **first row** of *Theme Colors*).
   d. Change the shape fill gradient to **From Center** (**second option** in the **second row** in the *Light Variations* category).

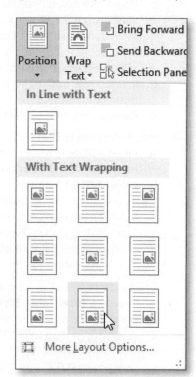

Figure 7-117 Position picture in the document

    e. Change the shape outline to **Olive Green, Accent 3** (**seventh color** in the **first row** of *Theme Colors*) and change the shape outline weight to **1½ pt**.

    f. Apply a shadow shape effect and select **Perspective: Upper Left** (**first option** in the **first row** of the *Perspective* category).

9. Position the shape and add text.

    a. Use the *Position* tab in the *Layout* dialog box to change the *Horizontal* **Alignment** to **Centered** *relative* to **Page** and change the *Vertical* **Absolute Position** to **0.2"** below the **Page**.

    b. Add text (not a text box) to the shape and type Life's Animal Shelter.

    c. Select the text in the shape and apply the following changes:

    Change the text color to **Olive Green, Accent 3, Darker 50%** (**seventh color** in the **last row** of *Theme Colors*).

    Change the font size to **22 pt**.

    Apply **bold** and **small caps** formatting.

    Change the *After* paragraph spacing to **0 pt**.

10. Save and close the document (Figure 7-118).

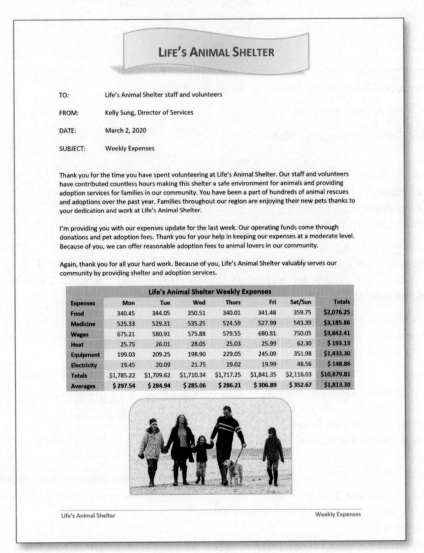

Figure 7-118 Word 7-4 completed

Independent Project 7-5

For this project, you modify a document of Microsoft Outlook shortcuts from Courtyard Medical Plaza. You convert text to a table, include tabs and indents in the table, modify the table, modify a table style, repeat header rows, insert and modify pictures, draw and modify a shape, and align and group objects.
[Student Learning Outcomes 7.1, 7.2, 7.3, 7.4, 7.5, 7.6]

Files Needed: **OutlookShortcuts-07.docx**, **CMP-logo-07.png**, and **Email-07.png** (Student data files are available in the Library of your SIMnet account.)
Completed Project File Name: **[your initials] Word 7-5.docx**

Skills Covered in This Project

- Change margins.
- Convert text to a table.
- Customize tabs and indents in the table.
- Insert a row and merge cells.
- Apply a table style.
- Modify a table style.
- Repeat header rows.
- Insert and resize a picture.
- Align and group pictures.
- Draw, resize, and modify a shape.
- Group selected objects.
- Edit a footer.

1. Open the **OutlookShortcuts-07** document from your student data files.

2. Save the document as [your initials] Word 7-5.

3. Change top, bottom, left, and right margins to **0.5"**.

4. Convert text to a table.
   a. Select all the text in the document and **Convert Text to Table**.
   b. Apply **AutoFit to window**.
   c. Separate text at **Paragraphs**.
   d. Change the number of columns to **2**.

5. Change tabs and indents in the table.
   a. Select the first column and set a **2.5" left** tab stop with a **broken line leader** (leader 3).
   b. Select the second column, set a **0.25" left indent** (*Paragraph* dialog box), and set a **2.6" left** tab stop with a **broken line leader**.

6. Add a row to the table and add text to the row.
   a. Add a row above the first row and type Microsoft Outlook Shortcuts in the first cell in the new row.
   b. Merge the cells in the new first row and change the *Left* indent to **0"**.

7. Change table style options and apply a table style.
   a. Select the table and set the *Table Style Options* to include a **Header Row** and **Banded Rows**.
   b. Apply the **List Table 4 - Accent 2** table style to the table (Figure 7-119).

Figure 7-119 Apply a table style

8. Modify the table style.
   a. Modify the **List Table 4 - Accent 2** table style.
   b. Apply the following formatting changes to the **Whole table**:
   Change the font size to **9 pt**.
   Change the text alignment to **Align Center Left**.
   Change the top and bottom cell margins to **0.02"** (*Hint: open the* Table Options *dialog box from the* Table Properties *dialog box*). Don't change the left and right cell margins.

c. Apply the following formatting changes to the table style to the **Header row**:
Change the font size to **16 pt**.
Change the text alignment to **Align Center**.

d. Apply the following formatting change to the table style to the **Odd banded rows**:
Change the *Fill Color* to **White, Background 1, Darker 5%** (**first color** in the **second row** of *Theme Colors*).

e. Click **OK** to accept the changes and to modify the table style.

9. Select the first row of the table and click **Repeat Header Rows** [*Table Tools Layout* tab, *Data* group]. The header row repeats at the top of each page.

10. Insert and resize pictures.
a. Place the insertion point at the end of the document and insert the ***CMP-logo-07*** picture.
b. Change the alt text to **CMP** logo.
c. Change the text wrapping to **Square**.
d. Drag the picture so it is approximately one inch below the table and one inch to the right of the left side of the table.
e. Place the insertion point at the end of the document and insert the ***Email-07*** picture.
f. Change the alt text to Graphic of an envelope in a circle.
g. Change the height of the email picture to **1.5"** and maintain aspect ratio.
h. Change the text wrapping to **Square**.
i. Drag the email picture so it is approximately one inch below the table and one inch to the left of the right side of the table.
j. Change the picture color to the **third option** in the **third row** in the *Recolor* area (**Red, Accent color 2 Light**).

11. Align and group the pictures.
a. Select both pictures.
b. Use the **Align** drop-down list [*Picture Tools Format* tab, *Arrange* group] to apply the following alignment changes:
Select **Align to Page**.
Select **Distribute Horizontally**.
Select **Align Selected Objects**.
Select **Align Middle**.
c. **Group** the selected objects.

12. Draw and modify a shape.
a. Draw a **Rectangle: Rounded Corners** shape (**second shape** in the *Rectangles* category) around the grouped objects.
b. Change the height to **2"** and the width to **6"**.
c. Select **Send to Back** from the *Send Backward* drop-down list so the shape displays behind the pictures.
d. Select the shape and apply the **Subtle Effect - Black, Dark 1** from the *Shape Styles* gallery (Figure 7-120).

Figure 7-120 Apply a shape style

13. Align and group the objects.
a. Select the shape and the grouped objects inside the shape.
b. Use the **Align** drop-down list [*Picture Tools Format* tab, *Arrange* group] to apply the following alignment changes:
Select **Align Selected Objects**.
Select **Align Center**.
Select **Align Middle**.
c. **Group** the selected objects.
d. Open the *Layout* dialog box and use the *Position* tab to change the *Horizontal* **Alignment** to **Centered** *relative to* **Margin** and change the *Vertical* **Absolute Position** to **7.5"** below the **Page**.

14. Edit the footer.
    a. Edit the footer, clear the existing right tab stop (6.5"), and set a **7.5" right** tab stop.
    b. Apply **bold** and **small caps** formatting to all the text in the footer and then close the footer.

15. Save and close the document (Figure 7-121).

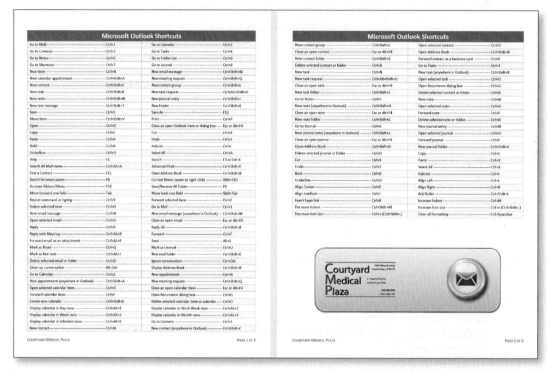

Figure 7-121 Word 7-5 completed

Independent Project 7-6

For this project, you create a cycling event calendar for the American River Cycling Club. You insert a table, modify the table structure, apply a table style, format and align text in the table, draw and modify shapes, add text to shapes, align shapes, and insert and modify a picture.
[Student Learning Outcomes 7.2, 7.3, 7.4, 7.6]

File Needed: ***ARCC-logo-07.png*** *(Student data files are available in the* Library *of your SIMnet account.)*
Completed Project File Name: ***[your initials] Word 7-6.docx***

Skills Covered in This Project

- Change margins and page orientation.
- Insert a table.
- Customize row height.
- Merge cells.
- Type and align text in a table.
- Apply a table style.
- Insert and modify a shape.
- Add text to a shape and modify text.
- Align shapes.
- Insert and modify a picture.
- Position a picture in the table.

---

1. Create a new blank Word document.

2. Save the document as [your initials] Word 7-6.

3. Change the page orientation to **Landscape**.

4. Change the top and bottom margins to **0.75"** and the left and right margins to **0.5"**. If you receive an error message about the margin settings, click **Ignore**.

5. Insert a table, modify table structure, and add text.
   a. Insert a **7x7** table.
   b. Change the row height to **1"** on all the rows.
   c. Merge the cells in the first row and type June.
   d. Change the row height of the second row to **0.3"**.
   e. Type the days of the week beginning with Sunday in the cells in the second row.
   f. Place the insertion point in the *Wednesday* column in the third row and type the day numbers beginning with 1. June has 30 days.

6. Set the table style options and apply a table style.
   a. Select the table and set the *Table Style Options* to include a **Header Row** and **Banded Rows**. All other options should be deselected.
   b. Apply the **Grid Table 4 - Accent 6** table style to the table.

7. Format text and text alignment in the table.
   a. Change the font size of the text in the first row to **72 pt**.
   b. Select the second row, change the font size to **14 pt.**, apply **bold** and **small caps** formatting, and change the text alignment to **Align Center** (center vertically and horizontally).
   c. Select rows 3–7, apply **bold** formatting, and change alignment to **Align Top Right**.

8. Add shapes to the table.
   a. Draw a **Rectangle: Folded Corner** shape (**fifth shape** in the **third row** in the *Basic Shapes* category) in the *Monday, June 6* cell.
   b. Change the height to **0.8"** and the width to **1"**.
   c. Apply the **Subtle Effect - Green, Accent 6** shape style (Figure 7-122).
   d. Add text to the shape (not a text box), type Morning Ride, press **Enter**, and type 6-8 a.m. You might not be able to see all the text you type; you format the text in the next step.
   e. Select all the text in the shape (**Ctrl+A**), change the font size to **10 pt**, apply **bold** formatting, and change the after paragraph spacing to **0 pt**.
   f. Select the shape, copy it, and paste it in the three cells below.
   g. Select the four shapes and, using the **Align** drop-down list, select **Align to Margin**, select **Align Left**, and select **Align Top**.

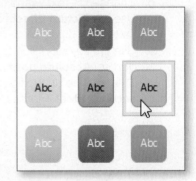

Figure 7-122 Apply a shape style

9. Add shapes to the table.
   a. Draw a **Plaque** shape (**tenth shape** in the **second row** in the *Basic Shapes* category) in the *Wednesday, June 1* cell.
   b. Change the height to **0.8"** and the width to **1"**.
   c. Apply the **Subtle Effect - Blue, Accent 1** shape style.
   d. Add text to the shape, type River Ride, press **Enter**, and then type 6-8 p.m.
   e. Select the text in the shape (**Ctrl+A**), change the font size to **10 pt.**, apply **bold** formatting, and change the after paragraph spacing to **0 pt**.
   f. Select and copy the shape and paste it in the four cells below.
   g. Select the five shapes, select **Align to Margin**, select **Align Left**, and then select **Align Top**.

10. Add shapes to the table.
    a. Draw an **Arrow: Pentagon** shape (**seventh shape** in the **second row** in the *Block Arrows* category) in the *Friday, June 3* cell.
    b. Change the height to **0.8"** and the width to **1"**.
    c. Apply the **Subtle Effect - Black, Dark 1** shape style.
    d. Add text to the shape, type Time Trial, press **Enter**, and then type 5-6 p.m.
    e. Select the text in the shape (**Ctrl+A**), change the font size to **10 pt**, apply **bold** formatting, and change the after paragraph spacing to **0 pt**.
    f. Select and copy the shape and paste it in the three cells below.
    g. Select the four shapes, select **Align to Margin**, select **Align Left**, and then select **Align Top**.

11. Add shapes to the table.
    a. Draw a **Flowchart: Document** shape (**seventh shape** in the **first row** in the *Flowchart* category) in the *Saturday, June 4* cell.
    b. Change the height to **0.8"** and the width to **1"**.
    c. Apply the **Subtle Effect - Gold, Accent 4** shape style.
    d. Add text to the shape, type Hilly Ride, press **Enter**, and then type 8-11 a.m.
    e. Select the text in the shape (**Ctrl+A**), change the font size to **10 pt**, apply **bold** formatting, and change the after paragraph spacing to **0 pt**.
    f. Select and copy the shape and paste it in the three cells below.
    g. Select the four shapes, select **Align to Margin**, select **Align Left**, and then select **Align Top**.

12. Insert a picture into the table.
    a. Insert the ***ARCC-logo-07*** picture in the first row.
    b. Change the alt text to ARCC logo.
    c. Change the height to **0.75"** and maintain the aspect ratio.
    d. Change the text wrapping to **In Front of Text**.
    e. Use the **Picture Effects** drop-down list to apply an **Offset Top** effect (*Shadow, Outer* category).
    f. Use the *Layout* dialog to set the *Horizontal* **Alignment** to **Right** *relative to* **Margin** and set the *Vertical* **Absolute position** to **0.3"** *below* **Margin**.
    g. Select "**June**" in the first row of the table and change the *Font Color* to the **last color** in the **second row** of *Theme Colors* (**Green, Accent 6, Lighter 80%**).

13. Save and close the document (Figure 7-123).

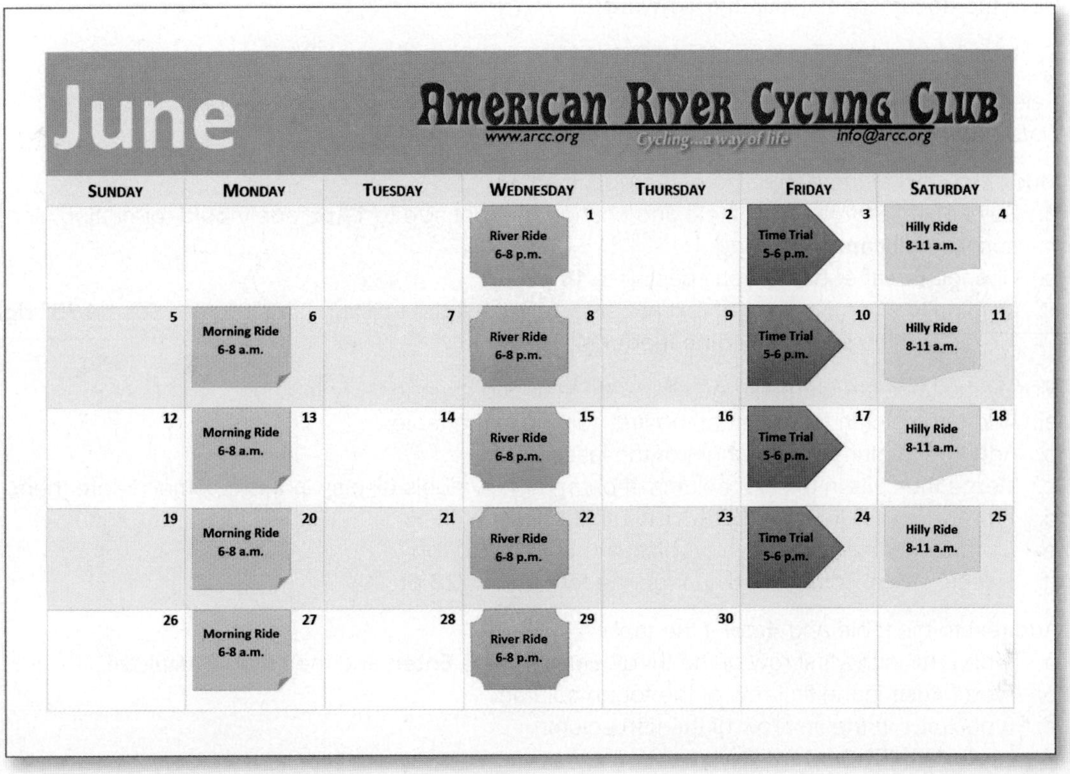

June

AMERICAN RIVER CYCLING CLUB

www.arcc.org Cycling...a way of life info@arcc.org

SUNDAY	MONDAY	TUESDAY	WEDNESDAY	THURSDAY	FRIDAY	SATURDAY
			1 River Ride 6-8 p.m.	2	3 Time Trial 5-6 p.m.	4 Hilly Ride 8-11 a.m.
5	6 Morning Ride 6-8 a.m.	7	8 River Ride 6-8 p.m.	9	10 Time Trial 5-6 p.m.	11 Hilly Ride 8-11 a.m.
12	13 Morning Ride 6-8 a.m.	14	15 River Ride 6-8 p.m.	16	17 Time Trial 5-6 p.m.	18 Hilly Ride 8-11 a.m.
19	20 Morning Ride 6-8 a.m.	21	22 River Ride 6-8 p.m.	23	24 Time Trial 5-6 p.m.	25 Hilly Ride 8-11 a.m.
26	27 Morning Ride 6-8 a.m.	28	29 River Ride 6-8 p.m.	30		

Figure 7-123 Word 7-6 completed

Improve It Project 7-7

For this project, you improve a buyer escrow checklist from Emma Cavalli at Placer Hills Real Estate. You split a table, convert a table to text, use bullets in the table, create a table style, apply a custom table style, and insert and modify pictures.
[Student Learning Outcomes 7.1, 7.2, 7.3, 7.4, 7.5]

Files Needed: ***BuyerEscrowChecklist-07.docx***, ***PHRE-logo-07.png***, and ***Checkmark-07.png*** *(Student data files are available in the* Library *of your SIMnet account.)*
Completed Project File Name: ***[your initials] Word 7-7.docx***

Skills Covered in This Project

- Split a table.
- Convert a table to text.
- Modify tab settings.
- Insert columns and merge cells.
- Change text direction.
- *AutoFit* a table to contents.
- Create a table style.
- Apply a custom table style.
- Modify column widths.
- Apply bullets to text in a table.
- Modify indents in a table.
- Insert and modify a picture.
- Group, align, and position pictures.

1. Open the **_BuyerEscrowChecklist-07_** document from your student data files.

2. Save the document as [your initials] Word 7-7.

3. Split the table at the "Task" row. "Task" should be in the first row of the second table.

4. Select the first table and convert the table to text (**Convert to Text** [_Table Tools Layout_ tab, _Data_ group]) using paragraph marks to separate text.

5. Modify the text at the beginning of the document.
   a. Select the first five lines of text and change the font size to **12 pt**, apply **bold** formatting, and apply **small caps** formatting.
   b. Change the after paragraph spacing to **18 pt**.
   c. Confirm the first five lines of text are selected, clear the existing tab stop, and set a **4.75" right** tab stop with a **solid underline leader** (4).

6. Modify the table structure, merge cells, add text, and change text direction.
   a. Add one column to the left of the first column in the table.
   b. Add three columns to the right of the last column.
   c. Merge the cells in the first column. If paragraph symbols display in this column, delete them.
   d. Type BUYER ESCROW CHECKLIST in the first column.
   e. Change the text direction to vertical from bottom to top.
   f. Select the first column and change the font size to **28 pt**.

7. Add text to the table and _AutoFit_ the table.
   a. Type Date in the first row of the third column, press **Enter**, and then type Completed.
   b. Type Initials in the first row of the fourth column.
   c. Type Notes in the first row of the fifth column.
   d. Apply **AutoFit Contents** to table.

8. Create and modify a table style.
   a. Create a new table style named PHRE table and base the style on the **Grid Table 5 Dark** table style.
   b. Apply the following changes to the **Whole table** in the new table style:
      Change the text alignment to **Align Center Left**.
      Change the top and bottom cell margins to **0.07"** (_Hint: use the_ Table Properties _dialog box_).
      Change the left and right cell margins to **0.1"**.
      Change the cell spacing to **0.04"**.
      Change the table alignment to **Center**.

9. Set table style options and apply a table style.
   a. Select the table and set the _Table Style Options_ to include a **Header Row** and **First Column**. All other options should be deselected.
   b. Apply the **PHRE** custom table style to the table.

10. Change the column widths in the table.
    a. Change the second column width to **3"**.
    b. Change the third column width to **1"**.
    c. Change the fifth column width to **1.2"**.

11. Apply bullets and change indents in the text in the table.
    a. Apply an open square bullet (_Wingdings_, character code 113) to the text in the second column below the "Task" column heading.
    b. Change the left indent of the bulleted list to **0"**.

12. Change font size and text alignment in the table.
    a. Select the first column and change the text alignment of the _First column_ to **Align Center**.
    b. Select the column headings in the first row (don't include the first column), change the font size to **12 pt**, apply **Small caps**, and change the text alignment to **Align Bottom Center**.

13. Delete the blank line between the tabbed text and the table.

14. Insert and modify pictures.
   a. Insert the **_PHRE-logo-07_** picture at the top of the document.
   b. Change the alt text to PHRE logo.
   c. Change the text wrapping to **Tight**.
   d. Drag the picture to the right of the tab leaders.
   e. Apply the **Offset: Bottom Right** shadow picture effect (**first option** in the _Outer_ category).
   f. Insert the **_Checkmark-07_** picture at the top of the document.
   g. Change the alt text to Checkmark graphic.
   h. Change the height to **1.5"** and maintain the aspect ratio.
   i. Change the text wrapping to **Tight**.
   j. Drag the picture to the right of the tab leaders and below the logo picture.
   k. Apply the **Offset: Bottom Right** shadow picture effect (**first option** in the _Outer_ category).
   l. Apply the **Pencil Grayscale** artistic effect (**third option** in the **first row**).

15. Align and group pictures.
   a. Select both pictures.
   b. Use the _Align_ drop-down list to select **Align Selected Objects** and select **Align Center**.
   c. Group the two pictures.
   d. Use the _Layout_ dialog box to set the _Horizontal_ **Absolute position** to **6.2"** _to the right of_ **Page** and set the _Vertical_ **Absolute position** to **0.3"** _below_ **Page**.

16. Save and close the document (Figure 7-124).

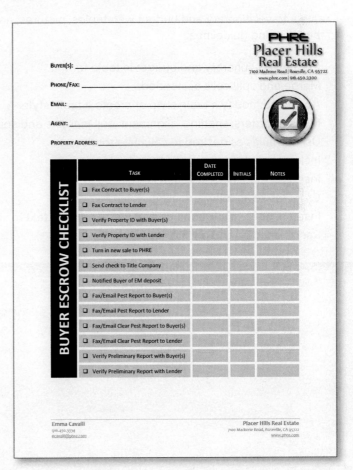

Figure 7-124 Word 7-7 completed

Challenge Project 7-8

We all look forward to vacations, and planning a vacation builds excitement and expectations. Create a travel itinerary and budget for an upcoming vacation, a trip, or your dream vacation.
[Student Learning Outcomes 7.1, 7.2, 7.3, 7.4, 7.5]

File Needed: None
Completed Project File Name: *[your initials] Word 7-8.docx*

Create a new blank document and save it as [your initials] Word 7-8.

A travel itinerary and budget include, but are not limited to, the following elements:

- Overall travel schedule
- Daily list of activities
- Description of activities
- To-do list
- Travel and accommodation information
- Pictures of destinations and hotels
- Estimated expenses

Create a travel itinerary and budget with tables, pictures, and shapes. Modify your document according to the following guidelines:

- Create your itinerary and budget in table format.
- Merge and split cells as needed.
- Apply and modify a table style or create a table style.
- Modify borders, shading, alignment, cell margins and spacing, and text direction.
- Use formulas as desired to calculate totals.
- Include bulleted and/or numbered lists.
- Insert pictures of destinations or places to visit.
- Crop, resize, modify, and align pictures.
- Insert shapes to surround objects or text or add text to shapes.
- Resize, modify, and position shapes.

Challenge Project 7-9

Most organizations prepare a calendar of events, or you might keep a personal calendar of upcoming assignments, tests, and projects for your classes. For this project, you create a monthly or weekly calendar of upcoming events for an organization you belong to or are familiar with, such as a non-profit organization, a professional organization, a student group, a school or work project team, a religious organization, or a sports team. Or, you can create a calendar for school work that is due in the next month.
[Student Learning Outcomes 7.1, 7.2, 7.3, 7.4, 7.5]

File Needed: None
Completed Project File Name: *[your initials] Word 7-9.docx*

Create a new blank document and save it as [your initials] Word 7-9.

Using tables, pictures, and shapes, create a calendar of events for an organization or upcoming class work. Modify your document according to the following guidelines:

- Create your events calendar in table format.
- Merge and split cells as needed.
- Resize columns and rows as needed.
- Add and align text.
- Apply and modify a table style or create a table style.
- Modify borders, shading, alignment, cell margins and spacing, and text direction.
- Insert shapes to surround objects or text or add text to shapes.
- Resize, modify, and position shapes.
- Insert an organization logo picture, picture of team members, or other appropriate pictures.
- Crop, resize, modify, and align pictures.

Challenge Project 7-10

Searching for a new car, motorcycle, bicycle, cell phone, cell phone plan, or any other expensive item can be a time-consuming task. When shopping for these high-cost items, researching product features and costs provides the information you need to make a decision. Create a product feature and cost comparison table to organize your research about a future purchase.
[Student Learning Outcomes 7.1, 7.2, 7.3, 7.4, 7.5]

File Needed: None
Completed Project File Name: *[your initials] Word 7-10.docx*

Create a new blank document and save it as [your initials] Word 7-10.

Your product feature and cost analysis can include, but is not limited to, the following elements:

- Product names
- Product features
- List of pros and cons for each product
- Cost comparison
- Cost of additional features
- Pictures of products

Create a document comparing the features and costs of different versions of a product you plan to purchase in the future. Include at least three comparable products. Modify your document according to the following guidelines:

- Create your product comparison in table format.
- Merge and split cells as needed.
- Apply and modify a table style or create a table style.
- Modify borders, shading, alignment, cell margins and spacing, and text direction.
- Use formulas as needed to calculate totals.
- Include bulleted and/or numbered lists.
- Insert pictures of products you plan to purchase.
- Crop, resize, modify, and align pictures.
- Insert shapes to surround objects or text or add text to shapes.
- Resize, modify, and position shapes.

Source of screenshots Microsoft Office 365 (2019): Word, Excel, Access, PowerPoint.

Using Desktop Publishing and Graphic Features

CHAPTER OVERVIEW

Microsoft Word is the leading word processing software on personal and business computers, and it is also a powerful desktop publishing application. Use Word to create professional-looking newsletters, brochures, advertisements, invitations, and a variety of documents that incorporate pictures, tables, columns, charts, text boxes, and other desktop publishing features. This chapter covers desktop publishing features in Word, including text boxes, custom themes, *SmartArt*, charts, and indexes.

STUDENT LEARNING OUTCOMES (SLOs)

After completing this chapter, you will be able to:

SLO 8.1 Apply desktop publishing features to a Word document (p. W8-482).

SLO 8.2 Customize an existing theme and create a custom theme (p. W8-491).

SLO 8.3 Insert and customize a built-in text box and create a custom text box (p. W8-492).

SLO 8.4 Insert and customize a *SmartArt* graphic (p. W8-498).

SLO 8.5 Insert and customize a chart (p. W8-503).

SLO 8.6 Mark index entries and insert and customize an index page (p. W8-512).

CASE STUDY

In the Pause & Practice projects in this chapter, you use desktop publishing features to enhance a handout given to the students in a freshman composition course at Sierra Pacific Community College District.

Pause & Practice 8-1: Enhance a document using custom page settings, a drop cap, page color, a watermark, and hyphenation.

Pause & Practice 8-2: Insert and customize a built-in text box, create a text box building

block, draw and customize a text box, and modify an existing theme to create a custom document theme.

Pause & Practice 8-3: Insert and modify a *SmartArt* graphic and a chart.

Pause & Practice 8-4: Mark index entries in a document and create and customize an index page.

Using Desktop Publishing Features

Word's desktop publishing features enable you to create engaging documents. For example, apply custom page settings, insert a drop cap, use page color, insert and customize a watermark, capture and insert a screenshot, use line numbering, and apply hyphenation to text. Moderately incorporating desktop publishing visual elements improves document readability and layout without overwhelming readers with too many formatting bells and whistles.

Custom Page Settings

In addition to changing margins, page orientation, and page size, you can apply a variety of custom page settings to multiple-page documents. *Gutter margins* and *mirror margins* are options for multi-page documents that you plan to print and bind on the left, right, or top. You can also change page settings to create *2 pages per sheet* or apply *book fold* to create a booklet. Table 8-1 lists and describes custom page settings:

Table 8-1: Custom Page Settings

Page Setting	Description
Gutter margins	Use to add extra margin space to the left or top of the document when you are planning to bind a document at the left or top. Gutter margins ensure text on bound edges displays correctly and margin spacing is even on multiple-page bound documents.
Mirror margins	Use on multi-page documents that print on both sides and have a binding at the left or right. When using mirror margins, the left and right margins become inside and outside margins. You can use a gutter margin with mirror margins to ensure additional space for binding the document.
2 pages per sheet	Use to split a page horizontally into two pages.
Book fold	Use to split a page vertically into two pages. Use book fold to create a booklet, menu, or invitation. When you use book fold, the page orientation of your document automatically changes to landscape.

▶ HOW TO: Apply Custom Page Settings

1. Click the **Margins** button [*Layout* tab, *Page Setup* group].
2. Select **Custom Margins** to open the *Page Setup* dialog box (Figure 8-1).
3. Change the **Gutter margin** setting and change the **Gutter position** to *Left* or *Top* in the *Margins* area on the *Margins* tab.
4. Click the **Multiple pages** drop-down list and select an option.
   - Adjust page gutter margins after you select a *Multiple pages* option.
   - The *Preview* area displays how the document will appear.
5. Click the **Apply to** drop-down list and select the part of the document where you want to apply the settings.
   - Options include *Whole document*, *This point forward*, or *Selected text*.
   - If you select *This point forward* or *Selected text*, Word inserts a section break to control page formatting.
6. Click **OK** to close the *Page Setup* dialog box.

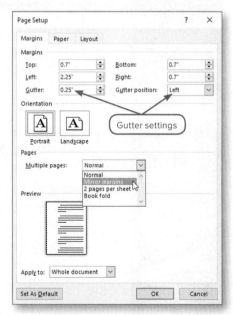

Figure 8-1 *Page Setup* dialog box

> **ANOTHER WAY**
>
> Click the **Page Setup** launcher [*Layout* tab] to open the *Page Setup* dialog box.

Drop Caps

A ***drop cap*** emphasizes the first letter of a paragraph (Figure 8-2). When applying this feature, the first letter of the paragraph becomes a graphic object, and you can customize its appearance and placement. You can also apply the drop cap format to the entire first word (not just the first letter) at the beginning of a paragraph.

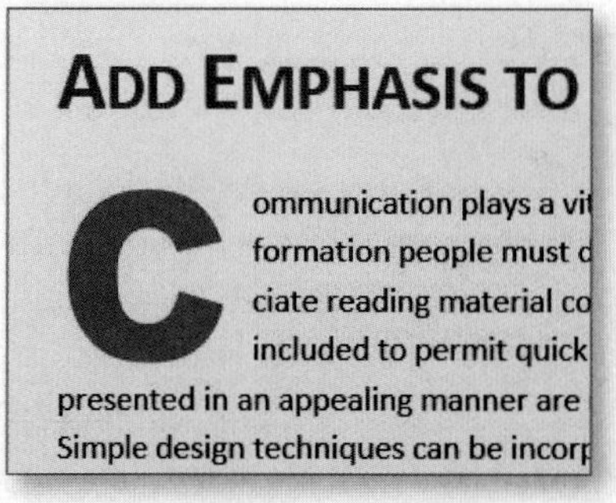

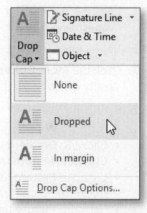

Figure 8-2 Drop cap applied to the first letter of a paragraph

▸HOW TO: Insert a Drop Cap

1. Place the insertion point in the paragraph to apply the drop cap.
   - By default, drop cap applies to the first letter of a paragraph.
   - Alternatively, select the first word of the paragraph and apply drop cap formatting to the first word of the paragraph rather than just the first letter.
2. Click the **Drop Cap** button [*Insert* tab, *Text* group] to display the list of drop cap choices (Figure 8-3).
3. Select a drop cap to apply to the first letter of the paragraph.
   - To remove an existing drop cap, click the **Drop Cap** button and select **None** from the drop-down list.

Figure 8-3 *Drop Cap* drop-down list

Drop Cap Options

After applying drop cap formatting to a letter or word in a paragraph, customize its appearance. Format the drop cap letter or word the same way you format text in a document by changing the drop cap's font, size, color, and style. Use the ***Drop Cap dialog box*** to customize the font and placement of the drop cap.

▸HOW TO: Customize a Drop Cap

1. Place the insertion point in the paragraph with the drop cap or select the drop cap.
2. Click the **Drop Cap** button [*Insert* tab, *Text* group] and select **Drop Cap Options**. The *Drop Cap* dialog box opens (Figure 8-4).
3. Select the position of the drop cap in the *Position* area.
4. Click the **Font** drop-down list to select a different font for the drop cap.
5. Click the **Lines to drop** text box and select the number of lines the drop cap should span.
   - The default *Lines to drop* is *3*.
6. Click the **Distance from text** text box and change the amount of space between the drop cap letter and the surrounding text.
   - The default *Distance from text* is *0"*.
7. Click **OK** to close the *Drop Cap* dialog box.

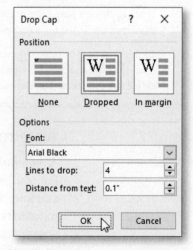

Figure 8-4 *Drop Cap* dialog box

Page Color

By default, a Word document has no page color. In previous chapters, you used shading and fill colors with borders, shapes, and other graphic objects. You can similarly change the *page color* of a document. When applying a page color, it applies to the entire document. Select a page color from theme colors or standard colors, or apply a gradient, texture, pattern, or picture as the background of a document.

▶**HOW TO: Apply and Customize Page Color**

1. Click the **Page Color** button [*Design* tab, *Page Background* group] to display the drop-down list of options (Figure 8-5).

2. Select from *Theme Colors* or *Standard Colors* to apply a page color.

3. Click the **More Colors** button to open the *Colors* dialog box to select from a variety of *Standard* or *Custom* colors.

4. Click the **Fill Effects** button to open the *Fill Effects* dialog box. Apply a *Gradient*, *Texture*, *Pattern*, or *Picture* as a page background for the document (Figure 8-6).

   - Click the **Gradient** tab to select gradient *Colors, Transparency,* and *Shading* styles.
   - Click the **Texture** tab to select a *Texture* to apply as the page background.
   - Click the **Pattern** tab to select a *Pattern* and change the *Foreground* and *Background* pattern colors.
   - Click the **Picture** tab to select a picture to use as the page background.

5. Click **OK** to close the *Fill Effects* dialog box and apply the fill as the page background.

   - Remove the page color by clicking the **Page Color** drop-down list and selecting **No Color**.

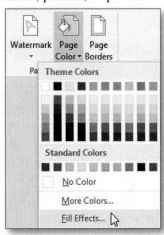

Figure 8-5 *Page Color* drop-down list

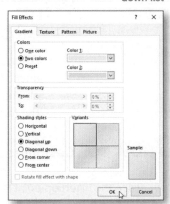

Figure 8-6 *Fill Effects* dialog box

Watermarks

A *watermark* is text or a picture that appears behind the text on every page in a document (Figure 8-7). For example, display the words "Draft" or "Sample" as a watermark behind the text as a notation for readers. A watermark text or picture does not affect the placement or wrapping of text or other objects in the document. Watermarks are typically in a lighter color than the other

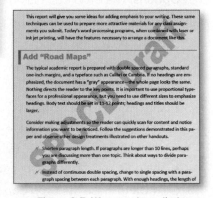

Figure 8-7 Watermark applied to a document

W8-484

text in the document and semitransparent so as not to affect the readability of the document. Insert a built-in watermark or a custom watermark.

Built-In Watermarks

Word provides a variety of built-in watermarks to insert into a document easily and quickly. Built-in watermarks display in categories on the *Watermark* drop-down list (Figure 8-8). Click the **Watermark** button in the *Page Background* group on the *Design* tab and select the built-in watermark to insert into your document.

Custom Watermarks

Alternatively, create your own custom watermark. A custom watermark can be text or a picture. You can change the font, size, color, and layout of the custom watermark.

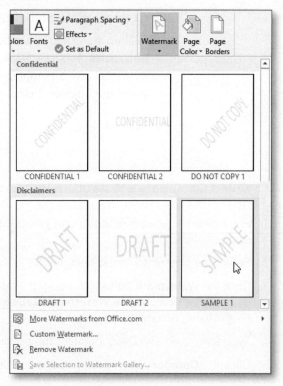

Figure 8-8 Insert a built-in watermark

▶HOW TO: Insert a Custom Watermark

1. Click the **Watermark** button [*Design* tab, *Page Background* group] and select **Custom Watermark**. The *Printed Watermark* dialog box opens (Figure 8-9).

2. Click the **Text watermark** radio button.

   • Alternatively, select the *Picture watermark* radio button and choose a picture to apply as a watermark.

3. Click the **Text** drop-down list and select from the text options in the list or type custom text for the watermark.

4. Click the **Font** drop-down list to select the font.

5. Click the **Size** drop-down list to select the font size.

   • *Auto* is the default font size, but you can choose a specific font size.

6. Click the **Color** drop-down list to select a color.

   • By default, the *Semitransparent* check box is selected. Deselect this check box to darken the watermark.

7. Select the **Diagonal** or **Horizontal** radio button in the *Layout* area.

8. Click **Apply** to add the watermark to your document.

9. Click **Close** to close the dialog box.

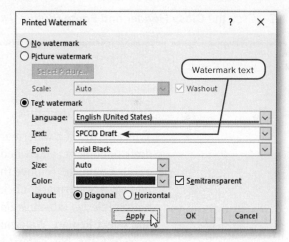

Figure 8-9 *Printed Watermark* dialog box

> **MORE INFO**
>
> Use the *Printed Watermark* dialog box to customize a built-in watermark.

Create a Watermark Building Block

Built-in watermarks are building blocks stored in the *Watermark* gallery. Creating a custom **watermark building block** is similar to creating a *Quick Part* or *Footer* building block. For example, save a company logo or a company name as a watermark building block to use in other documents. Select a custom watermark and save it in the *Watermark* building block gallery.

▶ HOW TO: Create a Watermark Building Block

1. Right-click the header or footer and select **Edit Header** or **Edit Footer** to open the header or footer.

2. Select the watermark in the document.

3. Click the **Watermark** button [*Design* tab, *Page Background* group] and select **Save Selection to Watermark Gallery**. The *Create New Building Block* dialog box opens (Figure 8-10).

4. Type the *Name* and *Description* for the building block.

5. Click the **Category** drop-down list and select a category or create a new category.

6. Click the **Save in** drop-down list and select the location to save the building block.

7. Click **OK** to create the watermark building block.

8. Click the **Close Header and Footer** button [*Header & Footer Tools Design* tab, *Close* group].

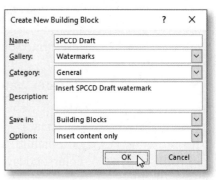

Figure 8-10 Create watermark building block

Remove a Watermark

Typically, insert a watermark on a sample or draft document, and when the review process is complete, remove the watermark. To remove a watermark, click the **Watermark** button [*Design* tab, *Page Background* group] and select **Remove Watermark** (Figure 8-11) or select the **No watermark** radio button in the *Printed Watermark* dialog box (see Figure 8-9).

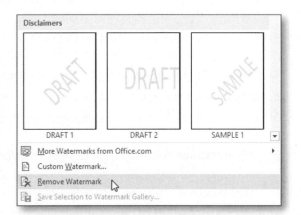

Figure 8-11 Remove a watermark

Screenshots

In Chapter 7, you inserted and customized pictures in documents. Another useful Word feature is *Screenshot*. Screenshot enables you to capture an open window on your computer such as an open document or an internet browser window. This screenshot becomes a picture that displays in your document, and you can resize, crop, arrange, and customize the screenshot.

▶ HOW TO: Insert a Screenshot

1. Open the file or internet browser window to use as a screenshot in your document.
2. Open the Word document and place the insertion point at the location to insert the screenshot.
3. Click the **Screenshot** button [*Insert* tab, *Illustrations* group] to display the drop-down list of available windows (Figure 8-12).
4. Select from the *Available Windows* to capture as a screenshot.
   - The screenshot displays as a picture in your document.
   - Resize, move, and customize the picture as desired.

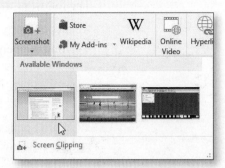

Figure 8-12 Select window to capture as a screenshot

> ### MORE INFO
> To save a picture in a document, right-click the picture and select **Save as Picture**.

Additionally, you can capture a portion of a window, which is called a *screen clipping*. When capturing a screen clipping, the pointer becomes a selection crosshair to select the portion of the window to capture.

▶ HOW TO: Insert a Screen Clipping

1. Open the window containing the content to capture.
2. Place the insertion point in the Word document at the location to insert the screen clipping.
3. Click the **Screenshot** button [*Insert* tab, *Illustrations* group] and select **Screen Clipping** from the drop-down list.
   - The window behind the Word document opens, and the pointer becomes a selection crosshair.
4. Click and drag over the region to capture as a screen clipping (Figure 8-13).
5. Release the pointer to capture the screen clipping.
   - The screen clipping displays as a picture in the document.
   - Resize, move, and customize the picture as desired.

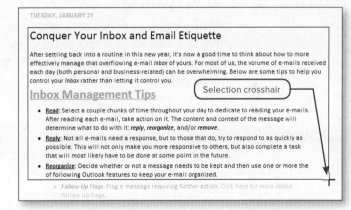

Figure 8-13 Select screen clipping

Hyphenation

Hyphenation is a Word feature used to divide words at the right margin of a column or page to balance line endings and use the space on each page more effectively. Word can automatically hyphenate your document, or you can manually choose the placement of the hyphen at the end of a line of text. Hyphenation is typically used when using multiple columns in a document. The following are basic hyphenation guidelines:

- Divide words between syllables.
- Don't hyphenate one-syllable words.
- Leave at least two letters and the hyphen at the end of a line and three letters on the carryover line.
- Don't divide proper nouns or proper adjectives.

Word applies these hyphenation guidelines when automatically hyphenating text, but it is a good idea to check your document for proper hyphenation.

▶ **HOW TO:** Automatically Hyphenate Text in a Document

1. Place the insertion point at the beginning of the document.
2. Click the **Hyphenation** button [*Layout* tab, *Page Setup* group].
3. Select **Automatic** to automatically hyphenate the entire document.
   - Click **Hyphenation Options** from the *Hyphenation* drop-down list to open the *Hyphenation* dialog box to customize hyphenation settings (Figure 8-14).
   - To remove hyphenation, click the **Hyphenation** button and select **None**.

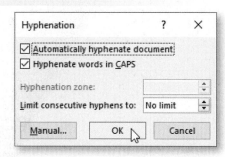

Figure 8-14 *Hyphenation* dialog box

Line Numbers

When reviewing or editing a long document with a team or in a meeting, it can be time consuming to locate specific text in the document and ensure everyone is viewing the same information. *Line numbers* display at the left side of each line and are a helpful reference when editing and reviewing a long document. Also, line numbers are commonly used on legal documents.

▶ **HOW TO:** Turn on Line Numbering

1. Click the **Line Numbers** button [*Layout* tab, *Page Setup* group].
2. Select from the drop-down list of options (Figure 8-15).
   - **Continuous**: Numbers lines consecutively throughout the document.
   - **Restart Each Page**: Numbers the lines on each page beginning with 1 and restarts each page with 1.
   - **Restart Each Section**: Numbers the lines in each section beginning with 1 and restarts each section with 1.
   - **Suppress for Current Paragraph**: Turns off numbering on the selected paragraph.
   - **Line Numbering Options**: Opens the *Page Setup* dialog box with the *Layout* tab displayed. Click the **Line Numbers** button to open the *Line Numbers* dialog box to customize line-numbering options.
3. Turn off line numbers by clicking the **Line Numbers** button and selecting **None**.

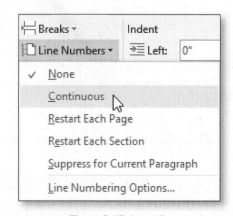

Figure 8-15 Insert line numbers

For this Pause & Practice project, you modify a handout Sierra Pacific Community College District gives to all its freshman composition students. You change margins, add a gutter margin, apply a drop cap, apply a page color, create a custom watermark, save a watermark as a building block, and apply hyphenation.

File Needed: **AddEmphasis-08.docx** *(Student data files are available in the Library of your SIMnet account.)*
Completed Project File Name: *[your initials] PP W8-1.docx*

1. Open the **AddEmphasis-08** document from your student data files.

2. Save the document as [your initials] PP W8-1.

3. Change the margins and add a gutter margin.
   a. Open the *Page Setup* dialog box, and change the *Top*, *Bottom*, and *Right* margins to **0.7"**.
   b. Change the *Left* margin to **2.25"**.
   c. Change the *Gutter* to **0.25"** and the *Gutter position* to **Left**.
   d. Click **OK** to close the *Page Setup* dialog box.

4. Apply styles to selected text.
   a. Apply the **Heading 1** style to all bolded (but not underlined) section headings. Don't apply the *Heading 1* style to the title.
   b. Apply the **Heading 2** style to all underlined headings.
   c. Apply the **List Paragraph** style to the two bulleted lists.

5. Add a gradient page color to the document.
   a. Click the **Page Color** button [*Design* tab, *Page Background* group] and select **Fill Effects**. The *Fill Effects* dialog box opens, and the *Gradient* tab displays (Figure 8-16).
   b. Click the **Two colors** radio button in the *Colors* area.
   c. Click the **Color 1** drop-down list and select the **last color** in the **second row** of *Theme Colors* (**Green, Accent 6, Lighter 80%**).
   d. Click the **Color 2** drop-down list and select the **last color** in the **third row** of *Theme Colors* (**Green, Accent 6, Lighter 60%**).
   e. Select the **Diagonal up** radio button in the *Shading styles* area.
   f. Select the upper left option In the *Variants* area.
   g. Click **OK** to close the dialog box and apply the page color.

6. Apply and customize a drop cap.
   a. Place the insertion point in the first paragraph below the title.
   b. Click the **Drop Cap** button [*Insert* tab, *Text* group] and click **Dropped**.
   c. Click the **Drop Cap** button again and select **Drop Cap Options**. The *Drop Cap* dialog box opens (Figure 8-17).
   d. Click the **Font** drop-down list and select **Arial Black**.
   e. Change the *Lines to drop* to **4**.
   f. Change the *Distance from text* to **0.1"**.
   g. Click **OK** to close the *Drop Cap* dialog box.
   h. Select the drop cap in the document and change the font color to the **fifth color** in the **last row** of *Theme Colors* (**Blue, Accent 1, Darker 50%**).
   i. Deselect the drop cap.

Figure 8-16 Apply gradient page color

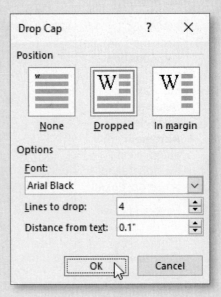

Figure 8-17 Modify drop cap options

7. Create a custom watermark.
   a. Click the **Watermark** button [*Design* tab, *Page Background* group] and select **Custom Watermark**. The *Printed Watermark* dialog box opens (Figure 8-18).
   b. Click the **Text watermark** radio button.
   c. Delete the existing text in the *Text* area, and type SPCCD Draft as the watermark text.
   d. Click the **Font** drop-down list and select **Arial Black**.
   e. Click the **Size** drop-down list and select **Auto** if it is not already selected.
   f. Click the **Color** drop-down list and select the **first color** in the *Standard Colors* area (**Dark Red**).
   g. Check the **Semitransparent** box and select the **Diagonal** radio button if they are not already checked and selected.
   h. Click **Apply** to insert the watermark.
   i. Click **Close** to close the dialog box.

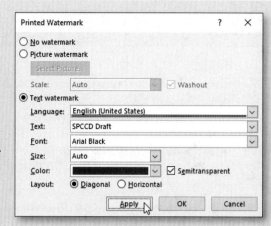

Figure 8-18 Create custom text watermark

8. Save the custom watermark as a building block.
   a. Edit the header on the first page.
   b. Select the watermark on the page.
   c. Click the **Watermark** button [*Design* tab, *Page Background* group (not *Header & Footer Tools Design* tab)] and select **Save Selection to Watermark Gallery**. The *Create New Building Block* dialog box opens (Figure 8-19).
   d. Add the following properties for the new building block:
      Name: SPCCD Draft
      Gallery: **Watermarks**
      Category: **General**
      Description: Insert SPCCD Draft watermark
      Save in: **Building Blocks**
      Options: **Insert content only**
   e. Click **OK** to close the dialog box and create the new building block.
   f. Close the header if it is still open.

Figure 8-19 Create watermark building block

9. Click the **Hyphenation** button [*Layout* tab, *Page Setup* group] and select **Automatic** to automatically hyphenate the entire document.

10. Save and close the document (Figure 8-20). Click **Save** if prompted to save changes to building blocks.

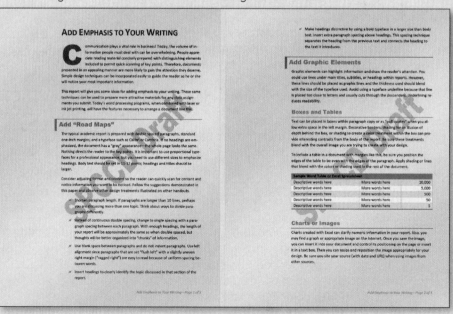

Figure 8-20 PP W8-1 completed (pages 1 and 2 of 3)

SLO 8.2 Customizing and Creating Themes

In *SLO 2.7: Using Styles and Themes*, you learned about themes and how a document theme controls the fonts, sizes, colors, line and paragraph spacing, and styles in a document. You can apply a *theme* to a document, customize an existing theme, or create a custom theme.

Theme Colors, Fonts, and Effects

When applying a theme to a document, Word automatically changes the *theme colors*, *theme fonts*, and *theme effects* to match the selected theme. Although the document theme controls the theme colors, fonts, and effects, you can customize a document theme by selecting different theme colors, fonts, and effects.

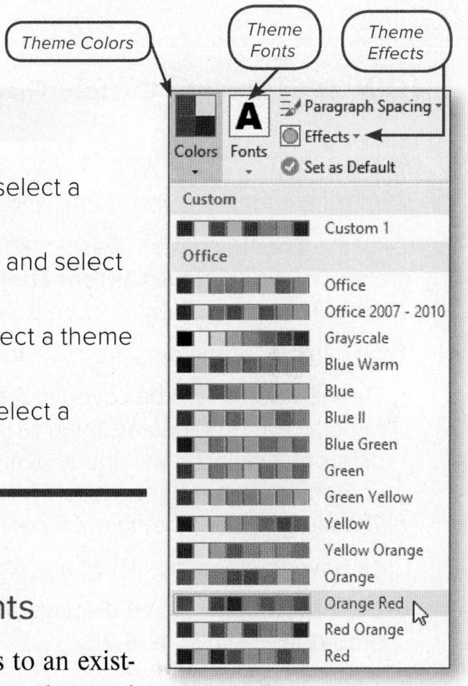

Figure 8-21 Select theme colors

▶ HOW TO: Customize a Theme

1. Click the **Themes** button [*Design* tab, *Document Formatting* group] and select a theme from the drop-down list.
2. Click the theme **Colors** button [*Design* tab, *Document Formatting* group] and select a theme color set (Figure 8-21).
3. Click the **Fonts** button [*Design* tab, *Document Formatting* group] and select a theme font set.
4. Click the **Effects** button [*Design* tab, *Document Formatting* group] and select a theme effects set.

Create Custom Theme Colors and Fonts

In addition to applying preset theme colors and fonts to an existing theme, you can also create your own custom theme colors and fonts. Select specific colors and fonts and save these custom color and font sets to apply to a document or document theme.

▶ HOW TO: Create New Theme Colors

1. Click the theme **Colors** button [*Design* tab, *Document Formatting* group].
2. Select **Customize Colors** from the drop-down list. The *Create New Theme Colors* dialog box opens (Figure 8-22).
3. Change the color of any item by selecting a color from the drop-down list in the *Theme colors* area.
   - The *Sample area* displays the theme colors.
4. Click the **Name** text box and type a name for the new theme colors.
5. Click **Save** to close the dialog box.
   - The new custom *Theme Colors* displays in the *Colors* drop-down list in the *Custom* category.

Figure 8-22 *Create New Theme Colors* dialog box

Creating new theme fonts is similar to creating new theme colors. Theme fonts contain two font sets: *Heading font* and *Body font*. Customize the new theme fonts and save the changes for future use (Figure 8-23).

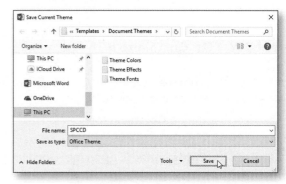

Figure 8-23 *Create New Theme Fonts* dialog box

Create a Custom Theme

After modifying theme fonts, colors, or effects, you can save these changes as a new document theme. Custom themes apply consistency among documents and save time. Custom themes display in the *Themes* drop-down list and can be applied to other documents.

▶ **HOW TO:** Create a Custom Theme

1. Apply a theme to a document.
2. Change the theme colors, fonts, and effects as desired.
3. Click the **Themes** button [*Design* tab, *Document Formatting* group] and select **Save Current Theme**. The *Save Current Theme* dialog box opens (Figure 8-24).
4. Type a name for the new theme in the *File name* area.
   - The new theme will be saved in the *Document Themes* folder on your computer. If you save the new theme in a different location, it will not be available in the drop-down list of themes in your documents.
   - The file type for a theme is *Office Theme*.
5. Click **Save** to close the dialog box and save your custom theme.
   - The new custom theme displays in the *Custom* category in the *Themes* drop-down list (Figure 8-25).

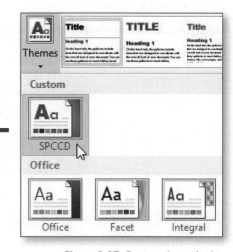

Figure 8-24 *Save Current Theme* dialog box

▶ MORE INFO

To delete a custom theme, right-click the custom theme in the *Themes* drop-down list and select **Delete**.

Figure 8-25 Custom theme in the *Themes* drop-down list

SLO 8.3

Using Text Boxes

Use a *text box* to draw attention to information in a document. Word includes many built-in text boxes, or you can draw your own text box. A text box is a graphic object that you can resize, arrange, and customize like a shape or picture. You can customize text in a text box and create a custom text box building block.

Built-In Text Boxes

A ***Built-in text box*** is preformatted with custom borders, fill, and effects. Built-in text boxes contain placeholder text in a ***content control field***. A content control field in a text box is a Word field where you insert and format custom text. After inserting a built-in text box into a document, customize both the text box format and the text box content.

The two main categories of built-in text boxes are *quotes* and *sidebars*. Use a quote text box to create a pull quote. A pull quote "pulls" content from the text to highlight and emphasize a point. Use sidebars to display additional information. Sidebars typically align at the left, right, top, or bottom of a page.

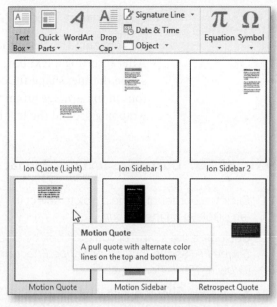

Figure 8-26 Built-in text boxes

▶ HOW TO: Insert a Built-In Text Box

1. Place the insertion point at the location to insert a text box.
2. Click the **Text Box** button [*Insert* tab, *Text* group].
3. Select a built-in text box from the drop-down list (Figure 8-26).
   - Select **More Text Boxes from Office.com** to view additional text box options.
4. Click the content control field of the text box and replace the placeholder text with custom text.

Customize Text Box Content

After inserting a built-in text box, replace the placeholder text with custom content. Type or paste information in the content control field or remove the content control field and type directly in the text box. Format text in the text box by changing the font, size, style, color, line spacing, and paragraph spacing using the font and spacing options on the *Home* tab. Alternatively, use the text options in the *WordArt Styles* and *Text* groups on the *Drawing Tools Format* tab to customize text.

▶ HOW TO: Customize Text Box Content

1. Click the placeholder text in the text box to select it (Figure 8-27).
2. Type text to replace the placeholder text or copy text and paste it in the content control field.
   - To remove the content control field, right-click the field and select **Remove Content Control** field from the context menu.
3. Select the text in the text box and customize as desired.
   - Use the *WordArt Styles* group [*Drawing Tools Format* tab] to modify the *WordArt Style*, *Text Fill*, *Text Outline*, and *Text Effects*.
   - Click the **Word Art Styles** launcher to open the *Format Shape* pane and to customize text. Adjust the text layout and internal margins in the *Text Options* area of the *Format Shape* pane.
   - Use the *Text* group [*Drawing Tools Format* tab] to change the *Text Direction*, *Align Text*, or *Create Link*. The *Create Link* option links text from one text box to another text box.

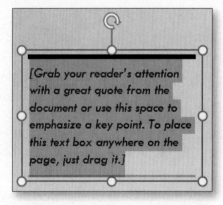

[Grab your reader's attention with a great quote from the document or use this space to emphasize a key point. To place this text box anywhere on the page, just drag it.]

Figure 8-27 Select placeholder text in the text box

Customize Text Box Format

Customizing the format of a text box is similar to customizing the format of other shapes. After inserting a text box, the *Drawing Tools Format* tab displays to customize the shape style, shape outline, shape fill, or shape effects of the text box. Use the *Position* and *Wrap Text* buttons in the *Arrange* group to customize the size and position of the text box and to control text wrapping around the text box.

▶**HOW TO:** Customize Text Box Format

1. Click the border of the text box to select it. The *Drawing Tools Format* tab displays on the *Ribbon*.

2. Customize the shape of your text box by modifying the *Shape Style, Shape Fill, Shape Outline,* or *Shape Effects* in the *Shape Styles* group [*Drawing Tools Format* tab].
   - Click the **Shape Styles** launcher to open the *Format Shape* pane and apply formatting changes to the shape of the text box (Figure 8-28).

3. Change the *Height* and *Width* of the text box shape in the *Size* group [*Drawing Tools Format* tab].
   - Alternatively, use the sizing handles to resize the text box shape.

4. Use the *Position, Wrap Text, Bring Forward, Send Backward, Align, Group,* or *Rotate* options [*Drawing Tools Format* tab, *Arrange* group] to customize the text box.
   - Click the **Size** launcher to open the *Layout* dialog box to customize *Position, Text Wrapping,* and *Size* of the text box.
   - Alternatively, click the **Layout Options** button to the right of the text box (see Figure 8-29) and select a text wrapping option.

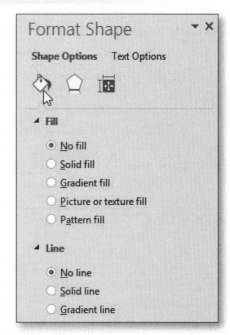

Figure 8-28 *Format Shape* pane

Draw a Text Box

Another way to insert a text box is to draw the text box. You can draw a text box in any shape anywhere in the document. After drawing a text box, insert and format text in the box and customize the text box shape.

▶**HOW TO:** Draw a Text Box

1. Click the **Text Box** button [*Insert* tab, *Text* group].

2. Select **Draw Text Box** from the drop-down list. The pointer becomes a drawing crosshair pointer.

3. Draw a text box in the document by dragging diagonally down and to the right (Figure 8-29). The insertion point displays in the text box.

4. Type or paste text in the text box.

5. Format the text in the text box as desired.

6. Use the *Drawing Tools Format* tab to customize the text box shape, alignment, text wrapping, size, and position.

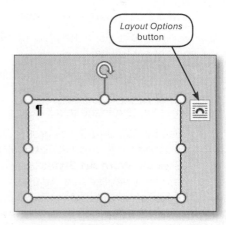

Figure 8-29 Draw a text box

Text Box Building Blocks

All built-in text boxes are building blocks in the *Text Box* gallery. Just like creating a watermark, header, footer, or table building block, you can create a text box building block. Once you have stored a custom text building block, you can insert it in other documents.

▶ **HOW TO:** Create a Text Box Building Block

1. Select a built-in or custom text box.
2. Click the **Text Box** button [*Insert* tab, *Text* group] and select **Save Selection to Text Box Gallery**. The *Create New Building Block* dialog box opens (Figure 8-30).
3. Type or select the *Name, Category, Description, Save in* area, and *Options* for the building block.
4. Click **OK** to create the text box building block.

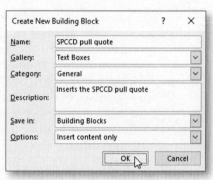

Figure 8-30 Create text box building block

PAUSE & PRACTICE: WORD 8-2

For this Pause & Practice project, you modify the document you edited in *Pause & Practice 8-1*. You customize an existing theme, create new theme fonts, create a new theme, insert and customize a built-in text box, draw and customize a text box, and create a text box building block.

File Needed: *[your initials] PP W8-1.docx*
Completed Project File Name: *[your initials] PP W8-2.docx*

1. Open the *[your initials] PP W8-1* document you completed in *Pause & Practice 8-1*.
2. Save the document as [your initials] PP W8-2.
3. Apply and customize a theme.
   a. Click the **Themes** button [*Design* tab, *Document Formatting* group] and select **Wisp** from the drop-down list.
   b. Click the theme **Colors** button [*Design* tab, *Document Formatting* group] and select **Orange Red** from the drop-down list.
   c. Click the **Effects** button [*Design* tab, *Document Formatting* group] and select **Subtle Solids** from the drop-down list.

4. Create new theme fonts.
   a. Click the **Fonts** button [*Design* tab, *Document Formatting* group] and select **Customize Fonts** from the drop-down list. The *Create New Theme Fonts* dialog box opens (Figure 8-31).
   b. Click the **Heading font** drop-down list and select **Arial Black**.
   c. Click the **Body font** drop-down list and select **Tw Cen MT**.
   d. Type SPCCD in the *Name* area.
   e. Click **Save** to create the new theme font and apply it to the current document theme.

Figure 8-31 *Create New Theme Fonts* dialog box

5. Create a new document theme.
   a. Click the **Themes** button [*Design* tab, *Document Formatting* group] and select **Save Current Theme** to open the *Save Current Theme* dialog box (Figure 8-32).
   b. Type SPCCD in the *File name* area. Don't change the save location.
   c. Click **Save** to close the dialog box and save the custom theme.

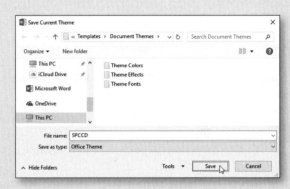

Figure 8-32 *Save Current Theme* dialog box

6. Insert and customize a built-in text box.
   a. Place the insertion point at the beginning of the first paragraph below the "Add "Road Maps"" heading.
   b. Click the **Text Box** button [*Insert* tab, *Text* group] and select **Motion Quote**. Don't be concerned about the text box placement; you will adjust this later.
   c. Select the last sentence in the first paragraph on the first page ("**Simple design techniques . . .**") and **copy** it. Don't include the paragraph mark at the end of the sentence when selecting it.
   d. Click the placeholder text in the text box to select it and press **Ctrl+V** to paste the copied text, which replaces the placeholder text.
   e. Select the text in the text box and apply **italic** formatting.
   f. Change the *Height* of the text box to **1.4"** and the *Width* to **1.9"** [*Drawing Tools Format* tab, *Size* group].
   g. Click the **Shape Effects** button [*Drawing Tools Format* tab, *Shape Styles* group], select **Preset**, and choose **Preset 2**.
   h. Click the **Position** button [*Drawing Tools Format* tab, *Arrange* group] and select **More Layout Options**. The *Layout* dialog box opens.
   i. Set the *Horizontal* **Absolute position** to **0.3"** *to the right of* **Page** and set the *Vertical* **Alignment** to **Centered** *relative to* **Page**.
   j. Click **OK** to close the *Layout* dialog box.

7. Create a text box building block.
   a. Select the text box you created in step 6 (Figure 8-33).
   b. Click the **Text Box** button [*Insert* tab, *Text* group] and select **Save Selection to Text Box Gallery**. The *Create New Building Block* dialog box opens.
   c. Add the following properties for the new building block:
      Name: SPCCD pull quote
      Gallery: **Text Boxes**
      Category: **General**
      Description: Inserts the SPCCD pull quote
      Save in: **Building Blocks**
      Options: **Insert content only**

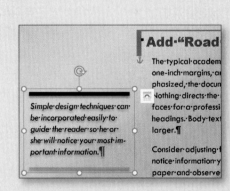

Figure 8-33 Text box positioned in the document

d. Click **OK** to close the dialog box and create the new building block.

8. Insert and customize a text box building block.
   a. Place the insertion point at the beginning of the first paragraph on the last page ("In writing, content . . .").
   b. Click the **Text Box** button [*Insert* tab, *Text* group] and select the **SPCCD pull quote** (Figure 8-34).
   c. Select the last sentence on the last page ("A design with graphic . . .") and copy it. Don't select the paragraph mark at the end of the sentence.
   d. Select the existing text in the text box, click the **Paste** drop-down arrow [*Home* tab, *Clipboard* group], and select the **Merge Formatting** paste option.
   e. Change the *Height* of the text box to **1.2"**.

General

SPCCD pull quote
Inserts the SPCCD pull quote

SPCCD pull quote

More Text Boxes from Office.com

Draw Text Box

Save Selection to Text Box Gallery

Figure 8-34 Insert text box building block

9. Draw a text box and customize the content.
   a. Place the insertion point on the second page.
   b. Click the **Text Box** button and select **Draw Text Box**. The pointer becomes a drawing crosshair pointer.
   c. Draw a text box (approximately 1" tall and 5" wide) over the second paragraph in the "Boxes and Tables" section.
   d. Change the *Height* to **0.8"** and the *Width* to **5.25"**.
   e. Type the following text in the text box:

   This is an example of a text box that was drawn between two paragraphs. Remember to adjust the text box's internal margins to leave space between the text and the text box. The format of this text box has been customized.

10. Customize the text box format.
    a. Select the text box.
    b. Click **More** button [*Drawing Tools Format* tab, *Shape Styles* group] to display the *Shape Styles* gallery and select **Subtle Effect – Dark Red, Accent 2 (third style** in the **fourth row** of *Theme Styles*).
    c. Click the **Shape Styles** launcher to open the *Format Shape* pane.
    d. Click **Layout & Properties** and select **Text Box** to expand this area (Figure 8-35).
    e. Change the *Vertical alignment* to **Middle**.
    f. Set the *Left*, *Right*, *Top*, and *Bottom* internal margins to **0.1"**.
    g. Click the **Alt Text** button [*Drawing Tools Format* tab, *Accessibility* group] and type Formatted text box in the text box.
    h. Close the *Alt Text* and *Format Shape* panes.
    i. Change the text wrapping to **Tight**.
    j. Drag the text box between the first and second paragraphs in the "Boxes and Tables" section.
    k. Click the **Align** button [*Drawing Tools Format* tab, *Arrange* group] and select **Align to Margin** (if it's not already selected).
    l. Click the **Align** button again and select **Align Left**.
    m. Use the up or down keyboard arrow key to align the text box evenly between the first and second paragraph, if necessary.

Format Shape

Shape Options   Text Options

Layout & Properties button

▲ **Text Box**

| Vertical alignment | Middle |
| Text direction | Horizontal |

☐ Do not rotate text

☐ Resize shape to fit text

Left margin	0.1"
Right margin	0.1"
Top margin	0.1"
Bottom margin	0.1"

☑ Wrap text in shape

Figure 8-35 *Format Shape* pane

11. Click at the beginning of the "Write Vertical Lists" heading and insert a **page break** (**Ctrl+Enter**).

12. Position the text box on the last page.
    a. Select the text box on the last page.
    b. Click the **Position** button [*Drawing Tools Format* tab, *Arrange* group] and select **More Layout Options**. The *Layout* dialog box opens.
    c. Set the *Vertical* **Absolute position** to **0.9"** below **Margin**. Don't change the *Horizontal* position.
    d. Click **OK** to close the *Layout* dialog box.

13. Save and close the document (Figure 8-36). Click **Save** if prompted to save changes to building blocks.

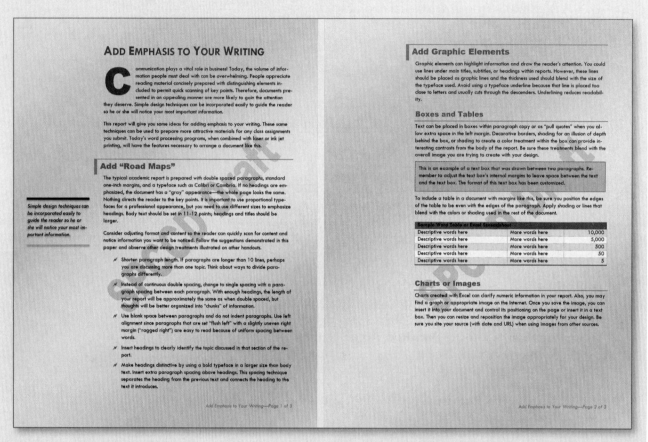

Figure 8-36 PP W8-2 completed (pages 1 and 2 of 3)

Using SmartArt

A *SmartArt* graphic is an excellent way to visually display information in a document. *SmartArt* graphics are a collection of customized shapes, lines, and text. Now that you have experience working with shapes and text boxes, you can apply this knowledge to customizing *SmartArt* graphics.

Insert a SmartArt Graphic

Word provides a variety of *SmartArt* categories, and each category has many built-in *SmartArt* graphics to insert in your document. Once you select and insert a *SmartArt* graphic, add text, customize the design, and customize the individual objects in the *SmartArt*.

▶ **HOW TO:** Insert a SmartArt Graphic

1. Place the insertion point in the document where you want to insert a *SmartArt* graphic.

2. Click the **SmartArt** button [*Insert* tab, *Illustrations* group] to open the *Choose a SmartArt Graphic* dialog box (Figure 8-37).

3. Select a category of *SmartArt* graphics on the left to view the options in that category.

4. Select a *SmartArt* graphic.

   - A preview and description of the graphic appears on the right.
   - The preview is the basic structure of the graphic; you can add to or remove graphic objects from this structure.

5. Click **OK** to close the dialog box and insert the *SmartArt* graphic.

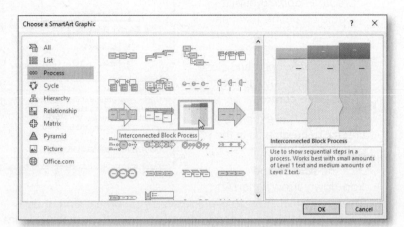

Figure 8-37 *Choose a SmartArt Graphic* dialog box

SmartArt Tools Tabs

After you insert a *SmartArt* graphic into a document, two *SmartArt* tabs become available: **SmartArt Tools Design** and **SmartArt Tools Format**. Use the *SmartArt Tools Design* tab to modify the design and structure of the *SmartArt* graphic. The following groups display on the *SmartArt Tools Design* tab: *Create Graphic*, *Layouts*, *SmartArt Styles*, and *Reset*.

Use the *SmartArt Tools Format* tab to format the shapes, text, arrangement, and size of the *SmartArt* graphic and the objects within the graphic. The following groups display on the *SmartArt Tools Format* tab: *Shapes*, *Shape Styles*, *WordArt Styles*, *Arrange*, and *Size*.

Customize SmartArt Text

Once a *SmartArt* graphic is inserted into your document, customize the graphic by adding shapes and bulleted text or removing these items. Type text directly in the *SmartArt* graphic or use the **Text pane** to enter and organize text. The *Create Graphic* group on the *SmartArt Tools Design* tab includes options to add a shape or bullet, promote or demote the level of items, move items up or down, switch the layout from right to left, or modify the layout.

Modify the text in the *SmartArt* graphic the same way you modify other text using the *Font* and *Paragraph* groups on the *Home* tab. You can also customize the text in the *SmartArt* graphic with the *WordArt Styles*, *Text Fill*, *Text Outline*, and *Text Effects* options in the *WordArt Styles* group on the *SmartArt Tools Format* tab.

▶HOW TO: Customize SmartArt Text

1. Select and insert a *SmartArt* graphic into your document.
   - Click the **Text Pane** button [*SmartArt Tools Design* tab, *Create Graphic* group] to toggle on/off the *Text* pane to the side of the *SmartArt* graphic (Figure 8-38).
   - Alternatively, open and close the *Text* pane by clicking the **Text pane control**.

2. Type text in the *Text* pane or directly in the objects in the *SmartArt* graphic.

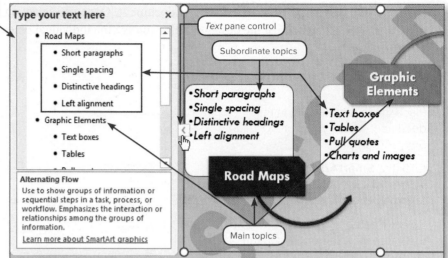

Figure 8-38 *SmartArt* graphic with *Text* pane displayed

3. Click the **Add Shape** drop-down arrow [*SmartArt Tools Design* tab, *Create Graphic* group] to add a shape after, before, above, or below the selected shape in the graphic (Figure 8-39).
   - The shapes and text in the graphics automatically resize when you add shapes to the *SmartArt* graphic.
   - Delete a shape or text by selecting it and pressing **Delete**.

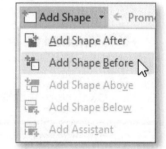

4. Click the **Add Bullet** button [*SmartArt Tools Design* tab, *Create Graphic* group] to add a subordinate topic to the list of topics.
   - Alternatively, press **Enter** at the end of a bulleted topic in the graphic or *Text* pane to add another bullet.

Figure 8-39 Add shape to *SmartArt* graphic

5. Click the **Promote** or **Demote** button [*SmartArt Tools Design* tab, *Create Graphic* group] to change a main topic to a subordinate topic or to change a subordinate topic to a main topic (Figure 8-40).

6. Click the **Move Up** or **Move Down** button [*SmartArt Tools Design* tab, *Create Graphic* group] to arrange topics in a list.
   - You can also select and drag or cut and paste topics in the *Text* pane to arrange them.

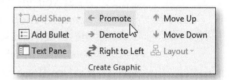

Figure 8-40 *Create Graphic* group on the *SmartArt Tools Design* tab

7. Click the **Right to Left** button [*SmartArt Tools Design* tab, *Create Graphic* group] to switch the layout of the *SmartArt* graphic from left to right or right to left.

8. Click the **WordArt Styles**, **Text Fill**, **Text Outline**, or **Text Effects** button to customize the appearance of the text [*SmartArt Tools Format* tab, *WordArt Styles* group] (Figure 8-41).
   - When customizing text, always select the text before applying formatting options.

9. Click the **Text Pane** button [*Table Tools Design* tab, *Create Graphic* group] or the **X** in the upper-right corner of the *Text* pane to close it.

Figure 8-41 *WordArt Styles* group on the *SmartArt Tools Format* tab

---

▶ **ANOTHER WAY**

Click the **Shape Styles** or **WordArt Styles** launcher [*SmartArt Tools Format* tab] to open the *Format Shape* pane to customize the *SmartArt* graphic.

Customize SmartArt Design

After typing and formatting the text in your *SmartArt* graphic, customize the overall design of the *SmartArt* graphic. Use options on the *SmartArt Tools Design* tab to change the layout of the *SmartArt* graphic, modify the colors of the objects, or apply a *SmartArt* style.

▶**HOW TO:** Customize SmartArt Design

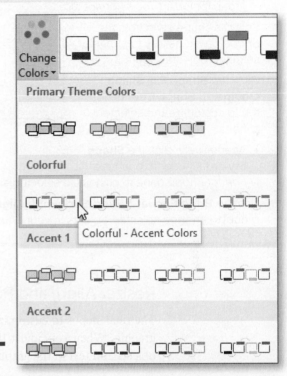

1. Select the *SmartArt* graphic and use the *Layouts* group [*SmartArt Tools Design* tab] to select a different *SmartArt* layout.
    - Click the **More** button in the *Layouts* group [*SmartArt Tools Design* tab] to display additional options in the *Layouts* gallery.
    - In the *Layouts* gallery, select **More Layouts** to open the *Choose a SmartArt Graphic* dialog box to change the *SmartArt* layout.
2. Click the **Change Colors** button [*SmartArt Tools Design* tab, *SmartArt Styles* group] to change the color of your *SmartArt* (Figure 8-42).
3. Select a *SmartArt* style [*SmartArt Tools Design* tab, *SmartArt Styles* group] to apply to the *SmartArt* graphic.
    - *SmartArt Styles* apply custom fill, outlines, and effects to your *SmartArt* graphic.
    - Click the **More** button [*SmartArt Tools Design* tab, *SmartArt Styles* group] to display additional style options.

Figure 8-42 Change the color of a *SmartArt* graphic

▶ MORE INFO

When you place the pointer on a layout, color, or style, Word temporarily applies the style or formatting to your *SmartArt* graphic to preview the change.

Customize SmartArt Objects

In addition to modifying *SmartArt* text and design, you can also customize individual objects within the *SmartArt* graphic. Change the size or shape of individual objects in a *SmartArt* graphic, apply a shape style, or customize a shape fill, outline, or effects. Apply changes to the individual objects in a *SmartArt* graphic similar to how you customize shapes.

▶**HOW TO:** Customize SmartArt Objects

1. Select the object to customize.
    - Use the **Ctrl** key to select multiple objects in your *SmartArt* graphic if you want to apply changes to more than one object.
    - You can also use the *Selection* pane [*SmartArt Tools Format* tab, *Arrange* group] to select objects in your *SmartArt* graphic.

2. Click the **Change Shape** button [*SmartArt Tools Format* tab, *Shapes* group] to select a different shape for the selected objects (Figure 8-43).

   - Word automatically applies the selected shape to the selected objects and adjusts the size of the text if needed.

3. Click the **Larger** or **Smaller** button [*SmartArt Tools Format* tab, *Shapes* group] to change the size of the selected objects.

   - Alternatively, change the size of an object by using the sizing handles or the *Size* group [*SmartArt Tools Format* tab].

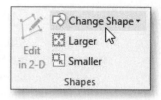

Figure 8-43 Shapes group on the *SmartArt Tools Format* tab

4. Select a shape style from the *Shape Styles* gallery to apply to selected objects (Figure 8-44).

5. Click the **Shape Fill**, **Shape Outline**, or **Shape Effects** button to customize the selected shapes.

   - Alternatively, click the **Shape Styles** launcher to open the *Format Shape* pane to customize selected shapes.

Figure 8-44 *Shape Styles* group on the *SmartArt Tools Format* tab

6. Use the **Bring Forward**, **Send Backward**, **Align**, **Group**, and **Rotate** buttons [*SmartArt Tool Format* tab, *Arrange* group] to arrange selected objects in your *SmartArt* graphic.

Resize, Align, and Position SmartArt

The final step is to customize the size, text wrapping, alignment, and position of the *SmartArt* graphic. When you adjust the size of your *SmartArt* graphic, Word automatically resizes the objects and text in the graphic.

▶ **HOW TO:** Resize, Align, and Position SmartArt

1. Select the *SmartArt* graphic and use the *Size* group [*SmartArt Tools Format* tab] or use the sizing handles to change the height and width of the graphic.

   - The sizing handles on a *SmartArt* graphic are the small circles on the sides and corners of the *SmartArt* frame.

2. Click the **Wrap Text** button [*SmartArt Tools Format* tab, *Arrange* group] to select a text wrap option.

3. Click and drag the frame of the *SmartArt* graphic to position it in your document.

   - When you place the pointer on the frame of the *SmartArt* graphic, the pointer becomes a four-pointed move pointer.
   - Alternatively, click the **Align** or **Position** button [*SmartArt Tools Format* tab, *Arrange* group] to align your *SmartArt* graphic in relation to the page or margins.

> **MORE INFO**
>
> Click the **Size** launcher [*SmartArt Tools Format* tab, *Size* group] to open the *Layout* dialog box to modify the position, text wrapping, and size.

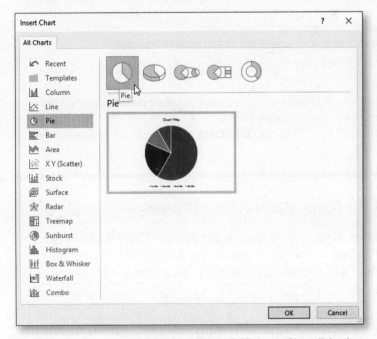

SLO 8.5

Using Charts

Use *Charts* to graphically display numerical data in Word documents, Excel worksheets, Access databases, and PowerPoint presentations. Insert a variety of different chart types and customize the data in the chart, the layout and elements of the chart, the chart design, and the format of the chart and chart elements.

Insert a Chart

When inserting a chart in a document, determine the type of chart that best displays the data you are presenting. The most common types of charts are *Column*, *Line*, *Pie*, and *Bar*. Word also offers other charts such as *Area*, *X Y (Scatter)*, *Stock*, *Surface*, *Doughnut*, *Bubble*, and *Radar*.

After inserting a chart, a chart containing sample data displays in the Word document. Also, a *Chart in Microsoft Word* worksheet opens in a new window and displays sample data. The information in the *Chart in Microsoft Word* worksheet displays in columns and rows, similar to a table (see Figure 8-46). As you edit the data in the worksheet, the chart in the Word document updates automatically.

▶HOW TO: Insert a Chart

1. Place the insertion point at the location to insert the chart.
2. Click the **Chart** button [*Insert* tab, *Illustrations* group]. The *Insert Chart* dialog box opens (Figure 8-45).

Figure 8-45 *Insert Chart* dialog box

3. Select the chart type to insert.
   - Chart categories display on the left.
   - The thumbnail graphics at the top display each chart structure, and a preview of a chart displays below the thumbnails.
4. Click **OK** to close the dialog box and to insert the chart.
   - The chart displays in the document and a *Chart in Microsoft Word* worksheet window opens (Figure 8-46).

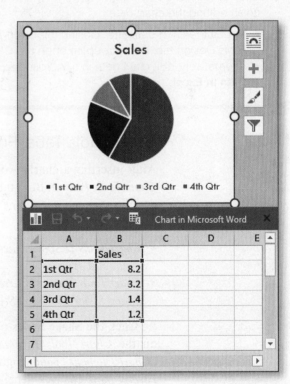

Figure 8-46 Chart inserted and *Chart in Microsoft Word* worksheet displayed

Customize Chart Data

After inserting a chart, the first step is to customize the data for the chart using the *Chart in Microsoft Word* worksheet (see Figure 8-46). Replace the sample data with your own data. Column and row headings describe the data and display as axes and legend labels in the chart.

The ***chart data range*** is the information in the *Chart in Microsoft Word* worksheet. A border displays around the chart data range as shown in Figure 8-47. Use the handle in the bottom-right corner of the chart data range border to adjust the chart data range. The information in the chart data range is used to generate the chart in the document.

▶HOW TO: Customize Chart Data

1. Type the chart data in the *Chart in Microsoft Word* worksheet (see Figure 8-47).

   - The data in the chart in the document updates automatically as you edit the *Chart in Microsoft Word* worksheet.
   - Include column and row headings to describe the data in the table. Columns are vertical, and rows are horizontal.
   - Drag the title bar of the *Chart in Microsoft Word* worksheet to reposition the window if needed.

2. Click and drag the **chart data range** handle (bottom-right corner of the chart data range border) to resize the chart data range (see Figure 8-47).

   - Verify that the chart data range contains no blank rows or columns. Blank rows or columns within the data range border display in the chart in the Word document.

3. Click the **X** in the upper-right corner of the *Chart in Microsoft Word* worksheet to close the window when you finish editing the chart data.

   - To edit the chart data after closing the *Chart in Microsoft Word* worksheet, click the **Edit Data** button [*Chart Tools Design* tab, *Data* group] to open the *Chart in Microsoft Word* window.
   - Alternatively, edit chart data in a Microsoft Excel worksheet. Click the **Edit Data** drop-down list and select **Edit Data in Excel**.

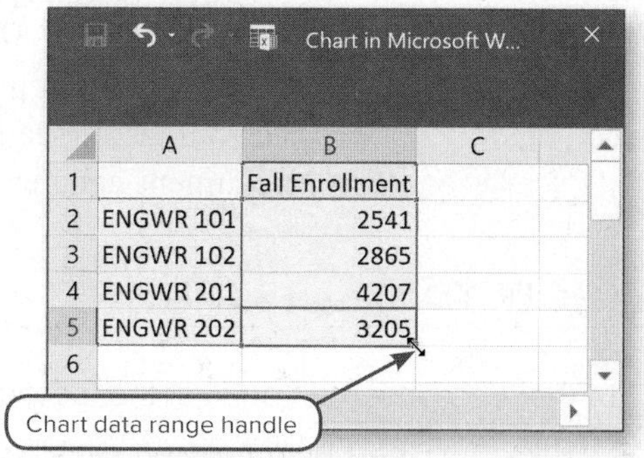

Figure 8-47 Edit chart data in the *Chart in Microsoft Word* worksheet

---

Chart Tools Tabs, Format Pane, and Format Buttons

After inserting a chart, two ***Chart Tools tabs*** display on the *Ribbon*: ***Chart Tools Design*** and ***Chart Tools Format***. Both tabs include options to customize the design and format of the chart and the elements within the chart. The following are the *Chart Tools* tabs and the groups available on each tab:

- ***Chart Tools Design***: *Chart Layouts, Chart Styles, Data,* and *Type*
- ***Chart Tools Format***: *Current Selection, Insert Shapes, Shape Styles, Word Art Styles, Arrange,* and *Size*

Click the **Shape Styles** or **WordArt Styles** launcher on the *Chart Tools Format* tab to open the ***Format "Chart Element" pane*** (Figure 8-48). The name of the *Format* pane changes depending on the chart element selected (for example, *Format Plot Area, Format Chart Title*). Click the **Chart Elements** drop-down list to select a chart element (see Figure 8-48). The *Format* pane

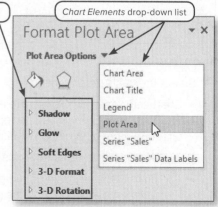

Figure 8-48 *Format "Chart Element"* pane

provides format categories (*Fill & Line*, *Effects*, *Layout & Properties*) and options within each category. The format categories and options vary depending on the chart element you select.

Additionally, four format buttons display on the right of a selected chart: *Layout Options*, *Chart Elements*, *Chart Styles*, and *Chart Filters*. These format buttons provide another method to customize chart design and format. Click any of these format buttons to display a list of options (Figure 8-49).

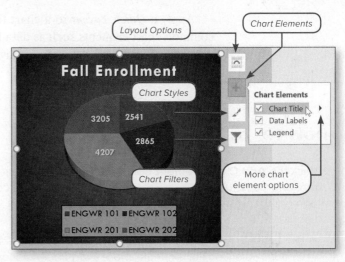

Figure 8-49 Chart format buttons

Customize Chart Layout

After inserting a chart and customizing the data to display in the chart, add or modify the elements of the chart. For example, add or modify the chart title, axis titles, legend, and data labels. Depending on the type of chart you are using, different chart element options are available. Click the **Add Chart Element** button on the *Chart Tools Design* tab in the *Chart Layouts* group to display the drop-down list of chart elements. Table 8-2 lists and describes the common chart elements:

Table 8-2: Chart Elements

Chart Element	Description
Axes	The horizontal axis (x-axis) and vertical axis (y-axis) that appear on charts. You can customize the scale and format of both axes.
Axis Titles	Text that describes the horizontal axis (x-axis) and vertical axis (y-axis).
Chart Title	Text that describes the chart's content and purpose.
Data Labels	Numerical labels on columns, bars, lines, or pie segments that display the number or percent for each value on the chart.
Data Table	A table below the chart that displays the data values.
Error Bars	Bars that display margins of error and standard deviations at a glance.
Gridlines	Vertical and horizontal lines that appear in the chart plot area to help readers distinguish values and data.
Legend	Text that describes the data represented in the chart and typically displays on the right or at the bottom of the chart.
Lines	Vertical lines that drop from data points to the x-axis or display vertical lines between high and low data points on line charts.
Plot Area	The area of the chart where the columns, bars, or lines display chart data.
Trendline	A line that charts the trend between data points.
Up/Down Bars	Bars that display between data points on a line chart.
Walls and Floors	Side and back walls and floors that display when using a 3-D chart.

Apply a *Quick Layout* to a chart to add common chart elements such as data labels or a data table. You can also change the chart type after you insert a chart.

Figure 8-50 *Add Chart Element* drop-down list

▶HOW TO: Customize Chart Layout

1. Click the **Add Chart Element** button [*Chart Tools Design* tab, *Chart Layouts* group], select the chart element to add or modify, and select an option within the chart element (Figure 8-50).
   - Most of the chart elements have a *More "Chart Element" Options* selection (for example, *More Data Label Options*) that opens the *Format "Chart Element"* pane to further modify the chart element (Figure 8-51).
   - Alternatively, click the **Chart Elements** button on the right of a chart and select or deselect a chart element (see Figure 8-49). Click the triangle on the right of each chart element in this menu to further customize each chart element.

2. Click the **Quick Layout** button [*Chart Tools Design* tab, *Chart Layouts* group] and select an option from the drop-down list to apply a *Quick Layout* to a chart.

3. Change the chart type by clicking the **Change Chart Type** button [*Chart Tools Design* tab, *Type* group] and selecting a different chart type in the *Change Chart Type* dialog box.

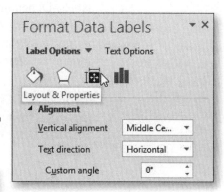

Figure 8-51 *Format Data Labels* pane

▶ MORE INFO
When you place your pointer on a chart element, a *ScreenTip* displays the name of the chart element.

Apply a Chart Style and Quick Color

After customizing the layout of your chart, you can apply a *Chart Style* and *Quick Colors*. A *Chart Style* is a combination of colors and chart elements applied to a chart with one click. *Quick Colors* are color sets that apply to the chart. The two different categories of *Quick Colors* are *Colorful* and *Monochromatic*. Both *Chart Styles* and *Quick Colors* apply to an entire chart.

▶HOW TO: Apply a Chart Style and Quick Color

1. Select the chart and click the **Chart Tools Design** tab.
2. Click the **More** button in the *Chart Styles* group to display the *Chart Styles* gallery (Figure 8-52).
   - Place the pointer on a selection in the *Chart Styles* gallery to display a preview of the style on the chart.

Figure 8-52 *Chart Styles* gallery

3. Click the **Change Colors** button [*Chart Tools Design* tab, *Chart Styles* group] and select a *Quick Color*.
   - Place your pointer on a selection in the *Quick Colors* drop-down list to display a preview of the *Quick Color* on the chart.

> **ANOTHER WAY**
>
> Click the **Chart Styles** button on the right of a chart to apply a *Chart Style* or *Quick Color*.

Customize Chart Elements

After inserting a chart and customizing the data, layout, and design, apply styles, fills, outlines, and effects to specific chart elements. For example, apply a fill color to the entire chart area, change the color of a column, apply an outline to the legend, or change the font on data labels.

▶ HOW TO: Customize Chart Elements

1. Select the chart element to modify.
   - Click the specific chart element in the chart or click the **Chart Elements** drop-down list [*Chart Tools Format* tab, *Current Selection* group] and select a chart element (Figure 8-53).

2. Click the **More** button in the *Shape Styles* gallery [*Chart Tools Format* tab, *Shape Styles* group] and apply a *Shape Style* to the chart element (Figure 8-54).

3. Click the **Shape Fill**, **Shape Outline**, or **Shape Effects** button [*Shape Styles* group] to apply a fill, outline, or effect to the chart element.
   - Click the **Shape Styles** launcher to open the *Format "Chart Element"* pane, which provides additional options. For example, select the chart data labels and click the *Shape Styles* launcher to open the *Format Data Labels* pane (see Figure 8-51).
   - Alternatively, right-click a chart element and select **Format "Chart Element"** from the context menu to open the *Format "Chart Element"* pane.

Figure 8-53 Select a chart element

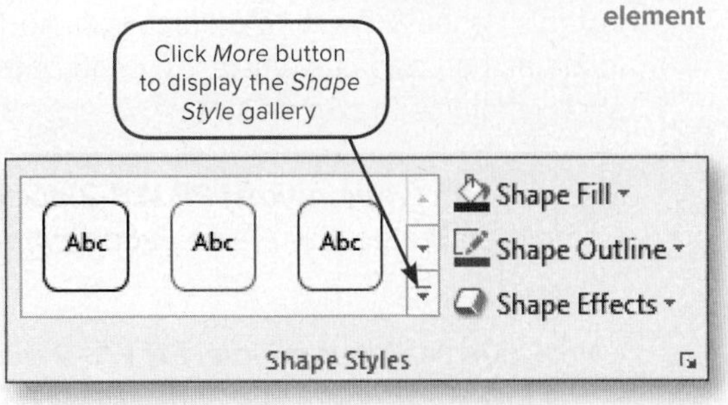

Figure 8-54 *Shape Styles* group on the *Chart Tools Format* tab

4. Click the **WordArt Styles**, **Text Fill**, **Text Outline**, or **Text Effects** button [*WordArt Styles* group] to customize the chart element text (Figure 8-55).
   - Click the **WordArt Styles** launcher to open the *Format* pane to customize the chart element.

Figure 8-55 *WordArt Styles* group on the *Chart Tools Format* tab

> ### ANOTHER WAY
> Use the arrow keys on the keyboard to scroll through and select chart elements.

Resize, Align, and Position a Chart

The final step is to customize the chart size, text wrapping, alignment, and position. Customizing the size and arrangement of the chart is similar to customizing *SmartArt* graphics, pictures, or shapes. Word automatically resizes chart elements when you adjust the size of the chart.

▶ HOW TO: Resize, Align, and Position a Chart

1. Select the chart.
2. Use the *Size* group [*Chart Tools Format* tab] or the sizing handles to change the height and width of the chart (Figure 8-56).
3. Click the **Wrap Text** button [*Chart Tools Format* tab, *Arrange* group] and select a text wrap option.

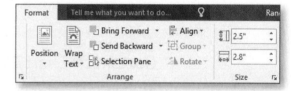

Figure 8-56 *Arrange* and *Size* groups on the *Chart Tools Format* tab

4. Click and drag the frame of the chart to position it in your document.
   - Place your pointer on the frame of the chart to display the four-pointed move pointer.
   - Click the **Align** or **Position** button [*Chart Tools Format* tab, *Arrange* group] to align your chart relative to the page or margins.
   - Alternatively, click the **Size** launcher [*Chart Tools Format* tab, *Size* group] to open the *Layout* dialog box to modify the position, text wrapping, and size of the chart.

PAUSE & PRACTICE: WORD 8-3

For this Pause & Practice project, you modify the document you created in *Pause & Practice 8-2*. You insert a chart and customize the chart data, layout, design, and format, and you insert a *SmartArt* graphic and customize the *SmartArt* text, design, and objects.

File Needed: *[your initials] PP W8-2.docx*
Completed Project File Name: *[your initials] PP W8-3.docx*

1. Open the *[your initials] PP W8-2* document you completed in *Pause & Practice 8-2*.
2. Save the document as [your initials] PP W8-3.

3. Insert a chart and customize the chart data.
   a. Place the insertion point at the end of the last paragraph on the second page.
   b. Click the **Chart** button [*Insert* tab, *Illustrations* group]. The *Insert Chart* dialog box opens (Figure 8-57).
   c. Click **Pie** on the left, select the **Pie** chart, and click **OK** to insert the chart and to open the *Chart in Microsoft Word* worksheet window. Don't be concerned with chart placement at this point; you will modify the placement later.
   d. Type the following data in the *Chart in Microsoft Word* worksheet (Figure 8-58):

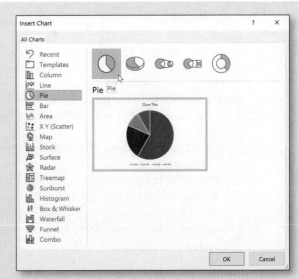

Figure 8-57 Insert pie chart

	A	B
1		Fall Enrollment
2	ENGWR 101	2541
3	ENGWR 102	2865
4	ENGWR 201	4207
5	ENGWR 202	3205

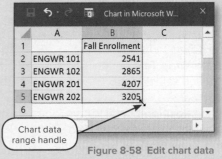

Chart data range handle

Figure 8-58 Edit chart data

   e. Adjust the chart data range (if necessary) by dragging the data range handle (bottom-right corner) to select A1:B5.
   f. Click the **X** in the upper-right corner of the *Chart in Microsoft Word* worksheet window to close it.

4. Modify the chart layout and design.
   a. Click the border of the chart to select the entire chart if it is not already selected.
   b. Click the **Add Chart Element** button [*Chart Tools Design* tab, *Chart Layouts* group], select **Data Labels**, and select **Center**.
   c. Click the **Change Chart Type** button [*Chart Tools Design* tab, *Type* group] to open the *Change Chart Type* dialog box.
   d. Select **3-D Pie** (second option) and click **OK** to close the dialog box and to change the chart type.
   e. Select **Style 7** in the *Chart Styles* gallery [*Chart Tools Design* tab, *Chart Styles* group]. You may need to click the **More** button in the *Chart Styles* group to display the *Chart Styles* gallery.

Figure 8-59 Select a chart element

5. Customize chart elements.
   a. Click the **Chart Elements** drop-down list [*Chart Tools Format* tab, *Current Selection* group] and select **Series "Fall Enrollment" Data Labels** (Figure 8-59).
   b. Apply **bold** formatting (**Ctrl+B**) to the selected data labels.
   c. Click the **Text Effects** button [*Chart Tools Format* tab, *WordArt Styles* group], select **Shadow**, and select **Offset: Bottom Right** (**first option** in the *Outer* category) (Figure 8-60).

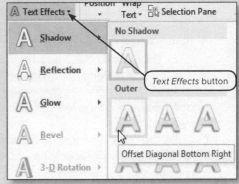

Figure 8-60 Apply a *Shadow* text effect

d. Click the title of the chart to select it and apply the **Offset: Bottom Right** shadow text effect.

e. Select the legend (rectangle box below the pie) in the chart.

f. Click the **More** button [*Chart Tools Format tab, Shape Styles* group] to display the *Shape Styles* gallery and select **Subtle Effect - Black, Dark 1** (**first style** in the **fourth row** of *Theme Styles*) (Figure 8-61).

Figure 8-61 Apply a Shape Style

g. Click the **Shape Styles** launcher to open the *Format* pane on the right.

h. Click the **Chart Elements** drop-down list near the top of the pane and select **Plot Area**.

i. Click the **Effects** button if it is not already selected and click **3-D Rotation** to open the *3-D Rotation* options area in the *Format Plot Area* pane (Figure 8-62).

j. Change the *Y Rotation* to **50°** and close the *Format Plot Area* pane.

6. Resize, change text wrapping, and position the chart.

a. Click the border of the chart to select the chart area. The tool tip displays *Chart Area* when you place the pointer on the border of the chart.

b. Change the *Height* to **2.5"** and the *Width* to **2.8"** in the *Size* group [*Chart Tools Format* tab].

c. Click the **Wrap Text** button [*Chart Tools Format* tab, *Arrange* group] and select **Tight**. The chart moves to the top of the second page.

d. Click the **Position** button [*Chart Tools Format* tab, *Arrange* group] and select **More Layout Options** to open the *Layout* dialog box.

e. Change the *Horizontal* **Alignment** to **Right** *relative to* **Margin**.

f. Change the *Vertical* **Absolute position** to **7.4"** *below* **Page**.

g. Click **OK** to close the dialog box. The chart displays near the bottom right of the second page (Figure 8-63).

7. Insert a *SmartArt* graphic and add text.

a. Position the insertion point at the end of the document (**Ctrl+End**).

b. Click the **SmartArt** button [*Insert* tab, *Illustrations* group] to open the *Choose a SmartArt Graphic* dialog box (Figure 8-64).

c. Click the **Process** button on the left.

d. Select **Interconnected Block Process** and click **OK** to insert the *SmartArt* graphic.

e. Click the **Text Pane** button [*SmartArt Tools Design* tab, *Create Graphic* group] to display the text pane on the left side of the *SmartArt* graphic.

f. Click the first main heading bullet in the *Text* pane of the *SmartArt* graphic and type Road Maps.

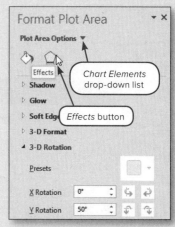

Figure 8-62 Change 3-D rotation

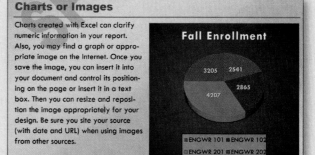

Figure 8-63 Customized chart

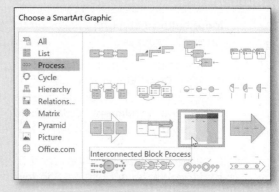

Figure 8-64 Insert a *SmartArt* graphic

g. Click the next bullet to move to the first subordinate topic bullet and type the following text, pressing **Enter** after each topic to add a new subordinate topic:
Short paragraphs
Single spacing
Distinctive headings
Left alignment

h. Add the following main and subordinate topics in the text pane (Figure 8-65):
Graphic Elements
   Text boxes
   Tables
   Pull quotes
   Charts and images
Vertical Lists
   Concise format
   Parallel structure
   Bulleted lists
   Numbered lists

i. Click the **X** in the upper-right corner of the *Text* pane to close the *Text* pane.

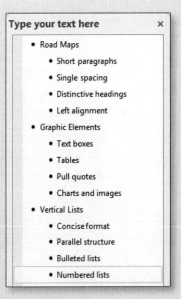

Figure 8-65 Add text using the *Text* pane

8. Change *SmartArt* layout and customize design.
   a. Click the border of the *SmartArt* graphic to select it if it is not already selected.
   b. Click the **More** button in the *Layouts* group [*SmartArt Tools Design* tab] to open the *Layouts* gallery.
   c. Select the **Alternating Flow** layout (Figure 8-66) to change the *SmartArt* graphic layout.
   d. Click the **Change Colors** button [*SmartArt Tools Design* tab, *SmartArt Styles* group] and select **Colorful - Accent Colors** (**first option** in the *Colorful* category).
   e. Click the **More** button in the *SmartArt Styles* group [*SmartArt Tools Design* tab] to open the *SmartArt Styles* gallery and select **Intense Effect** (**fifth style** in the **first row**) (Figure 8-67).

Figure 8-66 Change the *SmartArt* layout

9. Modify *SmartArt* objects.
   a. Press and hold the **Ctrl** key and click the border of the three main topics ("Road Maps," "Graphic Elements," and "Vertical Lists") to select all three.
   b. Click the **Change Shape** button [*SmartArt Tools Format* tab, *Shapes* group] and select the **fifth shape** in the *Rectangles* area (**Rectangle: Diagonal Corners Snipped**) (Figure 8-68).
   c. Confirm the three shapes are selected and apply **bold** formatting.
   d. Click the **Text Effects** button [*SmartArt Tools Format* tab, *WordArt Styles* group], select **Shadow**, and select **Offset: Bottom Right** in the *Outer* category.
   e. Click the border of the *SmartArt* graphic to deselect the three shapes.
   f. Select the three subordinate topic shapes (containing bulleted items) and apply **italic** formatting (**Ctrl+I**). Italics is applied to the text in the bulleted lists.

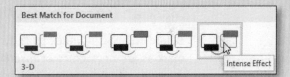

Figure 8-67 Apply a *SmartArt* style

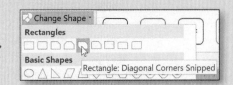

Figure 8-68 Change *SmartArt* shapes

10. Resize the *SmartArt* graphic.
    a. Click the frame of the *SmartArt* graphic to select it.
    b. Change the *Height* to **3"** and the *Width* to **5"** in the *Size* group [*SmartArt Tools Format* tab].

11. Save and close the document (Figure 8-69).

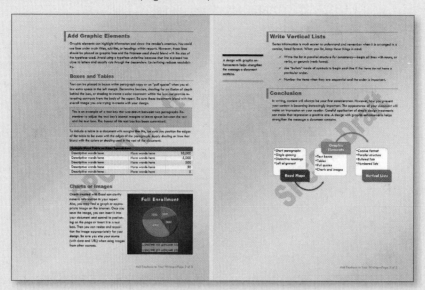

Figure 8-69 PP W8-3 completed (pages 2 and 3)

Creating an Index

An *index page* is a list of topic references in a long report or technical document. Readers use an index to look up the location of key words in a document. Mark *index entries* in a document and use these index entries to create an index page for the document. Word automatically generates an index page that displays index entries and page numbers. In this section, you learn how to insert an index entry, an index subentry, a cross-reference to an index entry, and an index page.

Mark an Index Entry

Before creating an index page, first mark index entries in the document. Select specific text to mark as an index entry or insert an index entry at a specific location in the document. When marking an index entry, Word inserts an *index field code* and automatically turns on *Show/Hide* if it is not already on to display the index field codes in the document. An index field code displays in braces following the index entry (Figure 8-70).

When creating index entries, spelling and capitalization are very important to maintain accuracy and consistency of index entries. If you make a spelling or capitalization error on an index entry, correct the error in the index code in the document (see Figure 8-70).

Figure 8-70 Index field code displayed in document

▶ **HOW TO:** Mark an Index Entry

1. Select the text or place the insertion point at the location to insert an index entry.

2. Click the **Mark Entry** button [*References* tab, *Index* group]. The *Mark Index Entry* dialog box opens (Figure 8-71).

   • If you select text before clicking the *Mark Entry* button, the text displays in the *Main entry* text box.

   • If you did not select text, the *Main entry* text box is empty.

3. Edit the text in the *Main entry* text box if necessary.
   - This is the text that will display on the index page.
4. Verify the **Current page** radio button in the *Options* area is selected.
5. Check the **Bold** or **Italic** box in the *Page number format* area to apply formatting to the page number on the index page.
   - For example, apply bold formatting to all main index entries.
6. Click the **Mark** or **Mark All** button. The index field code displays in braces following the index entry (see Figure 8-70).
   - *Mark* inserts an index field code on the selected text or location.
   - *Mark All* inserts an index field code on all instances of the word or words in the *Main entry* text box.
   - The *Mark Index* entry dialog box remains open so you can continue marking index entries in the document.
7. Click the **Close** button when you finish marking index entries.

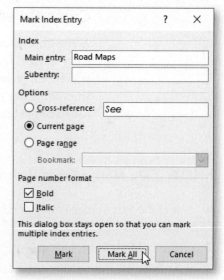

Figure 8-71 *Mark Index Entry* dialog box

MORE INFO

When *Show/Hide* is active, the index field codes affect pagination; don't be concerned about this. When *Show/Hide* is turned off, these hidden field codes do not affect pagination.

Mark an Index Subentry

An index *subentry* indexes items within a main index entry. For example, you can mark "Boxes," "Tables," and "Pull Quotes" as subentries for the main index entry of "Graphic Elements." When marking subentries, these entries display with an indent on the index page to visually indicate them as subentries to a main index entry.

▶**HOW TO: Mark an Index Subentry**

1. Select the text or place the insertion point at the location to insert the index subentry.
2. Click the **Mark Entry** button [*References* tab, *Index* group] to open the *Mark Index Entry* dialog box (Figure 8-72).
3. Type the main entry in the *Main entry* text box.
   - Spelling is very important when typing the main index entry because Word uses the exact spelling to index text on the index page.
4. Type the subentry in the *Subentry* text box.
5. Click **Mark** or **Mark All**.
6. Continue marking index entries or click **Close** to close the dialog box.

Figure 8-72 Mark an index subentry

Cross-Reference an Index Entry

A *cross-reference index entry* references another index entry rather than a page number. You can cross-reference a main index entry or a subentry. Figure 8-73 shows an index page with a cross-reference index entry (*See* Sample SmartArt).

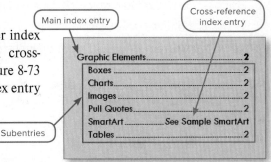

Figure 8-73 Index page with a main index entry, subentries, and a cross-reference index entry

▶HOW TO: Mark a Cross-Reference Index Entry

1. Select the text or place the insertion point at the location to create a cross-reference index entry.
2. Click the **Mark Entry** button [*References* tab, *Index* group].
3. Type the main entry in the *Main entry* text box.
    - Type the subentry in the *Subentry* text box also if the item is an index subentry.
4. Select the **Cross-reference** radio button in the *Options* area.
5. Click the *Cross-reference* text box after "*See*" and type the cross-reference text (Figure 8-74).
    - "*See*" automatically displays before the text in the *Cross-reference* text box.
6. Click **Mark**.
7. Continue marking index entries or click **Close** to close the dialog box.

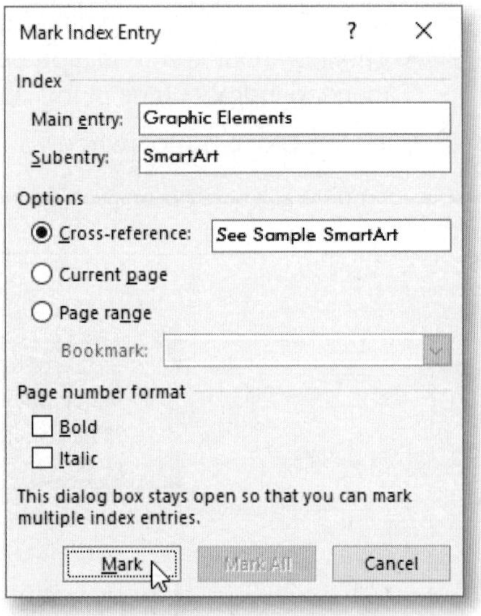

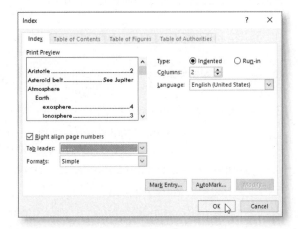

Figure 8-74 Create a cross-reference index entry

Insert an Index Page

After marking index entries in your document, insert an *index page*. Word provides a variety of index page formats. You can also customize the index page format to change the number of columns or page number alignment. It is usually best to insert the index page on a separate page at the end of your document.

▶HOW TO: Create an Index Page

1. Place the insertion point at the location to insert the index page.
    - Use a page break (**Ctrl+Enter**) to insert a blank page at the end of your document.
    - To include a title on the index page, type it and press **Enter** before inserting the index page.
2. Click the **Insert Index** button [*References* tab, *Index* group] to open the *Index* dialog box (Figure 8-75).
3. Click the **Formats** drop-down list and select an index page format.
    - A sample index page displays in the *Print Preview* area.

Figure 8-75 *Index* dialog box

4. Check the **Right align page numbers** box to align page numbers on the right (if desired).

5. Click the **Tab leader** drop-down list to select a tab leader.

6. Select the **Indented** or **Run-in** radio button in the *Type* area.

   - *Indented* places each subentry on a new line indented below the main entry. This is the default setting.
   - *Run-in* lists subentries on the same line. The document margins control how subentries wrap to the next line.

7. Type the number of columns in the *Columns* area.

8. Click the **OK** button to close the dialog box and to insert the index page (Figure 8-76).

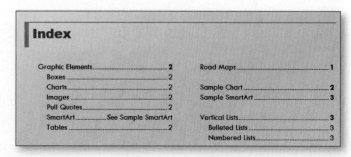

Figure 8-76 Index page

Update an Index Page

After inserting an index page, add, remove, or edit index entries if necessary. When modifying index entries or applying changes to a document that affect the pagination, update the index page to ensure index entries and page numbers are correct. Remember to turn off **Show/Hide** before updating the index page. Update the index page using one of the following methods:

Figure 8-77 Update index page

- Select the index page and click the **Update Index** button in the *Index* group on the *References* tab (Figure 8-77).
- Right-click the index page and select **Update Field** from the context menu.
- Select the index page and press **F9**.

Delete an Index Entry

To remove an index entry, delete the index field code in the document. When deleting an index entry, be very specific to select only the index field code and surrounding braces.

▶ **HOW TO:** Delete an Index Entry

1. Turn on **Show/Hide**.

2. Select the **index field code** to remove and press **Delete** (Figure 8-78).

   - Select both braces and the text between them ({XE "Road Maps" \b}).
   - After deleting the index entry, check the document to ensure you did not delete any other text, spaces, or paragraph marks.

Figure 8-78 Delete index field code

3. Turn off **Show/Hide**.

4. Click the **Update Index** button [*Reference* tab, *Index* group] to update your index page.

For this Pause & Practice project, you finalize the document for Sierra Pacific Community College District. You mark index entries including main entries, subentries, and a cross-reference entry. You also create and customize an index page.

File Needed: *[your initials] PP W8-3.docx*
Completed Project File Name: *[your initials] PP W8-4.docx*

1. Open the *[your initials] PP W8-3* document you saved in *Pause & Practice 8-3*.

2. Save the document as [your initials] PP W8-4.

3. Mark main index entries.
   a. Select "**Road Maps**" in the first section heading on the first page; don't include the quotation marks.
   b. Click the **Mark Entry** button [*References* tab, *Index* group] to open the *Mark Index Entry* dialog box (Figure 8-79). The text "Road Maps" displays in the *Main entry* text box.
   c. Check the **Bold** box in the *Page number format* area.
   d. Click **Mark All** to mark all instances of this text as a main index entry. Leave the *Mark Index Entry* dialog box open to mark additional index entries. Drag the title bar of the *Mark Index Entry* dialog box to move it if needed.
   e. Select "**Graphic Elements**" in the heading at the top of the second page; don't include the paragraph mark.
   f. Click the **Main entry** text box to display the selected text, confirm the **Bold** box is checked, and click **Mark All**.
   g. Select "**Vertical Lists**" in the "Write Vertical Lists" heading on the last page.
   h. Click the **Main entry** text box to display the selected text, confirm the **Bold** box is checked, and click **Mark All**.
   i. Leave the *Mark Index Entry* dialog box open to mark additional index entries. The index field codes affect pagination; this will be fixed later.

4. Mark index subentries.
   a. Select "**Boxes**" in the first subheading of the "Add Graphic Elements" section on the second page.
   b. Delete the existing text in the *Main entry* text box, type Graphic Elements, and type Boxes in the *Subentry* text box (Figure 8-80).
   c. Deselect the **Bold** check box and click **Mark All**.
   d. Repeat steps 4 a–c to mark the following index subentries in the "Add Graphic Elements" section. Type Graphic Elements as the *Main entry* for each subentry. Tables ("Boxes and Tables" heading)

Figure 8-79 *Mark Index Entry* dialog box

Figure 8-80 Mark index subentry

Pull Quotes (in the first sentence in the "Boxes and Tables" section; don't select quotation marks)

Charts ("Charts or Images" heading)

Images ("Charts or Images" heading)

e. Place the insertion point at the end of the second bulleted item in the "Write Vertical Lists" section on the last page.

f. Type Vertical Lists in the *Main entry* text box, type Bulleted Lists in the *Subentry* text box, and click **Mark**.

g. Place the insertion point at the end of the third bulleted item in the "Write Vertical Lists" section on the last page.

h. Type Vertical Lists in the *Main entry* text box, type Numbered Lists in the *Subentry* text box, and click **Mark**.

i. Click **Close** to close the *Mark Index Entry* dialog box.

5. Mark an area and an object as index entries.

a. Place the insertion point at the end of the body paragraph in the "Charts or Images" section.

b. Click the **Mark Entry** button [*References* tab, *Index* group] to open the *Mark Index Entry* dialog box (Figure 8-81).

c. Type Sample Chart in the *Main entry* text box, check the **Bold** box, and click **Mark**. Leave the *Mark Index Entry* dialog box open to mark an additional index entry.

d. Select the *SmartArt* graphic in the "Conclusion" section.

e. Type Sample SmartArt in the *Main entry* text box, check the **Bold** box (if necessary), and click **Mark**. Leave the *Mark Index Entry* dialog box open to mark an additional index entry.

Figure 8-81 Mark a chart as an index entry

6. Create a cross-reference index entry.

a. Select the word "**Images**" in the "Charts or Images" subheading.

b. Type Graphic Elements in the *Main entry* text box and type SmartArt in the *Subentry* text box (Figure 8-82).

c. Select the **Cross-reference** radio button and type Sample SmartArt after the word "*See*" in the text box.

d. Deselect the **Bold** check box and click **Mark**.

e. Click **Close** to close the *Mark Index Entry* dialog box.

7. Insert and customize an index page at the end of the document.

a. Place the insertion point at the end of the document (**Ctrl+End**) and insert a **page break** (**Ctrl+Enter**).

b. Type Index, apply the **Heading 1** style, and press **Enter**.

Figure 8-82 Create a cross-reference index entry

c. Click the **Insert Index** button [*References* tab, *Index* group] to open the *Index* dialog box (Figure 8-83).

d. Click the **Formats** drop-down list and select **Simple**.

e. Check the **Right align page numbers** box.

f. Click the **Tab leader** drop-down list and select the **dot leader**.

g. Confirm the *Type* is **Indented** and the number of *Columns* is **2**.

h. Click **OK** to close the dialog box and to insert the index.

8. Review the document and update the index page.

   a. Click the **Show/Hide** button [*Home* tab, *Paragraph* group] to turn it off.

   b. Review the document with *Show/Hide* turned off.

   c. Place the insertion point in the index on the last page and click the **Update Index** button [*References* tab, *Index* group].

9. Format the title of the document.

   a. Select the title of the document on the first page.

   b. Change the font to **Arial Black**.

   c. Change the left indent to **−2"** (negative 2").

10. Save and close the document (Figure 8-84).

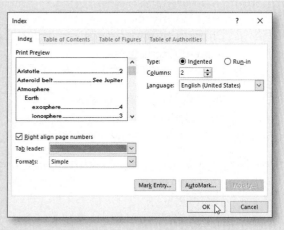

Figure 8-83 *Index* dialog box

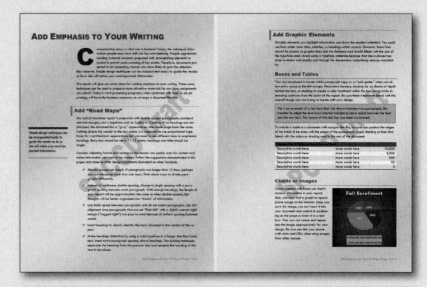

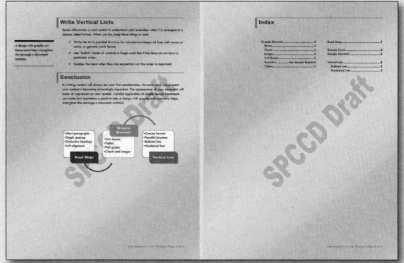

Figure 8-84 PP W8-4 completed

Chapter Summary

8.1 Apply desktop publishing features to a Word document (p. W8-482).

- *Gutter margins*, *mirror margins*, *2 pages per sheet*, and *book fold* customize page layout.
- A *drop cap* emphasizes the first letter or first word of a paragraph.
- Customize a drop cap to adjust the number of lines to drop and the distance from text.
- Add *page color* to the document and customize page color with a fill color, gradient color, texture, pattern, or picture.
- A *watermark* is text or a picture that appears behind the text in the document without affecting the layout of the document. Apply a built-in watermark, create a custom watermark, or use a picture as a watermark.
- Create a *watermark building block* to save and use in other documents.
- A *screenshot* or *screen clipping* captures and inserts a window or portion of a window as a picture in your document.
- The *hyphenation* feature automatically or manually hyphenates an entire document.
- Use *Line numbering* to insert line numbers on each line of a document. Line numbers are helpful when editing a long document or working with a group on document review.

8.2 Customize an existing theme and create a custom theme (p. W8-491).

- Apply a *theme* and customize *theme colors*, *theme fonts*, and *theme effects*.
- Save a custom theme, theme colors, theme fonts, and theme effects to use in other documents.

8.3 Insert and customize a built-in text box and create a custom text box (p. W8-492).

- *Text boxes* are shapes that display text.
- Insert built-in text boxes or draw custom text boxes.
- Customize text boxes by applying a *shape style*, *fill*, *outline*, or *effect*.
- Save a text box as a *building block* to use in other documents.

8.4 Insert and customize a *SmartArt* graphic (p. W8-498).

- *SmartArt* graphics are shapes and text that graphically present information in a document.
- Use the *SmartArt* **Text pane** to type information in the *SmartArt* graphic or type information directly in the graphic objects.
- Add shapes and add text in the shapes. Text in a *SmartArt* graphic can be reordered, promoted, or demoted.
- Customize the *SmartArt* graphic design by changing the layout, colors, or applying a *SmartArt* style using the **SmartArt Tools Design** tab.
- Customize the individual objects and text in a *SmartArt* graphic using the **SmartArt Tools Format** tab.
- Resize and arrange *SmartArt* graphics in the same way you resize and arrange pictures and shapes.

8.5 Insert and customize a chart (p. W8-503).

- Charts visually present numerical data.
- Use the **Chart in Microsoft Word** window to type the chart data and set the **chart data range**.
- Use the **Chart Tools Design** and **Chart Tools Format** tabs to customize the chart and its elements.
- Add and customize chart elements such as **chart title**, **axis titles**, **legend**, **data labels**, **data table**, and **gridlines**. Customize chart **axes**, **plot area**, **chart wall**, **chart floor**, and **3-D rotation**.
- Preset options are available for all chart elements. Further customize each element using the **Format "Chart Element" pane**.
- Resize and arrange charts in a document in the same way you resize and arrange *SmartArt* graphics, pictures, and shapes.

8.6 Mark index entries and insert and customize an index page (p. W8-512).

- Mark an *index entry* in your document and Word inserts an *index field code*.

- Use the **Mark Entry** dialog box to create a **main entry**, **subentry**, and a **cross-reference** index entry. The *Mark Entry* dialog box also includes options to customize the page number format and mark an individual entry or mark all instances of specific text.
- An **index** lists all index entries with a page number.
- Customize the layout and format of the index page.
- After adding or deleting index entries, update the index when content or pagination changes.

Check for Understanding

The SIMbook for this text (within your SIMnet account) provides the following resources for concept review:

- Multiple-choice questions
- Short answer questions
- Matching exercises

Guided Project 8-1

For this project, you convert a document about teen substance abuse from Courtyard Medical Plaza into a booklet. You adjust page setup and margins, apply desktop publishing features, insert and customize text boxes, apply and modify a theme, insert and modify a *SmartArt* graphic, and mark index entries and create an index page.
[Student Learning Outcomes 8.1, 8.2, 8.3, 8.4, 8.6]

File Needed: **SubstanceAbuse-08.docx** (*Student data files are available in the* Library *of your SIMnet account.*)
Completed Project File Name: *[your initials] Word 8-1.docx*

Skills Covered in This Project

- Use book fold layout and change margins.
- Apply, customize, and save a theme.
- Apply page color and hyphenation.
- Insert and customize a built-in text box.
- Insert and customize a *SmartArt* graphic.
- Use the *Find* feature.
- Mark index entries.
- Create an index page.
- Update an index.

1. Open the **SubstanceAbuse-08** document from your student data files.

2. Save the document as [your initials] Word 8-1.

3. Change page setup and margins.
    a. Open the *Page Setup* dialog box.
    b. Click the **Multiple pages** drop-down list and select **Book fold**.
    c. Click the **Sheets per booklet** drop-down list and select **All**.
    d. Change the *Top*, *Bottom*, *Inside*, and *Outside* margins to **0.5"**.
    e. Change the *Gutter* to **0.25"**.
    f. Click **OK** to close the *Page Setup* dialog box. Click **Ignore** if a dialog box opens informing you the margins are outside the printable area.

4. Apply and customize a theme.
    a. Apply the **Integral** theme [*Design* tab, *Document Formatting* group].
    b. Click the theme **Colors** button [*Design* tab, *Document Formatting* group] and select **Aspect**.
    c. Click the theme **Colors** button again and select **Customize Colors**. The *Create New Theme Colors* dialog box opens (Figure 8-85).
    d. Click the **Accent 1** drop-down list and select the **sixth color** in the **fifth row** of *Theme Colors* (**Red, Accent 2, Darker 25%**).
    e. Click the **Hyperlink** drop-down list and select the **sixth color** in the **first row** of *Theme Colors* (**Red, Accent 2**).

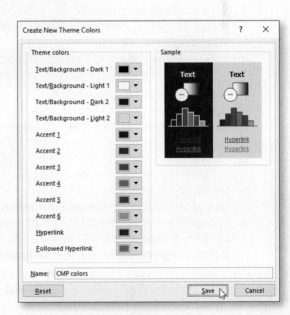

Figure 8-85 *Create New Theme Colors* dialog box

f. Type **CMP colors** in the *Name* text box.

g. Click **Save** to close the dialog box and save the new theme colors.

h. Click the **Themes** button and select **Save Current Theme**. The *Save Current Theme* dialog box opens.

i. Type **CMP** in the *File name* text box and click **Save** to save the custom theme. Don't change the save location.

5. Click the **Page Color** button [*Design* tab, *Page Background* group] and select the **first color** in the **second row** of *Theme Colors* (**White, Background 1, Darker 5%**).

6. Click the **Hyphenation** button [*Layout* tab, *Page Setup* group] and select **Automatic** to hyphenate the entire document.

7. Insert and customize a built-in text box.

a. Place the insertion point at the end of the first body paragraph in the "Why Do Teens Abuse Drugs and Alcohol?" section.

b. Click the **Text Box** button [*Insert* tab, *Text* group] and select **Simple Text Box**.

c. Select and copy the last three sentences (don't include the paragraph mark) in the first paragraph of the "What Is Teen Substance Abuse?" section (beginning with "Some teens try. . .").

d. Click the placeholder text in the text box to select it and press **Ctrl+V** to paste the text in the text box.

e. Select the text in the text box, apply **italic** formatting, change the line spacing to **1.5**, and change the *After* paragraph spacing to **0 pt**.

f. Click the **More** button [*Drawing Tools Format* tab, *Shape Styles* group] to display the *Shape Styles* gallery and select the **second style** in the **fifth row** of *Theme Styles* (**Moderate Effect – Dark Red, Accent 1**).

g. Click the **Edit Shape** button [*Drawing Tools Format* tab, *Insert Shape* group], select **Change Shape**, and select the **second shape** in the *Rectangles* category (**Rectangle: Rounded Corners**).

h. Change the *Height* to **1.6"** and the *Width* to **1.7"** [*Drawing Tools Format* tab, *Size* group].

i. Click the **Position** button [*Drawing Tools Format* tab, *Arrange* group] and select **Position in Middle Right with Square Text Wrapping** (Figure 8-86).

j. Turn on **Show/Hide**, and if a blank line displays in the "Why Do Teens Abuse Drugs and Alcohol?" section, delete it.

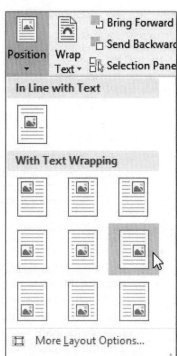

Figure 8-86 Position text box on the page

8. Insert and customize a built-in text box.

a. Select the text box and copy it.

b. Place the insertion point at the end of the last paragraph in the "What Should You Do If Your Teen Is Using?" section on the second page and press **Ctrl+V** to paste the shape.

c. Copy the first two sentences in the first body paragraph in the "What Should You Do if Your Teen Is Using?" section on the second page.

d. Select all the text in the text box, click the bottom half of the **Paste** button [*Home* tab, *Clipboard* group], and select the **Merge Formatting** option (**second** option).

e. Change the *Height* and *Width* to **1.8"** [*Drawing Tools Format* tab, *Size* group].

f. Click the **Position** button [*Drawing Tools Format* tab, *Arrange* group] and select **Position in Bottom Right with Square Text Wrapping**.

9. Place the insertion point at the beginning of the "Can Teen Substance Use and Abuse Be Prevented?" section and insert a **page break**.

10. Insert and customize a *SmartArt* graphic.

a. Place the insertion point at the end of the document.

b. Click the **SmartArt** button [*Insert* tab, *Illustrations* group] to open the *Choose a SmartArt Graphic* dialog box.

c. Click **Cycle** on the left, select **Continuous Cycle**, and click **OK** to close the dialog box and to insert the *SmartArt* graphic (Figure 8-87).

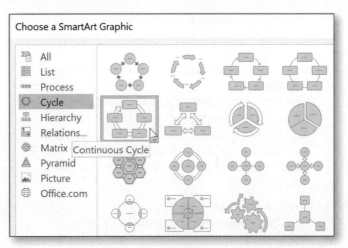

d. Beginning at the top and going clockwise, type the following text in the *SmartArt* graphic boxes:

Expectations
Activities
House Rules
Communication
Know Friends

Figure 8-87 Insert a *SmartArt* graphic

e. Apply the **Moderate Effect** (**fourth style** in the **first row** in the *SmartArt Styles* gallery) [*SmartArt Tools Design* tab] (Figure 8-88).

11. Mark index entries.

Figure 8-88 Apply a *SmartArt* style

a. Click the **Find** button [*Home* tab, *Editing* group] to open the *Navigation* pane to the left of the Word window.

b. Type alcohol in the search text box to find all instances of this word.

c. Select the first occurrence of "**alcohol**" in the body of the document.

d. Click the **Mark Entry** button [*References* tab, Index group] to open the *Mark Index Entry* dialog box. The word "alcohol" appears in the *Main entry* text box (Figure 8-89).

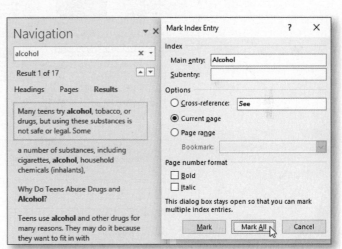

e. Capitalize the "A" in "alcohol" in the *Main entry* text box.

f. Click the **Mark All** button to mark all instances of this word as an index entry.

g. Continue this process to mark the following words as index entries. Capitalize the first letter of the first word in the *Main entry* text box.

Tobacco
Drugs
Drug abuse
Marijuana
Risk
Treatment

Figure 8-89 Find text in the *Navigation* pane and mark index entries

h. Click **Close** to close the *Mark Index Entry* dialog box and close the *Navigation* pane.

12. Create an index page.
a. Place the insertion point at the end of your document (**Ctrl+End**) and insert a page break (**Ctrl+Enter**).
b. Type Index, apply the **Heading 1** style, and press **Enter**.

c. Click the **Insert Index** button [*References* tab, *Index* group] to open the *Index* dialog box (Figure 8-90).

d. Click the **Formats** drop-down list and select **Simple**.

e. Check the **Right align page numbers** box.

f. Click the **Tab leader** drop-down list and select the **dot leader**.

g. Confirm the *Type* is **Indented** and *Columns* is **2**.

h. Click **OK** to close the dialog box and insert the index.

13. Update the index page.
    a. Turn off **Show/Hide** [*Home* tab, *Paragraph* group].
    b. Place the insertion point in the index and click the **Update Index** button [*References* tab, *Index* group].

14. Save and close the document (Figure 8-91).

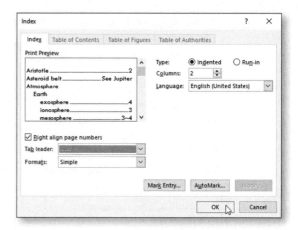

Figure 8-90 *Index* dialog box

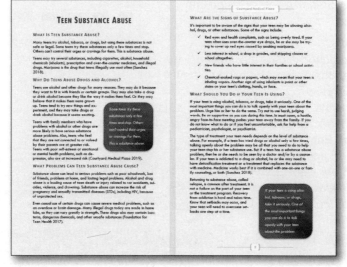

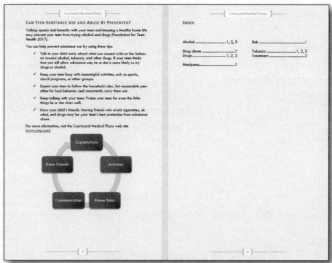

Figure 8-91 Word 8-1 completed

Guided Project 8-2

For this project, you modify a promotional flyer for Placer Hills Real Estate. You apply and modify a theme, apply a page color, create and customize a chart, insert and modify a *SmartArt* graphic, insert and customize a text box, and insert and position a watermark.
[Student Learning Outcomes 8.1, 8.2, 8.3, 8.4, 8.5]

File Needed: ***YourFirstHome-08.docx*** *(Student data files are available in the Library of your SIMnet account.)*
Completed Project File Name: *[your initials] Word 8-2.docx*

Skills Covered in This Project

- Apply, customize, and save a theme.
- Apply page color.
- Insert a chart and customize chart data.
- Insert an axis title and data labels.

- Modify a vertical axis.
- Customize chart elements.
- Resize a chart.
- Insert and customize a *SmartArt* graphic.
- Resize and arrange the *SmartArt* graphic.
- Insert, customize, and align a built-in text box.

---

1. Open the ***YourFirstHome-08*** document from your student data files.

2. Save the document as [your initials] Word 8-2.

3. Apply, customize, and save a theme.
   a. Apply the **Facet** theme [*Design* tab, *Document Formatting* group].
   b. Click the theme **Fonts** button [*Design* tab, *Document Formatting* group] and select **Tw Cen MT**.
   c. Click the theme **Colors** button [*Design* tab, *Document Formatting* group] and select **Green**.
   d. Click the **Themes** button and select **Save Current Theme**. The *Save Current Theme* dialog box opens.
   e. Type PHRE in the *File name* area and click **Save** to save the custom theme. Don't change the save location.

4. Click the **Page Color** button [*Design* tab, *Page Background* group] and select the **seventh color** in the **second row** of *Theme Colors* (**Lime, Accent 3, Lighter 80%**) (Figure 8-92).

5. Insert a chart and customize the chart data.
   a. Place the insertion point on the blank line below the "Fixed Mortgage Rate Averages" heading.
   b. Click the **Chart** button [*Insert* tab, *Illustrations* group]. The *Insert Chart* dialog box opens (Figure 8-93).
   c. Click **Line** on the left, select **Line with Markers** at the top, and click **OK** to insert the chart.
   d. Type the following information in the *Chart in Microsoft Word* worksheet to replace the sample chart data (Figure 8-94). If necessary, resize the worksheet window by clicking and dragging the bottom-right corner.

Figure 8-92 Apply a page color

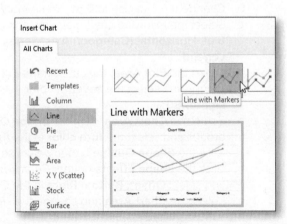

Figure 8-93 Insert a line chart

e. Click and drag the **chart data range** handle (bottom-right corner) so it appears around the chart data you typed (see Figure 8-94).

f. Click the **X** in the upper-right corner of the *Chart in Microsoft Word* window to close it.

	A	B	C
1	Year	Rate	Points
2	1978	11.2	1.6
3	1983	13.88	2.5
4	1988	10.32	2.1
5	1993	8.38	1.8
6	1998	7.44	1
7	2003	5.84	0.7
8	2008	5.04	0.7
9	2013	3.96	0.8
10	2018	4.16	1.1

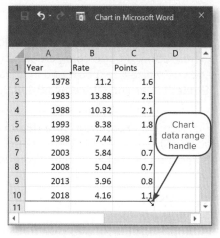

Figure 8-94 Type the chart data and select the chart data range

6. Add and customize chart elements.

   a. Click the "**Chart Title**" and type Historic Mortgage Rates and Points to replace the existing text.

   b. Click the **Add Chart Element** button [*Chart Tools Design* tab, *Chart Layouts* group], select **Axis Titles**, and select **Primary Vertical**.

   c. Type Percent to replace the placeholder text in the vertical axis title text box.

   d. Click the **Add Chart Element** button, select **Data Labels**, and select **Above**.

   e. Right-click the vertical axis numbers and select **Format Axis**. The *Format Axis* pane opens.

   f. Click the **Axis Options** button if it is not already selected (Figure 8-95).

   g. Type 1.0 in the *Minor* text box in the *Units* area.

   h. Click the **Tick Marks** heading.

   i. Click the **Minor type** drop-down list and select **Cross**.

   j. Close the *Format Axis* pane.

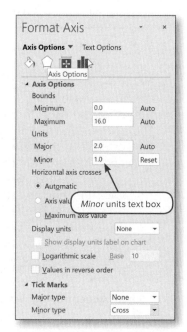

Figure 8-95 *Format Axis* pane

7. Customize chart elements.

   a. Click the **Chart Elements** drop-down list [*Chart Tools Format* tab, *Current Selection* group] and select **Vertical (Value) Axis** to select the vertical axis.

   b. Change the font size to **8 pt** [*Home* tab, *Font* group].

   c. Select the following chart elements and change the font size to **8 pt**: **Horizontal (Category) Axis**, **Series "Rate" Data Labels**, **Series "Points" Data Labels**, and **Legend**.

   d. Select the **Plot Area**, click the **Shape Fill** button [*Chart Tools Format* tab, *Shape Styles* group], and select the **seventh color** in the **second row** of *Theme Colors* (**Lime, Accent 3, Lighter 80%**).

   e. Select the **Chart Area**, click the **Shape Outline** button [*Chart Tools Format* tab, *Shape Styles* group], and select the **fifth color** in the **first row** of *Theme Colors* (**Green, Accent 1**).

   f. Click the **Shape Outline** button again, select **Weight**, and select **1½ pt**.

   g. Click the **Shape Effects** button [*Chart Tools Format* tab, *Shape Styles* group], select **Shadow**, and select **Offset: Bottom Right** in the *Outer* category.

   h. Select the **Chart Area** and change the *Height* to **3"** and the *Width* to **6.5"** [*Chart Tools Format* tab, *Size* group].

8. Insert and customize a *SmartArt* graphic.

   a. Place the insertion point at the end of the document (**Ctrl+End**).

b. Click the **SmartArt** button [*Insert* tab, *Illustrations* group]. The *Choose a SmartArt Graphic* dialog box opens (Figure 8-96).

c. Click **Process** on the left, select **Circle Process**, and then click **OK**.

d. Click the **Add Shape** button [*SmartArt Tools Design* tab, *Create Graphic* group] three times to add three more shapes to the graphic.

e. Beginning at the left, type the following text in the shapes:

Be patient
Be sure you are ready
Determine what you can afford
Get your credit in shape
Save for a down payment
Get mortgage pre-approval

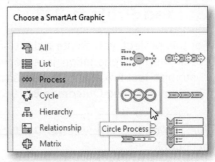

Figure 8-96 Insert *SmartArt* graphic

f. Click the **Change Colors** button and select **Dark 2 Fill** (**third option** in the *Primary Theme Colors* category).

g. Click the **SmartArt Styles** drop-down list and select **Inset** (**second option** in the *3-D* category).

h. Click directly above the text in the first text box to select the text box and then use **Ctrl+click** to select the other five text boxes.

i. Apply **bold** formatting to the selected text boxes.

9. Resize and arrange the *SmartArt* graphic.

a. Click the frame of the *SmartArt* graphic to select it and change the *Height* to **1.8"** and the *Width* to **7"** [*SmartArt Tools Format* tab, *Size* group].

b. Click the **Wrap Text** button [*SmartArt Tools Format* tab, *Arrange* group] and select **Behind Text**.

c. Click the **Position** button [*SmartArt Tools Format* tab, *Arrange* group] and select **More Layout Options** to open the *Layout* dialog box.

d. Set the *Horizontal* **Absolute position** to **0.7"** *to the right of* **Page**.

e. Set the *Vertical* **Absolute position** to **8"** *below* **Page**.

f. Click **OK** to close the dialog box.

10. Insert and customize a built-in text box.

a. Place the insertion point at the beginning of the document.

b. Click the **Text Box** button [*Insert* tab, *Text* group] and select **Semaphore Quote**.

c. Type HOME BUYING INFO FROM PLACER HILLS REAL ESTATE to replace the placeholder text in the text box.

d. Select the text, change the font size to **14 pt**, apply **bold** formatting, and change the *After* paragraph spacing to **0 pt**.

e. Change the *Height* of the text box to **0.8"** and the *Width* to **2.8"** [*Drawing Tools Format* tab, *Size* group].

f. Click the **Align** button [*Drawing Tools Format* tab, *Arrange* group] and select **Align to Margin** if it is not already checked.

g. Click the **Align** button again and select **Align Top**.

h. Turn on **Show/Hide**. If a blank line displays above the first line of text in the body of the document ("Learn about Mortgages"), delete it.

11. Save and close the document (Figure 8-97).

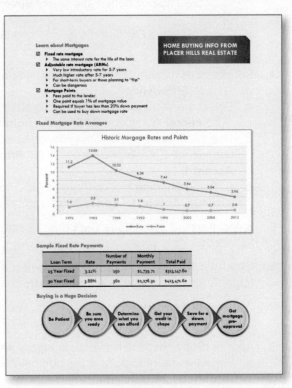

Figure 8-97 Word 8-2 completed

Guided Project 8-3

For this project, you create a draft of a newsletter for Central Sierra Insurance. You apply and modify a theme, apply hyphenation, insert a watermark, customize and apply a drop cap, use *WordArt*, insert and customize text boxes, and create and customize a chart.
[Student Learning Outcomes 8.1, 8.2, 8.3, 8.5]

File Needed: ***CSINewsletter-08.docx*** *(Student data files are available in the* Library *of your SIMnet account.)*
Completed Project File Name: *[your initials] Word 8-3.docx*

Skills Covered in This Project

- Apply, customize, and save a theme.
- Set tab stops.
- Apply a border and shading to selected text.
- Apply automatic hyphenation.
- Insert a built-in watermark.
- Apply and customize a drop cap.

- Insert, resize, and arrange *WordArt*.
- Draw a text box around selected text.
- Customize text box style and arrangement.
- Insert a chart and customize chart data.
- Resize and position a chart.
- Insert a chart title and data labels.
- Modify a vertical axis.
- Customize chart elements.

---

1. Open the ***CSINewsletter-08*** document from your student data files.

2. Save the document as [your initials] Word 8-3.

3. Apply, customize, and save a theme.
   a. Apply the **Integral** theme [*Design* tab, *Document Formatting* group].
   b. Click the theme **Colors** button [*Design* tab, *Document Formatting* group] and select **Yellow Orange**.
   c. Click the **Themes** button and select **Save Current Theme**. The *Save Current Theme* dialog box opens.
   d. Type CSI in the *File name* area and click **Save** to save the custom theme. Don't change the save location.

4. Set tab stops and apply a border and shading to selected text.
   a. Turn on **Show/Hide**.
   b. Select the second paragraph ("Issue No. XVII . . .") and apply **bold** formatting.
   c. Set a **center** tab stop at **3.75"** and a **right** tab stop at **7.5"**.
   d. Use the *Borders and Shading* dialog box to apply a **Box** border, change the *Width* to **1 pt**, and change the *Color* of the border to the **fifth color** in the **first row** of *Theme Colors* (**Orange, Accent 1**).
   e. Click the **Shading** tab, change the *Fill* color to the **fifth color** in the **second row** of *Theme Colors* (**Orange, Accent 1, Lighter 80%**), and click **OK** to close the dialog box.

5. Select the third paragraph ("CSI's Cost-Effective . . ."), change the font size to **22 pt**, and apply **bold** formatting.

6. Click anywhere in the document to deselect the text, click the **Hyphenation** button [*Layout* tab, *Page Setup* group], and select **Automatic**.

7. Click the **Watermark** button [*Design* tab, *Page Background* group] and select **Draft 1** in the *Disclaimers* category.

8. Apply a drop cap to the first letter in a paragraph.
   a. Place the insertion point at the beginning of the first paragraph in the section with two columns ("Now you can have . . .").

b. Click the **Drop Cap** button [*Insert* tab, *Text* group] and select **Drop Cap Options** to open the *Drop Cap* dialog box (Figure 8-98).

c. Select **Dropped** in the *Position* area.

d. Change the *Lines to drop* to **2** and change the *Distance from text* to **0.1"**.

e. Click **OK** to close the dialog box and to apply the drop cap.

9. Apply *WordArt* to the title and position the title.

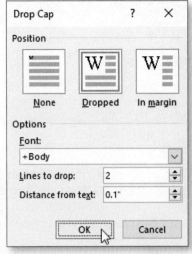

Figure 8-98 Customize and apply a drop cap

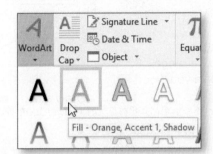

Figure 8-99 Apply *WordArt* to selected text

a. Select "**Central Sierra Insurance Newsletter**" at the top of the document.

b. Click the **WordArt** button [*Insert* tab, *Text* group] and select the **second option** in the **first row** (**Fill: Orange, Accent color 1; Shadow**) (Figure 8-99).

c. Click the **Wrap Text** button [*Drawing Tools Format* tab, *Arrange* group] and select **Tight**.

d. Click the **Position** button [*Drawing Tools Format* tab, *Arrange* group] and select **More Layout Options** to open the *Layout* dialog box.

e. Set the *Horizontal* **Alignment** to **Centered** *relative to* **Page**.

f. Set the *Vertical* **Absolute position** to **0.1"** *below* **Page**.

g. Click **OK** to close the dialog box.

10. Draw text boxes around selected text and customize the text boxes.

a. Select the paragraph of text beginning "**Picture mid-summer with temps . . .**"

b. Apply **bold** and **italic** formatting to the selected text.

c. Click the **Text Box** button [*Insert* tab, *Text* group] and select **Draw Text Box**. A text box appears around the selected text.

d. Click the **More** button [*Drawing Tools Format* tab, *Shape Styles* group] to display the *Shape Styles* gallery and select **Subtle Effect - Orange, Accent 1** (**second style** in the **fourth row** of *Theme Styles*) (Figure 8-100).

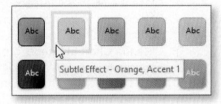

Figure 8-100 Apply shape style to text box

e. Change the *Width* of the text box to **7.5"** [*Drawing Tools Format* tab, *Size* group].

f. Select all the text in the second column.

g. Click the **Text Box** button [*Insert* tab, *Text* group] and select **Draw Text Box**. A text box appears around the selected text.

h. Click the **More** button [*Drawing Tools Format* tab, *Shape Styles* group] to display the *Shape Styles* gallery and select **Subtle Effect - Orange, Accent 1**.

11. Insert a chart and customize the chart data.

a. Place the insertion point at the end of the document (**Ctrl+End**).

b. Click the **Chart** button [*Insert* tab, *Illustrations* group] to open the *Insert Chart* dialog box.

c. Click **Column** on the left, select **Clustered Column** at the top, and click **OK** to insert the chart. A *Chart in Microsoft Word* worksheet also opens.

d. Type the following information in the *Chart in Microsoft Word* window to replace the sample chart data (Figure 8-101). Resize column width by clicking and dragging the right edge of a column heading.

	A	B	C
1		Repair Cost	Replacement Cost
2	Refrigerator	800	2000
3	Computer	225	1000
4	Water Heater	250	1200
5	Air Conditioner	500	4000

Figure 8-101 Type the chart data and select the chart data range

    e. Click and drag the **chart data range** handle around the chart data you typed (see Figure 8-101).

    f. Click the **X** in the upper-right corner of the *Chart in Microsoft Word* window to close it.

12. Customize the position and size of the chart.
    a. Select the border of the chart, click the **Position** button [*Chart Tools Format* tab, *Arrange* group] and select **Position in Bottom Center with Square Text Wrapping**.
    b. Change the *Height* of the chart to **2.8"** and the *Width* to **6"** [*Chart Tools Format* tab, *Size* group].

13. Customize the layout of the chart.
    a. Select the "**Chart Title**" and type Estimated Repair and Replacement Costs to replace the existing text.
    b. Click the **Add Chart Element** button [*Chart Tools Design* tab, *Chart Layouts* group], click the **Data Labels** button, and select **Outside End** to align data labels above each column.

14. Customize chart elements and design.
    a. Right-click the vertical axis numbers and select **Format Axis**. The *Format Axis* pane opens (Figure 8-102).
    b. Click the **Number** heading.
    c. Click the **Category** drop-down list and select **Currency**.
    d. Change *Decimal places* to **0** and confirm that the *Symbol* is **$**.
    e. Close the *Format Axis* pane.
    f. Select **Style 14** from the *Chart Styles* gallery [*Chart Tools Design* tab, *Chart Styles* group].
    g. Click the **Chart Elements** drop-down list [*Chart Tools Format* tab, *Current Selection* group] and select **Plot Area** to select the chart plot area.
    h. Click the **Shape Fill** button [*Chart Tools Format* tab, *Shape Styles* group] and select the **first color** in the **second row** of *Theme Colors* (**White, Background 1, Darker 5%**).
    i. Select the **Chart Area** from the *Chart Elements* drop-down list, click the **Shape Outline** button [*Chart Tools Format* tab, *Shape Styles* group], and select the **fifth color** in the **first row** of *Theme Colors* (**Orange, Accent 1**).
    j. Click the **Shape Outline** button again, select **Weight**, and then select **2¼ pt**.
    k. Click the **Shape Effects** button [*Chart Tools Format* tab, *Shape Styles* group], select **Shadow**, and then select **Offset: Center** (**second option** in the **second row** in the *Outer* category).

Figure 8-102 Customize vertical axis number format

15. Save and close the document (Figure 8-103).

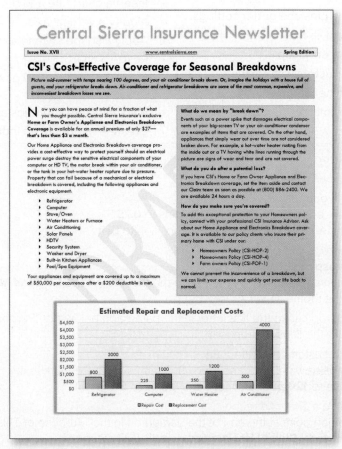

Figure 8-103 Word 8-3 completed

Independent Project 8-4

For this project, you customize a draft of a report for Sierra Pacific Community College District. You apply desktop publishing features, apply and customize a theme, insert and customize text boxes, insert and customize a *SmartArt* graphic and a chart, mark index entries, and create an index page. [**Student Learning Outcomes 8.1, 8.2, 8.3, 8.4, 8.5, 8.6**]

File Needed: ***OnlineLearning-08.docx*** *(Student data files are available in the* Library *of your SIMnet account.)*
Completed Project File Name: *[your initials] Word 8-4.docx*

Skills Covered in This Project

- Adjust document margins and gutter settings.
- Apply, customize, and save a theme.
- Use and customize a drop cap.
- Create and apply a custom watermark.
- Apply automatic hyphenation.
- Insert a built-in watermark.
- Insert and customize a *SmartArt* graphic.
- Insert a chart and customize chart data.
- Insert a chart title and data labels.
- Modify a vertical axis.
- Apply a shape style to a chart.
- Resize a chart.
- Insert, customize, and position built-in text boxes.
- Mark index main entries and subentries.
- Create and update an index page.

1. Open the **OnlineLearning-08** document from your student data files.
2. Save the document as [your initials] Word 8-4.
3. Adjust margins and gutter settings.
   a. Change the top, bottom, left, and right margins to **0.75"**.
   b. Change the gutter to **0.25"** and the gutter position to **Left**.
4. Apply and customize a theme.
   a. Apply the **Retrospect** theme.
   b. Change the theme *Colors* to **Grayscale** and the theme *Fonts* to **Gil Sans MT**.
   c. Save the current theme as SPCCD 2.
5. Apply a **Dropped** drop cap to the first letter in the paragraph below the "Purpose of This Plan" heading and modify the lines to drop to **2**.
6. Create and apply a custom text watermark.
   a. Insert a custom text watermark and type OL Draft as the watermark text.
   b. Change the size to **120 pt** and change the layout to **Diagonal**.
7. Insert and customize a *SmartArt* graphic.
   a. Place the insertion point at the end of the paragraph in the "Purpose of This Plan" section.
   b. Insert the **Horizontal Bullet List** *SmartArt* graphic (*List* category).
   c. Type the following main heading and bulleted information in the *SmartArt* graphic (Figure 8-104):

Online Learning Modes	Planning Process	SPCCD Online Learning
Online course	Program Selection	Course Offerings and Programs
Hybrid course	Leadership and Management	Student Support Services
Television or Tele-Web course		Faculty Training
Web-Enhanced course		Tech Support Services
		Current Research

d. Select the *SmartArt* border and change the height of the *SmartArt* graphic to **1.5"** and the width to **6.5"**.

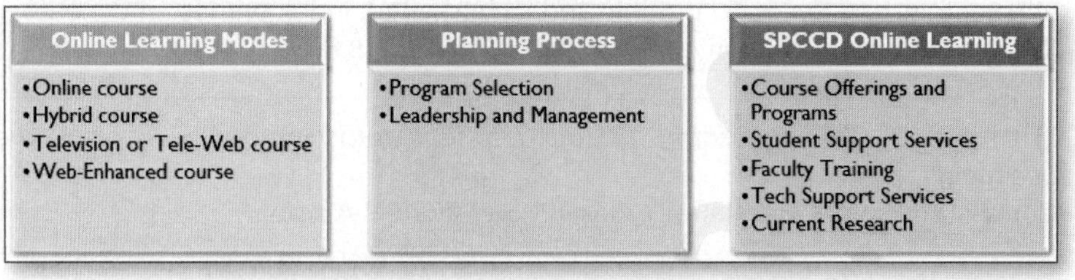

Figure 8-104 *SmartArt* graphic and text

e. **Change Colors** to **Colorful - Accent Colors** (**first option** in the *Colorful* category).
f. Apply the **Polished** *SmartArt* style (**first style** in the *3-D* category).
g. **Bold** the text in the three main headings of the *SmartArt* graphic.
h. Place the insertion point at the end of the paragraph above the *SmartArt* graphic and press **Enter**.

8. Insert and customize a chart.
   a. Place the insertion point at the end of the last paragraph in the "Course Offerings and Programs" section on the second page.
   b. Insert a **Clustered Column** chart.
   c. Type the following information in the *Chart in Microsoft Word* worksheet to replace the sample chart data (Figure 8-105):

	A	B	C
1	Year	OL Courses	Traditional Courses
2	2015	621	6900
3	2016	745	7842
4	2017	982	9352
5	2018	1106	9617
6	2019	1247	9856

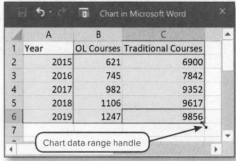

Figure 8-105 Type in the chart data and select the chart data range

   d. Adjust the chart data range as needed and close the *Chart in Microsoft Word* worksheet (see Figure 8-105).
   e. Type **SPCCD Course Offerings** as the chart title.
   f. Apply data labels to the **Outside End** of the columns.
   g. Apply the **Style 11** chart style.
   h. Format the vertical axis and change the number format to **Number** with **0** decimal places and a **1000 separator**.
   i. Select the **Chart Area** and apply the **Subtle Effect – Gray, Accent 4** shape style (**fifth style** in the **fourth row** of *Theme Styles*).
   j. Change the height of the chart to **2.5"** and the width to **6.5"**.
   k. Place the insertion point at the end of the paragraph above the chart and press **Enter**.
9. Insert and customize text boxes.
   a. Place the insertion point at the end of the paragraph in the "Planning Process" section on the first page and insert the **Austin Quote** built-in text box.
   b. Copy the second sentence in the paragraph in the "Purpose of This Plan" section ("This plan incorporates. . .") and paste (**Ctrl+V**) it in the text box to replace the placeholder text.
   c. Select the text box and apply the **Subtle Effect - Black, Dark 1** shape style (**first style** in the **fourth row** of *Theme Styles*).
   d. Change the height of the text box to **1.25"** and the width to **3.4"**.
   e. Set the *Position* [*Drawing Tools Format* tab, *Arrange* group] as **Position in Bottom Right with Square Text Wrapping**.
   f. Place the insertion point at the top of the third page and insert the **Austin Quote** built-in text box.
   g. Copy the first and second sentences in the first paragraph in the "Tech Support Services" section ("The ITC has trained. . .") and paste (**Ctrl+V**) it in the text box to replace the placeholder text.
   h. Select the text box and apply the **Subtle Effect - Black, Dark 1** shape style.
   i. Change the height of the text box to **1.6"** and the width to **2.3"**.
   j. Set the *Position* as **Position in Middle Right with Square Text Wrapping**.
10. Insert **page breaks** before the "Program Selection" and "Student Support Services" headings.
11. Mark index entries.
   a. Select and mark the four main section headings as a **Main entry**. Use **bold** page number format and click **Mark** (not *Mark All*).
   b. Select each of the types of online courses in the "Online Learning Modes" section and **Mark** (not *Mark All*) each as **Subentry**. Type **Online Learning Modes** as the *Main entry* and type the online course type as the *Subentry*. Deselect **Bold** page number format.
   c. Select each of the subheadings in the "Planning Process" section and mark as **Subentry**. Type **Planning Process** as the *Main entry* and the subheading as the *Subentry*. Deselect **Bold** page number format if necessary.

    d. Select each of the subheadings in the "SPCCD Online Learning" section and mark as **Subentry**. Type **SPCCD Online Learning** as the *Main entry* and the subheading as the *Subentry*. Deselect **Bold** page number format if necessary.

    e. Select the chart and create an index entry. Type **SPCCD Online Learning** as the *Main entry* and **Course Offerings Chart** as the *Subentry*. Deselect **Bold** page number format if necessary.

12. Create and update an index page.

    a. Place the insertion point at the end of the document and insert a **page break**.

    b. Type **Index**, apply the **Heading 1** style, and press **Enter**.

    c. Insert an index and use **Simple** format, **right align page** numbers, use a **dot leader**, and use **1** column.

    d. Turn off **Show/Hide** and update the index.

13. Save and close the document (Figure 8-106).

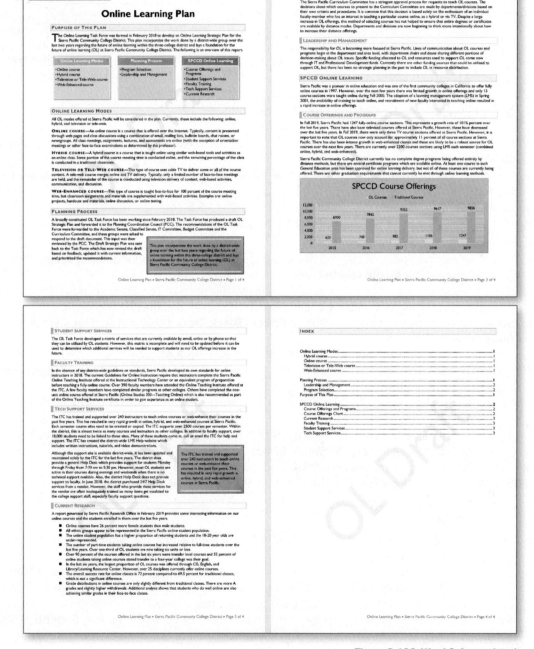

Figure 8-106 Word 8-4 completed

Independent Project 8-5

For this project, you customize an informational flyer for the Skiing Unlimited program. You apply desktop publishing features, apply and customize a theme, insert and customize a text box, insert and customize a *SmartArt* graphic, and insert a chart.
[Student Learning Outcomes 8.1, 8.2, 8.3, 8.4, 8.5]

Files Needed: ***SkiingUnlimited-08.docx*** and ***Snow-08.png*** *(Student data files are available in the* Library *of your SIMnet account.)*
Completed Project File Name: *[your initials] Word 8-5.docx*

Skills Covered in This Project

- Customize and save a theme.
- Use a picture as a page color.
- Insert and customize a built-in text box.
- Insert a chart and customize chart data.
- Insert data labels.
- Modify chart elements.
- Apply a chart and shape style to the chart.
- Resize the chart.
- Insert and customize a *SmartArt* graphic.
- Resize and arrange a *SmartArt* graphic.

1. Open the ***SkiingUnlimited-08*** document from your student data files.

2. Save the document as [your initials] Word 8-5.

3. Create a custom theme.
   a. Change the theme *Colors* to **Red**, theme *Fonts* to **Candara**, and theme *Effects* to **Grunge Texture**.
   b. Save the current theme as Skiing Unlimited.

4. Apply a picture as the page color.
   a. Apply a **Page Color** and use **Fill Effects**.
   b. Select the **Picture** tab of the *Fill Effects* dialog box and select the ***Snow-08*** picture from your student data files.

5. Insert and customize a built-in text box.
   a. Place the insertion point at the top of the document and insert the **Grid Quote** built-in text box.
   b. Type SKIING UNLIMITED, press **Enter**, and type LOOKING BACK. . .LOOKING FORWARD to replace the placeholder text in the text box.
   c. Change the height of the text box to **1.5"** and the width to **8.4"**.
   d. Select "**SKIING UNLIMITED**" in the text box, change the font size to **40 pt**, apply **bold** formatting, turn off **italic** formatting, and **left** align text.
   e. Select "**LOOKING BACK. . .LOOKING FORWARD**," change the font size to **16 pt**, and **right** align text.
   f. Use the *Position* tab in the *Layout* dialog box to change the *Horizontal* **Alignment** to **Centered** *relative to* **Page** and change the *Vertical* **Alignment** to **Top** *relative to* **Page**.
   g. Turn on **Show/Hide**, and if a blank line displays above the first body paragraph, delete it.
   h. Apply **10 pt** *Before* paragraph spacing on the first body paragraph below the text box.

6. Insert and customize a chart.
   a. Place the insertion point at the end of the first body paragraph in the document.
   b. Insert a **Clustered Bar** chart.
   c. Type the information in the table at the right in the *Chart in Microsoft Word* worksheet to replace the sample chart data (Figure 8-107):
   d. Adjust the chart data range and close the worksheet (see Figure 8-107).
   e. Type Skiing Unlimited to replace the existing text as the chart title.
   f. Add data labels to the **Outside End** of the bars.
   g. Apply the **Style 12** chart style.

	A	B	C
1		Participants	Volunteers
2	2016	41	104
3	2017	53	138
4	2018	61	186
5	2019	74	231

h. Select the **Chart Area** and apply the **Subtle Effect – Black, Dark 1** shape style (**first style** in the **fourth row** of *Theme Styles*).

i. Apply **bold** formatting to the data labels (participants and volunteers), vertical axis, horizontal axis, and legend.

j. Select the chart area and change the height of the chart to **2.5"** and the width to **6.5"**.

k. Place the insertion point at the end of the paragraph above the chart and press **Enter**.

7. Insert and customize a *SmartArt* graphic.

a. Place the insertion point at the end of the second body paragraph.

b. Insert the **Circle Arrow Process** *SmartArt* graphic (*Process* category).

c. Type the following information in the *SmartArt* graphic. Add shapes and use the *Text* pane as needed.

January 20
January 27
February 10
February 17
February 24

d. Apply **bold** formatting and **8 pt** font size to the text in the *SmartArt* graphic.

e. Select the border of the *SmartArt* and change the height to **3.5"** and the width to **2"**.

f. Change the color of the *SmartArt* graphic to **Dark 2 Fill** (**third color** in the *Primary Theme Colors* category).

g. Apply the **Subtle Effect** *SmartArt* style (**third style** in the **first row**).

h. Change the text wrapping to **Tight**.

i. Drag the *SmartArt* graphic to the bottom right of the first page. Use the alignment guides for placement.

j. Use the *Position* tab in the *Layout* dialog box to change the *Horizontal* **Absolute position** to **6"** *to the right of* **Page** and change the *Vertical* **Absolute position** to **7"** *below* **Page**.

8. Save and close the document (Figure 8-108).

Figure 8-107 Type in the chart data and select the chart data range

	A	B	C	D
1		Participants	Volunteers	
2	2016	41	104	
3	2017	53	138	
4	2018	61	186	
5	2019	74	231	
6				

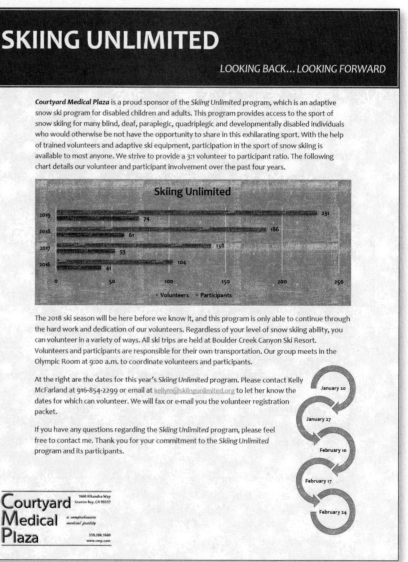

Figure 8-108 Word 8-5 completed

Independent Project 8-6

For this project, you customize a weekly expense report for Life's Animal Shelter. You apply desktop publishing features, apply and customize a theme, insert and customize text boxes, and insert and customize a chart.
[Student Learning Outcomes 8.1, 8.2, 8.3, 8.5]

File Needed: **WeeklyExpenses-08.docx** *(Student data files are available in the* Library *of your SIMnet account.)*
Completed Project File Name: *[your initials] Word 8-6.docx*

Skills Covered in This Project

- Customize and save a theme.
- Apply and customize a drop cap.
- Insert and customize built-in text boxes.
- Insert a chart and customize chart data.
- Customize the chart title.
- Modify chart elements.
- Apply a chart and shape style to the chart.
- Resize a chart.

1. Open the **WeeklyExpenses-08** document from your student data files.

2. Save this document as [your initials] Word 8-6.

3. Change the bottom margin to **0.5"**. Click **Ignore** if prompted about margins being outside of printable area.

4. Create a custom theme.
   a. Change the theme *Colors* to **Median**, theme *Fonts* to **Corbel**, and theme *Effects* to **Banded Edge**.
   b. Save the current theme as LAS.

5. Apply a **Dropped** drop cap to the first letter in the first body paragraph, modify it to drop **2** lines, and set the distance from text to **0.1"**.

6. Insert and customize a built-in text box.
   a. Place the insertion point at the top of the document and insert the **Grid Sidebar** built-in text box.
   b. Change the height to **11"** and the width to **2.5"**.
   c. Use the *Position* tab in the *Layout* dialog box to change the *Horizontal* **Alignment** to **Right** *relative to* **Page** and change the *Vertical* **Alignment** to **Top** *relative to* **Page**.
   d. Type Life's Animal Shelter to replace the first placeholder text ("Sidebar Title").
   e. Select "**Life's Animal Shelter**" in the text box, change the font size to **28 pt**, apply **bold** formatting (if not already applied), and apply the **Offset: Top Left** shadow text effect (**third option** in the **third row** in the *Outer category*).
   f. Click the second placeholder text in the text box and type the following, pressing **Enter** after each line except the last line:

      3429 Second Avenue North
      Park Rapids, MN 56470
      218.240.7880
      www.lifesanimalshelter.com
      "Serving our community through animal rescue and pet adoption"
      (Don't press *Enter* after this last line.)

   g. Select the address and phone number lines and change the *After* paragraph spacing to **0 pt**.
   h. Select the quoted text including the quotation marks ("**Serving our community . . .**"), change the line spacing to **1.5**, and apply **italic** formatting.
   i. Turn on **Show/Hide**, and if a blank line displays above the first body paragraph, delete it.

7. Insert and customize a chart.
   a. Place the insertion point at the end of the second body paragraph.
   b. Insert a **3-D Clustered Column** chart.
   c. Type the following information in the *Chart in Microsoft Word* worksheet to replace the sample chart data (Figure 8-109):

	A	B	C
1		Daily Total Expenses	Daily Average Expenses
2	Mon	1785	298
3	Tues	1709	285
4	Wed	1710	285
5	Thurs	1717	286
6	Fri	1841	307
7	Sat/Sun	2116	353

   d. Adjust the chart data range and close the worksheet (see Figure 8-109).
   e. Change the height of the chart to **3"** and the width to **4.5"**.
   f. Type **Daily Expenses** to replace the existing text in the chart title.
   g. Apply the **Style 6** chart style.
   h. Select the **Chart Area** and apply the **Brown, Text 2** shape fill color (**fourth color** in the **first row** of *Theme Colors*).
   i. Use the *Shape Fill* drop-down list to apply the **From Center** *Gradient* (**second option** in the **second row** in the *Dark Variations* category).
   j. Apply **bold** formatting to the legend and the horizontal axis.
   k. Place the insertion point at the end of the second body paragraph and press **Enter**.

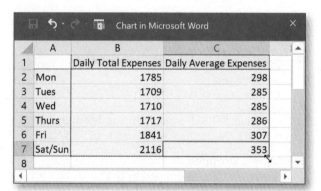
Figure 8-109 Type in the chart data and select the chart data range

8. Insert and customize a built-in text box.
   a. Select the last body paragraph (not including the paragraph mark) and cut (**Ctrl+X**) it from the document.
   b. Insert the **Motion Quote** built-in text box.
   c. Paste (**Ctrl+V**) the cut text in the text box to replace the placeholder text.
   d. Select the text in the text box and change the text alignment to **Center** [*Home* tab, *Paragraph* group].
   e. Apply the **Preset 2** shape effect.
   f. Change the height of the text box to **1"** and the width to **4"**.
   g. Use the *Position* tab in the *Layout* dialog box to change the *Horizontal* **Absolute Position** to **1.3"** *to the right of* **Page** and change the *Vertical* **Alignment** to **Bottom** *relative to* **Margin**.

9. Save and close the document (Figure 8-110).

Life's Animal Shelter

TO: Life's Animal Shelter staff and volunteers

FROM: Kelly Sung, Director of Services

DATE: March 14, 2020

SUBJECT: Weekly Expenses

Thank you for the time you have spent volunteering at Life's Animal Shelter. Our staff and volunteers have contributed countless hours making this shelter a safe environment for animals and providing adoption services for families in our community. You have been a part of hundreds of animal rescues and adoptions over the past year. Families throughout our region are enjoying their new pets thanks to your dedication and work at Life's Animal Shelter.

I'm providing you with our expenses update for the last week. Our operating funds come through donations and pet adoption fees. Thank you for your help in keeping our expenses at a moderate level. Because of you, we can offer reasonable adoption fees to animal lovers in our community.

3429 Second Avenue North
Park Rapids, MN 56470
218.240.7880
www.lifesanimalshelter.com

"Serving our community through animal rescue and pet adoption"

Again, thank you for all your hard work. Because of you, Life's Animal Shelter valuably serves our community providing pet rescue, shelter, and services.

Figure 8-110 Word 8-6 completed

Improve It Project 8-7

For this project, you customize a document from American River Cycling Club. You apply desktop publishing features, apply and customize a theme, and insert and customize text boxes, a *SmartArt* graphic, and a chart.
[Student Learning Outcomes 8.1, 8.2, 8.3, 8.4, 8.5]

File Needed: ***HeartRate-08.docx*** *(Student data files are available in the* Library *of your SIMnet account.)*
Completed Project File Name: *[your initials] Word 8-7.docx*

Skills Covered in This Project

- Adjust margins.
- Apply and customize a drop cap.
- Customize and save a theme.
- Draw and customize a text box.
- Align and group a picture and text box.

- Insert and customize a *SmartArt* graphic.
- Insert a chart and customize chart data.
- Resize a chart.
- Insert a chart title, axis titles, and data labels.
- Apply a chart and shape style to the chart.
- Modify chart elements.
- Insert, customize, and position a built-in text box.

---

1. Open the ***HeartRate-08*** document from your student data files.

2. Save the document as [your initials] Word 8-7.

3. Change the top margin to **0.75"**, the bottom margin to **0.5"**, the left margin to **1.75"**, and the right margin to **0.75"**. Click **Ignore** if prompted about margins being outside of printable area.

4. Apply a **Dropped** drop cap to the first letter in the first body paragraph and modify it to drop **2** lines.

5. Create a custom theme.
   a. Change the theme *Colors* to **Green Yellow** and theme *Fonts* to **Gil Sans MT**.
   b. Save the current theme as ARCC.

6. Draw a text box and customize it.
   a. **Draw Text Box** down the left side of your document.
   b. Change the height to **11"** and the width to **1.3"**.
   c. Apply the **Lime, Accent 1, Lighter 80%** shape fill (**fifth color** in the **second row** of *Theme Colors*).
   d. Remove the shape outline (**No Outline**).

7. Resize a picture and align and group a picture with a text box.
   a. Select the picture (logo) at the top of the document and change the width to **8.5"**. The height automatically adjusts.
   b. Select the picture (if necessary) and **Rotate Left 90°**.
   c. Drag the picture on top of the text box on the left and **Bring to Front** [*Picture Tools Format* tab, *Arrange* group].
   d. Use the **Ctrl** key to select the text box and picture.
   e. Align selected objects at **Align Center** and **Align Middle**.
   f. Confirm both objects are still selected and **Group** the two objects.
   g. Use the *Position* tab in the *Layout* dialog box to change the *Horizontal* **Absolute position** to **0"** to the right of **Page** and change the *Vertical* **Alignment** to **Top** *relative to* **Page**.

8. Insert and customize a *SmartArt* graphic.
   a. Place the insertion point at the end of the second body paragraph ("Example: a 40-year-old's . . .").
   b. Insert the **Equation** *SmartArt* graphic (*Process* category).

c. Type the following information in the *SmartArt* graphic:

220
Age
Max Heart Rate

d. Select the **plus** shape and **Change Shape** [*SmartArt Tools Format* tab, *Shapes* group] to **Minus Sign** (**second shape** in the *Equation Shapes* category).
e. Select the border of the *SmartArt* graphic and change the height to **1"** and the width to **4"**.
f. Apply the **Intense Effect** *SmartArt* style (**fifth style** in the **first row**).
g. Change the text wrapping to **Top and Bottom**.
h. Use the *Position* tab in the *Layout* dialog box to change the *Horizontal* **Alignment** to **Centered** *relative to* **Margin** and change the *Vertical* **Alignment** to **Top** *relative to* **Line**.
i. Select the sentence below the *SmartArt* graphic and **center** it.

9. Insert and customize a chart.
a. Select the tabbed text below the paragraphs (including the paragraph mark on the last row) and **Cut** (**Ctrl+X**) it.
b. Place the insertion point on the blank line below the last body paragraph and insert a **Line with Markers** chart.
c. Place the insertion point in cell **A1** in the *Chart in Microsoft Word* and **paste** (**Ctrl+V**) the content.
d. Adjust the chart data range and close the worksheet (Figure 8-111).
e. Change the height of the chart to **3.3"** and the width to **6"**.
f. Type Max and Target Heart Rates as the chart title.
g. Add a **Primary Horizontal** axis title and type Age in the text box.
h. Add a **Primary Vertical** axis title and type Heart Rate in the text box.

	A	B	C	
1	Age	Max Heart Rate	Target Heart Rate (75%)	
2	20	200	150	
3	25	195	146	
4	30	190	143	
5	35	185	139	
6	40	180	135	
7	45	175	131	
8	50	170	128	
9	55	165	124	
10	60	160	120	
11				

Figure 8-111 Paste the chart data and select the chart data range

10. Modify chart elements.
a. Apply the **Style 2** chart style.
b. Select the **Chart Area** and apply the **Subtle Effect – Lime, Accent 1** shape style (**second style** in the **fourth row** of *Theme Styles*).
c. Change the shape outline weight to **1½ pt**.
d. Apply the **Offset: Center** shadow shape effect (**second option** in the **second row** of the *Outer* category).
e. Select the legend and apply the **Subtle Effect – Lime, Accent 1** shape style.

11. Insert and customize a text box.
a. Place the insertion point at the end of the first paragraph in the "What Is Target Heart Rate?" section and insert the **Austin Quote** built-in text box.
b. **Copy** the first sentence in the second paragraph in the "What Is Target Heart Rate?" section and **paste** (**Ctrl+V**) it in the text box to replace the placeholder text.
c. Change the height of the text box to **1.6"** and the width to **2"**.
d. Select the text box and apply the **Subtle Effect – Lime, Accent 1** shape style.
e. Change the text wrapping to **Tight**.
f. Use the *Position* tab in the *Layout* dialog box to change the *Horizontal* **Absolute position** to **5.9"** *to the right of* **Page** and change the *Vertical* **Absolute position** to **3.4"** *below* **Page**.
g. Select the text in the text box, apply **italic** formatting, and change the text alignment to **center**.

h. Turn on **Show/Hide**, and if a blank line displays above the first body paragraph in the "What is Target Heart Rate" section, delete it.

12. Save and close the document (Figure 8-112).

WHAT IS MAXIMUM HEART RATE?

Maximum heart rate is the highest your pulse rate can get. To calculate your **predicted maximum heart rate**, use this formula:

(Example: a 40-year-old's predicted maximum heart rate is 180)

Your actual maximum heart rate can be determined by a graded exercise test. Please note that some medicines and medical conditions might affect your maximum heart rate. If you are taking medicines or have a medical condition (such as heart disease, high blood pressure, or diabetes), always ask your doctor if your maximum heart rate/target heart rate will be affected.

WHAT IS TARGET HEART RATE?

You gain the most benefits and decrease the risk of injury when you exercise in your target heart rate zone. Usually, this is when your exercise heart rate (pulse) is 60 percent to 85 percent of your maximum heart rate. Do not exercise for an extended amount of time above 85 percent of your maximum heart rate. This increases both cardiovascular and orthopedic risk and does not add any extra benefit.

> *When beginning an exercise program, you might need to gradually build up to a level that is within your target heart rate zone, especially if you have not exercised regularly before.*

When beginning an exercise program, you might need to gradually build up to a level that is within your target heart rate zone, especially if you have not exercised regularly before. If the exercise feels too hard, slow down. You will reduce your risk of injury and enjoy the exercise more if you don't try to overdo it.

To find out if you are exercising in your target zone (between 60 percent and 85 percent of your maximum heart rate), use your heart rate monitor to track your heart rate. If your pulse is below your target zone (see the chart below), increase your rate of exercise. If your pulse is above your target zone, decrease your rate of exercise.

The following chart displays maximum and target heart rates for different ages. Remember, these are estimated heart rates and will vary depending of fitness level and other physiological factors.

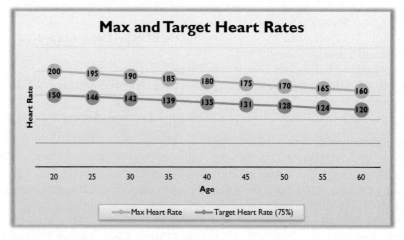

American River Cycling Club
Cycling... a way of life
info@arcc.org
www.arcc.org

Challenge Project 8-8

It is important to plan and budget for your college education. Create an education plan and budget using desktop publishing and graphics features discussed in this chapter. Use a *SmartArt* graphic to plan your courses for your remaining semesters and use a chart to visually display your estimated expenses.
[Student Learning Outcomes 8.1, 8.2, 8.3, 8.4, 8.5]

File Needed: None
Completed Project File Name: *[your initials] Word 8-8.docx*

Create a new blank document and save it as [your initials] Word 8-8. Create an education plan and budget using the Word features you learned in this chapter. Modify your document according to the following guidelines:

- Use a *SmartArt* graphic to display your education plan.
- Use a chart to display your estimated expenses.
- Apply and customize a theme and create a custom theme.
- Customize the *SmartArt* graphic and the chart layout and design.
- As appropriate, include a drop cap, page color, watermark, screenshot, and/or hyphenation.
- Insert a built-in text box or draw a text box and customize as needed.

Challenge Project 8-9

Apply desktop publishing features to improve readability and enhance the appearance of a report from one of your classes or from your job. Apply and customize a theme, mark index entries, and create an index page. You can also include a *SmartArt* graphic, a chart, and text boxes as appropriate.
[Student Learning Outcomes 8.1, 8.2, 8.3, 8.4, 8.5, 8.6]

File Needed: None
Completed Project File Name: *[your initials] Word 8-9.docx*

Open an existing report and save it as [your initials] Word 8-9. Modify your document according to the following guidelines:

- Apply and customize a theme and create a custom theme.
- Mark index entries, subentries, and cross-reference index entries.
- Create and customize an index page.
- Use built-in text boxes for pull quotes to emphasize important information in the report.
- Insert and customize a *SmartArt* graphic and/or chart as appropriate to visually display information.
- Include a drop cap, page color, watermark, screenshot, and/or hyphenation, as appropriate.

Challenge Project 8-10

Create a flyer, announcement, or invitation to an upcoming event for a student group or organization on campus, such as a blood drive, community service event, or food bank collection. Use desktop publishing and graphic features to enhance this document.
[Student Learning Outcomes 8.1, 8.2, 8.3, 8.4, 8.5]

File Needed: None
Completed Project File Name: *[your initials] Word 8-10.docx*

Create a new blank document and save it as [your initials] Word 8-10. Create a flyer, announcement, or invitation using Word features you learned in this chapter. Modify your document according to the following guidelines:

- Apply and customize a theme and create a custom theme.
- Appropriately include a drop cap, page color, watermark, screenshot, and/or hyphenation.
- Insert and customize text boxes to emphasize information in pull quotes.
- Insert and customize a *SmartArt* graphic and/or chart, as appropriate, to visually display information.
- Customize your *SmartArt* graphics and chart layout and design.

Source of screenshots Microsoft Office 365 (2019): Word, Excel, Access, PowerPoint.

Working Collaboratively and Integrating Applications

CHAPTER OVERVIEW

Microsoft Word provides tools that enable collaboration on documents. *Comments* and *Track Changes* are two valuable collaboration tools when editing documents with others. In addition to collaborating with multiple users, you can also integrate content from other Microsoft Office applications into a Word document. For example, insert a PowerPoint slide, a chart from Excel, or a table from Access in your Word documents. You can also merge data from Outlook, Excel, and Access into a Word document.

STUDENT LEARNING OUTCOMES (SLOs)

After completing this chapter, you will be able to:

SLO 9.1 Enhance collaboration by using advanced comments and track changes features and sharing documents (p. W9-546).

SLO 9.2 Use Word collaboration features to compare, combine, and protect documents (p. W9-553).

SLO 9.3 Embed and link content from other Microsoft Office applications into a Word document (p. W9-565).

SLO 9.4 Use mail merge rules to customize how data merges into a Word document from other Office applications (p. W9-574).

SLO 9.5 Insert bookmarks into a document (p. W9-576).

CASE STUDY

In the Pause & Practice projects in this chapter, you use collaboration and integration features available in Word to enhance an informational document from Hamilton Civic Center about their yoga classes.

Pause & Practice 9-1: Use advanced *Comments* and *Track Changes* features to edit a document and review a document that has comments and edits marked with tracked changes.

Pause & Practice 9-2: Prepare a document to be shared, combine changes from two documents, and protect a document.

Pause & Practice 9-3: Embed and link objects from PowerPoint and Excel into a Word document.

Pause & Practice 9-4: Add a bookmark to a document, merge recipients from Excel into a Word document, and use rules to customize a mail merge.

WORD

SLO 9.1 Advanced Collaboration Features

In chapter 3, you learned how to use comments and tracked changes to collaborate on a document. In this chapter, you will learn how to customize these features and use advanced collaboration features. Customize how comments and tracked changes display in a document, lock tracking, collaborate on an online document, and print document markup.

> **MORE INFO**
>
> Review comments and track changes in *SLO 3.1: Using Comments* and *SLO 3.2: Using Track Changes and Sharing.*

Customize Comment and Markup Color

Comments and tracked changes appear in a default color when you insert a comment or change a document using *Track Changes*. If multiple reviewers are commenting on the same document, Word uses a different color for each reviewer. Customize the colors to use for comments and markup in the *Track Changes Options* dialog box.

▶ **HOW TO:** Customize Comment and Markup Color

1. Click the **Tracking** launcher [*Review* tab, *Tracking* group] to open the *Track Changes Options* dialog box.

2. Click the **Advanced Options** button to open the *Advanced Track Changes Options* dialog box (Figure 9-1).

3. Click the **Insertions Color**, **Deletions Color**, or **Comments** drop-down lists and select a color for comments and markups.

   - Existing comments and markup edits change to the selected color.
   - By default, Word uses the *By author* option, which uses a different color for each author.

4. Click **OK** to close the *Advanced Track Changes Options* dialog box.

5. Click **OK** to close the *Track Changes Options* dialog box.

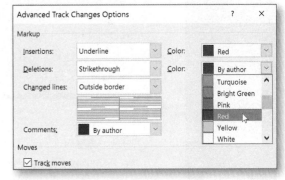

Figure 9-1 Change comment and markup color in the *Advanced Track Changes Options* dialog box

Customize Show Markup Options

Customize which markup displays, how it displays, and which reviewers' markup displays.

▶ **HOW TO:** Customize Show Markup Options

1. Click the **Show Markup** button [*Review* tab, *Tracking* group] to display the list of markup options.

2. Select the markup options to display or hide (*Comments*, *Insertions and Deletions*, and *Formatting*).

   - A check mark indicates a markup option displays.

3. Click **Balloons** and select one of the three balloons options: **Show Revisions in Balloons**, **Show All Revisions Inline**, or **Show Only Comments and Formatting in Balloons** (Figure 9-2).

- *Show Only Comments and Formatting in Balloons* is the default setting.

4. Click **Specific People** to display a list of reviewers and select or deselect reviewers as desired (Figure 9-3).

- When you deselect a reviewer, his or her comments and revisions do not display in the document.
- A check mark indicates a reviewer's comments and revisions display in the document.

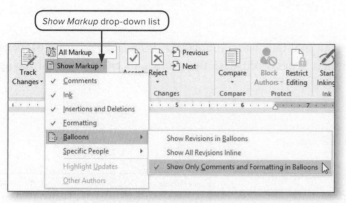

Figure 9-2 Customize *Show Markup* options

Figure 9-3 Select or deselect reviewers

Change Tracking Options

The *Track Changes Options* and *Advanced Track Changes Options* dialog boxes provide additional control over how changes and comments appear in a document. Customize how markups, moves, table cell highlighting, formatting, and balloons display in the document, and customize the color for each of these changes. Changes made in the *Track Changes Options* and *Advanced Track Changes Options* dialog boxes are global changes that affect all documents that use *Track Changes*.

▶ **HOW TO:** Change Tracking Options

1. Click the **Tracking** launcher [*Review* tab, *Tracking* group] to open the *Track Changes Options* dialog box.

2. Click the **Advanced Options** button to open the *Advanced Track Changes Options* dialog box (Figure 9-4).

3. Click the **Insertions**, **Deletions**, **Changed lines**, **Comments**, or **Color** drop-down list and change the appearance as desired.

4. Select or deselect the **Track moves** check box to determine if Word marks moved content as a tracked change.

- Use the drop-down lists to customize how *Moved from* and *Moved to* display in a document.
- Also in this area, customize how *Inserted cells*, *Deleted cells*, *Merged cells*, and *Split cells* display.

5. Select or deselect the **Track formatting** check box to determine if Word marks formatting changes as a tracked change.

- Customize how formatting changes display in the document and the *Markup* area.

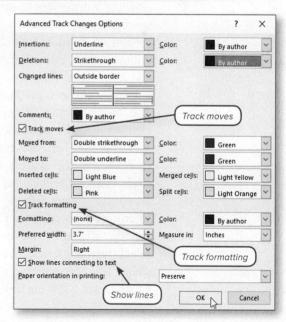

Figure 9-4 *Advanced Track Changes Options* dialog box

6. Select the **Show lines connecting to text** check box to display a line connecting the formatting change in the *Markup* area with highlighted text in the document.
7. Click **OK** to close the *Advanced Track Changes Options* dialog box.
8. Click **OK** to close the *Track Changes Options* dialog box.

Lock Tracking

When working on a document with multiple users, you can **Lock Tracking** so other users cannot turn off *Track Changes* without a password. Use this feature to ensure that all changes made by users are tracked.

▶ HOW TO: Lock Tracking

1. Click the bottom half of the **Track Changes** button [*Review* tab, *Tracking* group] and select **Lock Tracking**. The *Lock Tracking* dialog box opens (Figure 9-5).
2. Type a password in the *Enter password* text box.
   • If you don't type a password, users can turn off *Lock Tracking* without a password.
3. Type the same password in the *Reenter to confirm* text box.
4. Click **OK** to close the dialog box and lock tracking.

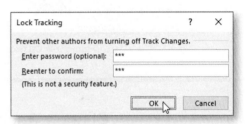

Figure 9-5 *Lock Tracking* dialog box

Real-Time Collaboration on a Shared Document

When a document is saved on *OneDrive*, an online storage area connected to your Microsoft account, you can share this document with others and collaborate online rather than emailing a document to others. Users can now simultaneously edit shared documents using the desktop version of Word 365 or 2019. Sharing a document online enables multiple users to edit a document and add comments. ***Real-time collaboration*** immediately displays changes users make on a shared document. The owner of the document can accept or reject changes made by other users.

Depending on the type of Microsoft account you're using, the sharing options display in a ***Send Link*** window (education and business Microsoft accounts) (Figure 9-6) or the ***Share*** pane (personal Microsoft account) (see Figure 9-9). The *Send Link* window or *Share* pane provides options to type or select recipients, set the permission level of the shared file, type a message recipients receive through email, or get a sharing link.

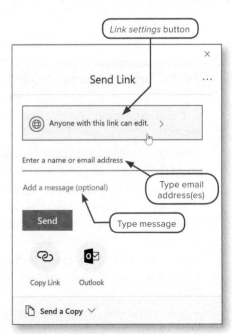

Figure 9-6 *Send Link* window

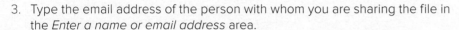

▶ HOW TO: Share an Online File (Education and Business Microsoft Accounts)

1. Open the file to share.
   - If the file is not saved in *OneDrive*, save the file to *OneDrive*.

Figure 9-7 *Share* button

2. Click the **Share** button (Figure 9-7) in the upper-right corner of the Word window to open the *Send Link* window (see Figure 9-6). The *Share* button icon may display differently in Office 2019.
   - Alternatively, click the **File** button to open the *Backstage* view, click **Share** on the left, select **Share with People**, and click the **Share with People** button. The *Backstage* view closes and the *Send Link* window opens in the Word document.

3. Type the email address of the person with whom you are sharing the file in the *Enter a name or email address* area.
   - If typing multiple email addresses, separate each with a semicolon.

4. Click the **Link settings** button to open the *Link settings* window (Figure 9-8).
   - Select who can use the sharing link.
   - Check the **Allow editing** box to enable recipients to edit the shared file. Deselect the **Allow editing** box to enable recipients to open and view the shared file, but restrict them from editing it.
   - Set an expiration date for the sharing link if desired (optional).

5. Click **Apply** to set the sharing link options and to return to the *Send Link* window.

6. Type a message to recipient(s) in the *Add a message* area. This is optional.

7. Click the **Send** button. An email is sent to people you invited.

8. Click the **X** to close the confirmation window.

Figure 9-8 *Link settings* window

If you're using a personal Microsoft account, the *Share* pane opens on the right after you click the *Share* button.

▶ HOW TO: Share an Online File (Personal Microsoft Account)

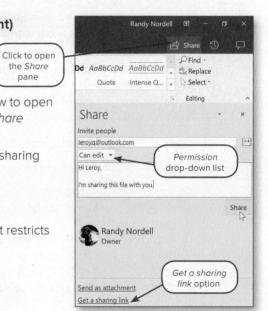

1. Open the file to share.
   - If the file is not saved in *OneDrive*, save the file to *OneDrive*.

2. Click the **Share** button in the upper-right corner of the Word window to open the *Share* pane to the right of the Word window (Figure 9-9). The *Share* button icon may display differently in Office 2019.

3. Type or select the email address of the person with whom you are sharing the file in the *Invite people* area.

4. Select **Can edit** or **Can view** from the *Permission* drop-down list.
   - *Can edit* enables users to edit a shared document.
   - *Can view* enables users to open and view a shared document but restricts users from editing the document.

5. Type a message to recipient(s) in the *Message* area.

6. Click the **Share** button. An email is sent to people you invited.

7. Click the **X** to close the *Share* pane.

Figure 9-9 Share a *OneDrive* file using the *Share* pane

> **MORE INFO**
>
> Sharing documents on *OneDrive* using Word Online is discussed further in chapter 12.

Print Document Markup

When you are working with a document containing tracked changes and comments, you have the option to print the markup.

> **HOW TO:** Print Document Markup

1. Click the **File** button to open the *Backstage* view.
2. Click the **Print** button on the left.
3. Click the first drop-down list in the *Settings* area and select **Print Markup** (Figure 9-10).
4. Click the **Print** button to print the document with markup.

Figure 9-10 *Print Markup* option in the *Settings* area

PAUSE & PRACTICE: WORD 9-1

For this Pause & Practice project, you work with two documents from Hamilton Civic Center. In the first document, you change user name and initials, add comments, and revise the document using *Track Changes*. In the second document, you review tracked changes, accept or reject changes, and delete comments.

Files Needed: **Yoga-09a.docx** and **Yoga-09b.docx** *(Student data files are available in the Library of your SIMnet account.)*
Completed Project File Names: **[your initials] PP W9-1a.docx** and **[your initials] PP W9-1b.docx**

---

1. Open the **Yoga-09a** document from your student data files.

2. Save the document as [your initials] PP W9-1a.

3. Change user name and initials.
   a. Click the **Tracking** launcher [*Review* tab, *Tracking* group] to open the *Track Changes Options* dialog box.
   b. Click the **Change User Name** button to open the *Word Options* dialog box.
   c. Type your first and last name in the *User name* text box and type your first and last initials in lowercase letters in the *Initials* text box in the *Personalize your copy of Microsoft Office* area.
   d. Check the **Always use these values regardless of sign in to Office** box.

e. Click **OK** to close the *Word Options* dialog box.
f. Click **OK** to close the *Track Changes Options* dialog box.

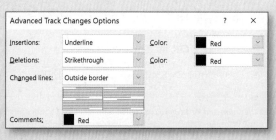

4. Change tracking and comment display options.
   a. Click the **Show Markup** drop-down list [*Review* tab, *Tracking* group], click **Balloons**, and select **Show Revisions in Balloons**.
   b. Click the **Tracking** launcher to open the *Track Changes Options* dialog box. Confirm that all of the boxes in the *Show* area are checked. Check any boxes that are not checked.
   c. Click the **Advanced Options** button to open the *Advanced Track Changes Options* dialog box.
   d. Change the **Color** of *Insertions*, *Deletions*, and *Comments* to **Red** (Figure 9-11).
   e. Click **OK** to close the *Advanced Track Changes Options* dialog box and click **OK** to close the *Track Changes Options* dialog box.
   f. Click the **Display for Review** drop-down list [*Review* tab, *Tracking* group] and select **All Markup** if it is not already selected (Figure 9-12).

Figure 9-11 Change settings in the *Advanced Track Changes Options* dialog box

Figure 9-12 Change *Display for Review* view

5. Add comments to the document.
   a. Select the word "**Registered**" in the first paragraph.
   b. Click the **New Comment** button [*Review* tab, *Comments* group] to open a new comment.
   c. Type What is Amanda's level of certification? in the comment balloon (Figure 9-13).

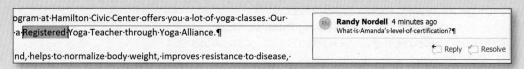

Figure 9-13 New comment inserted

   d. Place the insertion point in the first word in the last sentence of the last paragraph ("**We**").
   e. Click the **New Comment** button and type Is this closing okay? in the comment balloon.

6. Turn on *Track Changes* and revise the document.
   a. Click the top half of the **Track Changes** button [*Review* tab, *Tracking* group] to turn on track changes (or press **Ctrl+Shift+E**).
   b. Select the word "**lot**" in the first sentence of the first paragraph.
   c. Type variety to replace the selected word. Confirm one space displays before and after the word.
   d. Select and delete the first sentence in the last paragraph ("**Register at the front desk or by phone**. "), including the space after the period.
   e. Type the following sentence as the first sentence in the last paragraph:
   Register at the front desk, by phone (615-822-4965), or online (www.hccenter.org). Confirm one space displays after the period.
   f. Delete the comma (,) after the first instance of "members" in the second sentence in the last paragraph.

7. Lock the tracked changes in the document.
   a. Click the bottom half of the **Track Changes** button and select **Lock Tracking** to open the *Lock Tracking* dialog box (Figure 9-14).

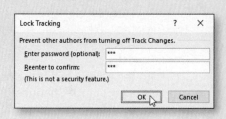

Figure 9-14 *Lock Tracking* dialog box

b. Type **HCC** in the *Enter password* text box and type **HCC** again in the *Reenter to confirm* text box.

c. Click **OK** to close the *Lock Tracking* dialog box.

8. Save and close the document (Figure 9-15).

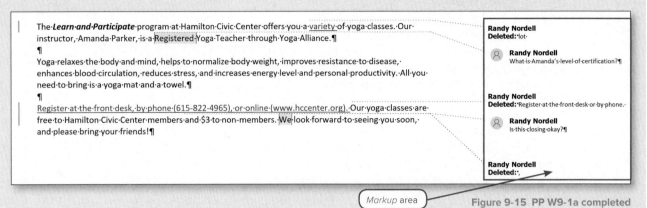

Markup area

Figure 9-15 PP W9-1a completed

9. Open the **Yoga-09b** document from your student data files.

10. Save the document as [your initials] PP W9-1b.

11. Click the **Display for Review** drop-down list [*Review* tab, *Tracking* group] and select **All Markup** if it is not already selected.

12. Display the *Reviewing* pane and reject changes.

a. Click the **Reviewing Pane** drop-down arrow [*Review* tab, *Tracking* group] and select **Reviewing Pane Vertical**. The *Reviewing* pane displays on the left side of the Word window.

b. Locate in the *Reviewing* pane where "*reduces stress,*" was inserted.

c. Right-click "**Rachel Gonzalves Inserted reduces stress,**" and select **Reject Insertion** from the context menu (Figure 9-16).

d. Locate in the *Reviewing* pane where "*reduces stress,*" was deleted.

e. Right-click "**Rachel Gonzalves Deleted reduces stress,**" and select **Reject Deletion** from the context menu.

f. Click the **X** in the upper-right corner of the *Reviewing* pane to close it.

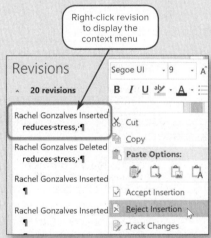

Right-click revision to display the context menu

Figure 9-16 Reject an insertion in the *Reviewing* pane

13. Accept changes in the document and delete comments.

a. Move to the top of the document (**Ctrl+Home**).

b. Click the **Next** button [*Review* tab, *Changes* group] to select the first change.

c. Click the top half of the **Accept** button [*Review* tab, *Changes* group] to accept the change and move to the next change.

d. Click the bottom half of the **Accept** button and select **Accept All Changes** from the drop-down list (Figure 9-17). All the remaining changes in the document are accepted.

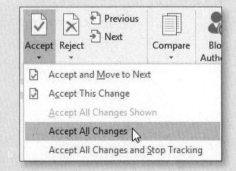

Figure 9-17 Accept all changes in the document

e. Click the bottom half of the **Delete** button [*Review* tab, *Comments* group] and select **Delete All Comments in Document** from the drop-down list to delete all comments.

14. Save and close the document (Figure 9-18).

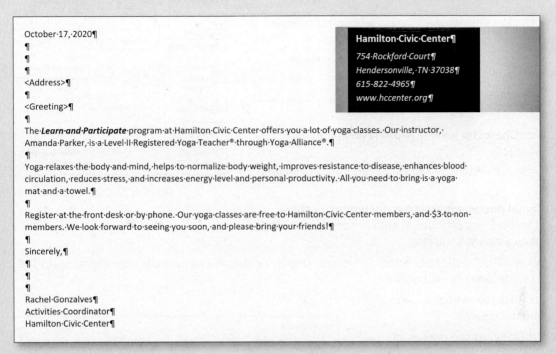

October·17,·2020¶
¶
¶
¶
<Address>¶
¶
<Greeting>¶
¶
The·**_Learn·and·Participate_**·program·at·Hamilton·Civic·Center·offers·you·a·lot·of·yoga·classes.·Our·instructor,·
Amanda·Parker,·is·a·Level·II·Registered·Yoga·Teacher®·through·Yoga·Alliance®.¶
¶
Yoga·relaxes·the·body·and·mind,·helps·to·normalize·body·weight,·improves·resistance·to·disease,·enhances·blood·
circulation,·reduces·stress,·and·increases·energy·level·and·personal·productivity.·All·you·need·to·bring·is·a·yoga·
mat·and·a·towel.¶
¶
Register·at·the·front·desk·or·by·phone.·Our·yoga·classes·are·free·to·Hamilton·Civic·Center·members,·and·$3·to·non-
members.·We·look·forward·to·seeing·you·soon,·and·please·bring·your·friends!¶
¶
Sincerely,¶
¶
¶
¶
Rachel·Gonzalves¶
Activities·Coordinator¶
Hamilton·Civic·Center¶

Hamilton·Civic·Center¶

754·Rockford·Court¶
Hendersonville,·TN·37038¶
615-822-4965¶
www.hccenter.org¶

Figure 9-18 PP W9-1b completed

SLO 9.2

Using Other Collaboration Features

In addition to *Comments* and *Track Changes*, Word provides additional features to manage documents when collaborating with others. The compare and combine features incorporate editing changes from multiple documents. Also, when finalizing a document, you can mark it as final, encrypt it with a password, restrict editing, and add a digital signature.

Compare Documents

Compare is a collaboration feature that compares different versions of a document and displays the differences marked with *Track Changes*. You can then review and accept or reject the tracked revisions. Use *Compare* to examine differences between an ***original document*** and a ***revised document***. You can customize which editing changes Word compares, and display comparison results in a new Word document, the original document, or the revised document.

▶HOW TO: Compare Documents

1. Click the **Compare** button [*Review* tab, *Compare* group] and select **Compare**. The *Compare Documents* dialog box opens (Figure 9-19).
   - Always save the documents before comparing.
2. Click the **Original document** drop-down list and select the original document or click the **Browse** button to locate and select the file.

- When you click the **Browse** button, the *Open* dialog box opens.

3. Click the **Revised document** drop-down list and select the revised document or click the **Browse** button to locate and select the file.

   - Type or change the reviewer name in the *Label changes with* text boxes.

4. Click the **More** or **Less** button to display more or fewer settings.

5. Select the revisions to compare by checking the boxes in the *Comparison settings* area.

6. Select either **Character level** or **Word level** in the *Show changes at* area.

   - Word displays comparison results by individual character or by word.

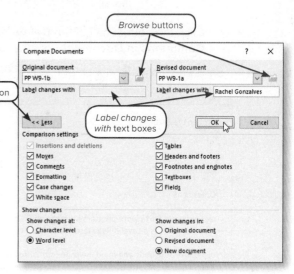

Figure 9-19 *Compare Documents* dialog box

7. Select **Original document**, **Revised document**, or **New document** in the *Show changes in* area to specify where the results of the comparison display.

   - *New document* is the default setting. This option displays changes in a new document and leaves the original and revised documents unchanged.

8. Click **OK** to close the dialog box and compare the documents.

   - If the original or revised document contains tracked changes, a dialog box opens and prompts you to accept the changes (Figure 9-20).
   - Tracked changes in both documents are accepted when the comparison is performed.
   - Click **Yes** to continue the comparison.
   - The differences between the two documents display as tracked changes. Accept or reject these proposed changes.

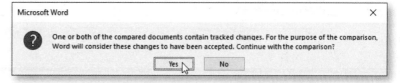

Figure 9-20 Accept changes before comparing documents

9. Save the compared document.

> **MORE INFO**
>
> When a document is saved on *OneDrive* the *Compare* drop-down list displays additional compare options: *Major Version*, *Last Version*, and *Specific Version*.

Show or Hide Source Documents

After comparing two documents, choose whether to show one or both of the source documents in the Word window or hide both source documents. If you show one or both source documents, they display on the right side of the Word window in the *Reviewing* pane. You can't edit the source documents when they display in a compared document; they display for review only.

▶HOW TO: Show or Hide Source Documents

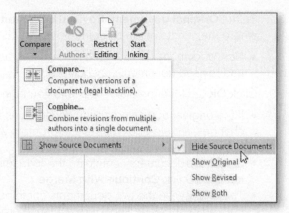

1. Click the **Compare** button [*Review* tab, *Compare* group].
2. Select **Show Source Documents** and select from one of the four options: **Hide Source Documents**, **Show Original**, **Show Revised**, or **Show Both** (Figure 9-21).
   - The last setting you choose applies the next time you compare documents.
3. Click the **X** in the upper-right corner of a source document to close it.

Figure 9-21 *Show Source Documents* options

Combine Documents

The *Combine* feature combines tracked changes from two documents into a single document. Whereas the *Compare* feature looks for just the *differences* between documents, the *Combine* feature incorporates *all* tracked changes from both documents into one document. You can then accept or reject the changes in the combined document, or combine all of the tracked changes in a new document, the original document, or the revised document.

> ### MORE INFO
>
> You can compare and combine only two documents at a time. If comparing or combining more than two documents, perform the feature multiple times.

▶HOW TO: Combine Documents

1. Click the **Compare** button [*Review* tab, *Compare* group] and select **Combine**. The *Combine Documents* dialog box opens (Figure 9-22).
   - Always save the documents before combining.
2. Click the **Original document** drop-down list and select the original document or click the **Browse** button to locate the file.
3. Click the **Revised document** drop-down list and select the revised document or click the **Browse** button to locate the file.
   - Type or change the reviewer name in the *Label unmarked changes with* text boxes.
4. Click the **More** or **Less** button to display more or fewer settings.
5. Select the revisions to compare by checking the boxes in the *Comparison settings* area.
6. Select either **Character level** or **Word level** in the *Show changes at* area.
   - Word displays combining results by individual character or by word.

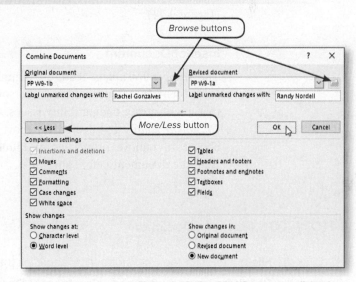

Figure 9-22 *Combine Documents* dialog box

7. Select **Original document**, **Revised document**, or **New document** in the *Show changes in* area. This determines where the results of the combined documents display.

   - *New document* is the default setting. This option displays changes in a new document and leaves the original and revised documents unchanged.

8. Click **OK** to close the dialog box and combine the documents.

   - If the original or revised document contains formatting changes, a dialog box opens and prompts you to select a document (Figure 9-23).
   - Select the document containing the formatting changes to keep and click **Continue with Merge**.
   - The changes in the two documents combine and display as tracked changes. Accept or reject these proposed changes.

9. Save the combined document.

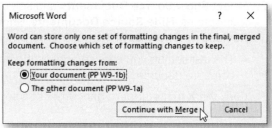

Figure 9-23 Keep formatting changes from a specific document

> **MORE INFO**
>
> Showing or hiding source documents functions the same when using either the *Compare* or *Combine* feature.

Check for Issues

Word provides tools to alert you to potential problems that may occur when sharing and collaborating on a document. The *Check for Issues* options include *Inspect Document*, *Check Accessibility*, and *Check Compatibility*. All of these options display on the *Backstage* view and *Check Accessibility* also displays on the *Ribbon* (Figure 9-24).

Inspect Document

The *Inspect Document* feature examines a document for hidden content, properties, or personal information that might create compatibility issues. Use the *Inspect Document* feature to generate a report where you can choose to remove properties or hidden information from the document before sharing it.

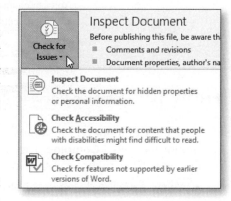

Figure 9-24 *Check for Issues* on the *Backstage* view

▶**HOW TO:** Inspect a Document

1. Click the **File** tab to open the *Backstage* view and click the **Info** button on the left.
2. Click the **Check for Issues** button and select **Inspect Document** from the drop-down list. The *Document Inspector* dialog box opens (Figure 9-25).
3. Select the document content to inspect by selecting or deselecting check boxes.
4. Click **Inspect**. The results display in the *Document Inspector* dialog box (Figure 9-26).

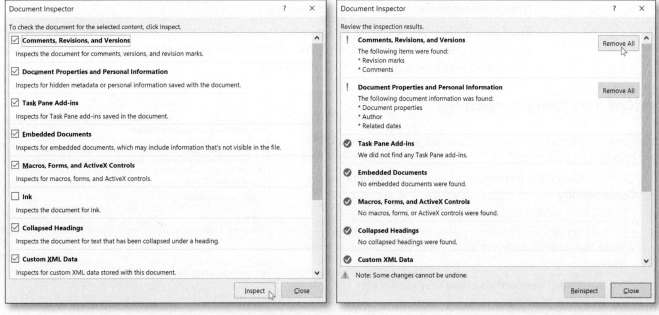

Figure 9-25 *Document Inspector* dialog box   Figure 9-26 Document inspection results

5. Click the **Remove All** button to remove selected information from the document.

6. Click the **Reinspect** button to inspect the document again after removing content.

7. Click the **Close** button to close the *Document Inspector* dialog box.

Check Accessibility

The ***Check Accessibility*** feature checks for potential issues that users with disabilities may have with your document. For example, users with visual impairments use document or screen readers to read the text in the document. A screen reader may not properly read objects in Word. The *Check Accessibility* feature alerts you to potential issues and provides you with recommended actions in the ***Accessibility Checker pane***.

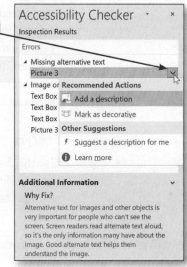

Figure 9-27 *Accessibility Checker pane*

▶**HOW TO:** Check Accessibility

1. Click the **Check Accessibility** button [*Review* tab, *Accessibility* group] to open the *Accessibility Checker* pane (Figure 9-27).
   - Alternatively, click the **Inspect Document** button in the *Info* area on the *Backstage* view and select **Check Accessibility**.

2. Click the triangle to the left of a heading in the *Inspection Results* area to display the results.

3. Select one of the results in the *Inspection Results* area.
   - Click the drop-down arrow to display *Recommended Actions* and *Other Suggestions*.
   - The *Additional Information* area displays why and how to fix the problems.

4. Click the **X** in the upper-right corner to close the *Accessibility Checker* pane.

Check Compatibility

The **Check Compatibility** feature searches for compatibility issues between the version of Word you are using and older or newer versions. This feature is useful when sharing documents with others who may have a different version of Word.

▶ **HOW TO:** Check Compatibility

1. Click the **File** tab to open the *Backstage* view and click the **Info** button on the left.
2. Click the **Check for Issues** button and select **Check Compatibility** from the drop-down list. The *Microsoft Word Compatibility Checker* dialog box opens (Figure 9-28).
   - The *Summary* area displays potential compatibility issues.
   - Based on the summary, change your document to correct these potential issues.
3. Click the **Select versions to show** drop-down list to select Word versions to check.
4. Click **OK** to close the dialog box.

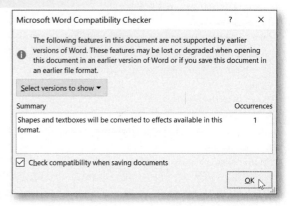

Figure 9-28 *Microsoft Word Compatibility Checker dialog box*

Protect Document

After sharing a document and making editing changes, finalize and protect your document. **Protect Document** options include *Always Open Read-Only*, *Encrypt with Password*, *Restrict Editing*, *Add a Digital Signature*, and *Mark as Final*. All of these options are available on the *Backstage* view (Figure 9-29).

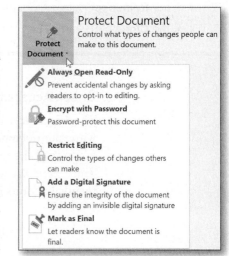

Figure 9-29 *Protect Document options*

Always Open Read-Only

A read-only file allows others to open the file but restricts editing of the file. Use the **Always Open Read-Only** when you want a document to remain unchanged. A user can open a read-only file, save the file with a different name, and edit the new file. Click the **File** tab to open the *Backstage* view, click the **Protect Document** button in the *Info* area, and select **Always Open Read-Only** to activate this feature.

Encrypt with Password

Use the **Encrypt with Password** feature to prevent users from opening and editing a document. When a document is encrypted with a password, a user receives a prompt to enter a password to open the document.

▶ **HOW TO:** Encrypt a Document with a Password

1. Click the **File** tab to open the *Backstage* view and click the **Info** button on the left.
2. Click the **Protect Document** button and select **Encrypt with Password**. The *Encrypt Document* dialog box opens (Figure 9-30).

3. Type a password in the *Password* text box and click **OK**. The *Confirm Password* dialog box opens.

   - Passwords are case sensitive.

4. Type the same password in the *Reenter password* text box and click **OK**.

   - A notation stating a password is required to open the document displays on the *Backstage* view in the *Protect Document* area.

5. Click the **Back** arrow to return to the document.

Figure 9-30 *Encrypt Document* dialog box

> ### MORE INFO
>
> Store document passwords in a secure location.

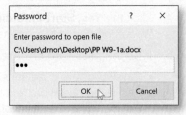

Figure 9-31 *Password* dialog box

When reopening a document encrypted with a password, a dialog box opens and prompts the user to enter the password (Figure 9-31). Type the password in the dialog box and click **OK** to open the document.

You can remove a document password after you have opened a document that is encrypted with a password.

▶ HOW TO: Remove a Document Password

1. Open the password encrypted document and type the password to open the document.

2. Click the **File** tab to open the *Backstage* view.

3. Click the **Protect Document** button and select **Encrypt with Password**. The *Encrypt Document* dialog box opens (Figure 9-32).

4. Delete the password in the *Password* text box and leave this text box blank.

5. Click **OK** to close the dialog box and remove the password.

Figure 9-32 Remove a document password

Restrict Editing

Another way to protect a document is to *restrict editing* of a document. This feature enables you to restrict what actions a user can perform in a document. Users can open the document without a password, but you control what content can be modified in the document. For example, restrict the editing of the entire document so the document becomes a read-only document, allow users to add comments or use *Track Changes*, or limit formatting changes to selected styles.

Remove restrictions on a document by clicking the **Stop Protection** button in the *Restrict Formatting and Editing* pane and entering the password.

▶ HOW TO: Restrict Editing of a Document

1. Click the **Restrict Editing** button [*Review* tab, *Protect* group] to open the *Restrict Editing* pane (Figure 9-33).
   - Alternatively, click the **Protect Document** button and select **Restrict Editing** in the *Info* area on the *Backstage* view.

2. Check **the Limit formatting to a selection of styles** box to limit editing to specific styles.
   - Click the **Settings** to select styles users can apply.

3. Check the **Allow only this type of editing in the document** box in the *Editing restrictions* area.
   - Click the drop-down list and select the type of editing to allow: *Tracked changes*, *Comments*, *Filling in forms*, or *No changes (Read only)* (see Figure 9-33).
   - *No changes (Read only)* restricts users from making any editing changes.

4. Click the **Yes, Start Enforcing Protection** button. The *Start Enforcing Protection* dialog box opens (Figure 9-34).

5. Type the password in the text box and reenter the password.
   - Passwords are case sensitive.
   - Leave the password text boxes blank to be able to turn off *Restrict Editing* without a password.

6. Click **OK** to close the dialog box and protect the document.

7. Click the **X** in the upper-right corner of the *Restrict Editing* pane to close it.

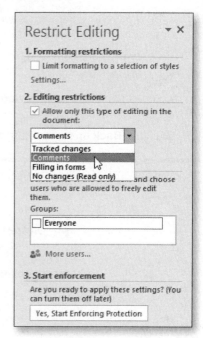

Figure 9-33 *Restrict Editing* pane

Figure 9-34 *Start Enforcing Protection* dialog box

Add a Digital Signature

The ***Add a Digital Signature*** feature ensures the integrity of a document by adding an invisible digital signature to the document. When you add a digital signature to your document, Word saves your document and marks it as final. This feature is useful when you are working with highly sensitive documents. This advanced security feature requires a digital ID that employers may provide. Third-party vendors also provide this security service.

Mark as Final

The ***Mark as Final*** feature marks a document as a final version and protects it from being edited. When a user opens a document that has been marked as final, the *Info* bar displays a message informing the user that the document has been marked as final.

▶ HOW TO: Mark a Document as Final

1. Save the document before marking it as final.

2. Click the **File** tab to open the *Backstage* view and click the **Info** button on the left.

3. Click the **Protect Document** button and select **Mark as Final** (see Figure 9-29).

4. Click **OK** in the dialog box that opens and informs you that the document will be marked as final and saved (Figure 9-35). Another dialog box opens.

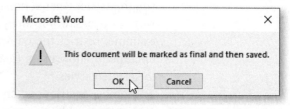

Figure 9-35 Confirm marked as final dialog box

5. Click **OK** in the dialog box that provides information about the final version (Figure 9-36).

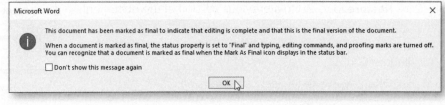

Figure 9-36 Marked as final dialog box

   - Check the **Don't show this message again** box to prevent this dialog box from displaying again.
   - A notation stating the document has been marked as final displays on the *Backstage* view (Figure 9-37).

Figure 9-37 *Marked as Final* notation on the *Backstage* view

6. Click the **Back** arrow to close the *Backstage* view and return to the document.

   - The *Info* bar between the *Ribbon* and the *Ruler* displays a notation indicating the document is marked as final (Figure 9-38).
   - The *Ribbon* is collapsed and the document is protected from editing.

Info bar

Figure 9-38 *Marked as Final* notation in the *Info* bar

When a document is marked as final, users can edit the document by turning off *Mark as Final*. Select one of the following to turn off *Mark as Final*:

- Click the **Edit Anyway** button in the *Info* bar (see Figure 9-38).
- Click the **File** tab to open the *Backstage* view, click the **Protect Document** button, and select **Mark as Final**.

Manage Versions

When you are working on a document, Word automatically saves your document every 10 minutes. You can use these ***autosaved versions*** to recover previous information or a previous version of your document. If Word or your computer crashes while working on a document, Word uses the most recent autosaved version to recover your document. The different saved versions of your document display in the *Versions* area in the *Backstage* view.

▶**HOW TO:** Recover Autosaved Versions of a Document

1. Click the **File** tab to open the *Backstage* view and click the **Info** button on the left.

2. Select one of the autosaved versions of the document in the *Manage Document* area (Figure 9-39). The autosaved document opens.

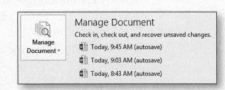

Figure 9-39 Autosaved versions of a document

   - The *Info* bar of the autosaved document displays two options: *Compare* and *Restore* (Figure 9-40).

3. Click the **Compare** button to compare the selected version with the most current version.

   - The most current version of the document opens so you can compare it to the selected previous version.

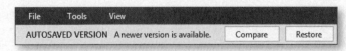

Figure 9-40 Version options on an autosaved document

4. Click **Restore** to revert to a previous version of the document.
   - A dialog box opens informing you that you are about to overwrite the last saved version of the document (Figure 9-41).
5. Click **OK** to overwrite the last saved version.

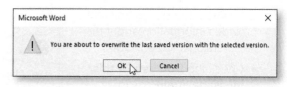

Figure 9-41 Overwrite most recent version with previous version

If an open document is saved on *OneDrive*, a *Version History* button displays near the upper-right corner of the Word window. Click the **Version History** button to open the *Version History* pane (Figure 9-42). Click **Open version** to open a previous version of the document.

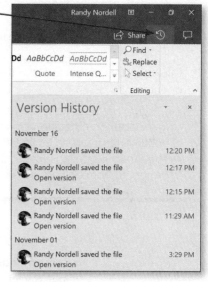

Figure 9-42 *Version History* pane

> **MORE INFO**
>
> Customize the frequency of autosave in the *Save* area of the *Word Options* dialog box.

PAUSE & PRACTICE: WORD 9-2

For this Pause & Practice project, you combine the two documents from *Pause & Practice 9-1* into a new document. You inspect the new document, check compatibility, restrict editing, encrypt the document with a password, and mark it as final.

Files Needed: *[your initials] PP W9-1a.docx* and *[your initials] PP W9-1b.docx*
Completed Project File Name: *[your initials] PP W9-2.docx*

1. Open a document and turn off *Lock Tracking*.
   a. Open *[your initials] PP W9-1a.docx*. If the document opens in *Reading* view, click the **View** tab in the upper left and select **Edit Document**.
   b. Click the bottom half of the **Track Changes** button [*Review* tab, *Tracking* group] and select **Lock Tracking** to open the *Unlock Tracking* dialog box.
   c. Type HCC in the *Password* text box and click **OK** to turn off *Lock Tracking*.
   d. Save and close the document. Leave Word open.

2. Combine documents.
   a. Click the **Compare** button [*Review* tab, *Compare* group] and select **Combine**. The *Combine Documents* dialog box opens (Figure 9-43).
   b. Click the **Browse** button in the *Original document* area to display the *Open* dialog box.
   c. Locate and select the *[your initials] PP W9-1b* document and click **Open**.
   d. Type Rachel Gonzalves in the *Label unmarked changes with* text box in the *Original document* area.

e. Click the **Browse** button in the *Revised document* area, select the *[your initials] PP W9-1a* document, and click **Open** to select the document.

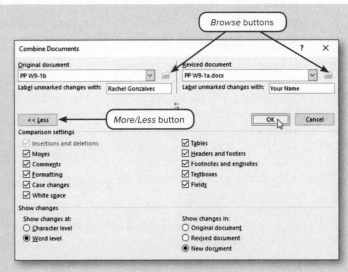

f. Type your first and last name in the *Label unmarked changes with* text box in the *Revised document* area.

g. Click the **More** button (if it displays) to display all settings options.

h. Confirm all check boxes are selected In the *Comparison settings* area.

i. Select the **Word level** radio button in the *Show changes at* area.

j. Select the **New document** radio button in the *Show changes in* area.

Figure 9-43 *Combine Documents* dialog box

k. Click **OK** to close the dialog box and to combine the documents into a new document. A dialog box opens and prompts you to keep the formatting changes from one of the documents (Figure 9-44).

l. Select the **Your document (PP W9-1b)** radio button and click **Continue with Merge**. The two documents are combined into a new Word document.

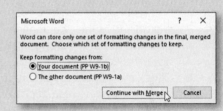

Figure 9-44 Keep formatting changes from a specific document

3. Save the combined document and hide source documents.
   a. Save this combined document as [your initials] PP W9-2.
   b. Hide the source documents if they display on the right. Click the **Compare** button, select **Show Source Documents**, and select **Hide Source Documents**.

4. Accept changes and delete comments.
   a. Click the bottom half of the **Accept** button [*Review* tab, *Changes* group] and select **Accept All Changes** to accept the remaining changes in the document.
   b. Click the bottom half of the **Delete** button [*Review* tab, *Comments* group] and select **Delete All Comments in Document** to delete all comments.
   c. Close the *Revisions* pane if it is open.
   d. Locate the registered trademark symbols in the second sentence in the first body paragraph. If a space displays before either of these symbols, delete the space, so the symbol displays directly after the word ("Teacher®" and "Alliance®").
   e. Save the document.

5. Inspect the document.
   a. Click the **File** tab to open the *Backstage* view.
   b. Click the **Check for Issues** button and select **Inspect Document** to open the *Document Inspector* dialog box.
   c. Deselect the **Document Properties and Personal Information** and **Custom XML Data** check boxes.
   d. Click **Inspect**. The *Document Inspector* dialog box opens and displays the inspection results (Figure 9-45). No issues should display.

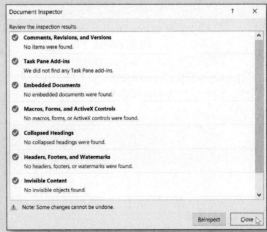

Figure 9-45 *Document Inspector* with inspection results displayed

e. Click **Close** to close the dialog box and click the **Back** arrow to return to the document.
   f. Save the document.

6. Check the compatibility and accessibility and add alt text.
   a. Click the **File** tab to open the *Backstage* view.
   b. Click the **Check for Issues** button and select **Check Compatibility**. The *Microsoft Word Compatibility Checker* dialog box opens.
   c. Review the compatibility issues and click **OK** to close the dialog box.
   d. Click the *Check Accessibility* button [*Review* tab, *Accessibility* group] to open the *Accessibility Checker* pane on the right.
   e. Click triangles in the *Errors* and *Warning* sections to expand these sections. Read the potential accessibility issues.
   f. Close the *Accessibility Checker* pane.
   g. Click the border of the text box near the upper-right corner to select it.
   h. Click the **Alt Text** button [*Drawing Tools Format* tab, *Accessibility* group].
   i. Type **Hamilton Civic Center information** in the text box.
   j. Close the *Alt Text* pane.

Figure 9-46 Restrict editing to only comments

7. Restrict editing of the document.
   a. Click the **Restrict Editing** button [*Review* tab, *Protect* group] to open the *Restrict Editing* pane.
   b. Check the **Allow only this type of editing in the document** box in the *Editing restrictions* area (Figure 9-46).
   c. Click the drop-down list and select **Comments**.
   d. Click the **Yes, Start Enforcing Protection** button. The *Start Enforcing Protection* dialog box opens (Figure 9-47).
   e. Type **HCC** in the *Enter new password* area.
   f. Type **HCC** in the *Reenter password to confirm* area.
   g. Click **OK** to close the dialog box.
   h. Close the *Restrict Editing* pane.

8. Encrypt the document with a password and mark the document as final.
   a. Click the **File** tab to open the *Backstage* view.
   b. Click the **Protect Document** button and select **Encrypt with Password**. The *Encrypt Document* dialog box opens.
   c. Type **HCC** in the *Password* text box and click **OK**. The *Confirm Password* dialog box opens.
   d. Type **HCC** in the *Reenter password* text box and click **OK**.
   e. Click the **Protect Document** button on the *Backstage* view and select **Mark as Final**.
   f. Click **OK** in the dialog box that informs you that the document will be marked as final and saved.
   g. Click **OK** to close the next informational dialog box.
   h. Click the **Back** arrow to close the *Backstage* view and return to the document.

Figure 9-47 Set protection password

9. Close the document (Figure 9-48).

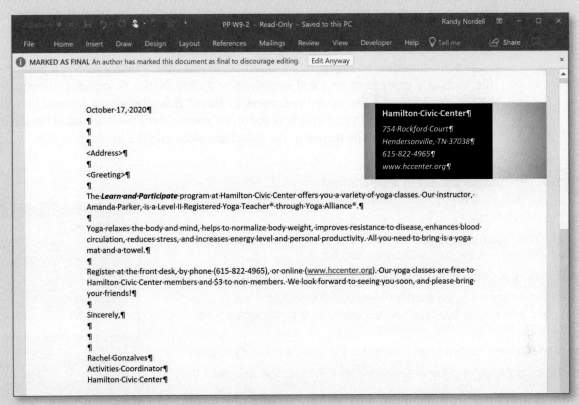

Figure 9-48 PP W9-2 completed

Integrating Office Applications

Microsoft Office provides the ability to integrate information between the different applications. For example, use data from an Excel worksheet in a Word document or PowerPoint presentation, export data from an Access database to use in an Excel worksheet or Word document, or insert slides from a PowerPoint presentation into a Word document.

Object Linking and Embedding

Object linking and embedding, also known as *OLE*, refers to Microsoft Office's ability to share information between the different Microsoft Office applications. The following terminology is important to know when using *OLE*:

- *Source program*: The Office application where you create the content
- *Destination program*: The Office application where you insert the object
- *Source file*: The file where the content is stored
- *Destination file*: The file where you insert the object

When using *OLE* to insert content from an Office application into a Word document, insert the content as an object and modify it in the Word document. Embedding and linking are two different ways to insert content from one application into another.

Embed an Object

Embedding inserts an object from one application into another. You can modify the object in the destination file independently of the source file. Use embedding when the source and destination files do not need to remain the same. When embedding an object into a Word document, the object retains the formatting from the source program.

When embedding an object into a Word document, you typically embed a portion of the file, such as a chart from an Excel worksheet or a slide from a PowerPoint presentation. To embed a portion of a file, copy the content to embed from the source file and then use the ***Paste Special*** dialog box to control how the object embeds into the destination file. Using this method, you select the file format of the object to embed into the destination file.

▶HOW TO: Embed an Object in a Document

1. Open the source file.
   - Use the source program to open the file or open the file from a *File Explorer* folder, which opens the source program and file.
2. Select the portion of the document to embed as an object (Figure 9-49).
   - To embed a chart, click the chart frame to select the *Chart Area*.
   - To embed a PowerPoint slide, select the entire slide by clicking a slide thumbnail in the *Navigation* area on the left.
3. **Copy (Ctrl+C)** the selected object and close the source file and program.
4. Place the insertion point in the destination file at the location to embed the object.
5. Click the bottom half of the **Paste** button [*Home* tab, *Clipboard* group] and select **Paste Special** (Figure 9-50). The *Paste Special* dialog box opens (Figure 9-51).
6. Select the **Paste** radio button.
7. Select the file type in the *As* area.
   - If you select the source program file type, the object retains the connection with the source program, and you can edit the object.
   - If you choose a different file type, such as a *Picture* or *Microsoft Office Graphic Object*, the object does not retain a connection with the source program, but rather connects to the destination program. You can edit this type of embedded object as you would a picture or graphic in Word.
8. Click **OK** to close the *Paste Special* dialog box and to embed the object in the destination file.

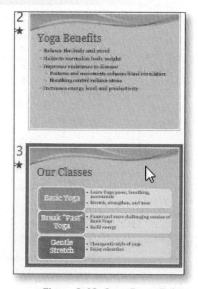

Figure 9-49 Copy PowerPoint slide to embed as an object

Figure 9-50 Open the *Paste Special* dialog box

Figure 9-51 *Paste Special* dialog box

▶ ANOTHER WAY

Alt+Ctrl+V opens the *Paste Special* dialog box.

Embed a File

You can also embed an entire file into a destination file. For example, embed an entire Excel worksheet or an entire PowerPoint presentation. When embedding an entire file into a Word document, the file retains the formatting from the source program.

▶HOW TO: Embed a File

1. Place the insertion point in your document at the location to insert the embedded file.
2. Click the **Object** button [*Insert* tab, *Text* group]. The *Object* dialog box opens.
3. Click the **Create from File** tab and click the **Browse** button to select a file to embed (Figure 9-52). The *Browse* dialog box opens.
4. Select the file to embed and click **Insert**.
5. Click **OK** to close the *Object* dialog box and embed the file.

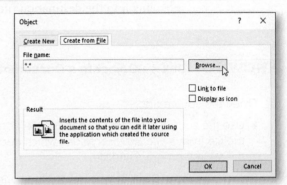

Figure 9-52 *Object* dialog box

> **MORE INFO**
>
> Be careful when embedding entire files because the destination file can become very large.

Modify an Embedded Object

Modifying an embedded object is similar to modifying other graphic objects in Word. The file type selected when embedding an object determines how the object is edited. For example, if you select the source program as the file type for the embedded object, the object retains the connection to the source program, and you edit it using the *Ribbon* from the source program. Double-click the object to display the *Ribbon* and tabs from the source program in Word. Use the *Ribbon* from the source program to modify the embedded object.

If you select a different file type for the embedded object, such as a picture or Microsoft Office Object, edit the object using the contextual tabs in Word.

▶HOW TO: Modify an Embedded Object

1. Select the embedded object. The contextual tab(s) associated with the object display.
   - If the object is connected with the source program, double-click the object to open the *Ribbon* from the source program.
2. Modify the size, text wrapping, and arrangement of the object.
3. Click outside the object area to deselect it.

Link an Object

Linking inserts an object from one application into another and creates a link between the object in the source and destination files. When you make changes to a linked object in the destination file, the object in the source file updates also because the objects are linked. In addition, if you change the object in the source file, the linked object in the destination file also changes. Linking is useful when you want the object in the source and destination files to remain the same in both locations.

To link an object, copy the object in the source file, and use the *Paste Special* dialog box to link it to the destination file.

▶HOW TO: Link an Object to a Document

1. Open the source file.
   - Use the source program to open the file or open the file from a *File Explorer* folder, which opens the source program and file.
2. Select and **copy** (**Ctrl+C**) an object in the source file (Figure 9-53).
   - To link a chart, click the chart frame to select the *Chart Area*.
   - To link a PowerPoint slide, select the entire slide by clicking a slide thumbnail in the *Navigation* area on the left.
   - To link an entire file, use the *Object* dialog box.
3. Place the insertion point in the destination file at the location to insert the linked object.
4. Click the bottom half of the **Paste** button [*Home* tab, *Clipboard* group] and select **Paste Special**. The *Paste Special* dialog box opens (Figure 9-54).
5. Select the **Paste link** radio button.
6. Select the file type in the *As* area.
7. Click **OK** to close the *Paste Special* dialog box and to insert the linked object in the destination file.

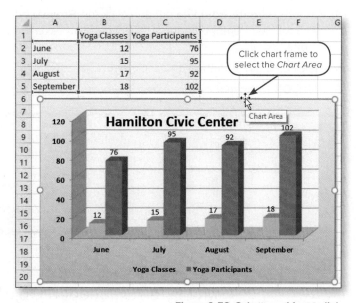

Figure 9-53 Select an object to link

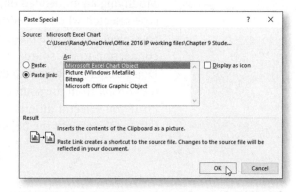

Figure 9-54 *Paste link* using the *Paste Special* dialog box

---

> ### ANOTHER WAY
> Select from one of the *Paste Options* available in the *Paste* drop-down list or context menu.

Open a Document Linked to an Object

When opening a document containing one or more linked objects, a dialog box opens and prompts you to update the links in the document, which updates the linked content in the destination file to match the content in the source file (Figure 9-55). Click **Yes** to update the link(s).

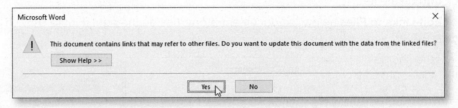

Modify the size, text wrapping, and arrangement of a linked object the same way you modify other graphic objects. In addition, you can modify the content of the linked object, modify the links in the document, or break the link between the linked object and the source file.

Modify Linked Object Content

A linked object in a Word document links directly to the source file. When you edit the linked object, the source file opens, and you can edit it. When you save the source file, the linked object in the destination file updates to reflect the current data from the source file.

▶ HOW TO: Modify Linked Object Content

1. Double-click the linked object to open the source program and file.
   - Alternatively, right-click the linked object, select **Linked [object type] Object**, and select **Edit Link** or **Open Link** to open the source program and file (Figure 9-56).
2. Edit the source file.
3. Save and close the source file.
   - Because both files are open, the linked object updates. If the linked object does not update, right-click the linked object and select **Update Link** from the context menu.

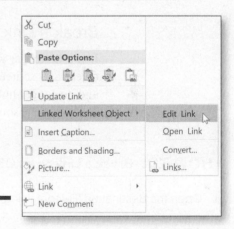

Figure 9-56 *Edit Link* from the context menu

You can also change the source file when the destination file is not open. When opening the destination file with the linked object, Word prompts you to update the linked object.

Modify a Link to an Object

A linked object in the destination file links to the source file on your computer. If you change the location of the source or destination file, Word cannot find the source file to update the linked object in the destination file. Edit the link to the destination file using the *Links* dialog box.

▶ **HOW TO:** Modify a Link to an Object

1. Open the destination file.
   - Word prompts you to update links in the document; click **Yes** to update links.
2. Click the **File** tab to open the *Backstage* view.
3. Click **Info** on the left.
4. Click **Edit Links to Files** below the document properties on the right (Figure 9-57). The *Links* dialog box opens (Figure 9-58).
5. Select the source file of the linked object in the *Source file* area.
   - If you have multiple linked objects in a document, multiple source files display in the *Source file* area.

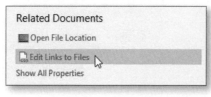

Figure 9-57 *Edit Links to Files* on the *Backstage* view

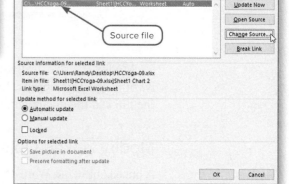

Figure 9-58 Change the source file in the *Links* dialog box

6. Click the **Change Source** button to open the *Change Source* dialog box.
7. Select the source file for the linked object and click **Open** to update the link and to close the *Change Source* dialog box.
8. Click **OK** to close the *Links* dialog box.
9. Click the **Back** arrow to return to the document.

Break a Link to an Object

If you no longer want a linked object to connect to the source file, break the link between the object and source file. When you do this, the linked object converts to an embedded object and no longer links directly to the source file. You can modify the embedded object without modifying the source file.

▶ **HOW TO:** Break a Link to an Object

1. Open the destination file containing the linked object.
2. Click the **File** tab to open the *Backstage* view.
3. Click the **Info** button on the left.
4. Click **Edit Links to Files** (see Figure 9-57). The *Links* dialog box opens (see Figure 9-58).
5. Select the source file of the linked object in the *Source file* area.
   - If you have multiple linked objects in a document, multiple source files display in the *Source file* area.
6. Click the **Break Link** button (see Figure 9-58). A dialog box opens confirming you want to break the selected link (Figure 9-59).
7. Click **Yes**. The *Links* dialog box closes automatically.
8. Click the **Back** arrow to return to the document.

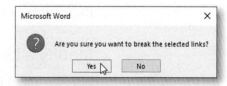

Figure 9-59 Confirm breaking links

PAUSE & PRACTICE: WORD 9-3

For this Pause & Practice project, you modify the document from *Pause & Practice 9-2*. You remove the document password and protection, insert a PowerPoint slide as an embedded object, modify the embedded object, insert an Excel chart as a linked object, and modify the linked object.

Files Needed: *[your initials] PP W9-2.docx*, *YogaPPT-09.pptx*, and *HCCYoga-09.xlsx* (*Student data files are available in the* Library *of your SIMnet account.*)
Completed Project File Name: *[your initials] PP W9-3.docx* and *[your initials] HCCYoga-09.xlsx*

---

1. Open the *[your initials] PP W9-2* document you saved in *Pause & Practice 9-2*.

2. Type HCC when prompted to enter a password and click **OK**. The open document is marked as final.

3. Click the **Edit Anyway** button on the *Info* bar to turn off *Mark as Final*.

4. Save the document as [your initials] PP W9-3.

5. Remove the document encryption password and disable restrict editing.
    a. Click the **File** tab to open the *Backstage* view.
    b. Click the **Protect Document** button and select **Encrypt with Password** to open the *Encrypt Document* dialog box (Figure 9-60).
    c. Delete the password in the *Password* text box and click **OK**.
    d. Click the **Protect Document** button again and select **Restrict Editing**. The *Restrict Editing* pane opens on the right.
    e. Click the **Stop Protection** button, type HCC in the *Password* text box, and click **OK**.
    f. Close the *Restrict Editing* pane.

Figure 9-60 Remove document encryption password

6. Insert a PowerPoint slide as an embedded object.
    a. Open your student data files from a *File Explorer* window and double-click **YogaPPT-09.pptx** to open this file in PowerPoint. Click the **Enable Editing** button on the *Message* bar if the file opens in *Protected* view.
    b. Select **slide 3** on the left in the *Slides* area, **copy** the slide from the *Slides* area, and close PowerPoint.
    c. Place the insertion point at the end of the third body paragraph in the *[your initials] PP W9-3* document.
    d. Click the bottom half of the **Paste** button [*Home* tab, *Clipboard* group] and select **Paste Special** to open the *Paste Special* dialog box (Figure 9-61).

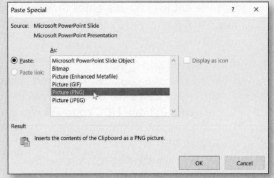

Figure 9-61 Paste embedded object

e. Click the **Paste** radio button.

f. Select **Picture (PNG)** in the *As* area.

g. Click **OK** to close the dialog box and to insert the slide as an embedded object.

7. Resize and position the embedded object.

a. Select the object and change the *Height* to **2.5"** [*Picture Tools Format* tab, *Size* group]. The width automatically changes.

b. Change the *Position* to **Position in Middle Right with Square Text Wrapping**.

c. Save the document.

8. Insert an Excel chart as a linked object.

a. Open your student data files from a *File Explorer* window and double-click **HCCYoga-09.xlsx** to open this worksheet in Excel. Click the **Enable Editing** button on the *Message* bar if the file opens in *Protected* view.

b. Save this file to your desktop and name it [your initials] HCCYoga-09.xlsx.

c. Select the frame of the chart to select the *Chart Area* (Figure 9-62) and **copy** the chart.

d. Return to your *[your initials] PP W9-3* document and place the insertion point at the end of the third body paragraph.

e. Press **Alt+Ctrl+V** to open the *Paste Special* dialog box (Figure 9-63).

f. Click the **Paste link** radio button.

g. Select **Microsoft Excel Chart Object** in the *As* area.

h. Click **OK** to close the dialog box and insert the chart as a linked object.

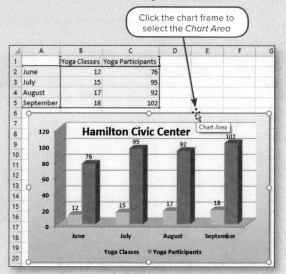

Figure 9-62 Select chart to copy

9. Modify the size, text wrapping, and position of the embedded chart.

a. Right-click the chart and select **Picture** to open the *Format Object* dialog box.

b. Click the **Size** tab, change the *Height* **Absolute** size to **2.8"**, and press **Tab**. The width automatically adjusts.

c. Click the **Layout** tab and click the **Advanced** button to open the *Layout* dialog box.

d. Select **Tight** on the **Text Wrapping** tab.

e. Click the **Position** tab and change the *Horizontal* **Alignment** to **Centered** *relative to* **Margin**.

f. Change the *Vertical* **Alignment** to **Bottom** *relative to* **Margin**.

g. Click **OK** to close the *Layout* dialog box.

h. Click **OK** to close the *Format Object* dialog box.

i. Save the document.

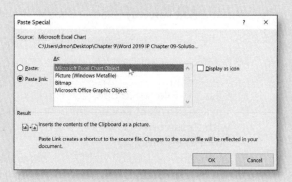

Figure 9-63 Paste link to an object

10. Modify linked object content.

a. Right-click the chart, select **Linked Worksheet Object**, and select **Edit Link** (or **Open Link**) to open the source file (*[your initials] HCCYoga-09.xlsx*) in Excel.

b. Change the number of *Yoga Classes* in *September* to 20 (cell **B5**).

c. Change the *Yoga Participants* in *September* to 115 (cell **C5**) (Figure 9-64).

d. Save the Excel worksheet and leave the file open.

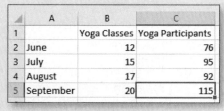

Figure 9-64 Change data in the source file

e. Return to the Word document, right-click the linked chart in the Word document, and select **Update Link** from the context menu. The values in the chart update to reflect the changed data in the source file.

f. Save the Word file.

11. Break the link between the linked chart and the source file.

Figure 9-65 Break link to source file

a. Click the **File** tab to open the *Info* area on *Backstage* view and select **Edit Links to Files** (near the bottom right) to open the *Links* dialog box (Figure 9-65).

b. Click the **Break Link** button. A dialog box opens confirming you want to break the selected link.

c. Click **Yes** to break the link to the source file.

d. Click the **Back** arrow to return to the document.

12. Save and close the Word document (Figure 9-66). Also, save and close the Excel file.

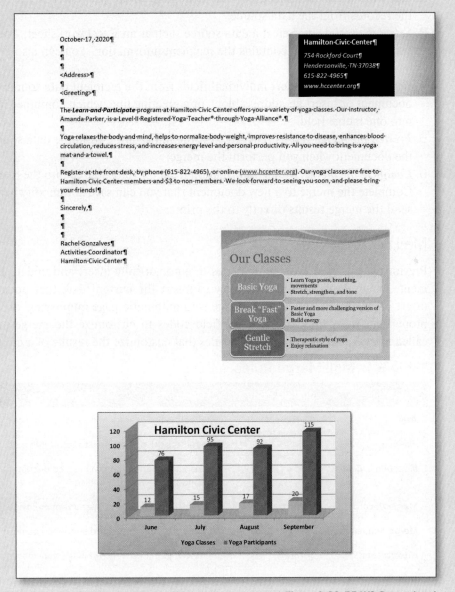
Figure 9-66 PP W9-3 completed

Using Mail Merge Rules

In chapter 5, you learned about mail merge and how to merge information from other Microsoft Office applications into a Word document (*SLO 5.4: Understanding Mail Merge*, *SLO 5.5: Merging Using the Mailing Tab*, and *SLO 5.6: Using the Mail Merge Wizard*). In chapter 6, you learned how to insert custom content into a document using Word field codes (*SLO 6.6: Using Document Properties and Word Fields*). This section reviews the merge process and presents advanced merge features using rules. Use rules, which are Word merge field codes, to customize and control the merge process.

Mail Merge Review

When merging content into a Word document, use the *Mailings* tab or the *Mail Merge Wizard* to create and customize the merge. The following are the six steps in the merge process:

1. *Select the type of merge*: Create merged letters, email messages, envelopes, labels, or a directory.
2. *Select the document*: Select the main document where you insert merge fields and merge the records from the data source.
3. *Select the recipients*: Select a data source such as an Excel worksheet, Access database, or Outlook contacts that contains the recipient information. You can also create and save a new data source.
4. *Insert merge fields*: Insert individual fields from the recipient data source into the main document or insert an address block or a greeting line, which combines individual fields into one merge field.
5. *Preview the merge results*: Display how the information from the data source will appear in the document when you perform the merge.
6. *Complete the merge*: Merge information from the data source into the main document. Complete the merge to a new document that you can save and modify before printing or send the merge results directly to the printer.

Mail Merge Rules

Previously, you used Word field codes to automatically insert and update content in a document. For example, you learned how to insert the current date that updates automatically, insert index entries and an index page with automatic page numbering, and insert document properties. You can also use Word field codes to customize the merge process, which are called *rules*. Table 9-1 describes the rules that customize the results of a merge:

Table 9-1: Mail Merge Rules

Rule	Field Code	Description
Ask	*Ask*	Prompts the user for text to assign to a bookmark
Fill-in	*Fill-in*	Prompts the user for text to insert into a document
If. . .Then. . .Else	*If*	Displays information in a merged document based on a logical condition being true or false
Merge Record #	*MergeRec*	Inserts the number of the current merge record
Merge Sequence #	*MergeSeq*	Inserts the merge record sequence number
Next Record	*Next*	Moves to the next record in the mail merge
Next Record If	*NextIf*	Moves to the next record in the mail merge if a condition is met
Set Bookmark	*Set*	Assigns new text to a bookmark
Skip Record If	*SkipIf*	Skips a record in the mail merge if a condition is met

For example, when creating a merged document, use the *If. . .Then. . .Else* rule to insert a specific sentence if the recipient is a member of the club and insert a different sentence if the recipient is not currently a member. Or, when creating a targeted mailing, use the *Skip Record If* rule to skip all records of individuals who do not live in a specific city.

Use the *Rules* button in the *Write & Insert Fields* group on the *Mailings* tab to insert merge rules into the main document or use the *Field* dialog box to insert a merge rule field.

> **HOW TO: Add a Rule to a Mail Merge**

1. Place the insertion point in the main mail merge document at the location to insert the rule.
   - Word populates the merge rule fields sequentially in your document starting at the beginning, so it is important to place the rule in the correct location.
2. Click the **Rules** button [*Mailings* tab, *Write & Insert Fields* group] and select the rule to insert (Figure 9-67). The *Insert Word Field: [Rule]* dialog box opens (Figure 9-68).
3. Enter the conditions for the rule.
   - Depending on the rule you insert, you may not need to fill in all conditions of the rule.
4. Click **OK** to close the dialog box and to insert the rule (field code).
   - Some field codes are hidden and do not display in the document. In the next section, you learn how to view field codes in a document.

Figure 9-67 Insert rule

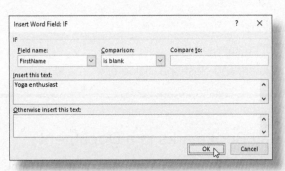

Figure 9-68 *Insert Word Field: IF* dialog box

View Merge Field Codes

Field codes display different from regular text and some field codes are hidden. For example, index field codes only appear when *Show/Hide* is turned on, property field codes display the text of the document property, and an address block field code displays "<<AddressBlock>>". The following are two ways to view field codes in a document:

- *View all field codes*: Press **Alt+F9** (Figure 9-69). **Alt+F9** toggles field codes display on/off.
- *View an individual field code*: Right-click the field and select **Toggle Field Codes** from the context menu. Repeat to toggle off the field code.

When editing a document, it is helpful to see the location of field codes. Delete or move field codes the same way you delete and move text or objects in your document.

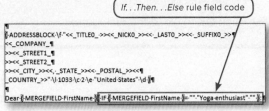

Figure 9-69 View codes for merge fields

SLO 9.5   Using Bookmarks

When working with documents, use a ***bookmark*** to mark a specific location, selected text, or an object in the document. After inserting a bookmark, create a hyperlink or a cross-reference to the bookmark to quickly move to this location in the document, or index the bookmark to include it on the index page.

Add a Bookmark

Add a bookmark in a Word document to mark a specific location, a word, selected text, or an object.

▶ **HOW TO:** Add a Bookmark

1. Position the insertion point at the location to insert a bookmark or select the text to bookmark.
2. Click the **Insert** tab.
3. Click the **Bookmark** button [*Links* group] to open the *Bookmark* dialog box (Figure 9-70).
4. Type the name of the bookmark.
   - Bookmark names cannot contain spaces.
5. Click **Add** to add the bookmark and close the dialog box.

Figure 9-70 *Bookmark* dialog box

Display Bookmarks in a Document

By default, bookmarks are not visible in a document. Display bookmarks in a document by changing a setting in the ***Word Options*** dialog box.

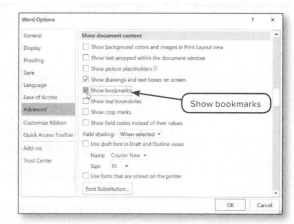

▶ **HOW TO:** Display Bookmarks in a Document

1. Click the **File** tab to open the *Backstage* view.
2. Click the **Options** button on the left to open the *Word Options* dialog box.
3. Select **Advanced** on the left of the *Word Options* dialog box (Figure 9-71).
4. Check the **Show bookmarks** check box in the *Show document content* area.
5. Click **OK** to close the dialog box.

Figure 9-71 Display bookmarks in document

When bookmarks display in a document, a gray I-beam marks the specific location of the bookmark (Figure 9-72), and gray brackets mark selected text (Figure 9-73).

Figure 9-72 Bookmark at specific location in the document

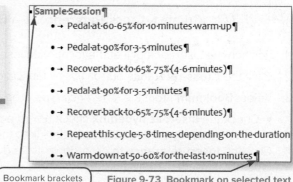

Figure 9-73 Bookmark on selected text

Bookmark brackets

Go To a Bookmark

The following are methods to quickly move to a bookmark in your document:

- *Insert Bookmark* [*Insert* tab, *Links* group]: Open the *Bookmark* dialog box, select the bookmark, and click **Go To**.
- *Find and Replace*: Click the **Find** drop-down arrow [*Home* tab, *Editing* group] and select the **Go To** tab. Select **Bookmark** in the *Go to what* area, select the bookmark, and click **Go To** (Figure 9-74).

Figure 9-74 Use *Go To* to find a selected bookmark

Hyperlink to a Bookmark

Create a *hyperlink* in your document that takes the reader to the bookmark.

> **HOW TO: Create a Hyperlink to a Bookmark**
>
> 1. Select the text on which to create a hyperlink to a bookmark.
> 2. Click the top half of the **Link** button [*Insert* tab, *Links* group] to open the *Insert Hyperlink* dialog box (Figure 9-75).
>   - Alternatively, press **Ctrl+K** or click the **Link** drop-down list and select **Insert Link** to open the *Insert Hyperlink* dialog box.
> 3. Choose **Place in This Document** in the *Link to* area.
> 4. Select the bookmark.
> 5. Click **OK** to insert the hyperlink and to close the dialog box.
>   - The hyperlinked text is blue and underlined.
>   - Press **Ctrl** and click the hyperlink to move to the bookmark.

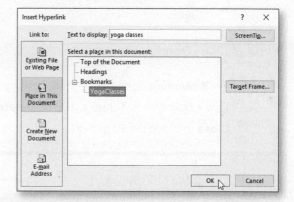

Figure 9-75 Insert a hyperlink to a bookmark

Cross-Reference a Bookmark

You can also *cross-reference* a bookmark. For example, insert a page number that references a bookmark at another location in the document ("Schedule rest days (*see page 3*)"). When a cross-reference page number links to a bookmark, the page number automatically updates if the bookmarked text moves to a different page.

▶HOW TO: Create a Cross-Reference to a Bookmark

1. Position the insertion point at the location to insert the cross-reference to a bookmark.
2. Click the **Cross-reference** button [*Insert* tab, *Links* group]. The *Cross-reference* dialog box opens (Figure 9-76).
3. Select **Bookmark** from the *Reference type* drop-down list.
   - Check the **Insert as hyperlink** check box to enable the cross-reference to function as a hyperlink to the bookmark.
4. Click the **Insert reference to** drop-down list and select the type of reference.
   - Insert a reference to a page number, the bookmarked text, or the words "above" or "below."
   - If you choose *Page number*, you can also include the words "above" or "below" after the page number (for example, *"see page 3 above"*).
5. Select the bookmark in the *For which bookmark* area.
6. Click **Insert** to insert the cross-reference.
7. Click **Close** to close the dialog box.

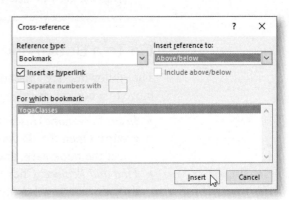

Figure 9-76 Insert a cross-reference to a bookmark

Use a Bookmark in a Formula

Bookmarks can also be variables in formulas. If a bookmark in a document is a value, you can insert the bookmark into a formula. Click the **Paste bookmark** drop-down list in the *Formula* dialog box to display the available bookmarks in your document.

Delete a Bookmark

When a bookmark is no longer needed in a document, delete the bookmark. After deleting a bookmark from a document, Word does not remove hyperlinks or cross-references associated with this bookmark. You must manually remove a hyperlink or cross-reference to a bookmark.

▶HOW TO: Delete a Bookmark

1. Click the **Bookmark** button [*Insert* tab, *Links* group]. The *Bookmark* dialog box opens.
2. Select the bookmark to delete and click **Delete**.
3. Click **Close** to close the *Bookmark* dialog box.

PAUSE & PRACTICE: WORD 9-4

For this Pause & Practice project, you add a bookmark, create a hyperlink and cross-reference to the bookmark, and merge the document from *Pause & Practice 9-3* with recipient data from an Excel worksheet. You select the type of merge, select recipients, insert merge fields, sort records, create rules, and share the document with your instructor.

Files Needed: **[your initials] PP W9-3.docx** and **HCCAddresses-09.xlsx** (Student data files are available in the Library of your SIMnet account.)
Completed Project File Names: **[your initials] PP W9-4.docx** and **[your initials] PP W9-4 merged.docx**

1. Open the **[your initials] PP W9-3** you completed in *Pause & Practice 9-3*.

2. Save the document as [your initials] PP W9-4.

3. Add a bookmark and display bookmarks in a document.
   a. Click the picture of the PowerPoint slide on the middle-right side of the document.
   b. Click the **Bookmark** button [*Insert* tab, *Links* group] to open the *Bookmark* dialog box (Figure 9-77).
   c. Type YogaClasses in the *Bookmark name* text box (no space between words).
   d. Click **Add** to add the bookmark.
   e. Click the **File** tab to open the *Backstage* view.
   f. Click **Options** to open the *Word Options* dialog box and click **Advanced** on the left.
   g. Check the **Show bookmarks** box in the *Show document content* area (Figure 9-78).
   h. Click **OK** to close the *Word Options* dialog box. The bookmark indicators display at the end of the last body paragraph in the letter.
   i. Click the PowerPoint slide picture (if necessary), drag the picture anchor from the beginning of the last body paragraph to "Sincerely," and notice how the bookmark indicator moves.

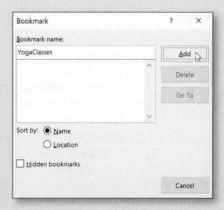

Figure 9-77 Add a bookmark

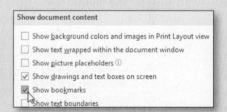

Figure 9-78 Show bookmarks in the document

4. Insert a hyperlink to a bookmark.
   a. Select "**yoga classes**" in the first sentence in the first body paragraph.
   b. Click the top half of the **Link** button [*Insert* tab, *Links* group] to open the *Insert Hyperlink* dialog box (Figure 9-79).
   c. Click **Place in This Document** on the left.
   d. Select the **YogaClasses** bookmark. If needed, click the plus sign (**+**) to the left of *Bookmarks* to display the bookmark.
   e. Click the **ScreenTip** button, type Types of yoga classes as the *ScreenTip*, and click **OK** to close the *Set Hyperlink ScreenTip* dialog box.
   f. Click **OK** to insert the hyperlink to the bookmark.

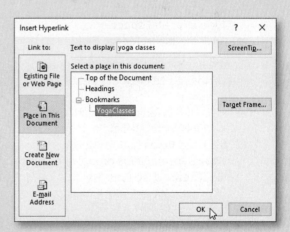

Figure 9-79 Insert a hyperlink to a bookmark

5. Insert a cross-reference to a bookmark.
   a. Place the insertion point after the "yoga classes" hyperlink and **space** once.
   b. Type (see and **space** once.
   c. Click the **Cross-reference** button [*Insert* tab, *Links* group] to open the *Cross-reference* dialog box (Figure 9-80).
   d. Click the **Reference type** drop-down list and select **Bookmark**.
   e. Check the **Insert as hyperlink** box (if necessary) and select **YogaClasses** in the *For which bookmark* area.
   f. Click the **Insert reference to** drop-down list and select **Above/below**.

g. Click **Insert** and then click **Close**.

h. Type **)** after "below" and before the period. Confirm proper spacing before and after the text in parentheses.

i. Save the document.

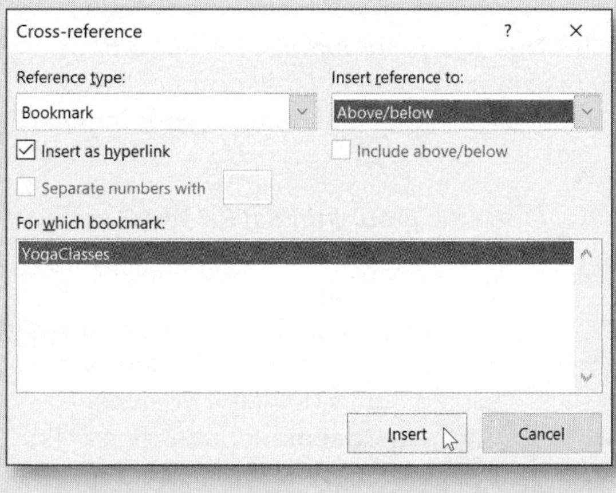

6. Start the mail merge, select recipients, and sort records.

   a. Click the **Start Mail Merge** button [*Mailings tab, Start Mail Merge* group] and select **Letters**.

   b. Click the **Select Recipients** button and select **Use an Existing List** to open the *Select Data Source* dialog box.

   c. Select the ***HCCAddresses-09*** file from your student data files and click **Open**. The *Select Table* dialog box opens.

   d. Select **MailingList** and click **OK**.

   e. Click the **Edit Recipient List** button to open the *Mail Merge Recipients* dialog box.

   f. Click the **LastName** column heading drop-down arrow, select **Sort Ascending**, and click **OK** to close the dialog box.

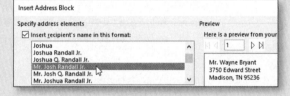

Figure 9-80 Insert a cross-reference to a bookmark

7. Insert an address block and greeting line field codes.

   a. Turn on **Show/Hide** if it is not already on.

   b. Select the **"<Address>"** placeholder and brackets and delete it. Don't delete the paragraph mark after the text.

   c. Click the **Address Block** button [*Mailings* tab, *Write & Insert Fields* group] to open the *Insert Address Block* dialog box (Figure 9-81).

   d. Select **Mr. Josh Randall Jr.** as the recipient's name format and click **OK** to close the dialog box and insert the address block.

   e. Select the **"<Greeting>"** placeholder and brackets and delete it. Don't delete the paragraph mark after the text.

   f. Type **Dear** and **space** once.

   g. Click the **Insert Merge Field** drop-down arrow, select **FirstName**, and type a colon (:).

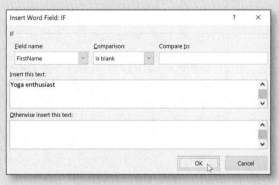

Figure 9-81 Insert *Address Block* merge field

8. Create a rule to insert a custom greeting if the recipient's first name is not available in the data source.

   a. Place the insertion point after the *<<FirstName>>* field and before the colon.

   b. Click the **Rules** button [*Mailings* tab, *Write & Insert Fields* group] and select **If. . .Then. . .Else** from the drop-down list. The *Insert Word Field: IF* dialog box opens (Figure 9-82).

   c. Click the **Field name** drop-down list and select **FirstName**.

   d. Click the **Comparison** drop-down list and select **is blank**.

   e. Type **Yoga enthusiast** in the *Insert this text* area.

   f. Click **OK** to close the dialog box and to insert the rule. This is a hidden field code and is visible only when field codes display.

Figure 9-82 Insert *If. . .Then. . .Else* rule

g. Press **Alt+F9** to display field codes in the document and confirm that the *If* field code is between the <<*FirstName*>> field and the colon. If you are using a laptop computer, you may have to press **Fn+Alt+F9**.

h. Press **Alt+F9** (or **Fn+Alt+F9**) again to toggle off field codes.

9. Create a rule to merge only those recipients from the city of Hendersonville.

a. Place the insertion point in front of the <<*AddressBlock*>> field.

b. Click the **Rules** button and select **Skip Record If** from the drop-down list. The *Insert Word Field: Skip Record If* dialog box opens (Figure 9-83).

c. Click the **Field name** drop-down list and select **City**.

d. Click the **Comparison** drop-down list and select **Not equal to**.

e. Type Hendersonville in the *Compare to* area.

f. Click **OK** to close the dialog box and to insert the rule. The rule displays in front of the <<*AddressBlock*>> field code.

Figure 9-83 Insert *Skip Record If* rule

10. Create a rule to insert a custom sentence based on each recipient's membership status.

a. Delete the last sentence in the last body paragraph of the letter ("We look forward . . ."). Don't delete the paragraph mark after the sentence.

b. Confirm that the insertion point is after the space after the period at the end of the third body paragraph.

c. Click the **Rules** button and select **If. . .Then. . .Else** from the drop-down list. The *Insert Word Field: IF* dialog box opens (Figure 9-84).

Figure 9-84 Insert *If. . .Then. . .Else* rule

d. Click the **Field name** drop-down list and select **MembershipDate**.

e. Click the **Comparison** drop-down list and select **is not blank**.

f. Type We look forward to seeing you again in our yoga classes. Next time you come, please feel free to bring your friends who are not yet members. in the *Insert this text* area.

g. Type We hope you will try one or more of our yoga classes. in the *Otherwise insert this text* area.

h. Click **OK** to close the dialog box and insert the rule. If the condition is true, the sentence displays in the document (see step 10f). When the document is merged, this sentence will change if the condition is false (no membership date).

11. Select the date line (first line of the document) and apply **18 pt** *Before* paragraph spacing.

12. Preview and finish the merge.
    a. Click the **Preview Results** button [*Mailings* tab, *Preview Results* group] to preview the merged document. *(Note: The* Skip Record If *rule is not applied until you finish the merge.)*
    b. Click the **Next Record** button [*Mailings* tab, *Preview Results* group] to preview the letters in the merge.
    c. Click the **Preview Results** button again to hide the recipient information and display the merge field codes.
    d. Save the document.
    e. Click the **Finish & Merge** button [*Mailings* tab, *Finish* group] and select **Edit Individual Documents**. The *Merge to New Document* dialog box opens.
    f. Click the **All** radio button and click **OK** to finish the merge. A new document opens, and the recipient information merges into the document. The document should contain four letters.

13. Save the merged document as [your initials] PP W9-4 merged (see Figure 9-87).

14. Share the document with your instructor.
    a. Save this document on *OneDrive* if you haven't already. If you don't have the ability to save to *OneDrive*, skip all of step 14.
    b. Click the **Share** button in the upper-right corner of the Word window to open the *Send Link* window (Figure 9-85). If you're using a personal Microsoft account, the *Share* pane displays on the right, and the sharing options differ slightly.
    c. Click the **Link settings** button to open the *Link settings* window (Figure 9-86).
    d. Click the **Anyone** button and check the **Allow editing** box (if necessary).
    e. Click **Apply** to close the *Link settings* window and return to the *Send Link* window.
    f. Type your instructor's email address in the *Enter a name or email address* area (see Figure 9-85).
    g. Type a brief message to your instructor and click the **Send** button.
    h. Click the **X** in the upper-right corner of the confirmation window to close it.

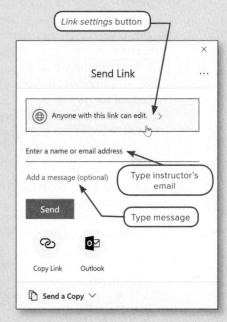

Figure 9-85 *Send Link* window

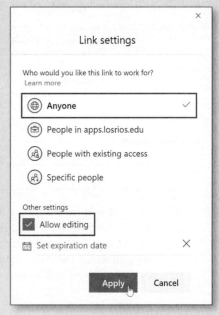

Figure 9-86 *Link settings* window

15. Save and close both documents (Figure 9-87).

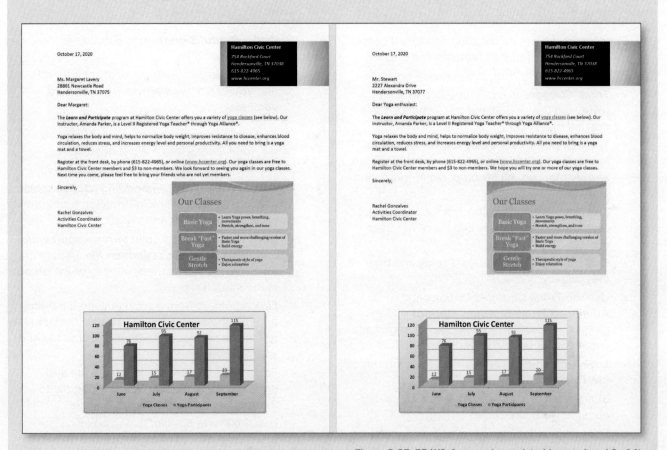

Figure 9-87 PP W9-4 merged completed (pages 1 and 2 of 4)

Chapter Summary

9.1 Enhance collaboration by using advanced comments and track changes features and sharing documents (p. W9-546).

- *Track Changes* is a collaboration tool that reviewers use to edit and track changes in a document.
- The four different *Display for Review* views to display tracked changes in a document are *Simple Markup*, *All Markup*, *No Markup*, and *Original*.
- Each change made using *Track Changes* is attributed to a reviewer and his or her user name.
- Customize which markups display and how they display.
- Use the *Track Changes Options* and *Advanced Track Changes Options* dialog boxes to customize how tracked changes and comments appear in your document.
- *Lock Tracking* prevents others from turning off the *Track Changes* feature.
- Share and collaborate with others by saving documents to OneDrive.
- *Real-time collaboration* immediately displays changes made to a shared document by multiple users.
- When printing a document, you can choose to print comments and markup.

9.2 Use Word collaboration features to compare, combine, and protect documents (p. W9-553).

- The *Compare* feature compares two versions of a document and displays the differences as tracked changes.
- The *Combine* feature combines two versions of a document.
- Word provides the following features to prepare your document for sharing with others: *Inspect Document*, *Check Accessibility*, and *Check Compatibility*.
- *Mark as Final* marks the document as a final version and protects it from editing.
- *Encrypt with Password* requires users to enter a password to open a document.
- Use *Restrict Editing* to control the type of changes made to a document. Restrict all editing or allow users to use comments, track changes, or fill in forms.

- *Add a Digital Signature* to a document to enhance security.
- Word autosaves documents at set intervals, and you can access previous *autosaved versions*.

9.3 Embed and link content from other Microsoft Office applications into a Word document (p. W9-565).

- *Object linking and embedding (OLE)* enables users to embed or link information from other Office applications into Word.
- Copy an embedded object from a *source file* and paste it into a *destination file*. Modify an embedded object independently of the object in the source file.
- *Link* an object from a source file to a destination file; the linked object in the destination file retains its connection with the source file and source program.
- Edit a linked object in the source file and update the object in the destination file to reflect the changes in the source file.
- Use the *Paste Special* dialog box to paste an embedded or linked object into the destination file.
- The process for resizing, arranging, or modifying embedded or linked objects in a Word document is similar to working with pictures, charts, *SmartArt*, or shapes.
- Modify or break the link between the object in the source and destination files.

9.4 Use mail merge rules to customize how data merges into a Word document from other Office applications (p. W9-574).

- Use mail merge to merge recipient information from other Office applications into a Word document.
- *Rules* are Word field codes that customize the output of a mail merge.
- View Word field codes in a document by pressing **Alt+F9**.

9.5 Insert bookmarks into a document (p. W9-576).

- Use a *bookmark* to mark a specific location or selected text in a document.
- Use the *Word Options* dialog box to control how bookmarks display in your documents.

- Use **Go To** to move to a bookmark in the document.
- Add a ***hyperlink*** to a bookmark to take users to the bookmark when they click the hyperlink.
- Press **Ctrl** and click a hyperlink to navigate to the linked area or object.
- Add a ***cross-reference*** to a bookmark to provide the page number or location of the bookmark in a document.

Check for Understanding

The SIMbook for this text (within your SIMnet account) provides the following resources for concept review:

- Multiple-choice questions
- Short answer questions
- Matching exercises

Guided Project 9-1

For this project, you edit a document from Kelly Sung at Life's Animal Shelter. You change how markup displays, accept and reject changes, review comments, edit the document, link and format slides from a PowerPoint presentation, finalize the document, and share the file with your instructor.
[Student Learning Outcomes 9.1, 9.2, 9.3]

Files Needed: ***LASSupportLetter-09.docx*** and ***LASSupportPPT-09.pptx*** *(Student data files are available in the* Library *of your SIMnet account.)*
Completed Project File Names: ***[your initials] Word 9-1.docx*** and ***[your initials] LASSupportPPT-09.pptx***

Skills Covered in This Project

- Change user name and initials.
- Change how markup displays.
- Change the color of insertions, deletions, and comments.
- Turn on *Track Changes* and edit a document.
- Review and delete comments.
- Reject and accept tracked changes.
- Insert the current date.
- Change the display for *Review* view.

- Accept and reject changes in a document.
- Link slides from a PowerPoint presentation to a Word document.
- Update text in a source file.
- Update a linked object in a destination file.
- Break links in the document.
- Resize and align pictures.
- Inspect a document and remove information.
- Mark a document as final.
- Share a file.

1. Open the ***LASSupportLetter-09*** document from your student data files.

2. Save the document as [your initials] Word 9-1.

3. Change user name and initials. Skip the following steps if your user name and initials are already in Word.
    a. Click the **Tracking** launcher [*Review* tab, *Tracking* group] to open the *Track Changes Options* dialog box.
    b. Click the **Change User Name** button to open the *Word Options* dialog box.
    c. Type your first and last name in the *User name* text box, type your initials in lowercase letters in the *Initials* text box, and check the **Always use these values regardless of sign in to Office** box.
    d. Click **OK** to close the *Word Options* dialog box and click **OK** to close the *Track Changes Options* dialog box.

4. Change how markup displays and the color of comments and markup.
    a. Click the **Display for Review** drop-down list [*Review* tab, *Tracking* group] and select **All Markup**.
    b. Click the **Show Markup** drop-down list [*Review* tab, *Tracking* group], click **Balloons**, and select **Show Revisions in Balloons**.
    c. Click the **Tracking** launcher to open the *Track Changes Options* dialog box.
    d. Click **Advanced Options** to open the *Advanced Track Changes Options* dialog box.

e. Change the *Color* of *Insertions*, *Deletions*, and *Comments* to **Red** (Figure 9-88).

f. Click **OK** to close the *Advanced Track Changes Options* dialog box and click **OK** to close the *Track Changes Options* dialog box.

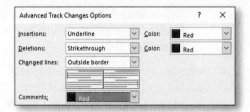

Figure 9-88 Change the color of insertions, deletions, and comments

5. Review comments and edit the document.

   a. Click the top half of the **Track Changes** button [*Review* tab, *Tracking* group] to turn on *Track Changes*.

   b. Click the **Next** button [*Review* tab, *Comments* group] to move to the first comment.

   c. Read the comment and click the top half of the **Delete** button [*Review* tab, *Comments* group] to delete the comment.

   d. Select "**[Insert Current Date]**", delete it, and insert the current date so it updates automatically. Use January 1, 2020 as the format for the date.

   e. Click the **Next** button [*Review* tab, *Comments* group] to move to the next comment and read the comment.

   f. Right-click the comment in the *Markup* area and select **Delete Comment**.

6. Accept and reject tracked changes.

   a. Click the top half of the **Track Changes** button to turn off *Track Changes*.

   b. Move to the top of the document (**Ctrl+Home**).

   c. Click the **Display for Review** drop-down list [*Review* tab, *Tracking* group] and select **No Markup** to display the final document with proposed changes accepted.

   d. Click the **Display for Review** drop-down list again and select **All Markup**.

   e. Click the **Next** button [*Review* tab, *Changes* group] to move to where the words "Kelly Sung," (including comma) were deleted. You have to click the **Next** button more than once to get to this deletion.

   f. Click the top half of the **Reject** button [*Review* tab, *Changes* group] to reject the deletion of the words "Kelly Sung,".

   g. Click the bottom half of the **Accept** button and select **Accept All Changes** to accept the remaining changes in the document.

7. Link slides from a PowerPoint presentation to the Word document.

   a. Open a *File Explorer* window, browse to your student data files, and open the ***LASSupportPPT-09.pptx*** PowerPoint presentation. Click the **Enable Editing** button on the *Message* bar if the file opens in *Protected* view.

   b. Save this file to your desktop and name it [your initials] LASSupportPPT-09.

   c. Select **slide 5** in the *Navigation* pane on the left and **copy** it.

   d. Return to your Word document and place the insertion point on the blank line below the last body paragraph. Turn on **Show/Hide** if necessary.

   e. Click the bottom half of the **Paste** button [*Home* tab, *Clipboard* group] and select **Paste Special** to open the *Paste Special* dialog box (Figure 9-89).

   f. Click the **Paste link** radio button, select **Microsoft PowerPoint Slide Object** in the *As* area, and click **OK** to insert the linked slide. The slide is placed on page 2; you will fix this later.

   g. Place the insertion point on the bottom right of the linked slide and press **Enter** once.

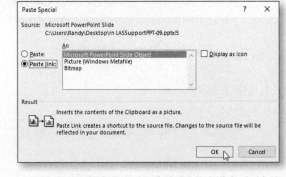

Figure 9-89 Paste copied slide as a linked object

h. Select **slide 6** in the PowerPoint file and **copy** it.
i. Return to the Word document, place the insertion point on the blank line below the first slide, and **Paste link** (repeat step 7f).

8. Modify content on the linked slides.
   a. Return to the PowerPoint presentation and select **slide 5** on the left.
   b. Select the title ("**Ways to Donate**") in the working area of PowerPoint (on the slide) and change the text to Donate to Life's Animal Shelter (Figure 9-90).

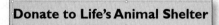

Donate to Life's Animal Shelter

Figure 9-90 Edit the slide title in the source file

   c. Select **slide 6** and change the title of the slide to Volunteer with Life's Animal Shelter.
   d. Save the PowerPoint presentation and leave it open.
   e. Return to the Word document, right-click the first slide, and select **Update Link** from the context menu. The title updates.
   f. Right-click the second slide and select **Update Link** from the context menu.
   g. Return to the PowerPoint presentation, save the presentation, and close PowerPoint.

9. Break the links between the source and destination files.
   a. Return to the Word document, click the **File** tab to open the *Backstage* view, and click **Info** on the left if it is not already selected.
   b. Click the **Edit Links to Files** button to open the *Links* dialog box (Figure 9-91).

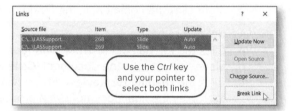

Figure 9-91 Break links using the *Links* dialog box

   c. Press the **Ctrl** key and click both of the items in the *Source file* area to select both items.
   d. Click the **Break Link** button. A dialog box opens confirming you want to break the selected links.
   e. Select **Yes** to break the links.
   f. Click the **Back** arrow to return to the document.

10. Format the slide pictures in the document.
    a. Select the first slide and change the *Height* to **2.5"** [*Picture Tools Format* tab, *Size* group]. The width automatically adjusts.
    b. Select the second slide and change the *Height* to **2.5"**.
    c. Click the first slide and click the **Center** alignment button [*Home* tab, *Paragraph* group].
    d. **Center** the second slide. Both slides display on the first page.

11. Save the document.

12. Inspect the document and mark as final.
    a. Click the **File** tab to open the *Backstage* view.
    b. Click the **Check for Issues** button and select **Inspect Document**. The *Document Inspector* dialog box opens.
    c. Click **Inspect**. The results display in the *Document Inspector* dialog box (Figure 9-92).

Figure 9-92 Inspection results displayed in the *Document Inspector* dialog box

d. Click the **Remove All** button in the *Custom XML Data* area.
  e. Click the **Close** button to close the *Document Inspector* dialog box.
  f. Click the **Protect Document** button on the *Backstage* view and select **Mark as Final**. A dialog box opens, informing you that the file will be saved and marked as final.
  g. Click **OK** to close the dialog box and click **OK** to close the next informational dialog box.
  h. Click the **Back** arrow to return to the document.

13. Share the document with your instructor.
  a. Save this document on *OneDrive* if you haven't already. If you don't have the ability to save to *OneDrive*, skip all of step 13.
  b. Click the **Share** button in the upper-right corner of the Word window to open the *Send Link* window (Figure 9-93). If you're using a personal Microsoft account, the *Share* pane displays on the right, and the sharing options differ slightly.
  c. Click the **Link settings** button to open the *Link settings* window (Figure 9-94).

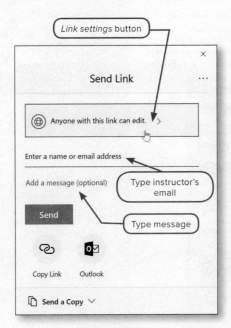

Figure 9-93 *Send Link* window

Figure 9-94 *Link settings* window

  d. Click the **Anyone** button and check the **Allow editing** box if necessary.
  e. Click **Apply** to close the *Link settings* window and return to the *Send Link* window.
  f. Type your instructor's email address in the *Enter a name or email address* area (see Figure 9-93).
  g. Type a brief message to your instructor and click the **Send** button.
  h. Click the **X** in the upper-right corner of the confirmation window to close it.

14. Close the document (Figure 9-95).

TO: Life's Animal Shelter Supporters

FROM: Kelly Sung, Director of Services

DATE: March 28, 2020

SUBJECT: Support Life's Animal Shelter

Thank you for your past support of Life's Animal Shelter. Because of supporters like you, this shelter is a safe environment for animals and provides pet adoption services for families in our community. Families throughout our region are enjoying their new pets thanks to your dedication and work at Life's Animal Shelter.

Would you again consider supporting Life's Animal Shelter through donating or volunteering? Our operating funds come through donations and pet adoption fees, which keeps our expenses at a moderate level. Because of supporters like you, we can offer reasonable adoption fees to animal lovers in our community.

Life's Animal Shelter

3429 2nd Avenue North
Park Rapids, MN 56470
218.240.7880
www.lifesanimalshelter.com

"Serving our community through animal rescue and pet adoption"

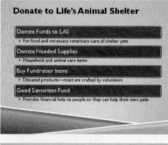

Figure 9-95 Word 9-1 completed

Guided Project 9-2

For this project, you edit two documents from American River Cycling Club. You revise a document and add comments, review and accept changes, combine two documents and accept changes, merge the combined document with an Access database table, create rules to customize the merge, and share the document with your instructor.
[Student Learning Outcomes 9.1, 9.2, 9.4]

Files Needed: ***ARCCCoaching-09a.docx***, ***ARCCCoaching-09b.docx***, and ***ARCC-09.accdb*** *(Student data files are available in the* Library *of your SIMnet account.)*
Completed Project File Names: *[your initials]* ***Word 9-2a.docx***, *[your initials]* ***Word 9-2b.docx***, *[your initials]* ***Word 9-2 combined.docx***, and *[your initials]* ***Word 9-2 merged.docx***

Skills Covered in This Project

- Change user name and initials.
- Change how markup displays.
- Change the color of insertions, deletions, and comments.
- Insert comments.
- Turn on *Track Changes* and edit a document.
- Change the display for *Review* view.
- Accept and reject changes in a document.
- Review and delete comments.
- Combine two documents and accept changes in the combined document.
- Start mail merge and select and edit recipients.
- Insert merge field codes.
- Create and insert rules to customize a merge.
- Finish and save the merged document.
- Share a file.

---

1. Open the ***ARCCCoaching-09a*** document from your student data files.

2. Save the document as [your initials] Word 9-2a.

3. Change user name and initials. Skip the following steps if your user name and initials are already in Word.
   a. Click the **Tracking** launcher [*Review* tab, *Tracking* group] to open the *Track Changes Options* dialog box.
   b. Click the **Change User Name** button to open the *Word Options* dialog box.
   c. Type your first and last name in the *User name* text box, type your initials in lowercase letters in the *Initials* text box, and check the **Always use these values regardless of sign in to Office** box.
   d. Click **OK** to close the *Word Options* dialog box and click **OK** to close the *Track Changes Options* dialog box.

4. Change how markup displays and the color of comments and markup.
   a. Click the **Display for Review** drop-down list [*Review* tab, *Tracking* group] and select **All Markup**.
   b. Click the **Show Markup** drop-down list [*Review* tab, *Tracking* group], click **Balloons**, and select **Show Only Comments and Formatting in Balloons**.
   c. Click the **Tracking** launcher to open the *Track Changes Options* dialog box.
   d. Click **Advanced Options** to open the *Advanced Track Changes Options* dialog box.
   e. Change the *Color* of *Insertions*, *Deletions*, and *Comments* to **Blue** (Figure 9-96).
   f. Click **OK** to close the *Advanced Track Changes Options* dialog box and click **OK** to close the *Track Changes Options* dialog box.

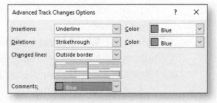

Figure 9-96 Change the color of insertions, deletions, and comments

5. Insert comments and track changes in the document.
   a. Select the date at the beginning of the document and click the **New Comment** button [*Review* tab, *Comments* group] to insert a new comment.
   b. Type Merge this letter with our database in the comment balloon.
   c. Select the first word in the last bulleted item ("**Be**") and click the **New Comment** button.
   d. Type Type a paragraph about the coach and include the coach's info in a table in the comment balloon.
   e. Click the top half of the **Track Changes** button [*Review* tab, *Tracking* group] to turn on *Track Changes*.
   f. Select and delete "**time trial, or century.**" in the first body paragraph (don't delete the paragraph mark) and type or time trial. (include the period).
   g. Select and delete "**General Guidelines**" including the paragraph mark.
   h. Delete the space between "off" and "season" in the first bulleted item, and type - (hyphen).
   i. Turn off **Track Changes**.

6. Save and close the document.

7. Open the ***ARCCCoaching-09b*** document from your student data files. Click the **Enable Editing** button on the *Message* bar if the file opens in *Protected* view.

8. Save the document as [your initials] Word 9-2b.

9. Review comments and changes and accept changes.
   a. Click the **Display for Review** drop-down list [*Review* tab, *Tracking* group] and select **Simple Markup** to display the document with proposed changes.
   b. Click the **Display for Review** drop-down list again and select **All Markup**.
   c. Click the bottom of the **Accept** button [*Review* tab, *Changes* group] and select **Accept All Changes**.
   d. Click the bottom half of the **Delete** button [*Review* tab, *Comments* group] and select **Delete All Comments in Document**.
   e. Save and close the document.

10. Combine the two edited documents.
    a. Click the **Compare** button [*Review* tab, *Compare* group] and select **Combine**. The *Combine Documents* dialog box opens (Figure 9-97).
    b. Click the **Browse** button in the *Original document* area. The *Open* dialog box opens.
    c. Select the *[your initials] Word 9-2a* document and click **Open**.
    d. Click the **Browse** button in the *Revised document* area, select the *[your initials] Word 9-2b* document, and click **Open**.
    e. Click the **More** button (if necessary) to display more options and confirm all boxes are checked.
    f. Select the **Word level** and the **New document** radio buttons In the *Show changes* area.
    g. Click **OK** to close the dialog box and combine the documents. The combined document displays in a new Word window.

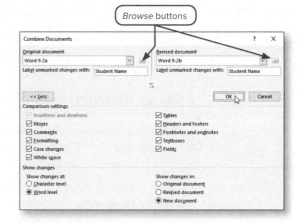

Figure 9-97 *Combine Documents* dialog box

11. Save the combined document as [your initials] Word 9-2 combined.

12. Hide source documents, accept changes, and delete comments.
    a. Confirm source documents don't display. If necessary, click the **Compare** button, click **Show Source Documents**, and select **Hide Source Documents**.

b. Click the bottom of the **Accept** button and select **Accept All Changes and Stop Tracking**.

c. Click the bottom half of the **Delete** button and select **Delete All Comments in Document**.

d. Close the *Reviewing* pane if it is open.

13. Start a merge and select recipients from an Access database.

 a. Click the **Start Mail Merge** button [*Mailings* tab, *Start Mail Merge* group] and select **Letters**.

 b. Click the **Select Recipients** button [*Mailings* tab, *Start Mail Merge* group] and select **Use an Existing List**. The *Select Data Source* dialog box opens.

 c. Select the ***ARCC-09*** database from your student data file and click **Open**.

 d. Click the **Edit Recipient List** button [*Mailings* tab, *Start Mail Merge* group] to open the *Mail Merge Recipients* dialog box.

 e. Click the **Last** column heading drop-down arrow and select **Sort Ascending**.

 f. Deselect the **check box** next to the following names so they are not included in the merge: **Roy Baxter**, **Rick Hermenn**, and **Kelsey Kroll**.

 g. Click **OK** to close the *Mail Merge Recipients* dialog box.

14. Insert merge fields.

 a. Select and delete "**<Name and address>**" (including the placeholder brackets). Don't delete the paragraph mark after these words.

 b. Click the **Address Block** button [*Mailings* tab, *Write & Insert Fields* group]. The *Insert Address Block* dialog box opens.

 c. Select **Joshua Randall Jr.** as the recipient's name format and click **OK** to close the dialog box and insert the *Address Block* merge field code.

 d. Place the insertion point after the space after "Dear".

 e. Click the **Insert Merge Field** drop-down arrow [*Mailings* tab, *Write & Insert Fields* group] and select **First** from the drop-down list.

 f. Place the insertion point in the first cell in the second row of the table.

 g. Click the **Insert Merge Field** drop-down arrow and select **Coach**.

15. Insert a rule to skip cyclists who are not racers.

 a. Place the insertion point in front of the *<<AddressBlock>>* merge field code.

 b. Click the **Rules** button [*Mailings* tab, *Write & Insert Fields* group] and select **Skip Record If**. The *Insert Word Field: Skip Record If* dialog box opens (Figure 9-98).

 c. Click the **Field name** drop-down list and select **Level**.

 d. Click the **Comparison** name drop-down list and select **Equal to**.

 e. Type Recreational in the *Compare to* text box and click **OK** to close the dialog box and to insert the rule.

Figure 9-98 Insert a *Skip Record If* rule

16. Insert a rule to insert the email address of the cyclist's coach, which is dependent upon the cyclist's gender (the men's and women's teams have different coaches).

 a. Place the insertion point in the third cell in the second row of the table (below "Email").

 b. Click the **Rules** button and select **If. . .Then. . .Else**. The *Insert Word Field: IF* dialog box opens (Figure 9-99).

 c. Click the **Field name** drop-down list and select **Gender**.

 d. Click the **Comparison** name drop-down list and select **Equal to**.

 e. Type Female in the *Compare to* area.

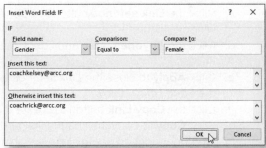

Figure 9-99 Insert an *If. . .Then. . .Else* rule

f. Type coachkelsey@arcc.org in the *Insert this text* area.

g. Type coachrick@arcc.org in the *Otherwise insert this text* area.

h. Click **OK** to close the dialog box and insert the rule. An email address displays in this cell.

17. Create a rule to insert the phone number of the cyclist's coach dependent upon the cyclist's gender.

a. Place the insertion point in the fourth cell in the second row of the table.

b. Click the **Rules** button and select **If. . .Then. . .Else**.

c. Click the **Field name** drop-down list and select **Gender**.

d. Click the **Comparison** name drop-down list and select **Equal to**.

e. Type Female in the *Compare to* area.

f. Type 916-453-2845 in the *Insert this text* area.

g. Type 916-451-9879 in the *Otherwise insert this text* area.

h. Click **OK** to close the dialog box and to insert the rule. A phone number displays in this cell.

i. Save the document.

18. Preview the results and finish the merge.

a. Click the **Preview Results** button [*Mailings* tab, *Preview Results* group] to preview your document.

b. Click the **Preview Results** button again to turn off preview.

c. Click the **Finish & Merge** button [*Mailings* tab, *Finish* group] and select **Edit Individual Documents**. The *Merge to New Document* dialog box opens.

d. Click the **All** radio button and click **OK** to finish the merge.

e. Save the merged document as [your initials] Word 9-2 merged (see Figure 9-103). The document should contain 13 letters.

19. Share the document with your instructor.

a. Save this document on *OneDrive* if you haven't already. If you don't have the ability to save to *OneDrive*, skip all of step 19.

b. Click the **Share** button in the upper-right corner of the Word window to open the *Send Link* window (Figure 9-100). If you're using a personal Microsoft account, the *Share* pane displays on the right, and the sharing options differ slightly.

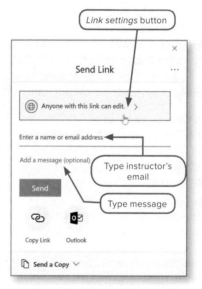

Figure 9-100 *Send Link* window

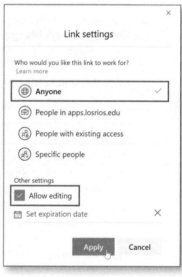

Figure 9-101 *Link settings* window

c. Click the **Link settings** button to open the *Link settings* window (Figure 9-101).

d. Click the **Anyone** button and check the **Allow editing** box if necessary.

e. Click **Apply** to close the *Link settings* window and return to the *Send Link* window.

f. Click the **Copy Link** button to create the sharing link.

g. Click **Copy** to copy the sharing link and click the **X** in the upper-right corner to close the sharing link window (Figure 9-102).

Figure 9-102 Copy sharing link

h. Use your email account to create a new email to your instructor. Include an appropriate subject line and a brief message in the body.

i. Press **Ctrl+V** to paste the sharing link to your document in the body of the email and send the email message.

20. Save and close all open documents (Figure 9-103).

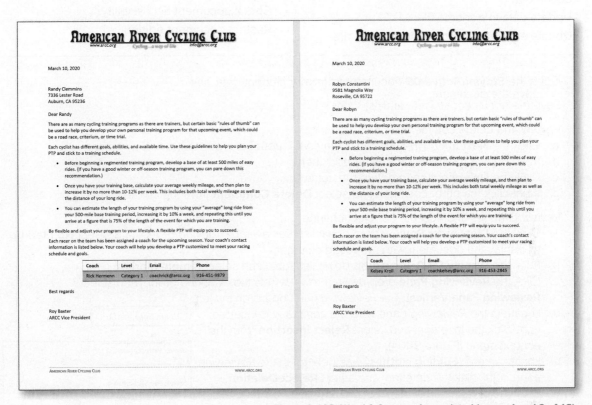

Figure 9-103 Word 9-2 merged completed (pages 1 and 2 of 13)

Guided Project 9-3

For this project, you edit a document from Sawyer Petrosky at Courtyard Medical Plaza. You review the document to accept and reject changes, review comments, edit the document, link and embed objects from Excel and PowerPoint, add a bookmark, create a hyperlink and cross-reference to a bookmark, prepare the document for sharing, and protect the document.
[Student Learning Outcomes 9.1, 9.2, 9.3, 9.5]

Files Needed: ***StayingActive-09.docx***, ***EstimatedCalories-09.xlsx***, and ***CMPStayingActive-09.pptx*** *(Student data files are available in the* Library *of your SIMnet account.)*
Completed Project File Names: *[**your initials**] Word 9-3.docx* and *[**your initials**] EstimatedCalories-09.xlsx*

Skills Covered in This Project

- Review and delete comments.
- Turn off *Track Changes* and use the *Reviewing* pane to accept and reject changes.
- Link a chart from an Excel worksheet to a Word document.
- Update data in a source file.
- Update a linked object in a destination file.
- Embed and format PowerPoint slides.
- Remove a watermark.
- Add a bookmark.
- Insert a hyperlink to a bookmark.
- Insert a cross-reference to a bookmark.
- Break a link to a linked chart.
- Check document accessibility.
- Restrict document editing.

---

1. Open the **StayingActive-09** document from your student data files.

2. Save the document as **[your initials] Word 9-3**.

3. Review and delete comments.
   a. Click the **Next** button [*Review* tab, *Comments* group] to move to the first comment.
   b. Read both of the comments in the document.
   c. Click the **Delete** button to delete the comment.
   d. Right-click the other comment and select **Delete Comment** from the context menu.

4. Review changes and accept and reject changes.
   a. Click the **Display for Review** drop-down list [*Review* tab, *Tracking* group] and select **No Markup** to display the document with proposed changes.
   b. Click the **Display for Review** drop-down list again and select **Simple Markup**.
   c. Click the **Reviewing Pane** drop-down arrow [*Review* tab, *Tracking* group] and select **Reviewing Pane Vertical**. The *Reviewing* pane opens on the left.
   d. Locate in the *Reviewing* pane where a comma was inserted, right-click the insertion, and select **Reject Insertion** from the context menu (Figure 9-104).
   e. Locate where "**Folding clothes**" was deleted in the *Reviewing* pane, right-click the deletion, and select **Reject Deletion**.
   f. Click the bottom half of the **Accept** button [*Review* tab, *Changes* group] and select **Accept All Changes** to accept the remaining changes.
   g. Click the **Reviewing Pane** button to close the *Reviewing* pane.

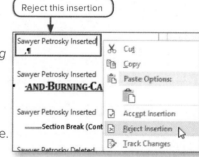

Figure 9-104 Reject an insertion

5. Paste a chart from an Excel worksheet as a link in the Word document.
   a. Open a *File Explorer* window, browse to your student data files, and open the **EstimatedCalories-09** Excel worksheet. Click the **Enable Editing** button on the *Message* bar if the file opens in *Protected* view.
   b. Save this file to your desktop and name it **[your initials] EstimatedCalories-09**.
   c. Select the frame of the chart and **copy** it.
   d. Return to your Word document and place the insertion point on the blank line above the "Keep Exercise Fun and Interesting" heading.
   e. Click the bottom half of the **Paste** button [*Home* tab, *Clipboard* group] and select **Paste Special**. The *Paste Special* dialog box opens (Figure 9-105).

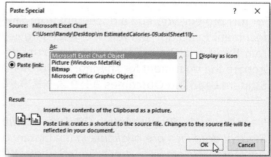

Figure 9-105 *Paste Special* dialog box

  f. Click the **Paste link** radio button and select **Microsoft Excel Chart Object** in the *As* area.

  g. Click **OK** to close the dialog box and to insert the linked chart.

  h. Click the chart to select it and **Center** [*Home* tab, *Paragraph* group] the chart horizontally.

6. Edit the source file and update the linked chart.

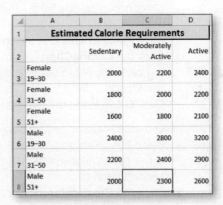

  a. Right-click the chart in the Word document, click **Linked Worksheet Object**, and select **Edit Link**. The linked Excel file opens.

  b. Click the **Moderately Active Male 31-50** cell (**C7**), type 2400, and press **Enter**.

  c. Click the **Moderately Active Male 51+** cell (**C8**), type 2300, and press **Enter** (Figure 9-106).

  d. Save the *[your initials] EstimatedCalories-09* worksheet.

  e. Return to the Word document, right-click the chart, and select **Update Link**. The data in the chart updates to match the source file.

Figure 9-106 Edit the source file

  f. Return to the Excel file, save the file, and exit Excel.

7. Embed slides from a PowerPoint presentation into the Word document.

  a. Open a *File Explorer* window, browse to your student data files, and open the ***CMPStayingActive-09*** PowerPoint presentation.

  b. Select **slide 2** on the left and **copy** it.

  c. Return to your Word document and place the insertion point on the blank line at the end of the second page.

  d. Click the bottom half of the **Paste** button [*Home* tab, *Clipboard* group] and select **Paste Special**. The *Paste Special* dialog box opens.

  e. Click the **Paste** radio button and select **Picture (PNG)** in the *As* area.

  f. Click **OK** to close the dialog box and insert the embedded picture.

  g. Place the insertion point at the end of the document (after the inserted slide) and press **Enter**.

  h. Repeat steps 7b–f to **copy** and embed **slide 8** below slide 2. Slide 8 displays on the third page.

  i. Return to PowerPoint and exit PowerPoint.

8. Resize and format the embedded slides.

  a. Return to the Word document, select the first slide (on second page), and change the *Height* to **3"** [*Picture Tools Format* tab, *Size* group]. The width automatically changes.

  b. Click the **Drop Shadow Rectangle** picture style in the *Picture Styles* gallery [*Picture Tools Format* tab, *Picture Styles* group].

  c. **Center** [*Home* tab, *Paragraph* group] the picture horizontally.

  d. Select the second slide and repeat steps 8a–c.

9. Click the **Watermark** button [*Design* tab, *Page Background* group] and select **Remove Watermark** from the drop-down list.

10. Add a bookmark to a chart.

  a. Select the chart at the bottom of the first page.

  b. Click the **Bookmark** button [*Insert* tab, *Links* group] to open the *Bookmark* dialog box (Figure 9-107).

  c. Type CalorieChart in the *Bookmark name* text box (no space between words).

  d. Click **Add** to add the bookmark.

Figure 9-107 Add a bookmark

11. Insert a hyperlink to a bookmark.
    a. Select the words "**calorie chart**" in the third bulleted item on the second page.
    b. Click the top half of the **Link** button [*Insert* tab, *Links* group] to open the *Insert Hyperlink* dialog box (Figure 9-108).
    c. Click **Place in This Document** on the left.
    d. Click the **CalorieChart** bookmark. If necessary, click the plus sign (+) to the left of *Bookmarks* to display the bookmark.
    e. Click **OK** to insert the hyperlink to the bookmark.

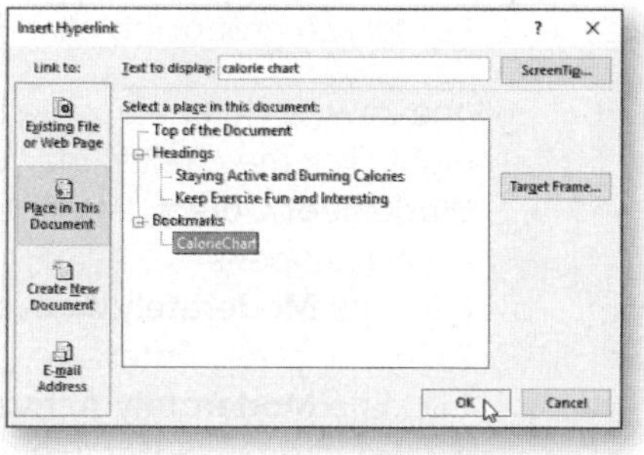

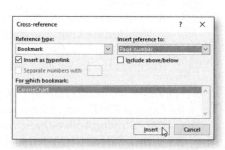

Figure 9-108 Insert a hyperlink to a bookmark

12. Insert a cross-reference to a bookmark.
    a. Place the insertion point after the space after "page" in the parentheses in the third bulleted item on the second page.
    b. Click the **Cross-reference** button [*Insert* tab, *Links* group] to open the *Cross-reference* dialog box (Figure 9-109).
    c. Click the **Reference** type drop-down list and select **Bookmark**.
    d. Check the **Insert as hyperlink** box (if needed) and select **CalorieChart** in the *For which bookmark* area.
    e. Click the **Insert reference to** drop-down list and select **Page number**.
    f. Click **Insert** and then click **Close**.

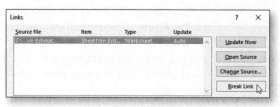

Figure 9-109 Insert a cross-reference to a bookmark

13. Break the link between the source and destination files.
    a. Click the **File** tab to open the *Backstage* view and click **Info** on the left if it is not already selected.
    b. Click the **Edit Links to Files** button to open the *Links* dialog box (Figure 9-110).
    c. Select the link and click the **Break Link** button. A dialog box opens confirming you want to break the link.
    d. Select **Yes** to break the links.
    e. Click the **Back** arrow to return to the document.

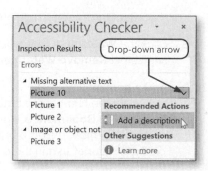

Figure 9-110 Break a link using the *Links* dialog box

14. Save the document.

15. Check document accessibility.
    a. Click the **Check Accessibility** button [*Review* tab, *Accessibility* group] to open the *Accessibility Checker* pane. Three items are missing alt text (Figure 9-111).
    b. Select the first item missing alt text in the *Accessibility Checker* pane. The chart in the document is selected.
    c. Click the drop-down arrow to the right of the first item and select **Add a description**. The *Format Picture* dialog box opens.
    d. Click the **Alt Text** tab and type Estimated calorie requirements chart in the *Alternative text* dialog box, and click **OK**.
    e. Right-click the first slide picture on the second page, select **Edit Alt Text**, and type A healthy lifestyle picture in the *Alt Text* pane.
    f. Select the second slide picture on the second page and type Exercise benefits and motivation picture in the *Alt Text* pane.
    g. Close the *Alt Text* and *Accessibility Checker* panes.

Figure 9-111 *Accessibility Checker* pane

16. Restrict editing of the document.
    a. Click the **Restrict Editing** button [*Review* tab, *Protect* group] to open the *Restrict Editing* pane (Figure 9-112).
    b. Check the **Allow only this type of editing in the document** box in the *Editing Restrictions* area.
    c. Click the drop-down list below the check box and select **Comments**.
    d. Click the **Yes, Start Enforcing Protection** button. The *Start Enforcing Protection* dialog box opens.
    e. Type **CMP** in the *Enter new password* text box.
    f. Type **CMP** in the *Reenter password to confirm* text box.
    g. Click **OK** to close the dialog box and begin enforcing protection.
    h. Close the *Restrict Editing* pane.

17. Save and close the document (Figure 9-113).

Figure 9-112 *Restrict Editing* pane

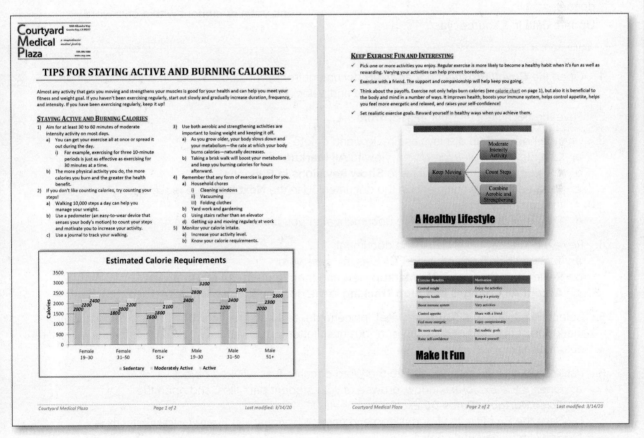

Figure 9-113 Word 9-3 completed

Independent Project 9-4

For this project, you edit a prospecting letter from Emma Cavalli at Placer Hills Real Estate. You track changes and insert comments, link an object from a source file, insert a bookmark, create a hyperlink to a bookmark, merge the document with a data source, apply merge rules, and encrypt the document. [Student Learning Outcomes 9.1, 9.2, 9.3, 9.4, 9.5]

Files Needed: *CavalliProspectingLetter-09.docx*, *FixedMortgageRates-09.xlsx*, and *CavalliPHRE-09.accdb (Student data files are available in the* Library *of your SIMnet account.)*
Completed Project File Names: *[your initials] Word 9-4.docx*,
[your initials] FixedMortgageRates-09.xlsx, and *[your initials] Word 9-4 merged.docx*

Skills Covered in This Project

- Change the *Display for Review* view.
- Change markup display.
- Review and delete comments.
- Turn off *Lock Tracking*.
- Accept changes in a document.
- Link a chart from an Excel worksheet to a Word document.
- Update data in a source file.

- Update a linked object in a destination file.
- Break a link to a linked chart.
- Add a bookmark.
- Insert a hyperlink to a bookmark.
- Start the mail merge and select and edit recipients.
- Insert merge field codes.
- Create and insert rules to customize a merge.
- Encrypt a document with a password.

1. Open the **CavalliProspectingLetter-09** document from your student data files. If this document opens in *Reading* view, click the **View** tab and select **Edit Document**.

2. Save the document as [your initials] Word 9-4.

3. Change how markup displays and review and delete comments.
   a. Change the *Display for Review* view to **All Markup**.
   b. Change how markup displays to **Show Revisions in Balloons**.
   c. Read each of the comments in the document. Use the **Next** button to move through the comments.
   d. Delete all the comments in the document after you finish reading them.

4. Review and accept changes in the document.
   a. Turn off **Lock Tracking**; type PHRE as the password.
   b. Review the changes in **No Markup** view and then return to **All Markup** view.
   c. **Accept All Changes and Stop Tracking** in the document.

5. Select and delete the "**[Current Date]**" placeholder text and brackets (don't delete the paragraph mark), insert the current date in proper business letter format (January 1, 2020), and set it to update automatically.

6. Paste an Excel worksheet chart into the Word document as a linked object.
   a. Open a *File Explorer* window, browse to your student data files, and open the **FixedMortgageRates-09** Excel worksheet.
   b. Save the Excel file to your desktop and name it [your initials] FixedMortgageRates-09.
   c. Select the chart and **copy** it.
   d. Return to the Word document and place the insertion point on the blank line below the "Fixed Mortgage Rate Averages" heading on the second page.
   e. **Paste link** as a **Microsoft Excel Chart Object**.

7. Update the source file for the linked chart.
   a. Return to the *[your initials] FixedMortgageRates-09* worksheet, change the *2019 Rate* to 4.62 and the *Points* to 0.9 and then save the worksheet.
   b. Update the chart in the destination Word file.
   c. Close Excel.
   d. Return to the Word document and break the link between the source file and the destination file.

8. Add a bookmark and create a hyperlink to a bookmark.
   a. Select the "**Sample Fixed Rate Payments**" heading on the second page.
   b. Add a bookmark and type SamplePayments as the *Bookmark name*.
   c. Change the *Word Options* to **Show bookmarks** [*Advanced* area of the *Word Options* dialog box].
   d. Select "**Sample Fixed Rate Payments**" in the second sentence of the second body paragraph on the first page.
   e. Create a hyperlink to the **SamplePayments** bookmark.

9. Start the mail merge.
   a. Select **Letters** as the type of mail merge.
   b. Select the **CavalliPHRE-09** Access database as the recipients.
   c. Edit the recipient list and sort in ascending order by last name.

10. Insert merge field codes.
    a. Delete the "**<Address>**" placeholder text and brackets on the first page. Don't delete the paragraph mark.
    b. Insert the **Address Block** merge field code and select the **Mr. Joshua Randall Jr.** format.
    c. Delete the "**<Greeting>**" placeholder text and brackets. Don't delete the colon.
    d. Insert the **Title** merge field code after "Dear", **space** once, and insert the **Last** merge field code. Confirm one space appears after "Dear" and between the *Title* and *Last* merge field codes, and a colon displays after the *Last* merge field code.
    e. Delete the "**<City>**" placeholder text and brackets in the first sentence in the first body paragraph.
    f. Insert the **City** merge field code.
    g. Check to ensure proper spacing around the merge field codes.

11. Insert rules to customize the merge.
    a. Place the insertion point on the blank line above the <<AddressBlock>> merge field code.
    b. Insert a **Skip Record If** rule to skip records where **City** is **Equal to** Roseville.
    c. Insert another **Skip Record If** rule to skip records where **City** is **Equal to** Rocklin.
    d. Insert another **Skip Record If** rule to skip records where **Status** is **Equal to** Sold.
    e. Delete "**has recently expired**" in the first sentence of the first body paragraph.
    f. Confirm one space displays after the <<City>> merge field code.
    g. Place the insertion point after the space after <<City>> and before the period.
    h. Insert an **If. . .Then. . .Else** rule and use the following settings for the rule: If the *Field name* **Expired** is **Equal to** True, insert has recently expired in the text box; otherwise, insert will expire soon in the text box.

12. Preview the merge results to see how the records will appear in your letter. Remember, the *Skip Record If* rule does not apply until you complete the merge.

13. Turn off the merge preview and save the Word document.

14. Finish the merge.
    a. Merge all the records to edit individual letters. The document should contain five letters (10 pages total).
    b. Save the new merged document as [your initials] Word 9-4 merged and close it (Figure 9-114).

15. Encrypt the *[your initials] Word 9-4* document with a password. Use PHRE as the password.

16. Save and close the document.

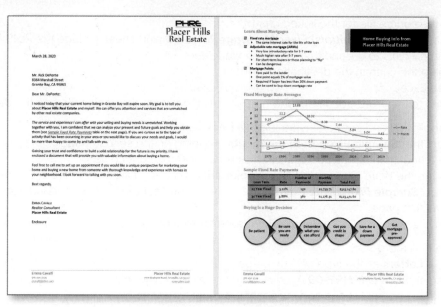

Figure 9-114 Word 9-4 merged completed (pages 1 and 2 of 10)

Independent Project 9-5

For this project, you edit an insurance renewal letter from Eva Skaar at Central Sierra Insurance. You use track changes, comments, and the combine feature; insert a bookmark, a hyperlink, and a cross-reference to a bookmark; perform a merge; and add merge rules and document protection. [Student Learning Outcomes 9.1, 9.2, 9.4, 9.5]

Files Needed: ***CSIRenewalLetter-09a.docx***, ***CSIRenewalLetter-09b.docx***, and ***SkaarCSIRenewals-09.accdb*** (*Student data files are available in the* Library *of your SIMnet account.*) Completed Project File Names: ***[your initials] Word 9-5a.docx***, ***[your initials] Word 9-5b.docx***, ***[your initials] Word 9-5 combined.docx***, and ***[your initials] Word 9-5 merged.docx***

Skills Covered in This Project

- Change how markup displays.
- Turn on *Track Changes* and edit a document.
- Insert comments.
- Remove a document encryption password.
- Review and delete comments.
- Change the *Display for Review* view.
- Accept changes in the document.
- Combine documents.
- Add a bookmark.
- Insert a cross-reference and hyperlink to a bookmark.
- Start the mail merge and select recipients.
- Insert merge field codes.
- Create and insert rules to customize a merge.
- Inspect a document and remove *Custom XML Data*.
- Merge to a new document.
- Mark a document as final.

1. Open the ***CSIRenewalLetter-09a*** document from your student data files.

2. Save the document as [your initials] Word 9-5a.

3. Change how markup and comments display.
   a. Change user name and initials to your name and initials.
   b. Use the *Advanced Track Changes Options* dialog box to change the insertions, deletions, and comments color to **Violet**.
   c. Change how markup displays to **Show Revisions in Balloons**.

4. Edit the document using *Track Changes* and add a comment.
   a. Turn on **Track Changes**.
   b. Type Central Sierra Insurance is to replace "I am" at the beginning of the first body paragraph.
   c. Delete the last sentence in the second body paragraph including the space at the beginning of the sentence ("**Due to changes . . .**"). Don't delete the paragraph mark at the end of the sentence.
   d. Place the insertion point after the space after "do not hesitate to call" in the last body paragraph, type (780-886-2464), and **space** once.
   e. Select the first word in the second body paragraph ("**Central**"), insert a comment, and type Insert a table with renewal information below this paragraph in the comment balloon.
   f. View the document with **Simple Markup** to review your revisions.
   g. Turn off **Track Changes** and save and close this document.

5. Open an encrypted document, remove password encryption, and save the document.
   a. Open the *CSIRenewalLetter-09b* document from your student data files.
   b. Use CSI as the password for this encrypted document.
   c. Remove the password encryption from the document using the **Protect Document** button on the *Backstage* view.
   d. Save the document as [your initials] Word 9-5b.

6. Review comments and accept tracked changes.
   a. View the document with **No Markup**, and then change the view back to **All Markup**.
   b. Read the comments in the document and then delete them.
   c. Accept all the changes in the document.
   d. Save and close the document.

7. Combine documents and review changes.
   a. Open the *Combine Documents* dialog box, select *[your initials] Word 9-5b* as the *Original* document, and select *[your initials] Word 9-5a* as the *Revised* document.
   b. Combine the documents into a **New document**.
   c. Hide source documents if they display.
   d. Accept all the changes in the document and delete all comments in the document.
   e. Save the combined document as [your initials] Word 9-5 combined.

8. Add a bookmark and create a cross-reference and hyperlink to a bookmark.
   a. Select the words "**Discounted Premium**" in the last cell of the first row of the table.
   b. Add a bookmark and type DiscountedPremium as the bookmark name.
   c. Place the insertion point at the end of the second body paragraph ("cost-effective renewal") and before the period.
   d. **Space** once, type (see, and **space** once again.
   e. Insert a cross-reference to the **DiscountedPremium** bookmark, **Insert as a hyperlink**, and *Insert reference to* **Above/below**. Insert the cross-reference and close the *Cross-reference* dialog box.
   f. Type) after "below."
   g. Select "**cost-effective renewal**" near the end of the second body paragraph and add a hyperlink to the **DiscountedPremium** bookmark.
   h. Save the document.

9. Start the mail merge and select recipients.
   a. Select **Letters** as the type of mail merge.
   b. Select the *SkaarCSIRenewals-09* Access database as the recipients.
   c. Edit the recipient list and sort in ascending order by last name.

10. Insert merge field codes.
    a. Delete the "**<Address>**" placeholder text (don't delete the paragraph mark), insert the **Address Block** merge field, and use the **Mr. Joshua Randall Jr.** format.
    b. Delete the "**<Salutation>**" placeholder text (don't delete the paragraph mark), insert the **Greeting Line** merge field, and use **Dear Mr. Randall:** as the format.
    c. Delete the "**<Policy Number>**" placeholder text and insert the **Policy_Number** merge field.
    d. Delete the "**<Company>**" placeholder text and insert the **Company** merge field.
    e. Delete the "**<Insurance Company>**" placeholder text and insert the **Insurance_Company** merge field.
    f. Delete the "**<First Name>**" placeholder text and insert the **First_Name** merge field.
    g. Place the insertion point in the first cell in the second row of the table and insert the **Policy_Description** merge field.
    h. Place the insertion point after the "$" in the second cell in the second row of the table and insert the **Premium_Basis** merge field.
    i. Place the insertion point after the "$" in the third cell in the second row of the table and insert the **Rate_per_1000** merge field.
    j. Use the **Highlight Merge Fields** feature and ensure proper spacing around the merge field codes. Turn off **Highlight Merge Fields** when finished reviewing.

11. Preview the merge results to see how the records will appear in your letter and then turn off preview.

12. Insert a rule to skip recipients who have paid online.
    a. Place the insertion point on the blank line above the <<*AddressBlock*>> merge field code.
    b. Insert a **Skip Record If** rule to skip records where **Paid_Online** is **Equal to** True [*Compare to* text box].
    c. Save the document.

13. Finish the merge.
    a. Merge all the records to edit individual letters. The document should contain five letters.
    b. Save the new merged document as **[your initials] Word 9-5 merged** and close it (Figure 9-115).

14. Mark the **[your initials] Word 9-5 combined** as final and then close the document.

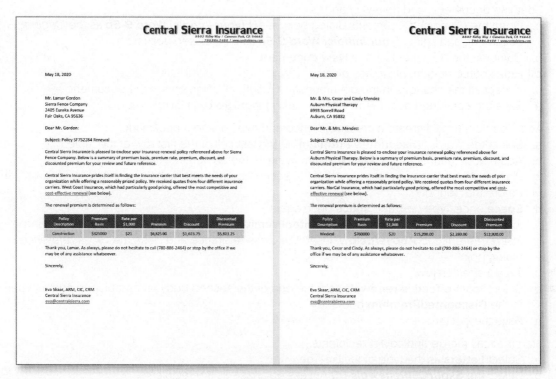

Figure 9-115 Word 9-5 merged completed (pages 1 and 2 of 5)

Independent Project 9-6

For this project, you edit a fax cover sheet for Kelly McFarland, director of Skiing Unlimited. You review the document to accept and reject changes, review comments, and edit the document, link a chart from Excel, protect the document, and share the file with your instructor.
[Student Learning Outcomes 9.1, 9.2, 9.3]

Files Needed: **SkiingUnlimitedFax-09.docx** and **SkiingUnlimitedParticipation-09.xlsx** (Student data files are available in the Library of your SIMnet account.)
Completed Project File Names: **[your initials] Word 9-6.docx** and
[your initials] SkiingUnlimitedParticipation-09.xlsx

Skills Covered in This Project

- Turn off *Lock Tracking*.
- Use the *Reviewing* pane to reject and accept changes.
- Turn off *Track Changes* and edit a document.
- Review and delete comments.
- Link a chart from an Excel worksheet to a Word document.
- Update data in the source file.
- Update a linked object in the destination file.
- Break links between documents.
- Encrypt a document with a password.
- Share a file.

---

1. Open the **SkiingUnlimitedFax-09** document from your student data files. If this document opens in *Reading* view, click the **View** tab and select **Edit Document**.

2. Save the document as **[your initials] Word 9-6**.

3. Review comments and changes.
   a. Turn off **Lock Tracking**. Use **CMP** as the password.
   b. Turn off **Track Changes**.
   c. Use the *Reviewing* pane to locate where "1" was deleted from the "PAGES" area and reject this deletion.
   d. Accept all remaining changes in the document.
   e. Read the two comments in the document and then delete them.
   f. Close the *Reviewing* pane.

4. Edit the document.
   a. Select the current date in the "*[Pick the date]*" field.
   b. Turn on **View Gridlines** to display table gridlines.
   c. Type **Seth Uribe** after "TO:".
   d. Type **916.450.9525** after "FAX:" in the first column of the second table.
   e. Type **916.450.9515** after "PHONE:" in the first column of the second table.
   f. Type your name in the "FROM:" area.

5. Paste a chart from an Excel worksheet as a linked object.
   a. Open a *File Explorer* window, browse to your student data files, and open the **SkiingUnlimitedParticipation-09** Excel worksheet.
   b. Save the Excel worksheet to your desktop and name it **[your initials] SkiingUnlimitedParticipation-09**.
   c. Select the chart and **copy** it.
   d. Return to the Word document and place the insertion point on the blank line below the second table.
   e. **Paste link** to the chart as a **Microsoft Excel Chart Object**.

6. Edit the source file and update the chart in the destination file.
   a. Return to the Excel worksheet and change the 2020 participants to 74 and the volunteers to 231.
   b. Save the Excel worksheet.
   c. Return to the Word document and update the linked chart.

d. Change the horizontal alignment of the chart in the destination file to **center**.

e. Close the Excel worksheet.

7. Break the link between the chart in the destination file and the source file.

8. Encrypt the document with a password. Use **CMP** as the password.

9. Turn off **View Gridlines**.

10. Share the document with your instructor.

a. Save this document on *OneDrive* if you haven't already. If you don't have the ability to save to *OneDrive*, skip all of step 10.

b. Click the **Share** button in the upper-right corner of the Word window to open the *Send Link* window. If you are using a personal Microsoft account, the *Share* pane opens on the right, and the sharing options differ slightly.

c. Edit the **Link settings** to **Allow editing** to **Anyone** and **Apply** these link settings.

d. Type your instructor's email address in the email area.

e. Type a brief message to your instructor and **Send** the sharing link.

f. Close the sharing confirmation window.

11. Save and close the document (Figure 9-116).

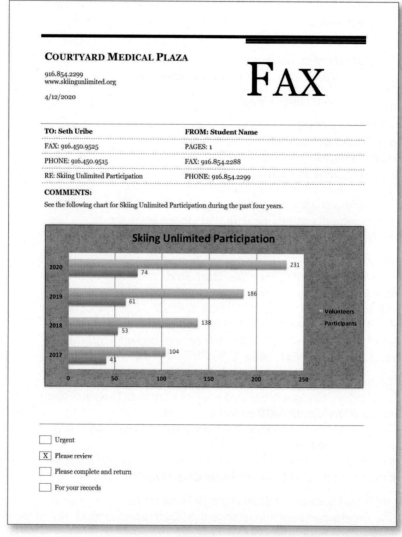

Figure 9-116 Word 9-6 completed

Improve It Project 9-7

For this project, you edit an insurance newsletter for Central Sierra Insurance. You use *Track Changes*, edit the document, accept changes, embed an Excel chart, format the chart, add a bookmark, insert a hyperlink to a bookmark, prepare the document for sharing, and mark the document as final.
[Student Learning Outcomes 9.1, 9.2, 9.3, 9.5]

Files Needed: *CSINewsletter-09.docx* and *EstimatedCosts-09.xlsx* (*Student data files are available in the* Library *of your SIMnet account.*)
Completed Project File Name: *[your initials] Word 9-7.docx*

Skills Covered in This Project

- Open a password-encrypted document.
- Remove a document password.
- Review and delete comments.
- Turn on *Track Changes* and edit a document.
- Change the *Display for Review* view.
- Change user name and initials.
- Change color of insertions, deletions, and comments.

- Accept and reject changes in a document.
- Embed and format a chart from an Excel worksheet to the Word document.
- Add a bookmark.
- Insert a hyperlink to a bookmark.
- Check accessibility.
- Edit alt text.
- Inspect a document.
- Mark a document as final.

---

1. Open the **CSINewsletter-09** document from your student data files. This document is encrypted with a password.
   a. Type **CSI** for the password.
   b. Remove the encryption password from this document.

2. Save the document as [your initials] Word 9-7.

3. Read the comments in the document and delete all comments.

4. Use *Track Changes* and edit the document.
   a. Turn on **Track Changes**.
   b. Change the user name and initials to your name and initials.
   c. Change the color of insertions, deletions, and comments to **Teal**.
   d. Change the *Display for Review* view to **Simple Markup**.
   e. Select the bordered text directly below the newsletter title ("**Issue No. XVII. . .**"), apply **Shading**, and select the first color in the second row of *Theme Colors* (**White, Background 1, Darker 5%**).
   f. Change hyphenation to **None**. This change will not be marked as a tracked change.
   g. Select the bulleted list in the first column and sort paragraphs in **ascending** order.
   h. Select "**Home Appliance and Electronics Breakdown coverage**" in the second paragraph in the first column and apply **bold** formatting.
   i. Apply **small caps** formatting to each of the three bolded headings in the text box in the second column.

5. Accept and reject changes.
   a. Change the *Display for Review* view to **All Markup**.
   b. Reject the three **Space After: 0 pt** formatting changes.
   c. Accept all other changes and stop tracking.

6. Select the text box in the second column and change the *Height* to **4.9"**.

7. Paste a chart from an Excel worksheet as an embedded object.
   a. Open a *File Explorer* window, browse to your student data files, and open the **EstimatedCosts-09** Excel worksheet.

b. Select the chart and copy it.

c. Close the Excel worksheet.

d. Return to the Word document and place the insertion point on the blank line below the text box in the second column.

e. Paste the copied chart as a **Picture (PNG)**. You will adjust the chart placement in the next step.

8. Format the chart.

a. Select the chart picture and change the text wrapping to **In Front of Text**.

b. Use the *Layout* dialog box to change the *Horizontal* **Alignment** to **Centered** *relative to* **Page** and change the *Vertical* **Alignment** to **Bottom** *relative to* **Margin**.

c. Change the *Width* of the chart picture to **7.5"**. The height adjusts automatically.

9. Add a bookmark and insert a hyperlink to a bookmark.

a. Select the chart and add a bookmark.

b. Type EstimatedCosts as the bookmark name.

c. Select "**cost-effective**" in the first sentence of the second paragraph in the first column.

d. Insert a hyperlink to the **EstimatedCosts** bookmark.

10. Check accessibility, edit alt text, and inspect the document.

a. **Check Accessibility** of the document and select the picture missing alt text.

b. **Edit Alt Text** and type Estimated repair and replacement costs picture as the alt text.

c. Close the *Alt Text* and *Accessibility Checker* panes.

d. Save the document.

e. **Inspect Document** and **Remove All** *Headers, Footers, and Watermarks*.

11. Save the document.

12. Mark the document as final and close the document (Figure 9-117).

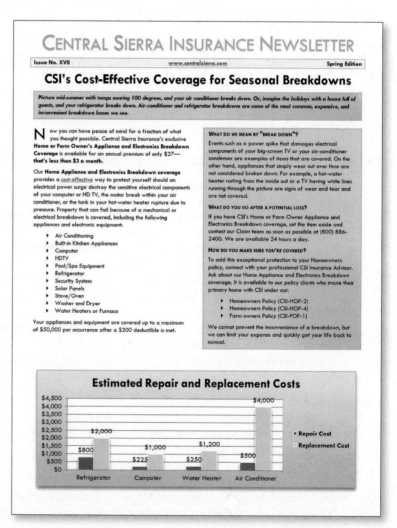

Figure 9-117 Word 9-7 completed

Challenge Project 9-8

People often work collaboratively with coworkers or classmates on projects. Use the Word collaboration tools in this chapter to work with others to modify a report, project, or document.
[Student Learning Outcomes 9.1, 9.2, 9.5]

File Needed: None
Completed Project File Name: *[your initials] Word 9-8.docx*

Open an existing document you are working on with others and save it as [your initials] Word 9-8. Modify your document according to the following guidelines:

- Customize your user name and initials.
- Insert comments.
- Use *Track Changes* to mark content and formatting changes.
- View the document in different *Display for Review* views.
- Customize tracking options.
- Add a bookmark to the document.
- Insert a hyperlink and/or a cross-reference to a bookmark.
- Prepare the document for sharing by inspecting the document, checking accessibility, and checking compatibility.
- Protect the document by using one or more of the protect document features. If you use a password to encrypt your document or restrict it from editing, send your instructor the password.

Challenge Project 9-9

For this project, you use the Word mail merge features to create a merged document. You can create mailing labels, a merged letter, an invitation, or other document that you can merge with recipients from a data source. Use an existing data source for recipients or create a new one. Use mail merge rules to customize your mail merge.
[Student Learning Outcome 9.1, 9.3, 9.5]

File Needed: None
Completed Project File Names: *[your initials] Word 9-9.docx* and *[your initials] Word 9-9 merged.docx*

Open a new or existing document and save it as [your initials] Word 9-9. Save your merged document as [your initials] Word 9-9 merged. Modify your documents according to the following guidelines:

- Use track changes and comments as necessary.
- Change track changes options.
- Edit the recipient list.
- Insert the *Address Block* and/or *Greeting Line* merge field codes.
- Insert individual merge fields.
- Use rules to customize the merge.
- Preview results and finish the merge.
- Inspect the main document and check accessibility.
- Mark the main document as final and encrypt with a password.

Challenge Project 9-10

Track changes, use comments and bookmarks, and link and embed objects to modify and enhance a document. For example, link your budget from an Excel worksheet to a Word document, embed your work or school schedule into a Word document, or link or embed slides from a PowerPoint presentation to a Word document to prepare a notes sheet for an upcoming presentation.
[Student Learning Outcome 9.1, 9.3, 9.5]

File Needed: None
Completed Project File Name: *[your initials] Word 9-10.docx*

Open a new or existing document and save it as [your initials] Word 9-10. Use the Word object linking and embedding features. Modify your document according to the following guidelines:

- Use track changes and comments.
- Customize how tracked changes and comments display.
- Embed an object from another application in a Word document.
- Link an object from another application to a Word document.
- Resize, arrange, and format linked or embedded objects.
- Update the source file and update the linked object.
- Break the object link between the source and destination files.
- Add a bookmark and insert a hyperlink and/or cross-reference to a bookmark.

CHAPTER 10

Automating Tasks Using Templates and Macros

CHAPTER OVERVIEW

Microsoft Word provides many tools to automate routine tasks and to work more efficiently. Templates store a common document structure, such as an agenda, check list, or company letterhead. Once you create a template, you can open a document based upon the template, modify the content, and save it with a new file name. The original template remains unchanged. Another tool available in Word is a macro. A macro is a stored set of instructions applied with a single command. Like templates, macros save time and add consistency to your documents.

STUDENT LEARNING OUTCOMES (SLOs)

After completing this chapter, you will be able to:

SLO 10.1 Create, save, and use a template to generate commonly used documents (p. W10-612).

SLO 10.2 Customize template content using a variety of Word fields and styles (p. W10-615).

SLO 10.3 Record a set of instructions as a macro and run and delete a macro (p. W10-622).

SLO 10.4 Copy and edit an existing macro using Visual Basic and add a keyboard and button shortcut to run a macro (p. W10-631).

SLO 10.5 Create and use a macro-enabled template to automate common tasks and copy a macro to another document (p. W10-638).

CASE STUDY

In the Pause & Practice projects in this chapter, you customize and use an agenda template for the student government at Sierra Pacific Community College District. You also create and use macros to automate common tasks used in Word documents.

Pause & Practice 10-1: Create and customize an agenda template and create a document based upon the template.

Pause & Practice 10-2: Create macros to store commonly used instructions and use these macros in the agenda template.

Pause & Practice 10-3: Edit existing macros, copy macros, assign a keyboard shortcut to a macro, and add macro buttons to the *Quick Access* toolbar.

Pause & Practice 10-4: Create a macro-enabled template, copy macros from another file, delete a macro, and create a document based upon the macro-enabled template.

Creating and Saving Templates

A *template* includes content and formatting and is used to create new documents quickly and with consistent format. You can create and customize new documents based on a template without modifying the structure and content of the original template file. For example, create an agenda template with formatting and placeholder text to use as the structure for a new agenda for each meeting. Use a template to avoid having to create a new agenda from scratch and to ensure the agendas have a consistent format.

A template file is a specific type of Word file that is different from a regular Word document. Template files have a *.dotx* file name extension, while regular Word document files have a .docx extension. You can save a new or existing document as a template or use a Word online template. Templates can also store styles, building blocks, and macros (macros are covered later in this chapter). Table 10-1 lists the types and extensions of the different Word files that you will be using in this chapter:

Table 10-1: Word Files

Word File Type	File Name Extension
Word Document	.docx
Word Template	.dotx
Word Macro-Enabled Document	.docm
Word Macro-Enabled Template	.dotm

Save a Document as a Template

When you create a new Word document, the document is, by default, a regular Word document (with a .docx extension). You can customize a new document and save it as a template file (with a .dotx extension) or save an existing document as a template file.

> ▶ **HOW TO:** Save a Document as a Template

1. Create a new document or open an existing document.
2. Click the **File** tab to open the *Backstage* view.
3. Click **Save As** on the left and click the **Browse** button to open the *Save As* dialog box (Figure 10-1).
4. Type the document name in the *File name* text box.
5. Click the **Save as type** drop-down list and select **Word Template**.
6. Browse to the location where you want to save your file.
   - When you select *Word Template* as the file type, the save location changes to the default location for templates. Be very specific where you save template files.
7. Click the **Save** button to close the dialog box and save the template.

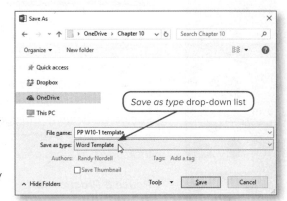

Figure 10-1 *Save As* dialog box

> ▶ ANOTHER WAY
>
> Press **F12** to open the *Save As* dialog box (when using a laptop computer, you may have to press **Fn+F12**).

Personal Templates

The *Custom Office Templates* folder is the default folder when saving a template file. After saving a template in this folder, it is available in the *Personal* templates area on the *Backstage* view. To view personal templates, open the *Backstage* view, click **New** on the left, and select **Personal** to view templates previously saved in the *Custom Office Templates* folder. Click a personal template to create a document based upon that template.

Online Word Templates

In addition to creating personal templates, Word provides a variety of online templates. Online templates are available in the *New* area on the *Backstage* view. Create a document based on an online template and customize it to meet your needs. Common templates are pinned to the list of templates in the *New* area. Search for other online templates by typing key words in the *Search for online templates* text box or clicking one of the *Suggested searches* links. Pin a template you use often to the template list or unpin templates from the existing list of templates. The *pin* icon displays in the bottom-right corner of the template.

After selecting an online template, a window opens that provides details about the template. When creating a file based upon a template, the file opens as a Word document (.docx).

▶ HOW TO: Use an Online Template

1. Click the **File** tab to open the *Backstage* view.
2. Click the **New** button on the left and click **Featured** to view the available online templates (Figure 10-2).
3. Search for online templates by clicking the **Search for online templates** text box and typing key words.
   - Alternatively, click one of the **Suggested searches** links to display related templates.
4. Select an online template to open a preview window (Figure 10-3).
   - A preview of the template appears on the left.
   - Details about the template appear on the right.
   - Click the **Previous** or **Next** button on the left or right to scroll through additional online templates in the same category.
   - Click the **pin** icon near the upper-right corner to pin a template to the *New* area on the *Backstage* view.
5. Click the **Create** button.
   - The online template opens as a Word document in a new window.
   - When you create a document based on an online template, the template is attached to the document.
6. Save the file as a template file or regular Word document.

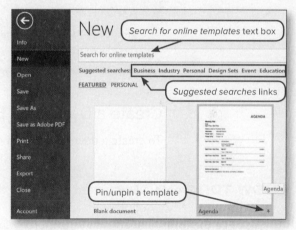

Figure 10-2 Online template in the *New* area on the *Backstage* view

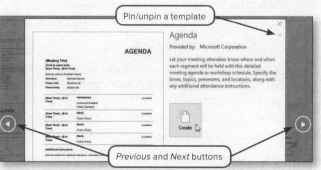

Figure 10-3 Template displayed in preview area

Edit a Template

When working with templates or documents based on templates, the method you use to open a file determines whether a file opens as a template or a document based on a template. You can open, edit, and customize a template file (.dotx). Alternatively, create a Word document (.docx) based on a template (see the next section, *Create a Document Based on a Template*).

▶HOW TO: Edit a Template

1. Click the **File** tab to open the *Backstage* view.
2. Click the **Open** button on the left.
3. Click **Browse** to display the *Open* dialog box (Figure 10-4).
   - The file icon for a template is different from the icon for a regular Word document. The file icon helps to distinguish the file type.
4. Locate and select the template you want to edit.
5. Click the **Open** button to display the template file for editing.
   - When you open a file, the file name appears in the title bar at the top center of the Word window.

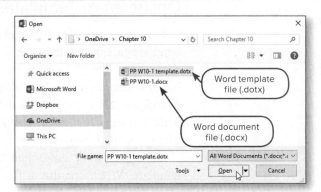

Figure 10-4 Open a template from the *Open* dialog box

▶ ANOTHER WAY

Press **Ctrl+F12** to display the *Open* dialog box (if you're using a laptop computer, you might have to press **Fn+Ctrl+F12**).

Create a Document Based on a Template

To create a document based on a template, always open the file from a *File Explorer* window.

▶HOW TO: Create a Document Based on a Template

1. Click **File Explorer** to open the *File Explorer* window.
   - The *File Explorer* button may be located on the Windows *Taskbar* or on the *Start* menu.
2. Browse to locate the template file (Figure 10-5).
3. Double-click the template file.
   - Alternatively, select the template file and press **Enter**.
   - Word opens a document (.docx) based upon the template and names the file with a generic file name (*Document1*), which displays in the title area of the Word window.
4. Save the new document.
   - Because this document is a new file based on a template, Word prompts you to save the document before closing it.

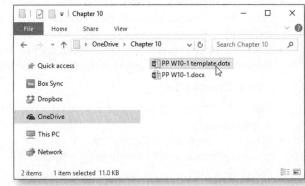

Figure 10-5 Open a document based on a template from a *File Explorer* window

SLO 10.2

Customizing and Using Templates

When creating a new document from an online template, content and formatting display in the document. Customize and format the template content to meet your needs. You can create a document based on a template or attach a template to an existing file. After attaching a template to a document, the styles and building blocks in the template are available in the document. You can also copy styles from one template to another template or document.

Customize Template Content

Online templates provide a basic structure and sample text for documents. Templates can also include content control fields, Word fields, and document property fields. You can add content, customize existing fields, add document property fields, or insert Word fields in a template.

Content Control Fields

Online templates include ***content control fields***. Content control fields are placeholders where users customize content such as enter text, select a date, or check a box. When you enter text in a content control field, the content control field is replaced by the text you type. You can move, copy, or delete these fields.

▶ **HOW TO:** Use Content Control Fields

1. Open the template or document with content control fields.
2. Click the **handle** of the content control field to select it (Figure 10-6).
   - Drag the field to a new location, copy it, or delete it.
   - Alternatively, right-click a content control field and select **Remove Content Control** to delete the field.
   - Deselect a content control field by pressing the **left** or **right** keyboard arrow key or clicking away from the content control field.
3. Type custom text in the content control field.
   - The content control field is replaced with the typed text.

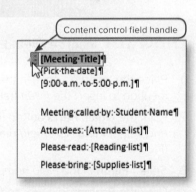

Figure 10-6 Content control field

Document Property Fields

Online templates typically include ***document property fields***. Document property fields are populated with content from the document properties. If the document property field is empty, the field displays the document property field name. You can add or remove document property fields.

▶ HOW TO: Customize and Insert Document Property Fields

1. Click the **handle** of the document property field to select it (Figure 10-7).
2. Type the content in the document property field.
   - The content you type populates the document property in the document.
   - Alternatively, click the **File** tab to open the *Backstage* view and edit document properties. This information displays in document property fields in the document.
3. Insert a document property field by placing the insertion point in the document at the desired location, clicking the **Quick Parts** button [*Insert* tab, *Text* group], clicking **Document Property**, and selecting the document property field to insert.
4. Remove a document property field by right-clicking the field and selecting **Remove Content Control**.
   - Alternatively, select the field handle and press **Delete**.

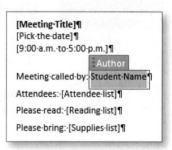

[Meeting·Title]¶
[Pick·the·date]¶
[9:00·a.m.·to·5:00·p.m.]¶
Author
Meeting·called·by:·Student·Name¶
Attendees:·[Attendee·list]¶
Please·read:·[Reading·list]¶
Please·bring:·[Supplies·list]¶

Figure 10-7 Document property field

Word Fields

Use Word fields in a template to automatically insert content. For example, use a Word field to automatically insert the last date the document was saved (*SaveDate*), add user name (*UserName*) or user initials (*UserInitials*), or include the file name of the document (*FileName*). Another useful field for templates is the ***Fill-in*** field. The *Fill-in* field prompts a user for information when a template or document based on a template opens.

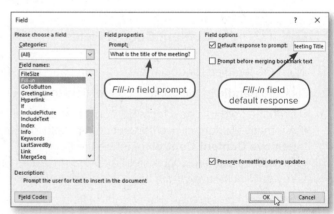

Figure 10-8 Insert a *Fill-in* field

▶ HOW TO: Insert a Fill-in Field

1. Place the insertion point in the template at the location to insert the *Fill-in* field.
2. Click the **Quick Parts** button [*Insert* tab, *Text* group] and select **Field**. The *Field* dialog box opens (Figure 10-8).
3. Select **Fill-in** in the *Field names* area.
4. Click the **Prompt** text box and type the prompt for the user.
5. Check the **Default response to prompt** check box in the *Field options* area and type a default response for the prompt.
   - The default response is text that displays in the field if the user does not type a response to the fill-in prompt.
6. Click **OK** to close the dialog box and to insert the field. A prompt dialog box opens (Figure 10-9).

Figure 10-9 *Fill-in* field prompt dialog box

7. Click **OK** to close the prompt dialog box and to insert the default text.
   - The default text displays in the *Fill-in* field (Figure 10-10).
   - When creating a document based on this template, the prompt dialog box opens (see Figure 10-9). The user accepts the default text or types text to replace the default response and to populate the *Fill-in* field.

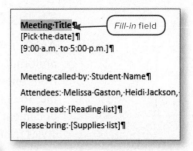

Figure 10-10 *Fill-in* field in the template

Attach a Template to a Document

When you create a document based on a template, the template automatically attaches to the document. Another way to connect a template to a document is to manually attach the template to the document. After attaching a template to a document, the styles, building blocks, and macros stored in the template become available in the document. Additionally, set the document to automatically update whenever changes are made to the template file.

▶ HOW TO: Attach a Template to a Document

1. Open the document on which you want to attach a template.
2. Click the **Document Template** button [*Developer* tab, *Templates* group]. The *Templates and Add-ins* dialog box opens (Figure 10-11).
   - If the *Developer* tab does not display on the *Ribbon*, click the **File** tab to open the *Backstage* view, select **Options** on the left to open the *Word Options* dialog box, click **Customize Ribbon**, check the **Developer** box on the right, and click **OK**.
3. Click the **Attach** button in the *Document template* area to open the *Attach Template* dialog box.
4. Select the template to attach and click **Open** to attach the template.
5. Check the **Automatically update document styles** box.

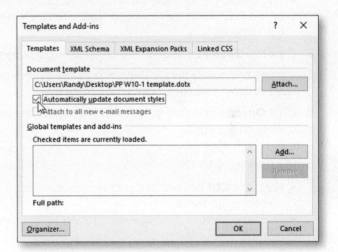

Figure 10-11 Attach a template to a document

   - If this box is checked, the styles in the document update each time styles are modified in the template.
   - If this box is not checked, the styles in the document do not update when the styles in the template are modified.
6. Click **OK** to close the *Templates and Add-ins* dialog box and attach the template to the document.

When creating a document based on a template, the template file automatically attaches to the document, but, by default, styles in the document do not automatically update when the styles in the template are modified. Change this setting by checking the **Automatically update document styles** box in the *Templates and Add-ins* dialog box.

Styles Organizer

Another way to automate tasks and create uniformity in documents is to copy styles from one document to another. For example, you can copy styles from a template or other document without attaching a template to a document or creating a document based on a template. Use the *Organizer* dialog box to copy styles from a template or document to another template or document.

> **MORE INFO**
>
> You cannot attach a template to a template file.

▶ HOW TO: Copy Styles into a Document

1. Open the document or template into which you want to copy styles.
2. Click the **Document Template** button [*Developer* tab, *Templates* group] to open the *Templates and Add-ins* dialog box.
3. Click the **Organizer** button to open the *Organizer* dialog box.
   - The open document displays on the left, and the styles display below the file name.
   - The template on which the document is based displays on the right. By default, new blank Word documents are based on the *Normal* template.
4. Click the **Close File** button below the styles in the document on the right (Figure 10-12).
   - This closes the template on which the document is based, and the *Close File* button becomes the *Open File* button.
5. Click the **Open File** button. The *Open* dialog box opens.
6. Browse and select the file that contains the styles you want to copy. This file is called the source file.
7. Click **Open** to open the source file. The source file styles display on the right.
8. Select the styles on the right to copy to the document on the left (Figure 10-13).
   - Press the **Ctrl** key and use your pointer to select non-adjacent styles.
   - Press the **Shift** key and use your pointer to select a range of adjacent styles.
9. Click the **Copy** button to copy the selected styles.
   - If the same style(s) exist in the document where you are copying the styles, a dialog box opens. Click **Yes** or **Yes to All** to overwrite the existing style(s).
10. Click the **Close** button to close the *Organizer* dialog box.
    - The copied styles display in the *Styles* gallery and *Styles* pane.

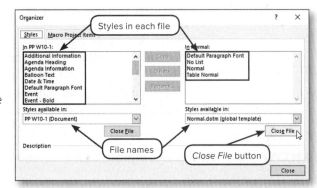

Figure 10-12 *Organizer* dialog box

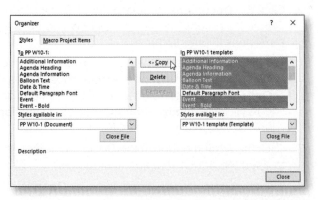

Figure 10-13 Copy selected styles

> **MORE INFO**
>
> Use the *Organizer* dialog box to delete styles from a document.

For this Pause & Practice project, you create and modify a template for Sierra Pacific Community College District student government meeting agendas. You save a document as a template, customize document property and content control fields, insert *Fill-in* fields, and create a document based on the template.

File Needed: **SPCCDAgenda-10.docx** *(Student data files are available in the* Library *of your SIMnet account.)*
Completed Project File Names: *[your initials] PP W10-1 template.dotx* and *[your initials] PP W10-1.docx*

1. Open the **SPCCDAgenda_10** document from your student data files.

2. Save the document as a Word template.
   a. Open the *Save As* dialog box (Figure 10-14).
   b. Type [your initials] PP W10-1 template in the *File name* text box.
   c. Click the **Save as type** drop-down list and select **Word Template**.
   d. Browse to the location where you want to save your file.
   e. Click **Save** to save the template.

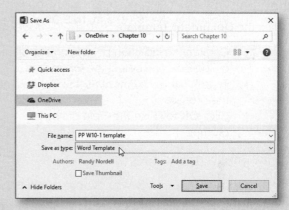
Figure 10-14 Save document as a Word template file

3. Customize the title.
   a. Select "**agenda**" and delete it. Don't delete the paragraph mark.
   b. Type SPCCD Student Government Agenda as the title.

4. Add content to document property and content control fields.
   a. Click the "**Author**" (*Student Name*) document property field handle to select the field (Figure 10-15).
   b. Type your first and last name to replace the existing document property.
   c. Select the "**Attendee list**" content control field and type the following text: Melissa Gaston, Heidi Jackson, Rachel Sanchez, Peter Zanko, Ron Costa, Roietta Molden, and Ravi Kumar.
   d. Select the "**Introduction**" content control field in the table and type Welcome and Meeting Overview to replace the placeholder text.
   e. Select the "**Wrap-up**" content control field and type Wrap-up and Adjourn to replace the placeholder text.

Figure 10-15 Document property field

5. Customize the table content.
   a. Place the insertion point on the blank line above the content control field in the third cell in the first row of the table (above "[Rainier Room]"). Turn on **View Gridline** to display table gridlines.
   b. Type Location as the heading.
   c. Select "**Location**" and apply the **Event – Bold** style [*Home* tab, *Styles* group].

6. Insert *Fill-in* fields.
   a. Select the "**Meeting Title**" content control field handle to select it and press **Delete** to remove the content control field.
   b. Confirm the insertion point is on the blank line above the "Pick the date" field.

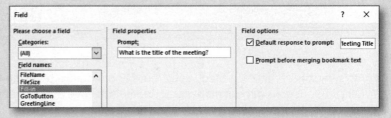

Figure 10-16 Insert *Fill-in* field

c. Click the **Quick Parts** button [*Insert* tab, *Text* group], and select **Field** to open the *Field* dialog box (Figure 10-16).

d. Select **Fill-in** in the *Field names* area.

e. Type What is the title of the meeting? in the *Prompt* text box.

f. Check the **Default response to prompt** box and type Meeting Title in the text box.

g. Click **OK** to close the *Field* dialog box and insert the *Fill-in* field. The prompt dialog box opens.

h. Click **OK** to accept the default response to the *Fill-in* prompt.

i. Right-click the "**9:00 a.m. to 5:00 p.m.**" content control field and select **Remove Content Control** from the context menu.

j. Confirm the insertion point is on the blank line below the "Pick the date" field, open the **Field** dialog box, and select the **Fill-in** field.

k. Type What is the time of the meeting? as the prompt and Meeting Time as the default response to the prompt.

l. Click **OK** to close the *Field* dialog box and click **OK** to accept the default response to the *Fill-in* prompt.

7. Save and close the template.

8. Open a *File Explorer* window, browse to the location of the *[your initials] PP W10-1 template* file, and double-click it to open a document based on the template.

9. Type custom content for *Fill-in* field prompts.
   a. Type Fall Welcome Day and click **OK** at the first prompt.
   b. Type 3 to 5 p.m. and click **OK** at the second prompt.

10. Save the document as a Word document and name it [your initials] PP W10-1. If prompted to save changes to the document template, click **Yes**.

11. Customize agenda content.
    a. Click the **[Pick the date]** field below "Fall Welcome Day" and select next Tuesday.
    b. Click the **Author** document property field to the right of "Meeting called by:" and type your first and last name (if it is not already entered).
    c. Click the **[Reading list]** field and type Fall Welcome Day Flyer and Welcome Day Guidelines to replace the content control field.
    d. Click the **[Supplies list]** field and type Same as above to replace the content control field.
    e. Click the **[9 a.m. – 10 a.m.]** field in the first cell in the table and type 3:00-3:15 to replace the content control field. If necessary, turn on **View Gridlines** [*Table Tools Layout* tab, *Table* group] to display table gridlines.
    f. Type the following times to replace the remaining time content control fields in the second, third, and fourth rows in the first column in the table.
       3:15-4:00
       4:00-4:45
       4:45-5:00

12. Customize headings and table content in the agenda.
    a. Click the content control field below "Welcome and Meeting Overview" in the second column in the first row and type your first and last name.
    b. Click the content control field below "Location" in the third column in the first row and type Sequoia Room to replace the content control field.

c. Click the **[Demos]** field (second column in the second row) and type Breakout Groups to replace the content control field.

d. Click the **[Working groups]** field (second column in the third row) and type Fall Welcome Day Planning to replace the content control field.

e. Click the content control field below "Breakout Groups" (second column in the second row) and type the following. Press **Enter** after each of the first two entries:
Club President: Melissa Gaston
Marketing: Peter Zanko
Facilities: Rachel Sanchez

f. Click the content control field in the third column in the second row and type the following. Press **Enter** after each of the first two entries:
Sequoia Room
Redwood Room
Oak Room

g. Click the content control field below "Fall Welcome Day Planning" in the second column in the third row and type To-do list and needs from each group to replace the content control field.

h. Click the content control field in the third column in the third row and type Sequoia Room to replace the content control field.

i. Click the content control field below "Wrap-up and Adjourn" in the second column in the fourth row and type Old business to replace the content control field.

j. Click the content control field in the third column in the fourth row and type Sequoia Room to replace the content control field.

k. Click the content control field below "Additional Information:" below the table and type Our next meeting is next Tuesday from 3 to 5 p.m. to replace the content control field.

l. Compare your document with Figure 10-17. Do not apply highlight format to the text you typed.

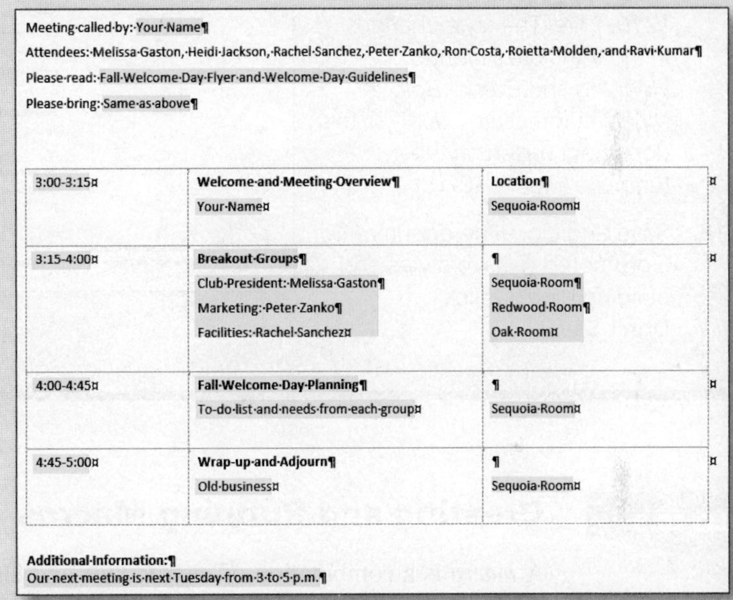

Meeting·called·by:·Your·Name¶
Attendees:·Melissa·Gaston,·Heidi·Jackson,·Rachel·Sanchez,·Peter·Zanko,·Ron·Costa,·Roietta·Molden,·and·Ravi·Kumar¶
Please·read:·Fall·Welcome·Day·Flyer·and·Welcome·Day·Guidelines¶
Please·bring:·Same·as·above¶

3:00-3:15¤	Welcome·and·Meeting·Overview¶ Your·Name¤	Location¶ Sequoia·Room¤	¤
3:15-4:00¤	Breakout·Groups¶ Club·President:·Melissa·Gaston¶ Marketing:·Peter·Zanko¶ Facilities:·Rachel·Sanchez¤	¶ Sequoia·Room¶ Redwood·Room¶ Oak·Room¤	¤
4:00-4:45¤	Fall·Welcome·Day·Planning¶ To-do·list·and·needs·from·each·group¤	¶ Sequoia·Room¤	¤
4:45-5:00¤	Wrap-up·and·Adjourn¶ Old·business¤	¶ Sequoia·Room¤	¤

Additional·Information:¶
Our·next·meeting·is·next·Tuesday·from·3·to·5·p.m.¶

Figure 10-17 Type text in content control fields

13. Change the document so styles are updated automatically if the template is modified.

a. Click the **Document Template** button [*Developer* tab, *Templates* group] to open the *Templates and Add-ins* dialog box.

b. Check the **Automatically update document styles** box and click **OK** to close the dialog box.

> **MORE INFO**
>
> If the *Developer* tab does not display on your *Ribbon*, click the **File** tab to open the *Backstage* view, select **Options** to open the *Word Options* dialog box, click **Customize Ribbon**, and then check the **Developer** box on the right.

14. Save and close the document. If prompted to save changes to the document template, click **Yes**.

15. Modify styles in the template file.
    a. Open the *[your initials] PP W10-1 template* file from within Word, not *File Explorer*.
    b. Select the title ("**SPCCD Student Government Agenda**").
    c. Change the font size to **28 pt** and apply **bold** and **small caps** formatting.
    d. Change line spacing to **Single** (1), *Before* paragraph spacing to **12 pt**, and *After* paragraph spacing to **0 pt**.
    e. Confirm the title is still selected, right-click the **Agenda Heading** style [*Home* tab, *Styles* group] and select **Update Agenda Heading to Match Selection** to update this style.
    f. Modify the **Event – Bold** style to apply **small caps** formatting. Each of the headings in the table changes to small caps.

16. Save and close the template file.

17. Open the *[your initials] PP W10-1* file. The style changes in the template (*Agenda Heading* and *Event - Bold* styles) automatically apply to this document based on the template (Figure 10-18).

18. Save and close the document. If prompted to save styles and building blocks, click **Don't Save**.

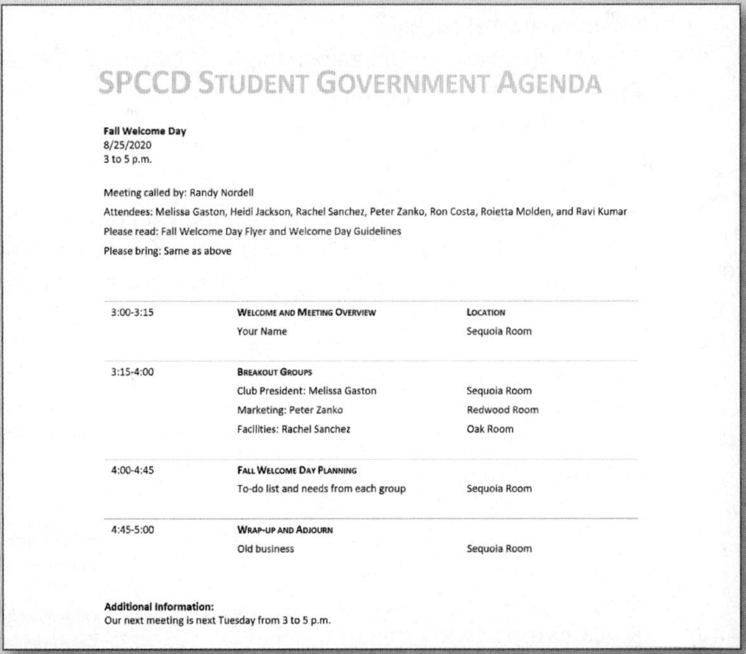

Figure 10-18 PP W10-1 completed

Creating and Running Macros

A *macro* is a combination of instructions and keystrokes that you store to use in future documents. Macros save time by recording and saving instructions you regularly use. For example, create a macro to insert and customize a header, to insert an *AutoText* building block, or to insert a custom watermark. Run macros quickly by assigning and using a keystroke combination or a button on the *Quick Access* toolbar. After creating a macro, it is available for other documents.

Plan a Macro

When creating a macro, plan what the macro will do, where you will store the macro, and how you will run the macro. Before creating a macro, ask yourself the following questions:

1. *What will my macro do?* A macro stores keystrokes and button selections. Carefully plan the macro keystrokes and commands before recording your macro.
2. *Where should I save my macro?* A macro can be stored in a template or in a document. If a macro is stored in a document, it is only available in that document. If a macro is stored in a template, the macro is available in the template and all documents based on that template. Alternatively, store a macro in the *Normal* template where it will be available in all new documents you create.

3. *How will I run my macro?* A macro can be assigned to a shortcut key such as **Ctrl+Shift+Alt+H** or a button on the *Quick Access* toolbar. Additionally, use the *Macros* dialog box to run a macro.

Record a Keyboard-Activated Macro

Similar to recording a video on a phone, a macro records the actions you perform and stores them for later use. After you plan what your macro will do, where it will be stored, and how it will run, you are ready to record the macro.

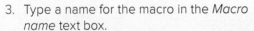

▶HOW TO: Record a Keyboard-Activated Macro

1. Place the insertion point at the location to record the macro.
   - When inserting text or an object, begin recording the macro with the insertion point at the location where the object will be inserted.
   - When inserting a header, footer, or watermark, the location of the insertion point is not important.

2. Click the **Record Macro** button [*Developer* tab, *Code* group] (Figure 10-19). The *Record Macro* dialog box opens (Figure 10-20).

3. Type a name for the macro in the *Macro name* text box.
   - Do not use spaces between words in a macro name. Use an underscore to separate words if necessary.
   - Macro names can include letters, numbers, and the underscore.

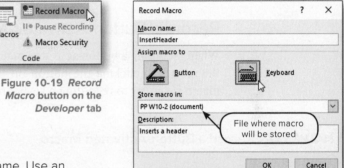

Figure 10-19 *Record Macro* button on the *Developer* tab

Figure 10-20 *Record Macro* dialog box

4. Click the **Store macro in** drop-down list and select the document or template where the macro will be stored.

5. Type a brief description for the macro in the *Description* text box (optional).

6. Click the **Keyboard** button to open the *Customize Keyboard* dialog box (Figure 10-21).

7. Click the **Save changes in** drop-down list and select the document or template where the keyboard shortcut will be saved.

8. Place the insertion point in the **Press new shortcut key** text box and press the keyboard sequence to use as the shortcut key for the macro.
   - Use a combination of **Ctrl**, **Shift**, **Alt**, and a letter or number for the shortcut key.
   - If the shortcut key is assigned to another command or macro, Word displays the macro or command to which the shortcut key is assigned in the *Currently assigned to* area.
   - If using a keyboard sequence that is already a keyboard shortcut (such as **Ctrl+S** for save), the keyboard sequence for the macro replaces the existing shortcut.
   - Choose a different shortcut key if the one you select is assigned to another command shortcut.

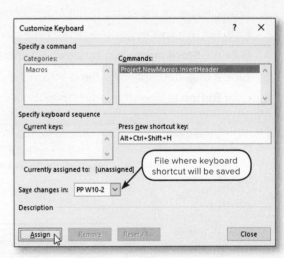

Figure 10-21 *Customize Keyboard* dialog box

9. Click the **Assign** button to assign the keyboard sequence as the macro shortcut.

10. Click the **Close** button to close the dialog box and to begin recording the macro. The pointer changes to a macro-recording pointer (Figure 10-22).

Figure 10-22 Record macro pointer

11. Perform the actions to record as a macro.

   - For example, edit a header, insert and format text in the header, and then close the header.
   - Click the **Pause Recording** button [*Developer* tab, *Code* group] to pause the recording. For example, use *Pause Recording* to perform an action you don't want recorded in the macro.

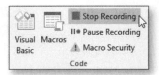

Figure 10-23 Stop recording the macro

12. Click the **Stop Recording** button [*Developer* tab, *Code* group] to stop recording the macro and store the macro (Figure 10-23).

▶ ANOTHER WAY

Click the bottom half of the **Macros** button [*View* tab, *Macros* group] and select **Record Macro**, or click the **Macros** button on the *Status* bar to open the *Record Macro* dialog box.

Record a Button-Activated Macro

When recording a button-activated macro, the button appears on the *Quick Access* toolbar. Run the macro by clicking the button on the *Quick Access* toolbar. Recording a button-activated macro is similar to recording a keyboard-activated macro.

▶HOW TO: Record a Button-Activated Macro

1. Place the insertion point at the location to record the macro.
2. Click the **Record Macro** button [*Developer* tab, *Code* group]. The *Record Macro* dialog box opens.
3. Type a name for the macro In the *Macro name* text box.
   - Do not use spaces between words in a macro name. If needed, use an underscore to separate words.
4. Click the **Store macro in** drop-down list and select the document or template where the macro will be stored.
5. Type a brief description for the macro in the *Description* text box (optional).
6. Click **Button** to open the *Word Options* dialog box (Figure 10-24).

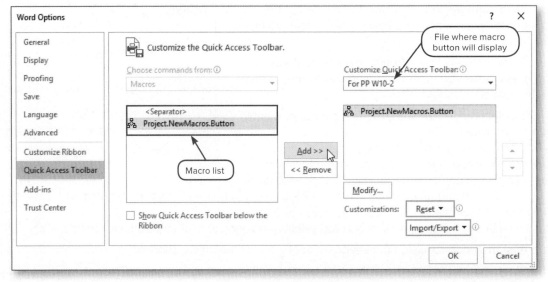

Figure 10-24 Add a macro to the *Quick Access* toolbar

7. Click the **Customize Quick Access Toolbar** drop-down list on the right and select the document or template where the macro button will be stored.

8. Select the **macro** in the list on the left (for example, **Project.NewMacro.Button**) and click the **Add** button (see Figure 10-24).

9. Click the **Modify** button. The *Modify Button* dialog box opens (Figure 10-25).

10. Type a name for the button in the *Display name* text box.

11. Select a symbol to use as the button. Word provides a variety of button symbol options.

12. Click **OK** to close the *Modify Button* dialog box.

13. Click the **OK** button to close the *Word Options* dialog box and begin recording the macro. The pointer changes to a macro-recording pointer.

14. Perform the actions to record as a macro.

15. Click the **Stop Recording** button [*Developer* tab, *Code* group] to stop recording the macro.

   - The macro button displays on the *Quick Access* toolbar (Figure 10-26).

Figure 10-25 *Modify Button* dialog box

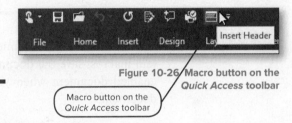

Figure 10-26 Macro button on the *Quick Access* toolbar

Macro button on the *Quick Access* toolbar

> **MORE INFO**
>
> Assigning a macro keyboard shortcut or adding a button on the *Quick Access* toolbar is not required. In this case, run the macro from the *Macros* dialog box.

Save a Macro-Enabled Document

After recording a macro, save the document as a macro-enabled document to store the macro in the document. When saving a document containing macros, Word prompts you to either save the document as a *Word Macro-Enabled Document* or remove the macros from the document. A Word macro-enabled document has a *.docm* file extension.

> **MORE INFO**
>
> If a document contains macros and is not saved as a macro-enabled document, Word removes the macros in the document.

▶ **HOW TO: Save as a Macro-Enabled Document**

1. Press **Ctrl+S** or click the **Save** button on the *Quick Access* toolbar to save a document containing a macro.

   - When you save a document that contains a macro, a dialog box opens and informs you the document contains macros (Figure 10-27).

2. Click **No** to open the *Save As* dialog box (Figure 10-28).

   - If you click *Yes*, the document is saved, and the macros are removed from the document.

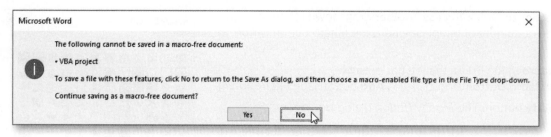

Figure 10-27 Dialog box prompting you to save as a macro-enabled document

3. Type a file name in the *File name* text box.

4. Click the **Save as type** drop-down list and select **Word Macro-Enabled Document**.

   - Saving a document as a macro-enabled template is covered in *SLO 10.5: Creating and Using Macro-Enabled Templates*.

5. Click the **Save** button.

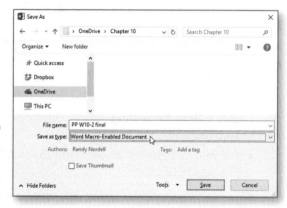

When creating a document that will contain macros, save the document as a macro-enabled document when you first save the document.

Figure 10-28 Save as a Word macro-enabled document

> **MORE INFO**
>
> The file icon for a macro-enabled document is different from the icon for a regular Word document and other Word file types.

Macro Security Settings

Because a macro is a program that runs within your document, Word provides security settings to control the action of macros when opening a document containing macros. The following are four different macro settings:

- *Disable all macros without notification*: All macros in the document are disabled without notification.
- *Disable all macros with notification*: All macros in the document are temporarily disabled and a security warning appears in the *Info* bar (Figure 10-29). Click the **Enable Content** button to enable macros in the document. This is the default setting, and the best setting to use.

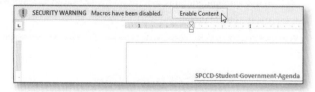

Figure 10-29 Click *Enable Content* to enable macros

- *Disable all macros except digitally signed macros*: All macros in the document are disabled except for digitally signed macros. Digitally signed macros are typically used in highly confidential documents and are not common.
- *Enable all macros*: All macros in the document are enabled. This is not recommended because of the potential danger of viruses encoded in a macro.

▶HOW TO: Change Macro Security Settings

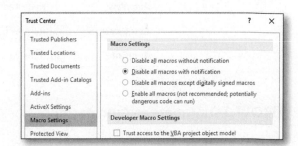

1. Click the **Macro Security** button [*Developer* tab, *Code* group]. The *Trust Center* dialog box opens (Figure 10-30).
   - Alternatively, open the *Trust Center* from the *Word Options* dialog box.
2. Select a macro setting in the *Macro Settings* area.
3. Click **OK** to close the *Trust Center* dialog box.

Figure 10-30 Macro settings in the *Trust Center* dialog box

Run a Macro

Running a macro inserts the recorded macro actions into the document. Run a keyboard-activated macro by pressing the keyboard shortcut key. Run a button-activated macro by clicking the macro button on the *Quick Access* toolbar. Alternatively, run a macro from the *Macros* dialog box.

▶HOW TO: Run a Macro from the Macros Dialog Box

1. Click the **Macros** button [*Developer* tab, *Code* group] to open the *Macros* dialog box (Figure 10-31).
2. Select the macro to run from the *Macro name* area.
3. Click the **Run** button.
   - The *Macros* dialog box automatically closes when you run a macro.

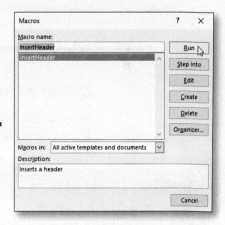

> **ANOTHER WAY**
>
> **Alt+F8** opens the *Macros* dialog box.

Figure 10-31 *Macros* dialog box

Create an AutoMacro

Word also provides *AutoMacros* that automatically run when you perform a specific action. For example, create an *AutoMacro* to insert the current date each time you open a document or remove a watermark when you save and close a document. Each *AutoMacro* uses a specific macro name that Word recognizes as a macro. Because *AutoMacros* run automatically, a macro button or keyboard shortcut is not necessary. Table 10-2 lists *AutoMacros* and a description of each:

Table 10-2: Types of AutoMacros

AutoMacro	Description
AutoExec	Runs when you open Word
AutoOpen	Runs each time you open a Word document
AutoNew	Runs each time you create a new Word document
AutoClose	Runs each time you close a Word document
AutoExit	Runs when you exit Word

▶ HOW TO: Create an AutoMacro

1. Click the **Record Macro** button to open the *Record Macro* dialog box (Figure 10-32).
2. Type the *AutoMacro* name in the *Macro name* text box.
3. Click the **Store macro in** drop-down list and select the document or template where you want to store the macro.
4. Type a brief description of the macro in the *Description* text box.
5. Click **OK** to begin recording the macro.
   - A macro button or keyboard shortcut is not necessary because an *AutoMacro* runs automatically when you perform an action such as open or close a document.
6. Perform the actions to be recorded in the *AutoMacro*.
7. Click the **Stop Recording** button [*Developer* tab, *Code* group].
   - The *AutoMacro* runs the next time you perform the specified action.
   - The *AutoMacro* displays in the *Macros* dialog box.

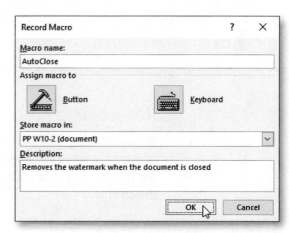

Figure 10-32 Record an *AutoMacro*

Delete a Macro

When a macro is no longer needed in a document or template, delete the macro using the *Macros* dialog box.

▶ HOW TO: Delete a Macro

1. Click the **Macros** button [*Developer* tab, *Code* group] to open the *Macros* dialog box.
2. Select the macro you want to delete from the list of macros in the *Macro name* area.
3. Click the **Delete** button. A dialog box opens asking if you want to delete the macro (Figure 10-33).
4. Click **Yes** to delete the macro.
5. **Close** the *Macros* dialog box.

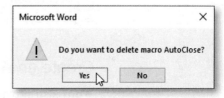

Figure 10-33 Delete a macro

For this Pause & Practice project, you modify the agenda document you created based on an agenda template. You create a macro to insert a header, create an *AutoMacro* to remove a watermark, save the agenda as a macro-enabled document, and delete a macro.

File Needed: *[your initials] PP W10-1.docx*
Completed Project File Names: *[your initials] PP W10-2.docx* and *[your initials] PP W10-2 final.docm*

1. Open the *[your initials] PP W10-1* document (not the template) completed in *Pause & Practice 10-1*.

2. Save the document as [your initials] PP W10-2 (regular Word document).

3. Create a keyboard-activated macro to insert a header.
   a. Click the **Record Macro** button [*Developer* tab, *Code* group] to open the *Record Macro* dialog box (Figure 10-34).
   b. Type InsertHeader (no spaces between words) in the *Macro name* text box.
   c. Click the **Store macro in** drop-down list and select **[your initials] PP W10-2 (document)**.
   d. Type Inserts a header in the *Description* text box.
   e. Click the **Keyboard** button to open the *Customize Keyboard* dialog box (Figure 10-35).
   f. Click the **Save changes in** drop-down list and select **[your initials] PP W10-2**.
   g. Place the insertion point in the **Press new shortcut key** text box and press **Alt+Ctrl+Shift+H**.
   h. Click the **Assign** button to assign the keyboard shortcut to the macro.
   i. Click the **Close** button to close the *Customize Keyboard* dialog box and to begin recording the macro.

4. Record a macro to insert a header.
   a. Click the **Header** button [*Insert* tab, *Header & Footer* group] and select **Edit Header** from the drop-down list to open the header.
   b. Click the **Bold** button [*Home* tab, *Font* group].
   c. Type SPCCD Student Government Agenda and press **Tab** two times to move the insertion point to the right margin.
   d. Type Last updated: and **space** once.
   e. Click the **Date & Time** button [*Header & Footer Tools Design* tab, *Insert* group] to open the *Date and Time* dialog box.
   f. Select the number date format (1/1/2020), check the **Update automatically** box, and click **OK** to close the dialog box and to insert the date.
   g. Click the **Borders** drop-down button [*Home* tab, *Paragraph* group] and select **Bottom Border**.
   h. Click the **Close Header and Footer** button [*Header & Footer Tools Design* tab, *Close* group] to close the header.
   i. Click the **Stop Recording** button [*Developer* tab, *Code* group].

Figure 10-34 Record a keyboard-activated macro

Figure 10-35 Assign a keyboard shortcut to the macro

5. Test the macro.
   a. Edit the header, delete all the information in the header (including the bottom border), and close the header.
   b. Press **Alt+Ctrl+Shift+H** to run the macro. The header displays in the document.

6. Click the **Watermark** button [*Design* tab, *Page Background* group] and select the **Draft 1** watermark.

7. Create and record an *AutoClose* macro that runs each time you close the document.

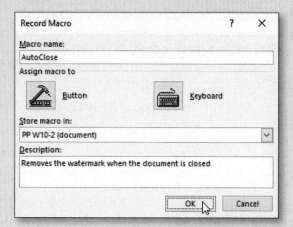

   a. Click the **Record Macro** button [*Developer* tab, *Code* group] to open the *Record Macro* dialog box (Figure 10-36).
   b. Type AutoClose (no spaces between words) in the *Macro name* text box.
   c. Click the **Store macro in** drop-down list and select **[your initials] PP W10-2 (document)**.
   d. Type Removes the watermark when the document is closed in the *Description* text box.
   e. Click the **OK** button to close the *Record Macro* dialog box and begin recording the macro.
   f. Click the **Watermark** button [*Design* tab, *Page Background* group] and select **Remove Watermark** from the drop-down list.

Figure 10-36 Record an *AutoClose* macro

   g. Click the **Stop Recording** button [*Developer* tab, *Code* group].

8. Click the **Watermark** button and select the **Draft 1** watermark to insert it.

9. Save the document as a macro-enabled document and close the document.

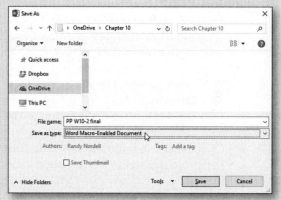

   a. Click the **Save** button or press **Ctrl+S** to save the document. A dialog box opens informing you that the macro cannot be saved in a macro-free document.
   b. Click **No** in the dialog box to open the *Save As* dialog box.
   c. Click the **Save as type** drop-down list and select **Word Macro-Enabled Document** (Figure 10-37).
   d. Type [your initials] PP W10-2 final in the *File name* text box.

Figure 10-37 Save the agenda as a macro-enabled document

   e. Select the location to save the document and click **Save** to save the macro-enabled document. If prompted to save changes to the template, click **Yes**.
   f. Close the document. The watermark is removed, and you are prompted to save the document.
   g. Click **Save** to save and close the document.

10. Open a macro-enabled document and enable the macro content.
    a. Open the **[your initials] PP W10-2 final** document. If this document does not display in the location where you saved the file, select **All Files** from the file type drop-down list (above the *Open* button) in the *Open* dialog box.
    b. Click **Enable Content** in the *Info* bar to enable the macros in the document (Figure 10-38) if a security warning displays in the *Info* bar. Notice that the watermark has been removed.

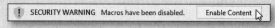

Figure 10-38 Enable macros in the document

11. Delete the *AutoClose* macro.
    a. Click the **Macros** button [*Developer* tab, *Code* group] to open the *Macros* dialog box.
    b. Select the **AutoClose** macro and click the **Delete** button. A dialog box opens asking if you want to delete the macro.
    c. Click **Yes** to delete the macro.
    d. Click **Close** to close the *Macros* dialog box.

12. Save and close the document (Figure 10-39). If prompted to save changes to the template, click **Yes**.

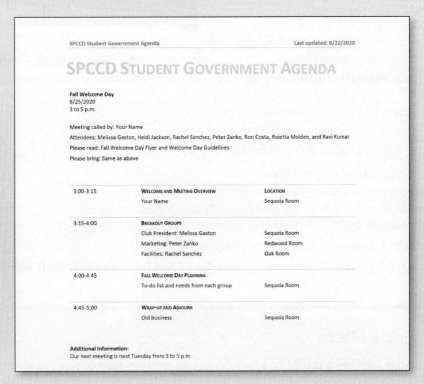

Figure 10-39 PP W10-2 final completed

Copying and Editing Macros

Macros are programs that run within Word, and they are coded in *Visual Basic* programming language. When recording a macro, Word automatically creates and stores the Visual Basic code in the macro. You can copy and edit a macro rather than creating another macro. The *Microsoft Visual Basic editor* is the program used to edit or copy a macro. You don't need knowledge of Visual Basic programming to copy a macro and do simple editing.

Copy a Macro

Copying and editing a macro can save time. For example, copy a macro that inserts a header and edit it so it inserts a footer instead. This section explains how to copy a macro, and the next section explains how to edit a macro. Copy a macro to create a macro that is similar to an existing macro. When creating a macro that is very different from an existing macro, it is easier to record a new macro.

▶ HOW TO: Copy a Macro

1. Click the **Macros** button [*Developer* tab, *Code* group] to open the *Macros* dialog box.
2. Select the macro to copy and click the **Edit** button. The *Microsoft Visual Basic* editor opens.
3. Select the Visual Basic code for the macro and click the **Copy** button or press **Ctrl+C** to copy it (Figure 10-40).
   - A macro begins with "Sub" and the name of the macro.
   - A macro ends with "End Sub."
   - The green text near the top is comment text that displays the macro name and description.
   - The coding in the middle describes the actions the macro performs.

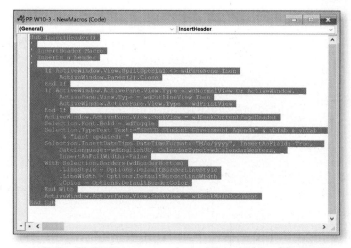

Figure 10-40 Copy a macro in the *Microsoft Visual Basic* editor

4. Place the insertion point on the blank line below "End Sub."
5. Click the **Paste** button or press **Ctrl+V** to paste the copied macro.
   - The copied macro appears below the original macro. A horizontal line separates the macros.
6. Change the name of the copied macro (Figure 10-41).
   - The macro name displays after "Sub" at the beginning of the macro code.
   - Don't delete the beginning and ending parentheses ( ) after the macro name.
   - The name of the macro is the macro name that appears in the *Macros* dialog box.

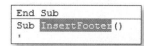

Figure 10-41 Change the macro name

7. Press **Ctrl+S** or click the **Save** button to save the macros.
8. Click the **File** menu in the upper-left corner and select **Close and Return to Microsoft Word** to return to your document.

Edit a Macro

After copying a macro or when editing an existing macro, edit the macro using the *Microsoft Visual Basic* editor. For example, change text in a macro, change the macro name or description, change a header to a footer, or change a border.

▶ HOW TO: Edit a Macro

1. Click the **Macros** button [*Developer* tab, *Code* group] to open the *Macros* dialog box.
2. Select the macro you want to edit and click the **Edit** button. The *Microsoft Visual Basic* editor opens (Figure 10-42).
3. Edit the existing code to customize the macro.
   - Figure 10-42 highlights edits to the macro. Highlighted text does not display when editing a macro in the Visual Basic editor.
4. Press **Ctrl+S** or click the **Save** button to save the macros.
5. Click the **File** menu in the upper-left corner and select **Close and Return to Microsoft Word** to return to your document.

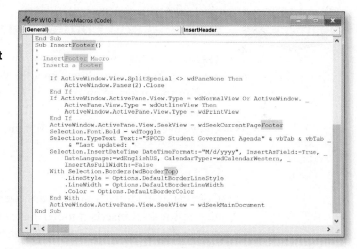

Figure 10-42 Edit the macro

W10-632

Assign a Shortcut Key to a Macro

After creating a macro, you can add a shortcut key or change the existing shortcut key. Use the ***Customize Keyboard*** dialog box to add or change a macros shortcut key.

▶HOW TO: Assign a Shortcut Key to a Macro

1. Click the **File** tab to open the *Backstage* view, select **Options** on the left to open the *Word Options* dialog box, and click **Customize Ribbon** on the left.
   - Alternatively, right-click a blank area on the *Ribbon* and select **Customize the Ribbon**.
2. Click the **Customize** button in the *Keyboard shortcuts* area. The *Customize Keyboard* dialog box opens (Figure 10-43).
3. Scroll down and select **Macros** in the *Categories* list.
4. Click the **Save changes in** drop-down list and select the document where the macro is stored.
5. Select the macro in the *Macros* list on which to add a shortcut key.
6. Place the insertion point in the *Press new shortcut key* text box.
7. Press the shortcut key (for example, **Alt+Ctrl+Shift+F**) to assign to the selected macro.

Figure 10-43 Assign a shortcut key to a macro

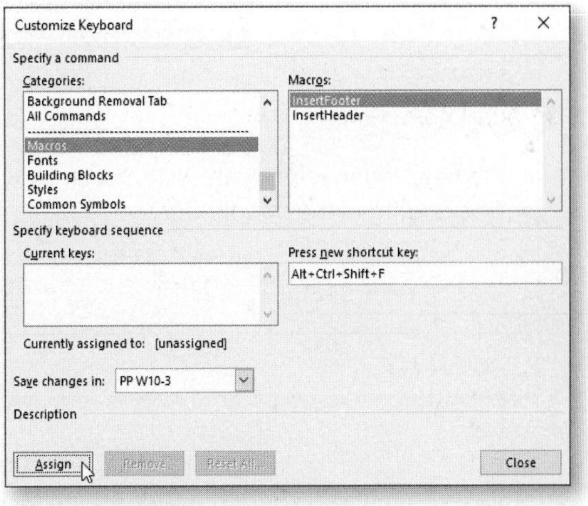

8. Click the **Assign** button.
   - The shortcut key displays in the *Current keys* area.
   - If the selected macro already has a shortcut key, the shortcut key displays in the *Current keys* area.
   - Remove a shortcut key by selecting it in the *Current keys* area and clicking the **Remove** button. After removing an existing shortcut key from a macro, you can add a new one.
9. Click **Close** to close the *Customize Keyboard* dialog box.
10. Click **OK** to close the *Word Options* dialog box.

Add a Macro Button to the Quick Access Toolbar

Recall that a button-activated macro runs when a user clicks the assigned macro button on the *Quick Access* toolbar. Edit an existing macro to add or edit a macro button on the *Quick Access* toolbar.

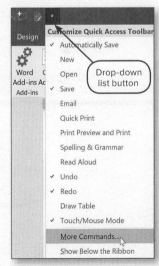

Figure 10-44 *Customize Quick Access Toolbar* drop-down list

▶HOW TO: Add a Macro Button to the Quick Access Toolbar

1. Click the **Customize Quick Access Toolbar** drop-down arrow (right side of the *Quick Access* toolbar) and select **More Commands** (Figure 10-44) to display the *Customize the Quick Access Toolbar* area of the *Word Options* dialog box (Figure 10-45).
   - Alternatively, click the **File** tab to open the *Backstage* view, select **Options** on the left to open the *Word Options* dialog box, and click **Quick Access Toolbar** on the left.
2. Click the **Choose commands from** drop-down list and select **Macros**.
3. Click the **Customize Quick Access Toolbar** drop-down list and select the document where the macro is stored.

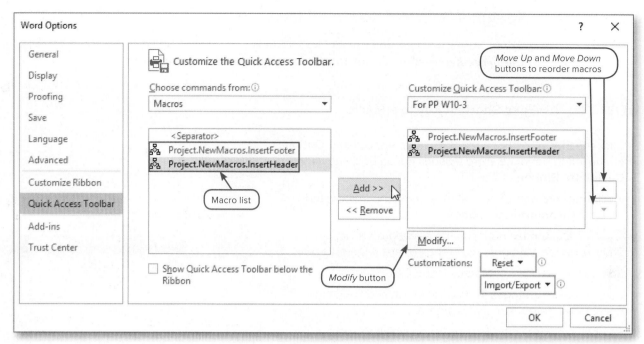

Figure 10-45 Add a macro button to the *Quick Access* toolbar

4. Select the macro to add to the *Quick Access* toolbar from the list of macros on the left and click the **Add** button.

- After adding macros to the *Quick Access* toolbar, reorder macros using the *Move Up* and *Move Down* buttons on the right side of the dialog box.

5. Click the **Modify** button to open the *Modify Button* dialog box (Figure 10-46).

- If a macro already has a *Quick Access* toolbar button, you can modify the display name or button symbol.

6. Type the display name for the macro button in the *Display name* text box.

- The display name is the tag that appears when you place the pointer on the button on the *Quick Access* toolbar.

7. Select a symbol to use as the button on the *Quick Access* toolbar.

8. Click **OK** to close the *Modify Button* dialog box.

9. Click **OK** to close the *Word Options* dialog box.

- The macro button appears on the *Quick Access* toolbar.

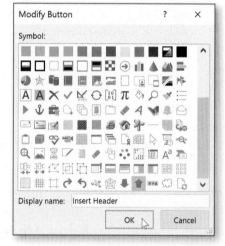

Figure 10-46 Modify the macro button and display name

> **ANOTHER WAY**
>
> Right-click a blank area on the **Ribbon** and select **Customize Quick Access Toolbar** to open the *Word Options* dialog box.

Remove a Macro Button from the Quick Access Toolbar

When deleting a macro that has a *Quick Access* toolbar button, the macro button on the *Quick Access* toolbar does not automatically delete. An error message displays when you click a macro button on the *Quick Access* toolbar after the macro has been deleted. It is best to remove the macro button from the *Quick Access* toolbar after deleting a macro. You can also remove a macro button from the *Quick Access* toolbar even if the macro has not been deleted.

The following are two different ways to remove a macro button from the *Quick Access* toolbar:

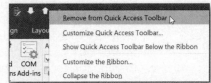

- Right-click the macro button on the *Quick Access* toolbar and select **Remove from Quick Access Toolbar** from the context menu (Figure 10-47).
- Open the *Customize the Quick Access Toolbar* area in the *Word Options* dialog box, select the macro button to remove, and click the **Remove** button.

Figure 10-47 Remove a macro button from the *Quick Access* toolbar

PAUSE & PRACTICE: WORD 10-3

For this Pause & Practice project, you modify the macro-enabled agenda document you created in *Pause & Practice 10-2*. You copy and edit a macro using the *Microsoft Visual Basic* editor, add a keyboard shortcut to a macro, and add macro buttons to the *Quick Access* toolbar.

File Needed: ***[your initials] PP W10-2 final.docm***
Completed Project File Name: ***[your initials] PP W10-3.docm***

1. Open the ***[your initials] PP W10-2 final*** macro-enabled document completed in *Pause & Practice 10-2*. If a security warning appears in the *Info* bar, click **Enable Content**.

2. Save the document as a **Word Macro-Enabled Document** named [your initials] PP W10-3. If prompted to save changes to the template, click **Yes**.

3. Copy the *InsertHeader* macro using the *Microsoft Visual Basic* editor.
   a. Click the **Macros** button [*Developer* tab, *Code* group] to open the *Macros* dialog box.
   b. Click the **Macros in** drop-down list and select **[your initials] PP W10-3 (document)**.
   c. Select the **InsertHeader** macro and click the **Edit** button. The *Microsoft Visual Basic* editor opens.
   d. Select the Visual Basic code for the macro beginning with "**Sub InsertHeader ( )**" and ending with "**End Sub**" (Figure 10-48).
   e. Click the **Copy** button or press **Ctrl+C** to copy the code for the macro.
   f. Place the insertion point on the blank line after "End Sub."
   g. Click the **Paste** button or press **Ctrl+V** to paste the copied macro. The copied macro displays below the original macro, and a horizontal line separates the two macros.

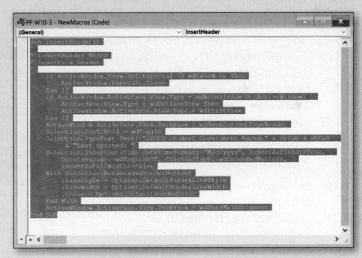

Figure 10-48 Select and copy macro Visual Basic code

4. Edit the *InsertFooter* macro.

   a. Change the word "Header" to Footer in the name of the copied macro (after "Sub" below the first macro) (Figure 10-49). The code should be "Sub InsertFooter ()" after the change.

Figure 10-49 Change the macro name

   b. Change the first comment line from "InsertHeader Macro" to InsertFooter Macro (Figure 10-50).

   c. Change the second comment line from "Inserts a header" to Inserts a footer.

   d. Change the word "Header" to Footer in the first line below the second "End If" section. The code should be "wdSeekCurrentPageFooter" after the change.

   e. Change the word "Bottom" to Top in the first line in the "With" section. The code should be "(wdBorderTop)" after the change.

   f. Press **Ctrl+S** or click the **Save** button to save the macros.

   g. Click the **File** menu and select **Close and Return to Microsoft Word** to return to your document.

   h. **Save** the document.

Figure 10-50 Edit the *InsertFooter* macro Visual Basic code

5. Test the *InsertFooter* macro.

   a. Click the **Macros** button to open the *Macros* dialog box.

   b. Select the **InsertFooter** macro and click the **Run** button. A footer with a top border displays in the document.

   c. Edit the header and footer in the document and delete all content in the header and footer (including the top and bottom borders).

   d. Close the header and footer area.

6. Add a keyboard shortcut to the *InsertFooter* macro.

   a. Click the **File** tab to open the *Backstage* view, select **Options** on the left to open the *Word Options* dialog box, and click **Customize Ribbon** on the left.

   b. Click the **Customize** button in the *Keyboard shortcuts* area. The *Customize Keyboard* dialog box opens (Figure 10-51).

   c. Scroll down and select **Macros** in the *Categories* area.

   d. Click the **Save changes in** drop-down list and select **[your initials] PP W10-3**.

   e. Select the **InsertFooter** macro in the *Macros* list.

   f. Place the insertion point in the *Press new shortcut key* text box and press **Alt+Ctrl+Shift+F**.

   g. Click the **Assign** button.

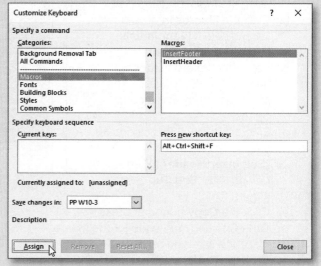

Figure 10-51 Add a shortcut key to the *InsertFooter* macro

h. Click **Close** to close the *Customize Keyboard* dialog box and click **OK** to close the *Word Options* dialog box.

7. Add macro buttons to the *Quick Access* toolbar.
   a. Click the **Customize Quick Access Toolbar** drop-down arrow (right side of the *Quick Access* toolbar) and select **More Commands** (Figure 10-52) to display the *Customize the Quick Access Toolbar* area of the *Word Options* dialog box (Figure 10-53).

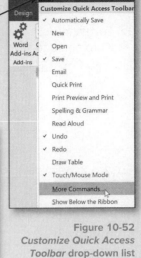

Figure 10-52
Customize Quick Access Toolbar drop-down list

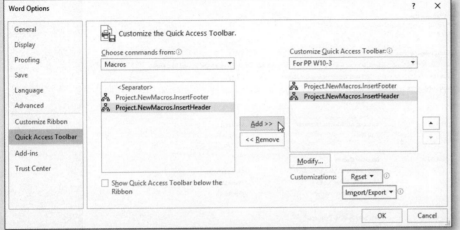

Figure 10-53 Add macro buttons to the *Quick Access* toolbar

   b. Click the **Choose commands from** drop-down list and select **Macros**.
   c. Click the **Customize Quick Access Toolbar** drop-down list and select **For [your initials] PP W10-3**.
   d. Select the **Project.NewMacros.InsertFooter** macro in the list of macros on the left and click the **Add** button.
   e. Select the **Project.NewMacros.InsertHeader** macro and click the **Add** button.
   f. Select the **Project.NewMacros.InsertHeader** macro in the list on the right and click the **Modify** button (see Figure 10-53) to open the *Modify Button* dialog box.
   g. Type Insert Header in the *Display name* text box, select the **blue up arrow** symbol on the last row, and click **OK** to close the *Modify Button* dialog box (Figure 10-54).
   h. Select the **Project.NewMacros.InsertFooter** macro in the list on the right and click the **Modify** button.
   i. Type Insert Footer in the *Display name* text box, select the **blue down arrow** symbol on the last row, and click **OK** to close the *Modify Button* dialog box.
   j. Click **OK** to close the *Word Options* dialog box. The two macro buttons display on the *Quick Access* toolbar.

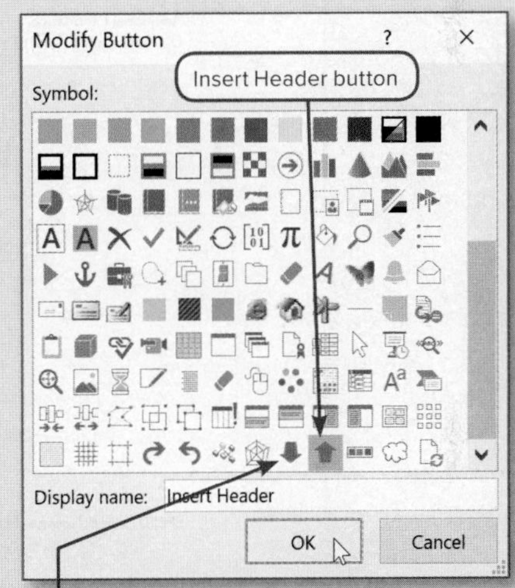

Figure 10-54 Modify the macro button and display name

8. Test a macro button and macro keyboard shortcut.
   a. Click the **Insert Header** button on the *Quick Access* toolbar to insert the header in the document (Figure 10-55).
   b. Press **Alt+Ctrl+Shift+F** to insert the footer.

Figure 10-55 *Insert Header* macro button on the *Quick Access* toolbar

c. Edit the header, delete all header content (including the bottom border), and close the header area. Do not delete the footer content.

9. Save and close the document (Figure 10-56). If prompted to save changes to the template, click **Yes**. If prompted to save styles and building blocks, click **Don't Save**.

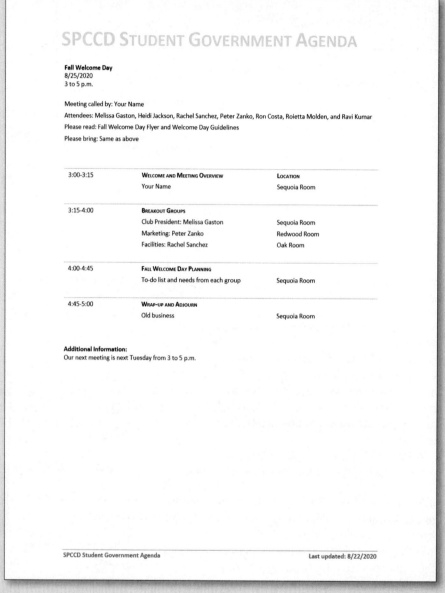

Figure 10-56 PP W10-3 completed

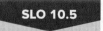
Creating and Using Macro-Enabled Templates

Storing macros in a Word template helps to further automate tasks. When creating a document based on a template or opening a document that has a template attached, the macros stored in the template are available in the document. You can also copy macros from a template or document to another template or document, so you don't have to re-create macros that exist in another file.

Save a Macro-Enabled Template

Similar to a Word document containing macros (macro-enabled document), a Word template containing macros must be saved as a *macro-enabled template* (*.dotm*) in order for the macros to function in the template and in documents you create based on the template.

▶ HOW TO: Save a Macro-Enabled Template

1. Open the file to save as a macro-enabled template or create a new document.
2. Open the *Save As* dialog box (Figure 10-57).
3. Type the name of the template in the *File name* text box.
4. Click the **Save as type** drop-down list and select **Word Macro-Enabled Template**.
5. Browse to the location on your computer to save the template.
   - Be specific when selecting the save location for templates because Word, by default, selects the default template location when you save a template file.
6. Click **Save** to close the dialog box and save the macro-enabled template.

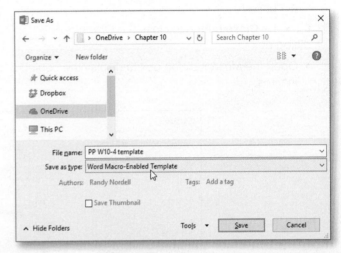

Figure 10-57 Save as a macro-enabled template

When you create macros in a template that is not macro-enabled and then save the template, a dialog box opens and informs you that the document cannot be saved in a macro-free environment. In this dialog box, click **No** to open the *Save As* dialog box. Save the file as a **Word Macro-Enabled Template** so the macros are available in the template.

Copy a Macro to Another File

Copying macros from one file to another file saves time. Copying macros is similar to copying styles. Use the *Organizer* dialog box to select the file containing the macros and the file where the macros will be copied. When copying macros from one file to another, Word copies the entire *macro project item*, which are all the macros stored in the file. After copying macros into a document, delete unwanted macros using the *Macros* dialog box.

▶ HOW TO: Copy Macros to Another Document

1. Open the document or template where you want to copy the macros.
2. Click the **Macros** button [*Developer* tab, *Code* group] to open the *Macros* dialog box.
3. Click the **Organizer** button. The *Organizer* dialog box opens and displays the *Macro Project Items* tab.
   - The open document displays on the left and the *Normal* template displays on the right.
4. Click the **Close File** button on the right to close the *Normal* template.
5. Click the **Open File** button on the right to display the *Open* dialog box (Figure 10-58).
6. Click the **File type** drop-down list to the right of the *File name* text box and select **All Word Documents**.

7. Browse to locate and select the file containing the macros and click **Open**.
   - The file appears on the right in the *Organizer* dialog box.

8. Select the macro project item (on the right) to copy to the open document (on the left) and click the **Copy** button (Figure 10-59).
   - The macro project item copies to the open document.

9. Click the **Close** button to close the *Organizer* dialog box.
   - Open the *Macros* dialog box to display the copied macros.

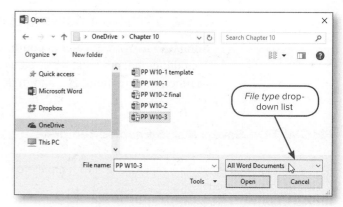

Figure 10-58 Open the document containing the macros

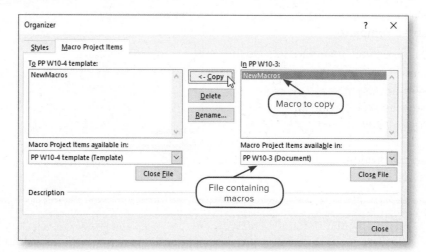

Figure 10-59 Copy macros from one file to another

> **MORE INFO**
>
> Use the *Organizer* dialog box to delete and rename macro project items.

Use a Macro-Enabled Template

Using a macro-enabled template is similar to using a template. After creating a new document based on a macro-enabled template, the macros in the template are available in the new document. The following describes how to create a new document based on a macro-enabled template and how to edit an existing macro-enabled template.

- *Create a new document based on a macro-enabled template*: Open a *File Explorer* window, locate the macro-enabled template, and double-click the file. A new document based on the macro-enabled template opens. A security warning appears in the *Info* bar informing you that macros are disabled. Click **Enable Content** to enable the macros in the new document (Figure 10-60).
- *Edit a macro-enabled template*: Open the macro-enabled template from within Word. A security warning appears in the *Info* bar. Click **Enable Content** to enable the macros in the macro-enabled template.

Figure 10-60 Enable macros in the document

> **MORE INFO**
>
> When opening files stored on *OneDrive* or other online locations, a dialog box may open prompting you to make the file a *Trusted Document*. If this dialog box opens, click **Yes**.

PAUSE & PRACTICE: WORD 10-4

For this Pause & Practice project, you modify the agenda template from *Pause & Practice 10-1*. You save the template as a macro-enabled template, copy macros from another document, delete a macro, assign a keyboard shortcut to a macro, create a macro, and create a document based on a macro-enabled template.

Files Needed: ***[your initials] PP W10-1 template.dotx, [your initials] PP W10-3.docm***, and ***SPCCDlogo-10.png*** *(Student data files are available in the* Library *of your SIMnet account.)*
Completed Project File Name: ***[your initials] PP W10-4 template.dotm***

1. Open Word, and from within Word, open the ***[your initials] PP W10-1 template*** Word template completed in *Pause & Practice 10-1*.

2. Save the template as a macro-enabled template.
   a. Open the *Save As* dialog box.
   b. Type [your initials] PP W10-4 template in the *File name* text box.
   c. Click the **Save as type** drop-down list and select **Word Macro-Enabled Template**.
   d. Browse to the location on your computer where you want to save the macro-enabled template.
   e. Click **Save** to close the dialog box and save the macro-enabled template.

3. Copy macros from a macro-enabled document into your macro-enabled template.
   a. Click the **Macros** button [*Developer* tab, *Code* group] to open the *Macros* dialog box.
   b. Click the **Organizer** button to open the *Organizer* dialog box.
   c. Click the **Close File** button on the right to close the *Normal* template.

d. Click the **Open File** button on the right to display the *Open* dialog box.

e. Click the **File type** drop-down list to the right of the *File name* text box and select **All Word Documents**.

f. Browse to locate and select the *[your initials]* **PP W10-3** macro-enabled document and click **Open** to close the dialog box and to return to the *Organizer* dialog box.

g. Select the **NewMacros** macro project item (on the right) and click the **Copy** button (Figure 10-61).

h. Click the **Close** button to close the *Organizer* dialog box.

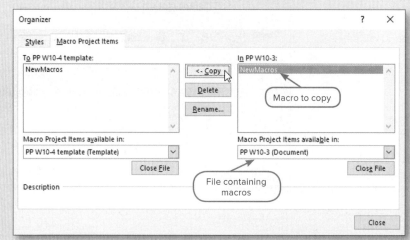

Figure 10-61 Copy macros from a macro-enabled document to a macro-enabled template

4. Delete the *InsertHeader* macro.

a. Click the **Macros** button [*Developer* tab, *Code* group] to open the *Macros* dialog box.

b. Click the **Macros in** drop-down list and select **PP W10-4 template (template)**.

c. Select the **InsertHeader** macro and click the **Delete** button.

d. Click **Yes** in the dialog box that opens and confirms the deletion of the macro.

e. Click **Close** to close the *Macros* dialog box.

5. Add a keyboard shortcut to the *InsertFooter* macro.

a. Click the **File** tab to open the *Backstage* view and select **Options** on the left to open the *Word Options* dialog box.

b. Click **Customize Ribbon** on the left and then click the **Customize** button in the *Keyboard shortcuts* area. The *Customize Keyboard* dialog box opens.

c. Scroll down and select **Macros** in the *Categories* list.

d. Click the **Save changes in** area and select **[your initials] PP W10-4 template**.

e. Select the **InsertFooter** macro in the *Macros* list.

f. Place the insertion point in the **Press new shortcut key** text box, press **Alt+Ctrl+Shift+F**, and click the **Assign** button.

g. Click **Close** to close the *Customize Keyboard* dialog box, and click **OK** to close the *Word Options* dialog box.

6. Create a keyboard-activated macro.

a. Place the insertion point after the content control field below the "Additional Information" heading and press **Enter** two times.

b. Click the **Record Macro** button [*Developer* tab, *Code* group] to open the *Record Macro* dialog box.

c. Type InsertPicture (no spaces between words) in the *Macro name* text box.

d. Click the **Store macro in** drop-down list and select **Documents Based On [your initials] PP W10-4 template**.

e. Type Inserts a picture in the *Description* text box.

f. Click the **Keyboard** button to open the *Customize Keyboard* dialog box.

g. Click the **Save changes in** drop-down list and select **[your initials] PP W10-4 template**.

h. Place the insertion point in the **Press new shortcut key** text box, press **Alt+Ctrl+Shift+P**, and click the **Assign** button.

i. Click the **Close** button to close the *Customize Keyboard* dialog box and to begin recording the macro.

7. Record a macro to insert a company logo picture.
   a. Click the **Pictures** button [*Insert* tab, *Illustrations* group] to open the *Insert Picture* dialog box.
   b. Browse to your student data files, select the ***SPCCDlogo-10*** picture, and click **Insert**.
   c. Click the **Stop Recording** button [*Developer* tab, *Code* group].

8. Select the inserted picture and delete it.

9. Save and close the macro-enabled template.

10. Create a document based on the macro-enabled template to confirm the template works properly.
   a. Open a *File Explorer* window, locate the ***[your initials] PP W10-4 template*** macro-enabled template, and double-click the file to create a new document based on the template.
   b. Click **OK** to accept the default responses to the two *Fill-in* field prompt dialog boxes.
   c. Click **Enable Content** on the security warning to enable the macros in the new document. If prompted to save styles and building blocks, click **Don't Save**.
   d. Press **Alt+Ctrl+Shift+F** to run the *InsertFooter* macro.
   e. Place the insertion point on the last blank line in the body of the document.
   f. Press **Alt+Ctrl+Shift+P** to run the *InsertPicture* macro.
   g. Examine the document to confirm that both the footer and logo display (Figure 10-62).

11. Close the document without saving.

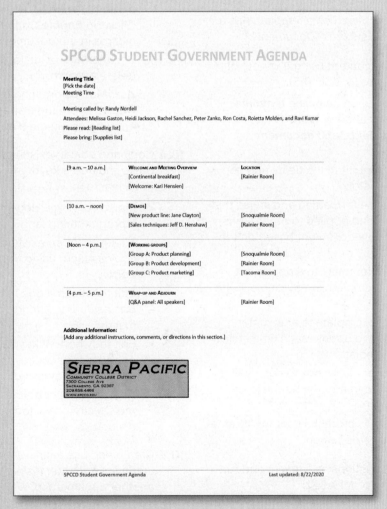

Figure 10-62 New document based on *PP Word 10-4 template* and macros inserted

Chapter Summary

10.1 Create, save, and use a template to generate commonly used documents (p. W10-612).

- A *template* is a type of Word file that stores content and formatting; create a document based on the contents of a template.
- A template file has a *.dotx* file name extension.
- Save an existing document or a new document as a template.
- A variety of online templates are available in Word in the *New* area on the *Backstage* view. Search for templates using key words.
- To edit a template, open the template file from within Word.
- To create a document based on a template, double-click the template file in a *File Explorer* window.
- A new document based on a template has a generic file name such as "*Document1.*"

10.2 Customize template content using a variety of Word fields and styles (p. W10-615).

- A document based on an online template includes a combination of **Word fields**, **content control fields**, and **document property fields**.
- Customize the content in the fields and copy, move, or delete fields.
- Templates also use formatting and styles that can be modified and applied to other areas of the template or a document based on the template.
- After attaching a template to a document, the styles in the template are available in the document.
- When attaching a template to a document, set the document to update each time styles change in the template.
- Use the **Organizer** dialog box to copy styles from one template to another template or document.
- Use a **Fill-in field** to prompt a user for information to insert into a document.

10.3 Record a set of instructions as a macro and run and delete a macro (p. W10-622).

- A *macro* is a combination of instructions and keystrokes that are stored and run in a document.

- Before creating and recording a macro, plan what the macro will do, where the macro will be stored, and how the macro will run.
- Use the **Record Macro** dialog box to create the macro and name it.
- Create a **keyboard-activated macro** or a **button-activated macro**. A keyboard-activated macro runs when you press a shortcut key. A button-activated macro runs when you click the macro button on the *Quick Access* toolbar.
- Save a document that contains macros as a **Word Macro-Enabled Document** in order for the macros to be stored in the document. A macro-enabled document has a *.docm* file name extension.
- When opening a document containing macros, a security warning appears in the *Info* bar. Click the **Enable Content** button to enable macros in the document.
- Use the **Macros** dialog box to run a macro or delete a macro.
- **AutoMacros** are macros that run automatically when performing a specific action such as opening or closing a document.

10.4 Copy and edit an existing macro using Visual Basic and add a keyboard and button shortcut to run a macro (p. W10-631).

- Macros are recorded in **Visual Basic**, which is a programming language.
- To duplicate an existing macro in a document, copy a macro using the **Microsoft Visual Basic editor**.
- Edit the macro code in the *Microsoft Visual Basic* editor to change an existing or copied macro.
- Edit the shortcut key assigned to a macro or add a shortcut key to a macro in the **Customize Keyboard** dialog box.
- Add, change, or delete a macro button from the *Quick Access* toolbar in *the Word Options* dialog box.

10.5 Create and use a macro-enabled template to automate common tasks and copy a macro to another document (p. W10-638).

- When you use a macro in a template, you must save the template as a macro-enabled template.

- A *macro-enabled template* has a *.dotm* file name extension.
- Copy a macro from one file to another using the *Organizer* dialog box.
- When you copy macros from one file to another, copy the *macro project item*, which is the set of macros stored in a file.
- A security warning displays in the *Info* bar when opening a template containing macros or a document based on a macro-enabled template.

Check for Understanding

The SIMbook for this text (within your SIMnet account) provides the following resources for concept review:

- Multiple-choice questions
- Short answer questions
- Matching exercises

Guided Project 10-1

For this project, you create a macro-enabled template from an existing Courtyard Medical Plaza document. You insert *Fill-in* fields, record a macro, assign a button to the macro, and create a document based on the template.
[Student Learning Outcomes 10.1, 10.2, 10.3, 10.4, 10.5]

File Needed: ***PrivacyNotice-10.docx*** *(Student data files are available in the* Library *of your SIMnet account.)*
Completed Project File Names: ***[your initials] Word 10-1 template.dotm*** and ***[your initials] Word 10-1.docm***

Skills Covered in This Project

- Save a document as a macro-enabled template.
- Insert a *Fill-in* field.
- Create a keyboard-activated macro.
- Add a macro button to the *Quick Access* toolbar.

- Create a new document based on a macro-enabled template.
- Insert information in a *Fill-in* field prompt dialog box.
- Enable the macro content in the document.
- Run a macro using the macro button on the *Quick Access* toolbar.

1. Open the ***PrivacyNotice-10*** document from your student data files.

2. Save the document as a macro-enabled template.
   a. Open the *Save As* dialog box.
   b. Type [your initials] Word 10-1 template in the *File name* text box.
   c. Click the **Save as type** drop-down list and select **Word Macro-Enabled Template**.
   d. Browse to the location on your computer where you want to save the file.
   e. Click **Save** to close the dialog box and save the macro-enabled template.

3. Turn on **Show/Hide** if needed and delete the information to the right of the tab on each line in the shaded heading area at the top of the document; don't delete the tab or the paragraph mark (Figure 10-63).

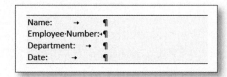

Figure 10-63 Remove text in the heading

4. Insert *Fill-in* fields to prompt users for information when a document is created based on the template.
   a. Place the insertion point after the tab and before the paragraph mark in the first line of the heading ("Name:").
   b. Click the **Quick Parts** button [*Insert* tab, *Text* group] and select **Field** from the drop-down list to open the *Field* dialog box (Figure 10-64).

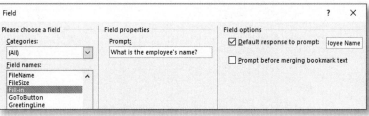

Figure 10-64 Insert *Fill-in* field

   c. Select **Fill-in** in the *Field names* list.
   d. Type What is the employee's name? in the *Prompt* text box.

e. Check the **Default response to prompt** box and type Employee Name in the text box.

f. Click **OK** to close the *Field* dialog box and to insert the *Fill-in* field. A dialog box opens prompting you for the employee's name.

g. Click **OK** to accept the default response to the prompt (Figure 10-65).

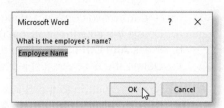

Figure 10-65 *Fill-in* field prompt dialog box

h. Place the insertion point after the tab on the second heading line ("Employee Number:") and insert another **Fill-in** field.

i. Type What is the employee's number? as the prompt and type Employee Number as the default response to the prompt.

j. Click **OK** to close the *Field* dialog box and **OK** to accept the default response at the prompt.

k. Place the insertion point after the tab on the third heading line ("Department:") and insert another **Fill-in** field.

l. Type What is the employee's department? as the prompt and type Employee Department as the default response to the prompt.

m. Click **OK** to close the *Field* dialog box and click **OK** to accept the default response at the prompt (Figure 10-66).

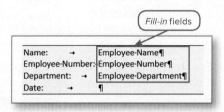

Figure 10-66 *Fill-in* fields inserted in the document

5. Record a keyboard-activated macro.

a. Place the insertion point after the tab on the fourth heading line ("Date:").

b. Click the **Record Macro** button [*Developer* tab, *Code* group]. The *Record Macro* dialog box opens (Figure 10-67).

c. Type InsertDate in the *Macro name* text box.

d. Click the **Store macro in** drop-down list and select **Documents Based On [your initials] Word 10-1 template**.

e. Type Inserts the date in the *Description* text box.

f. Click the **Keyboard** button. The *Customize Keyboard* dialog box opens (Figure 10-68).

g. Click the **Save changes in** drop-down list and select **[your initials] Word 10-1 template**.

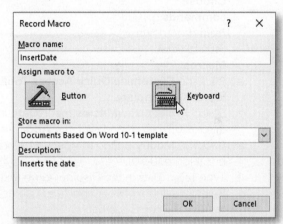

Figure 10-67 Record a keyboard-activated macro

h. Place the insertion point in the **Press new shortcut key** text box, press **Alt+Ctrl+Shift+D**, and click the **Assign** button to assign the keyboard shortcut to run the macro.

i. Click the **Close** button to close the dialog box and to begin recording your macro. Your pointer changes to a macro-recording pointer.

6. Record a macro to insert the date.

a. Click the **Date & Time** button [*Insert* tab, *Text* group] to open the *Date and Time* dialog box.

b. Select the spelled-out date format (January 1, 2020).

c. Deselect the **Update automatically** check box.

d. Click **OK** to close the dialog box and to insert the date.

e. Click the **Stop Recording** button [*Developer* tab, *Code* group] to stop recording the macro.

Figure 10-68 Assign a shortcut key to the macro

7. Test the macro to confirm it works properly.
   a. Delete the date that was inserted in the fourth heading line; don't delete the tab or paragraph mark.
   b. Press **Alt+Ctrl+Shift+D** to run the macro.
   c. Delete the date you just inserted.

8. Add a macro button to the *Quick Access* toolbar.
   a. Click the **Customize Quick Access Toolbar** drop-down arrow (right side of the *Quick Access* toolbar) and select **More Commands** to display the *Customize the Quick Access Toolbar* area of the *Word Options* dialog box (Figure 10-69).

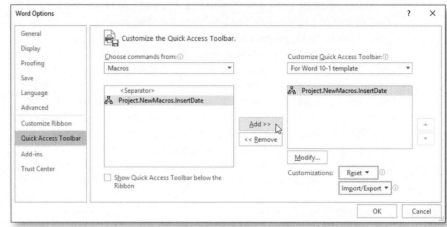

Figure 10-69 Add a macro button to the *Quick Access* toolbar

   b. Click the **Choose commands from** drop-down list and select **Macros**.
   c. Click the **Customize Quick Access Toolbar** drop-down list and select **For [your initials] Word 10-1 template**.
   d. Select **Project.NewMacros.InsertDate** in the list of macros on the left and click the **Add** button.
   e. Click the **Modify** button to open the *Modify Button* dialog box (Figure 10-70).
   f. Type Insert Date in the *Display name* text box.
   g. Select a symbol of your choice to use as the button on the *Quick Access* toolbar.
   h. Click **OK** to close the *Modify Button* dialog box.
   i. Click **OK** to close the *Word Options* dialog box.

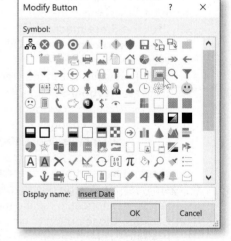

Figure 10-70 Modify the macro button and display name

9. Save and close the macro-enabled template.

10. Create a new document based on *[your initials] Word 10-1 template*.
    a. Open a *File Explorer* window and browse to locate the *[your initials] Word 10-1 template* file.
    b. Double-click the file to open a new document based on the template.
    c. Type Mrs. Karen Draper in the first prompt dialog box and click **OK**.
    d. Type 0001484 in the second prompt dialog box and click **OK**.
    e. Type Marketing in the third prompt dialog box and click **OK**.
    f. Click the **Enable Content** button in the security warning in the *Info* bar to enable the macro in the document. If prompted to save changes to the template, click **Save**.

11. Save the document as a **Word Macro-Enabled Document** named [your initials] Word 10-1. If prompted to save changes to the template, click **Yes**.

12. Run the macro to insert the date.
    a. Place the insertion point after the tab on the fourth line of the heading ("Date:").
    b. Click the **Insert Date** macro button on the *Quick Access* toolbar to insert the date.

13. Save and close the document (Figure 10-71).

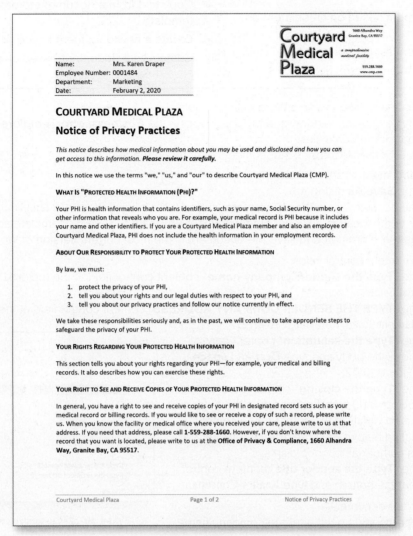

Figure 10-71 Word 10-1 completed (page 1 of 2)

Guided Project 10-2

For this project, you open an online Word template and create a letter template for Emma Cavalli at Placer Hills Real Estate. You customize content control fields, delete content control fields, insert text from another file, create a document based on the template, and customize the document.
[Student Learning Outcomes 10.1, 10.2]

Files Needed: **BusinessLetterTemplate-10** and **CavalliLetter-10.docx** (Student data files are available in the Library of your SIMnet account.)
Completed Project File Names: **[your initials] Word 10-2 template.dotx** and
[your initials] Word 10-2.docx

Skills Covered in This Project

- Create a document based on an online Word template.
- Save a document as a template.
- Customize a content control field.
- Delete a content control field.
- Copy text from a document to paste into a template.
- Create a new document based on a template.
- Customize a document based on a template.

---

1. Open a document based upon a Word online template.
   a. Open a *File Explorer* window and browse to locate the ***BusinessLetterTemplate-10*** template from your student data files.
   b. Double-click the file to open a document based upon the template.

2. Save this document as a template.
   a. Open the **Save As** dialog box.
   b. Save the document as a **Word Template** named [your initials] Word 10-2 template.
   c. Browse to the location on your computer where you want to save the template and click the **Save** button. If prompted to save the document in the most current version of Word, click **OK**.

3. Customize content control fields.
   a. Click the "**Type the sender company name**" content control field at the top, and type Placer Hills Real Estate.
   b. Click the "**TYPE THE SENDER COMPANY ADDRESS**" content control field at the top and type 7100 Madrone Road, Roseville, CA 95722.
   c. Click the "**Type the salutation**" content control field above the body and type Dear and **space** once. (Figure 10-72)
   d. Click the "**Type the closing**" content control field at the bottom and type Best regards in the field.
   e. Type Emma Cavalli in the author name content control field below "Best regards" to replace the existing author name if one displays.
   f. Click the "**Type the sender title**" content control field near the bottom and type Realtor Consultant.

4. Add text to the document.
   a. Place the insertion point after the company name at the bottom and press **Enter**.
   b. Type ecavalli@phre.com and press **Enter**.
   c. Type 916.450.3334 as the phone number.
   d. Right-click the email address above the phone number and select **Remove Hyperlink** from the context menu.

5. Delete content control field, copy text from another document, and paste it into the template.
   a. Right-click the body content control field (below "Dear") and select **Remove Content Control** from the context menu (Figure 10-73).
   b. Open the ***CavalliLetter-10*** document from your student data files.
   c. Select and **copy** all the text in the document and close the document.
   d. Place the insertion point on the blank line below "Dear."
   e. Click the bottom half of the **Paste** button and select **Use Destination Theme** to paste the text into the document (Figure 10-74).

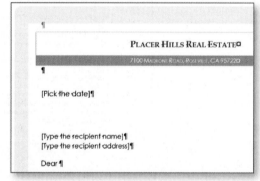

Figure 10-72 Customize content control fields

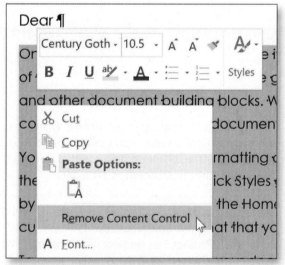

Figure 10-73 Delete content control field

    f. Delete the blank line below the pasted body text (above "Best regards").

    g. Select the four body paragraphs in the letter, change the line spacing to **1.15**, and change the *After* paragraph spacing to **12 pt**.

6. Save and close the template.

7. Create a new document based on *[your initials] Word 10-2 template*.

    a. Open a *File Explorer* window and browse to locate the *[your initials] Word 10-2 template* file.

    b. Double-click the file to open a new document based on the template.

Figure 10-74 Paste text using the destination theme

8. Save the file as a **Word Document** named [your initials] Word 10-2. If prompted to save the template file, click **Yes**.

9. Customize the document based on the template.

    a. Click the "**Pick the date**" content control field and select the current date.

    b. Click the "**Type the recipient name**" content control field and type Mr. and Mrs. Robert McCartney.

    c. Click the "**Type the recipient address**" content control field and type 7105 High Street, press **Enter**, and type Folsom, CA 93714.

    d. Place the insertion point after the space after "Dear" and type Robert and Lanita.

    e. Confirm that "Emma Cavalli" is the author name that appears in the content control field below "Best regards." If it is not, change it to Emma Cavalli.

10. Save and close the document (Figure 10-75). If prompted to save the template file, click **Yes**.

Figure 10-75 Word 10-2 completed

Guided Project 10-3

For this project, you modify a template and document for Sierra Pacific Community College District. You save a template as a macro-enabled template, record and edit a macro, copy and modify a macro, and attach a template to a document.
[Student Learning Outcomes 10.1, 10.2, 10.3, 10.4, 10.5]

Files Needed: ***SPCCDtemplate-10.dotx*** and ***SPCCDValues-10.docx*** *(Student data files are available in the* Library *of your SIMnet account.)*
Completed Project File Names: *[your initials] Word 10-3 template.dotm* and
[your initials] Word 10-3.docm

Skills Covered in This Project	• Add a keyboard shortcut to a macro.

Skills Covered in This Project

- Save a template as a macro-enabled template.
- Create a button-activated macro.
- Edit a macro in Visual Basic.
- Copy and modify a macro using the Visual Basic editor.

- Add a keyboard shortcut to a macro.
- Save a document as a macro-enabled document.
- Attach a template to a document.
- Enable macro content in the document.
- Run a macro in a document.

1. Open Word, and from within Word, open the ***SPCCDtemplate-10*** template from your student data files. If you don't find this file in your student data files, click the **File type** drop-down list in the *Open* dialog box and select **All Word Documents** to display all Word files.

2. Save the document as a macro-enabled template.
   a. Open the **Save As** dialog box.
   b. Save as a **Word Macro-Enabled Template** named [your initials] Word 10-3 template.
   c. Browse to the location on your computer where you want to save the macro-enabled template and click the **Save** button.

3. Create a button-activated macro.
   a. Place the insertion point anywhere in the words "*Two Columns*" in the document.
   b. Click the **Record Macro** button [*Developer* tab, *Code* group] to open the *Record Macro* dialog box (Figure 10-76).
   c. Type TwoColumns in the *Macro name* text box.
   d. Click the **Store macro in** drop-down list and select **Documents Based On [your initials] Word 10-3 template**.
   e. Type Change to two columns in the *Description* text box.
   f. Click the **Button** button to open the *Customize the Quick Access Toolbar* area of the *Word Options* dialog box.
   g. Click the **Customize Quick Access Toolbar** drop-down list and select **For [your initials] Word 10-3 template**.
   h. Select the **TemplateProject.NewMacros.TwoColums** macro and click the **Add** button (Figure 10-77).
   i. Click the **Modify** button to open the *Modify Button* dialog box (Figure 10-78).

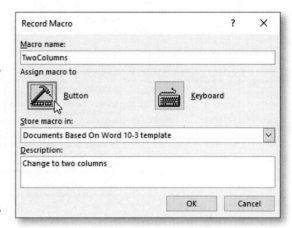

Figure 10-76 Record a button-activated macro

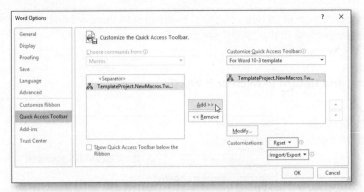

Figure 10-77 Add a macro button to the *Quick Access* toolbar

Figure 10-78 Modify the macro button and display name

    j. Type **Two Columns** in the *Display Name* text box and select a symbol of your choice.

    k. Click **OK** to close the *Modify Button* dialog box and click **OK** to close the *Word Options* dialog box and to begin recording the macro.

4. Record a macro to change the number of columns to two.

    a. Click the **Columns** button [*Layout* tab, *Page Setup* group] and select **Two** from the drop-down list.

    b. Click the **Stop Recording** button [*Developer* tab, *Code* group].

    c. **Save** the macro-enabled template.

5. Edit a macro so it will work on documents with different margins and page layout.

    a. Click the **Macros** button to open the *Macros* dialog box.

    b. Select the **TwoColumns** macro and click the **Edit** button. The Microsoft Visual Basic editor opens.

    c. Select "**.Width = InchesToPoints(6.5)**" and **delete** it. It is okay if a blank line displays where you deleted the code (Figure 10-79).

    d. Press **Ctrl+S** to save the macro code and leave the Microsoft Visual Basic editor open.

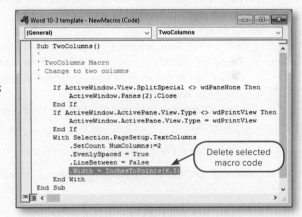

Figure 10-79 Delete macro code

6. Copy the macro and modify it to apply a three-column format.

    a. Select the *TwoColumns* macro code beginning with "**Sub TwoColumns ( )**" and ending with "**End Sub**" and press **Ctrl+C** to copy the code.

    b. Place the insertion point below "End Sub" and press **Ctrl+V** to paste the copied macro code.

    c. Change the word "Two" to **Three** in the name of the copied macro (after "Sub" below the first macro) (Figure 10-80). The code should be "Sub ThreeColumns ( )" after the change.

    d. Change the first comment line from "TwoColumns Macro" to **ThreeColumns Macro**.

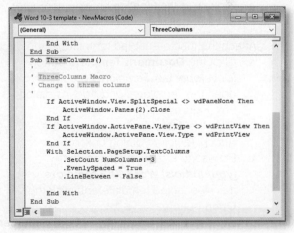

Figure 10-80 Modify the macro code

W10-653

e. Change the second comment line from "Change to two columns" to Change to three columns.

f. Change the number "2" to 3 in the second line in the "With" section. The code should be ".SetCount NumColumns:=3" after the change.

g. Press **Ctrl+S** to save the macro code.

h. Click the **File** menu and select **Close and Return to Microsoft Word**.

7. Assign a keyboard shortcut to a macro.

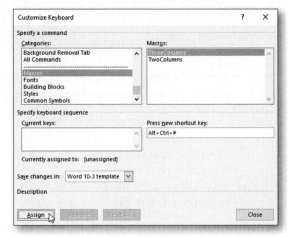

Figure 10-81 Add a shortcut key to a macro

a. Click the **File** tab to open the *Backstage* view and select **Options** on the left to open the *Word Options* dialog box.

b. Click **Customize Ribbon** on the left.

c. Click the **Customize** button in the *Keyboard shortcuts* area. The *Customize Keyboard* dialog box opens (Figure 10-81).

d. Scroll down and select **Macros** in the *Categories* area.

e. Click the **Save changes in** drop-down list and select **[your initials] Word 10-3 template**.

f. Select the **ThreeColumns** macro in the *Macros* list.

g. Place the insertion point in the **Press new shortcut key** text box and press **Alt+Ctrl+Shift+3** (*Alt+Ctrl+#* displays as the keyboard shortcut).

h. Click the **Assign** button.

i. Select the **TwoColumns** macro in the *Macros* list.

j. Place the insertion point in the **Press new shortcut key** text box and press **Alt+Ctrl+Shift+2** (*Alt+Ctrl+@* displays as the keyboard shortcut).

k. Click the **Assign** button.

l. Click **Close** to close the *Customize Keyboard* dialog box and click **OK** to close the *Word Options* dialog box.

8. Save and close the macro-enabled template.

9. Open the ***SPCCDValues-10*** document from your student data files.

10. Save this document as a macro-enabled document.

a. Open the **Save As** dialog box.

b. Save as a **Word Macro-Enabled Document** named [your initials] Word 10-3.

c. Browse to the location on your computer where you want to save the document and click the **Save** button.

11. Attach the macro-enabled template to the document.

a. Click the **Document Template** button [*Developer* tab, *Templates* group] to open the *Templates and Add-ins* dialog box (Figure 10-82).

b. Click the **Attach** button to open the *Attach Template* dialog box.

c. Browse to locate and select the **[your initials] Word 10-3 template** macro-enabled template and click the **Open** button.

d. Check the **Automatically update document styles** box.

Figure 10-82 Attach a template to a document

e. Click **OK** to close the *Templates and Add-ins* dialog box and to attach the template.
f. Click the **Enable Content** button if you are prompted to enable the macros in the document.

12. Run the macros in the document.
   a. Place the insertion point anywhere in the body of the document below the title.
   b. Click the **Two Columns** button on the *Quick Access* toolbar to apply a two-column format to the body of the document.
   c. Press **Alt+Ctrl+Shift+3** to apply a three-column format to the body of the document.

13. Save and close the document (Figure 10-83).

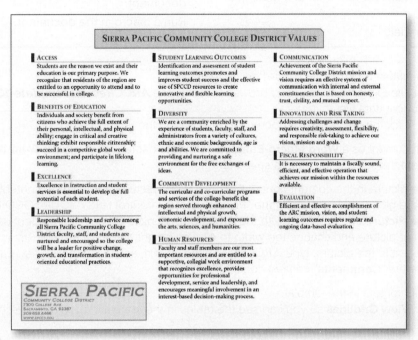

Figure 10-83 Word 10-3 completed

Independent Project 10-4

For this project, you create a receipt template for the American River Cycling Club from a Word template. You save the template as a macro-enabled template, modify the template format and structure, customize the template content, insert *Fill-in* fields, record and copy macros, and create a macro-enabled document based on the template.
[Student Learning Outcomes 10.1, 10.2, 10.3, 10.4 10.5]

Files Needed: ***ARCCReceiptTemplate-10*** and ***ARCClogo-10.png*** *(Student data files are available in the Library of your SIMnet account.)*
Completed Project File Names: *[your initials] Word 10-4 template.dotm* and
[your initials] Word 10-4.docm

Skills Covered in This Project

- Create a document based on a Word template.
- Save a document as a macro-enabled template.
- Insert and resize a picture.
- Delete and customize a content control field.
- Modify the structure and format of a table in a template.
- Insert a *Fill-in* field.
- Record a button-activated macro.
- Copy and modify a macro.
- Add a macro button to the *Quick Access* toolbar.
- Create a document based on a template.
- Respond to a *Fill-in* field prompt.
- Enable the macro content in the document.
- Save a document as a macro-enabled document.
- Run a macro in the document.

1. Open a document based upon a Word online template.
   a. Open a *File Explorer* window and browse to locate the ***ARCCReceiptTemplate-10*** template from your student data files.
   b. Double-click the file to open a document based upon the template.

2. Save the document as a **Word Macro-Enabled Template** named [your initials] Word 10-4 template. Be sure to select the specific location to save the template.

3. Change the picture in the content control field, resize the picture, and remove content control fields.
   a. Select the picture placeholder in the "Picture" content control field ("YOUR LOGO HERE").
   b. **Change Picture** and replace it with the ***ARCClogo-10*** picture from your student data files.
   c. Select the picture and change the width to **4"**. The height automatically adjusts.
   d. Add alt text to the picture, type ARCC logo as the alt text, and close the *Alt Text* pane.
   e. Remove the "**Comments**" content control field.

4. Modify table content in the template.
   a. Turn on **View Gridlines** so you can see the tables in the template (this template contains four tables).
   b. Delete the last row of the third table (beginning with "Fax:").
   c. Delete **From:** in the first row in the third table and type Date:.
   d. Insert the date in the cell to the right of "Date:". Use the spelled-out date format (January 1, 2020) and set it to update automatically.

5. Use the following information to customize the fax template content control fields in the second table.
   Your Company Name: Kelly Weatherby
   Street Address: P.O. Box 4472
   City, ST ZIP Code: Sacramento, CA 95841
   Phone: 916-450-3320
   Fax: 916-450-3301
   e-mail: kelly@arcc.org

6. Insert *Fill-in* fields in the third table.
   a. Insert a **Fill-in** field in the cell to the right of "To:". Type Who is the recipient? as the prompt and Recipient as the default response to the prompt. When prompted, click **OK** to accept the default response.
   b. Insert a **Fill-in** field in the cell to the right of "Phone:" in the third table. Type What is the recipient's phone number? as the prompt and Phone Number as the default response to the prompt. When prompted, click **OK** to accept the default response.
   c. Insert a **Fill-in** field in the cell to the right of "RE:". Type What type of receipt? as the prompt and Receipt Type as the default response to the prompt. When prompted, click **OK** to accept the default response.

7. Record a button-activated macro to insert text.
   a. Place the insertion point in the second row of the fourth table (below "For your records").
   b. Record a macro named MembershipReceipt and store it in **Documents Based On [your initials] Word 10-4 template**.
   c. Leave the *Description* blank.
   d. Click **Button** to assign a button to this macro.
   e. Select **For [your initials] Word 10-4 template** as the *Quick Access* toolbar to customize.
   f. **Add** the **Project.NewMacros.MembershipReceipt** macro.
   g. Modify the macro button to use Membership Receipt as the display name, select the **orange square** as the symbol for the button, and click **OK** to close the *Word Options* dialog box.
   h. Begin recording the macro. Confirm the insertion point is in the second row of the fourth table and type Thank you for renewing your $75 ARCC membership.
   i. **Stop Recording** the macro and delete the text you just typed.
   j. Test the macro by clicking the **Membership Receipt** macro button on the *Quick Access* toolbar.
   k. Delete the text inserted by the macro.

8. Copy and modify a macro.
   a. Open the *Macros* dialog box and edit the **MembershipReceipt** macro.
   b. Copy the macro code and paste it below the existing macro.
   c. Change the name of the copied macro (after "Sub" below the first macro) to ItalyReceipt () (Figure 10-84).
   d. Change the word "Membership" in the comment line to Italy The comment code should be " ItalyReceipt Macro" after the change.

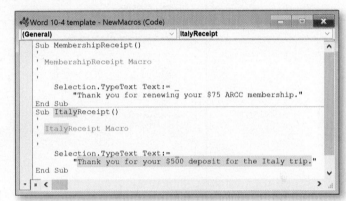

Figure 10-84 Modify the macro code

   e. Change the text after "Selection. TypeText . . ." to Thank you for your $500 deposit for the Italy trip. The text after the "Selection. TypeText . . ." code should display as "Thank you for your $500 deposit for the Italy trip."
   f. Save the macro code, and close and return to the Word document.

9. Customize the *Quick Access* toolbar for the **[your initials] Word 10-4 template** to add a macro button for the *ItalyReceipt* macro.
   a. Use Italy Receipt as the display name.
   b. Select the **green square** as the symbol for the button and click **OK** to close the *Word Options* dialog box.
   c. Place the insertion point in the second row of the fourth table and run the *ItalyReceipt* macro using the macro button on the *Quick Access* toolbar.
   d. Delete the text inserted by the macro.

10. Save and close the macro-enabled template.

11. Open a document based on the **[your initials] Word 10-4 template** (open from a *File Explorer* window).

12. Use the following information for the three *Fill-in* prompt dialog boxes.
    Recipient name: Rick Hermenn
    Recipient phone number: 916-452-9226
    Receipt type: Italy receipt

13. **Enable Content** in the document.

14. Save the document as a **Word Macro-Enabled Document** named [your initials] Word 10-4. If prompted to save the styles and building block, click **Don't Save**. If prompted to save changes to the template, click **Yes**.

15. Place the insertion point in the second row of the fourth table and run the *ItalyReceipt* macro using the button on the *Quick Access* toolbar.

16. Save and close the document (Figure 10-85).

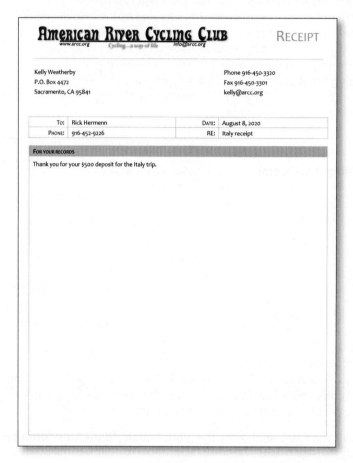

Figure 10-85 Word 10-4 completed

Independent Project 10-5

For this project, you modify a document from Courtyard Medical Plaza using macros you create in a different document. You create macros, copy and modify a macro, and copy macros to a document. [Student Learning Outcomes 10.3, 10.4, 10.5]

Files Needed: **CMPmacros-10.docx**, **VaccinationSchedule-10.docx**, and **CMPlogo-10.png** (Student data files are available in the Library of your SIMnet account.)
Completed Project File Names: **[your initials] Word 10-5 macros.docm** and **[your initials] Word 10-5.docm**

Skills Covered in This Project

- Save a document as a macro-enabled document.
- Insert and arrange a picture.
- Save a picture as an *AutoText* building block.
- Create a macro to insert an *AutoText* building block.
- Create a macro to apply and modify a table style.
- Copy and modify a macro.
- Use the *Organizer* dialog box to copy a macro from one file to another.
- Run a macro in a document.

---

1. Open the **CMPmacros-10** document from your student data files.

2. Save the document as a **Word Macro-Enabled Document** named [your initials] Word 10-5 macros.

3. Insert a picture and save it as an *AutoText* building block.
   a. Insert the **CMPlogo-10** picture on the blank line below the table.
   b. Change the text wrapping to **Tight**.
   c. Change the *Horizontal* **Absolute position** to **0.3"** *to the right of* **Page**.
   d. Change the *Vertical* **Absolute position** to **9.6"** *below* **Page**.
   e. Add alt text to the picture, type CMP logo as the alt text, and close the *Alt Text* pane.
   f. Select the picture and **Save Selection to AutoText Gallery**.
   g. Use Insert CMP logo as the name and save in the **Normal** template.
   h. Delete the picture from your document.

4. Create and record a macro to insert the *AutoText* building block into the footer.
   a. Place the insertion point on the blank line below the table.
   b. Record a macro named InsertLogoFooter and store the macro in **[your initials] Word 10-5 macros (document)**. Don't assign a button or keyboard shortcut to the macro and don't include a description.
   c. Begin recording the macro, **Edit Footer**, insert the **Insert CMP logo** *AutoText* building block, **Close Header and Footer**, and stop recording the macro.

5. Create and record a macro to apply and modify a table style.
   a. Place the insertion point in the table.
   b. Record a macro named GridTable2 and store the macro in **[your initials] Word 10-5 macros (document)**. Don't assign a button or keyboard shortcut to the macro and don't include a description.
   c. Begin recording the macro, check the **Header Row**, **Banded Rows**, and **First Column** boxes [*Table Tools Design* tab, *Table Style Options* group]. The other boxes should not be checked.
   d. Apply the **Grid Table 2 - Accent 2** table style to the table.
   e. Use the **Select** button [*Table Tools Layout* tab, *Table* group] to select the entire table.
   f. Open the *Table Properties* dialog box (**Properties**) [*Table Tools Layout* tab, *Table* group], click the **Cell** tab, change the vertical alignment to **Center**, and click **OK** to close the *Table Properties* dialog box.
   g. Stop recording the macro.

6. Copy and modify a macro.
   a. Open the *Macros* dialog box and edit the **GridTable2** macro.
   b. Select and copy the *GridTable2* macro code and paste it below the *GridTable2* macro.
   c. Change the name of the copied macro (after "Sub" below the *GridTable2* macro) to GridTable5 () (Figure 10-86).

```
Sub GridTable5()
'
' GridTable5 Macro
'
'
    Selection.Tables(1).ApplyStyleHeadingRows = Not Selection.Tables(1). _
        ApplyStyleHeadingRows
    Selection.Tables(1).ApplyStyleRowBands = Not Selection.Tables(1). _
        ApplyStyleRowBands
    Selection.Tables(1).ApplyStyleFirstColumn = Not Selection.Tables(1). _
        ApplyStyleFirstColumn
    Selection.Tables(1).Style = "Grid Table 5 Dark - Accent 2"
    Selection.Tables(1).Select
    Selection.Cells.VerticalAlignment = wdCellAlignVerticalCenter
End Sub
```

Figure 10-86 Modify the macro code

d. Change the number "2" in the first comment line to 5. The comment code should be "GridTable5 Macro" after the change.

e. Change the words "Grid Table 2" in the "Selection.Tables (1).Style. . ." line to **Grid Table 5 Dark**. The code should be "Grid Table 5 Dark - Accent 2" after the change.

f. Save the macro code and close and return to the Word document.

7. Place the insertion point in the table and run the **GridTable5** macro using the *Macros* dialog box.

8. Save and close the macro-enabled document.

9. Open the ***VaccinationSchedule-10*** document from your student data files.

10. Save this document as a **Word Macro-Enabled Document** named [your initials] Word 10-5.

11. Copy the macros from the ***[your initials] Word 10-5 macros*** document to ***[your initials] Word 10-5***.
a. Open the *Macros* dialog box and then open the *Organizer* dialog box (Figure 10-87).

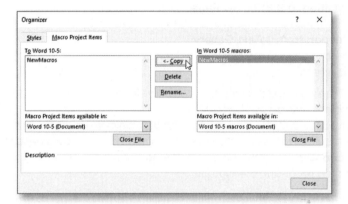

Figure 10-87 Copy macros from one file to another

b. Click the **Macro Project Items** tab if necessary.

c. **Close** the *Normal* template on the right and open the ***[your initials] Word 10-5 macros*** document. In the *Open* dialog box, select **All Word Documents** in the file type drop-down list to display all Word documents if necessary.

d. Select the **NewMacros** macro project item from **[your initials] Word 10-5 macros** (on the right) and **Copy** to **[your initials] Word 10-5** (on the left).

e. Close the *Organizer* dialog box.

12. Open the *Macros* dialog box and run the **InsertLogoFooter** macro to insert the footer into the document.

13. Place the insertion point in the table and run the **GridTable5** macro.

14. Place the insertion point in the table and run the **GridTable2** macro.

15. Save and close the document (Figure 10-88).

VACCINATION SCHEDULE

Think of vaccines as a coat of armor for your child. To keep it shiny and strong, you have to make sure your child's immunizations are up to date. Timely vaccinations help to prevent disease and keep your family and the community healthy. Some immunizations are given in a single shot, while others require a series of shots over a period of time.

Vaccines for children and teenagers are listed alphabetically below with their routinely recommended ages. Missed doses will be assessed by your child's physician and given if necessary. Keep a personal record of all immunizations and bring it with you to each office visit.

Don't neglect your vaccinations!

RECOMMENDED VACCINATION SCHEDULE

Name of Vaccine	When It's Recommended	Total Doses
Chickenpox (varicella)	At 12 months and 4-6 years	2
Diphtheria, tetanus, and pertussis (DTaP)	At 2, 4, 6 and 12-15 months, and 4-6 years	5
Haemophilus influenzae type b (Hib)	At 2, 4, 6, and 12 months	4
Hepatitis A (HepA)	At 12 and 18 months	3
Hepatitis B (HepB)	At birth, 1-2 months, and 6 months	3
Human papillomavirus (HPV)	3-dose series for girls at age 11-12 years	3
Inactivated influenza (flu shot)	Annually starting at age 6 months	Annually
Inactivated poliovirus (IPV)	At 2, 4, 6 months, and 4-6 years	4
Live intranasal influenza	Annually starting at age 2 years	Annually
Measles, mumps, and rubella (MMR)	At 12 months and 4-6 years	2
Meningococcal conjugate (MCV)	At 11-12 years	1
Pneumococcal conjugate (PCV)	At 2, 4, 6, and 12 months	4
Pneumococcal polysaccharide (PPSV)	At 2, 4, 6, and 12 months	4
Rotavirus (RV)	At 2, 4, and 6 months	3
Tetanus and diphtheria (Td)	At 11-12 years	1

These recommendations are for generally healthy children and teenagers and are for information only. If your child has ongoing health problems, special health needs or risks, or certain conditions that run in your family, talk with your child's physician. He or she may recommend additional vaccinations or schedules based on earlier immunizations and special health needs.

Courtyard
Medical
Plaza

1660 Alhandra Way
Granite Bay, CA 95517

a comprehensive medical facility

559.288.1660
www.cmp.com

Figure 10-88 Word 10-5 completed

Independent Project 10-6

For this project, you create an insurance renewal letter template for Central Sierra Insurance. You create a macro-enabled template, insert *Fill-in* fields, record a macro, copy and modify a macro, and create a document based on the template.
[Student Learning Outcomes 10.1, 10.2, 10.3, 10.4, 10.5]

File Needed: **CSIPolicyRenewal-10.docx** *(Student data files are available in the* Library *of your SIMnet account.)*
Completed Project File Names: *[your initials]* **Word 10-6 template.dotm** and
[your initials] **Word 10-6.docm**

Skills Covered in This Project

- Save a document as a macro-enabled template.
- Insert a *Fill-in* field.
- Create a keyboard-activated macro to insert the closing lines of a letter.
- Copy and modify a macro.
- Assign a keyboard shortcut to a macro.

- Create a document based on a macro-enabled template.
- Respond to a *Fill-in* field prompt.
- Enable the macro content in the document.
- Save a document as a macro-enabled document.
- Update formulas in a table.
- Run a macro in a document.

1. Open the **CSIPolicyRenewal-10** document from your student data files.

2. Save the document as a **Word Macro-Enabled Template** named [your initials] Word 10-6 template.

3. Insert *Fill-in* fields in the document.
   a. Use the following information in Table 10-3 for the five *Fill-in* fields to replace the bracketed placeholder text. Delete placeholder text and brackets.
   b. Accept the default response as you create each *Fill-in* field.

   Table 10-3:

Placeholder Text	Prompt	Default Response to Prompt
[Name and Address]	Type name, company, and address.	Name/Company/Address
[First Name]	Type client's first name.	First Name
[Insurance Company]	Type name of insurance company.	Insurance Company
[Premium Basis]	What is the premium basis?	Premium Basis
[Rate per $1000]	What is the rate per $1000?	Rate per $1000

4. Create and record a macro to insert the closing lines of the letter.
   a. Place the insertion point on the last blank line in the document.
   b. Record a macro named GretchenClosing and store the macro in **Documents Based On [your initials] Word 10-6 template**.
   c. Type Inserts Gretchen Souza closing lines as the description. Don't assign a keyboard shortcut or button to the macro.
   d. Begin recording the macro and type the following lines of text:
      Sincerely and press **Enter** four times
      Gretchen Souza, ARM, CIC, CRM and press **Enter**
      Central Sierra Insurance and press **Enter** gretchen@centralsierra.com
   e. Stop recording the macro and delete the text you just typed. Confirm two blank lines display below the last paragraph in the letter.

5. Copy and modify a macro.
   a. Edit the *GretchenClosing* macro, copy it, and paste it below the last line of macro code.
   b. Change the name of the copied macro (after "Sub" below the *GretchenClosing* macro) to **JuanClosing ()** (Figure 10-89).
   c. Change the word "Gretchen" in the first comment line to **Juan**. The comment code should be "JuanClosing Macro" after the change.
   d. Change the words "Gretchen Souza" in the second comment line to **Juan Taylor**. The comment code should be "Inserts Juan Taylor closing lines" after the change.

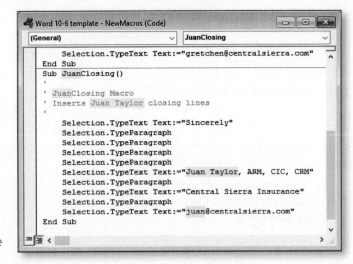

Figure 10-89 Modify the macro code

   e. Change the words "Gretchen Souza" in the second "Selection.TypeText Text:. . ." line to **Juan Taylor**. The code should be "Juan Taylor, ARM, CIC, CRM" after the change.
   f. Change the word "gretchen" in the email address in the last "Selection.TypeText Text:. . ." line to **juan**. The code should be "juan@centralsierra.com" after the change.
   g. Save the macro code and close and return to the Word document.

6. Assign a keyboard shortcut to the two macros.
   a. Open the *Customize Keyboard* dialog box and select **Macros** in the *Categories* area.
   b. Save changes in the **[your initials] Word 10-6 template**.
   c. Select the *GretchenClosing* macro and assign **Alt+Ctrl+Shift+G** as the keyboard shortcut.
   d. Select the *JuanClosing* macro and assign **Alt+Ctrl+Shift+J** as the keyboard shortcut.
   e. **Close** the *Customize Keyboard* dialog box and click **OK** to close the *Word Options* dialog box.

7. Test the macro and finalize the template.
   a. Use the keyboard shortcut to test the *GretchenClosing* macro.
   b. Delete the inserted macro text. Confirm that two blank lines display below the last paragraph in the letter.
   c. Use the keyboard shortcut to test the *JuanClosing* macro.
   d. Delete the inserted macro text. Confirm that two blank lines display below the last paragraph in the letter.

8. Check the spacing in the document around the *Fill-in* fields to ensure proper spacing.

9. Save and close the template.

10. Open a *File Explorer* window and create a new document based on **[your initials] Word 10-6 template**.

11. Use the following information for the *Fill-in* field prompts:
    Name/Company/Address:
    Mr. Lamar Gordon
    Sierra Fence Company
    2405 Eureka Avenue
    Fair Oaks, CA 95636

First Name: Lamar
Insurance Company: West Coast Insurance
Premium Basis: $325,000
Rate per $1000: $21

12. **Enable Content** in the document. If prompted to save the template, click **Save**.

13. Save the document as a **Word Macro-Enabled Document** named *[your initials] Word 10-6*. If prompted to save the template, click **Yes**.

14. Update the formulas in the last three cells in the second row of the table (right-click and **Update Field**).

15. Place the insertion point on the second blank line below the body and run the *JuanClosing* macro.

16. Save and close the document (Figure 10-90). If prompted to save the template, click **Save**.

Figure 10-90 Word 10-6 completed

Improve It Project 10-7

For this project, you create an invoice template for Eller Software Services from an online Word template. You save the template as a macro-enabled template, customize the template content, insert a *Fill-in* field, record macros in the template, and create a macro-enabled document based on the template.
[Student Learning Outcomes 10.1, 10.2, 10.3, 10.5]

Files Needed: ***Invoice* online Word template** and ***ESSlogo-10.png*** *(Student data files are available in the Library of your SIMnet account.)*
Completed Project File Names: ***[your initials] Word 10-7 template.dotm*** and ***[your initials] Word 10-7.docm***

Skills Covered in This Project

- Create a document based on a Word online template.
- Save a document as a macro-enabled template.
- Insert, resize, and arrange a picture.
- Customize a content control field.
- Delete a row from a table.
- Insert a *Fill-in* field.
- Insert a formula in a table.
- Record a button-activated macro.
- Create a document based on a template.
- Respond to a *Fill-in* field prompt.
- Enable the macro content in the document.
- Save a document as a macro-enabled document.
- Run a macro in a document.

1. Create a document from an online Word template.
   a. Search for online templates in the *New* area on the *Backstage* view and use invoice as the keyword.
   b. Select the **Invoice (Red design)** online Word template and create a document based on this template. If this template is not available in Word, open the ***Invoice-10*** file from your student data files.

2. Save the document as a **Word Macro-Enabled Template** named [your initials] Word 10-7 template.

3. Change the existing logo picture and resize and arrange the picture.
   a. **Change Picture** of the sample logo picture and replace it with ***ESSlogo-10*** from your student data files.
   b. Change the height to **0.6"** while maintaining the aspect ratio.
   c. Change the text wrapping to **In Front of Text**.
   d. Change the *Horizontal* **Alignment** to **Right** *relative to* **Margin**.
   e. Change the *Vertical* **Alignment** to **Top** *relative to* **Margin**.
   f. Add alt text to the picture, type ESS logo as the alt text, and close the *Alt Text* pane.

4. Customize the content of the template.
   a. Type Eller Software Services in the "Company" content control field.
   b. Type 3421 East Avenue, Saint Cloud, MN 56301 in the "Street Address, City, ST ZIP Code" content control field.
   c. Type Payment is due within 30 days after the invoice date. in the "Add additional instructions" content control field.
   d. Edit the footer, type the following information in the content control fields, and then close the footer:
      Telephone: 320.675.4100
      Fax: 320.675.4101
      Email: info@ellersoftware.com
      Web: www.ellersoftware.com
   e. Delete the next to last row in the third table in the body of the document ("Shipping & Handling").

5. Insert a *Fill-in* field.
   a. Remove the content control field below "To" and insert a **Fill-in** field.
   b. Type What is the client's name, company, and address? as the prompt and Client Info as the default response to the prompt.
   c. Accept the default response to the prompt.

6. Insert formulas in the table.
   a. Insert a formula in the cell to the right of "Subtotal" to **SUM** the cells **ABOVE** (Figure 10-91). Use the **$#,##0.00;($#,##0.00)** number format.
   b. Insert a formula in the cell to the right of "Sales Tax" to multiply cell **D13** by **7.5%** and use the same number format.
   c. Insert a formula in the cell to the right of "Total Due By [Date]" to add cells **D13** and **D14** and use the same number format.

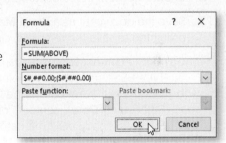

Figure 10-91 Insert a formula to add the cells above

7. Record a button-activated macro to insert a product into the invoice.
   a. Place the insertion point in the cell below "Quantity" in the table.
   b. Record a macro named ESS_Software and store it in **Documents Based On [your initials] Word 10-7 template**.
   c. Type Inserts ESS Accounting Software package as the *Description*.
   d. Assign the macro to a button and add the macro to the *Quick Access* toolbar **For [your initials] Word 10-7 template**.

e. Modify the button to use **ESS Software** as the display name and select a button symbol of your choice (Figure 10-92).
f. Begin recording the macro and type the following information in the first row of the table, pressing **Tab** to move from cell to cell:

    1   ESS Accounting Software $875.00 $875.00
g. Stop recording the macro.
h. Delete the text you typed in the table.

Figure 10-92 Assign a button to a macro

8. Record another button-activated macro to insert a product into the invoice.
   a. Place the insertion point in the cell below "Quantity".
   b. Record a macro named **ESS_Support** and store it in **Documents Based On [your initials] Word 10-7 template**.
   c. Type Inserts ESS Accounting Software Support package as the *Description*.
   d. Assign a button to the macro and add the macro to the *Quick Access* toolbar **For [your initials] Word 10-7 template**.
   e. Modify the button to use **ESS Support** as the display name and select a button symbol of your choice.
   f. Begin recording the macro and type the following information in the first row of the table, pressing **Tab** to move from cell to cell:

      8 hrs   ESS Accounting Software Support $75.00 $600.00
   g. Stop recording the macro.
   h. Delete the text you typed in the table.

9. Save and close the macro-enabled template.

10. Open a *File Explorer* window and create a new document based on the **[your initials] Word 10-7 template**.

11. Use the following information for the *Fill-in* field prompt:
    Ms. Amanda Mendez
    Paradise Lakes Resort
    1256 Raymond Drive
    Cass Lake, MN 56633

12. **Enable Content** in the document. If prompted to save styles and building blocks, click **Don't Save**.

13. Save the document as a **Word Macro-Enabled Document** named [your initials] Word 10-7. If prompted to save the template, click **Yes**.

14. Customize content control fields.
    a. Type ESS2305 in the invoice number content control field on the left ("[0000]").
    b. Select the current date in the "Click to select date" content control field.
    c. Select the "**[Date]**" content control field near the bottom of the last table in the body ("Total Due By [Date]") and select the date one month from today.

15. Run macros.
    a. Place the insertion point in the cell below "Quantity" and run the **ESS Software** macro using the button on the *Quick Access* toolbar.
    b. Place the insertion point in the first cell in the next row and run the **ESS Support** macro.

16. Update the three formulas in the table beginning with the "Subtotal" formula and continuing down (right-click and **Update Field**).

17. Select the total amount field in the last cell in the last row and apply **bold** format.

18. Save and close the document (Figure 10-93).

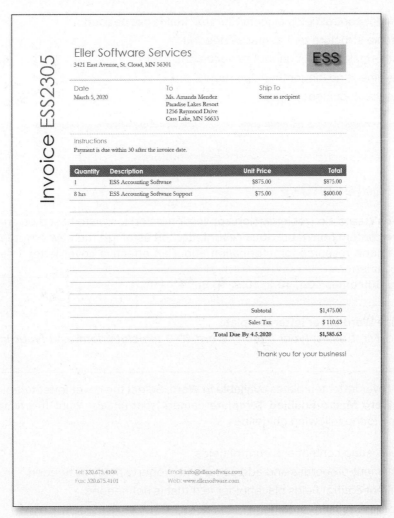

Figure 10-93 Word 10-7 completed

Challenge Project 10-8

For this project, you create a resume based on an online Word template. You can use content from a previous resume to customize the new resume. Your college career center is a good resource for information about an effective resume.
[**Student Learning Outcomes 10.1, 10.2**]

File Needed: **Online Word resume template**
Completed Project File Name: ***[your initials] Word 10-8.docx***

Search the online resume templates available in Word. Select the resume template of your choice and save the document as [your initials] Word 10-8. Modify your document according to the following guidelines:

- Customize the existing content control fields.
- Customize document properties and add document property fields as needed.

- Delete any content control fields placeholder text that is not needed.
- Modify the resume structure and format as needed.
- Use consistent formatting throughout the document.
- Ensure your resume is no longer than two pages.
- Save and close the document.

Challenge Project 10-9

For this project, you create a cover letter (job application letter) template based on an online Word template. You can use content from a previous cover letter to customize the new cover letter. Your college career center is a good resource for information about an effective cover letter. Use *Fill-in* fields and macros in your cover letter.
[Student Learning Outcomes 10.1, 10.2, 10.3, 10.5]

File Needed: **Online Word cover letter template**
Completed Project File Names: *[your initials] Word 10-9 template.dotm* and *[your initials] Word 10-9 .docm*

Search for online cover letter templates available in Word. Select the cover letter template of your choice and save it as a **Word Macro-Enabled Template** named [your initials] Word 10-9 template. Modify your template according to the following guidelines:

- Customize the existing content and control fields.
- Customize document properties and add document property fields as needed.
- Delete any content control fields placeholder text that is not needed.
- Use *Fill-in* fields for the recipient's name and address and the salutation.
- Record macros for paragraphs of information in the body of the letter. Store these macros in the template so you can customize future cover letters with information from the macros.
- Modify the cover letter structure and format as needed.
- Use consistent formatting and fit the cover letter on one page.
- Save and close the template.

Create a document based on your cover letter template. Customize information in the *Fill-in* field prompts and enable macro content. Insert content from macros as needed. Save the document as a macro-enabled document named [your initials] Word 10-9.

Challenge Project 10-10

Most of your classes have homework assignments, and your professors usually want you to turn in these assignments in a specific format. For example, you might have to include a header with your name, your professor's name, and the name of the assignment. In this project, create a macro-enabled template that you can use for your homework assignments.
[Student Learning Outcomes 10.2, 10.3, 10.4, 10.5]

Files Needed: None
Completed Project File Name: *[your initials] Word 10-10 template.dotm*

Create a new document and save it as a **Word Macro-Enabled Template** named [your initials] Word 10-10 template. Modify your template according to the following guidelines:

- Plan the macros you want to include in this document.
- Create and record macros for content to insert into your homework assignment document.
- If the macros are similar, copy and edit them to create new macros.
- Assign the macros to a button or keyboard shortcut.
- Include *Fill-in* fields as needed.
- Run macros to confirm they work properly.
- Include a heading to label each macro content in the document.

Working with Forms and Master Documents

CHAPTER OVERVIEW

In previous chapters, you used content control fields in templates and cover pages. This chapter covers how to insert and customize a variety of content control fields. Use content control fields and templates together to create fill-in forms. Also, group or protect forms so users can only edit the content control fields, which preserves the formatting of fillable forms.

In chapter 3, you worked with reports and long documents. This chapter also introduces how to manage long documents using a master document and subdocuments. Use *Outline* view and heading styles when working with a master document and subdocuments.

STUDENT LEARNING OUTCOMES (SLOs)

After completing this chapter, you will be able to:

SLO 11.1 Insert, customize, and arrange a variety of content control fields (p. W11-671).

SLO 11.2 Insert and customize advanced content control fields where a user selects from a list of choices (p. W11-679).

SLO 11.3 Edit a content control field to change the format and lock content and use *Design* mode to edit placeholder text (p. W11-681).

SLO 11.4 Group content control fields, protect and edit a form, create a form based on a template, fill in a form, and save a form based on a template (p. W11-686).

SLO 11.5 Manage a long document using a master document that contains subdocuments (p. W11-690).

CASE STUDY

In the first three Pause & Practice projects in this chapter, you create a registration form for Central Sierra Insurance using content control fields. In Pause & Practice 11-4, you manage a long report using a master document that contains subdocuments.

Pause & Practice 11-1: Customize a registration form using basic content control fields.

Pause & Practice 11-2: Insert and customize advanced content control fields where users select from options.

Pause & Practice 11-3: Group content control fields, save a form as a template, and create a new document based on the template.

Pause & Practice 11-4: Use a master document containing subdocuments to manage a long report.

WORD

Using Content Control Fields

You are familiar with customizing information in content control fields from *SLO 3.6: Inserting a Cover Page* and *SLO 10.2: Customizing and Using Templates*. This section covers how to insert and customize basic content control fields where users enter information such as their name and company, check a check box, pick a date, or insert a picture. Each content control field has a title and properties associated with it. Arrange content control fields in a document using a variety of formatting methods.

Content Control Fields

Recall that ***content control fields*** are containers for information or objects. Each content control field is designed to contain a specific type of information. Table 11-1 lists the basic content control fields and a description of each:

Table 11-1: Content Control Fields

Content Control Field	Use
Rich Text	User types text and the text can be formatted.
Plain Text	User types text and all the text is formatted the same way.
Check Box	User selects or deselects a check box.
Date Picker	User selects a date from a calendar thumbnail.
Picture	User inserts a picture into the content control field.

The size of *Rich Text* and *Plain Text* content control fields adjusts as a user types text in the fields. These content control fields can contain a few words or paragraphs of text. *Check Box* content control fields can be checked or unchecked by a user and do not change in size. *Date Picker* content control fields automatically adjust in size to fit the date format you select. *Picture* content control fields automatically resize to accommodate a picture.

Control Content Control Field Arrangement

When using content control fields in a document or form, the first step is to plan the arrangement of the fields. Use ***tab stops*** and ***indents*** to control the location of the fields and to control how the text wraps to the next line when you are using *Rich Text* or *Plain Text* content control fields.

Tables are also an effective way to arrange content control fields. Insert one or more content control fields in a cell and use horizontal and vertical alignment to align them in a cell. Use tab stops and indents to arrange content control fields in the cells of a table.

Insert a Rich Text Content Control Field

Use a ***Rich Text content control field*** where the user enters a single word, a sentence, or paragraphs of text. Users can also copy and paste text in a *Rich Text* content control field and apply formatting to individual words or all text in the content control field. For example, users can apply bold and italic formatting to a specific word or to all the text in a *Rich Text* content control field.

▶ HOW TO: Insert a Rich Text Content Control Field

1. Place the insertion point at the location to insert a content control field.
2. Click the **Rich Text Content Control** button [*Developer* tab, *Controls* group] (Figure 11-1). A *Rich Text* content control field displays in the document (Figure 11-2).

   - Click the **handle** of the content control field to select it.
   - Press the **left** or **right** keyboard arrow key to deselect the content control field and to move the insertion point to the left or right of the content control field.

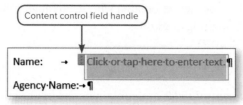
Figure 11-2 *Rich Text* content control field

Figure 11-1 Insert *Rich Text* content control field

   - Move a content control field by selecting the content control field handle and dragging it to a new location, or cut or copy the field and paste it in another location.

> ### ANOTHER WAY
>
> To copy a content control field, press and hold the **Ctrl** key and drag the content control field to another location.

Content Control Field Properties

After inserting a content control field, add a ***title*** and a ***tag*** to the content control field using the ***Content Control Properties*** dialog box so each content control field has a unique identifier. The content control field title, such as *Name*, *Address*, *Company*, or *Email*, displays on the handle of the field. A tag is a unique identifier that can connect to a database, and information from the form automatically populates fields in a database. Both *Title* and *Tag* fields are optional.

▶ HOW TO: Customize Content Control Field Properties

1. Select the content control field and click the **Properties** button [*Developer* tab, *Controls* group]. The *Content Control Properties* dialog box opens (Figure 11-3).
2. Click the **Title** text box and type a title for the content control field.
3. Click the **Tag** text box and type a tag for the content control field.

   - You do not have to include a tag unless you are connecting your form to a database.

4. Click **OK** to close the *Content Control Properties* dialog box.

   - The title of the content control field appears on the handle of the field (Figure 11-4).

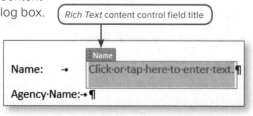
Figure 11-4 Content control field title displayed on the handle

Figure 11-3 *Content Control Properties* dialog box

Plain Text Content Control Field

The main differences between a *Rich Text* and a ***Plain Text content control field*** is how the text is formatted and how multiple paragraphs of text display in the field. In a *Rich Text* content control field, individual words can be formatted independently of other words in the field, but text in a *Plain Text* content control field is all formatted the same. You can apply bold, italic, or paragraph formatting, but all the text in a *Plain Text* content control field will have the same formatting.

In addition, *Plain Text* content control fields, by default, can contain only one paragraph of text. Change the properties of the *Plain Text* content control field to enable users to use *Enter* to type text on a new line or to include multiple paragraphs of text. Word automatically inserts a line break (*Shift+Enter*) rather than a paragraph break (*Enter*) when the user presses **Enter**.

▶ **HOW TO:** Insert and Customize a Plain Text Content Control Field

1. Place the insertion point at the location to insert a content control field.

2. Click the **Plain Text Content Control** button [*Developer* tab, *Controls* group] to insert a *Plain Text* content control field (Figure 11-5).

3. Select the content control field and click the **Properties** button [*Developer* tab, *Controls* group] to open the *Content Control Properties* dialog box (Figure 11-6).

4. Click the **Title** text box and type a title for the content control field.

5. Check the **Allow carriage returns (multiple paragraphs)** box to enable users to type multiple lines of text.

   • Check this box if you want users to be able to use *Enter* to insert a paragraph break between lines or paragraphs of text.

6. Click **OK** to close the *Content Control Properties* dialog box.

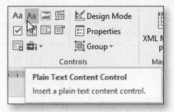

Figure 11-5 Insert a *Plain Text* content control field

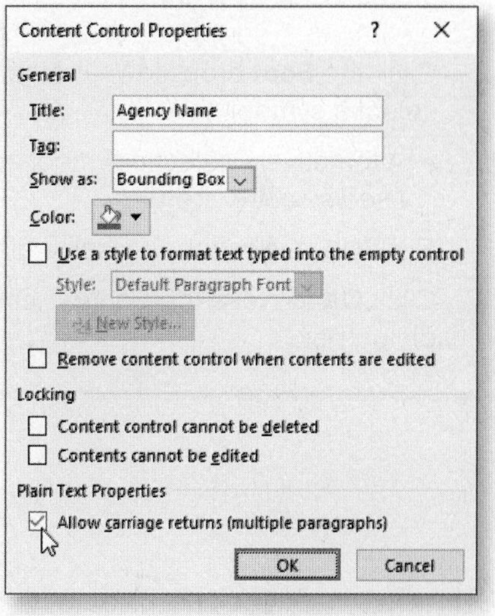

Figure 11-6 Allow multiple lines of text in a *Plain Text* content control field

Check Box Content Control Field

A ***Check Box content control field*** enables users to select an option by clicking a check box. A *Check Box* content control field limits users to only two options: checked or unchecked. By default, an unchecked *Check Box* content control field is an open box, and when a user checks the box, it displays an **X**. Customize how the unchecked and checked box display. For example, use a check mark symbol for a checked *Check Box* content control field.

1. Place the insertion point at the location to insert a content control field.

2. Click the **Check Box Content Control** button [*Developer* tab, *Controls* group] to insert a *Check Box* content control field (Figure 11-7).

   • By default, a *Check Box* content control field displays as unchecked.

3. Select the content control field and click the **Properties** button [*Developer* tab, *Controls* group] to open the *Content Control Properties* dialog box.

4. Click the **Title** text box and type the title of the content control field.

5. Change the checked or unchecked symbol by clicking the **Change** button (Figure 11-8). The *Symbol* dialog box opens (Figure 11-9).

Figure 11-7 Insert *Check Box* content control field

Figure 11-8 Change check box content control symbol

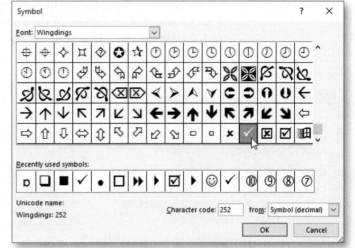

Figure 11-9 *Symbol* dialog box

6. Click the **Font** drop-down list, select a font set, and select a symbol.

   • Alternatively, select a symbol from the *Recently used symbols* area.

7. Click **OK** to close the *Symbols* dialog box.

8. Click **OK** to close the *Content Control Properties* dialog box.

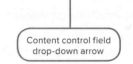

Content control field drop-down arrow

Figure 11-10 *Date Picker* content control field

Date Picker Content Control Field

A *Date Picker content control field* provides a calendar thumbnail where a user selects a date rather than typing a date (Figure 11-10). This ensures consistency in how dates display in the document. Customize the date format in the *Content Control Properties* dialog box.

1. Place the insertion point at the location to insert the content control field.

2. Click the **Date Picker Content Control** button [*Developer* tab, *Controls* group] to insert a *Date Picker* content control field (Figure 11-11).

3. Select the content control field and click the **Properties** button [*Developer* tab, *Controls* group] to open the *Content Control Properties* dialog box.

4. Click the **Title** text box and type a title for the content control field.

Figure 11-11 Insert *Date Picker* content control field

5. Select a date format from the list in the *Date Picker Properties* area in the *Content Control Properties* dialog box (Figure 11-12).

- Alternatively, customize the date field code. The date field code displays in the *Display the date like this* text box. For example, *MMMM d, yyyy* displays the date as January 1, 2010, *MMMM d* displays as January 1, and M/d/yy displays as 1/1/20.

6. Click **OK** to close the *Content Control Properties* dialog box.

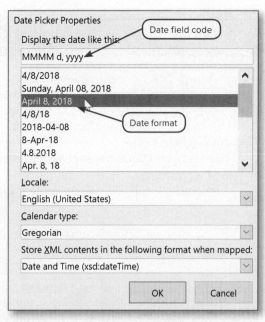

Figure 11-12 Select the date format

Picture Content Control Field

A ***Picture content control field*** enables users to insert a picture at a specific location in the document (Figure 11-13). For example, use a *Picture* content control field in a real estate listing template to display a picture of the home. A *Picture* content control field automatically resizes to fit the selected picture. Arrange a *Picture* content control field in a document the same way you arrange a picture with text wrapping and alignment.

When you use a *Picture* content control field, consider how an inserted picture will affect the layout of the existing text and content in the document. Position the *Picture* content control field in a location that does not adversely affect other text and fields in the document.

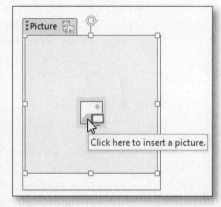

Figure 11-13 *Picture* content control field

▶ **HOW TO:** Insert and Customize a Picture Content Control Field

1. Place the insertion point at the location to insert the content control field.

2. Click the **Picture Content Control** button [*Developer* tab, *Controls* group] to insert a *Picture* content control field (Figure 11-14).

3. Select the content control field and click the **Properties** button [*Developer* tab, *Controls* group] to open the *Content Control Properties* dialog box.

4. Click the **Title** text box and type a title for the content control field.

5. Click **OK** to close the *Content Control Properties* dialog box.

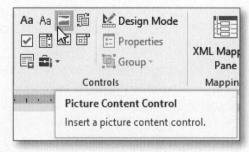

Figure 11-14 Insert a *Picture* content control field

For this Pause & Practice project, you modify an existing document from Central Sierra Insurance to create a fill-in registration form for a conference. Set a tab stop and indents to control alignment of content control fields and insert and customize content control fields.

File Needed: **CSIConferenceRegistration-11.docx** *(Student data files are available in the* Library *of your SIMnet account.)*
Completed Project File Name: ***[your initials] PP W11-1.docx***

---

1. Open the ***CSIConferenceRegistration-11*** document from your student data files.

2. Save the document as a Word document named [your initials] PP W11-1.

3. Add a tab stop and set a hanging indent.
   a. Check the **Ruler** box [*View* tab, *Show* group] to display the ruler if necessary.
   b. Select the "**Name:**" and "**Agency Name:**" paragraphs and set a **1" left** tab stop (not left indent).
   c. Select the next two paragraphs of text ("**Yes, . . .**" and "**No, . . .**"), set a **hanging** indent at **0.25"**, and set a **0.25" left** tab stop (not left indent).

4. Insert and customize *Rich Text* content control fields.
   a. Place the insertion point after "Name:" and press **Tab**.
   b. Click the **Rich Text Content Control** button [*Developer* tab, *Controls* group] to insert a *Rich Text* content control field.
   c. Select the content control field and click the **Properties** button [*Developer* tab, *Controls* group] to open the *Content Control Properties* dialog box (Figure 11-15).
   d. Type **Name** in the *Title* text box and click **OK** to close the dialog box.
   e. Place the insertion point after "Agency Name:" and press **Tab**.
   f. Insert a **Rich Text** content control field.
   g. Click the **Properties** button to open the *Content Control Properties* dialog box, type **Agency Name** as the *Title*, and click **OK**.
   h. Place the insertion point after "Arrival Time:" in the "Travel" section and press **Tab**.
   i. Insert a **Rich Text** content control field.
   j. Open the *Content Control Properties* dialog box, type **Arrival Time** as the *Title*, and click **OK**.
   k. Place the insertion point after "Departure Time:" and press **Tab**.
   l. Insert a **Rich Text** content control field.
   m. Open the *Content Control Properties* dialog box, type **Departure Time** as the *Title*, and click **OK**.

Figure 11-15 Add a title to the content control field

5. Insert *Check Box* content control fields, customize the properties, and change the symbol.
   a. Place the insertion point before "Yes, . . ." (below "Agency Name") and click the **Check Box Content Control** button [*Developer* tab, *Controls* group] to insert a *Check Box* content control field.
   b. Open the *Content Control Properties* dialog box and type **Attending** as the *Title*.
   c. Click the **Change** button to the right of *Checked symbol* (Figure 11-16). The *Symbol* dialog box opens.
   d. Click the **Font** drop-down list and select **Wingdings**.

Figure 11-16 Change the symbol for the
check box content control field

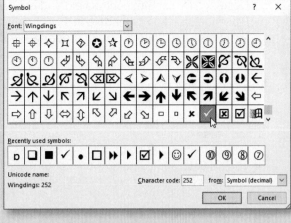

Figure 11-17 Select symbol for check box content control field

Check Box content control fields   Rich Text content control fields

Name: Click·or·tap·here·to·enter·text.¶

Agency·Name: Click·or·tap·here·to·enter·text.¶

☐ · Yes,·I·plan·to·attend·the·Agricultural·Insurance·

☐ · No,·I·won't·be·able·to·attend·this·year's·Agricu.·
        online·sessions.¶

Figure 11-18 Rich Text and Check Box
content control fields

e. Select the **check mark** symbol (character
   code 252) (Figure 11-17).
f. Click **OK** to close the *Symbol* dialog box and
   click **OK** to close the *Content Control Properties*
   dialog box.
g. Press the **right** arrow key two times to deselect
   the *Check Box* content control field and position
   the insertion point after the content control field
   and before the text ("Yes,").
h. Press **Tab**.
i. Place the insertion point before "No, . . ." and insert a **Check Box** content control field.
j. Open the *Content Control Properties* dialog box and type Not Attending as the *Title*.
k. Click the **Change** button to the right of *Checked symbol*, select the **check mark** symbol
   (*Wingdings* character code 252), click **OK** to close the *Symbol* dialog box, and click **OK** to close
   the *Content Control Properties* dialog box.
l. Press the **right** arrow key two times to deselect the content control field and position the insertion
   point after the content control field and before the text ("No,").
m. Press **Tab** (Figure 11-18).

6. Insert and customize *Check Box* content control fields.
   a. Place the insertion point before "I will be
      staying . . .", insert a **Check Box** content control
      field, and customize the content control properties
      to include Staying at Northgate as the *Title*. Note: Do
      not change the *Checked symbol* for all the *Check
      Box* content control fields in step 6.
   b. Use the **right** arrow key to deselect the content
      control field and position the insertion point
      between the content control field and the text,
      and press **Tab** (Figure 11-19).
   c. Place the insertion point before "I will not be
      staying . . .", insert a **Check Box** content control field,
      and customize the content control properties
      to include Not Staying at Northgate as the *Title*.

■ ACCOMMODATIONS¶
☐ · I·will·be·staying·at·the·Northgate·Resort.¶

Type·of·Room   ·   Type·of·Bed   ·
¶

☐ · I·will·not·be·staying·at·the·Northgate·Resort.¶

■ TRAVEL¶
Arrival·Date:¶

☐ · I·will·be·driving·to·the·conference.¶

☐ · I·will·be·flying·to·the·conference.¶
   · ☐ · I·need·a·shuttle·to·and·from·Northgate·Resort.¶
   · Airline:¶
   · Arrival·Time: · Click·or·tap·here·to·enter·text.¶
   · Departure·Time: · Click·or·tap·here·to·enter·text.¶

Figure 11-19 Check Box content control fields inserted

d. Deselect the content control field and press **Tab** between the content control field and the text.

e. Place the insertion point before "I will be driving . . .", insert a **Check Box** content control field, and customize the content control properties to include **Driving** as the *Title*.

f. Deselect the content control field and press **Tab** between the content control field and the text.

g. Place the insertion point before "I will be flying . . .", insert a **Check Box** content control field, and customize the content control properties to include **Flying** as the *Title*.

h. Deselect the content control field and press **Tab** between the content control field and the text.

i. Place the insertion point before "I need a shuttle . . ." and after the tab, insert a **Check Box** content control field, and customize the content control properties to include **Shuttle** as the *Title*.

j. Deselect the content control field and press **Tab** between the content control field and the text.

k. Review your document to confirm the correct placement of the check box content control fields (see Figure 11-19).

7. Insert and customize a *Date Picker* content control field.
   a. Place the insertion point after "Departure Date:" and press **Tab**.
   b. Click the **Date Picker Content Control** button.
   c. Open the *Content Control Properties* dialog box and type **Departure Date** as the *Title*.
   d. Click the **Display the date like this** text box, delete the existing text, and type **MMMM d** to display the month and day only (Figure 11-20).
   e. Click **OK** to close the dialog box.

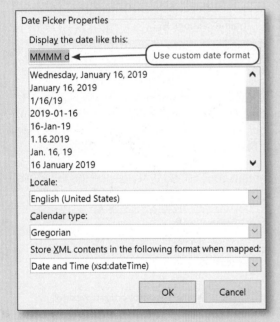

Figure 11-20 Type the specific date format

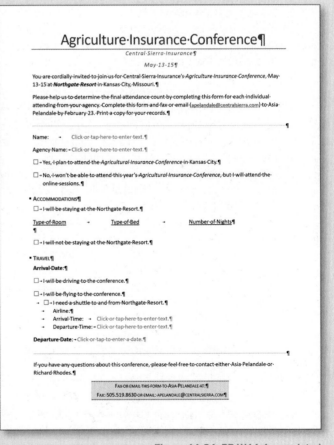

Figure 11-21 PP W11-1 completed

8. Confirm none of the *Check Box* content control fields are checked.

9. Save and close the document (Figure 11-21).

Using Advanced Content Control Fields

In addition to the content control fields you learned about in *SLO 11.1: Using Content Control Fields*, other content control fields enable users to select from pre-defined options. The *Combo Box* and *Drop-Down List* content control fields enable users to choose from a list of choices you create. These content control fields limit the responses of users and save users time by enabling them to select an option from the list rather than typing a response. The *Building Block Gallery* content control field lets users insert a building block. *Legacy Tools* are form fields that are available in older versions of Word.

Combo Box Content Control Field

A ***Combo Box content control field*** displays user selections in a drop-down list (Figure 11-22). When inserting a *Combo Box* content control field, create the list of options in the *Content Control Properties* dialog box. This content control field also provides users the option of typing

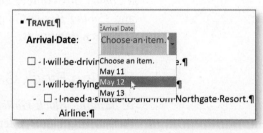

Figure 11-22 *Combo Box* content control field

their own responses in the field. For example, create a list of dates from which users can choose, but they also have the option of typing a different date.

▶ HOW TO: Insert and Customize a Combo Box Content Control Field

1. Place the insertion point at the location to insert a content control field.
2. Click the **Combo Box Content Control** button [*Developer* tab, *Controls* group] to insert a *Combo Box* content control field (Figure 11-23).
3. Select the content control field and click the **Properties** button [*Developer* tab, *Controls* group] to open the *Content Control Properties* dialog box.
4. Click the **Title** text box and type a title for the content control field.
5. Click the **Add** button in the *Drop-Down List Properties* area (Figure 11-24). The *Add Choice* dialog box opens (Figure 11-25).

Figure 11-23 Insert a *Combo Box* content control field

6. Click the **Display Name** text box and type a choice.

   • The *Value* field automatically displays the same text you type in the *Display Name* text box.

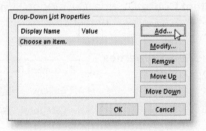

Figure 11-24 *Drop-Down List Properties*

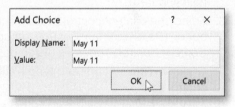

Figure 11-25 *Add Choice* dialog box

7. Click **OK** (or press **Enter**) to close the *Add Choice* dialog box.

   • Click the **Add** button to insert additional drop-down list choices to the *Combo Box*.
   • Alternatively, press **Enter** two times to add a choice and to open the *Add Choice* dialog box.

8. Customize the drop-down list to modify, remove, or reorder drop-down list choices.

   • Select an item in the list and click **Modify** to change an option in the list.
   • Select an item in the list and click **Remove** to remove an option from the list.
   • Select an item in the list and click **Move Up** or **Move Down** to reorder the list.
   • You can select and **Remove** the "Choose an item" option.

9. Click **OK** to close the *Content Control Properties* dialog box.

Drop-Down List Content Control Field

A **Drop-Down List content control field** is similar to a *Combo Box* content control field (Figure 11-26). However, users are limited to the options that display in the drop-down list; they cannot type a different response in the *Drop-Down List* content control field. Insert and customize a *Drop-Down List* content control field the same way you insert and customize a *Combo Box* content control field. *Drop-Down List* and *Combo Box* content control fields display the same in a document.

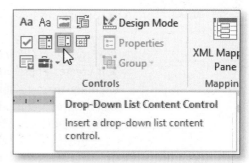

Figure 11-26 Insert a *Drop-Down List* content control field

Building Block Gallery Content Control Field

A **Building Block Gallery content control field** enables users to insert a building block from the building block gallery you specify (see *SLO 6.3: Understanding and Using Building Blocks*, *SLO 6.4: Creating and Using AutoText Building Blocks*, and *SLO 6.5: Using and Customizing Quick Parts Building Blocks* for information about building blocks). The advantage of using a *Building Block Gallery* content control field rather than just inserting a building block is that you control where the building block displays in the document. For example, if you create a form letter, you could save paragraphs of text as individual building blocks in *the AutoText* building block gallery and then insert a *Building Block Gallery* content control field. Users would then select the appropriate *AutoText* building block from the *Building Block Gallery* content control field to insert the building block in a specific location in the document.

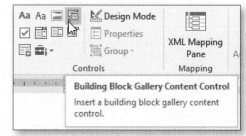

> ▶**HOW TO:** Insert and Customize a Building Block
> Gallery Content Control Field

1. Place the insertion point at the location to insert a content control field.
2. Click the **Building Block Gallery Content Control** button [*Developer* tab, *Controls* group] to insert a *Building Block Gallery* content control field (Figure 11-27).

Figure 11-27 Insert a *Building Block Gallery* content control field

3. Select the content control field and click the **Properties** button [*Developer* tab, *Controls* group] to open the *Content Control Properties* dialog box.
4. Click the **Title** text box and type a title for the content control field.
5. Click the **Gallery** drop-down list to select a building block gallery (Figure 11-28).

Figure 11-28 Select the *Building Block* gallery and category

   - *Quick Parts* is the default building block category when you insert a *Building Block Gallery* content control field.
   - To limit a user's choice to a specific category of building blocks, click the **Category** drop-down list and select a category.
6. Click **OK** to close the *Content Control Properties* dialog box.
   - Users click the drop-down list in the *Building Block Gallery* content control field to select a building block to insert (Figure 11-29).

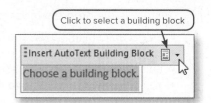

Figure 11-29 *Building Block Gallery* drop-down list

Legacy Tools

Legacy tools are a set of form fields from previous versions of Word that can still be used in current versions (Figure 11-30). Legacy tools function only in templates where *Restrict Editing* is turned on. Legacy tools include **Legacy Forms** and **ActiveX Controls** fields. Insert legacy form fields into forms, and they function similarly to content control fields (but they only function in a protected template). *ActiveX* control fields require macros to function and are usually used in web pages.

Figure 11-30 Legacy tools

SLO 11.3

Editing Content Control Fields

After creating a form and inserting content control fields, customize the color of the content control fields, how the content control fields display in the document, or how content control fields display after users enter information. You also have the option to lock content control fields and the content in these fields. Use *Design* mode to change the placeholder text for content control fields.

Apply a Style to a Content Control Field

The style of the paragraph containing a content control field controls how the text displays in the field. For example, if you insert a *Rich Text* or *Combo Box* content control field in a paragraph formatted with the *Normal* style, the text you type or select is formatted in *Normal* style. You can change the style that applies to the text typed or selected in a content control field.

▶ **HOW TO:** Apply a Style to a Content Control Field

1. Select the content control field to modify and click the **Properties** button [*Developer* tab, *Controls* group] to open the *Content Control Properties* dialog box (Figure 11-31).

2. Check the **Use a style to format text typed into the empty control** box.

3. Click the **Style** drop-down list and select a style to apply to the contents of the content control field.

   • Alternatively, you can click **New Style** to create a new style to apply.

4. Click **OK** to close the *Content Control Properties* dialog box.

   • The selected style does not apply to the placeholder text in the content control field; the selected style applies only to text that users type or select.

Figure 11-31 Apply a style to content control field contents

Change Content Control Display and Color

Change how content control fields display and the color of the content control field. When inserting a content control field, it is, by default, shown as a **bounding box**, which displays with a border and handle. You can change the settings to display the content control field with **start and end tags**, so the content control fields are more visible in the document. Content control fields can also display with no borders and no start and end tags, which is the *None* option. The *None* option displays the content control field with only shading.

▶HOW TO: Change Content Control Display and Color

1. Select the content control field to modify and click the **Properties** button [*Developer* tab, *Controls* group] to open the *Content Control Properties* dialog box (Figure 11-32).

2. Click the **Show as** drop-down list and select from the three options: **Bounding Box** (Figure 11-33), **Start/End Tag** (Figure 11-34), or **None** (Figure 11-35).

3. Click the **Color** drop-down list and select a color for the content control field.
   - By default, the theme of the document controls the color of content control fields.
   - To change the content control field to the original theme color, click the **Color** drop-down list and select **Automatic**.

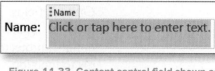

Figure 11-33 Content control field shown as a *Bounding Box* and a color applied

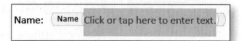

Figure 11-34 Content control field shown as *Start/End Tag* and a color applied

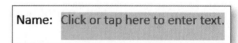

Figure 11-32 Modify content control field display and color

Figure 11-35 Content control field shown as *None* and a color applied

4. Click **OK** to close the *Content Control Properties* dialog box.

▶ **MORE INFO**

When a content control field is shown as *None*, no color applies to the content control field, even if you select a color. The color of the field remains gray.

User Interaction with Content Control Fields

By default, the content control field remains in a document when a user types or selects text. However, you can customize a content control field so the field is removed from the document when a user edits the contents of the field. In other words, the text a user enters or selects replaces the content control field. In many online templates, content control fields are removed when a user types text or selects an option.

Check the **Remove content control when contents are edited** box to remove the content control field when a user types or selects text (Figure 11-36). When using grouping or protection on forms (covered in *SLO 11.4: Using Forms*), do not check the *Remove content control*

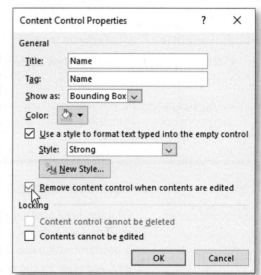

Figure 11-36 Remove content control when contents are edited

when contents are edited box in the *Content Control Properties* dialog box. Checking the box prevents users from typing information in the field.

Lock a Content Control Field

You have the ability to lock a content control field so a user cannot delete and/or edit it. The *Content control cannot be deleted* option in the *Locking* area of the *Content Control Properties* dialog box prevents users from inadvertently deleting a content control field. When this option is checked, a user can edit the contents of the content control but not delete it. The *Contents cannot be edited* option prevents users from editing the contents of the field.

▶HOW TO: Lock Content Control Fields

1. Select the content control field to modify and click the **Properties** button [*Developer* tab, *Controls* group] to open the *Content Control Properties* dialog box (Figure 11-37).

2. Check the **Content control cannot be deleted** box in the *Locking* area to prevent users from deleting the content control field.

3. Check the **Contents cannot be edited** box to prevent users from editing the content control field.

4. Click **OK** to close the *Content Control Properties* dialog box.

Content Control Properties	?	X

General

Title: Name
Tag: Name
Show as: Bounding Box
Color:
☑ Use a style to format text typed into the empty control
Style: Strong
⤷ New Style...
☐ Remove content control when contents are edited

Locking
☑ Content control cannot be deleted
☐ Contents cannot be edited

OK   Cancel

Figure 11-37 Lock a content control field

Design Mode

Use *Design mode* to view and edit content control fields in a document. After inserting a content control field in a document, Word automatically inserts placeholder text (such as "Click or tap here to enter text.") in the field (with the exception of *Picture* and *Check Box* content controls). Use *Design* mode to customize the placeholder text.

▶HOW TO: Use Design Mode to Edit Placeholder Text

1. Click the **Design Mode** button [*Developer* tab, *Controls* group] to turn on *Design* mode.
   - Start and end tags display in *Design* mode.
   - The start tag displays on the left below the title of the content control field.

2. Click the content control field **start tag** to select the placeholder text to modify (Figure 11-38).

3. Type the new placeholder text.

4. Click the **Design Mode** button to turn off *Design* mode.

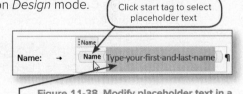

Click start tag to select placeholder text

Name: → Name Type your first and last name ¶

Figure 11-38 Modify placeholder text in a content control field

Customized placeholder text

> ### MORE INFO
>
> When using *Design* mode, the formatting and layout of your document may temporarily display differently. When you turn off *Design* mode, the formatting and layout displays correctly.

Delete a Content Control Field

When customizing a document or form containing content control fields, you may need to delete an existing content control field. The following are two different ways to remove a content control field:

- Click the handle of the content control field to select it and press **Delete**. This method deletes the content control field and the contents of the field.
- Right-click the content control field and select **Remove Content Control** from the context menu. This method removes the content control field but not the contents of the field if the contents have been edited. The edited contents of the field remain in the document.

PAUSE & PRACTICE: WORD 11-2

For this Pause & Practice project, you work with the form from *Pause & Practice 11-1*. You insert content control fields, modify the properties of the content control fields, and use *Design* mode to change the placeholder text.

File Needed: *[your initials] PP W11-1.docx*
Completed Project File Name: *[your initials] PP W11-2.docx*

1. Open the *[your initials] PP W11-1* you completed in *Pause & Practice 11-1*.

2. Save the document as [your initials] PP W11-2.

3. Insert and customize a *Drop-Down List* content control field.
   a. Place the insertion point on the blank line below "Type of Room" and click the **Drop-Down List Content Control** button [*Developer* tab, *Controls* group] to insert a *Drop-Down List* content control field.
   b. Click the **Properties** button [*Developer* tab, *Controls* group] to open the *Content Control Properties* dialog box (Figure 11-39).
   c. Type Room Type in the *Title* text box.
   d. Check the **Content control cannot be deleted** box.
   e. Click the **Add** button to open the *Add Choice* dialog box.
   f. Type Suite in the *Display Name* text box and press **Enter** (or click **OK**) to close the *Add Choice* dialog box.
   g. Press **Enter** again (or click **Add**) to open the *Add Choice* dialog box.
   h. Type Studio in the *Display Name* text box and press **Enter** to close the *Add Choice* dialog box.
   i. Select the **Choose an item** option in the *Drop-Down List Properties* area and click the **Remove** button to remove this option from the list (see Figure 11-39).
   j. Click **OK** to close the *Content Control Properties* dialog box.

Figure 11-39 Insert and customize a *Drop-Down List* content control field

   k. Press the **right** arrow key to deselect the *Drop-Down List* content control field and press **Tab** to position the insertion point below "Type of Bed."

4. Insert another *Drop-Down List* content control field.
   a. Insert a **Drop-Down List** content control field.
   b. Open the *Content Control Properties* dialog box, type **Bed Type** as the *Title*, and check the **Content control cannot be deleted** box.
   c. Add the following choices: **King**, **Queen**, and **Two Doubles**.
   d. Remove **Choose an item** from the list of choices and click **OK** to close the dialog box.
   e. Press the **right** arrow key to deselect the *Drop-Down List* content control field and press **Tab** to position the insertion point centered below "Number of Nights".

5. Insert *Combo Box* content control fields.
   a. Insert a **Combo Box** content control field.
   b. Open the *Content Control Properties* dialog box, type **Number of Nights** as the *Title*, and check the **Content control cannot be deleted** box.
   c. Add the following choices: **1, 2, 3,** and **4**.
   d. Remove **Choose an item** from the list of choices and click **OK** to close the dialog box. Don't be concerned if this field looks misaligned; it should begin near the middle of the heading above it.
   e. Place the insertion point after "Arrival Date:", press **Tab**, and insert a **Combo Box** content control field.
   f. Open the *Content Control Properties* dialog box, type **Arrival Date** as the *Title*, and check the **Content control cannot be deleted** box.
   g. Add the following choices: **May 11, May 12,** and **May 13**.
   h. Remove **Choose an item** from the list of choices and click **OK** to close the dialog box.
   i. Place the insertion point after "Airline:", press **Tab**, and insert a **Combo Box** content control field.
   j. Open the *Content Control Properties* dialog box, type **Airline** as the *Title*, and check the **Content control cannot be deleted** box.
   k. Add the following choices: **American, Delta, Southwest,** and **United**.
   l. Remove **Choose an item** from the list of choices and click **OK** to close the dialog box.

6. Apply a style and change the color of content control fields.
   a. Select the **Name** content control field and open the *Content Control Properties* dialog box (Figure 11-40).
   b. Click the **Color** drop-down list and select **sixth color** in the **third row** (**Gold**).
   c. Check the **Use a style to format text typed into the empty control** box.
   d. Click the **Style** drop-down list and select **Strong**.
   e. Click **OK** to close the *Content Control Properties* dialog box.
   f. Select the **Agency Name** content control field, change the *Color* to **Gold**, and apply the **Strong** style (see steps 6b–e above).
   g. Use the *Content Control Properties* dialog box to change the *Color* to **Gold** on all the remaining *Rich Text*, *Drop-Down List*, *Combo Box*, and *Date Picker* content control fields. Do not apply the *Strong* style and do not change the color on the *Check Box* content control fields.

Figure 11-40 Change the color and add a style to a content control field

7. Use *Design* mode to customize the placeholder text on content control fields.
   a. Click the **Design Mode** button [*Developer* tab, *Controls* group] to turn on *Design* mode.
   b. Click the **Name** start tag to select the placeholder text and type **Type your first and last name** as the placeholder text (Figure 11-41).

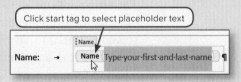

Figure 11-41 Customize placeholder text using *Design* mode

c. Use the following information to customize the placeholder text on other content control fields. Click the start tag on each field and type the customized placeholder text.
Agency Name: Type your agency name
Room Type: Select room type
Bed Type: Select bed type
Number of Nights: Select or type # of nights
Arrival Date: Select or type arrival date
Airline: Select or type airline
Arrival Time: Type arrival time
Departure Time: Type departure time
Departure Date: Select departure date

d. Click the **Design Mode** button to turn off *Design* mode.

8. Save and close the document (Figure 11-42).

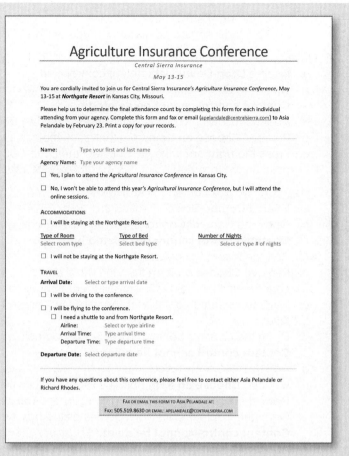

Figure 11-42 PP W11-2 completed

SLO 11.4

Using Forms

After inserting and customizing content control fields to create a form, determine how to set up the form so others can use it. Grouping form fields enables users to type or select content in the content control fields in the form but prevents users from modifying the form. Saving the form as a template enables users to create a new document based upon the form template so the original form is not modified. Additionally, use the protect feature to enable editing of content control fields while restricting editing on other parts of the form.

Group Content Control Fields

The **Group** feature locks all parts of a document except content control fields. An advantage of using the *Group* feature with content control fields is that users can fill in these fields, and you do not need to save the document as a template. For example, create a fillable registration form, save it as a document, and group the content control fields. You can then email the registration form to users, who can edit only the contents of the form fields and save and return the form.

▶HOW TO: Group Content Control Fields

1. Open a document containing content control fields.
2. Select the entire document (**Ctrl+A**).
3. Click the **Group** button [*Developer* tab, *Controls* group] and select **Group** from the drop-down list (Figure 11-43).

   - Grouping protects the text and formatting in the document but enables users to edit the contents of content control fields.
   - To turn off grouping, select the entire document, click the **Group** button, and select **Ungroup**.

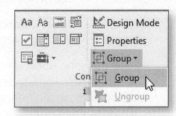

Figure 11-43 Group content control fields

Save a Form as a Template

Grouping content control fields is useful when the form is not going to be used again by the same person. Saving a form as a *template* is a good idea if the form is going to be reused. For example, a business can create an expense form that employees complete each month to report expenses. In this case, it is best to save the form as a template so the form can be reused, and employees can create a new expense report document based upon the template each month. This preserves the original template.

▶HOW TO: Save a Form as a Template

1. Open the form you want to save as a template.
2. Open the *Save As* dialog box.
3. Type a file name for the template in the *File name* text box.
4. Click the **Save as type** drop-down list and select **Word Template**.
5. Browse to the location on your computer or *OneDrive* where you want to save the document.
6. Click **Save** to close the dialog box and save the template.

Protect a Form

Similar to grouping, *Restrict Editing* is another way to protect a form. *Restrict Editing* is commonly used with forms that are saved as templates and controls what areas of the document or template can be edited. Use *Restrict Editing* to enable users to fill in forms while protecting the content and layout of the document.

▶HOW TO: Protect a Form

1. Open the form you want to protect.

   - A form cannot be protected when in *Design Mode*. Turn off **Design Mode** [*Developer* tab, *Controls* group] before protecting a document.

2. Click the **Restrict Editing** button [*Developer* or *Review* tab, *Protect* group]. The *Restrict Editing* pane opens on the right (Figure 11-44).

3. Check the **Allow only this type of editing in the document** box.

4. Click the drop-down list and select **Filling in forms**.

5. Click the **Yes, Start Enforcing Protection** button. The *Start Enforcing Protection* dialog box opens (Figure 11-45).

   - Protecting the document with a password is optional.
   - To use a password, type a password in the *Enter new password* text box and type it again in the *Reenter password to confirm* text box.
   - If you don't want to use a password, leave both of the text boxes blank.

6. Click **OK** to close the *Start Enforcing Protection* dialog box.

Figure 11-45 *Start Enforcing Protection dialog box*

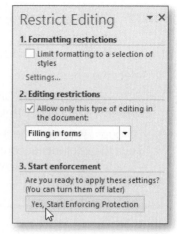

Figure 11-44 *Restrict Editing pane*

To turn off restrict editing, click the **Stop Protection** button in the *Restrict Editing* pane (Figure 11-46). If a password was used to restrict editing, Word prompts the user to type the password in the *Unprotect Document* dialog box to turn off restrict editing.

Figure 11-46 Stop protecting a document

> **MORE INFO**
>
> When using grouping or protection on forms, do not check the *Remove content control when contents are edited* box in the *Content Control Properties* dialog box. Checking the box prevents users from typing information in these fields.

Open and Fill in a Form

After creating your form, inserting and customizing content control fields, and grouping content control fields or protecting the form, you are ready to fill out the form by editing the contents of content control fields.

> **HOW TO: Open and Fill in a Form**

1. Open a form containing the content control fields.

   - If the form is a document, open from within Word.
   - If the form is a template, open a *File Explorer* window and double-click the template file to create a document based on the template.

2. Select a content control field and type information, check a box, or select from a drop-down list.

3. Select the next field or press the **Tab** key to move to the next field.

   - Don't press *Tab* after typing information in a *Rich Text* or *Plain Text* content control field, which inserts a tab after the text you typed. Instead, click the next field to fill in information.
   - On *Check Box* content control fields, click the box or press the **spacebar** to select or deselect the check box.

- On *Combo Box*, *Drop-Down List*, *Date Picker*, and *Building Block Gallery* content control fields, click the **drop-down arrow** on the right to view selections (Figure 11-47).
- On *Picture* content control fields, click the **icon** in the middle to select a picture to insert.

4. Save and close the document when you finish filling in the form.

Name:	**Jennie Owings**
Agency Name:	**Central Sierra Insurance**

✓ Yes, I plan to attend the *Agricultural Insurance Confe*

☐ No, I won't be able to attend this year's *Agricultural* online sessions.

ACCOMMODATIONS

☒ I will be staying at the Northgate Resort.

Room Type Room	Type of Bed
Select room type ▾	Select bed type

Suite   ying at the Northgate Resort.
Studio ▸

Figure 11-47 Filling in a form

Edit and Save a Form

You can add, copy, or move content control fields in an existing form. Also, customize the properties of each content control field or use *Design* mode to change the placeholder text. To edit a template, open the template from within Word, so the template file opens rather than creating a document based on the template. If grouping or restricted editing has been used, use **Ungroup** to ungroup content control fields or **Stop Protection** to edit the content control fields in the document. After editing your form, group content control fields or restrict editing of the document, and then save the document.

PAUSE & PRACTICE: WORD 11-3

For this Pause & Practice project, you finalize the form you modified in *Pause & Practice 11-2*. You save the form as a template, group content control fields, create a document based on the form template, and fill in content control fields.

File Needed: *[your initials] PP W11-2.docx*
Completed Project File Names: *[your initials] PP W11-3 form.dotx* and *[your initials] PP W11-3.docx*

---

1. Open the *[your initials] PP W11-2* file you completed in *Pause & Practice 11-2*.

2. Save the document as a **Word Template** named [your initials] PP W11-3 form and select the location to save the template.

3. Group content control fields.
   a. Select the entire document (**Ctrl+A**).
   b. Click the **Group** button [*Developer* tab, *Controls* group] and select **Group** from the drop-down list.

4. Save and close the template.

5. Create a new document based upon a template and save the new document.
   a. Open a *File Explorer* window and locate the *[your initials] PP W11-3 form* template.
   b. Double-click the template file to create a document based on the template.
   c. Save this new document as a *Word Document* named [your initials] PP W11-3. If prompted to save changes to the template, click **Yes**.

6. Fill in the conference registration form.
   a. Type Jennie Owings in the *Name* field.
   b. Type Central Sierra Insurance in the *Agency Name* field.
   c. Check the **Attending** box ("Yes, I plan to attend. . .").
   d. Check the **Staying at Northgate** box.
   e. Click the **Room Type** drop-down list and select **Studio**.
   f. Click the **Bed Type** drop-down list and select **King**.
   g. Click the **Number of Nights** drop-down list and select **4**.
   h. Click the **Arrival Date** drop-down list and select **May 12**.
   i. Check the **Flying** and **Shuttle** boxes.
   j. Type Alaska in the *Airline* field. Because "Alaska" is not a selection in the drop-down list, you must type the airline.
   k. Type 9:45 a.m. in the *Arrival Time* field.
   l. Type 6:20 p.m. in the *Departure Time* field.
   m. Click the **Departure Date** *Date Picker* field and select **May 16**.
7. Save and close the document (Figure 11-48). If prompted to save changes to the template, click **Yes**. If prompted to save styles and building blocks, click **Don't Save**.

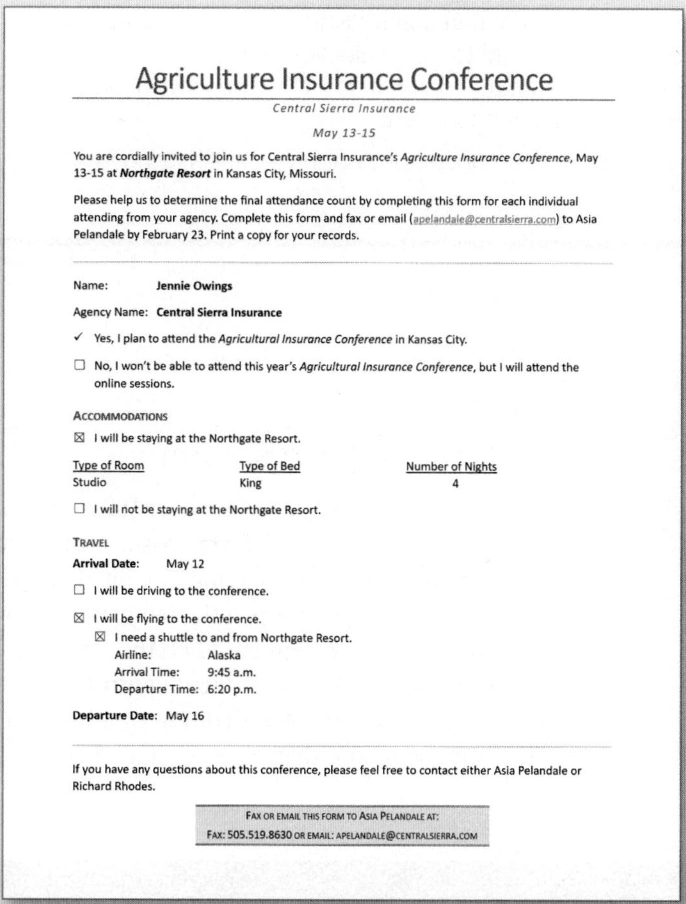

Agriculture Insurance Conference
Central Sierra Insurance

May 13-15

You are cordially invited to join us for Central Sierra Insurance's *Agriculture Insurance Conference*, May 13-15 at **Northgate Resort** in Kansas City, Missouri.

Please help us to determine the final attendance count by completing this form for each individual attending from your agency. Complete this form and fax or email (apelandale@centralsierra.com) to Asia Pelandale by February 23. Print a copy for your records.

Name:	**Jennie Owings**

Agency Name:	**Central Sierra Insurance**

✓ Yes, I plan to attend the *Agricultural Insurance Conference* in Kansas City.

☐ No, I won't be able to attend this year's *Agricultural Insurance Conference*, but I will attend the online sessions.

ACCOMMODATIONS

☒ I will be staying at the Northgate Resort.

Type of Room	Type of Bed	Number of Nights
Studio	King	4

☐ I will not be staying at the Northgate Resort.

TRAVEL

Arrival Date:	May 12

☐ I will be driving to the conference.

☒ I will be flying to the conference.
  ☒ I need a shuttle to and from Northgate Resort.
  Airline:	Alaska
  Arrival Time:	9:45 a.m.
  Departure Time:	6:20 p.m.

Departure Date:	May 16

If you have any questions about this conference, please feel free to contact either Asia Pelandale or Richard Rhodes.

FAX OR EMAIL THIS FORM TO ASIA PELANDALE AT:
FAX: 505.519.8630 OR EMAIL: APELANDALE@CENTRALSIERRA.COM

Figure 11-48 PP W11-3 completed

SLO 11.5

Working with a Master Document

When working with a long document, you can combine multiple documents into one *master document*. A master document can contain existing text and includes text from one or more *subdocuments*. A subdocument is a file you insert and link to a master document. For example, a market research report where team members each write a section of the report. Insert and link each person's document as a subdocument in the master document.

Outline View

In chapters 2 and 6, you applied styles to headings, such as *Heading 1* and *Heading 2*, to organize long documents and to create a table of contents based on the document headings. Apply heading styles to show the outline structure of your document. *Outline view* displays a document as an outline so you can easily rearrange sections of your document. For example, change a heading level by promoting it to a higher-level heading or demoting it to a lower-level heading. Also, add, delete, or edit text in *Outline* view. Use *Outline* view when working with master and subdocuments. When using *Outline* view, the *Outlining tab* displays.

▶ HOW TO: Use Outline View

1. Click the **Outline** button [*View* tab, *Views* group] to display the document in *Outline* view and to open the *Outlining* tab (Figure 11-49).
   - Text with a heading style applied has a *section selector* (plus icon) to the left.
   - Text with *Normal* style (*Body* style) or other styles applied has an open circle bullet to the left of the first line.

2. Click the **section selector** (plus icon) to the left of a heading to select the heading and text in that section.

3. Click the **Promote** or **Demote** button to change the level of a selected heading.
   - Alternatively, click the **Outline Level** drop-down list and select a heading level or click the **Promote to Heading 1** or **Demote to Body Text** button.

4. Click the **Move Up** or **Move Down** button to move selected text up or down in the outline.

5. Click the **Expand** or **Collapse** button to expand or collapse a section.
   - Alternatively, double-click the **section selector** to the left of a heading to expand or collapse a section.

6. Click the **Show Level** drop-down list to select which levels display in the outline.
   - By default, all levels display.

7. Check the **Show Text Formatting** check box to display the style formatting.
   - If this check box is not selected, text in the outline displays without styles applied.

8. Check the **Show First Line Only** box to display only one line of text for each heading in the outline.

9. Click the **Close Outline View** button to close *Outline* view.

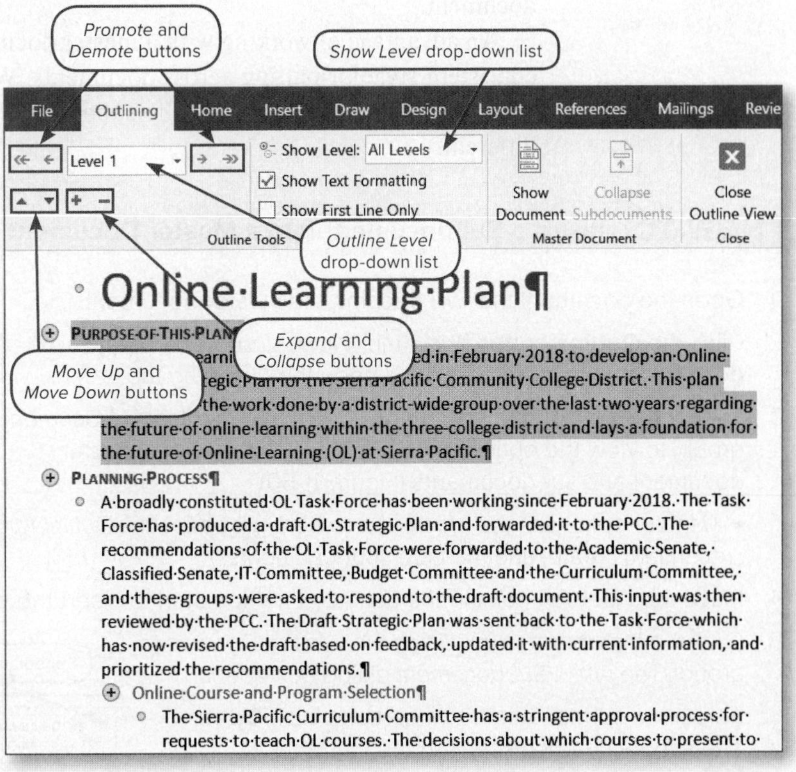

Figure 11-49 Using *Outline* view and the *Outlining* tab

▶ ANOTHER WAY

Press **Alt+Shift+Left** to promote to a higher level.
Press **Alt+Shift+Right** to demote to a lower level.
Press **Alt+Shift+Up** to move selected text up.
Press **Alt+Shift+Down** to move selected text down.

Insert a Subdocument into a Master Document

You can use any document as a master document. Use *Outline* view when working with master and subdocuments. After inserting a subdocument into a master document, the subdocument links to the master document. Word inserts section breaks before and after a subdocument.

Changes made to a linked subdocument in the master document automatically update in the subdocument file. Changes made to a subdocument file automatically update in the master document.

An advantage of working with a master document and subdocuments is the ability to apply consistent style formatting across documents. When inserting a subdocument, the styles from the master document apply to the subdocument even if the styles in the subdocuments are different.

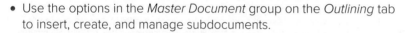

▶**HOW TO:** Insert a Subdocument into a Master Document

1. Open the document that will become the master document.

2. Click the **Outline** button [*View* tab, *Views* group] to display the document in *Outline* view and to open the *Outlining* tab.

3. Click the **Show Document** button [*Outlining* tab, *Master Document* group] to view the options available for working with a master document and subdocuments (Figure 11-50).

Figure 11-50 *Master Document* group on the *Outlining* tab

   • Use the options in the *Master Document* group on the *Outlining* tab to insert, create, and manage subdocuments.

4. Place the insertion point in the outline at the location to insert the subdocument.

5. Click the **Insert** button [*Outlining* tab, *Master Document* group]. The *Insert Subdocument* dialog box opens.

6. Select the subdocument to insert and click **Open**. The subdocument displays in the master document (Figure 11-51).

   • If the subdocument has heading styles applied, a dialog box opens asking if you want to rename the style(s) in the subdocument. Click **Yes** or **Yes to All** to rename the styles in the subdocument to match the styles in the master document. Click **No** or **No to All** if you do not want the styles in the subdocument to be renamed.
   • A next page section break displays before, and a continuous section break displays after, the subdocument.
   • Remove these section breaks in *Outline* view or in *Print Layout* view if desired.
   • A border displays around the subdocument in the view. This border does not display in *Print Layout* view.
   • A subdocument selector displays to the left of the first line of the subdocument. Click this icon to select the entire subdocument.

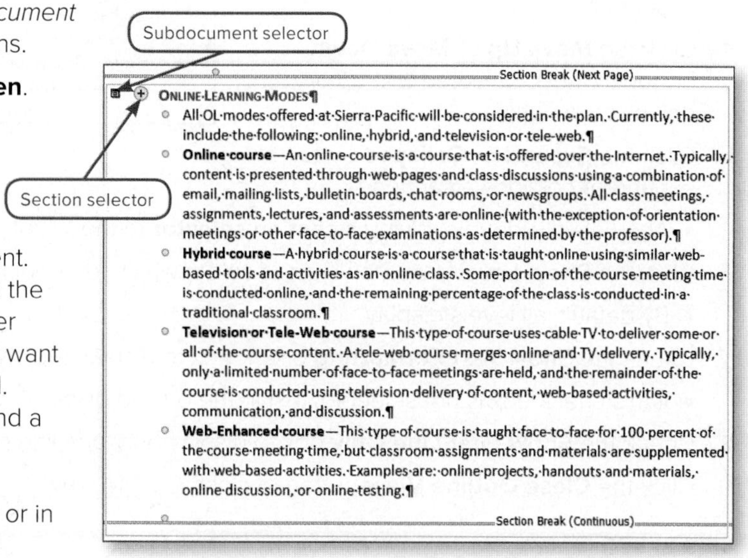

Figure 11-51 Subdocument inserted into a master document

7. Click the **Insert** button to insert another subdocument into the master document.

8. Click the **Close Outline View** button to close *Outline* view and to return to *Print Layout* view.

Create a Subdocument

In addition to inserting an existing subdocument file into a master document, you can create a subdocument in the master document in *Outline* view. When creating a subdocument in the master document, Word creates a separate file and saves it in the same location as the master document. Type the subdocument text in the master document or open the subdocument file and modify it.

▶HOW TO: Create a Subdocument

1. Open the master document and click the **Outline** button [*View* tab, *Views* group] to display the document in *Outline* view.

2. Place the insertion point in the outline at the location to create the subdocument.
   - You can only create a subdocument in the master document at a heading level (for example, *Heading 1* or *Heading 2*), not at the body level. You receive an error message if you try to create a subdocument at the body level.

3. Click the **Create** button [*Outlining* tab, *Master Document* group] to create a new subdocument (Figure 11-52).
   - The new subdocument is blank.
   - Section breaks display before and after the new subdocument and a border displays around the subdocument in *Outline* view.

4. Type content in the subdocument.
   - Use the **Promote** or **Demote** button to change heading levels.

5. Save the master document.
   - When you save the master document, all subdocuments are also saved.

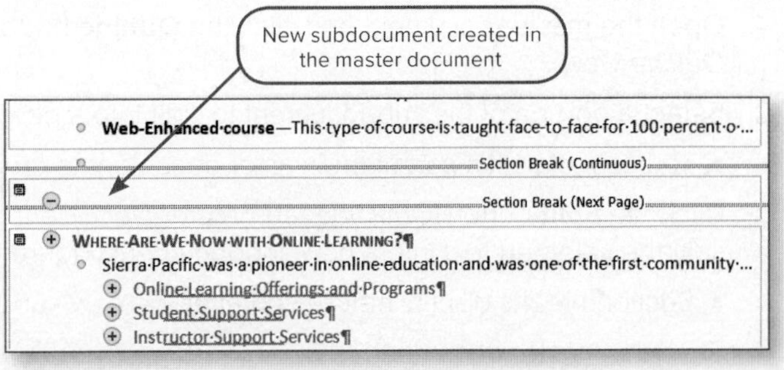

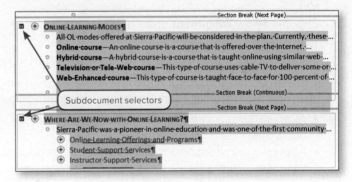

Figure 11-52 Create a new subdocument in the master document

Merge Subdocuments

After inserting subdocuments into your master document, you can merge two or more adjacent subdocuments into one subdocument. Word saves the new merged subdocument with the file name of the first subdocument. The other merged subdocument files remain on your computer, but they no longer link to the master document.

▶HOW TO: Merge Subdocuments

1. Open the master document and click the **Outline** button [*View* tab, *Views* group] to display the document in *Outline* view.

2. Select the subdocuments to merge.
   - Press the **Shift** key and click the **subdocument selectors** to select multiple subdocuments (Figure 11-53). Alternatively, click and drag to select subdocuments.
   - You can merge more than two subdocuments.
   - You cannot merge a subdocument with text in the master document or merge non-adjacent subdocuments.

Figure 11-53 Select subdocuments to merge

3. Click the **Merge** button [*Outlining* tab, *Master Document* group].
   - The section breaks between subdocuments are not removed.

4. Save the master document.
   - The contents of the merged subdocument save in the first subdocument file.
   - The other subdocument files no longer link to the master document, but the files remain in their original location.

Split a Subdocument

A portion of a subdocument in the master document can be split into a separate subdocument. When you split a subdocument, a new linked subdocument file is created and the selected text is removed from the original linked subdocument.

▶ **HOW TO:** Split a Subdocument

1. Open the master document and click the **Outline** button [*View* tab, *Views* group] to display the document in *Outline* view.
2. Select a portion of the subdocument to split into a new subdocument.
   - You cannot split a part of the master document to create a new subdocument.
3. Click the **Split** button [*Outlining* tab, *Master Document* group] to split the selected text into a new subdocument (Figure 11-54).
   - Section breaks display before and after the new subdocument.
4. Save the master document.
   - The new subdocument saves as a new file. The first heading of the new subdocument becomes the subdocument file name.

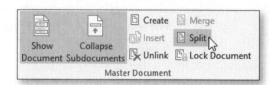

Figure 11-54 Split selected content into a separate subdocument

Unlink a Subdocument

Unlink a subdocument from the master document to break the connection between the two documents. After unlinking a subdocument, the text of the subdocument remains in the master document and becomes part of the master document. Because the documents are no longer linked, changes made in the subdocument file are not updated in the master document.

▶ **HOW TO:** Unlink a Subdocument

1. Open the master document and click the **Outline** button [*View* tab, *Views* group] to display the document in *Outline* view.
2. Click the **Show Document** button [*Outlining* tab, *Master Document* group] to display the borders around the subdocuments.
3. Click the **subdocument selector** or place the insertion point within a subdocument.
4. Click the **Unlink** button [*Outlining* tab, *Master Document* group] to unlink the subdocument from the master document (Figure 11-55).
   - After unlinking a subdocument, it becomes part of the master document.
   - After unlinking a subdocument from the master document, you cannot merge or split the text that was previously a subdocument.

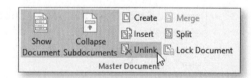

Figure 11-55 Unlink a subdocument from the master document

Arrange Text in an Outline

After inserting, merging, and splitting subdocuments, move subdocuments or sections within a subdocument or the master document in *Outline* view. Use the **Move Up (Alt+Shift+Up)** or **Move Down (Alt+Shift+Down)** button to move a selected subdocument or section up or down in the outline (Figure 11-56). You can also select a section and drag it to a different location in the outline.

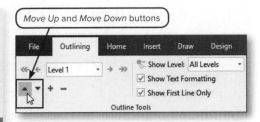

MORE INFO

When moving the contents of a subdocument into the master document text, the link between the subdocument and the master document is removed.

Figure 11-56 Use the *Move Up* or *Move Down* button to arrange sections of subdocuments

When working on a long document, click the **Collapse** button to collapse sections of the document to more easily rearrange subdocuments and selected sections (see Figure 11-55). After collapsing subdocuments, the text below a heading does not display in *Outline* view. Check the **Show First Line Only** box (see Figure 11-56) to display only the first line of text on each heading and body level so the document is less cluttered and easier to edit. Click the **Show Document** button to view borders around the subdocuments.

Lock a Subdocument

Lock a subdocument so changes cannot be made to the subdocument in the master document while using *Outline* view or *Print Layout* view. After locking a subdocument, you can still change the original subdocument file, and those changes update in the master document.

> **HOW TO:** Lock a Subdocument

1. Open the master document and click the **Outline** button [*View* tab, *Views* group] to display the document in *Outline* view.
2. Click the **Show Document** button [*Outlining* tab, *Master Document* group] to display the borders around the subdocuments.
3. Click the **subdocument selector** or place the insertion point within a subdocument.
4. Click the **Lock Document** button [*Outlining* tab, *Master Document* group] to lock the subdocument in the master document.
   - A lock icon appears below the subdocument icon (Figure 11-57).

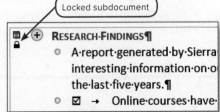

Figure 11-57 Locked subdocument

When a master document and a subdocument are both open in Word, the subdocument in the master document automatically locks in the master document. Changes to the subdocument can only be made in the subdocument file, not in the master document. When you close the subdocument file, the subdocument in the master document unlocks.

Save and Reopen a Master Document

When saving a master document, all the linked subdocuments also save. If you make changes to any of the subdocuments in the master document, those changes will save in the subdocument files when saving the master document. This ensures that linked subdocument files are consistent with the subdocument content in the master document.

You can modify subdocument files when the master document is closed. When you open the master document, the updated content from the subdocument files displays in the master document. When reopening a master document, the subdocuments display as hyperlinks

(Figure 11-58). Click a subdocument link to open the subdocument file. Click **Expand Subdocuments** in *Outline* view to display the text of the subdocuments.

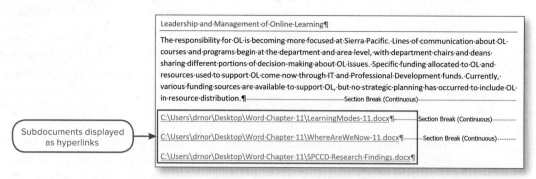

Figure 11-58 Subdocuments displayed as hyperlinks in the master document

> **HOW TO:** Reopen a Master Document and Display Subdocuments

1. Open the master document and click the **Outline** button [*View* tab, *Views* group] to display the document in *Outline* view.

   - Linked subdocuments by default display as hyperlinks in both *Print Layout* and *Outline* views (see Figure 11-58).

2. Click the **Show Document** button [*Outlining* tab, *Master Document* group].

3. Click the **Expand Subdocuments** button [*Outlining* tab, *Master Document* group] to display the contents of the subdocuments (Figure 11-59).

   Figure 11-59 Expand subdocuments to display subdocument text in the master document

   - This button toggles between *Expand Subdocuments* and *Collapse Subdocuments*.
   - When subdocuments are expanded, the options in the *Master Document* group become active.
   - Click **Collapse Subdocuments** to display hyperlinks to subdocuments.
   - Click a subdocument hyperlink to open the subdocument file.

4. Click **Close Outline View** to return to your document.

> **ANOTHER WAY**
>
> Ctrl+\ toggles between expanding documents and collapsing documents in any view.

PAUSE & PRACTICE: WORD 11-4

For this Pause & Practice project, you work with a master document and subdocuments. You insert subdocuments into a master document, split a subdocument, arrange subdocuments, modify subdocuments, reopen a master document, and unlink documents.

Files Needed: ***OnlineLearning-11.docx***, ***LearningModes-11.docx***, and ***WhereAreWeNow-11.docx***
(Student data files are available in the Library *of your SIMnet account.)*
Completed Project File Names: ***[your initials] PP W11-4.docx*** and ***SPCCD Research Findings*** (split subdocument)

1. Open the ***OnlineLearning-11*** file from your student data files.

2. Save the document as [your initials] PP W11-4.

3. Open a *File Explorer* window, locate the ***LearningModes-11*** and ***WhereAreWeNow-11*** files from your student data files. **Copy** and **paste** the files to the same location as you saved the ***[your initials] PP W11-4*** file.

4. Use *Outline* view to change heading level and arrange sections.
   a. Return to the ***[your initials] PP W11-4*** document in Word and turn on **Show/Hide** [*Home* tab, *Paragraph* group] if it is not already on.
   b. Click the **Outline** button [*View* tab, *Views* group] to display the document in *Outline* view.
   c. Click the **Show Level** drop-down list and select **All Levels** if it is not already selected.
   d. Confirm the **Show Text Formatting** box is checked and the **Show First Line Only** box is unchecked (Figure 11-60).

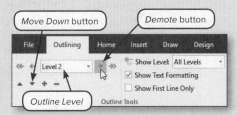

   e. Click the **section selector** (plus icon) to the left of the "Online Course and Program Selection" heading to select the heading and body text.
   f. Click the **Demote** button [*Outlining* tab, *Outline Tools* group] to demote the heading to *Level 2* (see Figure 11-60).

Figure 11-60 Demote heading to *Level 2*

   g. Click the **section selector** to the left of the "Leadership and Management of Online Learning" heading to select the heading and body text.
   h. Click the **Move Down** button twice [*Outlining* tab, *Outline Tools* group] (see Figure 11-60) to move this section below the "Online Course and Program Selection" heading and body text in the outline (Figure 11-61).

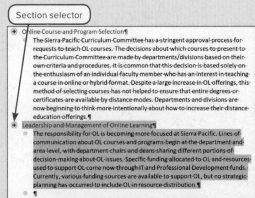

5. Insert subdocuments into the master document.
   a. Place the insertion point on the blank line below the last body paragraph in the outline.
   b. Click the **Show Document** button [*Outlining* tab, *Master Document* group].
   c. Click the **Insert** button [*Outlining* tab, *Master Document* group] to open the *Insert Subdocument* dialog box.
   d. Browse to the location where your master document and subdocuments are saved.

Figure 11-61 Heading demoted and section moved down

   e. Select the ***LearningModes-11*** file and click **Open** to insert the subdocument.
   f. Select the "**Online Learning Modes**" line in the subdocument (Figure 11-62).
   g. Click the **Outline Level** drop-down list [*Outlining* tab, *Outline Tools* group] and select **Level 1**.
   h. Place the insertion point on the last blank line in the outline (after the last section break).
   i. **Insert** the ***WhereAreWeNow-11*** file as a subdocument.
   j. Click **Yes to All** in the dialog box asking if you want to rename styles in the subdocument (Figure 11-63).

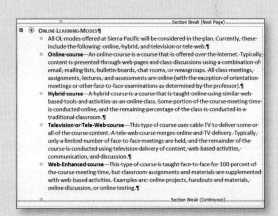

Figure 11-62 Subdocument inserted into the master document

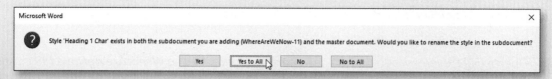

Figure 11-63 Rename styles in the subdocument file

6. Split a subdocument.
   a. Check the **Show First Line Only** box [*Outlining* tab, *Outline* Tools group] to display only the first line of text at each level.
   b. Click the **section selector** to the left of the "Research Findings" section in the second subdocument.
   c. Click the **Split** button [*Outlining* tab, *Master Document* group] to split the section into a new subdocument.
   d. Click the **section selector** to the left of the "Research Findings" section and click the **Promote** button once. The "Research Findings" heading changes to *Level 1*.
   e. Place the insertion point in front of the "RESEARCH FINDINGS" heading, type SPCCD, and **space** once (Figure 11-64).
   f. Click the **Close Outline View** button.

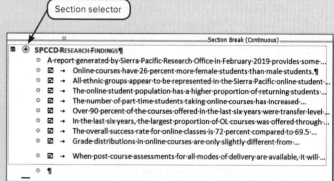

Figure 11-64 Split subdocument and promote heading

7. Save and close the *[your initials] PP W11-4* master document.

8. Modify a subdocument.
   a. Open the *WhereAreWeNow-11* document from the location where your master document and subdocuments are located.
   b. Change "Tech" to Instructor in the last subheading of this document ("Tech Support Services").
   c. Save and close the document.

9. Open the *[your initials] PP W11-4* master document.

10. Arrange a subdocument.
    a. Change to *Outline* view. The subdocuments display as hyperlinks.
    b. Click the **Show Document** button and the **Expand Subdocuments** button [*Outlining* tab, *Master Document* group].
    c. Click the **subdocument selector** to the left of "ONLINE LEARNING MODES" to select the entire subdocument (Figure 11-65).

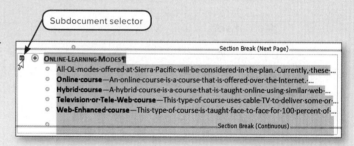

Figure 11-65 Select subdocument

    d. Click the **Move Up** button to move this subdocument above the "Planning Process" section. You will have to click the *Move Up* button multiple times. The moved subdocument becomes part of the master document and is no longer linked to the subdocument file.

11. Unlink subdocuments from the master document.
    a. Click the **subdocument selector** to the left of "Where Are We Now with Online Learning" to select the entire subdocument.
    b. Click the **Unlink** button [*Outlining* tab, *Master Document* group] to unlink this document from the subdocument file.

   c. Place the insertion point in the last subdocument ("SPCCD Research Findings").

   d. Click the **Unlink** button to unlink this document from the subdocument file.

12. Remove section breaks from the document.

   a. Deselect the **Show First Line Only** check box [*Outlining* tab, *Outline Tools* group] to display the entire outline.

   b. Place the insertion point on each of the section break indicators and press **Delete** to remove each of the section breaks in the document (including the section break at the end of the outline). Be careful not to delete any text.

   c. Confirm no blank lines or section breaks display between sections.

   d. Close *Outline* view and return to *Print Layout* view.

13. Insert **page breaks** before the "Online Course and Program Selection" and "Student Support Services" headings to keep the headings with the text that follows.

14. Save and close the document (Figure 11-66).

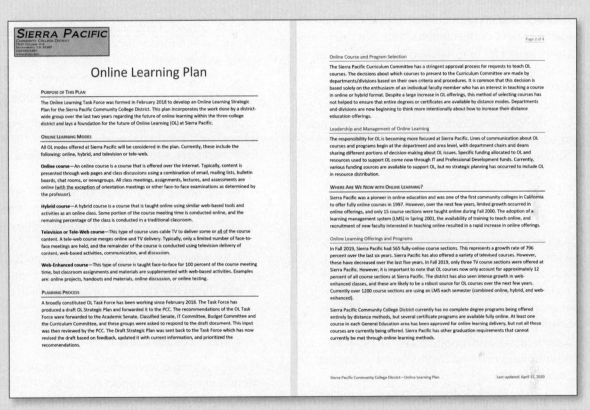

Figure 11-66 PP W11-4 completed (pages 1 and 2 of 4)

Chapter Summary

11.1 Insert, customize, and arrange a variety of content control fields (p. W11-671).

- **Content control fields** are containers in a document where users enter or select information.
- Use **tab stops**, **indents**, and **tables** to align and arrange content control fields in a document.
- Use **Rich Text** and **Plain Text** content control fields for open-ended responses from users.
- Users can apply formatting to specific text in a *Rich Text* content control field.
- A **Check Box** content control field enables a user to select or deselect a check box.
- Users select (or enter) a date in a **Date Picker** content control field.
- A **Picture** content control field prompts a user to insert a picture into a document.
- Use the **Content Control Properties** dialog box to add a **title** and modify the properties of a content control field.

11.2 Insert and customize advanced content control fields where a user selects from a list of choices (p. W11-679).

- A **Combo Box** content control field provides a list of choices, or users can type their own responses.
- A **Drop-Down List** content control field provides a list of choices. In a *Drop-Down List*, users cannot type their own responses.
- Add, remove, and modify users' choices in both *Combo Box* and *Drop-Down List* content control fields.
- A **Building Block Gallery** content control field lets users select a building block to insert into a document. Specify which building block gallery and category users can select.
- **Legacy Forms** and **ActiveX** control fields are other available form fields you can use in your Word documents.

11.3 Edit a content control field to change the format and lock content and use *Design* mode to edit placeholder text (p. W11-681).

- Apply a style to the contents of a content control field. Select from an existing style or create a new style.

- Change the color of content control fields. By default, the content control field color is controlled by the theme of the document.
- A content control field displays in the document as a **bounding box**, with **start and end tags**, or not shown at all (the *None* option). By default, content control fields display as bounding boxes.
- Set up a content control field so the field remains in the document when a user enters information or set it so the field is removed when a user enters information.
- Lock content control fields so the field cannot be deleted, or lock a field so it cannot be edited by users.
- Copy, move, or delete content control fields.
- Modify placeholder text in **Design mode**.

11.4 Group content control fields, protect and edit a form, create a form based on a template, fill in a form, and save a form based on a template (p. W11-686).

- **Group** content control fields so users enter or select information in content control fields but cannot edit the content or format of the other parts of the document.
- Save a form as a **template** so you can base a new document on the template without modifying the structure or content of the template.
- Use **Restrict Editing** so users can only fill in content control fields in forms.

11.5 Manage a long document using a master document that contains subdocuments (p. W11-690).

- A **master document** is useful when working with long documents.
- A **subdocument** is a Word document inserted and linked to a master document.
- Use **Outline view** when working with a master document and subdocuments.
- **Expand** or **collapse** and **promote** or **demote** headings using the **Outlining tab** in *Outline* view.
- **Merge** subdocuments to combine multiple subdocuments into one subdocument file.
- **Split** a portion of a subdocument to create a new subdocument.

- **Unlink** a subdocument from a master document. The changes made in the unlinked subdocument are not updated in the master document.
- Move subdocuments and sections of text in subdocuments and the master document in *Outline* view.
- **Lock** a subdocument to prevent subdocument text from being edited in the master document.

Check for Understanding

The SIMbook for this text (within your SIMnet account) provides the following resources for concept review:

- Multiple-choice questions
- Short answer questions
- Matching exercises

Guided Project 11-1

For this project, you create a form template for Emma Cavalli at Placer Hills Real Estate. You use content control fields, customize content control fields, protect the form, and create a new document based on the form template.
[Student Learning Outcomes 11.1, 11.2, 11.3, 11.4]

Files Needed: ***PHREAuthorizationLetter-11.docx*** and ***BurgessHome-11.jpg*** *(Student data files are available in the* Library *of your SIMnet account.)*
Completed Project File Names: ***[your initials] Word 11-1 form.dotx*** and ***[your initials] Word 11-1.docx***

Skills Covered in This Project

- Save a document as a template.
- Set a tab stop to align text and content control fields.
- Insert and customize *Date Picker*, *Combo Box*, *Rich Text*, *Plain Text*, and *Picture* content control fields.

- Use *Design* mode to customize placeholder text.
- Protect a form.
- Create a document based on a template.
- Fill in a content control field.

1. Open the ***PHREAuthorizationLetter-11*** document from your student data files.
2. Save the document as a **Word Template** named [your initials] Word 11-1 form.
3. Set tab stops to align text and content control fields.
    a. Turn on **Show/Hide** [*Home* tab, *Paragraph* group] if it is not already on.
    b. Select the lines of text beginning with "**Loan Application Date**" and ending with "**Street Address**" and set a **1.5" left** tab stop.
    c. Select the "**City**" line of text and set the following **left** tab stops: **0.4"**, **1.5"**, and **1.8"**.
    d. Place the insertion point after "City:", press **Tab** twice, and type ZIP:.
    e. Select the line of text that contains "**Sincerely,**" and set a **center** tab stop at **5.25"**.
4. Insert and customize a *Date Picker* content control field.
    a. Place the insertion point after "Loan Application Date:" and press **Tab**.
    b. Click the **Date Picker Content Control** button [*Developer* tab, *Controls* group] to insert a *Date Picker* content control field (Figure 11-67).
    c. Click the **Properties** button [*Developer* tab, *Controls* group] to open the *Content Control Properties* dialog box.
    d. Type Application Date in the *Title* text box.
    e. Select the spelled-out date format (January 1, 2020) in the *Date Picker Properties* area.
    f. Click **OK** to close the *Content Control Properties* dialog box.

Figure 11-67 Content control form fields

5. Insert and customize *Combo Box* content control fields.
    a. Place the insertion point after "Financial Institution:" and press **Tab**.
    b. Click the **Combo Box Content Control** button [*Developer* tab, *Controls* group] to insert a *Combo Box* content control field.

c. Click the **Properties** button to open the *Content Control Properties* dialog box.

d. Type Financial Institution in the *Title* text box.

e. Click the **Add** button in the *Drop-Down List Properties* area to open the *Add Choice* dialog box.

f. Type Bank of America in the *Display Name* text box and click **OK** to close the dialog box and add the choice.

g. Add two more choices: Chase Bank and Wells Fargo Bank.

h. Select **Choose an item** and click the **Remove** button (Figure 11-68).

i. Click **OK** to close the *Content Control Properties* dialog box.

j. Place the insertion point after the first tab after "City:" and insert a **Combo Box** content control field.

k. Open the *Content Control Properties* dialog box and type City as the *Title*.

l. Add Lincoln, Loomis, Rocklin, and Roseville as the choices, remove **Choose an item**, and click **OK** to close the dialog box.

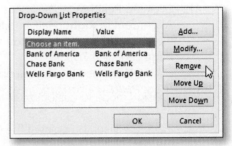

Figure 11-68 Add choices to the *Combo Box* and remove a choice

6. Insert and customize *Rich Text* content control fields.

a. Place the insertion point after "Loan Number:" and press **Tab**.

b. Click the **Rich Text Content Control** button [*Developer* tab, *Controls* group] to insert a *Rich Text* content control field.

c. Open the *Content Control Properties* dialog box and type Loan Number as the *Title* (Figure 11-69).

d. Click the **Show as** drop-down list and select **None**.

e. Check the **Use a style to format text typed into the empty control** box.

f. Click the **Style** drop-down list and select **Book Title**.

g. Click **OK** to close the dialog box.

h. Place the insertion point after "Borrower Name(s):" and press **Tab**.

i. Insert a **Rich Text** content control field.

j. Open the *Content Control Properties* dialog box, type Borrower Name as the title, and repeat steps 6d–g to customize the content control field.

Figure 11-69 Customize *Rich Text* content control field

7. Insert and customize *Plain Text* content control fields.

a. Place the insertion point after "Street Address:" and press **Tab**.

b. Click the **Plain Text Content Control** button [*Developer* tab, *Controls* group].

c. Open the *Content Control Properties* dialog box and type Street Address as the *Title*.

d. Click the **Show as** drop-down list, select **None**, and click **OK** to close the dialog box.

e. Place the insertion point after "ZIP:" and press **Tab**.

f. Insert a **Plain Text** content control field.

g. Open the *Content Control Properties* dialog box, type ZIP Code as the *Title*.

h. Click the **Show as** drop-down list, select **None**, and click **OK** to close the dialog box.

8. Insert and customize a *Picture* content control field.

a. Place the insertion point after "Sincerely," press **Tab**, and type Picture of the Property.

b. Place the insertion point on the blank line below the phone number at the end of the document.

c. Click the **Picture Content Control** button [*Developer* tab, *Controls* group] to insert a *Picture* content control field.

d. Open the *Content Control Properties* dialog box, type Property Picture as the *Title*, and click **OK** to close the dialog box.

e. Click the **Position** button [*Picture Tools Format* tab, *Arrange* group] and select **More Layout Options** from the drop-down list to open the *Layout* dialog box.

f. Click the **Size** tab and change the *Height* and *Width* to **2.5"**.

g. Click the **Text Wrapping** tab and select **Tight**.

h. Click the **Position** tab and set the *Horizontal* **Alignment** to **Right** relative to **Margin** and the *Vertical* **Absolute position** at **5.7"** below **Page** (Figure 11-70).

i. Click **OK** to close the *Layout* dialog box.

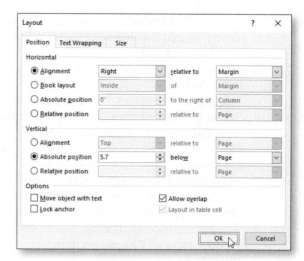

Figure 11-70 Customize the layout of the *Picture* content control field

9. Use *Design* mode to customize placeholder text.

a. Place the insertion point at the beginning of the document.

b. Click the **Design Mode** button [*Developer* tab, *Controls* group] to turn on *Design* mode.

c. Click the **Application Date** start tag and type Select date of loan application as the placeholder text (Figure 11-71).

d. Type Select or type financial institution as the placeholder text for the *Financial Institution* field.

e. Type Type loan number as the placeholder text for the *Loan Number* field.

f. Type Type borrower name(s) as the placeholder text for the *Borrower Name* field.

g. Type Type street address as the placeholder text for the *Street Address* field.

h. Type Select or type city as the placeholder text for the *City* field.

i. Type Type ZIP code as the placeholder text for the *ZIP Code* field.

j. Click the **Design Mode** button to turn off *Design* mode.

Figure 11-71 Customize field placeholder text

10. Protect the form template.

a. Click the **Restrict Editing** button [*Developer* tab, *Protect* group] to display the *Restrict Editing* pane on the right (Figure 11-72).

b. Check the **Allow only this type of editing in the document** box in the *Editing restrictions* area.

c. Click the drop-down list and select **Filling in forms**.

d. Click **Yes, Start Enforcing Protection**. The *Start Enforcing Protection* dialog box opens.

e. Click **OK** to protect the document without a password.

f. Close the *Restrict Editing* pane.

Figure 11-72 Restrict editing to *Filling in forms*

11. Save and close the form template.

12. Open a *File Explorer* window, locate the **[your initials] Word 11-1 form** template, and double-click the file to create a new document based on the template.

13. Save the document as [your initials] Word 11-1. If prompted to save changes to the template, click **Yes**.

14. Use the following information to fill in the content control fields:
    Application Date: Select the previous Monday
    Financial Institution: Chase Bank
    Loan Number: CB2003476
    Borrower Name(s): John and Robyn Burgess
    Street Address: 85741 Auberry Road
    City: Roseville
    ZIP Code: 95722

15. Insert a picture in the *Picture* content control field.
    a. Click the **icon** in the center of the *Property Picture* content control field to open the *Insert Pictures* dialog box.
    b. Select **From a File** to open the *Insert Picture* dialog box.
    c. Select the ***BurgessHome-11*** picture from your student data files and click **Insert**.

16. Save and close the document (Figure 11-73).

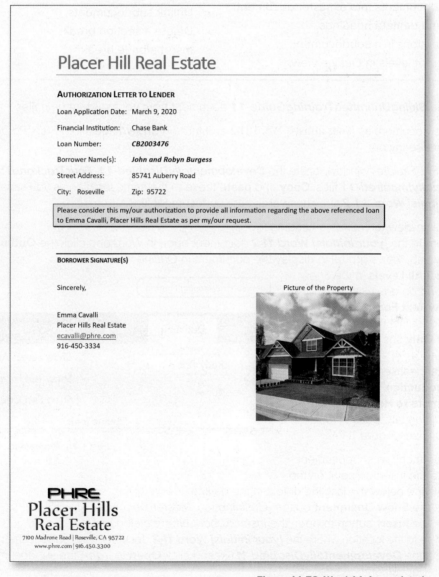

Figure 11-73 Word 11-1 completed

Guided Project 11-2

For this project, you use a master document and subdocuments to create a training guide for the Skiing Unlimited program. You insert subdocuments into a master document, split and merge subdocuments, change heading levels, and arrange sections of a subdocument.
[Student Learning Outcome 11.5]

Files Needed: **SkiingUnlimitedTrainingGuide-11.docx**, **DevelopmentallyDisabled-11.docx**, **FourTrackandThreeTrack-11.docx**, and **VisuallyImpaired-11.docx** (Student data files are available in the Library of your SIMnet account.)
Completed Project File Name: **[your initials] Word 11-2.docx**

Skills Covered in This Project

- Use *Outline* view.
- Insert subdocuments into a master document.
- Promote and demote headings.
- Arrange sections in a subdocument.
- View different levels in *Outline* view.
- Modify subdocument text.
- Merge two subdocuments.
- Split a subdocument into two subdocuments.
- Unlink subdocuments.
- Delete a section break.
- Insert a page break.

1. Open the **SkiingUnlimitedTrainingGuide-11** document from your student data files.

2. Save the document as [your initials] Word 11-2 and turn on **Show/Hide** [*Home* tab, *Paragraph* group] if it is not already on.

3. Open a *File Explorer* window, locate the **DevelopmentallyDisabled-11**, **FourTrackandThreeTrack-11**, and **VisuallyImpaired-11** files. **Copy** and **paste** these to the same location as you saved the **[your initials] Word 11-2** file. These are your subdocument files.

4. Use *Outline* view to change a heading level.
   a. Return to the **[your initials] Word 11-2** document open in Word and click the **Outline** button [*View* tab, *Views* group] to display the document in *Outline* view.
   b. Select **All Levels** in the *Show Level* drop-down list, check the **Show Text Formatting** box, and deselect the **Show First Line Only** box if necessary (Figure 11-74).
   c. Place the insertion point in "**Introduction**" and click the **Promote to Heading 1** button [*Outlining* tab, *Outline Tools* group] (see Figure 11-74).

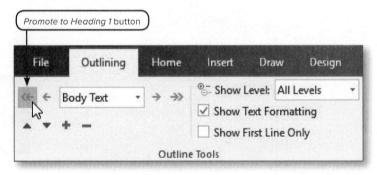

Figure 11-74 *Promote to Heading 1 button*

5. Insert and modify a subdocument.
   a. Place the insertion point on the blank line below the last line of text in the outline.
   b. Click the **Show Document** button [*Outlining* tab, *Master Document* group].
   c. Click the **Insert** button to open the *Insert Subdocument* dialog box.
   d. Browse to the location where the **[your initials] Word 11-2** document and subdocuments are located.
   e. Select the **DevelopmentallyDisabled-11** file and click **Open** to insert the subdocument into the master document.

f. Click **Yes to All** in the dialog box that opens and asks if you want to rename styles in the subdocument (Figure 11-75).

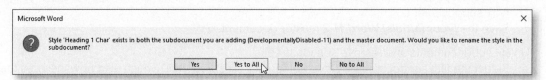

Figure 11-75 Rename styles in the subdocument file

g. Click the **section selector** to the left of "Disabilities" to select the heading and the text below the heading.

h. Click the **Demote** button [*Outlining* tab, *Outline Tools* group] to change the selected heading to *Level 2*.

i. **Demote** to *Level 2* each of the next three headings in the subdocument.

6. Insert and modify another subdocument.
   a. Place the insertion point on the last blank line in the outline.
   b. **Insert** the *VisuallyImpaired-11* file and click **Yes to All** in the dialog box that opens and asks if you want to rename styles in the subdocument.
   c. Click the **Show Level** drop-down list and select **Level 2** to display two levels of headings in the outline (Figure 11-76).
   d. Select the "**Disabilities**" section in the second subdocument ("Visually Impaired (VI)") and click the **Move Up** [*Outlining* tab, *Outline Tools* group] button to move this section above the "Physical Evaluation" section.

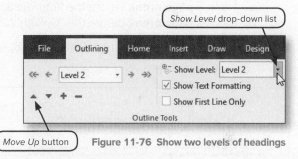

Figure 11-76 Show two levels of headings

7. Insert and modify another subdocument.
   a. Click the **Show Level** drop-down list and select **All Levels** to display all the text in the outline.
   b. Place the insertion point on the last blank line in the outline.
   c. **Insert** the *FourTrackandThreeTrack-11* file and click **Yes to All** in the dialog box that opens and asks if you want to rename styles in the subdocument.
   d. Select the "**Four-Track and Three-Track**" section heading at the top of this subdocument (don't select the entire section) and **promote** to *Level 1*.
   e. Select the "**Bi-Ski and Mono-Ski**" section heading in this subdocument and **promote** to *Level 1*.

8. Modify subdocuments.
   a. Click the **Show Level** drop-down list and select **Level 2**.
   b. Place the insertion point before "Disabilities" in the first subdocument ("Developmentally Disabled (DD)"), type Common, and then **space** once.
   c. Place the insertion point before "Disabilities" in the second subdocument ("Visually Impaired (VI)"), type Common, and then **space** once.

9. Merge subdocuments.
   a. Click the **subdocument selector** for the first subdocument ("Developmentally Disabled (DD)"), press the **Shift** key, and click the **subdocument selector** for the second subdocument ("Visually Impaired (VI)") to select both subdocuments (Figure 11-77).
   b. Click the **Merge** button [*Outlining* tab, *Master Document* group] to merge the two subdocuments.

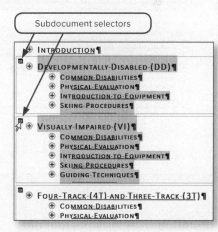

Figure 11-77 Select subdocuments to merge

10. Split a section of a subdocument to create a new subdocument.
    a. Select the "**Bi-Ski and Mono-Ski**" section.
    b. Click the **Split** button [*Outlining* tab, *Master Document* group] to split the selected section into a new subdocument.
    c. Save the ***[your initials] Word 11-2*** master document.

11. Unlink subdocuments and remove section breaks.
    a. Select the first subdocument ("Developmentally Disabled (DD)", which also now includes the merged "Visually Impaired (VI)" section) and click the **Unlink** button [*Outlining* tab, *Master Document* group] to break the link between the master document and the subdocument file.
    b. **Unlink** the other two subdocuments.
    c. Click the **Show Level** drop-down list and select **All Levels**.
    d. Move to the top of the outline, click the first section break, and press **Delete**.
    e. Delete all remaining section breaks in the document.
    f. Delete any blank lines between sections and at the end of the document.

12. Click the **Close Outline View** button [*Outlining* tab, *Close* group] to view the document in *Print Layout* view.

13. Insert page breaks to keep text with headings.
    a. Insert a **page break** before the "Introduction to Equipment" section at the bottom of page 4.
    b. Insert a **page break** before the "Gliding Wedge Turns" section at the bottom of page 5.

14. Save and close the document (Figure 11-78).

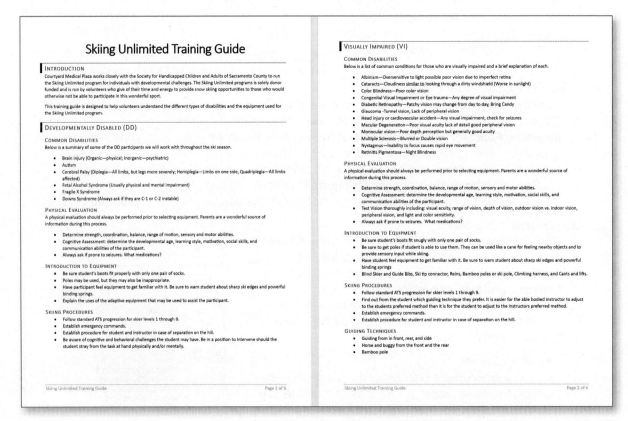

Figure 11-78 Word 11-2 completed (pages 1 and 2 of 6)

Guided Project 11-3

For this project, you create a volunteer form for Life's Animal Shelter. You insert content control fields, customize content control fields, group content control fields, and create a new document based on the form template.
[Student Learning Outcomes 11.1, 11.2, 11.3, 11.4]

File Needed: **LASVolunteerForm-11.docx** *(Student data files are available in the* Library *of your SIMnet account.)*
Completed Project File Names: *[your initials] Word 11-3 form.docx* and *[your initials] Word 11-3.docx*

Skills Covered in This Project

- Set a tab stop to align text and content control fields.
- Change table row height and text alignment.
- Insert and customize *Rich Text*, *Plain Text*, *Check Box*, *Drop-Down List*, and *Combo Box* content control fields.
- Copy and customize a content control field.
- Use *Design* mode to customize placeholder text.
- Group content control fields.
- Fill in a content control field.

---

1. Open the **LASVolunteerForm-11** document from your student data files.

2. Save the Word document as [your initials] Word 11-3 form.

3. Set a tab stop to align text and content control fields and modify the table.
   a. Select the last four rows of the table and set a **0.25" left** tab stop.
   b. Place the insertion point before the text in the fourth row of the table ("Yes, I can volunteer . . .") and press **Ctrl+Tab** to insert a tab before the text.
   c. Use **Ctrl+Tab** to insert a tab before the text in the last three rows of the table.
   d. Select the entire table, change the row height to **0.3"**, and change the text alignment to **Align Center Left**.

4. Insert and customize a *Rich Text* content control field.
   a. Place the insertion point in the second cell in the first row.
   b. Click the **Rich Text Content Control** button [*Developer* tab, *Controls* group] to insert a *Rich Text* content control field.
   c. Click the **Properties** button to open the *Content Control Properties* dialog box (Figure 11-79).
   d. Type Name as the *Title*.
   e. Click the **Color** drop-down list and select the **seventh color** in the **first row** (**Indigo**).
   f. Check the **Use a style to format text typed into the empty control** box.
   g. Click the **Style** drop-down list and select **Strong**.
   h. Check the **Content control cannot be deleted** box in the *Locking* area.
   i. Click **OK** to close the dialog box.

5. Insert and customize *Plain Text* content control fields.
   a. Place the insertion point in the second cell in the second row.
   b. Click the **Plain Text Content Control** button [*Developer* tab, *Controls* group] to insert a *Plain Text* content control field.

Figure 11-79 Customize a *Rich Text* content control field

c. Open the *Content Control Properties* dialog box and type Email Address as the *Title*.

d. Click the **Color** drop-down list and select **Indigo**.

e. Check the **Content control cannot be deleted** box in the *Locking* area.

f. Click **OK** to close the dialog box.

g. Place the insertion point in the second cell in the third row and insert a **Plain Text Content Control** field.

h. Open the *Content Control Properties* dialog box and type Phone Number as the *Title*.

i. Click the **Color** drop-down list and select **Indigo**, check the **Content control cannot be deleted** box, and click **OK** to close the dialog box.

6. Insert and customize *Check Box* content control fields.

   a. Place the insertion point before the tab in front of "Yes, I can volunteer . . ."

   b. Click the **Check Box Content Control** button [*Developer* tab, *Controls* group] to insert a *Check Box* content control field.

   c. Open the *Content Control Properties* dialog box and type Volunteer as the *Title*.

   d. Click the **Color** drop-down list and select **Indigo**.

   e. Click the **Change** button in the *Checked symbol* area (Figure 11-80) to open the *Symbol* dialog box.

   f. Click the **Font** drop-down list and select **Wingdings**.

   g. Select the **smiley face** icon (character code 74) and click **OK** to close the *Symbol* dialog box.

   h. Click **OK** to close the *Content Control Properties* dialog box.

Figure 11-80 Customize a *Check Box* content control field

   i. Place the insertion point before the tab in front of "Yes, I would like to donate . . ." and insert a **Check Box Content Control** field.

   j. Open the *Content Control Properties* dialog box and type Donate as the *Title*.

   k. Change the *Color* to **Indigo**, change the *Checked symbol* to the **smiley face** icon (character code 74), click **OK** to close the *Symbol* dialog box, and click **OK** to close the *Content Control Properties* dialog box.

7. Insert and customize a *Drop-Down List* content control field.

   a. Place the insertion point after "Hours per week I can volunteer:" and **space** once.

   b. Click the **Drop-Down List Content Control** button [*Developer* tab, *Controls* group] to insert a *Drop-Down List* content control field.

   c. Open the *Content Control Properties* dialog box and type Volunteer Hours as the *Title*.

   d. Click the **Color** drop-down list and select **Indigo**.

   e. Check the **Use a style to format text typed into the empty control** box.

   f. Click the **Style** drop-down list and select the **Strong** style.

   g. Check the **Content control cannot be deleted** box in the *Locking* area.

   h. Click the **Add** button in the *Drop-Down List Properties* area to open the *Add Choice* dialog box.

   i. Type 1-5 hours in the *Display Name* text box and click **OK** to close the dialog box and add the choice.

   j. Add three more choices: 6-10 hours, 11-15 hours, and 16-20 hours.

   k. Select **Choose an item** and click the **Remove** button (Figure 11-81).

   l. Click **OK** to close the *Content Control Properties* dialog box.

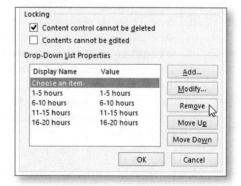

Figure 11-81 Add and remove choices from a *Drop-Down List* content control field

8. Insert and customize a *Combo Box* content control field.
   a. Place the insertion point after "Amount:" and **space** once.
   b. Click the **Combo Box Content Control** button [*Developer* tab, *Controls* group] to insert a *Combo Box* content control field.
   c. Open the *Content Control Properties* dialog box and type **Donation Amount** as the *Title*.
   d. Click the **Color** drop-down list and select **Indigo**.
   e. Check the **Use a style to format text typed into the empty control** box.
   f. Click the **Style** drop-down list and select the **Strong** style.
   g. Check the **Content control cannot be deleted** box in the *Locking* area.
   h. Add the following choices: $10, $25, $50, and $100.
   i. Select **Choose an item** and click the **Remove** button.
   j. Click **OK** to close the *Content Control Properties* dialog box.

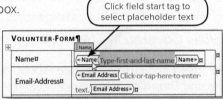

9. Use *Design* mode to customize placeholder text.
   a. Click the **Design Mode** button [*Developer* tab, *Controls* group] to turn on *Design* mode.
   b. Click the **Name** start tag and type **Type first and last name** as the placeholder text (Figure 11-82).
   c. Type **Type email address** as the placeholder text for the *Email Address* field.

Figure 11-82 Customize field placeholder text

   d. Type **Type phone number** as the placeholder text for the *Phone Number* field.
   e. Type **Select hours** as the placeholder text for the *Volunteer Hours* field.
   f. Type **Select or type donation amount** as the placeholder text for the *Donation Amount* field.
   g. Click the **Design Mode** button to turn off *Design* mode.

10. Group content control fields to lock the text in the document.
    a. Select the entire document (**Ctrl+A**).
    b. Click the **Group** button [*Developer* tab, *Controls* group] and select **Group** from the drop-down list.
    c. Click anywhere in the document to deselect the selected text.

11. Save the document, but do not close it.

12. Save the Word document as a different file name. Save it as [your initials] Word 11-3.

13. Use the following information to fill in the content control fields in the table:
    Name: Cammi Acevedo
    Email Address: cammi@live.com
    Phone Number: 218.285.3776
    Check the **Yes, I can volunteer. . .** box.
    Volunteer Hours: **6-10 hours**
    Check the **Yes, I would like to donate. . .** box.
    Donation Amount: type $40

14. Save and close the document (Figure 11-83).

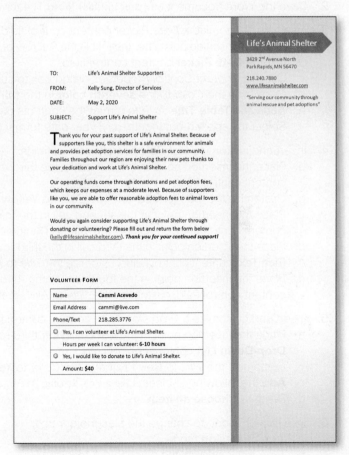

Figure 11-83 Word 11-3 completed

Independent Project 11-4

For this project, you create a training log form for the American River Cycling Club and then insert the form into a master document. You will insert and customize content control fields, copy and paste content control fields, insert a subdocument into a master document, and modify the contents of the master document.
[Student Learning Outcomes 11.1, 11.2, 11.3, 11.4, 11.5]

Files Needed: *TrainingLogForm-11.docx* and *TrainingLog-11.docx* (Student data files are available in the Library of your SIMnet account.)
Completed Project File Names: *[your initials] Word 11-4 form.docx* and *[your initials] Word 11-4.docx*

Skills Covered in This Project

- Insert and customize *Date Picker*, *Rich Text*, and *Drop-Down List* content control fields.
- Copy, paste, and modify a content control field.
- Use *Outline* view.
- Insert a subdocument into a master document.
- Remove a section break in an outline.
- Unlink a subdocument.
- Use *Design* mode to customize placeholder text.
- Group content control fields.

1. Open the *TrainingLogForm-11* document from your student data files.

2. Save the Word document as [your initials] Word 11-4 form.

3. Insert and customize a *Date Picker* content control field.
   a. Place the insertion point after the text in the first row of the table ("TRAINING LOG. . .") and **space** once.
   b. Insert a **Date Picker** content control field.
   c. Use the *Content Control Properties* dialog box to customize the *Title* to Training Week.
   d. Customize the *Color* to the **seventh color** in the **third row** (**Yellow**).
   e. Apply the **Table Title** style to format the contents of the content control field.
   f. Select the spelled-out month, day, year date format (January 1, 2020).

4. Insert and customize *Rich Text* content control fields.
   a. Place the insertion point in the first cell in the third row (below "Miles") and insert a **Rich Text** content control field.
   b. Customize the *Title* to Miles and the *Color* to **Yellow**.
   c. Place the insertion point in the second cell in the third row (below "Duration"), insert a **Rich Text** content control field, customize the *Title* to Duration, and change the *Color* to **Yellow**.
   d. Place the insertion point in the third cell in the third row (below "Average Speed"), insert a **Rich Text** content control field, customize the *Title* to Average Speed, and change the *Color* to **Yellow**.
   e. Place the insertion point in the fourth cell in the third row (below "Average HR"), insert a **Rich Text** content control field, customize the *Title* to Average HR, and change the *Color* to **Yellow**.

5. Insert and customize a *Drop-Down List* content control field.
   a. Place the insertion point in the last cell in the third row (below "How I Felt") and insert a **Drop-Down List** content control field.
   b. Customize the *Title* to How I Felt and the *Color* to **Yellow**.
   c. **Add** the following choices: Like a Pro, Strong, Average, and Tired.
   d. Remove **Choose an item**.

6. Use *Design* mode to change the placeholder text:
   a. Turn on **Design** mode.
   b. Type **Enter miles** as the placeholder text for *Miles*.

c. Type Enter hours as the placeholder text for *Duration*.
d. Type Enter avg. speed as the placeholder text for *Average Speed*.
e. Type Enter avg. HR as the placeholder text for *Average HR*.
f. Type Select how I felt as the placeholder text for *How I Felt*.
g. Turn off **Design** mode.

7. Copy and paste content control fields.
   a. Select the **Miles** content control field handle and **copy** the field.
   b. **Paste** the content control field in each of the six cells that are below its current location.
   c. Repeat the above steps for the remaining content control fields in the other columns (Figure 11-84).

TRANSING·LOG·FOR·THE·WEEK·OF·Click or tap to enter a date. ¤					¤
MILES¤	**DURATION¤**	**AVERAGE·SPEED¤**	**AVERAGE·HR¤**	**HOW·I·FELT¤**	¤
Enter·miles¤	Enter·hours¤	Enter·avg.·speed¤	Enter·avg.·HR¤	Select·how·I·felt¤	¤
Enter·miles¤	Enter·hours¤	Enter·avg.·speed¤	Enter·avg.·HR¤	Select·how·I·felt¤	¤
Enter·miles¤	Enter·hours¤	Enter·avg.·speed¤	Enter·avg.·HR¤	Select·how·I·felt¤	¤
Enter·miles¤	Enter·hours¤	Enter·avg.·speed¤	Enter·avg.·HR¤	Select·how·I·felt¤	¤
Enter·miles¤	Enter·hours¤	Enter·avg.·speed¤	Enter·avg.·HR¤	Select·how·I·felt¤	¤
Enter·miles¤	Enter·hours¤	Enter·avg.·speed¤	Enter·avg.·HR¤	Select·how·I·felt¤	¤
Enter·miles¤	Enter·hours¤	Enter·avg.·speed¤	Enter·avg.·HR¤	Select·how·I·felt¤	¤

Figure 11-84 Copy and paste content control fields

8. Save and close the document.

9. Open the ***TrainingLog-11*** document from your student data files.

10. Save the Word document as [your initials] Word 11-4.

11. Insert a subdocument into this master document, unlink subdocument, and change heading level.
    a. Change to **Outline** view and deselect the **Show First Line Only** check box if it is checked.
    b. Place the insertion point on the blank line at the end of the outline.
    c. Click the **Show Document** button and **Insert** the ***[your initials] Word 11-4 form*** as a subdocument. Click **Yes to All** when prompted to rename styles in the subdocument.
    d. Select the subdocument and **Unlink** it from the master document.
    e. Delete the section breaks in the outline.
    f. Change the "Training Intensity and Heart Rate" heading to **Level 1**.
    g. Close the *Outline* view and return to *Print Layout* view.

12. Select the entire document and **Group** the content controls fields.

13. Save and close the document (Figure 11-85).

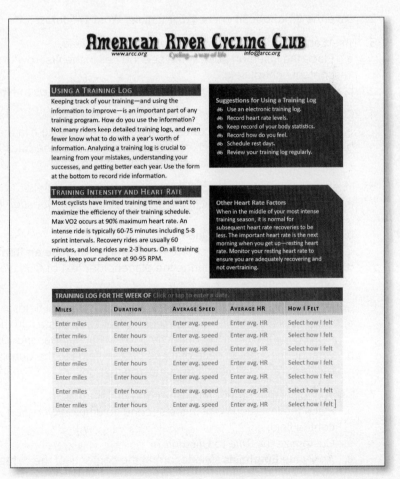

Figure 11-85 Word 11-4 completed

Independent Project 11-5

For this project, you create an insurance questionnaire for Central Sierra Insurance. You insert and customize content control fields, copy and modify content control fields, protect the document, create a new document based on the questionnaire, and fill in content control fields.
[Student Learning Outcomes 11.1, 11.2, 11.3, 11.4]

File Needed: ***InsuranceQuestionnaire-11.docx*** (*Student data files are available in the* Library *of your SIM-net account.*)
Completed Project File Names: *[your initials] **Word 11-5 form.docx*** and *[your initials] **Word 11-5.docx***

Skills Covered in This Project

- Insert and customize *Rich Text, Drop-Down List, Combo Box,* and *Date Picker* content control fields.
- Change the display for a content control field.
- Apply a style to a content control field.

- Copy, paste, and customize a content control field.
- Use *Design* mode to customize placeholder text.
- Restrict editing to filling in forms.
- Fill in a content control field.

---

1. Open the ***InsuranceQuestionnaire-11*** document from your student data files.

2. Save the Word document as [your initials] Word 11-5 form.

3. Insert and customize a *Rich Text* content control field.
   a. Place the insertion point in the second cell in the first row of the table and insert a **Rich Text** content control field.
   b. Customize the *Title* to **Question 1** and change *Show as* to **None**.

4. Copy, paste, and modify *Rich Text* content control fields.
   a. Copy the "Question 1" content control field and paste it in the second column for questions 2–5.
   b. Change the *Title* on each of these pasted fields to the question number (*Question 2, Question 3, etc.*) and remove the text from the *Tag* text box.

5. Insert and customize a *Drop-Down List* content control field.
   a. Place the insertion point in the second column on *Question 6* and insert a **Drop-Down List** content control field.
   b. Customize the *Title* to **Question 6**.
   c. **Add** Yes and No as the choices and remove **Choose an item**.
   d. Use *Design* mode to change the placeholder text of *Question 6* to **Select Yes or No** and then turn off *Design* mode.

6. Copy, paste, and modify *Drop-Down List* content control fields.
   a. Copy the "Question 6" content control field and paste it in the second column for questions 7–10. Don't copy the content control field to 7a, 8a, 9a, 10a, and 10b.
   b. Change the *Title* on each of these pasted fields to the question number (*Question 7, Question 8, etc.*) and remove the text from the *Tag* text box.

7. Insert and customize a *Combo Box* content control field.
   a. Place the insertion point in the second column on *Question 7a* and insert a **Combo Box** content control field.
   b. Customize the *Title* to **Question 7a**.
   c. Apply the **Emphasis** style to format the contents of the content control field.

d. **Add** N/A as the choice and remove **Choose an item**.

e. Use *Design* mode to change the placeholder text to **Type a response or select N/A** and then turn off *Design* mode.

8. Copy, paste, and modify *Combo Box* content control fields.

a. Copy the "Question 7a" content control field and paste it in the second column for *Questions 8a, 9a, 10a,* and *10b.*

b. Change the *Title* on each of these pasted fields to the question number (*Question 8a, Question 9a,* etc.) and remove the text from the *Tag* text box.

9. Insert and customize a *Date Picker* content control field.

a. Place the insertion point after "Date of Application:", **space** once, and insert a **Date Picker** content control field.

b. Customize the *Title* to **Application Date** and select the spelled-out date format (January 1, 2020).

c. Use *Design* mode to change the placeholder text to **Select date of application** and then turn off *Design* mode. Remember, content temporarily shifts when using *Design* mode and returns to normal when you turn off *Design* mode.

10. Restrict editing of the questionnaire.

a. Use the *Restrict Editing* pane to allow only **Filling in forms**.

b. Start enforcing protection and don't use a password. Close the *Restrict Editing* pane.

11. Save the document, but do not close it.

12. Save the Word document as a different file name. Save it as [your initials] Word 11-5.

13. Use the information in Table 11-2 to fill in the questionnaire:

Table 11-2: Content Control Fields

Question 1	Tish Waterson
Question 2	95002 North Avenue, Loomis, CA 96885
Question 3	916-528-6861
Question 4	CA3775409
Question 5	18
Question 6	**Yes**
Question 7	**Yes**
Question 7a	15%
Question 8	**No**
Question 8a	**N/A**
Question 9	**No**
Question 9a	**N/A**
Question 10	**No**
Question 10a	**N/A**
Question 10b	**N/A**
Application Date	**Select current date**

14. Save and close the document (Figure 11-86).

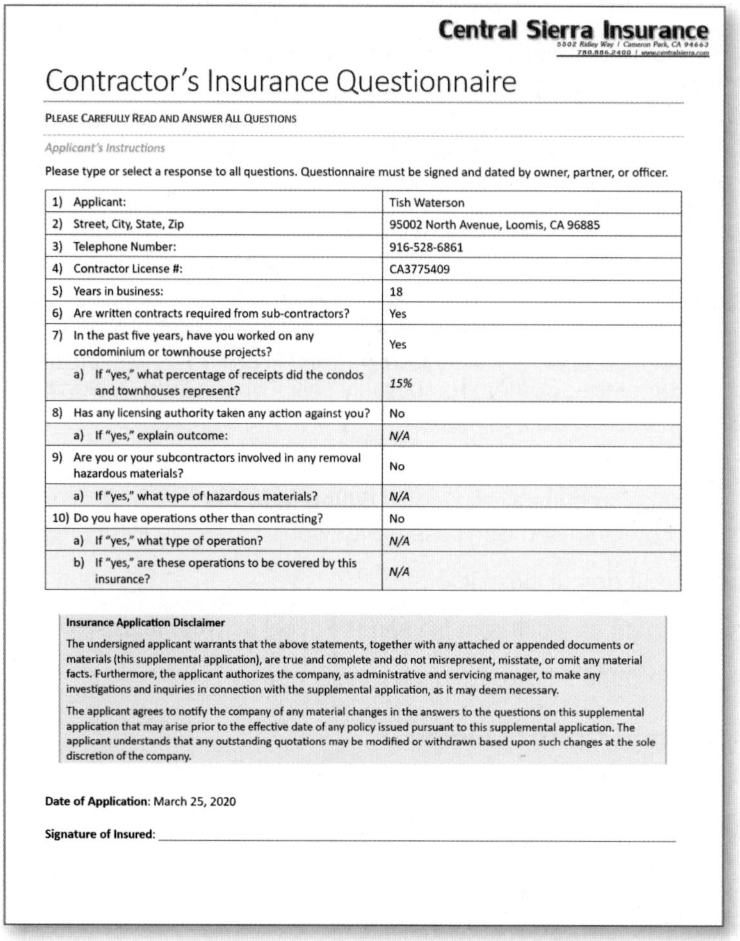

Central Sierra Insurance
5502 Ridley Way | Cameron Park, CA 94663
780.886.2400 | www.centralsierra.com

Contractor's Insurance Questionnaire

PLEASE CAREFULLY READ AND ANSWER ALL QUESTIONS

Applicant's Instructions

Please type or select a response to all questions. Questionnaire must be signed and dated by owner, partner, or officer.

1) Applicant:	Tish Waterson
2) Street, City, State, Zip	95002 North Avenue, Loomis, CA 96885
3) Telephone Number:	916-528-6861
4) Contractor License #:	CA3775409
5) Years in business:	18
6) Are written contracts required from sub-contractors?	Yes
7) In the past five years, have you worked on any condominium or townhouse projects?	Yes
a) If "yes," what percentage of receipts did the condos and townhouses represent?	*15%*
8) Has any licensing authority taken any action against you?	No
a) If "yes," explain outcome:	*N/A*
9) Are you or your subcontractors involved in any removal hazardous materials?	No
a) If "yes," what type of hazardous materials?	*N/A*
10) Do you have operations other than contracting?	No
a) If "yes," what type of operation?	*N/A*
b) If "yes," are these operations to be covered by this insurance?	*N/A*

Insurance Application Disclaimer

The undersigned applicant warrants that the above statements, together with any attached or appended documents or materials (this supplemental application), are true and complete and do not misrepresent, misstate, or omit any material facts. Furthermore, the applicant authorizes the company, as administrative and servicing manager, to make any investigations and inquiries in connection with the supplemental application, as it may deem necessary.

The applicant agrees to notify the company of any material changes in the answers to the questions on this supplemental application that may arise prior to the effective date of any policy issued pursuant to this supplemental application. The applicant understands that any outstanding quotations may be modified or withdrawn based upon such changes at the sole discretion of the company.

Date of Application: March 25, 2020

Signature of Insured: ______________________

Figure 11-86 Word 11-5 completed

Independent Project 11-6

For this project, you use a master document and subdocuments to create a report for Courtyard Medical Plaza. You insert subdocuments into a master document, split and merge subdocuments, change heading levels, unlink subdocuments, and arrange sections of a subdocument.
[Student Learning Outcome 11.5]

Files Needed: ***TeenSubstanceAbuse-11.docx***, ***SubstanceAbuse1-11.docx***, ***SubstanceAbuse2-11.docx***, ***SubstanceAbuse3-11.docx***, and ***SubstanceAbuse4-11.docx*** *(Student data files are available in the* Library *of your SIMnet account.)*
Completed Project File Name: ***[your initials] Word 11-6.docx***

Skills Covered in This Project

- Use *Outline* view.
- Insert a subdocument into a master document.
- Promote and demote headings.
- Merge subdocuments.
- Split a subdocument into two subdocuments.
- Show different levels in *Outline* view.
- Arrange sections in a subdocument.
- Unlink subdocuments.
- Delete a section break.
- Insert a page break.

1. Open the ***TeenSubstanceAbuse-11*** document from your student data files.

2. Save the document as [your initials] Word 11-6.

3. Open a *File Explorer* window, locate the ***SubstanceAbuse1-11.docx***, ***SubstanceAbuse2-11.docx***, ***SubstanceAbuse3-11.docx***, and ***SubstanceAbuse4-11.docx*** files from your student data files, and **copy** these to the same location as your *[your initials] Word 11-6* file. These are your subdocument files.

4. Return to the *[your initials] Word 11-6* document and display the document in **Outline** view.

5. Select the "**What Is Teen Substance Abuse?**" heading and change it to **Level 1**.

6. Insert subdocuments into the master document.
   a. Place the insertion point on the blank line at the end of the outline.
   b. Click the **Show Document** button and **Insert** the ***SubstanceAbuse1-11*** file. This file should be located in the same folder as *[your initials] Word 11-6* document.
   c. *Insert* each of the following subdocuments on the last blank line of the outline: ***SubstanceAbuse2-11.docx***, ***SubstanceAbuse3-11.docx***, and ***SubstanceAbuse4-11.docx***.

7. Change heading levels in the subdocuments.
   a. **Show First Line Only** in the outline.
   b. Change the "What Problems Can Teen Substance Abuse Cause?" heading in the first subdocument to **Level 2**.
   c. Change the "What Are the Signs of Substance Abuse?" heading in the second subdocument to **Level 2**.
   d. Change the "Why Do Teens Abuse Drugs and Alcohol?" heading in the third subdocument to **Level 1**.
   e. Change the "What Should You Do if Your Teen Is Using?" and "Bibliography" headings in the fourth subdocument to **Level 1**.
   f. Change the "Can Teen Substance Use and Abuse Be Prevented?" and "What Are the Treatment Options?" headings in the fourth subdocument to **Level 2**.

8. Merge and split subdocuments.
   a. Select the first three subdocuments and **merge** them into one subdocument. Use the **Shift** key and the **subdocument selectors** to select multiple subdocuments.
   b. Select the "**Bibliography**" section and **split** it into a separate subdocument.

9. Arrange sections in subdocuments, unlink subdocuments, and remove section breaks.
   a. Change the *Show Level* to display **Level 2**, which displays *Levels 1* and *2* in the outline.
   b. Move the *Level 1* heading ("Why Do Teens Abuse. . .") in the first subdocument above the *Level 2* headings.
   c. Move the second *Level 2* heading ("What Are the Treatment Options?") in the second subdocument above the first *Level 2* heading ("Can Teen Substance Use. . .") in that subdocument.
   d. **Unlink** the three subdocuments from the master document and show **All Levels**.
   e. Remove all section breaks from the master document.

10. Save the document.

11. Close *Outline* view to display the document in *Print Layout* view.

12. Finalize the document and insert page breaks.
    a. Place the insertion point in front of "Can Teen Substance Use and Abuse Be Prevented?" on the second page and insert a **page break**.
    b. Place the insertion point in front of the "Bibliography" heading and insert a **page break**. If a section break displays at the end of the bibliography, delete it.
    c. Delete any blank lines display in the document (if necessary).

13. Save and close the document (Figure 11-87).

TEEN SUBSTANCE ABUSE

WHAT IS TEEN SUBSTANCE ABUSE?

Many teens try alcohol, tobacco, or drugs, but using these substances is not safe or legal. Some teens try these substances only a few times and stop. Others can't control their urges or cravings for them. This is substance abuse.

Teens may try various substances, including cigarettes, alcohol, household chemicals (inhalants), prescription and over-the-counter medicines, and illegal drugs. Marijuana is the drug that teens use most often (Sanchez, 2018).

WHY DO TEENS ABUSE DRUGS AND ALCOHOL?

Teens use alcohol and other drugs for many reasons. They may do it because they want to fit in with friends or certain groups. They may also take a drug or drink alcohol because they like the way it makes them feel, or they may believe that it makes them more grown up. Teens tend to try new things and take risks, and they may take drugs or drink alcohol because it seems exciting.

Teens with family members who have problems with alcohol or other drugs are more likely to have serious substance abuse problems. Also, teens who feel that they are not connected with or valued by their parents are at greater risk. Teens with poor self-esteem or emotional or mental health problems, such as depression, also are at increased risk (Courtyard Medical Plaza, 2019).

What Problems Can Teen Substance Abuse Cause?

Substance abuse can lead to serious problems such as poor schoolwork, loss of friends, problems at home, and legal problems. Alcohol and drug abuse is a leading cause of teen death or injury related to car accidents, suicides, violence, and drowning. Substance abuse can increase the risk of pregnancy and sexually transmitted diseases (STDs), including HIV, because of unprotected sex.

Even casual use of certain drugs can cause severe medical problems, such as an overdose or brain damage. Many illegal drugs today are made in home labs, so they can vary greatly in strength. These drugs also may contain bacteria, dangerous chemicals, and other unsafe substances (Foundation for Teen Health, 2017).

What Are the Signs of Substance Abuse?

It's important to be aware of the signs that your teen may be abusing alcohol, drugs, or other substances. Some of the signs include:

▸ Red eyes and health complaints, such as being overly tired. If your teen often uses over-the-counter eye drops, he or she may be trying to cover up red eyes caused by smoking marijuana.
▸ Less interest in school, a drop in grades, and skipping classes or school altogether.
▸ New friends who have little interest in their families or school activities.
▸ Chemical-soaked rags or papers, which may mean that your teen is inhaling vapors. Another sign of using inhalants is paint or other stains on your teen's clothing, hands, or face.

WHAT SHOULD YOU DO IF YOUR TEEN IS USING?

If your teen is using alcohol, tobacco, or drugs, take it seriously. One of the most important things you can do is to talk openly with your teen about the problem. Urge him or her to do the same. Try not to use harsh, judging words. Be as supportive as you can during this time. In most cases, a hostile, angry face-to-face meeting pushes your teen away from the family. If you do not know what to do or if you feel uncomfortable, ask for help from a pediatrician, psychologist, or psychiatrist.

What Are the Treatment Options?

The type of treatment your teen needs depends on the level of substance abuse. For example, if a teen has tried drugs or alcohol only a few times, talking openly about the problem may be all that you need to do to help your teen stop his or her substance use. But if a teen has a substance abuse problem, then he or she needs to be seen by a doctor and/or by a counselor. If your teen is addicted to a drug or alcohol, he or she may need to have detoxification treatment or a treatment that replaces the substance with medicine. Medical treatment works best if it is combined with one-on-one or family counseling, or both (Sanchez, 2018).

Returning to substance abuse, called relapse, is common after treatment. It is not a failure on the part of your teen or the treatment program. Recovery from addiction is hard and takes time. Know that setbacks may occur, and your teen will need to overcome them one step at a time.

Courtyard Medical Plaza—Teen Substance Abuse

Figure 11-87 Word 11-6 completed (pages 1 and 2 of 4)

Improve It Project 11-7

For this project, you create a buyer escrow checklist form for Placer Hills Real Estate. You convert text to a table, modify the table, insert and customize content control fields, copy and modify content control fields, and group content control fields.
[Student Learning Outcomes 11.1, 11.2, 11.3, 11.4]

File Needed: ***BuyerEscrowCheckList-11.docx*** *(Student data files are available in the* Library *of your SIMnet account.)*
Completed Project File Name: ***[your initials] Word 11-7.docx***

Skills Covered in This Project

- Set tab stops to align text.
- Convert text to a table.
- Apply a table style.
- Modify row height and column width and change text alignment.
- Insert and customize *Rich Text*, *Plain Text*, *Combo Box*, and *Date Picker* content control fields.

- Change color and apply a style to a content control field.
- Copy, paste, and customize a content control field.
- Use *Design* mode to customize placeholder text.
- Group content control fields.

---

1. Open the **BuyerEscrowCheckList-11** document from your student data files.

2. Save the Word document as [your initials] Word 11-7.

3. Select the five lines beginning with "**Buyers(s):**" and ending with "**Property Address:**" and set **left** tab stops at **0.75"** and **1.25"**.

4. Convert text to a table and modify the table.
   a. Select the lines of text beginning with "**Task**" through the last line of the document.
   b. Convert the text to a table with **4** columns and **AutoFit to window**.
   c. Select the entire table if it is not already selected and change the font size to **10 pt**.
   d. Apply the **Grid Table 2** table style and set the table options to include a **Header Row**, **Banded Rows**, and **First Column**.
   e. Change the row height of the entire table to **0.3"** and change the text alignment to **Align Center Left**.
   f. Select the first column, change the width to **2.8"**, and set a **0.25" left** tab stop.
   g. Change the width of the second and third columns to **1"** and change the text alignment to **Align Center**.
   h. Change the width of the fourth column to **1.6"**.

5. Insert and customize a *Rich Text* content control field.
   a. Insert a **Rich Text** content control field after the tab following "Buyer(s):".
   b. Change the title to Buyer, change the color to the **second color** in the **second row** (**Green**), and apply the **Book Title** style.

6. Insert and customize a *Plain Text* content control field.
   a. Insert a **Plain Text** content control field after the tab following "Phone:".
   b. Change the title to Phone and change the color to **Green**.

7. Copy and modify *Plain Text* content control fields.
   a. Copy the *Plain Text* content control field ("Phone") and paste it after the tab following "Email" and "Property Address."
   b. Change the titles to Email and Address respectively and remove the text from the *Tag* field on the two copied fields.
   c. Copy and paste the "**Phone**" *Plain Text* content control field in cells below "Initials" and "Notes" in the table (paste only in the second row of the table).
   d. Change the titles to Initials and Notes respectively and remove the text from the *Tag* field.

8. Insert and customize a *Combo Box* content control field.
   a. Insert a **Combo Box** content control field after the tab following "Agent:".
   b. Change the title to Agent and change the color to **Green**.
   c. Add Emma Cavalli, Ames Bellah, Hudson Alves, and Simon Bidou as the choices and remove **Choose an item**.
   d. Use the **Move Up** and **Move Down** buttons to arrange these choices alphabetically by last name.

9. Insert and customize a *Date Picker* content control field.
   a. Insert a **Date Picker** content control field in the cell below "Date Completed" in the table.
   b. Change the title to Date Completed, change the color to **Green**, and select the number date format (1/1/2020).

10. Insert *Check Box* content control fields.
    a. Insert a **Check Box** content control field before "Fax Contract to Buyer(s)."
    b. Use the **right** arrow key to deselect the content control field. You may have to press the **right** arrow key more than once to deselect the content control field.
    c. Press **Ctrl+Tab** to insert a tab between the *Check Box* content control field and the text.
    d. Repeat steps 10a–c above on each of the remaining cells in the first column.

11. Use *Design* mode to customize the placeholder text.
    a. Turn on **Design** mode and customize the placeholder text on the following fields:
       Buyer: Type buyer's name(s)
       Phone: Type phone number
       Email: Type email address
       Agent: Select or type agent's name
       Property Address: Type property address
       Date Completed: Select date
       Initials: Type initials
       Notes: Type notes
    b. Turn off **Design** mode.

12. Copy each of the content control fields in the second, third, and fourth columns of the table to the cells below to fill the table with content control fields.

13. Select the second and third columns of the table and **Align Center**.

14. Select the fourth column of the table and **Align Center Left**.

15. Select the entire document and **group** the content control fields.

16. Save and close the document (Figure 11-88).

Buyer Escrow Checklist

Buyer(s):   Type buyer's name(s)

Phone: Type phone number

Email: Type email address

Agent: Select or type agent's name

Property Address: Type property addresss

Task	Date Completed	Initials	Notes
☐ Fax Contract to Buyer(s)	Select date	Type initials	Type notes
☐ Fax Contract to Lender	Select date	Type initials	Type notes
☐ Verify Property ID with Buyer(s)	Select date	Type initials	Type notes
☐ Verify Property ID with Lender	Select date	Type initials	Type notes
☐ Turn in new sale to PHRE	Select date	Type initials	Type notes
☐ Send check to Title Company	Select date	Type initials	Type notes
☐ Notified Buyer of EM deposit	Select date	Type initials	Type notes
☐ Fax/Email Pest Report to Buyer(s)	Select date	Type initials	Type notes
☐ Fax/Email Pest Report to Lender	Select date	Type initials	Type notes
☐ Fax/Email Clear Pest Report to Buyer(s)	Select date	Type initials	Type notes
☐ Fax/Email Clear Pest Report to Lender	Select date	Type initials	Type notes
☐ Verify Preliminary Report with Buyer(s)	Select date	Type initials	Type notes
☐ Verify Preliminary Report with Lender	Select date	Type initials	Type notes

Emma Cavalli
916.450.3334
ecavalli@phre.com

Placer Hills Real Estate
7100 Madrone Road, Roseville, CA 95722
www.phre.com

Figure 11-88 Word 11-7 completed

Challenge Project 11-8

Before each semester begins, you have a variety of tasks to accomplish so you are ready when classes begin. For example, register and pay for classes, complete financial aid paperwork, buy books and supplies, download and read the course syllabi, check professors' web sites, or log into learning management systems.

For this project, you create a form using content control fields to manage tasks you need to accomplish before the semester begins.
[Student Learning Outcomes 11.1, 11.2, 11.3, 11.4]

File Needed: None
Completed Project File Names: *[your initials] Word 11-8 checklist.dotx* and *[your initials] Word 11-8.docx*

Create a new document and save it as a template named [your initials] Word 11-8 checklist. Modify your document according to the following guidelines:

- List the text and content control fields you will need in this checklist based on the tasks you need to complete before the semester begins.
- Use tab stops, indents, and/or a table to control alignment of text and content control fields.
- Insert text and content control fields for the tasks you need to complete before the semester begins.
- Customize content control fields to include titles. Change the color and how the field displays. Apply a style and add choices to *Combo Box* and *Drop-Down List* content control fields.
- Copy and modify content control fields as needed.
- Use *Design* mode to customize placeholder text.
- Group the content control fields.

Create a new document based on the checklist template and save it as [your initials] Word 11-8.

- Fill in the content control fields.
- Save and close the document.

Challenge Project 11-9

For this project, you create a form to use for an upcoming conference or workshop or a membership form for a club or organization. Insert a variety of text and content control fields in this form.
[Student Learning Outcomes 11.1, 11.2, 11.3, 11.4]

File Needed: None
Completed Project File Name: *[your initials] Word 11-9 form.dotx*

Create a new document and save it as a template named [your initials] Word 11-9 form. Modify your document according to the following guidelines:

- List the text and content control fields you will need in this form.
- Use tab stops and indents to control alignment of text and content control fields.

- Insert text and content control fields for your form.
- Customize content control fields to include a title. Change the color and how the field displays, apply a style, and add choices to *Combo Box* and *Drop-Down List* content control fields.
- Copy and modify content control fields as needed.
- Use *Design* mode to customize placeholder text.
- Restrict editing of the document and protect with a password.

Challenge Project 11-10

It is important to create a budget and live within it. Track what you're spending in order to create an accurate budget and effectively control your finances. For this project, you create an expenditure template to track your weekly spending, and then create a document based upon the expenditure template. [Student Learning Outcomes 11.1, 11.2, 11.3, 11.4]

File Needed: None
Completed Project File Names: *[your initials] Word 11-10 template.dotx* and *[your initials] Word 11-10.docx*

Create a new document and save it as a template named [your initials] Word 11-10 template. Modify your template according to the following guidelines:

- List the text and content control fields you need in your weekly expenditure template.
- Use a table to control alignment of text and content control fields.
- Insert text and content control fields for expenses.
- Customize content control fields to include a title. Change the color and how the field displays, apply a style, and add choices to *Combo Box* and *Drop-Down List* content control fields.
- Copy and modify content control fields as needed.
- Use *Design* mode to customize placeholder text.
- Insert a formula at the bottom of the table to total your expenditures for the week.
- Group the content control fields.

Create a new document based on the expenditure template and save it as [your initials] Word 11-10.

- Fill in your weekly spending in the content control fields.
- Update the formula in the table to total expenses. Ungroup content control fields, if necessary, to update the formula.
- Save and close the document.

Customizing Word and Using OneDrive and Office Online

CHAPTER OVERVIEW

Now that you know how to use the many features of Word, this chapter will introduce Word settings and how to personalize the working environment. Office 365 and 2019 also integrates with "cloud" technology, which enables you to use your Office files in *OneDrive* and *Office Online*. Cloud services enable your files and Office settings to roam with you and enables you to share *OneDrive* files with others. With these online features, you are not limited to using Office on only one computer, and you don't have to save your files on a USB drive or portable hard drive to have access to your files.

STUDENT LEARNING OUTCOMES (SLOs)

After completing this chapter, you will be able to:

SLO 12.1 Customize Word options, the *Ribbon*, and the *Quick Access* toolbar to personalize your working environment (p. W12-724).

SLO 12.2 View and modify Office account settings and install an Office add-in (p. W12-734).

SLO 12.3 Use *OneDrive* to create, upload, move, copy, delete, and download files and folders (p. W12-740).

SLO 12.4 Share *OneDrive* files and folders (p. W12-745).

SLO 12.5 Use *Office Online* to edit, create, share, collaborate, and comment on a document (p. W12-751).

SLO 12.6 Explore other *Office Online* products and productivity tools (p. W12-758).

CASE STUDY

For the Pause & Practice projects in this chapter, you modify Word settings and use Microsoft cloud services to save, edit, and share documents for Courtyard Medical Plaza.

Pause & Practice 12-1: Customize the Word working environment and Office account settings and install an Office add-in.

Pause & Practice 12-2: Use *OneDrive* and *Word Online* to save, create, edit, and share documents.

Pause & Practice 12-3: Create and share a *Form* using *Office Online* and *OneDrive*.

Customizing Word

In previous chapters, you have used Word features to format and enhance a variety of documents. The focus of this section is to customize Word settings, which are global settings that apply to all files you create and edit. Customize Word settings in the *Word Options* dialog box, which you open from the *Backstage* view. Once implemented, these options apply to all documents.

Word Options

The *Word Options* dialog box displays settings in 11 categories. Within each category, you change individual settings by selecting or deselecting a check box or selecting from a drop-down list. Buttons in the *Word Options* dialog box open a dialog box to display additional customization settings. The following list includes the different categories in the *Word Options* dialog box:

- *General*
- *Display*
- *Proofing*
- *Save*
- *Language*
- *Ease of Access*
- *Advanced*
- *Customize Ribbon*
- *Quick Access Toolbar*
- *Add-ins*
- *Trust Center*

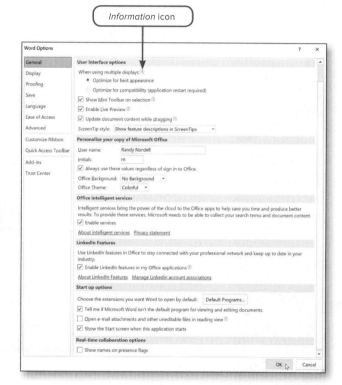

Figure 12-1 *Word Options* dialog box

▶ HOW TO: Customize Word Options

1. Click the **File** tab to open the *Backstage* view.
2. Click the **Options** button on the left to open the *Word Options* dialog box (Figure 12-1).
3. Click a category on the left to display the available options on the right.
4. Change options using check boxes, text boxes, drop-down lists, or buttons.
   - When you click a button, such as *Default Programs*, a dialog box with additional option settings opens.
5. Click **OK** to close the *Word Options* dialog box and apply the settings.

General

The *General* category includes the following areas: *User Interface options*, *Personalize your copy of Microsoft Office*, *Office intelligent services*, *LinkedIn Features*, *Start up options*, and *Real-time collaboration options* (see Figure 12-1).

In the *User Interface options* area, show/hide the mini toolbar display, enable/disable live preview, and turn on/off document content while dragging. You can also change the *ScreenTip* style.

MORE INFO

Place your pointer on the *Information* icon at the end of a selection to display information about that selection.

In the *Personalize your copy of Microsoft Office* area, change your user name and initials and change the Office background and theme. To use the current user name and initials as the default setting for all users, check the **Always use these values regardless of sign in to Office** box.

Enable the *Office intelligent services* and *LinkedIn Features* to use the *Researcher* and *Resume Assistant* features in Word.

In the *Start up options* area, set the default program, choose how email attachments display, and determine whether or not the *Start* screen displays when Word opens. The *Start* screen displays your recent documents and Word templates.

In the *Real-time collaboration options* area, display presence flags to indicate individuals collaborating on an online document. Sharing is covered in *SLO 12.4: Sharing OneDrive Files and Folders* and *SLO 12.5: Using Office Online* later in this chapter.

Display

The *Display* options category controls how document content displays on the screen and when it is printed (Figure 12-2). In the *Page display options* area, show or hide white space between pages in *Print Layout* view, highlighter marks, and document tooltips.

In the *Always show these formatting marks on the screen* area, select the formatting marks to display when *Show/Hide* is turned on. By default, object anchors and all formatting marks display. To customize which formatting marks display, deselect **Show all formatting marks** and check the individual marks next to the formatting marks you want *Show/Hide* to display.

In the *Printing options* area, specify elements to print by selecting the appropriate check box. You can also set Word to update fields and linked data before printing.

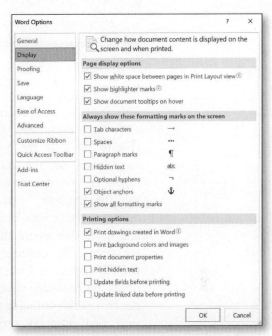

Figure 12-2 *Display* options in the *Word Options* dialog box

Proofing

The *Proofing* category controls how Word corrects and formats text (Figure 12-3). Click the **AutoCorrect options** button to open the *AutoCorrect* dialog box to change options in the *AutoCorrect, Math AutoCorrect, AutoFormat As You Type, AutoFormat,* and *Actions* categories.

In the *When correcting spelling in Microsoft Office programs* area, Word is, by default, set to ignore words in uppercase, words that contain numbers, and internet and file addresses. Click the **Custom Dictionaries** button to open the *Custom Dictionaries* dialog box to add, edit, or delete words from the custom dictionary.

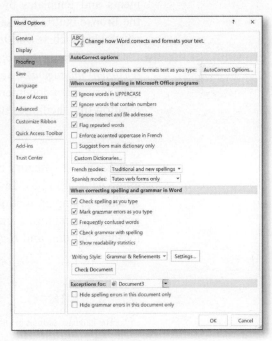

Figure 12-3 *Proofing* options in the *Word Options* dialog box

The options in the *When correcting spelling and grammar in Word* area control how and when the spelling and grammar check functions. You can also turn on ***readability statistics*** to display statistics about your document after you finish checking spelling and grammar. By default, Word checks spelling and grammar, but not style. To check grammar and style, click the **Settings** button to modify grammar and style settings.

In the *Exceptions for* area, hide spelling and grammatical errors in a selected document or in all new Word documents.

> ### ▶ MORE INFO
>
> Many options in the *Proofing* category apply to all Office applications and files.

Save

The *Save* category controls how and where documents are saved (Figure 12-4). In the *Save documents* area, set the default file format to save documents, establish the frequency that *AutoRecover* saves your open documents, and determine where these files are stored. By default, pressing **Ctrl+O** (*Open*) or **Ctrl+S** (*Save*) opens the *Backstage* view, but you can change this setting so the *Backstage* view does not show when opening or saving files. Change the default save location for documents and templates by clicking the **Browse** button and selecting a new folder, such as *OneDrive*.

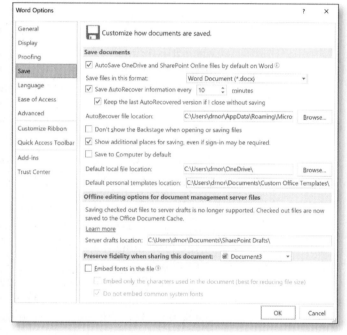

Figure 12-4 *Save* options in the *Word Options* dialog box

The *Offline editing options for document management server files* area pertains to documents shared on a web server (such as *OneDrive for Business*), which is a location that facilitates storage and sharing of files.

Language

The *Language* category controls the language preferences in Word and the other Office programs (Figure 12-5). In the *Choose Editing Languages* area, select the language to use for spelling, grammar, dictionaries, and sorting. Also, add a new language, set a different default language, or remove a language. In the *Choose Display Language* area, set the display language for tabs, buttons, and *Help.*

> ### ▶ MORE INFO
>
> The language settings in Office are determined by the default language you selected when you installed Windows.

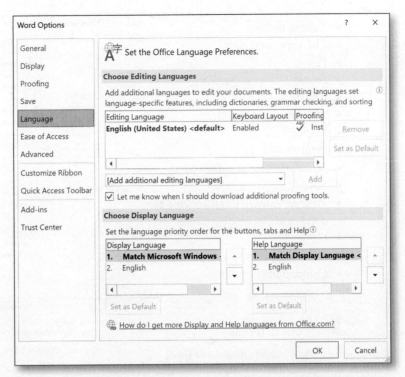

Figure 12-5 *Language* options in the *Word Options* dialog box

Ease of Access

The *Ease of Access* area provides options to make a document more accessible to those with disabilities (Figure 12-6). In the *Feedback options* and *Application display options* areas, select how feedback is provided to users and how *ScreenTips* display.

By default, Word automatically generates alt text descriptions for pictures in a document. However, you can edit the alt text that displays for each picture. If necessary, disable this option in the *Automatic Alt Text* area and manually insert alt text for each picture.

The *Document display options* control whether headings, such as Heading 1 and Heading 2, display expanded when a user opens a document.

Figure 12-6 *Ease of Access* options in the *Word Options* dialog box

Advanced

The *Advanced* category includes a variety of options such as controlling how text is selected, using drag and drop, following hyperlinks, controlling the format of pasted objects, displaying recent documents, scroll bars, and the vertical ruler (Figure 12-7). The following is a list of the different options in the *Advanced* category. Scroll through each of these areas to familiarize yourself with the options available.

- *Editing options*
- *Cut, copy, and paste*
- *Pen*
- *Image Size and Quality*
- *Chart*
- *Show document content*
- *Display*
- *Print*
- *When printing this document*
- *Save*
- *Preserve fidelity when sharing this document*
- *General*
- *Layout options*
- *Compatibility options*

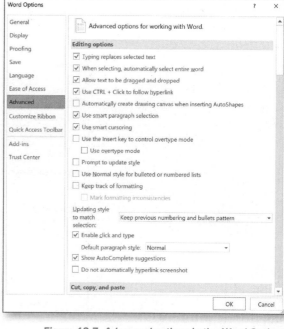

Figure 12-7 *Advanced* options in the *Word Options* dialog box

> **MORE INFO**
>
> The *Customize Ribbon* and *Quick Access Toolbar* options are covered later in this section.

Add-ins

Add-ins are programs that add functionality to your Office programs. Examples of add-in programs include Acrobat PDF Maker or Google Desktop.

In the *Add-ins* category in the *Word Options* dialog box, view the add-in programs that interact with Office (Figure 12-8). Enable or disable add-ins by clicking the **Manage** drop-down list, selecting a category, and clicking **Go**. A dialog box opens where you enable or disable add-ins.

Trust Center

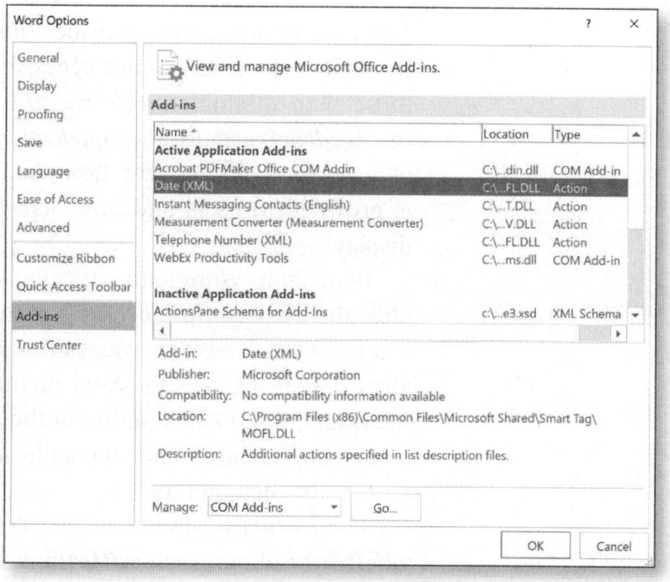

Figure 12-8 *Add-ins* options in the *Word Options* dialog box

Use the *Trust Center* to select options to keep your files safe and to prevent your files and computer from becoming infected with viruses. You can change the settings in the *Trust Center* dialog box, but it is generally recommended that you use the default settings in the *Trust Center*.

> **MORE INFO**
>
> For more information on macros and the *Trust Center*, see *SLO 10.3: Creating and Running Macros*.

HOW TO: Customize Trust Center Settings

1. Click the **File** tab to open the *Backstage* view.
2. Click the **Options** button on the left to open the *Word Options* dialog box.
3. Click the **Trust Center** button on the left.
4. Click the **Trust Center Settings** button to open the *Trust Center* dialog box (Figure 12-9).
5. Click the different categories on the left to view the available options and apply changes.
6. Click **OK** to close the *Trust Center* dialog box.
7. Click **OK** to close the *Word Options* dialog box.

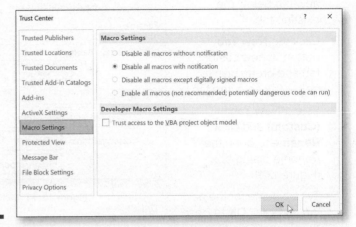

Figure 12-9 *Trust Center* dialog box

Customize the Ribbon

The *Ribbon* displays many of the common commands in Word, but not all available commands display on the *Ribbon*. Customize the *Ribbon* to add a new group to a tab or to add commands you commonly use. For example, create a new group on the *Home* tab that includes a button to open the *Tabs* dialog box or create a custom tab with groups containing commonly used commands.

> **MORE INFO**
>
> You can add commands to custom groups, but you cannot add or remove commands in existing groups.

HOW TO: Add a Tab, Group, and Commands to the Ribbon

1. Right-click anywhere on the **Ribbon** and select **Customize the Ribbon** from the context menu. The *Word Options* dialog box opens and displays the *Customize Ribbon* area (Figure 12-10).

   - Alternatively, click the **File** tab to open the *Backstage* view, click the **Options** button to open the *Word Options* dialog box, and select **Customize Ribbon**.
   - The left side lists available commands, and the right side lists the existing tabs and groups that display on the *Ribbon*.
   - The drop-down lists at the top of each of the lists provide you with other commands and tabs to display in these lists.

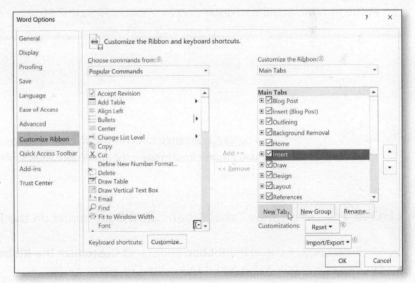

Figure 12-10 *Customize Ribbon* area of the *Word Options* dialog box

2. Click a tab on the right at the location to insert a new tab below the existing tab.

3. Click the **New Tab** button. A new custom tab and group display below the selected tab.

4. Select **New Tab (Custom)** and click **Rename** to open the *Rename* dialog box (Figure 12-11).

5. Type a name for the new tab and click **OK** to close the *Rename* dialog box.

Figure 12-11 Rename a new tab

Figure 12-12 Rename a new group

6. Select **New Group (Custom)** and click **Rename** to open the *Rename* dialog box (Figure 12-12).

7. Type a name for the new group in the *Display name* area, select a symbol (optional), and click **OK** to close the *Rename* dialog box.

8. Select a custom group on the right where you want to add a command.

   - Click the **plus** or **minus sign** by a tab or group to expand or collapse it.

9. Click the **Choose commands from** drop-down list on the left side and select **All Commands** to display all the available commands.

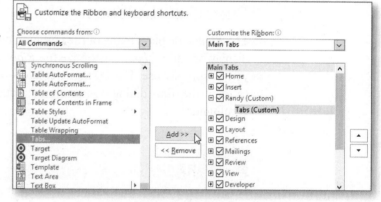

Figure 12-13 Add a command to a custom group

10. Select a command on the left to add to the custom group on the right and click the **Add** button to add the command to the group (Figure 12-13).

11. Click **OK** to close the *Word Options* dialog box.

   - The new tab and group display on the *Ribbon* (Figure 12-14).

Figure 12-14 Custom tab, group, and commands on the *Ribbon*

You can rearrange tabs on the *Ribbon*, groups on a tab, and commands in a custom group, but you cannot rearrange existing commands within existing groups.

▶ **HOW TO:** Rearrange Tabs, Groups, and Commands on the Ribbon

1. Right-click anywhere on the **Ribbon** and select **Customize the Ribbon** from the context menu. The *Word Options* dialog box opens and displays the *Customize Ribbon* area.

2. Select the command, group, or tab to rearrange.

3. Click the **Move Up** or **Move Down** button to rearrange the selected item (Figure 12-15).

4. Click **OK** to close the *Word Options* dialog box.

▶ ANOTHER WAY

In the *Customize Ribbon* area of the *Word Options* dialog box, right-click an item on the right side and select **Add New Tab**, **Add New Group**, **Rename**, **Move Up**, or **Move Down** from the context menu.

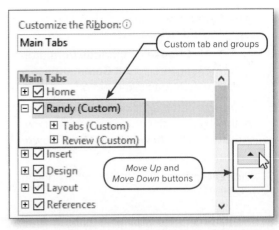

Figure 12-15 Rearrange a tab on the *Ribbon*

Customize the Quick Access Toolbar

In chapter 10, you added frequently used commands and macro buttons to the *Quick Access* toolbar. By default, the *Save*, *Undo*, *Redo*, and *Touch/Mouse Mode* (if the computer has a touch screen) commands display on the *Quick Access* toolbar. Add commonly used commands from the *Customize Quick Access Toolbar* drop-down list (Figure 12-16) or add other commands in the *Quick Access Toolbar* area in the *Word Options* dialog box.

When customizing the *Quick Access* toolbar, changes, by default, apply to all documents, but you can choose to customize the *Quick Access* toolbar for the current document only.

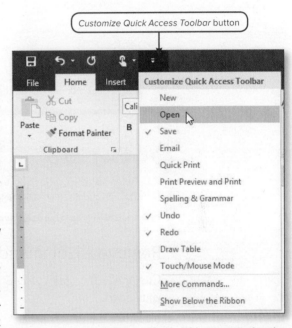

Figure 12-16 Add a command to the *Quick Access* toolbar

▶ HOW TO: Customize the Quick Access Toolbar

1. Click the **Customize Quick Access Toolbar** drop-down list on the right edge of the *Quick Access* toolbar (see Figure 12-16).

2. Select a command to add to the *Quick Access* toolbar. The command displays on the *Quick Access* toolbar.

   • Items on the *Customize Quick Access Toolbar* drop-down list with a check mark are commands that display on the *Quick Access* toolbar.

3. Add a command that is not listed on the *Customize Quick Access Toolbar* drop-down list by clicking the **Customize Quick Access Toolbar** drop-down list and selecting **More Commands**.

   • The *Word Options* dialog box opens and displays the *Quick Access Toolbar* area (Figure 12-17).

4. Click the **Customize Quick Access Toolbar** drop-down list on the right and select **For all documents** or the **For [current document]**.

   • If you select *For all documents* (which is the default setting), changes apply to the *Quick Access* toolbar for all documents you open in Word.

   • If you select the current document, changes apply to the *Quick Access* toolbar in that document only.

5. Select a command on the left to add and click the **Add** button.
   - Click the **Choose commands from** drop-down list and select **All Commands** to display more command options.

6. Rearrange commands on the *Quick Access* toolbar by selecting the command to move and clicking the **Move Up** or **Move Down** button.

7. Click **OK** to close the *Word Options* dialog box.

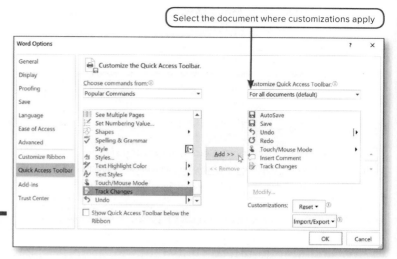

Select the document where customizations apply

Figure 12-17 Customize the *Quick Access* toolbar

> **ANOTHER WAY**
>
> Right-click a command on the *Ribbon* and select **Add to Quick Access Toolbar** from the context menu.

> **MORE INFO**
>
> To display the *Quick Access* toolbar below the *Ribbon*, click the **Customize Quick Access Toolbar** drop-down list and select **Show Below the Ribbon**.

Remove a Command from the Quick Access Toolbar

Customize the *Quick Access* toolbar to remove an existing command or remove a command you added.

▶HOW TO: Remove Commands from the Quick Access Toolbar

1. Right-click the item to remove on the *Quick Access* toolbar.
2. Select **Remove from Quick Access Toolbar** from the context menu (Figure 12-18).
   - Alternatively, click the **Customize Quick Access Toolbar** drop-down list and click a checked command to deselect it, which removes it from the *Quick Access* toolbar.
   - Also, remove commands from the *Quick Access* toolbar by opening the *Word Options* dialog box, selecting **Quick Access Toolbar**, selecting a command on the right, and clicking the **Remove** button.

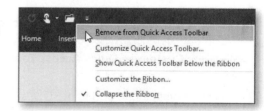

Figure 12-18 Context menu to remove a command from the *Quick Access* toolbar

Remove an Item from the Ribbon

To remove custom tabs, groups, or commands from the *Ribbon*, use the *Customize Ribbon* area of the *Word Options* dialog box. You cannot remove existing default tabs from Word, but you can deselect one or more tabs in the *Customize the Ribbon* area so they are hidden and do not display on the *Ribbon*. You can remove existing groups from a tab, but you cannot delete individual commands from an existing default group.

▶ HOW TO: Remove an Item from the Ribbon

1. Right-click anywhere on the **Ribbon** and select **Customize the Ribbon** from the context menu. The *Word Options* dialog box opens and displays the *Customize Ribbon* area (Figure 12-19).

   - Alternatively, click the **File** tab to open the *Backstage* view, click the **Options** button to open the *Word Options* dialog box, and select **Customize Ribbon**.

2. Hide a tab by clicking the check box to the left of the tab name to deselect the tab.

   - The tab still exists in the list, but it does not display on the *Ribbon*.

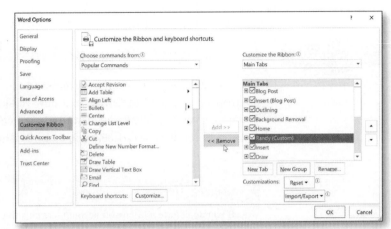

Figure 12-19 Remove a custom tab from the *Ribbon*

3. Select a custom tab, group, or command on the right and click the **Remove** button.

   - Click the **plus** or **minus sign** to the left of a tab or group to expand or collapse the tab and group.
   - Alternatively, right-click a tab or group and select **Remove** from the context menu.

4. Click **OK** to close the *Word Options* dialog box.

Reset the Ribbon and Quick Access Toolbar

Use the *Word Options* dialog box to reset the *Ribbon* or *Quick Access* toolbar to their original settings. When resetting the *Ribbon*, reset a specific tab or all *Ribbon* customizations.

▶ HOW TO: Reset the Ribbon and Quick Access Toolbar

1. Open the *Word Options* dialog box and select either **Customize Ribbon** or **Quick Access Toolbar**.

2. Click the **Reset** button at the bottom right and select from the available options (Figures 12-20 and 12-21).

   - To reset a specific tab, select the tab to reset before clicking the *Reset* button.
   - To reset the *Ribbon*, select **Reset only selected Ribbon tab** or **Reset all customizations**.
   - To reset the *Quick Access* toolbar, select **Reset only Quick Access Toolbar** or **Reset all customizations**.
   - Select **Reset all customizations** to both the *Ribbon* and the *Quick Access* toolbar.

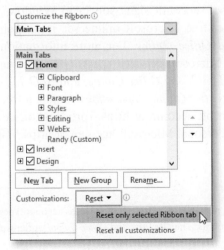

Figure 12-20 Reset the *Ribbon*

Figure 12-21 Reset the *Quick Access* toolbar

3. Click **Yes** if a dialog box opens to confirm you want to delete customizations (Figure 12-22).

4. Click **OK** to close the *Word Options* dialog box.

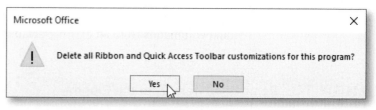

Microsoft Office   ✕

⚠ Delete all Ribbon and Quick Access Toolbar customizations for this program?

        Yes   No

Figure 12-22 Confirm to delete all customizations

SLO 12.2

Customizing Office and Installing Office Add-ins

Use your Microsoft account information to log in to both Windows and Office. When upgrading from one version of Office to a new version, many of your settings automatically transfer to the new version. View and customize Office account settings in the *Backstage* view, and add connected services to Office, such as LinkedIn or Twitter, as well as Office add-ins.

> **MORE INFO**
>
> If you don't have a Microsoft account, create a free account at the following web site: https://signup .live.com.

Microsoft Account Information

One of the many features of Office and Windows is the portability of your documents and account settings. Office settings and files can travel with you, which means you are not restricted to using just a single computer. For example, log in to Office on a computer at a computer lab on your college campus, at a public library, or at a friend's home, and your Office settings apply to that computer.

Use your Microsoft account (user name and password) when signing in to Windows on your computer. Microsoft Office uses this information to transfer your Office settings to the computer you are using. Your name displays in the upper-right corner of the Word window. Click your name to display a link to access your account settings (Figure 12-23).

Your Microsoft account signs you in to Windows, Office, and other free Microsoft online services, such as *OneDrive* and *Office Online*. For more information on these online Microsoft services, see *SLO 12.3: Using OneDrive, SLO 12.5: Using Office Online*, and *SLO 12.6: Exploring Other Office Online Applications*. Create a free education Microsoft account at https://products.office.com/en-us/student/office-in-education or create a free personal Microsoft account at https://signup.live.com.

Randy Nordell

Randy Nordell
drnordell@live.com

Change photo

About me

Account settings

Switch account

Figure 12-23 Microsoft account information

> **MORE INFO**
>
> Microsoft has personal, education, and business account types. This chapter focuses on educational Microsoft accounts. The *OneDrive* and *Office Online* working environments are slightly different when using a personal or business account.

▶ HOW TO: Use Your Microsoft Account in Office

1. Click your name or the log on area in the upper-right corner of the Word window (see Figure 12-23).
2. Click the **Account settings** link to open the *Account* area on the *Backstage* view (Figure 12-24).

   - Alternatively, click the **File** tab and select **Account** on the left.
   - Your account information displays.
   - If you are not signed in to Office with your Microsoft account, click the **Sign in** link in the upper-right corner of the Word window or on the *Backstage* view to open the *Sign in* dialog box.
   - Type your Microsoft account email address and click **Next**. Another *Sign in* dialog box opens (Figure 12-25).
   - Type your password and click **Sign in**.
   - If you don't have a Microsoft account, click the **Create one** link to create a free Microsoft account.
   - Also, use your Microsoft account to log in to *OneDrive* where you create, store, and share files and use *Office Online*.

Figure 12-24 *Account* area on the *Backstage* view

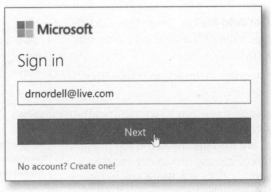

Figure 12-25 Sign in to Office using a Microsoft account

MORE INFO

If you are using a public computer, be sure to click the **Sign out** link in the *Account* area on the *Backstage* view to log out of your Microsoft account.

Customize Office Account Settings

Change the *Office Background* and *Office Theme* in the *Account* area on the *Backstage* view or in the *General* category in the *Word Options* dialog box. Click the **Office Background** or **Office Theme** drop-down list and select a background or theme (Figure 12-26). The background displays a graphic pattern in the upper-right corner of the Word window. The theme controls the colors of the working *Ribbon*, the *Backstage* view, and dialog boxes. The background and theme you select apply to all Office applications you use. The new default *Office Theme* for Office is *Colorful*.

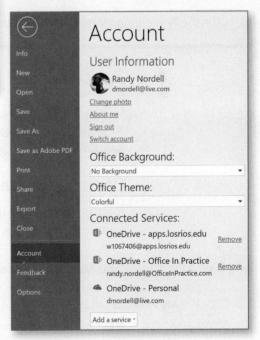

Figure 12-26 Customize Office *Account* settings

Office also enables you to connect to online services. In the *Account* area on the *Backstage* view, add online services you regularly use by clicking the **Add a service** drop-down list and selecting a service (see Figure 12-26). When adding a service, Office prompts you to enter your user name and password to connect to the online service. The services you are currently connected to are listed in the *Connected Service* area.

Office Add-ins

Another feature in Office is the ability to install *Office add-ins*. Similar to apps on your smartphone, Office add-ins are applications that add functionality to Office programs. For example, add a dictionary, encyclopedia, a news feed, or maps. When you add and open an Office add-in, the add-in opens in a pane at the right of the Word window.

▶ HOW TO: Install an Office Add-in

1. Click the **Get Add-ins** link [*Insert* tab, *Add-ins* group] to open the *Office Add-ins* dialog box (Figure 12-27).
2. Select a category on the left to display the available add-ins.
   - Use the *Search* text box to type keywords and search for matching add-ins.
   - Click the **My Add-ins** link at the top of the dialog box to display previously installed Office add-ins. Click the **Store** link to return to the list of add-ins.
3. Select an add-in to display a description.
4. Click the **Add** button to install the add-in.
   - An *Add-in* pane opens on the right (Figure 12-28).
   - Depending on the app you select, you may be taken to a web site to add the app.
5. Click the **X** in the upper-right corner to close the pane.

Figure 12-27 *Office Add-ins* dialog box

Figure 12-28 *Add-in* pane

> **MORE INFO**
>
> Check the *Office Add-ins* store for new and featured add-ins. New add-ins are added regularly.

Open and Manage Office Add-ins

After installing apps in Office, view installed add-ins, open an add-in pane at the right, and manage which add-ins are visible.

▶ HOW TO: Open and Manage Office Add-ins

1. Click the **My Add-ins** button [*Insert* tab, *Add-ins* group] to open the *Office Add-ins* dialog box (Figure 12-29).
2. Select an add-in to open and click **OK**. The add-in opens in a pane to the right of the Word window (see Figure 12-28).
   - Alternatively, click the **My Add-ins** drop-down arrow [*Insert* tab, *Add-ins* group] to display *Recently Used Add-ins*.

3. Manage available add-ins by clicking the **My Add-ins** button [*Insert* tab, *Add-ins* group] to open the *Office Add-ins* dialog box.

- Right-click an add-in (or click the ellipses in the upper-right corner) and select **Remove** to remove an add-in.
- Additionally, view add-in details or rate and review the add-in from this context menu.
- Click the **Store** link at the top of the dialog to search for and install other add-ins.

4. Click the **Manage My Add-ins** link in the *Office Add-ins* dialog box to open an internet browser window that displays your add-ins.

- Click the **Hide** link to hide an add-in.
- Click the **Hidden** link in the upper-right corner to display hidden add-ins. Click **Retrieve** to display the add-in.

Figure 12-29 Open an Office add-in

PAUSE & PRACTICE: WORD 12-1

For this project, you change Word options, add items to the *Ribbon* and the *Quick Access* toolbar, modify your Office account settings, and add an Office add-in.
Note: Use your education Microsoft account for this project. If you don't have an education Microsoft account, create one at https://products.office.com/en-us/student/office-in-education.

File Needed: ***StayingActive-12.docx*** *(Student data files are available in the* Library *of your SIMnet account.)*
Completed Project File Name: ***[your initials] PP W12-1.docx***

1. Open the ***StayingActive-12*** document from your student data files.

2. Save this document as [your initials] PP W12-1.

3. Log in to Office using your Microsoft account. Skip this step if you are already logged in with your Microsoft account.
   a. Click **Sign in** in the upper-right corner of the Word window.
   b. Log in to Office using your Microsoft account username and password. If you don't have a Microsoft account, go to https://products.office.com/en-us/student/office-in-education and follow the instructions to create a free education Microsoft account.

4. Customize Word options.
   a. Click the **File** tab to open the *Backstage* view and select **Options** to open the *Word Options* dialog box.
   b. Select **General** on the left, type your name and initials in the *User name* and *Initials* text boxes if they do not already display, and check the **Always use these values regardless of sign in to Office** box.
   c. Select **Display** on the left and check the **Update fields before printing** and **Update linked data before printing** boxes in the *Printing options* area.
   d. Select **Save** on the left and check the **Don't show the Backstage when opening or saving files** box in the *Save documents* area.

e. Select **Advanced** on the left and check the **Show bookmarks** box in the *Show document content* area if it is not already checked.

f. Click **OK** to close the *Word Options* dialog box and apply the changes.

5. Add and rename a custom tab and group.

a. Right-click anywhere on the **Ribbon** and select **Customize the Ribbon** from the context menu to open the *Word Options* dialog box and to display the *Customize Ribbon* area.

b. Click the **Home** tab on the right (under *Main Tabs*) and click the **New Tab** button. A new tab and group are inserted below the *Home* tab.

c. Select **New Tab (Custom)** and click the **Rename** button to open the *Rename* dialog box.

d. Type your first name and click **OK** to close the *Rename* dialog box.

e. Select **New Group (Custom)** and click the **Rename** button to open the *Rename* dialog box (Figure 12-30).

f. Select the smiley face symbol, type Common Commands in the *Display name* area, and click **OK** to close the *Rename* dialog box.

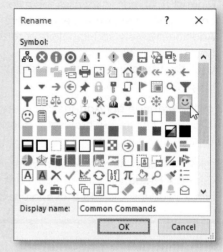

Figure 12-30 Rename new custom group

6. Add commands to a custom group on the *Ribbon*.

a. Select the new **Common Commands** group on the right.

b. Click the **Choose commands from** drop-down list on the left side and select **All Commands** to display all the available commands in the list on the left.

c. Scroll down and select the **Borders and Shading** command (the first one listed) and click the **Add** button to add the command to the group (Figure 12-31).

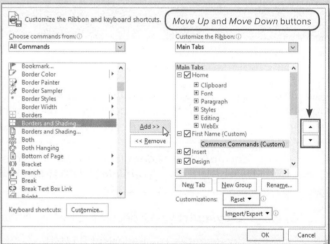

Figure 12-31 Add a command to a custom group

d. Select and add the **Tabs** and the **Custom Margins** commands to the *Common Commands* group.

e. Use the **Move Up** or **Move Down** button on the right to arrange the commands in alphabetical order.

f. Click **OK** to close the *Word Options* dialog box.

g. Click the **[your first name]** tab on the *Ribbon* (Figure 12-32).

7. Add commands to the *Quick Access* toolbar.

a. Click the **Customize Quick Access Toolbar** drop-down list and select **New** (Figure 12-33).

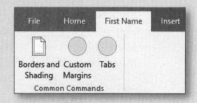

Figure 12-32 New tab and group

b. Add **Open** and **Quick Print** to the *Quick Access* toolbar from the *Customize Quick Access Toolbar* drop-down list.

c. Click the **Customize Quick Access Toolbar** drop-down list and select **More Commands** to open the *Word Options* dialog box and to display the *Quick Access Toolbar* area.

d. Scroll down the list on the left, select **Insert Comment**, and click the **Add** button (Figure 12-34).

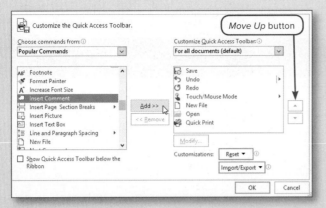

Figure 12-34 Add a command to the *Quick Access* toolbar

Figure 12-33 Add a command to the *Quick Access* toolbar

e. Select **Quick Print** on the right and use the **Move Up** button to rearrange it so it appears after *Save* in the *Quick Access* toolbar list of commands.

f. Click **OK** to close the *Word Options* dialog box.

8. Customize your Office account settings.

a. Click the **File** tab and select **Account** to display your account information on the *Backstage* view.

b. Click the **Office Background** drop-down list and select a background of your choice.

c. Click the **Office Theme** drop-down list and select a theme of your choice.

d. Click the **Add a service** drop-down list, select **Storage**, and click **Office 365 SharePoint** or **OneDrive**. Follow the prompts to connect your Microsoft account. Skip this step if your *SharePoint* or *OneDrive* is already connected.

e. Click the **Back** arrow to close the *Backstage* view.

9. Add an Office add-in. You must be logged in to your Microsoft account to add an add-in.

a. Click the **Get Add-ins** button [*Insert* tab, *Add-ins* group] to open the *Office Add-ins* dialog box (Figure 12-35).

b. Click **Editor's Picks** in the *Category* area to display the add-ins.

c. Select an add-in of your choice. A dialog box opens with information about the add-in.

d. Click **Add** to add the add-in. The add-in opens in the pane on the right. If the add-in does not automatically load in the *Add-ins* pane, click the **exclamation point** in the upper-left corner of the *Add-ins* pane to display information about the add-in, and then click the **Start** button to activate the add-in. Some add-ins display as a button on the *Ribbon*. Click the button to open the pane at the right.

e. Close the *Add-ins* pane.

Figure 12-35 Add an Office add-in

10. Save and close the document (Figure 12-36).

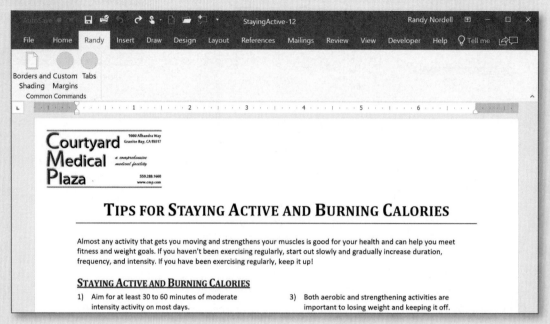

Figure 12-36 PP W12-1 completed (page 1 and customized *Ribbon* and *Quick Access* toolbar displayed)

Using OneDrive

Windows and Microsoft Office work in conjunction with your Microsoft account and **OneDrive** to provide online storage and access to your files from any computer. *OneDrive* is a secure "cloud" storage area. When you have or create a Microsoft account (Outlook.com, Live, Hotmail, MSN, Messenger, or other Microsoft service account), you also have a *OneDrive* account.

Use *OneDrive* to store files, create folders to organize stored files, and share files with others. Access your *OneDrive* files from a *File Explorer* window on your computer or access *OneDrive* online from any computer using an internet browser. If you don't have a Microsoft account, create a free education account at https://products.office.com/en-us/student/office-in-education or create a free personal account at https://signup.live.com.

> **MORE INFO**
>
> While *OneDrive* is secure and requires a user name and password to log in, no online accounts are 100 percent secure. Highly sensitive and confidential documents should not be stored online.

Use OneDrive in a File Explorer Window

When using Windows 10, *OneDrive* is one of the storage location folders, similar to the *Document* or *Pictures* folders (Figure 12-37). The **OneDrive folder** in a *File Explorer* window looks and functions similarly to other Windows folders. Save, open, and edit documents from the *OneDrive* folder. Also, create folders and rename, move, or delete files from your *OneDrive* folder. When opening the *Save As* or *Open* dialog box in Word, *OneDrive* is one of the available folders. In *Word Options*, you can set *OneDrive* as the default save location.

The primary difference between the *One-Drive* folder and other Windows folders is the physical location where files are stored. After saving a file in your *Documents* folder, the file is stored only on the hard drive on the computer, and you have access to this file only when working on your computer. When you save a document in your *OneDrive* folder, the file is stored on the computer and the *OneDrive* cloud, and you have access to the file from your computer *and* any other computer with internet access.

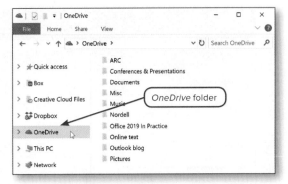

Figure 12-37 *OneDrive* folder displayed in a *File Explorer* window

> **MORE INFO**
>
> To access the *OneDrive* folder on your computer, you must be logged in using your Microsoft account.

Use OneDrive Online

The main benefit of using *OneDrive* to store files is the ability to access files from any computer with internet access. In addition to accessing *OneDrive* files from a *File Explorer* folder on your computer, access your *OneDrive* files from a web page using an internet browser. Sign in to the *OneDrive* web page (onedrive.com) using your Microsoft account.

> **MORE INFO**
>
> Depending on the internet browser you use (Chrome, Edge, or Firefox), the user interface, button options, and dialog boxes might be slightly different. Also, the *OneDrive* online environment changes regularly, so figures in this book might be slightly different from what is currently available.

▶ HOW TO: Use OneDrive Online

1. Open an internet browser window and go to the *OneDrive* web site (onedrive.com), which takes you to the *OneDrive* sign-in page.
   - You can use any internet browser to access *OneDrive* (Microsoft Edge, Google Chrome, or Mozilla Firefox).
2. Click the **Sign in** button, type your Microsoft account email address, and click **Next**.
3. Type your Microsoft account password and click **Sign in** to go to your *OneDrive* web page (Figure 12-38).
   - If using your own computer, check the **Keep me signed in** box to stay signed in to *OneDrive* when you return to the page.
   - The different areas of *OneDrive* display on the left side (*Files*, *Recent*, *Shared*, and *Recycle bin*) (Figure 12-39).
4. Choose from the view options on the *OneDrive* page in the upper-right corner of the window (Figure 12-40).
   - Click the **View** button to select from the different views: *List*, *Compact list*, or *Tiles*. Figure 12-39 displays *OneDrive* folders in *List* view.
   - Sort *OneDrive* files and folders by clicking the column heading and selecting a sort option.

Figure 12-38 Sign in to *OneDrive*

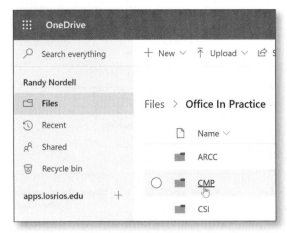

Figure 12-39 *OneDrive* online environment

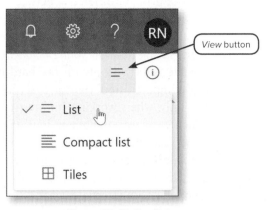

Figure 12-40 *OneDrive* view options

5. Click the **Files** button on the left to display your folders and files in the *Files* area on the right.

6. Click the **circle** to the left of a file or folder to select it (Figure 12-41).
   - Use the buttons and drop-down menus at the top to perform actions on selected files and folders.

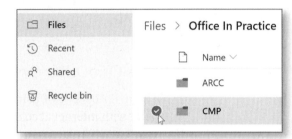

Figure 12-41 Select a *OneDrive* folder

7. Click a file or folder to open it (Figure 12-42).
   - Click an Office file to open the file in *Office Online* (see *SLO 12.5: Using Office Online*).
   - Click a folder to open the folder and display the folder contents. Click **Files** on the left or at the top to return to all *OneDrive* files.

8. Click your name or picture icon in the upper-right corner and select **Sign out** to sign out of *OneDrive*.

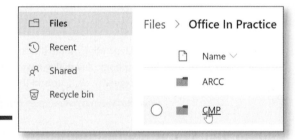

Figure 12-42 Open a *OneDrive* folder

> **MORE INFO**
> If you're using a personal or business Microsoft account, the *OneDrive* online environment and features differ slightly.

Create a OneDrive Folder

Create folders in *OneDrive* online to organize your files. The hierarchy of folders and files in *OneDrive* is similar to *File Explorer*.

▶ **HOW TO: Create a OneDrive Folder**

1. Sign in to *OneDrive* from an internet browser window (onedrive.com).
2. Click the **Files** button on the left to display the contents of your *OneDrive* folder in the *Files* area on the right.
3. Click the **New** button and select **Folder** from the drop-down list (Figure 12-43). A new folder window opens.

4. Type the name of the new folder and click **Create**.
   - An icon displays in the upper-left corner of the folder or file name to indicate a new *OneDrive* folder or file.
5. Click a folder to open it.
   - Create a new folder inside an existing folder or upload files to the folder (see the following *Upload a File* section).
6. Click **Files** on the left to return to the main *OneDrive* folder.

> **MORE INFO**
>
> After creating or uploading files or folders online in *OneDrive*, these changes also display in the *OneDrive* folder in *File Explorer* on your computer.

Figure 12-43 Create a new *OneDrive* folder

Upload a File or Folder

Upload files to *OneDrive* from a folder on your computer or a portable storage device. When uploading files to *OneDrive*, you are not removing the files from the original location, but rather copying them to *OneDrive*.

▶ **HOW TO: Upload a File or Folder to OneDrive**

1. Click **Files** on the left to display your files and folders in the *Files* area on the right.
   - If you are uploading a file to a specific folder, click the folder to open it.

2. Click the **Upload** button and select **File** or **Folder** (Figure 12-44).
   - The actions for this button may vary depending on the internet browser you use. Some browsers open a dialog box when you click the *Upload* button rather than displaying the *File* and *Folder* options.
   - The dialog box that opens varies depending on the browser you use and the upload choice you make.

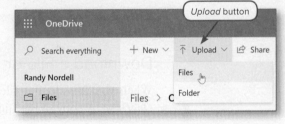

Figure 12-44 Upload a file to *OneDrive*

3. Select the file(s) or folder to upload to *OneDrive* and click **Open** (Figure 12-45).
   - You may have to click **OK** or **Select Folder** depending on the browser you use and whether you are uploading a file or folder.
   - You can upload more than one file at a time. Use the **Ctrl** key to select non-adjacent files, the **Shift** key to select a range of files, or **Ctrl+A** to select all files in a folder.
   - An upload status indicator appears in the upper-right corner when uploading files or a folder.

Figure 12-45 Select a file to upload to *OneDrive*

Move, Copy, or Delete a File or Folder

You can also move, copy, and delete files and folders online in *OneDrive*. When moving a file or folder, it is removed from its current location and moved to the new location you select. When copying a file or folder, it is copied to the new location you select, and the file or folder also remains in its original location.

Figure 12-46 Move or copy a *OneDrive* file

▶ **HOW TO:** Move, Copy, or Delete OneDrive Files

1. Check the **circle** to the left of the file or folder you want to move or copy.
   - Move multiple items by selecting the check boxes of all the items to move.
2. Click the **Move to** or **Copy to** button at the top (Figure 12-46). A *Move item to* or *Copy item to* pane opens on the right.
3. Select the **Your OneDrive** to display a list of *OneDrive* folders.
4. Select the folder where you want to move or copy the selected item(s).
   - Click **New folder** and type a folder name to create a new folder.
5. Click the **Move here** or **Copy here** button (Figure 12-47).
6. Delete a file or folder by checking the **circle** to the left of the item(s) to delete and then clicking the **Delete** button at the top.

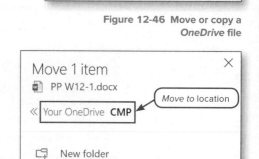

Figure 12-47 Move selected item(s)

▶ **MORE INFO**
If you are using a personal Microsoft account, the move and copy options differ slightly.

Download a File or Folder

When you download a file or folder from *OneDrive*, the file or folder is not removed from *OneDrive*. A copy of the file or folder is downloaded to the location you specify.

▶ **HOW TO:** Download a File or Folder from OneDrive

1. Check the **circle** to the left of the file or folder you want to download.
   - If you select more than one file or an entire folder to download, a compressed (zipped) folder downloads.
   - If you select a single file, *OneDrive* downloads the file.
2. Click the **Download** button at the top. Depending on the internet browser you use, the download actions differ slightly.
   - *Google Chrome*: Click the **Download** button and the *Save As* dialog box opens (Figure 12-48).
   - *Microsoft Edge*: Click the **Download** button, and the download options display at the bottom of the browser window.

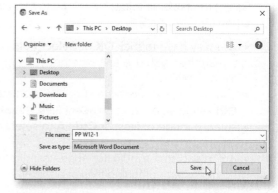

Figure 12-48 Save a downloaded file from *OneDrive*

- *Mozilla Firefox*: Click the **Download** button, and the *Opening [File name]* dialog box opens where you select the option to open or save the file or folder.

3. Select the location where you want to save the downloaded items.
4. Type a file name in the *File name* area if you want to rename the file.
5. Click the **Save** button to close the *Save As* dialog box and download the selected items.

Sharing OneDrive Files and Folders

In addition to being able to access all your *OneDrive* files from any computer or mobile device, you can also share files and folders. Sharing provides the ability to collaborate with others on individual files, or you can share a folder where others can view, download, upload, and edit files. When sharing files and folders, you control the users' level of access by selecting a permission level to allow users to view or edit files, or remove the sharing permission.

Share a File in Word

Within Word, you can share a file stored on *OneDrive* using the **Share** pane. If you try to share a file that is not saved in *OneDrive*, Word prompts you to save the file in *One-Drive* before sharing it. Depending on the type of Microsoft account you're using, the sharing options display in a **Send Link** window (education and business Microsoft accounts) (Figure 12-49) or the **Share** pane (personal Microsoft account). The *Send Link* window or *Share* pane displays a variety of sharing options.

Figure 12-49 *Send Link* window

▶**HOW TO:** Share a File in Word

1. Open the file to share.
   - If the file is not saved in *OneDrive*, save the file to *OneDrive*.
2. Click the **Share** button (Figure 12-50) in the upper-right corner of the Word window to open the *Send Link* window (see Figure 12-49). The *Share* button icon may display differently in Office 2019.
   - If you're using a personal Microsoft account, the *Share* pane opens at the right after you click the *Share* button.
3. Type the email address of the person with whom you are sharing the file in the *Enter a name or email address* area.
   - If typing multiple email addresses, separate each with a semicolon.
4. Click the **Link settings** button (see Figure 12-49) to open the *Link settings* window (Figure 12-51).
   - Select who can use the sharing link.
   - Check the **Allow editing** box to enable recipients to edit the shared file. Deselect the **Allow editing** box to enable recipients to open and view the shared file, but restrict them from editing it.
   - Set an expiration date for the sharing link if desired (optional).

Figure 12-50 *Share* button

5. Click **Apply** to set the sharing link options and to return to the *Send Link* window (see Figure 12-49).

6. Type a message to recipient(s) in the *Add a message* area. This is optional.

7. Click the **Send** button. An email is sent to people you invited.

8. Click the **X** to close the confirmation window.

Figure 12-51 *Link settings window*

> ► **ANOTHER WAY**
>
> You can also send a file as an attachment through email. Click the **Send a Copy** link at the bottom of the *Send Link* window and select **Word Document** or **PDF**.

Create a Sharing Link

Another way to share a file with others is to create a sharing link (hyperlink), copy it, and email the sharing link to recipients. Also, you can paste a sharing link in a Word document or other online location.

> ►**HOW TO:** Create a Sharing Link

1. Open the file to share.

   - If the file is not saved in *OneDrive*, you are prompted to save the file to *OneDrive*.

2. Click the **Share** button in the upper right of the Word window to open the *Send Link* window (Figure 12-52).

   - If you're using a personal Microsoft account, the *Share* pane opens at the right after you click the *Share* button.

3. Click the **Link settings** button to open the *Link settings* window (see Figure 12-51).

   - Select who can use the sharing link.
   - Check the **Allow editing** box to enable recipients to edit the shared file. Deselect the **Allow editing** box to enable recipients to open and view the shared file, but restrict them from editing it.
   - Set an expiration date for the sharing link if desired (optional).

4. Click **Apply** to set the sharing link options and to return to the *Send Link* window.

5. Click the **Copy Link** button (see Figure 12-52) to open the window that displays the sharing link (Figure 12-53).

6. Click the **Copy** button to copy the sharing link.

7. Click the **X** to close the confirmation window.

8. Paste the copied sharing link in an email, Word document, or other online location.

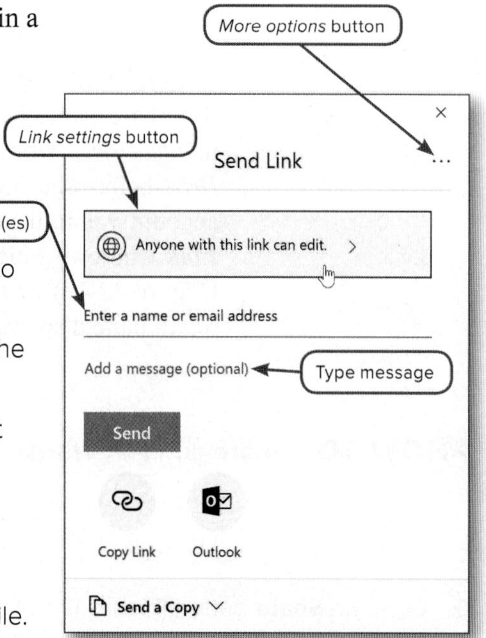

Figure 12-52 *Send Link window*

Figure 12-53 Copy a sharing link

Edit or Disable a Sharing Link

After sharing a file with others, you can edit the sharing permission or disable the sharing link.

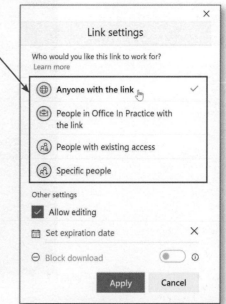

▶**HOW TO:** Edit or Disable a Sharing Link

1. Open the shared file.
2. Click the **Share** button in the upper-right corner of the Word window to open the *Send Link* window (see Figure 12-52).
   - If you're using a personal Microsoft account, the *Share* pane opens at the right after you click the *Share* button and the edit and disable options differ slightly.
3. Click the **Link settings** button to open the *Link settings* window (Figure 12-54).
   - Change who can access the sharing link.
   - Check or uncheck the **Allow editing** box to change sharing permission.
4. Click **Apply** to return to the *Send Link* window.
5. Disable a sharing link by clicking the **More options** button (ellipsis) and selecting **Manage Access** (Figure 12-55). The *Manage Access* window opens (Figure 12-56).
   - The *Manage Access* window displays sharing links and the owner of the file.

Figure 12-54 *Link settings* window

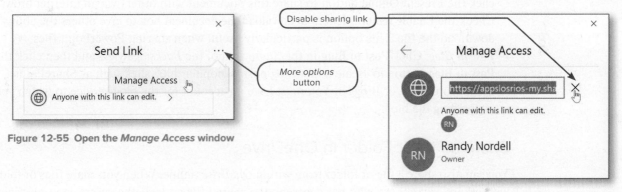

Figure 12-55 Open the *Manage Access* window

Figure 12-56 *Manage Access* window

6. Click the **X** to the right of a sharing link to disable the sharing link.
7. Click the **X** to close the *Manage Access* window.

Other Sharing Options in Word

Word also provides other ways to share files. You can email a file, email a PDF version of a file, present a file online, or post a file to a blog (web log). Click the **Share** button on the *Backstage* view to display and use the other sharing options.

- *Email*: Click the **Email** button in the *Share* area on the *Backstage* view to display the different email options (Figure 12-57). You can *Send as Attachment, Send a Link, Send as a PDF, Send as XPS,* and *Send as Internet Fax.* For the first four options to function, Microsoft Outlook must be set up on your computer. To *Send as Internet Fax,* you must first sign up with a fax service provider.

Figure 12-57 Share a file through email

- *Present Online*: Click **Present Online** in the *Share* area of the *Backstage* view and then click the **Present Online** button to share this document with others via an internet browser. Check the **Enable remote viewers to download the document** box to give others the ability to download the file. This option is particularly useful when sharing PowerPoint files.
- *Post to Blog*: Click **Post to Blog** in the *Share* area of the *Backstage* view and then click the **Post to Blog** button to create a new blog post to popular blog sites such as SharePoint Blog, WordPress, or Blogger. You must have an account for the blog service to which you are posting the blog.

Share a File or Folder in OneDrive

You can also share a file or folder from within *OneDrive* online. When you share files or folders with others, you choose who has access to the shared file and whether users can only view or edit the files and folders. When you share a file or folder in *OneDrive*, you have the option to send an email with a link to the shared item or generate a link to share with others.

> **MORE INFO**
>
> Microsoft regularly updates *OneDrive* online. Figures in this chapter may appear slightly different from how *OneDrive* displays in your internet browser. The figures in this section display *OneDrive* using the Google Chrome web browser.

▶HOW TO: Share a OneDrive File or Folder

1. Open an internet browser and log in to your *OneDrive* account (onedrive.com).
2. Select (check the circle) the file or folder you want to share.
   - If you share a folder, shared users have access to all the files in the folder.

3. Click the **Share** button at the top of the OneDrive window to open the *Send Link* window. If you're using a personal Microsoft account, the *Share* window opens and the sharing options differ slightly (Figure 12-58).

4. Click the **Link settings** button to open the *Link settings* window (Figure 12-59).

   - Select who can use the sharing link.
   - Check the **Allow editing** box to enable recipients to edit the shared file. Deselect the **Allow editing** box to enable recipients to open and view the shared file, but restrict them from editing it.
   - Set an expiration date for the sharing link if desired (optional).

5. Click **Apply** to return to the *Send Link* window.

6. Send a sharing link by typing recipient(s) email address(es), typing a brief message, and clicking the **Send** button (see Figure 12-58). Close the confirmation window.

7. Alternatively, create a sharing link by clicking the **Copy Link** button (see Figure 12-58) and clicking the **Copy** button in the window that opens (Figure 12-60). Close the copy link window.

Figure 12-58 Share a file or folder in *OneDrive*

Figure 12-59 *Link settings* window

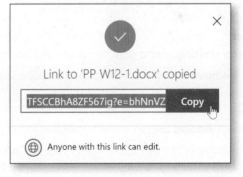

Figure 12-60 Copy a sharing link

Change OneDrive Sharing Permission

You can change the sharing permission or remove sharing on a file or folder from within OneDrive. The ***Information pane*** on the right displays properties of the selected file or folder.

▶HOW TO: Change or Remove OneDrive Sharing

1. Select the shared file or folder in *OneDrive* online (onedrive.com).
2. Click the **Information** button in the upper-right corner to open the *Details* pane on the right (Figure 12-61).
3. Click the **Manage access** link in the *Has Access* area to open the *Manage Access* area (Figure 12-62).
   - The *Manage Access* area in the *Details* pane lists sharing permissions for the selected file or folder.

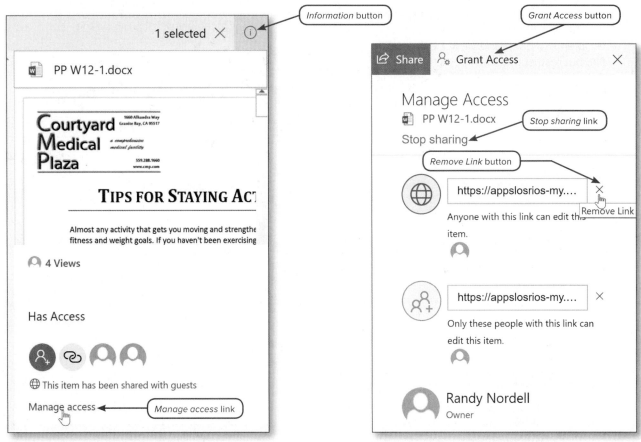

Figure 12-61 *Details pane in OneDrive*   Figure 12-62 *Manage Access pane*

4. Click the **Stop sharing** link to remove all sharing access to the file.
   - Click the **Remove Link** button (**X**) to the right of a specific sharing link to disable the sharing link (see Figure 12-62).
   - Copy a sharing link by clicking the link and pressing **Ctrl+C**.
5. Click the **Grant Access** button at the top of the *Manage Access* pane to open a *Grant Access* window.
   - Add email address(es), select permission level (**Can view** or **Can edit**), type a brief message, and click **Grant Access** to add recipients to the shared file.
6. Click the **X** in the upper-right corner of the *Manage Access* pane to close it and return to the *Details* pane.
7. Click the **Information** button to close the *Details* pane.

Using Office Online

Microsoft *Office Online* is a free online suite of apps that work in conjunction with your Microsoft account and your online *OneDrive* account. *Office Online* enables you to work with Office files online *without* installing the desktop version of Office 365 or 2019.

Office Online apps are available from your *OneDrive* account (onedrive.com) or Microsoft account web page (office.com) (Figure 12-63). *Office Online* is an online (internet browser-based) version of the desktop version of Office 365 or 2019 and not as robust in terms of features, but you can create, edit, print, share, and insert comments in files. If you need more advanced features, open an *Office Online* document in the desktop version of the Office application.

Click the *App launcher* button to display a menu of apps

Figure 12-63 *Office Online* apps

> **MORE INFO**
>
> Microsoft regularly updates the *Office Online* products and online environment. Figures in this chapter may appear slightly different from how *Office Online* displays in your internet browser. Also, Microsoft Access is not available in *Office Online*.

Edit an Office Online File

Use *Office Online* to open and edit Office files you have stored in *OneDrive*. The working environment in *Office Online* is very similar to Microsoft Office and has the familiar *Ribbon*, tabs, and groups. However, not as many features are available in *Office Online*. From within the *Office Online* apps, you can open and edit a file in the desktop application.

▶HOW TO: Edit an Office Online File

1. Log in to your *OneDrive* account in an internet browser window (onedrive.com).

2. Click an Office file (the file name, not the circle on the left) to open from *OneDrive* (Figure 12-64). The file displays in the *Office Online* app in your browser.

   • Alternatively, select a file (check circle), click the **Open** drop-down list, and select **Open in [Office application] Online** or **Open in [Office application]**.

3. Click the **Simplified Ribbon** button to toggle on or off the *Simplified Ribbon* (Figure 12-65).

   • The *Simplified Ribbon* may not be available on all *Office Online* apps.

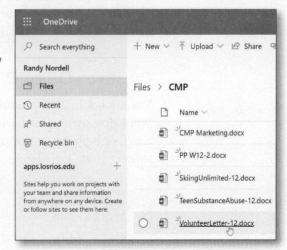

Figure 12-64 Open a *OneDrive* file in *Office Online*

- The *Simplified Ribbon* displays fewer options on the *Ribbon*. When this feature is turned off, more options display on the *Ribbon*, and the *Ribbon* appears similar to the *Ribbon* on the desktop applications.

Figure 12-65 *Simplified Ribbon*

4. Edit and apply formatting changes in *Office Online* (Figure 12-66).

- When using *Office Online*, advanced formatting such as text boxes, pictures, charts, and *SmartArt* might not display as they do when you open the file in the desktop version of Office 365 or 2019.
- *Word Online* automatically saves changes to files.

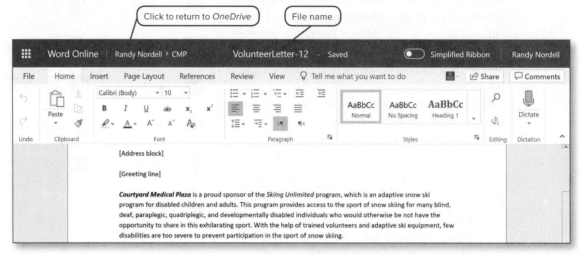

Figure 12-66 Edit a document in *Word Online*

5. Close the browser tab to close the *Office Online* document.

- When opening a file in *Office Online*, the file opens in a new tab and *OneDrive* remains open in the previous browser tab.
- Alternatively, click the **[Your Name]** link (or **Apps launcher**) near the top left to return to your *OneDrive* folders and files (see Figure 12-66).

> **MORE INFO**
>
> The *Simplified Ribbon* may not be available on all *Office Online* apps. The *Ribbon* in the *Office Online* apps may vary slightly depending on the type of Microsoft account you are using.

Create an Office Online File

You are not limited to editing existing documents in *Office Online*; you can also create a new Word document, Excel workbook, PowerPoint presentation, OneNote notebook, *Forms for Excel*, or a plain text document. When you create an *Office Online* file, the file automatically saves in your *OneDrive*.

> **MORE INFO**
>
> *OneNote* and *Forms* are discussed later in *SLO 12.6: Exploring Other Office Online Applications*.

▶HOW TO: Create an Office Online File

1. Select the location in *OneDrive* to create a new file.
2. Click the **New** button and select the type of file to create (**Word document**, **Excel workbook**, **PowerPoint presentation**, **OneNote notebook**, **Forms for Excel**, or **Plain text document**) (Figure 12-67). A new file opens in *edit* mode.
3. Type information in the file and apply formatting as desired.
   - *Office Online* automatically saves changes to the file.
4. Rename the file by clicking the default file name in the *Title* bar and typing a new file name (Figure 12-68).
   - Alternatively, click the **File** tab and select **Save As** for other saving options.

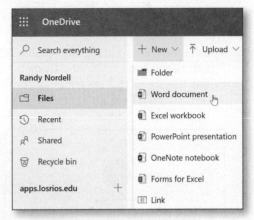

Figure 12-67 Create a *Word Online* document

Figure 12-68 Rename a document in *Word Online*

5. Close the browser tab to close the *Office Online* file.
   - Alternatively, click the *[Your Name]* link (top left) to return to your *OneDrive* folders and files (see Figure 12-68).

Share an Office Online File

In addition to sharing a file from *OneDrive*, you can also share an *Office Online* file. You have the option to send a sharing email or get a link to share the file. The process for sharing a file in *Office Online* is similar to sharing a file or folder in *OneDrive*.

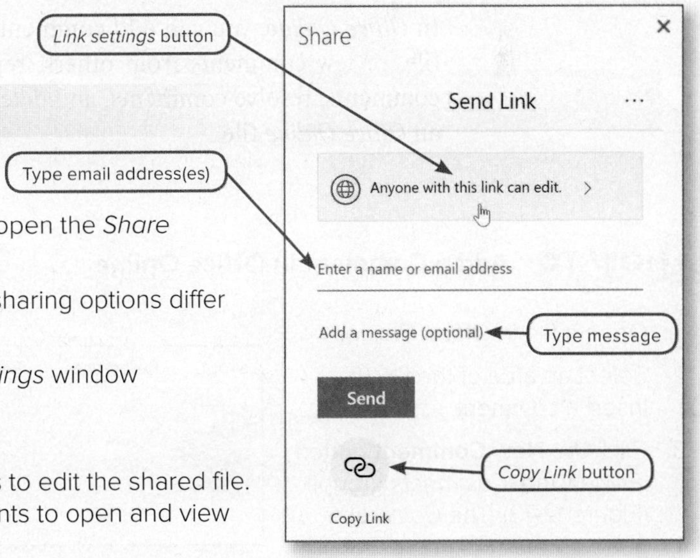

▶HOW TO: Share an Office Online File

1. Open a file in *Office Online*.
2. Click the **Share** button in the upper-right corner to open the *Share* window (Figure 12-69).
   - If you're using a personal Microsoft account, the sharing options differ slightly in the *Share* window.
3. Click the **Link settings** button to open the *Link settings* window (Figure 12-70).
   - Select who can use the sharing link.
   - Check the **Allow editing** box to enable recipients to edit the shared file. Deselect the **Allow editing** box to enable recipients to open and view the shared file, but restrict them from editing it.
   - Set an expiration date for the sharing link if desired (optional).

Figure 12-69 Share a file in *Office Online*

4. Click **Apply** to return to the *Share* window.

5. Send a sharing link by typing recipient(s) email address(es), typing a brief message, and clicking the **Send** button (see Figure 12-69). Close the confirmation window.

6. Alternatively, create a sharing link by clicking the **Copy Link** button (see Figure 12-69) and clicking the **Copy** button in the *Share* window that opens (Figure 12-71). Close the *Share* window.

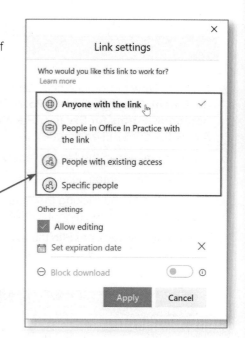

Figure 12-71 Copy a sharing link

Figure 12-70 *Link settings* window

Collaborate in Office Online

Use *Office Online* to collaborate with others who have permission to edit the shared Office file. If two or more users are working on the same file in *Office Online*, collaboration information displays as a tag in the *Office Online* file (Figure 12-72). Changes to the file automatically save and apply to the file.

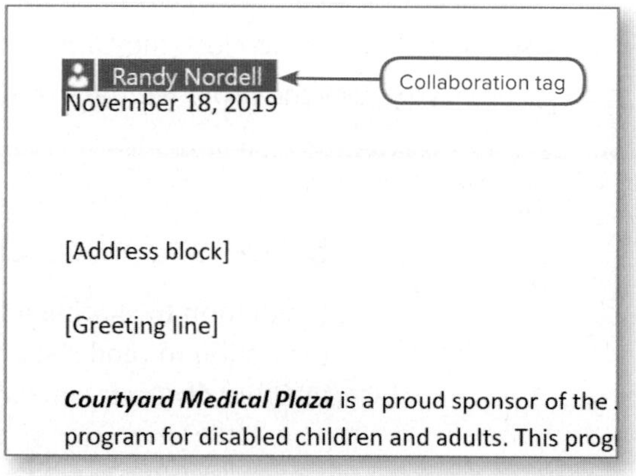

Use Comments in Office Online

In *Office Online*, you can add comments to a file, review comments from others, reply to comments, resolve comments, and delete comments. Use the *Review* tab to add a comment to an *Office Online* file.

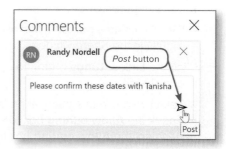

Figure 12-72 Collaborating on an *Office Online* file

▶ **HOW TO: Add a Comment in Office Online**

1. Open a file in *Office Online*.

2. Select an area of the file to insert a comment.

3. Click the **New Comment** button [*Review* tab, *Comments* group] (Figure 12-73). The *Comments* pane opens at the right (Figure 12-74).

Figure 12-73 Insert a *New Comment*

Figure 12-74 Post a comment in *Office Online*

4. Type a comment in the comment text box in the *Comments* pane and click the **Post** button to post the comment (see Figure 12-74).

5. Click the **X** in the upper-right corner of the *Comments* pane or click the **Show Comments** button [*Review* tab, *Comments* group] to close the pane.

Review Comments in Office Online

When reviewing your own comments or comments from others, click a comment balloon in the document or click the **Show Comments** button [*Review* tab, *Comments* group] to open the *Comments* pane on the right. Click the **More thread actions** button (ellipsis) in the upper-right corner of a comment to display comment actions (Figure 12-75). You can perform the following actions on existing comments:

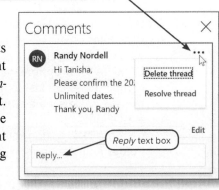

Figure 12-75 Comment actions

- Click the **Reply** text box, type a comment, and click the **Send** button.
- Click the **More thread actions** button and select **Resolve thread** to mark a comment as done after you have acted on the comment or when it is no longer relevant.
- Click the **More thread actions** button and select the **Delete thread** button to delete a comment.

PAUSE & PRACTICE: WORD 12-2

For this project, create a folder in *OneDrive*, upload files to *OneDrive*, edit a document in *Word Online*, create a *Word Online* document, and share a *OneDrive* folder.

Note to Instructor and Students:

Use your education Microsoft account for this project. If you don't have an education Microsoft account, create one at https://products.office.com/en-us/student/office-in-education.

Microsoft regularly updates the Office Online *products and* OneDrive *online environment. Instructions and figures in this project may differ slightly from how* Office Online *and* OneDrive *display in your internet browser. The Google Chrome web browser is used for instructions and figures in this project.*

Files Needed: **[your initials] PP W12-1.docx**, **SkiingUnlimited-12.docx**, **TeenSubstanceAbuse-12.docx**, and **VolunteerLetter-12** *(Student data files are available in the* Library *of your SIMnet account.)*
Completed Project Folder and File Names: **CMP** *OneDrive* folder containing the following five files: **CMP Marketing, [your initials] PP W12-2.docx, SkiingUnlimited-12.docx, TeenSubstanceAbuse-12.docx,** and **VolunteerLetter-12.docx**

1. Log in to *OneDrive* online using your education Microsoft account.
   a. Open an internet browser window and go to the *OneDrive* web site (onedrive.com), which takes you to the *OneDrive* sign-in page. You can use any internet browser to access *OneDrive* (Microsoft Edge, Google Chrome, or Mozilla Firefox).

b. Click the **Sign in** button, type your Microsoft account email address, and click **Next**.

c. Type your Microsoft account password and click **Sign in** to go to your *OneDrive* web page (Figure 12-76). If using your own computer, check the **Keep me signed in** box to stay signed in to *OneDrive* when you return to the page.

2. Create a new folder, upload files, and rename a file.
   a. Click **Files** on the left to display the contents of your *OneDrive* folder.
   b. Click the **View options** button in the upper-right corner and select **List** to display your folders and files in *List* view if they do not already display as a list (Figure 12-77).
   c. Click the **New** button at the top and select **Folder** from the drop-down list (Figure 12-78).

Figure 12-76 Sign in to *OneDrive*

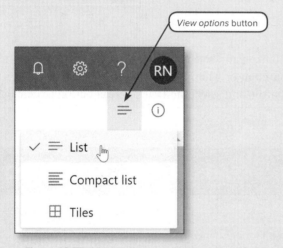
Figure 12-77 *View options* button in *OneDrive*

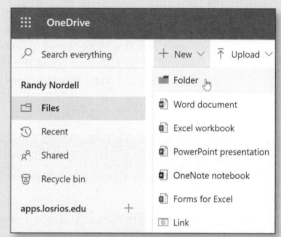
Figure 12-78 Create a new folder in *OneDrive*

d. Type **CMP** as the name for the new folder and click **Create**.
e. Click the **CMP** folder to open the folder.
f. Click the **Upload** button at the top and select **Files** to open an upload dialog box. The name of this dialog box may vary depending on the internet browser you are using.
g. Select the *[your initials] PP W12-1* file from *Pause & Practice 12-1* and click **Open** to upload this file to the **CMP** folder.
h. Repeat the above process to upload the **SkiingUnlimited-12**, **TeenSubstanceAbuse-12**, and **VolunteerLetter-12** files from your student data files (use the **Ctrl** key to select non-adjacent files). Four files should display in your **CMP** folder in *OneDrive*.
i. Check the circle to the left of the *[your initials] PP W12-1* file and click the **Rename** button to open the *Rename* dialog box. If the *Rename* button does not display at the top, click the **ellipsis** button to display additional options.
j. Change the file name to [your initials] PP W12-2 and click **Save**.

3. Edit a file in *Word Online*.
   a. Click the **VolunteerLetter-12** file in the **CMP** folder to open it in *Word Online*.
   b. Click the **Simplified Ribbon** button near the upper right to turn off the *Simplified Ribbon* (if necessary).

c. Replace the ski dates placeholder text and brackets in the bulleted list with the following dates:
   January 11
   January 25
   February 1
   February 8
   February 15

Figure 12-79 Add a comment

4. Add a comment to the document and close the document.
   a. Select the items in the bulleted list.
   b. Click the **New Comment** button [*Review* tab, *Comments* group] to open a new comment in the *Comments* pane on the right.
   c. Type **Please confirm these dates with Tanisha** in the comment text box and click the **Post** button (Figure 12-79).
   d. Click the **X** in the upper-right corner of the *Comments* pane to close the pane.
   e. Click the **X** on the ***VolunteerLetter-12*** tab of the browser to close the ***VolunteerLetter-12*** document (Figure 12-80).

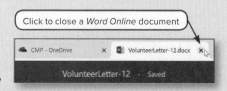
Figure 12-80 Close a *Word Online* document

5. Create a new Word document in *Word Online*.
   a. Confirm the ***CMP*** folder is open in *OneDrive* in the browser window. If not, open it.
   b. Deselect the ***VolunteerLetter-12*** if it is selected (checked).
   c. Click the **New** button and select **Word document**. A new document opens in *Word Online*.
   d. Select the file name at the top, type **CMP Marketing** as the new file name, and press **Enter**.

CMP Marketing
 • Skiing Unlimited (January and February)
 • Health Lifestyle Workshops (April and October)
 • Substance Abuse Prevention Conference (June)

Figure 12-81 *CMP Marketing* document in *Word Online*

   e. Place the insertion point in the document, type **CMP Marketing** on the first line of the document, and press **Enter**.

Figure 12-82 Return to the *OneDrive* folder

   f. Click the **Bullets** button [*Home* tab, *Paragraph* group] to turn on bullets and type the following three bulleted items:
   Skiing Unlimited (January and February)
   Healthy Lifestyle Workshops (April and October)
   Substance Abuse Prevention Conference (June)
   g. Select "**CMP Marketing**," apply the **Heading 1** style [*Home* tab, *Styles* group], and **bold** formatting (Figure 12-81).
   h. Click the **CMP** link near the upper-left corner of the *Word Online* window to return to the ***CMP*** folder in *OneDrive* (Figure 12-82). You should now have five files in your ***CMP*** folder in *OneDrive*.

6. Share the ***CMP*** folder with your instructor.
   a. Click **Files** on the left to return to your *OneDrive* folders and files.
   b. Check the circle to the left of the ***CMP*** folder to select the folder.
   c. Click **Share** at the top to open the *Send Link* window (Figure 12-83). If you are using a personal Microsoft account, sharing options differ.

Figure 12-83 *Send Link* window

d. Click the **Link settings** button to open the *Link settings* window (Figure 12-84).

e. Select the **Anyone with the link** option.

f. Deselect the **Allow editing** check box.

g. Click **Apply** to return to the *Send Link* window.

h. Type your instructor's email address in the **Enter a name or email address** area and type a brief message in the **Add a message** area.

i. Click **Send** to send your instructor the sharing link.

j. Click the **X** in the upper-right corner of the sharing confirmation window.

7. Return to *OneDrive* and sign out of your account. Figure 12-85 displays files in the **CMP** folder.

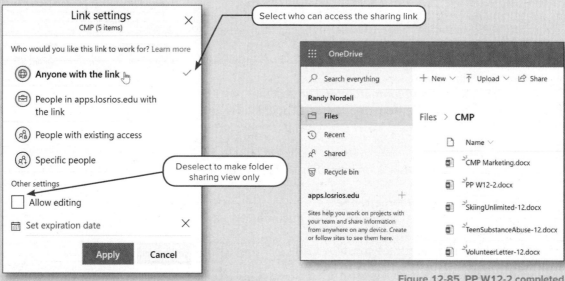

Figure 12-84 *Link settings* window

Figure 12-85 PP W12-2 completed (*CMP* folder in *OneDrive*)

Exploring Other Office Online Applications

A Microsoft account provides access to many Microsoft online applications in addition to *OneDrive* and *Word Online*. In *Office Online*, you have access to the main applications in Office 365 and 2019 (except Access) and additional online applications not available in the desktop version of Office such as *Forms* and *Sway*.

Office Online

Office Online provides online access to the most popular Office applications. All these programs are free with your Microsoft account. Each of these applications have the look and feel of the desktop version but do not include as many features.

Log in to *Office Online* (office. com) using your Microsoft account. The *Apps* area displays many of the available apps (Figure 12-86). You can

Figure 12-86 *Apps* area in *Office Online*

also click the **App launcher** button (Figure 12-87) in the upper-left corner of the *Office Online* to display and choose from the list of apps (the *App launcher* button is available in all areas of *Office Online* and *OneDrive*). The available options may display differently whether you access this menu from *Office Online* or *OneDrive*.

Forms

Office Online gives users the ability to create *Forms* to gather data. A form is essentially a survey or questionnaire. It is created in the *Forms* area in *Office Online* (Figure 12-88) and is shared via email or posted in an online environment. Respondents complete the online *Form* in an internet browser window, and responses to the *Form* are automatically added to the *Form* file in the *Forms* area of *Office Online*. The creator of the *Form* does not receive individual email survey responses but can easily view survey results in *Forms* or open and view the response data in the Excel desktop application.

Figure 12-87 List of *Office Online* apps

> **MORE INFO**
>
> *Forms* is now available in education, business, and personal Microsoft accounts. Previously, *Excel Survey* was available in personal Microsoft accounts.

Create and Share a Form

Forms provides a variety of question types, themes, and customization options for you to create a professional-looking survey. Before creating a *Form*, plan the questions to be asked and the types of questions to be used. After creating a form, create a sharing link to email to recipients.

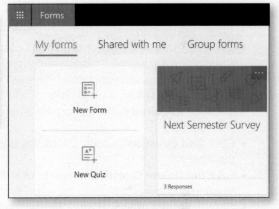

Figure 12-88 *Apps* area in *Office Online*

▶**HOW TO: Create and Share a Form**

1. Log in to *Office Online* (office.com) using your Microsoft account.
2. Click the **Forms** in the *Apps* area (see Figure 12-86) to open the *Forms* area (see Figure 12-88). If *Forms* does not display in the *Apps* area, click **Explore all your apps** to display all available *Office Online* apps.
   - Alternatively, if you're already logged in to *OneDrive* or *Office Online*, click the **App launcher** button and select **Forms** (see Figure 12-87).
3. Click **New Form** to create a new *Form*.

4. Enter a title and description (optional) for the form.

   - Click the **Insert image** button to search for or select an image to insert above the title.
   - *Forms* automatically saves the form as you make changes.

5. Click the **Add question** button to display a list of question types (Figure 12-89).

   - Click the **More question types** button to display additional question types.

6. Select a question type to add a question to the form (Figure 12-90).

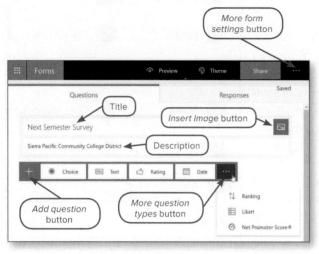

Figure 12-89 Add a question to a *Form*

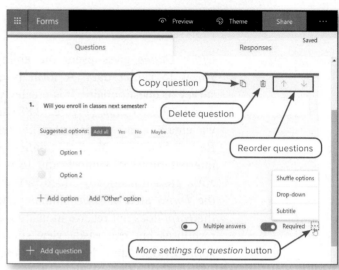

Figure 12-90 Type a question description and customize options

- Type the question text.
- Click the **More settings for question** button to add a subtitle and customize response options.
- Customize the response content. This will vary depending on the type of question.
- Click the **Required** button to require a response to the question.
- Click **Add question** to continue adding questions to the *Form*.
- Click the **Delete Question** button to delete an existing question.
- Click the **Move question up** or **Move question down** arrows to reorder questions.

7. Click the **Theme** button to apply a preset theme color or picture.

   - Click the **Custom theme** button (**+**) to select a picture or custom color.

8. Click the **Preview** button to view how your form will display to recipients.

   - Click the **Mobile** button to view how your form will display on a mobile device.
   - Click the **Back** button to return to the form editing area.

9. Click the **Share** button display sharing options (Figure 12-91).

   - Click the drop-down list to select who can respond to the form and select **Anyone with the link can respond** or **Only people in my organization can respond**.

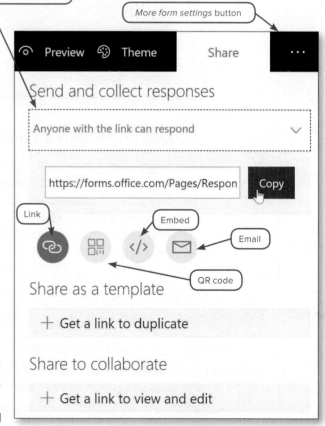

Figure 12-91 *Form* sharing options

- Click the **More form settings** button to display additional sharing options.
- In addition to creating a sharing link, you can also generate a QR or embed code or open an email with the sharing link (requires Microsoft Outlook).

10. Click the **Copy** button to copy the sharing link. Use your email to email the sharing link to recipients.

11. Click **Forms** to return to the *Forms* area or click the **App launcher** button and select **Office 365** or **OneDrive** to return to Office Online or *OneDrive*.

Respond to a Form

After emailing a *Form* sharing link to recipients, they can click the sharing link (or QR or embed code) to open the form on a computer, tablet, or mobile device. Recipients respond to the form questions and click the **Submit** button to record responses (Figure 12-92). Required questions are marked with a red asterisk and must be answered in order to submit the form. The responses are automatically stored in the *Form* rather than emailed to the creator of the form.

View Form Responses

Forms collect and consolidate responses from recipients. The results are stored and can be viewed in the *Forms* area in *Office Online*. *Forms* by default displays a summary of responses, but you can view individual responses or details about each question. Also, you can open and view responses in the Excel desktop application.

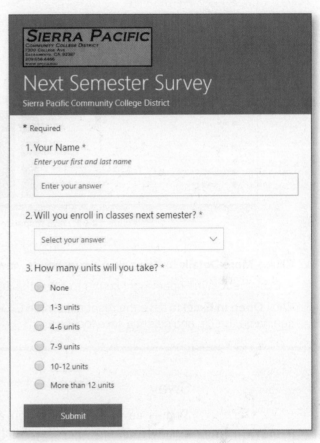

Figure 12-92 Complete and submit a *Form*

▶ **HOW TO: View Form Responses**

1. Log in to *Office Online* (office.com) using your Microsoft account and click **Forms** in the *Apps* area.
   - If you are in *OneDrive*, click the **App launcher** button and select **Forms** or **Forms for Excel**.

2. Click a form to open it and click the **Reponses** tab (Figure 12-93).
   - A summary of responses displays below the form title and details the number of responses, average time to complete, and status (*Active* or *Inactive*).
   - Click the **More options** button to display additional options: *Delete all responses*, *Print summary*, and *Create a summary link*.

3. Click the **View Results** button to display each individual response.
   - Scroll through individual results by clicking the **left** or **right** arrow.
   - Click the **Back** button to return to the summary of responses.

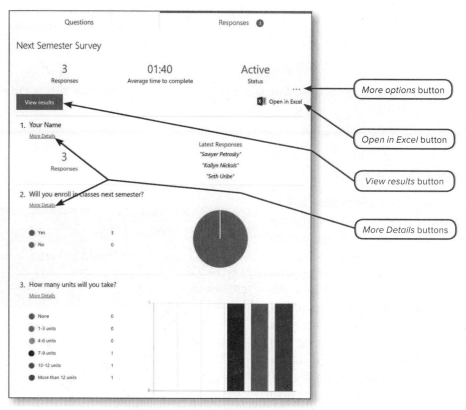

Figure 12-93 *Form* response summary

4. Click a **More Details** button below a question to view additional details about a question.
   • Click the **X** in the upper-right corner to close the *Details* window and return to the summary of responses.
5. Click **Open in Excel** to save the responses in an Excel worksheet. The *Save As* dialog box opens, where you can name the file and select a save location.

Sway

Sway is an online presentation application that is similar to PowerPoint and Prezi and is only available online through your Microsoft account (Figure 12-94). In *Sway*, you type text, import text or another file (Word, PowerPoint, PDF), add pictures, videos, charts, tweets, or embed links to other online sources. Each object in a *Sway* is called a *card*, and cards can be combined into a *group*. Share a *Sway* with others similar to how you share a *OneDrive* or *Office Online* file.

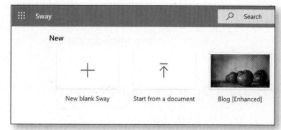

Figure 12-94 Create a *Sway* online presentation

> **MORE INFO**
>
> Click the **Tutorials** button in the upper-right corner of *Sway* to view an online tutorial video of this application. *Sway* is also available as a free app for Windows 10 from the Windows Store.

OneNote Online

OneNote Online is a powerful note-taking application that integrates with other Office applications. *OneNote* is organized into *Notebooks*, *Sections*, and *Pages* (Figure 12-95). You can insert text, pictures, links, and tables. *One-Note* uses text formatting features similar to those in Word. *OneNote* is also available as a Windows desktop application and an app for phones and tablets. *OneNote* syncs across all devices when connected to your Microsoft account.

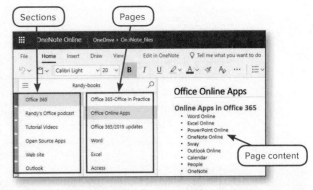

Figure 12-95 *OneNote* notebook, section, and page displayed

When opening *OneNote Online* for the first time, you are prompted to create a new notebook. Each subsequent time you log in, you are prompted to select the notebook to open. Click the **+ Section** or **+ Page** button to add a section or page to your notebook. Share your notebook to collaborate with others.

PAUSE & PRACTICE: WORD 12-3

For this project, you create a *Form* and share it with your professor and others.

Note to Instructor and Students:

Use your education Microsoft account for this project. If you don't have an education Microsoft account, create one at https://products.office.com/en-us/student/office-in-education.

File Needed: None
Completed Project File Name: ***Next Semester Survey***

1. Log in to *Office Online* (office.com) using your education Microsoft account.
   a. Click the **Sign in** button, type your education Microsoft account email address, and click **Next**.
   b. Type your Microsoft account password and click **Sign in** to go to your *OneDrive* web page.

2. Create a *Form* and add a question.
   a. Click **Forms** in the *Apps* area of *Office Online*. If *Forms* does not display in this area, click **Explore all your apps** to display all available *Office Online* apps.
   b. Click the **New Form** button.
   c. Type Next Semester Survey as the title for your form.
   d. Type Sierra Pacific Community College District as the description for your form.
   e. Click the **Add question** button and select **Text**.
   f. Type Your Name in the *Question* text box.
   g. Click the **More settings for question** button and select **Subtitle** (Figure 12-96).
   h. Type Enter your first and last name in the question subtitle text box.
   i. Click the **Required** button to make this a required question.

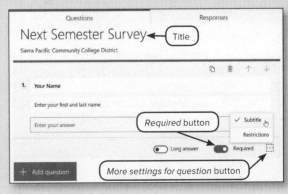

Figure 12-96 Add a *Text* question to a *Form*

3. Add a *Choice* question.
   a. Click the **Add question** button and select **Choice** (Figure 12-97).
   b. Type Will you enroll in classes next semester? in the *Question* text box.
   c. Click the **More settings for question** button and select **Subtitle** to turn off the subtitle option.
   d. Click **Yes** in the *Suggested options* area to add this as *Option 1*.
   e. Click **No** in the *Suggested options* area to add this as *Option 2*.
   f. Confirm that **Required** is on. If it is not, click the **Required** button.
   g. Click the **More settings for question** button and select **Drop-down** to make the response a drop-down list.

Figure 12-97 Add a *Choice* question to a *Form*

4. Add another *Choice* question.
   a. Click the **Add question** button and select **Choice** (Figure 12-98).
   b. Type How many units will you take? in the *Question* text box.
   c. Click the **Required** button to turn off the required option.
   d. Type None in the *Option 1* text box.
   e. Type 1-3 units in the *Option 2* text box.
   f. Click the **Add option** button four times to add four more options (*Options 3-6*).
   g. Type the following as *Options 3, 4, 5, and 6*:
      4-6 units
      7-9 units
      10-12 units
      More than 12 units

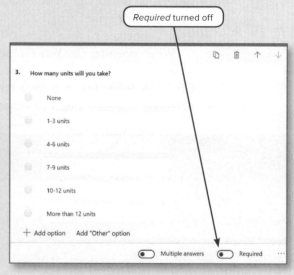

Figure 12-98 Add a *Choice* question to a *Form*

5. Apply a *Theme* to the *Form*.
   a. Click the **Theme** button and select a theme color or picture of your choice. If you want to add a custom picture or color, click the **Customize theme** button (+) and select a custom image or color.
   b. Click the **Theme** button to close the *Theme* area.

6. Preview the *Form*.
   a. Click the **Preview** button to view how the form will display on a computer (Figure 12-99).
   b. Click the **Mobile** button to view how the form will display on a mobile device.
   c. Click the **Back** button to return to the form.

Figure 12-99 PP W12-3 (Next Semester Survey Form) completed

7. Create and copy a sharing link for the *Form*.
   a. Click the **Share** button to display the *Send and collect responses* area.
   b. Click the drop-down list above the sharing link and select **Anyone with the link can respond** (Figure 12-100).
   c. Click the **Copy** button to copy the sharing link.
   d. Click the **Share** button to close the *Send and collect responses* area.

8. Click the **Forms** button to return to the main *Forms* area. The form you just created displays in the *Forms* area.

9. Email the *Form* sharing link to your professor and yourself.
   a. Open the email program you use and create a new email.
   b. Add your email address and your instructor's email address to the recipient list.
   c. Type *[your name]* **Form PP W12-3** as the subject.
   d. Type a brief message in the body of the message.
   e. Paste (**Ctrl+V**) the copied form link below the message in the body of the email.
   f. Type your name below the form sharing link.
   g. Send the email message.

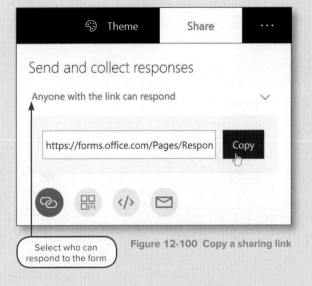

Select who can respond to the form

Figure 12-100 Copy a sharing link

Chapter Summary

12.1 Customize Word options, the *Ribbon,* and the *Quick Access* toolbar to personalize your working environment (p. W12-724).

- Use the **Word Options** dialog box to customize global settings in Word. Certain Word option settings apply to all Office programs.
- The *Word Options* dialog box features the following categories: *General, Display, Proofing, Save, Language, Ease of Access, Advanced, Customize Ribbon, Quick Access Toolbar, Add-ins,* and *Trust Center.*
- Use the *Word Options* dialog box to customize the *Ribbon.* Create a new tab or group, add commands to custom groups, rearrange existing tabs and groups, and rename existing and custom tabs and groups.
- Quickly customize and add commands to the *Quick Access* toolbar using the *Customize Quick Access Toolbar* drop-down list or add other commands using the *Word Options* dialog box.
- Both the *Ribbon* and the *Quick Access* toolbar can be reset to return them to their original settings. Reset the *Ribbon* or the *Quick Access* toolbar individually or reset all customizations, which resets both the *Ribbon* and the *Quick Access* toolbar.

12.2 View and modify Office account settings and install an Office add-in (p. W12-734).

- The *Account* area on the *Backstage* view provides information and account customization options.
- Office account information and settings are available whenever you log in to Word (or any Office application) using your Microsoft account.
- Change the **Office Background** in the *Account* area on the *Backstage* view.
- Add **Connected Services** to your account to access online services for **Images & Videos**, **Storage**, and **Sharing**.
- **Add-ins** are applications that provide additional functionality to Office. Office add-ins are available in the *Store,* and add-ins previously installed display in the *My Add-ins* area.

12.3 Use *OneDrive* to create, upload, move, copy, delete, and download files and folders (p. W12-740).

- **OneDrive** is a cloud storage area that provides you with online storage space for your files. If you have a Microsoft account (Live, Hotmail, MSN, Messenger, or other Microsoft service account), you have access to *OneDrive.*
- Access your *OneDrive* files from any computer that has internet access.
- Log in to *OneDrive* using your Microsoft account.
- Use *OneDrive* to add files, create folders, and move, copy, delete, and download files.

12.4 Share *OneDrive* files and folders (p. W12-745).

- Share *OneDrive* files with others. Determine the access other users have to view and/or edit your *OneDrive* files.
- Email a sharing request to others or create a sharing link that can be emailed, shared in a document, or posted to an online location.
- Other sharing options include **Email**, **Present Online**, and **Post to Blog**.
- Change sharing permission to view or edit a *OneDrive* file or folder or remove sharing permission.

12.5 Use *Office Online* to edit, create, share, collaborate, and comment on a document (p. W12-751).

- **Office Online** is free online software that works in conjunction with your Microsoft account and is available from your *OneDrive* web page.
- *Office Online* is similar to Microsoft Office 365 and 2019, but is less robust in available features.
- You can use *Office Online* without having Office 365 or 2019 installed on your computer.
- Edit existing files from your *OneDrive* account in *Office Online* and create new Office files using *Office Online.*
- Share *Office Online* files with others.
- More than one user can edit an *Office Online* file at the same time, which enables real-time collaboration on documents.

- Add comments, reply to comments, resolve the comment thread, or delete the comment thread on *Office Online* files.

12.6 Explore other *Office Online* products and productivity tools (p. W12-758).

- *Office Online* contains additional online productivity tools in addition to **Word Online**, **Excel Online**, and **PowerPoint Online**.
- **Forms** enable users to create a survey or questionnaire to share with others. *Forms* collect data and stores it in *Office Online*.
- **Sway** is an online presentation application available in *Office Online* and connected to your Microsoft account.

- **OneNote** is a note-taking program that is available in both *Office Online* and as a Windows desktop app.

Check for Understanding

The SIMbook for this text (within your SIMnet account) provides the following resources for concept review:

- Multiple-choice questions
- Short answer questions
- Matching exercises

Guided Project 12-1

For this project, you work on documents from the American River Cycling Club using *OneDrive, Word Online,* and *Forms.*
[Student Learning Outcomes 12.1, 12.2, 12.3, 12.4, 12.5, 12.6]

Note to Instructor and Students:

> *Use your education Microsoft account for this project. If you don't have an education Microsoft account, create one at https://products.office.com/en-us/student/office-in-education. See the* Microsoft Account Information *section in* SLO 12.2: Customizing Office and Installing Office Add-ins.

> *Microsoft regularly updates the* Office Online *products and* OneDrive *online environment. Instructions and figures in this project may differ slightly from how* Office Online *and* OneDrive *display in your internet browser. The Google Chrome web browser is used for instructions and figures in this project.*

Files Needed: ***TrainingLog-12.docx, ARCC-logo-12, ARCCCyclingCalendar-12.docx, FlexibilityExercises-12.docx,*** and ***HeartRate-12.docx*** *(Student data files are available in the* Library *of your SIMnet account.)*
Completed Project Folder and File Names: ***ARCC*** *(OneDrive folder) containing* ***ARCCCyclingCalendar-12.docx, FlexibilityExercises-12.docx, HeartRate-12.docx,*** and ***[your initials] Word 12-1.docx.*** Also, ***American River Cycling Club*** (Form).

Skills Covered in This Project

- Reset customizations to the *Ribbon* and *Quick Access* toolbar.
- Customize the *Quick Access* toolbar for the current document.
- Apply an Office background and theme.

- Log in to *OneDrive* and create a folder.
- Upload a file to your *OneDrive* folder.
- Open a document in *Word Online.*
- Add a comment to a *Word Online* document.
- Create and share a *Form.*
- Share a *OneDrive* folder.

---

1. Open the ***TrainingLog-12*** document from your student data files.

2. Save this document as *[your initials]* Word 12-1.

3. Reset the *Ribbon* and *Quick Access* toolbar.
    a. Click the **Customize Quick Access Toolbar** drop-down list on the *Quick Access* toolbar and select **More Commands** to open the *Word Options* dialog box and display the *Quick Access Toolbar* area (Figure 12-101).
    b. Click the **Reset** button and select **Reset all customizations**. A confirmation dialog box opens.
    c. Click **Yes** to delete all *Ribbon* and *Quick Access* toolbar customizations. Leave the *Word Options* dialog box open.

Select document where
Quick Access toolbar
customizations apply

Figure 12-101 Reset *Ribbon* and *Quick Access* toolbar customizations

4. Add commands to the *Quick Access* toolbar for this document only.
   a. Click the **Customize Quick Access Toolbar** drop-down list on the right and select **For [your initials] Word 12-1** (Figure 12-102).
   b. Select **Quick Print** in the list on the left and click **Add**.
   c. Add the **Spelling & Grammar** and the **Open** commands to the *Quick Access* toolbar.
   d. Click **OK** to close the *Word Options* dialog box.

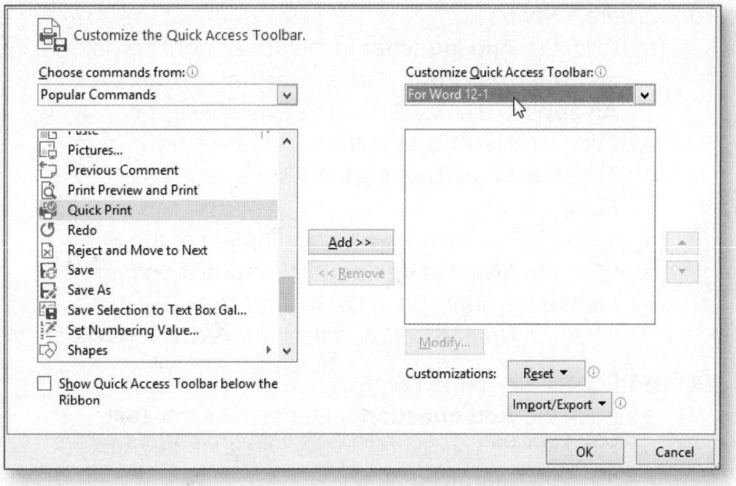

Customize the Quick Access Toolbar.

Choose commands from:
Popular Commands

Customize Quick Access Toolbar:
For Word 12-1

- Pictures...
- Previous Comment
- Print Preview and Print
- Quick Print
- Redo
- Reject and Move to Next
- Save
- Save As
- Save Selection to Text Box Gal...
- Set Numbering Value...
- Shapes

Add >>
<< Remove

Modify...

Customizations: Reset ▼

☐ Show Quick Access Toolbar below the Ribbon

Import/Export ▼

OK   Cancel

Figure 12-102 Add commands to the *Quick Access* toolbar on this document only

5. Apply an Office background and theme.
   a. Click the **File** tab to display the *Backstage* view and click **Account** on the left.
   b. Click the **Office Background** drop-down list and select a background of your choice.
   c. Click the **Office Theme** drop-down list and select a theme of your choice.
   d. Click the **Back** arrow to return to your document.

6. Save and close the document and exit Word.

7. Log in to *OneDrive* online using your Microsoft account.
   a. Open an internet browser window and go to the *OneDrive* web site (onedrive.com), which takes you to the *OneDrive* sign in page. You can use any internet browser to access *OneDrive*.
   b. Click the **Sign in** button, type your education Microsoft account email address, and click **Next**.
   c. Type your Microsoft account password and click **Sign in** to go to your *OneDrive* web page.

8. Create a folder and upload files to your *OneDrive*.
   a. Click the **Files** button on the left to display your *OneDrive* folders and files.
   b. Click the **View options** button in the upper-right corner and select **List** view if files and folders are not already displayed as a list.
   c. Click the **New** button and select **Folder** from the drop-down list.
   d. Type ARCC as the name of the new folder and click **Create**.
   e. Click the **ARCC** folder to open it.
   f. Click the **Upload** button and click **Files** to open an upload dialog box.
   g. Locate and select *[your initials] Word 12-1* and click **Open** to upload this file to the **ARCC** folder.
   h. Upload the following files to the **ARCC** folder from your student data files: **ARCCCycling Calendar-12**, **FlexibilityExercises-12**, and **HeartRate-12**. The **ARCC** folder in *OneDrive* should contain four files.

9. Add a comment to a document in *Word Online*.
   a. Click the **ARCCCyclingCalendar-12** document to open it in *Word Online*.
   b. Click the **Simplified Ribbon** button to turn off the *Simplified Ribbon* (if necessary).
   c. Select "**June**" in the upper right and click **New Comment** [*Review* tab, *Comments* group] to open the *Comments* pane at the right.
   d. Type Please email the June Cycling Calendar to ARCC members in the comments area and click **Post**.
   e. Click the **X** in the upper-right corner of the *Comments* pane to close the pane.
   f. Click the **X** on the browser tab to close the **ARCCCyclingCalendar-12** document and return to the **ARCC** folder in *OneDrive*.
   g. Deselect the **ARCCCyclingCalendar-12** if it is selected (check mark on the left).

10. Create a *Form*.
    a. Click the **App launcher** in the upper-right corner and select **Forms**. If *Forms* does not display, click **All apps** to display a list of all available apps.
    b. Click the **New Form** button to create a new *Form*.
    c. Type American River Cycling Club as the title of the *Form*.
    d. Type Cycling Survey as the description of the *Form*.
    e. Click the **Insert image** button to open the image area at the right (Figure 12-103).
    f. Click the **Upload** button, select the ***ARCC-logo-12*** file from your student data files, and click **Open**.

Figure 12-103 Insert image in a *Form*

11. Add questions to the *Form*.
    a. Click the **Add question** button and select **Text**.
    b. Type What's your name? in the *Question* text box.
    c. Click the **Required** button.
    d. Click **Add question** and select **Date**.
    e. Type When will you start racing this season? in the *Question* text box.
    f. Click **Add question** and select **Choice**.
    g. Type What is your racing category? in the *Question* text box.
    h. Type Pro/1/2 in the *Option 1* text box and type 3 in the *Option 2* text box.
    i. Click the **Add option** button two times to add two more options.
    j. Type 4 in the *Option 3* text box and type 5 in the *Option 4* text box.
    k. Click the **More settings for question** button and select **Drop-down** (Figure 12-104).
    l. Confirm the *Required* button is on (dark) for each of the three questions.

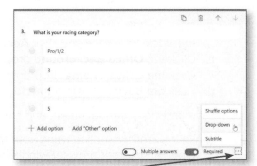

Figure 12-104 Add *Choice* question and customize settings

More settings for question button

12. Apply a *Theme* and preview the form.
    a. Click the **Theme** button and select a theme color or picture of your choice.
    b. Click the **Preview** button to preview your form (Figure 12-105).
    c. Click the **Back** button to return to the form.

13. Share a *Form*.
    a. Click the **Share** button to display the *Send and collect responses* area.
    b. Click the drop-down list above the sharing link and select **Anyone with the link can respond** (Figure 12-106).
    c. Click the **Copy** button to copy the sharing link.
    d. Click the **Share** button to close the *Send and collect responses* area.
    e. Click the **Forms** button to return to the main *Forms* area. The form you just created displays in the *Forms* area.

Figure 12-105 Preview the *Form*

14. Email the *Form* sharing link to your professor and yourself.
    a. Open the email program you use and create a new email.

b. Add your email address and your instructor's email address to the recipient list.

c. Type *[your name]* **Word 12-1 form** as the subject.

d. Type a brief message in the body of the message.

e. Paste (**Ctrl+V**) the copied sharing link below the message in the body of the email and type your name below the sharing link.

f. Send the email message.

15. Return to the *Forms* area in the internet browser window.

16. Click the **App launcher** button and select *OneDrive* to return to your *OneDrive*.

17. Share a *OneDrive* folder with your instructor.

a. Return to *OneDrive* in the internet browser and click **Files** at the left to display your *OneDrive* files.

b. Click the **circle** to the left of the ***ARCC*** folder to select it.

c. Click **Share** at the top to open the *Send Link* window.

d. Click the **Link settings** button, select **Anyone with the link**, deselect the **Allow editing** check box, and click **Apply** to return to the *Send Link* window.

e. Type your instructor's email address in the first text box and type a brief message in the body area.

f. Click **Send** to send the sharing email to your instructor.

18. Close the browser window (Figure 12-107).

Figure 12-106 Copy a sharing link

Select who can respond to the form

Figure 12-107 Word 12-1 completed (*ARCC* folder in *OneDrive*)

Guided Project 12-2

For this project, you use *OneDrive* and *Word Online* to customize a document for Hamilton Civic Center. [Student Learning Outcomes 12.1, 12.2, 12.3, 12.4, 12.5]

Note to Instructor and Students:

> *Use your education Microsoft account for this project. If you don't have an education Microsoft account, create one at https://products.office.com/en-us/student/office-in-education. See the* Microsoft Account Information *section in* SLO 12.2: Customizing Office and Installing Office Add-ins.

> *Microsoft regularly updates the* Office Online *products and* OneDrive *online environment. Instructions and figures in this project may differ slightly from how* Office Online *and* OneDrive *display in your internet browser. The Google Chrome web browser is used for instructions and figures in this project.*

File Needed: **YogaClasses-12.docx** (*Student data files are available in the* Library *of your SIMnet account.*)
Completed Project Folder and File Name: **HCC** (*OneDrive* folder) containing the file
[your initials] Word 12-2.docx

Skills Covered in This Project

- Apply an Office background and theme.
- Create a new group on the *Home* tab.
- Add and arrange commands in the custom group.
- Arrange a group on a tab.

- Upload a file to *OneDrive*.
- Create a folder in *OneDrive*.
- Move a file to a *OneDrive* folder.
- Edit a document in *Word Online*.
- Add a comment to a document in *Word Online*.
- Get a sharing link to a *OneDrive* file.

1. Open the **YogaClasses-12** document from your student data files. Open this file in the desktop application of Word, not *Word Online*.

2. Save this document as *[your initials]* Word 12-2.

3. Apply an Office background and theme.
   a. Click the **File** tab to display the *Backstage* view and click **Account** on the left.
   b. Click the **Office Background** drop-down list and select a background of your choice.
   c. Click the **Office Theme** drop-down list and select a theme of your choice.
   d. Click the **Back** arrow to return to your document.

4. Customize the *Ribbon* to add a group and commands.
   a. Right-click on a blank area on the **Ribbon** and select **Customize the Ribbon** from the context menu to open the *Word Options* dialog box and display the *Customize Ribbon* area.
   b. Click the **Home** tab on the right and click the **New Group** button. A new group appears below the existing groups on the *Home* tab.
   c. Select **New Group (Custom)** and click **Rename** to open the *Rename* dialog box.
   d. Type your first name as the group name in the *Display name* area and click **OK** to close the *Rename* dialog box.
   e. Select the **[your first name] (Custom)** group on the right.
   f. Click the **Choose commands from** drop-down list on the left side and select **All Commands** to display all the available commands in the list on the left.

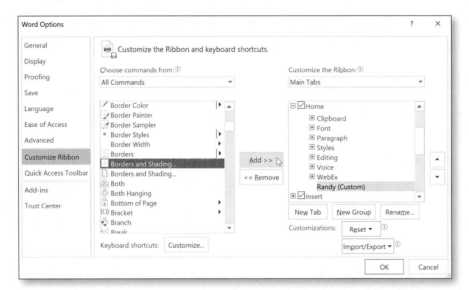

Figure 12-108 Add a custom group and commands to the *Home* tab

g. Select the **Borders and Shading** command (the first one) and click the **Add** button between the two lists to add the command to the group (Figure 12-108).

h. Add the **Tabs**, **Custom Margins**, and **Comment** commands to the *[your first name]* group.

i. Use the **Move Up** and **Move Down** buttons to arrange the commands in alphabetical order.

j. Select the *[your first name]* **(Custom)** group and click the **Move Up** button so it appears between the *Styles* and *Editing* groups.

k. Click **OK** to close the *Word Options* dialog box.

l. Click the **Home** tab to view your custom group (Figure 12-109).

Figure 12-109 Custom group displayed on the *Home* tab

5. Save and close the document and exit Word.

6. Log in to *OneDrive* online using your Microsoft account.
   a. Open an internet browser window and go to the *OneDrive* web site (onedrive.com), which takes you to the *OneDrive* sign-in page.
   b. Click the **Sign in** button.
   c. Type your Microsoft account email address and click **Next**.
   d. Type your Microsoft account password and click **Sign in** to go to your *OneDrive* web page.

7. Upload a file in *OneDrive*, create a folder, and move a file.
   a. Click the **Files** button on the left to display your *OneDrive* folders and files.
   b. Click the **Upload** button and select **Files** from the drop-down list to open an upload dialog box.
   c. Select *[your initials] Word 12-2* from your solutions files and click **Open** to upload this file to the *OneDrive* folder.
   d. Click the **New** button and select **Folder** from the drop-down list.
   e. Type HCC as the name of the new folder and click **Create**.
   f. Click the **circle** to the left of *[your initials] Word 12-2* to select this file.
   g. Click the **Move to** button at the top to open the *Move* pane on the right.
   h. Click **Your OneDrive**, select the **HCC** folder, and click **Move here** to close the page and move the file to the **HCC** folder (Figure 12-110).

8. Edit a document in *Word Online* and add a comment.
   a. Click the **HCC** folder to open it.
   b. Click the *[your initials] Word 12-2* file to open it in *Word Online*. The text box in the upper-right corner does not display correctly, and text wrapping around the picture might not display correctly. Don't try to repair the layout in *Word Online*.
   c. Click the **Simplified Ribbon** button to turn off the *Simplified Ribbon* (if necessary).
   d. Place the insertion point at the end of the second body paragraph (". . . yoga mat and towel.") and press **Enter** two times.
   e. Type Our yoga classes are taught on the following days and times: and press **Enter** two times.
   f. Click the **Bullets** button [*Home* tab, *Paragraph* group] and type the following three bulleted lines:
      Monday, Wednesday, and Friday at 6 and 8 a.m.
      Tuesday and Thursday at 7 a.m. and 12:30 p.m.
      Saturday and Sunday at 9 a.m.
   g. Select the sentence before the bulleted list.

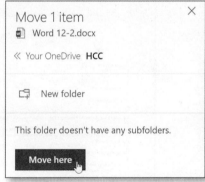

Figure 12-110 Move a file to a folder in *OneDrive*

h. Click the **New Comment** button [*Insert* tab, *Comments* group] to open the *Comments* pane on the right.

i. Type Rachel, please confirm with Amanda the days and times of the yoga classes in the new comment and click the **Post** button.

j. Click the **X** in the upper-right corner of the *Comments* pane to close the pane.

9. Share a file on *OneDrive* with your instructor.

Figure 12-111 Create a sharing link to a *OneDrive* file

a. Click the **Share** button at the top-right corner to open the *Send Link* window (Figure 12-111).

b. Click the **Link settings** button to open the *Link settings* window.

c. Select **Anyone with the link**, check the **Allow editing** box (if not already checked), and click **Apply** to return to the *Send Link* window (see Figure 12-111).

d. Click the **Copy Link** button. A *Share* window opens.

e. Click **Copy** and close the *Share* window.

f. Click the **X** on the browser tab to close the *[your initials] Word 12-2* file (Figure 12-112).

g. Close **X** in the upper-right corner of the browser window to close the internet browser.

10. Email the sharing link to your professor and yourself.

a. Open the email program you use and create a new email.

b. Type your email address and your instructor's email address in the *To* area.

c. Type *[your name]* Word 12-2 as the subject.

d. Type a brief message in the body of the message (be sure to include your name) and paste (**Ctrl+V**) the sharing link.

e. Send the message.

Figure 12-112 Word 12-2 completed (displayed in the desktop version of Word)

Guided Project 12-3

For this project, you customize the working environment in Word and use *OneDrive* and *Word Online* to modify files for Placer Hills Real Estate.
[Student Learning Outcomes 12.1, 12.2, 12.3, 12.4, 12.5]

Note to Instructor and Students:

> *Use your education Microsoft account for this project. If you don't have an education Microsoft account, create one at https://products.office.com/en-us/student/office-in-education. See the* Microsoft Account Information *section in* SLO 12.2: Customizing Office and Installing Office Add-ins.

> *Microsoft regularly updates the* Office Online *products and* OneDrive *online environment. Instructions and figures in this project may differ slightly from how* Office Online *and* OneDrive *display in your internet browser. The Google Chrome web browser is used for instructions and figures in this project.*

Files Needed: ***ExpirationLetter-12.docx***, ***EscrowChecklist-12.docx***, and ***HomeBuying-12.docx*** *(Student data files are available in the* Library *of your SIMnet account.)*
Completed Project Folder and File Names: ***PHRE*** *(OneDrive* folder) containing the following files: ***EscrowChecklist-12.docx***, ***HomeBuying-12.docx***, and *[your initials]* ***Word 12-3.docx***

Skills Covered in This Project

- Change default save location in Word.
- Reset the *Quick Access* toolbar.
- Add and rearrange commands on the *Quick Access* toolbar.

- Create a *OneDrive* folder.
- Upload files to a *OneDrive* folder.
- Edit a document in *Word Online*.
- Share a *OneDrive* folder.

---

1. Open the ***ExpirationLetter-12*** document from your student data files in the Word desktop application and save the file as *[your initials]* Word 12-3.

2. Change the default save location in Word.
   a. Click the **File** tab to open the *Backstage* view and click **Options** to open the *Word Options* dialog box.
   b. Click **Save** on the left to display save options (Figure 12-113).
   c. Click the **Browse** button to the right of *Default local file location*. The *Modify Location* dialog box opens.
   d. Select the **OneDrive** folder on the left and click **OK** to close *the Modify Location* dialog box and change the default save location. If the *OneDrive* folder is not available on the computer you are using, skip this step.
   e. Leave the *Word Options* dialog box open.

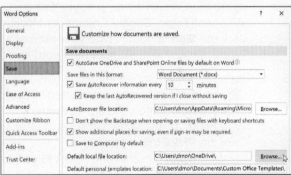

Figure 12-113 Change the default save location

3. Reset and modify the *Quick Access* toolbar.
   a. Select **Quick Access Toolbar** on the left in the *Word Options* dialog box.
   b. Click the **Reset** button and select **Reset only Quick Access Toolbar**. *Note: If your* Quick Access *toolbar is already at its original settings, the* Reset only Quick Access Toolbar *option is not active, and you can skip both this step and step 3c.*

   c. Click **Yes** in the dialog box that opens to confirm the reset.

   d. Click the **Customize Quick Access Toolbar** drop-down list in the list on the right and select **For *[your initials]* Word 12-3**.

   e. Select **Email** In the list of commands on the left and click the **Add** button to add it to the *Quick Access* toolbar.

   f. Add **Insert Comment**, **Quick Print**, and **Open** to the *Quick Access* toolbar.

   g. Select **Open** on the right and use the **Move Up** button to position it above *Quick Print* (Figure 12-114).

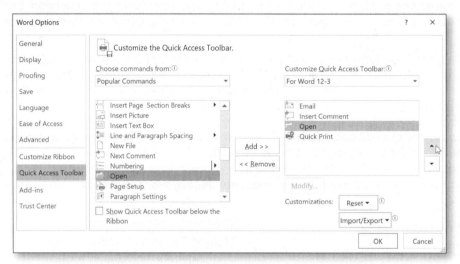

Figure 12-114 Add and rearrange commands on the *Quick Access* toolbar

   h. Click **OK** to close the *Word Options* dialog box.

   i. Save and close the document and exit Word.

4. Log in to *OneDrive* online using your education Microsoft account.

   a. Open an internet browser window and go to the *OneDrive* web site (onedrive.com), which takes you to the *OneDrive* sign in page. You can use any internet browser to access *OneDrive* (Microsoft Edge, Google Chrome, or Mozilla Firefox).

   b. Click the **Sign in** button, type your Microsoft account email address, and click **Next**.

   c. Type your Microsoft account password and click **Sign in** to go to your *OneDrive* web page.

5. Create a *OneDrive* folder and upload files.

   a. Click the **Files** button on the left to display your *OneDrive* folders and files.

   b. Click the **New** button and select **Folder** from the drop-down list.

   c. Type PHRE as the name of the new folder and click **Create**.

   d. Click the **PHRE** folder to open it.

   e. Click the **Upload** button and select **Files** from the drop-down list to open an upload dialog box.

   f. Select *[your initials] **Word 12-3**** from your solutions files and click **Open** to upload this file to the **PHRE** folder in *OneDrive*.

   g. Upload the **EscrowChecklist-12** and **HomeBuying-12** files from your student data files to the **PHRE** folder in *OneDrive*. The **PHRE** folder should contain three files.

6. Edit a document in *Word Online*.

   a. Click the *[your initials] **Word 12-3*** file to open it in *Word Online*.

   b. Replace the "<Address Block>" placeholder text with the following recipient address:

    Mr. Rick DePonte
    8364 Marshall Street
    Granite Bay, CA 95863

c. Replace the "*<Salutation>*" *placeholder text (don't delete the colon) with* **Mr. DePonte** as the salutation.

d. Click the **X** on the browser tab to close the *[your initials] Word 12-3* file and return to the *PHRE* folder in *OneDrive*.

7. Share a folder on *OneDrive* with your instructor.

   a. Click **Files** at the left to return to your *OneDrive* folders.

   b. Click the **circle** to the left of the *PHRE* folder to select it and click **Share** at the top to open the *Send Link* window (Figure 12-115).

   c. Click the **Link settings** button to open the *Link settings* window, select **Anyone with the link**, check the **Allow editing** box (if not already checked), and click **Apply** to return to the *Send Link* window.

   d. Type your instructor's email address in the first text box.

   e. Type a brief message and your name in the second text box.

   f. Click **Send** to send the sharing email to your instructor.

8. Close **X** in the upper-right corner of the browser window to close the internet browser. (Figure 12-116).

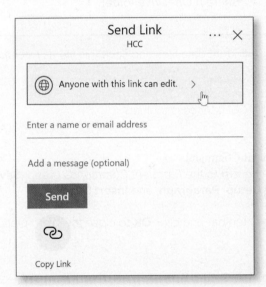

Figure 12-115 Share a *OneDrive* folder

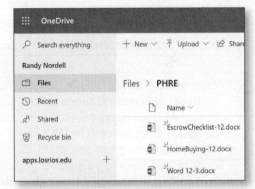

Figure 12-116 Word 12-3 completed (*PHRE* folder in *OneDrive*)

Independent Project 12-4

For this project, you customize the working environment in Word and use *OneDrive* and *Word Online* to create, store, edit, and share documents for Sierra Pacific Community College District.
[Student Learning Outcomes 12.1, 12.2, 12.3, 12.4, 12.5]

Note to Instructor and Students:

> *Use your education Microsoft account for this project. If you don't have an education Microsoft account, create one at https://products.office.com/en-us/student/office-in-education. See the* Microsoft Account Information *section in* SLO 12.2: Customizing Office and Installing Office Add-ins.

Microsoft regularly updates the Office Online *products and* OneDrive *online environment. Instructions and figures in this project may differ slightly from how* Office Online *and* OneDrive *display in your internet browser. The Google Chrome web browser is used for instructions and figures in this project.*

Files Needed: **OnlineLearning-12.docx, EmergencyProcedures-12.docx**, and **WritingTips-12.docx**
(Student data files are available in the Library *of your* SIMnet *account.)*
Completed Project Folder and File Names: **SPCCD** *(OneDrive folder)* containing the following files: **EmergencyProcedures-12.docx, [your initials] Word 12-4a.docx, [your initials] Word 12-4b.docx**, and **WritingTips-12.docx**

Skills Covered in This Project

- Reset the *Ribbon* and the *Quick Access* toolbar.
- Create a new tab and group on the *Ribbon*.
- Add and arrange commands in a custom group.
- Add commands to the *Quick Access* toolbar.
- Customize *Word Options*.

- Apply an Office background and theme.
- Create a *OneDrive* folder and upload files.
- Create a document in *Word Online* and apply formatting.
- Add a comment to a *Word Online* document.
- Share a *OneDrive* folder.

---

1. Open the **OnlineLearning-12** document from your student data files and save this file as *[your initials]* Word 12-4a.

2. Reset and customize the *Ribbon* and the *Quick Access* toolbar.
   a. **Reset all customizations** to the *Ribbon* and the *Quick Access* toolbar.
   b. Create a new tab after the *Home* tab.
   c. Rename the new tab to **SPCCD**.
   d. Rename new group in the *SPCCD* tab to **Frequent Commands**.
   e. Add the following commands (in *Popular Commands*) to the *Frequent Commands* group: **Save As, Spelling & Grammar, Insert Comment, Page Setup, Paragraph**, and **Insert Picture**.
   f. Arrange these commands in alphabetical order.
   g. Add **Open** and **Quick Print** to the *Quick Access* toolbar and click **OK** to close the *Word Options* dialog box.

3. Customize Word options.
   a. Open the *Word Options* dialog box and display the **General** area.
   b. Confirm that your *User name* and *Initials* are correct. Change them if necessary.
   c. Select an *Office Background* and *Office Theme* of your choice.
   d. Select the **Advanced** category on the left and check the **Expand all headings when opening a document** check box in the *Show document content* area.
   e. Click **OK** to close the *Word Options* dialog box.

4. Save and close the document and exit Word.

5. Create a *OneDrive* folder and upload files.
   a. Open an internet browser and log in to your education *OneDrive* account (onedrive.com).
   b. Create a new folder named **SPCCD** in the *Files* area.
   c. Open the **SPCCD** folder and upload the **[your initials] Word 12-4a** file.
   d. Upload the following files from your student data files: **EmergencyProcedures-12** and **WritingTips-12**.

6. Create a new Word document in *Word Online* and add a comment.
   a. Open the **SPCCD** folder in *OneDrive* if necessary.
   b. Create a new **Word document** using *Word Online* and name it *[your initials]* Word 12-4b.

c. Type SPCCD Fall Semester Important Dates and press **Enter** two times.

d. Turn on bullets and type the following five bulleted items:
August 22: Classes begin
August 30: Last day to register
October 1: Apply for Fall graduation
November 8: Last day to drop
December 14-18: Final exams

e. Apply **Heading 1** style, **bold** format, and **12 pt**. *After* paragraph spacing to the first line (Figure 12-117).

f. Select the bulleted list and insert a comment.

g. Type Please confirm these dates are correct in the comment and **Post** the comment.

h. Close the *[your initials] Word 12-4b* document and return to your **SPCCD** folder in *OneDrive* (Figure 12-118).

7. Share the **SPCCD** folder on *OneDrive* with your instructor.
a. Select the **SPCCD** folder and **Share** the folder.
b. Allow **Anyone with the link** to edit the folder.
c. Type your instructor's email address in the recipient area and type a brief message in the body area.
d. **Send** the folder sharing link to your instructor.

8. Sign out of *OneDrive* and close the internet browser window.

SPCCD Fall Semester Important Dates

- August 22: Classes begin
- August 30: Last day to register
- October 1: Apply for Fall graduation
- November 8: Last day to drop
- December 14-18: Final exams

Figure 12-117 Data for document in *Word Online*

Figure 12-118 Word 12-4 completed (*SPCCD* folder in *OneDrive*)

Independent Project 12-5

For this project, you use *OneDrive* and *Word Online* to customize, store, edit, and share documents for Life's Animal Shelter. You also create and share a *Form*.
[Student Learning Outcomes 12.3, 12.4, 12.5, 12.6]

Note to Instructor and Students:

Use your education Microsoft account for this project. If you don't have an education Microsoft account, create one at https://products.office.com/en-us/student/office-in-education. See the Microsoft Account Information *section in* SLO 12.2: Customizing Office and Installing Office Add-ins.

Microsoft regularly updates the Office Online *products and* OneDrive *online environment. Instructions and figures in this project may differ slightly from how* Office Online *and* OneDrive *display in your internet browser. The Google Chrome web browser is used for instructions and figures in this project.*

Files Needed: *LASExpenses-12.docx* and *LASSupportForm-12.docx* (*Student data files are available in the* Library *of your SIMnet account.*)
Completed Project Folder and File Names: *LAS* (*OneDrive* folder) containing the following files: *LASExpenses-12.docx*, *LASSupportForm-12.docx*, and *[your initials] Word 12-5.docx*. Also, *Life's Animal Shelter* (Form)

Skills Covered in This Project

- Create a *OneDrive* folder.
- Upload a file to a *OneDrive* folder.
- Edit a document in *Word Online*.
- Mark a comment as resolved.
- Create a document in *Word Online* and apply formatting.
- Create and share a *Form*.
- Share a *OneDrive* folder.

---

1. Create a *OneDrive* folder and upload files to the *OneDrive* folder.
   a. Open an internet browser and log in to your education *OneDrive* account (onedrive.com).
   b. Create a new folder name LAS in the *Files* area.
   c. Open the **LAS** folder and upload the **LASExpenses-12** and **LASSupportForm-12** files from your student data files to the **LAS** folder.

2. Edit a *Word Online* document and mark a comment as done.
   a. Open the **LASExpenses-12** document in *OneDrive*. The text and graphic objects in the document may not align properly; don't try to repair the alignment.
   b. Change the date in the "DATE" line to the current date.
   c. Click the **comment balloon** to the right of the date line to open the *Comments* pane.
   d. Click the **More thread actions** button, select **Resolve thread**, and close the *Comments* pane.
   e. Close the **LASExpenses-12** document and return to your **LAS** folder in *OneDrive*.

3. Create a new document in *Word Online*.
   a. Create a new **Word document** in *Word Online* in the **LAS** folder and type *[your initials]* Word 12-5 as the file name.
   b. Type New LAS Supporters as the title and press **Enter**.
   c. Insert a table and type the information in Table 12-1.

Table 12-1

Name	Email	Phone
Jennie Solara	jennies@live.com	208-773-2519
Ramon and Mary Clifton	cliftonrm@gmail.com	208-836-9914
Trevor Andrews	tandrews@outlook.com	208-228-3498

   d. Edit the email addresses so the first letter is not capitalized if necessary.
   e. Confirm **Header Row** and **Banded Rows** are selected in the *Table Style Options* group [*Table Tools Design* tab] and deselect other options.
   f. Apply the **Grid Table 5 Dark – Accent 1** table style to the table.
   g. Select the title ("**New LAS Supporters**"), apply **Heading 1** style, **bold** formatting, and **6 pt**. *After* paragraph spacing (Figure 12-119).
   h. Close the document and return to your **LAS** folder in *OneDrive*.

New LAS Supporters

Name	Email	Phone
Jennie Solara	jennies@live.com	208-773-2519
Ramon and Mary Clifton	cliftonrm@gmail.com	208-836-9914
Trevor Andrews	tandrews@outlook.com	208-228-3498

Figure 12-119 Word 12-5 *Word Online* document completed

4. Create and share a *Form*.
   a. Go to the *Forms* area in *Office Online* and create a **New Form**.
   b. Type Life's Animal Shelter as the title and Volunteer Survey as the description.
   c. Add a **Text** question, type Your Name as the question text, and make the question required.

d. Display a subtitle for the question and type Enter your first and last name as the subtitle.

e. Add a **Choice** question, type Can you volunteer at Life's Animal Shelter? as the question text, and make the question required.

f. Add **Yes** and **No** as the two options, make the options a **Drop-down** list, and turn off **Subtitle**.

g. Add another **Choice** question, type How many hours per week can you volunteer? as the question text, and make the question required.

h. Add the following four options:
1-5 hours
6-10 hours
11-15 hours
16-20 hours

i. Apply a **Theme** color or picture of your choice.

j. **Preview** the form in both **Computer** (Figure 12-120) and **Mobile** views and then go **Back** to the form.

k. **Share** the form, allow anyone with the link to respond, and **Copy** the sharing link.

l. Return to the **LAS** folder in *OneDrive* online.

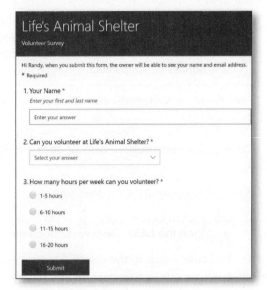

Figure 12-120 Preview the *Form*

5. Share a *Form*.

a. Open your email, create a new email message to your instructor, and use *[your name]* Word 12-5 Form as the subject line.

b. Type a brief message in the body, paste (**Ctrl+V**) the sharing link in the body of the email message, and send the message.

6. Share the **LAS** folder in *OneDrive* with your instructor.

a. Return to *OneDrive* and select the **LAS** folder.

b. **Share** the **LAS** folder and allow **Anyone with the link** to edit the folder.

c. Type your instructor's email address in the recipient area and type a brief message in the body area.

d. **Send** the sharing link.

7. Sign out of *OneDrive* and close the internet browser window (Figure 12-121).

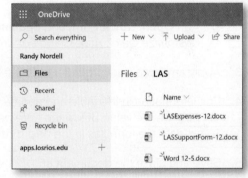

Figure 12-121 Word 12-5 completed
(*LAS* folder in *OneDrive*)

Independent Project 12-6

For this project, you customize the working environment in Word and use *OneDrive* and *Word Online* to customize, store, edit, and share documents for Central Sierra Insurance.
[Student Learning Outcomes 12.1, 12.2, 12.3, 12.4, 12.5]

Note to Instructor and Students:

> *Use your education Microsoft account for this project. If you don't have an education Microsoft account, create one at https://products.office.com/en-us/student/office-in-education. See the* Microsoft Account Information *section in* SLO 12.2: Customizing Office and Installing Office Add-ins.

Microsoft regularly updates the Office Online *products and* OneDrive *online environment. Instructions and figures in this project may differ slightly from how* Office Online *and* OneDrive *display in your internet browser. The Google Chrome web browser is used for instructions and figures in this project.*

Files Needed: ***RenewalLetter-12.docx*** and ***ConferenceRegistrationForm-12.docx*** *(Student data files are available in the* Library *of your SIMnet account.)*

Completed Project Folder and File Names: ***CSI*** *(OneDrive folder) containing the following files:* ***ConferenceRegistrationForm-12.docx*** *and [your initials] Word 12-6.docx*

Skills Covered in This Project

- Reset the *Ribbon* and the *Quick Access* toolbar.
- Add commands to the *Quick Access* toolbar.
- Apply an Office background and theme.
- Edit a document and update formulas.

- Log in to *OneDrive* and create a folder.
- Upload a file to a *OneDrive* folder.
- Delete and add a comment to a document in *Word Online*.
- Share a *OneDrive* folder.

---

1. Open the ***RenewalLetter-12*** document from your student data files in the desktop version of Word and save this file as *[your initials]* Word 12-6.

2. Reset the *Ribbon* and *Quick Access* toolbar and customize the *Quick Access* toolbar.
    a. **Reset all customizations** on the *Ribbon* and *Quick Access* toolbar and close the *Word Options* dialog box.
    b. Add **Open**, **Quick Print**, and **Spelling & Grammar** to the *Quick Access* toolbar from the *Customize Quick Access Toolbar* drop-down list.

3. Apply an *Office Background* and *Office Theme* of your choice.

4. Edit information in the table and update formulas.
    a. Change the value below the *Rate per $1,000* column heading in the table to $19.50.
    b. Update the formulas in the next three cells.

5. Save and close the document and exit Word.

6. Create a *OneDrive* folder and upload files to a *OneDrive* folder.
    a. Open an internet browser and log in to your education *OneDrive* account (onedrive.com).
    b. Create a new *OneDrive* folder named CSI.
    c. Open the ***CSI*** folder and upload the ***[your initials] Word 12-6*** file.
    d. Upload the ***ConferenceRegistrationForm-12*** file from your student data files to the ***CSI*** folder.

7. Use *Word Online* to delete a comment and add a comment.
    a. Open the ***[your initials] Word 12-6*** document in your ***CSI*** folder in *OneDrive*.
    b. Open the *Comments* pane and **Delete thread** to delete the comment.
    c. Close the ***[your initials] Word 12-6*** document and return to the ***CSI*** folder in *OneDrive*.
    d. Open the ***ConferenceRegistrationForm-12*** file in *Word Online* and select the title of the document.
    e. Add a new comment, type Please email this conference registration form to all CSI sales staff in the comment area, and post the comment.
    f. Close the ***ConferenceRegistrationForm-12*** document and return to your *OneDrive* folder.

8. Share the **CSI** folder in *OneDrive* with your instructor.
   a. Select the **CSI** folder and **Share** the folder.
   b. **Share** the **CSI** folder and allow **Anyone with the link** to edit the folder.
   c. Type your instructor's email address in the recipient area and type a brief message in the body area.
   d. **Send** the sharing link.
9. Sign out of *OneDrive* and close the internet browser window (Figure 12-122).

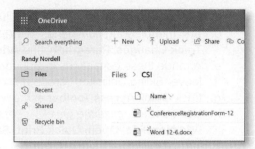

Figure 12-122 Word 12-6 completed
(*CSI* folder in *OneDrive*)

Improve It Project 12-7

For this project, you customize the working environment in Word and use *OneDrive* and *Word Online* to customize, store, edit, and share documents for Skiing Unlimited.
[Student Learning Outcomes 12.1, 12.2, 12.3, 12.4, 12.5]

Note to Instructor and Students:

> *Use your education Microsoft account for this project. If you don't have an education Microsoft account, create one at https://products.office.com/en-us/student/office-in-education. See the* Microsoft Account Information *section in* SLO 12.2: Customizing Office and Installing Office Add-ins.

> *Microsoft regularly updates the* Office Online *products and* OneDrive *online environment. Instructions and figures in this project may differ slightly from how* Office Online *and* OneDrive *display in your internet browser. The Google Chrome web browser is used for instructions and figures in this project.*

Files Needed: ***VolunteerLetter-12.docx***, ***SkiingUnlimited-12.docx***, and ***TrainingGuide-12.docx*** *(Student data files are available in the* Library *of your SIMnet account.)*
Completed Project Folder and File Names: ***Skiing Unlimited*** *(OneDrive folder)* containing the following files: ***SkiingUnlimited-12.docx***, ***TrainingGuide-12.docx***, and ***[your initials] Word 12-7.docx***

Skills Covered in This Project

- Create a *OneDrive* folder.
- Reset the *Ribbon* and *Quick Access* toolbar.
- Create a new group on an existing tab.
- Add commands to a custom group.
- Arrange a group on a tab.
- Add commands to the *Quick Access* toolbar.
- Create a *OneDrive* folder and upload a file.
- Edit a document in *Word Online*.
- Reply to and delete a comment in *Word Online*.
- Share a document in *OneDrive*.
- Customize group options.

1. Open the ***VolunteerLetter-12*** document from your student data files in the desktop version of Word and save this file as *[your initials]* Word 12-7.

2. Reset and customize the *Ribbon* and the *Quick Access* toolbar.
   a. **Reset all customizations** on the *Ribbon* and the *Quick Access* toolbar.
   b. Create a new group on the *Home* tab on the *Ribbon*.

    c. Rename the new custom group as Skiing Unlimited and select a symbol of your choice.
    d. Add the following commands to the *Skiing Unlimited* group: **Page Setup**, **Insert Comment**, **Track Changes**, **Paragraph**, and **Add Table**.
    e. Arrange these commands in alphabetical order.
    f. Move "Skiing Unlimited" group up so it appears between the *Paragraph* and *Styles* groups.
    g. Click **Quick Access Toolbar** at the left to display this area.
    h. Use the *Customize the Quick Access Toolbar* drop-down list and select **For Word 12-7**.
    i. Add **New File**, **Open**, **Quick Print**, **Save As**, and **Track Changes** to the *Quick Access* toolbar.

3. Apply an *Office Background* and *Office Theme* of your choice.

4. Save the document and exit Word.

5. Create a *OneDrive* folder and upload files.
    a. Open an internet browser and log in to your education *OneDrive* account (onedrive.com).
    b. Create a new *OneDrive* folder named Skiing Unlimited.
    c. Open the **Skiing Unlimited** folder and upload the **[your initials] Word 12-7** file.
    d. Upload the **SkiingUnlimited-12** and **TrainingGuide-12** files from your student data files to the **Skiing Unlimited** folder.

6. Edit a document in *Word Online*.
    a. Open the **[your initials] Word 12-7** document in *Word Online*.
    b. Replace the placeholder text and brackets in the bulleted list with the following dates:
        January 11
        January 25
        February 1
        February 8
        February 15
    c. Close the **[your initials] Word 12-7** document and return to your **Skiing Unlimited** folder in *OneDrive*.

7. Edit comments in *Word Online*.
    a. Open the **SkiingUnlimited-12** document in *Word Online*.
    b. Reply to the existing comment, type The dates are correct in the comment area, and post the comment.
    c. Close the **SkiingUnlimited-12** document and return to your **Skiing Unlimited** folder in *OneDrive*.
    d. Open the **TrainingGuide-12** document in *Word Online*.
    e. **Delete thread** of the existing comment and close the *Comments* pane.
    f. Close the **TrainingGuide-12** document and return to your *OneDrive* folder.

8. Share the **Skiing Unlimited** folder in *OneDrive* with your instructor using a sharing link.
    a. Select the **Skiing Unlimited** folder in *OneDrive* and share the folder.
    b. **Share** the **Skiing Unlimited** folder, allow **Anyone with the link** to edit the folder, and **Copy Link**.
    c. Open your email, create a new email message to your instructor and use *[your name]* Word 12-7 as the subject line.
    d. Type a brief message in the body, paste (**Ctrl+V**) the sharing link in the body of the email message, and send the email message.

9. Sign out of *OneDrive* and close the internet browser window (Figure 12-123).

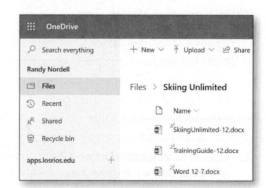

Figure 12-123 Word 12-7 completed
(*Skiing Unlimited* folder in *OneDrive*)

Challenge Project 12-8

OneDrive is an excellent online storage area to organize your school work. You can create a *OneDrive* folder and subfolders to store files from all your classes and share files or folders with classmates and instructors. Remember, it is recommended that you do not store files with highly sensitive information in online locations.
[Student Learning Outcomes 12.3, 12.4, 12.5]

Note to Instructor and Students:

> *Use your education Microsoft account for this project. If you don't have an education Microsoft account, create one at https://products.office.com/en-us/student/office-in-education. See the* Microsoft Account Information *section in* SLO 12.2: Customizing Office and Installing Office Add-ins.

File Needed: None
Completed Project File Name: New *OneDrive* folder, subfolder, and files

Create a *OneDrive* folder to store all files for all your classes. Modify your *OneDrive* folder according to the following guidelines:

- Create a *OneDrive* folder and name the folder your school name.
- Create subfolders for each of your classes and any other folders needed (for example, "Financial Aid," "Clubs," "Internships," etc.).
- Upload files to each of the folders.
- Use *Office Online* to edit a file.
- Share the folder for this class with your instructor.

Challenge Project 12-9

Now that you are familiar with many of the features and the working environment in Word, customize the working environment to meet your needs. For this project, customize the *Ribbon,* the *Quick Access* toolbar, and Word options to personalize your working environment in Word.
[Student Learning Outcomes 12.1, 12.4]

File Needed: None
Completed Project File Name: *[your initials] Word 12-9*

Create a new document and save it as *[your initials]* Word 12-9. List the top ten Word features you have learned in this class and create your *Word Top 10* list. Customize Word options, the *Ribbon*, and the *Quick Access* toolbar as desired. Modify your document according to the following guidelines:

- Create your *Word Top 10* list of features.
- Apply formatting and design principles to attractively format and arrange this document.
- Modify Word options to meet your needs.
- Reset the *Ribbon* and the *Quick Access* toolbar.

- Create a new tab and/or group and rename them.
- Add and arrange commands in the group.
- Add commands to the *Quick Access* toolbar.
- Save the file to *OneDrive* and share the file with your instructor.

Challenge Project 12-10

Office Online has many other applications you can use online to increase your personal productivity. For this project, create a *Form*.
[**Student Learning Outcomes 12.3, 12.5, 12.6**]

Note to Instructor and Students:

> *Use your education Microsoft account for this project. If you don't have an education Microsoft account, create one at https://products.office.com/en-us/student/office-in-education. See the* Microsoft Account Information *section in* SLO 12.2: Customizing Office and Installing Office Add-ins.

File Needed: None
Completed Project File Name: *[your initials] Word 12-10 form*

Create a new *Form* for a club, organization, work team, or student group. Modify your *Form* according to the following guidelines:

- Create a new *Form*.
- Include at least four questions and three different question types.
- Customize the content.
- Preview the results.
- Share the *Form* with your instructor and classmates.
- Review the compiled responses in *Forms*.

Source of screenshots Microsoft Office 365 (2019): Word, Excel, Access, PowerPoint.

appendices

Office Shortcuts

Using Function Keys on a Laptop

When using a laptop computer, function keys perform specific Windows actions on your laptop, such as increase or decrease speaker volume, open Windows *Settings*, or adjust the screen brightness. So when using a numbered function key in an Office application, such as **F12** as a shortcut to open the *Save As* dialog box, you may need to press the ***function key*** (**Fn** or **fn**) on your keyboard in conjunction with a numbered function key to activate the Office command (Figure Appendix A-1). The *function key* is typically located near the bottom left of your laptop keyboard next to the *Ctrl* key.

Appendix A-1
Function key

Common Office Keyboard Shortcuts

Action	Keyboard Shortcut
Save	Ctrl+S
Copy	Ctrl+C
Cut	Ctrl+X
Paste	Ctrl+V
Select All	Ctrl+A
Bold	Ctrl+B
Italic	Ctrl+I
Underline	Ctrl+U
Close *Start* page or *Backstage* view	Esc
Open *Help* dialog box	F1
Activate *Tell Me* feature	Alt+Q
Switch windows	Alt+Tab

Word Keyboard Shortcuts

Action	Keyboard Shortcut
File Management	
Open a new blank Word document	Ctrl+N
Save	Ctrl+S
Open *Save As* dialog box	F12
Open an existing document from the *Backstage* view	Ctrl+O
Open an existing document from the *Open* dialog box	Ctrl+F12
Close a document	Ctrl+W
Editing	
Toggle on/off *Show/Hide*	Ctrl+Shift+8

(continued)

Action	Keyboard Shortcut
Copy	**Ctrl+C**
Cut	**Ctrl+X**
Paste	**Ctrl+V**
Bold	**Ctrl+B**
Italic	**Ctrl+I**
Underline	**Ctrl+U**
Double underline	**Ctrl+Shift+D**
Small caps	**Ctrl+Shift+K**
All caps	**Ctrl+Shift+A**
Left align text	**Ctrl+L**
Center text	**Ctrl+E**
Right align text	**Ctrl+R**
Justify text	**Ctrl+J**
Single line spacing	**Ctrl+1**
Double line spacing	**Ctrl+2**
1.5 line spacing	**Ctrl+5**
Left Indent	**Ctrl+M**
Remove Left Indent	**Ctrl+Shift+M**
Undo	**Ctrl+Z**
Repeat/redo	**Ctrl+Y**
Insert line break	**Shift+Enter**
Insert page break	**Ctrl+Enter**
Insert column break	**Ctrl+Shift+Enter**
Insert non-breaking space	**Ctrl+Shift+spacebar**
Copy formatting	**Ctrl+Shift+C**
Paste formatting	**Ctrl+Shift+V**
Increase font size	**Ctrl+Shift+. (Ctrl+>)**
Decrease font size	**Ctrl+Shift+, (Ctrl+<)**
Insert an endnote	**Alt+Ctrl+D**
Insert a footnote	**Alt+Ctrl+F**
Update field	**F9**
Open Panes and Dialog Boxes	
Print area on the *Backstage* view	**Ctrl+P**
Open *Font* dialog box	**Ctrl+D**
Open *Editor* pane	**F7**
Open *Thesaurus* pane	**Shift+F7**

(continued)

Action	Keyboard Shortcut
Open *Navigation* pane	**Ctrl+F**
Open *Find and Replace* dialog box with the *Replace* tab selected	**Ctrl+H**
Open *Find and Replace* dialog box with the *Go To* tab selected	**Ctrl+G or F5**
Open *Insert Hyperlink* dialog box	**Ctrl+K**
Open Word Help dialog box	**F1**
Selection and Navigation	
Select all	**Ctrl+A**
Turn selection on (continue to press F8 to select word, sentence, paragraph, or document)	**F8**
Move the insertion point to the beginning of the document	**Ctrl+Home**
Move the insertion point to the end of the document	**Ctrl+End**
Move the insertion point to the beginning of a line	**Ctrl+left arrow**
Move the insertion point to the end of a line	**Ctrl+right arrow**
Switch window	**Alt+Tab**

glossary

.docx The file format of a Word 2016 document.

2 pages per sheet Custom page setting that splits a page horizontally into two pages.

3D Model A graphic object similar to a picture, but it can be rotated on its center axis to display the object at different angles.

A

Add Text Inserts text on a shape object.

Add-in Third-party application users can add to Office application programs to provide enhanced functionality.

Address Block Single merge field that groups individual merge fields to make a complete mailing address in mail merge.

alignment guides Vertical and horizontal green lines that appear when you drag a graphic object; help to align the object to margins, text, or other objects.

All apps An area of the *Start* menu in Windows 10 that displays all apps (applications) on the computer.

***All Markup* view** The *Display for Review* view that displays all tracked changes and comments in a document.

Alt Text Text used to describe a picture, table, or graphic object and is used by screen readers to provide an audio description of the graphic to make documents accessible for those with visual impairments. Also referred to as *Alternative* text.

app (application) The term used to describe a software application or program on a computer.

Artistic Effects Built-in formatting that can be applied to a picture.

ascending order Sort order that arranges data from lowest to highest for a numeric field or from A to Z for a text field.

aspect ratio The ratio of width of height; affects picture and object sizing.

AutoComplete Feature that fills in the complete day, month, or date as you type.

***AutoComplete* tag** The notation that displays and predicts what will be typed, such as a day, month, or date. When the tag appears, press **Enter** to automatically insert the text.

AutoCorrect Feature that corrects commonly misspelled words.

***AutoCorrect Options* smart tag** Tag that appears by a word that has been automatically corrected.

AutoFit Formatting option that automatically adjusts column width to adjust the width of a table.

AutoFormat Feature that controls the formatting of items such as numbered and bulleted lists, fractions, ordinal numbers, hyphens and dashes, quotes, indents, and hyperlinks.

AutoMacro A macro that automatically runs when an action, such as opening or closing a document, occurs.

AutoSave Automatically saves a file stored on OneDrive.

AutoText Building block gallery where you store information; you can insert *AutoText* building blocks in a document.

axis (pl. axes) Vertical or horizontal boundary on the plot area of line, column, and bar charts.

axis title Chart element that names the horizontal and vertical axes using placeholders or textboxes.

B

***Backstage* view** Area of an Office application where you perform common actions, such as *Save, Open, Print,* and *Share,* and change application options; document properties are displayed here.

balloon Object where comments display.

Banded Columns *Table Style* option featuring columns that have alternating colors.

Banded Rows *Table Style* option featuring rows that have alternating colors.

bar chart Chart type that is similar to a column chart with bars shown horizontally.

bar tab stop Tab that inserts a vertical line at the tab stop.

bibliography List of the sources used in a report.

bibliography style Style that determines the formatting of sources and citations in a report.

block format letter All parts of the letter begin at the left margin. No lines are indented or centered. Block format can be used on either business or personal business letters.

Book fold Custom page setting that splits a page vertically into two pages.

bookmark Location in a document that is electronically marked and can be linked to a hyperlink or cross-reference.

border Line around text, paragraph, page, cell, table, or graphic object.

Border Painter Pointer used to draw borders on a table.

Border Sampler Tool that applies an existing border style on a table to other areas of a table; similar to the *Format Painter.*

Border Style Built-in border color, weight, and format applied to selected boundaries of a table.

building block Text, formatting, and/or object that is saved and can be inserted into a document; there are a variety of different building block galleries (e.g., *Quick Parts, AutoText, Header, Footer,* or *Tables*).

***Building Block Gallery* content control field** Word field in which users insert a building block into the content control field.

bulleted list Unordered list of items; a bullet symbol precedes each item, and a left and hanging indent controls left alignment.

button Use to apply a command or open a dialog box in Office applications.

button-activated macro A macro that runs when a button on the *Quick Access* toolbar or *Ribbon* is pressed.

C

caption Descriptive text that appears above or below a graphic.

cell Intersection of a column and a row.

cell address Letter of the column and number of the row that represents the location of a cell; also referred to as a cell reference.

cell margins Space around the top, bottom, left, and right of the text inside a table cell.

cell reference Column letter and row number that represents the location of the cell; also referred to as a cell address.

cell spacing Amount of space between cells in a table.

center tab stop Tab that centers text at the tab stop.

Change Case Button used to change text from the case shown to a different case such as uppercase to lowercase.

Change Colors Gallery that lists different color combinations for *SmartArt* layouts that are based on theme colors.

character spacing Space between letters and words.

Character style Style that applies to selected text.

chart Object that displays numeric data in the form of a graph to compare data values or display data trends.

chart area One of several chart background elements; background area where the entire chart is displayed in a frame.

chart element One of the components that make up a chart, such as chart floor, chart area, data series, chart wall, etc.

chart floor Horizontal bottom area of a 3-D chart.

chart label A title, legend, or data table used to organize chart data.

chart object An object that represents a chart in a workbook.

Chart Styles Gallery that lists preset effects for chart elements.

chart title Chart element that names the chart using placeholders or text boxes.

chart type Category of charts that represent data using various shapes and subtypes.

chart walls Vertical side and back areas of a 3-D chart.

Check Accessibility Examines a document for potential issues that users with disabilities might have when using a screen reader or other adaptive resources.

check box Box that allows you to choose one or more from a group of options.

Check Box content control field Word field in which users select or deselect a check box.

Check Compatibility Examines a document for potential version compatibility issues.

child table Table inside parent table.

citation Abbreviated source information in the body of a report that credits the source of information referred to in the document.

Clear Formatting Command that removes formatting from selected text and formats the text in *Normal* style.

clip art Electronic graphical image.

Clipboard Location where multiple copied items from an Office file or other source such as a web page are stored.

Clipboard pane Pane that displays the contents of the *Clipboard*.

column Vertical grouping of cells in a table or a vertical area of text in a document.

column break Formatting option that ends a column and pushes subsequent text to the next column.

column selector Pointer that selects a column of a table.

Combine Tool that merges an original document and a revised document and displays differences between the two documents as marked changes.

Combo Box content control field Word field in which users select from a list of options or type in their own response.

Comment Word collaboration feature that allows users to add notations to a document without affecting text or objects in the document.

Compare Tool that reviews an original document and a revised document and displays differences between the two documents as marked changes.

Compress Picture Feature that reduces the resolution and file size of a picture or all pictures in a document.

connected services Third-party services users can add to Office application programs, such as Facebook, LinkedIn, and YouTube.

Content Control Display Options that control how content control fields are shown in the document; there are three display (*Show as*) options: *Bounding Box, Start/End Tag,* and *None.*

content control field Word field in which you type custom information such as the date or year.

Content Control Field Properties Unique identifiers, content, and format of a content control field.

context menu Menu of commands that appears when you right-click text or an object.

context-sensitive Describes menu options that change depending on what you have selected.

continuous section break Formatting option that divides a document into different sections on the same page so sections can be formatted independently of each other; can also be used at the end of columns to balance column length.

copy Duplicate text or other information.

Cortana The help feature in Windows 10 that responds to both keyboard and voice commands. *Cortana* searches not only the computer but also the Internet and displays search results in the *Cortana* menu.

crop Trim unwanted areas of a selected picture.

cropping handles Black handles that appear on the corners and sides of pictures that you can drag to remove part of the picture.

crosshair Large plus sign tool used to draw a shape.

cross-reference Note in a document that directs readers to another location in a document.

cross-reference index entry Index entry that references another index entry rather than a page number.

custom dictionary Location in Office where words that you add to the dictionary are stored.

cut Remove text or other information.

D

data label Numerical value on data plotted in a chart.

database An organized collection of integrated and related tables.

Date Picker content control field Word field in which users select a date from a calendar.

decimal tab stop Tab that aligns text at the decimal point at the tab stop.

default Setting that is automatically applied by an application unless you make specific changes.

descending order Sort order that arranges data from highest to lowest for a numeric field or from Z to A for a text field.

Design mode Setting that allows users to edit placeholder text in content control fields.

destination file File where an object is inserted.

destination program Office application where an object is inserted.

dialog box Window that opens and displays additional features.

Different First Page Formatting option that imposes first-page header or footer content that differs from the other headers and footers in a document.

Different Odd & Even Pages Formatting option that imposes headers and/or footers that differ on odd and even pages.

Display for Review View options that show tracked changes and comments in a document; there are four *Display for Review* views: *Simple Markup, All Markup, No Markup,* and *Original.*

Distribute Columns Table option that evenly distributes column width.

Distribute Rows Table option that evenly distributes row height.

document property Information about a file such as title, author name, subject, etc.

document property field Word field that displays the document property contents in the body, header, or footer of a document.

drag and drop A method to copy or move select text or an object.

Drop Cap Feature that changes the first letter or word of a paragraph to a larger font, graphic object.

drop-down list List of options that displays when you click a button.

Drop-Down List content control field Word field in which users select from a list of options and are limited to those selections; users cannot type in their own response as they can in a *Combo Box* content control field.

E

Edit link A hyperlink used when sharing a file with others that allows users to edit a shared file.

edit mode Office Online view where users can edit and save a file.

Editor Pane Displays at the right side of a Word document when using the *Spelling & Grammar* feature.

Effect Formatting feature such as shadow, glow, or soft edges added to an element.

embed Insert an object from an Office application into another file; an embedded object is no longer connected to the original file and can be modified independently without affecting the original object.

Enable Content Button that activates content blocked by Word macro security settings.

Encrypt with Password Protects a document from being opened and edited; a password is required to open the document.

endnote Reference, citation, or other text that appears at the end of a document.

eraser Pointer used to erase parts of a table.

extract Create a regular folder from a zipped folder.

F

field handle Area to select a document property of content control field.

field name Label associated with each field in a database or recipient list in mail merge.

File Explorer Window where you browse for, open, and manage files and folders (formerly called Windows Explorer).

file name extension A series of letters automatically added to a file name that identifies the type of file (e.g., *.docx, .dotx, .docm,* and *.dotm*).

fill Color or pattern used as a background.

Filter Feature used to select records in a recipients list that match specific criteria.

Find Feature that searches a file to locate specific text and/or formatting.

first line indent Horizontal space between the first line of a paragraph and the left margin.

folder A Windows feature used to store and organize files in a specific location.

font Named design of type for characters, punctuation, and symbols.

font color The color applied to selected text.

font face Specifies the shape of text.

font size Specifies the size of text.

font style Formatting applied to create bold, italics or underlined text.

footer Displays content at the bottom of a document page or object.

footnote Reference, citation, or other text that appears at the bottom of a page.

Format Painter Tool that duplicates formatting choices, such as font, font size, line spacing, indents, bullets, numbering, styles, etc., from one selection to another selection.

Forms An online survey or questionnaire tool that is available in the Office 365 online environment.

formula Mathematical syntax in a cell that calculates and updates results.

function Predefined formula that performs a specific task (e.g., *SUM* or *AVERAGE*).

function keys The numbered command keys (i.e., F1, F2, etc.) located near the top of the keyboard. Function keys can perform both Windows and Office application commands. Some laptops require the user to press the *Function key* (*Fn* or *fn*) on the keyboard in conjunction with a numbered function key to activate an Office command.

G

gallery Group of options on a tab.

Go To The feature that moves the insertion point to a specific location in a file, such as a page, bookmark, footnote, comment, or heading level.

Gradient Option that blends two or more colors or light and dark variations of the current fill color in different directions.

graphics Visual objects such as pictures, clip art, shapes, *SmartArt,* charts, and *WordArt.*

grayscale A range of shades of black in a display or printout.

Greeting Line Single merge field that groups individual merge fields to make a complete salutation in a business letter in mail merge.

gridlines Lines that visually frame rows and columns in a table.

group Area on a tab that contains related commands and options.

Group/Ungroup *Group* combines multiple graphic objects; *Ungroup* separates previously grouped objects into separate objects; also used with content control fields to restrict editing of a document and allow editing only of content control fields.

Gutter margins Custom page settings that add extra margin space at the top or left of a document to accommodate binding.

H

hanging indent Additional horizontal space between second and carry-over lines of a paragraph and the left margin.

header Displays content at the top of each page of a document.

header row First row of a table.

Highlight Merge Fields Feature used in mail merge to shade all merge fields in a document to visually identify the location of the merge fields.

horizontal alignment Content positioning option that aligns material in relation to the left, center, right, or middle (justified) of the margins, column, or cell; can also refer to the position of objects in relation to each other.

hyperlink Text or an object that a reader can click to be taken to another location in the document, to a web page, or to a different file.

Hyphenation Feature that automatically hyphenates text in a document; facilitates tighter text wrapping at the right margin.

I

Icon Small graphic image that can be inserted into a document.

Import/Export Styles Tool that copies styles from one document to another.

index Alphabetical list of key words with page number references for where they can be found in a document, typically found at the end of a document; also called an index page.

index entry Text, bookmark, or location in a document that is marked with a field code and is used to generate an index page.

index field code Word field code that marks an index entry.

Ink Comments Users write comments using a stylus or their finger on a touch-screen computer.

insert control Button that allows you to quickly insert a row or column into a table.

Inspect Document Examines a document for hidden content, properties, or personal information that might create document compatibility issues.

J

justified alignment Content positioning option that aligns material with both the left and right margins.

K

Kerning Space between letters in a proportional font.

keyboard shortcut Key or combination of keys that you press to apply a command.

keyboard-activated macro A macro that runs when a keystroke combination is pressed.

L

Labels Pre-defined table format used to arrange information so it prints correctly on a sheet of labels; can be used to create individual labels, a full sheet of the same label, or in mail merge.

landscape orientation Page layout option in which the page is oriented so it is wider than it is tall.

leader Series of dots or lines that fills the blank space between text and a tab stop.

Learning Tools An immersive editing environment that adjusts how text displays on the screen. The *Read Aloud* feature is also available on the *Immersive Learning Tools* tab.

left indent Horizontal space between a paragraph and the left margin.

left tab stop Tab that aligns text at the left of the tab stop.

Legacy Tools Content control fields available in previous versions of Word.

legend Descriptive text in a table that describes a data series and identifies it by color.

line break Formatting option that controls where lines begin and end; can be used to keep lines together in a bulleted or numbered list.

Line Numbers Feature that automatically numbers lines in a document; facilitates collaborative editing and reviewing process.

line spacing Amount of space between lines of text within a paragraph.

link Insert an object from an Office application file into another file; linking maintains a connection between the source file and the destination file, and when the original object is modified, the linked object updates automatically.

Linked style Style that applies to selected text or an entire paragraph.

List style Style that applies a numbered or bulleted list style to selected paragraphs.

live layout Feature that automatically and instantly rearranges text and other objects when you drag a graphic object to a different location.

live preview Display option that allows you to temporarily apply and view a style or formatting feature.

lock a subdocument Protect a subdocument from being modified within a master document; users can edit the original subdocument file, and changes are reflected in the master document.

Lock Tracking Keeps *Track Changes* turned on so all changes reviewers make are marked.

M

macro Recorded combination of instructions and keystrokes that are saved and can be inserted in other documents.

Macro Security Settings Options that control how macros are handled when a user opens a document.

macro-enabled document Word document that contains macros.

macro-enabled template Word template that contains macros; a document based on a macro-enabled template contains the macros that are stored in the template.

Mail Merge Feature that combines information from a recipient list into a main document, such as a letter or labels.

mail merge rule Controls the results of a mail merge by applying a condition and action to the merge.

Mail Merge Wizard Step-by-step instructions to guide a user to create a mail merge.

main document Document where a mail merge is performed, such as a letter or labels.

Manage Versions Allows users to recover a previous version of a document.

margin Blank space at the top, bottom, left, or right of a document; in a text box, the space between the outside of the box and the text within the box; in a table, the space between a cell border and the cell text.

Mark as Final Saves a document and prevents it from being edited.

markup area Area outside the right margin of a document where comments and tracked changes display.

master document File containing links to one or more subdocuments.

Match Fields Feature used in mail merge to select fields from a recipient list to match corresponding fields in an address block or greeting line.

mathematical order of operations Set of rules that establishes the sequence that operations are performed in multiple-operation expressions and formulas.

maximize Increase the size of the window of an open Office file so it fills the entire computer monitor.

Merge Completes a mail merge by inserting information from the recipient list into the merge fields in the main document.

Merge Cells Command that combines two or more cells in a row or column.

merge field An individual piece of information from a recipient list, such as first name, last name, or company name, that is inserted in the main document during a mail merge.

merge subdocuments Combine two or more subdocuments in a master document.

Microsoft Access The database software in the Microsoft Office suite of applications.

Microsoft account User profile used to log in to Windows and Microsoft Office; this free account also provides access to *OneDrive* and Office Online.

Microsoft Excel The spreadsheet software in the Microsoft Office suite of applications.

Microsoft Office 2016 The suite of Microsoft productivity software that typically includes Microsoft Word, Excel, Access, PowerPoint, OneNote, and Outlook.

Microsoft Office 365 The subscription version of Microsoft Office where users pay a monthly or yearly fee to install and use the Microsoft Office applications on a computer.

Microsoft OneNote The note-taking software in the Microsoft Office suite of applications.

Microsoft Outlook The personal information management software in the Microsoft Office suite of applications that includes email, calendar, contacts, and tasks.

Microsoft PowerPoint The presentation software in the Microsoft Office suite of applications.

Microsoft Store The online store where users can purchase and download a variety of apps (applications).

Microsoft Word The word processing software in the Microsoft Office suite of applications.

Microsoft Visual Basic editor Program used to edit macro code.

mini toolbar Toolbar listing formatting options that appears when you select text or right-click.

minimize Place an open Office file on the *Taskbar* so it is not displayed on the desktop.

Mirror **margins** Margin settings for multi-page documents that are printed on both sides; ensures consistent margin space when the document is bound on the left.

mixed punctuation Use a colon after the salutation (e.g., "Dear Ms. Vasquez:") and a comma after the complimentary close (e.g., "Best regards,"). Mixed or open punctuation can be used on either business or personal business letters.

modified block format letter Type the date line and closing lines [complimentary close, writer's name, writer's title, and return address (on personal business letters)] beginning at the horizontal midpoint. Typically, set a left tab stop at 3.25". Modified block format can be used on either business or personal business letters.

multilevel list Customized list that includes a combination of numbers, letters, or bullets.

N

Navigation **pane (Windows** *File Explorer*) The area on the left side of a *File Explorer* window that displays the different storage areas of the computer.

Navigation **pane (Word)** The pane at the left side of the Word window when the *Find* command is selected. The *Navigation* pane displays headings, pages, and search results.

nested table A table inside another table; the main table is the parent table, and tables inside the parent table are child tables.

No Markup **view** The *Display for Review* view that displays the final document with changes applied.

non-breaking space Formatting option that keeps words together so they are not separated by word wrap at the end of a line.

Normal **template** Predesigned and ready-to-use document that includes default fonts, font sizes, line and paragraph spacing, styles, and margins; new blank document.

numbered list List that arranges items in order; a number or letter precedes each item, and a left and hanging indent controls left alignment.

NumPages **field** Word field that lists the number of pages in a document.

O

Object Linking and Embedding (OLE) Integration feature to insert content from other Office application files into a Word document.

Office Background Graphic image display in the working environment of Word.

Office Clipboard Storage location for cut or copied data shared by all Office applications.

Office **desktop apps** The version of Microsoft Office that users download and install on a PC or Apple computer.

Office Online The online version of Microsoft Office that is available through a web browser.

Office **universal apps** The version of Microsoft Office that users download and install on tablets or mobile phone devices.

Office Theme Color of the working environment in Word.

OneDrive Online (cloud) storage area that is a part of your Microsoft account where you can store and access documents from any computer with an Internet connection.

OneDrive **folder** Windows folder that displays folders and files stored on a user's *OneDrive* account; synchronizes folders and files stored in the *OneDrive* folder with *OneDrive* cloud storage.

Online Video A graphic image that can be inserted into a document that links to an online video and can be played from within a Word document.

online Word template Preset template available on Office.com that users can use to create documents and customize content.

open punctuation Punctuation after the salutation and complimentary close are omitted. Mixed or open punctuation can be used on either business or personal business letters.

operating system Software that makes a computer function and controls the working environment.

operator Mathematical symbol used in formulas.

Original **view** The *Display for Review* view that displays the original document with none of the tracked changes applied.

outdent Negative indent that lines up information outside the left or right margins.

outline Border around selected element.

Outline **view** View option used to arrange and edit subdocuments in a master document.

P

page break Formatting option that controls where text on a page ends.

Page Color Fill color, color gradient, picture, or texture applied to the entire page(s) of a document.

page number field Word field that lists the page number.

page orientation The direction of the page. The two different orientation options are *Portrait* and *Landscape*.

paragraph alignment Formatting option that determines how a paragraph is positioned horizontally on the page.

paragraph break Formatting option that you insert when you press *Enter* at the end of a word, line, or paragraph.

paragraph spacing Amount of spacing before and after a paragraph.

Paragraph **style** Style that applies to an entire paragraph.

paragraph symbol Icon that indicates a paragraph break.

parent table The main table that has child tables inside of it.

Paste Place text or other objects that have been stored on the *Clipboard* in a new location.

Paste Options Gallery of choices for how data is copied.

Paste Special Dialog box that allows users to choose how a copied object or text is inserted into a document.

PDF (portable document format) File format used to convert a file into a static image.

pen Pointer used to draw a table or add columns, rows, or cells.

picture anchor Location in a document where an object connects to text.

Picture **content control field** Word field in which users insert a picture into the field.

Picture Correction Options Feature that sharpens, softens, or changes the brightness or contrast of a picture by a percentage of its original resolution.

Picture Effects Command used to apply effect options, such as *Shadow* or *Glow*, to pictures.

Picture Fill *Shape Fill* option that fills the *WordArt* or shape with a picture from a file or from the Office.com clip art collection.

placeholder Text that temporarily marks a spot in a document where a citation is missing and needs to be completed.

Plain Text content control field Word field in which users can type text; all of the text in the field is formatted the same way.

plot area Area of a chart that displays chart data.

pointer Small icon, such as a block plus sign, thin black plus sign, or white arrow, that appears and moves when you move your mouse or touch your touchpad.

points Font measurement of 1/72 of an inch.

portrait orientation Page layout option in which the page is oriented so it is taller than it is wide.

Position A character-spacing option that raises or lowers text by a designated number of points.

Preview Mail Merge Displays information from the recipient list in the merge fields in a main document in mail merge.

program options Area in each Office application where you can make changes to the program settings.

protection Layer of security you can apply to a document for form fields that allows various areas to be accessible while others are not.

Q

Quick access (Windows *File Explorer*) The area at the top of the *Navigation* pane in a *File Explorer* window that displays folders or locations on a computer so users can quickly access these item. Users can pin folders or locations on a computer to the *Quick access* area of a *File Explorer* window.

Quick Access toolbar Area located above the *Ribbon* with buttons you use to perform commonly used commands.

Quick Parts Building block gallery where you store information; you can insert *Quick Parts* building blocks in a document.

Quick Tables Gallery of built-in and custom table building blocks.

R

radio button Round button you click to choose one option from a list.

range Group of cells.

Read Aloud The Word feature that reads text out loud and highlights each word as it is read.

read-only mode *Office Online* view where users can view and add comments to a file.

Real-time collaboration The Word 2016 feature that allows multiple users to simultaneously edit a shared filed stored in an online location, such as *OneDrive*.

recipients Data that can be merged into a main document from an external source, such as an Excel worksheet, Access database, or text file, used in mail merge.

record Collection of related data fields used in mail merge.

Recycle Bin Location where deleted files and folders are stored.

Redo Repeat an action.

reference marker Number, letter, or symbol that marks a footnote or endnote in the body of a document.

Repeat The command to automatically repeat the previous command used.

Replace Feature that searches a file to locate specific text and/ or formatting and replace it with specified replacement text and/or formatting.

Researcher Search for quotes, citable sources, and images about a topic and displays information from journals and websites in the *Researcher* pane.

Reset Picture Command used to restore a picture's original characteristics and dimensions.

resize pointer Pointer that resizes a graphic object or a table column or row.

Resolve comment Marks a comment as resolved and replaces *Mark as Complete* on previous versions of Word.

restore down Decrease the size of the window of an open Office file so it does not fill the entire computer monitor.

Resume Assistant Connects with LinkedIn and provides assistance in Word when working on a resume.

Restrict Editing Protects an entire document or portions of a document; a user can customize to allow comments or tracked changes.

reviewer User who inserts comments and changes in a document; a document can have multiple reviewers.

Reviewing pane Area to the left of the Word window where tracked changes and comments display.

Ribbon Bar that appears at the top of an Office file window and displays available commands.

Ribbon Display Options A button is the upper right corner of an Office application window that controls how the *Ribbon* displays. The options include *Auto-hide Ribbon, Show Tabs,* and *Show Tabs and Commands.*

Rich Text content control field Word field in which users can type and format some or all of the text.

right indent Horizontal space between a paragraph and the right margin.

right tab stop Tab that aligns text at the right of the tab stop.

rotation handle A circular arrow used to rotate a graphic object.

row Horizontal grouping of cells.

row height Top to bottom measurement of a row.

row selector Pointer that selects a row of a table.

Ruler Vertical or horizontal guide that displays measurements within the margins of a document.

S

sans serif font One of several font typefaces with letters that do not include structural details (flair).

Save a Copy Option to save a file as a different file name when the file is saved on OneDrive.

Scale Character-spacing option that changes spacing by a designated percentage.

screen clipping A capture of a portion of an open window on your computer as a graphic object.

screenshot A capture of an open window on your computer as a graphic object.

ScreenTip Descriptive information about a button, drop-down list, launcher, or gallery selection that appears when you place your pointer on the item.

section break Formatting option used to break a document into different sections so sections can be formatted independently of each other.

Select Recipients Feature used in mail merge to choose the recipients that will be merged into the main document.

selection handle Four-pointed arrow that selects and moves objects.

Selection pane Window that displays graphic objects in a document; used to select, rearrange, group, or hide objects.

serif font One of several font typefaces with letters that feature structural details (flair).

Settings (Windows 10) The area of Windows 10 used to customize computer settings. The *Settings* area in Windows 10 is similar to the *Control Panel* in previous versions of Windows.

shading Fill color applied to text, paragraph, page, cell, table, or graphic object.

Shadow Style effect option that provides dimension by inserting a shadow behind or below text or an object.

shape Graphic object that can be drawn, such as a line, arrow, circle, or rectangle.

shape adjustment handle Yellow circle handle that changes the contour of a shape.

Shape Effects Command used to apply effect options, such as *Shadow, Reflection,* or *Glow,* to a graphic object.

Shape Fill Color, gradient color, picture, or texture applied to a graphic object.

Shape Outline Border, border color, and border weight applied to a graphic object.

Shape Style Set of built-in formats for shapes that include borders, fill colors, and effect components.

share Allow other users access to a file or folder saved in an online location, such as *OneDrive.*

Share (Windows 10 *File Explorer*) The feature in a *File Explorer* window that allows users to share files stored online with other users.

Share pane The pane at the right side of the Word, Excel, or Power-Point window that displays options to share a file.

Show/Hide Button that displays or hides paragraph breaks, line breaks, spaces, tabs, and other formatting symbols in a document.

Side to Side Page movement that scrolls horizontally through a multi-page document.

Simple Markup view The *Display for Review* view that displays the document with all tracked changes applied and a line at the left side of the document indicating where changes are made.

sizing handles Circles on the corners and sides of an object that resize the object.

Smart Lookup The feature that displays the definition and additional information from the Internet of a selected word or words.

Smart Lookup pane The pane on the right side of the Office application window that displays the definition and additional information from the Internet of a selected word or words when the *Smart Lookup* feature is used.

SmartArt graphics Diagram layouts used to illustrate concepts such as processes, cycles, or relationships.

SmartArt Styles Gallery that displays different effects for emphasizing shapes within *SmartArt* layouts.

Snap Assist The Windows feature that allows users to fill half or a quarter of the computer screen with an open application or window and select another open application or window to fill a different half or quadrant of the computer screen.

Soft Edges Style effect option that creates a feathered edge, which gradually blends into the background color.

soft page break Formatting option that allows text to flow to the next page when it reaches the bottom margin of a page.

Sort Feature that arranges text, table rows, or records in alphabetical or numerical order.

source Complete bibliographic reference for a book, journal article, or web page.

source data Cell range with values and labels graphed in a chart.

source documents The two documents (original and revised) used when comparing and combining documents.

source file File where linked content is stored.

source program Office application where content is created.

Spelling Feature that identifies misspelled words and gives the user word choice options to correct spelling.

split a subdocument Create a new subdocument from a portion of a subdocument.

split button Use to apply a command or display a drop-down list of additional commands depending on where you click the button.

Split Cells Command that divides a single cell into two or more cells.

Split Table Command that splits an existing table into two tables.

Start button (Windows 10) The button located on the left of the Windows *Taskbar* that opens the Windows *Start* menu.

Status bar The area at the bottom of an Office application that displays certain file information and application commands.

style Set of built-in formats, which include a variety of borders, shading, alignment, and other options.

Style gallery Collection of preset effects for text, shapes, pictures, or other objects.

Style Set Group of styles and formatting applied to an entire document.

style template Word template used to store styles; a new document based upon a style template contains the styles in the styles template; a style template can be attached to a document so styles are available and update automatically.

Styles Organizer Dialog box that allows users to copy styles from one document or template to another document or template; also referred to as the *Organizer* dialog box.

Styles pane Window that opens on the right and displays styles in a document where you can insert or modify styles.

subdocument File inserted into and linked to a master document.

subentry Index entry that is subordinate to a main index entry.

syntax Rules that dictate how the various parts of a formula must be written.

System tray The Windows area at the bottom right of the screen that displays Windows system icons.

T

tab Area on the *Ribbon* that lists groups of related commands and options; also a keyboard button that moves the insertion point to the next tab stop.

tab selector Button at the top of the vertical *Ruler* where you select the type of tab stop you want to set on the *Ruler.*

tab stop Marker that controls where the insertion point stops when *Tab* is pressed.

table Information arranged in columns and rows.

Table building block An entire table saved as a building block that can be inserted in a document; table building blocks are stored in the *Quick Tables* gallery.

table of contents List of topics in a document; lists headings in the document and related page numbers.

Table properties Alignment, text wrapping, size, and position options for an entire table.

table selector handle Handle that appears at the upper left of a table when the pointer is on a table.

Table Style Options Tool that applies table style formatting to specific areas of a table, such as header row, first column, or banded rows.

Table Styles Built-in formats for tables, which include a variety of borders, shading, alignment, and other options.

Tablet mode The Windows feature that optimizes the computer for use with a touch screen.

target frame Window where a reader is directed when a hyperlink document or web site opens.

task pane Area at the left or right of an Office application window where you can perform tasks.

Task View The feature in Windows 10 that displays all open windows as tiles on the desktop, and users can select an item to display as the active window on the desktop.

Taskbar Horizontal area at the bottom of the Windows desktop where you can launch programs or open folders.

Tell Me The new help feature in Office applications that displays both application commands and information about commands.

template Predesigned and ready-to-use file upon which other Word documents can be created and modified; a Word template has a .dotx file name extension.

text box Graphic object where you can type text; also an area in a dialog box where you can type text.

Text Effects Command used to apply effect options, such as *Shadow* or *Glow,* to text.

Text pane Area where you enter text for *SmartArt* shapes.

text wrapping Formatting option that controls how text wraps around a graphic.

Theme Collection of fonts, colors, and effects that you can apply to an entire document, workbook, or presentation; provides consistent background graphics.

Theme Colors Set of background and accent colors.

Theme Fonts Pair of fonts used in headings and body text.

Thesaurus Resource tool that lists synonyms for a selected word.

thumbnail Small picture of an image or layout.

tick marks Symbols that identify the categories, values, or series on an axis.

Touch Mode The Office applications feature that optimizes the software for use with a touch screen.

Track Changes Word feature that marks text and formatting changes in a document.

Track Changes Options Settings that customize how changes and comments are tracked and displayed in a document.

U

Undo Reverse an action.

unlink a subdocument Break the links between the master document and the subdocument file.

Update Labels Feature used in mail merge to insert merge fields that were inserted into the first label into the remaining labels.

V

value Number that you type in a cell for numbers, currency, dates, and percentages.

value axis (Y axis) Vertical border in the plot area that measures charted data.

vertical alignment Content positioning option that aligns material in relation to the top, bottom, or middle of the page; can also refer to the position of objects in relation to each other.

View-only link A hyperlink used when sharing a file with others that allows users to only view or download a shared file.

Visual Basic Programming language used to record and store macros.

W

watermark Background text or image that appears on every page of a document.

Watermark **building block** Saved watermark object that you can insert from the *Watermark* gallery.

Weight Thickness of an line or border measured in points.

white space Blank space around text and objects in a document; improves the readability of a document and prevents the document from appearing cluttered.

Windows 10 Operating system software that controls computer functions and the working environment.

Windows desktop Working area in Windows.

Windows *Start* menu Menu that displays when the *Start* button in the bottom left corner of the screen is clicked. Open applications and Windows features from the *Start* menu.

Word field Code inserted in a document that controls content display (e.g., a document property field, formula field, or page number field).

Word Options Dialog box that allows users to customize global Word settings.

word wrap Formatting option that ensures that text automatically continues to the next line when a line ends at the right margin.

WordArt Graphic object that visually enhances text.

worksheet Individual sheet within an Excel workbook; also referred to as a sheet; comparable to a page in a book.

wrap points Locations on a graphic object that function as boundaries for an object and determine where text wraps around the object; you can adjust wrap points for precise text wrapping.

Wrap Text Formatting tool that enables you to display the contents of a cell on multiple lines.

X

X axis Axis displayed horizontally, usually on the bottom of a chart; also called the category axis.

Y

Y axis Axis displayed vertically, usually on the left of a chart; also called the value axis.

Z

zip The Windows feature that combines files and/or folders into one compressed folder; also called a compressed folder.

zipped (compressed) folder Folder that has a reduced file size and can be attached to an email.

Zoom Change file display size.

index

Symbols
* (wildcard character), W2-101
? (wildcard character), W2-101

Numbers
2 pages per sheet, W8-482
3D Format, W1-24

A
Access
  object linking and embedding. *See* Object
    linking and embedding (OLE)
  recipients data source, W5-302 to W5-303
  tables, W5-303
Accessibility Checker pane, W9-557
Actions category, W12-725
ActiveX Controls, W11-681
Add a service drop-down list, W12-736
Add Chart Element button, W8-505
Add Chart Element drop-down list, W8-506
Add Choice dialog box, W11-679
Add Digital Signature, W9-559 to W9-560
Add macro button to Quick Access toolbar,
    W10-633 to W10-634
Add New Source, W3-157 to W3-158
Add question to form, W12-760
Add to Styles gallery box, W6-348, W6-349
Add-in pane, W12-736
Add-ins, W12-736 to W12-737
Add-ins category, W12-728
Address Block merge field, W5-306 to W5-307,
    W5-317
Advanced category, W12-727 to W12-728
Advanced Properties, W1-39
Advanced Track Changes Options dialog box,
    W9-546, W9-547
Alert dialog box, W5-311
Align button, W4-246, W7-433
Alignment
  charts, W8-508
  graphics, W4-246, W8-502
  guides, W7-433
  paragraph, W1-29
  shapes, W7-448 to W7-449
  table, W4-225
  vertical, W2-70
All caps, W1-22
All Markup view, W3-144
Alt text, W4-242
Always Open Read-Only, W9-558
Always show these formatting marks on the
    screen area, W12-725
Always use these values regardless of sign in to
    Office box, W12-725
American Psychological Association (APA) style,
    W3-156
APA style, W3-156
App launcher button, W12-758 to
    W12-759
Application display options area,
    W12-727
Apply picture border, W7-436 to W7-437
Apps area, W12-758 to W12-759

Apps for Office programs
  add-ins, W12-736 to W12-737
  collaboration features, W12-754 to W12-755
  create file, W12-752 to W12-753
  edit file, W12-751 to W12-752
  forms, W12-759 to W12-762
  Office Online, W12-751 to W12-755,
    W12-758 to W12-763
  OneNote Online, W12-763
  Sway, W12-762
Arithmetic operators, W4-248
Artistic Effects button, W7-439
Aspect ratio, W7-434
Asterisk (*), W2-101
Attach template to document, W6-359 to W6-360
Author, W3-139
AutoClose, W10-628
AutoComplete, W1-9
AutoComplete tag, W1-9
AutoCorrect, W1-9
AutoCorrect category, W12-725
AutoCorrect dialog box, W1-10
AutoCorrect Format As You Type category,
    W12-725
AutoCorrect Options button, W12-725
AutoCorrect Options dialog box, W1-9, W12-725
AutoCorrect Options smart tag, W1-9
AutoExec, W10-628
AutoExit, W10-628
AutoFit, W4-224
AutoFormat, W1-9
AutoFormat category, W12-725
AutoMacros, W10-627 to W10-628
Automatic Alt Text area, W12-727
Automatic capitalization, W1-9
Automatic hyphenation, W8-488
Automatically update document styles box,
    W10-617
AutoNew, W10-628
AutoOpen, W10-628
AutoSave, W1-5
Autosaved version recovery, W9-561 to W9-562
AutoText building blocks, W6-368 to W6-369,
    W10-622
AutoText gallery, W6-368 to W6-369
AVERAGE function, W7-412 to W7-413
Axes, W8-505
Axis titles, W8-505

B
Background Removal tab, W7-438
Balancing columns, W4-238, W4-239
Balloons
  comments, W3-139 to W3-140,
    W12-755
  customize, W9-547
  track changes, W3-142
Banded Columns, W4-232
Banded Rows, W4-232
Bar tab, W2-72
Bibliography button, W3-163
Bibliography style, W3-156 to W3-157, W3-157
Bibliography/references/work cited
  Add New Source, W3-157 to W3-158
  bibliography style, W3-156 to W3-157,
    W3-157

create bibliography/references/work cited
    pages, W3-162 to W3-163
  current/master list, W3-160, W3-161
  definitions, W3-156
  edit citations and sources, W3-161
  insert a citation, W3-159
  insert references, W3-162
  manage sources, W3-160 to W3-161
  placeholder, W3-159 to W3-160
  report styles, W3-156
  Source Manager dialog box, W3-160, W3-161
  table of contents, W3-163
  Use the Researcher, W3-162
Bing Image Search, W4-242
Bitmap (BMP), W4-241
Blank document, W1-3, W5-292
Block arrows, W4-248
Blog posts, W12-748
Blue double underline, W1-33
BMP (.bmp), W4-241
Bold, W1-20, W1-22
Bold and Italic, W1-22
Book fold, W8-482
Bookmark dialog box, W9-576
Bookmarks
  cross-reference, W9-577 to W9-578
  delete, W9-578
  display, W9-576 to W9-577
  in formulas, W9-578
  go to, W9-577
  hyperlink, W9-577
  insert, W9-576
  marker, W9-576 to W9-577
Border and Shading Options dialog box, W2-105
Border Painter, W7-422 to W7-423
Border Sampler, W7-423 to W7-424
Border Styles gallery, W7-423
Borders
  built-in, W2-104
  customize, W2-104 to W2-105
  default setting, W2-104
  page, W2-106
  picture, W7-436 to W7-437
  remove, W2-104
  table, W4-230
Borders and Shading dialog box, W2-104,
    W2-105 to W2-106, W4-230, W7-424
Borders button, W2-105
Borders drop-down list, W2-104, W4-230
Bottom, W2-70
Bounding box, W11-681, W11-682
Brown dotted underline, W1-33
Browse button, W12-726
Building block galleries, W6-367, W6-374,
    W7-427 to W7-428
Building Block Gallery content control field,
    W11-680
Building Block Gallery drop-down list, W11-680
Building block template, W6-365
Building blocks
  AutoText, W6-368 to W6-369, W10-622
  categories, W6-364
  create, W6-365 to W6-366, W6-368, W6-374
  delete, W6-367, W6-369, W6-375
  description, W6-364
  edit, W6-367, W6-369, W6-375
  insert, W6-366, W6-368 to W6-369,
    W6-374, W7-427, W11-680